5500

Logic Programming

Logic Programming
Ehud Shapiro, editor
Koichi Furukawa, Jean-Louis Lassez, Fernando Pereira, and David H. D. Warren, associate editors

The Art of Prolog: Advanced Programming Techniques, Leon Sterling and Ehud Shapiro, 1986

Logic Programming: Proceedings of the Fourth International Conference (volumes 1 and 2), edited by Jean-Louis Lassez, 1987

Concurrent Prolog: Collected Papers (volumes 1 and 2), edited by Ehud Shapiro, 1987

Logic Programming: Proceedings of the Fifth International Conference and Symposium (volumes 1 and 2), edited by Robert A. Kowalski and Kenneth A. Bowen, 1988

Constraint Satisfaction in Logic Programming, Pascal Van Hentenryck, 1989

Logic-Based Knowledge Representation, edited by Peter Jackson, Han Reichgelt, and Frank van Harmelen, 1989

Logic Programming: Proceedings of the Sixth International Conference, edited by Giorgio Levi and Maurizio Martelli, 1989

Meta-Programming in Logic Programming, edited by Harvey Abramson and M. H. Rogers, 1989

Logic Programming: Proceedings of the North American Conference 1989 (volumes 1 and 2), edited by Ewing L. Lusk and Ross A. Overbeek, 1989

PROLOG and Its Applications, edited by Alan Bond and Basuki Soetarman, 1990

Logic Programming: Proceedings of the 1990 North American Conference, edited by Saumya Debray and Manuel Hermenegildo, 1990

Concurrent Constraint Programming Languages, Vijay A. Saraswat, 1990

Logic Programming: Proceedings of the Seventh International Conference, edited by David H. D. Warren and Peter Szeredi, 1990

Prolog VLSI Implementations, Pierluigi Civera, Gianluca Piccinini, and Maurizio Zamboni, 1990

The Craft of Prolog, Richard A. O'Keefe, 1990

Logic Programming

Proceedings of the 1990 North American Conference

edited by Saumya Debray and Manuel Hermenegildo

The MIT Press
Cambridge, Massachusetts
London, England

This book was printed and bound in the United States of America.

Library of Congress Cataloging-in-Publication Data

Logic programming: proceedings of the 1990 North American conference / edited by Saumya Debray and Manuel Hermenegildo.
p. cm. -- (Logic programming)
Papers presented at the 1990 North American Conference on Logic Programming held in Austin, Texas, Oct. 29 - Nov. 1, 1990; sponsored by the Association of Logic Programming, in collaboration with the IEEE Computer Society, ACM, and ESPRIT.
Includes bibliographical references and index.
ISBN 0-262-54058-4
1. Logic programming--Congresses. I. Debray, Saumya. II. Hermenegildo, Manuel. III. North American Conference on Logic Programming (1990: Austin, Tex.) IV. Association for Logic Programming. V. Series.
QA76.63.L634 1990
006.3--dc20 90-13352
CIP

Contents

Constraints and their Applications

Concurrency

Databases

Implementation II

Partial Evaluation

Constraints

Theory

Program Analysis

Proof Theory

Parallelism I

Negation

Parallelism II

Abstracts of Invited Lectures

Abstracts of Advanced Tutorials

Program Committee

Saumya Debray, Co-Chair	University of Arizona, United States
Manuel Hermenegildo, Co-Chair	Universidad Politecnica de Madrid, Spain
Hassan Aït-Kaci	Digital Paris Research Laboratory, France
Krzysztof Apt	Centre for Mathematics and Computer Science, The Netherlands
Mats Carlsson	SICS, Sweden
Doug DeGroot	Texas Instruments, United States
Atsuhiro Goto	ICOT, Japan
Steve Gregory	University of Bristol, United Kingdom
Joxan Jaffar	IBM, United States
Ken Kahn	Xerox PARC, United States
Laximant V. Kalé	University of Illinois, United States
Paris Kanellakis	Brown University, United States
Vipin Kumar	University of Minnesota, United States
Ken Kunen	University of Wisconsin, United States
Georgio Levi	Universita di Pisa, Italy
Jack Minker	University of Maryland, United States
Gopalan Nadathur	Duke University, United States
Richard O'Keefe	Royal Melbourne Institute of Technology, Australia
Raghu Ramakrishnan	University of Wisconsin, United States
Vijay Saraswat	Xerox PARC, United States
Stuart Shieber	Harvard University, United States
Hidehiko Tanaka	University of Tokyo, Japan
Evan Tick	University of Oregon, United States
Carlo Zaniolo, Conference Chair	MCC, United States

Series Foreword

The logic programming approach to computing investigates the use of logic as a programming language and explores computational models based on controlled deduction.

The field of logic programming has seen a tremendous growth in the last several years, both in depth and in scope. This growth is reflected in the number of articles, journals, theses, books, workshops, and conferences devoted to the subject. The MIT Press series in logic programming was created to accommodate this development and to nurture it. It is dedicated to the publication of high-quality textbooks, monographs, collections, and proceedings in logic programming.

Ehud Shapiro
The Weizmann Institute of Science
Rehovot, Israel

Preface

This volume contains the papers presented at the 1990 North American Conference on Logic Programming, held in Austin, Texas, from October 29 to November 1, 1990. The conference was sponsored by the Association for Logic Programming, in collaboration with the IEEE Computer Society, ACM, and ESPRIT. The previous meetings of this conference, and its predecessor, the Symposium on Logic Programming, were in Atlantic City (1984), Boston (1985), Salt Lake City (1986), San Francisco (1987), Seattle (1988), and Cleveland (1989).

We received 171 papers from 19 countries all over the world. The Program Committee met May 21 and 22 in Flagstaff, Arizona. Most of the papers submitted were of high quality and merit. A significant number of quality submissions could not be included in the program, as we could accommodate only 42 papers. In addition to the contributed papers, invited talks were given by Fernando Pereira (AT&T Bell Laboratories), Jon Barwise (Indiana University), and Ugo Montanari (University of Pisa, Italy). The keynote speech of the conference was given by Bob Boyer (University of Texas at Austin). Raymond Smullian accepted our invitation to speak at the conference banquet. The conference also included five advanced tutorials, by Uday Reddy (University of Illinois), Vijay Saraswat (Xerox PARC), Carlo Zaniolo (MCC), Andrzej Ciepielewski (Southern Methodist University), and Pascal Van Hentenryck (Brown University).

We would like to thank the program committee members, who handled the high number of submissions with industry and grace. Apart from the program committee members, many other referees also contributed to the reviewing. Their names are listed separately in this volume. Finally, very special thanks are due to Fosca Giannotti, Nai-Wei Lin, Roger Nasr, and Francesca Rossi for their help with numerous organizational and artistic aspects.

Saumya Debray, Tucson, Arizona
Manuel Hermenegildo, Madrid, Spain
July 1990

Referees

Piero A. Bonatti
Akira Aiba
Hassan Aït-Kaci
Krzysztof Apt
S. Auwatanamongkol
Shiva Azadegan
Chitta Baral
R. Barbuti
D. Barker-Plummer
Prasenjit Biswas
Antonio Brogi
Alastair Burt
Mats Carlsson
Bob Carpenter
Andrea Corradini
Damian Chu
Andrzej Ciepielewski
John Conery
Jim Crammond
Danny De Schreye
Doug DeGroot
Saumya Debray
Bart Demoen
C. F. Fan
Barry Fagin
Jose-Alberto Fernandez
Nissim Francez
Torkel Franzen
Alan Frisch
Hiroshi Fujita
John Gallagher
Giorgio Gallo
Dipayan Gangopadhyay
Mark Giuliano
Atsuhiro Goto
Shigeki Goto
Eric Gregoire
Steve Gregory
Toshiyuki Hama
John Hannan
Ryuzo Hasegawa
Bogumil Hausman
David Hawley
Nevin Heintze
Richard Helm
Manuel Hermenegildo
Keiji Hirata
Bruce Holmer
Kenji Horiuchi
Matthew Huntbach
Tien Huynh
Nobuyuki Ichiyoshi
Akira Imai
Dean Jacobs
Joxan Jaffar
Bharat Jayaraman
R. K. Shyamasundar
Ken Kahn
Laximant V. Kalé
Tadashi Kanamori
Paris Kanellakis
Hirofumi Katsuno
Taro Kawagishi
Tadashi Kawamura
Bob Keller
Delia Kesner
Michael Kifer
H. Koike
Seiichi Kondo
Mark Korsloot
Sarit Kraus
Per Kreuger
Vipin Kumar
Ken Kunen
Arun Lakhotia
Anno Langen
Catherine Lassez
Jean-Louis Lassez
Giorgio Levi
Vladimir Lifschitz
Nai-Wei Lin
Zheng Lin
Tim Lindholm
Yuan Liu
John Lloyd
Jorge Lobo
P. M. Hill
Michael Maher
Paolo Mancarella
Joe Marks
Kimbal Marriott
Maurizio Martelli
Yuji Matsumoto
Spiro Michaylov
Dale Miller
Kathleen Milsted
Jack Minker
Nobuyoshi Miyazaki
Toshihiko Miyazaki
Fumio Mizoguchi
Ugo Montanari
Shinichi Morishita
Yukihiro Morita
Kuniaki Mukai
Masaki Murakami
Gopalan Nadathur
Hiroshi Nakashima
Raymond Ng

Martin Nilsson	Uday S. Reddy	Mark Stickel
Katsumi Nitta	V. S. Subramanian	Peter Stuckey
Richard O'Keefe	Fariba Sadri	Askander Suarez
Mitsuhiro Okada	Dan Sahlin	R. Sundararajan
A. Okumura	V. A. Saletore	Peter Szeredi
Catuscia Palamidessi	Ko Sakai	Akikazu Takeuchi
Dino Pedreșchi	Yasubumi Sakakibara	Hidehiko Tanaka
Fernando Pereira	Chiaki Sakama	Jiro Tanaka
Don Perlis	Vijay Saraswat	Evan Tick
Andreas Podelski	Taisuke Sato	F. Turini
Teodor Przymusinski	David Sehr	Pascal Van Hentenryck
Lawrence Puel	Hirohisa Seki	Peter Van Roy
Arcot Rajasekar	Kiyoshi Shibayama	Donald W. Loveland
Sanjay Rajopadhye	Stuart Shieber	Kenichi Yamazaki
Raghu Ramakrishnan	Thomas Sjoland	Roland Yap
Balkrishna Ramkumar	Gert Smolka	Hiroto Yasuura
Kazuaki Rokusawa	Wayne Snyder	Kazumasa Yokota
Francesca Rossi	Harald Søndergaard	Wlodek Zadrozny
Enrique Ruspini	Leon Sterling	Yuli Zhou

Semantics

Failure and Success made Symmetric *

Giorgio Levi[1], Maurizio Martelli[2], and Catuscia Palamidessi[1]

[1]Dipartimento di Informatica, Università di Pisa,
Corso Italia 40, 56125 Pisa, Italy

[2]Dipartimento di Matematica, Università di Genova,
via L.B. Alberti 4, 16132 Genova, Italy

June 27, 1990

Abstract

The treatment of success and failure in the semantics of positive logic programs presents some asymmetric aspects. The paper presents a solution to this problem by first giving a symmetric characterization of the set of non-ground atoms which result in a successful computation and the set of those which result in a finitely failed computation.

Moreover, we extend the usual notions of Herbrand Universe, Base and Interpretations to continuous ones, thus allowing the characterization of infinite computations. In this extended setting a transformation (the immediate consequence operator defined on continuous interpretations) is presented, which has an interesting property, namely that its greatest fixpoint is reached in ω steps. This result allows to symmetrically characterize the above introduced sets also from the point of view of the fixpoint semantics. In fact, the set of non-ground atoms which result in a successful computation is obtained as the least fixpoint of this transformation, while the set of those which result in a finitely failed computation is given by the complement (with respect to the set of all atoms) of its greatest fixpoint.

Key words and phrases: logic programming, finite failure, downward continuity, greatest fixpoint.

*Partially supported by the ESPRIT Basic Research Action P3020 ("Integration")

1 Introduction.

Some recent papers [FLMP89a],[FLMP89b] have developed a new approach to the operational, fixpoint and model-theoretic semantics, which allows the declarative semantics to capture various operational properties.

This effort was first applied to positive logic programs and should be applied to general logic programs. A first step in this direction is to look at the problem of characterizing finitely failed atoms and goals. In the literature the set of finitely failed atoms is well characterized from an operational, fixpoint and model-theoretic point of view, only in the ground atom case. In this paper we characterize also the set of non ground finitely failed atoms using some of the results developed in [FLMP89a], where we studied the set of atomic consequences of a given program.

The introduction of the set of non ground finitely failed atoms into our reconstruction of the semantics of logic programs shows a first asymmetry, namely the fact that this set is not the negative counterpart of the atomic consequences set. Thus we introduce the notion of non-ground success set which characterizes exactly the set of atoms which have a successful computation (with any computed answer substitution).

As soon as we introduce negative information into the picture, another asymmetry shows up in the fixpoint semantics. As pointed out in [JLM86] we have an asymmetric theory in the following sense. A ground atom A belongs to the success set iff, given the immediate consequence operator from Herbrand interpretations to Herbrand interpretations T, $A \in T \uparrow \omega = lfp(T)$. If we consider finitely failed ground atoms, a ground atom A belongs to the finite failure set iff $A \notin T \downarrow \omega$. On the other end, $gfp(T) = T \downarrow \omega$ holds for *canonical* programs only, and not all programs are canonical. Jaffar and Stuckey [JaS86] studied canonical programs and proved that every logic program is equivalent to a canonical program. Blair and Brown in [BlB90] choose a specific pre-interpretation for which the corresponding transformation T is such that $gfp(T) = T \downarrow \omega$.

In this paper, we tackle the same problem considered by [BlB90] and we show that it is possible to give a greatest fixpoint characterization of the set of non-ground finitely failed atoms.

Let us discuss which kind of structures we need. It is well known that the greatest fixpoint of a monotonic transformation T on a complete lattice always exists. Moreover, if T is downward continuous then the greatest fixpoint can be reached in ω steps starting from the top of the lattice. In general, downward continuity requires certain additional topological properties on the elements of the lattice. Namely, those elements must be closed (in topological sense). This requires the underlying structure to be a complete domain. In the case of the Herbrand interpretations, we have therefore to perform a completion of the Herbrand universe (i.e. we have to embed the Herbrand universe in a complete domain). In the literature there are examples of this kind of construction. See, for instance, the metric method of [Abd84], and the approach based on a partial ordering (completion by ideals) of [Gol88]. The metric topologies have less *discriminating power* than the CPO-based topologies, in the sense that the former identify more elements. For instance, the sequences $\{p(f^n(x), f^n(x))\}_{n \geq 0}$ and $\{p(f^n(x), f^{n+1}(x))\}_{n \geq 0}$ converge to the same metric limit $p(f^\omega, f^\omega)$, whilst they have different *lubs* when considered as chains of ideals. The same applies to the sequences $\{p(f^n(a))\}_{n \geq 0}$ and $\{p(f^n(x))\}_{n \geq 0}$ (to be more precise, $\{p(f^n(a))\}_{n \geq 0}$ does not correspond to any chain and has no *lub*). To solve our problem, we need to discriminate the first two sequences. Intuitively, this is because we want to model the difference between the program

$$\{p(f(x), f(x)) \leftarrow p(x, x)\}$$

and the program

$$\{p(f(x), f(f((x))) \leftarrow p(x, f(x))\}$$

since the goal $\leftarrow p(x, x)$ finitely fails in the second but not in the first. On the other side, we must introduce limits for sequences like $\{p(f^n(a))\}_{n \geq 0}$. More precisely, we must force interpretations to be closed (i.e. to contain the limits) with respect to these sequences. Intuitively, this is because the immediate consequence operator associated to a program like

$$\begin{aligned} \{\ & q \leftarrow p(x) \\ & p(f(x)) \leftarrow p(x)\ \ \} \end{aligned} \tag{1}$$

is not downward continuous on the descending chain of interpretations

$$\{p(f^k(a) \mid k \geq n\}_{n \geq 0},$$

since its intersection is empty (see [AvE82]). To obtain downward continuity it is sufficient to add the limit element. The chain becomes

$$\{\{p(f^k(a) \mid k \geq n\} \cup \{p(f^\omega\}\}_{n \geq 0}$$

which has a non empty intersection.

In order to get this "intermediate" discrimination power, we suggest a method based on the combination of both approaches. More precisely we define a metric topology on top of the space obtained as completion by ideals. We believe that an approach based on ideals only cannot meet the above requirements. In the construction proposed by Golson [Gol88], downward continuity holds for programs which do not contain local variables only. Note that program (1) has local variables.

The metric structure also provides a method, alternative to downward continuity, to prove that a program is canonical (the function T associated to the program is such that $T \downarrow \omega = gfp(T)$). Indeed, it is sufficient to prove that $\{T \downarrow n\}_{n \geq 0}$ is a Cauchy sequence, having limit $T \downarrow \omega$, and that T is continuous in the metric sense. In our paper, we follow this approach.

In the following sections, we define a complete Herbrand universe with the above described technique (our explicit notion of domain for interpretations is another difference with respect to the approach of [Gol88]) and we extend the transformation T_v on the new lattice of interpretations defined in [FLMP89a]. Finally, we show that the new transformation is continuous (in the metric sense), and that the greatest fixpoint of this new transformation corresponds to (the complement of) the set of non-ground finitely failed atoms.

2 Preliminaries.

The reader is assumed to be familiar with the terminology and the basic results in the semantics of logic programs [Llo87], [Apt88].

Let the language L consist of: a finite set *Con* of *data constructors*, a finite set *Pred* of *predicate symbols*, a denumerable set *Var* of *variable symbols*. The sets *Con* and *Pred* are partitioned with respect to the arity. Con_n and $Pred_n$ denote function and predicate symbols of arity n.

Let *Term* be the set of terms built on *Con* and *Var*. The Herbrand Universe U is the set of all the ground terms. A substitution is a mapping $\vartheta : Var \rightarrow Term$ such that the set $dom(\vartheta) = \{X | \vartheta(X) \neq X\}$ (*domain* of ϑ) is finite. ε denotes the empty substitution. The composition $\vartheta\sigma$ of the substitutions ϑ and σ is defined as the functional composition. The preordering $\leq$ on substitutions is such that $\vartheta \leq \sigma$ iff there exists ϑ' such that $\vartheta\vartheta' = \sigma$.

An *atom* A is an object of the form $p(t_1, \ldots, t_n)$, where $p \in Pred_n$ and $t_1, \ldots, t_n \in Term$. The Herbrand Base B is the set of all ground atoms. The application of the substitution ϑ to the atom A is denoted by $A\vartheta$. We define $A \leq A'$ (A is more general than A') iff there exists ϑ such that $A\vartheta = A'$. The relation $\leq$ is a preorder. Let $\approx$ be the associated equivalence relation (*renaming*).

A *definite clause* is a formula $H \leftarrow B_1, \ldots, B_n$ $(n \geq 0)$, where H and the B_i's are atoms, "$\leftarrow$" and "," denote logic implication and conjunction respectively, and all variables are universally quantified. A is the *head* of the clause and $B_1, \ldots, B_n$ is the *body*. If the body is empty the clause is a *unit clause*. A *program* is a finite set of definite clauses $W = \{C_1, \ldots, C_n\}$. A *goal statement* is a formula $\leftarrow A_1, \ldots, A_m$, where each A_i is an atom. $G \stackrel{\vartheta}{\longmapsto} \Box$ will denote the SLD-refutation of a goal G with computed answer substitution ϑ.

An SLD-derivation is called *failed* if it is finite and it is not a refutation. An SLD-tree, given a program W and a goal G, is a way of representing the SLD-derivations for G via a selection rule R. An SLD-tree is *successful* if it contains the empty clause, and it is *finitely failed* if it is finite and not successful.

The following definitions are all related to a given program W.

Let us first recall the basic operational characterizations of atoms which have a successful and a finitely failed computation. In the classical approach ([Llo87], [Apt88]) the following sets have been studied and characterized. The (ground) success set:

$$SS = \{A \mid A \text{ is ground and } \leftarrow A \overset{\varepsilon}{\longmapsto} \square\}$$

The (ground) finite failure set:

$$FF = \{A \mid A \text{ is ground and } \leftarrow A \text{ has a finitely failed SLD-tree}\}$$

In [FLMP89a] we gave a formal treatment of another important set, the atomic consequence set:

$$ACS = \{A \mid \leftarrow A \overset{\varepsilon}{\longmapsto} \square\}$$

In this paper we want to characterize also the set of non-ground atoms which have a finitely failed computation. This is not the counterpart of the set *ACS*, which is the set of those atoms with a successful computation, and an empty computed answer substitution. Thus we will discuss about a larger set of successful atoms, which have a successful computation with any computed answer substitution (the existential quantification of the atom is proved). The operational concepts that we characterize are the following. The non-ground success set:

$$NGSS = \{A \mid \leftarrow A \overset{\vartheta}{\longmapsto} \square\}$$

The non-ground finite failure set:

$$NGFF = \{A \mid \leftarrow A \text{ has a finitely failed SLD-tree}\}$$

2.1 Interpretations and models.

We introduce here a definition of interpretations and models slightly different from (but equivalent to) the standard one. The idea is to extend the notion of domain so to include tuples in the domain itself [1]. This will help in the definition of an appropriate continuous domain.

A *domain* is a pair (D, π), where D is a set and $\pi = \{\pi_n\}_{n \geq 0}$ is a partition of D, i.e.

- $\forall n \; \pi_n \subseteq D$,
- $\forall m, n \; [\pi_m \cap \pi_n = \emptyset]$,
- $\bigcup_{n \geq 0} \pi_n = D$,

we additionally require

- $\pi_0 = \emptyset$.

[1]This idea was suggested by H. Blair.

An *interpretation* for the language L is given by a domain (D, π) and a function I such that

- $\forall f \in Con_n$, $I(f)$ is a function from π_n to π_1
- $\forall p \in Pred_n$, $I(p)$ is a function from π_n to $\{true, false\}$.

When the domain is clear from the context, we will denote an interpretation simply by I.

The correspondence with the standard notion is immediate. For instance, a standard Herbrand interpretation I (a subset of the Herbrand Base) can be viewed as an interpretation whose domain is (U^*, π), where

- U is the standard Herbrand domain,
- $U^* = \bigcup_{n \geq 0} U^n$, where U^n is the cartesian product $U \times \ldots \times U$ n times,
- $\pi_n = U^n$

and

- $\forall f \in Con_n$, $I(f)\langle t_1, \ldots, t_n\rangle = \langle f(t_1), \ldots, f(t_n)\rangle$
- $\forall p \in Pred_n$,

$$I(p)\langle t_1, \ldots, t_n\rangle = \begin{cases} true & \text{if } p(t_1, \ldots, t_n) \in I \\ false & \text{if } p(t_1, \ldots, t_n) \notin I \end{cases}$$

We will use a bar to denote generic tuples and sequences. For instance, $\bar{t}$ stands for a tuple of terms, $\bar{A}$ for a sequence of atoms, etc. The truth value of a formula of L in I is defined as usual. A model M of a set $\mathcal{F}$ of formulae in L ($M \models \mathcal{F}$) is an interpretation in which all elements of $\mathcal{F}$ are true. We write $\mathcal{F} \models \mathcal{A}$ to denote the validity of $\mathcal{A}$, namely that $\mathcal{A}$ is true in every model of $\mathcal{F}$.

2.2 Herbrand structures and the immediate consequence operator

The set of Herbrand interpretations, ordered by set inclusion, is a complete lattice. On this structure, the immediate consequence operator T [Llo87], [Apt88], defined by:

$$\begin{aligned} T(I) = \{A \mid\ & \exists H \leftarrow \bar{B} \in W \\ & \exists \vartheta \text{ grounding} \\ & \bar{B}\vartheta \in I \\ & A = H\vartheta\} \end{aligned}$$

is continuous. We recall the following definitions

- $T\uparrow 0 = \emptyset$
- $T\uparrow n+1 = T(T\uparrow n)$
- $T\uparrow\omega = \bigcup_{n\geq 0}(T\uparrow n)$

and

- $T\downarrow 0 = B$
- $T\downarrow n+1 = T(T\downarrow n)$
- $T\downarrow\omega = \bigcap_{n\geq 0}(T\downarrow n)$

By monotonicity of T, there exist the least and the greatest fixpoints of T, $lfp(T)$ and $gfp(T)$, and

$$T\uparrow\omega \subseteq lfp(T) \subseteq gfp(T) \subseteq T\downarrow\omega$$

hold. Moreover, by continuity of T, $lfp(T) = T\uparrow\omega$, whilst the converse, $gfp(T) = T\downarrow\omega$ in general does not hold.

The program (1) in the introduction is a well known example of this fact. Note that $T\downarrow\omega = \{q\}$, while $gfp(T) = T\downarrow\omega + 1 = \emptyset$.

We recall the basic results:

- Model-theoretic and fixpoint characterization of the success set

$$\begin{aligned} SS &= \{A \mid A \text{ is ground and } W \models A\} \\ &= M \text{ (the least Herbrand model)} \\ &= T\uparrow\omega \end{aligned} \tag{2}$$

- Fixpoint characterization of the finite failure set

$$FF = B\backslash T\downarrow\omega \tag{3}$$

2.3 Herbrand structures enriched with variables and the extended immediate consequence operator

The definitions and the results of previous sections have been extended, first by Clark [Cla79] and then by Falaschi et al. [FLMP89a], to interpretations and models whose domain is obtained by enriching the Herbrand universe with elements corresponding to the names of variables. To be more precise, in [FLMP89a] the actual structure is the quotient set with respect to variable renaming. We follow here the approach of [FLMP89a].

Let U_v be the set of all terms ("Herbrand universe with variables"). The domain we consider is $((U_v{}^*)_{/\approx}, \pi_v)$, where $\pi_{v_n} = (U_v{}^n)_{/\approx}$ [2]. For the sake of simplicity, we will denote the equivalence class of a tuple with the tuple itself. The "Herbrand base with variables" B_v is the set

[2] Note that $(U_v{}^*)_{/\approx}$ is not isomorphic to $(U_{v/\approx})^*$. This is the first reason why we introduce in section 2.1 the new notion of interpretation. The other reason is the kind of completion we define in section 4.

$$\{p(\bar{t}) \mid p \in Pred_n \wedge \bar{t} \in \pi_{v_n}\}$$

We introduce the following operators on subsets I_v of B_v

- $Down(I_v) = \{A \mid \exists A' \in I_v\ [A \leq A']\}$
- $Up(I_v) = \{A \mid \exists A' \in I_v\ [A' \leq A]\}$
- $Ground(I_v) = \{A \mid A \in I_v \wedge A \text{ is ground}\}$

The interpretations on this domain ("Herbrand interpretations with variables"), are those subsets I_v of B_v that are *upward closed*, i.e., $I_v = Up(I_v)$. The set $\mathcal{I}_v$ of interpretations, ordered by set inclusion, is a complete lattice. B_v is the supremum. On this structure, the extended immediate consequence operator T_v, defined by

$$T_v(I_v) = \{H\vartheta \mid \begin{array}{l} H \leftarrow \bar{B} \in W \\ \bar{B}\vartheta \in I_v\} \end{array}$$

is continuous. Again, by monotonicity of T_v, there exist the least and the greatest fixpoints of T_v, $lfp(T_v)$ and $gfp(T_v)$, and

$$T_v{\uparrow}\omega \subseteq lfp(T_v) \subseteq gfp(T_v) \subseteq T_v{\downarrow}\omega$$

hold. Moreover, by continuity of T_v, $lfp(T_v) = T_v \uparrow \omega$ holds, whilst the converse, $gfp(T_v) = T_v{\downarrow}\omega$ in general does not hold. Again the program (1) shows this fact.

We recall the basic results, that extend the ones listed in (2), i.e. the model-theoretic and fixpoint characterization of the atomic consequence set ACS

$$\begin{aligned} ACS &= \{A \mid W \models A\} \\ &= M_v \text{ (the least Herbrand model with variables)} \\ &= T_v{\uparrow}\omega \end{aligned} \quad (4)$$

Until now, there was no counterpart of the result in (3) characterizing the non-ground finite failure set. This can be considered one main contribution of this paper. As an example, the program (1) is such that $T_v \downarrow \omega = \{q\}$, and we see that the simple solution of defining $NGFF$ as $B_v \backslash T_v{\downarrow}\omega$ does not work. In fact $NGFF$ would contain atoms like $p(x)$ which are not finitely failed.

In the following we will show the relation between ACS and $NGSS$. This last notion represents all successful computations, and thus it is the notion which is really symmetric with respect to $NGFF$.

3 Non-ground finite failure and success sets and the transformations on Herbrand interpretations.

In this section we present a characterization of the non-ground success set and the non-ground finite failure set in terms of the least upper bound and the greatest lower bound of two chains of interpretations. The elements of the chains can be obtained by repeatedly applying the immediate consequence operator T starting from the empty set and the Herbrand base, and then by performing the downward closure. The same construction can be done by using T_v instead of T. We will characterize the two sets by using T_v, because the extension that we will propose in the following sections (transformation on complete Herbrand interpretations) is based on T_v. Nevertheless, in the technical proofs we will use both T_v and T, according to convenience. Let us first consider the relation between the non-ground success set and these transformations.

Theorem 3.1

$$NGSS = Down(ACS) = Down(lfp(T_v))$$

Proof From [Cla79], [FLMP89a] we know that

$$\begin{aligned} lfp(T_v) &= \{A \mid \leftarrow A \overset{\varepsilon}{\longmapsto} \square\} \\ &= \{A \mid W \models A\} \end{aligned}$$

$\subseteq$) Let $A \in NGSS$. Let ϑ be a computed answer substitution for $\leftarrow A$. Then $W \models A\vartheta$ ([Cla79]). Hence $A\vartheta \in lfp(T_v)$ and therefore $A \in Down(lfp(T_v))$.

$\supseteq$) Let $A \in Down(lfp(T_v))$. Then there exists $A' \in lfp(T_v)$ such that $A \leq A'$. Hence $\leftarrow A'$ has a successful SLD-derivation with empty computed answer substitution, and therefore, by the lifting lemma ([Llo87]), $\leftarrow A$ has a successful SLD-derivation, i.e. $A \in NGSS$.

$\square$

Note that it could easily be shown that $NGSS$ is also equal to $Down(SS)$ and $Down(lfp(T))$, while a model-theoretic characterization of $NGSS$ results to be $\{A \mid W \models \exists A\}$, i.e., the set of atoms whose existential quantification is a logical consequence of the program.

Proposition 3.2 *Down is continuous with respect to the lattice $(\mathcal{I}_v, \subseteq)$, i.e. for every chain of interpretations $\{I_{v_i}\}_{i\geq 0}$, $Down(\bigcup_{i\geq 0} I_{v_i}) = \bigcup_{i\geq 0} Down(I_{v_i})$ holds.*

Proof

$\subseteq$) Let $A \in Down(\bigcup_{i\geq 0} I_{v_i})$. Then there exists $i \geq 0, A' \in I_{v_i}$ such that $A \leq A'$. Therefore $A \in Down(I_{v_i})$, hence $A \in \bigcup_{i\geq 0} Down(I_{v_i})$.

$\supseteq$) Let $A \in \bigcup_{i\geq 0} Down(I_{v_i})$. Then there exists $i \geq 0, A' \in I_{v_i}$ such that $A \leq A'$. Therefore $A \in Down(\bigcup_{i\geq 0} I_{v_i})$.

□

Corollary 3.3

$$NGSS = Down(lfp(T_v)) = Down(\bigcup_{n\geq 0} T_v \uparrow n) = \bigcup_{n\geq 0} Down(T_v \uparrow n)$$

To characterize *NGFF*, let us recall two results from [Apt88].

Lemma 3.4 (Apt [Apt88], lemma 5.7) *Let A be an atom and let ϑ be a substitution. If $\leftarrow A$ has a finitely failed SLD-tree of depth $\leq n$ then so has $\leftarrow A\vartheta$.*

Lemma 3.5 (Apt [Apt88], lemma 5.9) *Let A be a ground atom. If $\leftarrow A$ has a finitely failed SLD-tree of depth $\leq n$ then $A \in T \downarrow n$.*

The following lemma corresponds to a classical result.

Lemma 3.6 *Let A be an atom. If $\leftarrow A$ has an infinite fair SLD-tree then for every $n \geq 0$ there exists a (grounding) substitution ϑ such that $A\vartheta \in T \downarrow n$.*

Proof It is an immediate consequence of lemma 5.10 in [Apt88].

□

We present now our construction. We give first the definition of the elements of the chain that allow to characterize *NGFF*.

Definition 3.7

- *For every $n \geq 0$ define $I_n = Down(T \downarrow n)$.*
- $I_\omega = \bigcap_{n\geq 0} I_n$.

Then we have the following result, which is the non-ground counterpart of theorem 5.6 in [Apt88].

Theorem 3.8 *The following three statements are equivalent*

1. *$A \in NGFF$.*
2. *$A \notin I_\omega$.*
3. *Every fair SLD-tree for $\leftarrow A$ is finitely failed.*

Proof

1⇒2) We prove a stronger property, corresponding to lemma 3.5 for non-ground atoms. Namely, we prove that if $\leftarrow A$ has a finitely failed SLD-tree of depth $\leq n$ then $A \notin Down(T\downarrow n)$. Assume (by contradiction) that $A \in Down(T\downarrow n)$. Then there exists a grounding substitution ϑ such that $A\vartheta \in T\downarrow n$. Then, by lemma 3.5, $\leftarrow A\vartheta$ has no finitely failed SLD-trees of depth $\leq n$. By lemma 3.4, also $\leftarrow A$ has no finitely failed SLD-trees of depth $\leq n$ (contradiction).

2⇒3) Assume, by contradiction, that there exists a fair SLD-tree for $\leftarrow A$ which is not finitely failed. There are two cases.

i) The tree contains an empty clause. In this case, the computed answer substitution ϑ is a correct answer substitution, therefore for any grounding substitution ϑ' we have $A\vartheta\vartheta' \in T\uparrow\omega$. Since $T\uparrow\omega \subseteq T\downarrow\omega$ [Apt88], and

$$\begin{array}{rcl} T\downarrow\omega & = & \bigcap_{n\geq 0} T\downarrow n \\ & \subseteq & \bigcap_{n\geq 0} Down(T\downarrow n) \\ & = & \bigcap_{n\geq 0} I_n \\ & = & I_\omega \end{array}$$

we have $A\vartheta\vartheta' \in I_\omega$. Since I_ω is downward closed, then $A \in I_\omega$ (contradiction).

ii) The tree is infinite. In this case, for every $n \geq 0$ there exists a (grounding) substitution ϑ such that $A\vartheta \in T\downarrow n$. Therefore for every $n \geq 0$ $A \in Down(T\downarrow n)$. Hence $A \in I_\omega$ (contradiction).

3⇒1) Immediate.

□

Let us note that I_ω can be obtained by using T_v instead of T.

Lemma 3.9 *For every n, $T\downarrow n = Ground(T_v\downarrow n)$ holds.*

Proof Immediate, by induction on n. □

Lemma 3.10 *If there exists at least one constant symbol, then for every interpretation I_v,*

$$Down(Ground(Up(I_v))) = Down(Up(I_v)).$$

Proof

⊆) Immediate, since $Ground(Up(I_v)) \subseteq Up(I_v)$.

⊇) Let $A \in Down(Up(I_v))$. Then $\exists A' \in Up(I_v)$ such that $A \leq A'$. Let ϑ be a grounding substitution for A'. Then $A \leq A'\vartheta$ and $A'\vartheta \in Ground(Up(I_v))$. □

Proposition 3.11 *For every n, $Down(T\downarrow n) = Down(T_v\downarrow n)$ holds.*

Proof

$$\begin{aligned} Down(T\downarrow n) &= Down(Ground(T_v\downarrow n)) \text{ (by lemma 3.9)} \\ &= Down(Ground(Up(T_v\downarrow n))) \\ &\quad \text{(since } T_v\downarrow n \text{ is upward closed)} \\ &= Down(Up(T_v\downarrow n)) \text{ (by lemma 3.10)} \\ &= Down(T_v\downarrow n). \text{ (since } T_v\downarrow n \text{ is upward closed)} \end{aligned}$$

□

From this proposition the relation between I_ω (and therefore $NGFF$) and T_v follows immediately.

Corollary 3.12 $NGFF = B_v \backslash I_\omega = B_v \backslash \bigcap_{n\geq 0} Down(T_v\downarrow n)$

Example 3.13 *Let us give an example of this result using program (1).*

$$T_v\downarrow 1 = \{p(s^n(0)), p(s^n(x)), q \mid n \geq 1\}$$

$$Down(T_v\downarrow 1) = T_v\downarrow 1 \bigcup \{p(x), q\}$$

$$T_v\downarrow k = \{p(s^n(0)), p(s^n(x)), q \mid n \geq k\}$$

$$Down(T_v\downarrow k) = T_v\downarrow k \bigcup \{p(s^n(x)), q \mid n < k\}$$

$$T_v\downarrow \omega = \{q\}$$

$$\bigcap_{n\geq 0} Down(T_v\downarrow n) = \{p(s^n(x)), q \mid n \geq 0\}$$

$$NGFF = \{p(s^n(0)) \mid n \geq 0\}$$

A first symmetry can be noted looking at corollaries 3.3 and 3.12. $NGSS$ is characterized as the union of an infinite chain whose elements are obtainable using $T_v\uparrow n$, while $NGFF$ is the complement of a set characterized as the intersection of an infinite chain whose elements are obtainable using $T_v\downarrow n$.

4 Continuous Herbrand domain, interpretations and models.

In the following sections, we will show that it is possible to give a greatest fixpoint characterization of $NGFF$.

We define a complete Herbrand universe and we extend the transformation T_v on the new lattice of interpretations. Finally, we show that the new transformation is continuous (in the metric sense), and that the greatest fixpoint of this transformation corresponds to (the complement of) $NGFF$.

We first recall some basic definitions.

4.1 Completion by ideals

Let $(P, \leq)$ be a preorder. A *directed set* in P is a subset D of P such that

$$\forall a, b \in D\ \exists c \in D\ [a \leq c\ \wedge\ b \leq c].$$

An *ideal* S is a directed set which is *downward closed*, i.e. such that

$$\forall a \in S\ [b \leq a \Rightarrow b \in S].$$

The set of ideals of P, ordered by set inclusion, will be denoted by $(Id(P), \subseteq)$. It is well known that it is a Complete Partial Order (CPO) and that it contains a sub-CPO isomorphic to $(P_{/\approx}, \leq)$, where $\approx$ is the equivalence relation induced by $\leq$.

Every atom $p(t)$ is characterized by the ideal with $p(t)$ as the top element, i.e., the set $\{A \mid A \leq p(t)\}$. Infinite elements come also into the picture with set such as $\{p(s^n(x)) \mid n \geq 0\}$, which represents an infinite element $p(s^\omega)$.

4.2 Complete metric spaces

A metric space is a pair (S, d) where S is a non empty set and the distance function $d : S \times S \to [0, 1]$ satisfies the following properties

1. $\forall x, y \in S\ [d(x, y) = 0 \text{ iff } x = y]$
2. $\forall x, y \in S\ [d(x, y) = d(y, x)]$
3. $\forall x, y, z \in S\ [d(x, z) \leq d(x, y) + d(y, z)]$

A sequence $\{x_i\}_{i \geq 0}$ of elements of S is a *Cauchy sequence* iff

$$\forall \delta > 0\ \exists k\ \forall m, n \geq k\ [d(x_m, x_n) \leq \delta]$$

The sequence $\{x_i\}_{i \geq 0}$ *converges* to a limit x (notation: $lim_{i \to \infty} x_i = x$) iff

$$\forall \delta > 0\ \exists k\ \forall n \geq k\ [d(x_n, x) \leq \delta]$$

Two Cauchy sequences $\{x_n\}_{n \geq 0}$ and $\{y_n\}_{n \geq 0}$ are *equivalent* iff

$$\forall \delta > 0\ \exists k\ \forall n \geq k\ [d(x_n, y_n) < \delta].$$

A metric space (S, d) is *complete* (or *closed*) iff each Cauchy sequence converges (to a limit in S) and it is *compact* iff each sequence $\{x_i\}_{i \geq 0}$ contains a converging subsequence $\{x_{i_j}\}_{j \geq 0}$. Given a metric space (S, d), there is a standard way to embed it into a complete metric space, that consists of adding the limits of the all Cauchy sequences. Formally, this is done by considering the quotient of the space of all the sequences, with respect to the above defined equivalence. The distance between two sequences is given by the limit of the distances on individuals.

A mapping $\mathcal{F}$ on metric spaces (S, d), (S', d') is *continuous* iff for each Cauchy sequence $\{x_i\}_{i \geq 0}$ in (S, d), $\{\mathcal{F}(x_i)\}_{i \geq 0}$ is a Cauchy sequence in (S', d'), and

$$lim_{i \to \infty} \mathcal{F}(x_i) = \mathcal{F}(lim_{i \to \infty}(x_i))$$

Let (S, d) be a complete metric space and let $\mathcal{P}(S)$ denote the set of subsets of S. The *Hausdorff distance* $d_H : \mathcal{P}(S) \times \mathcal{P}(S) \to [0, 1]$ is defined as follows

$$d_H(X, Y) = \begin{cases} max\{sup_{x \in X} d_S(x, Y), sup_{y \in Y} d_S(X, y)\} & \text{if } X, Y \neq \emptyset \\ 0 & \text{if } X = Y = \emptyset \\ 1 & \text{otherwise} \end{cases}$$

where

$$d_S(x, Y) = inf_{y \in Y} d(x, y)$$

Let $\mathcal{P}_{co}(S)$ denote the set of the complete subsets of S. Then $(\mathcal{P}_{co}(S), d_H)$ is a complete metric space.

We define a distance d on atoms as follows

$$d(A, B) = \begin{cases} 0 & \text{if } A = B \\ 2^{-max\{n | (A)_n = (B)_n\}} & \text{otherwise} \end{cases}$$

where $(A)_n$ represents the cut at height n of the atom A (viewed as a tree).

Definition 4.1 (Complete Herbrand domain) *The Complete Herbrand Domain* (U_c, π_c) *is defined by:*

$$U_c = Id(U_v^*),$$

where $\leq$ *on* U_v^* *is the usual ordering on tuples of terms, and*

$$\pi_{c_n} = Id(U_v^n).$$

According to the results reported in section 4.1, $(U_c, \subseteq)$ contains a sub-CPO isomorphic to the CPO $((U_v^*)_{/\approx}, \subseteq)$, (the Herbrand universe with variables defined in section 2.3). In other words, there is an isomorphism $\mathcal{F}$ between $((U_v^*)_{/\approx}, \subseteq)$ and a subset of $(U_c, \subseteq)$ that preserves the ordering. This isomorphism also preserves the function π_v, namely $\pi_{c_n} = \mathcal{F}(\pi_{v_n})$. In fact

$$\begin{aligned} \pi_{c_n} &= Id(U_v^n) \text{ (by definition)} \\ &= \mathcal{F}((U_v^n)_{/\approx}) \text{(tuples of different length are not comparable)} \\ &= \mathcal{F}(\pi_{v_n}) \end{aligned}$$

Let *Dsubst* be the set of *directed sets* of substitutions, with typical elements $\Theta, \Psi, \ldots$. We define the application of Θ to the tuple $\bar{t}$ by

$$\bar{t}\Theta = \{\bar{u} \mid \exists \vartheta \in \Theta \; [\bar{u} \leq \bar{t}\vartheta]\}$$

Lemma 4.2 (Representation Lemma) *Any element* α *of* U_c *can be represented by a tuple of terms and an ideal of substitutions. More formally*

$$\forall \alpha \in U_c \; \exists \bar{t} \in U_v^* \; \exists \Theta \in Dsubst \; [\alpha = \bar{t}\Theta]$$

Proof See [Gol88].

Definition 4.3 (Continuous Herbrand base) *The continuous Herbrand base B_c is defined as*

$$\{p(\bar{t}\Theta) \mid p \in Pred_n \ \wedge \ \bar{t}\Theta \in \pi_{c_n}\}$$

Because of the representation lemma, every element of B_c can be represented as $A\Theta$, where A is an appropriate atom and Θ is an appropriate directed set of substitutions.

Lemma 4.4 *Let d_H be the Hausdorff distance on B_c, based on the distance d between atoms defined in section 4.2. Then (B_c, d_H) is a complete metric space.*

The operator *Up* of section 2.3 is extended to the subsets I_c of B_c as follows:

$$Up_c(I_c) = \{\alpha \mid \exists \alpha' \in I_c\ [\alpha' \subseteq \alpha]\}$$

Definition 4.5 *The distance d_c on the subsets of B_c is defined as the Hausdorff distance based on the metric space (B_c, d_H).*

Definition 4.6 (Complete Herbrand interpretations) *A complete Herbrand interpretation I_c is any upward closed (i.e. $I_c = Up_c(I_c)$) and complete*[3] *(w.r.t. the distance d_c of definition 4.5) subset of B_c. We will denote by $\mathcal{I}_c$ the set of complete Herbrand interpretations.*

It is possible to prove that the set $\mathcal{I}_c$, ordered by set inclusion, is a complete lattice. The greatest lower bound (*glb*) is given by the set intersection $\cap$ and the least upper bound (*lub*) is given by the metric closure of the set union, i.e. for every set of interpretations $\mathcal{L}$, $lub(\mathcal{L}) = Cl(\bigcup_{I_c \in \mathcal{L}} I_c)$. The function $Cl : \mathcal{I}_c \rightarrow \mathcal{I}_c$ adds to an interpretation all the limits of the Cauchy sequences. Moreover, according to the results reported in section 4.2, $(\mathcal{I}_c, d_c)$ is a complete metric space.

There is a "natural" correspondence Ω between $\mathcal{I}_v$ and $\mathcal{I}_c$, that amounts to perform the completion. This correspondence is defined as:

$$\Omega(I_v) = Cl(\{Down(A) \mid A \in I_v\})$$

Notice that it is immediate to see that Ω is a poset omomorphism, i.e., it preserves the set inclusion ordering. Namely

$$I_v \subseteq I'_v \Rightarrow \Omega(I_v) \subseteq \Omega(I'_v)$$

[3] the completeness is the main difference with the approach of Golson [Gol88], and the reason why the transformation we define in section 5 has the property of a transformation associated to a canonical program, without the need of any additional restriction on the programs.

The lattice of (upward closed) interpretations with variables, however, is not a sublattice of $(\mathcal{I}_c, \subseteq)$. In fact, the natural correspondence Ω does not preserve the *glb* operation. This is the point in which we gain in expressivity: the *glb* of a descending chain in $(\mathcal{I}_c, \subseteq)$ contains here more information than the corresponding chain of standard interpretations.

Example 4.7 *Let $\{I_{v_i}\}_{i\geq 0}$ be the descending chain of interpretations with variables defined by $I_{v_i} = Up(\{p(f^j(x)) \mid j \geq i\}) = \{p(f^j(t)) \mid t \in U_c, j \geq i\}$. We have*

$$\Omega(I_{v_i}) = Cl(\{p(x)\Theta_{t,j} \mid t \in U_c, j \geq i\}),$$

where

$$\Theta_{t,j} = \{\varepsilon, \{x/f(x)\}, \ldots, \{x/f^j(t)\}\},$$

Note now that all Chauchy sequences in this set have as limit $p(x)\Theta$, with

$$\Theta = \{\varepsilon, \{x/f(x)\}, \ldots, \{x/f^j(x)\}, \ldots\}.$$

Therefore

$$\Omega(I_{v_i}) = \{p(x)\Theta_{t,j} \mid t \in U_c, j \geq i\} \cup \{p(x)\Theta\}$$

Hence

$$\bigcap_{i\geq 0} \Omega(I_{v_i}) = \{p(x)\Theta\},$$

whilst

$$\bigcap_{i\geq 0} I_{v_i} = \emptyset.$$

In this case, Golson [Gol88] finds the same result, since it would be sufficient to consider the upward closure to get the limit element. In fact:

$$p(x)\Theta \in Up_c(\{p(x)\Theta_{x,j}\}),$$

However, we can show a similar example in which our approach differs from the Golson's one:

Example 4.8 *Let $\{I_{v_i}\}_{i\geq 0}$ be the descending chain of interpretations with variables defined by $I_{v_i} = \{p(f^j(a)) \mid j \geq i\}$. We have*

$$\Omega(I_{v_i}) = Cl(\{p(x)\Theta_j\}),$$

where

$$\Theta_j = \{\varepsilon, \{x/f(x)\}, \ldots, \{x/f^j(a)\}\},$$

All Cauchy sequences converge to the limit $p(x)\Theta$, with Θ defined as in example 4.7. Hence

$$\Omega(I_{v_i}) = \{p(x)\Theta_j \mid j \geq i\} \cup \{p(x)\Theta\}$$

and

$$\bigcap_{i\geq 0} \Omega(I_{v_i}) = \{p(x)\Theta\},$$

In [Gol88] the metric limit is not required, and

$$p(x)\Theta \notin Up_c(\{p(x)\Theta_j\})$$

Hence the corresponding sequence would be $I'_i = \{p(x)\Theta_j \mid j \geq i\}$ so obtaining

$$\bigcap_{i\geq 0} I'_i = \emptyset,$$

Note that the objects I'_i's are not allowed as interpretations in our definition, since they are not complete.

Intuitively, the metric structure allows to add the limit of the sequence $\{p(f^i(a))\}_{i\geq 0}$, in the same way as in the case $\{p(f^i(x))\}_{i\geq 0}$, since these sequences are equivalent (in the metric sense).

However, our approach has still more discrimination power than in the pure metric approaches. This is shown in the following example.

Example 4.9 *Consider the sequences*

$$\{p(f^i(x), f^i(x))\}_{i\geq 0}$$

and

$$\{p(f^{i+1}(x), f^i(x))\}_{i\geq 0}.$$

These sequences are equivalent in the metric (B_v, d) *and their limit is* $p(f^\omega, f^\omega)$.

Consider now the corresponding sequences

$$\{I_i\}_{i\geq 0} = \{Down(p(f^i(x), f^i(x)))\}_{i\geq 0}$$

and

$$\{I'_i\}_{i\geq 0} = \{Down(p(f^{i+1}(x), f^i(x)))\}_{i\geq 0}$$

in (B_c, d_H). *They are not equivalent, in fact*

$$\forall i\, [p(x,x) \in I_i \setminus I'_i]$$

and

$$\forall i\, [p(f(x), x) \in I'_i \setminus I_i]$$

therefore

$$\forall i\, [d_H(I_i, I'_i) = \frac{1}{2}]$$

5 Fixpoint characterization of non-ground success set and non-ground finite failure set.

This section presents the fixpoint characterization of *NGSS* and *NGFF*. We will give only a survey of the results that would need quite lengthy and complicate proofs.

We extend the immediate consequence operator on $\mathcal{I}_c$ as follows

$$T_c(I_c) = \{H\Theta \mid \exists H \leftarrow \bar{B} \in W \\ \bar{B}\Theta \in I_c\}$$

The following results present the most important characteristics of this transformation.

Proposition 5.1 *T_c is continuous with respect to the metric d_c.*

Proposition 5.2

1. *For each chain $\{I_{c_i}\}_{i\geq 0}$ that is a Cauchy sequence, $lub_{i\geq 0} I_{c_i} = lim_{i\to\infty} I_{c_i}$ holds.*
2. *For each descending chain $\{I_{c_i}\}_{i\geq 0}$ that is a Cauchy sequence, $glb_{i\geq 0} I_{c_i} = lim_{i\to\infty} I_{c_i}$ holds.*

Lemma 5.3

1. *$\{T_c\uparrow n\}_{n\geq 0}$ is a Cauchy sequence.*
2. *$\{T_c\downarrow n\}_{n\geq 0}$ is a Cauchy sequence.*

Corollary 5.4

1. *$lfp(T_c) = T_c\uparrow\omega$*
2. *$gfp(T_c) = T_c\downarrow\omega$*

The following result shows that T_c extends T_v.

Proposition 5.5 *For every n,*

1. *$T_c\uparrow n = \Omega(T_v\uparrow n)$,*
2. *$T_c\downarrow n = \Omega(T_v\downarrow n)$.*

The following definition allows to obtain corresponding usual interpretations from the continuous ones.

Definition 5.6 *The function $\mho : \mathcal{I}_c \to \mathcal{I}_v$ is defined as*

$$\mho(I_c) = \bigcup_{\alpha \in I_c} \alpha$$

Lemma 5.7 *For every n,*

1. $Down(T_v \uparrow n) = \mho(T_c \uparrow n)$,
2. $Down(T_v \downarrow n) = \mho(T_c \downarrow n)$.

We state, finally, the main results that relate this new construction to *NGSS* and *NGFF*.

Proposition 5.8

1. $\bigcup_{n \geq 0} Down(T_v \uparrow n) = \mho(lub_{n \geq 0} T_c \uparrow n)$
2. $\bigcap_{n \geq 0} Down(T_v \downarrow n) = \mho(glb_{n \geq 0} T_v \downarrow n)$

Theorem 5.9 $NGSS = \mho(lfp(T_c))$.

Proof

$$\begin{array}{rcl} NGSS & = & Down(lfp(T_v)) \text{ (by theorem 3.1)} \\ & = & \bigcup_{n \geq 0} Down(T_v \uparrow n) \text{ (by corollary 3.3)} \\ & = & \mho(\overline{lub}_{n \geq 0} T_c \uparrow n) \text{ (by proposition 5.8 (part 1))} \\ & = & \mho(lfp(T_c)) \text{ (by corollary 5.4 (part 1))} \end{array}$$

□

Theorem 5.10 $NGFF = B_v \setminus \mho(gfp(T_c))$

Proof

$$\begin{array}{rcl} NGFF & = & B_v \setminus \bigcup_{n \geq 0} Down(T_v \downarrow n) \text{ (by corollary 3.12)} \\ & = & B_v \setminus \mho(\overline{lub}_{n \geq 0} T_c \downarrow n) \text{ (by proposition 5.8 (part 2))} \\ & = & B_v \setminus \mho(gfp(T_c)) \text{ (by corollary 5.4 (part 2))} \end{array}$$

□

6 Conclusions.

In this paper we have studied various properties of the non-ground finitely failed atoms and we have proved that *NGFF* is the complement of the greatest fixpoint of the immediate consequence operator extended to complete Herbrand interpretations.

This is the first step tewards an extension to general goals and programs of the approach presented in [FLMP89b].

References

[Abd84] M.A. Nait Abdallah. On the interpretation of infinite computations in logic programming. In J. Paredaens, editor, *Automata, Languages and Programming, LNCS*, 172, Springer Verlag, 1984.

[Apt88] K.R. Apt. Introduction to logic programming (revised and extended version). Techn. Report CS-R8826, Centre for Mathematics and Computer Science, Amsterdam, 1988.

[AvE82] K.R. Apt and M.H. van Emden. Contributions to the theory of logic programming. *JACM*, 29(3):841–862, 1982.

[BlB90] H.A. Blair and A.L. Brown. Definite clause programs *are* canonical (over a suitable domain). To appear on *Annals of Mathematics and Artificial Intelligence.*

[Cla79] K.L. Clark. Predicate logic as a computational formalism. Res. Report DOC 79/59, Imperial College, Dept. of Computing, London, 1979.

[FLMP89a] M. Falaschi, G. Levi, M. Martelli, and C. Palamidessi. Declarative modeling of the operational behaviour of logic languages. *Theoretical Computer Science*, 69(3):289–318, 1989.

[FLMP89b] M. Falaschi, G. Levi, M. Martelli, and C. Palamidessi. A model-theoretic reconstruction of the operational semantics of logic programs. Techn. Report TR-32/89, Dip. di Informatica, Univ. of Pisa, 1989.

[Gol88] W.G. Golson. Toward a declarative semantics for infinite objects in logic programming. *Journal of Logic Programming*, 5:151–164, 1988.

[JLM86] J. Jaffar, J.-L. Lassez and M. Maher. Some issues and trends in the semantics of logic programming. *Proc. Third Int. Conf. on Logic Programming, LNCS*, 225:223-241, Springer Verlag, 1986.

[JaS86] J. Jaffar and P.J. Stuckey. Canonical logic programs. *Journal of Logic Programming*, 3:143–155, 1986.

[Llo87] J.W. Lloyd. *Foundations of Logic Programming.* Springer Verlag, 1987. Second edition.

Algebraic Properties of a Class of Logic Programs

Paolo Mancarella, Dino Pedreschi[§], Marina Rondinelli, and Marco Tagliatti
Dipartimento di Informatica
Università di Pisa
Corso Italia, 40
I-56100 Pisa, Italy
{paolo, pedre}@dipisa.di.unipi.it

Abstract

Three operators for manipulating definite logic programs were introduced in [18], which relate to set-theoretic union, intersection and complementation. In the present paper, these operators and their properties are extended to deal with a broader class of programs, which allows an arbitrary use of negation in clause bodies, still prohibiting the introduction of local variables. The paper presents the natural declarative meaning of the three operators, together with their properties which qualify the class of programs as a constructive boolean algebra. From the operational side, two alternative query evaluation procedures are shown equivalent for computing with programs in the class: SLDNF-resolution, and ordinary SLD-resolution augmented with intensional negation (which is one of the approaches to constructive negation). As a byproduct, a novel completeness result for SLDNF is established. The practical impact of the achieved results is sketched.

1 Introduction

This paper is aimed at studying the properties of a class of logic programs. This class is rather restrictive in a sense, since each clause A:-B in a program of the class is constrained to use in its body B only variables occurring in its head A. In another sense, such a class is rather liberal, since it allows an arbitrary use of the negation connective "¬" in clause bodies. Programs in this class are called *non variable introducing* (nvi) in [7]. From the expressiveness viewpoint, the class is not trivial: first, even without negation, the programs in this class are enough to emulate any (variable-introducing) logic program [18], and hence to compute any

---

§ Work performed while this author was with the Department of Computer Sciences, University of Texas at Austin, Austin, Texas 78712-1188. D. Pedreschi also acknowledges support from C.N.R. — Italian National Research Council.

computable function. Second, programs with negation find useful applications in common-sense and non-monotonic reasoning [6]. From a theoretical viewpoint, the class is interesting at least for the following considerations.

First, three natural operators over programs can be defined, which correspond to the union (*lub*), intersection (*glb*) and complementation operators in a boolean algebra; these operators provide mechanisms for composing programs together, and possess a natural declarative interpretation. The programs which such operators act upon may be viewed in two different ways: i) as programs where the connective "¬" is adopted, or ii) as pairs of *definite* programs, where the connective "¬" has been removed. More precisely, a program P (in case ii) is identified with a pair of definite programs $<P^+, P^->$, termed the positive and negative component of P (resp.), defining predicates p and $\tilde{p}$ which explicitly represent the positive and negative information of predicate p in P. The technique for transforming P into $<P^+, P^->$ is called *intensional negation* in [3, 4, 17]. Under this assumption, a semantics may be envisaged for a program P by considering the *immediate consequences operator* $T_{<P^+, P^->}$ associated to the corresponding pair $<P^+, P^->$ [1]. This semantics allows to characterize the program algebra, equipped with the three operators, as a constructive version of a boolean algebra.

The second motivation is that two equivalent, alternative operational semantics are available to evaluate the programs in the class, in correspondence to the two different possibilities of looking at a program as either P or $<P^+, P^->$. One is SLDNF-resolution performed on P, i.e. SLD-resolution augmented with the negation-as-failure rule [2, 9, 15, 20]. The other one is just SLD-resolution *without* negation-as-failure, performed on $<P^+, P^->$. The two approaches turn out to be equivalent (i.e. they allows to compute the same information), thus justifying the identification of P and $<P^+, P^->$. Moreover, they are sound and complete with respect to a suitable declarative meaning associated to the program, based on 3-valued logic. As a byproduct, a completeness result for SLDNF-resolution is established with reference to a new class of programs.

The present paper represents the current farest point where the ideas underlying the algebra of logic programs and intensional negation have been pushed. [3,4,17] showed how intensional negation can be applied to all *definite* programs, while [18,19] showed how an algebraic structure can be devised for non-variable-introducing, *definite* programs. The present paper improves on all of them in that it shows how intensional negation extends to some *non-definite* programs, and how the algebraic structure extends to non-variable-introducing, *non-definite* programs. With [18, 19], this paper shares the aim of individuating a compositional, homomorphic semantics for logic programming, which enables to assign the meaning to a complex program P as a function of the meaning of the subcomponents of P. In the authors' opinion, such a program algebra is an important tool for addressing modularity and meta-level issues. In fact, it provided the foundations for the *Logical ML* project, aimed at developing a functional language which acts as a meta-level environment for logic programming in-the-large [5, 8, 16, 19].

The paper is organized as follows. Sec. 2 introduces the union, intersection and complementation operators, while Sec. 3 discusses their declarative meaning with respect to the completed version of the program. Sec. 4 explains how a program can be represented by a pair of definite programs expressing the positive and negative information of the original one. With reference to these two alternative representations of programs, Sec. 5 introduces two query evaluation procedures and discusses how they relate each other; Sec. 6 discusses completeness of the query evaluation procedures. Sec. 7 presents the algebraic properties of the operators, under the assumption that a program is identified with its *immediate consequence* operator. Finally, Sec. 8 concludes the paper discussing some practical impacts of the ideas presented in the paper.

2 Operators over logic programs

A *program clause* is of the form A :- $B_1,\ldots,B_k$, $k\geq 0$, where A is an atom (i.e. a positive literal) and $B_1,\ldots,B_k$ is a conjunction of (positive or negative) literals; the clause is said to be *definite* if $B_1,\ldots,B_k$ are all positive literals. Variables occurring in the body but not in the head of a clause are named *local variables*. Throughout this paper, we use the term (logic) *program* referring to a collection of clauses *without local variables*; moreover, if all the clauses are definite, the program is referred to as *definite program*. We will use P, Q, possibly with subscripts, to range over programs. An ordinary *Horn definite program* is then a collection of definite clauses, possibly *with* local variables.

The class of logic programs can be equipped with three operators which enjoy standard algebraic properties and qualify it as a kind of boolean algebra. These operators are termed *juxtaposition* (or union), *junction* (or intersection) and *negation* and they are denoted $\cup$, $\cap$ and Not (for the first two, we chose to overload the set-theoretic counterpart). These operators are indeed a straightforward extension of those introduced in [18, 19] for the class of definite programs. The $\cup$ and $\cap$ operators are defined as follows.

Definition 1
Given two programs P and Q:
a) (P $\cup$ Q) is the program obtained as the union of the clauses of P and Q.
b) (P $\cap$ Q) is the program obtained as follows:

if H :- $A_1,\ldots,A_n$ is a clause of P
and H' :- $B_1,\ldots,B_k$ is a clause of Q
and there exists θ=mgu(H,H')
then (H :- $A_1,\ldots,A_n,B_1,\ldots,B_k)\theta$ is a clause of (P $\cap$ Q).

$\cup$ and $\cap$ are two means for combining logic programs together: The former has the simple effect of taking the set-theoretic union the clauses of the argument programs, while the latter is the dual operator, which performs a sort of intersection of the argument programs. Some simple examples:

- (p(x,a):-¬q(x)) $\cap$ (p(b,y):-r(y)) = (p(b,a):-¬q(b),r(a))
- (p(a):-q(b)) $\cap$ (p(b)) = $\emptyset$
- ((p(a):-q(b)) $\cup$ p(b)) $\cap$ (p(a):-¬q(c)) = (p(a):-q(b),¬q(c)).

Of course, every program can be viewed as the *juxtaposition* of its clauses. Given the set of programs S = $\{P_1,\ldots,P_n\}$, the shorthands $\bigcup S$ and $\bigcap S$ will be used for $P_1 \cup \ldots \cup P_n$ and $P_1 \cap \ldots \cap P_n$.

Before defining the negation operator, a further remark is due. For technical reasons which will be explained shortly, a slight complication must be tackled, namely that only *left-linear* programs will be taken into account, that is programs such that each clause head does not contain multiple occurrences of the same variable. Following the terminology in [14] an atom satisfying the above property is said to be *unrestricted*. It is worth noting that each program can be easily transformed into a left-linear form, provided that an equality predicate eq is given, the definition of which contains the single, non left-linear clause eq(x,x). For example the clause p(x,f(x)) :- B can be transformed into p(x,f(y)) :- eq(x,y), B. Hereafter the term *program* will identify a set of *left-linear* clauses, possibly augmented with the only non left-linear clause eq(x,x) defining equality. These considerations are summarized in the following

Definition 2

Given a first order language L=<Π (set of predicate names),Σ (set of function names)>, with the binary predicate symbol eq$\in\Pi$, the class of logic programs over L is inductively defined as follows:

i) 0 is a program (the empty program);

ii) EQ: eq(x,x) is a program;

iii) p(t) :- $B_1,\ldots,B_k$, $k\geq 0$, is a program, where p is a symbol in Π different from eq, p(t) is an unrestricted atom, and $B_1,\ldots,B_k$ is a conjunction of literals in L.

iv) P $\cup$ Q is a program, if P and Q are.

The motivation for considering only left-linear programs is that the transformation technique presented in [3, 4 , 17], upon which the negation operator is defined, is based on the notion of *term complementation*. This notion makes sense only if *unrestricted* (tuples of) terms are taken into account. In this context, referring to the underlying signature Σ, it is easy to define a function *neg* which, given an unrestricted term t, computes a *finite* set $\{t_1,\ldots,t_n\}$ of unrestricted terms such that *ground*(t) = HU \ $\bigcup_{i=1,\ldots,n}$ *ground*(t_i), that is $t_1,\ldots,t_n$ represent the whole (set-theoretic) complement of *ground*(t) [4, 19][1]. More precisely, the terms in *neg*(t) are the most general terms which do not unify with t itself. A similar technique is used in [11]. When needed, we will denote by *ground*(*neg*(t)) the set HU*ground*(t). What follows is a definition of *neg* referring to the underlying signature Σ:

$neg(x) = \{\}$, if x is a variable term

$neg(f(t_1,\ldots,t_n)) = \{ g(x_1,\ldots,x_k) \mid g \text{ in } \Sigma, g \neq f\} \cup$
$\{ f(x_1,\ldots,x_{i-1},t',x_{i+1},\ldots,x_n) \mid i \in [1,n], t' \in neg(t_i) \}$,
if f is an n–adic constructor in Σ.

Obviously, the second rule collapses into

$$neg(f) = \{g(x_1,\ldots,x_n) \mid g \text{ in } \Sigma, g \neq f\}$$

if f is a constant symbol. Moreover the variables introduced by *neg* are distinct each other, that is if $neg(t) = \{t_1,\ldots,t_k\}$ then $<t_1,\ldots,t_k>$ is an unrestricted tuple. As pointed out in [14], it is not possible to represent the complement of a restricted term, like f(x,x), by means of a finite set of other terms: this is the motivation underlying the restriction to left-linear programs, which compels us to an ad-hoc treatment of equality in the algebra of programs.

We are now in the position of defining the negation operator Not, referring to the various ways programs are constructed as in Def.2.

Definition 3

i) $Not(0) = \cup \{p(x) \mid p \in \Pi\} = 1$

ii) $Not(p(t) :- B_1,\ldots,B_k) =$

$$\bigcup \{p(t_j) \mid t_j \in neg(t)\} \cup$$
$$\bigcup \{p(t) :- B_i \mid i \in 1,\ldots,k \} \cup$$
$$\bigcup \{q(x) \mid q \neq p, q \in \Pi \}$$

iii) $Not(P \cup Q) = Not(P) \cap Not(Q)$

iv) $Not(EQ) =$

$$\bigcup \{eq(f(x), g(y)) \mid f,g \in \Sigma, f \neq g \} \cup$$
$$\bigcup \{eq(f(x_1,\ldots,x_n),f(y_1,\ldots,y_n)) :- eq(x_i, y_i) \mid f \in \Sigma, i = 1,\ldots,n \}$$

v) $Not(Not(EQ)) = EQ$.

Informally, Not(P) is intended to represent explicitly the negative information of P, in the sense that, for each predicate name p, p in Not(P) *is the same as* ¬p in P, and vice versa. This will be made precise in the next section, where the declarative meaning of the operators ∪, ∩ and Not will be

[1] HU and HB denote the Herbrand universe and the Herbrand base (resp.), wrt to the underlying f.o.l. $L=<\Pi,\Sigma>$.

characterized with respect to the notion of completed program.

As an example, consider the program P defining the even natural numbers, represented as usual by the constant 0 and the unary constructor s:

$$P = (\ p(0).\ \cup\ \ p(s(x)) :- \neg p(x)\ )$$

By the Def. 3, Not(P) is obtained as follows:

$$\text{Not}\ (p(0)) \cap \text{Not}\ (p(s(x)) :- \neg p(x))$$

$$= p(s(x)) \cap (p(0) \cup p(s(x)) :- \neg p(x))$$

$$= p(s(x)) :- \neg p(x)$$

In [3, 4, 19] the negation technique is defined for the whole class of definite Horn programs (possibly *with* local variables), but the transformed programs in general are *not* Horn programs. This is due to the fact that the negation of a clause containing local variables is not a Horn clause any longer. On the contrary, this problem does not arise if, as in the present case, only programs without local variables are considered, since this class of programs is *closed* wrt the Not operator.

3 Declarative meaning of the $\cup$, $\cap$ and Not operators

A logical interpretation to the $\cup$, $\cap$ and Not operators may be assigned with reference to the *completed version* comp(P) (or *completion*) of a program P. comp(P) is a simple transformation of a program P, intuitively aimed at expressing the fact that P includes *all and only* the knowledge about the problem at hand. Originally introduced in [9] and later used in [12] for explaining the adoption of the *negation-as-failure* rule, comp(P) consists in replacing the various clauses for each predicate p in P with a single axiom of the kind ($p \leftrightarrow \Psi$). This is accomplished as follows. First, an equality theory corresponding to unification is introduced, i.e. a theory EQ such that i) EQ $\vdash \exists(t=u)$ iff t and u are unifiable, and ii) EQ $\vdash \forall(t\neq u)$ iff t and u are not unifiable. Second, each clause $p(t_1,\ldots,t_n)$:- Body is transformed into its *normalized version*, using the equality symbol defined in EQ:

$$p(x_1,\ldots,x_n) :- \exists y_1,\ldots,y_h\ (x_1=t_1,\ldots,x_n=t_n,\text{Body})$$

where $y_1,\ldots,y_h$ are the variable occurring in $t_1,\ldots,t_n$, and $x_1,\ldots,x_n$ are fresh variables. If there are $m\geq0$ clauses for predicate p in the program, then the *completed definition* of p is:

$$\forall x_1,\ldots,x_n\ (\ p(x_1,\ldots,x_n) \leftrightarrow \psi_1 \vee \ldots \vee \psi_m)$$

where each $p(x_1,\ldots,x_n)$:- ψ_i is the normalization of a clause for p. In the special case m=0, the completed definition of p collapses to $\forall x_1,\ldots,x_n$ ($\neg p(x_1,\ldots,x_n)$). Finally, comp(P) is defined to be the set of axioms EQ together with the completed definitions of all predicate symbols.

The following results relate $\cup$, $\cap$ and Not with disjunction, conjunction and negation (resp.) in the completed version of a program.

Proposition 1
Let $\forall x_1,\ldots,x_n\ (p(x_1,\ldots,x_n) \leftrightarrow \Psi)$ be the completed definition of predicate p in comp(P), and $\forall x_1,\ldots,x_n\ (p(x_1,\ldots,x_n) \leftrightarrow \Phi)$ be the completed definition of predicate p in comp(Q);

then

i. $\forall x_1,\ldots,x_n(p(x_1,\ldots,x_n) \leftrightarrow \Lambda)$ is the completed definition of p in comp($P \cup Q$),

and $\Lambda \leftrightarrow (\Psi \vee \Phi)$;

ii. $\forall x_1,\ldots,x_n(p(x_1,\ldots,x_n) \leftrightarrow \Lambda)$ is the completed definition of p in comp($P \cap Q$),

and $\Lambda \leftrightarrow (\Psi \wedge \Phi)$.

Proposition 2

Let A be a ground atom in HB. Then

i) comp(P) $\models$ A *iff* comp(Not(P)) $\models \neg$A

ii) comp(P) $\models \neg$A *iff* comp(Not(P)) $\models$ A.

4 Programs as pairs of (definite) programs

Let us now introduce an alternative way of defining the complement of a program, which is based on the idea of looking at negation as a particular kind of ordinary, positive information. The aim is to view a negative literal $\neg p(t)$ as a positive one, involving the new predicate symbol "$\neg p$": to avoid confusion, such a new symbol will be written $\tilde{p}$. To this extent, the underlying f.o.l. $L=\langle\Pi,\Sigma\rangle$ must be extended to $L'=\langle\Pi\cup\tilde{\Pi},\Sigma\rangle$ where $\tilde{\Pi}=\{\tilde{p}\}_{p\in\Pi}$. By an abuse of language, atoms involving a predicate symbol in Π will be referred to as *positive literals*, whereas atoms involving a predicate symbol in $\tilde{\Pi}$ will be referred to as *negative literals*. Moreover, definite programs whose clause heads are positive (resp. negative) literals will be referred to as *positive* (resp. *negative*) *programs*. Also, we need to distinguish between 0, the empty *positive* program, and 1, the empty *negative* program. We will use M, N to range over positive and negative programs, P^+, Q^+ to range over positive programs, and P^-, Q^- to range over negative programs. A *complementation* operator is defined over positive (resp. negative) programs, yielding a negative (resp. positive) program which explicitly expresses the complementary knowledge implicitly embodied in the original program. Given a (positive or negative) program M, its complement is denoted by $\overline{M}$ and it is defined inductively, rephrasing Def. 3.

Definition 4

Let M be a (positive or negative) program over $L'=<\Pi\cup\tilde{\Pi},\Sigma>$. Then $\overline{M}$ is defined by induction on the structure of M as follows.

i) $\overline{0} = \bigcup\{\tilde{p}(x) \mid \tilde{p}\in\tilde{\Pi}\}$

$\overline{1} = \bigcup\{p(x) \mid p\in\Pi\}$

ii) $\overline{(p(t) :\text{-}\ B_1,\dots,B_k)} =$

$\bigcup\{\tilde{p}(t_j) \mid t_j \in \mathit{neg}(t)\} \cup$

$\bigcup\{\tilde{p}(t) :- \tilde{B}_i \mid i\in 1,\dots,k\} \cup$

$\bigcup\{\tilde{q}(x) \mid \tilde{q}\neq\tilde{p},\ \tilde{q}\in\tilde{\Pi}\}$

$\overline{(\tilde{p}(t) :\text{-}\ B_1,\dots,B_k)} =$

$\bigcup\{p(t_j) \mid t_j \in \mathit{neg}(t)\} \cup$

$\bigcup\{p(t) :- \tilde{B}_i \mid i\in 1,\dots,k\} \cup$

$\bigcup\{q(x) \mid q\neq p,\ q\in\Pi\}$

$$\text{where } \tilde{B}_i = \begin{cases} q(s) & \text{if } B_i = \tilde{q}(s) \\ \tilde{q}(s) & \text{if } B_i = q(s) \end{cases}$$

iii) $\overline{M_1 \cup M_2} = \overline{M_1} \cap \overline{M_2}$

iv) $\overline{EQ} =$

$\bigcup\{\widetilde{eq}(f(x), g(y)) \mid f,g\in\Sigma,\ f\neq g\} \cup$

$\bigcup\{\widetilde{eq}(f(x_1,\dots,x_n),f(y_1,\dots,y_n)) :- \widetilde{eq}(x_i, y_i) \mid f\in\Sigma,\ i=1,\dots,n\}$

v) $\overline{\overline{EQ}} = EQ.$

The idea now is to transform a program P over the language $L=<\Pi,\Sigma>$ into a pair $<P^+,P^->$ of definite programs over the extended language $L'=<\Pi\cup\tilde{\Pi},\Sigma>$ such that P^+ is the positive program which represents the positive information of by P, whereas P^- is the negative program which makes the negative information of P explicit. This is achieved by the following

Definition 5

Let P be a program. Then

a) P^+ is obtained from P replacing each negative literal $\neg q(t)$ by $\tilde{q}(t)$;

b) $P^- = \overline{P^+}$.

Referring back to Def. 2, it is worth noting that an atom of the kind $\tilde{p}(t)$ in P^+ corresponds to $\neg p(t)$ in P, while $\tilde{p}(t)$ in P^- corresponds to p(t) in Not(P). Analogously, an atom of the kind p(t) in P^+ corresponds to p(t) in P, while p(t) in P^- corresponds to $\neg p(t)$ in Not(P). Applying the transformation on program P of the previous even/odd example, we obtain:

P^+: p(0) $\qquad\qquad$ P^-: $\tilde{p}(s(x))$:- p(x)

$\quad$ p(s(x)) :- $\tilde{p}(x)$

In the next Sections 5 and 6, arguments will be provided which allow us to consistently view a program P as the corresponding pair <P^+, P^->. Actually, it will turn out that P and <P^+, P^-> are equivalent both in a declarative and in a computational sense. This will substantiate the claim that P^+ embodies the positive information and P^- embodies the negative information about the original predicates of P.

5 Negation-as-failure and intensional negation

SLDNF, i.e. SLD-resolution augmented with the negation-as-finite-failure rule to deal with negative subgoals, is the best known query evaluation procedure for logic programs with negation [1, 9, 15]. In a derivation, SLDNF is constrained to select a negative literal only if this is fully instantiated. If a goal is only made of negative non-ground literals, then SLDNF fails to proceed further: this is known as the floundering problem. In our programs, the absence of local variables is sufficient to ensure that the evaluation of a ground initial goal will never flounder, since no uninstantiated variables will be introduced. Let $SS_{SLDNF}(P)$ (resp. $FF_{SLDNF}(P)$) the set of ground atoms succeeding (resp. finitely failing) using SLDNF-resolution wrt program P. It is well known that SLDNF is sound and complete wrt to comp(P) in the case of definite programs, i.e.:

comp(P) $\models$ q(u) *iff* $q(u) \in SS_{SLDNF}(P)$

comp(P) $\models$ $\neg$q(u) *iff* $q(u) \in FF_{SLDNF}(P)$

but this is not true in general. For instance, consider P = (p :- q) $\cup$ (p:-$\neg$q) $\cup$ (q:-q). Then comp(P) $\models$ p, but any SLDNF-evaluation of the goal p diverges. Thus, in the general case, only the if part of the above statement holds. Nevertheless, the following proposition establishes a complete duality between SLDNF-success wrt to a program P and SLDNF-failure wrt to the complementary program Not(P).

Proposition 3

For every ground atom A :

i) $A \in SS_{SLDNF}(P)$ *iff* $A \in FF_{SLDNF}(Not(P))$

ii) $A \in FF_{SLDNF}(P)$ *iff* $A \in SS_{SLDNF}(Not(P))$.

Prop. 3 suggests an alternative query evaluation process: if a negative subgoal $\neg q(u)$ is selected in a derivation, the corresponding query $q(u)$ on Not(P) can be evaluated instead of using the finite failure of $q(u)$ in P to establish $\neg q(u)$; the converse action will occur when a negative subgoal is selected during a derivation on Not(P).This is the operational intuition underlying Def. 4: predicates p and $\tilde{p}$ in $<P^+, P^->$ make explicit the different rôles of predicate p in P and Not(P). As a consequence, the negation-as-failure rule has been eliminated from the query evaluation procedure, i.e. SLDNF over P has been replaced by ordinary SLD-resolution over $<P^+, P^->$ (or, equivalently, $P^+ \cup P^-$). As an example, considering the even/odd program $P = p(0). \cup p(s(x))$:- $\neg p(x)$, we obtain

$P^+ = p(0). \cup p(s(x))$:- $\tilde{p}(x)$ $\qquad\qquad$ $P^- = \tilde{p}(s(x))$:- $p(x)$

thus $p(s(s(0))) \rightarrow \tilde{p}(s(0)) \rightarrow p(0) \rightarrow true$ is a SLD-refutation over $<P^+, P^->$ corresponding to the following SLDNF-refutation over P: $p(s(s(0))) \rightarrow true$ since $p(s(0))$ fails since $p(0) \rightarrow true$. Indeed, these two query evaluation procedures are equivalent, as established in the following:

Proposition 4

For every ground atom $q(u)$ in HB:

i) $\quad q(u) \in SS_{SLDNF}(P)$ *iff* $q(u) \in SS_{SLD}(P^+ \cup P^-)$

ii) $\quad q(u) \in FF_{SLDNF}(P)$ *iff* $\tilde{q}(u) \in SS_{SLD}(P^+ \cup P^-)$.

Here, $SS_{SLD}(P^+ \cup P^-)$ denotes the ordinary SLD success set of the definite program $P^+ \cup P^-$, which coincides with the minimum model of $P^+ \cup P^-$, as well as with the least fixed point $T_{P+\cup P-}\uparrow\omega$ of its immediate consequences operator $T_{P+\cup P-}$ [1, 15, 21].

SLD-resolution over $P^+ \cup P^-$ was termed *intensional negation* in [3, 4, 17]; it is essentially a way of getting rid of negation-as-failure, by replacing the latter with a constructive procedure, able to infer substitutions for negative goals as well. In the example of even/odd numbers, SLDNF over P can only be adopted to check the validity of ground queries like $p(s(s(0)))$ or $\neg p(s(0))$, while it will flounder on open queries like $p(x)$; on the contrary, SLD over $P^+ \cup P^-$ is able to produce answer substitutions for the queries $p(x)$ or $\tilde{p}(x)$ — the even and the odd numbers, in the example. In general, the well known completeness results for SLD over definite programs enable us to conclude that, if $q(u) \in SS_{SLDNF}(P)$ then the open SLD-query $q(x)$ over $P^+ \cup P^-$ will produce an answer substitution θ such that $q(u)$ is an instance of $q(x)\theta$.

Thus the novel procedure restores symmetry in the treatment of positive and negative information. Nevertheless, the semantic equivalence with SLDNF allows to use either procedure interchangeably, whenever desired or appropriate. Thus, the constructive procedure may be adopted when inference of negative information is crucial, whilst SLDNF may be adopted when the constructive approach is unpractical, e.g. in large database-like programs, where a blind adoption of the complementary program may yield huge P^- components.

The following is the dual of Prop. 4:

Proposition 5

For every ground atom q(u) in HB:

i) $q(u) \in FF_{SLDNF}(P)$ *iff* $q(u) \in FF_{SLD}(P^+ \cup P^-)$

ii) $q(u) \in SS_{SLDNF}(P)$ *iff* $\tilde{q}(u) \in FF_{SLD}(P^+ \cup P^-)$.

So we get the following relation between success and failure set of $P^+ \cup P^-$:

Proposition 6

For every ground atom q(u) in HB:

i) $\tilde{q}(u) \in SS_{SLD}(P^+ \cup P^-)$ *iff* $q(u) \in FF_{SLD}(P^+ \cup P^-)$

ii) $q(u) \in SS_{SLD}(P^+ \cup P^-)$ *iff* $\tilde{q}(u) \in FF_{SLD}(P^+ \cup P^-)$.

6 Three-valued logic and completeness results

A logical, declarative characterization of SLD over $P^+ \cup P^-$, and hence of SLDNF over P, can be devised considering the 3-valued semantics of comp(P). Kleene's 3-valued logic has been applied to logic programming by several authors [10, 13]. In 3-valued (Herbrand) interpretations, an atom A may receive truth value true, false or undefined. Ordinary 2-valued models are also 3-valued ones, and thus 3 valued logical consequences are a subset of 2-valued ones. comp(P) is always consistent wrt 3-valued logic, while this is not the case in 2-valued logic (e.g., consider P = (p :- ¬p)). Relying on the results in [10, 13], it is possible to show that the facts inferred using intensional negation, i.e. SLD over $P^+ \cup P^-$, coincide with the 3-valued logical consequences of comp(P), i.e. that SLD over $P^+ \cup P^-$ (and hence SLDNF over P) is *sound* and *complete* wrt the 3-valued semantics of comp(P). This is expressed in the following:

Proposition 7

For every ground atom q(u) in HB:

ii) $q(u) \in SS_{SLD}(P^+ \cup P^-)$ *iff* $comp(P) \mid=_3 q(u)$.

i) $\tilde{q}(u) \in SS_{SLD}(P^+ \cup P^-)$ *iff* $comp(P) \mid=_3 \neg q(u)$.

Although the proof of the above proposition turns out to be surprisingly simple, it is omitted in the present short version of the paper, since its presentation requires the introduction of the details concerning the application of 3-valued logic to logic programming.

Finally, it is worth noting that Prop. 4 and 7 combined together allow us to establish another completeness result for SLDNF resolution. In fact, Kunen proved recently that 2- and 3- valued semantics coincide in the case of *strict* programs, i.e. programs in which no predicate symbol p depend both positively and negatively from another predicate q. If P is a strict program, we have the following chain of equivalences:

$$\text{comp}(P) \models_2 q(u)$$

iff (Kunen's result)

$$\text{comp}(P) \models_3 q(u)$$

iff (Prop. 7)

$$q(u) \in SS_{SLD}(P^+ \cup P^-)$$

iff (Prop. 5)

$$q(u) \in SS_{SLDNF}(P).$$

Analogously:

$$\text{comp}(P) \models_2 \neg q(u) \textit{ iff}$$

$$\text{comp}(P) \models_3 \neg q(u) \textit{ iff}$$

$$\tilde{q}(u) \in SS_{SLD}(P^+ \cup P^-) \textit{iff}$$

$$q(u) \in FF_{SLDNF}(P).$$

As a consequence, for strict programs and ground queries, SLDNF is sound and complete with respect to the 2-valued semantics of the completed program. Notice that this result is not covered by the current most general completeness theorems for SLDNF, since they require the program and the query being *allowed*, which is not the case here.

7 The program algebra

In [18, 19] the semantics of a definite program P is defined to be its immediate consequences transformation T_P [1]. This approach accounted for the superposition of a rich algebraic structure over the class of definite programs. In the previous sections, we provided declarative and operational arguments supporting the statement that a program P should be actually viewed as the pair of definite programs $<P^+,P^->$. Coherently with this approach, P can be modelled by the transformation $T_{P^+ \cup P^-}$, representing the single deductive step of $<P^+,P^->$. In this way, $T_{P^+ \cup P^-}$ can be consistently understood as the immediate consequences transformation associated to P. Notice that such a transformation is continuous over the lattice of Herbrand interpretations, while this is not the case if it is directly defined in the Apt-vanEmden style, since P uses negation within clause bodies.

Hence, [P], [$<P^+,P^->$], T_P and $T_{P^+ \cup P^-}$ are all legal ways of denoting the same transformation over the Herbrand base of the extended language L'. In the rest of this section we show how this assumption allows to extend the algebraic structure of [18, 19] to our larger class of programs. Hereafter, P=Q will stand for [P]=[Q]; hence $P \cup Q = <(P \cup Q)^+, (P \cup Q)^->$ and $P \cap Q = <(P \cap Q)^+, (P \cap Q)^->$.

Proposition 8

Let P and Q be programs.

a) $(P \cup Q) = <P^+ \cup Q^+, P^- \cap Q^->$

b) $(P \cap Q) = <P^+ \cap Q^+, P^- \cup Q^->$

c) $Not(P) = <P^-, P^+>[p/\tilde{p}, \tilde{p}/p]_{p \in \Pi}$.

The above proposition states that: (a) juxtaposing programs P and Q is the same as taking the union of P^+ and Q^+ while taking the intersection of P^- and Q^-; (b) states a dual property for $\cap$. (c) states that complementing program P is the same as swapping P^+ and P^- and exchanging p with $\tilde{p}$. Prop. 8 suggests an incremental, efficient way of computing the new negative component of a derived program from the negative components of the argument programs, avoiding the recomputation of the negative component from scratch.

The following tables present a collection of rules which point out the algebraic nature of the class of programs with respect to $\cup$, $\cap$ and Not. P, P_1, P_2 and P_3 are programs.

1	$P \cup P = P$
	$P \cap P = P$
2	$P_1 \cup P_2 = P_2 \cup P_1$
	$P_1 \cap P_2 = P_2 \cap P_1$
3	$(P_1 \cup P_2) \cup P_3 = P_1 \cup (P_2 \cup P_3)$
	$(P_1 \cap P_2) \cap P_3 = P_1 \cap (P_2 \cap P_3)$
4	$P_1 \cup (P_2 \cap P_3) = (P_1 \cup P_2) \cap (P_1 \cup P_3)$
	$P_1 \cap (P_2 \cup P_3) = (P_1 \cap P_2) \cup (P_1 \cap P_3)$
5	$Not(Not(P)) = P$
6	$Not(P_1 \cup P_2) = Not(P_1) \cap Not(P_2)$
	$Not(P_1 \cap P_2) = Not(P_1) \cup Not(P_2)$

Moreover, let Id be the following program:

$<\cup\{p(x){:-}\ p(x)\}_{p\in\Pi}, \cup\{\tilde{p}(x) :- \tilde{p}(x)\}_{p\in\Pi}>$.

Recall that programs 0 (the empty positive program) and 1 (the empty negative one) are:

$0 = <\{\},\cup\{\tilde{p}(x)\}_{p\in\Pi}>$ $\qquad$ $1 = <\cup\{p(x)\}_{p\in\Pi}, \{\}>$

7	$0 \cup P = P$		$1 \cup P = 1$
8	$0 \cap P = 0$		$1 \cap P = P$
		9 Id= Not(Id)	
10	Not(0) = 1		Not(1) = 0

As a consequence, logic programs are essentially a boolean algebra, with the only exception of rule 9, which states that Id is a fixed point of Not; indeed, Id is a counterexample for the *excluded middle* rules: P∪Not(P) = 1 and P∩Not(P) = 0, which thus are missing. This highlights the nature of this class of programs as a constructive version of a boolean algebra, since its complementation operator has a distinct computational interpretation.

The next table summarizes the relations between the various operators and the atom inferred in the success set using intensional negation or, by Prop. 4, SLDNF. Here:

$SS^+(P)=\{p(t) \mid p(t)\in SS_{SLD}(P^+\cup P^-)\}$, $SS^-(P)=\{\tilde{p}(t) \mid \tilde{p}(t)\in SS_{SLD}(P^+\cup P^-)\}$, $HB^+=\{p(t) \mid p(t)\in HB\}$ and $HB^-=\{\tilde{p}(t) \mid \tilde{p}(t)\in HB\}$.

11	$SS^+(1)=HB^+$
	$SS^-(1)=\varnothing$
12	$SS^+(0)=\varnothing$
	$SS^-(0)=HB^-$
13	$SS^+(Id)=\varnothing$
	$SS^-(Id)=\varnothing$
14	$SS^+(Not(P)) = SS^-(P)$
	$SS^-(Not(P)) = SS^+(P)$

The following extra rules also hold when positive programs are considered:

15	$SS^+(P_1 \cup P_2) \supseteq SS^+(P_1) \cup SS^+(P_2)$
	$SS^-(P_1) \cap SS^-(P_2) \supseteq SS^-(P_1 \cup P_2)$
16	$SS^+(P_1) \cap SS^+(P_2) \supseteq SS^+(P_1 \cap P_2)$
	$SS^-(P_1 \cap P_2) \supseteq SS^-(P_1) \cup SS^-(P_2)$

8 Concluding remarks

The algebraic properties of the class of non-variable-introducing programs have been presented, along with two alternative, equivalent operational semantics to evaluate such programs. The program-transforming operators of the algebra represent basic means for composing logic programs together, aimed at addressing the modular construction of knowledge-based systems. These operators are indeed the basis on top of which the language *Logical ML* has been designed to serve as a programming environment for logic programming in-the-large [5, 8, 16, 19].

As an example of application of the ideas contained in this paper, consider the situation in which the programmer is interested in defining a predicate p about which some positive knowledge (i.e., cases in which p holds) and some negative knowledge (i.e., cases in which p does not hold) is available. It is then possible to collect the positive knowledge in a program P_1 containing clauses of the kind p(t) :- ..., and the negative knowledge in (the negative component of) a program P_2 containing clauses with negated heads, i.e. clauses of the kind $\tilde{p}(t)$:- ... . Basically, the programmer is free to provide either the positive or the negative component of a program, the system being able to construct the missing component from the available one. In the example, the programmer provides P_1^+ and P_2^-, and it is the system's task to derive the complete definitions $P_1 = \langle P_1^+, P_1^- \rangle$ and $P_2 = \langle P_2^+, P_2^- \rangle$. Finally, intersecting the two programs will accomplish the task of putting the two pieces together in a single theory which summarizes the overall knowledge about predicate p:

$$P = P_1 \cap P_2 = \langle P_1^+ \cap P_2^+, P_1^- \cup P_2^- \rangle.$$

An instance of this way of specifying programs typically occurs in dealing with *defaults* and *exceptions*: consider the standard, oversimplified problem of specifying, with respect to a population of birds, the *normal* definition of the predicate "fly", together with some exceptions to the general law. Let theory B represent the population of birds by means of a collection of facts like bird(sparrow), bird(hawk), bird(ostrich), ..., and define:

D^+ = (fly(x):-bird(x).) $\qquad\qquad$ E^- = (¬fly(ostrich).)

Here, program D expresses the default knowledge, whereas E the exceptional one. Now, the expression:

$$B \cup (D \cap E)$$

has the effect of putting the separate information together in a theory in which only birds that are not an ostrich can fly. This solution, although appealingly simple, has the disadvantage that, due to the intensional negation process as defined in the present paper, the theory E^+ contains a fact fly(b) for each individual bird b which is not an ostrich, and so does $(D \cap E)$. Nevertheless, in the actual implementation of the algebra, the complementation of a term (like "ostrich" in the example) during the intensional negation process is not eagerly performed, but rather inequalities are left unsolved and carried along the evaluation using standard constraint logic programming techniques (see [3]). Thus the system is actually able to produce the following code for $(D \cap E)$:

$$D \cap E \;=\; (\text{ fly(x) :- bird(x), x}{\neq}\text{ostrich. })$$

Theory definitions like $B \cup (D \cap E)$ can be expressed in *Logical ML*, which is essentially a functional language with polymorphic types built on top of the algebra of logic programs. Its prototype is currently being exploited to verify the practical effectiveness of the ideas presented in this paper.

Acknowledgements

The authors are indebted with Krzysztof Apt for many helpful discussions. Thanks are also owed to the other members of the LML project at the University of Pisa: Antonio Brogi, Chiara Meo and Franco Turini.

References

[1] Apt,K.R., van Emden, M.H. "Contribution to the Theory of Logic Programming". *Journal of the ACM*, 29 (3) 841–862, 1982.

[2] Apt,K.R. "Introduction to Logic Programming". To appear in *Handbook of Theoretical Computer Science* (J. van Leeuwen Ed.) North–Holland, 1990.

[3] Barbuti,R., Mancarella,P., Pedreschi,D., Turini,F. "Intensional Negation of Logic Programs: examples and implementation techniques". Proc. TAPSOFT '87, LNCS 250, 96–110, 1987.

[4] Barbuti,R., Mancarella,P., Pedreschi,D., Turini,F. "A Transformational Approach to Negation in Logic Programming". *Journal of Logic Programming* , 8, 201-208, 1990,.

[5] Bertolino, B., Mancarella, P., Meo, L., Nini, L., Pedreschi, D., Turini, F. "A progress report on the LML project". Proc. FGCS'88 Fifth Generation Comp. Sys. Conf., ICOT, 675-684, 1988.

[6] Bezem, M., Apt,K.R. "Acyclic programs". Proc. 7th Int. Conf. on Logic Programming, 617-633, 1990.

[7] Bol, R.N., Apt,K.R., Klop, J.W. "An analysis of loop checking algorithms for logic programs". Tech. rep. TR-89-32, Dept. of Comp. Sci., Univ. of Texas at Austin, 1989.

[8] Brogi, A., Mancarella, P., Pedreschi, D., Turini, F. "Hierarchies through Basic Meta-level Operators". Proc. META90 - 2nd Workshop on Meta-programming in Logic, Leuven, 381-396, 1990.

[9] Clark,K.L. "Negation as Failure". In *Logic and Data Bases* (Gallaire, H. e Minker,J. Eds.) Plenum, New York, 293–322, 1978.

[10] Fitting, M.R. "A Kripke-Kleene semantics for logic programs". *J. Logic Programming,* 2, 295-312, 1985.

[11] Giannotti,F., Matteucci,A., Pedreschi,D., Turini,F. "Symbolic Evaluation with Structural Recursive Symbolic Constants". *Science of Computer Programming* 9, 161–177, 1987.

[12] Jaffar,J., Lassez,J.–L., Lloyd,J.W. "Completeness of the Negation–as–Failure Rule". Proc. IJCAI-8, Karlsruhe, 500–506, 1983.

[13] Kunen, K. "Negation in logic programming". *J. Logic Programming* 4, 289-308, 1987.

[14] Lassez,J.–L., Marriot,K. "Explicit and Implicit Representation of Terms Defined by Counter Examples". *Journal of Automated Reasoning*, 1987.

[15] Lloyd,J.W. *Foundations of Logic Programming*. Springer Symbolic Computation Series, Berlin, 1984.

[16] Mancarella,P., Pedreschi,D., Turini,F. "Functional Metalevel for Logic Programming". In *Metalevel Architectures and Reflection* (P.Maes and D.Nardi, Eds.) North–Holland, 329-344, 1987.

[17] Mancarella,P. "Intensional Negation of Logic Programs". Ph.D. Thesis (in Italian), Dip. di Informatica, Univ. di Pisa, 1988.

[18] Mancarella,P., Pedreschi, D., "An Algebra of Logic Programs". Proc. 5th Int. Conf. and Symp. on Logic Programming, Seattle, 1006-1023, 1988.

[19] Pedreschi,D. "Logic Programming: Compositional Semantics, Algebraic Structures and Program Completions". Ph.D. Thesis (in Italian), Dip. di Informatica, Univ. di Pisa, 1988.

[20] Shepherdson,J.C. "Negation in Logic Programming". In *Foundations of Deductive Databases and Logic Programming* (J.Minker, Ed.) Morgan Kaufmann, Los Altos, 1987.

[21] vanEmden,M.H., Kowalski,R.A. "The Semantics of Predicate Logic as a Programming Language". *Journal of the ACM* 23, 733–742, 1976.

Stationary Semantics for Disjunctive Logic Programs and Deductive Databases

Teodor C. Przymusinski
Department of Mathematical Sciences
The University of Texas at El Paso
teodor%utep.uucp@cs.utexas.edu

Abstract

We extend the *well-founded semantics*, defined originally for normal (non-disjunctive) logic programs, to the class of *all disjunctive* logic programs and deductive databases. The new semantics, which we call the *stationary semantics*, has the following properties:

- It is *constructively* defined for *all disjunctive logic programs* and deductive databases at the same time providing a precise formalization of the *negation as failure* operator used in logic programs.

- For normal (i.e., non-disjunctive) logic programs the stationary semantics coincides with the *well-founded semantics*. It also leads to the notion of a *dynamic stratification* of an arbitrary disjunctive program.

- The stationary semantics also naturally extends the *3-valued stable model semantics*. In fact, it can be equivalently defined by introducing the so called *stationary states*, which are generalizations of 3-valued stable models.

- For *stratified* disjunctive programs, the stationary semantics coincides with the *perfect model semantics*. In particular, for positive disjunctive programs, it is equivalent to the *minimal model semantics*.

- The stationary semantics is the *only* known semantics which is defined for all disjunctive programs and extends both the well-founded semantics of normal programs and the perfect model semantics of stratified disjunctive programs. In particular, the stationary semantics differs from the semantics proposed earlier by K. Ross as well as from the semantics proposed by J.Minker et.al.

- The stationary semantics can be shown to be equivalent to suitable forms of two powerful *non-monotonic formalisms*, namely, autoepistemic logic and default theory.

- The stationary semantics has its *weak* version which uses *inclusive* rather than *exclusive* interpretation of disjunctions. It is also well-defined for programs using the so called *"classical negation"*, in addition to the usual "negation as failure".

1 Introduction

The *well-founded* semantics has been introduced in [Van Gelder *et al.*, 1990] for the class of *all normal* (non-disjunctive) logic programs as an extension of the *perfect model semantics* of (locally) stratified programs [Apt *et al.*, 1988; Van Gelder, 1989b] (see also [Przymusinski, 1988]). The well-founded semantics has many of the features of the perfect model semantics [Przymusinski, 1989a], has several natural, yet equivalent, definitions (see [Van Gelder *et al.*, 1990; Przymusinski, 1989a; Van Gelder, 1989a; Bry, 1989]), is equivalent to *3-valued stable model semantics* [Przymusinski, 1990a; Przymusinski, 1989c] and coincides with natural forms of all major non-monotonic formalisms [Przymusinski, 1989b].

The well-founded semantics also has a realistic, computationally based proof theory. Namely, both the *SLS-resolution* [Przymusinski, 1989a] and D.S. Warren's *ET-algorithm* provide sound and complete procedural mechanisms for the well-founded semantics. Recently, D. S. Warren developed the *Extended Warren Abstract Machine* (XWAM) [Warren, 1989] and an elegant interpreter (in Prolog) for the well-founded semantics (see [Przymusinski and Warren, 1990] for more details).

In summary, the well-founded semantics appears to be the *most suitable semantics for normal* logic programs (see [Przymusinska and Przymusinski, 1990] for an overview), avoiding various drawbacks of *Clark's predicate completion semantics* [Clark, 1978; Lloyd, 1984; Fitting, 1985; Kunen, 1987; Kunen, 1988]. The latter, however, can be viewed as a natural and computationally less expensive *approximation* to the well-founded semantics, in the sense that any answers given by the Fitting-Kunen 3-valued extension of Clark's semantics [Fitting, 1985; Kunen, 1987] (or by SLDNF-resolution) are *correct* with respect to the well-founded semantics (but not vice versa).

For the broader class of *disjunctive* logic programs and deductive databases the situation seemed less clear. For *positive* disjunctive programs, the *minimal model semantics* is the most natural choice. It is determined by the set of all minimal models of the program, corresponds to the Generalized Closed World Assumption (GCWA), due to [Minker, 1982], and extends the *least model semantics* of positive normal programs [Van Emden and Kowalski, 1976]. In [Przymusinski, 1988] the *perfect model semantics* has been extended to *stratified disjunctive* programs. This semantics extends both the perfect model semantics of stratified normal programs and the minimal model semantics of positive disjunctive programs, has those same natural features as its restriction to normal programs [Przymusinski, 1988] and appears to be a suitable semantics for stratified disjunctive programs.

Until now, however, no suitable semantics was known that would be defined for *all* disjunctive programs and extend *both* the well-founded semantics of normal programs and the perfect model semantics of disjunctive logic programs. Indeed, the *3-valued stable model semantics* introduced in [Przymusinski, 1990a] and shown to be an extension of both the perfect model semantics and the well-founded semantics was defined only for a subclass of the class of all disjunctive problems.

In this paper, we introduce the so called *stationary semantics*, which is defined for *all* disjunctive logic programs and extends the well-founded semantics of normal programs, the perfect model semantics of stratified disjunctive programs and the (3-valued) stable model semantics. The stationary semantics constitutes therefore an *extension of all previously discussed semantics* and provides a natural semantics for *all* disjunctive logic programs and deductive databases.

The definition of stationary semantics is given by providing a mathematically precise *formalization of the "negation as failure" operator* used in logic programming and thus, hopefully, establishes a clear semantic foundation for logic programming. The lack of clarity as to the precise meaning of negation as failure has been the single most important obstacle to finding a suitable semantics for logic programs.

As it was the case with the well-founded semantics, the stationary semantics is *equivalent* to natural forms of *non-monotonic formalisms*, namely, autoepistemic logic and default theory. More precisely, after translation of the program P into an autoepistemic (resp. default) theory $\hat{P}$ the stationary semantics of P coincides with the suitable autoepistemic (resp. default) semantics of $\hat{P}$ (see [Przymusinski, 1990b] for details). The stationary semantics also immediately leads to the notion of a *dynamic stratification* of an arbitrary disjunctive program.

The stationary semantics is the *only* known semantics which is defined for all disjunctive programs and extends both the well-founded semantics of normal programs and the perfect model semantics of stratified disjunctive programs. In particular, the stationary semantics is different from the extended well-founded semantics proposed earlier in [Ross, 1989] because Ross' semantics does *not* extend the perfect model semantics (see Example 3.4). The stationary semantics is closely related to the generalized well-founded (GWF) semantics proposed in [Baral *et al.*, 1990; Baral *et al.*, 1989]. However, the two semantics are essentially different, because the GWF-semantics does *not* extend the well-founded semantics, treats clauses of the form $A \leftarrow \neg B$ as somewhat equivalent to disjunctions $A \vee B$ (see [Przymusinski, 1989c] and Example 3.6) and handles negative disjunctions differently.

The stationary semantics is introduced in this paper by constructing, for any disjunctive program P, its unique *canonical stationary state* S_P and defining the stationary semantics $STAT(P)$ of P to be the set of all sentences satisfied in S_P. The canonical stationary state generalizes the well-founded model of a program and for normal programs it coincides with the well-founded model M_P of P.

An alternative approach, pursued in [Przymusinski, 1990c], is to associate with any program P the class of ***all stationary states*** of P and to define the semantics $STAT(P)$ as the set of sentences satisfied in *all* stationary states of P. The two approaches are equivalent, i.e., they lead to the same semantics. Stationary states generalize the concept of 3-valued stable models and the canonical stationary state turns out to simply be the ***smallest*** stationary state, thus extending the analogous result relating well-founded and 3-valued stable models of normal programs [Przymusinski, 1989c; Przymusinski, 1990a].

The stationary semantics is quite flexible and can be easily adapted to support additional requirements. For example, the original semantics interprets disjunctions of atoms appearing in the heads of clauses as ***exclusive*** disjunctions, so that, for example, when applied to the program $A \vee B$ it implies $\neg A \vee \neg B$. In many applications, an ***inclusive*** interpretation of disjunctions (or some mixture of exclusive and inclusive interpretations) may be more appropriate. Accordingly, one can define a ***weak stationary semantics*** (see [Przymusinski, 1990c]) which interprets disjunctions inclusively and extends both the well-founded semantics of normal programs and the inclusive semantics of stratified disjunctive programs proposed in [Ross and Topor, 1988; Rajasekar *et al.*, 1989].

Similarly, following the method described in [Przymusinski, 1989c; Przymusinski, 1990a], the stationary semantics can be also immediately extended to the broader class of programs, first introduced in [Gelfond and Lifschitz, 1989], that allows the use of "classical negation" $\neg$ in addition to the use of negation as failure $\sim$ (see [Przymusinski, 1990c]).

Finally, let us point out that our approach strongly benefits from earlier important contributions to the semantics of logic programs and would certainly be impossible without them. In addition to the basic work by [Van Gelder *et al.*, 1990] and the older and already classical works, such as [Clark, 1978; Van Emden and Kowalski, 1976; Reiter, 1978; Minker, 1982; Fitting, 1985; Kunen, 1987; Apt *et al.*, 1988; Van Gelder, 1989b], the following two recent and yet fundamental approaches played a particularly important role in our investigation:

- The work of [Gelfond, 1987] who first[1] provided a mathematically precise formalization of the "negation as failure" by translating logic programs into corresponding autoepistemic theories obtained by replacing all negative premises "**not** A" by "$\neg\mathbf{L}A$", i.e., by replacing the "negation as failure of A", which before has been given only an informal or intuitive meaning, into a formally defined statement "don't believe in A" in autoepistemic logic; here $\mathbf{L}$ denotes the autoepistemic ***belief***

[1]Naturally, with the exception of Clark's work on program completion.

operator. A parallel work in default logic was done by [Bidoit and Froidevaux, 1988].

Gelfond's work led to the introduction of the ***stable model semantics*** in [Gelfond and Lifschitz, 1988], which extends the perfect model semantics to a class of programs significantly broader than the class of stratified programs and has an elegant and simple fixed point definition. The stable model semantics has been received with great interest in the logic programming community and accepted by many researchers as a correct and important step towards the ultimate solution of the problem of semantics.

Unfortunately, while eliminating the positive recursion problem suffered by Clark's semantics, the stable model semantics ***suffers from essentially the same negative recursion problem as the Clark completion semantics***. Namely, first of all, it is not defined for many programs involving negative recursion, thus making it impossible to extract from them all the potentially valuable information and, secondly, even in those cases when the stable semantics is defined it does not always lead to the expected (intended) meaning of the program (see [Van Gelder *et al.*, 1990; Przymusinska and Przymusinski, 1990; Przymusinski and Warren, 1990] for a more detailed discussion).

Moreover, the stable model semantics is computationally intractable. As it was proven in [Marek and Truszczynski, 1988], just determining whether a propositional program ***has*** a stable model is *NP-complete*. In contrast, the well-founded model of such a program can be found in ***polynomial*** time [Van Gelder *et al.*, 1990].

The ***3-valued stable semantics*** introduced in [Przymusinski, 1989c; Przymusinski, 1990a] eliminated those problems and was shown to be equivalent to the well-founded semantics. In spite of those shortcomings, Gelfond's approach has a fundamental value and plays a significant role in our considerations.

- The recent work by J. Minker and his students (see, e.g.,[Minker and Rajasekar, 1990; Baral *et al.*, 1990; Baral *et al.*, 1989]), and, to a lesser degree, the parallel work by [Belegrinos, 1988], where the concept of a 'generalized Herbrand interpretation' was introduced and called a (Herbrand) ***state***. A state consists of ***disjunctions of literals*** rather than just single literals.

  In addition to providing elegant and new fixed point characterizations of the least model semantics and the perfect model semantics, Minker and his students proposed various generalizations of the well-founded semantics and showed that the best way to properly define semantics of disjunctive programs is to use states rather than standard Herbrand interpretations.

> This is a very important idea which plays a crucial role in our approach. In fact, we believe that a proper semantics of disjunctive programs *cannot* be defined by using standard Herbrand models.

The term "stationary semantics" is supposed to reflect those two important ideas, namely, our stationary states are ***states*** which are, in some specific sense which is explained later, ***stable***.

The paper is organized as follows. In Section 2 we define disjunctive logic programs and their Herbrand models and states and in Section 3 we introduce stationary states and stationary semantics and establish their basic properties. Due to the page limitation, proofs of the results contained in this paper will appear elsewhere. The specific autoepistemic logic corresponding to our approach is introduced and investigated in [Przymusinski, 1990b] and the class of all stationary states of a program is introduced in [Przymusinski, 1990c].

2 Disjunctive Programs and Their Models

In this section we define ***logic programs*** and their ***partial interpretations and models***. We closely follow the approach developed in [Przymusinski, 1989a; Przymusinska and Przymusinski, 1990] with some important modifications, though. Namely, we introduce ***belief predicates*** $\mathcal{B}A$, which are closely related to the autoepistemic belief operator **L**, but correspond to a different and more expressive autoepistemic logic (see [Przymusinski, 1990b] for details). Belief predicates are no different from standard predicate symbols except that they have a specific ***intended meaning***, which is informally discussed below and formally defined in the next section. As discussed in the introduction, we will also define the notion of a ***Herbrand state***, essentially generalizing the notion of a Herbrand interpretation.

By an ***alphabet*** $\mathcal{A}$ of a first order language $\mathcal{L}$ we mean a (finite or countably infinite) set of ***constant***, ***predicate*** and ***function*** symbols. In addition, any alphabet is assumed to contain a countably infinite set of ***variable*** symbols, the connectives $\wedge, \vee, \neg, \leftarrow$ and quantifiers $\exists, \forall$ and the usual punctuation symbols.

Moreover, we assume that for ***every*** predicate symbol A in our alphabet[2] there is also the corresponding predicate symbol $\mathcal{B}A$, which is called a ***belief predicate***. Predicate symbols which are ***not*** belief predicates are called ***objective*** predicates. While belief predicates are ***no different*** from objective predicate symbols and should therefore be treated like any other predicate symbol, they are assigned a ***special intended meaning*** which guarantees their special role. Namely:

- A given theory P is supposed to logically imply $\mathcal{B}A$ if and only if A is ***believed***, or, more precisely, if and only if all ground instances of A are

[2]More precisely, for every *objective* predicate – see below.

logical consequences of the theory;

- A given theory P is supposed to logically imply $\neg\mathcal{B}A$ if and only if A is *disbelieved* (false by default or negation as failure), or, more precisely, if and only if all ground instances of A are false in all *minimal models* of the theory.

In other words, for a given theory P we are supposed to have[3]:

$$P \models \mathcal{B}A \quad \text{iff} \quad GCWA(P) \models A$$

$$P \models \neg\mathcal{B}A \quad \text{iff} \quad GCWA(P) \models \neg A.$$

More generally, similar rules are supposed to apply to disjunctions[4], namely:

$$P \models \mathcal{B}A_1 \vee \ldots \vee \mathcal{B}A_n \quad \text{iff} \quad GCWA(P) \models A_1 \vee \ldots \vee A_n$$

$$P \models \neg\mathcal{B}A_1 \vee \ldots \vee \neg\mathcal{B}A_n \quad \text{iff} \quad GCWA(P) \models \neg A_1 \vee \ldots \vee \neg A_n$$

The *stationary states* or models of a program, which will be defined in the next section, will be precisely those states or models of the program that *enforce the intended meaning of belief predicates.* In logic programs, whenever we would normally use "$\sim A$", meaning the "negation as failure of A" we will use "$\neg\mathcal{B}A$" instead (see [Gelfond, 1987]).

The *first order language* $\mathcal{L}$ over the alphabet $\mathcal{A}$ is defined as the set of all well-formed first order formulae that can be built by starting from the atoms and using connectives, quantifiers and punctuation symbols in a standard way. A *literal* is either an atom A or its negation $\neg A$. An expression is called *ground* if it does not contain any variables. If G is a quantifier-free formula, then by its *ground instance* we mean any ground formula obtained from G by substituting ground terms for all variables. For a given formula G of $\mathcal{L}$ its *universal closure* or just *closure* is obtained by universally quantifying all variables in G which are not bound by any quantifier.

Definition 2.1 *By a* (partial) Herbrand interpretation *I of the language $\mathcal{L}$ we mean any* set of ground literals. *An interpretation is* total *if for every ground atom A either A or $\neg A$ belongs to I.*

An interpretation is *consistent* if there is no atom A such that both A and $\neg A$ belong to I and no atom A such that both A and $\neg\mathcal{B}A$ belong to I. The last requirement stems from our intended interpretation of belief atoms.

For example a (consistent) interpretation I is given by

$$A, \neg C, \mathcal{B}A, \neg\mathcal{B}B, \neg\mathcal{B}C$$

[3]Recall, that an atom is a logical consequence of a theory if and only if it is true in all of its minimal models.

[4]It would be more natural to talk about, say, believing $\neg A_1 \vee \ldots \vee \neg A_n$, i.e., about $\mathcal{B}(\neg A_1 \vee \ldots \vee \neg A_n)$ rather than about $\neg\mathcal{B}A_1 \vee \ldots \vee \neg\mathcal{B}A_n$. However, the first approach leads to a more complex formalization and therefore is not used here.

meaning that, A and $\mathcal{B}A$ are true while C, $\mathcal{B}B$ and $\mathcal{B}C$ are false. The status of the remaining proposition B, is undefined.

Suppose that I is an interpretation and F and G are arbitrary closed formulae (i.e., *sentences*). We now recursively define what it means for a sentence (i.e., a closed formula) to be *true* or *false* in I:

- A ground atom A is true in I if it belongs to I and it is false in I if $\neg A$ belongs to I.
- $\neg F$ is true (resp. false) in I if and only if F if false (resp. true) in I.
- $F \vee G$ is true (resp. false) in I if and only if either F or G is true in I (resp. if both F and G are false in I).
- $F \wedge G$ is true (resp. false) in I if and only if both F and G are true in I (resp. if either F or G is false in I).
- $F \leftarrow G$ is true in I if: (a) F is true in I whenever G is true in I and (b) G is false in I whenever F is false in I. Otherwise, $F \leftarrow G$ is false in I.
- $\exists x\ F(x)$ is true in I if one of ground instances of $F(x)$ is true in I and it is false in I if all of its ground instances are false in I (as usual, we assume that x is the only free variable in $F(x)$).
- $\forall x\ F(x)$ is true in I if all ground instances of $F(x)$ are true in I and it is false in I if one of its ground instances is false in I.

The connective $\leftarrow$ represents what we call a *constructive implication*. It is easy to see that the formula $F \leftarrow G$ is *not* equivalent to $F \vee \neg G$. Indeed, $F \leftarrow G$ is always true if G is *not* true and F is not false, while $F \vee \neg G$ is true if and only if either F is true or G is false. The constructive implication connective $\leftarrow$ will be used in the definition of logic programs.

Definition 2.2 *If a closed formula F is true in a consistent interpretation M then we write $M \models F$ and say that M is a* model *of F or that F is* satisfied *in M. By a* theory *T we mean a (finite or infinite) set of closed formulae. A (partial or total) interpretation M is a (partial or total)* model *of a theory T if all formulae from T are satisfied in M, i.e., if $M \models F$, for all F in T.*

We say that a theory T logically implies *a sentence F if F is satisfied in all partial models M of T. In this case we also write $T \models F$.*

Example 2.1 *Suppose that $I = \{A, \neg\mathcal{B}C\}$ is an interpretation. Then:*

- *$A \vee B$, $\neg\mathcal{B}C \vee \neg B$ and $A \wedge \neg\mathcal{B}C$ are true, $\neg A \vee \mathcal{B}C$ and $\neg A \wedge B$ are false, but $B \vee \neg B$ and $A \wedge B$ are undefined, i.e., neither true nor false.*
- *$B \leftarrow \neg B$, $B \leftarrow B$ and $A \leftarrow B$ are true, but $\neg A \leftarrow B$ and $\mathcal{B}C \leftarrow A$ are false.*

Definition 2.3 *By a* disjunctive logic program *we mean a set of universally closed* clauses *of the form*

$$A_1 \vee \ldots \vee A_k \leftarrow B_1 \wedge \ldots \wedge B_m \wedge \neg \mathcal{B}C_1 \wedge \ldots \wedge \neg \mathcal{B}C_n,$$

where $k > 0$, $m, n \geq 0$, $\mathcal{B}C_j$'s are belief predicates and A_i's and B_i's are objective predicates. Conforming to a standard convention, conjunctions are replaced by commas and therefore clauses are usually written in the form

$$A_1 \vee \ldots \vee A_k \leftarrow L_1, \ldots, L_k.$$

A program is called normal *or* non-disjunctive *if k=1 in all clauses of P. A program is called* positive *if none of its clauses contains negative premises.*

Observe that programs defined above do *not* use classical negation $\neg A$ except when applied to believe atoms. As we pointed out in the introduction, our approach can be easily extended to programs allowing general classical negation. If P is a program then, unless stated otherwise, we will assume that the alphabet $\mathcal{A}$ used to write P consists precisely of all the constant, predicate and function symbols that explicitly *appear* in P and thus $\mathcal{A} = \mathcal{A}_P$ is completely determined[5] by the program P. The following proposition is obvious.

Proposition 2.1 *A (partial or total) interpretation M is a model of a program P if and only if for all ground instances of its clauses*

$$A_1 \vee \ldots \vee A_k \leftarrow L_1, \ldots, L_k,$$

if all L_i's are true in M then at least one A_i is true in M and if all A_i's are false in M then at least one of the L_i's is also false in M.

By a *ground instantiation* of a logic program P we mean the (possibly infinite) theory consisting of all ground instances of clauses from P. It is easy to see that a Herbrand interpretation M is a model of a program P if and only if it is a model of its ground instantiation. Therefore, as long as only Herbrand interpretations are considered, one can identify any program P with its ground instantiation. Whenever convenient, we will assume, without further mention, that the program P has already been instantiated. This will allow us to essentially restrict our considerations to a *propositional language*.

For any interpretation I we will denote by $Pos(I)$ the set of all positive literals (atoms) in I and by $Neg(I)$ the set of all negative literals in I (in both cases including belief literals). In other words, $Pos(I)$ represents the set of atoms which are *true* in I (i.e., those that belong to I) and $Neg(I)$ represents the set of atoms which are *false* in I (i.e., those whose negation belongs to I). Clearly, for any interpretation I, we have

$$I = Pos(I) \cup Neg(I).$$

[5]If there are no constants in P then one is added to the alphabet.

This immediately leads to a *natural ordering* between interpretations defined as follows:

Definition 2.4 *[Przymusinski, 1989a] Suppose that $I = Pos(I) \cup Neg(I)$ and $J = Pos(J) \cup Neg(J)$ are two interpretations. We define:*

$$I \preceq J \quad \textit{if} \quad Pos(I) \subseteq Pos(J) \quad \textit{and} \quad Neg(I) \supseteq Neg(J).$$

Models which are $\preceq$-minimal or $\preceq$-least will be simply called minimal or least models, respectively.

Thus one interpretation is less than another if it contains less positive facts and more negative facts. In other words, the ordering $\preceq$ minimizes the *degree of truth* of atoms, by minimizing the set $Pos(M)$ of true atoms and maximizing the set $Neg(M)$ of false atoms.

Example 2.2 *Suppose that the program P is given by:*

$$A \leftarrow \neg \mathcal{B}C.$$

The program has the following minimal models $\{\neg C, \ \neg\mathcal{B}C, \ A\}$, $\{\neg C, \ \mathcal{B}C, \ \neg A, \ \neg\mathcal{B}A\}$ and $\{\neg C, \ \neg\mathcal{B}A\}$. Observe that in all of them C is false. We recall that a model cannot contain both A and $\neg\mathcal{B}A$. On the other hand, the program:

$$A \leftarrow \neg \mathcal{B}A$$

has only two minimal models: one is empty $\{\}$ and the other is $\{\mathcal{B}A, \ \neg A\}$.

Finally, we introduce the notion of a *Herbrand state* of a program. Our definition is similar to the definition of a state in [Baral *et al.*, 1989] and is closely related to the ideas developed in [Belegrinos, 1988]. By a *positive belief disjunction* we mean any disjunction $\mathcal{B}A_1 \vee \ldots \vee \mathcal{B}A_k$ of belief atoms and by a *negative belief disjunction* we mean any disjunction $\neg\mathcal{B}A_1 \vee \ldots \vee \neg\mathcal{B}A_k$ of negative belief atoms.

Definition 2.5 *By an* Herbrand state *S of the language $\mathcal{L}$ we mean any consistent (i.e., having a model) set of positive and negative belief disjunctions.*

The set $S = \{\mathcal{B}A \vee \mathcal{B}C, \neg\mathcal{B}A \vee \neg\mathcal{B}C\}$ is an example of a consistent state and intuitively says that we believe in $A \vee B$ and in $\neg A \vee \neg B$. In the next section we will construct a unique (canonical) state of any disjunctive program.

Observe that, as opposed to interpretations, a state contains only disjunctions of *belief* atoms. The reason is the following:

Positive information: The intended meaning of the objective disjunction $A_1 \vee \ldots \vee A_k$ is equivalent to the corresponding belief disjunction $\mathcal{B} A_1 \vee \ldots \vee \mathcal{B} A_k$ and therefore it does not matter which of the two forms is actually used.

Negative information: Obviously, strictly negative facts, i.e., objective disjunctions of the form $\neg A_1 \vee \ldots \vee \neg A_n$, *cannot* be inferred from logic programs since the interpretation in which all atoms are true is clearly a model of any logic program. Therefore only facts obtained by using negation or failure or negation by default, i.e., precisely facts of the form $\neg \mathcal{B} A_1 \vee \ldots \vee \neg \mathcal{B} A_k$, are derivable from logic programs.

Observe that every *positive* disjunctive logic program P has a unique *least state* $LEAST(P) = POS(P) \cup NEG(P)$, where:

$$POS(P) = \{\mathcal{B} A_1 \vee \ldots \vee \mathcal{B} A_k : GCWA(P) \models A_1 \vee \ldots \vee A_k\};$$

$$NEG(P) = \{\neg \mathcal{B} A_1 \vee \ldots \vee \neg \mathcal{B} A_k : GCWA(P) \models \neg A_1 \vee \ldots \vee \neg A_k\}.$$

This least state coincides (when belief symbols $\mathcal{B}$ are removed) with the *least state* of a disjunctive program defined in [Minker and Rajasekar, 1990] as a generalization of the notion of the least model of a positive normal program. As we will see in Theorem 3.3 below, for positive disjunctive programs P, canonical stationary states S_P always coincide with least states $LEAST(P)$.

3 The Stationary Semantics

In this section we will define, for every disjunctive logic program P, its unique *canonical stationary state* S_P which is a generalization of the well-founded model of normal (non-disjunctive) programs. The canonical stationary state S_P is the *smallest*, in the sense of containing the least amount of information, state S with the property that the theory $\frac{P}{S} = P \cup S$ obtained by adding the state S to the program P *satisfies the intended meaning of belief predicates*, i.e., satisfies the following *stability conditions* for all disjunctions:

$$\frac{P}{S} \models \mathcal{B} A_1 \vee \ldots \vee \mathcal{B} A_n \quad \text{iff} \quad GCWA(\frac{P}{S}) \models A_1 \vee \ldots \vee A_n;$$

$$\frac{P}{S} \models \neg \mathcal{B} A_1 \vee \ldots \vee \neg \mathcal{B} A_n \quad \text{iff} \quad GCWA(\frac{P}{S}) \models \neg A_1 \vee \ldots \vee \neg A_n.$$

Remark 3.1 *In [Przymusinski, 1990c] we investigate the class of* all stationary states, *i.e., all states of a program satisfying the above stability conditions, and we show that stationary states generalize 3-valued stable models and lead to the same semantics of logic programs.*

Now we define the *canonical stationary state* S_P of an arbitrary disjunctive logic program P. We apply the iterative approach originally used in

[Van Gelder *et al.*, 1990] to define well-founded models and later used in [Przymusinski, 1989a] to give their constructive fixed point definition.

The construction of the ***canonical stationary state*** of a program P is conceptually very simple. We start from scratch, i.e., with the initial program $P_0 = P$ and an empty initial state $S_0 = \emptyset$ and recursively construct an ***increasing*** sequence $S_0 \subseteq S_1 \subseteq \ldots S_\alpha \subseteq \ldots$ of states which eventually reaches a fixed point $S_\lambda = S_{\lambda+1}$. This fixed point state S_λ is defined as the canonical stationary state S_P of the program and is shown to satisfy the two ***stability conditions*** given above.

The recursive construction proceeds as follows. Suppose that we have already constructed states S_α, for $\alpha < \beta$. We now define S_β as follows:

- If β is a limit ordinal we define

$$S_\beta = \bigcup_{\alpha<\beta} S_\alpha,$$

  i.e., we take the union of all the previously defined states.

- If $\beta = \alpha + 1$ is a successor ordinal then we define

$$P_\alpha = \frac{P}{S_\alpha} = P \cup S_\alpha \quad \text{and} \quad S_\beta = POS(P_\alpha) \cup NEG(P_\alpha)$$

  where, for any theory T,

$$POS(T) = \{\mathcal{B}A_1 \vee \ldots \vee \mathcal{B}A_n : GCWA(T) \models A_1 \vee \ldots \vee A_n\};$$

$$NEG(T) = \{\neg\mathcal{B}A_1 \vee \ldots \vee \neg\mathcal{B}A_n : GCWA(T) \models \neg A_1 \vee \ldots \vee \neg A_n\}.$$

  Thus $POS(T)$ denotes the set of all positive beliefs about T and $NEG(T)$ denotes the set of all negative beliefs about T.

In other words, at every successor step we add the set of all ***positive belief disjunctions*** $\mathcal{B}A_1 \vee \ldots \vee \mathcal{B}A_n$ with the property that $A_1 \vee \ldots \vee A_n$ can be logically derived from the theory $P_\alpha = P \cup S_\alpha$ and the set of all ***negative belief disjunctions*** $\neg\mathcal{B}A_1 \vee \ldots \vee \neg\mathcal{B}A_n$ with the property that $\neg A_1 \vee \ldots \vee \neg A_n$ is true in all minimal models of P_α. Therefore, at every successor step we add to our previously constructed state all those positive and negative belief disjunctions that must be satisfied if the two ***stability conditions*** are supposed to hold true.

Remark 3.2 *We have developed a* proof theory *for the 3-valued (or partial model) logic used in this paper, which resembles standard resolution theory. It allows us to give* constructive definitions *of both $POS(P)$ and $NEG(P)$. We will not discuss this further in this paper.*

It is easy to prove that the sequence S_α of states is increasing and therefore must have a ***fixed point***, i.e., there must exist a λ such that $S_\lambda = S_{\lambda+1}$. We define this state $S_P = S_\lambda$ to be the unique ***canonical stationary state*** of P. It turns out that S_P is the ***smallest state*** of the program P which satisifies the stability conditions.

Theorem 3.1 *For any disjunctive logic program P the unique* canonical stationary state S_P *of P is well defined and is the* smallest state *of the program P, in the sense of containing the least amount of information, which satisfies the stability conditions, i.e., the smallest state S with the property that the theory $\frac{P}{S} = P \cup S$ obtained by adding S to the program P satisfies, for all disjunctions, the conditions:*

$$\frac{P}{S} \models \mathcal{B}A_1 \vee \ldots \vee \mathcal{B}A_n \quad \text{iff} \quad GCWA(\frac{P}{S}) \models A_1 \vee \ldots \vee A_n;$$

$$\frac{P}{S} \models \neg\mathcal{B}A_1 \vee \ldots \vee \neg\mathcal{B}A_n \quad \text{iff} \quad GCWA(\frac{P}{S}) \models \neg A_1 \vee \ldots \vee \neg A_n.$$

Definition 3.1 *The* stationary semantics $STAT(P)$ *of the program P is defined as the set of all sentences logically derivable from the stationary state S_P.*

Now it is time to look at some examples.

Example 3.1 *Let us construct the canonical stationary state of the simple program*

$$A \leftarrow \neg\mathcal{B}C$$

discussed in Example 2.2. We begin with the empty state S_0 and define:

$$P_0 = P \cup S_0 = P \quad \text{and} \quad S_1 = POS(P) \cup NEG(P)$$

where

$$POS(P) = \{\mathcal{B}A_1 \vee \ldots \vee \mathcal{B}A_n : GCWA(P) \models A_1 \vee \ldots \vee A_n\};$$

$$NEG(P) = \{\neg\mathcal{B}A_1 \vee \ldots \vee \neg\mathcal{B}A_n : GCWA(P) \models \neg A_1 \vee \ldots \vee \neg A_n\}.$$

Since it is clear that the program P does not logically imply any objective *disjunctions $A_1 \vee \ldots \vee A_n$, the set $POS(P)$ is empty. On the other hand, as we have seen in Example 2.2, all minimal models of P contain $\neg C$ and therefore $NEG(P) = \{\neg\mathcal{B}C\} = S_1$. Thus we have:*

$$P_1 = P \cup S_1 = P \cup \{\neg\mathcal{B}C\} \quad \text{and} \quad S_2 = POS(P_1) \cup NEG(P_1)$$

where

$$POS(P_1) = \{\mathcal{B}A_1 \vee \ldots \vee \mathcal{B}A_n : GCWA(P_1) \models A_1 \vee \ldots \vee A_n\};$$

$$NEG(P_1) = \{\neg\mathcal{B}A_1 \vee \ldots \vee \neg\mathcal{B}A_n : GCWA(P_1) \models \neg A_1 \vee \ldots \vee \neg A_n\}.$$

Clearly, $P_1 \models A$ and therefore $POS(P_1) = \{\mathcal{B}A\}$ and $NEG(P_1) = NEG(P)$. It follows that

$$S_2 = \{\mathcal{B}A,\ \neg\mathcal{B}C\}$$

and it is easy to see that $S_3 = S_2$. We conclude that $S_P = S_2 = \{\mathcal{B}A,\ \neg\mathcal{B}C\}$ is the canonical stationary state of P. It obviously coincides (when belief symbols $\mathcal{B}$ are removed) with the perfect or well-founded model M_P of the program, namely, $M_P = \{A,\ \neg C\}$.

Recall again that for any theory T and any positive disjunction $A_1 \vee \ldots \vee A_n$ we always have:

$$T \models A_1 \vee \ldots \vee A_n \text{ iff } GCWA(T) \models A_1 \vee \ldots \vee A_n.$$

This implies that for all positive disjunctions we have:

$$\frac{P}{S} \models \mathcal{B}A_1 \vee \ldots \vee \mathcal{B}A_n \quad \text{iff} \quad \frac{P}{S} \models A_1 \vee \ldots \vee A_n;$$

and therefore in all states belief disjunctions $\mathcal{B}A_1 \vee \ldots \vee \mathcal{B}A_n$ can be always equivalently replaced by the corresponding objective disjunctions $A_1 \vee \ldots \vee A_n$. Similarly, as a matter of notation, we could introduce an abbreviation, say, $\sim A \equiv \neg\mathcal{B}A$ and then negative belief disjunctions would be simply written as $\sim A_1 \vee \ldots \vee \sim A_n$. For example, the canonical state in the previous example would be simply written as $\{A, \ \sim C\}$.

Example 3.2 *Suppose now that P is given by:*

$$\begin{aligned} A &\leftarrow \neg\mathcal{B}C \\ D &\leftarrow \neg\mathcal{B}A. \end{aligned}$$

Again, we begin with the empty state S_0 and set $P_0 = P \cup S_0 = P$ and $S_1 = POS(P) \cup NEG(P)$ and we again observe that $POS(P)$ is empty and $NEG(P) = \{\neg\mathcal{B}C\} = S_1$. Thus we have $P_1 = P \cup S_1 = P \cup \{\neg\mathcal{B}C\}$ and $S_2 = POS(P_1) \cup NEG(P_1)$. As before, $P_1 \models A$, $POS(P_1) = \{\mathcal{B}A\}$ and $NEG(P_1) = NEG(P)$. Therefore, $S_2 = \{\mathcal{B}A, \ \neg\mathcal{B}C\}$.

Now we take $P_2 = P \cup S_2 = P \cup \{\mathcal{B}A, \ \neg\mathcal{B}C\}$ and $S_3 = POS(P_2) \cup NEG(P_2)$. Since P_2 contains $\mathcal{B}A$, all of its minimal models must clearly contain $\neg D$ and thus $NEG(P_2) = \{\neg\mathcal{B}C, \ \neg\mathcal{B}D\}$ and $POS(P_2) = POS(P_1)$. Therefore, $S_3 = \{\mathcal{B}A, \ \neg\mathcal{B}C, \ \neg\mathcal{B}D\}$ and it is easy to see that $S_3 = S_4$. We conclude that $S_P = S_3 = \{\mathcal{B}A, \ \neg\mathcal{B}C, \ \neg\mathcal{B}C\}$ is the canonical stationary state of P. Again it coincides (when belief symbols $\mathcal{B}$ are removed) with the perfect or well-founded model M_P of the program, namely, $M_P = \{A, \ \neg C, \ \neg D\}$.

Now we can state the second main result of the paper.

Theorem 3.2 *For any normal logic program P the canonical stationary state S_P coincides (when belief symbols $\mathcal{B}$ are removed) with the well-founded model M_P of P. Consequently, the stationary semantics $STAT(P)$ of P coincides (again, when belief symbols $\mathcal{B}$ are removed) with the well-founded (or 3-valued stable) semantics of P.*

Example 3.3 *Consider now the following simple positive disjunctive program:*

$$A \vee C.$$

Since $P \models A \vee C$ we have $POS(P) = \{\mathcal{B}A \vee \mathcal{B}C\}$ and since $\neg A \vee \neg C$ holds in all minimal models of P, we have $NEG(P) = \{\neg\mathcal{B}A \vee \neg\mathcal{B}C\}$. Thus

$$S_1 = \{\mathcal{B}A \vee \mathcal{B}C,\ \neg\mathcal{B}A \vee \neg\mathcal{B}C\}.$$

It is easy to see that $S_2 = S_1$. We conclude that $S_P = S_1 = \{\mathcal{B}A \vee \mathcal{B}C,\ \neg\mathcal{B}A \vee \neg\mathcal{B}C\}$ is the canonical stationary state of P. It clearly coincides (when belief symbols $\mathcal{B}$ are removed) with the least state $LEAST(P) = \{A \vee C,\ \neg A \vee \neg C\}$ of the program introduced at the end of the previous section. Similarly, the stationary semantics $STAT(P)$ coincides with the minimal model semantics $MIN(P)$ of P.

Observe that the stationary state or the least state *encode in compact form all minimal models of the program.* This leads us to the next result of the paper.

Theorem 3.3 *For any positive disjunctive logic program P the canonical stationary state S_P coincides (when belief symbols $\mathcal{B}$ are removed) with the least state $LEAST(P)$ of P. The stationary semantics $STAT(P)$ of P coincides (again, when belief symbols $\mathcal{B}$ are removed) with the minimal model semantics of P.*

Example 3.4 *Consider now the following stratified disjunctive program:*

$$\begin{array}{lcl} A \vee C & & \\ \quad D & \leftarrow & \neg\mathcal{B}A \\ \quad D & \leftarrow & \neg\mathcal{B}C. \end{array}$$

As before we show that

$$S_1 = \{\mathcal{B}A \vee \mathcal{B}C,\ \neg\mathcal{B}A \vee \neg\mathcal{B}C\}.$$

Let $P_1 = P \cup S_1$. Since $P_1 \models C$, we have

$$S_2 = \{\mathcal{B}C,\ \mathcal{B}A \vee \mathcal{B}C,\ \neg\mathcal{B}A \vee \neg\mathcal{B}C\}.$$

Again, it is easy to see that $S_2 = S_3$ and we conclude that $S_P = S_2 = \{\mathcal{B}C,\ \mathcal{B}A \vee \mathcal{B}C,\ \neg\mathcal{B}A \vee \neg\mathcal{B}C\}$ is the canonical stationary state of P. Observe that S_P again encodes in a compact form all perfect models of the program, namely $\{A,\ \neg B,\ C\}$ and $\{B,\ \neg A,\ C\}$ and therefore the stationary semantics $STAT(P)$ of P coincides with the perfect model semantics $PERF(P)$ of P [Przymusinski, 1988]. It should be pointed out here that Ross's extended well-founded semantics [Ross, 1989] applied to P leads to different results.

This allows us to state the third main result of the paper.

Theorem 3.4 *For any stratified disjunctive logic program P the stationary semantics $STAT(P)$ of P coincides (when belief symbols $\mathcal{B}$ are removed) with the perfect model semantics of P.*

Observe that, as it was the case with the well-founded model [Przymusinski, 1989a], the canonical stationary state leads to a natural *dynamic stratification* of the program. Namely, in the previous example, the first *dynamic stratum* of P is $\{\mathcal{B}A \vee \mathcal{B}C,\ \neg\mathcal{B}A \vee \neg\mathcal{B}C\}$, i.e., the set of disjunctions obtained at the first level of iteration, and the *second stratum* contains $\mathcal{B}C$, which was obtained at the second level.

Example 3.5 *Consider now the program P*

$$\begin{array}{lcl} D & & \\ A & \leftarrow & \neg\mathcal{B}A \end{array}$$

involving negative recursion. Since P implies D, but neither A nor $\neg A$ *are true in all minimal models of P, therefore* $POS(P) = \{\mathcal{B}D\}$*, while* $NEG(P)$ *is empty. Therefore* $S_1 = \{\mathcal{B}D\}$*. Addition of* S_1 *to P does not allow us to conclude any new information and therefore* $S_2 = S_1$ *and* $S_P = S_1 = \{\mathcal{B}D\}$ *is the canonical stationary model of P. It coincides (when belief symbols* $\mathcal{B}$ *are removed) with the well-founded (or 3-valued stable) model* M_P *of the program, namely,* $M_P = \{D\}$*. Obviously, the program does not have any (2-valued) stable models.*

Example 3.6 *The canonical stationary model of the program*

$$\begin{array}{lcl} A & \leftarrow & \neg\mathcal{B}C \\ C & \leftarrow & \neg\mathcal{B}A \\ D & \leftarrow & A \\ D & \leftarrow & C \end{array}$$

is empty. Indeed, the program does not logically imply any objective positive disjunctions and there are no negative objective disjunctions which are true in all of its minimal models and therefore $S_1 = S_0 = \{\}$*.*

This example illustrates differences between our semantics and the semantics introduced in [Baral et al.*, 1989], which in this case implies,* $A \vee C$ *and thus D, and, in general, to some extent treats clauses of the form* $A \leftarrow \neg\mathcal{B}C$ *as disjunctions* $A \vee C$ *(see the remarks below). Obviously, the program does not have any (2-valued) stable models.*

Finally, consider the program discussed in [Przymusinski, 1990a] which does not have any 2- or 3-valued stable models.

Example 3.7

$$\begin{array}{rcl} \multicolumn{3}{l}{work \vee tired \vee sleep} \\ work & \leftarrow & \sim tired \\ sleep & \leftarrow & \sim work \\ tired & \leftarrow & \sim sleep \\ angry & \leftarrow & \sim paid, work \\ paid & \leftarrow & \end{array}$$

It easy to see that the canonical stationary state S_P of the program contains:

$$\{\mathcal{B}work \vee \mathcal{B}tired \vee \mathcal{B}sleep,\ \mathcal{B}paid,\ \neg\mathcal{B}angry\}$$

which seems to fully agree with our intuitions.

It seems that most researchers agree that the program

$$\begin{array}{lll} A & \leftarrow & \neg\mathcal{B}A \\ D & & \end{array}$$

discussed in Example 2.2 should *not* imply A, while it clearly should imply D. This is due to the fact that neither the connective $\leftarrow$ nor the negation symbol $\neg\mathcal{B}$ represent classical implication or negation and also to the fact that in logic programming we only accept answers which can be derived, in some sense, in a *constructive way*. Clearly A cannot be false either and therefore some researchers propose not to assign any semantics to programs with this kind of *negative recursion* while others assign the semantics in which D is true but the truth value of A is undefined.

The last solution seems *greatly superior*, because it allows us to assign reasonable semantics to more programs, and thus prevents us from loosing useful information contained in the program (in this case, the fact that D is true). This is the solution adopted by the well-founded semantics, by the stationary semantics and also by Fitting and Kunen's 3-valued extension of Clark's semantics.

At the same time a number of researchers (e.g., [Baral *et al.*, 1990; Baral and Subrahmanian, 1990]) argue that the program P discussed in Example 3.6:

$$\begin{array}{lll} A & \leftarrow & \neg\mathcal{B}C \\ C & \leftarrow & \neg\mathcal{B}A \\ D & \leftarrow & A \\ D & \leftarrow & C \end{array}$$

should be viewed as representing a disjunction $A \vee C$ and thus should imply D.

As we have seen, the well-founded and the stationary semantics, as well as Fitting-Kunen's semantics do not derive either $A \vee C$ or D and we believe that this is a *correct* approach. Let us try to explain this statement:

First of all, if we really wanted to express disjunction $A \vee C$, we should do so explicitely, rather than use this conspicuous way.

Secondly, it seems that in logic programming we only accept answers which can be derived, in some sense, in a *constructive way* and it appears that this condition is not satisfied here for $A \vee C$ and D.

Thirdly, if for any propositions A and C the above program is to be viewed as representing a disjunction $A \vee C$ and thus should imply D then it would be natural to expect that, in particular, this should be true for A being equal to C. However, this immediately leads to the conclusion that the program:

$$\begin{array}{lll} A & \leftarrow & \neg\mathcal{B}A \\ D & \leftarrow & A \end{array}$$

should imply both D and A, which contradicts the dominating view that the clause $A \leftarrow \neg\mathcal{B}A$ is not equivalent to A.

Finally, we should view the above clauses as representing a disjunction $A \vee C$ only if we view our knowledge about the world as, in some sense, *complete*, i.e., if we believe that in any possible model of the world every fact is always known to be either *true* or *false*. We then argue that since A must be either true or false, C must be, respectively, false or true and, consequently, either A or C must always be true. However, the assumption that our knowledge about the world is complete in this sense is not only unintuitive, but it also prevents us, as pointed out above, from assigning sensible meaning to large classes of programs and thus should be rejected. Once we agree that portions of our knowledge might be incomplete and some facts may be neither true nor false, but rather undefined, there is no longer any reason to view the program P above as somehow representing a disjunction $A \vee C$, because it is quite possible that both A and C might be undefined (and so can be D).

Acknowledgements

The author acknowledges support from the National Science Foundation under grant #IRI-89-10729 and from the Army Research Office under grant #27079-EL-SAH. The author also expresses gratitude to the anonymous referees of this paper for their helpful comments.

References

[Apt *et al.*, 1988] K. Apt, H. Blair, and A. Walker. Towards a theory of declarative knowledge. In J. Minker, editor, *Foundations of Deductive Databases and Logic Programming*, pages 89–142, Morgan Kaufmann, Los Altos, CA., 1988.

[Baral and Subrahmanian, 1990] C. Baral and V.S. Subrahmanian. *Stable and Extension Class Theory for Logic Programs and Default Logics.* Research report, University of Maryland, 1990.

[Baral *et al.*, 1989] C. Baral, J. Lobo, and J. Minker. *Generalized Disjunctive Well-Founded Semantics for Logic Programs: Declarative Semantics.* Research report UMIACS TR 90-39, CS TR 2436, University of Maryland, College Park, Maryland 20742, 1989.

[Baral *et al.*, 1990] C. Baral, J. Lobo, and J. Minker. Generalized well-founded semantics for logic programs. In *10th International Conference on Automated Deduction, West Germany*, 1990.

[Belegrinos, 1988] N. Belegrinos. *Clauses, Partial Interpretations and the Closed World Assumption.* Research report #13, Melbourne University, 1988.

[Bidoit and Froidevaux, 1988] N. Bidoit and C. Froidevaux. General logical databases and programs: default logic semantics and stratification. *Journal of Information and Computation*, 1988. In print.

[Bry, 1989] F. Bry. Logic programming as constructivism: a formalization and its application to databases. In *Proceedings of the Symposium on Principles of Database Systems*, pages 34–50, ACM SIGACT-SIGMOD, 1989.

[Clark, 1978] K.L. Clark. Negation as failure. In H. Gallaire and J. Minker, editors, *Logic and Data Bases*, pages 293–322, Plenum Press, New York, 1978.

[Fitting, 1985] M. Fitting. A Kripke-Kleene semantics for logic programs. *Journal of Logic Programming*, 2(4):295–312, 1985.

[Gelfond, 1987] M. Gelfond. On stratified autoepistemic theories. In *Proceedings AAAI-87*, pages 207–211, American Association for Artificial Intelligence, Morgan Kaufmann, Los Altos, CA, 1987.

[Gelfond and Lifschitz, 1988] M. Gelfond and V. Lifschitz. The stable model semantics for logic programming. In R. Kowalski and K. Bowen, editors, *Proceedings of the Fifth Logic Programming Symposium*, pages 1070–1080, Association for Logic Programming, MIT Press, Cambridge, Mass., 1988.

[Gelfond and Lifschitz, 1989] M. Gelfond and V. Lifschitz. *Logic Programs with Classical Negation*. Research report, UT El Paso and Stanford University, 1989.

[Kunen, 1987] K. Kunen. Negation in logic programming. *Journal of Logic Programming*, 4(4):289–308, 1987.

[Kunen, 1988] K. Kunen. Some remarks on the completed database. In R. Kowalski and K. Bowen, editors, *Proceedings of the Fifth Logic Programming Symposium*, pages 978–992, Association for Logic Programming, MIT Press, Cambridge, Mass., 1988.

[Lloyd, 1984] J.W. Lloyd. *Foundations of Logic Programming*. Springer Verlag, New York, N.Y., first edition, 1984.

[Marek and Truszczynski, 1988] W. Marek and M. Truszczynski. *Autoepistemic Logic*. Research report, University of Kentucky, University of Kentucky, 1988.

[Minker, 1982] J. Minker. On indefinite data bases and the closed world assumption. In *Proc. 6-th Conference on Automated Deduction*, pages 292–308, Springer Verlag, New York, 1982.

[Minker and Rajasekar, 1990] J. Minker and A. Rajasekar. A fixpoint semantics for disjunctive logic programs. *Journal of Logic Programming*, :(to appear), 1990.

[Przymusinska and Przymusinski, 1990] H. Przymusinska and T. Przymusinski. Semantic issues in deductive databases and logic programs. In R. Banerji, editor, *Formal Techniques in Artificial Intelligence*, pages 321–367, North-Holland, Amsterdam, 1990.

[Przymusinski, 1988] T. Przymusinski. On the declarative semantics of stratified deductive databases and logic programs. In J. Minker, editor, *Foundations of Deductive Databases and Logic Programming*, pages 193–216, Morgan Kaufmann, Los Altos, CA., 1988.

[Przymusinski, 1989a] T. Przymusinski. Every logic program has a natural stratification and an iterated fixed point model. In *Proceedings of the Eighth Symposium on Principles of Database Systems*, pages 11–21, ACM SIGACT-SIGMOD, 1989.

[Przymusinski, 1989b] T. Przymusinski. *Three-Valued Non-Monotonic Formalisms And Semantics of Logic Programs*. Research report, University of Texas at El Paso, 1989. (Extended abstract appeared in: T. Przymusinski. Three-valued non-monotonic formalisms and logic programming. In R. Brachman, H. Leveque, and R. Reiter, editors, *Proceedings of the First International Conference on Principles of Knowledge Representation and Reasoning (KR'89), Toronto, Canada*, pages 341–348, Morgan Kaufmann, 1989.).

[Przymusinski, 1989c] T. Przymusinski. The well-founded semantics coincides with the three-valued stable semantics. *Fundamenta Informaticae*, 1989. (In print).

[Przymusinski, 1990a] T. Przymusinski. Extended stable semantics for normal and disjunctive logic programs. In *Proceedings of the Seventh International Logic Programming Programming Conference, Jerusalem, Israel*, Association for Logic Programming, MIT Press, Cambridge, Mass., 1990. (In print).

[Przymusinski, 1990b] T. C. Przymusinski. *Autoepistemis Logic for Reasoning About Disjunctive Information.* Research report, University of Texas at El Paso, 1990. (in preparation).

[Przymusinski, 1990c] T. C. Przymusinski. *Stationary States of Logic Programs.* Research report, University of Texas at El Paso, 1990. (in preparation).

[Przymusinski and Warren, 1990] T. C. Przymusinski and D. S. Warren. *Well-founded Semantics: Theory and Implementation.* Research report, UT at El Paso and SUNY at Stony Brook, 1990. (in preparation).

[Rajasekar *et al.*, 1989] A. Rajasekar, J. Lobo, and J. Minker. Weak generalized closed world assumption. *Journal of Automated Reasoning*, (5):293–307, 1989.

[Reiter, 1978] R. Reiter. On closed-world data bases. In H. Gallaire and J. Minker, editors, *Logic and Data Bases*, pages 55–76, Plenum Press, New York, 1978.

[Ross, 1989] K. Ross. The well founded semantics for disjunctive logic programs. In *Proceedings of the First International Conference on Deductive and Object Oriented Databases*, pages 352–369, 1989.

[Ross and Topor, 1988] K. Ross and R. Topor. Inferring negative information from disjunctive databases. *Journal of Automated Reasoning*, (4):397–424, 1988.

[Van Emden and Kowalski, 1976] M. Van Emden and R. Kowalski. The semantics of predicate logic as a programming language. *Journal of the ACM*, 23(4):733–742, 1976.

[Van Gelder, 1989a] A. Van Gelder. The alternating fixpoint of logic programs with negation. In *Proceedings of the Symposium on Principles of Database Systems*, pages 1–10, ACM SIGACT-SIGMOD, 1989.

[Van Gelder, 1989b] A. Van Gelder. Negation as failure using tight derivations for general logic programs. *Journal of Logic Programming*, 6(1):109–133, 1989. Preliminary versions appeared in *Third IEEE Symp. on Logic Programming* (1986), and *Foundations of Deductive Databases and Logic Programming*, J. Minker, ed., Morgan Kaufmann, 1988.

[Van Gelder *et al.*, 1990] A. Van Gelder, K. A. Ross, and J. S. Schlipf. The well-founded semantics for general logic programs. *Journal of the ACM*, 1990. (to appear). Preliminary abstract appeared in Seventh ACM Symposium on Principles of Database Systems, March 1988, pp. 221–230.

[Warren, 1989] David S. Warren. *The XWAM: A Machine that Integrates Prolog and Deductive Database Query Evaluation.* Technical report #25, SUNY at Stony Brook, 1989.

Implementation I

Compilation of Compound Terms in Prolog

Micha Meier
European Computer-Industry Research Centre (ECRC),
Arabellastr.17, 8000 Munich 81, West Germany
micha%ecrc.de@pyramid.com, micha@ecrc.de

Abstract

The execution of a compiled Prolog program can spend a significant amount of time in the unification of compound terms. We show that in the Warren Abstract Machine [7], the approach to compile this unification may be unnecessarily inefficient. When we analyse what are the redundant operations that the WAM executes, we can see that the inefficiency is mainly caused by the *breadth-first* approach to traverse the structures during the unification. We present here a method to compile the unification of compound terms which is based on a *depth-first* approach and show that it is both more general and more efficient than that of the original WAM. Furthermore we present a more efficient approach to compile compound terms in the body and also describe several possible optimizations. Our method was used in the implementation of the SEPIA system [4] developed at ECRC.

1 Introduction

The execution of Prolog programs consists mainly of procedure invocation and unification. The unification itself is estimated to account for about 70 % - 80 % of the execution time. The unification of compound terms, i.e. expressions $f(arg_1, \ldots, arg_n)$, may consume a considerable amount of time, because during the unification these compound terms have to be constructed or scanned. For example, on a set of 15 large benchmark programs measured with an emulator-based Prolog system [4], about 25 % of all emulated abstract instructions accounted for the unification of compound terms.

The WAM [7] presents a complete and compact scheme to compile compound terms, both in head and subgoal arguments. We have analyzed the WAM behavior during the unification of compound terms and have found that sometimes it is not efficient enough, because redundant operations are executed. We will first describe the problems in the WAM and then present a different scheme which tries to avoid them. The reader is assumed to be fluent in the WAM, for a good introduction see e.g. [1].

2 Compound Argument Unification in the WAM

In compiled Prolog, the compound arguments are handled differently in the head and in the body of a clause. A compound term in the clause body is compiled into a sequence of instructions that actually create this term on the heap and put a reference to it into an argument register. A compound term in the head is compiled into instructions which perform the unification with the corresponding argument in the register. The unification is a general two-way matching procedure, which can result in binding variables both in the caller and in the callee. Therefore, the unification instructions must be able to both decompose the caller argument and check if it matches with the clause head, and to create the representation of a compound term on the heap in case that the corresponding slot in the caller argument is a variable. This is the so-called *structure copying* as opposed to *structure sharing* where new structures are not explicitly created, but shared instead.

2.1 Head Arguments

A compound head argument represents a tree structure which has to be traversed during the unification with the caller. The main contribution of the WAM here is the introduction of the **mode** flag to which some instructions are sensitive. This makes it possible to generate only one instruction per source item and the bytecode is very compact. If the procedure argument is being decomposed in the unification, that is, when its main functor is identical with the main functor of the head argument, the machine is said to be in **read** mode. Conversely, if the caller argument is a variable, the machine is in **write** mode where the structure will be constructed on the heap. The **unify** instructions that are emitted for the arguments of the structure depend on the current mode: in the **read** mode they test the type of the caller argument, in the **write** mode the argument is created on the heap. The arguments of a structure are unified in the same mode as the structure functor. When the structure is being constructed on the heap, its arguments are pushed using the heap top pointer **H**, when an existing structure is decomposed, the **S** pointer is used to point to the currently unified argument. For example, the head structure in

p(f(g(...), h(...), k(...))) :- ...

is in the WAM compiled into

get_structure	$f/3$, A_1
unify_variable	X_1
unify_variable	X_2
unify_variable	X_3
get_structure	g/n_1, X_1

```
unify_ ...          <arguments of g>
...
get_structure       h/n2, X2
unify_ ...          <arguments of h>
...
get_structure       k/n3, X3
unify_ ...          <arguments of k>
...
```

If this procedure is called with **?- p(f(g(a), B, C))**, the first and second block of **unify** instructions is executed in **read** mode because the head compound term matches the corresponding functors **f/3** and $\mathbf{g/n_1}$ in the caller. The remaining two blocks of **unify** instructions are executed in **write** mode, because the structures $\mathbf{h/n_2}$ and $\mathbf{k/n_3}$ must be constructed and bound to **B** and **C** respectively.

Let us consider this example from another point of view. We can see that the code generated by the WAM is the same as the code for (when **=/2** is expanded in-line)

p(f(X1, X2, X3)) :- X1 = g(...), X2 = h(...), X3 = k(...).

where **X1**, **X2** and **X3** are temporary variables. The unification of the main structure is completely separated from the unification of its compound arguments. As the unification of the temporaries can be written in any order, the traversal of the rest of the tree can be made in any manner, as long as this way of assigning compound arguments to temporaries is kept.

This model is very easy to understand and efficient enough to implement on bytecode emulators, however it has several inherent problems:

- The **write** mode is not propagated to the substructures. Whenever a structure is unified in **write** mode, it is clear that all its substructures will also be unified in **write** mode. The WAM does not use this property, in a substructure in **write** mode the following is executed:
  - the instruction **unify_variable** pushes a new free variable on the heap and stores a pointer to it in a temporary variable
  - The instruction **get_structure** later dereferences this variable, finds out that it is uninstantiated (although this is known at compile time), and thus it sets the **write** mode. The variable is then bound to a new structure on the heap and for this binding even a trail test has to be performed.

  Several memory accesses, dereferencing, tag test and trail test are redundant. This is the consequence of the fact that the unification of a term is completely separated from the unification of its compound arguments.

- References to all substructures are saved into temporary variables. Although Prolog programmers do not seem to like deeply nested structures (except for tail-recursive ones like lists), often their arity might be quite high [3] and so many temporaries are necessary. This increases the number of used registers, or causes additional memory accesses for temporaries allocated in memory.

- Every **unify** instruction must test the **mode** bit. In fact every **unify** instruction is just a shorthand for two different instructions, one **read** and one **write**. In native code implementations, and especially on processors with an instruction pipeline, these frequent tests break the instruction flow and slow down the execution. Most commercial systems split the **unify** instructions explicitly to avoid the tests.

- In a term like **f(g(a), h(b), i(c))**, the code starts with

get_structure	**f/3,** $\mathbf{A}_i$
unify_variable	X_1
unify_variable	X_2
unify_variable	X_3

  If the caller argument is **f(g(b), B, C)**, the unification of **g(a)** and **g(b)** fails and so the two **unify_variable** instructions were useless. The same effect could be achieved by just saving a *pointer* to the second argument.

- If the information about the instantiations of the arguments is available, e.g. in the form of mode declarations, it can be used only if the **unify** instructions are explicitly divided into **read** and **write** instructions. The compiler can then suppress generation of code that would never be executed.

- This sort of breadth-first traversal can be always simulated using a bounded depth-first traversal, however the converse is not true. Therefore the depth-first is more general and a better candidate for the compilation technique.

2.2 Body Arguments

In the WAM, compound terms in subgoal arguments are compiled using the same **unify** instructions like in the clause head. The only difference is that the structures are built *bottom-up*, without the **get** instructions, so that dereferencing and trail tests are avoided. The other problems remain, though. Although it is known that the instructions will be executed in **write** mode, each **unify** instruction tests the mode flag. It is also necessary to use temporary variables to build the structure. However, it is known at compile time that the structure will be created in consecutive locations at the heap top, and all pointer offsets are fixed. Therefore, no temporary variables are really necessary to create the structure.

3 Depth-First Method

Our method has the following differences compared to the WAM:

- an explicit distinction between **read** and **write** instructions is made, the compiler generates separate **read** and **write** mode sequences,
- nested structures are unified in a *depth-first* manner,
- no code is duplicated, the execution can switch from the **read** to the **write** sequence and back,
- the body compound arguments are built *top-down* in a *breadth-first* manner, no temporary variables are necessary.

3.1 Head Arguments

While the WAM saves all compound arguments into temporary variables, in the depth-first approach it is enough to save a *pointer* to the argument following a compound one. No temporary variable is needed for the last structure argument. Note for example, that no temporaries are necessary to unify a list containing only constants. The temporaries can be viewed as a return stack whose depth is known at compile time. When the unification of a substructure is finished, the execution proceeds with the next argument whose address is saved in the corresponding temporary variable.

Since the two sequences are now compiled separately, the **get_structure** and **get_list** instructions are slightly modified. For the **write** mode the execution continues in sequence, for **read** mode a branch to a given label is executed. At the end of the **write** mode sequence there is a **branch** instruction that causes a branch to the end of the **read** mode sequence.

Even when the two sequences are split, it is not possible to avoid some tests. Since part of the structure may be unified in **read** and part in **write** mode, branches from one sequence to the other one might be necessary (unless one wants to duplicate the code, but this is exactly what we try to avoid when compiling into native code). The basic observation is as follows: If a structure is unified in **read** mode, all its parent and sibling structures are also unified in **read** mode. Therefore, when the unification of this structure is finished, the execution continues directly in the **read** mode sequence. This is the *upward propagation* of the **read** mode. The compound arguments of a structure, however, might have to be unified in **write** mode if they are matched with a free variable. Hence at the *beginning* of the unification of a structure in **read** mode it is necessary to perform a test and possibly branch into the **write** mode sequence.

If a structure is unified in **write** mode, all its substructures are also unified in **write** mode, i.e. the **write** mode is propagated *downwards*, but its parent structure might be unified in **read** mode. Therefore, at the end of each structure unified in **write** mode the system has to test if a branch back into the **read** mode sequence has to be made. The condition when to jump from the **write** mode sequence back to the **read** sequence is as follows: at the end of every compound term the address of the next argument to unify is obtained from a temporary variable. The tag of this variable stores a flag which decides whether to jump back to the **read** mode sequence or whether to continue with the next instruction.

In **write** mode the whole structure skeleton has to be pushed on the heap at once since the structure arguments are not unified and accessed consecutively. Therefore the **write_structure** pushes the functor on the heap and increments **H** by the arity of the structure. To access structure arguments, both in **read** and **write** mode the **S** register is used. The **read** and **write** mode instruction sequences are very similar except that the former contains the **read** and the latter the **write** variants of the unification instructions.

Below we present an example how to implement our method in the WAM. Note that for bytecode emulators these instructions are too low-level, several instructions could be merged into one to avoid the dispatching overhead. For native code, on the other hand, the generated code must be postprocessed to remove redundant operations.

read_down $\mathbf{X}_i$

This instruction is generated before a compound term which is not the last argument. A reference to the next argument is stored into the temporary.

```
Xi = S + 1;
```

write_down $\mathbf{X}_i$

Like **read_down**, but the mode **write** is marked into the tag of the temporary.

```
Xi = tag_struct(S + 1);
```

read_structure F

A substructure in **read** mode. If the term pointed to by **S** is a structure pointer and the functor of the structure is equal to F, **S** is set to point to its first argument, else a failure occurs.

```
if (tag(*S) != tag_struct ||
    S = val(*S), *S++ != F)
    Fail;
```

write_structure F

A substructure in **write** mode. A pointer to a new structure skeleton with functor F is stored in the location pointed to by **S** and **S** is set to point to the first argument of the new structure skeleton.

```
*S = tag_struct(H);
H++ = F;
S = H;
H += arity(F);
```

read_up X_i
This instruction is generated at the end of a structure which is itself a (not last) argument of a compound term. The **S** pointer is restored from the temporary.

```
S = Xi;
```

read_list
Corresponds to **read_structure** for lists.

```
if (tag(*S) == tag_list)
    S = val(*S);
else
    Fail;
```

read_test LabW
This instruction precedes a substructure in **read** mode. S is dereferenced. If the result of dereferencing is a free variable, it is trailed if necessary and a jump to **LabW** is executed.

```
S = Deref(S);
if (tag(S) == tag_ref) {
    trail(S);
    P = LabW;
}
```

read_constant C
A constant argument of a compound term in **read** mode. The contents of S is dereferenced and unified with C. After a successful unification S is incremented.

```
if (Unify(*Deref(S), C))
    S++;
else
    Fail;
```

write_up X_i
This instruction is generated at the end of a structure in **write** mode which is not the last argument. The S pointer is restored from the temporary.

```
S = val(Xi);
```

write_list
Corresponds to **write_structure** for lists.

```
*S = tag_list(H);
S = H;
H += 2;
```

write_test X_i, LabR
This instruction is generated after a **write_up** instruction. If the tag of X_i is not **write**, a jump to LabR is executed.

```
if (tag(Xi) != tag_struct)
    P = LabR;
```

write_constant C
A constant argument of a compound term in **write** mode. **C** is stored into the location pointed to by S and S is incremented.

```
*S++ = C;
```

3.1.1 Compilation Example

Note that the WAM uses less abstract instructions, however they are more complicated than ours. When expanded, the WAM code is always longer.

f(g(X), b)

	Our Code		WAM Code	
	get_structure	A_i, LabR	get_structure	A_i
	write_down	X_1	unify_variable	X_1
W1:	write_structure	g/1	unify_constant	b
	write_variable	Y_1	get_structure	g/1, X_1
	write_up	X_1	unify_variable	Y_1
	write_test	X_1, R1		
	write_constant	b		
	branch	Ends		
LabR:	read_down	X_1		
	read_test	W1		
	read_structure	g/1		
	read_variable	Y_1		
	read_up	X_1		
R1:	read_constant	b		
Ends:				

As we can see, the code generated for **read** and **write** mode is very similar, temporary variables are the same in both sequences and the correspondence of labels for branches between the two sequences is straightforward.

3.2 Body Arguments

Unlike head arguments, the compound terms to be constructed in the clause body are known at compile time, they are going to be pushed onto consecutive heap locations. Therefore, when the compound term is created top-down, in a breadth-first manner, one pointer is completely sufficient to build it, no temporary variables are necessary.

The instructions work as follows: the generation starts with the topmost structure, first the functor is pushed at the heap top using the **H** pointer, then the structure arguments are pushed, followed by the next substructure etc. Whenever a compound subargument is encountered, a structure pointer to it is pushed on the heap and then the next argument is built. Thus each new structure is put at the end of a queue and built when it is at its beginning.

put_structure F, A_i This instruction corresponds to the beginning of a compound argument of a body subgoal. A functor is pushed on the heap, a structure pointer to it is stored into $\mathbf{A}_i$.

A_i = tag_struct(H);

***H++ = F;**

push_constant C The constant C is pushed on the heap. Note that C can also be a functor of a compound term.

```
*H++ = C;
```

push_structure Offset This instruction corresponds to a compound subargument. A structure pointer to **H + Offset** is pushed on the heap top.

```
*H = tag_struct(H + Offset);
H++;
```

push_list Offset This instruction corresponds to a compound subargument which is a list.

```
*H = tag_list(H + Offset);
H++;
```

An example of a body goal compilation:
test :- do(parse(s(np, vp), [birds, fly], [])).

Our Code		WAM Code (from [7])	
put_structure	parse/3, A_1	put_structure	s/2, X_2
push_structure	3	unify_constant	np
push_list	5	unify_constant	vp
push_constant	[]	put_list	X_4
push_constant	s/2	unify_constant	fly
push_constant	np	unify_nil	
push_constant	vp	put_list	X_3
push_constant	birds	unify_constant	birds
push_list	1	unify_value	X_4
push_constant	fly	put_structure	parse/3, A_1
push_constant	[]	unify_value	X_2
execute	do/1	unify_value	X_3
		unify_nil	
		execute	do/1

It can be seen that to achieve the same effect the WAM needs 3 temporary variables and more code than our method.

4 Optimizations

The above presented methods are the basic schemata only, there are many optimizations to be applied on them.

In the sequence of **up**, **down** and **test** abstract instructions in the generated native code usually several machine instructions can be omitted, which is easy to do in a peephole optimizer.

The **unify_local_value** WAM instruction has only its **write** counterpart, in the **read** sequence the normal **read_value** instruction is used.

- When the head structure contains void variables, it is often possible to omit part of the **read** sequence, provided that no nonvoid argument follows the void one(s). For example, the term

  [_|_]

  can be simply compiled into

```
        get_list     Ai, Ends
        write_void   2
Ends:
```

- Ground compound terms in the clause body should not be compiled into a sequence of instructions - even with a *structure copying* method they can be shared. The compound term can be created once at compile time and in the clause body the **put_constant** instruction just puts a corresponding structure or list pointer to it.

  Similarly, ground compound terms in the head should be constructed at compile time and treated like constants in the **write** sequence, e.g. **f(g(a), g(b))** is compiled into

```
        get_structure    f/2, Ai, LR
        write_constant   < g(a) >
        write_constant   < g(b) >
        branch           Ends
LR:     read_down        X1
        ...
Ends:
```

- If the compound argument is the indexed one, a branch directly to the **read** sequence can be executed:

```
append([], L, L).
append([X|L1], L2, [X|L3]) :-
    append(L1, L2, L3).
```

	Our Code			WAM Code	
La:	switch_on_type	A_1, list:Ll, nil:Ln, default:fail		switch_on_type	A_1, list:Ll, nil:Ln, default:fail
Lv:	get_nil	A_1	Lv:	get_nil	A_1

```
Ln: get_value        A2, A3          Ln: get_value        A2, A3
    proceed                              proceed

    get_list         A1, Ll          Ll: get_list         A1
    write_variable   X4                  unify_variable   X4
    write_variable   A1                  unify_variable   A1
    branch           E1                  get_list         A3
Ll: read_variable    X4                  unify_value      X4
    read_variable    A1                  unify_variable   A3
E1: get_list         A3, Lr              execute          append/3
    write_value      X4
    write_variable   A3
    branch           La
Lr: read_value       X4
    read_variable    A3
    branch           La
```

- When more information is available about the instantiation of the caller arguments, e.g. from abstract interpretation, the compiler can omit certain instructions and regroup the others, so that a simple peephole optimization yields optimal native code. For example, if the clause

  p(g(f(X), h(X))).

  is always called with an instantiated argument, but the arguments of **g/2** are known to be unbound, a mixture of **read** and **write** sequence can be generated, the compiler can replace some of the **read** instructions by **write** ones:

  g(f(X), h(X))

```
          Default                              Mixture

    get_structure    g/2, Ai, LR        get_structure    g/2, Ai, L1
    write_down       X1             L1: read_down        X1
W1: write_structure  f/1                read_test        L2
    write_variable   X2                 write_structure  f/1
    write_up         X1                 write_variable   X2
    write_test       X1, R1             read_up          X1
W2: write_structure  h/1                read_test        X1, L3
    write_value      X2             L3: write_structure  h/1
    branch           Ends               write_value      X2
```

```
LR: read_down       X1
    read_test       W1
    read_structure  f/1
    read_value      X2
    read_up         X1

R1: read_test       W2
    read_structure  h/1
    read_value      X2
Ends:
```

Note also that the depth-first approach is even more flexible - the compiler might decide to compile e.g. the last argument depth-first and the other ones breadth-first etc.

5 Discussion

Optimizing the unification of compound terms in Prolog is a challenging task. One of the problems of Prolog efficiency is exactly this - inefficient handling of structures. Often a compound term is created before calling a goal only to decompose it in the called procedure, which is a severe overhead. The *structure sharing* systems have an advantage here, because the structures do not have to be explicitly created. On the other hand, structure sharing has other disadvantages like poor locality of references and creating long reference chains, so that the only way currently being followed is to optimize the structure copying mechanism.

Despite the problems in the WAM handling of compound terms, there has been very little work published about alternative approaches[1]. Current emulated systems seem to use the WAM code since it is compact, but the emulator contains separate versions of the **unify** instructions for **read** and **write** mode. The mode flag is not used because each concerned instruction knows to which version of the next instruction it should continue.

Native code systems often use a scheme similar to [6], where explicit **read** and **write** sequences are generated, e.g. for **f(g(a), g(b))**

```
     get_structure   f/2, Ai, LR
     write_variable  X1
     write_variable  X2
     branch          S1
LR:  read_variable   X1
     read_variable   X2
S1:  get_structure   g/1, X1
     ...
```

In this way the use of the mode flag is not necessary, however nested

[1]Our work presented in this paper is based on [2].

structures are still unified separately from the main term and so all the problems with the **write** mode remain. If the last argument is compound, it can be unified directly, without a **write_variable** instruction and so the **write** mode can be propagated to it. Propagating the **write** mode to other substructures is obviously difficult with *breadth-first* traversal, but it is a trivial task when the *depth-first* approach is used.

Turk [6] describes an approach where the **write** mode is propagated using a branch into the middle of the **get** instruction, to omit dereferencing and testing. The **write** mode can thus be directly propagated only to the first compound argument, its first compound subargument etc. The following arguments have to push a free variable on the heap and the **get** instruction has to dereference and test it like in the basic WAM. In our method the number of branches depends on the actual data, how often it is necessary to switch between the two sequences; the **write** mode is propagated everywhere.

Recently, Van Roy [5] described a lower-level abstract language for the unification which generates separate sequences for the **read** and **write** mode. The **write** mode sequences use a breadth-first approach similar to ours for body terms, but the whole skeleton is pushed at once, so that some of the **push** instructions need two offsets as arguments, which is less efficient for bytecode and for some machines. The **read** mode sequences use depth-first traversal, but the code is not shared between the two sequences, except for the last argument, and so the **write** mode instructions appear also inside the **read** mode sequence. In this way, Van Roy's **write** mode sequence does not contain any redundant operations, however for the expense that this code cannot be shared. For complex structures the size of the generated code grows exponentially. When we use the **push** instructions instead of the **write** ones, except for the last argument, and generate an additional **write** sequence for every label in **read_test** using the **push** instructions, we obtain a method which is very similar to the Van Roy's one.

Our methods have the following advantages over the WAM or the above derivatives:

- Since we are using the depth-first approach, our method for head unification needs less temporary variables than the WAM for wide or shallow structures.

- We generate explicit **read** and **write** sequences and for every source item (including parentheses) there is at most one **read** and one **write** instruction. The code size is proportional to the term size, no code is duplicated.

- The **write** mode is automatically propagated to all head substructures, no intermediate free variables are pushed on the heap in order to save and restore the mode information. If it is necessary to save the mode information, most often this is done in a register. Our method thus performs less memory accesses than the pure WAM.

- Our method uses the **H** and **S** register in a uniform way both in **read** and **write** instructions. It is therefore possible to jump from one sequence tothe other one, or generate directly mixed code.
- Our method can be used both for depth-first and breadth-first structure traversal. After performing the global analysis of the program, the compiler can generate the appropriate code and omit sequences or parts of them which are not necessary.
- The code for constructing compound terms in the body is optimal. For general head terms the length of our code is (after postprocessing) minimal.

The drawbacks of our method concern the following cases:

- For left-balanced head structures like **f(g(h(a), b), c)** where each structure has only one compound argument which is not the last one, our method needs more temporary variables than the WAM. Prolog programmers normally prefer right-balanced structures which can be processed using tail-recursive loops.
- When a structure is unified in **read** mode and all its arguments are unified in **write** mode, two branches are executed for each argument. In this case, either breadth-first approach can be used, or the compiler can generate a mixture of **read** and **write** sequences.

Acknowledgements

The author would like to thank to Dominique Henry de Villeneuve, Alexander Herold, Jacques Noye, Bruno Poterie and Joachim Schimpf for fruitful discussions about this topic and for commenting previous versions of this paper and to the referees of the submitted paper for interesting comments about up-to-date systems. Many of the ideas presented here are probably already part of Prolog folklore and so the author would also like to acknowledge all people that have contributed to their development.

References

[1] John Gabriel, Tim Lindholm, E.L. Lusk, and R. A. Overbeek. A Tutorial on the Warren Abstract Machine for Computational Logic. Technical Report ANL-84-84, Argonne National Laboratory, 1984.

[2] Micha Meier. The Compilation of Compound Term Unification in Prolog. Internal Report IR-LP/lpp1, ECRC, May 1987.

[3] Micha Meier. Analysis of Prolog Procedures for Indexing Purposes. In ICOT, editor, *Proceedings of the International Conference on Fifth Generation Computer Systems*, pages 800–807, Tokyo, November 1988.

[4] Micha Meier, Abderrahmane Aggoun, David Chan, Pierre Dufresne, Reinhard Enders, Dominique Henry de Villeneuve, Alexander Herold, Philip Kay, Bruno Perez, Emmanuel van Rossum, and Joachim Schipf. SEPIA - an Extendible Prolog System. In *Proceedings of the 11th World Computer Congress IFIP'89*, San Francisco, August 1989.

[5] Peter Van Roy. An Intermediate Language to Support Prolog's Unification. In Ewing L. Lusk and Ross A. Overbeek, editors, *Proceedings of the NACLP'89*, pages 1148–1164, Cleveland, October 1989.

[6] Andrew K. Turk. Compiler Optimizations for the WAM. In *Third International Conference on Logic Programming*, pages 657–662, London, July 1986.

[7] David H. D. Warren. An Abstract Prolog Instruction Set. Technical Note 309, SRI, October 1983.

A Program to Compile Compound Terms

```
% Compile a head compound term
head(Term) :-
    functor(Term, F, A),
    compile_args(Term, 1, A, 1, Code,
         [branch(lab(_)), label(LR)|ReadCode]),
    read_seq(Code, ReadCode, []),
    pwrite([get_structure(F/A, reg(i), lab(LR))|Code]).

% Compile a compound subgoal argument
body(Term) :-
    functor(Term, F, A),
    A1 is A + 1,
    compile_body([Term|Cont], Cont, A1, [_|Code], []),
    pwrite([put_structure(F/A, reg(i))|Code]).

% Write sequence for the arguments of a compound term
compile_args(Term, A, A, Reg) -->
    {arg(A, Term, Arg)},
    compile_arg(Arg, Reg, last).
compile_args(Term, I, A, Reg) -->
    {I < A, arg(I, Term, Arg), I1 is I + 1},
    compile_arg(Arg, Reg, notlast),
    compile_args(Term, I1, A, Reg).

% Generate the write sequence for one argument
compile_arg(Struct, Reg, last) -->
    {compound(Struct), functor(Struct, F, A)},
```

```
    [label(_), write_structure(F/A)],
    compile_args(Struct, 1, A, Reg).
compile_arg(Struct, Reg, notlast) -->
    {compound(Struct), functor(Struct, F, A), Reg1 is Reg+1},
    [write_down(reg(Reg)), label(_), write_structure(F/A)],
    compile_args(Struct, 1, A, Reg1),
    [write_up(reg(Reg)), write_test(lab(_))].
compile_arg(Const, _, _) -->
    {atomic(Const)},
    [write_constant(Const)].

% Generate the read sequence and fill in the labels
read_seq([branch(lab(L))|_]) -->
    [label(L)].
read_seq([write_down(R)|T]) -->
    [read_down(R)],
    read_seq(T).
read_seq([label(L), write_structure(S)|T]) -->
    [read_test(lab(L)), read_structure(S)],
    read_seq(T).
read_seq([write_up(R), write_test(lab(L))|T]) -->
    [read_up(R), label(L)],
    read_seq(T).
read_seq([write_constant(C)|T]) -->
    [read_constant(C)],
    read_seq(T).

% Compile a queue of body structures
compile_body([], [], _) --> {true}.
compile_body([Struct|Rest], Cont, Off) -->
    {functor(Struct, F, A), Off1 is Off - 1},
    [push_constant(F/A)],
    compile_struct(Struct, 1, A, Off1, NewOff, Cont, NewCont),
    compile_body(Rest, NewCont, NewOff).

% Compile one body structure
compile_struct(Struct, A, A, Off, NewOff, Cont, NewCont) -->
    {arg(A, Struct, Arg)},
    compile_body_arg(Arg, Off, NewOff, Cont, NewCont).
compile_struct(Struct, I, A, Off, NewOff, Cont, NewCont) -->
    {I < A, arg(I, Struct, Arg), I1 is I + 1},
    compile_body_arg(Arg, Off, NO, Cont, NC),
    compile_struct(Struct, I1, A, NO, NewOff, NC, NewCont).

% Compile one argument of a body structure
```

```
compile_body_arg(Const, Off, NewOff, C, C) -->
    {atomic(Const), NewOff is Off - 1},
    [push_constant(Const)].
compile_body_arg(Struct, Off, NewOff, [Struct|C], C) -->
    {compound(Struct), functor(Struct, _, A),
        NewOff is Off + A},
    [push_structure(Off)].

% Print the generated code
pwrite([]).
pwrite([label(Lab)|Rest]) :-
    write(Lab),
    write(:),
    pwrite(Rest).
pwrite([Instr|Rest]) :-
    put(9),
    functor(Instr, F, A),
    write(F),
    name(F, LS),
    length(LS, Length),
    tab(20-Length),
    writeargs(Instr, 1, A),
    nl,
    pwrite(Rest).

writeargs(Instr, A, A) :-
    arg(A, Instr, Arg),
    writearg(Arg).
writeargs(Instr, I, A) :-
    I < A,
    arg(I, Instr, Arg),
    writearg(Arg),
    write(', '),
    I1 is I + 1,
    writeargs(Instr, I1, A).

writearg(lab(L)) :-
    write(L).
writearg(reg(R)) :-
    write('X'),
    write(R).
writearg(Arg) :-
    write(Arg).
```

Finding Advantageous Orders for Argument Unification for the Prolog WAM

Zerksis D. Umrigar
Department of Computer Science
SUNY, Binghamton, NY 13901
(607) 777-4311
umrigar@bingvaxu.cc.binghamton.edu

Abstract

Unification has the property that the result of unifying two structures is independent of the order in which the arguments of those structures are unified. This paper represents an attempt to systematically find an order for argument unification which attempts to minimize the use of instructions and temporary storage on the the Warren Abstract Machine (WAM) [7] for Prolog.

This paper shows that by changing the order of unification of the arguments for certain types of terms, there are simple compilation algorithms which are guaranteed to produce both a minimum number of instructions and use a minimum number of registers. For more general terms, we give a general algorithm called *reordering unification* for unification scheduling which minimizes the number of instructions while attempting to minimize the number of temporary registers. Instead of allocating a register to a variable when it is first encountered, it is advantageous to defer the allocation until more information becomes available. Hence our general algorithm does code generation before register allocation, with the code generation phase producing a set of constraints on register allocation. When these constraints are subsequently solved, the resulting register allocation is backpatched into the previously generated code.

1 Introduction

The Warren Abstract Machine for Prolog [7] is an architecture for Prolog which has been extremely influential and forms the basis of many existing Prolog implementations. Among its many optimizations, the WAM attempts to reduce memory bandwidth requirements by using registers for both parameter passing and temporary storage. Hence to realize the full potential of this architecture, it is desirable to optimize the use of these registers.

The original WAM report [7] and much subsequent work implicitly assumes that the arguments within Prolog terms are unified in a strict left-to-right order. There is no reason for such a restriction, as the results of the unification of two structures is independent of the order in which the arguments of the structures are unified. This paper explores some of the alternative approaches which result when we remove this restriction.

In the next section, we review those aspects of using argument registers on the WAM which are germane to the topic of this paper. We then outline a framework for this inquiry by explicating the assumptions we are making. We then review how previous work fits in within this framework. This is followed by a discussion of how conventional compiler optimization techniques fit our problem. We then motivate our approach by considering several examples. With that done, we are prepared to present the major results of this paper.

We first show how certain restricted classes of terms can be compiled in an optimal way. We then discuss the sources of register allocation conflicts and how such conflicts may be avoided. We then present our reordering unification algorithm.

We conclude the paper with a brief discussion of how we can use searching to generate optimal code for unrestricted terms and point to directions for future work.

This paper does not give a formal presentation of the algorithms. Instead it gives an informal account which attempts to convey to the reader the intuition on which those algorithms are based. The reader is assumed to be familiar with the details of the WAM as described in [7] or [3].

2 · The Use of the WAM Argument Registers

As defined in [2], a *chunk* is a sequence of inline goals followed by a user goal. We define a *temporary variable* in a Prolog clause to be one which has all its occurrences in a single chunk (the head being counted as part of the first chunk.) A *permanent variable* is any variable which is not temporary. Permanent variables need to be stored in a clause's environment, whereas temporary variables can be stored using the argument registers. Finally, we define a *permanent term*[1] as a Prolog term which does not contain any temporary variables.

Note that our definition of temporary and permanent variables is different and simpler than that given in [7] and [2], and is similar to that in [6] and [4]. The advantage of this definition is that our temporary variables are a superset of those given by Warren's definition. This implies that fewer variables are permanent which leads to smaller environments.

The argument registers in the WAM are used for three distinct purposes:

1. Passing arguments to a procedure. This is their primary purpose.
2. Storing the temporary variables which occur in a Prolog clause. We will call the temporary variables which actually appear in a source

[1]This is similar to the *known terms* used by [4].

clause *source temporaries*.

3. For temporary storage during the unification of nested structures. This is because WAM instructions are not capable of directly handling nested structures — substructures are processed by associating them with new temporary variables called *structure temporaries*. For example, the nested structure in the chunk `p(f(g(a)))` can be replaced by introducing the new structure temporary `X` in the chunk `X=g(a), p(f(X))`.

Structure and source temporaries do not appear to be all that different. However there is a major difference, in that there are exactly two references to a structure temporary, whereas there may be any number of references to a source temporary. Considering a Prolog term as a graph, terms containing only structure temporaries can be represented as trees, whereas terms containing source temporaries will, in general, be DAGs. It turns out that allocating the structure temporaries is relatively easy while allocating the source temporaries is difficult.

The WAM capitalizes on the fact that most Prolog programs rarely use the full power of unrestricted unification to unify deeply nested structures. It specializes the general unification algorithm to the structures which are present in the source code. This is done by compiling clause heads into a sequence of `get` and `unify` instructions which match the source arguments with the incoming arguments contained in the argument registers. Similarly a goal is compiled into a sequence of `put` and `unify` instructions which load the argument registers for the call about to be made. The details of exactly how structures are compiled follows:

Head (goal) structures of a Prolog clause are compiled using the instruction `get_structure` (`put_structure`), followed **immediately** by a sequence of `unify` instructions for the arguments. The code for a structure argument which itself is a structure, is linked to the `unify` instruction for that argument using a structure temporary assigned to some argument register.

When we `get` some structure in the head, we are not interested in preserving a pointer to that structure. Assume that we wish to `get` a structure S without `get`ting any of its substructures. Also assume that S has m arguments which are structures or unallocated source temporaries. Then we will need $m - 1$ new registers since the register which was originally pointing to the structure can immediately be reused for `unify`ing with one of the arguments. After the `get` of the structure and its arguments has been completed, m registers will be occupied, containing the substructures or previously unallocated source temporaries.

On the other hand, when we `put` some structure in a goal, we are interested in preserving a pointer to that structure. Assume that we wish to `put` a structure S without `put`ting any of its substructures. Also assume that S has m arguments which are structures or unallocated source temporaries. Then we will need m new registers since the register which was originally pointing to the structure cannot be immediately reused for `unifying` with any of the arguments. Hence to `put` the entire structure we will need a total of $m + 1$ registers.

In the sequel, we will be interested in the *level* at which source temporaries occur. We the top-level at which an argument can occur level 0, the next level 1 and so on. For example, in the goal `p(f(X),X,Y)` `X` has both level 0 and level 1 occurrences, whereas `Y` only has a level 0 occurrence.

3 Assumptions

We assume that we always want a clause to fail as soon as possible. Hence we do not consider possibilities of interspersing the code for the head and the code for the first goal.

We also assume that we do not want to build duplicate structures. This assumption restricts us to traversing head arguments in a strictly top-down manner. If we did not do so, the WAM may unnecessarily enter write-mode, building a structure on the heap only to match it subsequently with a similar structure pointed to by an incoming argument register.

We do not attempt to allocate permanent variables to registers in an attempt to reduce the cost of accessing them in the environment. We also do not attempt to determine when to spill the argument registers if there are not enough of them to meet all the demands for temporary storage. It is felt that the algorithms given in this paper could be extended to handle those situations.

Finally, what do we mean by optimization? The WAM is already highly optimized to Prolog — usually each instruction corresponds to a non-punctuation token in the source program. The scope for optimization within the constraints described above is relatively limited. Hence the prioritized goals for our compilation algorithms are

1. Minimization of the number of instructions when compiling the first chunk.

2. Minimization of the number of registers used.

with 1 being our primary goal.

4 Previous Work

In [6], Van Roy allocates temporaries to any available free register without much consideration of the issues involved. He does however mention that processing substructures in different orders can lead to better code, but seems to imply that finding those orders is inefficient. This is in contrast to the efficient algorithms for special kinds of terms presented in this paper.

[2] gives serious consideration to the register allocation problem for temporary variables. No consideration was given to the possibility of producing

better code by varying the order in which structure arguments are unified. This becomes readily apparent by considering one of the examples from that paper which we shall do subsequently.

The earliest work known to this author where different orders for processing arguments were considered was [1]. The authors constructed a directed graph on subsets of the argument registers where there was a directed edge from a subset I to a subset O if some variable in a head argument belonging to I was used in a goal argument belonging to O. The presence of cycles in the directed graph signalled a conflict which was resolved by allocating a register. The ordering constraints used seem to be overly conservative, and it also appears that the algorithm produces interspersed code for the head and first goal.

The work which is closest to that reported here is the *adaptive unification* algorithm of [4]. In that paper, the authors attempted to vary the processing order for the arguments of a head or goal to minimize the number of WAM instructions. They did not attempt to schedule the substructures of the arguments. They also did not make any attempt to minimize the number of temporary registers. This paper differs from that paper in the following ways:

1. We present an algorithm for processing permanent terms which uses both a minimum number of instructions **and a minimum number of registers**.

2. We consider a source of register conflict caused by occurrences of level-1 source temporaries in the first goal.

3. We consider different orders of processing among permanent terms — something which was explicitly mentioned as omitted in [4].

4. We show how it is possible to eliminate an overly conservative policy of register allocation while still resolving conflicts. In general, this would lead to fewer registers being used.

As we progress through this paper, we will discuss how our approach differs from that used by them.

5 Conventional Optimization and the WAM

The Prolog clause `p(a,b,f(a,g(X))):- q(c,X)` is equivalent to

```
p(AH1,AH2,AH3):-
  AH1=a, AH2=b, AH3=f(a,T1), T1=g(X),
  AG1=c, AG2=X,
  q(AG1,AG2).
```

Our reordering unification algorithm presented later in the paper does this transformation incrementally as it is processing chunks. The two lines containing the equalities above are similar to the *basic blocks* containing only straight-line assignments used in conventional optimization. However, there is an important difference — since = denotes unification rather than assignment, there is no restriction on the order in which these unifications are done. Hence, when we consider Prolog terms as DAGs, there is no restriction that children be evaluated before parents. This removes a constraint on ordering which is present in conventional optimization. The removal of this constraint represents an opportunity for greater optimization, but also tends to make the optimization problem harder.

Even with these differences, it is interesting to view the similarities. We will show in this paper that there are efficient algorithms for optimally compiling Prolog terms which are trees — these are terms which are permanent terms. This does not appear to be the case for compiling Prolog terms which are unrestricted DAGs (nonpermanent terms which share one or more source temporaries). These results are similar to the result in conventional optimization that there are efficient algorithms for compiling arithmetic expressions which are trees, but not for those which are unrestricted DAGs.

6 Some Example Code Sequences

In this section, we consider examples of code sequences for some Prolog clauses produced by using compilation algorithms previously published in the literature, and also the corresponding code sequences produced by varying the order of unification of arguments.

Consider the following example taken from [2]. The clause

```
p(X,Y,f(Z)):- q(a,b,Z,g(X,Y)).
```

The code sequence shown below on the left is produced by the most informed of the three algorithms presented in [2], whereas the code sequence on the right is produced by allowing arguments to be processed in an appropriate order.

```
get_structure   f/1,A3          get_structure   f/1,A3
unify_variable  A3              unify_variable  A3
move_register   A1,A5           put_structure   g/2,A4
put_constant    a,A1            unify_value     A1
move_register   A2,A6           unify_value     A2
put_constant    b,A2            put_constant    a,A1
put_structure   g/2,A4          put_constant    b,A2
unify_value     A5              execute         q/4
unify_value     A6
execute         q/4
```

The improved version uses 8 instructions and 4 registers versus 10 instructions and 6 registers for the original version.

The following example is given in [4].

```
head(f(T),g(T)):- goal(a,T).
```

Our implementation of the algorithm described there generated the code sequence shown below on the left, whereas the code sequence shown on the right can be generated by allowing an appropriate unification order.

```
get_structure    f/1,A1          get_structure    g/1,A2
unify_variable   A1              unify_variable   A2
get_structure    g/1,A2          get_structure    f/1,A1
unify_value      A1              unify_value      A2
move_register    A1,A2           put_constant     a,A1
put_constant     a,A1            execute          goal/2
execute          goal/2
```

Note the extra `move_register` instruction in the first code sequence which is avoided in the second sequence by *unloading* register `A2` before assigning a register to `T`.

For the clause

```
p(f(X)):- q(g(X)).
```

our implementation of the adaptive unification algorithm from [4] produced the code sequence shown on the left below, whereas the code sequence shown on the right can be produced by predicting a register conflict not considered in [4].

```
get_structure    f/1,A1          get_structure    f/1,A1
unify_variable   A1              unify_variable   A2
move_register    A1,A2           put_structure    g/1,A1
put_structure    g/1,A1          unify_value      A2
unify_value      A2              execute          q/1
execute          q/1
```

Examining the goal and recollecting that the functor of a structure is `put` immediately preceeding its arguments, it should be clear that in the leftmost code sequence `X` should not have been assigned to register `A1`. Since the adaptive unification algorithm does not consider such sources of register conflicts, it goes ahead and makes this allocation which results in the extra `move_register` instruction.

By analyzing these and similar examples, the following facts emerge:

- It is never disadvantageous to `get` (`put`) any head (goal) argument which is a permanent term without nested structures before (after) all other arguments. Doing so makes the argument register available for use as a temporary while processing other arguments.

- It is never disadvantageous to `get` any head argument which is a permanent term with upto one nested structure per level before all other more complex arguments. The same argument register can be used as the structure temporary necessary to `get` the nested substructures.

- It is never disadvantageous to `get` (`put`) repeated top-level head (goal) source variable arguments before (after) all other arguments. If there are m top-level occurrences of a particular variable, then doing this frees $m-1$ to m argument registers for use as temporaries while processing other arguments.

- It *may* be preferable to `get` (`put`) any head (goal) argument which is a permanent term before (after) all other arguments. This depends on exactly how many substructures the argument has versus the number of source temporaries in the other arguments.

- If a source temporary has an occurrence at level 0 in the goal, it is preferable to allocate that argument register to the source temporary. If that argument position is still occupied by an incoming head argument, then attempt to unload that argument.

- A source temporary `X` should not be allocated to a register A_i if `X` has an occurrence at level 1 in argument position i in the goal.

A useful side-effect of attempting to `put` arguments which are structures before arguments which are permanent variables, is that it may be possible to avoid `put_unsafe_value` instructions. The reason for this is that if the permanent variable occurs inside a structure it will be initialized to a safe variable on the heap using a `unify_variable` instruction.

7 Handling Permanent Terms

In this section we show how a goal which contains only permanent terms can be compiled. In that case all terms can be considered to be trees. The algorithm builds terms from the bottom-up and is optimal in both its use of temporary storage and in the count of generated WAM instructions. The procedure used turns out to be similar to that given in [5].

Considering a structure as a tree, we label the nodes of the tree with non-negative integers. The label associated with a node is intended to correspond to the minimum number of temporary registers required to `put` the complete substructure rooted at that node. The labelling is done using a bottom-up procedure. The label associated with a node N is determined using one of the following two rules:

1. If N is a leaf (corresponding to a constant or permanent variable), then it is assigned the label 0.

2. If N is a non-leaf (corresponding to some n-ary structure), and its n children have been assigned the labels $L_1, \ldots, L_n$ and that m of these n children are themselves structures. Let $\mathbf{\Pi}$ be a permutation $\langle \pi_1, \ldots, \pi_n \rangle$ of $\langle 1 \ldots n \rangle$ such that $L_{\pi_i} \geq L_{\pi_j}$ for $i < j$. Let

$p = \max(L_{\pi_1}, L_{\pi_2} + 1, L_{\pi_3} + 2, \ldots L_{\pi_m} + (m-1))$, where $\max(\emptyset) = 0$. Then N is assigned the label $\max(m+1, p)$.

We now present an algorithm to **put** a labelled structure S which uses a minimum number of temporary registers:

To put a structure S into register A_s:

1. If the label corresponding to S is 1 (all of S's arguments are constants or permanent variables), then **put** S into A_s. No other registers are required.

2. If the label corresponding to S is > 1 and it has n children with labels $L_1, \ldots, L_n$, then let $\mathbf{\Pi}$ and m be as defined as in step (2) of the labelling procedure. Recursively **put** the substructures rooted at arguments $\pi_1, \ldots, \pi_m$ (**in that order**) into m free registers. Add A_s to the list of free registers when **put**ting the arguments these substructures. Then **put** the main structure S into A_s using the m temporary registers and then free the m temporary registers.

For example, assume that we wish to **put** the structure

```
f(g(a), g(h(a),h(b)), g(h(a),h(b),h(c)) )
```

into register `A1` with all other registers available. The labelling of the substructures is

```
4(1(0), 3(1(0),1(0)), 4(1(0),1(0),1(0)) ).
```

We show on the left below the code sequence resulting from the normal left-to-right processing of arguments, whereas the code sequence shown on the right results from the above algorithm and uses 2 fewer registers.

```
put_structure   g/1,A2          put_structure   h/1,A1
unify_constant  a               unify_constant  a
put_structure   h/1,A1          put_structure   h/1,A3
unify_constant  a               unify_constant  b
put_structure   h/1,A4          put_structure   h/1,A4
unify_constant  b               unify_constant  c
put_structure   g/2,A3          put_structure   g/3,A2
unify_value     A1              unify_value     A1
unify_value     A4              unify_value     A3
put_structure   h/1,A1          unify_value     A4
unify_constant  a               put_structure   h/1,A1
put_structure   h/1,A5          unify_constant  a
unify_constant  b               put_structure   h/1,A4
put_structure   h/1,A6          unify_constant  b
unify_constant  c               put_structure   g/2,A3
put_structure   g/3,A4          unify_value     A1
unify_value     A1              unify_value     A4
unify_value     A5              put_structure   g/1,A4
unify_value     A6              unify_constant  a
put_structure   f/3,A1          put_structure   f/3,A1
unify_value     A2              unify_value     A4
unify_value     A3              unify_value     A3
unify_value     A4              unify_value     A2
```

A similar algorithm can be used to compile heads which contain only permanent terms. It is similar to the above except for the following:

- The final expression for the label of a substructure is $\max(1, m, p)$ rather than $\max(m + 1, p)$.
- Structures are traversed from the top-down.
- It first works on easier structures (with a lower label).

8 Preventing Register Conflicts

The only situation where non-trivial register conflicts can arise is the compilation for a first chunk with both a head and a goal. In this situation, source temporaries sometimes have a natural affinity for one or more specific registers where they have 0-level occurrences. Unfortunately that affinity cannot always be accomodated — this gives rise to conflicts.

For analyzing register conflicts, it is important to consider the head arguments which are source temporaries [2], as well as the goal arguments which are source temporaries [2,4]. As well as these 0-level occurrences of source temporaries, we will show that it is also necessary to consider level 1 occurrences of source temporaries. Hence we define

$$\begin{aligned} \text{head}(\mathtt{X}, L) &= \{\mathtt{A}_i \mid \text{Head contains } \mathtt{X} \text{ at level } L \text{ in argument position } i.\} \\ \text{goal}(\mathtt{X}, L) &= \{\mathtt{A}_i \mid \text{Goal contains } \mathtt{X} \text{ at level } L \text{ in argument position } i.\} \end{aligned}$$

As identified by [2] and [4], if for source temporary X $\text{goal}(\mathtt{X}, 0) \neq \emptyset$, then some register $\mathtt{A}_i \in \text{goal}(\mathtt{X}, 0)$ is a natural choice for assigning to X. There are two problems to be solved for this to be possible:

1. $\mathtt{A}_i$ must be free when code for X is first generated. This is necessary to avoid the use of extra `move_register` instructions.
2. If $|\text{goal}(\mathtt{X}, 0)| > 1$, then there is a choice of which $\mathtt{A}_i \in \text{goal}(\mathtt{X}, 0)$ must be chosen.

If the chosen $\mathtt{A}_i$ is occupied, then its contents must be copied elsewhere so that $\mathtt{A}_i$ can then be freed. [4] takes care of attempting to free the register when it is occupied by another variable but does not consider the situation when it is occupied by an incoming non-permanent head argument which has not yet been processed. The adaptive unification algorithm described there handles the situation where the variable stored in $\mathtt{A}_i$ has a similar natural register, by recursively attempting to free that register. It also handles the situation which results when this cascade of attempts is impossible due to a cycle resulting in another attempt to free $\mathtt{A}_i$.

To ensure that variables $\mathtt{Y} \neq \mathtt{X}$ are not allocated to some register in goal($\mathtt{X}, 0$), [4] does not allow any variables except incoming head arguments to be allocated to any register in goal($\mathtt{X}, 0$). This strategy is overly conservative whenever $|\text{goal}(\mathtt{X}, 0) - \text{head}(\mathtt{X}, 0)| > 1$ as all but one of those registers could have been used for storing other temporaries, without generating any extra instructions. Hence their strategy may lead to extra registers being used.

[4] ignores another source of conflict. If when compiling the goal `p(f(X))`, it is found that `X` has been assigned to register `A1`, then it will have to be copied elsewhere before the `put` for the first argument can be commenced. This will require another `move_register` instruction. The principle exemplified here is that it is necessary that `X` should not be allocated to any register $\mathtt{A}_i \in \text{goal}(\mathtt{X}, 1)$.

If $\text{goal}(\mathtt{X}, 0) = \emptyset$ but $\text{head}(\mathtt{X}, 0) \neq \emptyset$, then it is natural to allocate some register in head($\mathtt{X}, 0$) to `X` — this means that one would like to keep the incoming argument register unchanged as long as possible. If we are lucky, `X` will be dead before that argument register is needed for something else and we will have saved a `move_register` instruction.

We use Free to represent the set of registers which are currently unused. We use Goal0 to represent the assignments of source variables `X` to a **single** register in goal($X, 0$). Initially we set Free to the set of argument registers less the set of head argument registers, and the set Goal0 to $\emptyset$.

If S is some set, we use $S^0_{\mathtt{X}}$ to indicate the contents of S just **before** `X` is **first** encountered, $S^{0+}_{\mathtt{X}}$ to indicate the contents of S just **after** the code for `X`'s **first** encounter is completed, $S^{\infty-}_{\mathtt{X}}$ to indicate the contents of S just **before** the code for `X`'s **last** occurrence is generated and $S^{\infty}_{\mathtt{X}}$ just **after** the code for `X`'s **last** occurrence is generated.

We now present our strategy for register allocation when the first occurrence of a variable `X` is encountered. We do not show the details of the code generated.

1. If $\text{goal}(\mathtt{X}, 0) = \emptyset$ then go to step 2. Else for some $\mathtt{A}_i \in \text{goal}(\mathtt{X}, 0)$ attempt to unload($\mathtt{X}, \mathtt{A}_i$). If this attempt succeeds, then add the pair $\langle \mathtt{X}, \mathtt{A}_i \rangle$ to $\text{Goal0}^0_{\mathtt{X}}$ to get Goal0^{0+}_{X} and remove $\mathtt{A}_i$ from $\text{Free}^0_{\mathtt{X}}$ to get $\text{Free}^{0+}_{\mathtt{X}}$. Else go to the next step.

2. If $\text{head}(\mathtt{X}, 0) = \emptyset$ then go to step 3. Else check whether there is some $\mathtt{A}_i \in \text{head}(\mathtt{X}, 0) \cap (\text{Free}^0_{\mathtt{X}} - \text{Goal0}^{\infty}_{\mathtt{X}})$ such that feasible($\mathtt{X}, \mathtt{A}_i$). If this attempt succeeds then remove $\mathtt{A}_i$ from $\text{Free}^0_{\mathtt{X}}$ to get $\text{Free}^{0+}_{\mathtt{X}}$. Else go to the next step.

3. Allocate some $\mathtt{A}_i \in (\text{Free}^0_{\mathtt{X}} - \text{Goal0}^{\infty}_{\mathtt{X}})$ to `X` such that feasible($\mathtt{X}, \mathtt{A}_i$). Remove $\mathtt{A}_i$ from $\text{Free}^0_{\mathtt{X}}$ to get $\text{Free}^{0+}_{\mathtt{X}}$.

It is possible to unload a register $\mathtt{A}_i$ for variable `X` if:

1. If $\mathtt{A}_i$ is free.

2. If A_i is occupied by a source temporary Y and either goal(Y, 0) = $\emptyset$ or it is possible to recursively unload Y into some register in goal(Y, 0) without attempting to unload X again. (This is similar to the *release* procedure in [4].)

3. If A_i is occupied by a structure and it is possible to recursive unload all source temporaries Y such that head(Y, 1) = A_i and goal(Y, 0) $\neq \emptyset$ into some register in goal(Y, 0) without attempting to unload X again.

Feasibility is a similar idea concerned with goal arguments. It is infeasible to use A_i to store X if $A_i \in$ goal(X, 1). For a feasible assignment the argument register A_i must be loaded with its final call argument only after all the registers in goal(X, 1) have been loaded. It is possible to defer the loading of A_i only if the loading of the registers assigned to its level-1 source temporaries can be deferred even later. More formally:

A_i is feasible for storing X if both the following conditions are satisfied:

1. $A_i \notin$ goal(X, 1).

2. If there is a Y such that goal(Y, 1) = A_i and Y is allocated to some register A_j, then the loading of A_i can precede the loading of A_j.

The loading of A_i can precede the loading of A_j if

1. A_j does not contain any level 1 temporary variables which have been allocated a register.

2. If A_j contains a level 1 source temporary allocated a register A_k, then A_k must be different from any registers in the precedence chain we are currently establishing and the loading of A_j can precede the loading of A_k.

For example, consider the clause

```
p(f(X),g(Y),Y,Y)):- q(f(Y),X,h(Y),X).
```

Natural choices for allocating X are to either A2 or A4 corresponding to its top-level occurrences in the goal. The natural choices for allocating Y are to either A3 or A4 corresponding to its top-level occurrences in the head. If we allocate X to A2 we have to unload A2 first — this can be done. If we try to allocate Y to A3, we find the allocation infeasible. Hence we allocate Y to A4. With these allocations the code can be generated as follows:

```
get_structure    g/1,A2          %Unloading of A2
unify_value      A4
get_structure    f/1,A1
unify_variable   A2
get_value        A3,A4
put_structure    f/1,A1
unify_value      A4
put_structure    h/1,A3
unify_value      A4
move_register    A2,A4
execute          q/4
```

9 The Reordering Unification Algorithm

The general reordering unification algorithm presented in this section has the optimal algorithm used for permanent terms as a special case — hence it will still produce optimal code for those special cases. For the more general case, its performance will, in general, be suboptimal, though it uses several methods to reduce its use of registers, while minimizing the instruction count.

Since code generation for a fact, or for a goal different from the first is just a special case of generating code for a first chunk which contains both a head and goal, we consider only the latter.

The algorithm is divided into several phases:

1. *Information Collection*: In this phase, each chunk is analyzed and the number of occurrences of each source temporary is noted, as are the level 0 and level 1 occurrences of each source temporary. Also the labellings for the structures are generated. This phase can be combined with one which collects information about permanent variables.

2. *Code Generation*: This phase produces the code. If a source temporary `X` can be assigned to some register in goal(`X`, 0) then that assignment is made. No other kinds of register allocation is done in this phase. For the unallocated source temporaries, constraints are produced for the final allocation.

3. *Constraint Solving*: The constraints produced in the previous phase are solved. This will allocate all the previously unallocated registers.

4. *Cleanup*: This phase may or may not be necessary depending on the exact implementation of the previous two phases. If necessary, it will be a simple peephole optimizer which processes the generated code and removes instructions which may have become redundant due to the register allocation in the previous phase.

Before code generation starts, for each source temporary `X` in the chunk we compute home(`X`) = head(`X`, 0) $\cap$ goal(`X`, 0). If home(`X`) $\neq \emptyset$, then we assign some arbitrary register from home(`X`) to `X`, record the assignment in Goal0 and ensure that we never attempt to assign **any** register in home(`X`) to any source temporary during the subsequent code generation.

We label structures and substructures with a label which is an ordered pair `<NSourceT,NStructT>` where `NStructT` is a label derived as for permanent terms (with source temporaries being assigned `0`) and `NSourceT` the number of source temporaries contained within the structure. Note that this labelling process is conservative, because when the processing of a structure is complete, not all the source temporaries in its substructures may still be live — the labelling process assumes that this is indeed the case. Note that permanent terms will always have the first component of the term as `0`. We use standard lexicographic ordering to compare labels.

Code generation uses *agendas* of outstanding argument registers which remain to be processed. Code generation is first done for the head, and then for the goal, with each of the subphases using a separate agenda. Each item on a agenda represents the contents of an argument register, along with a label (which is a pair as defined earlier). The register allocation considerations of the last section impose a partial order on the order in which agenda items should be processed. Within this partial order, the head agenda is kept sorted in non-decreasing order by the label, while the goal agenda is sorted in non-increasing order.

When generating code, we process permanent terms in a depth-first manner — i.e. we process a subterm and all its substructures completely before proceeding to its siblings. Unless dictated by the considerations of the last section, non-permanent terms are processed in increasing order of their pair label for the head and in decreasing order for the goal.

The general idea behind the agenda is illustrated by considering the head agenda. It is initialized to the list of head arguments (suitably annotated to contain the labellings, variable information, etc.) Considerations of the last section may impose a partial order on the agenda items. As code generation commences, the first (least) agenda item is removed and code is generated for its top-level components. If the selected item has substructures, then code is **immediately** generated for all those substructures which are permanent terms (in the order requested by their labels), while the remaining substructures are *inserted* back onto the agenda. This process of reducing the topmost agenda item continues until it is empty. Note that the only non-compound terms which will ever enter the agenda will be those resulting from the occurrences of non-compound terms in the top-level of the head.

Note also how the ordering within the agenda enforces the orderings previously discussed. We will first process those terms with label `<0,0>` which correspond precisely to atomic terms. We then process terms of the form `<0,X>` with `X` $>$ 0 which correspond to permanent terms. Note that because of the insistence that permanent substructures are processed as soon as they are accessed, the algorithm plunges into the structures in a manner similar to that of the optimal algorithm discussed earlier. Unless dictated by the register allocations of the last section, terms having fewer source temporaries are processed before those which have more.

The ideas used for managing the goal agenda are similar.

Note that the register allocation for a source temporary is done when that source temporary is first encountered. Note also that the method used for allocating a register to a source temporary uses the contents of the Goal0 set at the last occurrence of the source temporary. This is not known when the variable is first encountered. Hence a suitable constraint is generated.

For example, assume that `X` is first encountered with free registers `FreeX` and last encountered with Goal0 `Goal0X`. Then a constraint similar to the following is generated:

```
delete(RX,FreeX,FreeX1), not member(RX,Goal0X), feasible(RX,X)
```

where FreeX1 is the set Free after the first encounter with `X`, `RX` is the assigned register, `delete(X,Xs,Zs)` is true if `X` $\in$ `Xs` and `Xs` $=$ `{X}` $\cup$ `Zs` and `Xs` $\neq$ `Zs`, `member/2` has the usual meaning and feasible is as defined previously. Note that this constraint cannot be run in an efficient way when the variable is first encountered because `Goal0X` is unknown. Nor can it can be run when the variable is last encountered because `FreeX` may still be unknown — this occurs if a variable which was born earlier than the current variable is still alive. After code generation is completed, the constraints are run in the order the variables were first encountered.

Note the advantage of deferring this register allocation. Unlike [4] we allow a source temporary to use a variable from the set of goal arguments which are variables, as long as the lifetimes of these variables do not interesect. Note also that since we allocate only a single register to a particular source temporary, remaining top-level arguments in the goal which contain the same source temporary are available for other uses right until the call is imminent.

10 Optimal Code Generation

As pointed out, the above algorithm is suboptimal in its use of temporary registers. Sometimes it may be necessary to compare its performance with an optimal register allocation. In this section we discuss a method for searching for an optimal register allocation. Unfortunately, because of the combinatorics of the search space, it is extremely unlikely that this method would prove practical for any but fairly small problems.

The basic method is to order the agenda used by the algorithm in all *feasible* ways. Restricting the feasible ways will obviously reduce the combinatorics of the search space. If we assume that we have arguments of uniform depth d and uniform arity n, then insisting that arguments be processed strictly top-down or bottom-up reduces the number of potential orderings from $O((n^d)!)$ to $O(n^d)$. However such an exponential will still make all but the smallest problems impractical.

We can reduce the feasible orderings still further by imposing the first-order considerations which were discussed earlier. Finally by noting that we can derive a lower bound on the number of registers required, we can search for an optimal assignment using iterative deepening, starting with the minimal number of registers and incrementing the number of permitted registers at each stage of the search.

11 Future Work

At this time we have a partial implementation of some of the ideas described here. We intend to complete the implementation and compare the quality of the generated code with that generated using the ideas in [4] of which we have a complete implementation.

Our present algorithm uses the number of source temporaries in a term as the first component of the label associated with that term. A more informed number would probably be better — the number of unallocated source temporaries in the term would meet that criterion, but would be more costly to implement since it would entail updating labels after each register allocation. Another alternative is to use a heuristic which attempts to process a agenda item if doing so releases more registers than it consumes — this can be predicted by comparing the number of allocated source temporaries with no occurrence outside the term, with the number of unallocated source temporaries with occurrences outside the term. Such a heuristic would tend to favor clusters of source temporaries.

A more interesting and useful exercise would be to remove the assumption that we have an unlimited number of registers, and to see how code should be generated with a fixed number of registers.

12 Conclusions

The algorithms used by present compilers for translating from Prolog code to WAM code are probably fairly adequate for non-complex predicate arguments, which are typical of most human-produced Prolog code, and the techniques discussed here may represent an overkill. However the same may not be true for machine-produced code or for a very high-performance WAM implementation with real high-speed hardware registers.

The techniques suggested here are an improvement on previously published techniques: We have shown how permanent terms can be compiled optimally (in both number of instructions and number of registers); We have identified additional sources of conflict in register assignments on the WAM and outlined how these conflicts can be eliminated; We have shown how doing register allocation after code generation, can produce better register allocations.

Acknowledgements

The author would like to thank the anonymous referees for this conference for their valuable comments. He would also like to thank the referee for the 17th SIGACT-SIGPLAN Symposium on Principles of Programming Languages for drawing his attention to [1] and [4] when given an earlier draft of this paper. Finally he would like to thank Mr. Kym Horsell for reading a draft of this paper.

References

[1] Shigeo Abe, Ken-ichi Kurosawa, and Kaoru Kiriyama. A new optimization technique for a prolog machine. In *COMPCON 86*, pages 241–245, 1986.

[2] Saumya K. Debray. Register allocation in a prolog machine. In *1986 Symposium on Logic Programming*, pages 267–275, September 1986.

[3] John Gabriel, Tim Lindholm, E. L. Lusk, and R. A. Overbeek. *A Tutorial on the Warren Abstract Machine for Computational Logic.* Technical Report ANL-84-84, Argonne National Laboratory, June 1985.

[4] Gerda Janssens, Bart Demoen, and Andre Marien. Improving the register allocation in wam by reordering unification. In *1988 5th International Conference on Logic Programming*, pages 1388–1402, August 1988.

[5] R. R Redziejowski. On arithmetic expressions and trees. *CACM*, 12(2):81–84, February 1969.

[6] Peter Van Roy. *A Prolog Compiler for the PLM.* Technical Report UCB/CSD 84/203, EECS, University of California at Berkeley, November 1984.

[7] David H. D. Warren. *An Abstract Prolog Instruction Set.* Technical Report 309, SRI International, October 1983.

From Decision Trees to Decision Graphs

Shmuel Kliger and Ehud Shapiro

Department of Computer Science
The Weizmann Institute of Science
Rehovot 76100, Israel

Abstract

In an earlier paper we reported on a decision tree compilation method for concurrent logic languages. Its theoretical analysis showed that under certain circumstances exponential size decision trees might be constructed. Experience showed that such trees do, in fact, occur in practice. The decision graph method was developed, based on similar principles, to overcome this problem.

Decision graphs offer a better time/space tradeoff than both decision trees and standard WAM-like code. The size of a decision graph is at most linear in the size of the source program. When decision trees behave well (i.e. don't exhibit exponential blowup) they are essentially identical to the corresponding decision graphs. When decision trees are exponential the corresponding decision graphs, in the worst case, degenerate to WAM code.

In this paper we describe the decision graph principles and compilation algorithm and present experimental results comparing decision graphs to decision trees. A compiler based on the decision graph method has been implemented. Measuring real large programs reveals substantial savings in code size relative to the decision trees and substantial speedup in run time relative to the WAM-like compilation method.

1 Introduction

Flat Concurrent Logic Programming (FCLP) languages are amenable to special compilation techniques for two reasons. First, these languages limit their non-determinism to primitive operations by having only simple pre-defined predicates in the guard of a clause. Second, in most of these languages, like FCP(:,?) [22] and its subset FCP(:), the guard can be separated into an *ask part*, that only tests the environment using input matching and primitive tests, and a *tell part*, that can also affect the environment using general unification and other primitives [15]. Furthermore, in related languages, such as Flat GHC [7,18] and Strand [3], the tell part is performed only after commit.

1.1 FCLP Abstract Machine

There are several implementations of FCLP languages [2,6,7]. All employ some variant of an abstract machine developed at the Weizmann Institute, first incorporated in an interpreter for FCP [10] and later refined and integrated with techniques for compiling unification, developed by Warren [20], within a compiler/emulator based implementation [6].

The basic concepts of the machine are as follows. The machine represents the goal by an active queue and a set of suspension lists. Each process in the goal is either in the active queue or in one or more suspension lists. The basic operation of the machine is to dequeue a process from the active queue, and to try to reduce it with some clause in the program. This operation is called a *process try* and it is composed of a sequence of clause tries. The clause try succeeds if the goal atom is an instance of the clause head, and if the guard, instantiated by the matching substitution of the goal atom and the clause head, succeeds. It fails if either the goal atom and the clause head are not unifiable or the goal atom is an instance of the clause head but the guard, instantiated by the matching substitution, fails. Otherwise, the clause try suspends. A process try succeeds if one of its clause tries succeeds, suspends if none succeeds, but at least one suspends, and fails if all clause tries fail.

A compiler that compiles the process try into a sequence of clause tries was developed [6]. Like in Warren's design [20], there is a one-to-one mapping between the source procedure's clauses and the target abstract program: each clause in the source procedure is compiled into a sequence of abstract machine instructions in the target abstract program that computes the clause try. For example, the following binary *merge* procedure in FCP(:):

(*a*) *merge*([X|Xs],Ys,Zs) ← true : Zs = [X|Zs′] | *merge*(Ys,Xs,Zs′).
(*b*) *merge*(Xs,[Y|Ys],Zs) ← true : Zs = [Y|Zs′] | *merge*(Xs,Ys,Zs′).
(*c*) *merge*([],Ys,Zs) ← true : Zs = Ys | true.
(*d*) *merge*(Xs,[],Zs) ← true : Zs = Xs | true.

is compiled to the following sequence of abstract instructions:

MERGE:
    try_me_else C2
    code for head matching and tell unification of clause (a)
    commit
    allocate args of body goal
    execute MERGE
C2: try_me_else C3
    code for clause (b), similar to clause (a)
C3: try_me_else C4
    code for head matching of clause (c)
    commit
    halt
C4: try_me_else S
    code for clause (d), similar to clause (c)
S: suspend

1.2 Overview of the Decision Tree Compilation Method

When compiling FCP(:,?) and related languages one can do better than Warren's scheme. The clause try in these languages can be separated into two steps. The first step, the *validation step*, only validates the environment using input matching and primitive tests, collectively called the ask component of the guard. By jointly compiling the ask component of a set of clauses in the same procedure into a decision tree [9], the validation step can be executed efficiently. This is achieved by combining shared ask operations to find the set of applicable clauses, compiling away redundant tests which occur during a process try in the WAM-like compilations.

A decision tree is a labelled tree in which the internal vertices are labelled with tests, the edges are labelled with test results and the leaves are labelled with sequences of instructions. For example, a typical vertex in the decision tree is labelled by a value check of some argument and the outgoing edges are labelled by the different values the argument might have. The execution of the decision tree begins at the root and follows a path in the tree until it reaches a leaf. At each vertex the test is performed and a path is deterministically chosen based on the test result. Upon reaching a leaf, the sequence of instructions at the leaf are executed. A successful transition in the decision tree is a sequence of tests that leads to a reduction to body goals in a leaf, corresponding to a successful clause try. A failure transition is a sequence of tests that leads to a failure operation, corresponding to a failed process try. Similarly, a suspend transition is a sequence of tests that leads to a suspend operation, corresponding to a suspended process try.

A decision tree for the afore-mentioned *merge* procedure looks like this:

case(value(1))
  list : **case**(value(2))
      list : **try**(a); **try**(b) ; **suspend**
      nil : **try**(a); **try**(d) ; **suspend**
      otherwise : **try**(a); **suspend**
  nil : **case**(value(2))
      list : **try**(b); **try**(c) ; **suspend**
      nil : **try**(c); **try**(d) ; **suspend**
      otherwise : **try**(c); **suspend**
  otherwise : **case**(value(2))
      list : **try**(b); **suspend**
      nil : **try**(d); **suspend**
      otherwise : **suspend**

It is clear that the tree for the *merge* procedure is not linear. The decision tree of an n-ary merge will be of size $O(2^n)$.

The decision tree construction algorithm, defined in [9], is a recursive algorithm that receives as input a procedure and returns a decision tree. At each iteration, the algorithm invokes an *indexing function* (described in

Section 1.2.2) to compute the label of the current node, i.e., the next test to be compiled. For each outgoing edge the algorithm computes the residual of the procedure, which is a set of the residuals of the clauses of the procedure, and recursively constructs the subtrees. A residual of a clause C by a test g is the remainder of the clause to be used in constructing the subtree of the g. The residual of a clause C by a test g is empty if there exists a test g' in C such that g implies $\neg g'$. If there exists a test g' in C such that g implies g' and there is no test g'' in C such that g implies $\neg g''$ then the residual is C minus the set of all tests that are implied by g. Otherwise, the residual is identical to C. The algorithm terminates, creating a leaf, when there exists a clause with an empty ask in the procedure.

1.2.1 Examples

The *connect_guard/4* is part of the compiler that compiles FCP(:,?) into decision trees/graphs. The *connect_guard/4* identifies the ask guard kernel predicates of FCP(:,?) and defines the input/output relations between their arguments. The procedure consists of 45 clauses, each of which matches the first two arguments and determines the corresponding input/output relation. The procedure looks like this:

```
(a)    connect_guard(2, _, Conn, Check) ← ...
(b)    connect_guard(3, arity, Conn, Check) ← ...
(c)    connect_guard(3, make_tuple, Conn, Check) ← ...
                 ⋮
(d)    connect_guard(4, arg, Conn, Check) ← ...
(e)    connect_guard(4, plus, Conn, Check) ← ...
                 ⋮
(f)    connect_guard(5, freeze, Conn, Check) ← ...
(g)    connect_guard(5, make_procedure, Conn, Check) ← ...
                 ⋮
```

A decision tree for the above procedure looks like this:

```
case(value(1))
  2 : clause (a)
  3 : case(value(2))
        arity : clause (b)
        make_tuple : clause (c)
        ⋮
  4 : case(value(2))
        arg : clause (d)
        plus : clause (e)
        ⋮
```

5 : **case**(value(2))
    freeze : clause (f)
    make_procedure : clause (g)
    ⋮
otherwise : **suspend**

It is clear that the size of the decision tree for the above procedure is linear in the size of the procedure. The tree consists of 45 paths that are induced by the 45 clauses of the procedure and each path is of length equal to the length of each of the clauses, i.e., 2, and in two tests a clause is chosen.

The *comm/5* procedure is part of the distributed unification algorithm [8]. The procedure is responsible for communication among processors. The input matching part of the procedure looks like this:

(a) comm([unify(_,_,_,_)|L], C, M, H, P) ← unknown(M),...
(b) comm([become(_,_,_)|L], C, M, H, P) ← unknown(M),...
(c) comm([], C, _, HT, _) ← ...
(d) comm(CIn, C, [unify(_,_,_,_)|L], H, P) ← ...
(e) comm(CIn, C, [become(_,_)|L], H, P) ← ...
(f) comm(CIn, C, [to_hash(_)|L], H, P) ← ...
(g) comm(_, C, [], HT, _) ← ...

A decision tree for the above procedure looks like this:

case(value(3))
  list : **case**(value(3.1))
    tuple/5 : a subtree induced by clauses (c) and (d)
    tuple/3 : a subtree induced by clauses (c) and (e)
    tuple/2 : a subtree induced by clauses (c) and (f)
    otherwise : a subtree induced by clause (c)
  nil : **case**(value(1))
    nil : a subtree induced by clauses (c) and (g)
    otherwise : a subtree induced by clause (g)
  otherwise : **case**(value(1))
    list : a subtree induced by clauses (a) and (b)
    nil : a subtree induced by clause (c)
    otherwise : **suspend**

The run-time complexity of the above decision tree is linearly bounded in the number of arguments that are input matched in the procedure, since along a path an argument is tested at most once. However, the decision tree exhibits an exponential blowup in size since some clauses of the procedure induce more than one path in the tree. Note that if the *unknown/1* guard[1] in clauses (a) and (b) were omitted, a greater blowup would occur since every clause of the procedure would induce more than one path in the tree.

[1] *unknown(X)* succeeds if the value of X is yet unknown and fails otherwise.

1.2.2 The Indexing Function

The *indexing function* is used by the construction algorithm at each iteration to choose the next test to be compiled. This test will label the current vertex. The function receives a procedure and returns a test from the procedure that can label the vertex. The test returned by the function must use arguments that were previously defined along the path from the root to the current vertex.

The indexing function determines the order of the tests in the decision tree and thus plays an important role in shaping the tree, affecting both the run-time complexity and the size of the tree. For example, let us examine the following procedure:

(1) p(1, 1, 1, ..., 1) ← ...
(2) p(_, 2, 2, ..., 2) ← ...
(3) p(_, _, 3, ..., 3) ← ...
⋮
(n) p(_, ..., _, n) ← ...

One possible sequence of tests is "left-to-right" in which the root of the decision tree is labelled by a test of the first argument, the root of each subtree is labelled by a test of the second argument and so on. The size of this decision tree is exponential in n and, since the length of each path in the tree is n, both the worst case and the average case run-time is n.

An alternative sequence is "right-to-left", in which the root of the decision tree is labelled by a test of the last argument. It is easy to see that in the "right-to-left" order, the size of the decision tree is n^2, the worst case run-time remains n but the average case run-time is reduced to $\frac{n}{2}$.

A good indexing function can reduce the size of the decision tree, effectively achieving common subexpression elimination by propagating common tests up the tree. For example, the procedure

p(a,t).
p(b,t). ,

where t is a large compound term, can be compiled either in a "left-to-right" order creating two identical big subtrees, each of which input matches the second argument against t, or in a "right-to-left" order creating a smaller tree that first input matches the second argument against t and only at the end input matches the first argument. The size of the latter decision tree is half the size of the former.

Finding the optimal sequence for compiling a procedure is not an easy task in the general case. A similar problem appears when constructing a binary decision tree from a decision table [11,12,13,14,16]. Constructing an optimal binary decision tree from a decision table has been proven to be an NP-complete problem [14]. Hickey shows in [5] that constructing a *switching tree* (a different name for decision tree) from a Prolog program is an NP-complete problem by reducing it to the set-covering problem [4]. Hence, the indexing function invites the use of heuristic methods to try to optimize the decision tree by choosing the "best" next test. We have adopted the following heuristic. A clause C *cares about* a test g if there is a test g' in the ask part of C such that one of $\{g' \wedge g, g' \wedge \neg g\}$ is consistent and the other inconsistent; if such a test does not exist in C then we say that C *doesn't care about* g (the notion of consistency is defined in Section 2). A *max-care* heuristic returns a test g, such that the number of clauses of the procedure that care about g is maximized. If there is more than one such maximizing test then the *min-variability* heuristic chooses a test with minimal variability, i.e., a test with the smallest number of different possible results, leading to a minimum number of subtrees. The combined max-care min-variability heuristic method is proven sufficient in most practical examples and is incorporated in our working compiler. In particular, for the above examples it produces optimal decision trees.

1.3 Decision Graph Concepts

Theoretical analysis has shown that under certain circumstances exponential size decision trees can be constructed. Such decision trees occur as a result of compiling procedures with clauses that don't care about different combinations of tests, so that an optimal sequence of tests is difficult to find.

Although it would seem that only contrived procedures produce exponential size decision trees, experience has shown that such trees do, in fact, occur in practice. In order to overcome this problem, the decision graph method was developed as an extension to the decision tree method.

A decision graph is a labelled directed acyclic graph in which the labels are as in the decision tree with the following modifications. Internal vertices can be labelled by sequences of instructions induced by tell parts and bodies of clauses. The graph contains an additional edge labelled *continue*, used to connect the subgraphs emanating from a vertex to their *otherwise* sibling. The general structure of the decision graph is sketched in Figure 1. The abstract machine of the decision graph is similar to that of the decision tree. The only difference stems from the fact that internal vertices can be labelled by instructions induced by tell parts and bodies of clauses. The execution of this type of vertex might lead to a successful transition, if a reducible clause is found.

One can see from the above examples that a clause may induce an exponential number of paths in the decision tree resulting in an exponential size tree. The main idea of the decision graph method is that each clause induces at most one path in the graph, where this path is linear in the size of the clause. Hence, the size of the decision graph is linearly bounded by the size of the source procedure.

The decision graph construction algorithm is based on the decision tree

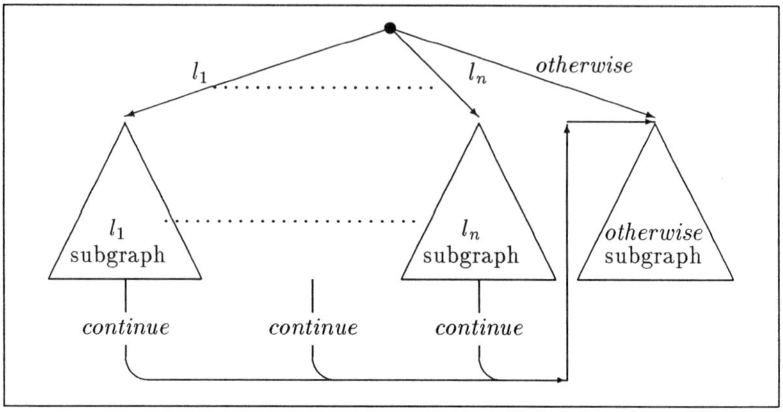

Figure 1: Decision Graph General Structure

algorithm. The key modification is that a clause is propagated from a vertex to at most one edge. If a clause does not care about the test in the vertex then in the decision tree method it is propagated to every subtree, whereas in the decision graph method it is propagated only to the *otherwise* subgraph. A continuation edge is associated with all the subgraphs. While the continuation edge associated with the *otherwise* subgraph is the one associated with the entire graph, the continuation edge of all the other immediate subgraphs point to the *otherwise* subgraph.

It is important to observe some inherent characteristics of the decision graph. If we delete all the continuation edges from the decision graph we get a tree, but not a legal decision tree for the source procedure. However, if we unfold all the continuation edges, i.e., replace each such edge by the subgraph it leads to, then we get a legal decision tree for the source procedure, but an inefficient one since tests are repeated along a path. If we partially evaluate this unfolded decision tree, eliminating redundant tests, we get essentially the decision tree provided by our earlier algorithm [9].

1.3.1 Examples

The afore-mentioned *merge/3* procedure is compiled to the 7 node decision graph described in Figure 2, while a decision tree for this procedure, described in Section 1.2.1, consists of 13 nodes and exhibits an exponential blowup in size.

The afore-mentioned *comm/5* procedure is compiled to the following decision graph:

case(value(3))

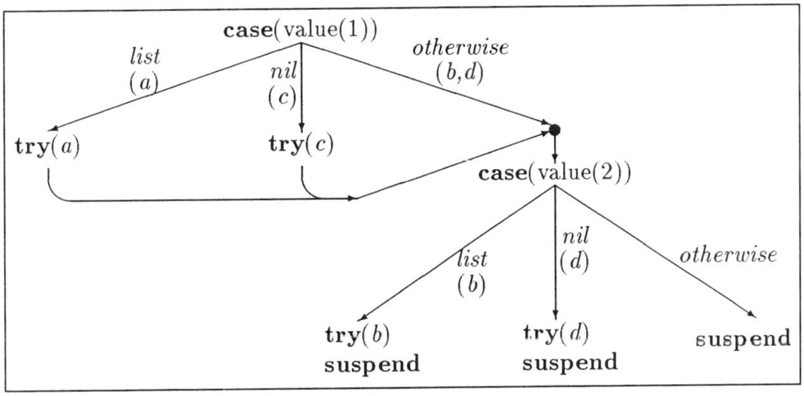

Figure 2: A Decision Graph for Merge

list : **case**(value(3.1))
  tuple/5 : a subgraph for clause (d) connected to *otherwise.1*
  tuple/3 : a subgraph for clause (e) connected to *otherwise.1*
  tuple/2 : a subgraph for clasue (f) connected to *otherwise.1*
  otherwise : **goto**(*otherwise.1*)
nil : **case**(value(1))
  nil : a subgraph for clause (g) connected to *otherwise.1*
  otherwise : **goto**(*otherwise.1*)
otherwise.1 : **case**(value(1))
    list : a subgraph induced by clause (a) and (b)
    nil : a subtree induced by clause (c)
    otherwise : **suspend**

The size of the decision graph is linearly bounded by the length of the procedure since each clause induces at most one path of linear length.

2 Decision Graph Construction Algorithm

In this section we present an algorithm for constructing a decision graph from an FCLP procedure, analyze its runtime complexity, and analyze the complexity of the generated decision graph. We first define notions used by the algorithm.

Canonical Clauses

The only compound data-structure we consider in our definitions is the tuple. An *n-ary tuple* with arguments $T_1, \ldots, T_n$ is represented as $\{T_1, \ldots, T_n\}$. The term $f(T_1,\ldots,T_n)$ is represented by $\{f, T_1, \ldots, T_n\}$, and the list [X|Xs] is equivalent to $\{X, Xs\}$.

We assume pre-defined sets of *ask* and *tell* predicates. An *ask guard* (*tell guard*) is an atom whose predicate is an ask predicate (tell predicate).

An *ask-tell clause* is a guarded Horn clause of the form:

$$H \leftarrow A_1, \ldots, A_n : T_1, \ldots, T_m \mid B_1, \ldots, B_k \qquad m, n, k \geq 0.$$

where H is called the *head* of the clause, $A_1, \ldots, A_n : T_1, \ldots, T_m$ the *guard* and $B_1, \ldots, B_k$ the *body*. Each A_i is an *ask guard* and $A_1, \ldots, A_n$ is called the *ask part*, and each T_i is a *tell guard* and $T_1, \ldots, T_m$ is called the *tell part.*

Notation: Given a syntactic object T, $vars(T)$ denotes the set of the variables that occur in T.

Definition: A *simple term* is either a constant, a variable or a tuple in which the arguments are pairwise different variables.

Definition: A *normalized ask-tell clause* is an ask-tell clause in which the head of the clause is an atom $P(X_1 \ldots, X_n)$, $n \geq 0$, where P is a predicate name and $X_1,\ldots,X_n$ are pairwise different variables, and each argument of an ask predicate in the ask part of the clause is a simple term.

Definition: Given a normalized ask-tell clause C, we associate with C a tree with labelled vertices and edges, denoted *Tree*(C), which represents the clause head and ask part structure. *Tree*(C) consists of a root with n outgoing edges labelled $1, \ldots, n$ leading to n subtrees $ST_C(X_1),\ldots,ST_C(X_n)$, respectively, where each $ST_C(X_i)$ is constructed recursively as follows:

1. If there exists $X_i = \{X_{i1}, \ldots, X_{ik}\}$ or $\{X_{i1}, \ldots, X_{ik}\} = X_i$ in the ask part of C then $ST_C(X_i)$ consists of a root labelled X_i with k outgoing edges labelled $1, \ldots, k$ leading to n subtrees $ST_C(X_{i1}),\ldots,ST_C(X_{ik})$, respectively.

2. Otherwise, $ST_C(X_i)$ is a vertex labelled by X_i.

An example of a clause and its tree is described in Figure 3.

We assume a set of *canonical variables* $V_{can} = \{Z_\rho \mid \rho \in I^*\}$, where I is the set of integers, that is distinct from the variables used in programs.

Definition: Given a normalized ask-tell clause C, $V(C)$ denotes the set of vertices of *Tree*(C), and $\mathcal{S}(X)$ denotes a sequence of labels from the root of *Tree*(C) to a node (an internal node or a leaf) labelled X in *Tree*(C). The *position renaming* substitution ψ_c of C is:

$$\psi_c : vars(C) \longrightarrow V_{can} \bigcup vars(C),$$

such that

$$\psi_c(X) = \begin{cases} Z_{\mathcal{S}(X)} & \text{if } X \in V(C) \\ X & \text{otherwise} \end{cases}$$

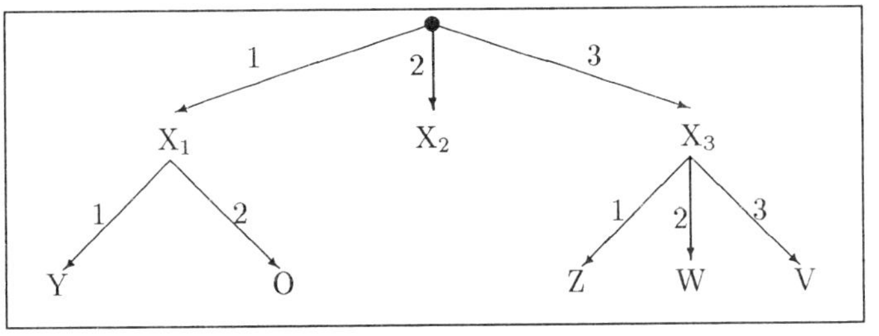

Figure 3: $Tree(P(X_1, X_2, X_3) \leftarrow X_1 = \{Y, O\}, O = 5, X_3 = \{Z, W, V\}, make\_tuple(3, T) | \ldots)$

In the clause of Figure 3, $\psi_c(X_1) = Z_1$, $\psi_c(X_2) = Z_2$, $\psi_c(X_3) = Z_3$, $\psi_c(Y) = Z_{1.1}$, $\psi_c(O) = Z_{1.2}$, $\psi_c(Z) = Z_{3.1}$, $\psi_c(W) = Z_{3.2}$ and $\psi_c(V) = Z_{3.3}$, $\psi_c(T) = T$.

Definition: The *canonical form* of a normalized ask-tell clause $C = H \leftarrow A : T \mid B$ is the triple $\langle A\psi_c, T\psi_c, B\psi_c \rangle$. A *canonical procedure* is a set of canonical clauses in which the non-canonical variables are renamed apart.

Residuals

Our compilation technique merges consistent guards taken from different clauses. Checking the consistency of a set of guards is, in general, difficult. Hence, in the compilation process we employ a simpler check, explained below.

The meaning of the guard predicates is given via a fixed set of ground atoms $\mathbf{T}$ over these predicates. An example can be found in [22]. A guard predicate g is *true* in $\mathbf{T}$ iff every ground instance of g is in $\mathbf{T}$, *false* in $\mathbf{T}$ if no ground instance of g is in $\mathbf{T}$, and has no truth value otherwise. Since $\mathbf{T}$ is fixed it is not mentioned in the following. For example, $3 < 5$ and $integer(4)$ are true, $5 < 3$ and $integer(s)$ are false, while $X < 5$ and $integer(X)$ are neither true nor false.

A *guard formula* consists of guards and logical connectives. A guard formula is *consistent* iff it has a true instance. For two guards g, g', we say that $g \Longrightarrow g'$ if for every substitution θ, $g\theta$ is true implies that $g'\theta$ is true.

Notation: Let G, G_1 and G_2 be sets of guards, then $\neg G = \{\neg g \mid g \in G\}$ and $G_1 \bigwedge G_2 = \{g_1 \wedge g_2 \mid g_1 \in G_1, g_2 \in G_2\}$.

We say that a set of guard formulas is *elementwise consistent* iff every formula in the set is consistent. Note that a set of guard formulas being elementwise consistent does not imply that its conjunction is consistent.

Definition: The *residual* of a canonical clause $C = \langle A, T, B \rangle$ by a test g, denoted $\Re(C,g)$, is:

$$\Re(C,g) = \begin{cases} \langle A \backslash \{g' | g \Longrightarrow g'\}, T, B\rangle & A \bigwedge\{g\} \text{ is elementwise consistent and} \\ & A \bigwedge\{\neg g\} \text{ is not elementwise consistent} \\ \emptyset & \text{otherwise} \end{cases}$$

Examples:

1. $\Re(\langle\{\ldots, Z_\rho = 3, \ldots\}, T, B\rangle, Z_\rho = 5) = \emptyset$.
2. $\Re(\langle\{\ldots, Z_\rho > 4, \ldots\}, T, B\rangle, Z_\rho = 5) = \emptyset$.
3. $\Re(\langle\{Z_\rho = 5\}, T, B\rangle, Z_\rho = 5) = \langle\emptyset, T, B\rangle$.
4. $\Re(\langle\{Z_{\rho1} = 4, Z_{\rho2} = 5\}, T, B\rangle, Z_\rho = 5) = \emptyset$.
5. $\Re(\langle\{\ldots, Z_\rho \leq 5, \ldots\}, T, B\rangle, Z_\rho > 5) = \emptyset$.
6. $\Re(\langle\{Z_\rho > 6\}, T, B\rangle, Z_\rho > 5) = \langle\{Z_\rho > 6\}, T, B\rangle$.
7. $\Re(\langle\{Z_\rho > 3\}, T, B\rangle, Z_\rho > 5) = \emptyset$.

Definition: The *otherwise-residual* of a canonical clause $C = \langle A, T, B\rangle$ by a set of tests Γ, denoted $\Re_{ow}(C,\Gamma)$, is:

$$\Re_{ow}(C,\Gamma) = \begin{cases} \langle A, T, B\rangle & A \bigwedge \neg\Gamma \text{ is elementwise consistent} \\ \emptyset & \text{otherwise} \end{cases}$$

It is easy to see that if Γ is pairwise inconsistent then for any clause C and for every $g \in \Gamma$, $\Re(C,g) \bigcap \Re_{ow}(C,\Gamma) = \emptyset$. If $\Re(C,g) \bigcup \Re_{ow}(C,\Gamma) = \emptyset$ then the ask part of C is inconsistent, and this error can be reported.

Definition: The *residual* of a canonical procedure P by a test g, denoted $\Re(P,g)$, is $\{\Re(C,g) \mid C \in P\}$.

Definition: The *otherwise-residual* of a canonical procedure P by a set of tests Γ, denoted $\Re_{ow}(P,\Gamma)$, is $\{\Re_{ow}(C,\Gamma) \mid C \in P\}$.

2.1 The Construction Algorithm

In this section we present the algorithm for constructing the decision graph. This recursive algorithm receives as input a canonical procedure P and a continuation $\mathcal{F}$, and returns a decision graph for P.

At each iteration, the algorithm invokes the **indexing function** to compute the next test to be compiled for the current node. The indexing function returns a set Γ that is either $\{Z_\rho = t_1, \ldots, Z_\rho = t_n\}$ where each t_i is a simple term or $\{g, \neg g\}$ for some ask guard. The correctness of the algorithm depends on Γ being pairwise inconsistent.

For each outgoing edge the associated residual of P and the continuation are computed, and the subgraph is recursively generated. The continuation

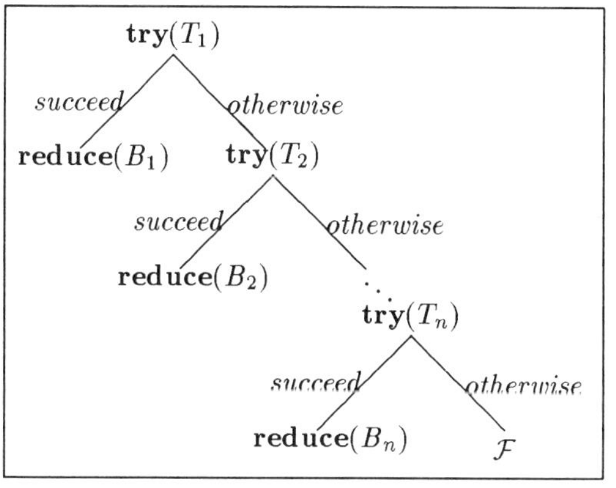

Figure 4: The Clause Try Graph – $C_{try}(C_s, \mathcal{F})$

for the *otherwise* subgraph is $\mathcal{F}$ while the continuation for all the other subgraphs is the *otherwise* subgraph. The recursion stops if either the residual of P is empty or all the ask parts in the residual of P are empty. In the first case a leaf $\mathcal{F}$ is constructed while in the second case a *clause try graph* is constructed. A *clause try graph* of a set of clauses $C_s = \{C_1, \ldots, C_n\}$, where each $C_i = \langle\emptyset, T_i, B_i\rangle$, and a continuation $\mathcal{F}$, denoted by $C_{try}(C_s, \mathcal{F})$, is the graph described in Figure 4. If there exists a C_i with an empty T_i then $C_{try}(C_s, \mathcal{F})$ is a single node labelled by **reduce**(B_i).

Figure 5 presents the decision graph construction algorithm. Given a procedure P and a continuation $\mathcal{F}$, a decision graph for P is created, denoted **decision_graph**($P, \mathcal{F}$).

Note that all the non-*otherwise* subgraphs of a vertex are always connected to the *otherwise* subgraph. There are many cases in which there is no need to connect the subgraphs. In such cases a simple data-flow analysis of the decision graph will eliminate redundant continuation edges.

It is easy to prove that the run-time complexity, i.e., the longest path in the graph, and the size of the decision graph are both linearly bounded by the length of the procedure, and in almost all cases they are strictly smaller than the procedure's length. In fact, only when the set of positions matched by each clause of the procedure are pairwise disjoint, the run-time complexity and the size are equal to the length of the procedure. In all other cases they are strictly smaller then the source procedure's length. Therefore, for most procedures P, the decision graph is more efficient, both in run-time complexity and code-size, than WAM based code.

Note that if at each iteration there is a test which all the clauses in the residual care about, then the decision graph is identical to the decision tree provided by the decision tree construction algorithm [9]. Furthermore, only when there is a saving in size, i.e., the size of the decision graph is smaller than the size of the decision tree, the run-time complexity of the decision

function **decision_graph**$(P, \mathcal{F} : \textit{pointer})$;
if $P = \emptyset$ *then* **decision_graph**$(P, \mathcal{F}) := \mathcal{F}$;
if $\forall C \in P.C = \langle \emptyset, T, B \rangle$ *then* **decision_graph**$(P, \mathcal{F}) := C_{try}(P, \mathcal{F})$;
if $\exists \langle A, T, B \rangle \in P.A \neq \emptyset$ *then do*
$\Gamma :=$ **indexing_function**(P);
if $\Gamma = \{Z_\rho = t_1, \ldots, Z_\rho = t_n\}$ *then*

decision_graph$(P, \mathcal{F}) :=$

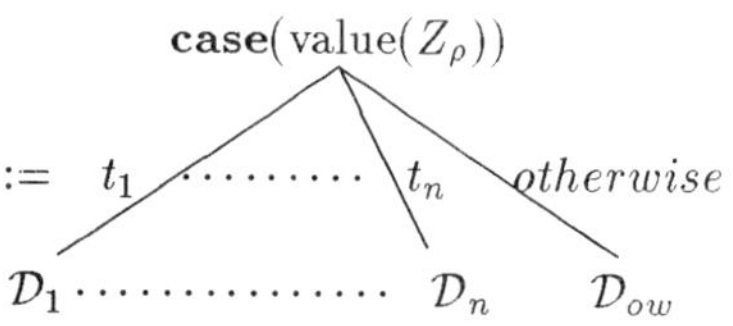

$\mathcal{D}_i :=$ **decision_graph**$(\Re(P, Z_\rho = t_i), \mathcal{D}_{ow})$
$\mathcal{D}_{ow} :=$ **decision_graph**$(\Re_{ow}(P, \Gamma), \mathcal{F})$

if $\Gamma = \{g, \neg g\}$ *then*

decision_graph$(P, \mathcal{F}) :=$

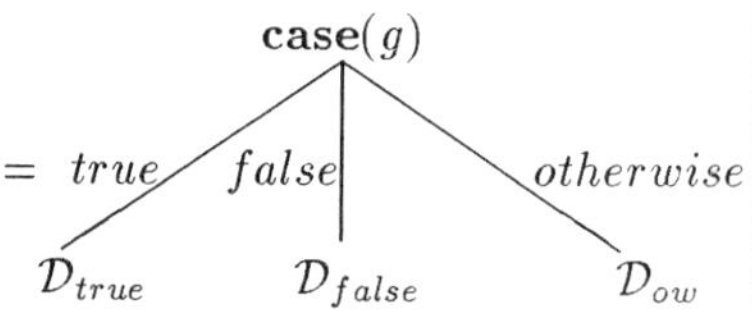

$\mathcal{D}_{true} :=$ **decision_graph**$(\Re(P, g), \mathcal{D}_{ow})$
$\mathcal{D}_{false} :=$ **decision_graph**$(\Re(P, \neg g), \mathcal{D}_{ow})$
$\mathcal{D}_{ow} :=$ **decision_graph**$(\Re_{ow}(P, \Gamma), \mathcal{F})$

Figure 5: The Decision Graph Construction Algorithm

graph is worse than that of the decision tree. When the size of the decision tree is linearly bounded by the size of the procedure the decision graph is identical to the decision tree.

We analyze the complexity of the decision graph construction algorithm. We denote the length of a procedure P by $l_p(P)$ and the length of a clause C by $l_c(C)$. It is clear that in constructing each node the construction algorithm scans the residual of the procedure a constant number of times. Since the size of the graph is linearly bounded by the length of the source program then the complexity of the construction algorithm is $O(l_p(P)^2)$. Furthermore, a tighter bound can be computed based on the fact that the length of the residual at a node v is greater than the sum of all the lengths of the residuals of the sons of v. It immediately follows that the complexity of the algorithm is $O(l_p(P) \times \max_{C \in P} l_c(C))$.

Module	Ps	Cs	DGS	DTS	Ratio
var_mon	13	55	278	3865	.07
winston	8	76	250	4031	.06
andorra	6	23	78	87	.89
automaton	31	71	232	323	.71
comm	7	21	99	125	.79
equivalent	19	61	237	312	.75
intersection	15	65	245	302	.81
stream	26	66	244	288	.77
domain_server	92	377	1313	2651	.49

Table 1: Comparing the Size of the Decision Graphs and Decision Trees

3 Experimental analysis

We have implemented a two-phase compiler, written in FCP(:,?), based on the decision graph/tree algorithms. The first phase compiles an FCP(:,?) into a decision graph or a decision tree. The second phase translates the decision graph/tree into an intermediate language, called Compiler Target Language (CTL). The emulator used in [6] was extended to implement the CTL's instructions.

In this section we present experimental results of compiling large real programs. First, we show the size improvement achieved due to the decision graph algorithm with respect to the decision tree algorithm. Second, we present the run time performance of the code produced by the decision graph compiler and compare it with the performance of the code produced by WAM-like compilation.

3.1 Comparing the Size of Decision Graphs with Decision Trees

We compare the sizes of the decision graphs and the decision trees of the following programs. The *andorra* module is a working Andorra [21] interpreter. The *automaton*, *equivalent* and *intersection* modules are parts of the working implementation of the type-checker [23] in FCP(:,?). The *comm* and *var_mon* are working parts of the distributed unification algorithm [8]. The *domain_server* and *stream* modules are part of the Logix system [19]. The first is responsible for routing requests among system services and the latter is a collection of system stream utilities. *winston* is a large test program used for testing the Andorra interpreter that marks edges with constraints. Table 1 summarizes the results. The columns marked **Ps** and **Cs** denote the number of procedures the module consists of and the total number of clauses in the module, respectively. The columns marked **DGS** and **DTS** denote the sizes, i.e., the number of nodes, of the decision graphs and decision trees, re-

Version	Source Size	Compilation Time			Binary Code Size		
		WAM (1)	DG (2)	(2)/ (1)	WAM (3)	DG (4)	(4)/ (3)
primitive	24246	16.603	22.460	1.35	45020	246640	5.47
hybrid	9985	7.279	11.592	1.59	17120	57850	3.37
hand-optimized	7884	5.355	8.912	1.66	12790	33260	2.60

Version	Reduc- tions	CPU Time		Reductions per Second		
		WAM	DG	WAM	DG	DG/ WAM
primitive	70414	178.070	4.200	390	16770	43.00
hybrid	70414	52.750	5.700	1340	12350	9.21
hand-optimized	83760	11.400	7.070	7350	11840	1.61

Table 2: The tokenizer - code size, compilation time and run time comparison

spectively, produced for the module. The last column marked **Ratio** denotes the ratio between the two sizes.

Observing the above examples, one can see that in most cases a saving of 20-25% in size is achieved by the decision graph algorithm relative to the decision tree algorithm. In extreme cases the size of the decision tree is so large that it is impractical to generate.

3.2 Run Time Performance

In this section we present preliminary measurements of some large modules compiled by the decision graph compiler and compare them with the earlier WAM-like compiler [6]. All of the measurements were computed on a Sun/4 SPARC station. The time units are in seconds and the size units are in bytes.

3.2.1 The Tokenizer

The *tokenizer* is a module used by both the decision graph compiler and the WAM-like compiler to parse and tokenize source FCP(:,?) modules.

Three different versions of the *tokenizer* have been compiled by the WAM-like and decision graph compilers and various measurements have been produced. The first version, referred to as *primitive* below, reverts to a naive approach to character recognition, where a clause is provided for each ascii character in each procedure where it is recognized. The second version, referred to as *hybrid*, uses range tests to recognize major groups of characters to reduce source code redundancy. The third version, referred to as *hand-optimized* below, is the current tokenizer in the Logix system [19], which has been revised several times to perform optimally under the WAM-like compilation. These revisions are: range-division ascii character recognition, use of

	Binary Size	Installation	
		CPU	RPS
WAM	1066198	14.220	3711.04
DG	1395120	7.090	7443.02
DG/WAM	1.30	0.49	2.00

Table 3: The Logix system - Installation comparison

multiple procedural levels, and rearrangement of clauses within procedures to minimize tokenizing time.

The results are summarized in Table 2. The top part of Table 2 presents compilation measurments for each of the three versions. The bottom part summarizes the run-time measurements of the compiled code tokenizing the *domain_server*[2]. The measurements presented in these tables indicate that the decision graph method offers a better time/space tradeoff than WAM-like code.

3.2.2 The Logix System

The Logix system [19], consisting of 198 module of FCP(:,?) and comprising 55414 lines of code, has been compiled by the decision graph compiler. Table 3 summarizes the comparison made between the installation of a system compiled by the decision graph compiler with one compiled by the WAM-like compiler. A two-fold speedup is realized by the decision graph compilation. This speedup seems to appear throughout all Logix system operations.

3.2.3 The Decision Graph Compiler

The decision graph compiler has been bootstrapped through the following stages:

1. Source compiled by WAM-like compiler, yielding binary module K_0.

2. Source compiled by K_0, yielding binary module K_1.

3. Source compiled by K_1, yielding binary module K_2.

4. Source compiled by K_2, yielding binary module K_3.

Table 4 summarizes the measurements taken for steps 1,2 and 4. A comparison between steps 2 and 4 indicates that while the run-time of the code produced by the decision graph compiler improved by 78% relative to that of the WAM-like compiler, the code size increased by only 16%. This comparison confirms that the decision graph method offers a better time/space tradeoff than the WAM-like compilation.

[2]The *domain_server* consists of 2062 lines of FCP(:,?), 7400 words and 55083 characters.

Step	Reductions	CPU	Bin Size	RPS
1	2982396	558	192643	5344.79
2	7213173	1364	225024	5288.25
4	7211796	765	225080	9427.18

Table 4: Bootstrapping the decision graph compiler

4 Future Work

Decision graph compilation invites the use of many optimization techniques, promising an improvement over the WAM based compilations, both in code size and in run-time complexity. Some of the optimizations are known techniques, like common subexpressions elimination, copy propagation, dead-code elimination, tail recursion, loop-invariant computations etc. [1]. In addition, the method calls for the development of specific optimization techniques based on top-down abstract interpretation, partial evaluation of the decision graphs and inter-procedure data flow analysis. These optimizations, together with deeper static analysis of guards and body goals, are very promising and are part of our ongoing research.

Acknowledgments

Bill Silverman helped in implementing, debugging and measuring the compiler, and implemented its assembler. Avshalom Houri has implemented the CTL's abstract machine emulator. Their contribution is gratefully acknowledged.

References

[1] A. V. Aho, R. Sethi, and J. Ullman. *Compilers Principles, Techniques, and Tools.* Addison-Wesley, 1986.

[2] I. Foster and S. Taylor. Flat PARLOG: a basis for comparison. *Int. Journal of Parallel Programming*, 16(2), 1987.

[3] I. Foster and S. Taylor. Strand: a pratical parallel programming tool. In E.L. Lusk and R. Overbeek, editors, *Proc. of the North American Conf. on Logic Programming*, pages 497–512, MIT Press, 1989.

[4] M. Garey and D. Johnson. *Computers and Intractability: A Guide to the Theory of NP-Completeness.* Freeman,San Francisco, 1979.

[5] T. Hickey and S. Mudambi. Global compilation of Prolog. *Journal of Logic Programming*, 7(3):193–230, November 1989.

[6] A. Houri and E. Shapiro. *A sequential abstract machine for Flat Concurrent Prolog.* Tech. Rep. CS86-20, Dep. of Computer Science, Weizmann Institute, Rehovot, 1986. Also Chapter 38 in [17].

[7] Y. Kimura and T. Chikayama. An abstract KL/1 machine and its instruction set. In *Proc. of 1987 Symp. of Logic Programming*, pages 468–477, IEEE, 1987.

[8] A. Kleinman. *Topics in Distributed Execution of Concurrent Logic Programming Languages with Atomic Unification.* Master's thesis, Dep. of Computer Science, Weizmann Institute, Rehovot, December 1989.

[9] S. Kliger and E. Shapiro. A decision tree compilation algorithm for FCP(:,?). In K. Bowen and R. A. Kowalski, editors, *Proc. of the 5th Int. Conf. of Logic Programming and Symp. of Logic Programming*, pages 1315–1336, MIT Press, 1988.

[10] C. Mierowsky, S. Taylor, E. Shapiro, J. Levy, and M. Safra. *The design and implementation of Flat Concurrent Prolog.* Tech. Rep. CS85-09, Dep. of Computer Science, Weizmann Institute, Rehovot, 1986.

[11] M. Miyakawa. Optimum decision trees - an optimal variable theorem and its related applications. *Acta Information*, 22:475–498, 1985.

[12] L. T. Reinwald and R. M. Soland. Conversion of limited-entry decision tables to optimal computer programs I : minimum average processing time. *Journal of the ACM*, 13(3):339–358, July 1966.

[13] L. T. Reinwald and R. M. Soland. Conversion of limited-entry decision tables to optimal computer programs II : minimum storage requirement. *Journal of the ACM*, 14(4):742–755, October 1967.

[14] R. L. Rivest and L. Hyafil. Constructing optimal binary decision trees is NP-complete. *Information Processing Letters*, 5(1):15–17, May 1976.

[15] V. A. Saraswat. A somewhat logical formulation of CLP synchronization primitives. In K. Bowen and R.A. Kowalski, editors, *Proc. of the 5th Int. Conf. of Logic Programming and Symp. of Logic Programming*, pages 1298–1314, MIT Press, 1988.

[16] H. Schumacher and K. C. Sevcik. The synthetic approach to decision table conversion. *Comm. of the ACM*, 19(6):343–351, June 1976.

[17] E. Shapiro, editor. *Concurrent Prolog, Collected Papers.* MIT Press, 1987.

[18] K. Ueda. *Guarded Horn Clauses.* Tech. Rep. TR-103, ICOT, 1985. Also Chapter 4 in [17].

[19] M. Hirsch W. Siverman, A. Houri, and E. Shapiro. *The Logix System User Manual, Version 1.3.* Rehovot, 1988. Technical Report, CS-21, Also Chapter 21 in [17].

[20] D.H.D. Warren. *An abstract Prolog instruction set.* Tech. Rep. 309, Artificial Intelligence Center, SRI International, 1983.

[21] R. Yang. Solving simple substitution ciphers in parallel logic system Andorra-I. In G. Levi and M. Martelli, editors, *Proc. of the 6th International Conf. of Logic Programming*, pages 113–128, Lisbon, July 1989.

[22] E. Yardeni, S. Kliger, and E. Shapiro. The languages FCP(:,?) and FCP(:). *New Generation Computing*, 7(2,3):89–107, 1990.

[23] E. Yardeni and E. Shapiro. *A Type System for Logic Programs.* Tech. Rep. CS87-05, Dep. of Computer Science, Weizmann Institute, Rehovot, 1986. Also Chapter 28 in [17].

Constraints and their Applications

Partial Evaluation of a CLP Language

Donald A. Smith dsmith@cs.brandeis.edu
Timothy J. Hickey tim@cs.brandeis.edu

Department of Computer Science
Brandeis University
Waltham, MA 02254

Abstract

This work extends previous research in partial evaluation in two directions by (1) providing an algorithm for partial evaluation of CLP($\mathcal{FT}$) — Prolog with universally quantified disequality constraints on finite trees; and (2) improving the handling of loops to guarantee the termination of partial evaluation. This work can be viewed as a first step toward the development of a CLP model of partial evaluation. In order to detect loops (recursion), our algorithm uses two operations on constraints: projection and equivalence. Combined with the *delayed unification* technique, a form of generalization, the algorithm guarantees that partial evaluation terminates and that the residue of partial evaluation contains no clauses from the original program. Our partial evaluator utilizes the additional optimization techniques of *reparameterization*, *constraint lifting* (an extension of Nakagawa's idea of common feature extraction), and *factorization*. Results of applying our method to the English language parser from the 'Chat' database query system are presented.

1 Introduction

Partial evaluation (PE) is a program transformation technique which can be used to improve the efficiency of programs. The basic idea is to perform computations which are independent of the input data at PE time, thereby transforming the original *subject* program into an equivalent but more efficient *residual* program. Publications which offer an overview of partial evaluation include [Futamura], [JSS], [KC], and [NGC]. Recently PE has attracted widespread interest among researchers in logic programming. Articles in [AR] and [NGC] as well as [BL], [CvES], [LS], [Kom], and [Owen] offer a sample of research on partial evaluation of logic programs.

In Section 1.1, as motivation for our algorithm, we review research by Hiroshi Fujita that divides partial evaluation of Prolog into two phases. We show how, by using constraints and by introducing a simple change to his algorithm, the two phases can be combined into a single phase while increasing the efficiency of PE. The section also introduces several concepts used later in the paper: reparameterization, specialization, eager unfolding, and iterated partial evaluation. Section 2 describes CLP($\mathcal{FT}$) and the U-constraint syntax for universally quantified disequality constraints; it then presents our PE algorithm, including constraint operations for loop (recursion) detection. Section 3 covers several extensions and optimizations, including delayed unification, constraint lifting, and factorization. In Section 4, we contrast our work with previous work in partial evaluation. Finally, in the appendix, we present benchmark results that demonstrate the use of our PE method on the 'Chat' database query system [WP].

1.1 A Two Stage Partial Evaluator for Prolog

In this section, as motivation for our PE algorithm, we describe previous research by Hiroshi Fujita that divides partial evaluation into two stages: one stage for specialization and another stage for removal of inconsistencies and inefficiencies in the output of the first stage. We will show how to eliminate the second stage and increase the efficiency of PE by incorporation of disequality constraints into the first stage using a CLP model of PE (Section 1.2) and by a simple change to the algorithm (Section 1.3).

In [Fujita], Hiroshi Fujita uses PE to transform a naive string matcher into an efficient program which runs in time linear in the length of the text string. The effect can be summarized by the claim that PE 'automatically' performed the optimization central to the Knuth-Morris-Pratt (KMP) string matching algorithm ([KMP], [HS]). [1] The program input to Fujita's partial evaluator is the following:

```
match(P,T):- match(P,T,P,T).
  /* match(Pattern, Text, OriginalPattern, OriginalText) */
match([A|Ps],[B|Ts], P, T):- A=B,match(Ps,Ts,P,T).
match([A|Ps],[B|Ts],P,[_|T]):- A\==B, match(P,T,P,T).
match([],_,_,_).
```

Notice the use of the non-logical disequality operator `\==` in clause 2 of `match/4`. When the pattern `P=[a,a,a,b]` is known at PE time, the partial evaluator transforms the preceding program into the much more efficient one:

```
match_2([a|A]):-match_3(A).   match_2([A|B]):-a\==A,match_2(B).
match_3([a|A]):-match_4(A).   match_3([A|B]):-a\==A,match_2(B).
match_4([a|A]):-match_5(A).   match_4([A|B]):-a\==A,match_2(B).
match_5([b|A]).               match_5([A|B]):-b\==A,match_9(B).
match_9(a,A):- match_5(A).    match_9(A,B):-  a\==A,match_2(B).
```

[1] By now the derivation of KMP has become a standard example in the PE literature. Consel and Danvy describe a similar result in [CD], where a string matcher written in Lisp is partially evaluated to obtain a KMP-like matcher. However, the input matcher was not so naive and required an unintuitive auxiliary function. P. Kursawe derives KMP for Prolog, but again the code is complex and, like Fujita, he uses the non-logical operator `\==` instead of `dif` constraints [Kursawe]. We believe that the incorporation of constraints leads to a natural and elegant derivation.

The generated program never 'backs up' on the text string: when a mismatch is detected, matching continues from the point of mismatch in the text string and at an appropriate location in the pattern string.

It is important to stress, though, that the efficient program is the result of a two stage process in Fujita's method: specialization and shortcutting. During specialization, a set of new residual clauses is generated. Shortcutting unfolds certain of these clauses and deletes others that are inconsistent. The following is a *rough* and intuitive description of how specialization of a goal G into a residual goal G' is carried out (cf. [Fujita, p. 3]). In Section 2 we present a more rigorous description of a (generalized) partial evaluator.

1. (Primitive) If G is a primitive then
   - If G is unevaluable (e.g., `X\== a`) then $G' = G$.
   - Else (e.g., `X=a` or `a\==b` or `a\==a`) execute G; if G succeeds, then let the residue $G' = true$, else $G' = fail$.
2. (Conjunction) If G is a conjunction $(G1, G2)$, recursively specialize $G1$ and $G2$ and let $G' = (G1', G2')$.
3. (Loop Detection and Memoization-lookup) If G is a procedure call (an atom) which is identical modulo variable renaming to a previously unfolded call P then let $G' = P'$, where P' is a call to the (memoized) residual procedure associated with P.
4. (Specialization) Else (G must be a non-looping procedure call), let G' be a new procedure call with a new predicate symbol and all variables occurring in G as arguments (e.g., $G =$`p(X,f(X,Y))` and $G' =$`p_1(X,Y)`); for each clause H_i`:-`B_i such that $G = H_i$ is solvable with mgu θ_i, specialize $B_i\theta_i$ getting residual goal B_i' and substitution θ_i'; add $G'\theta_i\theta_i'$`:-`B_i' to the set of residual clauses.

Step 3 above serves two purposes. First, if the unfolding of P and the creation of its residual procedure P' have completed, then the specializer avoids repeating work by using a call to P' as the specialization of G. Secondly and more importantly, suppose P is in fact an *ancestor* call of G — one whose specialization has *not* finished in step 4. Then, PE is about to enter a loop, and returning residue $G' = A'$ avoids the loop. Of course, this sort of loop detection does not detect all loops, and partial evaluators typically have various termination heuristics as well. We will have more to say about these topics in later sections.

In step 4 (Specialization), the distinct variables appearing in G are collected and made the arguments of G'. We call this transformation *reparameterization.* It is important for reducing the overhead of parameter passing and unification at run time, since known arguments and functors can be 'factored out' when creating residual clauses. Reparameterization resembles but is more general than the operation of 'pushing down of meta arguments'

(PDMA) mentioned in [Owen] and [SB]. Furthemore, it is performed during specialization, whereas in [SB] it occurs as a separate pass.

The clauses output by the specializer above contain some inefficiencies (*trivial* predicates which have only a single clause) and some inconsistencies (calls which are doomed to fail due to incompatible constraints). Only during the second stage, shortcutting, are these redundancies and inconsistencies removed.

1.2 The Desirability of Using a CLP Model of PE

Because Fujita used the non-logical operator `\==` instead of the logical constraint `dif`, the residual program output by stage 1 contains inconsistencies, clauses which are doomed to fail [Fujita, p 7]:

```
match_11(a,B):- match_4(B).
match_11(A,B):- a \== A,match_12(A,B).
match_12(a,A):- ....  % This fails when called by match_11.
match_12(A,B):- a \== A, ....
```

The second clause of `match_11` makes a call to `match_12` after executing `a \== A`. But if the program is called with a ground text list, the first clause of `match_12` cannot possibly succeed, given the condition `a \== A`. Hence any work done specializing the body of this clause would be wasted. In general, an arbitrarily large amount of time could be lost due to such inefficiency.

Fujita's second stage, shortcutting, deletes such inconsistent clauses. Yet using the constraint `dif(a,A)` and a CLP model of PE allows us to generate the efficient KMP matcher without a post-processing stage for propagating constraints. Our algorithm incorporates constraints as an integral part of the partial evaluator and thereby avoids generating the inconsistent clauses in the first place. (For example, if `dif(a,A)` is used in the body of `match_11` above, then the first clause of `match_12` never gets created, since the call is doomed to fail.) This allows PE to be more time and space efficient, since fewer branches of the search tree need be traversed.

1.3 Trivial Predicates, Eager Unfolding, & Iterated PE

A trivial predicate is simply a predicate with only a single clause in its definition. Stage 2 of Fujita's algorithm unfolds calls to such predicates (much like in-line coding of functions in Lisp). But a simple change to the algorithm causes stage 1 to do such shortcutting automatically. If specialization of a goal G has resulted in a trivial predicate with the single clause `H:- B`, then unfold (resolve) by unifying the call G' with `H` and replacing the call with `B`, with variables bound from the unification. (See Section 2.) As in the last section, this optimization can save an arbitrarily large amount of PE time.

In fact, such in-line unfolding could be done even for non-trivial predicates, by unfolding once for each residual clause. We call this option of unfolding a call with multiple clauses *eager unfolding*. It may however lead to a large increase in code size.[2] For example, given the clause `q(X,Y):- int(X),int(Y)` with facts `int(0)...int(9)`, the residue would be 100 clauses `q_1(0,0)...q_1(9,9)`. And for the string matcher, eager unfolding yields a large program that does not correspond to KMP.

In contrast to eager unfolding, our default option is as follows: when a call specializes to a predicate with multiple clauses, the call is replaced by a call to the new predicate, which is used as a 'buffer' for storing the multiple choices. (The residue for `q` above is then isomorphic to the original.) Following [Owen], we call this option *(auxiliary) call creation.* Call creation sometimes results in less efficient programs, when inconsistent bindings between different residual calls are not detected until run time. We allow the user to specify via program declarations that certain calls should be eagerly unfolded.

In certain cases, especially with call creation, *re*-partially evaluating the residue of one iteration of PE gives more efficient results. (See the Appendix.) This suggests that *iterated partial evaluation* can be used, until a fixed point is reached or until we run out of patience. However, there are programs for which a fixed point does not exist: at every iteration of PE, the residue changes. One such program is the following:

```
even(0).  even(s(X)):- odd(X).   odd(s(X)):- even(X).
query(X):- even(X),odd(X).
```

When `even` and `odd` are eagerly unfolded, the loop detection of partial evaluation prevents the infinite loop that would occur during normal evaluation of `query(X)`. Still, each iteration of PE binds `X` to $s^i(0)$ for greater and greater i, so a fixed point is never reached. Furthermore, it is not hard to concoct, for any n, a program which requires n iterations of partial evaluation to reach the fixed point.

The benefits of partial evaluation come from at least three operations: pruning of the search tree due to failure detection (resulting from either specialization or unfolding); compression of inference chains due to unfolding; and constraint simplification (including reparameterization and the technique of Section 3.3). All three operations can be combined in a single algorithm.

2 Partial Evaluation of CLP($\mathcal{FT}$)

In this section we present our basic algorithm for partial evaluation of CLP($\mathcal{FT}$) with specialization, unfolding, loop detection, and memoization. In Section 3 we introduce several enhancements to the basic algorithm.

---

[2] In addition, eager unfolding has the disadvantage that residual clauses may share *common prefixes*. This happens when the first n goals in conjunction use call creation and the $n+1$st goal is eagerly unfolded: residues of the first n goals appear in each clause resulting from eager unfolding (cf. [Owen], p. 321).

2.1 The Language CLP($\mathcal{FT}$).

CLP($\mathcal{FT}$) refers to Prolog with disequality constraints on finite trees ([JL]). The CLP domain $\mathcal{FT}$ is the domain whose model is the set of all finite trees over an infinite alphabet (with infinitely many function symbols of every arity) and it is axiomatized by Clark's Equality Theory E^*. The only difference between this domain and the domains used by Prolog and Prolog II is that we allow universally quantified disequalities, in addition to equations and simple disequalities between terms.[3] Universally quantified disequalities are of the form $\forall X_1, \ldots, X_n X \neq T$ where T is a term. For programming we adopt a more convenient notation, called the U-constraint notation, in which universally quantified variables are denoted by terms of the form `?V`, and disequality is denoted by `<>`. For example, the universally quantified constraint $\forall Y, Z.X \neq f(Y, W, g(Y, Z))$ corresponds to the following U-constraint `X<>f(?Y,W,g(?Y,?Z))`. A CLP($\mathcal{FT}$) program is then a set of clauses of the usual form where the constraints are allowed to be equations, disequations, and U-constraints.

The restrictions to finite trees, an infinite Herbrand universe, and U-constraints are not strictly necessary, as even the more general cases have complete axiomizations [Maher]; however, our implemented partial evaluator deals only with the restricted case. Applications of U-constraints, including elimination of cuts and constructive negation, are discussed in [SmHi].

2.2 The PE Algorithm

The PE algorithm handles only 'pure', definite clause CLP($\mathcal{FT}$) programs — those without cuts, non-logical primitives and negative literals (other than disequalities). We believe that many of the ideas will be relevant for less 'pure' languages, as well as for other CLP domains (by replacing E^* with some other satisfaction complete theory). In fact, we have used essentially the same algorithm for partial evaluation of CLP(Bool) and (with modifications to restrict unfolding) of Prolog with cuts.

Partial evaluation takes as input a list L of clauses, a goal G, and a set C of constraints. Unbound variables appearing in constraint sets are implicitly existentially quantified. We call a set C of constraints *satisfiable* and write $\models C$ iff $\mathcal{FT} \models \mathcal{C}$ (or equivalently $E^* \models C$). The output of PE is a list L' of residual clauses, and a possibly empty list $R = [r_1, \ldots r_n]$, where each r_i is a pair $\langle G_i, C_i \rangle$; each G_i is a goal; and each C_i is a set of constraints. The intention is (roughly) that for any constraint $\hat{C}$ the answer constraints of the query $\leftarrow G, C \bigcup \hat{C}$ with respect to L are the same as the union of the answer constraints of the queries $\leftarrow G_i, C_i \bigcup \hat{C}$ with respect to L'. Furthermore,

[3] In the standard definition of CLP languages [JL], constraints are conjunctions of atomic formulas. Thus, to be precise, we need to introduce a new predicate symbol $d_T(X, Y)$ for each universally quantified disequality $\forall Z.X \neq T(Y, Z)$ where Y, Z are tuples of variables and $T(Y, Z)$ is a term. The axiom defining d_T is simply $\forall X, Y.d_T(X, Y, Z) \Leftrightarrow \forall Z.X \neq T(Y, Z)$.

the residual program will return answers in the same order under a standard depth-first interpreter, as long as use of eager unfolding is restricted to leading or deterministic calls. (Eager unfolding can permute the order of answers; see [HiSm]).

Partial evaluation can prune failure nodes associated with infinite branches of the search tree. (For example, `append([1|X],Y,U),append(U,Z,[2|W])` would loop in a normal depth-first Prolog system. But since $1 \neq 2$ and thanks to loop detection, the failure of the goal is detected at PE time.) As a result, the corresponding successful and finitely failed queries of the subject and residual programs may differ under a depth-first interpreter. Certain queries which would loop in the original program will finitely fail in the residual program; this in turn will allow other queries to succeed by avoiding those infinite derivations. If this is undesirable, one can restrict the various transformations to yield exact equivalence. Formal proofs of correctness of our partial evaluator can be found in [HiSm], where these issues are discussed in greater detail and for a more general class of CLP languages.

Notice that the minimal Herbrand models of the subject and residual programs ([Lloyd]) will in general *not* be identical, even for instances of the query G, because of reparameterization. But one can add clauses like G:-G_i (for example, `match([a,a,a,b],L):- match_1(L).`) so that at least for instances of the query, the same calls can be used. For goals other than the G_i and C_i no promise is made about completeness.

To detect loops, we make use of an equivalence relation $\cong$ that holds between goal-constraint pairs. We say that $\langle G, C\rangle \cong \langle G', C'\rangle$ iff, modulo variable renaming, G and G' are identical and C and C', restricted to the variables appearing in G and G' respectively, define identical constraints. We make the definition of $\cong$ more precise in Section 2.3.

To define reparameterization, we need the following notation. If G is a procedure call (a non-constraint atom), then $Pred(G)$ is the predicate symbol of G, $Args(G)$ is the list of arguments in G, and $Vars(G)$ is the *set* of variables in G ordered by first appearance in a left-right, depth-first traversal of G. For example, if G =`p(X,f(A,B),X)`, then $Pred(G) = p$, $Args(G) = [X, f(A, B), X]$, and $Vars(G) = \{X, A, B\}$. The function *reparam* takes three arguments: a predicate symbol p, the old procedure call G, and a solvable set of constraints C. $reparam(p, G, C)$ returns a new procedure call G' where $Pred(G') = p$ and $Args(G') = Vars(G\sigma)$, where σ is an idempotent mgu corresponding to the equations in C. Thus, if G is as above and $C = \{B = a\}$, then $reparam(p_{new}, G, C) = p_{new}(X, A)$.

Finally, we represent clauses in the form H:-C, B, where C is a set of constraints and B is a conjunction of atoms (procedure calls). Compared to the standard format for clauses, in which individual constraints can appear scattered throughout the body, the new format permits a more concise and higher level description of the algorithm.

To compute the partial evaluation of G, C, and L, initialize global variable L' to $\emptyset$ and invoke procedure *pe*, passing goal G and constraints C as parameters. $pe(G, C)$ returns a list $R = [r_1, \ldots r_k]$ of goal-constraints pairs as defined above. L' will contain the list of residual clauses, which can be filtered by removing any clauses not reachable from G in the dependency graph for L'. Figure 1 contains the pseudo-code for *pe*.

The reader may notice one problem with the algorithm as presented: it may not terminate. One solution is to use termination heuristics that cut off specialization and return $G' = G$ and $C' = C$ when certain conditions hold. (We must then initialize L' to L.) For many applications, including string matching and 'compilation' of many interpreted programs via PE, termination heuristics are not needed. We postpone until Section 3.2 discussion of a technique which eliminates the need for termination heuristics as it guarantees termination in such a way that no clauses from L are needed to execute the residual program.

2.3 Loop (Recursion) Detection

We distinguish two types of loops that can occur during PE: simple and non-simple loops. Intuitively, a *simple* loop occurs if while specializing a certain atomic goal, an attempt is made to specialize another goal which is identical to the first (modulo renaming). Hence simple loops can be detected by comparing the current goal with ancestor goals in the (partial) proof tree of the query. The technique is standard in the PE literature (e.g., [BL]); it allows partial evaluators to 'discover' recursions in the input program and to create recursive residual clauses. We suggest that 'loop detection' is a misnomer and 'recursion detection' is a more appropriate name for the operation.

Like simple loops, *non-simple loops* also arise from recursions in the subject program. However, unlike simple loops, (constraints on) one or more arguments differ compared to the ancestor, and the current call cannot in general be replaced by a call to an ancestor's residual predicate. We refer to such calls having non-isomorphic ancestor calls of the same predicate and arity as *non-simple loop calls*. In this and the next two subsections we concentrate on detection of simple loops. In Section 3.1 we consider a generalization which can handle some non-simple loops.

Notice, by the way, that loop detection is not a matter of whether a call should be *unfolded*; rather, it is a matter of whether a call should be *specialized*. Unfolding is a separate question. We suspect that this distinction is often overlooked.

2.4 Testing Equivalence of Goal-Constraint Pairs

In this section, we present a precise definition of simple loops and discuss algorithms for their detection. In standard Prolog, where the only constraints are equality constraints, equation solving is effected by substitution. Thus, the test for a (simple) loop is quite simple: is there an atomic ancestor goal G' which is syntactically identical to the current goal G, modulo variable renaming? For CLP($\mathcal{FT}$), we want to know whether $\langle G, C\rangle \cong \langle G', C'\rangle$,

$pe(G,C)$ = case $\langle G,C\rangle$:

1. (Base Case) If $G = true$ then return $[\langle true, C\rangle]$.

2. (Conjunction) If G is a conjunction (G_1, G_2), then recursively invoke $pe(G_1, C)$, getting the list R_1 of residual pairs. Let $R_1 = [\langle g_{11}, c_{11}\rangle, \ldots, \langle g_{1n}, c_{1n}\rangle]$, $n \geq 0$. For each pair $\langle g_{1i}, c_{1i}\rangle \in R_1$, invoke $pe(G_2, c_{1i} \bigcup C)$, getting the list R_{2i} of residual pairs. Let $R_{2i} = [\langle g_{2i1}, c_{2i1}\rangle, \ldots, \langle g_{2im_i}, c_{2im_i}\rangle]$. Return the list R of pairs such that $\langle G', C'\rangle \in R$ iff G' is the conjunction (g_{1i}, g_{2ik}) and $C' = c_{1i} \bigcup c_{2ik} \bigcup C$ for some $i \leq n$, $k \leq m_i$.

3. (Loop Detection) If G is a procedure call such that there exists a pair $\langle A, C_A\rangle$ whose partial evaluation has *not* finished (A is an *ancestor* call) and $\langle G, C\rangle \cong \langle A, C_A\rangle$, then let A' be the residual call associated with A. Return $R = [\langle G', C\rangle]$, where $G' = reparam(Pred(A'), G, C)$.

4. (Memoization Lookup and Unfolding) If G is a procedure call such that there exists a pair $\langle P, C_P\rangle$ whose partial evaluation *has* finished and $\langle G, C\rangle \cong \langle P, C_P\rangle$, then let P' be the residual call associated with P and $G' = reparam(Pred(P'), G, C)$. Let $[H_1\text{:-}C_1, B_1, \ldots, H_n\text{:-}C_n, B_n]$ be (a new renaming of) the list of clauses for P' in L', and $R = [\langle B_1, C_1 \bigcup \{G' = H_1\}\rangle, \ldots, \langle B_n, C_n \bigcup \{G' = H_n\}\rangle]$.

   If $R = []$ (P failed) or $|R| = 1$ (trivial predicate) or G is to be *eagerly unfolded*, then return R. Else return $[\langle G', C\rangle]$.

5. (Specialization and Unfolding)

   Let $[H_1\text{:-}C_1, B_1, \ldots, H_n\text{:-}C_n, B_n]$ be (a new renaming of) the list of clauses such that $C_i' = C \bigcup \{G = H_i\} \bigcup C_i$ is satisfiable. If this list is empty (G failed) return $[]$.

   Else, let $G' = reparam(p_{new}, G, C)$, for some new predicate symbol p_{new}. For each i such that $1 \leq i \leq n$, recursively specialize by invoking $pe(B_i, C_i')$ getting list R_i of residual pairs. Let $R = concat_i R_i$. For each $\langle B', C'\rangle \in R$, add $G'\text{:-}C', B'$ to L', the list of new, residual clauses (for memoization and auxiliary call creation).

   If $R = []$ (G failed) or $|R| = 1$ (trivial predicate) or G is to be *eagerly unfolded*, then return R. Else return $[\langle G', C\rangle]$.

Figure 1: Partial Evaluation Algorithm (unoptimized)

where $\cong$ is the equivalence relation that holds between semantically equivalent (modulo variable renaming) goal-constraint pairs. (We assume that the implementation treats semantically equivalent goals the same.)

Maher's quantifier elimination algorithm [MAHER] can be used to test for equivalence of $\langle G, C\rangle$ and $\langle G'C'\rangle$ as follows: Let $V = Vars(G)$, $W = Var(C) - V$; similarly, let $V' = Vars(G')$, $W' = Var(C') - V'$. Then $\langle G, C\rangle \cong \langle G', C'\rangle$ iff

$$\exists V, V'(G = G') \wedge \forall V, V'(G = G' \rightarrow (\exists W.C \iff \exists W'.C'))$$

and Maher's algorithm can be used to test the satisfiability of this first order formula in the equality theory of finite trees.

A more efficient approach would be to define a canonical form $I(C)$ for each constraint set C such that two constraints are logically equivalent iff their canonical forms are identical. One can then test for equivalence of goal-constraint pairs using a projection operator π_V such that for any constraint set C with variables $V \cup W$, $\pi_V(C)$ is a constraint set which is logically equivalent to $\exists W.C$. ($\pi_V(C)$ projects from C only those constraints that are 'relevant' to V.) The two pairs $\langle G, C\rangle$ and $\langle G', C'\rangle$ are then equivalent iff $I(\pi_V(C)) = I(\pi_{V'}(C'))$. This is the approach we have taken in implementing our partial evaluator [SmHi].

Projecting and testing equivalence of constraints are important not just for recursion detection. Goal-constraint pairs also have to be compared for equivalence during memoization lookup (case 4). And the partial evaluator has to collect and represent constraints during the creation of residual clauses in case 5; for the sake of efficiency, it is desirable that a simplified and minimal representation of constraints appear in residual clauses. (Hence instead of storing C' in the bodies of residual clauses in case 5 of the PE algorithm, *pe* should store the projection of C' onto the variables appearing in the clause.) Finally, projection is needed at the top level, when Prolog prints out the answer constraints on the set of goal variables.

3 Optimizations and Variations

At the end of the previous section we suggested one optimization for the PE algorithm: storing only relevant constraints in residual clauses. Another optimization is to maintain constraint sets C in solved form (e.g., replacing $\{f(X) \neq f(Y), Z = Z\}$ with $\{X \neq Y\}$; see [SmHi]) and to replace equations in C with substitutions (mgus). In this section, we consider some additional optimizations and variations on the PE algorithm.

3.1 Using 'Instance-of' for Loop Detection and Memoization Lookup

We have assumed that a loop occurs when the current atomic goal-constraint pair is *identical* modulo variable renaming to an ancestor pair (simple loop).

Yet one could use a condition weaker than identity modulo variable renaming for detecting loops and for memoization lookup. If the current goal-constraint pair $\langle G, C\rangle$ is an *instance* of pair $\langle A, C_A\rangle$ then it is correct to use the residual goal A' associated with the latter as the new residue.[4] For example, $\langle$`p(a)`$,\emptyset\rangle$ is an instance of $\langle$`p(X)`$,\emptyset\rangle$ and it would be correct to use the memoized residue, say `p_1(X)`, associated with the latter pair (with `X` bound to `a`) as the specialization of the former call.

Using 'instance-of' to check for loops will cause the partial evaluator to loop less often, since it will inhibit specialization more often. However, PE will output a less efficient residual program in certain cases. For example, `p(a)` is an instance of `p(X)`, but it could happen that the former always fails though not the latter. If during the specialization of `p(X)`, a call `p(a)` were encountered, and if 'instance-of' were used to test for a loop, then `p(a)` would not be specialized and its failure would not be detected until run time.

Section 3.3 describes how to test the instance-of relation for dif and U-constraints.

3.2 Delayed Unification

In this section we describe a general technique, delayed unification,[5] that prevents partial evaluation from looping, guarantees that the residue of partial evaluation contains no clauses from the original program, and appears to perform well in practice (see appendix). In Section 4, we will compare the technique with some related work.

We illustrate the technique with an example. Without delayed unification, our partial evaluator would enter a loop given the following (non-naive) program for reversing a list:

```
query(L,R):- rev([a,b,c|L],R).
rev(L,R):- rev_aux(L,[],R).
rev_aux([],R,R).   rev_aux([H|T],In,R):- rev_aux(T,[H|In],R).
```

A goal like `query(L,R)` will cause PE to loop because in the recursive call in the body of the second clause for `rev_aux`, the second argument `[H|In]` (the accumulator) increases in size. In contrast, the naive reverse program (using `append`) would have no such problem since the recursion acts on a smaller sub-list of the input.

Using delayed unification, we create a variant of the second clause for `rev_aux` in which the output unification for the second argument of the recursive call is moved to a point after the call: `rev_aux([H|T],In,R):- rev_aux(T,Two,R),eq(Two,[H|In])`. The transformed program is equivalent to the original program, given the unit clause `eq(X,X)`. And when we

[4]The same idea appeared in [BL]. Compare also the idea of *partial definitions* in [FN].

[5]We thank an anonymous referee for directing us to the technical report [BL], where a similar idea due to John Gallagher was mentioned very briefly and offered as a "solution to the problem of non-termination". The model of PE in that report is quite different from ours. We will discuss the differences in Section 4.

partially evaluate the new program, recursion detection allows us to obtain the following efficient program:

```
query_1(L,R):- rev_aux_4(L,[c,b,a],R).
rev_aux_4([],R,R). rev_aux_4([H|T],In,R):- rev_aux_4(T,[H|In],R).
```

The residual clause for `query_1` reflects the fact that the reversal of a list beginning with `[a,b,c]` is a list ending with `[c,b,a]`.

The technique of delayed unification is based on the shortening operation which replaces arguments in non-simple loop calls with 'smaller' arguments (by substituting variables for subterms of arguments) and adds an equation after the call to 'make up the difference'. If program analysis can determine that partial evaluation will converge even without shortening, then delayed unification is not needed at all. In other cases, certain arguments must be shortened. As the example with `rev_aux` suggests, mode information can be utilized to determine which arguments to shorten: the second argument is, in effect, an output parameter. (See also [Sestoft], where only calls satisfying a 'structural induction property' that assures termination are unfolded.) In our current implementation, however, we do the transformation dynamically at run time, shortening those arguments which have 'grown' since an ancestor call.

Fix the Herbrand universe to include only those functors and atoms appearing in the program and let $|T|$ denote the size of term T based on some measure. The measure should have the property that there are only a finite number of T with $|T| \leq n$ for all n and if $m < n$ then the number of T with $|T| \leq m$ is less than the number of T with $|T| \leq n$. Typical measures are depth or size of terms regarded as finite trees. Then, delayed unification replaces `p(T)` with `p(U),V=S` where $|U| < |T|$ and $X = T$ iff $(X = U \wedge V = S)$. Furthermore, we can prove that the technique guarantees termination of PE, leaving no clauses from the original program. Briefly, this is because a program contains only a finite number of function symbols and there are only a finite number of terms (modulo variable names) of a certain size. Thus, any infinite branch in the search tree would contain a simple loop which would be detected in step 3 of the algorithm. We are investigating extending the technique of delayed unification to allow shortening of disequality and other constraints.

We have used the technique on the English language parser (`sentence/5`) from the 'Chat' ([WP]) database query system. Without delayed unification, our partial evaluator would fail to terminate. To prevent looping, we tried two shortening heuristics. With both heuristics, shortening is performed only when the current call to be specialized has a non-isomorphic ancestor of the same predicate and arity. The first heuristic potentially shortens every argument in such a call; only those arguments which have grown since the ancestor call are shortened. The second heuristic shortens all applicable calls to a fixed depth of term size. Depending on the shortening heuristic and the number of iterations of PE, parsing runs up to 44% faster with residual code

3 times the size of the input. Furthermore, clauses from the original input program are totally eliminated from the residue. Best results occurred when (equality) constraint lifting from Section 3.3 and iterated PE were used. (See the appendix.) There are other non-trivial examples (not discussed here) in which we have obtained a sixfold speedup and a decrease in code size.

We note, finally, that delayed unification is natural for unification-based languages like Prolog: certain subterms are replaced with unbound variables. Thanks to the logical variable, delayed unification can be realized within the object language. In Lisp, the analogous technique must be performed in the meta-language of the partial evaluator: certain variables are marked 'unknown' or 'dynamic' [Jones]. This is a reflection of the general ease with which partial evaluation can be performed for logic programming languages.

3.3 Constraint Lifting and LCA

Consider a call to a residual procedure such that each clause contains a certain constraint on a goal variable (e.g., each clause for `p_1(X)` contains $X = f(Y)$ for some Y). It should be possible to 'lift' the constraint up to the parent residue, possibly leading to an earlier detection of failure. This optimization is similar to H. Nakagawa's *common feature extraction*, which applies only to equality constraints [Nakagawa]. We call the corresponding optimization for CLP *constraint lifting*.

In the case of equality constraints, constraint lifting can be based on anti-unification, as described in [LMM]. Using the anti-unification algorithm, one can calculate the least common anti-instance (lca) of a set of terms. The lca (dual of the mgu) of a set of terms is that unique (up to variable renaming) term such that every term in the set is an instance of the lca — that is, the lca is an anti-instance of the set of terms — and the lca is an instance of any (other) anti-instance — that is, the lca is the *least* such term. For example, the lca of `f(X,g(a,b,a))` and `f(1,g(d,b,d))` is `f(X,g(Y,b,Y))`. The lca of `f(a)` and `g(b)` is X (anything) since in the lattice of terms there is no term below X (the 'top' of the lattice) with these terms as instances.

It should be realized that the lca of a set of terms is an abstraction of the set of ground solutions represented by that set. By this we mean that the lca is in general an *overestimate* of the union of solutions of the terms in the set. Thus, `f(_)`, the lca of `f(a)` and `f(b)`, includes as an instance `f(c)` and other terms not in {`f(a)`} $\bigcup$ {`f(b)`}.

We will see that the notion of lca does not easily extend to disequality constraints. Yet constraint lifting can still be performed. It is useful to adopt notation from [LM], where instead of `X=f(Y),Y<>a,Y<>f(?)`, one writes `X=f(Y)`\{`f(a)`,`f(f(_))`}. The notation $T\backslash\{T_1, T_2, \ldots, T_n\}$ (which we call the *backslash notation*) indicates the subset of ground terms in the Herbrand universe $\mathcal{H}$ which are instances of T but not instances of any T_i. Without loss of generality we can assume that for each T_i there is a substitution θ_i such that $T_i = T\theta_i$. It is helpful to regard the items to the right of the \

as 'holes' (subsets of $\mathcal{H}$ which are to be excluded from the set). [6] We will use $-$ for $\backslash$ when the items are to be regarded as sets rather than terms.

Let us also adopt some terminology from [Kunen] for referring to subsets of $\mathcal{H}$. We use the term *basic set* to refer to the set of ground terms which are instances of a Prolog term (an equality constraint). Call a subset represented by a backslash expression such as $T\backslash\{T_1, T_2, \ldots, T_n\}$ a *miniset* set. Lastly, let *elementary set* refer to a set representable by a finite union of minisets.

If we let $b(T)$ denote the basic set corresponding to a term T, and let $t(B)$ denote the unique term (up to variable renaming) corresponding to a basic set B, then the lca of a set of terms $T_1, \ldots, T_n$ can be defined as $t(B)$, where B is the intersection of all basic sets containing $b(T_1), \ldots, b(T_n)$. This definition makes sense because it can be shown that the set B is a basic set. Moreover, it is clear from the definition that B is the least basic set containing the $b(T_i)$.

We can attempt to extend this definition to minisets but a difficulty arises from the fact that the intersection of all minisets M containing a given union $M_1 \cup \ldots \cup M_r$ is not itself a miniset. For example, the intersection of all minisets containing $M_1 = f(a)$ and $M_2 = f(b)$ is simply the union of M_1 and M_2 which is an elementary set and not a miniset.

Two solutions to this problem can be seen. One is to observe that the definition of lca extends very easily to elementary sets since the finite union of elementary sets is itself an elementary set. Thus the lca of a collection of elementary sets is simply their union. One could then generalize the CLP language so that disjunctions of constraints are allowed and could use elementary sets for constraint lifting. The disadvantage of this approach is that it greatly increases the complexity of the partial evaluation algorithm.

A second approach is to use a lifting algorithm which constructs a miniset which is a common anti-instance (although not necessarily a least common anti-instance). For example, if $M_1, \ldots, M_n$ is a collection of minisets, with $M_i = b(T_i) - \{b(S_{i1}), \ldots, b(S_{ir_i})\}$, one can form a common anti-instance $M = b(T) - \{R_1, \ldots, R_m\}$ by letting T be the lca of the T_i and letting the R_i be formed as follows.

Let $Q = \{b(S_{ij}) : i = 1, \ldots, n,\ j = 1, \ldots, r_i\}$, and for each $U \subseteq Q$, let $R(U) = \bigcap_{B \in U} B$ be the basic set formed by intersecting all basic sets in U. We then let $\{R_i\}$ be the set of all $R(U)$ such that $R(U)$ does not intersect M_i for any i. Observe that $M = T - \{R_i\}$ contains each M_i (as T contains M_i and each R_j is in M_i^c). Thus, M is a common anti-instance of the M_i; in fact, M is the smallest common anti-instance of the M_i such that the R_j are formed from intersections of the $b(S_{ij})$ [SmHi].

Finally, using the notation in this section we can now show how to test for the subset relation for dif constraints, as promised in Section 3.1. Let

[6] Equivalently, we can regard the item to the left of the $\backslash$ as a continent and the items to the right as lakes. We do not allow — and our syntax for U-constraints does not express — islands within the lakes: deeper nestings of set difference expressions. U-constraints express exactly the minisets.

$\alpha = A\backslash\{A_1, \ldots, A_n\}$ and $\beta = B\backslash\{B_1, \ldots, B_m\}$, with α, β nonempty. Then

$$\begin{aligned}
\alpha \subseteq \beta \ &\text{iff}\ \ \alpha \bigcap \beta^C = \emptyset \\
&\text{iff}\ \ \alpha \bigcap (B^C \bigcup (\bigcup_j B_j)) = \emptyset \\
&\text{iff}\ \ \alpha \bigcap B^C = \emptyset \text{ and } \forall_j (\alpha \bigcap B_j) = \emptyset \\
&\text{iff}\ \ A\backslash\{A_1, \ldots, A_n, B\} = \emptyset \text{ and } \forall_j mgu(A, B_j)\backslash\{A_1, \ldots, A_n\} = \emptyset \\
&\text{iff}\ \ A\backslash\{B\} = \emptyset \text{ and } \forall_j \exists_i mgu(A, B_j)\backslash\{A_i\} = \emptyset \ \ \text{(since } \alpha \text{ is nonempty)}
\end{aligned}$$

The last line of the derivation determines a test whether miniset α is a subset of miniset β. Furthermore, the test is expressible within the backslash notation and thus requires no new operations besides those already used for unification (mgu) and disequality (dif).

3.4 Factorization

In this section we introduce the factorization optimization. Given a set of residual clauses, constraint lifting determines a constraint $\hat{C}$ which is a common anti-instance of the constraints in each clause. After constraint lifting, it is desirable for efficiency to remove the common part $\hat{C}$ from each residual clause. To see this, consider the following contrived program and its residue after constraint lifting:

```
q(A) :- A<>1,A<>2,r(A,B).
r(A,f(1)) :- A<>3,A<>5.        r(A,f(2)) :- A<>1,A<>4,A<>5.
```

```
q_1(A) :- A<>1,A<>2,A<>5,r_1(A,f(C)).
r_1(A,f(1)) :- A<>1,A<>2,A<>3,A<>5.
r_1(A,f(2)) :- A<>1,A<>2,A<>4,A<>5.
```

Notice first that constraint lifting lifted the constraints `A<>5` and `B=f(C)` up to the call in the clause for `q_1`. Secondly, notice that the constraints `A<>1` and `A<>2` were 'inherited' from the call and appear in the clauses for `r_1`. (Thus, even without constraint lifting, factorization is useful.) Whenever `r_1` is invoked in the body of clause `q_1`, the constraints on `A` have already been successfully executed. Yet both clauses for `r_1` include those constraints in their bodies. This repetition is clearly wasteful since those constraints will already be in force whenever `r_1` is called.

To solve these problems, we introduce the semantic difference operation $-$ on constraint sets. Given constraint sets C_1 and C_2, where $Vars(C_2) \subseteq Vars(C_1) = V$ and $\forall V(C_1 \Rightarrow C_2)$, let $C_1 - C_2$ be a (simplified) set of constraints such that $((C_1 - C_2) \bigcup C_2) \Leftrightarrow C_1$. In the example above, if $C_2 = \{A \neq 1, A \neq 2, A \neq 5\}$ and in the first clause for `r_1` $C_1 = C_2 \bigcup \{A \neq 3\}$, then $C_1 - C_2 = \{A \neq 3\}$. (In this case $-$ corresponds to set difference; but this is not necessarily so.)

In step 5 of the algorithm, let $\hat{C}$ be the lifted constraints common to the residual pairs in R. Instead of adding $G'\text{:-}C', B'$ to L', the list of residual clauses, add $G'\text{:-}\pi_V(\check{C}'), B'$, where $V = Vars(G') \bigcup Vars(B')$ and $\check{C}' = C' - (C \bigcup \hat{C})$.[7] Use of $-$ guarantees that only new, 'local', constraints which were not lifted or inherited from the caller are included in the residual clause. The idea is that in every call to G' we know that $C \bigcup \hat{C}$ will always hold, so we can 'specialize' the residual C' first by 'subtracting out' any constraints implied by C or $\hat{C}$ and then by projecting on the variables appearing in the clause [HiSm].

Returning to our contrived example above, the application of the factorization operation during creation of the clauses for `r_1` yields the following clauses: `r_1(A,f(1)) :- A<>3` and `r_1(A,f(2)) :- A<>4`, as desired.

The reader may have noticed that due to the binding of `B` to `f(C)`, the call `r_1(A,f(C))` can be reparameterized. This would yield a new call, say, `r_2(A,C)` and then a new set of clauses for `r_2` without the `f(_)` in the heads. But if `r_1` were called recursively in a clause reachable from `r_1`, then reparameterizing would lead to code expansion, unless such recursive calls were reparameterized as well.

4 Related Work

Several researchers on partial evaluation ([CvES], [Kom], [LS], [BL], and [Kursawe]) share a similar model in which partial evaluation is viewed as a variation on SLD resolution and where residual clauses use the same predicate names as input clauses. This is in contrast to our approach, in which PE is rather viewed as a program transformation involving specialization, reparameterization, constraint lifting, etc. We call the model shared by the several researchers the 'standard view' of PE. In our description we will initially follow [CvES]. Also, for simplicity and since the other researchers did not deal with CLP languages, we will consider only standard Prolog and thus, for example, talk of answer substitutions instead of answer constraints.

In contrast to SLD, partial evaluation constructs (according to the standard view) a *partial* derivation tree from a query Q: a tree whose root is Q and whose leaves can be unresolved goals. Instead of returning only unconditional answer substitutions as the output of a query, PE returns also conditional answer substitutions such as $Q\theta{:-}B$: answers conditionalized on the successful resolution of the residual goals B at the leaves. (Lloyd and Shepherdson's term for such a conditional answer is *resultant.*) The correctness of SLD resolution guarantees that $\tilde{\forall} Q\theta{:-}B$ is a logical consequence of the clauses. The list of (un)conditional answers corresponding to leaf nodes of a partial derivation tree is called a frontier.

In order for the frontiers created by unfolding to be 'complete', the au-

[7] It is necessary also to associate the lifted constraints $\hat{C}$ with the set of clauses of G' for use during memoization lookup (case 4).

thors of [CvES] require that every goal appearing in a residue be an *instance of* the root of some frontier. (The analogous concept for [LS] and [BL] is the *closedness* condition.) To guarantee completeness, they suggest repeatedly creating frontiers for goals violating this condition, starting with the query, until a complete set is obtained. (Termination is not addressed.) However, if the root of some frontier is an instance of another root, the former must be deleted to avoid redundant answers. (The analogous concept for [LS] and [BL] is *independence*.) This guarantees completeness, since any goal will be an instance of some root of a frontier, but has the disadvantage that some of the benefits of PE are lost when 'instance-of' is used, since variable bindings are not utilized to prune the search tree.

The closedness, independence, and well-structuredness (see [BL]) requirements are, we believe, an artifact of the standard model of partial evaluation, in which the residual program uses the same predicate names and arities as the original program. (The basic problem is that there can be only one procedure of a given predicate and arity.) In contrast, we employ reparameterization[8] and create specialized procedures for each call (polyvariancy), stopping for loop detection and memoization. Accordingly, a disadvantage of our method is the increased code size of the residual program (see the appendix). The advantages are that failure can be detected more often, residual clauses are more finely specialized to their callers, and the overhead of parameter passing and unification is (often vastly) reduced. Moreover, the closedness and independence conditions are trivially maintained, since each call form is specialized into a new procedure, with new predicate name, 'tailor-made' for its arguments. Even if non-independent calls are partially evaluated or if the user specifies via 'suspension' declarations that certain calls not be specialized, the residual program is irredundant and complete since residues from different calls do not interfere and needed clauses from the original program are automatically incorporated [HiSm].

To avoid PE time loops, we use recursion detection to detect simple loops and delayed unification to generalize certain calls via shortening. But instead of generalizing calls to their most general form, or to a call which is an anti-instance of calls being partially evaluated ([BL], [CvES], [Kursawe]), our method generalizes them only part of the way. Again, this leads to more highly specialized residues while still guaranteeing termination.

Delayed unification resembles but is independent of several published techniques. Tamaki and Sato used term-depth abstraction, which is similar to shortening, for limiting the number of tabulated predicates in OLDT resolution, an alternative to SLD resolution incorporating aspects of breadth-first search and bottom-up execution [TS]. In [GCS], programs are specialized by using abstract OLDT resolution with term-depth abstraction as the finite abstract domain of computation. Residual clauses are constructed from sequences of clauses in the OLDT trees. In contrast, we perform PE in the

[8]The 'renaming transformation' from [BL] is similar to but not as general as reparameterization.

concrete domain of the program and perform delayed unification (abstraction) only at non-simple loop nodes. Unlike these works, we incorporate constraints, reparameterization, constraint lifting, and factorization. Delayed unification is also related to binding time analysis [Jones], whereby Lisp expressions are classified as static (known at PE time) or dynamic (unknown at PE time).

Several researchers have suggested combining partial evaluation with more powerful transformation techniques like folding ([Owen], [Kom], [BCD].) or theorem proving ([FN]). The cost is that such techniques require (substantial) advice from the user to guide the program transformation [Kom, p 8ff]. In contrast, pure partial evaluation is relatively automatic; and optimizations which on first glance appear to require the power of a theorem prover can sometimes, as for KMP in Section 1, be accomplished directly in the host language via CLP operations.

In [FOF], Fujita et. al. present a method of partial evaluation of GHC programs which incorporates constraints. But, as was the case with Fujita's research described in Section 1.1, the constraint solver is 'added on top of' the partial evaluator, as a separate step in the algorithm. The authors of [FOF] contrasted their method with what might be achievable using CLP and suggested that CLP and partial evaluation may 'cross-fertilize' so that "partial evaluation of CLP programs may be introduced in a very natural way" [FOF,p 938]. Our work can be seen as a partial fulfillment of this suggestion.

Acknowledgements: We would like to thank Jacques Cohen for reading and editing several rough drafts. Thanks are also due to Harry Mairson for helpful discussions and to an anonymous referee for directing us to relevant publications. This work was supported by the National Science Foundation under Grant CCR-871 8989.

5 Bibliography

[AHU]. Aho, A., Hopcroft, J., and Ullman, J.. *The Design and Analysis of Computer Algorithms.* Addison-Wesley, 1974.

[AR]. Abramson, H. and Rogers, M., eds. *Meta-Programming in Logic Programming.* MIT Press, 1989.

[BCD]. Bossi, A., Cocco, N. and Dulli, S. "A Method for Specializing Logic Programs". *ACM Transactions on Programming Languages*, Vol. 12, No. 2, April 1990.

[BEJ]. Bjorner, D., Ershov, A.P. and Jones, N.D., *Partial Evaluation and Mixed Computation.* (North-Holland), 1988.

[BL] Benkerimi, K. and Lloyd, J.W. "A Procedure for the Partial Evaluation of Logic Programs". TR-89-04, University of Bristol, 1989.

[CD] Consel, C., and Danvy, O.. "Partial Evaluation of Pattern Matching in Strings". Manuscript, 1988.

[CvES] Cheng, M., van Emden M., and Strooper, P. "Complete Sets of Frontiers in Logic-based Program Transformation" in [AR], p. 282-297.

[FN]. Futatmura, Y, and Nogi, K. "Generalized Partial Computation", in [BEJ], p 133.

[FOF] Fujita, H., Okumura, A. and Furukawa, K. "Partial Evaluation of GHC Programs Based on the UR-set with Constraints". *Logic Programming: Proceedings of the Fifth International Conference and Symposium*, Vol 2, p 924.

[Fujita] Fujita, H.. "An Algorithm for Partial Evaluation with Constraints". ICOT Technical Memo. TM-0367, ICOT, Tokyo, 1987.

[Futamura]. Futamura, Y.. "Partial Evaluation of Computation Process — an Approach to a Compiler-Compiler", *Systems, Computers, Controls*, Vol. 2, No. 5, pp 45-50,1977.

[GCS] Gallagher, J., Codish, M., and Shapiro, E. "Specialization of Prolog and FCP Programs Using Abstract Interpretation", in [NGC].

[HiSm] Hickey, Timothy and Smith, Donald A. "Partial Evaluation and Constraint Logic Programming". Technical Report, Brandeis University, 1990.

[HS]. Horowitz, E. and Sahni, S.. *Fundamentals of Data Structures*. C.S. Press, 1983.

[JL]. Jaffar, J., Lassez, J.-L., "Constraint Logic Programming". *Proceedings of the 14th ACM Symposium on the Principles of Programming Languages*, 1987, pp 111-119.

[Jones]. Jones, N.D., "Re-examination of Automatic Program Specialization", in [BEJ].

[JSS] Jones, N.D., Sestoft, P., and Sondergaard, H.. "An Experiment in Partial Evaluation: The Generation of a Compiler Generator". *First International Conference on Rewriting Techniques and Applications*. Dijon, France, 1985.

[KC]. Kahn, K., and Carlsson, M.. "The Compilation of Prolog Programs without the Use of a Prolog Compiler". *Proceedings of the International Conference on Fifth Generation Computer Systems*, (ed., ICOT), 1984.

[KMP] Knuth, D.E., Morris, J.H., and Pratt, V.R. "Fast Pattern Matching in Strings". *SIAM Journal on Computing* Vol. 6, No 2, pp 323-350 (June, 1977).

[Kom] Komorowski, Jan. "Synthesis of Programs in the Framework of Partial Deduction". Technical Report, Department of Computer Science, Abo Akademi, Abo Finland, 1989.

[Kursawe]. Kursawe, P. "Pure Partial Evaluation and Instantiation", in [BEJ].

[LM]. Lassez, J. and Marriott, K. "Explicit Representation of Terms Defined by Counter Examples". *Journal of Automated Reasoning*, 3:301-317, 1986.

[LMM] Lassez, J., Maher, M.J., and Marriott, K. ''Unification Revisited" in Minker J., ed, *Foundations of Deductive Databases and Logic Programming*.

[Lloyd] Lloyd, J.W. *Foundations of Logic Programming*, Springer, 1987.

[LS] Lloyd, J., Shepherdson, J. "Partial Evaluation in Logic Programming". Technical report CS-87-09, University of Bristol, Bristol, U.K.

[Maher] Maher, M.J. "Complete Axiomatizations of the Algebras of Finite, Rational and Infinite Trees". Report, IBM T.J. Watson Research Center, Yorktown Heights, NY. 1988.

[Nakagawa]. Nakagawa, H. "A Prolog Program Transformation System". *Program Specification and Transformation*, ed. by L.G.L.T. Meertens. (North-Holland), 1987.

[NGC]. *New Generation Computing*, 6 (1988). The entire issue of the journal is devoted to partial evaluation and mixed computation. Besides the articles, the issue contains an extensive, annotated bibliography and a glossary of terms.

[Owen]. Owen, Stephen. "Issues in the Partial Evaluation of Meta-Interpreters", in *Meta-PRogramming in Logic Programming*, p 319-339.

[SB]. Sterling, L. and Beer, R.D. "Metainterpreters for Expert System Construction". *J Logic Programming* 1989: pp 163-178.

[Sestoft]. Sestoft, P. "Automatic Call Unfolding in a Partial Evaluator" in [BEJ].

[SmHi] Smith, D. and Hickey, T., "Constraint Operations for Partial Evaluation of CLP($\mathcal{FT}$)". Technical Report, Brandeis University, 1990.

[TS] Tamaki, H. and Sato, T. "OLD Resolution with Tabulation", Proc. 3rd ICLP, LNCS 225, 1986.

[WP]. Warren, D.H.D., and Pereira, F.C.N. "An Efficient Easily Adaptable System for Interpreting Natural Language Queries". *IJCAI-81*, Vancouver, Canada, 1981

Appendix: Benchmark results for PE of 'Chat' parser

constraint lifting?	p.e. iterations	heuristic	time	% savings	code size
-	-	(original)	143	0%	64,000
No	1	MGF	137	4%	118,000
No	1	global (1)	112	22%	93,000
No	1	global (4)	107	25%	115,000
No	1	ancestor	106	26%	114,000
No	2	global (1)	107	25%	118,000
No	2	global (4)	107	25%	169,000
No	2	ancestor	107	25%	126,000
Yes	1	global (1)	109	24%	124,000
Yes	1	global (4)	93	35%	164,000
Yes	1	ancestor	93	35%	163,000
Yes	2	global (1)	86	40%	186,000
Yes	2	global (4)	82	43%	291,000
Yes	2	ancestor	81	43%	165,000
Yes	3	ancestor	80	44%	175,000

Time is as reported by Quintus Prolog's `statistics` predicate, with rounding to the nearest second. The benchmark measured the time for 10 repetitions of finding all parses of the 23 example sentences in `ed/3` from file chattop.pl. Code size is in bytes, rounded to nearest 1000, as reported by Quintus' `compile` predicate. It includes those clauses reachable from (the residue of) `sentence/5`. No eager unfolding was performed and no 'suspend' annotations were used.

All three heuristics are performed only on non-simple loop calls. The *MGF* heuristic generalizes the call all the way to the most general form. For the *ancestor heuristic*, each argument of the call is (possibly) shortened to a tree depth no greater than 3+ the depth of the corresponding argument of the (oldest) ancestor. For example, `p(f(g([a,b])))` with ancestor `p(X)` is shortened to `p(f(g([A|B])))`; the delayed part of the unification is `[A|B]=[a,b]`. The *global* heuristic shortens each argument in a non-simple loop call to a depth no greater than a fixed quantity; in the table above the numbers in parentheses after 'global' indicate the maximum term depth allowed. Smarter heuristics based on program/mode analysis are clearly needed.

The results indicate a time-space tradeoff, the usefulness of constraint lifting, and the importance of iterated PE when used with constraint lifting: later passes of PE utilize lifted constraints for pruning, reparameterization, and removal of data abstractions. We see a need for tools for measuring and determining the causes of speedup and code expansion. We are encouraged by these results since we were able to obtain speedups on a moderate sized application program despite the use of simple heuristics.

A Constraint Logic Programming Approach for Maintaining Consistency in User-Interface Design

Hayato Ohwada and Fumio Mizoguchi
Dept. of Industrial Administration, Science University of Tokyo
Noda, Chiba 278, Japan

Abstract

This paper outlines an approach for building graphical user-interfaces through a constraint logic programming framework. In this approach, Horn clause logic can be used as a picture specification language for explicitly describing graphical objects and their relations on the screen. Triton is a constraint logic programming language which handles linear arithmetic expressions and represents objects. Using Triton, picture specifications are executable as constraint logic programs. The advantage of this approach is maintaining consistency between the underlying relations in a picture. When a user change any attribute value or relation between objects, Triton provides automatic reconstruction of the picture by propagating the change. Default constraints on the basis of negation by failure are useful for not only drawing pictures without complete information, but updating the pictures by the addition of preferable default constraints. Because such desired constraints are incrementally added as queries, Triton decreases the imposition of the user-interface design process by means of the constraint satisfier.

1 Introduction

The goal of this paper is to simplify the user-interface design process by using formal logic. Formal logic can be used as a specification language for explicitly describing objects and their relations in pictures without regard to a precise sequence of low-level operations [6] [11]. Although the logic programming language Prolog can be viewed as an executable specification language and is widely used to represent knowledge of many kinds, we still believe that it is not adequate for handling mathematical relations and representing structural objects, because it is based on unification that can be viewed as testing the satisfiability of equalities over the Herbrand Universe.

Constraint Logic Programming is a scheme for generalizing logic programming which includes constraints [7]. In this scheme, we can design various constraint logic programming languages according to the choice of the domain of constraints. We have designed a constraint logic programming language, namely Triton whose domain is both real numbers and structural objects. Using Triton, picture specifications consisting of Horn clauses are executable as constraint logic programs.

Constraints are widely used for building graphical user-interfaces [1]. A constraint is a declarative description that must hold within a picture. In constraint-based tools for drawing the picture, the constraint satisfier maintains consistency between constraints. In Triton, constraints are directly specified in terms of logical expressions, and are executed by using the constraint satisfaction mechanism of Triton. This capability provides automatic reconstruction of the picture by changing desired attribute values or relations without changing a sequence of instructions for drawing the picture.

We use default constraints on the basis of negation by failure. A default constraint defines an implicit relation that may be maintained in a picture. It is useful for drawing pictures without complete information that enable graphic primitives executable. It is also used for updating the pictures by the incremental addition of preferable default constraints. Thus Triton provides a basis toward realizing an interactive user-interface builder by means of the expressive power of constraint logic programming.

2 A Logic-based Approach

We take a logic-based approach to simplifying the time-consuming process of building graphical user-interfaces. The advantages of this approach are described below.

1. Formal logic gives relevant descriptions of the properties and constraints of user interfaces. We often start with a specification for building graphical user-interfaces. This specification includes graphical items, objects consisting of such items, and mathematical relations between them. Formal logic can directly specify such things as logical descriptions. Logical descriptions give information for arrangement of items on the screen without regard to a precise sequence of low-level operations. They are also used for viewing a set of graphical terms as a single logical expression. For example, the structural object *Box* can be referred as a logical term rather than a collection of graphical operations as shown in the next section. This feature of formal logic is useful for defining and re-using user-interface components.

2. Logic specifications are abstract. Because logic specifications are machine and language independent, they are ideally suitable for the general description of the user-interface. They can also be written without taking data structures of objects into account. We naturally think of objects as a set of graphical terms that may be decomposed into simpler terms. A complex object, however can be specified as a simple term rather than a hierarchical data structure by using an elegant notation in the specification. We will use functional notations to refer sub-components of objects.

3. Logic specifications are executable as constraint logic programs. In this paper, objects and relations between them are defined as a set of Horn clauses with constraints. Triton is based on SLD-resolution with constraint solving. The constraint solver deals with linear arithmetic expressions and structural objects. Therefore logic specifications are executable under the computation mechanism of Triton. This property means that there is no distinction between specification and program [9].

4. Logic specifications are declarative. We do not need to consider the data flow of computation. We specify what relations are to hold without specifying how to calculate attribute values for drawing pictures. This means that there is no ordering relations between logical descriptions, and therefore we can put and remove arbitrary logical descriptions at any place. In contrast, procedural languages impose the heavy load that requires careful updating of the specification for providing the desired operations.

5. The constraint satisfier automatically maintains consistency among constraints. A constraint must be satisfied bidirectionally by the constraint satisfier. There is no input-output distinction between variables in the constraints. Thus we have no restriction on the way to put and update the values of the variables. This means that we do not need to consider the data dependency among the variables. Instead, the constraint satisfier seeks the data dependency at run time, then maintains consistency so as to satisfy the constraints. If the constraints are unidirectional, we must care for the ordering of the constraints in updating the values.

6. Logic programming is incremental. If a goal statement is divided into several statements, each statement can be regarded as a goal and these statements can be incrementally given. This framework called incremental query [5] provides an opportunity to observe the current state of computation through answer substitutions and to add the new query that is desirable for interactive problem solving. The construction of user-interfaces needs the facility of interactive editing. Incremental query plays a role of such facility.

3 A Logic Specification

A simple example will illustrate the above advantages of logic specification. Consider the following graphical objects:

- Horizontal line(HL) has two endpoints whose y-coordinates are equal.
- Vertical line(VL) has two endpoints whose x-coordinates are equal.
- Line with the midpoint(L) has a midpoint whose x(y)-coordinate is the average of x(y)-coordinates of the endpoints.
- Cross lines(CLS) has a horizontal line and a vertical line that cross at the midpoints.

Each statement defines objects, attributes and constraints implicitly. We clarify these terms. Each object has several items:

- CLS has HL and VL.

- HL and VL has two endpoints($P1$,$P2$) and the midpoint(MP) respectively.
- $P1$, $P2$, MP has values of the x-coordinates and y-coordinates respectively.

These items may also be regarded as components or attributes of objects. An object can be represented as a set of pairs that consists of the name and the value of an item. The name of the item is the identifier used to access the value. Therefore we deal with the name of the item as an access function. More formally, an object is denoted as follows :

$$object = \{(fun, val) | val = fun(object)\}$$

The objects in the example are represented below.

$$\begin{array}{ll} cls & = \{(hl, hl(cls)), (vl, vl(cls))\} \\ hl & = \{(p1, p1(hl)), (p2, p2(hl)), (mp, mp(hl))\} \\ vl & = \{(p1, p1(vl)), (p2, p2(vl)), (mp, mp(vl))\} \\ p1 & = \{(x, x(p1)), (y, y(p1))\} \\ p2 & = \{(x, x(p2)), (y, y(p2))\} \end{array}$$

Here, access functions of an object are not fixed. They are dynamically created by unification between objects mentioned below.

According to the above formulation, logic specifications for defining graphical components has the following structure:

- The domain is the union of real numbers and a set of objects. In the example, variables are instantiated to an element of $R \cup \{ cls, hl, vl, p1, p2, mp \}$.
- The functions are the union of a set of arithmetic functions and a set of access functions. The example has the functions $\{ +, -, *, /, sin, cos, \cdots \} \cup \{ hl, vl, p1, p2, mp, x, y \}$.
- The relations are $\{ =, \neq, <, \leq \}$.

By using this structure, a logic specification of the example can be written as the following Horn clauses:

```
HL(hl)     if   y(p1(hl))=y(p2(hl))                      C1
VL(vl)     if   x(p1(vl))=x(p2(vl))                      C2
ML(ml)     if   x(mp(ml))=(x(p1(ml))+x(p2(ml)))/2        C3
           and  y(mp(ml))=(y(p1(ml))+y(p2(ml)))/2
CLS(cls)   if   HL(hl(cls))                              C4
           and  VL(vl(cls))
           and  ML(hl(cls))
           and  ML(vl(cls))
           and  mp(hl(cls))=mp(vl(cls))
```

The syntax is based on a conventional symbolic notation in which a predicate name is denoted as a upper-case string and a function is a lower-case string. The symbol "=" signify the identification between terms. It also specify the identification of objects. The constraint `mp(hl(cls))=mp(vl(cls))` describes the same position by unifying the two objects.

4 Execution of the Logic Specification

Clauses $C1-4$ can be executed as a constraint logic program. The execution is based on SLD-resolution with constraint simplification. In contrast, Prolog is based on SLD-resolution with constraint evaluation. Evaluation is done in a passive manner, while simplification is active processing. Constraint simplification is the transformation from a set of constraints to more simplified constraint set. Although the process is widely used in constraint logic programming languages, we describe the procedural semantics for the comparison with default constraint processing presented in Section 6.

Suppose that a clause is of the form:

$$A\ if\ A_1\ and\ A_2\ and\ \cdots\ A_k$$

where $A_m (1 \leq m \leq k)$ is an atom or a constraint. As selecting a goal A_m, it is proved by the rule:

(1) derive a new goal if A_m is an atom,
(2) simplify A_m if is a constraint.

The derivation is characterized by the notion of resolvent. We consider a resolvent R which has the form:

$$< A_1, \cdots, A_m, \cdots, A_k; CS >$$

where $A_m (1 \leq m \leq k)$ is an atom or constraint, and CS is a set of constraints. Here, R' is a new resolvent of R if the following conditions hold.

1. If A_m is a constraint, $R' = < A1, \cdots, A_{m-1}, A_{m+1}, \cdots, A_k; CS' >$ where $CS' = simplify(\{A_m\} \cup CS)$

2. Let C be $B\ if\ B_1\ and\ \cdots\ B_q$ where variables in B are distinct. If A_m is an atom and θ is a mgu of B and A_m, $R' = (A_1, \cdots, A_{m-1}, B_1, \cdots, B_q, A_{m+1}, \cdots, A_k)\theta$

In this derivation, finite failure occurs when an atom can not be derived or a constraint set can not be simplified.

Constraint simplification is realized by the two constraint solvers: *equation solver* and *inequation solver*. Equation solver transforms a set of linear equations to a solved form of the original set. The solved form is a set of equations in which the left-hand sides of the equations are all distinct variables that never appear in the right-hand sides. These variables are called eliminated variables. To obtain the solved form, we use the rules: *variable elimination*, *tree rewriting*, *equation anteposition* and *back substitution* [8]. After solving equations, inequation solver checks consistency of a set of inequations that have no eliminated variables. The algorithm is based on SUP-INF method which calculates greatest lower bounds and least upper bounds for each variable [12].

In addition to equation and inequation solver, we must introduce the procedure of unification between objects into constraint simplification. Suppose that two objects are represented as follows:

$$x = \{(fx_1, vx_1), \cdots, (fx_n, vx_n)\}$$
$$y = \{(fy_1, vy_1), \cdots, (fy_m, vy_m)\}$$

where fx_i and fy_i are functions such that $vx_i = fx_i(x)$, $vy_j = fy_j(y)$. The constraint $x = y$ is solved by the following rule:

1. If $fx_i = fy_j$, then $vx_i = vy_j$
2. If $fx_i \notin \{fy_1, \cdots, fy_m\}$,
   then $v_{new} = vx_i$ and $y = \{(fy_1, vy_1), \cdots, (fy_m, vy_m), (fx_i, v_{new})\}$
3. If $fy_j \notin \{fx_1, \cdots, fx_n\}$,
   then $v_{new} = vy_j$ and $x = \{(fx_1, vx_1), \cdots, (fx_n, vx_n), (fy_j, v_{new})\}$
   where v_{new} is a distinct variable.

This procedure creates new items of objects at the unification process. Thus we do not need to pre-enumerate the items of the objects. We can incrementally define the objects that can not be entirely characterized for the sake of the partial information. This idea for characterizing the objects under partial information is similar to CIL [10].

Unification between objects provides two useful mechanisms: *inheritance of attributes and constraints*, and *composite object creation*. Suppose that we pose the query

```
HL(line) and ML(line)
```

using $C1-4$. The derivation proceeds as follows:

```
< HL(line),ML(line)  ;  {}>
              ↓          C1
< ML(line)  ;  { y(p1(line))=y(p2(line)) }>
              ↓          C3
< □ ; { y(p1(line))=y(p2(line)),
        x(mp(line))=(x(p1(line))+x(p2(line)))/2,
        y(mp(line))=y(p2(line)) } >
```

Here, the object line is represented by the attribute set {p1,p2,mp} that is the union of that of HL and ML. It also have the three constraints that specify the property of a horizontal line with the midpoint.

To create a composite object easily, we rewrite the clause $C4$ to $C4'$.

```
CLS(cls)  if  HL(hl(cls)) and VL(vl(cls))        C4'
```

When we pose the query

```
CLS(cls),
```

it is solved as follows:

```
< CLS(cls) ; {} >
          ↓       C4'
< HL(hl(cls),VL(vl(cls)) ; {} >
          ↓       C1
< VL(vl(cls)) ; { y(p1(hl(cls)))=y(p2(hl(cls))) } >
          ↓       C2
< □ ; { y(p1(hl(cls)))=y(p2(hl(cls))),
        x(p1(vl(cls)))=x(p2(vl(cls))) } >
```

The composite object can be created by using the functional notation.

5 The Constraint Logic Programming Language: Triton

Triton is the extension of CS-Prolog we developed [8]. It provides constraint solving for linear arithmetic expressions, object representation and meta-level predicates (ex. assert and retract). The meta predicates are used for saving objects that are created at editing sessions. Triton is currently implemented on top of Prolog and ESP (developed by ICOT).

Logic specifications are easily translated into Triton programs. The syntax is the same as most Prolog systems. The only difference is adopting the dot notation which specify an access function of objects. The expression `Object.Slot` denotes the value the access function `Slot` of the object `Object`. Nested dot notations are also allowed. For example, clauses $C1-4$ are coded as follows:

```
h_line(Line)   :-  Line.p1.x=Line.p2.x.                    P1
v_line(Line)   :-  Line.p1.y=Line.p2.y.                    P2
mp_line(Line)  :-  Line.mp.x=(Line.p1.x+Line.p2.x)/2,      P3
                   Line.mp.y=(Line.p1.y+Line.p2.y)/2.
cross_line(C)  :-  C.line1=Line1, C.line2=Line2,           P4
                   h_line(Line1), mp_line(Line1),
                   v_line(Line2), mp_line(Line2),
                   Line1.mp=Line2.mp.
```

This program is translated into Prolog programs, then it is executed by the Prolog system.

So far, we do not deal with graphic primitives. Because picture drawing is performed by a sequence of graphic primitives, we must call them within a declarative program. We have two approaches to using them. The first approach is based on *event-processing*. In this case, graphic primitives are directly called and may be delayed until executable. For example, graphic primitives are added into the clause $P3$ as follows:

```
mp_line(Line)  :-  Line.p1.x=X1, Line.p2.x=X2,
                   Line.p1.y=Y1, Line.p2.y=Y2,
                   Line.mp.x=MX, Line.mp.y=MY,
                   MX=(X1+X2)/2, MY=(Y1+Y2)/2,
                   draw_line(X1,Y1,X2,Y2),
                   draw_point(MX,MY).
```

The predicates"**draw_line**" and "**draw_point**" are graphic primitives and are delayed by using "freeze" mechanism such as Prolog-II [4]. These primitives are executed when all the variables are instantiated. Thus we can not specify the ordering relations among the primitives within a logic specification.

The second approach is based on *stream-processing*. In this approach, graphic primitives are indirectly called, and a sequence of the primitives are described as the data structure "list". Since the primitives are totally ordered, we can explicitly specify the ordering relations. Instead of indirect calling, the special predicate, namely "outstream" is used for interpreting the sequence of the primitives. This predicate plays a role of calling them. Suppose that clause $P3$ is rewritten into the clause

```
mp_line(Line,S0,S1)  :-  Line.p1.x=X1,Line.p2.x=X2,
                         Line.p1.y=Y1, Line.p2.y=Y2,
                         Line.mp.x=MX, Line.mp.y=MY,
                         MX=(X1+X2)/2, MY=(Y1+Y2)/2,
                         S0=[draw_line(X1,Y1,X2,Y2),
                             draw_point(MX,MY)|S1].
```

where the variable **S0**, **S1** is head and tail of the stream respectively. Given the query

```
?-  mp_line(Line,S,[]),
    Line.p1.x=100, Line.p1.y=100,
    Line.p2.x=200, Line.p2.y=300,
    outstream(S).
```

the line with the midpoint is drawn.

Here, we note that in the first approach a picture is drawn with "xor" operation in order to efficiently recover the screen image on backtracking, while the second approach makes the screen clear and re-executes the sequence of the primitives. Although the second one seems to be less efficient, we take the approach for easily maintaining the screen image.

6 Default Constraints

There still exists a serious problem in the logic-based approach mentioned above. The problem is due to the fact that we must give a complete specification for drawing the desired picture. We often start with an incomplete specification. We want to make the complete specification through the interactive editing process. This process contains the following properties:

- Pictures can be drawn in the absence of information to specify the positions of the pictures on the screen.
- Pictures can be updated by adding preferable constraints that may be inconsistent with the constraints already added.

To realize the above properties, we introduce the notion of *default constraint*. A default constraint specifies an implicit relation that may be maintained. The notion of preference is included in the default constraint for describing the strength of the default constraint. Default constraints are used for the following situations:

- Graphic primitives are not executable due to the lack of information.
- Pre-specified relations on the screen should be updated for specifying more preferable relations.

The notion of default constraint has already been introduced in ThingLab and HCLP [2] [3]. The main feature of their systems are to find the best solution using the pre-specified comparator. This approach is intuitive to get the most plausible solution by competing default constraints. However, it may be not logical and be inefficient in logic programming framework, since variants representing solutions must be created and compared on the multiple variable binding environments.

Our approach is based on negation by failure rule. The usage of this rule is similar to default reasoning. The meaning of a default constraint is given the rule

$$Constraint\ if\ A_1\ and\ \cdots\ A_k\ and\ not\ \overline{Constraint} \qquad DR$$

where $\overline{Constraint}$ is the complement of *Constraint*. This statement indicates that if the goals A_1 *and* $\cdots$ A_k holds and $\overline{Constraint}$ can not be shown then *Constraint* holds. This rule gives a default within the expression "can not be shown". It also has a "non-monotonic" character in which derived formulas are invalid if contradictory information is added later. Examples below help to understand the meaning clearly.

```
x(p1(line))=100  if  Line(line) and not x(p1(line))≠100
y(p1(line))=100  if  Line(line) and not y(p1(line))≠100
x(p2(line))=200  if  Line(line) and not x(p2(line))≠200
y(p2(line))=200  if  Line(line) and not y(p2(line))≠200
```

Using the clause $C3$ which defines a line with the midpoint, the line can be drawn by using the default constraints that are consistent with $C3$.

The above example shows how to set default values using default constraints. The next example uses essentially default constraints.

```
y(p1(line))=y(p2(line))        if  Line100(line)
                               and not y(p1(line))≠y(p2(line))
x(p2(line))-x(p1(line))=100    if  Line100(line)
                               and not
                                   x(p2(line)-x(p1(line))≠100
```

When we give the fact

```
Line100(line) and x(p1(line))=100 and y(p1(line))=300
```

a horizontal line with the length 100 appears on the screen.

It is well-known that default reasoning has a problem called *multiple extensi n problem.* The problem is that default reasoning has a number of interpretations with respect to default rules. If a subset of default rules is inconsistent, the truth of a default rule is dependent to priority of the choice of rules. Suppose that the following default constraints are given.

```
x(p1(line))=100 if  Line(line) and not x(p1(line))≠100   D1
y(p1(line))=100 if  Line(line) and not y(p1(line))≠100   D2
x(p2(line))=200 if  Line(line) and not x(p2(line))≠200   D3
y(p2(line))=200 if  Line(line) and not y(p2(line))≠200   D4
```

Under the fact

```
Line(hl) and HL(hl) ,
```

the above default constrains are inconsistent. In this case, two interpretations exists. The first one is the extension $D1$, $D2$, $D3$ hold, while the second one is the extension $D1$, $D3$, $D4$ hold. The difference between the interpretations are made by priority between $D2$ and $D4$, because the constraint $D2$ and $D4$ are inconsistent under the constraint of the horizontal line. Thus, priority among default constraints concerns with the meaning of a logic specification with default constraints.

We avoid the multiple extension problem by making a set of default constraints hierarchical. This treatment eliminates the interaction among default constraints and produces the single extension of them.

A default constraint set is hierarchical if it has a level mapping from a set of constraints to the non-negative integers, such that the level of $\overline{Constraint}$ in DR is less than that of $Constraint$. To show the level of $Constraint$ explicitly, we rewrite DR to the following clause:

$$Default(constraint\ level)\ if\ A_1\ and\ \cdots\ and\ A_k$$

where *level* is the level of *constraint*. The level of the normal constraints (not default constraints) is zero.

Now we give the declarative meaning of a default constraint. Let $cs(k)$ be a set of default constraints from the level 0 to the level k, and $soln(cs(k))$ be the solution set of the constraint set $cs(k)$. The declarative meaning is defined by the rule

$$constraint\ if\ Default(constraint\ level)\ and\ soln(cs(level)) \neq \phi.$$

The rule implies the following statement:

> If the set of default constraints at *level* are inconsistent, then all default constraints at the level which is greater than or equal to *level* are withdrawn.

This statement guarantees that the multiple extension problem never occurs.

Examples of hierarchical default constraints are described below.

```
Default(x(p1(line))=100 1)  if  Line(line)        D5
Default(y(p1(line))=100 2)  if  Line(line)        D6
Default(x(p2(line))=200 3)  if  Line(line)        D7
Default(y(p2(line))=200 4)  if  Line(line)        D8
```

Given the fact

```
Line(line) and HL(hl) ,
```

the default constraint $D8$ is withdrawn. The following example is pathological.

```
Default(x(p1(line))=100 1)  if  Line(line)        D9
Default(y(p1(line))=100 1)  if  Line(line)        D10
Default(x(p2(line))=200 1)  if  Line(line)        D11
Default(y(p2(line))=200 1)  if  Line(line)        D12
```

When we give the same facts as the above, all the default constraints are withdrawn. Therefore we should specify the distinction of preference for making default constraints useful.

7 Execution of a Logic Specification with Default Constraints

Before executing logic programs with default constraints, we collect the default constraints scattered in the program. Mostly a default constraint specifies an implicit relation that may hold in the underlying object. Here, we restrict the form of the definition of the default constraint as follows:

$$Default(constraint_1\ level_1) \quad if\ A \qquad F1$$

$$\vdots$$

$$Default(constraint_n\ level_n) \quad if\ A \qquad F2$$

where the clause A declares the object. All default constraints presented above are of this form. Suppose that the program contains the clause

$$A \quad if \ A_1 \ and \ \cdots \ A_k \qquad F3$$

The object A associated with the default constraints are represented as the clause

$$\begin{array}{ll} A \ \ if & A_1 \ and \ \cdots \ A_k \\ & and \ Default(constraint_1 \ level_1) \\ & \qquad \vdots \\ & and \ Default(constraint_n \ level_n) \end{array} \qquad F4$$

The clause $F4$ can be obtained by translating the clauses $F1-3$ under the completed definition of A.

The derivation of log:c programs with default constraints is characterized by the definition of resolvent. This definition extends the derivation of constraint logic programs shown in section 4. We consider the following form of resolvent R:

$$< A_1, \cdots, A_m, \cdots, A_k; CS; DS >$$

where DS is a set of default constraints.

The new resolvent is produced by the following algorithm:

Step1 *Normal derivation process*

1. If A_m is a default constraint, $R' = < A_1, \cdots, A_{m-1}, A_{m+1}, \cdots, A_k ; CS ; \{A_m\} \cup DS >$.
2. If a goal is empty, go step2.
3. Otherwise the derivation is the same as that of a normal program.

Step2 *Default constraint simplification process*

1. Put $i = 0$, $CS_0 = CS$, $DS_0 = DS$.
2. Find the default constraint set DC_i at the level i.
3. If DS_i is not empty and the constraint set $DC_i \cup CS$ can be simplified, put $CS_{i+1} = simplify(DC_i \cup CS)$, $DS_{i+1} = DS_i - DC_i$, increment i and go to 2. Otherwise stop.

The success set of a program with default constraints is the same as the program without them. The difference of the two programs is that the program with the default constraints obtains more specific answer substitutions by using the default constraints.

Suppose that a horizontal line is defined as follows:

```
HL(hl)    if    y(p1(hl))=y(p2(hl))
          and   Default(x(p1(hl))=100 1)
          and   Default(y(p1(hl))=100 2)
          and   Default(x(p2(hl))=200 3)
          and   Default(y(p2(hl))=200 4)
```

The derivation process is shown below.

```
<HL(hl) ; {} ; {}>
        ↓
<y(p1(hl))=y(p2(hl)),Default(x(p1(hl))=100 1), ··· ; {} ; {}>
        ↓
<Default(x(p1(hl))=100 1), ··· ; {y(p1(hl))=y(p2(hl))} ; {}>
        ↓
<□ ; {y(p1(hl))=y(p2(hl))} ; {Default(x(p1(hl))=100 1), ··· }>
        ↓
<□ ; {y(p1(hl))=y(p2(hl)),x(p1(hl))=100} ; { ··· }>
        ↓
<□ ; {x(p1(hl))=100,y(p1(hl)=100,y(p2(hl))=200} ; { ··· }>
        ↓
<□ ; {x(p1(hl))=100,y(p1(hl)=100,y(p2(hl))=200,
     x(p2(hl))=200} ; {··· }>
```

Now we incorporate default constraints into Triton. We think that users want to specify rather the strength of the default constraints than the level. The relation between the strength and the level is monotonic decrease. In triton, a default constraint with the strength is specified as follows:

$$A \ \text{:-} \ \cdots, default(C, S_i, S_j), \cdots$$

where $S_j = S_i + 1$, S_i indicates the strength of the constraint C, and S_j is used for specifying stronger constraints than C.

We show an illustrative example of the use of default constrains. The example is incremental editing.

```
?-  mp_line(L),                                  Q1
    default(L.p1.x=200,S0,S1),
    default(L.p1.y=400,S1,S2),
    default(L.p2.x=400,S2,S3),
    default(L.p2.x=400,S3,S4).

?-  default(L.p1.y=200,S4,S5).                   Q2
?-  default(L.p1.y=L.p2.y,S5,S6).                Q3
?-  default(L.p1.y=600,S6,S7).                   Q4
```

The default constraints in $Q1$ are used to set default values of the positions at the endpoints. Given $Q2$, the point $p1$ moves and the midpoints automatically moves. The line is horizontal through $Q3$, and then both endpoints move up by the constraints $Q4$ and $Q3$. Thus the picture is incrementally updated by adding new default constraints.

After solving each query, Triton automatically releases variable bindings that are made by default constraints. The default constraints are entirely re-solved in adding a new query, while normal constraints are solved incrementally. This constraint solving strategy becomes less efficient when there exists many independent default constraints. However considering realistic applications, most graphical user-interfaces consists of graphical objects that are tightly connected each other. Therefore the strategy seems to be reasonable for interactively building user-interfaces. Moreover, implementation techniques such as dependency-directed backtracking for creating new variable bindings may be expensive for the realistic case.

8 Concluding Remarks

In this paper, we attempt to provide a constraint logic programming framework for building graphical user-interfaces. This framework is based on the intimate relation between logic specification and logic program. Triton has been designed for executing logic specifications as constraint logic programs.

We introduce default constraints into logic programming for the purpose of realizing an interactive user-interface builder. The advantage of the default constraints is to draw and update pictures under incomplete specifications. The semantics of logic programs with default constraints has an augmented feature to obtain more specific answer substitutions by using the default constraints. We believe that this feature provides a general expressive power for designing interactive problem solving systems.

In order to make the present approach more powerful, Triton has two additional functions that are not mentioned in this paper. One is to saving edited objects for the purpose of re-use. The meta-predicate "assert" built in Triton collects constraints that must hold within an object, and save the constraints as a program. The other is to generate procedures for drawing the object efficiently. The procedure is produced as a sequence of graphic primitives by interpreting the declarative programs. We hope that these functions provide user-interface design environments for rapid prototyping.

We do not use inequations for constructing user-interfaces. If inequations are contained in the program, a picture may not be drawn. This is due to the fact that default constraints determining the position of the picture are inconsistent with the inequations. To solve this problem, we will introduce the mechanism of constraint relaxation that changes the condition of a default constraint automatically. For example, a default value should be changed so as to satisfy the inequations. Such constraint satisfier will be provided near future.

References

[1] A. Borning, R. Duisberg. Constraint-Based Tools for Building User Interfaces, ACM Transactions on Graphics, Vol. 5, No. 4, pp. 345-374, Oct. 1986.

[2] A. Borning, R. Duisberg, B. Freeman-Benson, A. Kramer, and M. Woolf. Constraint Hierarchies. In *Proc. of the 1987 ACM Conference on Object-Oriented Programming Systems, Languages and Applications*, pp. 48-60. ACM, October 1987.

[3] A. Borning, M. Maher, A. Martindale, and M. Wilson. Constraint Hierarchies and Logic Programming. In *Proc. of the Sixth International Conference on Logic Programming*, pp. 149-164, June 1989.

[4] A. Colmerauer. *PROLOG II: Manuel de Reference et Modele Theorique.* Tech. Report, GIA - Faculte de Sciences de Luminy, March 1982.

[5] M.H. van Emden, M. Ohki, A. Takeuchi. Spreadsheet with Incremental Queries as a User Interface for Logic Programming, *New Generation Computing*, Vol. 4, No. 3, 1986.

[6] R. Helm and K. Marriott. Declarative Graphics. In *Proc. of the Third International Conference on Logic Programming*, pp. 513-527, April 1986.

[7] J. Jaffar and J-L. Lassez. Constraint Logic Programming. In *Proc. of the 14th ACM Principles of Programming Languages Conference*, Munich, January 1987. ACM.

[8] T. Kawamura, H. Ohwada, and F. Mizoguchi. CS-Prolog: A Generalized Unification Based Constraint Solver. In *Proc. of Logic Programming'87, LNCS 315*, Springer Verlag, pp. 19-39, June 1987.

[9] R. Kowalski. The relation between logic programming and logic specification, C.A.R. Hoare and J.C. Shepherdson (eds.), *Mathematical Logic and Programming Languages*, pp. 11-24, 1984.

[10] K. Mukai. Partially Specified Term in Logic Programming for Linguistic Analysis. In *Proc. of the International Conference on Fifth Generation Computer Systems*, pp. 479-488, 1988.

[11] F. Pereira. Can Drawing be liberated from the Von Neumann Style? Tech. Note 282, AI Center, SRI International. June 1983.

[12] R. E. Shostak. On the SUP-INF Method for Proving Presburger Formulas, *J.ACM 24*, pp. 529-543, 1977.

Constraint Logic Programming Applied to Hypothetical Reasoning in Chemistry

Jean Jourdan and Raúl E. Valdés-Pérez
School of Computer Science
Carnegie Mellon University
Pittsburgh, PA 15213 - USA
{jjourdan,valdes}@cs.cmu.edu

Abstract

We have applied the new constraint-logic-programming (CLP) language PrologIII to the real, complex problem of devising chemical reaction-pathway hypotheses.
The problem statement is organized as a set of informal premises that acceptable hypotheses must fulfill, including two key premises that specify the numbers of reaction steps and chemical species to be allowed in a pathway. Our approach to the problem involves formalizing these diverse premises as boolean, numerical, and other PrologIII constraint types.
The resulting program is a clear improvement in terms of scope and flexibility on its immediate predecessor developed in a procedural language. The program is part of ongoing research, since automation of the chemistry problem has not previously been realized.
Our application has involved in a natural way constraints of both boolean and numerical character; previous reported CLP applications have exploited only one or the other language ability. The current program illustrates how the combination of such constraints can be achieved. Our result also constitutes evidence that the wholly separate processing of boolean and numerical constraints in PrologIII is not an important obstacle to the solution of tasks presenting both aspects.
From our experience we extract some observations on PrologIII and CLP applications programming, with emphasis on factors that increase program efficiency.

1 Introduction

A constraint logic programming (CLP) language [1] integrates logic programming and constraint handling. This integration allows problems having a numerical and/or logical character to be tackled in a declarative way with non-deterministic computation. Thus it extends the scope of logic programming and enables finer control over a logic program.
Several existing CLP languages are CLP(R) [2], CHIP [3], and PrologIII [4, 5, 6]. These new languages are Prolog-like logic programming languages extended by constraint-handling techniques. Aside from the Herbrand domain, which they share, they differ by the remaining domains on which constraints can be expressed. For example, CLP(R) only permits constraints on real terms, PrologIII on linear rational and on boolean terms, and CHIP on linear rational, boolean, and finite-domain terms.
The published applications have not exploited within one program the ability offered by CLP languages to express and combine constraints on several computational

domains including boolean and numeric. Many reported applications concern diagnosis, testing, verification, and design of digital circuits. Two CHIP applications treat the problems of generating focused tests to detect faults [7] and of diagnosing faults in digital circuits [8] using boolean constraints. A CLP(R) application to several electrical engineering problems [9, 10], including circuit design, uses only numerical constraints. Other application domains are as follows. Two CHIP papers in scheduling, allocation, and planning [11, 12] have involved numerical and "symbolic" (finite domain) constraints. The financial options-trading O.T.A.S system [13], written in CLP(R), automatically generates and analyzes investment strategies using numerical constraints. None of these applications combines boolean with numerical constraints in a same program.

A contribution of this paper is to demonstrate that the combination of several types of constraint can arise naturally on real problems, and to illustrate the programming involved. Our approach exploits most of the expressible constraint types in PrologIII, and shows how numerical and boolean constraints work together to narrow the search for solutions.

Our application domain is chemistry, which has not yet been explored by CLP. Our PrologIII implementation greatly extends the scope of an earlier Lisp-based implementation, thanks to the flexibility of declarative programming. The increased scope enables the study of chemical reactions which were beyond the scope of the earlier program. Also, the implementation is quite short and transparent, involving about three pages of code. We add that this application is ongoing research; automation of the task carried out by these two programs has not been done before.

The rest of this paper is organized as follows. Section 2 surveys briefly the PrologIII language. Section 3 describes the task and our earlier experiences with a Lisp-based implementation, and poses a practical question which is addressed by the PrologIII re-implementation. Section 4 explains in detail how the problem is handled in PrologIII. Finally, section 5 evaluates our result and discusses some insights gained into CLP application.

2 PrologIII - A CLP Language

A CLP language combines the declarativeness of logic programming with the efficiency of constraint-handling techniques. The unification concept of logic programming is replaced by the concept of constraint-handling, which treats unification as just another constraint.

CLP advances *logic programming* by extending the domains of expression to include subsets of ordinary algebra, as well as propositional logic. CLP also permits better control over a logic program by constraining the possible unifications through explicit constraints. CLP improves on *constraint programming* because it supports the dynamic generation of constraints, e.g., sets of rules can devise appropriate constraints by examining the problem instance.

PrologIII is a CLP language that enables expression of linear numerical constraints, boolean constraints, and a generalization of the inequality relation to include all PrologIII object types.

PrologIII terms are formed using constants, variables, and operators. The constants are those of propositional logic $[1', 0']$, the non-negative integers, and the empty list $\langle\rangle$. There are three types of operator on these terms: boolean operators $[\wedge, \vee, \neg]$, numerical operators [*, /, +, -], several constructive operators [$\langle\rangle$, .], and others. These operators are typed, so only certain operands are legal. An important point

is that any variable appearing in a boolean expression is typed **boolean**, so the variable cannot be unified with a non-boolean expression. Two examples of PrologIII terms are $2+3/5$, $\langle 1,2,3\rangle$, and $(\neg a \vee b)$.
Constraints in PrologIII are formulated using typed relations. Examples of the numerical relations are $<$, $>$, $\geq$, $\leq$. A numerical constraint using these relations is $2*x < 4*7+2$. An example of a boolean relation is the logical implication $\Rightarrow$. A boolean constraint using implication is $(a \wedge b) \Rightarrow c$. PrologIII also allows constraints on the composite object **tree** using the equality ($=$) and inequality ($\neq$) relations. Finally, there are unary relations to restrict the type of a variable, for example, $l : 5$ restricts the type of variable l to a list of length 5. One can specify a set of constraints to be satisfied simultaneously. An example of such a set is: $\{x \geq y,\ y > 10,\ a \Rightarrow (c \vee d),\ v = tree(u),\ x \neq 5/3\}$.[1] Within a rule, the predicates and constraints are separated by a comma; if a rule has constraints but not predicates, then $\rightarrow$, appears.
It is important to note some representational limitations. First, PrologIII cannot treat an expression like $x < y$ as boolean. Hence, a boolean variable cannot unify with such an expression. This inability is due to the wholly separate processing of boolean and numerical constraints. A second limitation is that numerical constraints refer to the domain of rational numbers; a variable's domain cannot be restricted to the integers. Forcing a variable to be integral is achieved indirectly, for example by using the system predicate **integer(x)** which assigns an integer value to **x**. Numerical constraints are required to be linear.
A PrologIII program is a finite collection of rules of the form: $Q_0 \rightarrow Q_1 Q_2 \dots Q_p, S$ where $Q_0 Q_1 Q_2 \dots Q_p$ are terms as defined above, and S is a set of constraints to be satisfied. Like Prolog, PrologIII can be regarded as a non-deterministic machine. One state of this machine is represented by the triplet $(W, T_0 T_1 T_2 \dots T_q, S)$ where $T_0 T_1 T_2 \dots T_q$ is a suite of terms called goals, S is a set of satisfiable constraints, and W is a set of variables. The state change is represented as follows:

$$\begin{array}{rcl} state_n & : & (W,\ T_0\, T_1\, \dots\, T_q,\ S) \\ chosen\ rule & : & Q_0 \rightarrow Q_1\, Q_2\, \dots\, Q_p, S' \\ state_{n+1} & : & (W,\ Q_1\, Q_2\, \dots\, Q_p\, T_1\, T_2\, \dots\, T_q,\ S \cup S' \cup \{Q_0 = T_0\}) \end{array}$$

The PrologIII machine will go from $state_n$ to $state_{n+1}$ if and only if the set of constraints $S \cup S' \cup \{Q_0 = T_0\}$ can be satisfied. Within this state change the PrologIII machine will simplify the set of constraints. When the list of goals is exhausted, PrologIII succeeds, and outputs the set of variables W together with a collection of simplified constraints holding on the variables.

3 The Task

The CLP application described here is part of an effort directed at partially automating the elucidation of chemical-reaction pathways [14, 15] The elucidation problem is the following: Given an *instantiation* of the (two-reagent) reaction schema $A + B \rightsquigarrow T + P_1 + \dots + P_{k \geq 0}$, ascertain the pathway, i.e., the set of constituent reaction steps, as well as the other species[2] $P_{k+1}, \dots, P_n$ (possibly none) formed during the reaction, but not yet identified. For example, an (unbalanced)

[1] In this paper we use standard mathematical notation rather than PrologIII notation for these symbols: $\rightarrow, \Rightarrow, \wedge, \vee, \neg, \neq, \geq$. Some differences between the Edinburgh notation and ours in this paper are: '$\rightarrow$' vs. ':-', '$\langle x,y,z,t\rangle$' vs. '$[x,y,z,t]$', '$\langle x\rangle.y$' vs. '$[x|y]$'.

[2] For our purposes, a species is a distinct molecular formula, e.g., CH_2O.

overall reaction such as $C_7H_9N + CH_2O \rightsquigarrow C_{17}H_{18}N_2 + H_2O$ may consist of this three-step pathway:

$$\begin{array}{rcl} C_7H_9N + CH_2O & \rightarrow & H_2O + \lfloor C_8H_9N \rfloor \\ \lfloor C_8H_9N \rfloor + \lfloor C_8H_9N \rfloor & \rightarrow & \lfloor C_{16}H_{18}N_2 \rfloor \\ \lfloor C_8H_9N \rfloor + \lfloor C_{16}H_{18}N_2 \rfloor & \rightarrow & C_{17}H_{18}N_2 + C_7H_9N \end{array}$$

in which there appear the two previously unidentified species C_8H_9N and $C_{16}H_{18}N_2$, shown within $\lfloor\ \rfloor$. Supporting such an hypothesis with evidence is partly an experimental process, outside the scope of this paper. Here we examine only the problem of forming initial pathway hypotheses for a particular reaction.

3.1 Task knowledge

Our approach has organized the task of forming pathway hypotheses as a sound deduction from premises. These premises refer to necessary properties at the level of species, steps, pathways, and sets of pathways. We shall discuss these premises in that order; chemical justification of them is given in [14], but is omitted here. (Hereafter, formula shall be synonymous with 'molecular formula.')

Premise referring to individual species.

- A formula consists of non-negative integers, not all zero (such a formula is called legal).

Premises referring to a pathway step.

- For each chemical element, the number of its reactant atoms in any step equals the number of its product atoms in the same step. That is, steps must be (chemically) balanced.
- All reaction steps have either one or two reactant molecules.
- All reaction steps have either one or two product molecules.
- No formula appears both among the reactants and among the products of a single reaction step.

Premises referring to a pathway (set of steps).

- The pathway is an instantiation of the reaction schema $A+B \rightsquigarrow T+(products)$. That is, the reagents A, B are the starting materials, forming the target product T.
- Neither reagent alone suffices to form the target product T.
- Any pathway has present exactly $\mathcal{S}$ distinct species formulas, which must include the starting materials and known products ($\mathcal{S}$ is a fixed integer parameter).
- There are exactly $\mathcal{R}$ reaction steps, all distinct ($\mathcal{R}$ is a fixed integer parameter).
- All pathway species must be formable from the two reagents A, B.
- For any pathway containing variables (i.e., unknown species), there must exist an assignment of legal formulas to the variables such that the steps are balanced.

Premise referring to a set of pathways.

- No two pathways are identical, nor become identical under any of the following transformations: 1. permuting the reactants (or products) within a step, 2. switching the reactants and products within a step, and 3. permuting two steps.

3.2 Experience with a previous implementation

We wrote previously a Common Lisp program to enumerate all distinct, *schematic*, reaction pathways below a certain complexity. These were collected into a catalogue; for example, one entry having six species ($\mathcal{S}=6$) and two reaction steps ($\mathcal{R}=2$) is this:

$$\begin{aligned} A+B &\rightarrow Y+Z \\ Z &\rightarrow T+X \end{aligned}$$

Over the total program scope of $\mathcal{R} \leq 3, \mathcal{S} \leq 8$, there were 15 494 catalogue entries. This catalogue permits forming pathway hypotheses in the following manner. The elucidation task presupposes that the reagents, and at least one product, are known, implying that their formulas are available. Some of a pathway's variables could be instantiated with these formulas, and the remaining unknowns inferred if possible. If the resulting instantiated pathway were legal, then the pathway would be a legitimate hypothesis, later to be confirmed or not with other evidence.
We illustrate this procedure with an instantiation resulting in an *illegal* pathway. Assume again that the (unbalanced) reaction scheme is: $C_7H_9N + CH_2O \rightsquigarrow C_{17}H_{18}N_2 + H_2O$, so two products of the reaction are already known. The variables of the schematic pathway shown next are bound to the reagents and products:

$$\begin{array}{rcl|rcl rcl} A+B &\rightarrow& X+Y & A &=& C_7H_9N & T &=& C_{17}H_{18}N_2 \\ X+X &\rightarrow& Z & B &=& CH_2O & W &=& H_2O \\ Z+Z &\rightarrow& T+W & & & & & & \end{array}$$

After binding, there remain the three undetermined species X, Y, Z, and three constraint equations for each chemical element, one equation arising from each step. Solving these equations, we obtain the following illegal pathway:

$$\begin{aligned} C_7H_9N + CH_2O &\rightarrow C_{17/4}H_5N_{1/2}O_{1/4} + C_{15/4}H_6N_{1/2}O_{3/4} \\ C_{17/4}H_5N_{1/2}O_{1/4} + C_{17/4}H_5N_{1/2}O_{1/4} &\rightarrow C_{17/2}H_{10}NO_{1/2} \\ C_{17/2}H_{10}NO_{1/2} + C_{17/2}H_{10}NO_{1/2} &\rightarrow C_{17}H_{18}N_2 + H_2O \end{aligned}$$

The pathway conjectures illegal formulas having a fractional number of elemental atoms.[3]
Experience with the above procedure soon showed that on many reaction schemes, the number of *simplest* pathways accounting for the transformation of reagents into products were quite few. For example, on the current reaction scheme, no legal hypotheses having fewer than six species and three reaction steps (6s3r) were found. In the class 6s3r, only five pathways were output, of the 6 773 stored. It became clear that the formulas of reagents/products, together with elemental conservation (i.e., that the total number of atoms of each element is constant), constituted an extremely powerful constraint.
At that point, the goal became to design an algorithm to exploit the formulas and elemental conservation *earlier in the generation phase*. Doing so would expand the scope of the reactions handled, which because of the catalogue approach seemed

[3] "Multiplying through" by 4 results in eight reactant molecules for the first step, exceeding the ceiling of two molecules stipulated by a task premise.

limited practically to three reaction steps, even with dedicated use of an engineering workstation. The reason was this: even though the catalogue had only 15 494 entries, many more were constructed, then rejected, in the course of generating the catalogue, and the number rejected would explode combinatorially if the catalogue scope were increased.

After moderate effort, no satisfactory algorithm was found. Finally, we perceived that constraint logic programming was an advantageous approach to the problem, in brief: How to express the constraints and apply them as early as possible in the generation of legal, pathway hypotheses?

4 A PrologIII Solution

This section describes our PrologIII answer to the question of how to express the task premises of section 3.1 and apply them to achieve an efficient search for reaction-pathway hypotheses.

A pathway-generation problem consists of the number $\mathcal{S}$ (of pathway species), the number $\mathcal{R}$ (of pathway steps), and a list of species of length $\mathcal{S}$, some of which are instantiated.[4] The remaining task premises do not vary from one problem to the next. $\mathcal{S}$ and $\mathcal{R}$ shall turn out to be pervasive parameters in the sense that their magnitudes determine the sizes of various program data structures.

The core idea underlying the program is to build a pathway template from the parameters $\mathcal{S}, \mathcal{R}$. To build a template means to generate a pathway data structure containing only variables, while attaching sets of constraints on those variables. The template is built deterministically, in order not to permit any backtracking on constraint generation.

Then the values of certain pathway variables are enumerated non-deterministically to find all consistent instantiated pathways, i.e., pathways in terms of formulas. All backtracking is confined to this enumeration stage.

First we describe in subsection 4.1 how the domain objects (species, formula, step, and pathway) are represented. Then subsection 4.2 shows how the pathway template is built and constrained. Finally, subsection 4.3 discusses how the pathways are enumerated.

4.1 Representation of domain objects

A formula is a vector of integers, one integer for each chemical element, e.g., $C_{13}H_{18}NI$ is represented by $\langle 13, 18, 1, 1\rangle$. An unknown formula is a vector of numeric variables.

A species is a quintuplet $\langle n, x, a, b, f\rangle$. The following gives some notion of their types and meaning; we shall adhere to this naming convention below.

n An identifier between 1 (or 0) and $\mathcal{S}$.
x A numeric variable.
a,b Two boolean variables.
f The species formula.

A step is a list of integer species-identifiers; an unknown step is a list of unknown identifiers. The main purpose of the identifiers is to serve as convenient species place-holders; however, their arithmetic properties are used to express the constraint derived from Proposition 1 below. Each identifier corresponds to a distinct species,

[4] The number of instantiated species (reagents and known products) need not equal $\mathcal{S}$, since not all the species formulas need be known beforehand.

hence also to a distinct formula. According to the premises of section 3.1, a step has at most two reactant and two product molecules, so we represent the general step $R_1 + R_2 \rightarrow P_1 + P_2$ by the identifier quadruplet $\langle r_1, r_2, p_1, p_2 \rangle$. A pathway is a list of steps of length $\mathcal{R}$.
The top-level goal is the following PrologIII rule.

```
Pathway(R, S, p, q) →
   All_formulas_are_distinct(p)
   Pathway_template(S, R, q, v, u)
   All_distinct_steps(q)
   Need_both_reagents(p)
   Enumerate_the_species(v, p, u);
```

The rule's first four subordinate predicates build the pathway template while constraining its variables. The last predicate **Enumerate_the_species** performs the enumeration. The four parameters to **Pathway** are these:

- $\mathcal{R}$ The number of reaction steps.
- $\mathcal{S}$ The number of species.
- **p** A list (of length $\mathcal{S}$) of species, including the initially unknown species.
- **q** A list (of length $\mathcal{R}$) of steps.

An $\mathcal{S}$=4 example of **p** on the scheme $O + H_2 \leadsto OH$ is:

$$\langle\langle 1, x1, a1, b1, \langle 1, 0\rangle\rangle, \langle 2, x2, a2, b2, \langle 0, 2\rangle\rangle, \langle 3, x3, a3, b3, \langle 1, 1\rangle\rangle, \langle 4, x4, a4, b4, f4\rangle\rangle$$

An $\mathcal{R}$=3 example of **q** is $\langle\langle r_1, r_2, p_1, p_2\rangle, \langle r_3, r_4, p_3, p_4\rangle, \langle r_5, r_6, p_5, p_6\rangle\rangle$.

4.2 Creating and constraining the pathway template

The description below of how task premises are expressed as constraints follows this pattern: one or more premises (or parts of a premise) from section 3.1 appear, preceded by a ♣. Then appear PrologIII fragments expressing the premises, justified more formally if the correctness of the fragment seems unclear.

4.2.1 Constraints on formulas

♣ *Any pathway has present exactly $\mathcal{S}$ distinct species (formulas) which must include the starting materials and known products.*

The first predicate in the *Pathway* rule above serves as our first example of a constraint expression within a PrologIII rule. The recursive rules below require all $\mathcal{S}$ species formulas to be distinct ($f1 \neq f2$). (The other aspects of the premise are expressed later, not here).
If all $\mathcal{S}$ formulas are input to the program, then the rules have little effect. The purpose is really to ensure that when $\mathcal{S}$ is greater than the number of known formulas, the newly conjectured formulas are unique.

```
All_formulas_are_distinct(⟨⟩) →;
All_formulas_are_distinct(⟨e⟩.l) →
   Pairwise_distinct_formulas(e, l)
   All_formulas_are_distinct(l);

Pairwise_distinct_formulas(e, ⟨⟩) →;
Pairwise_distinct_formulas(⟨n1, x1, a1, b1, f1⟩, ⟨⟨n2, x2, a2, b2, f2⟩⟩.l) →
   Pairwise_distinct_formulas(⟨n1, x1, a1, b1, f1⟩, l),
   {f1 ≠ f2};
```

These simple rules illustrate the ability of the language to pose constraints using recursion.

are made to pathway species via the **integer(n)** predicate, within the predicate **Instantiate_species** below. That is, the program was designed so that the entire process of placing constraints on the pathway template involves no choice points, therefore no backtracking to place different constraints is possible. This localized backtracking proved an important contributor to efficiency, given our experience with alternate designs that did involve backtracking to template generation.

A general rule is that enumeration is more efficient when the variable of enumeration is more constrained. The pathway species are considerably constrained, as shown in previous sections. Hence, this aspect also contributes to overall efficiency.

The enumeration process is summarized by the following two PrologIII rules, where **l** is the list of $\mathcal{S}$ *assignable* species, **v** is the list of *pathway* species, and **u** is a list of available identifiers, i.e., reagents or previously formed products.

```
Enumerate_the_species(v, p, ⟨0, 1, 2⟩.u) →
    Instantiate_species(v, p, u);

Instantiate_species(⟨⟩, p, k) →;
Instantiate_species(⟨⟨n, x, a, b, f⟩⟩.v, p, u) →
    integer(n)
    belong_to(⟨n, x, a, b, f⟩, p)
    eq(u, ⟨n⟩.k)
    Instantiate_species(v, p, k);
```

To better understand the role of the constraints during enumeration, we should look at the predicate **belong_to**. At the start of enumeration, the only active constraints are those on the variables being enumerated; these constraints are explicitly taken into account by the predicate **integer(n)**. The remaining constraints become active only when a pathway species is unified with an assignable species.

The binding between the pathway species and the species identifiers is achieved by the predicate **belong_to**.

```
belong_to(⟨0, 0, 1', 1', f⟩, l) →
    coefficients_all_zero(f);

belong_to(⟨n, x, a, b, f⟩, ⟨⟨n, x, a, b, f⟩⟩.l) →,
    {n ≠ 0, x ≥ 1};
belong_to(⟨n, x, a, b, f⟩, ⟨⟨n', x', a', b', f'⟩⟩.l) →
    belong_to(⟨n, x, a, b, f⟩, l),
    {n ≠ 0, n ≠ n'};
```

The first rule below is used on species having the zero identifier, i.e., null species; their attached variables are bound to appropriate dummy values.

We shall illustrate how constraints become active with a two-step pathway template. Four independent sets of pathway constraints are shown below (these are only a subset of the actual constraints, omitting for example the **Need_both_reagents** constraints, to keep the example small).

species identifiers			numerical equations		
n_r11 + n_r12	→	n_p11 + n_p12	x_r11 + x_r12	=	x_p11 + x_p12
n_r21 + n_r22	→	n_p21 + n_p22	x_r21 + x_r22	=	x_p21 + x_p22

set of *a*-clauses			elemental balance		
a_r11 ∧ a_r12	⇒	a_p11	f_r11 + f_r12	=	f_p11 + f_p12
a_r11 ∧ a_r12	⇒	a_p12	f_r21 + f_r22	=	f_p21 + f_p22
a_r21 ∧ a_r22	⇒	a_p21			
a_r21 ∧ a_r22	⇒	a_p22			

4.2.2 Constraints on species identifiers

♣ *Any pathway has present exactly $\mathcal{S}$ distinct species formulas.*

This pathway premise can be re-directed as a constraint on species identifiers, since each identifier corresponds to a unique formula. Actually, the *exactly $\mathcal{S}$* is not captured; the following constraint expresses instead *at most $\mathcal{S}$*.

$$r_1, r_2, p_1, p_2 \leq \mathcal{S}$$

♣ *All reaction steps have either one or two reactant molecules. All reaction steps have either one or two product molecules.*

These premises are taken into account by our representation of a general step as the identifier quadruplet $\langle r_1, r_2, p_1, p_2 \rangle$. The species identifier '0' represents the absence of a species, e.g., if $r_1 = 0$, then the step has only one reactant molecule.

$$r_1, p_1 \geq 0, \quad r_2, p_2 \geq 1$$

r_2 and p_2 are non-zero, so every step has at least one reactant and product.

♣ *No reaction step involves a same molecular formula among both its reactants and products.*

This is easily rendered as a numerical constraint at the reaction step level, in terms of species identifiers:

$$r_1 \neq p_1, \quad r_1 \neq p_2, \quad r_2 \neq p_1, \quad r_2 \neq p_2$$

We emphasize that these inequalities are over the domain of species identifiers, not of formulas, although the effect is the same, since the formulas differ if the identifiers do. This constraint prohibits steps of form $R \rightarrow P$.
The above constraints wholly capture the effect of the premise. However, the goal of *highly constrained* enumeration is served by including another constraint *entailed by* the premise. For example, a step of form $R + R \rightarrow P + P$ must result eventually in a violation of the premise, because the formula of R must equal that of P for the step to balance. This form is prohibited by making use of a special-purpose proposition:

Proposition 1 *A step is of the form $R + R \rightarrow P + P$ if and only if $(r_1 + r_2) + (p_1 + p_2) * 1000 \;=\; 2r_2 + 2p_2 * 1000$ and $\mathcal{S} < 1000$.*

Proof. If the step is $R + R \rightarrow P + P$, then in our representation we have $r_1 = r_2$ and $p_1 = p_2$, and the equation follows immediately. Conversely, if we assume the equation and that $\mathcal{S} < 1000$ (in practice, a safe assumption), then we see that $r_1 + r_2 = 2r_2$ and $p_1 + p_2 = 2p_2$. Therefore, $r_1 = r_2$ and $p_1 = p_2$, and the proof is complete.

♣ *No two pathways are identical, nor become identical under any of the following transformations: 1. permuting the reactants (or products) within a step.*

The following numerical constraint enforces a unique ordering on the reactants and products via the species identifiers.

$$r_1 \leq r_2, \quad p_1 \leq p_2$$

This ordering prevents any permutation of reactants or products.

We can collect all the identifier constraints so far in a PrologIII rule:

$$
\begin{array}{l}
Step\_template(\langle r_1, r_2, p_1, p_2\rangle, \mathcal{S}) \rightarrow, \\
\quad \{ \\
\quad 0 \leq r_1 \leq \mathcal{S}, \\
\quad 1 \leq r_2 \leq \mathcal{S}, \\
\quad 0 \leq p_1 \leq \mathcal{S}, \\
\quad 1 \leq p_2 \leq \mathcal{S}, \\
\quad (r_1 + r_2) + (p_1 + p_2) * 1000 \neq 2r_2 + 2p_2 * 1000, \ /* \ prohibit\ R{+}R \rightarrow P{+}P \ */ \\
\quad r_1 \neq p_1, r_1 \neq p_2, \\
\quad r_2 \neq p_1, r_2 \neq p_2, \ /* \ reactants\ and\ products\ are\ distinct \ */ \\
\quad r_1 \leq r_2, p_1 \leq p_2 \ /* \ ordering\ on\ the\ identifiers \ */ \\
\quad \};
\end{array}
$$

4.2.3 Constraints on steps

♣ *For each chemical element, the number of its reactant atoms in any step equals the number of its product atoms in the same step. That is, steps must be (chemically) balanced.*

The premise that the number of elemental atoms must balance is handled easily. Each chemical element gives rise to a separate balance constraint, expressed by the following PrologIII rule:

$$
\begin{array}{l}
Balanced\_step(\langle\langle\rangle, \langle\rangle, \langle\rangle, \langle\rangle\rangle) \rightarrow; \\
Balanced\_step(\langle\langle a\rangle.f\_r1, \langle b\rangle.f\_r2, \langle c\rangle.f\_p1, \langle d\rangle.f\_p2\rangle) \rightarrow \\
\quad freeze(a, integer(a)) \\
\quad freeze(b, integer(b)) \\
\quad freeze(c, integer(c)) \\
\quad freeze(d, integer(d)) \\
\quad Balanced\_step(\langle f\_r1, f\_r2, f\_p1, f\_p2\rangle), \\
\quad \{a + b = c + d, a \geq 0, b \geq 0, c \geq 0, d \geq 0\};
\end{array}
$$

The restriction to integral formulas is accomplished using the well-known freeze primitive generally found in versions of Prolog.

4.2.4 Constraints on pathways

♣ *For any pathway containing unknown species (i.e., variables), there must exist an assignment of legal formulas to the unknowns such that the steps are balanced.*

The existence of an assignment is testable as shown by the following proposition.

Proposition 2 *A pathway containing variables is consistent if and only if there exists a satisfying positive-integer assignment to the variables of the corresponding numerical equations.*[5]

The numerical equations corresponding to a pathway are those obtained by changing the domain to that of the integers, and replacing the '→' symbols by '=.' So, each pathway will have PrologIII constraints of numerical equations, one equation for each $\langle r1, r2, p1, p2\rangle$ step.

$$
\begin{array}{l}
Attached\_equation\_system(\langle x\_r1, x\_r2, x\_p1, x\_p2\rangle) \rightarrow, \\
\quad \{x\_r1 + x\_r2 = x\_p1 + x\_p2\};
\end{array}
$$

The rule's parameter is not a step, rather a list of numeric variables attached to the species of a step in the quintuplet representation, reached via the identifier.

[5] A proof of the result is in [14].

The numerical-constraint processing algorithm will test whether these constraints are soluble in the rationals. If these equations have a rational solution, then they have also an integer solution, since they are homogeneous. Positive solutions are enforced by adding the constraints $x\_i \geq 1$.[6]

♣ *There are exactly $\mathcal{R}$ reaction steps, all distinct.*

For our purpose, two steps are distinct if their species formulas are both: 1. not identical, symbol for symbol, and 2. not identical after switching the roles of reactant/product in the step. For example, the steps $C_7H_9N + CH_2O \rightarrow H_2O + C_8H_9N$ and $H_2O + C_8H_9N \rightarrow C_7H_9N + CH_2O$ are not distinct because they fail the second requirement. The requirements are expressed on the identifiers domain by:

$$(\forall\, step_i, step_j \in pathway)\ (step_i \neq step_j) \wedge (step_i \neq switch\_roles(step_j))$$

rendered thus in PrologIII:

$All\_distinct\_steps(\langle\rangle) \rightarrow;$
$All\_distinct\_steps(\langle\langle r1, r2, p1, p2\rangle\rangle.l) \rightarrow$
$\quad Pairwise\_distinct\_steps(\langle r1, r2, p1, p2\rangle, l)$
$\quad All\_distinct\_steps(l);$

$Pairwise\_distinct\_steps(e, \langle\rangle) \rightarrow;$
$Pairwise\_distinct\_steps(\langle r1, r2, p1, p2\rangle, \langle\langle r3, r4, p3, p4\rangle\rangle.l) \rightarrow$
$\quad Pairwise\_distinct\_steps(\langle r1, r2, p1, p2\rangle, l),$
$\quad \{\langle r1, r2, p1, p2\rangle \neq \langle r3, r4, p3, p4\rangle,\ \langle r1, r2, p1, p2\rangle \neq \langle p3, p4, r3, r4\rangle\};$

4.2.5 Path-oriented constraints on pathways

This section treats premises that refer to paths from reagents to various species; certain paths must or must not exist in an acceptable pathway. This section provides our first use of *boolean constraints*; all previous constraints have been numerical.

♣ *Neither reagent alone suffices to form the target product T.*

A key to formulating the premise is perceiving the analogy between a set of chemical reactions and a propositional proof. The reaction step $R_1 + R_2 \rightarrow P_1 + P_2$ corresponds to the logical implication $r_1 \wedge r_2 \Rightarrow p_1 \wedge p_2$. Here is a full pathway example:

$A + B$	$\rightarrow$	$X + Y$	$a \wedge b$	$\Rightarrow$	$x \wedge y$
$X + X$	$\rightarrow$	Z	x	$\Rightarrow$	z
$Z + Z$	$\rightarrow$	$T + W$	z	$\Rightarrow$	$t \wedge w$

The clause-form implications associated with a pathway will be referred to as $\mathcal{C}$. We proceed to re-express the above premise as a statement about propositional proofs.

Proposition 3 *In a pathway, species X_1 by itself does not form species X_2 if and only if the corresponding set of clauses $\mathcal{C}$ does not derive $x_1 \Rightarrow x_2$. That is, if and only if $\mathcal{C} \nvdash \{\neg x_1 \vee x_2\}$.*

We combine this statement with the refutation theorem $\mathcal{C} \vdash f \Leftrightarrow \mathcal{C} \cup \{\neg f\} \vdash \emptyset$ to express the desired conditions. A pathway satisfies our formability premise if and only if both these statements are true:
1. $\mathcal{C} \cup \{\neg(\neg reagent_1 \vee target)\} \nvdash \emptyset$ (or, $\mathcal{C} \cup \{reagent_1\} \cup \{\neg target\} \nvdash \emptyset$)
2. $\mathcal{C} \cup \{\neg(\neg reagent_2 \vee target)\} \nvdash \emptyset$ (or, $\mathcal{C} \cup \{reagent_2\} \cup \{\neg target\} \nvdash \emptyset$)

[6] These constraints are actually placed in the predicate **belong_to**, described in section 4.3, because here a null species is possible, and its attached x would need to equal zero.

Since the two sets of clauses are not independent, they must be implemented separately, otherwise the theorems of one set can - incorrectly - be used by the other set. Therefore, we shall use two independent sets of clauses: a and b sets; each receives its own version of $\mathcal{C}$, $\neg target$, and $reagent_1/reagent_2$.
The following rule attaches independent boolean constraints from a single pathway step to the a and b clause-sets.

$$\begin{aligned}&Attached\_clause\_system(\langle a\_r1,\ a\_r2,\ a\_p1,\ a\_p2\rangle,\ \langle b\_r1,\ b\_r2,\ b\_p1,\ b\_p2\rangle) \rightarrow,\\ &\quad \{a\_r1 \wedge a\_r2 \Rightarrow a\_p1,\quad a\_r1 \wedge a\_r2 \Rightarrow a\_p2,\\ &\quad\ b\_r1 \wedge b\_r2 \Rightarrow b\_p1,\quad b\_r1 \wedge b\_r2 \Rightarrow b\_p2\};\end{aligned}$$

The expression of the conditions is completed by adding to the a-set its copies $\{a_1\}, \{\neg a_3\}$ of the clauses $\{reagent_1\}$, $\{\neg target\}$, and to the b-set its copies $\{b_1\}$, $\{\neg b_3\}$ of the clauses $\{reagent_2\}$, $\{\neg target\}$, via this rule:

$$\begin{aligned}&Need\_both\_reagents(\langle\langle 1,x1,a1,b1,f1\rangle.\langle 2,x2,a2,b2,f2\rangle.\langle 3,x3,a3,b3,f3\rangle\rangle.l) \rightarrow,\\ &\quad \{a1 = 1',\ a3 = 0',\ b2 = 1',\ b3 = 0'\};\end{aligned}$$

$\langle 1, x1, a1, b1, f1\rangle$ represents the first reagent, $\langle 2, x2, a2, b2, f2\rangle$ the second reagent, and $\langle 3, x3, a3, b3, f3\rangle$ the target product; by convention they head the list of species. The third and fourth entries of a quintuplet serve to attach boolean clauses to the species, to enforce respectively that the first and second reagents alone not form the target product.
If instead we considered three-reagent reactions, we would need six sets of independent clauses instead of two to express the following conditions:

$$(\forall\, i,j,k \in (1,2,3))\ \ reagent_i \not\Rightarrow target,\ \ reagent_j \wedge reagent_k \not\Rightarrow target$$

♣ *All pathway species must be formable from the two reagents A, B.*

The intent of this second path-oriented premise is to exclude spurious pathways such as $A + B \rightarrow T$, $Y \rightarrow X$. We take account of this premise *as a by-product of* a quite powerful constraint on pathway generation, which is motivated next. Informally, a next pathway step is "executable" only if its reactants are available, either as starting materials or as products of "previous" steps. For example, at a reaction's start, only steps involving the two reagents can react. This availability criterion induces a partial order on the steps of a pathway. We shall restrict pathway generation to those pathways that are a legitimate linear path through the partial order. This restriction, accomplished with the **freeze** primitive, turns out to have a powerful beneficial impact on total generation time. A binding to the reactants is not propagated until it is verified that the binding is available from the pool of species created by the previous reaction steps. The constraint is expressed by modifying the *step_template* rule of section 4.2.2 thus:

$$\begin{aligned}&Step\_template(\langle r_1, r_2, p_1, p_2\rangle, \mathcal{S}, u) \rightarrow\\ &\quad available(r_1, u)\\ &\quad available(r_2, u),\\ &\quad \{[constraints \ldots]\};\\ &available(e, l) \rightarrow freeze(e, member(e, l));\end{aligned}$$

where u is the list of available species identifiers, which is initialized to $\langle 0, 1, 2\rangle$, meaning that the two reagents and the null species are the only ones initially available.
All of the constraints described above are used in the two rules below, which build the pathway template via recursion on the list of step templates. All the numerical

and boolean systems that constrain the pathway template are formulated by these rules.

$Pathway\_template(\mathcal{S}, 0, \langle\rangle, \langle\rangle, u) \rightarrow;$

$Pathway\_template(\mathcal{S}, r, \langle\langle r1, r2, p1, p2\rangle\rangle.l, \langle\langle r1, x1, a1, b1, f1\rangle, \langle r2, x2, a2, b2, f2\rangle,$
$\langle p1, x3, a3, b3, f3\rangle, \langle p2, x4, a4, b4, f4\rangle\rangle.v, u) \rightarrow$
$Step\_template(\langle r1, r2, p1, p2\rangle, \mathcal{S}, u)$
$Attached\_equation\_system(\langle x1, x2, x3, x4\rangle)$
$Balanced\_step(\langle f1, f2, f3, f4\rangle)$
$Attached\_clause\_system(\langle a1, a2, a3, a4\rangle, \langle b1, b2, b3, b4\rangle)$
$Pathway\_template(\mathcal{S}, r-1, l, v, u);$

4.2.6 Unexpressed premises

♣ *Any pathway has present exactly $\mathcal{S}$ distinct species formulas.*

By itself, this premise makes a statement about acceptable *completed* pathways; hence, it has little potential to reject partially generated pathways. We were content to express the premise as a PrologIII verification, rather than constraint.

♣ *No two pathways are identical, nor become identical under any of the following transformations: 3. permuting two steps.*

One attempt to express the premise involves defining an order on the steps. We formulated such constraints by placing an order on steps, but this order interfered with the partial order of section 4.2.5, so we did not express the premise.

4.3 Species enumeration

The rules of the previous sections created a pathway template of a fixed number of steps $\mathcal{R}$ having constraints on the pathway species and their attached variables (numeric, boolean etc.). At this point the template contains no constants. To obtain our goal of a pathway in terms of known formulas, we must instantiate some of the template variables while taking into account the $\mathcal{S}$ available species, some of whose formulas are already known. The obvious course is to choose a set of variables and enumerate all of their legal values, in order to find all consistent instantiated pathways.

Enumeration is better understood with reference to two separate lists: 1. the assignable species, i.e., the list of $\mathcal{S}$ species, some of which come initially instantiated (e.g. see the input parameter to rule **Pathway** in section 4.1), and 2. the pathway species, i.e., the list (of length $4\mathcal{R}$) of species quintuplets in the pathway template, four quintuplets per step.

We recall that each *assignable* species has as unique identifier an integer from 1 to $\mathcal{S}$. Then, enumeration proceeds by assigning an *assignable* species to a *pathway* species via the identifiers, thus unifying their attached constraint variables in the quintuplet representation. Unification is done by the predicate **belong_to**, which is like a typical **member** predicate. When all the pathway species have been unified with the identifiers, and no constraint is violated, then this good pathway is printed, and the remaining solutions are found by continuing the enumeration using backtracking.

Pathway-species enumeration uses the predefined PrologIII predicate **integer(n)**, which serves to enumerate all integer assignments to **n** that satisfy accompanying constraints. Backtracking is done at this predicate; each backtrack on **integer(n)** yields another value for **n**, to be checked as always against the constraints. It is important to note that the program is deterministic up to when assignments

These constraints hold over the following domains: **n** integers (species identifiers); **a** boolean values; **x** rationals; **f** vector of integers (formulas).
Suppose that an enumeration step unifies n_r11 with 1, i.e., n_r11 is bound to the first-reagent identifier. The only immediate affect on the constraints is to unify f_r11 with the formula of the first reagent. Suppose the next step also unifies n_r12 with 1. Now the affect on the constraints is broader: we have the unification $a\_r11 = a\_r12$, which simplifies the set of boolean constraints; we have $x\_r11 = x\_r12$, transforming the first numerical equation into $2 * x\_r11 = x\_p11 + x\_p12$, and similarly for the elemental balance equations. As illustrated, the constraints become stronger as enumeration proceeds.
Occasionally during enumeration the constraints become inconsistent. Proceeding with the example, suppose the next enumeration steps unify n_p11 with 0 (the null species) and n_p12 with 3 (the target product). The first a-clause becomes $\{a_1 \Rightarrow a_3\}$ where a_1 is a boolean variable attached to the first reagent and a_3 is attached to the target product. The conjunction of this clause with constraints introduced by **Need_both_reagents** is inconsistent: $\{a_1 \Rightarrow a_3,\ a_1 = 1',\ a_3 = 0'\}$.
After each unification, PrologIII checks that the resulting constraints sets are consistent; if not, backtracking occurs, resulting in unifying a pathway species with a different species identifier.

5 Evaluation

Our purpose in this paper has been to demonstrate the practical power of PrologIII, and to illustrate its programming with special reference to combining constraints over different computational domains. The next section extracts some general observations from this experience. First we will justify the assertion that our program is a practical success.
The previous Lisp-based program, called STOICH, is limited to reactions of at most three steps ($\mathcal{R} \leq 3$), for the reasons given in section 3.2. In contrast, increasing $\mathcal{R}$ in our PrologIII program (let's call it STOICH/CLP) from $\mathcal{R}_1$ to $\mathcal{R}_2$ involves a trivial change within the initial goal from a list $\langle w_1, w_2, \ldots, w_{\mathcal{R}_1}\rangle$ to a list $\langle w_1, w_2, \ldots, w_{\mathcal{R}_2}\rangle$. Increasing the number of pathway species $\mathcal{S}$ is also only a trivial change to the sizes of lists in the initial goal.
A second limitation of STOICH is its pervasive assumption of a two-reagent reaction. Changing this assumption so it can handle one-reagent or three-reagent reactions could involve weeks of work, and hasn't been attempted. In contrast, STOICH/CLP was designed with the same assumption, but has been changed to handle a three-reagent reaction currently under study; this effort took only one hour.
The correctness of STOICH/CLP has been confirmed by comparing its output with that of STOICH. Finally, the speeds of the two programs are roughly comparable within the $\mathcal{R} \leq 3$ scope of STOICH, although STOICH/CLP fares better. Outside that scope, there is no other program to compare STOICH/CLP against, since we are the first to automate this task.
The execution time of STOICH/CLP is found to be modest when the number of unknown species is 0 or 1. For constant $\mathcal{S}$, increasing the number of steps does not appreciably change the time. However, the Macintosh II execution time of STOICH/CLP increases (from $\approx$ 10 min to $\approx$ 10 hours) when the number of initially unknown species (equal to $\mathcal{S}$ minus the number of known formulas) goes from one to two.[7] The reason seems to be that many promising partial pathways have to

[7]This result is from an 8-species/5-step problem for which 6 of the species formulas are known.

be considered, i.e., there are fewer early search cutoffs. It is unclear yet whether the same jump in execution time will be observed when going from two to three unknown species.

5.1 Observations on use of PrologIII

PrologIII, as a logic programming language, has shown that its declarativeness contributes to flexibility, for the reasons of the previous section. Also, only about twenty PrologIII rules were needed to express the task premises efficiently. As also seen above, the PrologIII implementation improved the scope and speed of our approach to hypothetical reasoning in reaction chemistry. We have proved the ability of PrologIII to handle naturally a complex, non-academic, research problem.
We can point out some general ideas about programming in PrologIII, and CLP in general. First, there exists a programming tradeoff illustrated by the following two extremes. In one extreme, all task knowledge is formulated as *verifications*, causing inefficiency because no early search pruning is possible. In the other extreme, all knowledge is formulated as *constraints*, causing inefficiency because the resulting large constraint expressions are handled poorly by exponential algorithms. Hence, there is a tradeoff between these two factors, although the ideas of the next paragraph can shift the trade in favor of constraints.
The execution time of a CLP program can be large, due to the ability to express constraints whose internal manipulation involves exponential algorithms. This problem can be greatly lessened by taking care to formulate the constraints as several independent sets, i.e., that share no variables, in order to manipulate them without amassing one giant constraint. The general inspiration is the classic one of dividing an exponential problem into $\alpha > 1$ sub-problems, so that an x^n problem reduces to an $\alpha x^{n/\alpha}$ problem, where $\alpha x^{n/\alpha} \ll x^n$. We add that forming independent constraints seems easier when the language supports expression over separate computational domains, as PrologIII does.
We have observed that often it is beneficial to incorporate redundant constraints into one's program. To illustrate, we consider a premise P that states a property required of an acceptable, completed object (e.g., a reaction pathway must have $\mathcal{S}$ species). Expressing P directly may yield little ability to prune unfruitful partial objects (e.g., a partial pathway of less than $\mathcal{R}$ steps), since it expresses a property of completed objects. However, P together with another premise P_2 may entail a property that does directly constrain partial objects, enabling earlier search cutoffs. Continuing with our example, P_2 states that a step has at most two products. Hence, if s, r are respectively the number of species and steps of a partial pathway, then the property $s + 2(\mathcal{R} - r) \geq S$ must hold for any partial pathway. In this way we derive a constraint usable earlier in the generation process.
Finally, our work strongly suggests that the wholly separate processing of numerical and boolean constraints in PrologIII, illustrated by the inability of $x < y$ to unify with a boolean variable, is not a large obstacle to the solution of tasks presenting both aspects.

Acknowledgment. We thank Profs. Herbert Simon, Tom Mitchell, and Bruce Buchanan for guiding this research on automated chemistry. We thank Prof. Mitchell for hosting the first author at CMU. PrologIA graciously allowed us to use PrologIII before its release. Nevin Heintze discussed with us our ideas on CLP, and commented in detail on a draft of this paper.

Simpler examples take less time.

The first author acknowledges research support from the French Conseil Regional PACA, and from G.I.A Marseille Luminy. The second author is supported by a Graduate Fellowship from the Avionics Laboratory at Wright-Patterson Air Force Base, awarded by Universal Energy Systems.

References

[1] J. Jaffar and J.-L. Lassez, "Constraint logic programming," in *Proc. of Conf. on Principles of Programming Languages*, January 1987.

[2] J. Jaffar and S. Michaylov, "Methodology and implementation of a CLP system," in *Proc. of 4th Int. Conf. on Logic Programming*, May 1987.

[3] M. Dincbas, H. Simonis, and P. van Hentenryck, "Extending equation solving and constraint handling in logic programming," in *Colloquium on Resolution of Equations in Algebraic Structures* (MCC, ed.), May 1987.

[4] A. Colmerauer, "Opening the Prolog III universe," *Byte*, pp. 177–182, August 1987.

[5] A. Colmerauer, "Une introduction a Prolog III," rapport technique, Groupe d'Intelligence Artificielle, Faculté des Sciences de Luminy, Marseille, France, 1989.

[6] A. Colmerauer, "Notes sur Prolog III," actes du seminair: programmation en logique, CNET Tregastel, France, May 1986.

[7] H. Simonis, "Test generation using the constraint logic programming language CHIP," in *Proc. of 6th Int. Conf. on Logic Programming*, 1989.

[8] H. Simonis and M. Dincbas, "Using logic programming for fault diagnosis in digital circuits," in *German Workshop on Artificial Intelligence*, pp. 139–148, September 1987.

[9] N. Heintze, S. Michaylov, and P. Stuckey, "CLP(R) and some electrical engineering problems," in *Proc. of 4th Int. Conf. on Logic Programming*, pp. 675–703, 1987. To appear in J. of Logic Programming.

[10] N. Heintze, S. Michaylov, and P. Stuckey, "CLP(R) and some electrical engineering problems," Technical Report CMU-CS-89-139, Carnegie Mellon University, 1989.

[11] M. Dincbas, H. Simonis, and P. van Hentenryck, "Solving the car-sequencing problem in constraint logic programming," in *Proc. of European Conf. on Artificial Intelligence*, 1988.

[12] M. Dincbas, P. van Hentenryck, H. Simonis, A. Aggous, and T. Graf, "Applications of CHIP to industrial and engineering problems," in *1st Int. Conf. on Industrial and Engineering Applications of Artificial Intelligence and Expert Systems*, June 1988.

[13] C. Lassez, "An application of constraint logic programming in finance." To appear in Systems and Control Encyclopedia.

[14] R. E. Valdés-Pérez, "Deductive assistance for elucidation of chemical reaction pathways," Technical Report CMU-CS-90-104, Carnegie Mellon University, 1990.

[15] R. E. Valdés-Pérez, "Deductive assistance for elucidation of reaction pathways." Accepted to Annual Meeting of American Institute of Chemical Engineers, 1990.

A Example

Our example is the following two-reagent reaction,

$$C_{13}H_{18}NX \;+\; C_{17}H_{17}N_2X \;\rightsquigarrow\; C_{31}H_{37}N_2X \;+\; C_{24}H_{27}N_2X \;+\; C_6H_7N \;+\; HX$$

which specifies four products that have been identified (X is an alias for either of the halogens I or Cl). The target is the first product, a blue dye of much commercial value. The program outputs these ten simplest pathway hypotheses, all having seven species and three steps (schematic versions are shown at the right).

1.
$$\begin{array}{rcl@{\qquad}rcl} C_{17}H_{17}N_2X & \rightarrow & C_6H_7N + C_{11}H_{10}NX & B & \rightarrow & W + Y \\ C_{13}H_{18}NX + C_{11}H_{10}NX & \rightarrow & HX + C_{24}H_{27}N_2X & A + W & \rightarrow & X + Z \\ 2C_{24}H_{27}N_2X & \rightarrow & C_{17}H_{17}N_2X + C_{31}H_{37}N_2X & 2X & \rightarrow & T + B \end{array}$$

2.
$$\begin{array}{rcl@{\qquad}rcl} C_{17}H_{17}N_2X & \rightarrow & HX + C_{17}H_{16}N_2 & B & \rightarrow & W + Z \\ C_{13}H_{18}NX + C_{17}H_{16}N_2 & \rightarrow & C_6H_7N + C_{24}H_{27}N_2X & A + W & \rightarrow & X + Y \\ 2C_{24}H_{27}N_2X & \rightarrow & C_{17}H_{17}N_2X + C_{31}H_{37}N_2X & 2X & \rightarrow & T + B \end{array}$$

3.
$$\begin{array}{rcl@{\qquad}rcl} C_{13}H_{18}NX & \rightarrow & HX + C_{13}H_{17}N & A & \rightarrow & W + Z \\ 2C_{24}H_{27}N_2X & \rightarrow & C_{17}H_{17}N_2X + C_{31}H_{37}N_2X & B + W & \rightarrow & X + Y \\ C_{17}H_{17}N_2X + C_{13}H_{17}N & \rightarrow & C_6H_7N + C_{24}H_{27}N_2X & 2X & \rightarrow & T + B \end{array}$$

4.
$$\begin{array}{rcl@{\qquad}rcl} C_{13}H_{18}NX & \rightarrow & C_6H_7N + C_7H_{11}X & A & \rightarrow & W + Y \\ C_{17}H_{17}N_2X + C_7H_{11}X & \rightarrow & HX + C_{24}H_{27}N_2X & B + W & \rightarrow & X + Z \\ 2C_{24}H_{27}N_2X & \rightarrow & C_{17}H_{17}N_2X + C_{31}H_{37}N_2X & 2X & \rightarrow & T + B \end{array}$$

5.
$$\begin{array}{rcl@{\qquad}rcl} C_{13}H_{18}NX & \rightarrow & HX + C_{13}H_{17}N & A & \rightarrow & W + Z \\ C_{17}H_{17}N_2X + C_{13}H_{17}N & \rightarrow & C_6H_7N + C_{24}H_{27}N_2X & B + W & \rightarrow & X + Y \\ C_{13}H_{17}N + C_{24}H_{27}N_2X & \rightarrow & C_6H_7N + C_{31}H_{37}N_2X & W + X & \rightarrow & T + Y \end{array}$$

6.
$$\begin{array}{rcl@{\qquad}rcl} C_{13}H_{18}NX & \rightarrow & C_6H_7N + C_7H_{11}X & A & \rightarrow & W + Y \\ C_{17}H_{17}N_2X + C_7H_{11}X & \rightarrow & HX + C_{24}H_{27}N_2X & B + W & \rightarrow & X + Z \\ C_7H_{11}X + C_{24}H_{27}N_2X & \rightarrow & HX + C_{31}H_{37}N_2X & W + X & \rightarrow & T + Z \end{array}$$

7.
$$\begin{array}{rcl@{\qquad}rcl} C_{13}H_{18}NX + C_{17}H_{17}N_2X & \rightarrow & C_6H_8NX + C_{24}H_{27}N_2X & A + B & \rightarrow & W + X \\ 2C_{24}H_{27}N_2X & \rightarrow & C_{17}H_{17}N_2X + C_{31}H_{37}N_2X & 2X & \rightarrow & T + B \\ C_6H_8NX & \rightarrow & HX + C_6H_7N & W & \rightarrow & Y + Z \end{array}$$

8.
$$\begin{array}{rcl@{\qquad}rcl} C_{13}H_{18}NX + C_{17}H_{17}N_2X & \rightarrow & HX + C_{30}H_{34}N_3X & A + B & \rightarrow & W + Z \\ 2C_{24}H_{27}N_2X & \rightarrow & C_{17}H_{17}N_2X + C_{31}H_{37}N_2X & 2X & \rightarrow & T + B \\ C_{30}H_{34}N_3X & \rightarrow & C_6H_7N + C_{24}H_{27}N_2X & W & \rightarrow & X + Y \end{array}$$

9.
$$\begin{array}{rcl@{\qquad}rcl} C_{13}H_{18}NX + C_{17}H_{17}N_2X & \rightarrow & C_6H_7N + C_{24}H_{28}N_2X_2 & A + B & \rightarrow & W + Y \\ 2C_{24}H_{27}N_2X & \rightarrow & C_{17}H_{17}N_2X + C_{31}H_{37}N_2X & 2X & \rightarrow & T + B \\ C_{24}H_{28}N_2X_2 & \rightarrow & HX + C_{24}H_{27}N_2X & W & \rightarrow & X + Z \end{array}$$

10.
$$\begin{array}{rcl@{\qquad}rcl} C_{13}H_{18}NX + C_{17}H_{17}N_2X & \rightarrow & C_6H_8NX + C_{24}H_{27}N_2X & A + B & \rightarrow & W + X \\ C_{13}H_{18}NX + C_{24}H_{27}N_2X & \rightarrow & C_6H_8NX + C_{31}H_{37}N_2X & A + X & \rightarrow & T + W \\ C_6H_8NX & \rightarrow & HX + C_6H_7N & W & \rightarrow & Y + Z \end{array}$$

B Program listing

This is a complete listing of the PrologIII fragments in the body of the paper, presented here in depth-first rule order. The program has been simplified somewhat for this paper, but it is very close to the actual program.

```
Pathway(R, S, p, q) →
  All_formulas_are_distinct(p)
  Pathway_template(S, R, q, v, u)
  All_distinct_steps(q)
  Need_both_reagents(p)
  Enumerate_the_species(v, p, u);

All_formulas_are_distinct(⟨⟩) →;
All_formulas_are_distinct(⟨e⟩.l) →
  Pairwise_distinct_formulas(e, l)
  All_formulas_are_distinct(l);

Pairwise_distinct_formulas(e, ⟨⟩) →;
Pairwise_distinct_formulas(⟨n1, x1, a1, b1, f1⟩, ⟨⟨n2, x2, a2, b2, f2⟩⟩.l) →
  Pairwise_distinct_formulas(⟨n1, x1, a1, b1, f1⟩, l),
  {f1 ≠ f2};

Pathway_template(S, 0, ⟨⟩, ⟨⟩, u) →;

Pathway_template(S, r, ⟨⟨r1, r2, p1, p2⟩⟩.l, ⟨⟨r1, x1, a1, b1, f1⟩,
⟨r2, x2, a2, b2, f2⟩, ⟨p1, x3, a3, b3, f3⟩, ⟨p2, x4, a4, b4, f4⟩⟩.v, u) →
  Step_template(⟨r1, r2, p1, p2⟩, S, u)
  Attached_equation_system(⟨x1, x2, x3, x4⟩)
  Balanced_step(⟨f1, f2, f3, f4⟩)
  Attached_clause_system(⟨a1, a2, a3, a4⟩, ⟨b1, b2, b3, b4⟩)
  Pathway_template(S, r−1, l, v, u);

Step_template(⟨r₁, r₂, p₁, p₂⟩, S, u) →,
  available(r₁, u)
  available(r₂, u),
  {
  0 ≤ r₁ ≤ S,
  1 ≤ r₂ ≤ S,
  0 ≤ p₁ ≤ S,
  1 ≤ p₂ ≤ S,
  /* next, prohibit R + R → P + P */
  (r₁ + r₂) + (p₁ + p₂) * 1000 ≠ 2r₂ + 2p₂ * 1000,
  r₁ ≠ p₁, r₁ ≠ p₂,
  r₂ ≠ p₁, r₂ ≠ p₂,  /* reactants and products are distinct */
  r₁ ≤ r₂, p₁ ≤ p₂  /* ordering on the identifiers */
  };
```

$available(e,l) \rightarrow freeze(e, member(e,l));$

$Attached\_equation\_system(\langle x\_r1, x\_r2, x\_p1, x\_p2\rangle) \rightarrow,$
$\{x\_r1 + x\_r2 = x\_p1 + x\_p2\};$

$Balanced\_step(\langle\langle\rangle, \langle\rangle, \langle\rangle, \langle\rangle\rangle) \rightarrow;$
$Balanced\_step(\langle\langle a\rangle.f\_r1, \langle b\rangle.f\_r2, \langle c\rangle.f\_p1, \langle d\rangle.f\_p2\rangle) \rightarrow$
$Balanced\_step(\langle f\_r1, f\_r2, f\_p1, f\_p2\rangle),$
$freeze(a, integer(a))\ freeze(b, integer(b))$
$freeze(c, integer(c))\ freeze(d, integer(d))$
$\{a + b = c + d, a \geq 0, b \geq 0, c \geq 0, d \geq 0\};$

$Attached\_clause\_system(\langle a\_r1, a\_r2, a\_p1, a\_p2\rangle, \langle b\_r1, b\_r2, b\_p1, b\_p2\rangle) \rightarrow,$
$\{a\_r1 \wedge a\_r2 \Rightarrow a\_p1, \quad a\_r1 \wedge a\_r2 \Rightarrow a\_p2,$
$b\_r1 \wedge b\_r2 \Rightarrow b\_p1, \quad b\_r1 \wedge b\_r2 \Rightarrow b\_p2\};$

$All\_distinct\_steps(\langle\rangle) \rightarrow;$
$All\_distinct\_steps(\langle\langle r1, r2, p1, p2\rangle\rangle.l) \rightarrow$
$Pairwise\_distinct\_steps(\langle r1, r2, p1, p2\rangle, l)$
$All\_distinct\_steps(l);$

$Pairwise\_distinct\_steps(e, \langle\rangle) \rightarrow;$
$Pairwise\_distinct\_steps(\langle r1, r2, p1, p2\rangle, \langle\langle r3, r4, p3, p4\rangle\rangle.l) \rightarrow$
$Pairwise\_distinct\_steps(\langle r1, r2, p1, p2\rangle, l),$
$\{\langle r1, r2, p1, p2\rangle \neq \langle r3, r4, p3, p4\rangle, \langle r1, r2, p1, p2\rangle \neq \langle p3, p4, r3, r4\rangle\};$

$Need\_both\_reagents(\langle\langle 1, x1, a1, b1, f1\rangle.\langle 2, x2, a2, b2, f2\rangle.$
$\langle 3, x3, a3, b3, f3\rangle\rangle.l) \rightarrow,$
$\{a1 = 1', a3 = 0', b2 = 1', b3 = 0'\};$

$Enumerate\_the\_species(v, p, \langle 0, 1, 2\rangle.u) \rightarrow$
$Instantiate\_species(v, p, u);$

$Instantiate\_species(\langle\rangle, p, k) \rightarrow;$
$Instantiate\_species(\langle\langle n, x, a, b, f\rangle\rangle.v, p, u) \rightarrow$
$integer(n)$
$belong\_to(\langle n, x, a, b, f\rangle, p)$
$eq(u, \langle n\rangle.k)$
$Instantiate\_species(v, p, k);$

$belong\_to(\langle 0, 0, 1', 1', f\rangle, l) \rightarrow$
$coefficients\_all\_zero(f);$

$belong\_to(\langle n, x, a, b, f\rangle, \langle\langle n, x, a, b, f\rangle\rangle.l) \rightarrow,$
$\{n \neq 0,\ x \geq 1\};$

$belong\_to(\langle n, x, a, b, f\rangle, \langle\langle n', x', a', b', f'\rangle\rangle.l) \rightarrow$
$belong\_to(\langle n, x, a, b, f\rangle, l),$
$\{n \neq 0, n \neq n'\};$

$coefficients\_all\_zero(\langle\rangle) \rightarrow;$
$coefficients\_all\_zero(\langle 0\rangle.l) \rightarrow$
$coefficients\_all\_zero(l);$

Concurrency

Concurrent Logic Programming: Asynchronism and Language Comparison [1]

Frank S. de Boer
Technische Universiteit Eindhoven,
P.O. Box 513, 5600 MB Eindhoven, The Netherlands
wsinfdb@win.tue.nl

Catuscia Palamidessi
Dipartimento di Informatica,
Università di Pisa, Corso Italia 40, 56125 Pisa, Italy
katuscia@dipisa.unipi.di.it

Abstract

The first contribution of this paper is to show that the nature of the communication mechanism of concurrent logic languages is essentially different from imperative concurrent languages. We prove that it is possible to model compositionally the successful, failing and suspending computations by means of sequences of input-output substitutions. This is to be contrasted with the compositionality in languages like CCS and TCSP, which requires less abstract (i.e. more complicated) structures, like trees and failure sets. The simple model we develop is based on a transition system containing a rule that does not exists in CCS, reflecting the asynchronous communication of bindings between AND-processes. Our approach is therefore basically different from previous ones, in which the compositional semantics for Concurrent Logic Languages is obtained by applying the standard techniques (failure sets, bisimulation etc.) for imperative languages.

The second contribution regards the comparison of Concurrent Logic Languages We start from the basic definition of embeddability given by Shapiro. This definition is too weak, since it is satisfied by any pair of Turing-equivalent languages. We show that this is not the case anymore if we additionally require the "separate compilation" of (AND-parallel) processes, and the preservation of the termination modes. In particular we prove, by means of the simple model above introduced, that Flat CP cannot be embedded in Flat GHC. Since Flat GHC is obviously Turing-equivalent, this result can be regarded as a proof that the definition of Shapiro (with the additional restrictions we propose) is more refined than the notion of language simulation in the classical computability theory.

1 Introduction

Compositionality is usually considered one of the most desiderable characteristics of a formal semantics, since it provides a foundation of program verification and modular design. The difficulty in obtaining this property depends upon the *operators* for composing programs, the behaviour we want

[1]Part of this work is supported by the ESPRIT BRA project "Integration".

to describe (*observables*), and the degree of ***abstractness*** we want to reach. Abstractness is related to the simplicity of the elements of the semantic domain, and to the ability to make no useless distinctions among programs. A compositional model is called *fully abstract* (with respect to some operators and observables) if it identifies programs that behave in the same way under all the possible contexts. In other words, it is the *most abstract* among the compositional (and correct) models.

In the field of logic languages there are basically two operators for composing programs: the conjunction of goals and the union of clauses. The observables are usually related to the finite result: computed answer substitutions and *termination modes* (success or failure). In [12], [13], Gaifman and Shapiro study the possible combinations of these parameters and present various fully abstract models for the pure Horn Clause Logic (HCL). Most of the previous models for HCL were compositional only with respect to the first operation, for instance the declarative models of [27] and [9], and the denotational ones of [6]. All of them were based on simple structures like sets of atoms or substitutions.

For Concurrent Logic Languages compositionality has been studied mainly with respect to the conjunction of goals, whilst union of clauses has been considered only in simple cases (union of *disjoint* programs [14], and union of *neatly intersecting* [2] programs [11]). This is rather natural since in a concurrent framework the main operation is the parallel composition of processes. In the following, we will consider only this operation. On the other hand, the class of observables has to be enriched by *suspension* (or *deadlock*).

In Concurrent Logic Languages, even when the observables are restricted to the successful cases, compositionality requires structures more complicated than the ones for HCL. It can be shown that (at least) sequences of input-output substitutions (i.e. substitutions labeled by input/output annotations) are necessary [22], [4], [5]. When also failure and suspension come into the picture, the general feeling is that the semantics structures must be further enriched. This is probably due to the influence of the classic results in the theory of concurrency. For languages like CCS [21] and TCSP [2], indeed, it has been shown that sequences are not sufficient (for modeling the deadlock behaviour). The following is a classical counterexample

Example 1.1 *Let* $p_1 ::= a(b+c)$ *and* $p_2 ::= ab + ac$*. The symbols* a, b, c *are actions,* ab *means that* a *is followed by* b *(sequential composition) and* $+$ *is the nondeterministic choice. The processes* p_1 *and* p_2 *give rise to the same set of sequences* $\{ab, ac\}$*, whilst they behave differently when they interact with the process* $p ::= \bar{a}\bar{b}$*, where* $\bar{a}$ *denotes the complement of the action* a*. Indeed, as in CCS parallel processes synchronize on the complementary actions (communications), we have that* p_1 *will always terminate whilst* p_2 *can deadlock (by choosing the branch* ac*).*

[2]Two programs P and P' are neatly intersecting if each predicate that occur in both programs is defined by the same clauses in P and P'.

In general, a compositional semantics can be obtained by using tree-like structures. On the other hand, trees encode often redundant branching information. In order to abstract from it, different approaches have been proposed. The most well known consist of defining an appropriate equivalence relation on trees (see, for instance, bisimulation [21]), and of grouping the *branching information* in *failure sets* [2]. In general, failure set semantics is more abstract than bisimulation and it is proved to be fully abstract in the case of TCSP.

Until now, with respect to compositionality, Concurrent Logic Languages have been regarded just as a particular case of the the classic paradigms. Therefore, the problem has been approached by applying the standard methods. De Bakker and Kok ([3], [17]) and De Boer et al. ([4], [5]) use trees labeled with functions on substitutions. More simple tree-like structures, labeled by constraints, are used by Gabbrielli and Levi ([10]) and by Saraswat and Rinard ([24]) (in the second one, the authors also define an equivalence relation on trees, based on bisimulation). In [14] and in [11] the authors approach the problem of full abstractness by refining the failure set semantics of TCSP.

One of the results of this paper is to show that compositionality in Concurrent Logic Languages doesn't require those complicated structures: sequences of input-output substitutions are sufficient! This is due to the different nature of the communication mechanism. Let's illustrate why.

In Logic Languages communication is based on *production* and *consumption* of bindings (substitutions) on shared variables. We can translate CCS processes by interpreting the action a as the production of a binding on a variable x_a and the action $\bar{a}$ as the consumption of this binding. The main difference is that the behaviour of complementary actions is not symmetrical as it is in CCS and in TCSP. Indeed, the production of a binding can always proceed, whilst the consumption has to wait. In other terms, the communication mechanism of concurrent logic languages is intrinsically *asynchronous*. The following example shows that this leads to an essentially different deadlock behaviour [3].

Example 1.2 *Let* $p_1 ::= \bar{a}\bar{b}+\bar{a}\bar{c}+\bar{a}\bar{d}$ *and* $p_2 ::= \bar{a}\bar{b}+\bar{a}(\bar{c}+\bar{d})$. *The failure set semantics distinguishes these two processes. Indeed, in case of synchronous communication, they behave differently under the context* $p ::= a(b+c)$. *The process* p_1 *can deadlock, by choosing the third branch, whilst* p_2 *cannot. In the case of asynchronous communication however, both processes have the same deadlock behaviour. The process* p_2 *can now deadlock by choosing the second branch, because* p *can independently decide to produce* b *(after* a*). In the formalism of concurrent logic languages, this example can be translated*

[3]The term *deadlock* is used here with its classical meaning in the theory of concurrency. In concurrent logic programming, this kind of *deadlock* can correspond both to *failure* or to *suspension* (whilst, in the current terminology, it is associated only to *suspension*). In example 1.2 it correspond to *suspension*.

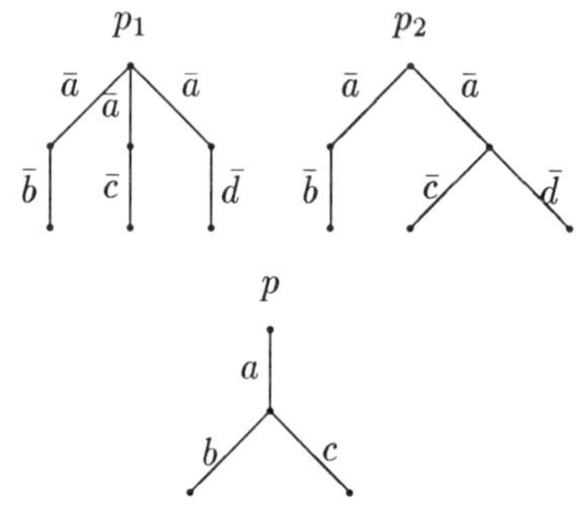

Figure 1: In logic programming p_1 and p_2 cannot be distinguished by p.

as follows (we use here the syntax of [11]. ask($t = u$) represents the consumption of a substitution satisfying the equation $t = u$, whilst tell($t = u$) represents the production of the most general substitution satisfying $t = u$, and | is the commit operator). Figure 1 illustrates this example.

$$\begin{array}{l} \{\ p_1(x_a, x_b, x_c, x_d) : -ask(x_a = a) \mid ask(x_b = b) \\ \quad p_1(x_a, x_b, x_c, x_d) : -ask(x_a = a) \mid ask(x_c = c) \\ \quad p_1(x_a, x_b, x_c, x_d) : -ask(x_a = a) \mid ask(x_d = d)\ \ \} \end{array}$$

$$\begin{array}{l} \{\ p_2(x_a, x_b, x_c, x_d) : -ask(x_a = a) \mid ask(x_b = b) \\ \quad p_2(x_a, x_b, x_c, x_d) : -ask(x_a = a) \mid p_3(x_c, x_d) \\ \quad p_3(x_c, x_d) : -ask(x_c = c) \mid \\ \quad p_3(x_c, x_d) : -ask(x_d = d) \mid \qquad\qquad\qquad \} \end{array}$$

$$\begin{array}{l} \{\ p(x_a, x_b, x_c, x_d) : -tell(x_a = a) \mid p'(x_b, x_c) \\ \quad p'(x_b, x_c) : -tell(x_b = b) \mid \\ \quad p'(x_b, x_c) : -tell(x_c = c) \mid \qquad\qquad \} \end{array}$$

This example indicates that in the asynchronous case the failure set semantics (at least as it is defined in [2]) contains redundant information. The essence of this redundancy relies in the following observation:

Example 1.3 *In the asynchronous case, $p_1 ::= a(b + c)$ is equivalent to $p_2 ::= ab + ac$ under every context. This is due to the fact that the choice present in p_1 does not depend upon the environment. After the production of a, p_1 can proceed to produce either b or c in the same way as p_2.*

This example may induce to believe that simple sequences of bindings are sufficient for obtaining compositionality. However this is not true in general, because of the different behaviour of the complementary (consuming) case. Consider the following example:

Example 1.4 *The process* $p_1 ::= \bar{a}(\bar{b}+\bar{c})$ *is not equivalent to* $p_2 ::= \bar{a}\bar{b}+\bar{a}\bar{c}$. *They are distinguished by the context* $p := ab$ *(*p_2 *can deadlock whilst* p_1 *cannot). This is due to the fact that the choice present in* p_1 *does depend upon the environment. This dependency is, however, of a different nature from the synchronous case. Here it is related only to the past behaviour of the environment, i.e. to the bindings that have already been produced.*

This last remark indicates a possible way to solve the problem. Given a sequence of substitutions representing the computation of a process with respect to an arbitrary environment, we add the information about who is the producer of each substitution (the process or its environment). From this information we can directly retrieve the past behaviour of the environment, upon which the present behaviour of the process completely depends.

We will show that we can describe compositionally the behaviour of a process by means of a Plotkin-like transition system, labeled by input-output substitutions. The behaviour of the possible environments are modeled by transitions labeled with input substitutions. This kind of transition step does not occur in the usual transition system for CCS, and it allows here to obtain directly a compositional operational semantics based on (sets of) sequences. These sequences are essentially different from the *scenarios* of [22], where input substitutions correspond to assumptions about the environment which are necessary for the process to proceed. As a consequence, compositionality is there obtained only for the success set. The input-output sequences we use are similar to the ones introduced in [14] as one component of the domain of the denotational semantics, the other ingredient being the suspension set. Because of what is stated above, this first component would have already been sufficient to define there a compositional (hence denotational) semantics.

One may believe that the model we develop, being so simple, has good chances to be fully abstract. This is not the case. The main reason (in languages with monotonic guards) is that sequences contain informations about the particular order of production of bindings, order that cannot be sensed by monotonic contexts. In [7] we show how to abstract from this redundancy, so to obtain a fully abstract model. In the same paper we also show that sequences contain already redundant information in the non-monotonic case, and that therefore its fully abstract model, whenever it exists, must be something in between (i.e. at an intermediate abstraction level of) the model we present here and the refined version we define there.

For generality reasons we consider a class of Flat Concurrent Logic Languages. This class will be denoted by HC($\mathcal{A},\mathcal{T}$), where HC stands for Horn Clauses and $\mathcal{A},\mathcal{T}$ are parameters which denote the set of primitives that can occur in the guards. We consider the following possibilities: $\mathcal{A} = \emptyset$ or $\mathcal{A} = Ask$, where

$$Ask = \{ask(E) \mid E \textit{ is a set of equations in the Herbrand universe}\}$$

and $\mathcal{T} = \emptyset$ or $\mathcal{T} = Tell$, where

$$Tell = \{tell(E) \mid E \textit{ is a set of equations in the Herbrand universe}\}.$$

This class includes, for instance, Oc [15] (HC($\emptyset, \emptyset$)), Flat GHC [26] (HC($Ask, \emptyset$)), ccH [10] and the language of [11](HC(Ask, $Tell$)), that is a refined version of Flat CP [25]. HC($\mathcal{A}, \mathcal{T}$) can be seen as a particular instance of the cc/Herbrand framework [24]. For example, HC($Ask, \emptyset$) corresponds to Eventual Herbrand and HC(Ask, $Tell$) corresponds to atomic Herbrand. We are mainly concerned with the following instances: HC($Ask, \emptyset$) and HC(Ask, $Tell$).

The model we obtain is rather simple, therefore it is suitable to investigate the properties of the different languages of this class. In particular, we use this model to prove that Flat CP is not embeddable in Flat GHC. The first definition of embeddability, given by Shapiro [25], is the following. A language L is embeddable into a language L' if there exists a mapping $\mathcal{F}$ (compiler) from programs of L to programs of L', and a mapping $\mathcal{V}$ (decoder) from the observables Obs' of L' to the observables Obs of L such that for every program P in L we have

$$\mathcal{V}(Obs'(\mathcal{F}(P))) = Obs(P)$$

This notion however is too weak since the above relation is satisfied by any language Turing-equivalent. For instance, it is possible to define $\mathcal{F}$ and $\mathcal{V}$ in such a way to embed in a simple language like Oc any other logic language [4]. To strengthen this notion, Shapiro adds some requirements concerning the complexity of the compilation function $\mathcal{F}$ (in practice he imposes the target language to *absorb* the unification mechanism of the object language). Our approach is orthogonal to the one of Shapiro, and (we think) more close to his original definition.

We start from the idea that, in a concurrent framework, at compile time we cannot make any assumption about the code of the processes that will be present in the environment. Therefore it is reasonable to require the "separate compilation" of the (AND) parallel processes. The above relation becomes then

$$\mathcal{V}(Obs'(\mathcal{F}(C_{||})[\mathcal{F}(P)])) = Obs(C_{||}[P])$$

for every context of parallel processes $C_{||}$ in L. (Here $\mathcal{F}$ is generalized to contexts.) An other point is that the compilation must preserve the behaviour of the original process with respect to deadlock and success. In fact these notions have, in a sense, an absolute meaning in any concurrent system. Therefore we require the termination mode of the target language not to be

[4]Due to space limitations, we don't prove this statement here. The idea is to code a program P into a term $c(P)$, and to define in Oc a general program that generates all the the observables of the form $\langle\{x/c(P), y/n\}, ss\rangle$, where ss stands for the successful termination mode. Then define $\mathcal{V}$ so that $\mathcal{V}(\langle\{x/c(P), y/n\}, ss\rangle) = \langle\vartheta_n, \alpha_n\rangle \in Obs(P)$.

affected by the decoder. In other words, a failure in $\mathcal{F}(P)$ must correspond to a failure in P, a success to a success, and a suspension to a suspension.

We show that this new definition "makes sense" by proving that Flat CP is not embeddable into Flat GHC. As far as we now, this was never formally proved before (also not with respect to other definitions of embeddability, like Shapiro's second one).

In general, it is easy to prove that L is embeddable into L' by showing how to translate all the operators of L into L' (for instance, it is easy to show that Flat GHC is embeddable into Oc), but it is not clear how to prove that L is *not* embeddable into L'. In fact, in principle we should check that the equation above does not hold for all the possible translations $\mathcal{F}$. The method we use here can maybe be regarded as a first step towards the development of a general technique. Using the compositional operational model defined above, we prove that the semantics of Flat GHC programs satisfies certain closure properties that are in general not satisfied by Flat CP. These closure properties give rise to an observable distinction that cannot be hidden by the decoder, when separate compilation is required.

This paper is organized as follows. Next section recalls some basic notions about substitutions, unification, and constraints. Section 3 introduces the class HC($\mathcal{A},\mathcal{T}$) and its informal semantics. Section 4 presents the new transition system for this class of languages, from which we derive the compositional semantics based on sequences. Finally, in section 6 we present the notion of embeddability, we prove that Flat CP is not embeddable in Flat CP and we discuss the scope of this result.

Due to space restrictions, all proofs are omitted.

2 Preliminaries

In this section we briefly recall some basic notions and results about substitutions and unification. We will use (mainly) the terminology of [1], [19], [18], and [8], to which we refer for a more detailed presentation of these topics.

2.1 Substitutions

Let *Var* be a non empty set of *variables*, with typical elements $x, y, z, \ldots$. Let *Cons* be a set of *constructors*, with typical elements $a, b, c, \ldots$ (constructors with 0 arguments, or *constants*), and $f, g, h, \ldots$ (constructors with one or more arguments). We assume the presence of at least one constant.

The set *Term*, with typical elements $t, u, \ldots$, is the set of all the *terms* built on *Var* and on *Cons*. Examples of terms are $f(a), f(x), g(f(a), f(x)), \ldots$. The set of variables occurring in t is denoted by $var(t)$.

The set of *substitutions*, *Subst*, with typical elements $\vartheta, \sigma, \ldots$, consists of all the mappings ϑ from *Var* into *Term* such that the domain of ϑ, $dom(\vartheta) =$

$\{x \in Var \mid \vartheta(x) \neq x\}$, is finite. We will use the set-theoretic notation $\{x/t \mid x \in dom(\vartheta) \wedge \vartheta(x) \equiv t\}$ to represent ϑ.

The *application* $t\vartheta$ of ϑ to t is defined as the term obtained by replacing each variable x in t by $\vartheta(x)$. The set $ran(\vartheta)$ (range of ϑ) is defined as $\bigcup_{x\in dom(\vartheta)} var(\vartheta(x))$. The substitution ϑ is *ground* iff $ran(\vartheta) = \emptyset$.

The *composition* $\vartheta\vartheta'$ of ϑ and ϑ' is defined by $(\vartheta\vartheta')(x) \equiv (\vartheta(x))\vartheta'$. We recall that the composition is associative, the empty substitution ϵ is the neutral element, and, for each term t, $t(\vartheta\vartheta') \equiv (t\vartheta)\vartheta'$ holds.

The restriction $\vartheta_{|V}$ of ϑ to a set of variables V is the substitution $\vartheta_{|V}(x) = \vartheta(x)$ for $x \in V$ and $\vartheta_{|V}(x) = x$ otherwise.

2.2 Unification

An *equation* is an expression of the form $t = u$, where t and u are terms. The set of sets of equations, with typical element E, will be denoted by *Eqn*. A set of equations E is *unifiable* iff there exists ϑ such that for all $t = u$ in E, $t\vartheta \equiv u\vartheta$ holds, where $\equiv$ is the syntactic identity on terms. ϑ is then called an *unifier* of E. The set of all the unifiers of E will be denoted by $unif(E)$. The set of all the *most general unifiers* of E is given by $mgu(E) = \{\vartheta \in unif(E) \mid \forall\vartheta' \in unif(E)\ \exists\sigma.\ \vartheta\sigma = \vartheta'\}$. It is well known that all the most general unifiers of a set E are equivalent, and this explains why, in the literature, we often find the terminology "*the* mgu of E".

2.3 Constraints on the Herbrand Universe

A constraint system is essentially a system of partial information that supports the notion of consistency and entailment. The notion of *constraint* was introduced in Logic Programming by Jaffar and Lassez [16]. Maher [20] suggested the use of constraints to model logically the synchronization and communication mechanisms of concurrent logic languages. We restrict here to a particular class of constraints: the *ask* and *tell* constraints on the Herbrand universe [23]. They are of the form $ask(E)$ and $tell(E)$ respectively, where E is a set of equations. A constraint of the form $ask(E)$ or $tell(E)$ is *solved* by a substitution ϑ if $\vartheta = mgu(E)$. We use the following notations: $Ask = \{ask(E) \mid E \in Eqn\}$ and $Tell = \{tell(E) \mid E \in Eqn\}$.

3 The class HC($\mathcal{A},\mathcal{T}$). Syntax and informal operational semantics.

The (parametric) sets $\mathcal{A}$ and $\mathcal{T}$ specify the set of *primitives* used in the guards. We restrict here to the following cases: $\mathcal{A} = \emptyset$ or $\mathcal{A} = Ask$, and $\mathcal{T} = \emptyset$ or $\mathcal{T} = Tell$.

Let *Pred* be a set of *predicates*, with typical elements $p, q, r, \ldots$. The set *Atom*, with typical elements $A, B, H \ldots$, is the set of all the *atomic formulas* built on *Pred* and on *Term*, and of the primitives of the form $tell(E)$. In the following, we use the abbreviations $\bar{A}, \bar{x}$ etc. to denote conjunctions of atoms, variables etc.

A *clause* C of HC($\mathcal{A}, \mathcal{T}$) is a formula of the form $H \leftarrow g_1{:}g_2 \mid \bar{B}$, where $g_1 \in \mathcal{A}$ and $g_2 \in \mathcal{T}$. The atom H is the head, $g_1{:}g_2$ is the guard and $\bar{B}$ is the body of the clause. A *goal statement* G is a formula of the form $\leftarrow \bar{A}$. The empty goal statement is denoted by $\Box$. A HC($\mathcal{A}, \mathcal{T}$) program P is a (finite) set of clauses.

An atom A in a goal G is seen as an (AND-) process. If A is of the form $tell(E)$ then:

- if E is unifiable then A *succeeds* producing the substitution $\vartheta = mgu(E)$, and the remaining goal $G \setminus A$ is istantiated by ϑ.
- if E is not unifiable then A and the whole goal *fails*

If A is an atomic formula, its computation proceeds by looking for a candidate clause in P.

Definition 3.1 *Let A be an atomic formula and let $C \equiv H \leftarrow g_1{:}g_2 \mid \bar{B}$ be a clause in P, renamed in order to have no variables in common with A. Then the clause C*

- is candidate *if*
  1. $\exists mgu(H = A) = \vartheta$,
  2. $\vartheta_{|A} = \epsilon$ *(where $\vartheta_{|A}$ denotes $\vartheta_{|var(A)}$),*
  3. $\exists \vartheta_1$ *such that $g_1\vartheta$ is solved by ϑ_1,*
  4. $\vartheta_{1|A} = \epsilon$,
  5. $\exists \vartheta_2$ *such that $g_2\sigma$ is solved by ϑ_2, where $\sigma = \vartheta\vartheta_1$.*
- suspends *if (1) is satisfied but (2) is not satisfied, or (1), (2) and (3) are satisfied but (4) is not satisfied.*
- fails *in all the other cases.*

If there are candidate clauses, then the computation of A *commits* to one of them (i.e. no backtracking will take place), A is replaced by $\bar{B}\sigma\vartheta_2$, and the rest of the goal is instantiated by ϑ_2. If all the clauses for A fail, then A and the whole goal fail. If no clauses are candidate and at least one clause suspends, then A *suspends*. A can be *resumed* when its arguments get bound by other processes in the goal. If all the processes in the goal suspend, then the goal suspends.

4 Compositional semantics for HC($\mathcal{A}, \mathcal{T}$).

To define the meaning of a goal in terms of its subgoals, we describe the behaviour of a goal as a sequence of *interactions* with its environment. Interactions are modeled as *input/output* substitutions. An input substitution is provided by the environment, whereas an output substitution is produced by the goal itself.

Definition 4.1

- *The set of input substitutions is* $Subst_I = \{\vartheta^I \mid \vartheta \in Subst\}$.
- *The set of output substitutions is* $Subst_O = \{\vartheta^O \mid \vartheta \in Subst\}$.
- *The set of input/output substitutions, with typical element* ϑ^ℓ, *is* $Subst_{IO} = Subst_I \cup Subst_O$.

The operational semantics we define is based on a transition system T labeled on $Subst_{IO}$. The *configurations* of T are pairs consisting of a goal and an infinite set of fresh variables (representing the variables still available for the renaming mechanism). To obtain a compositional operational semantics we need a compositional renaming mechanism. We propose the following (formal) solution. Let $\mathcal{P}_i(Var)$ be the set of all the infinite sets of variables. We assume the existence of a *partitionating* function $Part : \mathcal{P}_i(Var) \to \mathcal{P}_i(Var) \times \mathcal{P}_i(Var)$ such that

$$\forall V \in \mathcal{P}_i(Var)\ [\langle V_1, V_2\rangle = Part(V) \Rightarrow (V_1 \cup V_2 \subseteq V\ \wedge\ V_1 \cap V_2 = \emptyset)]$$

In this way we can split the "available variables" among the subgoals so to avoid clash of variables among the subcomputations.

Table 1 gives the rules for T describing the "successful" computation steps. We call them *computation rules.*

Table 1: The Transition System T. Computation Rules

C1 $\langle A, V\rangle \xrightarrow{\vartheta_2^O} \langle \bar{B}\sigma\vartheta_2, W\rangle$ **if** $\exists C \in P_V\ [C \text{ is candidate }] \wedge W = V \setminus var(P_V)$

C2 $\langle tell(E), V\rangle \xrightarrow{\vartheta^O} \langle \Box, V\rangle$ **if** $\exists \vartheta = mgu(E)$

C3 $\langle A, V\rangle \xrightarrow{\vartheta^I} \langle A\vartheta, V\rangle$ **where** A is either an atomic formula or $tell(E)$

C4 $$\frac{\langle \bar{A}_1, V_1\rangle \xrightarrow{\vartheta^I} \langle \bar{B}_1, W_1\rangle \quad \langle \bar{A}_2, V_2\rangle \xrightarrow{\vartheta^\ell} \langle \bar{B}_2, W_2\rangle}{\langle \bar{A}_1, \bar{A}_2, V\rangle \xrightarrow{\vartheta^\ell} \langle \bar{B}_1, \bar{B}_2, W_1 \cup W_2\rangle}$$ **where** $\langle V_1, V_2\rangle = Part(V)$

The rule **C1** describes the normal atomic reduction step. The symbols $C, \bar{B}, \sigma$, and ϑ_2 are the ones of definition 3.1, whilst P_V denotes the program P renamed with the variables in V.

The rule **C2** describes the output of the substitution satisfying an atom of the form *tell*(E). Note that in the case of HC$(\mathcal{A}, \emptyset)$ this is the only rule that allows to produce bindings on the (shared) variables of the goal.

The rule **C3** describes the input of a substitution produced by the external environment. Note that ϑ is any substitution, namely it represents a *free assumption* on the environment. In other words, it does not depend upon what the goal needs to proceed, and wether or not it will fail after this input. This is the point in which our transition system essentially differs from the semantics described in [22] and in [11], and this is why our sequences contain information enough to achieve compositionality.

Finally, **C4** describe the transition of a goal in terms of the transitions of the subgoals. Note that this is the rule that allows to check that the input assumptions really correspond to the outputs done by the environment.

Table 2 and table 3 illustrate the rules for failure and suspension respectively. We need to introduce in our configurations the symbols *fail* and *susp*, with the obvious meaning.

Table 2: The Transition System T. Failure Rules

F1	$\langle A, V\rangle \xrightarrow{\epsilon^O} \langle fail, V\rangle$ **if** $\forall C \in P_V$ [C fails]	
F2	$\langle tell(E), V\rangle \xrightarrow{\epsilon^O} \langle fail, V\rangle$ **if** $\not\exists mgu(E)$	
F3	$\dfrac{\langle A, V\rangle \xrightarrow{\epsilon^O} \langle fail, V\rangle}{\langle A, \bar{B}, V \cup W\rangle \xrightarrow{\epsilon^O} \langle fail, V \cup W\rangle}$	**where** A is an atomic formula or *tell*(E)

Table 3: The Transition System T. Suspension Rules

S1	$\langle A, V\rangle \xrightarrow{\epsilon^O} \langle susp, V\rangle$ **if** $\exists C \in P_V$ [C suspends] $\wedge$ $\forall C \in P_V$ [C is not candidate]	
S2	$\dfrac{\langle \bar{A}_1, V_1\rangle \xrightarrow{\epsilon_1^O} \langle susp, V_1\rangle \quad \langle \bar{A}_2, V_2\rangle \xrightarrow{\epsilon_1^O} \langle susp, V_2\rangle}{\langle \bar{A}_1, \bar{A}_2, V\rangle \xrightarrow{\epsilon_1^O} \langle susp, V_1 \cup V_2\rangle}$	**where** $\langle V_1, V_2\rangle = Part(V)$

The operational semantics $\mathcal{O}$ based on this transition system T delivers sets of sequences s of input/output substitutions, ended by a *termination mode* or by $\perp$. We denote the set of these sequences as $Seq = Subst_{IO}{}^*.\{ss, ff, dd, \perp\}$. The set $Subst_{IO}{}^*$, with typical element c, denotes the sequences of substitutions generated during the computation, whilst the symbols ss, ff, and dd represent the possible ways in which a process can terminate: *success*, *failure* and *suspension* (or *deadlock*) respectively. The symbol $\perp$ stands for *unfinished.* It is introduced in order to associate a non empty semantics to infinite processes. In fact, even if we are interested only in finite computations, this is necessary for modelling failure compositionally. The symbol α will denote an element ranging over the set $\{ss, ff, dd, \perp\}$.

Definition 4.2 (Operational Semantics) *The operational semantics* $\mathcal{O}$: $Goal \rightarrow [\mathcal{P}_i(Var) \rightarrow Seq]$ *is given by*

$$\begin{array}{lcl} \mathcal{O}[\![\Box]\!](V) & = & \{ss, \perp\} \\ \mathcal{O}[\![fail]\!](V) & = & \{ff, \perp\} \\ \mathcal{O}[\![susp]\!](V) & = & \{dd, \perp\} \\ \mathcal{O}[\![\bar{A}]\!](V) & = & \{\vartheta^\ell.\mathcal{O}[\![\bar{B}]\!](W) \mid \langle \bar{A}, V\rangle \xrightarrow{\vartheta^\ell} \langle \bar{B}, W\rangle\} \cup \{\perp\} \end{array}$$

In the following, when $V = Var \setminus var(A)$, we will write simply $\mathcal{O}[\![\bar{A}]\!]$ instead of $\mathcal{O}[\![\bar{A}]\!](V)$.

Note that definition 4.2 is recursive. We consider $\mathcal{O}$ as the least fixpoint of the transformation (continuous with respect to set inclusion) associated with its defining equations.

From this operational semantics we obtain our observation criterium as follows:

Definition 4.3 (Observables) *We define* $Obs(\bar{A}) = Result_{\bar{A}}(\mathcal{O}[\![\bar{A}]\!])$, *where* $Result_{\bar{A}}(S) = \{\langle \vartheta_{c|\bar{A}}, \alpha\rangle \mid c.\alpha \in S \wedge c \in Subst_O \wedge \alpha \in \{ss, ff, dd\}\}$, *and* ϑ_c *is the substitution obtained by composing all the elements of* c*:* $\vartheta_\lambda = \epsilon$ *and* $\vartheta_{\sigma.c} = \sigma\vartheta_c$.

Note that in this definition we pick up the sequences entirely composed by output substitutions. This amounts to require that each substitution we observe has been really produced. It is easy to see that this notion of observables, based on T, corresponds to the set of *finite results* (computed answer substitution, termination mode) that can be derived by the classical operational semantics described in section 3.

To show the compositionality of the operational semantics we define the *parallel composition* $\|$. This operator, first introduced in [14], allows to combine sequences of input/output substitutions that are equal at each point, apart from the labels, so modeling the interaction of a process with its environment. It corresponds to apply iteratively the rule **C4** of the transition system T.

Definition 4.4 (Parallel composition operator) *The partial operator* $\|$: $Seq \times Seq \rightarrow Seq$ *is defined by* $s_1 \parallel s_2 = s_2 \parallel s_1$, $\vartheta^I.s_1 \parallel \vartheta^\ell.s_2 = \vartheta^\ell.(s_1 \parallel s_2)$, $s \parallel ss = s$, $\alpha \parallel ff = ff$, $dd \parallel dd = dd$, *and* $\bot \| \bot = \bot$.

The natural extension of $\|$ *on sets will be still denoted by* $\|$.

The following result shows the compositionality of our operational semantics with respect to goal conjunction. The compositionality with respect to the union of disjoint programs (or neatly intersecting programs) is obviously given by the set union.

Theorem 4.5 (Compositionality of $\mathcal{O}$)

$$\mathcal{O}[\![\bar{A}_1, \bar{A}_1]\!](V) = \mathcal{O}[\![\bar{A}_1]\!](V_1) \parallel \mathcal{O}[\![\bar{A}_1]\!](V_2), \quad where\ \langle V_1, V_2\rangle = Part(V).$$

Note that $\mathcal{O}$ is also a *denotational semantics*, since it is compositional and it is defined as the fixpoint of an (higher order) operator.

Example 4.6 *Consider the following program*

$p(x,y) : -ask(x = a){:}tell(y = b) \mid .$

We have

$$\begin{array}{llll}\mathcal{O}[\![p(x,y)]\!] = \{ & \{x/a\}^I.\{y/b\}^O.ss\ , & \{x/a, y/b\}^I\epsilon^O.ss\ , & \dots \\ & \{x/b\}^I\epsilon^O.ff\ , & \{x/a, y/a\}^I\epsilon^O.ff\ , & \dots \\ & \epsilon^O.dd\ , & \{y/b\}^I\epsilon^O.dd\ , & \dots \ \}\end{array}$$

$$Obs(p(x,y)) = \{\langle\epsilon, dd\rangle\}.$$

Consider now the program

$q(x,y) : -tell(x = a) \mid r(y).$ $r(y) : -ask(y = b) \mid .$

We have

$$\begin{array}{llll}\mathcal{O}[\![q(x,y)]\!] = \{ & \{x/a\}^O.\{y/b\}^I.ss\ , & \{x/a, y/b\}^I.\epsilon^O.ss\ , & \dots \\ & \{x/b\}^I.\epsilon^O.ff\ , & \{x/a, y/a\}^I.\epsilon^O.ff\ , & \dots \\ & \{x/a\}^O.dd\ , & \{x/a\}^I.\epsilon^O.dd\ , & \dots \ \}\end{array}$$

$$Obs(q(x,y)) = \{\langle\{x/a\}, dd\rangle\}$$

We consider now the union of the two programs and the goal $p(x,y),q(x,y)$. *We get*

$$\begin{array}{lll}\mathcal{O}[\![p(x,y), q(x,y)]\!] & = & \mathcal{O}[\![p(x,y)]\!] \parallel \mathcal{O}[\![q(x,y)]\!] \\ & = & \{\ \{x/a\}^O.\{y/b\}^O.ss\ ,\quad \{x/a, y/b\}^I.\epsilon^O.ss\ ,\ \dots \\ & & \quad \{x/b\}^I\epsilon^O.ff\ ,\quad \{x/a, y/a\}^I.\epsilon^O.ff\ ,\ \dots\ \}\end{array}$$

$$Obs(p(x,y), q(x,y)) = \{\langle\{x/a, y/b\}, ss\rangle\}.$$

The following example, corresponding to example 1.4 in the introduction, shows the compositionality of our semantics with respect to the *failures*. If we apply to it the translation of example 1.2, we get also an example showing the compositionality for the *suspensions*.

Example 4.7 *Consider the two programs*

$$\begin{array}{|l|}\hline p_1(x,y) :- ask(x=a) \mid q_1(y). \\ q_1(y) :- ask(y=b) \mid . \\ q_1(y) :- ask(y=c) \mid . \\ \hline \end{array}$$

$$\begin{array}{|l|}\hline p_2(x,y) :- ask(x=a) \mid q_2(y). \\ p_2(x,y) :- ask(x=a) \mid r_2(y). \\ q_2(y) :- ask(y=b) \mid . \\ r_2(y) :- ask(y=c) \mid . \\ \hline \end{array}$$

We have:

$$\mathcal{O}[\![p_1(x,y)]\!] = \{\ \{x/a\}^I.\{y/b\}^I.ss\ ,\quad \{x/a\}^I.\{y/c\}^I.ss\ ,\quad \ldots\ \}$$

$$\begin{aligned}\mathcal{O}[\![p_2(x,y)]\!] = \{\ &\{x/a\}^I.\{y/b\}^I.ss\ ,\quad \{x/a\}^I.\{y/c\}^I.ss\ ,\quad \ldots \\ &\{x/a\}^I.\{y/b\}^I.ff\ ,\quad \{x/a\}^I.\{y/c\}^I.ff\ ,\quad \ldots\ \}\end{aligned}$$

Consider now the program

$$\begin{array}{|l|}\hline p(x,y) :- tell(x=a) \mid tell(y=b). \\ \hline \end{array}$$

we have

$$\mathcal{O}[\![p(x,y)]\!] = \{\ \{x/a\}^O.\{y/b\}^O.ss\ ,\quad \ldots\ \}$$

Therefore

$$\begin{aligned}\mathcal{O}[\![p(x,y), p_1(x,y)]\!] &= \mathcal{O}[\![p(x,y)]\!] \parallel \mathcal{O}[\![p_1(x,y)]\!] \\ &= \{\ \{x/a\}^O.\{y/b\}^O.ss\ ,\quad \ldots\ \}\end{aligned}$$

whilst

$$\begin{aligned}\mathcal{O}[\![p(x,y), p_2(x,y)]\!] &= \mathcal{O}[\![p(x,y)]\!] \parallel \mathcal{O}[\![p_2(x,y)]\!] \\ &= \{\ \{x/a\}^O.\{y/b\}^O.ss\ ,\quad \ldots \\ &\qquad \{x/a\}^O.\{y/b\}^O.ff\ ,\quad \ldots\ \}\end{aligned}$$

5 On the notion of embeddability

In this section we discuss the notion of *embeddability* proposed by Shapiro in [25]. We define the notion of *uniform embeddability* by requiring the compositionality of the compilation function with respect to parallel processes, and the preservation of the termination mode. Finally, we prove that Flat CP is not uniformly embeddable into Flat GHC.

We start with recalling the definition of Shapiro. For simplicity, we assume each program P to be associated to a goal G_P (*initialized program*,[14]), *IProg* will denote the set of initialized programs.

Definition 5.1 (Embeddability (Shapiro, [25])) *Let L, L' be two languages and let $Obs : IProg(L) \rightarrow O$, $Obs' : IProg(L') \rightarrow O'$ be their* observation criteria. *The language L is* embeddable *in L' iff there exists a* compiler *from initialized programs of L to initialized programs of L', (i.e. a mapping $\mathcal{F} : IProg(L) \rightarrow IProg(L')$), and a decoder from observables of L' to observables in L (i.e. a mapping $\mathcal{V} : O' \rightarrow O$) such that, for every $G_P \in IProg(L)$, $\mathcal{V}(Obs'(\mathcal{F}(G_P))) = Obs(G_P)$*

As observed in the introduction, this definition is "too weak", in the sense that it is satisfied by any pair of Turing-equivalent languages, and any "reasonable" logic language obviously is Turing-equivalent.

In the same paper, Shapiro has given a stronger definition of embeddability by requiring the decoder $\mathcal{V}$ to be *natural*:

$$\text{for all atoms } A \text{ in } P,\ \mathcal{V}(Obs'(\mathcal{F}(A))) = Obs'(\mathcal{F}(A))$$

i.e., $\mathcal{V}$, restricted to observables of atoms corresponding to the original atoms of P, is the identity. This prevents the simulation of the variables of the source language with constants of the target language. In other terms the embedding must *absorb* the basic execution mechanism of logic languages, the unification.

This approach suggests a method of comparison between logic languages based on the complexity of the compilation function. This is probably the most interesting parameter to be considered in practical cases, when choosing a "good language" in which to "reuse" the software available in other languages.

However, we think that definition 5.1 suggests also other considerations. Our approach, orthogonal to the one of Shapiro, starts from the point of view that the notion of *observables* (that is a parameter in definition 5.1) can be more powerful than the usual *input-output functionality* associated to programs in classical sequential languages. In particular, the definition of observables given in previous section (to which we will refer from now on), involves notions like failure and suspension that reflect the *interaction capabilities* of a process. In a concurrent framework it is necessary to consider, when compiling a process, how this process is able to interact with its environment. The interactions capabilities must be preserved in the compilation. So, for instance, we must take into account the *deadlock behaviour*. The compilation "is not good" if the process in the target language gives rise to more deadlock possibilities than the one in the source language. Hence it is reasonable to assign to these notions an absolute meaning, by requiring the decoder to preserve the termination modes. Namely, to map failure into failure, suspension into suspension, and success into success.

Definition 5.2 *A decoder $\mathcal{V}$ is* termination invariant *if it is the identity on the second component of the observation pairs, i.e.*

$$\forall\vartheta\ \forall\alpha\ \exists\sigma\ [\mathcal{V}(\langle\vartheta,\alpha\rangle) = \langle\sigma,\alpha\rangle]$$

As a second point, we think that in a concurrent framework it is reasonable to require the "separate compilation" of each component of a given system. To formalize this idea, we introduce the following (general) definition.

Definition 5.3 *A compiler $\mathcal{F} : Prog(L) \rightarrow Prog(L')$ is* compositional *with respect to an n-ary operator op of L iff there exists an n-ary operator op′ in L′ such that for all the constructs $P_1, \ldots P_n$ in L:*

$$\mathcal{F}(op(P_1, \ldots P_n)) = op'(\mathcal{F}(P_1), \ldots \mathcal{F}(P_n))$$

A *op*-context $C_{op}[\,]$ (in the language L) is an object of the form

1. $[\,]$, *the empty context*, or
2. $op(P_1, \ldots P_{i-1}, [\,], P_{i+1}, \ldots P_n)$

Given a context $C_{op}[\,]$, the construct $C_{op}[P]$ is defined, as usual, by "filling the hole" of $C_{op}[\,]$ with P.

If $\mathcal{F}$ is compositional then we can extend $\mathcal{F}$ on *op*-contexts as follows:

1. $\mathcal{F}([\,]) = [\,]$, *the empty context* in L', or
2. $\mathcal{F}(op(P_1, \ldots P_{i-1}, [\,], P_{i+1}, \ldots P_n)) =$
   $op'(\mathcal{F}(P_1), \ldots \mathcal{F}(P_{i-1}), [\,], \mathcal{F}(P_{i+1}), \ldots \mathcal{F}(P_n))$

We indicate by $\mathcal{F}(C_{op}[\,])[\,]$ the op'-context in L' obtained by applying $\mathcal{F}$ to $C_{op}[\,]$. This extension satisfies the following property

Proposition 5.4 *If $\mathcal{F}$ is compositional then for every context $C_{op}[\,]$, and for every construct P in L, $\mathcal{F}(C_{op}[P]) = \mathcal{F}(C_{op}[\,])[\mathcal{F}(P)]$ holds.*

As explained before, we will require the compositionality of the compiler with respect to the parallelism operator. In terms of logic languages, this amounts to require the compositionality of $\mathcal{F}$ with respect to goal conjunction (compositionality with respect to conjunction in the body is not necessary) The construct $G_P, G'_{P'}$ corresponds to $(G, G')_{P \cup P'}$ if P, P' are disjoint or neatly intersecting, (otherwise we just rename G' and P').

To prove that Flat CP is not embeddable in Flat GHC we need still an other assumption about $\mathcal{V}$, that is the following:

Definition 5.5 *The decoder $\mathcal{V}$ is* compatibility invariant *iff* $\forall\vartheta\,\forall\vartheta'$: *if* $\mathcal{V}(\langle\vartheta,\alpha\rangle) = \langle\sigma,\alpha\rangle, \mathcal{V}(\langle\vartheta',\alpha\rangle) = \langle\sigma',\alpha\rangle$, *and* σ,σ' *are incompatible, (i.e.* $\nexists mgu(\mathcal{E}(\sigma),\mathcal{E}(\sigma'))$*), then* ϑ,ϑ' *are incompatible.* $\mathcal{E}(\vartheta)$ *is the equation set associated to a substitution, i.e.* $\{x = \vartheta(x) \mid x \in dom(\vartheta)\}$.

We think that this condition derives as a consequence from the other assumptions about $\mathcal{V}$ and $\mathcal{F}$, however wen haven't been able yet to prove it. Therefore we state it as a conjecture

Conjecture 5.6 *If $\mathcal{F}$ is compositional, $\mathcal{V}$ is termination invariant, and L is embeddable in L', then $\mathcal{V}$ is compatibility invariant.*

Note, however, that the condition of Shapiro on $\mathcal{V}$ (*naturality*) implies termination invariance and compatibility invariance.

Definition 5.7 (Uniform embeddability) *A language L is* uniformly embeddable *in L' iff there exists a AND-compositional compiler $\mathcal{F}$, and a decoder $\mathcal{V}$, termination invariant and compatibility invariant, such that* $\forall G_P \in IProg(L)[\mathcal{V}(Obs'(\mathcal{F}(G_P)) = Obs(G_P)]$

If L and L' are both logic languages, then we consider the observables defined in previous sections. The condition becomes $\mathcal{V}(Obs(\mathcal{F}(G_P)) = Obs(G_P)$ where the range of *Obs* is the set of pairs ⟨computed answer substitution, termination mode⟩.

5.1 Non-embeddability of Flat Cp in Flat GHC.

The key of our proof relies on the following closure property, satisfied by HC(*Ask*, ∅) (Flat GHC) and not by HC(*Ask*, *Tell*) (Flat CP). This property forces a particular observable behaviour, namely it causes more failure cases.

Proposition 5.8 *Let G be a goal in HC(Ask, ∅). Then*

$$[c.\vartheta^{O}.s \in \mathcal{O}(G) \wedge \nexists mgu(\mathcal{E}(\vartheta) \cup \mathcal{E}(\vartheta'))] \Rightarrow [c.\vartheta'^{I}.ff \in \mathcal{O}(G)]$$

Proposition 5.9 *If a language L is* uniformly embeddable *in L' via $\mathcal{F}$ and $\mathcal{V}$, then for every $G_P \in IProg(L)$ and for every AND-parallel context $C_{||}[\,]$,* $\mathcal{V}(Obs(\mathcal{F}(C_{||}[\,])[\mathcal{F}(G_P)])) = Obs(C_{||}[G_P])$ *holds.*

Theorem 5.10 *HC(Ask, Tell) cannot be uniformly embedded in HC(Ask, ∅).*

5.2 Interpretation of the result.

One consequence of theorem 5.10 is that Flat CP is strictly more expressive than Flat GHC: the so-called atomic unification (tell constraints in the guard) cannot be simulated by languages that have tell constraints only in the body (at least, if we want to preserve the same interaction capabilities).

An other consequence is that, even if definition 5.1 is satisfied by any pair of Turing-equivalent languages this is obviously not the case for definition 5.7. It is interesting to understand why. Let's recall the definition of "simulation" in classical sequential languages:

Definition 5.11 *A language L can be simulated by L' iff there exists an encoder $\mathcal{C}$, from the inputs of L to the inputs of L', a compiler $\mathcal{F}$ from the programs of L to the programs of L', and a decoder $\mathcal{D}$ from the outputs of L' to the outputs of L such that, for every program P in L and for every input i: $\mathcal{D}(\mathcal{F}(P)(\mathcal{C}(i))) = P(i)$.*

There are various reasons why definition 5.7 is stronger then definition 5.11:

- The notion of observables is more powerful than the notion of input-output behaviour. Indeed, the possibility to observe also failure and suspension (beside success) gives more information about the internal structure of the program [5]. In other words, whilst the success set is completely characterized by the minimal model (that is related to the extensional definition of a function) failure and suspension require to consider also other models. A program containing a loop can have the same minimal model (and the same success set) of a program with no loops, but the other models (and their failure sets) are different.
- The notion of indeterminism in concurrent languages is different from the notion of nondeterminism in sequential languages. The nondeterministic Turing machines are equivalent to the deterministic ones, in the sense that they compute the same class of functions. But only the successful cases are take into account. On the other side, in concurrency, deadlock cases are relevant. Therefore it is reasonable to require deadlock to be decoded as deadlock, that is one of the strenghtening factors.
- The requirement of compositionality of $\mathcal{F}$ with respect to parallel processes is an other strengthening factor. On the other side, it seems quite reasonable to require the "separate compilation" of processes. At compilation time, we cannot make assumptions about the code of the other processes that will be present in the environment.

As a conclusion, we have the feeling that Shapiro's definition of embeddability (with some additional restriction) is the basis of a theory for comparing Concurrent (logic) languages "more refined" than the the classic theory of computability (in the sense that the former is able to sense differencies that are not captured by the second), and orthogonal to the classic theory of complexity (since these differencies mainly rely not on algorithmic complexity, but on the interaction capabilities of a process with its environment).

[5] This observation is due to H. Blair.

6 Future work

We are extending the transition system modeling the communication mechanism, and the compositional semantics presented here (and its fully abstract refinement presented in [7]) to logic languages with general constraints, and to the class ccL of [23]. The main modification is the replacement of substitutions in the sequences with (existentially quantified) constraints on arbitrary domain. With respect to full abstractness, the result presented in [7]) can be extended if the set of constraints we consider is well founded, in the sense that each element can be decomposed into a finite set of minimal elements. For the other kinds of contraints, full abstractness is still under investigation.

On the side of language comparison, we are trying to characterize the minimal conditions under which the definition of embeddability is not trivial. in particular, we are trying to prove conjecture 5.6.

Aknowledgements The motivations for this paper arose from the joint work with Joost Kok and Jan Rutten.

References

[1] K.R. Apt. Introduction to logic programming (revised and extended version). Technical Report CS-R8826,CWI, Amsterdam, 1988.

[2] S.D. Brookes, C.A.R. Hoare, and W. Roscoe. A theory of communicating sequential processes. *Journal of ACM*, 31:499–560, 1984.

[3] J.W. de Bakker and J.N. Kok. Uniform abstraction, atomicity and contractions in the comparative semantics of Concurrent Prolog. In *Proc. of FGCS*, Tokyo, 1988, 347–355.

[4] F.S. de Boer, J.N. Kok, C. Palamidessi, and J.J.M.M. Rutten. Control flow versus logic: a denotational and a declarative model for Guarded Horn Clauses. In *Proc. of the Symposium on MFCS, LNCS 379*, 1989,165–176.

[5] F.S. de Boer, J.N. Kok, C. Palamidessi, and J.J.M.M. Rutten. Semantic models for a version of PARLOG. In *Proc. of ICLP*, Lisboa, 1989, 621–636. The MIT Press. Extended version to appear in *TCS*.

[6] F.S. de Boer, J.N. Kok, C. Palamidessi, and J.J.M.M. Rutten. From failure to success: Comparing a denotational and a declarative semantics for Horn Clause Logic. In *Proc. of the International Workshop on Semantics for Concurrency, LNCS*, Leicester, 1990.

[7] F.S. de Boer and C. Palamidessi. On the asynchronous nature of communication in concurrent logic languages: A fully abstract model based on sequences. In *Proc. of Concur 90, LNCS*, The Netherlands, 1990. Full version available as report at the Technische Universiteit Eindhoven.

[8] E. Eder. Properties of substitutions and unifications. *Journal of Symbolic Computation*, 1:31–46, 1985.

[9] M. Falaschi, G. Levi, M. Martelli, and C. Palamidessi. Declarative modeling of the operational behaviour of logic languages. *TCS*, 69(3):289–318, 1989.

[10] M. Gabbrielli and G. Levi. Unfolding and Fixpoint Semantics for Concurrent Constraint Logic programs. In *Proc. of the Second Int. Conf. on Algebraic and Logic Programming, LNCS*, Nancy, France, 1990.

[11] H. Gaifman, M. J. Maher, and E. Shapiro. Reactive Behaviour semantics for Concurrent Constraint Logic Programs. In *Proc. of NACLP*, 1989.

[12] H. Gaifman and E. Shapiro. Fully abstract compositional semantics for logic programs. In *Proc. of POPL*, 1989, 134–142.

[13] H. Gaifman and E. Shapiro. Proof theory and semantics of logic programs. In *Proc. of LICS*, 1989, 50–62.

[14] R. Gerth, M. Codish, Y. Lichtenstein, and E. Shapiro. Fully abstract denotational semantics for Concurrent Prolog. In *Proc. of LICS*, 1988, 320–335.

[15] M. Hirata. Parallel list processing language Oc and its self-description. *Computing Software*, 4(3):41–64, 1987. In Japanese.

[16] J. Jaffar and J.-L. Lassez. Constraint Logic Programming. In *Proc. of POPL*, Munich, 1987, 111–119.

[17] J.N. Kok. A compositional semantics for Concurrent Prolog. In *Proc. of STACS, LNCS 294*, 1988, 373–388.

[18] J. L. Lassez, M. J. Maher, and K. Marriot. Unification Revisited. In J. Minker, editor, *Foundations of Deductive Databases and Logic Programming.* Morgann Kaufmann, 1988.

[19] J.W. Lloyd. *Foundations of logic programming.* Springer-Verlag, second edition, 1987.

[20] M. J. Maher. Logic semantics for a class of committed-choice programs. In *Proc. of ICLP*, 1987, 858–876. The MIT Press.

[21] Robin Milner. Calculi for synchrony and asynchrony. *TCS*, 25:267–310, 1983.

[22] V.A. Saraswat. Partial Correctness Semantics for CP($\emptyset, |, \&$). In *Proc. of the Conference on Foundations of Software Computing and Theoretical Computer Science, LNCS 206*, 1985, 347–368.

[23] V.A. Saraswat. *Concurrent Constraint Programming Languages.* PhD thesis, january 1989. To be published by the MIT Press.

[24] V.A. Saraswat and M. Rinard. Concurrent constraint programming. In *Proc. of POPL*, 1990.

[25] E.Y. Shapiro. The family of concurrent logic programming languages. *ACM Computing Surveys*, 21(3):412–510, 1989.

[26] K. Ueda. Guarded Horn Clauses. In E. Y. Shapiro, editor, *Concurrent Prolog: Collected Papers.* The MIT Press, 1987.

[27] M.H. van Emden and R.A. Kowalski. The semantics of predicate logic as a programming language. *Journal of ACM*, 23(4):733–742, 1976.

Comparative Semantics for a Parallel Contextual Logic Programming Language[1]

Jean-Marie Jacquet[2] and Luís Monteiro[3]

Abstract

The purpose of this paper is to present and compare six semantics, ranging in the operational, declarative and denotational types, for a parallel version of contextual logic programming. Three operational semantics are first discussed. They all rest on a transition system but differ in their ability of describing success sets, failure sets, infinite computations and of handling multiple occurrences of computations. Two declarative semantics are then described. They extend, respectively, the Herbrand interpretation and the immediate consequence operator to our contextual framework. Finally, a denotational semantics based on processes, structured as trees, is given. The mathematical tools mainly used for these semantics are complete lattices for the declarative semantics and metric spaces for the other ones.

The parallel logic language under consideration is an elementary one: it uses or-parallelism and and-parallelism in an unrestricted manner. A reconciliation calculus is provided as a way of combining substitutions resulting from the reductions of conjoined goals. Despite its simplicity, we believe that the parallel language still constitutes a model of interest since it captures the basis of contextual logic programming and of parallel logic programming.

1 Introduction

Contextual logic programming ([MP89]) is an extension of the logic programming paradigm based on the idea of having both local and context-dependent predicate definitions. A language is proposed for supporting local definitions of predicates of the kind provided by systems of modules, and context-dependency in the form of predicate definitions implicitly supplied by the context. On the one hand, the clauses comprising a program are distributed over several modules (or "units", as they will be called here), and in that sense a predicate definition is local to the unit where the corresponding clauses occur. On the other hand, the definition of a predicate may depend on predicates not defined in the same unit, and in that case the definitions available in the context for those predicates are assumed by default.

We turn in this paper to a quite simple parallel version of the contextual logic programming framework. It just involves and-parallelism and or-parallelism without any concern for guard-like constructs, commitment, read-only annotations, mode declarations or other suspension constructs. We shall also not tackle negation here. However, our purpose is not to provide the reader with a practical parallel contextual logic language nor to discuss some parallel implementation. It is semantical and, more precisely, it consists of presenting and of relating semantical models for it.

---

[1]Part of this work was carried out in the context of ESPRIT Basic Research Action (3020) Integration.

[2]Centre for Mathematics and Computer Science, P.O. Box 4079, 1009 AB Amsterdam, The Netherlands.

[3]Departamento de Informática, Universidade Nova de Lisboa,2825 Monte da Caparica, Portugal.

With respect to this aim, we believe that the parallel contextual logic language treated here—subsequently referred to as CLL—is of interest since it captures the basis of contextual logic programming and of parallel logic programming. As an additional argument, our future research (under development) for more practical and more elaborated concurrent contextual logic languages will be based on the results exposed here.

The paper presents and compares six semantics issued from the logic programming and imperative traditions and ranging in the classical operational, declarative and denotational types. And-parallelism is treated in a quite close way to real concurrent executions : to allow a goal to progress from one step, it is sufficient that one of its subgoals performs one step, although all of them are allowed to do so. Restated in other terms, in contrast with work such as [BKRP89], our modelling of and-parallelism includes the interleaving perception of parallel computations as well as the true concurrent one. For simplicity of the exposition, or-parallelism is not treated in the same way but more implicitly as a choice. Some parallelism is however still captured in the sense that no order is imposed on the way clauses should be selected for reduction. It should also be noted that our modelling of or-parallelism and and-parallelism allows to capture the different (concurrently executed) and/or search subtrees, corresponding, in the parallel framework, to SLD-derivation paths. Repetition of such subtrees is furthermore taken into account in some semantics by means of multi-sets.

Our six semantics are composed of three operational semantics, two declarative semantics and one denotational semantics. Four of them, namely the operational semantics O_{bu} and O_{td}, and the two declarative semantics $Decl_m$ and $Decl_f$, take place in the logic programming tradition. The other ones, called O_{ch} and Den, are issued from the imperative tradition, especially from its metric branch.

The operational semantics O_{bu} rests on the so-called bottom-up derivation relation. It describes successful derivations of goals in a bottom-up fashion but does not produce any substitution. It is however interesting since it is close to the declarative reading of the clauses and thus help, in the one hand, in understanding the declarative semantics and, on the other hand, in relating the operational and declarative semantics.

The operational semantics O_{td} also rests on a derivation relation. It describes the derivation in a top-down manner and associates a computed answer substitution with each of them. It thus corresponds to the classical success set and failure set characterizations of programs.

The two declarative semantics $Decl_m$ and $Decl_f$, are based on model and fixed-point theory, respectively. They generalize the notions of Herbrand interpretation and consequence operator for classical Horn clause logic in order to take into account the context dependency of the truth of formulae. As suggested, an effort has been made to keep these semantics as simple as possible as well as in the main streams of logic programming semantics. However, context-dependency and parallel executions raise new problems, for which fresh solutions are proposed.

The third operational semantics O_{ch} completes the operational description of O_{bu} and O_{td} by handling multiple occurrences of computations as well as infinite computations. It furthermore tackles more closely the computation steps and, therefore, makes the modelling of and-parallelism fully apparent. Technically speaking, it is based on computation histories represented as streams of actions. Multiplicity of occurrences is handled by means of multi-sets.

The denotational semantics Den, defined as usual compositionally, further details the computation by handling choice-points i.e. points of possible alternatives of use of unifiable clauses. It uses (as usual, too), processes organized in tree-like structures.

Although they are of classical inspiration, these last two semantics still present some originality with related work ([BZ82], [BKMOZ86], [BM88], [B88], [KR88], [BK88], [BKRP89], ...). It arises essentially from the four following points :

i) our concern with contextual logic programming, which has not been done before and which requires new solutions;
ii) the novel way (including interleaving and true concurrency) in which parallelism is modelled;
iii) the handling of multiple occurrences of computations;
iv) our use of local state and of reconciliation to combine them, which allows to define the denotational semantics more simply; in particular, the processes are expressed here just in terms of very intuitive computation steps - input substitutions, actions and output substitutions - rather than functions.

The semantical tools mainly used in this paper are of four types : sets, multi-sets, complete lattices and metric spaces. Despite this variety, the semantics have been related throughout the paper. Lack of space prevents us however from giving proofs. Nevertheless, all the propositions stated hereafter have been proved in [Mo89] and [Ja90].

The remainder of this paper is organized into 8 Sections. Section 2 describes the basic constructs of the language and explains our terminology. Section 3 recalls the basic semantical tools used in the paper. Section 4 presents (and compares) the three operational semantics according to their power of expression : O_{bu}, O_{td} and O_{ch}. Section 5 discusses the declarative models $Decl_m$ and $Decl_f$ and connects them with the operational semantics. Section 6 specifies the denotational semantics Den and compares it with the operational semantics O_{ch} and, consequently, in view of previous results, to the other semantics. Finally, section 7 sums up the relationship established in the paper and gives our conclusions.

2 The language CLL

As usual in logic programming, the language CLL comprises denumerably infinite sets of *variables*, *functions* and *predicates*, subsequently referred to as *Svar*, *Sfunct* and *Spred*, respectively. It also includes a set *Sunit* of so-called *unit names*, characterized by the property that every element u has attached a finite subset of Spred, called the *sort* of u and denoted by *sort(u)*. The sets Svar, Sfunct, Spred and Sunit are assumed to be pairwise disjoint.

The notions of term, atom, clause, substitution, unification, ... are defined as usual. We do not recall them here but rather specify some contextual related notions as well as some useful notations.

An *extension formula* is a formula of the form $u \gg \overline{G}$ where u is a unit name and $\overline{G}$ is a finite conjunction of atomic or extension formulae. A *general atom* (*g-atom*) is an atomic or an extension formula. It is typically denoted by the letters A, B, C, ... A *general goal* (*g-goal*) is a finite conjunction of g-atoms. It is typically denoted by the symbols $\overline{A}$, $\overline{B}$, $\overline{C}$, ..., $\overline{G}$, ... The empty g-goal is denoted by the $\triangle$ letter. Clauses take here the form $H \leftarrow \overline{B}$ and allow extension formulae to take place in their bodies. Given an atom $A = p(t_1,\dots,t_m)$, we denote by *name(A)* the predicate name of A, namely p. A set of clauses is said to *define* a predicate p if it contains a clause whose head's name is p.

A *unit* is a formula of the form u : U, where u $\in$ Sunit and U is a finite set of clauses such that the set of predicates defined in U is sort(u). We call u the *name* or *head* of the unit and U its *body*. A *system of units* is a set $\mathcal{U}$ of units such that no two distinct units in $\mathcal{U}$ have the same name. For a unit in $\mathcal{U}$ with name u, we denote its body by $|u|_{\mathcal{U}}$, or simply |u| if $\mathcal{U}$ is understood. In the sequel we will often abuse language and refer to u as a unit in $\mathcal{U}$ when in fact we mean the unit u : |u|. The set of systems is subsequently referred to as *Ssyst*.

A *context* is a stack of units. It is referred to by its name, consisting of an arbitrary sequence of unit names. The set of context names, *Scontext*, is thus the free monoid $\text{Sunit}^{<\omega}$. Context names are represented by juxtaposition, as in uv. The empty sequence λ is employed as the name of the *empty* context. The context resulting from *extending* the context c with unit u (i.e. by putting u on top of the stack) is denoted by uc.

3 Mathematical preliminaries

3.1 Sets and multi-sets

Executions may result in computing a same answer or a same computation path several times. Multi-sets, allowing an element to be repeated, are used subsequently to capture this repetition. To clearly distinguish them from sets, they are denoted by adding the *ms* label to the $\{\ldots\}$ brackets, as in $\{a,a,b\}_{ms}$, whereas sets are denoted by the *s* label, as in $\{a,b\}_s$. The union symbol $\cup$ is also subscripted in this way for the same purpose. To avoid any ambiguity, let us further precise that, given two multi-sets S and T, we denote by $S \cup_{ms} T$ the collection of all elements of S and T repeated as many times as they occur in S and T.

The usual notations $\mathcal{P}(E)$ and $\mathcal{M}(E)$ are used to denote, respectively, the set of sets and multi-sets, with elements from E. The notations $\mathcal{P}_\pi(E)$ and $\mathcal{M}_\pi(E)$ are moreover employed to denote those sets and multi-sets verifying the property π. For instance, $\mathcal{M}_{nf}(E)$ (resp. $\mathcal{M}_{nco}(E)$) denotes the set of non-empty and finite[4] multi-sets (resp. the non-empty and compact multi-sets) with elements from E.

3.2 Reconciliation of substitutions

Full use of and-parallelism requires a way of combining substitutions issued from the concurrent reductions of subgoals of a g-goal in order to form answer substitutions for the whole g-goal. It has been provided under the name of *reconciliation of substitutions* in [Ja89] and has been extensively studied there. Concurrently, an equivalent notion, named parallel composition of substitutions, has been developed in [Pa88] and [Pa90]. We briefly recall this notion here for the sake of completeness. The reader is referred to the above three references for more details.

The reconciliation of substitutions is based on the interpretation of substitutions in equational terms. Precisely, any substitution $\theta = \{X_1/t_1, \ldots, X_m/t_m\}_s$ is associated with the system of the equations $X_1 = t_1, \ldots, X_m = t_m$, subsequently referred to as *syst(θ)*. Reconciling substitutions then consists of solving systems composed of the associated equations.

Concepts of unifiers and mgus can be defined for these systems in a straightforward way. It is furthermore possible to relate the unification of systems of equations

[4]To avoid confusion, we precise that a multi-set is finite iff it contains only a finite number of elements (and thus not iff any element occurs a finite number of times).

with that of terms in such a way that all properties of the unification of terms transpose to the unification of systems of equations. In particular, mgus of systems can be proved to be equal modulo renaming. We consequently use, in the following, the classical abuse of language and speak of *the* mgu of a unifiable system. It is referred to as *mgu_syst(S)*, where S is the system under consideration.

We are now in a position to define the notion of reconciliation of substitutions.

Definition 1 *The substitutions $\theta_1, \ldots, \theta_m$ ($m \geq 1$) are reconcilable iff the system composed of the equations of syst(θ_1), ..., syst(θ_m) is unifiable. When so, its mgu is called the* reconciliation *of the substitutions. It is denoted by $\rho(\theta_1, \ldots, \theta_m)$.* ∎

The equational interpretation of substitutions requires, at some point, the idempotence of the substitutions. This is not a real restriction since any unifiable terms or systems of equations admit an idempotent mgu. It is furthermore to our point of view the natural one. For ease of the discussion, we will take the convention of using, from now on, idempotent substitutions only. Their set is referred to as *Ssubst*.

3.3 Complete lattices and metric spaces

Complete lattices and metric spaces will be used as important semantical tools. The reader is assumed to be familiar with them as well as with their related notions of convergent sequences, directed, closed and compact subsets, completeness, continuous and contracting functions .... He is also assumed to be familiar with Tarski's lemma, describing the set of prefixed points of continuous functions of complete lattices, and Banach's theorem, stating the existence of a unique fixed point of contractions in complete metric spaces. He is referred to [Ll87] and [En77], when need be. Furthermore, lack of space prevents us from describing all the metrics used in this paper. We will however employ essentially the classical ones and refer to [B88] for such a description. The only exception to this rule concerns the metric on multi-sets that we now make precise.

Proposition 2 *Let E be some set and let $\perp$ be an element not in E. Let furthermore*[5] *$.[.] : E \times \mathbf{N} \rightarrow E \cup_s \{\perp\}_s$ be a function such that,*

i) for any $e \in E$: $e[0] = \perp$;
ii) for any $e, f \in E$:if $e[n] = f[n]$, for all $n \in \mathbf{N}$, then $e=f$;
iii) for any $e \in E, m, n \in \mathbf{N}$: $(e[m])[n]=e[min\{m,n\}_s]$.

Such a function is subsequently called truncation. Define, for any $S \in \mathcal{M}(E)$ and $n \in \mathbf{N}$, $S[n]$ as the multi-set $\{s[n] : s \in S\}_{ms}$. Furthermore, define, for any $e, f \in E$, $S, T \in \mathcal{M}(E)$,

$$d_E(e,f) = 2^{-sup\{n: e[n]=f[n]\}_s};$$

$$d_{ms}(S,T) = 2^{-sup\{n: S[n]=T[n]\}_s}.$$

Then, the space (E, d_E) is a metric space. Moreover, the spaces $(\mathcal{M}_{nf}(E), d_{ms})$ and $(\mathcal{M}_{nco}(E), d_{ms})$, where compactness[6] *is taken with respect to d_E, are metric spaces. They are complete if (E, d_E) is complete.* ∎

[5] We denote by $\mathbf{N}$ the set of non negative integers.

[6] Compactness is extended straightforwardly from sets to multi-sets : a mutli-set M is compact iff any sequence of elements of M contains a subsequence converging to an element of M.

4 Operational semantics

4.1 Bottom-up derivation

The first characterization of the operational semantics of CLL is expressed in terms of the notion of bottom-up derivation. Its interest arises from its closeness to the "declarative" reading of clauses. It is twofold. On the one hand, it helps in understanding the declarative semantics, to be presented in section 5. On the other hand, it helps in proving the equivalence between the operational and the declarative semantics.

The notion of bottom-up derivation is characterized indirectly by defining a "bottom-up derivation relation". It takes the form $c \overset{bu}{\vdash}_{\mathcal{U}} \overline{G}$, for a system of units $\mathcal{U}$, a context name c and a g-goal $\overline{G}$. The intended meaning is that *every* ground instance of $\overline{G}$ is true in the situation represented by the context c. The relation $\overset{bu}{\vdash}_{\mathcal{U}}$ is defined more formally by means of rules of the form

$$\frac{\text{Assumptions}}{\text{Conclusion}} \quad \textit{if} \ \text{Conditions},$$

asserting the Conclusion whenever the Assumptions and Conditions hold. (Note that Assumptions and Conditions may be absent from some rules.) Precisely, it is defined as the smallest relation of Ssyst × Scontext × Sgoal satisfying the following rules (N-B) to (E-B), by case analysis on the form of $\overline{G}$. The notation *Sinst(U)* is used to denote the set of all (possibly non-ground) instances of clauses in U, and $\overset{bu}{\vdash}_{\mathcal{U}}$ is written simply as $\overset{bu}{\vdash}$, for readability.

Null formula

(N-B) $$\frac{}{c \overset{bu}{\vdash} \Delta}$$

Conjunction

(C-B) $$\frac{c \overset{bu}{\vdash} A_1, \ldots, c \overset{bu}{\vdash} A_m}{c \overset{bu}{\vdash} A_1, \ldots, A_m}$$

Atomic formula—local reduction

(R-B) $$\frac{uc \overset{bu}{\vdash} \overline{B}}{uc \overset{bu}{\vdash} H} \quad \textit{if} \ \ H \leftarrow \overline{B} \in \text{Sinst}(|u|)$$

Atomic formula—contextual definition

(X-B) $$\frac{c \overset{bu}{\vdash} A}{uc \overset{bu}{\vdash} A} \quad \textit{if} \ \ \text{name}(A) \notin \text{sort}(u)$$

Extension formula

(E-B) $$\frac{uc \overset{bu}{\vdash} \overline{G}}{c \overset{bu}{\vdash} u \gg \overline{G}}$$

The first three rules are essentially the same as for Horn clause logic. They state, respectively, that true can be derived in any context, that a conjunction is derivable if its conjuncts are, and that the head of a clause is derivable if its body is. The rule (X-B) explains the meaning of contextual definition: an atom is derivable in a context whose top unit does not define the atom's predicate name if the atom is derivable in the context with the top unit removed. The last rule (E-B) characterizes context extension: an extension formula is derivable in a context if the "inner" conjunction is derivable in the context extended with the unit mentioned in the extension formula.

Definition 3 *Let δ^- and δ^+ be two fresh symbols. The* bottom-up operational semantics *of CLL is the function O_{bu} : Ssyst $\longrightarrow$ Scontext $\longrightarrow$ Sgoal $\longrightarrow$ $\{\delta^-, \delta^+\}_s$ defined as follows: for any $\mathcal{U}\in$Ssyst, c$\in$Scontext and $\overline{G}\in$Sgoal,*

$$O_{bu}(\mathcal{U})(c)(\overline{G}) = \begin{cases} \delta^+, & \textit{if } c \overset{bu}{\vdash}_{\mathcal{U}} \overline{G} \\ \delta^-, & \textit{otherwise} \end{cases}$$ ■

4.2 Top-down derivation

The operational semantics O_{bu} does not deliver that much information, just the possible existence of a successful derivation. The purpose of any computation is however far more richer: to compute bindings for the variables of the query. The notion of successful top-down derivation allows precisely to capture such an idea. Given a system of units $\mathcal{U}$ and a g-goal $\overline{G}$, it consists of a sequence of steps reducing $\overline{G}$ to the null conjunction. Associated with it, there is a substitution θ representing the values computed for the variables of $\overline{G}$. The expected result (presented in section 5) is that the universal closure of $\overline{G}\theta$ is a logical consequence of $\mathcal{U}$, and that any instance of $\overline{G}$ which is a consequence of $\mathcal{U}$ can be obtained as instance of $\overline{G}\theta$ for some computed substitution θ.

As before, the top-down derivation is not specified directly, but by means of a top-down derivation relation. For any context name c and g-goal $\overline{G}$, $c \overset{td}{\vdash}_{\mathcal{U}} \overline{G}\ [\theta]$, or more simply $c \overset{td}{\vdash} \overline{G}\ [\theta]$ when $\mathcal{U}$ is understood, denotes the fact that there is a (successful) *top-down derivation of* $\overline{G}$ *in* c *from* $\mathcal{U}$ *with substitution* θ. Again, $\overset{td}{\vdash}_{\mathcal{U}}$ is formally defined as the smallest relation of Ssyst × Scontext × Sgoal × Ssubst satisfying the rules below. The symbol ϵ denotes the empty (identity) substitution.

Null formula

(N-T) $$\frac{}{c \overset{td}{\vdash} \Delta\ [\epsilon]}$$

Conjunction

(C-T) $$\frac{c \overset{td}{\vdash} A_1\ [\theta_1], \ldots, c \overset{td}{\vdash} A_m\ [\theta_m]}{c \overset{td}{\vdash} A_1,\ldots,A_m\ [\rho(\theta_1, \ldots, \theta_m)]}$$

Atomic formula—local reduction

(R-T) $$\frac{uc \overset{td}{\vdash} \overline{B}\theta\ [\sigma]}{uc \overset{td}{\vdash} A\ [\theta\sigma]} \quad \textit{if} \quad \begin{cases} H \leftarrow \overline{B} \in |u|^7 \\ \theta = \text{mgu}(A,H) \end{cases}$$

Atomic formula—contextual definition

(X-T) $$\frac{c \overset{td}{\vdash} A\ [\theta]}{uc \overset{td}{\vdash} A\ [\theta]} \quad \textit{if} \quad \text{name}(A) \notin \text{sort}(u)$$

Extension formula

(E-T) $$\frac{uc \overset{td}{\vdash} G\ [\theta]}{c \overset{td}{\vdash} u \gg \overline{G}\ [\theta]}$$

These rules have a reading similar to the bottom-up case. For example, rule (C-T) states that in order to derive a g-goal we must derive each g-atom and then reconcile the resulting substitutions.

The relationship between the top-down and bottom-up derivations is established by the following proposition.

[7] As usual, a suitable renaming of the clauses is assumed.

Proposition 4 *If* $c \overset{td}{\vdash} \overline{G}\ [\theta]$ *then* $c \overset{bu}{\vdash} \overline{G}\theta$. *Conversely, if* $c \overset{bu}{\vdash} \overline{G_o}$ *and* $\overline{G_o}$ *is an instance of* $\overline{G}$, *there is a substitution* θ *such that* $c \overset{td}{\vdash} \overline{G}\ [\theta]$ *and* $\overline{G_o}$ *is an instance of* $\overline{G}\theta$. ∎

The *top-down operational semantics* can now be characterized. As may be seen in the following definition, it corresponds to the usual notion of success set and failure set.

Definition 5 *Define the* top-down operational semantics *as the following function* $O_{td} : Ssyst \rightarrow Scontext \rightarrow Sgoal \rightarrow \mathcal{P}(Ssubst)$: *for any* $\mathcal{U} \in Ssyst$, $c \in Scontext$, *and* $\overline{G} \in Sgoal$, $O_{td}(\mathcal{U})(c)(\overline{G}) = \{\theta : c \overset{td}{\vdash}_{\mathcal{U}} \overline{G}\ [\theta]\}_s$. ∎

The following result relating O_{bu} and O_{td} is an immediate consequence of the previous proposition.

Proposition 6 *Let* $\alpha_1 : \mathcal{P}(Subst) \rightarrow \{\delta^-, \delta^+\}_s$ *be the function defined as*

i) $\alpha_1(\emptyset) = \delta^-$
ii) $\alpha_1(\Sigma) = \delta^+$, *if* $\Sigma \neq \emptyset$

One has $O_{bu} = \alpha_1 \circ O_{td}$. ∎

4.3 Computation histories

Although more powerful than O_{bu}, the operational semantics O_{td} suffers from two problems: it cannot cope with infinite computations and cannot distinguish multiple occurrences of computations. The operational semantics O_{ch} is introduced as a remedy. It essentially delivers the histories of the computations rather than just their results and collects all their repetitions. The main technicalities used for that purpose are as follows. Repetition is captured by using multi-sets rather than sets. Histories are modelled by words whose elements represent the multi-set of unifications and context updates (namely the basic operations of CLL) performed at each step, as well as the two termination status, failure and success. These histories are formally identified by means of a labelled transition system, in the style of [Pl81], whose labels correspond to the multi-sets of basic actions and whose configurations are some generalization of the goals. This extension is justified by the fact that, in order to represent truly concurrent executions, any g-atom of any g-goal must operate in a private working memory space, namely its own state and its own context.

This intuition given, let us define O_{ch} more precisely. The following notation and definitions specify the concepts sketched above.

Notation 7 (Histories) *The notations* unif(A,B), cxt_ext(c,u) *and* cxt_pop(c) *are used to represent the actions of unifying the atoms A and B, of extending the context c by the unit u, and of poping the context c, respectively. The set of such* basic actions *is referred to as* Sact. *The set of words formed from* $\mathcal{M}_{nf}(Sact)$ *and which finite elements are ended by one of the terminator operators* δ^-, *representing failure, and* δ^+, *representing success, is referred to as* Shist. *Elements of Shist are called* histories. ∎

Definition 8 (Extended g-atoms and goals) Extended g-atoms (eg-atoms) *are constructs of the form* A in $< \sigma, c >$ *where A is a g-atom, σ is a substitution and c is a context. They are typically denoted by the letters* $\widehat{A}$, $\widehat{B}$, $\widehat{C}$, ... Extended g-goals (eg-goals) *are conjunctions of eg-atoms. They are typically referred to as* $\widetilde{A}$, $\widetilde{B}$, $\widetilde{C}$, ..., $\widetilde{G}$, ... *The empty eg-goal is denoted by the* Δ_{ext} *symbol. The set of eg-goals is referred to by* Sextgoal. *Finally,* $(A_1,\ldots,A_m)$ in $<\sigma, c>$ *is defined as the eg-goal* $(A_1$ in $<\sigma,c>)$, ..., $(A_m$ in $<\sigma,c>)$. ■

Definition 9 (Transition relation) *The transition relation used for specifying the operational semantics* O_{ch} *is defined as the smallest relation* $\rightarrow$ *of* $Ssyst \times Sextgoal \times \mathcal{M}_{nf}(Sact) \times Sextgoal$ *satisfying the following rules (R-H) to (C-*H_3*). For ease of reading, the more suggestive notation* $\widetilde{G} \stackrel{l}{\longrightarrow} \widetilde{G^*}$ *is employed instead of* $(\mathcal{U},\widetilde{G},l,\widetilde{G^*})$.

Atomic formula - local reduction

$$(R\text{-}H) \quad \frac{}{A \text{ in } <\sigma, uc> \stackrel{l}{\longrightarrow} \overline{B} \text{ in } <\sigma^*, uc>} \quad \text{if} \left\{ \begin{array}{l} (H \leftarrow \overline{B}) \in |u|^8 \\ A\sigma \text{ and } H \text{ are unifiable} \\ \sigma^* = \sigma \circ mgu(A\sigma, H) \\ l = \{unif(A\sigma, H)\}_{ms} \end{array} \right.$$

Atomic formula—contextual definition

$$(X\text{-}H) \quad \frac{}{A \text{ in } <\sigma, uc> \stackrel{l}{\longrightarrow} A \text{ in } <\sigma^*, c>} \quad \text{if} \left\{ \begin{array}{l} name(A) \notin sort(u) \\ l = \{cxt\_pop(uc)\}_{ms} \end{array} \right.$$

Extension formula

$$(E\text{-}H) \quad \frac{}{u \gg \overline{G} \text{ in } <\sigma, c> \stackrel{l}{\longrightarrow} \overline{G} \text{ in } <\sigma, uc>} \quad \text{if } \; l = \{cxt\_ext(c, u)\}_{ms}$$

Conjunction

$$(C\text{-}H_1) \quad \frac{\widetilde{A} \stackrel{l}{\longrightarrow} \widetilde{A^*}}{\widetilde{A},\widetilde{B} \stackrel{l}{\longrightarrow} \widetilde{A^*},\widetilde{B}} \qquad\qquad (C\text{-}H_2) \quad \frac{\widetilde{B} \stackrel{l}{\longrightarrow} \widetilde{B^*}}{\widetilde{A},\widetilde{B} \stackrel{l}{\longrightarrow} \widetilde{A},\widetilde{B^*}}$$

$$(C\text{-}H_3) \quad \frac{\widetilde{A} \stackrel{l_1}{\longrightarrow} \widetilde{A^*};\widetilde{B} \stackrel{l_2}{\longrightarrow} \widetilde{B^*}}{\widetilde{A},\widetilde{B} \stackrel{l_1 \cup_{ms} l_2}{\longrightarrow} \widetilde{A^*},\widetilde{B^*}}$$

■

Rules (R-H), (X-H) and (E-H) essentially rephrase the rules (R-T), (X-T) and (E-T) defining how atoms and extension formulae should be treated. Rules (C-H_1), (C-H_2) and (C-H_3) define the and-parallel execution of conjoined eg-atoms. It is worth noting that, thanks to rules (CH_1)and (C-H_2), all eg-atoms need not be reduced in one step in order to allow the whole conjunction to perform one reduction step. Such maximal parallel executions can however take place thanks to rule (C-H_3). Our modelling of and-parallelism is thus very close to the real practical operational executions: it expresses concurrent executions waiting for some processing resource as well as the fully concurrent executions when enough computing resources are available. Reformulated in a more conceptual level, our modelling of and-parallelism subsumes the interleaving approach to concurrency as well as the truly concurrent one (assuming, as usual, that all unfications take the same amount of time). Notice finally that no reconciliation takes place in the rule (C-H_3). Indeed, conjoined eg-atoms of a g-goal are first reduced before reconciliation is performed to determine the answer susbstitution for the whole g-goal. Hence, no reconciliation is present in the computation histories, capturing the only computed unifications and context operations. It will however be used to relate O_{td} and O_{ch}.

[8] As usual, a suitable renaming of the clauses is assumed.

We are now in position to define the operational semantics O_{ch}. Note that the finitely branching property of the transition relation is not sufficient to ensure that the codomain of $\mathbf{O}$ and O_{ch} is composed of non-empty and finite multi-sets of histories. However, it is strong enough to ensure that it is composed of compact ones.

Definition 10

1) Define $\mathbf{O} : Ssyst \rightarrow Sextgoal \rightarrow \mathcal{M}_{nco}(Shist)$ *as follows : for any* $\mathcal{U} \in Ssyst$, *any* $\widetilde{G} \in Sextgoal$[9],

$$\begin{aligned}\mathbf{O}(\mathcal{U})(\widetilde{G}) &= \{l_1.l_2.\cdots.l_n.\delta^- : \widetilde{G} \xrightarrow{l_1} \widetilde{A_1} \xrightarrow{l_2} \ldots \xrightarrow{l_n} \widetilde{A_n} \neq \Delta_{ext}, \widetilde{A_n} \not\rightarrow\}_{ms} \\ &\cup_{ms}\{l_1.l_2.\cdots.l_n.\delta^+ : \widetilde{G} \xrightarrow{l_1} \widetilde{A_1} \xrightarrow{l_2} \ldots \xrightarrow{l_n} \Delta_{ext}\}_{ms} \\ &\cup_{ms}\{l_1.l_2.\cdots.l_n.\cdots : \widetilde{G} \xrightarrow{l_1} \widetilde{A_1} \xrightarrow{l_2} \ldots \xrightarrow{l_n} \widetilde{A_n} \xrightarrow{l_{n+1}} \ldots\}_{ms}.\end{aligned}$$

2) Define the computational history operational semantics *as the following function* $O_{ch} : Ssyst \rightarrow Scontext \rightarrow Ssubst \rightarrow Sgoal \rightarrow \mathcal{M}_{nco}(Shist)$: *for any* $\mathcal{U} \in Ssyst$, *any* $c \in Scontext$, *any* $\sigma \in Ssubst$, *any* $\overline{G} \in Sgoals$,

$$O_{ch}(\mathcal{U})(c)(\sigma)(\overline{G}) = \mathbf{O}(\mathcal{U})(\overline{G} \text{ in } <\sigma, c>). \qquad \blacksquare$$

It is worth noting that the auxiliary function $\mathbf{O}$ can be related to the fixed point of the following higher-order contraction Ψ_{op} reflecting the recursive nature of $\mathbf{O}$. This property combined with the fortunate circumstance that contractions have one fixed point will be usefull later to relate O_{ch} with the denotational semantics Den.

Definition 11 *Define* $\Psi_{op} : [Ssyst \rightarrow Sextgoal \rightarrow \mathcal{P}_{nco}(Shist)] \rightarrow [Ssyst \rightarrow Sextgoal \rightarrow \mathcal{P}(Shist)]$ *as follows: for any* $F \in [Ssyst \rightarrow Sextgoal \rightarrow \mathcal{P}_{nco}(Shist)]$, *any* $\mathcal{U} \in Ssyst$, *any* $\widetilde{G} \in Sextgoal$,

$$\begin{aligned}\Psi_{op}(F)(\mathcal{U})(\widetilde{G}) &= \{\delta^- : \widetilde{G} \neq \Delta_{ext}, \widetilde{G} \not\rightarrow\}_s \cup_s \{\delta^+ : \widetilde{G} = \Delta_{ext}\}_s \\ &\cup_s\{l.h : \widetilde{G} \xrightarrow{l} \widetilde{G^*}, h \in F(\mathcal{U})(\widetilde{G^*})\}_s.\end{aligned} \qquad \blacksquare$$

Proposition 12

1) The function Ψ_{op} *is a contraction from* $[Ssyst \rightarrow Sextgoal \rightarrow \mathcal{P}_{nco}(Shist)]$ *to* $[Ssyst \rightarrow Sextgoal \rightarrow \mathcal{P}_{nco}(Shist)]$.

2) Let $\beta : \mathcal{M}(Shist) \rightarrow \mathcal{P}(Shist)$ *be the function that transforms any multi-set in the corresponding set, namely the function defined by* $\beta(M) = \{m : m \in M\}_s$ *for any* $M \in \mathcal{M}(Shist)$. *The function* $\beta \circ \mathbf{O}$ *is a fixed point of* Ψ_{op}. $\blacksquare$

It is here worth noting that using multi-sets instead of sets in the above definition makes Ψ_{op} a non-contracting function. In fact, this multi-set version, say Ψ^*_{op}, has an infinite number of fixed points, obtained by progressively duplicating computation paths in $\mathbf{O}$. Hence, multiplicity cannot be handled suitably at the stream level by contractions. This fact will force us to use two arguments to relate O_{ch} and Den: the classical contracting argument to establish that elements are preserved and an additional argument to prove that the multiplicity of occurrence of elements is also conserved.

[9]The multiplicity of occurences of elements of the multi-sets is left unformal and intuitive for the sake of clarity. A precise formal definition can however be stated by extending the transition relation with an additional argument specifying the points of duplication of transitions.

We conclude this section by relating the operational semantics O_{td} and O_{ch}. Roughly speaking, all we have to do is, for each history, to perform all the unifications it contains and to reconcile the results. This is more precisely achieved by means of the three following functions.

Definition 13
1) Define eq_act *as follows: for any* $l \in Sact$,

$$eq\_act(l) = \begin{cases} \{A = B\}_s & \text{if } l = unif(A,B) \\ \emptyset & \text{if } l = cxt\_ext(c,u) \text{ or } l = cxt\_pop(c) \end{cases} .$$

2) Define mgu_syst_hist *as follows: for any* $h \in Shist$, $mgu\_syst\_hist(h)$ *is*

$$\begin{cases} \{mgu\_syst(\bigcup_{s\; i=1,\ldots,m} \bigcup_{s\; a \in l_i} eq\_act(a))\}_s, \text{ if } h = l_1.\ldots.l_m.\delta^+ \\ \emptyset, \text{ if } h = l_1.\ldots.l_m.\delta^- \text{ or if } h \text{ is infinite} \end{cases}$$

3) Define α_2 *as follows: for any* $MH \in \mathcal{M}_{nco}(Ssyst)$,

$$\alpha_2(MH) = \bigcup_{s\; h \in MH} \{mgu\_syst\_hist(h)\}_s.$$

■

Relating O_{td} and O_{ch} then consists of noting, by an inductive reasoning on reductions and histories, that, for any system $\mathcal{U}$, any context c and any g-goal $\overline{G}$, $O_{td}(\mathcal{U})(c)(\overline{G})$ and $[\alpha_2 \circ O_{ch}](\mathcal{U})(c)(\epsilon)(\overline{G})$ are identical.

Proposition 14 *For any* $\mathcal{U} \in Ssyst$, *any* $c \in Scontext$, $\overline{G} \in Sgoal$, *one has*

$$O_{td}(\mathcal{U})(c)(\overline{G}) = [\alpha_2 \circ O_{ch}](\mathcal{U})(c)(\epsilon)(\overline{G}).$$

■

5 Declarative semantics

5.1 Model theory

The operational semantics is concerned with proof, the declarative semantics with truth. The declarative semantics of a system of units is characterized by the set of g-goals that are true in every model of the system of units. The purpose of this section is to show how such semantics can be defined.

The first task is to find an appropriate notion of interpretation for CLL. An interpretation of Horn clause logic is a subset of the Herbrand base, intended to record the set of all facts that are true under the interpretation. In CLL, which facts are true depend on the context. An interpretation of CLL must thus provide a way to associate a subset of the Herbrand base with every context. Such subsets are called "situations".

Let $S_I(c)$ be the situation associated with the context c under the interpretation I. One must have $S_I(\lambda)=\emptyset$ since no facts are true in the empty context. Moreover, the situation $S_I(uc)$ must be the "update" by u of the previous situation $S_I(c)$, and consequently the equality $S_I(uc)=I_u(S_I(c))$ must hold for some function I_u depending on u. A unit name u is then interpreted as a "situation update" I_u, formalized as a mapping from situations to situations. Furthermore, given the intended meaning of context extension, such a function must redefine the predicates defined in the unit and leave the other predicates unchanged. The required notion of interpretation is then a family of updates I_u indexed by u ∈ Sunit. These ideas are now made precise.

Definition 15 *The Herbrand base of CLL is as usual the set HB of all ground atoms built with Sfunct and Spred. A* situation *is a subset of HB. If* $P \subseteq$ *Spred and* $S \subseteq$ *HB, the* restriction *of S to P is the set* $S \downarrow [P] = \{p(t_1,\ldots,t_n) \in S : p \in P\}_s$. *To simplify the notation,* $S \downarrow [Spred\text{-}P]$ *is abbreviated to* $S \downarrow [\text{-}P]$. ∎

Definition 16 *A continuous mapping* $t : \mathcal{P}(HB) \rightarrow \mathcal{P}(HB)$ *is called an* update *with respect to* $P \subseteq$ *Spred if, for every* $S \subseteq$ *HB, it satisfies the two following conditions:*

i) Preservation: $t(S) \downarrow [\text{-}P] = S \downarrow [\text{-}P]$ *(atoms with names not in P are preserved by t).*

ii) Dependency: $t(S) = t(S \downarrow [\text{-}P])$ *(the update depends only on the preserved atoms).* ∎

Definition 17 *An* interpretation *I of CLL is a family* $I = (I_u)_{u \in Sunit}$, *where each* I_u *is an update with respect to sort(u).* ∎

Definition 18 *Given a situation S, a finite set F of formulae and an interpretation I, the fact that* the formulae in *F* are true in *S* with respect to *I*, *denoted* $S \models_I F$, *is defined by the cases below. Let ground(F) be the set of all ground instances of formulae in F. Let us furthermore write* $S \models_I f$ *instead of* $S \models_I \{f\}_s$.

i) Sets: $S \models_I F$ *if and only if* $S \models_I f$ *for every* $f \in F$.

ii) Units: $S \models_I u{:}U$ *if and only if* $I_u(S) \models_I \overline{U}$.

iii) Clauses : $S \models_I H \leftarrow \overline{B}$ *if and only if* $S \models_I H_0 \leftarrow \overline{B}_0$ *for all* $(H_0 \leftarrow \overline{B}_0) \in$ *ground*$(H \leftarrow \overline{B})$.

iv) Ground clauses : $S \models_I H \leftarrow \overline{B}$ *if and only if* $S \models_I H$ *whenever* $S \models_I \overline{B}$.

v) Ground extension formulae : $S \models_I u \gg \overline{G}$ *if and only if* $I_u(S) \models_I \overline{G}$.

vi) Ground atomic formulae : $S \models_I A$ *if and only if* $A \in S$. ∎

The way this relation is defined is standard, with the possible exception of units and ground extension formulae. A unit is true in a given situation if the body is true in the situation updated by the denotation of the unit name. Extension formulae are interpreted similarly.

The notion of model, central for the declarative semantics, can now be defined.

Definition 19 *An interpretation I is a* model *of a set F of formulae if* $S \models_I F$ *for every* $S \subseteq$ *HB. A formula f is a* consequence *of F, denoted* $F \models f$, *if every model of F is a model of f.* ∎

The case of interest is when F is a system of units $\mathcal{U}$ and f is a g-goal $\overline{G}$. The (model-theoretic) declarative semantics will now be defined for this case. In the next definition, for a context name $c = u_1 \ldots u_n$, $c \gg \overline{G}$ will be used as a shorthand for the extension formula $u_n \gg \ldots \gg u_1 \gg \overline{G}$.

Definition 20 *Define the* declarative semantics $Decl_m$: *Ssyst* $\rightarrow$ *Scontext* $\rightarrow$ *Sgoal* $\rightarrow \mathcal{P}(Ssubst)$ *as follows: for any* $\mathcal{U} \in$ *Ssyst,* $c \in$ *Scontext, and* $\overline{G} \in$ *Sgoal:*

$$Decl_m(\mathcal{U})(c)(\overline{G}) = \{\theta : \forall \overline{G}_0 \in ground(\overline{G}\theta), \mathcal{U} \models c \gg \overline{G_0}\}_s.$$ ∎

5.2 Fixed-point theory

The models of a system of units $\mathcal{U}$ can be characterized as the prefixed points of a continuous operator $T_{\mathcal{U}}$: Sint $\rightarrow$ Sint associated with $\mathcal{U}$, where Sint is the set (complete lattice) of all interpretations. This characterization has two important consequences that follow directly from Tarski's lemma. The first is that $\mathcal{U}$ always has a minimal model $M_{\mathcal{U}}$, given by the least fixed point of $T_{\mathcal{U}}$. The second is that there is a standard iterative procedure for computing the least fixed point of $T_{\mathcal{U}}$, and hence $M_{\mathcal{U}}$. These facts are used to define a fixed-point semantics $Decl_f$.

First, note that the set Sint of all interpretations $I = (I_u)_{u \in Sunit}$, partially ordered by $I \leq J$ if and only if $I_u(S) \subseteq J_u(S)$ for every $u \in$ Sunit and $S \subseteq HB$, is a complete lattice. The mapping $T_{\mathcal{U}}$: Sint $\rightarrow$ Sint associated with $\mathcal{U}$ can now be defined.

Definition 21 *Let $T_{\mathcal{U}} : Sint \rightarrow Sint$ be the mapping defined as follows : for every interpretation I, $T_{\mathcal{U}}(I)$ is the interpretation J such that*

$$J_u(S) = (S \downarrow \lfloor\text{-}sort(u)\rfloor) \cup_s \{A : \exists(A \leftarrow \overline{B}) \in ground(|u|), I_u(S) \models_I \overline{B}\}_s$$

for every $u \in Sunit$ and $S \subseteq HB$. ∎

This mapping is well defined (that is $T_{\mathcal{U}}(I)$ is an interpretation, for every interpretation I) and continuous. Moreover, it can be shown that an interpretation I is a model of $\mathcal{U}$ if and only if $T_{\mathcal{U}}(I) \leq I$. By Tarski's lemma, $T_{\mathcal{U}}$ has a least fixed point, which therefore is also the least model of $\mathcal{U}$. This statement is the contents of the next proposition.

Proposition 22 *Every system of units $\mathcal{U}$ has a minimal model $M_{\mathcal{U}}$, given as the least fixed point of $T_{\mathcal{U}}$.* ∎

The fixed-point semantics is defined in terms of the least fixed point of $T_{\mathcal{U}}$, as usual.

Definition 23 *Define the* fixed-point semantics *$Decl_f$: Ssyst $\rightarrow$ Scontext $\rightarrow$ Sgoal $\rightarrow \mathcal{P}(Ssubst)$ as follows: for any $\mathcal{U} \in Ssyst$, $c \in Scontext$, and $\overline{G} \in Sgoal$:*

$$Decl_f(\mathcal{U})(c)(\overline{G}) = \{\theta \,.\, \forall \overline{G_0} \subset ground(\overline{G}\theta), \emptyset \models_{M_{\mathcal{U}}} c \gg \overline{G_0}\}_s,$$

where $M_{\mathcal{U}}$ is the minimal model of $\mathcal{U}$. ∎

The equivalence between the declarative and the fixed-point semantics is based on the following observation. There are two quantifications involved in the consequence relation $\mathcal{U} \models \overline{G}$, one over all models of $\mathcal{U}$ and the other over all situations. It is possible to eliminate both, by considering only the minimal model of $\mathcal{U}$ and the truth of $\overline{G}$ in the empty situation with respect to that model.

Proposition 24 *For every system of units $\mathcal{U}$ and g-goal $\overline{G}$, $\mathcal{U} \models \overline{G}$ if and only if $\emptyset \models_{M_{\mathcal{U}}} \overline{G}$. In particular, the declarative and the fixed-point semantics coincide, that is $Decl_m = Decl_f$.* ∎

The remainder of this section describes the connection between the operational and the declarative semantics. The relationship between the bottom-up derivation and the consequence relation $\models$ is established via the association of a situation with every context.

Definition 25 *Let I be an interpretation of a system of units $\mathcal{U}$. For every context name c, the* situation $S_I(c)$ determined by c under *I is defined inductively as follows:*

i) $S_I(\lambda) = \emptyset$,

ii) $S_I(uc) = I_u(S_I(c))$. ■

Proposition 26 *Given a system of units $\mathcal{U}$ with minimal model M, a context name c and a g-goal $\overline{G}$, one has $c \vdash^{bu}_{\mathcal{U}} \overline{G}$ if and only if $S_M(c) \models_M \overline{G_0}$ for every $\overline{G_0} \in ground(\overline{G})$.* ■

The equivalence between the bottom-up operational semantics and the declarative semantics is an easy consequence of the previous result.

Proposition 27 *One has $O_{bu} = \alpha_1 \circ Decl_m$.* ■

The next result relates the consequence relation to the top-down derivation relation.

Proposition 28 *If $\overline{G_0}$ is a ground instance of a g-goal $\overline{G}$ and if c is a context name, then $S_M(c) \models_M \overline{G_0}$ if and only if $c \vdash^{td}_{\mathcal{U}} \overline{G}[\theta]$ for some substitution θ such that $\overline{G_0}$ is an instance of $\overline{G}\theta$.* ■

It is now easy to establish the equivalence between the top-down operational semantics and the declarative semantics.

Proposition 29 *Let $\alpha_3 : \mathcal{P}(Ssubst) \rightarrow \mathcal{P}(Ssubst)$ be defined as follows: for every $\Sigma \in \mathcal{P}(Ssubst)$, $\alpha_3(\Sigma) = \{\sigma\theta : \sigma \in \Sigma, \theta \in Ssubst\}_s$. One has $Decl_m = \alpha_3 \circ O_{td}$.* ■

6 Denotational semantics

This section introduces our last semantics. It makes no use of transition systems and no reference to any declarative paradigm but is defined compositionally on the basis of processes. They may be formally described as multi-sets of computation steps followed by new processes, each computation step being described as an input multi-set of substitutions, a multi-set of basic actions[10] and an output multi-set of substitutions. They are organised in tree-like structures to capture the place of the various choice of use of clauses. Two auxiliary processes, $p^+$and p^-, are furthermore introduced to indicate termination in the successful and failure status. In view of this rough introduction, the set of processes Sproc could be recursively defined by the equation

$$\text{Sproc} = \{p^+, p^-\}_s \cup_s \mathcal{M}_{nf}(\text{Scstep} \times \text{Sproc}) \quad (1)$$

where Scstep[11] is $\mathcal{M}_{nf}(\text{Ssubst}) \times \mathcal{M}_{nf}(\text{Sact}) \times \mathcal{M}_{nf}(\text{Ssubst})$. Recursive equations of this type have been solved in a metric setting in [BZ82] and [AR89]. The careful reader will however note that no multi-sets are tackled in these references and, furthermore, that, to apply their results, $\mathcal{M}_{nf}(\text{Scstep} \times \text{Sproc})$ should be endowed with a distance, which cannot be inferred from previous definitions unless a truncation on Scstep × Sproc is clearly specified. Anyway, the simplicity of the equation (1) allows us to solve it directly. This is achieved as in [BZ82], by first defining an auxiliary space Sfproc, by then endowing it with a distance d and by finally defining the metric space Sproc as the completion of (Sfproc,d). We will furthermore take profit of this direct solving to restrict the processes to those verifying the following property:

> the multi-sets of the initial substitutions of the first computation steps are identical. (2)

[10] Recall notation 7 of section 4.3.

[11] Read Scstep as the set of computation steps.

Definition 30 *Define the set of finite processes Sfproc inductively by the following rules :*

i) $p^+, p^- \in Sfproc$

ii) *if* $\omega_1 = (\Lambda_1, S_1, \Upsilon_1), \ldots, \omega_m = (\Lambda_m, S_m, \Upsilon_m) \in Scstep$, $p_1, \ldots, p_m \in Sfproc$, $m > 0$ *and* $\Lambda_1 = \ldots = \Lambda_m$, *then* $\{(\omega_1, p_1), \ldots, (\omega_m, p_m)\}_{ms} \in Sfproc$. ∎

Endowing Sfproc with a distance can be achieved by considering the union of the equation (1) as disjoint and by defining the truncation function .[.] on processes.

Definition 31 *Define the truncation function .[.] on Sfproc by the following rules:*

i) $p[0] = \perp$, *for any* $p \in Sfproc$,

ii) $p^+[n] = p^+$, *for any* $n > 0$,

iii) $p^-[n] = p^-$, *for any* $n > 0$,

iv) $\{(\omega_1, p_1), \ldots, (\omega_m, p_m)\}_{ms}[1] = \{\omega_1, \ldots, \omega_m\}_{ms}$,
for any $\omega_1, \ldots, \omega_m \in Scstep$, $p_1, \ldots, p_m \in Sfproc$,

v) $\{(\omega_1, p_1), \ldots, (\omega_m, p_m)\}_{ms}[n] = \{(\omega_1, p_1[n-1]), \ldots, (\omega_m, p_m[n-1])\}_{ms}$,
for any $\omega_1, \ldots, \omega_m \in Scstep$, $p_1, \ldots, p_m \in Sfproc$, $n > 1$. ∎

Definition 32 *Define the metric on Sfproc as follows:*

i) $d(p^+, p^+) = d(p^-, p^-) = 0$,

ii) $d(p^-, p) = 1 = d(p, p^-)$, *for any* $p \in Sfproc$, *distinct from* p^-,

iii) $d(p^+, p) = 1 = d(p, p^+)$, *for any* $p \in Sfproc$, *distinct from* p^+,

iv) $d(p_1, p_2) = d_{ms}(p_1, p_2)$, *for any* $p_1, p_2 \in Sfproc$, *distinct from* p^+ *and* p^-. ∎

The metric space of processes Sproc is then defined from the space of finite processes Sfproc by taking in addition all limits of Cauchy sequences of Sfproc. This is achieved precisely by defining Sproc as the completion of (Sfproc,d). Two interesting properties of these new processes is that their structure ressemble that of finite processes and that they do verify property (2). The common value of these Λ_i's of any process p is subsequently referred to as *init(p)*.

Defining a compositional semantics requires to define an operator $\tilde{\|}$ equivalent at the denotational level to the parallel composition operator "," between g- atoms. It is defined according to our modelling of parallel composition of section 4.3 and by means of a suitable contraction to handle correctly recursivity with infinite structures. Note that, because of the tree-like structure of the processes, the contractivity problems of Ψ^*_{op} do not occur here.

Definition 33 *Define* $\Psi_{\|} : [Sproc \times Sproc \rightarrow Sproc] \rightarrow [Sproc \times Sproc \rightarrow Sproc]$ *as follows: for any* $F \in [Sproc \times Sproc \rightarrow Sproc]$, *for any* $p \in Sproc$, *for any* $p_1, p_2 \in Sproc \setminus \{p^+, p^-\}_s$:

i) $\Psi_{\|}(F)(p^-, p) = p^- = \Psi_{\|}(F)(p, p^-)$;

ii) $\Psi_{\|}(F)(p^+, p) = p = \Psi_{\|}(F)(p, p^+)$;

iii) $\Psi_{\|}(F)(p_1, p_2) =$

$$\begin{aligned}
&\{(\omega*, F(p'_1, p'_2)) : ((\Lambda_1, S_1, \Upsilon_1), p'_1) \in p_1, ((\Lambda_2, S_2, \Upsilon_2), p'_2) \in p_2,\\
&\quad \omega* = ((\Lambda_1 \cup_{ms} \Lambda_2), S_1 \cup_{ms} S_2, (\Upsilon_1 \cup_{ms} \Upsilon_2))\}_{ms}\\
&\cup_{ms} \{(\omega*, F(p'_1, p_2)) : ((\Lambda_1, S_1, \Upsilon_1), p'_1) \in p_1, \Lambda_2 = init(p_2),\\
&\quad \omega* = ((\Lambda_1 \cup_{ms} \Lambda_2), S_1, (\Upsilon_1 \cup_{ms} \Lambda_2))\}_{ms}\\
&\cup_{ms} \{(\omega*, F(p_1, p'_2)) : ((\Lambda_2, S_2, \Upsilon_2), p'_2) \in p_2, \Lambda_1 = init(p_1),\\
&\quad \omega* = ((\Lambda_1 \cup_{ms} \Lambda_2), S_2, (\Upsilon_2 \cup_{ms} \Lambda_1))\}_{ms}.
\end{aligned}$$ ∎

Proposition 34 *The function* $\Psi_{\|}$ *is well-defined and is a contraction.* ∎

Definition 35 *Define the function* $\tilde{\|}$: *Sproc* $\times$ *Sproc* $\rightarrow$ *Sproc as the fixed point of* $\Psi_{\|}$. ∎

Proposition 36 *For any* $p_1, p_2, p_3 \in$ *Sproc*, $(p_1 \,\tilde{\|}\, p_2) \,\tilde{\|}\, p_3 = p_1 \,\tilde{\|}\, (p_2 \,\tilde{\|}\, p_3)$. ∎

We are now in position to specify the denotational semantics Den. In view of its compositional nature, it is mainly defined by stating the denotational meaning of the basic cases, namely the empty g-goal and the g-goal reduced to one g-atom, which is quite straightforward in view of the preceeding sections. As before, undesirable problems with recursivity are avoided by means of a (well-defined) higher-order contraction Ψ_{den}. It is stated in terms of extended g-goals rather than g-goals in order to ease the relationship between O_{ch} and Den. Nevertheless, a similar contraction can be defined directly on g-goals (in a similar way) and its fixed point can be proved equal to Den, defined as the following restriction of **D**.

Definition 37 *Define* Ψ_{den} : [*Ssyst* $\rightarrow$ *Sextgoal* $\rightarrow$ *Sproc*] $\rightarrow$ [*Ssyst* $\rightarrow$ *Sextgoal* $\rightarrow$ *Sproc*] *as follows: for any* $F \in$ [*Ssyst* $\rightarrow$ *Sextgoal* $\rightarrow$ *Sproc*], *for any* $\mathcal{U} \in$ *Ssyst*,

i) $\Psi_{den}(F)(\mathcal{U})(\Delta_{ext}) = p^{+}$

ii) $\Psi_{den}(F)(\mathcal{U})(A \text{ in } <\sigma, c>) = p^{-}$, *if* $c=\lambda$ *or if the following conditions holds:* $c = uc'$, $name(A) \in sort(u)$, *no clause of u unifiable with A.*

iii) $\Psi_{den}(F)(\mathcal{U})(A \text{ in } <\sigma, c>) = \{(\omega_1, F(\mathcal{U})(\widetilde{B_1})), \ldots, (\omega_m, F(\mathcal{U})(\widetilde{B_m}))\}_{ms}$, *if the following conditions holds :*

- $c = uc'$,
- $name(A) \in sort(u)$,
- $H_1 \leftarrow \overline{B_1}, \ldots, H_m \leftarrow \overline{B_m}$ *are all the clauses of u unifiable with* $A\sigma$, *say with (idempotent) mgu* $\theta_1, \ldots, \theta_m$, *respectively,*
- $\omega_i = (\{\sigma\}_{ms}, \{unif(A\sigma, H_i)\}_{ms}, \{\sigma\circ\theta_i\}_{ms})$, *for all i,*
- $\widetilde{B_i} = \overline{B_i} \text{ in } <\sigma\circ\theta_i, c>$.

iv) $\Psi_{den}(F)(\mathcal{U})(A \text{ in } <\sigma, c>) = \{(\omega, F(\mathcal{U})(A \text{ in } <\sigma, c'>)\}_{ms}$,
if $c=uc'$, $name(A) \notin sort(u)$, $\omega = (\{\sigma\}_{ms}, \{cxt\_pop(c)\}_{ms}, \{\sigma\}_{ms})$.

v) $\Psi_{den}(F)(\mathcal{U})(u \gg \overline{G} \text{ in } <\sigma, c>) = \{(\omega, F(\mathcal{U})(\overline{G} \text{ in } <\sigma, uc>)\}_{ms}$,
where $\omega = (\{\sigma\}_{ms}, \{cxt\_ext(c,u)\}_{ms}, \{\sigma\}_{ms})$.

vi) $\Psi_{den}(F)(\mathcal{U})((\widehat{A_1}, \ldots, \widehat{A_m}) \text{ in } <\sigma, c>)$
$= \Psi_{den}(F)(\mathcal{U})(\widehat{A_1} \text{ in } <\sigma, c>) \,\tilde{\|}\, \ldots \,\tilde{\|}\, \Psi_{den}(F)(\mathcal{U})(\widehat{A_m} \text{ in } <\sigma, c>)$. ∎

Proposition 38 *The function* Ψ_{den} *is well-defined and is a contraction.* ∎

Definition 39

1) Define **D** : *Ssyst* $\rightarrow$ *Sextgoal* $\rightarrow$ *Sproc as the (unique) fixed point of* Ψ_{den}.

2) Define the denotational semantics *Den* : *Ssyst* $\rightarrow$ *Scontext* $\rightarrow$ *Ssubst* $\rightarrow$ *Sgoal* $\rightarrow$ *Sproc as follows: for any* $\mathcal{U} \in$ *Ssyst, any* $c \in$ *Scontext, any* $\sigma \in$ *Ssubst, any* $\overline{G} \in$ *Sgoal*, $Den(\mathcal{U})(c)(\sigma)(\overline{G}) = \mathbf{D}(\mathcal{U})(\overline{G} \text{ in } <\sigma, c>)$. ∎

We conclude this section by relating Den with the operational semantics O_{ch}. This achieved by relating the auxiliary functions **O** and **D**. Function **O** handles linear structures whereas function **D** manipulates tree-like structures. To relate them, we thus first need to introduce a function that, given some tree, produces the streams it contains. We then need to select the appropriate part of the computational set of O_{ch}, namely the action multiset part. This is the purpose of the following function α_4. Its recursive nature suggests to define it as the fixed point of some higher-order contraction. However, because of the stream structure of the results, contractivity problems already encountered for Ψ^*_{op} makes the definition of such a contraction impossible. Anyway, the function α_4 can be defined correctly by taking advantage of the tree-like structure of the processes, especially by defining a notion corresponding to that of predecessors in trees. This is subsequently denoted by $\omega \hookrightarrow_p \omega^*$, $\omega \hookrightarrow_p \delta^+$, $\omega \hookrightarrow_p \delta^-$, with respective meaning that ω is a predecessor of ω^*, of δ^+ and of δ^- in p.

Definition 40 *Define $\alpha_4 : Sproc \to \mathcal{M}(Shist)$ as follows:*

i) $\alpha_4(p^-) = \{\delta^-\}_{ms}$,

ii) $\alpha_4(p^+) = \{\delta^+\}_{ms}$,

iii) $\alpha_4(p) = \{S_1.\cdots.S_m.\delta : (\Lambda_1, S_1, \Upsilon_1) \hookrightarrow_p \ldots \hookrightarrow_p (\Lambda_m, S_m, \Upsilon_m) \hookrightarrow_p \delta,$
$((\Lambda_1, S_1, \Upsilon_1), p^*) \in p, \delta \in \{\delta^+, \delta^-\}_s\}_{ms}$
$\cup_{ms} \{S_1.\cdots.S_m.\cdots : (\Lambda_1, S_1, \Upsilon_1) \hookrightarrow_p \ldots (\Lambda_m, S_m, \Upsilon_m) \hookrightarrow_p \cdots,$
$((\Lambda_1, S_1, \Upsilon_1), p^*) \in p\}_{ms}$[12]

for any $p \in Sproc \setminus \{p^+, p^-\}_s$. ■

Proposition 41 *For any $p \in Sproc$, $\alpha_4(p)$ is non-empty and compact.* ■

Relating **O** and **D** consists of proving two properties :

i) firstly that the function $\alpha_4 \hat{\circ} \mathbf{D}$: Ssyst $\to$ Sextgoal $\to \mathcal{M}_{nco}$(Shist) defined as

$$(\alpha_4 \hat{\circ} \mathbf{D})(\mathcal{U})(\widetilde{\mathrm{G}}) = \alpha_4(\mathbf{D}(\mathcal{U})(\widetilde{\mathrm{G}}))$$

is, after composition with the function β[13], a fixed point of Ψ_{op}. As $\beta \circ \mathbf{O}$ is also a fixed point of Ψ_{op}(see proposition 12) and since contractions have only one fixed point, it is then proved that the functions **O** and $\alpha_4 \hat{\circ} \mathbf{D}$ return the same elements. Hence, so are the corresponding restrictions O_{ch} and $\alpha_4 \hat{\circ}$Den (the function $\alpha_4 \hat{\circ}$Den is defined similarly to $\alpha_4 \hat{\circ} \mathbf{D}$).

ii) secondly, that the sources of duplication of elements are the same in **O** and $\alpha_4 \hat{\circ} \mathbf{D}$. If so, the elements of the multi-sets delivered by **O** and $\alpha_4 \hat{\circ} \mathbf{D}$ occur with the same multiplicity. Taking the respective restrictions, the same property then also holds for O_{ch} and $\alpha_4 \hat{\circ}$Den.

These two properties can indeed be proved so that one can claim the following proposition.

Proposition 42 *One has $\mathbf{O} = \alpha_4 \hat{\circ} \mathbf{D}$ and therefore $O_{ch} = \alpha_4 \hat{\circ} Den$.* ■

7 Comparison and conclusion

The paper has presented six semantics ranging in the operational, declarative and denotational types. Four of them are inspired by the traditional logic programming paradigm. They consist of the operational semantics O_{bu} and O_{td}, based on the notions of bottom-up and top-down derivations, respectively, and of the declarative semantics Decl_m and Decl_f, based on model theory and fixed-point theory, respectively. The two other semantics are issued from the imperative tradition, and, more

[12]As in definition 10, the multiplicity of elements of the multi-sets is left informal and intuitive for the sake of clarity. A formal definition can however be achieved by inserting an additional argument in the predecessor relation that distinguishes the nodes of the process tree.

[13]Recall the function β introduced in proposition 12.

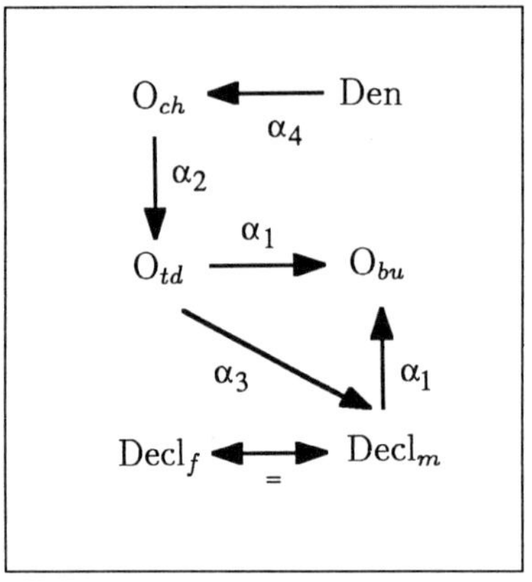

a) The minimal relations

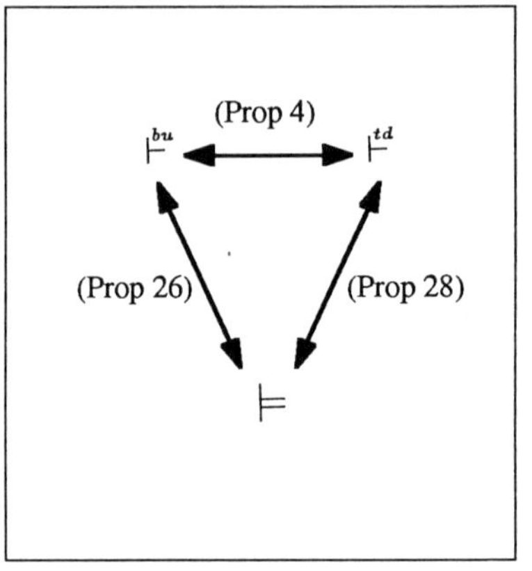

b) Equivalence of the bottom-up derivation, top-down derivation and satisfaction relation

Figure 1: Relations between the semantics

particularly, from its metric semantical branch ([BZ82], [BKMOZ86], [BM88], [B88], [KR88], [BK88], ...). They consist of the operational semantics O_{ch}, characterizing computations by means of streams, and of the denotational semantics Den, characterizing them, in a compositional way, via tree-like structures. All these semantics have been related throughout the paper, thanks to propositions 6, 14, 24, 27, 29, 42. They are summed up in figure 1a).

The minimal relations have only been stated in the paper. From them, it is possible to deduce other relations, for instance to connect Den with $Decl_f$. It is furthermore impossible to add nonredundant relations. For instance, it is impossible to relate O_{td} and O_{ch} since the former essentially delivers the results of the computation and the latter basically delivers histories of the computation. Similarly, it seems impossible to guess the choice point to build Den from O_{ch}. However, it is worth noting that although the semantics are different, it is possible to further connect the bottom-up derivation, the top-down derivation and the model theory. Propositions 4, 26, 28 and have, respectively, established the equivalence between the bottom-up and top-down derivations, the equivalence between the bottom-up derivation and the satisfaction relation, and the equivalence between the top-down derivation and the satisfaction relation. Hence, figure 1a) can be completed by figure 1b).

The parallel version of contextual logic programming presented in this paper is quite simple: it just includes or-parallelism and and-parallelism. It is not considered as a practical language to program with but rather as a first case study model. It is however quite interesting in the sense that it captures both the basis of contextual logic programming and of parallel logic programming. Our future work, under development, will be based on the results presented in this paper. It will be concerned with more elaborated versions including inheritance, guard-like constructs with related commitment operations, suspension conditions and some other more elaborated mechanisms (under development) for communication and concurrency. Also, we are trying to develop semantics closer to real computation in treating or-parallelism as real parallelism and not just as non-deterministic choice as in the paper. Finally, we are investigating the relationship of our model with semantics of the partial order type such as pomsets or event structures (see e.g. [Gr81], [Pr86], [BW90]).

Acknowledgments

The idea of contextual logic programming has been developed in joint work with A. Porto, with whom we have discussed many of the topics of this paper. We also thank the C.W.I. concurrency group, composed by J.W. de Bakker, F. de Boer, F. van Breughel, A. de Bruin, E. Horita, P. Knijnenburg, J. Kok, J. Rutten, E. de Vink and J. Warmerdam, for comments on a previous version of this paper. In particular, the first author wishes to thank E. Horita and J. Warmerdam for their "every-day" intensive discussions.

The research reported herein has been partially supported by Esprit BRA 3020 (Integration). The first author likes to thank also the Belgian National Fund for Scientific Research as well as the University of Namur for having supported his past research, from which some ideas of this paper have arisen. The second author also thanks the Instituto Nacional de Investigação Científica for partial support.

References

[AR89] America P., Rutten J.J.M.M., Solving reflexive domain equations in a category of complete metric spaces, *Journal of Computer and System Sciences*, Vol 39, no. 3, 1989, pp. 343-375.

[B88] de Bakker J.W., Comparative Semantics for Flow of Control in Logic Programming without Logic, Report CS-R8840, Center for Mathematics and Computer Science, Amsterdam, The Netherlands, 1988, to appear in *Information and Computation.*

[BK88] de Bakker J.W., Kok J.N., Uniform Abstraction, Atomicity and Contractions in the Comparative Semantics of Concurrent Prolog, *Proc. of FGCS*, 1988, pp. 347-355.

[BKMOZ86] de Bakker J.W., Kok J.N., Meyer J.-J.Ch, Olderog E.-R., Zucker J.I., Contrasting Themes in the Semantics of Imperative Concurrency, in *Current Trends in Concurrency : Overviews and Tutorials* (J.W. de Bakker, W.P. de Roever, G. Rozengerg, eds.), Lecture Notes in Computer Science, Vol. 224, Springer-Verlag, 1986, pp. 51-121.

[BKRP89] de Boer F.S., Kok J.N., Palamidessi C., Rutten J.J.M.M., Semantic Models for a Version of PARLOG, *Proc. of the 6th Int. Conf. on Logic Programming*, 1989, pp. 621-636.

[BM88] de Bakker J.W., Meyer J.-J.Ch., Metric Semantics for Concurrency, *BIT*, 28, 1988, pp. 504-529.

[BW90] de Bakker J.W., Warmerdam J., Metric Pomset Semantics for a Concurrent Language with Recursion, to appear in *Proc. of the 18e Ecole de Printemps d'Informatique Théorique*, La Roche-Posay, France, 1990.

[BZ82] de Bakker J.W., Zucker J.I., Processes and the Denotational Semantics of Concurrency, *Information and Control* 54, 1982, pp.70-120.

[En77] Engelking R., *General Topology*, Polish Scientific Publishers, 1977.

[Gr81] Grabowski J., On Partial Languages, *Fundamenta Informaticae* IV.2, 1981, pp. 427-498.

[Ja89] Jacquet J.-M., *Conclog : a Methodological Approach to Concurrent Logic Programming*, Ph.D. Thesis, University of Namur, Belgium, 1989, to appear as Lecture Notes in Computer Science, Springer-Verlag.

[Ja90] Jacquet J.-M., *Semantics for a Concurrent Contextual Logic Programming Language*, to appear as Technical Report, Center for Mathematics and Computer Science, Amsterdam, The Netherlands.

[KR88] Kok J.N., Rutten J.J.M.M., Contractions in Comparing Concurrency Semantics, *Proc. 15th ICALP* (T. Leistö, A. Salomaa, eds.), Lecture Notes in Computer Science, Vol. 317, Springer-Verlag, 1988, to appear in *Theoretical Computer Science*.

[Ll89] Lloyd J., *Foundations of Logic Programming*, Springer-Verlag, 1987.

[M86] Miller D., A Theory of Modules for Logic Programming, *Proc. of the 1986 Symposium on Logic Programming*, 1986, pp. 106-114.

[M89] Miller D., A Logical Analysis of Modules in Logic Programming, *Journal of Logic Programming* (6), 1989, pp. 79-108.

[Mo89] Monteiro L., *The Semantics of Contextual Logic Programming*, Technical Report UNL DI-5/89, Departamento de Informática, Universidade Nova de Lisboa, Portugal, 1989.

[MP89] Monteiro L., Porto A., Contextual Logic Programming, *Proc. of the 6th Int. Conf. on Logic Programming*, 1989, pp. 284-299.

[Pa88] Palamidessi C., *A Fixpoint Semantics for Guarded Horn Clauses*, Technical Report CS-R8833, Center for Mathematics and Computer Science, Amsterdam, The Netherlands, 1988.

[Pa90] Palamidessi C., Algebraic Properties of Idempotent Substitutions, Technical Report TR-32/89, Dipartimento di Informatica, University of Pisa, Pisa, Italy, 1989, to appear in *Proc. of the 17th ICALP*, 1990.

[Pl81] Plotkin G.D., *A Structural Approach to Operational Semantics*, Technical Report DAIMI FN-19, Computer Science Department, Aarhus University, 1981.

[Pr86] Pratt V., Modelling Concurrency with Partial Orders, *Int. Journal of Parallel Programming*, 15, 1986, pp. 33-71.

Abstract Interpretation for Concurrent Logic Languages

Christian Codognet
LIENS, 45 rue d'Ulm, 75230 PARIS Cedex 05, France
and University of Paris-XIII
codognet@ens.ens.fr

Philippe Codognet
INRIA, B.P. 105, 78153 LE CHESNAY Cedex, France
codognet@minos.inria.fr

Marc-Michel Corsini
LaBRI, 351, Cours de la libération, 33405 TALENCE Cedex, France
and University of Bordeaux-II
corsini@geocub.greco-prog.fr

Abstract

Abstract interpretation provides a general theoretical framework for statically computing information about the dynamic behavior of programs. We propose a general framework for Abstract Interpretation for Concurrent Logic Languages, in particular for FCP(:). Two main features of Concurrent Logic Languages have to be taken into account : synchronization between processes, consisting in suspending matching and in communication by shared variables, and don't care non-determinism, consisting in guarded clauses with a commit operator. We will present a meta-algorithm that simulates Stream-and parallelism by mimicing every possible computation, i.e. interleaving of atomic actions. The termination and correctness of the algorithm will be sketched. We also present a simpler one allowing to factorize several computations into a single one provided that the abstract domain enjoys a simple monotonicity property.

As an application, we will instanciate our meta-algorithm with an abstract domain detecting possible deadlocks in FCP(:) programs. This domain will basically consist in groundness and sharing information on variables together with a special structure recording possible suspension of processes. An important point to mention is that we need to include some information on variables in order to accurately simulate possible executions. This application will be illustrated with two simple FCP(:) programs.

1 Introduction

Abstract interpretation provides a general theoretical framework for statically computing information about the dynamic behavior of programs. Such information about a program will be used either to optimize it or to establish run-time properties (which are undecidable in the general case). The seminal work on abstract interpretation (for imperative languages) is due to the Cousots [CC 77, Cou 78], and its translation/adaptation to logic programming (read : Prolog) has proved very fecund [Mel 86, JS 87, KK 87, Bru 88, SM 89, CF 89]. This paper is based on the framework initiated in [CCF 86] and developed in [Cor 89, CF 89], which departs from the collecting semantics principle [JS 87, SM 89] and from abstract AND/OR trees [Bru 88]. [CF 89] presents a meta-algorithm whose correctness is proved w.r.t. SLD-derivations, i.e. the usual operational semantics for Prolog. This algorithm is a "meta"-version of that of [MU 87], and it is also close to that of [KK 87] as it combines top-down and bottom-up analysis. It has to be instantiated by a particular abstract domain to perform a particular analysis. The elements of the abstract domain are called abstract states and they approximate real substitutions. The task of a particular abstract interpretation is to associate to every clause c of the original logic program P a set S of abstract states such that for every possible real substitution which c may be called with during the execution of P, there is an element of S safely (i.e. pessimistically) approximating it.

In this paper we extend the framework of [CF 89] to Concurrent Logic Languages [Sha 89, CCRS 89], taking one of the offsprings of Flat Concurrent Prolog, FCP(:)[Sha 89], as a basis of this study. FCP(:) uses the Ask and Tell framework of [Sar 88, 89] and have atomic test unification.

Two main features of CLLs have to be taken into account : synchronization between processes on the one hand, consisting in suspending matching and in communication by shared variables, and don't care non-determinism on the other hand, consisting in guarded clauses with a commit operator. The second point will be treated in a way similar to don't know non-determinism in Prolog, as abstract interpretation has to consider every possible computation in order to be correct. On the contrary, the first point will lead to the design of two different algorithms : a general one intented to mimic every possible computation (i.e. interleaving of atomic actions), and a simpler one allowing to factorize several computations into a single one provided that the abstract domain enjoys a simple monotonicity property. Remark that these abstract simulations of synchronization and communication mechanisms are not treated in [GCS 88] where FCP programs are abstractly executed in the traditional left-to-right order of Prolog and the restrictions of abstract computations due to synchronization are ignored.

As an application, we will instanciate our meta-algorithm with an abstract domain detecting possible deadlocks in FCP(:) programs. Of course, we will only state sufficient conditions for a program to be deadlock-free. This domain will basically consists in groundness and sharing information on variables together with a special structure recording possible suspension of processes. An important point to mention is that we need to include some information on variables in order to accurately simulate possible executions.

This paper is organized as follows. Section 2 presents Concurrent Logic Languages and more precisely the syntax and operational semantics of FCP(:). Section 3 describes the basic definitions and the meta-algorithms for abstract interpretation of FCP(:) programs. Two algorithms are proposed, one general and one simpler that requires the abstract domain to enjoy a simple monotonicity property. In section 4, a particular abstract domain is presented, and it is used to detect possible deadlocks in FCP(:) programs. Possible extensions and perspectives are addressed in section 5 that ends the paper.

2 Concurrent Logic Languages

The reader is assumed to be familiar with the classical notions of logic programming, see for instance [Llo 87]. Throughout this paper, we will restrict ourselves to FCP(:). This language illustrates the basic execution mechanisms of Concurrent Logic Programming and can be given a simple operational semantics.

2.1 Syntax of FCP(:)

- An FCP(:) *program* is a finite set of guarded clauses. [1]
- a *guarded clause* is a formula of the form :

$$H \leftarrow Ask_1, ..., Ask_m : Tell_1, ..., Tell_n \mid B_1, ..., B_p. \quad n, m, p \geq 0$$

  where $H, B_1, ..., B_p$ are atoms, $Ask_1, ..., Ask_m$ are guard test predicates, and $Tell_1, ..., Tell_n$ are guard unifications. H is called the *head* of the clause, $Ask_1, ..., Ask_m : Tell_1, ..., Tell_n$ the *guard*, and $B_1, ..., B_p$ the body. If the guard is empty, the commit operator (|) is omitted. A *fact* is a guarded clause whose body is empty.

- we assume a finite set of *guard test predicates*, including $X = Y$, $X \neq Y$, $X < Y$, $X \leq Y$, *number(X)*. These predicates require their arguments to be ground and therefore all variables appearing in the guard of a clause have to appear in the head.

2.2 Operational semantics

While Prolog is a don't know nondeterministic sequential language (whose basic operation is unification), FCP(:) is a don't care nondeterministic concurrent language. According to the "process interpretation" of CLLs [Sha 83], the atoms of the current goal are concurrent processes whose synchronization is achieved through suspending matching and communication through shared variables. Don't care nondeterminism amounts to choose a guarded clause among those defining a predicate : any such that the evaluation of its head and guard succeeds (i.e. neither suspends nor fails). Observe that the selected clause is unique (i.e. the subsequent computation is committed to that choice).

Following [Pnu 86] and [Cha 88], [Sha 89] models concurrency by the nondeterministic interleaving of the atomic actions of the processes participating to a computation, where valid atomic action are defined by a *transition system*. It proposes a simple operational semantics for various CLLs, including FCP(:), close to the usual operational semantics of logic programs : indeed SLD-resolution can be rephrased as a transition system. As given in [Sha 89] :

Definitions

- A *transition system* for a program P of a language $\mathcal{L}$ is a couple $< \mathcal{S}; \mathcal{T} >$ where :

- $\mathcal{S}$ is a set of *states* $< G; \sigma >$. The goal G is either a sequence of atoms or *fail* and σ is a substitution.
- $\mathcal{T}$ is a set of *transitions*, i.e. of functions from $\mathcal{S}$ to $2^{\mathcal{S}}$. For states S, S' and transition t, $S \xrightarrow{t} S'$ is a notation for $S' \in t(S)$.

- A transition is *enabled* on a state S if $t(S) \neq \emptyset$. A *terminal state* is a state on which no transition is enabled. A terminal state of the form $< true; \sigma >$ is called a *success state* and $< fail; \sigma >$ a failure state.

- A *computation of a program P on goal G* is a (possibly infinite) sequence of states

[1] a sequence would be necessary if order-dependent guard predicates, eg. *otherwise*, are allowed.

$c = S_1, S_2, ..., S_i, ...$ s.t. :
$S_1 =< G; \epsilon >$ (where ϵ is the empty substitution).
$\forall k, S_k \in t(S_{k-1})$ for some transition t.
c is finite and of length k only if S_k is terminal.

The transition system for a Prolog program P will be given by the two following transitions :

• $< A_1, ..., A_n; \theta > \overset{Reduce_{prolog}}{\longrightarrow} < (B_1, ..., B_k, A_2, ..., A_n)\theta'; \theta \circ \theta' >$
if $mgu(A_1, A) = \theta'$ for a variant $A \leftarrow B_1, ..., B_k$ of some clause of P,
where $mgu(A, A')$ is the most general unifier of A and A'

• $< A_1, ..., A_n; \theta > \overset{fail_{prolog}}{\longrightarrow} < fail; \theta >$
if $mgu(A_1, A) = fail$ for variants $A \leftarrow B_1, ..., B_k$ of all clauses of P.

To define the transition system for a FCP(:) program P we only need to allow any atom to be reduced and to replace unification by suspending matching and guard checking. We will use the following functions :

$$match(A, A') = \begin{cases} \theta & \text{if } \theta \text{ is the most general substitution s.t. } A = A'\theta \\ fail & \text{if } mgu(A, A') = fail \\ suspend & \text{otherwise} \end{cases}$$

$$try(A, A' \leftarrow Ask : Tell | B) = \begin{cases} \theta \circ \theta' & \text{if } match(A, A') = \theta \\ & \quad \wedge \text{ checking } Ask\theta \text{ succeeds} \\ & \quad \wedge\ mgu(Tell\theta) = \theta' \\ fail & \text{if } match(A, A') = fail \\ & \quad \vee\ match(A, A') = \theta \\ & \qquad \wedge \text{ checking } Ask\theta \text{ fails} \\ & \quad \vee\ match(A, A') = \theta \\ & \qquad \wedge \text{ checking } Ask\theta \text{ succeed} \\ & \qquad \wedge\ mgu(Tell\theta) = fail \\ suspend & \text{otherwise} \end{cases}$$

in order to now define the transitions :

• $< A_1, ..., A_n; \theta > \overset{Reduce_{FCP(:)}}{\longrightarrow} < (A_1, ..., A_{i-1}, B_1, ..., B_k, A_{i+1}, ..., A_n)\theta'; \theta \circ \theta' >$ if for some i, $try(A_i, C) = \theta'$ for a variant $C = A \leftarrow Ask : Tell | B_1, ..., B_k$ of some clause of P.

• $< A_1, ..., A_n; \theta > \overset{fail_{FCP(:)}}{\longrightarrow} < fail; \theta >$
if for some i $try(A_i, C) = fail$ for variants C of all clauses of P.

3 Abstract Interpretation for Concurrent Logic Languages

In this section, we present a general framework for abstract interpretation of Concurrent Logic Languages, which is based on the one developed for Prolog in [CF 89].

The specification of a technique based on Abstract Interpretation is the giving of an *abstract domain* D, elements of which are *abstract states* that approximate substitutions and of abstract operations on these elements that approximate composition of substitutions. Its task is to analyze any logic program P and goal (or set of goals),

in order to associate to each clause c of P a set $S(c)$ of abstract states such that, if, during the execution of P, c is called with a substitution σ, there exists an element of $S(c)$ that approximates σ. In this case the specification is said to be safe (or correct).
In our mind a general framework for Abstract Interpretation consist of:
- an algorithm to realize whatever specification one may want to do
- some clear conditions that guarantee the correctness of this algorithm
We present a meta-algorithm AbInt-FCP(T), where T is a triple $(D, \uparrow\prod, \downarrow\prod)$: T specifies the abstract domain D and the abstract operations on D to be used in the algorithm. For ensuring the termination of any AbInt-FCP(T) we need the finiteness of the abstract domain D [2], and the correctness of any AbInt-FCP(T) is shown by comparing the abstract computations with the concrete FCP ones.
Basically, the meta-algorithm will try to simulate the computation mechanisms of Concurrent Logic Languages on abstract states. Observe that abstract interpretation for CLLs will thus differ from abstract interpretation for Prolog in the same measure that CLLs differ from Prolog. There are two main differences:

- suspending matching and guard checking are used for each computation step instead of unification. This mechanism will be simulated by the $\downarrow\prod$ function that is peculiar to the abstract domain.
- stream and-parallelism obliges to immediately propagate any new binding to all other literals/processes sharing this variable. We will design two algorithms that simulate this communication mechanism : a general one that mimics every possible computation, i.e. every interleaving of atomic actions, and a simpler one factorizing several computations into a single one provided that the abstract domain enjoys a simple monotonicity property.

3.1 Preliminaries

Definition
Given a program P, the *specification* of a technique based on Abstract Interpretation for P is a triple $T=(D, \uparrow\prod, \downarrow\prod)$. D is the abstract domain containing special elements $\perp$, *fail* and *suspend*, representing respectively absence of information, sure failure and sure suspension. The functions $\uparrow\prod$ and $\downarrow\prod$ are abstract operations of type $literal \times D \times D \times clause \rightarrow D$ and $literal \times D \times clause \rightarrow D$ respectively.

The abstract operation $\downarrow\prod$ will simulate the checking of the (ask and tell) guard, and can be seen as an abstract *try* function (recall 2.2). If a clause try surely suspends (resp. fails) then $\downarrow\prod$ returns *suspend* (resp. *fail*); computations reaching such states can obviously be ignored. $\uparrow\prod$ corresponds to the communication of a partial instantiation to the calling literal.

Three notions are at the basis of AbInt-FCP(T) : call pattern, success pattern and call/success tree.

Definitions
Let P be a program, $T=(D, \uparrow\prod, \downarrow\prod)$ a specification. A *call pattern* for P in T

[2] Recall that D depends on P. Moreover, we only need that the subset of D used for analyzing a program P is finite. In such an extension, the abstract computation has to enforce that any new abstract state belongs to the authorized finite subset, by approximating non-authorized elements by authorized ones if necessary, see [Che 90].

is a couple (A,Δ) where A is a literal of P and Δ ∈ D. A *success pattern* is a triple (A,Δ,Δ') where A is a literal of P and Δ, Δ' ∈ D. A *call/success tree* is a tree whose root is a call pattern, and whose nodes are either call or success patterns.

Intuitively, a call/success tree t is a tree where the root is labeled (A,Δ), and the leaves are (normally) labeled (A,Δ,Δ'). t approximates all real FCP-computations starting with $< A; \delta >$ where Δ is an approximation of δ. The states Δ' at the leaves approximate the answer substitutions δ' of the success states $< true; \delta' >$.

3.2 The algorithm AbInt-FCP(T)

The algorithm consists of a main program *analyze* and two procedures *create_tree* and *derive*. The task of *create_tree* is to create, for a given call pattern, a new call/success tree whose root is labeled by this call pattern. A branch is started with a success pattern for each alternative clause, according to the checking of its guard part. Then, each success pattern whose third component is not *fail* or *suspend* (i.e. the corresponding guard check neither suspends nor fails) is given as many sons (call patterns) as there are literals in the body of the clause. We thus simulate the beginning of all possible subcomputations.
The procedure *derive*, given a node m labeled (A_j, Δ) and success pattern sp=(A_j, Δ, Δ'), expands the call/success tree where m appears in order to propagate a new abstract state Δ' to related processes, i.e. possible consumers, and thus simulate Stream And-parallelism. This is achieved by creating a success pattern $(A, \Delta_0, \uparrow \prod(A, \Delta_0, \Delta', c))$ for the head literal A, in order to recursively propagate the new abstract state Δ'. For each brother literal A_i, $(i \neq j)$, a new call pattern (A_i, Δ') is also creating. This computation will go on until the same call pattern is found for the second time on a branch of the call/success tree, ensuring the local termination.
It is important to note that our success patterns correspond to partial computations (basic FCP observables, due to Stream-parallelism), but not to completed successful computations as in Prolog (basic Prolog observables, due to sequentiality).
It is interesting to compare this *derive* procedure, that mimics the FCP computation, to the derive procedure of [CF 89] that mimics Prolog computation which goes as follows : if A_j is the last literal of the clause then a success pattern $(A, \Delta_0, \uparrow \prod(A, \Delta_0, \Delta', c))$ corresponding to the call pattern (A, Δ_0) is created, else there is a literal A_{j+1} and a son node labeled by (A_{j+1}, Δ') is created.

INPUT : a program P and a goal *goal* [3]
OUTPUT : a set of call/success trees for P in T

In the sequel *cp* and *sp* denote a call and a success pattern, respectively; if cp=(A,Δ) and sp=(A,Δ,Δ'), sp will often be denoted by (cp,Δ'). For a clause c and an integer i, $< c, i >$ will denote the ith literal of c. For a node n of a call/success tree t, lab(n) is its label, which is either a call or success pattern. root(n) is the label of the root of t.
The following variables are used in the algorithm :
- **CP** the list of the call patterns labeling the root of a call/success tree
- **SP(cp)** the list of the success patterns labeling the leaves of the call/success tree with root labeled by cp

[3] we will only consider goals containing a single literal, without loss of generality as one can always augment P with $goal \leftarrow l_1, ..., l_n$ for handling a query $\leftarrow l_1, ..., l_n$.

– **Node(cp)** the list of the nodes labeled by cp
– **Active** the list of the nodes that need to be processed

```
program analyze
begin
Active:={(goal,⊥)}   * initial call pattern for the query *
CP := ∅
while Active ≠ ∅ do
   begin
   let m ∈ Active
   Active := Active - { m }
   case lab(m) of
   cp=(A,Δ) : add m to Node(cp)
              if cp ∉ CP then create_tree(cp)
              else forall sp ∈ SP(cp) do derive(m,sp)
   sp=(A,Δ,Δ') : let cp=(A,Δ)
                 if sp ∉ SP(cp) then
                    begin
                    add sp to SP(cp)
                    for each k ∈ Node(cp) do derive(k,sp)
                    end
   endcase
   end
end analyze.

procedure create_tree(cp:call pattern)
begin
let cp = (A,Δ)
add cp to CP
SP(cp):=∅
create a node n with lab(n)=cp
forall clause c with same head predicate than A do
   begin
   Δ' := ↓ ∏(A, Δ, c)
   create a node m and make it son of n
   lab(m) := (cp,↑ ∏(A, Δ, Δ', c))
   if Δ' ≠ fail ∧ Δ' ≠ suspend then
      begin
      add m to Active
      forall literal l of c do
            begin
            create a node m' and make it son of m
            lab(m'):=(l,Δ')
            add m' to Active
            end
      end
endcase
end create_tree
```

The *derive* procedure, defined below, uses a procedure déjà_vu(cp:call pattern) that checks if cp already appears on the current branch of the call/success tree.

procedure derive(m:node;sp:success pattern)
begin
let lab(m)=($\langle c,j\rangle$,Δ)
let sp=($\langle c,j\rangle$,Δ,Δ')
let lab(root(m))=(A,Δ_0)
create two new nodes r_1 and r_2
make r_1 a son of m and r_2 a son of r_1
lab(r_1):=sp
lab(r_2):=(A,Δ_0,$\uparrow\prod(A,\Delta_0,\Delta',c)$)
add r_2 to Active
forall literal l of c except $\langle c,j\rangle$ **do**
    if not *déjà_vu*(l,Δ') **then**
        begin
        create a node r and make it son of r_2
        lab(r):=(l,Δ')
        add r to Active
        end
    end
end derive

Observe that well-known techniques for decreasing the complexity of Abstract Interpretation, as using a maximum function among success patterns for a given call pattern instead of keeping the set of all of them, can be used in our framework as well, obviously paying the price for precision.

3.3 Termination and correctness of AbInt-FCP(T)

Let P be a program and T=(D,$\uparrow\prod$,$\downarrow\prod$) a specification for P. We note H the Herbrand universe for P, and S the set of suspending substitutions from a countable set V of variables to $H\cup\{fail, suspend\}$.
The termination and correctness of the algorithm will rely on the five following properties :

1. (D,≤) is a finite poset containing three special elements ⊥ , *fail* and *suspend* ordered as follows :
   - ⊥ is the least element
   - *fail* is a maximal element
   - $\forall\Delta\in D-\{\bot, fail\}$, $suspend\leq\Delta$
2. There exist two functions ABS (abstraction), from S to D, and CONC (concretization), from D to 2^S, which form a Galois insertion, i.e :
   - $\forall\Delta\in D,\ ABS(CONC(\Delta))=\Delta$
   - $\forall\delta\in S,\ CONC(ABS(\delta))\geq\delta$
3. $\uparrow\prod$ and $\downarrow\prod$ are monotonic, i.e. for any literal l, any clause c of P, and $\Delta_1,\Delta_2,\Delta_1',\Delta_2'$ *s.t.* $\Delta_1\leq\Delta_1'$ and $\Delta_2\leq\Delta_2'$ we have $\uparrow\prod(l,\Delta_1,\Delta_2,c)\leq\uparrow\prod(l,\Delta_1',\Delta_2',c)$ and similarly for $\downarrow\prod$.

4. Consider two unifiable literals A and B=$\langle c, 0\rangle$. Let σ_1 and σ_2 be two substitutions, let Δ_1=ABS(Aσ_1) and Δ_2=ABS(Bσ_2). The following two points must hold :
   a. $\uparrow\prod(A, \Delta_1, \Delta_2, c) \leq$ ABS(mgu(Aσ_1,Bσ_2))
   b. $\downarrow\prod(A, \Delta_1, c) \leq$ ABS(mgu(Aσ_1,B))

5. $\downarrow\prod$ must correctly simulate guard checking :
   - $\downarrow\prod(A, \Delta, c) = \mathit{fail} \Rightarrow \forall\delta \in CONC(\Delta),\ try(A\delta, c) = \mathit{fail}$
   - $\downarrow\prod(A, \Delta, c) = \mathit{suspend} \Rightarrow \forall\delta \in CONC(\Delta),\ try(A\delta, c) = \mathit{suspend}$

3.3.1 Termination of AbInt-FCP(T)

The termination only relies on property (1) :
First observe that each call/success tree is finite for the following reasons. First, there is a finite number of clauses and of literals inside a clause, thus there is finitely many branches. Second, each branch is finite as the number of distinct call patterns (l, Δ) is finite, because the number of literals in a clause is finite and D is finite, and we have the *déjà_vu* check. As each of call/success tree has a finite number of nodes and as Active grows only when a call/success tree grows, this shows that AbInt-FCP(T) stops.

3.3.2 Correctness of AbInt-FCP(T)

The following theorem establishes the correctness of the algorithm

Theorem
Let P be a program and T=(D,$\uparrow\prod$,$\downarrow\prod$) a specification of a technique based on Abstract Interpretation that satisfies the 5 conditions stated above.
For every computation of P starting with a goal $< goal; \epsilon >$ and ending with a success state $< true; \theta >$, there exists a success pattern $(goal, \perp, \Delta)$ s.t. $\Delta \leq ABS(\theta)$.
Sketch of the proof
The proof is similar to that of [CF 89] for the framework of Abstract Interpretation for Prolog. By induction on the length of the FCP-computations, one can show that each partial proof-tree produced by such computations is correctly approximated, i.e. we have the following fact :
<u>*Fact :*</u> for each FCP-computation $S_1, \ldots, S_k, S_{k+1}, \ldots$ of P,
where $S_k =< A_1, \ldots, A_i, \ldots, A_n; \theta >$
and $S_{k+1} =< (A_1, \ldots, A_{i-1}, B_1, \ldots, B_p, A_{i+1}, \ldots, A_n)\sigma; \theta \circ \sigma >$,
the set of call/success trees produced by the algorithm contains a tree t such that :
1. the root is labeled by (A_i,Δ), where $\Delta \leq ABS(\theta)$
2. there is a leaf labeled by (A_i, Δ, Δ'), with $\Delta' \leq ABS(\theta \circ \sigma)$

□

3.4 A simpler algorithm : AbInt-FCP'(T)

We will now propose a simpler algorithm allowing to factorize several computations in a single one provided that the abstract domain enjoys a simple monotonicity property. This algorithm will be very close to the one developed for Prolog in [CF 89]. Namely, a success pattern $(A_i, \Delta_{i-1}, \Delta_i)$ will create a call pattern (A_{i+1}, Δ_i) according to the order of the literals in the clause, excepted for the success pattern

$(A_n, \Delta_{n-1}, \Delta_n)$ of the last literal A_n which will be reinjected to A_1, by creating a call pattern (A_1, Δ_n), instead of giving rise to a success pattern for the calling literal as in Prolog. One can figure this process as a token passed among all brother literals of the clause, each of them updating it with new information. The synchronization and communication among literals in FCP(:) obliges to reinject the token from the last literal (Δ_n) to the beginning of the clause as some literal A_i may be waken-up (and thus update the current token) by the work done by some A_j, $j > i$ (recorded in Δ_n). This loop will go on until the same call pattern is found for the second time in the current computation, i.e. on the current branch of a call/success tree, representing the fact that no work can proceed any more. This achieves indeed a local fixpoint computation of the token, and gives a success pattern for the calling literal : (A,Δ,Δ').

This simulation of the synchronization and communication among literals/processes factorize several abstract FCP-computations in a single branch of a call/success tree and is thus much simpler that what is done by the previous algorithm where each branch represents a single abstract FCP-computation. Indeed, independent sub-computations (w.r.t. synchronization) are now executed in a somewhat left to right manner, and thus factorized as we do not consider all possible interleavings any more. Whereas the first algorithm started, upon a success pattern (A_i, Δ, Δ'), call patterns and new branches of the call/success tree for each brother literal A_j $(j \neq i)$ in order to simulate the immediate communication of the new instantiation, the simpler algorithm only creates a call pattern (A_{i+1}, Δ') and thus simulates the communication from A_i to A_{i+1}. However, A_{i+1} will communicate its successes to A_{i+2} and so on with $A_{i+3}, ..., A_n, A_1, ..., A_i, ...$, so that every processes that could be waken-up and proceed will do so.
However, this simplification is correct if the $\downarrow \prod$ function satisfies :

$$\Delta' \geq \Delta \Rightarrow \ (\downarrow \prod(A, \Delta', c) = \mathit{fail} \vee \mathit{suspend} \Rightarrow \downarrow \prod(A, \Delta, c) = \mathit{fail} \vee \mathit{suspend} \ )$$

This property ensures that overwork is not harmful.

The algorithm AbInt-FCP'(T) consists again of a main program *analyze* identical to the previous one and of two procedures *create_tree'* and *derive'*. *create_tree'* is also mainly identical to the previous one, except that the **if** construct is changed to :

if Δ ≠ *fail* **then**
  begin
  add m to Active
  create a node m' and make it son of m
  lab(m'):=($\langle c, 1\rangle$,$\downarrow \prod(A, \Delta, c)$)
  add m' to Active
  end

procedure derive'(m:node;sp:success pattern)
begin
let lab(m)=($\langle c, j\rangle$,Δ)
let sp=($\langle c, j\rangle$,Δ,Δ')
let lab(root(m))=(A,Δ_0)
create two new nodes r_1 and r_2
make r_1 a son of m and r_2 a son of r_1

```
lab(r1):=sp
if the body of c has j literals then l:=⟨c, 1⟩
else l:=⟨c, j + 1⟩
if déjà_vu(l,Δ') then
   begin
   lab(r2):=(A,Δ0,↑ ∏(A, Δ0, Δ', c))
   add r2 to Active
   end
else begin
     if Δ'=suspend then lab(r2)=(l,Δ) else lab(r2):=(l,Δ')
     add r2 to Active
     end
end derive'
```

4 Application to deadlock detection

We have to define the specification (D,$\uparrow \prod$,$\downarrow \prod$) that we want to use for detecting deadlock-free programs. The abstract domain D has to give efficient groundness information on variables as this information will then be used by $\downarrow \prod$ for determining possible suspensions during matching and guard check. The accuracy of the abstract states in approximating substitutions (instanciations of variables of a clause) will be crucial for the abstract derivations to realistically represent possible concrete ones, and hence for the deadlock detection not to be too pessimistic. We have thus preferred to use for this purpose a quite sophisticated structure called a *contexts* [Cor 89, CF 89], instead of a simple one as used in [Mel 86] for example. A similar analysis could be done with the abstract domain of [JL 89]. The abstract domain will consist in tuples (α, flag), where α approximates a substitution and contains groundness and sharing information on variables, and *flag* is an element of {*suspendible, committable, committable-or-failed*} that will be used to record suspension.

4.1 Groundness and sharing information

[Cor 89, CF 89] introduces *contexts* that approximate substitutions and contain precise information about groundness and covering relations among variables that we will now define.

Definition
Let σ be a substitution, S_1 and S_2 two subsets of the domain of $\sigma$and V_{S_i} be the set $\{X/\exists Z, \in S_1 \cup S_2 s.t. X \in Var(\sigma(Z))\}$

- S_1 covers S_2 wrt σ if $V_{S_1} \supseteq V_{S_2}$
- S_1 and S_2 are variable-equivalent wrt σ if $V_{S_1} = V_{S_2}$

Consider, for example, the substitution σ={ W/A, X/A, Y/B, Z/f(A,B) }:
{Z} covers {X} and also {Y}, {Z} and {X,Y} are variable-equivalent and {W} and {X} are variable-equivalent.
It is easy to see that the definition above allows efficient groundness propagation. For example, if we know that Z is ground, we can infer that X, Y and W are ground as well, conversely if X and Y are ground, we are able to infer that W and Z are ground too.

Definition
Let $\mathcal{F}$ be the set of the function symbols occurring in the program, with their arity, as for example g/2. This set will be used to record the principal functor of a ground variable; we also need a distinct special symbol ξ (for non-ground variables) and a symbol ν identifying variables bound to arithmetic expressions (recall the guard test predicates of 2.1). Let $\mathcal{F}_* = \mathcal{F} \cup \{\xi, \nu\}$ A *context* α is a 5-tuple of the form (V, T, GR, K, F) where :

1. V is a finite subset of the variables of the program that will form the domain of α.

2. T is a labeling of the domain with principal functor information, and is thus a subset of $V \times F_*$.

3. $GR \subseteq V$ is the set of ground variables.

4. K contains the variable equivalence information, and is thus a subset of $V \times 2^V$.

5. $F \subseteq V \times V$ contains the covering information.

A partial order can be naturally introduced among contexts. Intuitively, the smaller will contain less ground variables or less covering arcs (i.e. less information). Unfortunately, in order to compare two contexts, one needs to remove useless covering information concerning ground variables, hence the notion of *coherence* below.

Definitions
Given two contexts α_i=(V_i,T_i,GR_i,,K_i,F_i) $i \in \{1,2\}$, we say :

1. α_1 is *coherent* wrt α_2 if for every (X,Y)$\in F_1$, whenever X is in GR_2 then Y is in GR_2, and for every (X,S)$\in K_1$, whenever $S \subseteq GR_2$, X$\in GR_2$.

2. $\alpha_1 \leq \alpha_2$ whenever:
 - α_1 is coherent wrt α_2,
 - V_1=V_2,
 - $GR_1 \subseteq GR_2$,
 - $K_1/\alpha_2 \subseteq K_2$,
 - $F_1/\alpha_2 \subseteq F_2$
 where F_1/τ_2={(X,Y) st (X,Y)$\in F_1$ and $\{X,Y\} \cap GR_2 = \emptyset$}
 and K_1/τ_2={(X,S') st (X,S)$\in K_1$, X$\notin GR_2$ and S'=S$-GR_2$}

4.2 Abstract domain

The abstract domain D will consist in tuples (α, *flag*), where α is an context containing groundness and sharing information as described in section 4.1, and *flag* is an element of S ={*suspendible, committable, committable-or-failed*} called a *suspension flag*. The lexicographical order is used on D, taking the previously defined order on contexts and *suspendible* < *committable-or-failed* < *committable*. Abstraction and concretization functions are simple to define and have obviously the desired property, see [CF 89].

The $\uparrow \prod$ and $\downarrow \prod$ functions operating on D can be easily defined by using the notion of *templates*, approximating the unification of two atoms. For instance, the template corresponding to the unification :

$$append(X_1, Y_1, [a, b]) = append([X_2 \,.\, L_2], Y_2, [X_2 : H_2])$$

can be depicted as :

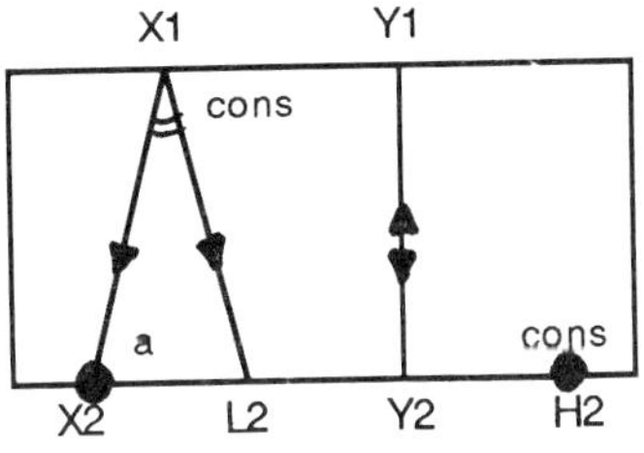

Black circles correspond to ground variables, whose principal functor is shown above, and oriented arcs represent covering information : an hyper-arc is put between a variable and all the variables appearing in its subterms, and a double oriented arc represents variable-equivalent variables.

$\downarrow \prod$ projects abstract states (instantiations) to the lower part of the template : $\downarrow \prod(A, \Delta, c)$ will compute a new context Δ' using Δ and the template corresponding to the unification of A and the head of c, by computing paths in the graph corresponding to the "gluing" of Δ and the template. For example, black nodes (ground variables) are propagated along directed arcs, and also in reverse direction if a node has all its successors black. Propagating covering relation is a bit more complex, see [CF 89] for a complete description and formalization.
Moreover, $\downarrow \prod$ has to compute the suspension flag in the following way :
Let A be an atom, c a clause of P and $\Delta = (\alpha, s) \in$ D.
$\downarrow \prod(A, \Delta, c) = (\alpha', s')$ such that .

$$s' = \begin{cases} \textit{committable} & \text{only if } \forall \delta \in CONC(\Delta),\ try(A\delta, c) = \theta \\ \textit{committable-or-failed} & \text{only if } \forall \delta \in CONC(\Delta),\ try(A\delta, c) = fail \vee \theta \\ & \quad \wedge\ \exists \delta' \in CONC(\Delta),\ try(A\delta', c) = fail \\ \textit{suspendible} & \text{otherwise} \end{cases}$$

Computing the suspension flag will correspond to check for simple properties of paths in the gluing of the context and the template, eg. that no node of the upper part (variable of the calling literal) becomes black or source of a path containing a directed arc, etc. Observe that for each guard test predicate authorized in the guard in addition to matching, one must define a corresponding abstract operation and check for suspension, eg. that the nodes corresponding to inputs are black.
$\uparrow \prod$ is defined similarly to $\downarrow \prod$ on contexts and let the suspension flag unchanged in order to conveniently define *deadlock-free trees* next section.

4.3 Analysis

Definitions

- Consider a call/success tree t for (A,Δ) and two distinct nodes n' and n" are labeled with (B,Δ') and (B,Δ") respectively. n' is *subsumed by* n" if the father of n' is a node labeled by (A,Δ,Δ') which is an ancestor of n".

- A branch of a call/success tree for (A,Δ) is *deadlock-free* if it ends with a success (A,Δ,Δ') and, for any call pattern (B, Δ_B) which is not subsumed, the call/success tree for (B, Δ_B) is deadlock-free. [4]

- A call/success tree t is *deadlock-free* if :

  (i) Consider the success patterns which are sons of the root (corresponding to the checking of the guards) and which are not labeled by (A,Δ,*fail*). Either there exists a success pattern labeled by (_,_,(_,*committable*)), or all success patterns are labeled by (_,_,(_, *committable-or-failed*)).

  (ii) Each branch of t not ended by (_,_,*fail*) or (_,_,*suspend*) is either deadlock-free or ended by a node (labeled by a call pattern) subsumed by a node of a deadlock-free branch.

Condition *(i)* ensures that the guard check cannot lead to suspension, while condition *(ii)* ensures that any computation will not leave any suspended subprocess : this is done by firstly discarding the branches corresponding to non-maximal (*subsumed*) computations and by secondly (recursively) inspecting the call/success tree of the last call pattern for each literal of the clause.

Checking a program for possible run-time deadlocks can be done in two steps : first the algorithm is run on the program with $(goal, \Delta)$ and call/success trees are collected; second the call/success tree with root $(goal, \Delta)$ is checked to be deadlock-free.
This ensures that, for each call occurring during the program execution, among all the alternative guards, either one guard will succeed, or all guards will succeed or fail, but anyhow the call will not be suspended forever.

This deadlock-check is valid for the call/success trees produced by both algorithms, but it however can be more simply formulated for the second algorithm as, in this case, a node can only subsume its ancestors. Hence the definition of a deadlock-free branch can be reformulated thanks to footnote 4, and *(ii)* will simply require that all branches are deadlock-free.

Let us illustrate the use of all this machinery by a simple example. Consider the well known [Pal 89, Sha 89] *merge* program defined below.

```
merge([X|In1],In2,Out) <- Out=[X|Out'], merge(In1,In2,Out') .
merge(In1,[X|In2],Out) <- Out=[X|Out'], merge(In1,In2,Out') .
merge([],In2,Out) <- Out=In2 .
merge(In1,[],Out) <- Out=In1 .

p(X) <- X=[a|X'], p(X') .
p(X) <- X=[] .

q(Y) <- Y=[b|Y'], q(Y') .
q(Y) <- Y=[] .
```

and the goal :

[4]Observe that, due to the déjà_vu check, the branch is indeed ended by : $(A_1, \Delta'), (A_1, \Delta', \Delta'), (A, \Delta, \Delta'), ..., (A_n, \Delta'), (A_n, \Delta', \Delta'), (A, \Delta, \Delta')$, where $A_1, ..., A_n$ are the (permuted) literals of the considered clause and that these call patterns (A_i, Δ') are the only non-subsumed ones on the branch.

```
goal <- p(X), q(Y), merge(X,Y,Z) .
```

Observe that the clauses have no guards and that the synchronization will be induced by the non-variable terms in the head of the *merge* clauses via matching. *merge* outputs a nondeterministic interleaving of the (possibly infinite) streams produced by p and q.

As D satisfies the monotonicity property, we can use the simple algorithm AbInt-FCP'(D) to determine that this program is deadlock-free, i.e. no call will be suspended forever during program execution.
The call/success tree for the goal will have branchs consisting in alternating call and success patterns for p, q, *merge*, until the same call pattern is found for the second time (local fixpoint computation). Intuitively, the algorithm will determine that p makes X ground in any case (and does not suspend), the same for q with Y, and thus that *merge* will not suspend. In this simple example, synchronization follows the order of the literals in the goal clause and thus only one round is necessary for *derive'* to compute success patterns for the goal. Observe nevertheless that this models synchronization between not only brother literals inside a clause but also between "cousins" in the computation tree.
Also observe that in this example we indeed consider infinitely many finite computations corresponding to all lists produced by p. We however do not take into account infinite computations (producing infinite streams) as for example if the unit clause $p([])$ is deleted.

Complex synchronization mechanisms can be accurately simulated, as for example back-communication protocol between processes. A producer sends a message with an unbound reply variable R and waits for R to be instanciated. The receiver replies by instanciating R, and the sender can proceed.
This kind of synchronization leads to several rounds in the *derive'* procedure. Let us illustrate this mechanism with an example presenting a simple mutual exclusion protocol taken from [Sha 89] :

```
mutex([lock(Reply)|In]) <- Reply=granted, mutex'(In) .

mutex'([lock(Reply)|In]) <- Reply=denied, mutex'(In) .
mutex'([]) .

p(lock(granted),X) <- X=p .
p(lock(denied),X) .

q(lock(granted),X) <- X=q .
q(lock(denied),X) .

faster(X) <- p(lock(R1),X), q(lock(R2),X),
     merge([lock(R1)],[lock(R2)],L),
     mutex(L) .
```

and the goal :

```
<- faster(Y) .
```

Let us detail once more the work of *derive'* on the clause defining *faster* where the synchronization takes place. The call/success tree for *faster* will have branchs

consisting in alternating call and success patterns for p, q, *merge* and *mutex*.
Let us intuitively detail what happens on each branch. The algorithm will determine that p suspends and then that q suspends. *merge* can proceed and produces L partially instanciated so that *mutex* proceed and make L ground. Then p will proceed as q (making X ground) and one more round *merge*, *mutex*, p, q that will make no change to the context will be necessary (recall the *deja_vu* function) to give a success pattern for *faster*, with a suspension flag *committable* or *committable-or-failed* but in no case *suspendible*.

5 Conclusion and future work

We have presented a general framework for abstract interpretation for FCP(:), a simple concurrent logic language. This framework derives from that of [CF 89], developed for Prolog, that has been naturally extended to cope with the new computation mechanisms. Other versions of this framework for more complex concurrent languages are easily adaptable as they share their basic execution mechanisms with FCP(:). One has however to be careful with the predicates allowed to appear in the guard, for example predicates such as *var(X)* or *otherwise* would cause some trouble (as they do for Prolog) and would prevent from using the simpler algorithm of 3.4, as the property on the $\downarrow\prod$ function would no more hold. An interesting perspective is to extend this framework for languages that encompass both Prolog and CLLs, such as Kernel Andorra Prolog [HJ 90] (this addresses the problem of dealing with deep guards instead of flat ones).
A particular abstract domain designed for determining possible deadlocks in FCP(:) programs has been proposed. It uses both sophisticated groundness and sharing information and specific information on clause matching for deadlocks. This domain enjoys the necessary property so that a simple algorithm can be used. More accurate analyses would have been possible with more complex domains. As always, a trade-off has to be done between accuracy and complexity of computation. On "toy" examples, the proposed abstract interpretation technique is sufficient to determine the deadlock-freeness property and it should be interesting to see what happens with larger programs.

Acknowledgments

We gratefully thank Gilberto Filè and Laura Semini for many helpful discussions.

References

[Bru 88] M. Bruynooghe : "A practical framework for the abstract interpretation of logic programs", research report K. U. Leuven, Belgium, 1988.

[CC 77] P. Cousot and R. Cousot : "Abstract interpretation : a unified framework for static analysis of programs by approximation of fixpoints", proc 4th ACM Symposium on Principles of Programming Languages, 1977.

[CCF 86] C. Codognet, M-M. Corsini and G. Filè : "Optimizations of logic programs based on their static analysis", research report 8624, University of Bordeaux-I, France 1986, and proc. GULP 88, Italy 1988.

[CCFS 89] P. Codognet, J. Chassin de Kergommeaux, P. Robert and J-C Syre: "Parallel Logic Programming" (in French), T.S.I. vol 8 no 3 & 4, 1989.

[CF 89] M.M. Corsini and G. Filè : "A complete framework for the abstract interpretation of logic programs : theory and application", research report, Universita di Padova, Italy, 1989.

[Cha 88] K. M. Chandy and J. A. Misra : "Parallel Program Design", Addison-Wesley 1988.

[Che 90] P-H. Cheong : "Type inference by abstract interpretation" (in French), Ph.D. dissertation, LIENS, Paris, 1990, forthcoming.

[Cor 89] M.M. Corsini : "Abstract interpretation in logic programming : theory and applications" (in French), Ph.D. dissertation, University of Bordeaux-I, France, 1989.

[Cou 78] P. Cousot : "méthodes itératives de construction et d'approximation de points fixes d'opérateurs monotones sur un treillis, analyse sémantique des programmes", Doctorate Thesis, University of Grenoble-I, 1978.

[GCS 88] J. Gallagher, M. Codish and E. Shapiro : "Specialization of Prolog and FCP Programs using abstract interpretation", New Generation Computing 6 pp 159-186, 1988.

[HJ 90] S. Haridi and S. Janson : "Kernel Andorra Prolog and its computation model", proc. 7th International Conference on Logic Programming, Jerusalem, MIT Press 1990.

[JL 89] D. Jacobs and A. Langen : "Accurate and efficient approximation of variable aliasing in logic programs", proc. NACLP 89, Cleveland, MIT Press 1989.

[JS 87] N. Jones and H. Sondergaard : " A semantic-based framework for the abstract interpretation of Prolog", in "Abstract Interpretation of Declarative Languages", S. Abramsky and C. Hankin (Eds), Ellis Horwood 1987.

[KK 87] T. Kanamori and T. Kawamura : "Analyzing success patterns of logic program by abstract hybrid interpretation", technical report TR-279, ICOT, Japan, 1987.

[Llo 87] J. Lloyd : "Foundations of Logic Programming", (2nd edition), Springer Verlag 1987.

[MU 87] H. Mannila and E. Ukkonen : "Flow analysis of Prolog programs", proc. Symposium on Logic Programming, San Francisco, 1987.

[Mel 86] C. S. Mellish : Abstract Interpretation of Prolog Programs", proc. 3rd International Conference on Logic Programming, London, LNCS 225, Springer Verlag 1986.

[Pal 89] C. Palamidessi : "A Theory for Modeling the Synchronization Mechanisms of Concurrent Logic Languages", draft, 1989.

[Pnu 86] A. Pnueli : "Application of temporal logic to the specification and verification of reactive systems : a survey of current trends", in "Current trends in concurrency", J. W. De Bakker, W. P. De Roever and G. Rozenberg (Eds), LNCS 224, Springer Verlag 1986.

[Sar 88] V. J. Saraswat : "A somewhat logical formulation of CLP synchronization primitives", proc of the 5th ICLP/SLP, Seattle, MIT Press 1988.

[Sar 89] V. J. Saraswat : "Concurrent Constraint Programming Languages", research report CMU-CS-89-108, Carnegie Mellon University, 1989.

[Sha 83] E. Shapiro : "A subset of Concurrent Prolog and its interpreter", technical report TR-003, ICOT, Japan, 1983.

[Sha 89] E. Shapiro : "The family of Concurrent Logic Programming Languages", ACM computing surveys, Vol. 21, No. 3, September 1989.

[SM 89] H. Sondergaard and K. Marriot : "Abstract Interpretation on Logic Programs", tutorial notes, North-American Conference on Logic Programming, 1989.

Databases

Is There Anything Better than Magic?

Yehoshua Sagiv[1]
Hebrew University and Stanford University
sagiv@cs.stanford.edu

Abstract

Envelopes are defined and an algorithm for creating envelopes is described. Envelopes are similar to magic sets in the sense that they restrict evaluation of a query just to relevant facts, but envelopes do not necessarily restrict computation to the same set of relevant facts as magic sets. One advantage of envelopes is that several different envelopes can be used to restrict a program, even if each envelope is created from a different adorned program. Another advantage of envelopes is that their size (i.e., number of facts) can be limited to the size of the EDB. In many cases, restricting an evaluation according to envelopes is more efficient than using the magic-set method. The method of envelopes is applicable also to programs with stratified negation.

1 Introduction

In recent years, the magic-set method and its variants [BMSU86, BeR87, DW87, Ker89, Ram88, RLK86, Seki89, VG86, Vie86, Vie89] have become the standard facility for evaluation of queries in deductive database systems [LV89, MNSUV87, MUV86, NT88, Zan88]. The attractiveness of this method lies in its generality and efficiency. The magic-set method is guaranteed to terminate when there are no function symbols; it does not duplicate work, since each subquery is solved only once; and it is efficient, since it focuses only on the portion of the database that is relevant to the given query.

Recently, it was shown [Bry89, Ull89a] that the magic-set method and its variants mentioned above are all equivalent in the sense that they generate the same set of queries (or magic facts) and the same set of facts for IDB predicates. Essentially, all these methods simulate top-down evaluation with memoing and, hence, generate the same set of queries and the same set of answers to those queries as top-down evaluation. Of course, counting just the number of facts (including magic facts) is not a complete cost measure, but it is a good indication of the relative efficiency of a method. Calculating the exact cost measure is hard to do, since it depends also on properties of

[1]Work supported by NSF grant IRI-87-22886, AFOSR grant 88-0266, and a grant of IBM Corp.

the data, such as join selectivities, etc., and so, it has never been done analytically. Simulation results comparing some of these methods are discussed in [BaR86].

Other methods that have been investigated include the counting methods [AO89, Brig87, BMSU86, BeR87, GSS87, HN88, HH89, HN84, SZ86, SZ87], one-sided recursions [Nau87], separable recursions [Nau88], and factorizing methods [NRSU89a, NRSU89b]. These methods could be more efficient than the magic-set method in certain cases, but they are applicable only in special cases.

There are also dynamic methods [KL86, Loz85]; that is, methods that determine how to restrict the search to relevant data during computation time rather than during compilation time. These methods determine relevant facts (for evaluating a query) differently from the magic-set method. A compile-time approach that uses a similar idea is described in [SS88]. The method of [SS88] generates at least as many IDB facts as the magic-set method, but the rules for computing the magic sets are simpler (i.e., the rules are "regular"); in particular, the rules for the magic predicates do not depend on any IDB predicate and, therefore, can be computed before computing any IDB fact. The advantage of this approach, as argued in [SS88], is that magic facts might be computed faster, because the rules are simpler and the IDB facts do not have to be used (note that this may also reduce the required space).

In view of the extensive research on query evaluation, one might think that this subject is well understood and it is unlikely that better methods would be found. However, we will show that there are still some very basic misconceptions about the magic-set method. The most striking one is the common belief that more bound columns is always better than fewer. As we will show in Section 3, in many cases just the opposite is true, i.e., given a query $?-\ p(a,b)$, it is sometimes better to evaluate the query $?-\ p(a,Y)$ and check whether b is in the answer as compared to evaluating the query $?-\ p(a,b)$ directly.

In this paper, we present an evaluation method that in many cases may be better than the magic-set method. This method is as general as the magic-set method, i.e., it can be applied to any program. However, whether the method is better than the magic-set method depends, in general, not just on the query and program, but also on the given EDB relations (i.e., the input to the program). Therefore, methods for estimating sizes of IDB relations, such as the method of [LN90], are needed in order to determine which method is better for a given program, query, and EDB relations. We illustrate on examples when our method is better than the magic-set method. Our method is also applicable to stratified programs, and in many cases it may result in a more efficient evaluation than the existing variety of magic-set transformations for stratified programs [BMR88, BPR87, BRSS90, KT88, KP88, Ross90].

$$sg(X,Z) \ :- \ flat(X,Z).$$
$$sg(X,Z) \ :- \ up(X,U),\ sg(U,V),\ flat(V,W),\ sg(W,Y),\ down(Y,Z).$$

Figure 1: Nonlinear same-generation.

$$m\_sg^{bf}(a).$$
$$m\_sg^{bf}(U) \ :- \ m\_sg^{bf}(X),\ up(X,U).$$
$$m\_sg^{bf}(W) \ :- \ m\_sg^{bf}(X),\ up(X,U),\ sg^{bf}(U,V),\ flat(V,W).$$

$$sg^{bf}(X,Z) \ :- \ m\_sg^{bf}(X),\ flat(X,Z).$$
$$sg^{bf}(X,Z) \ :- \ m\_sg^{bf}(X),\ up(X,U),\ sg^{bf}(U,V),\ flat(V,W),\ sg^{bf}(W,Y),\ down(Y,Z).$$

Figure 2: Magic program for a bf query.

2 Preliminaries

We consider *datalog programs,* i.e., programs consisting of Horn-clause rules with no function symbols. We assume that rules are *safe,* i.e., variables in the head of a rule must also appear in the body. It is important to distinguish between the *EDB* (extensional database) and the *IDB* (intensional database). A program has *IDB predicates,* which are the predicates that appear in the heads of rules (and may also appear in bodies of rules), and *EDB predicates,* which are the predicates that appear only in bodies of rules.

An EDB consists of a set of ground facts for EDB predicates, and it serves as an input to a given program. The output of the program is the IDB and it consists of ground facts for IDB predicates. The IDB is obtained by applying the rules of the program bottom-up to the EDB.

A query is of the form $?-\ q(\alpha_1, \ldots, \alpha_m)$, where q is an IDB predicate and each α_i is either a variable or a constant. The set of answers to the query consists of all IDB facts that match $q(\alpha_1, \ldots, \alpha_m)$.

The *magic-set* method is a method for transforming a given program and query to a *magic program,* such that the magic program computes all the answers as efficiently as a top-down evaluation. Note that the magic-set transformation depends only on the given program and query, but not on the EDB. We assume familiarity with the notion of an *adorned program* and the magic-set transformation, as described in [BeR87, Ull89b].

$$
\begin{array}{lll}
m\_sg^{fb}(c). & & \\
m\_sg^{fb}(Y) & :- & m\_sg^{fb}(Z),\ down(Y,Z). \\
m\_sg^{fb}(V) & :- & m\_sg^{fb}(Z),\ down(Y,Z),\ sg^{fb}(W,Y),\ flat(V,W). \\
 & & \\
sg^{fb}(X,Z) & :- & m\_sg^{fb}(Z),\ flat(X,Z). \\
sg^{fb}(X,Z) & :- & m\_sg^{fb}(Z),\ down(Y,Z),\ sg^{fb}(W,Y),\ flat(V,W), \\
 & & sg^{fb}(U,V),\ up(X,U).
\end{array}
$$

Figure 3: Magic program for an fb query.

3 Motivation

Consider the nonlinear same-generation program shown in Figure 1. A magic program for the query $?- sg(a,Z)$ is shown in Figure 2. Note that the order of subgoals in Figure 2 seems to be the best, since each subgoal has a bound column (i.e., argument position). Similarly, Figure 3 shows a magic program for the query $sg(X,c)$.

Now suppose that the query is $sg(a,c)$, i.e., both columns are bound. Thus the head of the recursive rule (in Figure 1) becomes sg^{bb}, but only one recursive subgoal can get the adornment bb. There are two symmetrical orderings, and Figure 4 shows the one that has $sg^{bf}(U,V)$ as the first recursive subgoal and $sg^{bb}(W,Y)$ as the second. Since we get the adornment bf in the body, we must also create rules with $sg^{bf}(X,Z)$ in the head. In addition to that, Figure 4 also shows the rules for the two magic predicates m_sg^{bf} and m_sg^{bb}. The magic program of Figure 4 is more complicated than either that of Figure 2 or Figure 3, but presumably it should take advantage of the fact that both columns of the query are bound and, hence, be more efficient than the other two programs. However, this not always the case. The program of Figure 4 contains every rule that appears in Figure 2, except for the fact $m\_sg^{bf}(a)$ that appears only in Figure 2. Suppose that the fact $up(a,a)$ is in the EDB. In this case, $m\_sg^{bf}(a)$ is generated by the first rule for m_sg^{bf} in Figure 4, and hence, the program of Figure 4 generates every fact generated by the program of Figure 4; in addition to that, the program of Figure 4 also generates facts for m_sg^{bb} and sg^{bb}. Thus, the program of Figure 4 is clearly less efficient than the program of Figure 2 when $up(a,a)$ is in the EDB. Even if $up(a,a)$ is not in the EDB, the program of Figure 4 could still generate (for some EDBs) many more facts than the program of Figure 2.

In order to get a program that takes advantage of the fact that both columns of the query are bound, one might do the following: Compute the magic predicates m_sg^{bf} and m_sg^{fb} using the rules of Figure 2 and Figure 3, respectively, and then use both predicates in the same recursive rule for sg, as shown in Figure 5. Note that the idea is that m_sg^{bf} would restrict the

$$
\begin{array}{lll}
m\_sg^{bb}(a,c). & & \\
m\_sg^{bb}(W,Y) & :- & m\_sg^{bb}(X,Z),\ up(X,U),\ sg^{bf}(U,V), \\
 & & flat(V,W),\ down(Y,Z). \\
 & & \\
m\_sg^{bf}(U) & :- & m\_sg^{bb}(X,Z),\ up(X,U). \\
m\_sg^{bf}(U) & :- & m\_sg^{bf}(X),\ up(X,U). \\
m\_sg^{bf}(W) & :- & m\_sg^{bf}(X),\ up(X,U),\ sg^{bf}(U,V),\ flat(V,W). \\
 & & \\
sg^{bb}(X,Z) & :- & m\_sg^{bb}(X,Z),\ flat(X,Z). \\
sg^{bb}(X,Z) & :- & m\_sg^{bb}(X,Z),\ up(X,U),\ sg^{bf}(U,V),\ flat(V,W), \\
 & & down(Y,Z),\ sg^{bb}(W,Y). \\
 & & \\
sg^{bf}(X,Z) & :- & m\_sg^{bf}(X),\ flat(X,Z). \\
sg^{bf}(X,Z) & :- & m\_sg^{bf}(X),\ up(X,U),\ sg^{bf}(U,V),\ flat(V,W), \\
 & & sg^{bf}(W,Y),\ down(Y,Z).
\end{array}
$$

Figure 4: Magic program for a *bb* query.

first column of sg and m_sg^{fb} would restrict the second. But the program of Figure 5 is incorrect; the EDB of Figure 6 shows that it does not compute all the answers, since $sg(a,c)$ can be derived from this EDB, but not by the program of Figure 5. Note that in Figure 6, up arrows denote facts for the EDB predicate *up*, flat arrows denote facts for *flat*, and down arrows denote facts for *down*.

4 Envelopes

The program of Figure 5 is incorrect, since the magic predicates depend on sg and, so, we cannot just take the rules for m_sg^{bf} and m_sg^{fb} from Figure 2 and Figure 3, respectively. If we also add the rules for sg^{bf} and sg^{fb}, then we get a correct program, but it is not more efficient, since the rules for either sg^{bf} or sg^{fb} solve the query. Generally, however, if the magic predicates do not depend on the IDB predicates, then we can restrict a computation according to magic predicates obtained from several programs (while taking from each program only the rules for the magic predicates). Even if some magic predicates depend upon some IDB predicates, we may still gain efficiency by combining magic predicates from several programs (while taking, of course, all rules that the magic predicates depend upon). This may happen when the magic predicates depend upon some (but not all)

$$
\begin{aligned}
&m\_sg^{bf}(a). \\
&m\_sg^{bf}(U) \ :- \ m\_sg^{bf}(X),\ up(X,U). \\
&m\_sg^{bf}(W) \ :- \ m\_sg^{bf}(X),\ up(X,U),\ sg(U,V),\ flat(V,W).
\end{aligned}
$$

$$
\begin{aligned}
&m\_sg^{fb}(c). \\
&m\_sg^{fb}(Y) \ :- \ m\_sg^{fb}(Z),\ down(Y,Z). \\
&m\_sg^{fb}(V) \ :- \ m\_sg^{fb}(Z),\ down(Y,Z),\ sg(W,Y),\ flat(V,W).
\end{aligned}
$$

$$
\begin{aligned}
sg(X,Z) \ &:- \ m\_sg^{bf}(X),\ m\_sg^{fb}(Z),\ flat(X,Z). \\
sg(X,Z) \ &:- \ m\_sg^{bf}(X),\ m\_sg^{fb}(Z),\ up(X,U),\ sg(U,V), \\
&\qquad flat(V,W),\ sg(W,Y),\ down(Y,Z).
\end{aligned}
$$

Figure 5: Combining magic predicates from different programs.

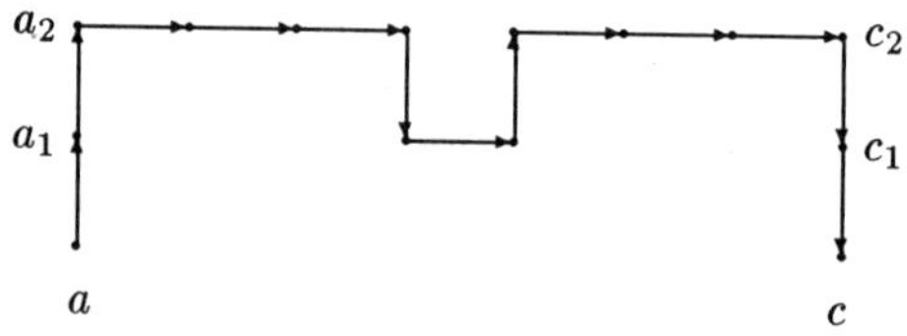

Figure 6: An EDB for nonlinear same-generation.

IDB predicates, or depend upon some (but not all) columns of IDB predicates (in the latter case, we can apply the existential optimization of [RBK88] to the rules that the magic predicates depend upon).

In general, we need a method for computing "magic sets" that do not depend on IDB predicates. In this section, we will define formally the concept of *envelopes*. Envelopes are similar to magic predicates, in the sense that they describe a set of "relevant facts" that are sufficient for evaluating a query. However, envelopes are not identical to magic predicates, since they do not necessarily describe the same set of relevant facts as magic predicates. In fact, magic predicates are a special case of envelopes. After defining envelopes formally, we will state a theorem that describes how several envelopes can be combined in one computation, and later we will describe a method for computing envelopes that do not depend upon IDB predicates.

A *factor* of a predicate p is a predicate that corresponds to a subset of the columns of p. We shall usually denote a factor as β_p, where β is a list of columns of p. For example,[2] 13_p is a factor corresponding to the first and third columns of p. A *factorization* of p is a collection of factors such that each column of p is represented in exactly one factor. For example, if p has 5 columns, then 13_p, 24_p, and 5_p is a factorization of p.

Consider an atom $p(\alpha_1, \ldots, \alpha_m)$, where each α_i is either a variable or a constant, and let $\mathcal{F}$ denote a factorization $\beta_1\_p, \ldots, \beta_k\_p$ of p. The *factorized conjunction* of $p(\alpha_1, \ldots, \alpha_m)$, denoted $\mathcal{F}\langle p(\alpha_1, \ldots, \alpha_m)\rangle$, is the conjunction of the predicates $\beta_1\_p, \ldots, \beta_k\_p$, such that the arguments of β_i_p $(i = 1, \ldots, k)$ are those α_j's that appear in the columns of β_i. For example, given the factorization 13_p, 24_p, and 5_p, the factorized conjunction of the atom $p(U, V, X, Y, Z)$ is $13\_p(U, X)$, $24\_p(V, Y)$, $5\_p(Z)$.

Next, consider a program $\mathcal{P}$ and a query $?-\, q(\alpha_1, \ldots, \alpha_m)$. An *answer tree* of $\mathcal{P}$ and $?-\, q(\alpha_1, \ldots, \alpha_m)$ with respect to an EDB D is a tree labeled by ground atoms, such that the following is true. First, the root is labeled by an atom of q that matches $q(\alpha_1, \ldots, \alpha_m)$. Second, leaves are labeled by atoms of the EDB D. Third, for each nonleaf node v there is a ground instance of some rule of $\mathcal{P}$, such that the head labels v and the atoms of the body label the children of v. Essentially, an answer tree shows that the atom labeling the root is an answer to the query, given the EDB D.

Consider a program $\mathcal{P}$, and suppose that $\mathcal{E}$ is a set of rules with predicates as follows. The EDB predicates of $\mathcal{E}$ are also EDB predicates of $\mathcal{P}$. For each IDB predicate p of $\mathcal{P}$, a unique factorization of p, denoted $\mathcal{F}_p$, appears among the IDB predicates of $\mathcal{E}$. In addition to that, $\mathcal{E}$ may have IDB predicates that do not appear in $\mathcal{P}$. We say that $\mathcal{E}$ computes an *envelope* of $\mathcal{P}$ with respect to a query $?-\, q(\alpha_1, \ldots, \alpha_m)$ (or simply that $\mathcal{E}$ is an *envelope* of $\mathcal{P}$) if for all EDBs D the following is true. If $p(c_1, \ldots, c_m)$ is an IDB atom labeling a node of an answer tree (of $\mathcal{P}$ and $?-\, q(\alpha_1, \ldots, \alpha_m)$ with respect to D), then each atom in the factorized conjunction $\mathcal{F}_p\langle p(c_1, \ldots, c_m)\rangle$ can be derived from D using $\mathcal{E}$.

Now consider a rule ρ that has an atom $p(\alpha_1, \ldots, \alpha_m)$ in its head. The *restriction* of ρ according to a given factorization $\mathcal{F}$ of p is obtained from ρ by adding the factorized conjunction $\mathcal{F}\langle p(\alpha_1, \ldots, \alpha_m)\rangle$ to the body. Essentially, the restriction has the effect of allowing ρ to generate only those facts for p, such that their projections on $\beta_1, \ldots, \beta_k$ are among the facts for $\beta_1\_p, \ldots, \beta_k\_p$, respectively. The *restriction* of $\mathcal{P}$ according to an envelope $\mathcal{E}$ is obtained by restricting each rule ρ of $\mathcal{P}$ according to the factorization that appears in $\mathcal{E}$ for the head predicate of ρ.

Proposition 4.1 *Consider a program $\mathcal{P}$ and a query $?-\, q(\alpha_1, \ldots, \alpha_m)$. If $\mathcal{E}$ is an envelope of $\mathcal{P}$ with respect to this query, then all answers to the query are computed by the program consisting of $\mathcal{E}$ and the restriction of $\mathcal{P}$ according to $\mathcal{E}$.*

[2] For simplicity, instances of lists are written just as strings of numbers, e.g., 13 denotes the list [1, 3]. Since examples never have predicates with 10 or more columns, there is no ambiguity in this notation.

The following theorem describes how several envelopes can be used in the same evaluation. Essentially, it implies that a program $\mathcal{P}$ can be restricted according to any number of envelopes.[3] However, the exact statement of the theorem is more general than that.

Theorem 4.1 *Consider a program $\mathcal{P}_0$ and a query $?- q(\alpha_1, \ldots, \alpha_m)$, and suppose that $\mathcal{P}_0, \mathcal{P}_1, \ldots, \mathcal{P}_n$ and $\mathcal{E}_1, \ldots, \mathcal{E}_{n-1}$ satisfy the following. For $i = 1, 2, \ldots, n-1$, program $\mathcal{P}_i$ is the restriction of $\mathcal{P}_{i-1}$ according to $\mathcal{E}_i$, where $\mathcal{E}_i$ is an envelope of either $\mathcal{P}_0$ or $\mathcal{P}_{i-1}$. Moreover, $\mathcal{P}_n$ is either $\mathcal{P}_{n-1}$ or obtained from $\mathcal{P}_{n-1}$ by the magic-set transformation. Then the program consisting of $\mathcal{P}_n$ and $\mathcal{E}_1, \ldots, \mathcal{E}_{n-1}$ computes all answers to the query.*

According to Theorem 4.1, if $\mathcal{E}_1$ is an envelope of $\mathcal{P}_0$, then we can restrict $\mathcal{P}_0$ according to $\mathcal{E}_1$ before producing the next envelope, and so on. It should be realized that only the restricted rules of $\mathcal{P}_0$, which are denoted as $\mathcal{P}_1$, are used to produce the next envelope (and the IDB predicates of $\mathcal{E}_1$ that appear in $\mathcal{P}_1$ are treated as EDB predicates). To achieve maximal restriction in the next envelope to be produced, we should restrict rules of $\mathcal{P}_0$ not just according to their heads, but also according to the IDB atoms in their bodies. Moreover, seeds[4] of the new envelope can be restricted according to previous envelopes. Examples are given at the end of this section.

In the remainder of this section, we will describe a method for obtaining envelopes. We start with a program $\mathcal{P}$ and a query $?- q(\alpha_1, \ldots, \alpha_m)$. The first step is to obtain an adorned program, as described in [BeR87, Ull89b]. We assume (as in [Ull89b]) that IDB predicates are renamed (if necessary) so that each IDB predicate has a unique adornment. Moreover, there is no need to use "full sips;" that is, we may adorn a column as free even if it is actually bound. For example, consider the rule

$$t(X,Z) \quad :- \quad e(X,Y),\ p(X,Z),\ t(Y,Z).$$

with the adornment bf for the head. Both columns of the last subgoal are bound, but we may choose to adorn that subgoal as t^{bf}.

The next step is to apply the magic-set transformation to the adorned program, as described in [BeR87, Ull89b], and then to choose a unique factorization for each IDB predicate p. Every factorization of p is permitted provided that each factor has only bound columns or only free columns, according to the unique adornment of p. As a convenient notation, a factor β_i_p will be denoted as $b\beta_i\_p$ if all its columns are bound, and as $f\beta_i\_p$ if all its columns are free. A factor $b\beta_i\_p$ is called a *bound factor,* and a factor $f\beta_j\_p$ is called a *free factor.* Note that once we choose a factorization for an

[3]When several envelopes are used to restrict the same program, we assume that IDB predicates are renamed so that distinct envelopes do not share any IDB predicate.

[4]A *seed* is a rule with an empty body that is obtained from the constants of the query; e.g., the first rule of Figure 2 is a seed.

IDB predicate p, the bound factors of p form a factorization of the magic predicate m_p of p.

The final step is to transform the magic program as follows. First, atoms of either IDB or magic predicates are replaced in bodies of rules with their factorized conjunctions. Next, heads of rules are also replaced with their factorized conjunctions (however, if the head is an IDB predicate, then it is replaced only with the conjunction of the free factors). Since each head is now a conjunction of atoms (and formally this is not a rule), we create a separate rule for each atom in the head by making copies of the body.

Theorem 4.2 *Given a program and a query, the above transformation creates a set of rules that computes an envelope.*

As an example, consider the magic program of Figure 2, and suppose that we factorize sg^{bf} into $b1\_sg$ and $f2\_sg$. Thus, the second rule for sg^{bf} is transformed into

$$\begin{aligned} f2\_sg(Z) \ :- \ & b1\_sg(X),\ up(X,U),\ b1\_sg(U),\ f2\_sg(V),\ flat(V,W), \\ & b1\_sg(W),\ f2\_sg(Y),\ down(Y,Z). \end{aligned}$$

Note that the head is replaced with a single conjunct (since there is only one free factor), and so, the result is just one rule.

The above rule has in its body atoms that are not connected to the head. Formally, an atom is *connected* to the head if it shares a variable either with the head or with another atom that is connected to the head. The result of deleting atoms not connected to the head is the following rule.

$$f2\_sg(Z) \ :- \ f2\_sg(Y),\ down(Y,Z).$$

Note that this deletion does not necessarily preserve equivalence. However, it can only increase the set of facts generated for the head. In this paper, we shall always delete atoms not connected to the head, since it produces shorter rules. If one wants to preserve equivalence, then this deletion should be applied during execution time to rules that have generated at least one fact. After transforming all the rules of Figure 2 (and deleting atoms not connected to heads), we get the program of Figure 7. Since this program computes just an envelope, we should also restrict the original program according to this envelope, i.e., add the following two rules.

$$\begin{aligned} sg(X,Z) \ :- \ & b1\_sg(X),\ f2\_sg(Z),\ flat(X,Z). \\ sg(X,Z) \ :- \ & b1\_sg(X),\ f2\_sg(Z),\ up(X,U),\ sg(U,V),\ flat(V,W), \\ & sg(W,Y),\ down(Y,Z). \end{aligned}$$

Figure 8 shows an envelope obtained from Figure 3 by factorizing sg^{fb} into $f1\_sg$ and $b2\_sg$. Restricting the original program of Figure 1 according to the envelopes of both Figure 7 and Figure 8 yields the program of Figure 9.

$$
\begin{array}{lll}
b1\_sg(a). & & \\
b1\_sg(U) & :- & b1\_sg(X),\ up(X,U). \\
b1\_sg(W) & :- & f2\_sg(V),\ flat(V,W). \\
f2\_sg(Z) & :- & b1\_sg(X),\ flat(X,Z). \\
f2\_sg(Z) & :- & f2\_sg(Y),\ down(Y,Z).
\end{array}
$$

Figure 7: An envelope for a bf query.

$$
\begin{array}{lll}
b2\_sg(c). & & \\
b2\_sg(Y) & :- & b2\_sg(Z),\ down(Y,Z). \\
b2\_sg(V) & :- & f1\_sg(W),\ flat(V,W). \\
f1\_sg(X) & :- & b2\_sg(Z),\ flat(X,Z). \\
f1\_sg(X) & :- & f2\_sg(U),\ up(X,U).
\end{array}
$$

Figure 8: An envelope for an fb query.

As stated in Theorem 4.1, we can also restrict the original program according to the envelope of Figure 8, and then apply the magic-set transformation for a bf query. The result is the program of Figure 10 (of course, the envelope of Figure 8 should be included as well).

When envelopes are constructed according to the method of this section, it is sometimes sufficient to restrict just according to bound factors. For example, in Figure 10 the free factors are redundant in the rules for sg^{bf}; however, not all the free factors are redundant in the rules for m_sg^{bf}. Exact details will be given in the full version of this paper.

5 Efficiency of Envelopes vs. Magic Sets

We have seen several programs for computing the answer to the query $?- sg(a,c)$ and the natural question is which one is better? It is hard to compute the exact cost of evaluation, and so, we will only consider the num-

$$
\begin{array}{lll}
sg(X,Z) & :- & b1\_sg(X),\ f1\_sg(X),\ b2\_sg(Z),\ f2\_sg(Z),\ flat(X,Z). \\
sg(X,Z) & :- & b1\_sg(X),\ f1\_sg(X),\ b2\_sg(Z),\ f2\_sg(Z), \\
& & up(X,U),\ sg(U,V),\ flat(V,W),\ sg(W,Y),\ down(Y,Z).
\end{array}
$$

Figure 9: Computing the query using the intersection of two envelopes.

$$
\begin{array}{lll}
m\_sg^{bf}(a) & :- & f1\_sg(a). \\
m\_sg^{bf}(U) & :- & m\_sg^{bf}(X),\ f1\_sg(X),\ up(X,U),\ f1\_sg(U). \\
m\_sg^{bf}(W) & :- & m\_sg^{bf}(X),\ f1\_sg(X),\ up(X,U),\ sg^{bf}(U,V), \\
 & & flat(V,W),\ f1\_sg(W).
\end{array}
$$

$$
\begin{array}{lll}
sg^{bf}(X,Z) & :- & m\_sg^{bf}(X),\ f1\_sg(X),\ b2\_sg(Z),\ flat(X,Z). \\
sg^{bf}(X,Z) & :- & m\_sg^{bf}(X),\ f1\_sg(X),\ b2\_sg(Z),\ up(X,U),\ sg^{bf}(U,V), \\
 & & flat(V,W),\ sg^{bf}(W,Y),\ down(Y,Z).
\end{array}
$$

Figure 10: A combination of an envelope and a magic program.

ber of facts generated by each program. It is important to include not just the number of facts for IDB predicates, but also the number of facts for envelope and magic predicates. There is a common assumption that magic sets are small, but this assumption has never been proved either theoretically or empirically. We doubt the validity of this assumption, and believe that in many cases the size of magic sets dominates the evaluation cost. As an example, consider the program of Figure 4. This program has a binary magic predicate m_sg^{bb}. If the size of the EDB is n, then $O(n^2)$ facts may be generated for m_sg^{bb} in the worst case, even when only $O(n)$ facts are generated for sg. Thus, the cost of generating magic facts may dominate the cost of the whole computation. In comparison, the program of Figure 2 has only a unary magic predicate and, so, only $O(n)$ facts can be generated for that predicate. However, the program of Figure 2 is not always more efficient than the program of Figure 4, since $O(n^2)$ facts could be generated for sg^{bf}.

A detailed comparison of the various programs for $?-\ sg(a,c)$ is lengthy, and we will only state a few points. If the program of Figure 4 generates more facts than the program of Figure 2, then the difference between the two programs could be $O(n^2)$ facts (recall that n is the size of the EDB). However, if the program of Figure 2 generates more facts, then the difference is no more than $O(n)$ facts.

The program of Figure 10 has the advantage that it never generates more facts for sg and m_sg^{bf} than that of Figure 2, and the number of facts it generates for the envelope predicates (i.e., $f1\_sg$ and $b2\_sg$) is no more than $O(n)$. Therefore, the difference between the two programs is no more than $O(n)$ if the program of Figure 10 is worse, but it could be $O(n^2)$ if the program of Figure 2 is worse.

The program of Figure 9 uses two envelopes rather than an envelope and a magic set, and hence, has simpler rules (that are easier to evaluate), as compared to the program of Figure 10. However, in some cases the program

$$
\begin{array}{lll}
b1\_sg(a). & & \\
b2\_sg(c). & & \\
b1\_sg(U) & :- & b1\_sg(X),\ up(X,U). \\
b2\_sg(V) & :- & b2\_sg(Z),\ down(V,Z). \\
 & & \\
sg(X,Z) & :- & b1\_sg(X),\ b2\_sg(Z),\ flat(X,Z). \\
sg(X,Z) & :- & b1\_sg(X),\ b2\_sg(Z),\ up(X,U),\ sg(U,V),\ down(V,Z).
\end{array}
$$

Figure 11: Linear same-generation restricted by an envelope.

of Figure 9 generates $O(n^2)$ facts while that of Figure 10 generates only $O(n)$ facts. Clearly, the program of of Figure 10 never generates more facts than the program of Figure 9.

In summary, the program of Figure 10 could not be worse by more than $O(n)$ facts, but could be better by $O(n^2)$ facts, as compared to the programs of Figures 2, 4, and 9.

As another example, consider the linear same-generation program

$$
\begin{array}{lll}
sg(X,Z) & :- & flat(X,Z). \\
sg(X,Z) & :- & up(X,U),\ sg(U,V),\ down(V,Z).
\end{array}
$$

with the query $?-sg(a,b)$. An adorned program is the following.

$$
\begin{array}{lll}
sg^{bb}(X,Z) & :- & flat(X,Z). \\
sg^{bb}(X,Z) & :- & up(X,U),\ down(V,Z),\ sg^{bb}(U,V).
\end{array}
$$

This program is right-linear and can be evaluated very efficiently [NRSU89a]. Essentially, the only recursive part in the evaluation is computing the magic predicate m_sg^{bb} according to the following rules.

$$
\begin{array}{lll}
m\_sg^{bb}(a,c). & & \\
m\_sg^{bb}(U,V) & :- & m\_sg^{bb}(X,Z),\ up(X,U),\ down(V,Z).
\end{array}
$$

However, the number of facts generated for m_sg^{bb} could be $O(n^2)$, where n is the size of the EDB.

If instead of computing the magic set m_sg^{bb}, we factor predicate sg into $b1\_sg$ and $b2\_sg$, then we get the program of Figure 11. The number of facts for $b1\_sg$ and $b2\_sg$ generated by this program is only $O(n)$.

Let D be an EDB consisting of the following facts: $up(a_1, d_i)$, $up(d_i, a_2)$, $down(c_2, e_i)$, and $down(e_i, c_1)$, for $i = 1, 2, \ldots, n$. Suppose that D_1 consists of D and the facts $up(a, a_1)$, $up(a_2, a_3)$, $up(a_3, a_4)$, $up(a_4, a_5)$, $down(c_1, c)$, and $flat(a_5, c_2)$. When D_1 is the EDB, the magic predicate m_sg^{bb} has $O(n^2)$ facts, but the program of Figure 11 creates only $O(n)$ facts. Next, consider a slightly different EDB D_2 that consists of D and the facts $down(c_1, c)$, $up(a_3, a_1)$, $up(a_4, a_3)$, $up(a, a_4)$, and $flat(a_2, c_2)$. When D_2 is the EDB, the magic predicate m_sg^{bb} has only $O(n)$ facts, and the program of Figure 11 creates $O(n^2)$ facts.

The above example indicates that ignoring the arity of magic predicates is wrong. The common approach of "bound is better" maximizes the arity of magic predicates, and consequently, the number of magic facts may be very large, and even larger than the size of the IDB. The above example shows that even a small change in the EDB may increase the number of facts for m_sg^{bb} from $O(n)$ to $O(n^2)$, and it undermines the common belief that magic sets are small in comparison to the size of the IDB.

The approach of using envelope predicates of small arities may be better in many cases than using magic sets of large arities. In particular, it could be better when several different envelopes could be used for the same query. However, determining the most efficient approach generally depends on the EDB, and hence, requires a method for estimating sizes of magic, envelope, and IDB predicates, such as the method of [LN90].

If we only consider chain rules (all predicates are binary), then the worst case time complexity of evaluating programs with unary envelope predicates is better than the worst case time complexity of evaluating programs with binary magic predicates (note that this is the complexity of the actual evaluation and not just the number of generated facts). This follows from a recent result of [Yan90].

One possible approach is to use envelope predicates that are guaranteed to have no more than $O(n)$ facts, where n is the size of the EDB. Clearly, unary envelope predicates have this property. However, in many cases we can choose envelope predicates of larger arities that have this property. In particular, there is a simple algorithm that uses only syntactical properties of the given program in order to generate envelope predicates with no more than $O(n)$ facts and with "maximal" arities. In the full version of this paper, we will describe this algorithm and define formally the meaning of "maximal" arities.

6 Reducing Envelopes

In this section, we will show how an envelope can be used to restrict itself. As an example, consider the program of Figure 12, which is a transitive closure with permissions; that is, if there is an arc from X to Y and a path from Y to Z, then there is a path from X to Z provided that the the fact $p(X, Z)$ is in the EDB.

Suppose that the query is $?-t(a, Z)$. According to the given order of subgoals, we get the adornments bf and bb for t. We could also get only the adornment bf if we put the subgoal $t(Y, Z)$ before $p(X, Z)$, but this is clearly not a good choice, since it would create a magic set for t^{bf} which is

$$
\begin{array}{lll}
t(X,Z) & :- & e(X,Z). \\
t(X,Z) & :- & e(X,Y),\ p(X,Z),\ t(Y,Z).
\end{array}
$$

Figure 12: Transitive closure with permissions.

$$
\begin{array}{lll}
b1\_t(a). & & \\
f2\_t(Z) & :- & b1\_t(X),\ e(X,Z). \\
b1\_t(Y) & :- & b1\_t(X),\ e(X,Y),\ p(X,Z). \\
 & & \\
t(X,Z) & :- & b1\_t(X),\ f2\_t(Z),\ e(X,Z). \\
t(X,Z) & :- & b1\_t(X),\ f2\_t(Z),\ e(X,Y),\ p(X,Z),\ t(Y,Z).
\end{array}
$$

Figure 13: Transitive closure with permissions restricted by $b1\_t$ and $f2\_t$.

the same as for ordinary transitive closure (i.e., without permissions). But the problem with having also the adornment bb for t is that the number of facts generated for m_t^{bb} might be quadratic in the size of the EDB. So, an alternative is to leave the order of subgoals as is, but to use the adornment bf (instead of bb) for the subgoal $t(Y,Z)$, and to factor t into $b1\_t(X)$ and $f2\_t(Z)$. The result is shown in Figure 13. Formally, there is also the following rule:

$$
f2\_t(Z) \;:-\; b1\_t(X),\ e(X,Y),\ p(X,Z),\ b1\_t(Y),\ f2\_t(Z).
$$

But this rule is redundant, since the atom of the head also appears in the body (the algorithm of [Sag87] can discover redundancies of this type).

We can further restrict the computation to relevant facts using the following idea. After computing the facts for $b1\_t$ and $f2\_t$, we restrict each occurrence of t in the original program. For example, in the recursive rule of Figure 12, we restrict both the head $t(X,Z)$ and the recursive subgoal $t(Y,Z)$, and the result is the following rule.

$$
\begin{array}{lll}
t(X,Z) & :- & b1\_t^{old}(X),\ f2\_t^{old}(Z),\ e(X,Y),\ p(X,Z), \\
 & & b1\_t^{old}(Y),\ f2\_t^{old}(Z),\ t(Y,Z).
\end{array}
$$

The superscript *old* associated with $b1\_t^{old}$ and $f2\_t^{old}$ means that these are the predicates of the old envelope computed by the rules of Figure 13. Now we generate a new envelope from the restricted program, and so, we get the following envelope rules.

$$
\begin{array}{lll}
b1\_t(a). & & \\
f2\_t(Z) & :- & b1\_t(X),\ b1\_t^{old}(X),\ f2\_t^{old}(Z),\ e(X,Z). \\
b1\_t(Y) & :- & b1\_t(X),\ b1\_t^{old}(X),\ e(X,Y),\ p(X,Z),\ b1\_t^{old}(Y),\ f2\_t^{old}(Z).
\end{array}
$$

$$\begin{array}{rcl} sg(X,Z) & :- & flat(X,Z). \\ sg(X,Z) & :- & up(X,U),\ sg(U,V),\ down(V,Z). \\ t(X,Z) & :- & e(X,Z). \\ t(X,Z) & :- & e(X,Y),\ t(Y,Z),\ \neg sg(X,Z). \end{array}$$

Figure 14: A stratified program.

The above envelope rules can generate successive fixpoints for $b1\_t$ and $f2\_t$ as follows. First, we assume that $b1\_t^{old}$ and $f2\_t^{old}$ are always true, and compute all facts for $b1\_t$ and $f2\_t$ that can be derived from these rules. Next, we use the facts computed for $b1\_t$ and $f2\_t$ as the extension of $b1\_t^{old}$ and $f2\_t^{old}$, respectively, and compute a new set of facts for $b1\_t$ and $f2\_t$. We iterate until the set of facts for $b1\_t$ and $f2\_t$ is the same as in the previous iteration.

The above process has the flavor of semi-joins [Ull89b]. Note that the number of facts for $b1\_t$ and $f2\_t$ is always at most $O(n)$, and at most $O(n)$ iterations can be done (n is the size of the EDB). Thus, in the worst case this approach is not better than applying the magic-set transformation with the adornments bf and bb for t. However, a few observations can be made. First, there is no need to continue the process until termination; at any point, the current set of facts for $b1\_t$ and $f2\_t$ can be used to restrict the computation of the original program. Second, it is easy to find examples in which this approach is more efficient than the magic program ($O(n)$ vs. $O(n^2)$), and there are examples in which the magic program is better. Thus, determining which method is better requires estimating the number of facts generated by each program.

In principle, every envelope can be used to restrict itself. However, this does not always result in reducing the number of envelope facts. For example, restricting the envelope of Figure 7 according to itself does not reduce the number of envelope facts.

7 Stratified Programs

Our method can also be applied to programs with stratified negation. However, when generating an envelope, it is incorrect to replace a negated subgoal with its factors. Therefore, one possible approach is to ignore negated subgoals. More specifically, first we generate a magic program in the usual way, then we delete all negated subgoals, and finally we factorize predicates in order to get an envelope. Clearly, this is a correct approach, since ignoring negated subgoals can only increase the number of facts generated by the envelope. It may seem, however, that ignoring negated subgoals makes this approach less efficient than the magic-set transformation for stratified

$$
\begin{array}{lll}
b1\_t(a). & & \\
b1\_t(Y) & :- & b1\_t(X),\ e(X,Y). \\
f2\_t(Z) & :- & b1\_t(X),\ e(X,Z). \\
\\
b1\_sg(X) & :- & b1\_t(X),\ e(X,Y),\ b1\_t(Y). \\
b2\_sg(Z) & :- & f2\_t(Z). \\
b1\_sg(U) & :- & b1\_sg(X),\ up(X,U). \\
b2\_sg(V) & :- & b2\_sg(Z),\ down(V,Z). \\
\\
sg(X,Z) & :- & b1\_sg(X),\ b2\_sg(Z),\ flat(X,Z). \\
sg(X,Z) & :- & b1\_sg(X),\ b2\_sg(Z),\ up(X,U),\ sg(U,V),\ down(V,Z). \\
t(X,Z) & :- & b1\_t(X),\ f2\_t(Z),\ e(X,Z). \\
t(X,Z) & :- & b1\_t(X),\ f2\_t(Z),\ e(X,Y),\ t(Y,Z),\ \neg sg(X,Z).
\end{array}
$$

Figure 15: A stratified program restricted by an envelope.

programs [BMR88, BPR87, BRSS90, KT88, KP88, Ross90]. But this is not necessarily the case.

Consider, for example, the program of Figure 14, and let the query be $?- t(a,Z)$. We can create an envelope by factorizing t^{bf} into $b1\_t$ and $f2\_t$, and factorizing sg^{bb} into $b1\_sg^{bb}$ and $b2\_sg^{bb}$. The envelope rules and the restriction of the program according to this envelope are shown in Figure 15. Note that if the magic-set method is used, m_sg^{bb} has the following rules:

$$
\begin{array}{lll}
m\_sg^{bb}(U,V) & :- & m\_sg^{bb}(X,Z),\ up(X,U),\ down(V,Z). \\
m\_sg^{bb}(X,Z) & :- & m\_t^{bf}(X),\ e(X,Y),\ t(Y,Z).
\end{array}
$$

Thus, now there are two rules that potentially may create $O(n^2)$ facts, and that is certainly an additional argument in favor of factorizing sg^{bb} into $b1\_sg^{bb}$ and $b2\_sg^{bb}$.

Note that the magic program for Figure 14 is not stratified, and that introduces an additional overhead in some of the magic-set methods for stratified programs [BMR88, BPR87, BRSS90, KT88, KP88, Ross90]. In comparison, the program of Figure 15 is stratified, since envelope predicates never depend on IDB predicates. We believe that in most cases, the program of Figure 15 is more efficient than those produced by the above methods.

8 Conclusion and Related Work

We have presented a method for creating envelopes. One advantage of envelopes, as compared to magic sets, is that several envelopes can be used to restrict the same program, even if each envelope is created from a different adorned program. Another advantage is the ability to limit the number of facts generated for envelope predicates to $O(n)$, where n is the size of the EDB. Consequently, we can obtain programs that in many cases are more efficient than those created by the magic-set transformation. However, more work is needed in order to develop methods for determining the envelopes (or magic sets) that should be used to restrict the computation of a given program and query. Part of the problem is that determining the best evaluation method depends on the given EDB, and therefore, methods for estimating sizes of predicates are required. One method for size estimation is described in [LN90]; however, the cost of estimating sizes according to this method might be prohibitive.

Although we have considered only datalog rules, the method we described can also handle rules with function symbols. Moreover, we can also generalize it to envelopes that compute predicates that may have nonground tuples, similarly to the magic-set extensions described in [Ker89, Ram88, Seki89].

As for related work, envelopes were first introduced in [SS88]. However, the method of [SS88] produces envelopes that are not always as tight as those produced by the method of Section 4. For example, for the nonlinear same-generation with a *bf* query, the method of [SS88] generates the rules of Figure 7 and two additional rules (that produce facts that are not produced by the rules of Figure 7). In a recent paper [SS90], the authors describe how to use multiple sips. Their method is essentially an intersection of several envelopes obtained from different adorned programs. In comparison, our approach, and in particular Theorem 4.1, provides a more general framework than the one described in [SS90]. The work reported in [SS90] and the work described in this paper were done independently of each other.

Factorization was also considered in [NRSU89a, NRSU89b]. However, these papers investigated when an envelope alone computes the exact answer to a query. Clearly, this is a property that holds only in special cases.

Acknowledgment

The author is grateful to Raghu Ramakrishnan and Jeff Ullman for valuable comments and discussions.

References

[AO89] Aly, H., and Z. M. Ozsoyoglu, "Synchronized Counting Method," *Proc. Fifth Int. Conf. on Data Engineering,* 1989, pp. 366–373.

[Brig87] Briggs, D. A., "A Reconsideration of the Termination Conditions of the Henschen-Naqvi Technique," COINS Tech. Rept. 87–11, University of Mass. at Amherst, 1987.

[BMR88] Balbin, I., K. Meenakshi, and K. Ramamohanarao, "An Efficient Labeling Algorithm for Magic Set Computation on Stratified Databases," Tech. Rept. 88/1, Dept. of CS, University of Melbourne, 1988.

[BPR87] Balbin, I., G. S. Port, and K. Ramamohanarao, "Magic Set Computations for Stratified Databases," Tech. Rept. 87/3, Dept. of CS, University of Melbourne, 1987.

[BMSU86] Bancilhon, F., D. Maier, Y. Sagiv, and J. D. Ullman, "Magic Sets and Other Strange Ways to Implement Logic Programs," *Proc. ACM SIGACT-SIGMOD Symp. on Principles of Database Systems,* 1986, pp. 1–15.

[BaR86] Bancilhon, F., R. Ramakrishnan, "An Amateur's Introduction to Recursive Query Processing Strategies," *Proc. ACM-SIGMOD Int. Conf. on Management of Data,* 1986, pp. 16–52.

[BRSS90] Beeri, C., R. Ramakrishnan, D. Srivastava, and S. Sudarshan, "Magic Implementation of Stratified Logic Programs," unpublished manuscript.

[BeR87] Beeri, C., and R. Ramakrishnan, "On the Power of Magic," *Proc. ACM SIGACT-SIGMOD-SIGART Symp. on Principles of Database Systems,* 1987, pp. 269–283.

[Bry89] Bry, F., "Query Evaluation in Recursive Databases: Bottom-Up and Top-Down Reconciled," *Proc. First Int. Conf. on Deductive and Object-Oriented Databases,* Kyoto, Japan, 1989, pp. 20–39.

[DW87] Dietrich, S. W., and D. S. Warren, "Extension Tables: Memo Relations in Logic Programming," *Proc. Symp. on Logic Programming,* 1987, pp. 264–272.

[GSS87] Grahne, G., S. Sippu, and E. Soisalon-Soininen, "Efficient Evaluation for a Subset of Recursive Queries," *Proc. ACM SIGACT-SIGART-SIGMOD Symp. on Principles of Database Systems,* 1987, pp. 284–293.

[HN88] Haddad, R. W., and J. F. Naughton, "Counting Methods for Cyclic Relations," *Proc. ACM SIGACT-SIGART-SIGMOD Symp. on Principles of Database Systems,* 1988, pp. 333–340.

[HH89] Han, J., and L. J. Henschen, "The Level-Cycle Merging Method," *Proc. First Int. Conf. on Deductive and Object-Oriented Databases,* Kyoto, Japan, 1989, pp. 113–129.

[HN84] Henschen, L. J., and S. A. Naqvi, "On Compiling Queries in Recursive First-Order Databases," *J. ACM,* **31**:1(1984), pp. 47–85.

[KT88] Kemp, D. B., and R. W. Topor, "Completeness of a Top-Down Query Evaluation Procedure for Stratified Databases," *Proc. Int. Conf. and Symp. on Logic Programming,* 1988, pp. 178–194.

[Ker89] Kerisit, J.-M., "A Relational Approach to Logic Programming: The Extended Alexander Method," *Theoretical Computer Science,* **69**:1(1989), pp. 55–68.

[KP88] Kerisit, J.-M., and J. M. Pugin, "Efficient Query Answering on Stratified Databases," *Proc. Int. Conf. on Fifth Generation Computer Systems,* 1988, pp. 719–726.

[KL86] Kifer, M., and E. L. Lozinskii, "A Framework for an Efficient Implementation of Deductive Databases," *Proc. 6th Advanced Database Symp.,* Tokyo, Japan, 1986, pp. 109–116.

[LV89] Lefebvre A., and L. Vieille, "On Deductive Query Evaluation in the DedGin* System," *Proc. First Int. Conf. on Deductive and Object-Oriented Databases,* Kyoto, Japan, 1989, pp. 225–246.

[LN90] Lipton, R. J., and J. F. Naughton, "Query Size Estimation by Adaptive Sampling," *Proc. ACM SIGACT-SIGART-SIGMOD Symp. on Principles of Database Systems,* 1990, pp. 40–46.

[Loz85] Lozinskii, E. L., "Evaluating Queries in Deductive Databases by Generating," *Proc. Int. Joint Conf. on Artificial Intelligence,* 1985, pp. 173–177.

[MNSUV87] Morris, K., J. F. Naughton, Y. Saraiya, J. D. Ullman, and A. Van Gelder, "YAWN! (Yet Another Window on NAIL!)," *Data Engineering,* **10**:4(1987), pp. 28–43.

[MUV86] Morris, K., J. D. Ullman, and A. Van Gelder, "Design Overview of the NAIL! System," *Proc. Third Int. Conf. on Logic Programming,* 1986, pp. 554–568.

[NT88] Naqvi, S. A., and S. Tsur, *A Logic Language for Data and Knowledge Bases,* Computer Science Press, Rockville, MD, 1988.

[Nau87] Naughton, J. F., "One-Sided Recursions," *Proc. ACM SIGACT-SIGART-SIGMOD Symp. on Principles of Database Systems,* 1987, pp. 340–348.

[Nau88] Naughton, J. F., "Compiling Separable Recursions," *Proc. ACM-SIGMOD Int. Conf. on Management of Data,* 1988, pp. 312–319.

[NRSU89a] Naughton, J. F., R. Ramakrishnan, Y. Sagiv, and J. D. Ullman, "Efficient Evaluation of Right-, Left-, and Multi-Linear Rules," *Proc. ACM-SIGMOD Int. Conf. on Management of Data,* 1989, pp. 235–242.

[NRSU89b] Naughton, J. F., R. Ramakrishnan, Y. Sagiv, and J. D. Ullman, "Argument Reduction through Factoring," *Proceedings of the Fifteenth International Conference on Very Large Databases,* 1989, pp. 173–182.

[Ram88] R. Ramakrishnan, "Magic Templates: A Spellbinding Approach to Logic Programs," *Proc. Int. Conf. and Symp. on Logic Programming,* 1988, pp. 140–159.

[RBK88] R. Ramakrishnan, C. Beeri, and R. Krishnamurthy, "Optimizing Existential Datalog Queries," *Proc. ACM SIGACT-SIGMOD-SIGART Symp. on Principles of Database Systems,* 1988, pp. 89–102.

[RLK86] Rohmer, J., R. Lescoeur, and J.-M. Kerisit, "The Alexander Method: A Technique for the Processing of Recursive Axioms in Deductive Databases," *New Generation Computing,* **4**:3(1986), pp. 273–285

[Ross90] Ross, K. A., "Modular Stratification and Magic Sets for DATALOG Programs with Negation," *Proc. ACM SIGACT-SIGART-SIGMOD Symp. on Principles of Database Systems,* 1990, pp. 161–171.

[SZ86] Sacca, D., and C. Zaniolo, "The Generalized Counting Method for Recursive Queries," *Proc. First Int. Conf. on Database Theory,* Rome, Italy, 1986, pp. 31–53.

[SZ87] Sacca, D., and C. Zaniolo, "Magic Counting Methods," *Proc. ACM-SIGMOD Int. Conf. on Management of Data,* 1987, pp. 49–59.

[Sag87] Sagiv, Y., "Optimizing Datalog Programs," *Foundations of Deductive Databases and Logic Programming,* (J. Minker, Ed.), Morgan Kaufmann Publishers, Los Altos, CA 94022, 1988, pp. 659–698. Extended Abstract appeared in *Proc. ACM SIGACT-SIGART-SIGMOD Symp. on Principles of Database Systems,* 1987, pp. 349–362.

[Seki89] Seki, H., "On the Power of Alexander Templates," *Proc. ACM SIGACT-SIGMOD-SIGART Symp. on Principles of Database Systems,* 1989, pp. 150–159.

[SS88] Sippu, S., and E. Soisalon-Soininen, "An Optimization Strategy for Recursive Queries in Logic Databases," *Proc. Int. Conf. on Data Engineering,* 1988, pp. 470–477.

[SS90] Sippu, S., and E. Soisalon-Soininen, "Multiple SIP Strategies and Bottom-Up Adorning in Logic Query Optimization," to appear in *Int. Conf. on Database Theory,* 1990, Paris, France.

[Ull89a] Ullman, J. D., "Bottom-Up Beats Top-Down for Datalog," *Proc. ACM SIGACT-SIGMOD-SIGART Symp. on Principles of Database Systems,* 1989, pp. 140–149.

[Ull89b] Ullman, J. D., *Principles of Database and Knowledge-Base Systems, Volume II: The New Technologies,* Computer Science Press, Rockville, MD 20850, 1989.

[VG86] Van Gelder, A., "A Message Passing Framework for Logical Query Evaluation," *Proc. ACM-SIGMOD Int. Conf. on Management of Data,* 1986, pp. 155–165.

[Vie86] Vieille, L., "Recursive Axioms in Deductive Databases: The Query/SubQuery Approach," *Proc. First Int. Conf. on Expert Database Systems,* 1986, pp. 179–193.

[Vie89] Vieille, L., "Recursive Query Processing: The Power of Logic," *Theoretical Computer Science,* **69**:1(1989), pp. 1–53.

[Yan90] Yannakakis, M., "Graph-Theoretic Methods in Database Theory," *Proc. ACM SIGACT-SIGMOD-SIGART Symp. on Principles of Database Systems,* 1990, pp. 230–242.

[Zan88] Zaniolo, C., "Design and Implementation of a Logic Based Language for Data Intensive Applications," *Proc. Int. Conf. and Symp. on Logic Programming,* 1988, pp. 1666–1687.

Reasoning in Inconsistent Databases

Shamim A. Naqvi
Bell Communications Research
445 South Street
Morristown, NJ 07960
shamim@bellcore.com

Francesca Rossi
University of Pisa
Computer Science Department
Corso Italia 40
56100 Pisa, Italy
rossi@dipisa.di.unipi.it

Abstract

We consider the problem of adding (possibly) non-Horn clauses to a database that is initially described by a set of Definite Horn clauses. In our model, information is always added to the database, and never deleted. Examples of such databases are stock market and consumer product databases. We show that this model of databases provides new functionality by allowing reasoning over inconsistent data, and also supports temporal, hypothetical and counter-factual queries. We provide a new procedural semantics for such queries that is novel in that rather than defining a new multi-valued logic or an ad-hoc truth maintenance method, we define a proof procedure that operates on the simple idea that earlier information is superseded by later information. We argue that the added functionality provided by our model is a strong reason for a logical treatment of databases since current database technology is quite adequate in supporting simple data retrieval requests. It is only in these more advanced functional requirements that the power of the logical view of databases can be demonstrated and justified.

1 Motivation

> A man comes upon another who is lying on the banks of a river, playing with a fishing line. Perturbed by this easy approach to fishing, he suggests the use of two fishing lines.
>
> "Why should I do that?" asks the irritated fisherman. The bystander explains painstakingly that in this way he can catch twice as many fish.
>
> "Then, what?" says the fisherman, who by now is even more irritated. Stung by the fellow's business ineptitude, the bystander explains that with the extra

> money he can hire people to fish for him, that he can soon buy boats to go fish in the ocean, and that pretty soon he will own a large fishing fleet.
>
> "What will I do then," says the fisherman persisting in his doggedness.
>
> "Well, nothing, my dear chap. You relax and go fishing."
>
> "And what do you think I am doing now"? asks the fisherman.

Since the inception of logic programming, it has been recognized that databases form a good application arena, undoubtedly because of the close connections between relational calculus and first-order logic. However, this view has received considerable opposition from other approaches, most notably the object-oriented approach. We claim that the reasons usually touted in support of adopting a logical approach to databases are unconvincing. The reasons one most often reads are that a logical treatment of databases affords a formal semantics, that any implementation faithful to the logical semantics can be chosen, that queries can be stated declaratively, and that application programs written as logic programs would be more concise and hopefully less prone to errors. The situation is further exacerbated by demonstrations of the power of logic programming which show how traditional database activities such as concurrency control, constraint checking, etc. can be couched as logic programs. We do not see much point in these demonstrations, for even if considered successful, they do not convert any users since no new problems are solved and database technology is adequate for traditional problems. For example, research in deductive databases started out in a promising direction, namely providing the extra expressive power of recursive queries to database query languages. However, since recursion can be relegated to the host language, many users remain unconvinced. They do not see a strong enough reason to abandon their current systems just for recursive queries. In short, we believe that contesting relational and object-oriented databases on their own turf is self-defeating— merely pointing out that logic programs can do what they can already accomplish is hardly a selling point. It would be more fruitful to draw these adversative approaches to unfamiliar terrain, and show actions that they may find difficult to emulate.

We claim that it is only by providing additional functionality, above and beyond relational and object-oriented approaches, that a logical framework can be sold, and that it is through this avenue that users can be compelled to eschew their current technologies.

A problem of considerable importance and excitement to the user community is the area of reasoning over inconsistent data. For example, in financial (stock market) and consumer product databases, new data is continually added to the system. Old data is never deleted. Quite often the new data is in direct contradiction to the older data. The question is whether new forms of query processing can be defined in such databases. The solution, incidentally, practiced by the users is to give priority to the newer information. Can this simple maxim be incorporated into query processing? Moreover, users of such databases frequently engage in hypothetical and counter-factual reasoning. Examples abound: If Coca-Cola Classic is put on sale will it take market share from Pepsi or from New Coke? If kosher hot dogs are put on sale will the sales volume of Grey Poupon mustard increase? If IBM had been down yesterday rather than up, what would the price of my technology portfolio be today? If the Dow Jones Industrial Average were up by 30, what would the weekly movement of DEC be? Notice that these queries posit information that is either contradictory to existing data or is to be hypothetically assumed and its consequences interrogated.

Current database technology is ill-equipped to handle this additional functionality. In the absence of well-defined and formal approaches, it is relegated to ad-hoc programming. Bevies of application programmers hand-code programs for market researchers and managers (the myth of managers posing ad-hoc queries to a database has long been exploded). It is in this unfamiliar arena that the relational and object-oriented approaches flounder and that a logical approach may hold sway over users.

One weakness of the above argument is that advanced functionality will probably come at the expense of performance. This is unfortunate but in the long run, functionality will provide the impetus for developing better optimization, compilation and execution technologies. The practical solution for database applications may be in providing the right balance between functionality and performance.

2 Inconsistency in Databases

Two different notions of inconsistency apply to databases. A state of the database is *semantically inconsistent* if it violates one or more integrity constraints. For example, a database state in which the age of employees is given by negative integers may violate the constraint that age must be a positive integer. The second notion of inconsistency is that of *logical inconsistency* where a database state may imply a proposition and its negation simultaneously.

Whereas techniques for maintaining semantic consistency have been the subject of intense and numerous investigations, the logical inconsistency problem has been solved by requiring that the database state must be logically consistent initially, and that subsequent operations on the data must maintain this consistency. Since detection of logical consistency is in general undecidable, the above requirement is satisfied by limiting the expressive power of the operations on the data, i.e., the transaction language and/or the data manipulation language are designed in such a way that inconsistent information cannot be expressed. For example, Definite Clause logic is never inconsistent since negation is disallowed. Similarly, in relational algebra negation is partially simulated by set difference.

In database theory, maintaining consistency in face of new contradictory information has been studied mostly in the context of the view update problem ([FUV83, FKUV88, BS81, DB82, RN89, Wil88]). Artificial Intelligence research in this area has led to non-monotonic formalisms, i.e., truth-maintenance systems (see [Prz89] for a logic programming perspective on non-monotonic reasoning and a list of related references). In such systems previously derived information may be contradicted by more recent inferences.

Previous approaches to this problem can be divided into two coarse categories. One involves the definition of a multi-valued logic, usually 3- or 4-valued [Fit85, Bel75]. But, as has been noticed by Kifer *et al.* [KL89], since there is no notion of a tautology, it is very hard to define a refutation procedure for such a logic. Another problem with such logics is that a multi-valued interpretation of logical implication is fraught with paradoxical perils. In the second direction towards this problem, a modal or two-part logic is proposed by some authors. A recent example is the RI logic of Kifer and Lozinskii [KL89]. There, an epistemic and an ontological level are defined, allowing modal inconsistency and contradictory knowledge at the epistemic level. Kifer *et al.* show a sound and complete inference procedure for their logic.

In this paper we consider the occurrence of logical inconsistency in data bases that admit insertions only; information once entered in the database is never deleted. We assume that our database consists of a set DB of *Definite Horn clauses*, plus a set C of possibly non-Horn clauses, related to the clauses in DB by a sort of unfolding of the completion of the database *COMP(DB)* (see [Clark78]). More precisely, a clause in C is either a fact, or the instantiation of the body of a clause in the unfolding of *COMP(DB)*, or the negation of one of the above. We treat DB as a theory T, i.e., a finite set of closed sentences, and denote the set of logical consequences of T by T^*. By considering now the set of possibly non-Horn clauses C, the set T^* could change. In particular, previously provable propositions may no longer have a proof. This non-monotonic behavior of the model of the database is implemented by a new definition of the database $NDB = DB \cup C$, called a *combined database*, and by a new inference procedure, called *SLIL-resolution*. It is easy to see that the set NDB may be logically inconsistent. The novelty of our approach is that we relegate the inconsistency problem to the inference procedure. Thus the special inference procedure, SLIL-resolution, must be able to effectively handle sets of inconsistent clauses. It accomplishes this objective by storing the clauses C in a priority structure and using them at different points in the process of constructing the proof tree. A proof is found if and only if no later information in the priority queue contradicts some part of the proof tree. Thus, new information supersedes previous information in SLIL-refutations.

Example 2.1 *Suppose that the database DB consists of the two clauses*[1]*:*

[1]The "Tweety-Fly" example has become obligatory in papers on non-monotonic reasoning, just as the "Student-Grade" example in databases, and the "append" in logic

$fly(x) : -bird(x)$ and $fly(x) : -plane(x)$. Obviously, nothing can be derived in this state. In fact, no query will succeed in SLIL-resolution, because SLIL in the case of definite clauses works just like SLD-resolution.

Now we consider the non-Horn clause $c_1 : bird(Tweety) \vee plane(Tweety)$. Note that this clause is a ground instance of the body of the clause $fly(x) : -bird(x) \vee plane(x)$ which is in COMP(DB) (note that here the unfolding of such clause returns the same clause, since there is no clause defining predicates "bird" and "plane"). The intuitive idea is that now (in the combined database $DB \cup c_1$), we would like to derive that Tweety can fly. In fact, the query $: -fly(Tweety)$ is the only one which will succeed in SLIL-resolution. More precisely, the priority structure of our resolution procedure contains the two rules in the first level, and the new added clause in the second level. Although the database is now indefinite, it is still consistent because of the presence of positive information only, so it is easy to see that $fly(Tweety)$ can be deduced without any need to check for inconsistency.

Let us now consider two more clauses (c_2 and c_3): $\neg bird(Tweety)$ and $\neg plane(Tweety)$. Again, note that these clauses are the negation of the body of a clause in COMP(DB) (again, unfolding doesn't change COMP(DB)). The idea is that we don't want to derive $fly(Tweety)$ any more, because we now know that Tweety is neither a bird nor a plane. SLIL-resolution puts these two new clauses in the third level of the priority structure, tries to prove $fly(Tweety)$ by using the first and the second level, but discovers that the third level contradicts the second one (and it also has a higher priority), so the proof fails.■

Note that the combined theory $NDB = DB \cup C$ of the above example was built incrementally, by starting with DB and then adding one or more clauses of C over time. In fact, only in this way could we give some priority to the different clauses of C, in order to resolve the possible inconsistencies. In other words, the clauses in C must be ordered in disjoint subsets, each one of which may contain only positive or only negative clauses, thus eliminating the possibility of any inconsistency within any subset.

Further note that, in contrast to truth-maintenance systems, we allow our combined database $DB \cup C$ to be logically inconsistent. It is the associated inference procedure, SLIL-resolution, that maintains the consistency of logical consequences from the database. This may be termed as "on demand" testing for consistency as opposed to maintaining a consistent set of formulae.

In Section 5 we shall show that this simple behavior of the combined database NDB outlined above gives intuitive semantics for view updates (as shown in [RN89]), for certain classes of temporal queries (e.g., Is it always the case that $X > 3$ and sometimes less than 6?), and hypothetical and counter-factual queries (e.g., If resistor 3241 would have not been in the circuit, what would the voltage be at gate 3162?). We present declarative

programs.

and procedural semantics for such queries based upon our model of the database. A major problem, apart from testing the validity of such queries, is to develop a calculus for them since, for example, transitivity of counter-factual inferences does not hold, i.e., from $(p \rightarrow q)$ and $(q \rightarrow r)$ it need not necessarily follow that $(p \rightarrow r)$.

An outline of the paper is as follows. In Section 3 we give the basic notions and the definition of a combined database. Section 4 presents SLIL-resolution and shows its soundness and completeness with respect to the class of combined databases. Section 5 shows the usefulness of our approach by describing its application to temporal, hypothetical, and counter-factual queries.

3 Combined Databases

A *(definite) database DB* is a finite collection of Definite Clauses (rules). A *fact* is a ground (i.e., variable-free) rule with an empty body. A *positive* clause is a clause free of negated literals, and a *negative* clause is a clause free of positive literals. A *positive* (respectively, *negative set*) of clauses is a set of positive (negative) clauses. A *p/n set* of clauses is either a positive or a negative set of clauses. A query is a headless rule (thus it is a negative clause). Given a definite database *DB* we let *COMP(DB)* denote the Clark completion of *DB*([Clark78]) and *COMP-IF(DB)* the if version of *COMP(DB)* (clauses are implications instead of if-and-only-if).

We define now the unfolding of a given database DB, written $UNF(DB)$, as follows: for every clause $c \in DB$, for all predicates p such that

- p appears in the body of c in the literal L, and
- p does not appear in the head of c, and
- there exist a rule defining p in DB, say c'

replace L by the body of c'.

In words, $UNF(DB)$ is obtained from DB by expanding each literal in the body of each clause of DB by its definition in DB.

We now set $UNFOLD(DB) = UNF^n(DB)$ such that $UNF^n(DB) = UNF^{n+1}(DB)$. I.e., we iterate the unfolding procedure described above until no more changes can be done to DB.

Example 3.1 *Consider the database DB consisting of the clauses*
$p :- q.$
$p :- b2, p.$
$q :- b1.$
Then, $COMP-IF(DB)$ is
$p :- q \vee (b2 \wedge p).$
$q :- b1.$

Thus UNF(COMP-IF(DB)) is
$p : -b1 \vee (b2 \wedge p)$.
$q : -b1$.
In this case, UNFOLD(COMP-IF(DB)) = UNF(COMP-IF(DB)), since there is no definition for b1 or b2 in COMP-IF(DB). ∎

A *combined database* NDB is a definite database DB, plus an ordered set of p/n-sets of clauses $C = \{C_1, \ldots, C_n\}$, such that a clause $c \in C_i$ for some i iff:

- c is a base fact;
- $\exists$ a clause $a : -c'$ in *UNFOLD(COMP-IF(DB))* and c is an instantiation of c';
- c is the negation of one of the above.

Both declarative and procedural semantics of such databases, restricted to their use in the view update context, is provided in [RN89]. The problem in giving any semantics to a database $NDB = DB \cup C$ is obviously that the set NDB may be logically inconsistent. However, as far as the declarative semantics is concerned, it is possible to construct, given $NDB = DB \cup C$, a new theory NDB' which has the intended meaning (of DB plus the additional indefinite information in C), and whose possible consequences are contained in the set NDB'^* (recall that NDB'^* denotes the set of logical consequences of NDB'). For the procedural semantics, a new inference procedure, called *SLIL-resolution*, is described that operates on DB and the clauses of C in a particular manner. The underlying maxim of SLIL is to give priority to new information over older, maybe contradictory information. Subsets of clauses in C are viewed in terms of a priority structure, and a step of inference succeeds if and only if no subsequent contradictory information in the priority queue is found.

4 Procedural Semantics of Combined Databases

The SLIL-refutation procedure is based on the SLI-refutation introduced in [LRM89]. The changes from SLI-refutation involve a new notation, new rules of inference, and a new data structure, called the *priority queue*, that holds the clauses added to the original database. The result is called SLIL-resolution (Linear resolution with Selection function for Indefinite clauses and Levels). It was already presented, in the context of view updates only, in [RN89]; here we will present it in the more general setting of combined databases.

Given a combined database $NDB = DB \cup C$, where DB is a database and C is an ordered set of p/n-sets of clauses $C_1, \ldots, C_n$, we now want to answer a query $: -q_1, \ldots, q_n$.

The order-dependence of the p/n-sets of clauses $C_1, \ldots, C_n$ can be motivated by noticing that a set of clauses C_i may undo the effects of another set of clauses C_j, with $j < i$. The data structure that takes care of this problem is a sequence $SEQ = (L_1, \ldots, L_n)$ of levels, where each level L_i contains C_i. This structure may be changed (not in the number of the levels, but in the content of each one of them) during the development of a proof. Note that, due to the restriction on the sets C_i, each L_i can contain either clauses with only positive literals, or clauses with only negative literals, thus eliminating the possibility of inconsistency in any single level.

Let

$NEG = \{c \mid \exists \text{a negative level L and} c \in L\}$

$POS = \{c \mid \exists \text{a positive level L and} c \in L\}$

We associate a level number with each Horn clause or positive non-Horn clause C, called the *level number*, ln, such that $ln(c) = 0$ if $c \in DB$, otherwise $ln(c) = i$ if $c \in L_i$.

The main idea of SLIL-resolution is to resolve a literal A in the current resolvent with some clause in some level, say L_i, and then to check, before replacing A, if there is some clause in some negative level among $L_{i+1}, \ldots, L_n$ that contradicts this action. Checking of only the levels after L_i is based on the fact that a clause may contradict only some past clauses, but none of the future ones. So there is nothing in $L_1, \ldots, L_{i-1}$ that can contradict the chosen literal in L_i.

At each step $i, i = 1, \ldots, m$, of the resolution procedure we have a goal G_i and a sequence $SEQ_i = (L_1, \ldots, L_n)$ of levels of non-Horn clauses. We also have a set of negative clauses CON_i that constrain the execution of the step.

The initial goal G_0 is set to the given query Q, and SEQ_0 is set to the given SEQ. The general current goal G_i will be $g_1 \vee \ldots \vee g_n$. The set of clauses to be considered for resolving the current goal is $DB \cup POS \cup NEG \cup Q$.

We have two rules of inference:

(*Factoring*): $\exists$ subgoals g_j, g_k, with $1 \leq j < k \leq n$ and a substitution θ_i such that $g_j\theta_i = g_k\theta_i$. Then

$$G_{i+1} = (g_1 \vee \ldots \vee g_{k-1} \vee g_{k+1} \vee \ldots \vee g_n)\theta_i$$

and $SEQ_{i+1} = SEQ_i$. ∎

(*Substitution*): there may be two cases:

- if g_1 is a positive atom, and $\exists B_1 \vee \ldots \vee B_m \in (DB \cup NEG)$ and θ_i such that $\neg g_1\theta_i = B_1\theta_i$, then

$$G_{i+1} = (B_2 \vee \ldots \vee B_m \vee g_2 \vee \ldots \vee g_n)\theta_i.$$

If $B_1 \vee \ldots \vee B_m \in L_i$, then $L_i := L_i \setminus \{B_1 \vee \ldots \vee B_m\}$ and SEQ_{i+1} is set to the current sequence $(L_1, \ldots, L_n)$;

- if g_1 is a negative atom, and $\exists B_1 \vee \ldots \vee B_m \in (DB \cup POS)$ and θ_i such that $\neg g_1\theta_i = B_1\theta_i$, then set $level = ln(B_1 \vee \ldots \vee B_m)$ and

$$CON_i = \{c \mid c \in L_k, k > level, c = \neg d_1 \vee \ldots \vee \neg d_h, \neg g_1\theta_i = d_1\theta_i\}$$

If $CON_i \neq \emptyset$, then the levels are changed as follows. All levels from L_1 to L_{level} remain unchanged. All negative levels from $L_{level+1}$ to L_n are changed using the following iterative algorithm:

for all $c = \neg d_1 \vee \ldots \vee \neg d_h \in CON_i$, if $c \in L_j$, then $L_j := L_j \setminus \{c\} \cup \{(\neg d_2 \vee \ldots \vee \neg d_n)\theta_i\}$.

Now, if $\Box \notin L_i \forall i$ (i.e. there is no empty clause in any of the levels), then

$$G_{i+1} = (B_2 \vee \ldots \vee B_m \vee g_2 \vee \ldots \vee g_n)\theta$$

and SEQ_{i+1} is set to the current sequence $(L_1, \ldots, L_n)$. ∎

An *SLIL-refutation* from $DB \cup SEQ$ of goal Q is a finite SLIL-derivation of the empty clause $\Box$.

Example 4.1 *Let us consider in more detail the example given in Section 1. The database DB consists of the two clauses $fly(x) : -bird(x)$ and $fly(x) : -plane(x)$. The first p/n-set of clauses (in the given order for C) is $C_1 = \{bird(Tweety) \vee plane(Tweety)\}$ and the second one is $C_2 = \{\neg bird(Tweety), \neg plane(Tweety)\}$. The query is : $-fly(Tweety)$.*

In this case we have $SEQ = (L_1, L_2)$, where

$$L_1 = \{bird(Tweety) \vee plane(Tweety)\}$$

and

$$L_2 = \{\neg bird(Tweety), \neg plane(Tweety)\}$$

$G_0 = \neg fly(Tweety)$ and $SEQ_0 = SEQ$. Now, $fly(Tweety)$ unifies with the head of the first rule with mgu $\theta = \{x/Tweety\}$, so $level = 0$ and $CON_0 = \emptyset$. This means that no level is changed. Moreover, no level contains the empty clause, so $G_1 = \neg bird(Tweety)$ and $SEQ_1 = SEQ_0$.

Now, $bird(Tweety)$ unifies with a literal in L_1, so the level number is 1 and $CON_1 = \{\neg bird(Tweety)\}$. Thus $L_2 := L_2 \setminus \{\neg bird(Tweety)\} \cup \{\Box\} = \{\neg plane(Tweety), \Box\}$. So, L_2 contains the empty clause. This means that a clause in level 1 is contradicted by a clause in level 2, and thus the proof fails. But we may note that any other branch will lead us to a similar situation, so the entire proof of $fly(Tweety)$ fails.

Let us now consider the case when the order of the two p/n-sets C_1 and C_2 is reversed. The intuitive meaning is now that, unlike the previous query, we want this one to succeed, i.e., we want to be able to deduce $fly(Tweety)$.

Following SLIL-resolution, we have $SEQ = (L_1, L_2)$, where now

$$L_1 = \{\neg bird(Tweety), \neg plane(Tweety)\}$$

and

$$L_2 = \{bird(Tweety) \vee plane(Tweety)\}$$

The first step is as in the previous case, so we end up with $G_1 = \neg bird(Tweety)$ *and* $SEQ_1 = SEQ$. *Then,* $bird(Tweety)$ *matches with a literal in* L_2, *so* $level = 2$ *and* $CON_1 = \emptyset$. *This means that no level is changed, so* $G_2 = plane(Tweety)$ *and* $SEQ_2 = SEQ$.

Now, $\neg plane(Tweety)$ *unifies with a literal in* L_1, *so*

$$L_1 := L_1 \setminus \{\neg plane(Tweety)\} = \{\neg bird(Tweety)\}$$

$G_{i+1} = \Box$ *and no level contains the empty clause, i.e, no contradictions have been found. Thus, the proof succeeds, i.e. that* $fly(Tweety)$ *can be deduced from the database.*■

Given the combined database $NDB = DB \cup C$, we said in Section 3 that it is possible to give a declarative semantics to the theory NDB'(see [RN89]), obtained from NDB by eliminating the inconsistencies while accomplishing all the updates in the right sequence. We will now restate the results (from [RN89]) that show that the SLIL-resolution procedure provides a procedural semantics which is equivalent to the declarative one, in the sense that it is sound and complete w.r.t. the set of logical consequences of NDB'.

Theorem 4.2 (from [RN89]) *Given* DB *and* C, *let us consider* NDB' *and* SEQ *(the sequence of levels corresponding to* C*). Then, for any ground positive atom* A, $NDB' \vdash A$ *if* A *has a SLIL-refutation from* $DB \cup SEQ$.
Proof Sketch: *Induction on the length of the SLIL-derivation.* ■

It must be noted that the above theorem states that every positive literal provable under SLIL is also logically entailed by NDB'. Thus, the soundness of SLIL is shown with respect to NDB'. In particular, we cannot consider the soundness issue based on the clauses in DB together with the clauses in the levels since this collective set may be inconsistent.

SLIL-resolution is also complete in the sense that every positive literal that is logically entailed by NDB' has a corresponding SLIL-proof. Let us define M_{atoms} $(NDB') = \{A \mid NDB' \vdash A$ and A is a ground positive atom$\}$.

Theorem 4.3 (from [RN89]) *Given* DB *and* C, *let us consider* NDB' *and* SEQ *(the sequence of levels corresponding to* C*). Then, a ground positive atom* A *can be deduced from* DB *and* SEQ *using SLIL-resolution if* $A \in M_{atoms}(NDB')$. ■
Proof Sketch: *By contradiction with atoms of* $M_{atoms}(NDB')$.

A special case of the SLIL proof procedure arises when the clauses of C are disjoint. In fact, it can be proved that in this case we do not need the entire sequence of n levels, but only one level L_1 for all the positive clauses and another level L_2 containing all the negative clauses.

When a large number of clauses have been added to DB, an equally large number of levels have to be considered by SLIL-resolution. In this case, some heuristic techniques can be of help in collapsing some of the levels and still preserve correctness. Also, ancestry resolution and factoring, which are the main culprits for the high cost of complete proof procedures for non-Horn programs, could be partially eliminated in the case of disjunctive programs by looking at the dependency graph (see [RLM89]).

Finally, SLIL-resolution may pay a heavy price in time because whenever we use the substitution rule we have to check all the negative clauses and their number may be very large. We can solve this problem by using an efficient pattern matching search technique that avoids looking at all the negative clauses (in fact we have to only look for all the clauses matching some already found base literal).

5 Applications of SLIL-resolution

We now turn our attention to applications of the model of databases NDB, and the associated inference method, SLIL-resolution. In a less general setting, the application of NDB and SLIL-resolution to the problem of view updates has been shown in [RN89]. In the next subsections we show applications that rely on this more general definition of NDB and SLIL-resolution.

5.1 Temporal Reasoning

Our objective is to provide semantics for temporal queries over NDB. Some examples of the kind of queries we have in mind are "Is $p(a)$ true at time t_1 and $q(X)$ true at a later time?", or "Is it always the case that $p(X,Y), Y > 3$ and sometimes $p(X,Y), Y < 6$?."

First we define the syntax of temporal queries. We start with Horn clause queries and add two temporal operators, $\Box$ (always), and $\bigcirc$ (next). Both of these operators can apply to formulae. A temporal query is a pair (s, Q) where s is a state (intuitively a point on the time line of the database) and Q is a formula over predicates, and the operators $\Box$ and $\bigcirc$. Thus,

$$:-(s, \Box(p(a), q(X)))$$

$$:-(s, (\Box p(a), \bigcirc q(a)))$$

are valid queries. The variables are implicitly existential.

The intuitive meaning of $(s, \Box\alpha)$ is that α is true for all states subsequent to state s, and that of $(s, \bigcirc\alpha)$ is that α is true in the state immediately after s. It is possible to define other, more conventional operators from $\Box$ and $\bigcirc$. Thus, the operator $\Diamond$ may be defined as

$$(s, \Diamond\alpha) \equiv_{def} (s, \neg\Box\neg\alpha)$$

Hence, $\Diamond\alpha$ has the intuitive meaning that α is eventually true in some state after s.

Our model of temporal queries associates time with states of the database. As a new *p/n-clause* is added to the database, a new time instant is created. Thus, corresponding to insertions of *p/n-clauses* $c_1, \ldots, c_n$ there is a series of time instants $t_1, \ldots, t_n$. The initial time instant t_0 is associated with the definite database DB.

Example 5.1 *The query "Is $p(a)$ true at time t_1 and $q(X)$ true at a later time?" stated above may be expressed in the query language as*

$$: -(t_1, (p(a), \Diamond q(X)))$$

The query "Is it always the case that $p(X,Y), Y > 3$ and sometimes $p(X,Y)$, $Y < 6$?" may be expressed as

$$: -(t_0, (\Box(p(X,Y), Y > 3), \Diamond(p(X,Y), Y < 6)))$$

■

We now present the declarative semantics for this class of queries. Our treatment is based upon that used in Interval Temporal Logic [Mos86]. We define a *state* as the set of logical consequences of a given database, then it can be seen that as clauses are added to DB in levels $L_1, L_2, \ldots, L_n$, there is a sequence of corresponding states $s_0, s_1, \ldots, s_n$, where s_0 is the state corresponding to the database DB, s_1 is the state corresponding to the database $DB \cup L_1$, s_2 is the state corresponding to $DB \cup L_1 \cup L_2$, etc. Let Σ be the set of all states. We define intervals of time as elements of Σ^+ where Σ^+ is the set of all non-empty finite sequences of states [MM84, Mos86]. If s, t are states then

$$\langle st \rangle, \langle ssttst \rangle$$

are possible intervals. An interval always contains at least one state. As in [Mos86] we define the length of an interval to be one less than the number of states in it. Thus, the interval $\sigma = \langle ssttt \rangle$ has the length 4, denoted $\mid \sigma \mid = 4$. The individual states of an interval σ are denoted $\sigma_0, \sigma_1, \ldots, \sigma_{|\sigma|}$.

A *model* of a temporal formula is a triple (D, Σ, M) where D is a data domain, Σ a set of states, and M an interpretation assigning meanings to the formulae of the language. A *state* can also be viewed as a function mapping variables to values in D; Σ is the set of all such functions. If s is a state and X a variable then let $s[[X]]$ denote the value of X in state s. Each n-place predicate p has an interpretation which is a function mapping n elements in D to a single truth value:

$$M[[p]] \in (D^n \rightarrow \{\text{true,false}\})$$

We now extend the interpretation M to assign meanings to formulae over intervals. In the following we consider an interval $\sigma = \langle \sigma_0, \sigma_1, \ldots, \sigma_n \rangle$ and let $s = \sigma_j$ for some $j, 0 \leq j \leq n$. The notation $M_\sigma[[s, w]]$ shall denote the truth value of the formula w in state s over the interval σ.

- $M_\sigma[[s,X]] = s[[X]]$, where X is a variable.
Thus the value of a variable on an interval is the value of that variable in state s of the interval.

- $M_\sigma[[s,p(e_1,\ldots,e_n)]] = M[[s,p]](M_\sigma[[s,e_1]],\ldots,M_\sigma[[s,e_n]])$. The interpretation of the predicate symbol p is applied to the interpretations of $e_1,\ldots,e_n$.

- $M_\sigma[[s,\neg w]] =$ true iff $M_\sigma[[s,w]] =$ false.

- $M_\sigma[[s,(w_1,w_2)]] =$ true iff $M_\sigma[[s,w_1]] =$ true and $M_\sigma[[s,w_2]] =$ true.

- $M_\sigma[[s,\bigcirc w]] =$ true iff $\mid \sigma \mid \geq j+1$ and $M_\sigma[[\sigma_{j+1},w]] =$ true.
Thus, $(s,\bigcirc w)$ is true over an interval if and only if it is true in the state immediately after state s of that interval (remember that $s = \sigma_j$).

- $M_\sigma[[s,\Box w]] =$ true iff $\forall j+1 \leq i \leq\mid \sigma \mid, M_{\sigma_i}[[s,w]] =$ true.
Thus, $(s,\Box w)$ is true over an interval if and only if it is true in all states of the interval after state s.

Example 5.2 *Let s,t and u be states such that $p(a)$ is true in s, $p(b)$ is true in t, and $p(c)$ is true in u, only. Then the query*

$$:-(s,(p(a),\bigcirc p(b)))$$

is true on an interval σ of length ≥ 1, if $p(a)$ is true in $\sigma_0 = s$, and $p(b)$ is true in the next state. Thus, the query is true over the interval $\langle stu\rangle$. On the other hand the query is false over the interval $\langle tt\rangle$. The query

$$:-(s,(p(a),\bigcirc p(b),\Diamond p(c)))$$

is true over an interval if $p(a)$ is true in $\sigma_0 = s$, $p(b)$ is true in the next state, and $p(c)$ is true in some subsequent state of the interval. For example, the query is true over the interval $\langle sttts sutt\rangle$.■

In processing a temporal query (t,Q) over NDB, we associate with $NDB = DB \cup L_1 \cup L_2 \cup \ldots \cup L_n$ the corresponding interval $\langle s_0,s_1,\ldots,s_n\rangle$ where s_0 is the state corresponding to the database DB, s_1 is the state corresponding to the database $DB \cup L_1$, s_2 is the state corresponding to the database $DB \cup L_1 \cup L_2$, etc. The truth of the query (t,Q) is then determined by the interpretation given above. More precisely, whenever we need to know the truth value of a formula over a state s_i, we apply SLIL resolution to the set of clauses corresponding to that state, i.e., to $DB \cup L_1 \cup \ldots \cup L_i$.

5.2 Hypothetical and Counter-factual Reasoning

The possibility of making hypothesis about the current world is of great interest both in databases and AI. *What-if* queries, in fact, permit us to investigate a possible future state of a dynamic world, thus giving some hints about the consequences of actions. Such hypothesis on a world can be either consistent or inconsistent with the current state of the world, accounting for the difference between hypothetical ([Sto80]) and counter-factual assumptions ([Gin86, Lew73]):

- hypothetical assumptions are always consistent with the current world;
- counter-factual assumptions are always inconsistent with the current world.

More precisely, we can say that, given the theory T, and the assumption A, if either $T \vdash A$ or $(\neg(T \vdash A)$ and $\neg(T \vdash \neg A))$, then $T \cup A$ is consistent, so A is an hypothetical assumption. On the contrary, if $T \vdash \neg A$, then $T \cup A$ is obviously inconsistent, so A is a counter-factual assumption.

Example 5.3 *[McC81]: In English, the difference between a hypothetical and a counter-factual proposition can be seen in the use of the verb mood: indicative vs. subjunctive. In fact, for example, the sentence "If Bill left at 2:00, he is in Pittsburgh by now" is a hypothetical conditional, while the sentence "If Carter had been born in Russia, he would have been a communist" is a counter-factual conditional.*■

A hypothetical or counter-factual query is a pair of the form (A, Q), where A is a hypothetical (respectively, counter-factual) assumption, called the premise of the query, and Q is a formula. To determine the validity of such a query (A, Q) in a database state DB it is reasonable to obtain a consistent database DB' that differs minimally from DB and such that $DB' \vdash A$, and then determine the satisfaction of Q in DB'.

In our framework, this same idea can be rephrased as follows. Given the current database NDB, defined by a set of Horn clauses plus some levels of p/n-clauses $L_1, \ldots, L_n$, we handle the hypothetical (or counter-factual) query $:-(A, Q)$ by storing in a new level L_{n+1} the assumption A and by then using SLIL-resolution on $NDB \cup L_{n+1}$ to answer the query Q.

Note that A can be stored in a level in two ways: explicitly (i.e., the level really contains A), or implicitly, in which case the level contains a set of clauses C such that $(DB \cup C) \vdash A$. More precisely, such sets of clauses can be obtained by unfolding the definition of A until the base relation level. If for example we have the two rules $p(x) :- b_1(x)$ and $p(x) :- b_2(x)$ in DB and $A = p(a)$, then the clause $b_1(a) \vee b_2(a)$ will be stored in the new level. We believe that this second alternative is more attractive, since rules may define different derived relations in terms of intersecting sets of base relations, and we would like the assumptions to be seen by all "relevant" relations in the database. The unfolding algorithm can be found in [RN89]. We shall not discuss it further here.

Although hypothetical and counter-factual queries appear to be similar since they are interpreted in the same way, this is true only when a single query is asked. In fact, in the case of a sequence of queries with an intersecting "domain", they can lead to different conclusions since hypothetical reasoning satisfies the transitive property while counter-factual reasoning does not. More precisely, let us consider the two queries $:-(A, B)$ and $:-(B, C)$ and let us suppose that they are both true. Then, if these queries are hypothetical, we can safely deduce the validity of the query $:-(A, C)$. If on the contrary they are counter-factual, then it may not be the case, i.e., it may be that $:-(A, C)$ fails.

Example 5.4 *[McC81]: Given the two hypothetical conditionals "If Bill left at 2:00, he is in Pittsburgh by now" and "If Bill is in Pittsburgh by now, he can go to Ted's birthday party," we can infer the new hypothetical conditional "If Bill left at 2:00, he can go to Ted's birthday party."*

On the contrary, given the two counter-factual conditionals "If Carter had been born in Russia, he would have been a communist" and "If Carter had been a communist, he would have been a traitor," we obviously cannot infer "If Carter had been born in Russia, he would have been a traitor." ∎

The reason why counter-factual reasoning does not satisfy the transitivity law can be intuitively explained by considering the following. Given an initial database DB, after the first counter-factual (A, B) has been proved we are in a new database DB' where now B can be proved. Now the second query, $:-(B, C)$, is not a counter-factual query because B is not in contradiction with DB'. Thus, to be able to correctly treat (B, C), we have to make it a counter-factual. Our solution to this problem is to go back to some database state where B creates a contradiction. More precisely, given a series of counter-factual queries $(A_1, A_2), (A_2, A_3), \ldots, (A_{n-1}, A_n)$ and a current database $NDB = DB \cup L_1 \cup \ldots \cup L_i$, we will create new levels as follows:

$$
\begin{aligned}
&L_{i+1} := A_1;\\
&L_{i+2} := \neg A_1 \wedge A_2;\\
&L_{i+3} := \neg A_1 \wedge \neg A_2 \wedge A_3;\\
&\vdots\\
&L_{i+n-1} := \neg A_1 \wedge \ldots \wedge \neg A_{n-2} \wedge A_{n-1}.
\end{aligned}
$$

Then we will use SLIL resolution to answer each query (A_j, A_{j+1}) in the database $DB \cup L_1 \cup \ldots \cup L_{i+j}$.

Since hypothetical conditionals satisfy the transitivity law, each premise in a series of hypothetical queries remains hypothetical (in the sense that it does not contradict the current database). Thus, we do not need to invalidate all the previous conditionals to be able to correctly answer the current hypothetical query. This means that, given the sequence of hypothetical queries $(A_1, A_2), (A_2, A_3), \ldots, (A_{n-1}, A_n)$ and a current database $NDB = DB \cup L_1 \cup \ldots \cup L_i$, we will create new levels as follows:

$$
\begin{aligned}
&L_{i+1} := A_1;\\
&L_{i+2} := A_2;
\end{aligned}
$$

$L_{i+3} := A_3;$

$\vdots$

$L_{i+n-1} := A_{n-1}.$

As above, to answer the query (A_j, A_{j+1}), we will try to prove it by using SLIL-resolution on the database $DB \cup L_1 \cup \ldots \cup L_{i+j}$.

6 Conclusions

The contributions of this paper are as follows:

- We have argued that the logic programming approach to database should emphasize additional functionality, above and beyond that provided by the relational and object-oriented approaches.
- Towards this objective, we identified a class of problems that are commonly faced in the user community, and which are not satisfactorily handled by the relational and object-oriented approaches. This class of problems deals with answering queries over inconsistent databases. The inconsistency here is not general; rather it is of a restricted and special nature and occurs in databases that allow incremental addition of data only. In this sense the problem is a more general version of the database update problem, in that now certain special kinds of clauses can be allowed to be added to the database.
- We have proposed a new model of databases NDB and an inference procedure, *SLIL-resolution*, that incorporates the common maxim of taking newer information as true over prior information. While this maxim may not always be true, the model proposed herein is sufficiently interesting to capture classes of temporal, hypothetical, and counter-factual queries. These queries provide some of the additional functionality we are desirous of attaining to make the logical approach viable in databases.

Acknowledgements

This work was initiated while Francesca Rossi was at MCC, Austin, Texas.

References

[Bel75] N. Belnap. *A Useful Four-Valued Logic.* D. Reidel Publishing Co., 1975.

[BS81] F. Bancilhon and N. Spyratos. Update semantics of relational views. *Association of Computing Machinery Transactions on Database Systems*, 6(4):557–575, 1981.

[Clark78] K. L. Clark. Negation as Failure. In H. Gallaire and J. Minker editors, *Logic and Databases*, Plenum Press, New York,1978.

[DB82] U. Dayal and P. Bernstein. On the correct translation of update operations on relational views. *Association of Computing Machinery Transactions on Database Systems*, 8(3):381–416, 1982.

[Fit85] M. Fitting. A kripke-kleene semantics for logic programs. *Journal of Logic Programming*, 2(4):295–312, 1985.

[FKUV88] R. Fagin, G. Kuper, J. Ullman, and M. Vardi. Updating logical databases. In P. Kanellakis, editor, *Advances in Computing Research*, Morgan-Kaufman, Los Altos, CA, Los Altos, CA, 1988.

[FUV83] R. Fagin, J. Ullman, and M. Vardi. On the semantics of updates in databases. In *Proceedings of the 2nd Annual Association of Computing Machinery Symposium on Principles of Database Systems*, 1983.

[Gin86] M. Ginsberg. Counterfactuals. *Artificial Intelligence*, 30:35–79, 1986.

[KL89] M. Kifer and E. Lozinskii. RI: a logic for reasoning with inconsistency. In *Proc. of Conference on Logics for Computer Science*, 1989.

[Lew73] D. Lewis. *Counterfactuals*. Harvard University Press, 1973.

[LRM89] J. Lobo, A. Rajasekar, and J. Minker. Extending the semantics of logic programs to disjunctive logic programs. In *Proc. of 6th International Conference on Logic Programming*, 1989.

[McC81] J. McCawley. *Everything that linguists have always wanted to know about logic but were ashamed to ask*. University of Chicago, 1981.

[MM84] B. Moszkowski and Z. Manna. *Reasoning in interval temporal logic. Lecture Notes in Computer Science 164*, Springer-Verlag, 1984. Also in Proc. of Workshop on Logics of Programs, Berlin, 1984.

[Mos86] B. Moszkowski. *Executing Temporal Logic Programs*. Cambridge University Press, 1986.

[Prz89] T. Przymusinski. Non-monotonic formalisms and logic programming. In *Proc. of 6th International Conference on Logic Programming*, 1989.

[RLM89] A. Rajasekar, J. Lobo, and J. Minker. Skeptical reasoning and disjunctive programs. In *Proc. of First International Conf. on Principles of Knowledge Representation and Reasoning*, 1989.

[RN89] F. Rossi and S. Naqvi. Contributions to the view update problem. In *Proc. of 6th International Conference on Logic Programming*, 1989.

[Sto80] M. Stonebraker. Hypothetical queries in database systems. In *Proc. of International Conference on Very Large Data Bases*, 1980.

[Wil88] M. Wilkins. A framework for comparison of update semantics. In *Proc. of 7th Association of Computing Machinery Conference on Principles of Database Systems*, 1988.

Null Values in Definite Programs

Yuan Liu

Computer Science Department
University of Maryland
College Park, MD 20742
liu@brillig.umd.edu

ABSTRACT

Null values are a special kind of incomplete information that appear in database applications. There are several kinds of null values. The one modeled in this paper are those that represent entities that are known to exist but whose exact values are only known to be in a finite subset of constants in a given domain. For example, if we know that Paul is the fraternal grandfather of John, then we know that there is someone who is the father of John and a child of Paul. If we further assume that there are only finitely many individuals, then this someone can be represented by the kind of null value mentioned here.

In this paper we incorporate these null values into definite programs by using a new kind of symbols called S-constants. We present model theoretic, proof theoretic and fixpoint semantics for such programs. In the above example, given the additional knowledge that Mike is the father of Joe, these semantics allow us to answer the question "Are John and Joe brothers?" by "Yes, if the (unknown) father of John is Mike."

The proposed semantics reduce to the usual semantics for definite programs (e.g. [11]) when there are no null values present.

Keywords: *incomplete information, null values, definite program semantics*

1. Introduction

A particular kind of incomplete information, called null values, often emerges in relational database applications. These represent the information "entity exists but value at present unknown".

They can be subdivided into two subtly different categories. The first contains those null values whose actual values can only be in a known domain. For example, if we know that Joe has a father but we do not know who he is, then Joe's father can be represented by a null value, say ω, in a father-son relation. If we further know that D is the set of all male names, then we know that Joe's father must be one of them, i.e. $\omega \in D$. These null values are similar to what is termed OR-object in [8] which are used to denote a special class of disjunctive facts in relational databases. Lipski's incomplete information [9] is a generalization of such null values.

The second category are those null values whose actual values can be either in a set of known constants or can be entirely new constants. The null values in Reiter's work [13] fall into this category.

Most of the previous work on query answering in databases with null values, deal with extensional databases only, i.e. there are no deductive rules. Some of these try to extend the relational algebra operators to accommodate the appearance of null values, e.g. [1, 2, 3, 4, 5, 7, 14, 17]. Others use a proof-theoretic approach which treats databases as sets of first order theories and queries as theorems to be derived from these theories, e.g. [12, 13, 16, 6, 15].

In this paper, we consider the problem of adding to a definite program, incomplete information represented by the first kind of null values. One way of achieving this is to use disjunctive clauses. For example, in [6], the information 'the unknown father of Joe is one of Dave, Mike or Smith' is represented by the clause 'Father(Dave,Joe) ∨ Father(Mike,Joe) ∨ Father(Smith,Joe)'. However, this means that we need to deal with the full complexity of disjunctive logic programs, although the clauses we use are just a very special subset of disjunctive clauses.

Instead, we preserve the definiteness of our clauses by introducing a new kind of symbol, called an S-constant, to represent these null values. This also allows us to define a refutation procedure that has the appearance of the SLD refutation. Our language is basically the same as that of first order logic. A *term* in our language can be one of the following: a variable, a constant, an S-constant, or a functional term. A functional term is a term of the form $f(t_1,...,t_n)$, where f is an n-ary function symbol, $n \geq 1$, and $t_1,...,t_n$ are terms. Other than the definition of terms, the definitions for constructs like atoms or formulas exactly parallel those for a first order language. A formula (term) is ground if it contains no variables.

In order to model null values whose actual values are in some known domains, we attach a specification of these domains to each formula in a program.

Definition D1.1 (***Program***) Let **L** be a language with constants D, and S-constants Σ.

- An ***extended program clause***, is a two-tuple (C;R). C is a formula of the form $A \leftarrow B_1,...,B_m$, where $m \geq 0$, A and B_j, $1 \leq j \leq m$, are atoms. R is a set of the form $\{\{\sigma_1\} \subseteq D_1,...,\{\sigma_n\} \subseteq D_n\}$ where for $1 \leq i \leq n$, σ_i is an S-constant that appears in C and D_i is a non-empty subset of D. We call 'A', '$B_1,...,B_m$' and 'R', respectively, the ***head***, the ***body***, and the ***domain specification*** of the extended program clause. D_i is called the ***range*** of σ_i in R. If there is no S-constant in a clause, then $R = \emptyset$.
- A ***program*** **P** is a set of extended program clauses that satisfy the following: if an S-constant, σ, appears in two different clauses, $(C_1;R_1)$ and $(C_2;R_2)$, then σ has the same range in R_1 and R_2. Let this range be r_σ. We say r_σ is the range of σ in program **P**. We will also call r_σ the ***initial range*** of σ. ■

We will see an example of a program in the next section.

We also need to modify the definition of a substitution.

Definition D1.2 (***Substitution***) Let < be an arbitrary ordering on the S-constants of our language so that the S-constants are represented by $\sigma_1, \sigma_2,...$ etc, and $\sigma_i < \sigma_j$ iff $i<j$. A ***substitution*** θ is a finite set of the form $\{t_1/v_1,...,t_n/v_n\}$, where each v_i is either a variable or an S-constant, and $v_i \neq v_j$ for $i \neq j$. Each v_i does not appear in the corresponding t_i. Also, if v_i is a variable, then t_i is an arbitrary term, and if v_i is an S-constant, say σ_m, then t_i can only be either a (normal) constant or another S-

constant σ_n such that $\sigma_m < \sigma_n$. The special substitution $\varepsilon = \{\}$, is called the ***identity substitution***.

The ***application*** of a substitution θ to a formula (or a term) H, written as $H\theta$, is the formula (term) obtained by simultaneously replacing all the v_i's in H by their corresponding t_i's. ■

The reason for imposing an arbitrary ordering on the S-constants will be made clear in the next section.

In the above definition, we do not allow substitutions of the form $\{t/\sigma\}$ where σ is an S-constant and t is a functional term other than a constant. The reason is that we consider function symbols to be distinct from constants, and as we will see in the next section, substitutions of S-constants express conditions that the S-constants must satisfy. Since we limit S-constants to have only constants as their initial values, a substitution of S-constant by a functional term, expressing that the S-constant be equal to the term, can never be satisfied. Therefore, we do not consider S-constants to be replaceable by functional terms.

In the following sections, we present model semantics, fixpoint semantics, and procedural semantics for our programs. Finally, we summarize our results and propose future work. A version of this paper with proofs of all the theorems can be found in [10].

2. Model Semantics

For logic programs without null values, the Herbrand Base of a program is an integral part of their declarative semantics. Therefore, in order to define a formal semantics for logic programs with null values we extend the classical Herbrand Base to include S-constants.

2.1. Herbrand Base with Null Values

First, we have the following straightforward extension to the Herbrand Base:

Definition D2.1 (*Null-Extended Herbrand Universe and Quasi Herbrand Base*) Let **P** be a program, and Σ be the set of S-constants in **P**.

- The Herbrand Universe with null values $_N U_P$ is the set of all ground terms that can be formed from constants, S-constants, and functions appearing in **P**. If no constant appears in **P** then we add an arbitrary constant, say a, to form ground terms.
- The *quasi*-Herbrand Base qHB(**P**) is the set $\{ P(c_1,\dots,c_n) \mid P$ is an n-ary predicate symbol in **P** $, c_i, i=1,\dots,n,$ are elements in $_N U_P \}$ ■

We note that when there is no S-constant, i.e. $\Sigma = \emptyset$, the quasi Herbrand Base reduces to the (classical) Herbrand Base.

The quasi Herbrand Base alone is not adequate for our purpose because it contains no information about the incompleteness of the S-constants. The following example illustrates what additional information we need by showing how we might want to respond to queries on a program containing such information. It exemplifies the kind of information we want to derive from a program.

Example 2.1

Consider the following program, where σ_1 and σ_2 are S-constants.

$$(\text{Father}(\sigma_1,\text{John});\{\{\sigma_1\} \Subset \{\text{Mike},\text{Smith},\text{Joe}\}\}) \quad \text{(E2.1.1)}$$

$$(\text{Father}(\text{Paul},\sigma_1);\{\{\sigma_1\} \Subset \{\text{Mike},\text{Smith},\text{Joe}\}\}) \quad \text{(E2.1.2)}$$

$(\text{Father}(\sigma_2,\text{George});\{\{\sigma_2\} \Subset \{\text{Dave,Mike,Smith}\}\})$ (E2.1.3)

$(\text{Father}(\text{Dave,Paul});\emptyset)$ (E2.1.4)

$(\text{Sib}(x,y) \leftarrow \text{Father}(z,x),\text{Father}(z,y);\emptyset)$ (E2.1.5)

Informally, (E2.1.1) and (E2.1.2) together specify that someone, represented here by σ_1, is both the father of John and the son of Paul, i.e. Paul is the fraternal grandfather of John, and the domain specifications say that this "someone" can only be Mike, Smith or Joe. The third clause, (E2.1.3), says that someone, represented by σ_2, is the father of George, and the domain specification restricts his identity to Dave, Mike or Smith. (E2.1.4) is an assertion that Dave is the father of Paul with no conditions associated with the statement.

In order for George and Paul to be siblings, σ_2 must be equal to Dave. This is possible since Dave is in the range of σ_2. On the other hand, for John and Paul to be siblings, σ_1 has to be Dave. However, this is in conflict with what we know from the program since the range of σ_1 specifies that it can only be one of Mike, Smith or Joe. Now consider John and George. In order for them to be siblings, σ_1 and σ_2 must have the same value(s). This is possible since there are common elements, Mike and Smith, in their ranges.

Let us now add the clause '$(\text{SR}(x,y,u,v) \leftarrow \text{Father}(x,y),\text{Sib}(u,v);\emptyset)$' to the program. Then in order for SR(Paul,Mike,John,George) to be true, Paul must be the father of Mike and John must be a sibling of George. As we see above, John and George are siblings under the condition that $\sigma_1=\sigma_2$. On the other hand, for Paul to be Mike's father, σ_1 must be Mike (by (E2.1.2)). Therefore, the tuple (Paul,Mike,John,George) satisfies the relation SR if both of these conditions are true, i.e. $\sigma_1=\sigma_2$ and $\sigma_1=\text{Mike}$. Similarly, for the tuple (Paul,Joe,John,George) to be in relation SR, Paul must be the father of Joe and John must be a sibling of George. As before, for Sib(John,George) to be true, σ_1 must be equal to σ_2 while for Father(Paul,Joe) to be true, σ_1 must be Joe. Here, however, we see that the condition $\sigma_1=\sigma_2 \wedge \sigma_1=\text{Joe}$ can not be satisfied, because $\sigma_1=\sigma_2$ implies that both σ_1 and σ_2 can only be either Mike or Smith, therefore, although Joe is in the original range of σ_1, the condition $\sigma_1=\sigma_2$ precludes it from the values σ_1 can take. ■

The first two queries in the above example involve restricting the range of an S-constant to a single element; while the third one requires that we reconcile the values of two S-constants. The last two queries in the example illustrates two points. First, we must record the conditions necessary to derive an answer, e.g. the condition $\sigma_1=\sigma_2$ for deriving Sib(John,George). In addition, we must also record how these conditions restrict the ranges of the S-constants involved in order to detect an unsatisfiable condition.

Definition D2.2 (*Assignment*) Let **P** be a program. Let $\Sigma = \{\sigma_1,\ldots,\sigma_m\}$ be the set of S-constants in **P**, D be the set of constants in **P**, and the range of σ_i in **P** be r_{σ_i}. An ***assignment*** is a set of the form $\{S_1 \Subset V_1,\ldots,S_n \Subset V_n\}$ where $S_i \subseteq \Sigma$ and $V_i \subseteq D$ for $1 \le i \le n$, and $S_i \cap S_j = \emptyset$ for $1 \le i,j \le n$, $i \ne j$. We also define $\perp$ as a special assignment. An assignment w is ***strict*** if it does not contain elements of the form $\{\sigma\} \Subset r_\sigma$, where σ is any S-constant, and if it satisfies the condition that, for $1 \le i \le m$, $V_i \subseteq \bigcap_{\sigma \in S_i} r_\sigma$.

The ***range*** of an S-constant σ in an assignment w, written as $\text{Ran}(\sigma,w)$, and the

class of σ in w, written as $Cla(\sigma,w)$, are defined as follows:

For the special assignment ⊥, $Cla(\sigma,\bot)=\emptyset$, and $Ran(\sigma,\bot)=\emptyset$. For all other assignment w, if there is an element $S \in V$ in w such that σ is a member of S, then $Ran(\sigma,w)=V$, and $Cla(\sigma,w)=S$, otherwise $Ran(\sigma,w)=r_\sigma$, $Cla(\sigma,w)=\{\sigma\}$. ■

Two things to note about this definition. The first is that the special assignment ⊥ is used to represent the case when we have an unsatisfiable condition. The second is that a domain specification is an assignment but not a strict assignment. Intuitively, an element of the form $\{\sigma\} \in r_\sigma$ merely expresses the initial constraint on the S-constant σ specified in the program, i.e. that σ has range r_σ and that whether σ is identical to any other S-constant is unknown. A strict assignment is one that does not contain such redundant information.

In defining a program with null values, we introduced extended program clauses. They are nothing more than ordered pairs of Horn clauses and domain specifications. Since domain specifications are a special kind of assignments, we can further define the following extensions:

Definition D2.3 (***Extended Clauses and Extended Goals***) Let **P** be a program and let w be an assignment. An ***extended clause*** is an ordered pair (C;w) where C is a clause. An ***extended goal*** is an extended clause (C;w) where C is a clause with no positive literals. ■

Following are some operations related to assignments.

Definition D2.4 (***Combining Assignments***) Let **P** be a program. Let $\Sigma = \{\sigma_1,...,\sigma_m\}$ be the set of S-constants in **P**, and let the initial range of σ_i in **P** be r_{σ_i} for $1 \le i \le m$. Let w_1 and w_2 be assignments. The ***combination*** of w_1 and w_2, written as w_1w_2, is defined inductively as follows:

1. If w_1 or w_2 is ⊥, then $w_1w_2=\bot$.
2. If neither w_1 nor w_2 are ⊥ and w_1 (resp. w_2) is ∅, then w_1w_2 is w_2 (resp. w_1).
3. Let $w_1=\{S_1 \in V_1\}$ and $w_2=\{S_2 \in V_2\}$. If $S_1 \cap S_2=\emptyset$ then $w_1w_2=w_1 \cup w_2$. If $S_1 \cap S_2 \ne \emptyset$ and $V_1 \cap V_2 \ne \emptyset$ then $w_1w_2 = \{S_1 \cup S_2 \in V_1 \cap V_2\}$. Otherwise ($S_1 \cap S_2 \ne \emptyset$ and $V_1 \cap V_2=\emptyset$), $w_1w_2=\bot$.
4. If $w_1=\{S_{11} \in V_{11},...,S_{1p} \in V_{1p}\}$ where $p>1$, then $w_1w_2=u(vw_2)$ where u is $\{S_{11} \in V_{11},...,S_{1p-1} \in V_{1p-1}\}$ and v is $\{S_{1p} \in V_{1p}\}$.
5. If $w_1=\{S_{11} \in V_{11}\}$, and $w_2=\{S_{21} \in V_{21},...,S_{2q} \in V_{2q}\}$ where $q>1$, then $w_1w_2=(w_1u)v$ where u is $\{S_{21} \in V_{21}\}$ and v is $\{S_{22} \in V_{22},...,S_{2q} \in V_{2q}\}$.

If $w_1w_2 \ne \bot$, then the assignments w_1 and w_2 are ***compatible***, otherwise, they are *incompatible*. ■

We note from Example 2.1 that, in general, any condition that we need to record can be seen as the result of applying a sequence of substitutions to the initial constraints specified in the program. For example, the substitution $\{\sigma_2/\sigma_1\}$ results in the condition $\sigma_1=\sigma_2$, and $\{Mike/\sigma_1\}$, results in the condition $\sigma_1=Mike$. This suggests that applying a substitution to a formula, has the same effect as attaching an assignment to that formula. Therefore, we have the following definitions:

Definition D2.5 (***Substitutions as Assignments***) Let **P** be a program, and $\Sigma = \{\sigma_1,...,\sigma_m\}$ be the set of S-constants in **P**, and the range of σ_i in **P** be r_{σ_i}. Let $[\,]_A$ be a mapping from substitutions to assignments. Then, let θ be a substitution, the assignment $[\theta]_A$ is called the ***equivalent assignment*** of θ, and is defined inductively as:

If $\theta = \varepsilon = \{\}$ is the identity substitution: $[\theta]_A=\emptyset$

If $\theta = \{t/v\}$, where v is a variable: $[\theta]_A = \varnothing$
If $\theta = \{t/v\}$, where v is an S-constant and t is a constant:
If $v \in \Sigma$ and $t \in r_v$ then $[\theta]_A = \{v \Subset \{t\}\}$. Otherwise, $[\theta]_A = \perp$.
If $\theta = \{t/v\}$, where v and t are both S-constants:
If $v \in \Sigma$, $t \in \Sigma$, and $r_v \cap r_t \neq \varnothing$ then $[\theta]_A = \{\{v,t\} \Subset r_v \cap r_t\}$. Otherwise, $[\theta]_A = \perp$.
If $\theta = \{t_1/v_1, \ldots, t_n/v_n\}$ where $n>1$: $[\theta]_A = [\lambda]_A[\mu]_A$ where λ is $\{t_1/v_1\}$ and μ is $\{t_2/v_2, \ldots, t_n/v_n\}$
If $[\theta]_A \neq \perp$ then we say that θ is ***applicable*** (w.r.t. **P**). Otherwise, it is inapplicable. Also, we say that $[\theta]_A$ is an assignment *expressible* by the substitution θ. ■

We see that if a substitution contains no substitutions for S-constant, then its equivalent assignment is $\varnothing$, which essentially represents the condition "true", i.e. "no additional restriction on the values of the S-constants". The reason we impose an ordering on the S-constants is that the two forms of substitutions $\{\sigma_i/\sigma_j\}$ and $\{\sigma_j/\sigma_i\}$ both express the condition that σ_1 and σ_2 are equal, and the ordering allows us to consistently choose one of them. Also, we note that given a substitution θ if $[\theta]_A \neq \perp$ then $[\theta]_A$ is strict.

A dual of the above mapping is the following:

Definition D2.6 (***Assignment as Substitution***) Let $[\,]_S$ be a mapping from strict assignments to substitutions. Then, let $w=\{S_1 \Subset V_1, \ldots, S_n \Subset V_n\}$ be a strict assignment, the substitution $[w]_S$ is called the ***equivalent substitution*** for w, and is defined inductively as follows:
$[\varnothing]_S = \varepsilon$, the identity substitution.
V_1 is a singleton set of constant c. Then $[w]_S = \{c/\tau \mid \tau \in S_1\} \cup [w - \{S_1 \Subset V_1\}]_S$
V_1 is not a singleton, and S_1 is the set $\{\sigma_{i_1}, \ldots, \sigma_{i_m}\}$, where $i_j < i_k$ for $j<k$. Then
$[w]_S = \{\sigma_{i_m}/\sigma_{i_j} \mid 1 \leq j < m\} \cup [w - \{S_1 \Subset V_1\}]_S$ ■

In the above definition, since $S_i \cap S_j = \varnothing$ for $i \neq j$, the order in which we convert the elements in an assignment w is irrelevant.

In defining a model semantics of a logic program with null values, we only need to consider assignments that are expressible by substitutions:

Definition D2.7 (***Assignment Universe***) Let **P** be a program. The ***assignment*** *universe* of **P** is the set $\{[\theta]_A \mid \theta$ is applicable w.r.t. **P** $\}$. ■

From now on, unless specified otherwise, an assignment always refers to one that is in the assignment universe.

Finally, we have the definition of the Herbrand Base with null values:

Definition D2.8 (***Herbrand Base with Null Values***) Let **P** be a program, qHB(**P**) be its quasi-Herbrand Base, and W be its assignment universe. The ***Herbrand Base with null values*** for program **P**, HBNV(**P**), is the set of ordered-pairs (A;w) where $A \in$ qHB(**P**), $w \in W$. We call elements in HBNV(**P**) *(null-)extended atoms.* ■

Below is an example that illustrates some of the definitions in this section.

Example 2.2

Consider the program **P** which contains the following :

$(F(\sigma_1,e)\,;\{\{\sigma_1\} \Subset \{e,f,g\}\})$

$(F(\sigma_2,f)\,;\{\{\sigma_2\} \Subset \{f,g,h\}\})$

$(S(x,y) \leftarrow F(z,x),F(z,y)\,;\varnothing)$

Then U_P is the set $\{e,f,g,h,\sigma_1,\sigma_2\}$. So,

$qHB(\mathbf{P})=\{F(e,e),F(e,f),F(e,g),F(e,h),F(e,\sigma_1),F(e,\sigma_2),F(f,e),...,F(f,\sigma_1),F(f,\sigma_2),..., F(\sigma_1,e),...,F(\sigma_1,\sigma_1),F(\sigma_1,\sigma_2),F(\sigma_2,e),...,F(\sigma_2,\sigma_1),F(\sigma_2,\sigma_2), S(e,e),...,S(f,e),...,S(\sigma_1,e),...,S(\sigma_2,e),...,S(\sigma_2,\sigma_2)\}$

and the assignment universe is:

$W=\{\varnothing,\{\{\sigma_1\}\in\{e\}\},\{\{\sigma_1\}\in\{f\}\},\{\{\sigma_1\}\in\{g\}\},\{\{\sigma_2\}\in\{f\}\},\{\{\sigma_2\}\in\{g\}\}, \{\{\sigma_2\}\in\{h\}\},\{\{\sigma_1\}\in\{e\},\{\sigma_2\}\in\{f\}\},\{\{\sigma_1\}\in\{e\},\{\sigma_2\}\in\{g\}\}, \{\{\sigma_1\}\in\{e\},\{\sigma_2\}\in\{h\}\},\{\{\sigma_1\}\in\{f\},\{\sigma_2\}\in\{f\}\},\{\{\sigma_1\}\in\{f\},\{\sigma_2\}\in\{g\}\}, \{\{\sigma_1\}\in\{f\},\{\sigma_2\}\in\{h\}\},\{\{\sigma_1\}\in\{g\},\{\sigma_2\}\in\{f\}\},\{\{\sigma_1\}\in\{g\},\{\sigma_2\}\in\{g\}\}, \{\{\sigma_1\}\in\{g\},\{\sigma_2\}\in\{h\}\},\{\{\sigma_1,\sigma_2\}\in\{f,g\}\},\{\{\sigma_1,\sigma_2\}\in\{f\}\},\{\{\sigma_1,\sigma_2\}\in\{g\}\}\}$

We will not list all the elements of HBNV(**P**) here. As we will see later, some of the elements of HBNV(**P**) that will be in the "model" of the program are:
$(F(\sigma_1,e);\varnothing), (F(\sigma_2,f);\varnothing), (S(e,e);\varnothing),(S(f,f);\varnothing),$
$(S(e,f);\{\{\sigma_1,\sigma_2\}\in\{f,g\}\}), (S(f,e);\{\{\sigma_1,\sigma_2\}\in\{f,g\}\}).$ ■

2.2. State and Model State

A program with null values can be viewed as a compact way of representing a set of possible worlds. For instance, if **P** has the following extended program clauses: $(P(\sigma_1);\{\{\sigma_1\}\in\{a,b\}\})$, $(Q(\sigma_2);\{\{\sigma_2\}\in\{c,d\}\})$, and $(R(e);\varnothing)$; which means that either a or b is in relation P, either c or d is in relation Q, and e is in relation R. We can view **P** as representing the four possible worlds: $\mathbf{P}_1$: {P(a),Q(c),R(e)}, $\mathbf{P}_2$: {P(a),Q(d),R(e)}, $\mathbf{P}_3$: {P(b),Q(c),R(e)}, $\mathbf{P}_4$: {P(b),Q(d),R(e)}. These are obtained from **P** by assigning to each null value one of the constant in the range of the null value. Each possible world can therefore be identified with a particular substitution. For instance, $\mathbf{P}_1$ can be identified with the substitution "a for σ_1 and c for σ_2", and $\mathbf{P}_2$ the substitution "a for σ_1 and d for σ_2", etc.

This above discussion motivates the following definitions.

Definition D2.9 (*S-Mapping*) Let **P** be a program, and let $\Sigma=\{\sigma_1,...,\sigma_n\}$ be the set of S-constants appearing in **P** and D be the set of constants appearing in **P**. A function V from Σ to D is an ***S-mapping*** iff V maps each element σ_i of Σ to a constant c_{ij} in the initial range of σ_i. We write an S-mapping V as a set of values $\{a_1,...,a_n\}$ to represent the fact that $V(\sigma_1)=a_1$, $V(\sigma_2)=a_2,...,V(\sigma_n)=a_n$. ■

Definition D2.10 (*S-Mapping Substitution and Possible Worlds*) Let **P** be a program and Σ be the set of S-constants appearing in **P**. Let V be an S-mapping, then the ***substitution corresponding to an S-mapping*** V is the substitution $\{V(\sigma_1)/\sigma_1,...,V(\sigma_n)/\sigma_n\}$, usually written as ρ_V.
Let S be a set of extended clauses, the ***image*** of S in the S-mapping V, written as S_V, is the set of first order formula: $\{R\rho_V \mid (R;w)\in S \wedge w[\rho_V]_A\neq\perp\}$ The ***possible world*** represented by **P** and the S-mapping V is the image of **P** in V, $\mathbf{P}_V$. ■

Let **P** be a program and V be an S-mapping, then the image of **P** in V is a set of definite clauses. Also, the image of any subset I of HBNV(**P**) in V is a set of ground atoms. Therefore, I_V can serve as a Herbrand interpretation of $\mathbf{P}_V$.

Definition D2.11 (*States*) Let **P** be a program, V be an S-mapping, and S be a subset of HBNV(**P**). Let (C; w) be an extended clause such that $w[\rho_V]_A\neq\perp$, then the value of (C; w)in V w.r.t. S is the Herbrand interpretation of $C\rho_V$ w.r.t. the set S_V. S is a ***state*** of **P** iff for every extended clause (C; w) in **P**, (C; w) has the same value w.r.t. S in every S-mapping. ■

It is easy to see that if w is a domain specification, then $w[\rho_V]_A \neq \perp$ for any S-mapping V. Therefore, every extended program clause in a program has a value in every S-mapping w.r.t. every subset of HBNV(**P**). A state, then, is just a collection of "consistent" interpretations. By this we mean that a clause is interpreted consistently in every possible world, i.e. we do not want to have a clause being interpreted as "true" under one S-mapping while interpreted as "false" under another S-mapping.

The definition of state has a shortcoming which is inherent in the format of HBNV: two apparently different subsets of HBNV can represent the same state, i.e. they have the same image in all S-mappings. For instance, consider the program **P** at the begining of this section with the four S-mappings $V_1 = \{a,c\}$, $V_2 = \{a,d\}$, $V_3 = \{b,c\}$, and $V_4 = \{b,d\}$. Although the following two sets $I_1 = \{(P(a);\{\{\sigma_1\} \subseteq \{a\}\}),(P(b);\{\{\sigma_1\} \subseteq \{b\}\})\}$ and $I_2 = \{(P(\sigma_1);\emptyset)\}$, look quite different, their images in every S-mapping is the same, i.e. both are $\{P(a)\}$ in V_1 and V_2, and both are $\{P(b)\}$ in V_3 and V_4. Therefore, there is no practical difference between the two. To deal with this shortcoming, we define the following relation

Definition D2.12 (***Equivalence Relation for States***) Let **P** be a program and let S and T be two subsets of HBNV(**P**). We say that S and T are ***equivalent***, written as $S \equiv_m T$, iff for every S-mapping V, $S_V = T_V$. ■

It is obvious that $\equiv_m$ is an equivalence relation. Similar to the definition of Herbrand models, we have the following.

Definition D2.13 (***Model State***) Let **P** be a program and I be a state of **P**. I is a ***model state*** of an extended clause (C; w) iff for every S-mapping V, if $w[\rho_V]_A \neq \perp$ then I_V is a Herbrand model of $C\rho_V$. I is a ***model state*** of **P** iff I is a model state of every extended clause in **P**, and for every state J such that $J \equiv_m I$, $J \subseteq I$. ■

The last condition in the above definition can be understood in another way. Since $\equiv_m$ is an equivalence relation, the set of all the states can be divided into equivalence classes. Given any state I, suppose that I belongs to the equivalence class E, then it is easy to see that the union of all the elements in E is itself a state, and moreover, this union is also equivalent to I and hence also a member of E. That is, $(\bigcup_{J \in E} J) \equiv_m I$, and hence $(\bigcup_{J \in E} J) \in E$. Let us call this union M. From the definition of model state of extended clauses, if I is the model state of an extended clause, then every member in E is also a model state of that clause. Therefore, if I is a model state of all the extended clauses in a program **P**, then so is M, and since all other states in E are subsets of M, M is a model state of **P**.

The following proposition concerns the existence of such a model state.

Proposition P2.1 Let **P** be a program, and let $V_1,...,V_n$ be all the possible S-mappings. If $M_1,...,M_n$ are Herbrand models of $\mathbf{P}_{V_1}, ..., \mathbf{P}_{V_n}$, respectively, then there exists a unique model state S of **P** such that $S_{V_1}=M_1, ..., S_{V_n}=M_n$.

Proof:

We prove this by constructing S. Let J_i be the set $\{(A;[\rho_{V_i}]_A) \mid A \in M_i\}$, then the image of J_i in V_i is exactly the set M_i. Let J be the set $\bigcup_{1 \le i \le n} J_i$, then J is a subset of HBNV(**P**) and J is a model state for every extended clause in **P**. Therefore, the set $S = \bigcup_{K \equiv_m J} K$ is a model state of **P**. Also, S is unique, since for any other state S', if $S'_{V_i}=M_i$ then $S' \equiv_m J$ and hence $S' \subseteq S$. *Q.E.D.*

Next, we introduce the concept of a minimal model state. Given a program **P**, for any S-mapping V, $\mathbf{P}_V$ is a definite program. Hence for each V, $\mathbf{P}_V$ has a unique least model. By proposition P2.1, there is a unique model state whose image in V is this least model.

Proposition P2.2 (*Least Model State*) Let **P** be a program with null values. There is a unique model state S of **P** such that S_V is the least Herbrand model of $\mathbf{P}_V$ for any S-mapping V. Furthermore, $S=\bigcap\{K \mid K \text{ is a model state of } \mathbf{P}\}$. ■

Example 2.3

Consider the following program **P**:

$$(F(\sigma_1,e)\,;\{\{\sigma_1\}\subseteq\{e,f,g\}\})$$
$$(F(\sigma_2,f)\,;\{\{\sigma_2\}\subseteq\{f,g,h\}\})$$
$$(S(x,y)\leftarrow F(z,x),F(z,y)\,;\varnothing)$$

It is easy to see that the state

$$M=\{\,(F(\sigma_1,e);\varnothing),(F(\sigma_2,f);\varnothing),(S(e,e);\varnothing),(S(f,f);\varnothing),$$
$$(S(e,f);\{\,\{\sigma_1,\sigma_2\}\subseteq\{f,g\}\,\}),(S(f,e);\{\,\{\sigma_1,\sigma_2\}\subseteq\{f,g\}\,\})\,\}$$

is a model state of all the extended clauses in **P**. To see this, consider, for instance, the S-mapping $V_1=\{e,f\}$. The image of **P** in V_1 is $\mathbf{P}_{V_1}=\{F(e,e),F(f,f),S(x,y)\leftarrow F(z,x),F(z,y)\}$ and $M_{V_1}=\{F(e,e),F(f,f),S(e,e),S(f,f)\}$ is a Herbrand model of $\mathbf{P}_{V_1}$. Furthermore, we see that if we remove any element from M_{V_1} then it is no longer a model of $\mathbf{P}_{V_1}$, i.e. M_{V_1} is the least model of $\mathbf{P}_{V_1}$. This result applies to all other eight S-mappings. Therefore, we can conclude that the largest equivalent state of M is the least model state of **P**. The part of this model state that is equivalent to the extended atom $(F(\sigma_1,e);\varnothing)$ is shown in Fig. 1. ■

$$\{\,(F(\sigma_1,e);\varnothing),(F(e,e);\{\,\{\sigma_1\}\subseteq\{e\}\,\}),(F(f,e);\{\,\{\sigma_1\}\subseteq\{f\}\,\}),(F(g,e);\{\,\{\sigma_1\}\subseteq\{g\}\,\}),$$
$$(F(\sigma_1,e);\{\,\{\sigma_2\}\subseteq\{f\}\,\}),(F(\sigma_1,e);\{\,\{\sigma_2\}\subseteq\{g\}\,\}),(F(\sigma_1,e);\{\,\{\sigma_2\}\subseteq\{h\}\,\}),$$
$$(F(e,e);\{\,\{\sigma_1\}\subseteq\{e\},\{\sigma_2\}\subseteq\{f\}\,\}),(F(f,e);\{\,\{\sigma_1\}\subseteq\{f\},\{\sigma_2\}\subseteq\{f\}\,\}),$$
$$(F(g,e);\{\,\{\sigma_1\}\subseteq\{g\},\{\sigma_2\}\subseteq\{f\}\,\}),(F(e,e);\{\,\{\sigma_1\}\subseteq\{e\},\{\sigma_2\}\subseteq\{g\}\,\}),$$
$$(F(f,e);\{\,\{\sigma_1\}\subseteq\{f\},\{\sigma_2\}\subseteq\{g\}\,\}),(F(g,e);\{\,\{\sigma_1\}\subseteq\{g\},\{\sigma_2\}\subseteq\{g\}\,\}),$$
$$(F(e,e);\{\,\{\sigma_1\}\subseteq\{e\},\{\sigma_2\}\subseteq\{h\}\,\}),(F(f,e);\{\,\{\sigma_1\}\subseteq\{f\},\{\sigma_2\}\subseteq\{h\}\,\}),$$
$$(F(g,e);\{\,\{\sigma_1\}\subseteq\{g\},\{\sigma_2\}\subseteq\{h\}\,\}),(F(\sigma_2,e);\{\,\{\sigma_1,\sigma_2\}\subseteq\{f,g\}\,\}),$$
$$(F(\sigma_2,e);\{\,\{\sigma_1,\sigma_2\}\subseteq\{f\}\,\}),(F(\sigma_2,e);\{\,\{\sigma_1,\sigma_2\}\subseteq\{g\}\,\}),$$
$$(F(f,e);\{\,\{\sigma_1,\sigma_2\}\subseteq\{f\}\,\}),(F(g,e);\{\,\{\sigma_1,\sigma_2\}\subseteq\{g\}\,\})\,\}$$

Fig. 1 (Example 2.3) Part of the Least Model State of Program **P**.

The following definition is analogous to the definition for "logical consequence" in first order logic.

Definition D2.14 ($\models_N$) Let **P** be a program. If every model state M of **P** is a model state of an extended clause (C; w), then we say that $\mathbf{P} \models_N (C;w)$. ■

We denote the unique model state in the above proposition as M_P^N. The following theorem argues strongly for using M_P^N as the declarative semantics for **P**.

Theorem T2.1 Let **P** be a program and (A;u) be an element in HBNV(**P**). Then $\mathbf{P}\models_N (A;u)$ iff $(A;u)\in M_P^N$.

Proof:

$\mathbf{P}\models_N (A;u)$

iff for any model state S of **P**, and for all S-mapping V such that $u[\rho_V]_A \neq \perp$, $S_V \models A\rho_V$.

iff for any model state S of **P**, and for all S-mapping V such that $u[\rho_V]_A \neq \perp$, $A\rho_V \in S_V$. ($\because$ $A\rho_V$ is ground)

iff for any model state S of **P**, $\bigcup_V \{(A\rho_V;[\rho_V]_A)\} \subseteq S$.

iff for any model state S of **P**, $(A;u)\in S$. $\quad$ ($\because$ $\{(A;u)\} \equiv_m \bigcup_V \{(A\rho_V;[\rho_V]_A)\}$)

iff $(A;u)\in M_P^N$. $\quad$ (proposition P2.2) $\quad$ *Q.E.D.*

3. Fixpoint Semantics

In this section, we provide a fixpoint characterization of M_P^N. First, we need some definitions.

Definition D3.1 (***Ground Instances of Extended Program Clauses***) Let **P** be a program, (C;d) be an extended program clause in **P**, and $\theta=\theta_v\theta_s$ be a substitution, where θ_v is a variable substitution, and θ_s is an applicable substitution w.r.t. **P**. Then $(C\theta;[\theta]_A)$ is a ground instance of (C;d) iff $C\theta$ contains no variable. Gnd(**P**) is the set of all the ground instances of the extended clauses in **P**. ■

Note that d in the above definition is a domain specification, and as such, is of the form $\{\{\sigma_1\}\subseteq D_1,\ldots,\{\sigma_n\}\subseteq D_n\}$, where for $1\leq i\leq n$, D_i is the initial range of σ_i. Since d is not an element of the assignment universe, we can not define the ground instance of (C;d) to be $(C\theta;d[\theta]_A)$. However, since d specifies the same condition as the empty assignment $\varnothing$, $(C\theta;[\theta]_A)$ is all we need.

Definition D3.2 (***Equivalence Closure***) Let **P** be a program, and I be a subset of HBNV(**P**). The *equivalence closure* (or *E-closure*) of I, equ(I), is the set $\bigcup_{J\equiv_m I} J$. ■

Since the only subset of the HBNV that is equivalent to the empty set $\varnothing$ is the empty set itself, we have equ($\varnothing$)=$\varnothing$. In general, equ(I) is much larger than I, as illustrated by the following example.

Example 3.1

Consider the program in example 2.3. Let $I=\{(F(\sigma_1,e);\varnothing)\}$. Then Figure 1 is the E-closure of I. ■

Definition D3.3 (***Fixpoint Operator***) Let **P** be a program $_NT_P$ is a mapping from the power set of HBNV(**P**) to the power set of HBNV(**P**). If $I\subseteq$HBNV(**P**), then $_NT_P(I)=\text{equ}(I)\cup T_P(I)$ where

$$T_P(I)=\{(A;w)\mid (A\leftarrow B_1,\ldots,B_n;w)\in \text{Gnd}(\mathbf{P}),$$

$$\text{and there are } (B_1';w_1),\ldots,(B_n';w_n) \text{ in I, such that } w=w_1\ldots w_n\neq\perp$$

$$\text{and } B_i'[w]_S=B_i \text{ for } 1\leq i\leq n\}$$

We also define $_NT_P\uparrow n$ and $T_P\uparrow n$ inductively as

$_NT_P\uparrow 0=\varnothing$ $\quad$ $_NT_P\uparrow n={}_NT_P({}_NT_P\uparrow(n-1))$ for n>0.

$T_P\uparrow 0=\varnothing$ $\quad$ $T_P\uparrow n=T_P(T_P\uparrow(n-1))$ for n>0. ■

Both T_P and $_NT_P$ are continuous, and since the power set of HBNV(**P**) is a complete lattice, this means that $_NT_P\uparrow\omega$ (resp. $T_p\uparrow\omega$) is the least fixpoint of $_NT_P$ (resp.

T_P).

The next proposition states that the model state of a program is identical to the pre-fixpoints of ${}_NT_P$.

Proposition P3.1 Let **P** be a program. I is a model state of **P** iff ${}_NT_P(I) \subseteq I$. ■

In proving the following theorem we use a property of complete lattices and fixpoint operators ([11]), namely,

Proposition P3.2 If L is a complete lattice, and T is an operator on this lattice, then the least fixpoint of T is equal to the greatest lower bound (glb) of the set $\{I \in L \mid T(I) \subseteq I\}$ ■

Theorem T3.1 (*Fixpoint Characterization of Least Model State*) Let **P** be a program. Then

(1) the least model state, M_P^N of **P** equals the least fixpoint of the operator ${}_NT_P$, ${}_NT_P\uparrow\omega$.

(2) $T_P\uparrow\omega \equiv_m {}_NT_P\uparrow\omega$.

Proof:

Part 1: $M_P^N = \bigcap\{K \mid K$ is a model state of P$\}$ = glb$\{K \mid K$ is a model state of P$\}$
= glb$\{K \mid {}_NT_P(K) \subseteq K\}$ = lfp$({}_NT_P)$ = ${}_NT_P\uparrow\omega$.

Part 2: (sketch) We prove by showing that for $n \geq 0$, $T_P\uparrow n \equiv_m {}_NT_P\uparrow n$.

We can show that for any subset I of HBNV(**P**) and any $n > 0$, if $T_P\uparrow n \equiv_m I$ and $T_P\uparrow n \subseteq I$, then $T_P\uparrow(n+1) \equiv_m T_P(I)$.

Since $T_P\uparrow(k-1) \subseteq {}_NT_P\uparrow(k-1)$ and by the induction hypothesis, $T_P\uparrow(k-1) \equiv_m {}_NT_P\uparrow(k-1)$, we have $T_P\uparrow k \equiv_m T_P({}_NT_P\uparrow(k-1))$. In any S-mapping V, $({}_NT_P\uparrow k)_V = ({}_NT_P\uparrow(k-1))_V \cup (T_P({}_NT_P\uparrow(k-1))_V$. Since ${}_NT_P\uparrow(k-1) \equiv_m T_P\uparrow(k-1)$ and $T_P({}_NT_P\uparrow(k-1)) \equiv_m T_P\uparrow k$, we have $({}_NT_P\uparrow k)_V = (T_P\uparrow(k-1))_V \cup (T_P\uparrow k)_V$. And since T_P is continuous, $T_P\uparrow(k-1) \subseteq T_P\uparrow k$. So, $({}_NT_P\uparrow k)_V = (T_P\uparrow k)_V$, and hence ${}_NT_P\uparrow k \equiv_m T_P\uparrow k$. *Q.E.D.*

Since the most useful information contained in a least model state of a program is the "images" of that model state in each possible world, (2) above tells us that it is adequate to calculate the least fixpoint of the T_P operator.

4. Procedural Semantics

In this section, we present a refutation procedure for Horn programs with null values, called NSLD refutation, which is a generalization of SLD refutation. But first, we need to extended the concept of unifiers.

Definition D4.1 (*Unifiers for Extended Atoms*) A set of extended atoms **T** = $\{(A_1;u_1),\ldots,(A_n;u_n)\}$ is unifiable if there is a substitution θ such that $A_i\theta = A_j\theta$ for $1 \leq i,j \leq n$, and $[\theta]_A u_1 \ldots u_n \neq \bot$. θ is called a unifier of **T**. A unifier θ of **T** is an mgu iff for each unifier ρ of **T**, there is a substitution μ such that $\rho = \theta\mu$. ■

Example 4.1

Let $\theta = \{f(y)/x, \sigma_2/\sigma_1\}$, then
$\{(P(g(\sigma_1),f(y));\{\{\sigma_1\} \Subset \{a,b,c\}\}),(P(g(\sigma_2),x);\{\{\sigma_2\} \Subset \{b,c,d\}\})\}$ is unifiable with θ as an mgu, since $[\theta]_A\{\{\sigma_1\} \Subset \{a,b,c\}\}\{\{\sigma_2\} \Subset \{c,d,e\}\} = \{\{\sigma_1,\sigma_2\} \Subset \{c\}\} \neq \bot$.

On the other hand, $\{(P(\sigma_1,f(y));\{\{\sigma_1\} \Subset \{a,b,c\}\}),(P(\sigma_2,x);\{\{\sigma_2\} \Subset \{e,f,g,\}\})\}$ is not unifiable since $[\theta]_A\{\{\sigma_1\} \Subset \{a,b,c\}\}\{\{\sigma_2\} \Subset \{e,f,g\}\} = \bot$. ■

Definition D4.2 (*NSLD-Derivation*) Let **P** be a program and $G = (\leftarrow A_1,\ldots,A_k; w)$ be an extended goal clause. An *NSLD-derivation* of $\mathbf{P} \cup \{G\}$ is a sequence of extended goal clauses G_0, G_1 ... where $G_0 = G$ and for all $i \geq 0$, G_{i+1} is obtained from G_i as follow:

(1) G_i is $(\leftarrow A_{i1},...,A_{im},...,A_{ik_i}\,;w_i)$
(2) $C_{i+1}=(A\leftarrow B_1,...,B_q\,;u)$ is an extended program clause in **P**
(3) $A_{im}\theta_{i+1}=A\theta_{i+1}$, where θ_{i+1} is an mgu of A and A_{im}.
(4) $w_{i+1}=w_i[\theta_{i+1}]_A\neq\bot$
(5) G_{i+1} is $(\leftarrow(A_{i1},...,A_{im-1},B_1,...,B_q,A_{im+1},...,A_{ik_i})\theta_{i+1}\,;w_{i+1})$

We call C_{i+1} the *input clause* to the i+1-st step. ■

Note that by (4) above, a sequence of extended goal clauses is an NSLD derivation only if the assignment part of each clause is not $\bot$.

Definition D4.3 (***NSLD-Refutation***) Let **P** be a program, and G=(g;u) be an extended goal clause. An ***NSLD-refutation*** of **P** $\cup$ {G} is a finite NSLD-derivation of **P** $\cup$ {G} such that $G_n=(\Box;u[\theta_1]_A...[\theta_n]_A)$, where θ_i, $1\leq i\leq n$, are the mgu's in the derivation. We say the refutation has length n. ■

Example 4.2

Consider the program in Example 2.3:

(1) $(F(\sigma_1,e)\,;\{\{\sigma_1\}\Subset\{e,f,g\}\})$

(2) $(F(\sigma_2,f)\,;\{\{\sigma_2\}\Subset\{f,g,h\}\})$

(3) $(S(x,y)\leftarrow F(z,x),F(z,y)\,;\emptyset)$

Let G be the goal $(\leftarrow S(e,f)\,;\emptyset)$. One possible NSLD-refutation is as follows:

Step 1: G_0 is $(\leftarrow S(e,f)\,;\emptyset)$. We choose S(e,f) and use clause (3) to calculate G_1. The mgu for the two atoms is $\theta_1=\{e/x,f/y\}$. Since there is no S-constant in θ_1, $w_1=[\theta_1]_A=\emptyset$. And G_1 is $(\leftarrow F(z,e),F(z,f)\,;\emptyset)$.

Step 2: Choose F(z,e) and use clause (1). The mgu is $\theta_2=\{\sigma_1/z\}$. This does not involve substitution of S-constants, therefore, w_2 is still $\emptyset$. And G_2 is $(\leftarrow F(\sigma_1,f)\,;\emptyset)$.

Step 3: The only atom left is $F(\sigma_1,f)$. We use clause (2). The mgu is $\theta_3=\{\sigma_2/\sigma_1\}$. $w_3=w_2[\theta_3]_A$ which is $\{\{\sigma_1,\sigma_2\}\Subset\{f,g\}\}$. And G_3 is the extended null clause $(\Box\,;w_3)$.

This is, therefore, an NSLD-refutation of length 3. ■

A computed answer is defined as follows.

Definition D4.4 (***Computed Answer***) Let **P** be a program, G=(g;u) be an extended goal. If there is an n-length NSLD refutation of **P** $\cup$ {G} with mgu's $\theta_1,...,\theta_n$, then a ***computed answer substitution*** θ for **P** $\cup$ {G} is the substitution obtained by restricting the variables in the composition $\theta_1...\theta_n$ to the variables that appear in g, and a *computed answer assignment* is the assignment $[\theta_1]_A...[\theta_n]_A$. ■

In example 4.2 the computed answer substitution is ε, and computer answer assignment is $[\theta_1]_A[\theta_2]_A[\theta_3]_A=\emptyset\emptyset[\theta_3]_A=[\theta_3]_A=\{\{\sigma_1,\sigma_2\}\Subset\{f,g\}\}$.

4.1. Soundness of NSLD-Resolution

NSLD refutation is sound with respect to the declarative semantics presented in the previous sections.

The following lemmas are used in the proof of the soundness theorem.

Lemma L4.1 Let **P** be a program, and **C** = (C;w) be an extended clause. Let $\mathbf{P}\models_N \mathbf{C}$.

(1) If u is an assignment such that $uw\neq\bot$ then $\mathbf{P}\models_N (C;uw)$.

(2) If θ is a substitution such that $w[\theta]_A\neq\bot$, then $\mathbf{P}\models_N (C\theta;w[\theta]_A)$. ■

Lemma L4.2 Let **P** be a program. Then

(1) (a) If $\mathbf{P}\models_N (A \wedge B\,;w)$ then $\mathbf{P}\models_N (A\,;w)$ and $\mathbf{P}\models_N (B\,;w)$

(b) If $\mathbf{P}\models_N (A\,;u)$ and $\mathbf{P}\models_N (B\,;w)$ and $uw \neq \bot$ then $\mathbf{P}\models_N (A \wedge B\,;uw)$

(2) $\mathbf{P}\models_N (A \leftarrow B\,;w)$ and $\mathbf{P}\models_N (B\,;w)$ implies $\mathbf{P}\models_N (A\,;w)$ ■

Theorem T4.1 (***Soundness***) Let **P** be a definite program, and $G=(\leftarrow C;u)$ be an extended goal clause. If there is an NSLD-refutation for $\mathbf{P} \cup \{G\}$ with computed answer substitution Θ and computed answer assignment w, then $\mathbf{P}\models_N (C\Theta;uw)$.

Proof:

Let $G=(\leftarrow C;u)=(\leftarrow A_1,\ldots,A_m;u)$. Let the $\mathbf{P} \cup \{G\}$ has an NSLD refutation with length n, and mgu's $\theta_1,\ldots,\theta_n$. Then $w=[\theta_1]_A\ldots[\theta_n]_A$. We prove the theorem by induction on the length n.

$n=1$: $C=A_1$, $\Theta=\theta_1$, $w=[\theta_1]_A$ and there is $(A;v)$ in **P** such that $A\theta_1=A_1\theta_1$ and $u[\theta]_{A,}\neq\bot$. Since $(A;v)$ is an extended assertion in **P**, $\mathbf{P}\models_N (A;\emptyset)$. By lemma L4.1(2), $\mathbf{P}\models_N (A\theta_1;\emptyset[\theta_1]_A)$. Since $u[\theta_1]_A\neq\bot$, by lemma L4.1(1), $\mathbf{P}\models_N (A\theta_1;u[\theta_1]_A)=(A_1\theta_1;uw)=(C\Theta;uw)$

$n<k$: Assume that the theorem is true for $n<k$.

$n=k$: Let the first input clause be $(A\leftarrow B_1,\ldots,B_p;v)$ in **P** and the atom chosen from G_0 be A_i and θ_1 is such that $A\theta_1=A_i\theta_1$ and $u[\theta_1]_A\neq\bot$. Then G_1 is

$(\leftarrow C_1;w_1) = (\leftarrow(A_1,\ldots,A_{i-1},B_1,\ldots,B_p,A_{i+1},\ldots,A_m)\theta_1;u[\theta_1]_A)$.

$G_1,\ldots,G_n$ is a length $n-1$ NSLD-refutation for $\mathbf{P} \cup \{G_1\}$, with mgu's $\theta_2,\ldots,\theta_n$. By the induction hypothesis, $\mathbf{P}\models_N (C_1\theta_2\ldots\theta_n;w_1[\theta_2]_A\ldots[\theta_n]_A)$. By lemma L4.2(1), $\mathbf{P}\models_N ((B_1,\ldots,B_p)\theta_1\theta_2\ldots\theta_n;w_1[\theta_2]_A\ldots[\theta_n]_A)=((B_1,\ldots,B_p)\Theta;uw)$.

Since $(A\leftarrow B_1,\ldots,B_p;v)$ is an extended clause in **P**, $\mathbf{P}\models_N (A\leftarrow B_1,\ldots,B_p;\emptyset)$. By lemma L4.1(1), $\mathbf{P}\models_N (A\leftarrow B_1,\ldots,B_p;u)$. Since $uw=u[\theta_1]_A\ldots[\theta_n]_A\neq\bot$, by lemma L4.1(1), $\mathbf{P}\models_N ((A\leftarrow B_1,\ldots,B_p)\Theta;uw)$. So by lemma L4.2(2), $\mathbf{P}\models_N (A\Theta;uw)$.

Also, by lemma L4.2(1), $\mathbf{P}\models_N ((A_1,\ldots,A_{i-1},A_{i+1},\ldots,A_m)\Theta;uw)$. So, $\mathbf{P}\models_N ((A_1,\ldots,A_m)\Theta;uw)$. *Q.E.D.*

4.2. Completeness of NSLD-Resolution

In this section we prove some completeness results of NSLD refutation. The main technique used in the proofs is combining refutations to form a larger one. However, the presence of S-constants complicates the proof in the following way. Without S-constants, the (SLD) refutation of a ground goal will always yield an answer substitution that is the identity substitution ε, and the refutations of two ground atoms can be easily combined to form a refutation for the conjunction of the two atoms. However, if there are S-constants in a ground goal, an NSLD refutation may produce an answer substitution that contains terms of the form c/σ or σ_1/σ_2, where c is a constant and σ,σ_1,σ_2 are S-constants. Therefore, we need the following lemma.

Lemma L4.3 Let **P** be a program with null values. Let $(B_i;w)$, $1\leq i\leq n$, be extended atoms in HBNV(**P**). If $\mathbf{P} \cup \{(\leftarrow B_i;w)\}$ has an NSLD-refutation with computed answer substitution ε and computed answer assignment w, for $1\leq i\leq n$, then $\mathbf{P} \cup \{(\leftarrow B_1,\ldots,B_n;w)\}$ also has an NSLD-refutation with computed answer substitution ε and computed answer assignment w. ■

The following property of the fixpoint operator T_p makes the proof of completeness much easier.

Proposition P4.1 Let **P** be a program with null values. Then $T_P\uparrow n$ can be refor-

mulated as $T_P\uparrow 1=T_P(\varnothing)$
$T_P\uparrow k=\{(A;w) \mid (A\leftarrow B_1,\ldots,B_m;w)\in Gnd(\mathbf{P})$,and there are $(B_1;w),\ldots,(B_m;w)$ in $T_P\uparrow(k-1)\}$, $k>1$. ■

Note that the above reformulation only applies to the upward powers of T_P, and not to the definition of T_P itself.

Theorem T4.2 (***Completeness***) Let **P** be a program with null values. Let $(A;w)$ be an element in $T_P\uparrow\omega$, then $\mathbf{P}\cup\{(\leftarrow A;w)\}$ has an NSLD-refutation such that the computed answer substitution is ε and the computed answer assignment is w.

(***Sketch***) Let $(A;w)$ be an element in $T_P\uparrow n$. We prove by induction on n.

$n=1$: $(A;w)\in T_P\uparrow 1$. $(A\leftarrow;w)\in Gnd(\mathbf{P})$. That is, there is a unit clause $(A'\leftarrow;u)$ in **P** and a pair of substitutions θ_v and θ_s, where θ_v contains only variable substitutions and θ_s contains only S-constant substitutions, such that $A'\theta_v\theta_s=A$ and $[\theta_s]_A=w$. Since $A'\theta_v\theta_s=A'\theta_s(\theta_v\theta_s)=A$, and $[w]_S=\theta_s$, therefore, there is an NSLD-refutation of length 1 where the unifier is $\theta_v\theta_s$.

$n>1$: Let $(A;w)$ be an element in $T_P\uparrow n$. Then there is $(A\leftarrow B_1,\ldots,B_m;w)\in Gnd(\mathbf{P})$, such that for $1\le i\le m$, $(B_i;w)\in T_P\uparrow(n-1)$. By the definition of Gnd(**P**), there exist an extended clause $C=(A'\leftarrow B_1',\ldots,B_m';u)$ in **P**, a variable substitution θ_v, and an S-constant substitution θ_s such that $[\theta_s]_A=w$ and $A'\theta_v\theta_s=A$, and $B_i'\theta_v\theta_s=B_i$ for $1\le i\le m$. $A'\theta_v\theta_s=A'\theta_s(\theta_v\theta_s)=A$ and $B'\theta_v\theta_s=B'\theta_s(\theta_v\theta_s)=B_i$ for $1\le i\le m$. Therefore, A and the head of the extended clause $C_w\equiv(A'[w]_S\leftarrow B_1'[w]_S,\ldots,B_m'[w]_S;uw)=(A'\theta_s\leftarrow B_1'\theta_s,\ldots,B_m'\theta_s;w)$ unifies with mgu $\theta_v\theta_s$. If we let $G_0=(\leftarrow A;w)$, and use C as the input clause, then we have $G_1=(\leftarrow(B_1'\theta_s,\ldots,B_m'\theta_s)(\theta_v\theta_s);[\theta_s]_A)=(\leftarrow B_1,\ldots,B_m;w)$. Since $(B_i;w)\in T_P\uparrow(n-1)$, by the induction hypothesis, each $(B_i;w)$ has an NSLD-refutation with computed answer substitution ε and computed answer assignment w. Using lemma L4.3, we have our result. ■

Furthermore, from theorem T3.1(2), we have the following (weak) completeness regarding ${}_NT_P$.

Theorem T4.3 (***Weak Completeness***) Let **P** be a program with null values. Let $(A;w)$ be an element in M_P^N, then there are m NSLD-refutation, $m\ge 1$, for $\mathbf{P}\cup\{(\leftarrow A;w)\}$ with computed answer substitutions $\Theta_1,\ldots,\Theta_m$, and computed answer assignments $u_1,\ldots,u_m$, such that $\{(A;w)\}\equiv_m \bigcup_{1\le i\le m}\{(A\Theta_i;wu_i)\}$. ■

This result states that NSLD can calculate the images for every element in M_P^N, but it might not be able to calculate the elements directly. For example, if a program contains the following clauses: $(P(x)\leftarrow Q(x,y),R(y);\varnothing)$, $(Q(a,\sigma);\{\{\sigma\}\Subset\{b,c\}\})$, $(R(b);\varnothing)$ and $(R(c);\varnothing)$. Then $(P(a);\varnothing)$ is in M_P^N. However, $(\leftarrow P(a);\varnothing)$ only have two NSLD refutations, with computed answer assignments $w_1=\{\{\sigma\}\Subset\{b\}\}$ and $w_2=\{\{\sigma\}\Subset\{c\}\}$, respectively. It is easy to see that
$\{(P(a);\varnothing)\}\equiv_m\{(P(a);w_1),(P(a);w_2)\}$.

5. Conclusion

In this paper, we consider the problems of representing, in definite logic programs, a class of indefinite information called null values, and of computing answers to queries in such programs.

To achieve this, we add to first order logic a new type of objects called S-constants. Together with other extensions, these S-constants are used to formulate the incompleteness represented by null values.

We then defined an extension to Herbrand models that gives our logic a model-theoretic semantics. Two operators are then defined to give a fixpoint characterization of this same semantics. One of the operator has a least fixpoint that corresponds exactly to the model semantics. The other operator captures the essential information contained in the model semantics and is much easier to compute than the first one. A proof procedure that is very similar in form to SLD resolution is also developed, with the proper soundness and completeness results.

Future work is to develop an appropriate semantics and proof procedure for inferring negative information from a program that contains null values. We then plan to investigate how to extend these work on null values to general Horn programs, i.e. programs that allow negative literals in the rule bodies. We would also like to pursue some other issues related to this work, e.g. the computational complexity of NSLD refutation, whether our represention of null values can be extended to model null values of other sorts, in particular, those whose actual values can be either in a set of known constants or can be entirely new constants as investigate by Reiter [13].

Acknowledgement

I wish to thank Professor Jack Minker for the insightful discussions throughout the various stages in the formulation of this paper, and for his patience in proofreading the different versions of the paper. I am also grateful to Dr. John Grant, Dr. Arcot Rajasekar, Dr. Jorge Lobo and the referees for their helpful suggestions. This work is done under the financial support of National Science Foundation (grant no. IRI-86-09170), the Army Research Office (grant no. DAAL-03-88-K0087), and the Air Force Office of Scientific Research (grant no. AFOSR-88-0152).

REFERENCES

1. BISKUP, J. A Formal Approach to Null Values in Database Relations, *Advances in Data Base Theory, vol. 1*, H. Gallaire, J. Minker, and J. M. Nicolas (eds.), Plenum Press, New York, 1981 , pp. 299-341.
2. BISKUP, J. A Foundation of Codd's Relational Maybe-operations, *XP2 Work-shop on Relational Database Theory* (University Park, June). Pennsylvania State Univ., 1981.
3. CODD, E. F. Understanding Relations (Installment #7), *FDT Bull. of ACM-SIGMOD 7*, 3-4 (Dec. 1975) , pp. 23-28.
4. CODD, E. F. Extending the Database Relational Model to Capture More Meaning, *ACM Trans. Database Systems 4*, 4 (Dec. 1979) , pp. 397-434.
5. GRANT, J. Null Values in a Relational Data Base, *Information Processing Letters 6*, 5 (Oct. 1977) , pp. 156-157.
6. GRANT, J. AND J. MINKER Answering Queries in Indefinite Databases and the Null Value Problem, *Advances in Computing Research 3* (1986) , pp. 247-267.
7. IMIELINSKI, T. AND W. LIPSKI Incomplete Information in Relational Databases, *J. ACM 31*, 4 (Oct. 1984) , pp. 761-791.
8. IMIELINSKI, T. AND K. VADAPARTY Complexity of Query Processing in Databases with OR-Objects, *Proceedings of the 8th ACM SIGACT-SIGMOD-SIGART Symposium on Principles of Database Systems* (Philadelphia, PA, March 29-31). ACM Press, 1989, pp. 51-65.

9. LIPSKI, W. On Semantic Issues Connected with Incomplete Information Databases, *ACM Trans. Database Systems 4*, 3 (Sept. 1979), pp. 262-296.
10. LIU, Y. AND J. MINKER Null Values in Definite Programs. Technical Report, CS-TR-2447, UMIACS-TR-90-48, University of Maryland, College Park. April, 1990.
11. LLOYD, J. W. *Foundations of Logic Programming*, Springer-Verlag, New York, 1984.
12. REITER, R. Towards a logical reconstruction of relational database theory, *On Conceptual Modelling, Perspectives from Artificial Intelligence, Databases and Programming Languages*, M. L. Brodie, J. Mylopoulos, and J. Schmidt (eds.), Springer-Verlag New York, 1984, pp. 191-233.
13. REITER, R. A Sound and Sometimes Complete Query Evaluation Algorithm for Relational Databases with Null Values, *J. ACM 33*, 2 (April 1986), pp. 349-370.
14. SIKLOSSY, L. Efficient Query Evaluation in Relational Databases with Missing Values, *Information Processing Letters 13*, 4-5 (1981), pp. 160-163.
15. VARDI, M. Querying Logical Databases, *Proceedings of the 4th ACM SIGACT-SIGMOD Symposium on Principles of Database Systems* (Portland, OR, Mar. 25-27). ACM, New York, 1985, pp. 57-65.
16. YUAN, L. Y. AND D. A. CHIANG A Sound and Complete Query Evaluation Algorithm for Relational Databases with Null Values, *Proceedings of the ACM SIGMOD International Conference on Management of Data* (Chicago, June). ACM, New York, 1988, pp. 74-81.
17. ZANIOLO, C. Database Relations with Null Values, *J. Comp. Sys. Sci. 28* (1984), pp. 142-166.

Implementation II

Generation Type Garbage Collection for Parallel Logic Languages

Toshihiro Ozawa, Akira Hosoi, and Akira Hattori
Fujitsu Limited
1015 Kamikodanaka, Nakahara-ku, Kawasaki 211, Japan

Abstract

This paper presents the characteristics of memory consumption of parallel logic languages and a garbage collection (GC) method for them. Parallel logic languages require large amounts of data since logic variables can have only one value, and thus efficient memory management is important for an efficient language processor.

We have evaluated the characteristics of memory consumption of the parallel logic language Flat Guarded Horn Clauses (FGHC). In FGHC, the amount of live data is always small compared to the total amount of data allocated. There are two kinds of data: short-term and long-term. From the observation, we concluded that garbage collection using only two generations best suits this kind of language.

We call our garbage collection method "two-generation garbage collection". Short-term data is garbage collected back in the 1st generation garbage collection and long-term data is collected in the 2nd generation garbage collection. This method is efficient independent of the ratio of the amount of live data to the size of data allocation area (heap). When this ratio is high, our method is especially good, reducing the amount of data copied by a factor of 10, compared to simple copying garbage collection.

1 Introduction

We paid special attention to logic languages[18][6][15] because of their semantic clarity and the simplicity of their execution model.

We have developed a language system for the parallel logic language FGHC on a shared memory multiprocessor as part of the Japanese Fifth Generation Computer Systems (FGCS) project. In the FGCS project, parallel inference machine (PIM) systems are being developed, whose kernel language KL1 is based on FGHC. This language system is being used for finding the characteristics of FGHC programs to design a PIM pilot machine (PIM/p)[16], which contains 128 processor elements connected in a hierarchical structure.

In parallel logic languages, many processes are produced which communicate with each other using shared variables. Many variables must be allocated since each variable can have only one value. Because the order of execution changes dynamically, the lifetime of data can't be determined beforehand. Efficient, automatic memory reclamation is needed. It must be designed based on the characteristics of memory consumption. These are well known in Lisp[5] and Prolog[3], but not in parallel logic languages.

Using this language system, we evaluated the performance and the memory consumption of FGHC, especially the lifetime of data. From the observation, generation type garbage collection would be well suited, compared to reference-counting scheme[4][8] or sliding-compaction scheme[12][7]. Several generation type garbage collection algorithms have been studied [11] [2] [19] [13], but there are still several design decisions to be made for parallel logic languages. For example, the number of generations, how to decide which generation is garbage collected, and how to execute in parallel. We have designed a garbage collection system we call two-generation garbage collection. It is a variation of generation type garbage collection optimized for this kind of language. It is efficient at any ratio of the amount of live data to heap size.

2 The parallel logic programming language FGHC

FGHC is a subset of the parallel logic programming language GHC. An FGHC program is a finite set of guarded Horn clauses consisting of a head, guard goals, a commitment operator (|), and body goals. In FGHC, guard goals are restricted to built-in goals in order to achieve higher efficiency.

$$Head :- Guard_1, Guard_2, \ldots | Body_1, Body_2, \ldots.$$

passive part active part

The combination of the head and guard goals represents the conditions under which the body goals can be executed. During execution of these tests, no assignments to the caller goal arguments can be made. The head and guard goals also play a part in passing arguments. If there are clauses whose conditions are satisfied, the execution of the caller goal is finished, one of them is chosen randomly, and the body goals are executed in parallel. During execution of body goals, assignment to caller goal arguments is allowed. If there is no clause that satisfies its conditions because some arguments of the caller goal are not yet instantiated, execution of the caller goal is suspended until the conditions are satisfied by the execution of other goals. Execution of one goal is called a reduction.

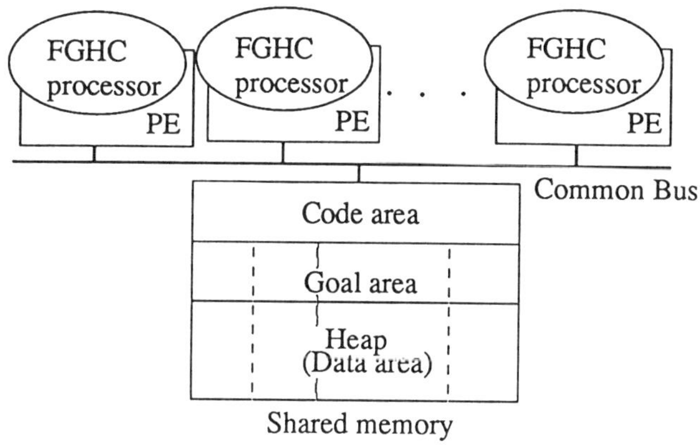

Figure 1. The FGHC processor

3 An FGHC processor on a shared memory multiprocessor

3.1 Structure and execution mechanism

Figure 1 shows the structure of our FGHC processor. The shared memory is divided into three parts. The first part is used for storing the clause definitions and is called the code area. The second part is the goal area. Because the order of execution of FGHC goals is nondeterministic, a goal can't be managed by the stack mechanism normally used in sequential languages. A goal is represented by a goal record[10][9]. Arguments and corresponding clause definitions are referenced by the goal record. These records are stored in this area. Many goals are created during execution[14] [17], and when execution of a goal is completed, the goal record can be reclaimed.

This is done with a free goal list, which is a linked list of currently unused goal records.

The last part is the heap area, used for allocation of data such as variables, lists, vectors, atoms, etc. The last of the heap used is pointed to by a heap allocation pointer, which is incremented when allocating new data. Data is represented by a cell that consists of a value field, a tag field for data typing, a garbage collection field, and a lock field for exclusive access. Data cells are allocated dynamically during execution and this area is reclaimed by garbage collection.

The free goal list and the heap are common resources. To avoid contention for access to the free goal list and heap allocation pointer, we assign a free goal list and a heap allocation pointer for each processor. Individual goal record areas and heap areas are distributed to each processor prior to execution. These common resources are redistributed if a processor runs out.

When a goal record is created, it is put into a scheduling queue. A processing element (PE) retrieves the goal record from the scheduling queue and tests the conditions of the corresponding clauses against the goal's arguments. If all tests in a clause succeed, its body goals are created and put into the scheduling queue. If the tests in all clauses fail, the goal fails. If a clause exists with tests that neither succeed nor fail because one or more of the goal's arguments are not yet instantiated, execution of the goal is suspended. The goal is bound to the uninstantiated arguments to be able to resume when one of them is instantiated. A goal is resumed by re-inserting it into the scheduling queue.

Like free goal lists, scheduling queues are distributed to each PE to reduce contention for retrieving goals. Each PE has its own scheduling queue, called a local-queue, which only it can access. For dynamic load balancing, there is an extra scheduling queue, which can be accessed by all PEs. Usually, a PE retrieves from and puts goals into its local-queue. However, if the local-queue becomes too long or another PE's local-queue is empty, the PE takes goals from its local-queue and puts them into the extra queue. A PE whose local-queue becomes empty will try to retrieve a goal from the extra queue. All PEs are informed by a flag in shared memory when one of the PEs has an empty local-queue. This flag is set by a PE when its local-queue and the extra queue are empty. Each PE checks it at the beginning of every goal execution, and resets it if it puts goals into the extra queue.

4 Performance evaluation

We evaluated the FGHC processor to determine the speed increase per additional processor used, and to investigate its memory consumption.

We used the following benchmarks:

- BUP

  This is a bottom up parser which searches all alternatives of a parse tree.

- DB1

  This is an OR parallel meta-interpreter for searching a database.

- MAXF

  This program finds the maximum flow in a network when the flow in each link is restricted.

- PRIME

  This program generates a list of sequential numbers and searches it for primes.

Table 1: Reduction and data allocation characteristics of benchmark programs

Benchmark	BUP	DB1	MAXF	PRIME	QUEEN
Number of reductions	36K	724K	69K	33K	39K
Total allocated data (K words)	73	1700	266	32	40

Table 2: Execution time for 1 processor

Benchmark	BUP	DB1	MAXF	PRIME	QUEEN
Execution time (s)	13.7	198	69.2	10.6	13.3

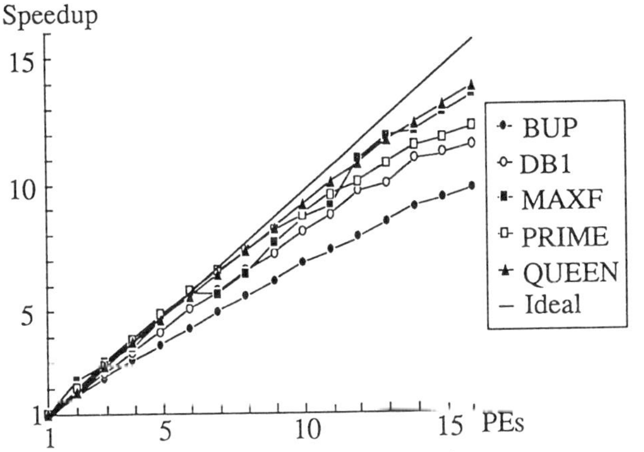

Figure 2. Execution Speed

- QUEEN

  This program searches for all solutions to the eight-queens problem.

Table 1 lists the reduction and data allocation characteristics of these benchmarks.

Table 2 gives the execution time for each benchmark using only one processor and ignoring garbage collection by providing ample memory. Figure 2 shows the relationship between the number of processors and the execution speed when more than one processor is used. We can speed up the system by adding PEs. Idle time, when no goal can be found in the local-queue or extra queue, is very small (about 1% of total execution time) for this load balancing method.

Table 3 shows how the ratio of the number of suspensions to the num-

Table 3: Suspension ratio

Benchmark		BUP	DB1	MAXF	PRIME	QUEEN
Suspension ratio (%)	1PE	1	11	42	0	0
	8PE	38	26	42	4	0
	16PE	35	26	41	12	1

ber of reductions (suspension ratio) varies with the number of processors. In BUP and DB1, the suspension ratio increases dramatically, resulting in a smaller increase in speed when adding processors. This indicates that a significant overhead due to suspensions exists when executing FGHC in parallel. Reducing the number of suspensions is difficult to do using only dynamic load balancing. To achieve a substantial overall reduction requires static program analysis.

5 Memory consumption

We have evaluated the memory consumption of FGHC using copying garbage collection[1]. When one processor exhausts its heap area, it stops the other processors. After all processors stop, they begin to collect garbage sequentially.

Table 4 shows the total amount of data allocated during execution and the mean and maximum amount of live data which is active at the time. This was measured by invoking garbage collection after every 2K words of new data was allocated. A lot of data is allocated, but the amount of live data is always small compared with the amount of data allocated. The distribution of live data in the memory space would be quite sparse if data compaction was not done. Compaction is needed to eliminate page faults and achieve high performance.

We also measured the lifetime of data. Figure 3 gives examples. Each line on the graph shows the percentage of data allocated between the (N-1)th and the Nth garbage collection that remains live as more data is allocated. Most data is thrown away quickly. This is because a large portion of the data is used only to pass information between goals. But, data with lifetimes longer than a certain period is generally alive until the program ends. All benchmarks we tried have the same characteristics. The time is almost the same for all generations in all benchmarks. So, data can be divided clearly into two types. Data with short lifetimes used mainly to pass information between goals, and data with longer lifetimes. This should be true for all parallel logic languages and other parallel languages that create a lot of processes that communicate with each other.

Table 4: Total allocated data and live data

Benchmark		BUP	DB1	MAXF	PRIME	QUEEN
Total allocated data (K words)		73	1700	266	32	40
Mean live data (K words)	1PE	6.7	11.2	42.6	0.3	0.7
	8PE	7.1	10.8	10.8	0.3	0.8
	16PE	7.0	11.0	11.9	0.3	1.0
Max live data (K words)	1PE	13.6	17.4	78.2	2.0	1.4
	8PE	13.7	18.6	17.0	0.7	1.3
	16PE	13.4	19.0	19.1	0.7	1.5

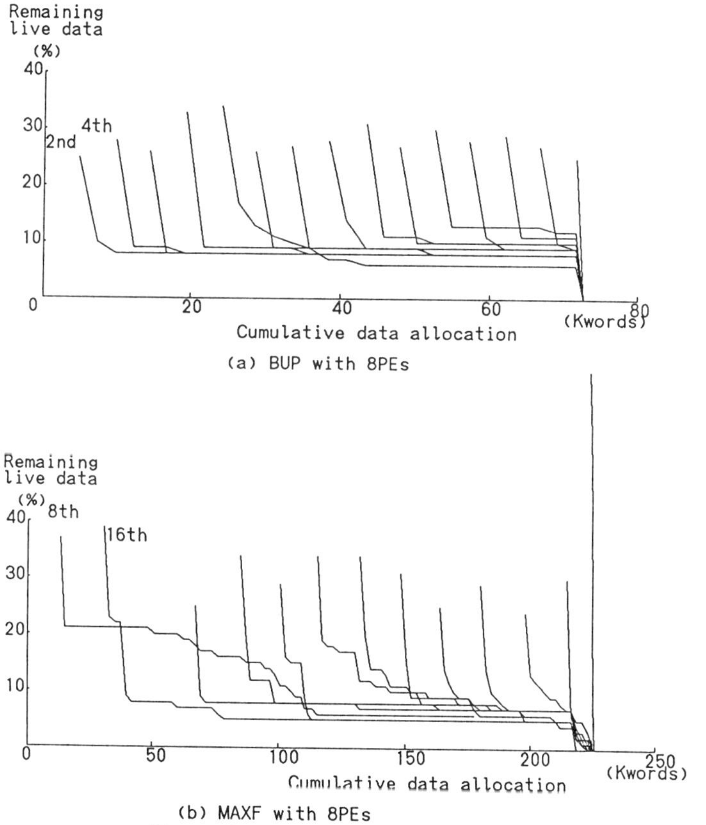

(a) BUP with 8PEs

(b) MAXF with 8PEs

Figure 3. Lifetime of data

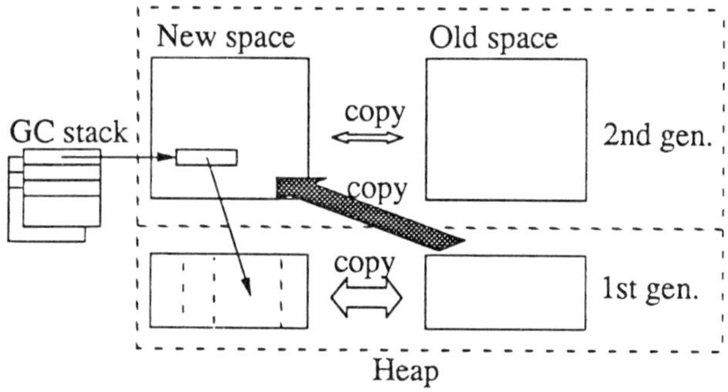

Figure 4. Structure of two-generation GC(1)

6 Garbage collection for parallel logic languages

We can use the characteristics of memory consumption to choose the best type of garbage collection for parallel logic languages. Using reference-counting scheme, the cost of the management of free list would be high, because a lot of data are discarded. Although this scheme has an advantage in terms of memory access locality, it is not practical without hardware support. Sliding-compaction scheme preserves the order of data in the heap, but the whole heap must be scanned. In our implementation of FGHC, the order of data need not be preserved. This scheme is too expensive for our FGHC processor.

Generation type garbage collection would suit this kind of language well. This type of garbage collection compacts data and uses the lifetime characteristics to reclaim garbage efficiently. Our observations show that two generations are enough. The 1st generation is for reclaiming data with short lifetimes, and the 2nd generation is for storing data with long lifetimes. Each generation has its own heap area. More than two generations would be redundant since there are only two types of data. The memory configuration is shown in Figure 4. In each generation, the heap area is divided into two regions, the new space and the old space. Each PE has a GC stack in which it records pointers in the 2nd generation which point to data in the 1st generation. When such a pointer is created, its address is put into a GC stack by the PE that created it.

Data allocation and generation garbage collection are done as follows.

1. The new space of the 1st generation is distributed evenly among all PEs prior to execution. Each PE has its own heap allocation pointer to avoid contention for data allocation. Each PE allocates new data from its 1st generation new space.

2. When a PE exhausts its 1st generation new space, it sets a flag in shared memory to notify the other PEs. All PEs check this flag before

executing a goal. If the flag is set, execution stops until all other PEs stop. Then, the PE that originally set the flag, decides which generation is garbage collected. If the 2nd generation is almost full, 2nd generation garbage collection is done. If not, 1st generation garbage collection is invoked. Almost full is a tunable parameter. It then switches the roles of the new and the old space. This is called a flip. All PEs then begin garbage collection together.

3. 1st generation garbage collection scavenges only the 1st generation, so only the 1st generation is flipped. All live data in the 1st generation can be traversed, starting from the goals in the scheduling queues, GC stacks, and the registers of the PEs. Each PE performs garbage collection locally at the same time by following the pointers in its scheduling queue, GC stack, and registers to find live first generation data and copy them. The data in the 2nd generation is not traversed at all. It then follows the pointers of goals in the extra queue which have not yet been followed by any PEs. If any of this data has been alive for a certain amount of time, T, it is copied into the new space of the 2nd generation. If not, it is copied into the new space of the 1st generation. If data copied to the 2nd generation points to data in the 1st generation, the address of the 2nd generation data is put into the GC stack. This threshold time, T, is the lifetime of short term data. The only exception to this occurs if the new space of the 2nd generation is exhausted during garbage collection. In this case, all data which would have gone there is copied into the new space of the 1st generation.

4. In 2nd generation garbage collection, both the 1st and 2nd generation are flipped, and all live data is copied to the appropriate new space. All live data in the 1st or 2nd generation can be traversed from the scheduling queues and the PE registers. The GC stack is redundant in this case. Each PE traverses the pointers contained in the scheduling queue goals and in the PE registers, copying data into the new space in the same way as for the 1st generation garbage collection. Since the 1st and 2nd generation are being collected together, if the 2nd generation fills up data from the 2nd generation could be copied into the 1st generation. But this would only occur shortly before running out of memory, so it does not affect normal operation.

The threshold time, T, is the minimum time a piece of data is guaranteed to be in the 1st generation. The passage of time is measured by the amount of data allocated. One way to do this is to attach a generation field to each piece of data indicating how many times it has survived a garbage collection. The amount of data allocated between each garbage collection is also recorded. With this information we can determine a lower boundary for how much data has been allocated since the creation of the data in question.

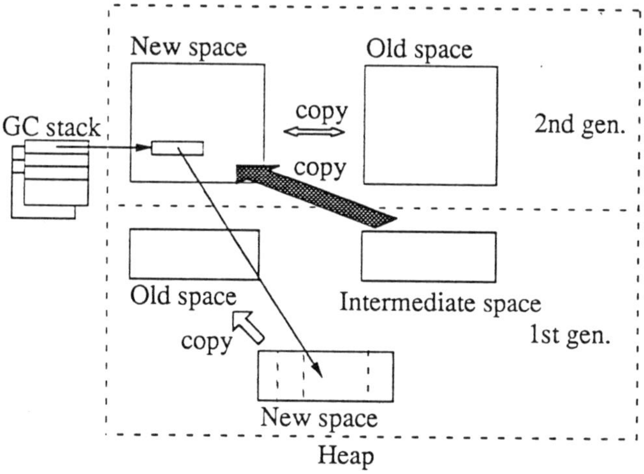

Figure 5. Structure of two-generation GC (2)

If the value of the generation field is N, then the lower bound is the amount of data allocated since the Nth previous garbage collection. This value is compared to T to determine whether a piece of data is short or long term.

Another way to measure the passage of time is to divide the 1st generation memory into 3 areas as in Figure 5.

Each area is equal to T. New data is allocated from the new space, and data which has not yet encountered a garbage collection is copied into the old space. The intermediate space is used for storing data which has survived one garbage collection. Garbage collection is invoked when the new space is exhausted. A flip is done and the name of the old and intermediate spaces are changed, the new space is not changed. The live data in the new space, which has not yet encountered a garbage collection, is copied into the old space and the live data in the intermediate space, which has survived one garbage collection, is copied into the 2nd generation new space. Since the new space is empty immediately after garbage collection, and the new space is the same size as T, invocation of garbage collection marks the passage of t. The live data copied into the 2nd generation has been in the 1st generation for at least T. This method requires more memory, but does not require a generation field in the data.

To execute a garbage collection in parallel, each PE traverses the live data from the goals in its local queue and GC stack (if it is a 1st generation garbage collection). When a PE is finished processing all its own live data, it chooses an untraversed goals in the extra queue and tries to traverse the live data attached to it. Garbage collection and goal execution all use the extra queue for load balancing.

7 Evaluation of two-generation garbage collection

We compared our two-generation garbage collection with simple copying garbage collection, with the same heap size. In the simple copying garbage collection, the heap is divided equally between the new and old spaces. In our two-generation garbage collection, the 2nd generation is twice the size of the maximum amount of live data observed in our tests (Table 4). This is divided equally among the new and old spaces. Whatever remains in the heap is allocated evenly between the three areas of the 1st generation (Figure 5).

Figure 6 compares the total amount of data copied by each of the two methods. We measured the amount of data copied instead of the garbage collection time because we cannot measure the two-generation garbage collection time exactly. The 1st generation garbage collection takes less than 100 ms. Since the total garbage collection time is proportional to the total amount of data copied, we can use this to estimate efficiency. This also eliminates effects due to parallelism. Figure 7 shows how the garbage collections performed. All tests were run using 8 PEs. In two-generation garbage collection, execution of goals is about 5 % slower than in simple copying garbage collection because two-generation garbage collection must record pointers from the 2nd generation to the 1st generation.

When the heap is large, the efficiency of simple copying garbage collection is about the same as that of two-generation garbage collection because there are only a few garbage collections. When the heap is small, there are many garbage collections, and the efficiency of two-generation garbage collection is about 10 times that of simple copying garbage collection. In simple copying garbage collection, the total amount of data copied depends on the size of the heap. When heap is small, the ratio of the amount of live data to the size of the heap is high and data with long lifetime is copied many times. In 2nd generation garbage collection the total amount of data copied is independent of the size of the heap. This means that data with long lifetime is efficiently divided and moved to the 2nd generation area. The shorter time required for each garbage collection and the compactness of live data within the memory space are other advantages of generation type garbage collection. We can conclude that two-generation garbage collection is an efficient method independent of the ratio of the amount of live data to heap size.

During any parallel garbage collection, one of the PEs will copy the maximum amount of data, which is some percentage of the total amount of data copied. One whole garbage collection time is proportional to this percentage. From the average, we can calculate the increase in speed that results from using parallelism in garbage collection. Figure 8 shows the relationship between the number of processors and garbage collection speed. The speed increase of garbage collection saturates at about 4 times, even if we use more than 4 PEs. This is because the amount of data traversed from

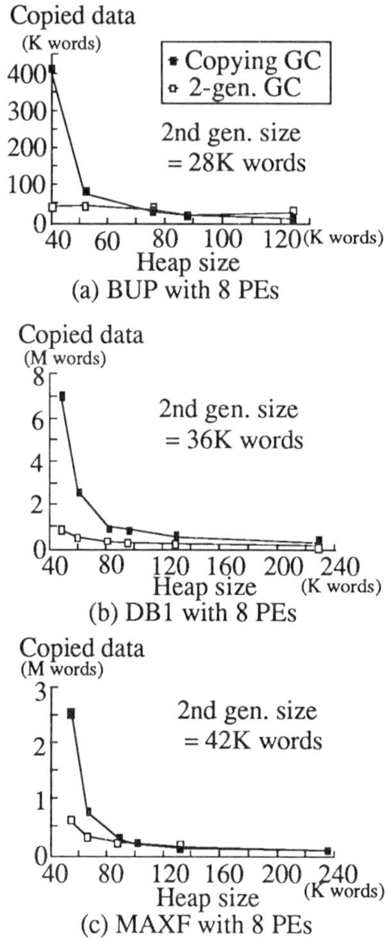

Figure 6. Performance of GCs

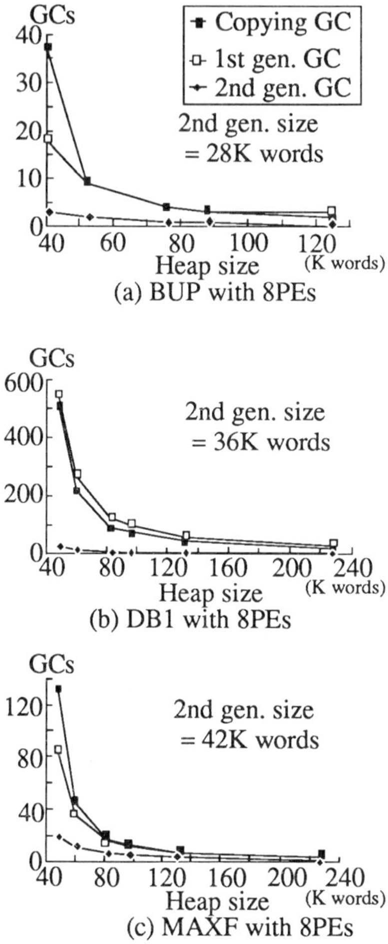

Figure 7. Number of GCs

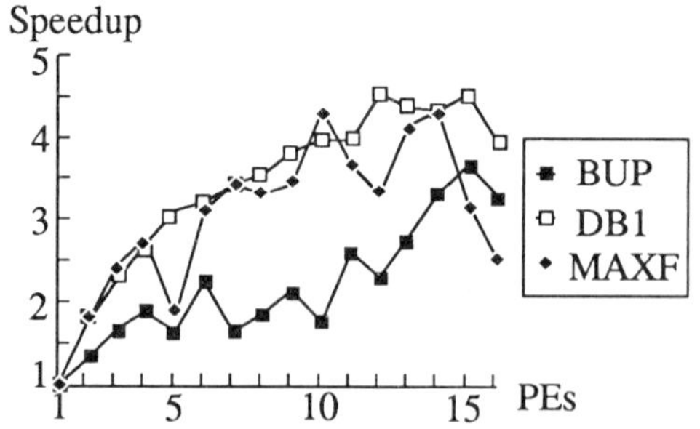

Figure 8. GC Speedup

different goals varies greatly. If there is one goal from which a lot of data can be traversed in the extra queue, garbage collection time is dominated by it. To improve the performance of parallel garbage collection, the unit size of execution must be made smaller. This is where our research will focus next.

8 Conclusions

We evaluated the memory consumption of the parallel logic language FGHC. There are two kind of data: short-term and long-term, and they are clearly distinguishable. Since these results come from the fact that a lot of processes are created and a large amount of data is consumed in passing information, these results should be valid for other similar parallel languages, especially logic languages.

The generation type garbage collection seems to suit this kind of language well. Using only 2 generations, we constructed an efficient garbage collection method which is independent of the ratio of the amount of live data to the size of the heap.

Acknowledgements

We would like to thank Manager Hiromu Hayashi and General Manager Junichi Tanahashi for their encouragement. We also thank our colleagues at Fujitsu and the members of the first research laboratory at ICOT for their discussions, and especially Mark Feldman for helpful suggestions after reading draft version of this paper.

References

[1] Baker, H. G., *List Processing in Real Time on a Serial Computer.* Comm. ACM, Vol. 21, No. 4, pp. 280-294, 1978.

[2] Ballard, S. and S. Shirron, *The Design and Implementation of VAX/Smalltalk-80.* Smalltalk-80: Bits of History, Words of Advice, G. Krasner(editor), Addison Wesley, pp. 127-150, 1983.

[3] Bruynooghe, M., *Towards a real time garbage collection for Prolog* Proceedings the Second Symposium on Logic Programming, 1985.

[4] Chikayama, T. and Y. Kimura, *Multiple Reference Management in Flat GHC* Proceeding of International Logic Programming '87.

[5] Clark, D. W. and C. C. Green, *An empirical study of list structure in LISP.* Comm. ACM, Vol. 20, No. 2, 1977.

[6] Clark, K. L. and S. Gregory, *Parlog: Parallel programming in logic.* ACM Trans. On Prog. Lang. and Syst., 1986.

[7] Crammond, J., *A Garbage Collection Algorithm for Shared Memory Parallel Processors.* Research Report PAR88/21 Dep. of Computing, Imperial College, London, 1988.

[8] Goto, A., Y. Kimura, T. Nakagawa and T. Chikayama, *Lazy Reference Counting: An Incremental Garbage Collection Method for Parallel Inference Machine.* Proceeding of International Logic Programming '88.

[9] Ichiyoshi, N., T. Miyazaki, and K. Taki, *A Distributed Implementation of Flat GHC on the Multi-PSI.* Proceeding of the Fourth International Conference on Logic Programming, 1987.

[10] Kimura, Y. and T. Chikayama, *An Abstract KL1 Machine and Its Instruction Set.* Proceedings of 1987 Symposium on Logic Programming, 1987.

[11] Lieberman, H. and C. Hewitt, *A Real-Time Garbage Collector Based on the Lifetimes of Objects.* Comm. of the ACM, Vol. 26, No.6, 1983.

[12] Morris, F. L., *A Time- and Space-Efficient Garbage Collection Algorithm.* Comm. ACM, Vol. 21, No. 8, 1978.

[13] Nakajima, K., *Piling GC — Efficient Garbage Collection for AI Languages.* Proceedings of the IFIP WG 10.3 Working Conference on Parallel Processing, pp. 201-204, 1988.

[14] Sato, M. and A. Goto, *Evaluation of the KL1 Parallel System on a Shared Memory Multiprocessor.* IFIP WG 10.3 Working Conference on Parallel Processing in Pisa, Italy, 1988.

[15] Shapiro, E., *Concurrent Prolog: A Progress Report.* IEEE Computer, August 1986.

[16] Shinogi, T., K. Kumon and A. Hattori, *MACRO-CALL INSTRUCTION FOR THE EFFICIENT KL1 IMPLEMENTATION ON PIM.* Proceedings the International Conference on Fifth Generation Computer Systems 1988.

[17] Sugie, M., M. Yoneyama and A. Goto, *Analysis of Parallel Inference Machines to Achieve Dynamic Load Balancing.* Proceeding of International Workshop Artificial Intelligence for Industrial Applications, 1988.

[18] Ueda, K., *Guarded Horn Clauses.* Technical Report TR-103,ICOT, 1985.

[19] Ungar, D., *Generation Scavenging: A Non-disruptive High Performance Storage Reclamation Algorithm.* Proceedings of the ACM SIGSOFT/SIGPLAN Software Engineering Symposium on Practical Software Development Environments, pp. 157-167, 1984.

A la Recherche de la Mémoire Perdue

or:

Memory Compaction for Shared Memory Multiprocessors

Design and Specification

Patrick Weemeeuw†

Bart Demoen‡

Abstract

We propose an adaptation of Morris' compaction algorithm to allow its parallel execution on shared memory multiprocessors: multiple processors cooperate on the compaction of one shared data area. The data area doesn't need to be contiguous. This makes the algorithm well suited for situations where the data is unevenly distributed among the processors, i.e. when data partitioning is not appropriate.

First, we point out which parts are inherently sequential in the original algorithm. Then we propose an extension of the notion 'relocation chain' (this is a data structure linking together all memory cells containing a reference to a particular cell), and explain how this allows parallel execution.

The algorithm is then presented as an UNITY program. UNITY is a programming theory consisting of a computational model and a proof system, and is applicable to a wide range of algorithms and architectures.

The UNITY program can be seen as a (high level) specification which can be proved correct and which can be tuned to a particular application.

The algorithm is still space efficient (3 bits for each cell); the time characteristics depend on the properties of the data and the tuning of the algorithm. The main drawback of the algorithm is the locking overhead, which is independent of the number of processors.

1. Introduction

For several kinds of applications, dynamically allocated data structures may become inaccessible during execution. Several techniques, known under the general term *Garbage Collection*, can be used to reclaim the wasted memory space. Memory compaction is an often used technique. We propose a parallel algorithm for the actual compaction phase on shared memory multiprocessors; i.e. we suppose that it is already known (from the marking phase) which cells are accessible and which are not.

The memory compaction problem can then be described as follows: given an area of storage containing scattered marked cells, then it is the intention to rearrange them into a compact mass at one end of the area. The order of the cells has to be preserved, and internal references (from one cell to another in the storage area) have to be updated accordingly. The influence on normal execution should be minimal.

Morris' compaction algorithm [Morris] performs this task in linear time relative to the size of the storage area, and in a space of the order of one extra bit for each reference (besides the mark bit).

In this report, we propose an adaptation of Morris' compaction algorithm to allow its parallel execution on shared memory multiprocessors. First we will informally

---

†K.U. Leuven, Department of Computer Science. Celestijnenlaan 200 A, B-3030 Heverlee, Belgium. E-mail address: patrick@cs.kuleuven.ac.be

‡K.U. Leuven, Department of Computer Science. E-mail address: bimbart@ cs.kuleuven.ac.be

describe Morris' algorithm, because its understanding is crucial for the following sections. Then we identify the parts in the algorithm that inhibit its parallel execution, and we propose informally an extension to the notion relocation chain to allow multiple processors to compact concurrently one shared data space.
In the next section, we present our algorithm as a UNITY program, together with parts of its correctness proof. Due to space limitations, we assume that the reader has already some knowledge about UNITY. See [Chandy & Misra] for a thorough treatment. A short introduction can also be found in [Weemeeuw & Demoen].
A later section describes how several refinements can be used to tune the algorithm to particular applications.
The application we have in mind is garbage collection for the Aurora system [Lusk et al.]. Aurora is an OR-parallel Prolog system, based on the SRI model [Warren 87], which is an OR parallel extension of the WAM [Warren 83]. Morris' compaction algorithm is very popular in sequential WAM based Prolog implementations [Pittomvils et al., Appleby et al.], because it preserves the possibility for cheap memory reclamation through backtracking. We wish to keep this important property, what excludes copying algorithms [Baker] or techniques based on reference counting [Glaser et al.]. [Ali & Haridi] presented an algorithm for distributed systems.
Although each processor administers its own data spaces in the Aurora system, global garbage collectors as described in [Crammond] which allow each processor to collect its own memory space in parallel, taking into account pointers from one heap to another, are not appropriate here. Since the shared data structures may be very unevenly spread across the different memory areas, such an algorithm would cause an unbalanced load. Furthermore, since the data areas are operated upon as stacks, we may wish to restrict the garbage collection to the memory space that actually runs out of space. Because the shared data is temporarily inconsistent during this process, the other processors have to stop normal execution, and they can better be involved in the garbage collection.

2. The algorithm of Morris

We start our description of Morris' algorithm with the definition of the notion 'relocation chain', followed by an outline of the three basic operations: insert, update and move.
A relocation chain of a cell is a data structure linking together all cells (the *members*) containing initially a reference to that cell (the *head*). The chain also contains the value originally stored in the head. For simplicity, we assume throughout this paper that external references are already included in the relocation chains of the cells they refer to. This imposes no restrictions on the generality.

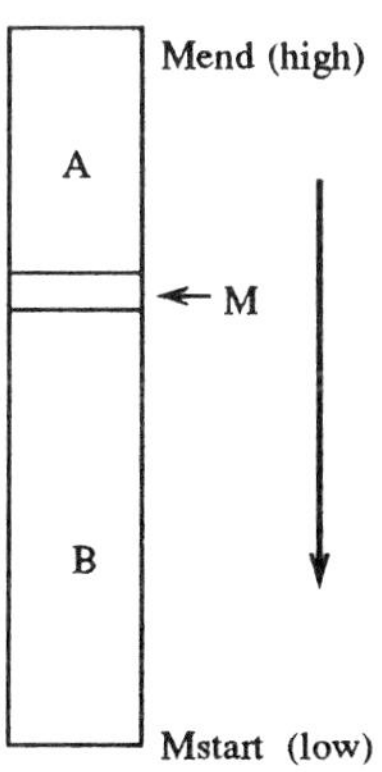

Figure 1.

The basic operations are then defined as follows:
<u>insert(A)</u>: if cell A is marked and cell A contains a reference to cell B, then include A in the relocation chain of B (or initialize the chain of B with A as the only member), else do nothing;
<u>update(A)</u>: if cell A is marked and cell A has a relocation chain, then update all cells member of the relocation chain with a reference to the new location of cell A and restore the original contents of cell A, else do nothing.
<u>move(A)</u>: if cell A is marked, then copy its contents to the new location of A and reset the mark bit, else do nothing.
By a careful succession of these basic operations, the memory can be correctly compacted in a space- and time-efficient way on sequential machines, as is described next.
The non-garbage cells are collected at the lower end of the

area. The algorithm is then divided in two successive phases: a downward and an upward one. The downward one takes care of updating all downward references, without moving the cells; the upward one does the actual compaction, while updating the upward references. For each phase, the insert operation is restricted to references in the current direction.

During the downward phase, the memory area is scanned from high towards low addresses (see figure 1). Whenever a marked cell M is encountered, it includes already in its relocation chain all the cells containing initially a downward reference to it. We know at this moment the new location of cell M: it is Mstart plus the total number of marked cells minus the number of marked cells already encountered during the downward phase. Thus we can update all the cells in the relocation chain of cell M with the new location of cell M, and we restore the original contents of cell M.

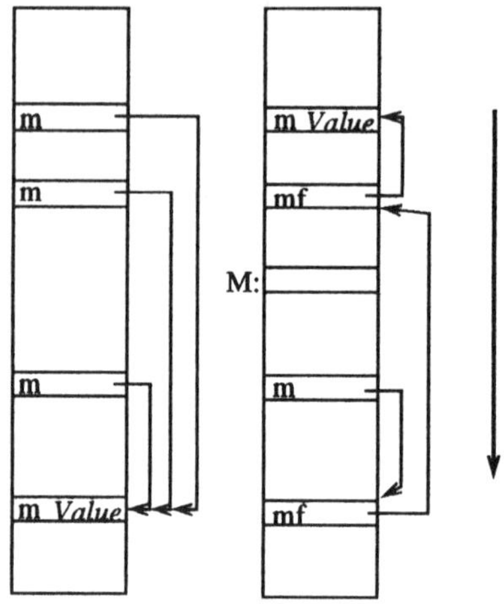

Initial situation Situation when handling cell M in the downward phase

Figure 2.

Then cell M is checked to see if it contains a downward reference, and if so, it is inserted in the relocation chain of the cell it refers to.

This way, the memory space A is converted incrementally into space B by moving the index M downwards. In space A holds the following invariant: if a marked cell contained initially a reference into space B, it is included in the relocation chain of that cell; otherwise, if it contained initially a downward reference to a cell in A, it contains now a reference to the new location of that cell. Marked cells containing no references remain unchanged.

Memory area B is governed by the following invariant: all marked cells initially referred to by one or more cells in area A, contain these and only these cells as members in their relocation chains.

After the downward phase, all downward references are updated.

The upward phase takes care of the upward references in an analogous manner and of the actual compaction. The memory area is scanned in the opposite direction, and each cell is moved to its new location after the update of its relocation chain and before it is inserted in another relocation chain.

The algorithm can be described schematically as follows:

```
{ downward phase }
for i := Mend downto Mstart
begin update(i); insert(i) end;
{ upward phase }
for i:= Mstart to Mend
begin update(i); move(i); insert(i) end;
```

An important characteristic of this ordering of the basic operations is that a cell never has a relocation chain and is included in another relocation chain at the same time. This allows us to represent the cells in a relocation chain at a cost of only one extra bit for each cell (the f-bit), besides the m-bit used to mark the reachable cells, and to run the algorithm in a linear time relative to the size of the storage area. The head and the members of a relocation chain are linked together in a linear list (the *chain*) starting at the head. The last cell in this chain contains the original contents of the head of the relocation chain. All cells in the chain have their f-bit set, except the last one (see figure 2). This allows an efficient implementation of the insert and update operations.

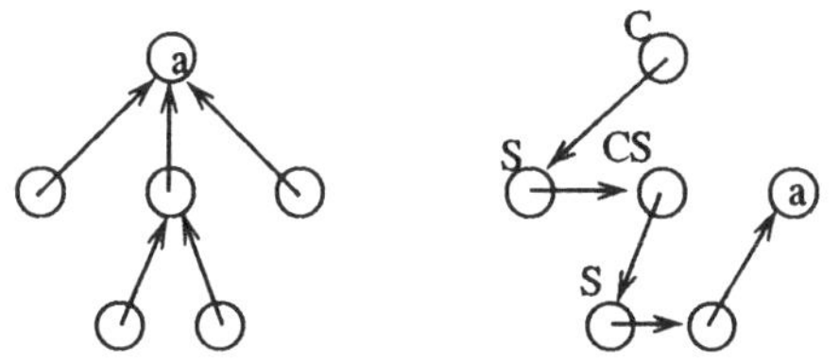

Figure 3: Equivalent data representations

3. Removing the restrictions on the parallelism

The main restrictions for parallel execution in the algorithm of Morris are:

- update can only be done when the relocation chain is complete (i.e. all the cells containing initially a reference to the head (in the current direction) must be member of the relocation chain);
- the cell containing initially a reference can not be inserted in a relocation chain before its own relocation chain is updated;
- the destination of a cell must be known before the update can be done.

The first and third restriction are inherent to the problem; we will remove the second restriction by allowing relocation chains to be nested one into another. The crux of the algorithm is based on the observation that a tree can also be represented as an annotated linear list without losing information [Knuth].

If we take the cells in the data area as vertices, and the pointers as edges, the references between cells form a graph structure. For the moment we assume that there are no references from a cell to itself. When this graph contains no loops, or if we restrict our attention to the upward (or downward) references only, the internal references form unordered trees, the references being the father pointers.

Every tree can be alternatively represented as an annotated linear list (figure 3). A tree consisting of only one cell is represented by that cell. A tree consisting of a topmost cell and n subtrees, is represented by a chain starting at the topmost cell, and continued by each of the linear representations of its subtrees (i.e.: the cells are linked in the chain in prefix order). The last cell in the chain then contains the information stored in the topmost cell of the tree.

The annotations C and S, possibly combined, disambiguate the linear chain. The C annotation means that the cell contains a reference to its first child. The S annotation means that the next cell in the linear list is a sibling cell of this cell (the cell doesn't have any children). Both annotations can occur together as CS: the cell contains a reference to its first child, and there is a sibling cell somewhere further in

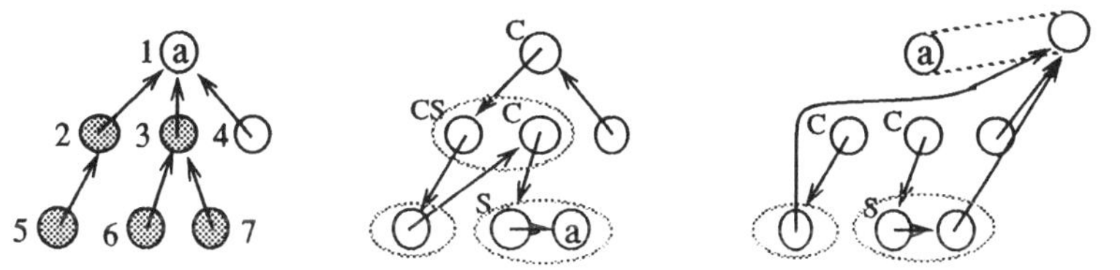

Initial situation. All cells are marked with the M annotation.

Situation when the shaded cells have undergone an insert operation. Annotations not shown are equal to M.

Situation after the update of the topmost cell. Its children now point directly or indirectly to its new location.

a b c

Figure 4: Equivalent data representations. Ellipses surround cells momentarily occurring in the same relocation chain.

the chain. Other cells in the relocation chains keep their M annotation.
Our insert and update operations will partially convert our data structure between those two representations, as is illustrated in Figure 4. At the same time, the update operation will update the references to the new destination of the header cell.
A M-marked cell occurring in a relocation chain (e.g. cell 5 in figure 4b) can not immediately be disambiguated from a marked cell *not* occurring in a relocation chain (cell 4): its interpretation depends on the annotations of the preceding cells in the enclosing relocation chains (if any). As each cell is only inserted once, this causes no further problems.
By removing a number of interdependencies between the different basic operations, scope for parallelism emerges. E.g.: all insert operations can be done concurrently, and the update operations can be done for a cell as soon as its relocation chain is complete. Moreover, a particular order in which the insert, update and move operations are to be done may be imposed in order to tune the algorithm to the particular characteristics of the data structure, while still enough parallelism remains. All this will be illustrated in section 7.

4. The program

In this section, we propose a program for the compaction phase. The correctness of the highest level is proven. We will not prove the correctness of the lower levels (the basic operations), but merely present the UNITY code for them, as the actual implementation is dependent of the application and the architecture. The interested reader can easily verify that the UNITY code for the basic operations meets the specifications. Also, the main objective of this paper is to show that there are several degrees of freedom in the ordering of the low level operations.

4.1 Informal Description.

We will derive our program as follows. First, the initial condition, an invariant and a progress condition will be proposed, which ensure a solution for the compaction problem.
Then, we will present the UNITY program in terms of the basic operations insert, update and move. The specification of these operations is given too. The actual proof that the invariant and the progress condition are satisfied can be found in [Weemeeuw & Demoen]. This proof is complicated because the predicates have to take the complete compaction area in consideration, which isn't exactly a narrow interface between the basic operations, and the expressions deal with different levels of describing the interface (relations about individual memory cells, references and relocation chains).
Finally, an implementation for the basic operations will be presented in the next section.
However, the UNITY program will serve only as a template for further refinements. The UNITY program states the necessary dependencies between the executions of the basic operations in order to guarantee a correct result. It does so by means of the additional boolean variables inserted[i], updated[i] and moved[i], which become true when the corresponding basic operation has been executed. An actual implementation will choose a particular sequencing of the basic operations, that satisfies the ordering expressed in the UNITY program, making these boolean variables and conditions implicit. The particular sequencing chosen will depend on the application.

4.2 Specification of the compaction algorithm

We first introduce some notational conventions. We denote a cell in the compaction area by M[i], i ranging from Mstart up to Mend. Each cell M[i], or cell i for short, has an annotation (the subfield .ant, which is initially U for unmarked or M for marked) and a contents (.cts). It is assumed that a contents with a pointer value can be discerned from other values. Because we do not want to elaborate on too specific implementation details, we simply state that pdt(i,j) holds iff cell i contains a reference to cell j: pdt(i,j) $\Leftrightarrow$ M[i].cts = ref(j) $\wedge$ M[i].ant = M. pdt stands for 'points directly to'. The relation in_rc(i,j) is used to denote that cell i is member of the relocation chain of cell j. We can now state the initial condition:

Initial condition:

$\forall$ i : Mstart $\leq$ i $\leq$ Mend ::
  M[i].ant = U
  $\vee$ (M[i].ant = M $\wedge$ (pdt(i,j) $\Rightarrow$ M[j].ant = M))
$\forall$ i,j : Mstart $\leq$ i $\leq$ Mend, Mstart $\leq$ j $\leq$ Mend :: $\neg$in_rc(i,j)
$\forall$ i : Mstart $\leq$ i $\leq$ Mend :: inserted[i] = updated[i] = moved[i] = *false*

Informally, this means that every cell is either marked or unmarked, and that all cells reachable from marked cells are marked as well. There are no relocation chains initially. No insert, update or move operation has been done.

Before we present the invariant, we need some further notational machinery and auxiliary functions.

The initial contents of the compaction area is denoted by the (constant) array M^0. Of course we have initially M = M^0. A reference from cell i to cell j in the initial situation is indicated by the (constant) relation pit(i,j) (*p*oints *i*nitially *t*o). pit(i,j) subsumes that i is marked.

The location after the compaction phase of cell i is denoted by dest(i), or i' for short. It is defined as follows (in UNITY, '~' is used to separate alternatives in conditional expressions):

dest(i) $\equiv$ i' $\equiv$ Mstart + Σ(j : Mstart $\leq$ j < i :: 1 if (M^0[j].ant=M)
  ~ 0 if (M^0[j].ant=U))

Remark that i' $\leq$ i.

Value(i) is the value associated with cell i. It is undefined for unmarked cells; for marked cells, if not a pointer, it is the original contents of the cell, otherwise, depending on whether the cell pointed to (j) is updated, it is a pointer to j (ref(j)) or to j' (ref(j')). Formally:

value(i) $\equiv$ M^0[i].cts if M^0[i].ant = M $\wedge$ $\neg$ $\langle$ $\exists$ j :: pit(i,j) $\rangle$
  ~ ref(j') if M^0[i].ant = M $\wedge$ pit(i,j) $\wedge$ updated[j]
  ~ ref(j) if M^0[i].ant = M $\wedge$ pit(i,j) $\wedge$ $\neg$updated[j]

Value(i) is not necessarily stored in cell i itself: it may be stored in the relocation chain of cell i, or in cell i', or implicitly be known because cell i itself is part of a relocation chain.

rc(j) is the set of cells which are member of the relocation chain of cell j (i.e. the children of j already in the chain). rc_value(j) is the value 'stored' in the relocation chain of cell j. This value is explicitly stored as the last cell of the linear chain if j is not embedded in another relocation chain; otherwise rc_value(j) is implicitly known because j $\in$ rc(k) for some k. If cell j does not have a relocation chain, rc_value(j) is undefined; otherwise rc_value(j) = value(j) always holds. The two functions rc() and rc_value() will be further specified in section 7, because they depend on the implementation of relocation chains. We illustrate this by a few examples (see figure 4b):

rc(1) = {2,3}	rc(3) = {6,7}	rc(4) = undefined
value(1) = a	value(3) = ref(1)	value(4) = ref(1)
rc_value(1) = a	rc_value(3) = ref(1)	rc_value(4) = undefined

Then, we will use in_rc(i,j) for 'j has a relocation chain and i is a member of it':

in_rc(i,j) $\equiv$ rc_value(j) = value(j) $\wedge$ i $\in$ rc(j)

Has_rc(j) is a shorthand for $\langle$ $\exists$ i :: in_rc(i,j) $\rangle$.

The relation pt(i,j) stands for 'cell i points to cell j', and is a generalization of the pdt-relation. It holds if either i points directly to j (i.e. pdt(i,j)), or i has a relocation chain with a reference to j stored as value in the relocation chain, but is not member of the relocation chain of j (cell i is the root of an outmost relocation chain):

$pt(i,j) \equiv (pdt(i,j) \vee (has\_rc(i) \wedge rc\_value(i) = ref(j))) \wedge \neg\, in\_rc(i,j)$

We have pt(2,1') in figure 4c, but not pt(2,1) in figure 4b, since in_rc(2,1) holds.

The invariant consists of 3 parts: one for each basic operation describing the relations holding between the initial and current configuration after the basic operation is performed on a particular cell. A configuration is completely defined by M[i], inserted[i], updated[i] and moved[i], for all i.

Invariant: $I \equiv \forall\, i : Mstart \leq i \leq Mend :: I1(i) \wedge I2(i) \wedge I3(i)$

I1(i) states that a cell i, initially pointing to some cell j, is included in the relocation chain of cell j if cell i has undergone an insert operation and cell j not yet an update operation:

$I1(i) \equiv inserted[i] \Rightarrow \langle\, pit(i,j) \wedge \neg updated[j] \Rightarrow in\_rc(i,j) \,\rangle$

We define (the relocation chain of) cell j to be complete if all cells initially pointing to j have undergone an insert operation:

$complete(j) \equiv \forall\, i : pit(i,j) :: inserted[i]$

Then, I2(j) states that, after an update operation of cell j, for each cell i containing initially a reference to cell j, either cell i contains directly or via its relocation chain a reference to cell j', or i has already been moved. Also, cell j can not be updated before its relocation chain is complete. If cell j did not initially contain a reference to another cell, then cell j contains its original contents after the update operation if it has not yet been moved.

$$\begin{aligned} I2(j) \equiv updated[j] \Rightarrow\ & \langle\, \forall\, i : pit(i,j) :: \neg moved[i] \Rightarrow pt(i,j') \,\rangle \\ & \wedge complete(j) \\ & \wedge (\neg \langle\, \exists\, k :: pit(j,k) \,\rangle \wedge \neg moved[j] \Rightarrow M[j].cts = M^0[j].cts) \end{aligned}$$

I3(i) states that when a move operation is done on an initially marked cell i, the cell is unmarked and its contents copied to destination i'. If the initial contents is a reference, the reference has been updated to the new location of the cell it referred initially to. Cell i is always unmarked after the move operation. The latter is necessary to guarantee that each cell in the free space collected at the upper end of the compaction area is unmarked after the compaction.

$$\begin{aligned} I3(i) \equiv moved[i] \Rightarrow\ & (M^0[i].ant = M \Rightarrow \\ & \quad M[i'].ant = U \\ & \quad \wedge (pit(i,j) \Rightarrow pdt(i',j')) \\ & \quad \wedge (\neg \langle\, \exists\, j :: pit(i,j) \,\rangle \Rightarrow M[i'].cts = M^0[i].cts)) \\ & \wedge M[i].ant = U \end{aligned}$$

The progress condition states that the fix-point in the computation FP will be reached.

Progress condition: *true* $\longrightarrow$ FP

where $FP \equiv \forall\, i :: inserted[i] \wedge updated[i] \wedge moved[i]$.

<u>Proof of the correctness of the solution strategy</u>

In this section, we prove that the invariant ensures a correct solution when the fixpoint is reached, given the initial condition. The invariant is trivially satisfied initially, since inserted[i], updated[i] and moved[i] are false for all i.

At the fixpoint, we have $I \wedge FP$.

$I1 \wedge FP \equiv I2 \wedge FP \equiv$ *true*.

$I3 \wedge FP$ simplifies to

$$\forall i,j :: \; M[i].ant = U \wedge (M^0[i].ant = M \Rightarrow \; (pit(i,j) \Rightarrow pdt(i',j')) \wedge (\neg\langle \exists j :: pit(i,j) \rangle \Rightarrow M[i'].cts = M^0[i].cts))$$

Taking into account the definition of i', we have that, at the fixpoint, every mark bit is cleared, that all cells initially marked are compacted into one contiguous block, and that the ordering of the cells, as well as the internal pointers, are preserved.

4.3 A program that satisfies the specifications

4.3.1 The program

The program Compaction is presented next. It uses the basic operations insert(i), update(i) and move(i) as primitives. All three basic operations consist of one assignment statement. This allows us to consider them for the moment as atomic actions. The initially section defines initial values for some of the variables. The assign section specifies the operations to be done. As all statements are separated by □, they can be done in any order that satisfies the corresponding conditions. || denotes concurrent execution. As each basic operation is executed concurrently while setting the corresponding boolean variable, all operations are executed exactly once.

```
Program Compaction
  declare
    i: integer;
    inserted, updated, moved: array[Mstart..Mend] of Boolean;
    M: array[Mstart..Mend] of Cell;
  initially
    ⟨ || i : Mstart ≤ i ≤ Mend ::
           inserted[i] = updated[i] = moved[i] = false ⟩
    || ⟨ || i : Mstart ≤ i ≤ Mend ::
                  M[i] = M⁰[i] ⟩
  assign
    ⟨ □ i : Mstart ≤ i ≤ Mend ::
          ⟨ insert(i) || inserted[i] := true ⟩ if ¬inserted[i]
    ⟩
  □ ⟨ □ i : Mstart ≤ i ≤ Mend ::
          ⟨ update(i) || updated[i] := true ⟩ if complete(i) ∧ ¬updated[i]
    ⟩
  □ ⟨ □ i : Mstart ≤ i ≤ Mend ::
          ⟨ move(i) || moved[i] := true ⟩
                if ¬moved[i] ∧ updated[i] ∧ inserted[i]
                  ∧ ⟨pit(i,j) ⇒ updated[j] ⟩ ∧ movable(i)
    ⟩
end
where:
  movable(i) ≡ (free(i') ∨ i = i' ∨ M⁰[i].ant=U)
  free(j) ≡ moved[j]
```

Remark that an expression as pit(i,j) cannot be evaluated by the program, since there is no copy of the initial configuration. Such expressions have to be eliminated too by choosing a particular order that makes this condition implicit.

4.3.2 Properties of the basic operations

We introduce a set of properties any implementation of the basic operations should possess. We do this without referring to the implementation of the relocation chains.

4.3.2.1 Properties of insert(i):

Nothing is removed from relocation chains:

$\forall$ j ,k :: *stable* in_rc(j,k) *in1a*

Cells different from i are not added to relocation chains:

$\forall$ j ,k : j $\neq$ i :: *stable* $\neg$in_rc(j,k) *in1b*

If cell i contains a reference to cell j then all cells different from i, from j and from the members of the nested relocation chains of i, remain unchanged. In_rc$^+$ is the anti-reflexive transitive closure of in_rc.

$\forall$ k : pt(i,j) $\wedge$ k $\neq$ i $\wedge$ k $\neq$ j $\wedge$ $\neg$in_rc$^+$(k,i) :: *constant* M[k] *in2a*

If cell i does not contain a reference to some cell j, then all cells remain unchanged:

$\neg\langle \exists$ j :: pt(i,j) $\rangle \Rightarrow \forall$ k :: *constant* M[k] *in2b*

Pairs (j,k) cannot be removed from the pt-relation unless j = i.

$\forall$ j,k : j $\neq$ i :: *stable* pt(j,k) *in3a*

Nothing is added to the pt-relation.

$\forall$ j,k :: *stable* $\neg$pt(j,k) *in3b*

Insert(i) adds i to the relocation chain of j when pt(i,j) holds (notice that pt(i,j) no longer holds after the insert operation):

$\forall$ i,j :: { pt(i,j) } insert(i) { in_rc(i,j) } *in4a*

Insert(i) does not add i to the relocation chain of j when pt(i,j) does not hold:

$\forall$ i,j :: { $\neg$pt(i,j) } insert(i) { $\neg$in_rc(i,j) } *in4b*

Finally, in5 states that an U annotation is preserved.

$\forall$ j :: *stable* M[j].ant = U *in5*

4.3.2.2 Properties of update(i):

Nothing is removed from relocation chains of cells different from i:

$\forall$ j,k : k $\neq$ i :: *stable* in_rc(j,k) *up1a*

Nothing is added to relocation chains:

$\forall$ j,k :: *stable* $\neg$in_rc(j,k) *up1b*

Cells different from i and not in the nested relocation chain of i remain unchanged.

$\forall$ j : $\neg$in_rc$^+$(j,i) $\wedge$ j $\neq$ i :: *constant* M[j] *up2a*

Everything remains unchanged when i does not have a relocation chain:

$\neg\langle \exists$ j :: in_rc(j,i) $\rangle \Rightarrow \langle \forall$ k :: *constant* M[k] $\rangle$ *up2b*

Pairs (j,k) cannot be removed from the pt-relation:

$\forall$ j,k :: *stable* pt(j,k) *up3a*

Pairs (j,k) are not added to the pt-relation unless j is in the relocation chain of i and k is the destination of i.

$\forall$ j,k : k $\neq$ i' $\vee$ $\neg$in_rc(j,i) :: *stable* $\neg$pt(j,k) *up3b*

Cells j in the relocation chain of i are removed from the chain and refer to i', the destination of i:

$\forall$ i,j :: { in_rc(j,i) } update(i) { pt(j,i') $\wedge$ $\neg$in_rc(j,i) } *up4a*

If i is the topmost cell of a (nested) relocation chain, then update stores in cell i the value which was stored in the relocation chain:

$\forall$ i :: { has_rc(i) $\wedge$ $\neg\langle \exists$ k :: in_rc(i,k) $\rangle$ $\wedge$ rc_value(i) = v }
update(i) { M[i].cts = v } *up4b*

Finally, up5 states that an U annotation remains unchanged by the update operation.

$\forall$ j :: *stable* M[j].ant = U *up5*

4.3.2.3 Properties of move(i):

The move operation preserves the in_rc-relation for all the cells:

$\forall$ j,k :: *constant* in_rc(j,k) *mo1*

All cells different from i and i' remain unchanged:

$\forall$ j : j $\neq$ i, j $\neq$ i' :: *constant* M[j] *mo2a*

All cells remain unchanged when cell i has annotation U:

$\forall$ j : M[i].ant = U :: *constant* M[j] *mo2b*

The pt-relation remains constant in all pairs (k,l) with k $\neq$ i' when cell i contains a reference to another cell:

pdt(i,j) $\Rightarrow$ $\forall$ k,l : k $\neq$ i' :: *constant* pt(k,l) *mo3a*

The pt-relation is constant when cell i does not contain a reference to another cell:

$\neg\langle \exists$ j :: pdt(i,j) $\rangle \Rightarrow \forall$ k,l :: *constant* pt(k,l) *mo3b*

The operation copies the contents of the marked cell i to cell i', and resets the annotation:

{ M[i].cts = v $\wedge$ M[i].ant = M }

move(i) { M[i'].cts = v $\wedge$ M[i'].ant = U } *mo4*

Finally, mo5 states that every U annotation remains unchanged by the move operation.

$\forall$ j :: *stable* M[j].ant = U *mo5*

4.3.3 Correctness proof

Given the program and starting from these properties, one can prove that the invariants are preserved and that the fixpoint is reached. Details can be found in [Weemeeuw & Demoen].

5. Refinement of the basic operations

5.1 The basic operations

In this section, we give an UNITY implementation for the basic operations. Several auxiliary functions depending on the representation of relocation chains, are here formally specified too.

As already mentioned informally in a previous section, a relocation chain is represented by a linear annotated list of cells, containing the cells in the relocation chain itself and all the embedded relocation chains. We call the part of the linear list representing the relocation chain of cell i and all its embedded relocation chains, the *segment* of cell i.

We define the functions dealing with the relocation chains below. These definitions depend on the equivalent data representations as proposed in section 3.

The set of cells in the relocation chain of cell i is defined as rc(i). Therefore it is assumed that has_rc(i) is true. The function end(i) gives the index of the last cell of the segment of cell i. E.g.: in figure 4b we have: end(1) = 7, end(2) = 5 and end(5) = 5. The function end_of_subchains(i) gives the index of the last cell of the segment of the cell j with i $\in$ rc(j); i.e. end_of_subchains(i) $\equiv$ end(j) with i $\in$ rc(j). We now give these definitions in terms of the implementation of the relocation chains.

Has_rc(i) is true if cell i contains C in its annotation:

has_rc(i) $\equiv$ M[i].ant $\in$ {C,CS}

The set rc(j) is defined as follows. Since cell j has a relocation chain, its contents points to the first member of the relocation chain. Then, let k be a member of the relocation chain that has a sibling cell (there is a S in the annotation). The next member can be found by inspecting the cts-field of the last cell in the segment of k: this is a reference to the next sibling.

rc(j) $\equiv$ { i : Mstart $\leq$ i $\leq$ Mend ::

M[j].cts=ref(i) $\vee$ $\langle \exists$k : k$\in$ rc(j)$\wedge$M[k].ant$\in$ {CS,S} :: M[end(k)].cts=ref(i) $\rangle$

}

The end function applied to a cell i yields i if i hasn't a relocation chain; otherwise it yields the result of applying end_of_subchains to the first member of the relocation chain of cell i.

end(i) ≡ i if ¬has_rc(i)
    ~ end_of_subchains(M[i].cts) if has_rc(i)

For the function end_of_subchains(i), we consider four cases, depending on whether cell i is or is not the last member in the relocation chain (S in the annotation), and on whether cell i has a relocation chain itself or not (C in the annotation). It is defined as follows:

end_of_subchains(i) ≡
  i if M[i].ant = M
  { i is the last member and has no relocation chain }
  ~ end(i) if M[i].ant = C
  { last member, has_rc(i): the end of the segment of its enclosing relocation chain is the end of its own subchain }
  ~ end_of_subchains(M[i].cts) if M[i].ant = S
  { not last member, ¬has_rc(i): take the end_of_subchains of the next member }
  ~ end_of_subchains(M[end(i)].cts) if M[i].ant = CS
  { not last member, has_rc(i): find the next member (pointed to by M[end(i)].cts) and take the end_of_subchains of that cell }

rc_value(i) is not used in the implementation below, but it can be defined as follows:

rc_value(i) ≡ M[end(i)].cts if has_rc(i) ∧ ¬ ⟨ ∃ j :: in_rc(i,j) ⟩ *{ outermost chain }*
    ~ ref(j) if has_rc(i) ∧ in_rc(i,j) *{ nested chain }*

If ¬has_rc(i), rc_value(i) is undefined.

We now give the implementation of the basic operations.

insert(i) ≡ ⟨ M[end(i)].cts := M[M[end(i)].cts].cts *{ change contents of end(i) }*
  ‖ M[M[end(i)].cts].cts := ref(i)
    { change contents of the head of the enclosing relocation chain }
  ‖ M[M[end(i)].cts].ant :=
      C if M[M[end(i)].cts].ant ∈ {M,C}
      ~ SC if M[M[end(i)].cts].ant ∈ {S,SC}
      { change annotation of the head of the enclosing relocation chain
  ‖ M[i].ant := {S} ∪ M[i].ant
      if M[M[end(i)].cts].ant ∈ {SC,C}
      { change annotation of i }
  ⟩ if M[i].ant ≠ U ∧ is_ref(end(i))

Basically, the insert operation consists of 4 assignments. Of course, the computation of end(i) has only to be done once. The computation of end(i) will be the main factor influencing the computing time if the relocation chains have a high nesting degree.

We illustrate the most complicated case (both i and the cell it refers to have a relocation chain) in figure 5. The annotation of the cells is given in italics. The segments representing the nested relocation chains are shown as triangles. After insertion, the segment of i is embedded in the segment of the cell it initially referred to. The simpler case (when there are no nested relocation chains) reduces to the insert operation in Morris' algorithm. In that case, i and end(i) refer to the same cell.

The update operation is presented below.

update(i) ≡ ⟨ M[i].ant := *{ change the annotation of the header:*
      M if M[i].ant = C *S if not the last member of an enclosing*
      ~ S if M[i].ant = CS *relocation chain; otherwise M }*
  ‖ M[i].cts := M[end(i)].cts *{ restore the appropriate value }*
  ‖ ⟨ ‖ j : j ∈ rc(i) :: *{ for each member:*

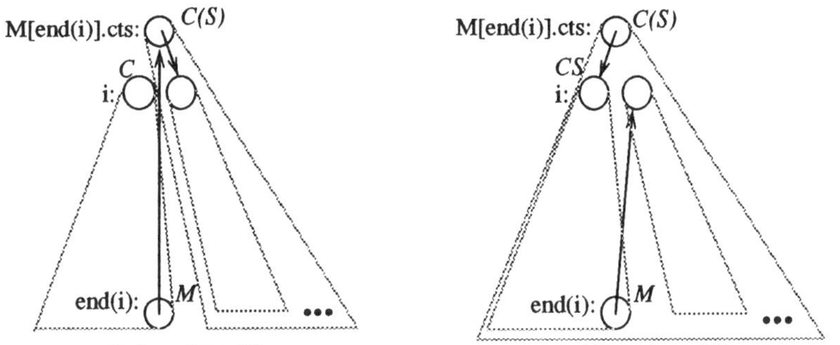

Before insert(i) After insert(i)

Figure 5

M[end(j)].cts := ref(i') *make it refer to the new location of i;*
|| M[j].ant := *clear the S in the annotation }*
C if M[j].ant ∈ {C,CS}
~ M if M[j].ant ∈ {S,M}
⟩
⟩ if M[i].ant ∈ {C,CS}

Also in this case, the computation of the end function is highly dependent of the nesting level of the relocation chains.

Finally, we present the code for the move operation.

move(i) ≡ ⟨ M[i'].cts, M[i'].ant, M[i].ant := M(i).cts, U, U if M[i].ant = M ⟩

It can easily be verified that the code, in combination with the definitions of the auxiliary functions, meets the specifications.

6. Discussion

The basic operations as given, can not handle cyclic structures in general. The reason for this is that it is not possible to represent a general graph structure as a linear annotated list.

There are two types of cyclic structures that need our attention. Cyclic structures without cells containing a reference to itself, can be handled by dividing the algorithm in an upward and a downward phase. All the operations and relations used can be partitioned in two components: an upward and a downward one, and the correctness of the algorithm can be proved accordingly. Cells containing a reference to itself can be coped with by a careful extension of the insert and the update operations. The insert operation should leave such cells alone, and the update operation should check whether the value of the updated cell is a reference to itself, and substitute it with a reference to the new location when appropriate. By combining these two extensions, all kinds of structures can be handled.

When the basic operations are executed atomically, we need three bits for each cell to store the five annotations (M, U, C, S and CS). However, for parallel execution we want to execute them concurrently. Therefor, we will need a sixth annotation to indicate the state 'locked' A cell can simply be locked by atomically exchanging its annotation with the annotation 'locked'. To avoid deadlock, a particular order can be imposed on the acquiring of locks on cells: firstly according to the nesting level (top down), and secondly according to the order of the cells in the relocation chains (left to right). Locking can be simplified a lot while inserting external references. We will elaborate further on the issue of locking in the next section.

Since we use in total only six annotations out of the eight ones possible with three bits, we may introduce some extra annotations to improve efficiency. For example, the C annotation can be split into a C- and a C'-annotation, depending on whether the rc_value of the relocation chain is a reference to another cell or not. This would reduce the insert operation to a no-operation if the value of the cell is not a reference to another cell.

Although the algorithm as presented assumes contiguous memory, this is not necessary and does not need any extension. Only when the compaction is split into an upward and a downward phase, there is the extra requirement of a total ordering over the address space, which is easily satisfied.

7. Scheduling aspects

In this section, we present two clear cut scheduling orders for the basic operations, and discuss how this influences the implementation of those operations.

As already mentioned before, it is the intention to arrange the basic operations in such an order that the precondition for their execution is true, and thus has not to be checked. Of course, there has to remain enough parallelism.

7.1 The in mass approach

In this approach, the whole compaction space is first converted into the intermediate format by the insert operations. Then, after synchronization, each cell of the compaction area is updated, and finally, again after synchronization, each cell is moved to its final destination.

This way, the relocation chains are always complete before an update operation is done. Only the condition movable(i) has still to be checked.

The main drawback of this approach is that the nesting level of the relocation chains is clearly maximal, but this drawback depends largely on the characteristics of the represented data. On the other hand, the implementation of the basic operations can be simplified, because there is only one type of operation executed at the same time. This means that e.g. the insert operation should only be prepared for interference of other insert operations occurring at the same time. This simplifies the mutual exclusion problem and reduces the overhead necessary for locking.

There is also no need to have a separate upward and downward phase, if there are no cyclic structures.

7.2 The chasing approach

In this approach, the compaction area is partitioned in a number of segments. The number of marked cells must be known for each segment. There is an upward and a downward phase, separated by a synchronization point. Processors can dynamically switch between three states: inserting, updating or moving a segment (the latter only in the second phase).

All the processors take each a segment at one end of the compaction area, and perform the insert operation on each cell of their segment. A segment can be updated as soon as it is completely inserted and all preceding segments have been inserted, because all the cells in the segment then have complete relocation chains. A similar condition holds for moving a segment during the second phase.

This approach has the advantage that pointer chains are kept short: the insert operation possibly increases the nesting level, but at the same time the update operation reduces the nesting level.

Also, the possible bottleneck at the beginning of the moving of cells (the destination must be free, what may cause quasi-sequential execution initially) can be avoided by allowing a processor to start early moving of a segment.

On the other hand, possible interference between concurrent operations is much bigger now.

8. Application to the Aurora System

The suitability of our algorithm depends highly on the characteristics of the data structures. In Prolog, pointer chains are very short in general ([Tick]), and can be collapsed ([Sahlin]). For Aurora, the pointer chains will be still shorter, because they may be broken by a conditional binding. A conditional binding goes through the Binding Arrays, and can be treated therefore as an external reference. Remark also that our algorithm is only less efficient than the original algorithm of Morris in the case of nested relocation chains (making abstraction of the (constant) locking overhead).

The data may be very irregularly spread among the stacks of the processors. Therefore, our algorithm may prove to be more efficient in this situation than other approaches that rely on data partitioning among the processors (each processor collecting its own stacks). It is also possible to determine after the marking phase which approach is best suited for the compaction.

We want also to keep the possibility to compact only the stack that actually runs out of space. Our algorithm is well suited for such situations.

For Aurora, we expect that our algorithm will run in almost linear time relative to the size of the storage area divided by the number of processors. The algorithm is currently being implemented, in order to give some definite answers on performance questions.

9. Conclusion

We presented a parallel compaction algorithm of which the correctness is proven. We deemed a correctness proof necessary because of the complexity of the parallel transformations of the data structures. The correctness is guaranteed for every execution order that meets the specified dependencies between the basic operations.

The main characteristic of the algorithm is that it allows processors to cooperate in the compaction of a shared (non contiguous) compaction space with a dynamic load distribution. The algorithm can be tuned to the characteristics of the data in the compaction space. It is expected to be time efficient when there are relatively little pointer chains; in such situations it will run in nearly linear time relative to the size of the compaction space. Locking overhead is constant and can be reduced substantially when an atomic exchange instruction for one cell is available. The algorithm runs in constant space (3 bits for each memory cell).

10. Acknowledgments

The authors wish to thank M. Bruynooghe and H. Van Acker for reading earlier versions of this paper. The first author is also indebted to several people at SICS for helpful discussions.

This research was supported by ESPRIT Project 2471 (PEPMA) and the RFO-AI-02 project, sponsored by DPWB.

11. References

[Ali & Haridi] Ali, K. A. M. and S. Haridi, "Global Garbage Collection for Distributed Heap Storage Systems," International Journal of Parallel Programming, vol. 15, no. 5, pp. 339 - 388, October 1986.

[Appleby et al.] Appleby, K., M. Carlsson, S. Haridi, and D. Sahlin, "Garbage Collection for Prolog based on WAM," Communications of the ACM, vol. 31, no. 6, pp. 719 - 741, June 1988.

[Baker] Baker, H. G. Jr., "List processing in real time on a serial computer," Communications of the ACM, vol. 21, no. 4, pp. 280 - 294, April 1978.

[Chandi & Misra] Chandi, K. M. and J. Misra, Parallel Program Design - A Foundation, Addisson-Wesley Publishing Company, August 1988.

[Crammond] Crammond, Jim, "A Garbage Collection Algorithm for Shared Memory Parallel Processors," International Journal of Parallel Programming 17 (6), pp. 497 - 522, December 1988.

[Glaser et al.] Glaser, H., M. Reeve, and S. Wright, "An Analysis of Reference Count Garbage Collection Schemes for Declarative Languages," in Proceedings of the International Computer Science Conference 88, AI: Theory and Applications, pp. 641 - 648, Hong Kong, 19 - 21 December 88.

[Knuth] Knuth, E., The art of Computer Programming, Vol. 1: Fundamental Algorithms, Addison Wesley, Reading, May 1968.

[Lusk et al.] Lusk, E., R. Butler, T. Disz, R. Olson, R. Overbeek, R. Stevens, D. H. D. Warren, A. Calderwood, P. Szeredi, S. Haridi, P. Brand, M. Carlsson, A. Ciepielewski, and B. Hausman, "The Aurora Or-parallel Prolog System," in Proceedings of the International Conference on Fifth Generation Computer Systems, pp. 819 - 830, 1988.

[Morris] Morris, F. L., "A time- and space efficient garbage compaction algorithm," Communications of the ACM, vol. 21, no. 8, pp. 662 - 665, August 1978.

[Pittomvils et al.] Pittomvils, E., M. Bruynooghe and Y. Willems, "Towards a real time garbage collector for Prolog," in Proceedings of the Second Symposium on Logic Programming, pp. 185 -198, Boston, 1985.

[Sahlin] Sahlin, Dan, "Collapsing variable chains in Prolog," SICS Research Report R89003.

[Tick] Tick, E., Memory Performance of Prolog Architectures, Kluwer Academic Publishers, 1988.

[Warren 83] Warren, D. H. D., "An Abstract Prolog Instruction Set," Technical Report, SRI International, Artificial Intelligence Center, August 1983.

[Warren 87] Warren, David H. D., "The SRI model for OR parallel execution of Prolog - abstract design and implementation," in Proceedings of the Symposium on Logic Programming, pp. 92 - 102, San Francisco, 1987.

[Weemeeuw & Demoen] Weemeeuw, P. and B. Demoen, "A la recherche de la mémoire perdue, or: Memory Compaction for Shared Memory Multiprocessors," CW report 112, Department of Computer Science, K. U. Leuven.

FCP Sequential Abstract Machine Characteristics for the Systems Development Workload

Leon Alkalaj
Jet Propulsion Laboratory
California Institute of Technology
Pasadena, CA. 91109

Tomás Lang
Computer Science Department
University of California, Los Angeles
Westwood, CA, 90024

Ehud Shapiro
Weizmann Institute of Science
Applied Mathematics Department
Rehovot, 76100, Israel

Abstract

Our motivation for performance analysis of FCP implementations is the design a special-purpose processor architecture for the efficient execution of FCP. We characterize algorithmic features of FCP program execution at the abstract machine level using an instrumented version of the abstract machine emulator. Results are obtained using benchmarks that are representative of a ***Systems Development Workload*** currently in use. The analysis of the goal management behavior shows a higher complexity of goal ***suspension*** and ***activation*** compared to the previously reported results. In addition, goal management operations occur on the average 1.3 times per goal reduction. These results motivate architectural support for goal management in a special-purpose environment. Furthermore, our results indicate that the average fraction of ***redundantly selected clauses*** during a goal reduction is 77%. This motivates the need for advanced compilation techniques for clause-indexing. Other results that characterize goal management and goal reduction are also presented, and ways of reducing their execution time are discussed.

1 Introduction

Current implementations of Flat Concurrent Prolog (FCP) on general-purpose processors execute by emulating the FCP sequential abstract machine [9]. Similar abstract machines have been proposed for the implementation of other concurrent logic programming languages such as Parlog [8] and GHC

	FCP Benchmark Programs						
	Cmp	Sim1	Sim2	Dbg	Slv	Distr	Logix
Mode	T	T	I	T	I	I	T
Size (lines)	3885	2066	2066	1670	676	6376	10000
Reductions (10^6)	7.1	3.0	7.7	1.6	0.4	0.3	1.5

Table 1: FCP Benchmark Information

[17]. Performance analysis of these implementations may be conducted at levels ranging from the very low machine level to the higher abstract machine level. Selecting the appropriate implementation level depends on the objectives of the performance analysis [5]. If the motivation is to improve the performance of the specific implementation, both low-level and high-level characteristics are meaningful. If the objective is to improve the performance of other implementations that use the same abstract machine but different emulation language or physical machine, then the performance analysis must yield results that are general enough. The tradeoff is between the amount of detail that one can measure, and the generality of the results.

Our motivation for performance analysis is the design of a *special-purpose* processor architecture for the efficient execution of FCP [1]. We analyze FCP program execution at the abstract machine level using an instrumented version of the Logix operating system [15]. The analysis characterizes the dynamic behavior of seven unoptimized FCP programs that are used for system development and prototyping. We refer to this set of programs as the *Sytems Development Workload*. The programs are large in source code size and execute over lengthy periods of time, thus achieving a reasonable average of program behavior. In Table 1 we show the size of the programs and the number of goal reductions performed. Programs executing in *interpret* mode (I) report failure and can be interpreted and debugged, while programs in *trust* mode (T) execute expecting all goals to succeed.

A *typical* workload session is described as follows. Two simulators are being developed using *Logix*. One is a simulator of a special-purpose FCP processor *Sim1* (*Sim2* is the same as *Sim1* but executes in *interpret* mode), and the second is a simulator of a distributed ring-architecture for the execution of FCP, *Dist*. Programs are debugged using the *Debugger* (Dbg) and compiled using the *Compiler* (Cmp). Program control flow analysis using abstract interpretation is performed using the *Solve* program (Slv). All programs are equally weighed even though they vary in size and execution time. This is justified by assuming that the user will use all of the applications equally while prototyping the system.

Two previously reported performance evaluations of concurrent logic programming languages are discussed here. In [7], the motivation for analysis is also the design of a special-purpose processor architecture for FCP. Program execution is analyzed at the host machine level using the Unix *gprof* profiling tools to determine time consuming events of the emulator. These results depend on the implementation on which the analysis was performed. In [16], an analysis of AND-parallel committed-choice execution of FGHC is compared to the OR-parallel uncommitted-choice execution of Aurora, running on the same multiprocessor machine. Program analysis is performed at the abstract machine level but the main emphasis is at the machine-level. Since both FGHC and Aurora are being optimized on the same multiprocessor machine, low-level analysis is meaningful.

Our approach for performance analysis differs from the two previously described. With the work described in [7] we share the motivation but not the approach, since our analysis is only at the abstract machine level rather than being machine dependent. With the analysis performed in [16] we share the approach but not the motivation, since we are concerned with a special-purpose processor architecture. Our work differs from both approaches in the selection of the workload which is representative of an existing working environment.

Several features of FCP program execution are given special attention in this paper. In Section 2 we characterize the dynamic behavior of goals, including goal creation, termination and asynchronous communication via goal suspension and data-driven activation. We reaffirm the suggestion made in [6] that the complexity and frequency of goal suspension and activation is a potential source of implementation inefficiency. We quantify our results using metrics that describe the frequency and complexity of goal management. Our measurements indicate that the Systems Development Workload exhibits a degree of goal management activity higher than previously observed in simple applications. These results motivate special-purpose architectural support for goal management [2].

In Section 3 we present selected characteristics of dynamic goal reduction. We evaluate the degree of redundant clause selection performed during clause-head matching. Quantifying redundant clause selection is important to understand the potential for performance improvement available if advanced clause-indexing compilation techniques are applied. Our measurements indicate that an average of 77% of all clause-tries are redundant in the considered workload.

2 The Dynamic Behavior of Goals in FCP

FCP is a parallel programming language with ***goals*** as the main unit of concurrency. Goals are analogous to ***processes*** in a multiprocessing system [13], ***objects*** in an object-oriented system, or concurrent ***threads*** of program control [4]. The execution of a goal is referred to as ***goal reduction***. A goal reduction may result in the creation of new goals, it may communicate with

	FCP Benchmark Programs						
	Cmp	Siml	Sim2	Dbg	Slv	Distr	Logix
Create	1890235	1133169	2501064	573869	156491	104799	477568
Halt	1887576	1131614	2499518	572005	155306	97184	474729
Suspend	887590	1892561	2513692	502659	52448	83315	306450
Activate	884945	1891022	2512160	500816	51277	75714	303625

Table 2: Goal Management Statistics

other goals using shared logical variables as communication channels, or terminate execution. FCP program execution consists of the non-deterministic reduction of concurrent goals.

The behavior of a goal is described using a set of guarded clauses. If more than one clause has a guard that is satisfied, program execution commits to any one clause, and disregards all alternatives. This aspect of FCP program execution is referred to as ***committed-choice*** execution. Goals defined in the body of a clause share data such as logical variables, lists, integers, or more complex structures. A logical variable is used to denote one object at a time, including other logical variables. If two (or more) goals share a logical variable, only one goal may be the producer of the value, while the other goal(s) can only receive the value. To control the access to shared logical variables, suspension rules are defined. In FCP, the user can annotate shared variables using the read-only operator '?'. A goal with variable *X?* can only read its value, while the goal that has the writable occurrence of *X* can assign a value. If a goal that has the read-only variable attempts to use the value before it is available, it will suspend waiting for that value. Other implicit suspension rules have been defined that do not require user annotation [14]. In general, a goal ***suspends*** if there is insufficient data to perform successful goal-head unification whereas the reduction may succeed when the data becomes available. In the FCP abstract machine, goal suspension is implemented using ***suspension lists*** associated with each suspending variable. Data-driven activation is implemented by rescheduling the suspended goals when the suspending variables receive data.

There are several outcomes of a goal reduction which we refer to as its ***dynamic*** behavior. A goal may ***create*** new goals, ***terminate*** execution, ***suspend*** if there is insufficient data to complete a goal reduction, and a goal is ***activated*** when the data is available. In the FCP abstract machine, goals are spawned at the end of the goal queue, except for the left-most goal in the clause which is used for iteration. For this scheduling policy, in Table 2 we show the total number of goals created, terminated, suspended and activated, and in Table 1 the total number of reductions. To better characterize the dynamic behavior of FCP goals we define the following three parameters. The average number of reductions (ANR) of a goal is the number of goal reductions per created goal; the average suspension rate

(ASR) is the number of suspensions per goal reduction; and the average goal management activity (AGM) is the number of goal creations, terminations, suspensions and activations per goal reduction.

In table 3, we show these parameters for the selected programs. For each parameter we compute the average value (Ave), the standard deviation (SD) and the coefficient of variation (CV). An average of 2.9 goal reductions are performed prior to goal termination. Therefore, in terms of goal reductions, one can characterize the workload as consisting of ***light weight*** or ***short-lived*** computations that iterate on the average just over three reductions prior to termination. The average goal suspension rate, ASR, varies more significantly, with the mean value equal to 0.27 suspensions per reduction, and the coefficient of variation 0.56. In other words, a goal suspends every 3.7 reductions. The benchmarks used in [16] recorded a smaller value for the suspension rate, that is, between 0 and 0.09. Whereas this value is closer to the characteristic behavior of the *Compiler* program, the Systems Development workload exhibits 3 times their maximum value. The average goal management activity per goal reduction, AGM, is evaluated to be 1.3 goal management operations per reduction. The high degree of goal management activity motivates architectural support in a special-purpose processor. Later in this paper, we will briefly review the approach proposed in [2].

Active Goal Queue

We now consider the distribution of the size of the goal queue used for scheduling ready goals. This distribution indicates the number of goals that could be shared and reduced concurrently in a parallel implementation. However, since the reducible goals differ in size and complexity, one can not simply correlate the size of the active queue with the degree of parallelism available in the program. Moreover, there are data dependencies between the goals that share logical variables, so some of the ready goals may in fact suspend if scheduled immediately.

In Figure 1 we show the distribution of the active queue size for values between 0 and 30. For all programs the maximum value of the distribution is less than 10. In Table 4 we show the maximum queue size, the average queue size and the percentage of the queue size distribution (R) not accounted for

	FCP Benchmark Programs							Workload		
	Cmp	Sim1	Sim2	Dbg	Slv	Distr	Logix	Ave	SD	CV
ANR	3.7	2.6	3.1	2.8	2.6	2.5	3.1	2.9	0.4	0.1
ASR	0.1	0.6	0.3	0.3	0.1	0.3	0.2	0.3	0.2	0.6
AGM	0.8	2.0	1.3	1.3	1.3	1.2	1.1	1.3	0.3	0.2

Table 3: Goal Management Parameters

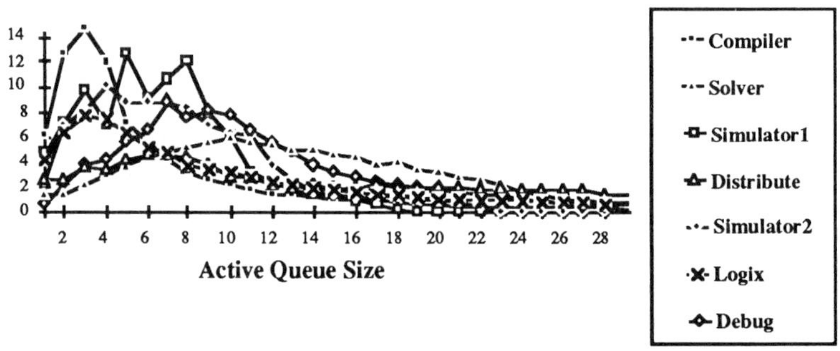

Figure 1: Distribution of FCP Active Queue Size

	FCP Benchmark Programs							Workload		
	Cmp	Sim1	Sim2	Dbg	Slv	Distr	Logix	Ave	SD	CV
Max	3195	72	56	50	51	148	200	538	1085	2
R (%)	10	0.2	0.8	1.2	2.4	24	20.5	8.5	9.3	1.1
Ave	6	7	8	11	13	10	7.5	9	2.3	0.3
SD	5.8	3.6	4.8	5.9	6.7	7.9	6.9			
CV	1	0.5	0.6	0.5	0.5	0.8	0.9			

Table 4: FCP Active Queue Size

in Figure 1. The *Compiler* program reached a maximum queue size of 3195, whereas other programs had values between 50 and 200. Despite the large number of spawned goals in all the programs, the average active queue size ranges from 6 to 13. The selected FCP programs are not known for their parallelism nor was data chosen to increase concurrency. The potential parallelism shown in Figure 1 and Table 4 are only due to the FCP programming model. The workload average for the active goal queue size is 9, with a standard deviation from the average being 2.3, and a coefficient of variation equal to 0.25. If we assume that the granularity of all goal reductions is of the same order of magnitude, the general observation is that the average active goal queue size for the Systems Development Workload implies that small scale parallelism is appropriate.

Goal Suspension Complexity, N_{susp}

Goal suspension occurs after it is determined that a set of value-to-variable assignments satisfy the ***suspension rules***. A goal may suspend on more than one variable, and more than one goal may suspend on a single variable. The complexity of the goal suspension mechanism is proportional to the num-

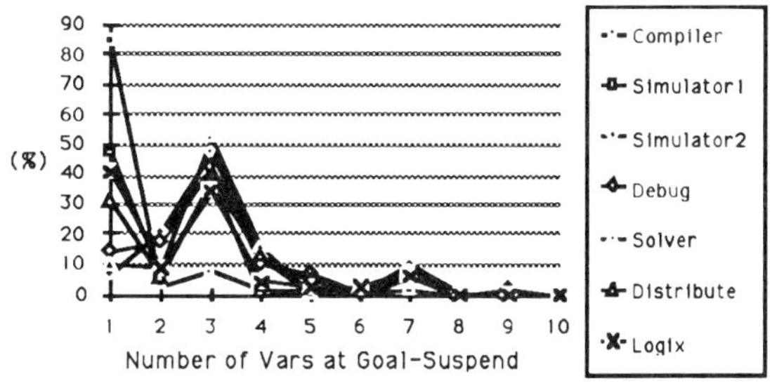

Figure 2: Distribution of the Number of Suspension Variables

ber of variables a goal suspends on, N_{susp}. For each variable, a ***suspension note*** is allocated and placed on the suspension list. In Figure 2 we show the distribution of the number of variables a goal suspends on during program execution. The results indicate that suspension generally occurs on few variables and that the average number suspension variables per goal suspension for the considered workload is $N_{susp} = 2.6$.

This result is higher than expected. The assumption that suspension occurs mostly on 1 or 2 variables was made by observing small applications that do not exhibit the program complexity characteristic of the workload we consider. However, it may be the case that better programming as well as more advanced compilation techniques will be able to eliminate unnecessary suspensions on more variables. Such compilation techniques are reported in [10], [11],[12]. The complexity of goal suspension is also affected by the goal scheduling policy of the abstract machine. Alternative scheduling policies may have impact on the number of goal suspensions as well as the suspension cost.

In Table 5 we show the total number of goal suspension variables, (the number of goal suspensions is shown in Table 2) the maximum number of variables used during a single goal suspension, the precentage of goal suspension lists of size between one and four, as well as the average number of suspension variables, the standard deviation and the coefficient of variation. Note that the maximum value for the number of suspension variables ranges from 8 to 15. This indicates that the goal suspensions complexity may even be unexpectedly high, which may reduce system performance. However, on the average 89% of all goal suspensions occurred with 4 or less variables. In the abstract machine, a suspension variable table is used to store the addresses of the suspending variables. In the FCP processor architecture described in [1], processor registers are used. In this case, having 4 registers will be sufficient for 89% of all goal suspensions. If there are more than 4 variables during goal suspension, additional space is allocated in memory.

	FCP Benchmark Programs							Workload		
	Cmp	Sim1	Sim2	Dbg	Slv	Distr	Logix	Ave	SD	CV
Max	8	9	12	14	14	10	15	12	3	0.2
(1-4)	0.97	0.9	0.9	0.8	0.9	0.9	0.9	0.9	0.4	0.4
Ave	1.4	2.3	3.3	3.1	3.3	2.8	2.5	2.6	0.6	0.2
SD	1	1.6	1.6	1.7	1.5	1.7	1.7			
CV	0.8	0.7	0.5	0.5	0.5	0.6	0.7			

Table 5: Suspending Variables at Goal Suspension

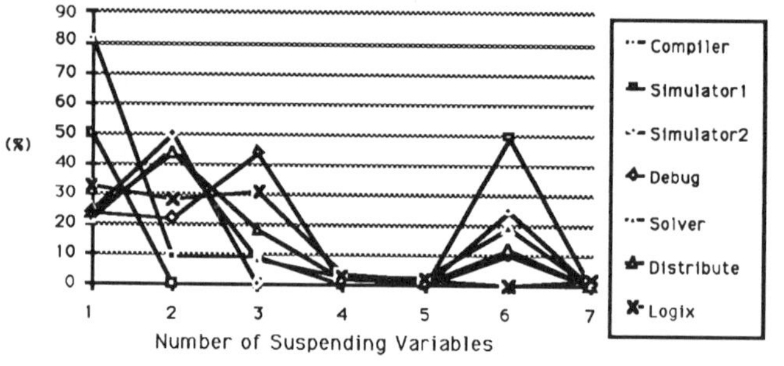

Figure 3: Distribution of Goals Suspension Variables at Clause-Commit

Redundant Suspension Note Allocation

A clause-try that suspends does not immediately result in the suspension of the goal since there may be another clause that can succeed. The goal suspension mechanism used in the sequential abstract machine allocates suspension notes as if the clause-try will suspend. If it does not suspend, the allocated notes are ***redundant*** (R), and are discarded. We refer to the suspension notes allocated during a clause-try that results in goal suspension as ***essential*** (E).

In Figure 3 we show the distribution of the number of goal suspension variables in the non-empty suspension table when there is a clause to commit to. In Table 6 we show that an average of 95% of all clause-commits occurred without allocating redundant suspension notes. The average number of suspension notes allocated per clause-suspension is 2.5, and the maximum number is 7. Of all the allocated suspension notes (E+R), 16% were redundantly allocated. An optimization of the suspension algorithm allocates suspension notes only after goal suspension is determined. This change has already been integrated into the abstract machine as a result of this analysis.

	FCP Benchmark Programs							Workload		
	Cmp	Sim1	Sim2	Dbg	Slv	Distr	Logix	Ave	SD	CV
Empty	0.98	0.9	0.9	0.9	0.97	0.95	0.97	0.95	0.3	0.3
R/(E+R)	0.1	0.16	0.16	0.2	0.2	0.1	0.2	0.16	0.1	0.8
Max	3	6	6	6	6	6	7	5.7	1.2	0.2
Ave	1.3	3.5	2.8	2.6	2.8	2.5	2.3	2.5	1.6	0.6
SD	0.6	2.5	1.9	1.4	1.8	1.5	1			
CV	0.5	0.7	0.7	0.5	0.6	0.6	0.4			

Table 6: Suspending Variables at Clause-Commit

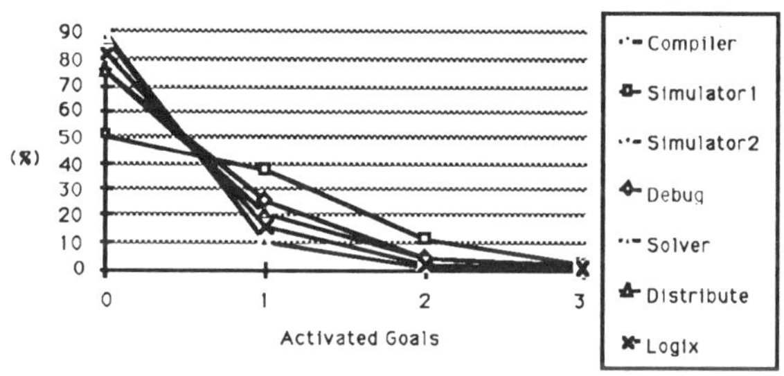

Figure 4: Distribution of the Number of Goals Activated at Clause-Commit

Goal Activation Complexity, N_{act}

Suspended goals are activated upon a successful clause-head unification and guard evaluation, that is, after a clause commits. When a clause-try succeeds, all variables that received new assignments and have goals suspended waiting for these values, are activated. The complexity of goal activation is proportional to the number of goals activated, N_{act}. In Figure 4 we show the distribution of the number of activated goals at clause-commit. In most cases, a clause-commit will not activate any goal. Either there were no new assignments made during the clause-head unification and guard evaluation, or, if there were assignments made, there were no goals suspended waiting for these values.

In Table 7 we show that the average number of goals activated per non-empty clause-commit is $N_{act} = 1.2$. However, the maximum number of goals activated may be unexpectedly high. In the ***Logix*** program the maximum number of goals activated was 142 and in ***Compiler*** 192. In the FCP abstract machine, activated goals are placed at the end of the goal queue. An alternative is to favor goals that have just received data and to schedule them at the front of the queue. This may result in less frequent goal suspensions.

	FCP Benchmark Programs							Workload		
	Cmp	Sim1	Sim2	Dbg	Slv	Distr	Logix	Ave	SD	CV
Max	192	12	23	10	4	20	142	72	72	1
Ave	1.1	1.3	1.3	1.2	1.1	1.2	1.2	1.2	0.1	0.1
SD	0.03	0.05	0.06	0.05	0.03	0.04	0.04			
CV	0.03	0.04	0.05	0.04	0.03	0.03	0.04			

Table 7: Activated Goals at Clause-Commit

2.1 Support for Goal Management

The dynamic goal management behavior of the Systems Development Workload exhibits a complexity higher than reported in previous performance evaluations of simple applications. However, our measurements were performed for one scheduling policy, where iteration is performed on the left-most goal, and the remaing goals in the clause-body as well as newly activated goals are spawned at the end of the goal queue. It would be interesting to consider how the goal management behavior depends on alternative goal scheduling policies.

Nevertheless, the previously described complexity and frequency of goal management operations motivate the use of architectural support in a special-purpose environment. In [3], the overlapped execution of goal management and goal reduction is described. The efficient execution of goal management operations is performed using a separate Goal Management Unit and a Goal Cache as part of the special-purpose processor [2]. The goal management operations **halt**, **spawn**, **suspend** and **commit** are decoupled from goal reduction instructions, and overlapped in the Goal Management Unit. The Goal Cache is used to store recently spawned goals in fixed-sized goal-windows. Switching and scheduling goals from the Goal Cache is efficiently implemented by manipulating goal window pointers and status bits. The overlapped execution mechanism allows only one goal mangement instruction to be overlapped at a time. Therefore, a delay results if a second goal management instruction is encountered before the previous one completes. Otherwise, all goal management instructions execute concurrently with the execution of goal reduction instructions.

A detailed performance analysis of overlapped goal management execution for the Systems Development Workload, shows that almost all of the goal management operations can overlap with goal reduction, without significant delay. This resulted in a speedup of almost two. However, it is also shown that other workloads that have a higher complexity of goal managment, that is, higher ratio of goal management granularity to goal reduction granularity, result in speedups greater than two when overlapped using the Goal Management Unit and Goal Cache [2].

3 Goal Reduction Statistics

The reduction of a goal consists of attempting to find a clause in the program that can be used for further program continuation. In the FCP abstract machine, clause-tries are performed sequentially. Each clause-try consists of matching (unifying) the individual arguments of the goal with arguments in the clause. The unification procedure consists of first dereferencing each argument, and then performing specific operations depending on the dereferenced argument type. If, during unification, varaiables are assigned values, these values are ***trailed***, just in case the clause-try does not commit. In case of clause-try failure or suspension, the trail stack is used to undo all assignments to memory. In this paper we present the following selected results that describe goal reduction:

- The number of ***redundant*** clause-tries prior to a clause-commit.
- The average number of arguments in the scheduled goal reductions.
- The average length of the dereference chain.
- The distribution of dereferenced data types.
- The amount of variable trailing performed during each clause-try.

The number of clause-tries prior to a commit indicates the degree of searching (shallow-backtracking) taking place before a successful clause-try is found. Improving the search strategy using clause-indexing techniques is an active area of research [10],[11],[12]. The average number of arguments in a scheduled goal helps determine the fixed size of goal templates used in the abstract machine, and in the fixed-sized goal windows used in the Goal Cache of a special-purpose processor [1]. Since the goal size (N) is known to the compiler, a goal that has $(M > N)$ arguments is represented by having the Nth argument denote a compacted set of $(M - N)$ arguments. Argument dereferencing is a common operation in logic programming languages. In [7], it is reported that 22% of the execution time is spent performing the dereference operation. We also determine the distribution of dereferenced data types useful to a probabilistic branch prediction strategy. In [7] it is reported that all of the data types are of similar probability. Finally, we analyze in detail clause-trailing since other similar languages like Parlog and GHC do not have trailing. Moreover, trailing is often cited as a potential source of performance degradation.

Redundant Clause Selection

We consider ***useful*** clause-tries to be all clause-tries that result in goal reduction and all clause-suspensions that result in goal suspension. Therefore,

	FCP Benchmark Programs							Workload		
	Cmp	Sim1	Sim2	Dbg	Slv	Distr	Logix	Ave	SD	CV
CR/CT	0.35	0.16	0.16	0.21	0.09	0.10	0.25	0.18	0.1	0.5
CF/CT	0.50	0.19	0.51	0.39	0.84	0.69	0.49	0.52	0.2	0.4
CS/CT	0.10	0.65	0.33	0.39	0.07	0.20	0.26	0.29	0.2	0.6
GS/CS	0.37	0.15	0.15	0.17	0.16	0.15	0.20	0.19	0.1	0.4
GS/CT	0.04	0.10	0.05	0.07	0.01	0.03	0.05	0.05	0.0	0.5
F^r_{ct}	0.60	0.74	0.79	0.82	0.90	0.87	0.69	0.77	0.1	0.13

Table 8: Clause-Try Statistics

all clause-failures and all clause-suspensions that result in goal reduction are ***redundant*** clause-tries. Since the total number of clause tries, CT, is equal to the sum of the clause reductions, failures and clause suspensions, ($CT = CR + CF + CS$), and if GS denotes the total number of goal suspensions, the fraction of redundant clause-tries, F^r_{ct} is expressed as:

$$F^r_{ct} = 1 - (\frac{CR}{CT} + \frac{GS}{CT}) \tag{1}$$

In Table 8 we show the number of reductions per clause-try CR/CT, goal suspensions per clause-try GS/CT, clause-suspension per clause-try CS/CT, clause-failures per clause-try CF/CT, as well as goal suspensions per clause-suspension GS/CS. The average number of redundant clauses selected is as high as $F^r_{ct} = 77\%$ for the Systems Development Workload.

It seems, at first, counter intuitive that a goal reduction performs an average of more than 50% of all clause-tries trying to commit. However, in the FCP abstract machine clauses are tried sequentially, and before a goal can suspend, all of the clauses must be tried to make sure that none of them can commit. It is precisely this issue of the large overhead of the redundant clause-selection that is addressed in the decision-tree (decision-graphs) compilation techniques proposed in [10].

FCP Goal Arguments

In Figure 5 we show the distribution of the number of goal arguments found in the selected FCP benchmarks. The goal size indicates the number of arguments and does not include the program counter (or perhaps some other system parameters that may be stored as part of a goal).

In Table 9 we also show the total number of allocated arguments, the maximum number of arguments found in a single goal and the average number of arguments per created goal. From the distribution of the number of goal arguments shown in Figure 5 we see that most goals have less than 7 arguments. Whereas the maximum number of goal arguments is between

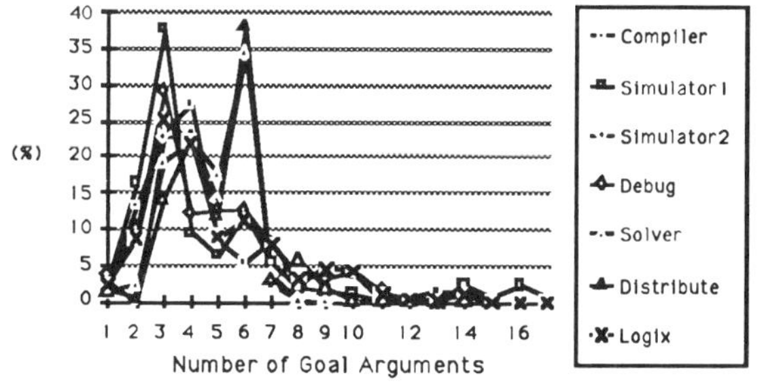

Figure 5: Distribution of the Number of Goal Arguments

	FCP Benchmark Programs							Workload		
	Cmp	Sim1	Sim2	Dbg	Slv	Distr	Logix	Ave	SD	CV
Max	14	17	14	14	14	14	14	15	1.2	0.1
1-8 (%)	88.5	92	99.9	91	99.7	98	89	94	4.6	0.1
Ave	4.9	4.5	4.6	4.7	4.7	5.1	4.9	4.8	0.2	0.0
SD	2.8	2.6	1.4	2.3	1.4	1.6	2.5			
CV	0.6	0.6	0.3	0.5	0.3	0.3	0.5			

Table 9: Goal Arguments

14 and 17, they occur very rarely. For the Systems Development Workload, the average maximum number of arguments is 15, whereas the average number arguments is close to 5. This average is also quite similar for all of the benchmark programs.

Also shown in Table 9 is the percentage of all goal reductions that had 8 or less goal arguments. On the average, this was in 94% of the cases. If we consider that a goal record also contains (besides goal arguments) the program counter (PC) and a time slice value (TS), then a goal record size of 10 words is sufficient for 94% of the spawned goals.

Argument Dereferencing

Goal head unification consist of matching arguments in the calling goal with the corresponding arguments of a called goal. A goal argument is denoted as a reference to a program data structure or as a reference to another reference. An argument reference is ***dereferenced*** prior to matching. This consists of following the chain of pointers until a non reference is encountered. It is performed not only during goal-head unification for matching goal arguments, but also prior to the assignment of a value to a variable.

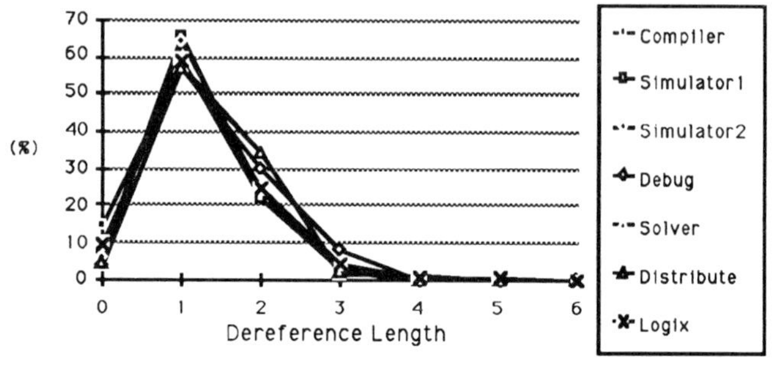

Figure 6: Distribution of Dereference Length

	FCP Benchmark Programs							Workload		
	Cmp	Sim1	Sim2	Dbg	Slv	Distr	Logix	Ave	SD	CV
$\frac{L}{D}$	1.3	2.5	2.8	1.7	2.0	2.7	1.9	2.1	0.5	0.2
$\frac{D}{CT}$	4.3	3.9	3.6	9.1	3.1	3.3	4.4	4.5	1.9	0.4

Table 10: Dereferencing Statistics

In Figure 6 we show the distribution of the dereference chain length, which are mostly less than 3. In Table 10 we show the ratio of the total length of the dereference chain (L) and the number of dereference calls (D). The average dereference length per dereference call is equal to 2.1. This value is higher than reported in [7] (average of 1.2) where simpler FCP programs were measured. However, in the Systems Development Workload, very large dereference chains can be created. For example, the repeated ***variable-to-variable*** unification used to implement the ***short-circuit*** technique of program termination detection results in long dereference chains. In the sampled programs, the maximum dereference length reached 400 and more.

In Table 10 we show that the average number of dereference calls per clause-try (D/CT) is equal to 4.5. Since arguments can be complex data structures, each argument unification may result in several dereference calls. However, a clasue-try does not attempt to unify arguments (which includes dereferencing) if the unification of the previous arguments fails. On the average, the number of dereference calls per clause-try is approximately equal to the average number of arguments in a scheduled goal (4.8).

One solution to lengthy dereference chains is to shorten references. That is, a dereference operation could be followed by an assignment operation that would assign the final dereference location to the intial reference pointer. This has as an overhead the additional memory access, but, it will result in shorter dereference lengths. However, in a special-purpose system, reference shortenning can be overlapped with dereferencing, and can be considered as

	FCP Benchmark Programs							Workload		
	Cmp	Sim1	Sim2	Dbg	Slv	Distr	Logix	Ave	SD	CV
Var	23	32	32	21	37	38	30	30	6	21
RO Var	5	12	11	5	3	7	8	7	3	46
Int	17	5	4	4	7	5	10	7	5	66
Real	0	0	0	0	0	0	0	0	0	0
Str	15	16	16	23	13	14	16	16	3	20
Nil	3	1	1	2	1	1	2	2	1	41
Car Ref	13	6	7	10	4	5	7	7	3	50
Car Int	7	1	2	2	0	0	5	2	2	100
Car Nil	0	0	0	0	0	0	0	0	0	0
Tuple	16	26	24	32	35	30	20	26	6	30
Vector	1	1	1	2	0	2	1	2	3	130

Table 11: Distribution of Dereferenced Data Types (%)

a way to reduce the average execution time of the dereference operation.

Branching on Dereference Types

Dereferencing an argument is followed by a polymorphic operation. To see the ***spectrum*** of dereferenced data types, we show in Table 11 their dynamic distribution. The most frequently dereferenced data structures in the Systems Development Workload are the logical variable (Var) (30%), the tuple (Tup) (26.3%), and the string (Str) (16%) data types. Therefore, for the Systems Development Workload it is clear that not all of the data types are dereferenced equally often. The variable, tuple and string data types account for an average of 72% of all the dereferenced data objects. A multiway branch prediction strategy, or the choice of a tag code, may make use of this uneven data type distribution.

Clause Trailing

The bindings produced during a clause-try that succeeds are correctly visible to the programming environment. However, if a clause-try fails or suspends, the assignments must be undone so that a new clause-try starts with the same memory state that preceded the clause-try. It is for this reason that the assignments to memory are trailed during a clause-try. This is referred to as ***clause-trailing***, and consists of pushing the address and previous value of a trailed variable into a stack. In case of clause-try failure or suspension, the entries are poped from the stack, and the old memory state is restored. We distinguish three cases of clause trailing, depending on whether a clause-try succeeds, suspends or fails. In Figure 7 we show the distribution of the trail size at clause-commit. In most programs the trail size is less than 7

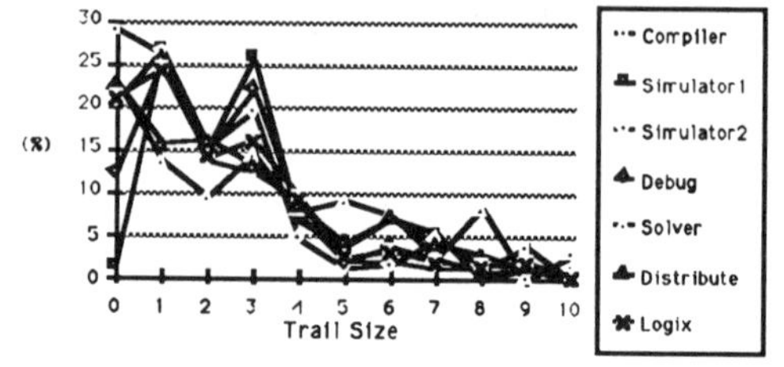

Figure 7: Distribution of Trail Size at Clause-Commit

Figure 8: Distribution of Trail Size at Clause-Suspend

entries, and in Table 12 we show the average number of trailed entries to be 5. Note that the maximum number of trailed entries is a high as 163 for the ***Distribute*** program, whereas the average maximum for the workload is 63.

In Figure 8 we show the distribution of the trail size at clause-suspend. It is similar for all the selected programs and in most cases is less than 4 entries. In Table 12 we show the maximum and average size of the trail. Compared to a clause-try that commits, the trail size is significantly smaller, with the average being 1.4, and the average maximum 29. This can be explained as follows. A clause-try that commits must perform complete goal-head unification that includes all of the arguments in the clause, where the unification of each pair of arguments may require trailing. Moreover, only the committing clause is the one communicating variable bindings into the programming environment, and the suspending clause is the one expecting bindings. So, from a programming point of view, it seems that less trailing can be expected in suspending clauses compared to committing clauses. Note that the averge trail size at clause-commit is close to the average number of arguments in a clause. Even though clause arguments may consist of

	FCP Benchmark Programs							Workload		
	Cmp	Sim1	Sim2	Dbg	Slv	Distr	Logix	Ave	SD	CV
Trailing at Clause-Commit										
Max	36	47	22	35	54	163	87	63	45	0.7
Ave	3.4	6.8	4.7	6.1	5.6	5.5	4.6	5	1	0.2
SD	2.6	4.2	3.2	4	3.6	3.6	3			
CV	0.8	0.6	0.7	0.7	0.6	0.7	0.7			
Trailing at Clause-Suspend										
Max	12	16	18	21	21	26	92	29	27	1
Ave	1.1	1.1	1.2	1.6	1.5	1.7	1.4	1.4	0.2	0.2
SD	0.6	0.5	0.6	1.5	1.3	1	1.1			
CV	0.5	0.5	0.5	1	0.8	0.6	0.8			
Trailing at Clause-Fail										
Max	38	10	12	20	46	18	81	32	24	0.7
Ave	0.2	0.4	0.5	0.4	0.9	0.8	0.5	0.5	0.2	0.5
SD	0.7	1	0.7	0.9	0.5	0.6	1			
CV	3.7	3	1.4	2.3	0.6	0.7	2.1			

Table 12: Trailing at Clause Commit, Suspend and Fail

nested data structures that require several trailings, improved compilation techniques may reduce the amount of trailing.

In Figure 9 we show the distribution of the trail size at clause-failure. In most cases it is less than 2 entries. In Table 12 we can see that the average trail size is 0.5, however the average maximum number of trailed variable assignments is 32. The amount of trailing for a clause-try that fails is significantly smaller than during a clause-try that commits or suspends since the complete clause-try is aborted as soon as the unification of a pair of arguments fail.

From the distributions of the trail sizes during a clause-try one can con-

Figure 9: Trailing at Clause-Failure

clude the following. Most trailing occurs in clause-tries than succeed. In fact, an order of magnitude more than during the clause-tries that fail. In other words, most clause-tries fail before they require much trailing and clause-tries that suspend, perform less trailing that clasue-tries that succeed. This implies that even if one could reduce the number of clause-tries that fail or suspend, (for example using better indexing techniques), the majority of trailing would remain during the clause-tries that result in clause-commit.

4 Conclusion

The motivation for the performance analysis presented in this paper is the design of a special-purpose processor architecture for the efficient execution of FCP. The analysis is performed at the abstract machine level by instrumenting the existing FCP abstract machine emulator. We define a specific Systems Development Workload that consists of seven large programs used during the prototyping of new systems. The workload is representative of an existing working environment. We conclude that the complexity and frequency of goal management activity for the specific workload is higher when compared to previously used benchmarks. These results motivate special-purpose architectural support for goal management operations halt, spawn, suspend and activate. Our measurements also show that there is a high degree of redundant clause-selection performed (77%); the average dereference length is larger due to the ***short-circuit*** programming technique used for termination detection; and an average of 5 variables are trailed during clause-tries that commit. These results further motivate the need for advanced clause-indexing techniques, dereference shortening and compilation techniques to avoid unnecessary trailing.

References

[1] L. Alkalaj. Architectural Support for Concurrent Logic Programming Languages. Doctoral Dissertation UCLA/CSD 890047, University of California, Los Angeles, June 1989.

[2] L. Alkalaj, T. Lang, and M. Ercegovac. Architectural Support for Tightly-Coupled Fine-Grain Goals in Flat Concurrent Prolog. In *Proceedings of the 17th International Symposium on Computer Architecture*, pages 292–301, May 1990.

[3] L. Alkalaj and E. Shapiro. An Architectural Model for a Flat Concurrent Prolog Processor. In *Proceedings of the 5th International Conference/Symposium on Logic Programming*, pages 1277–1297, August 1988.

[4] E. C. Cooper and R. P. Draves. C Threads. Technical Report CMU-CS-88-154, Carnegie Mellon University, June 1988.

[5] D. Ferrari. Workload Characterization of Tightly-Coupled and Loosley-Coupled Systems. In *Proceedings of the 1989 ACM SIGMETRICS and PERFORMANCE 89*, page 210, May 1989.

[6] I. Foster and S. Taylor. Flat Parlog: A Basis for Comparison. *International Journal of Parallel Programming*, 16(2), 1987.

[7] R. Ginosar and A. Harsat. Profiling LOGIX: A Step Towards a Flat Concurrent Prolog Processor. EE Pub. Technical Report No. 617, Technion Institute of Technology, Haifa, January 1987.

[8] S. Gregory. *Parallel Logic Programming in PARLOG, The Language and its Implementation*. Addison-Wesley, 1987.

[9] A. Houri and E. Shapiro. The Sequential Abstract Machine for Flat Concurrent Prolog. *Journal of Logic Programming*, (7):85–123, 1989.

[10] S. Kliger. Towards a Native Code Compiler for Flat Concurrent Prolog. Master's Thesis CS 87, Weizmann Institute of Science, Applied Mathematics Department, July 1987.

[11] S. Kliger and E. Shapiro. A Decision Tree Compilation Algorithm for FCP(:,?). In *Proceedings of the 5th International Conference/Symposium on Logic Programming*, pages 1315 – 1336, Aug 1988.

[12] S. Kliger and E. Shapiro. From Decision Trees to Decision Graphs. In *Proceedings of the North American Conference on Logic Programming*, October 1990.

[13] E. Shapiro. Concurrent Prolog: A Progress Report. *IEEE Computer*, 18(6):76 – 92, August 1986.

[14] E. Shapiro. The Family of Concurrent Logic Programming Languages. *ACM Computing Surveys*, 21(3):412–510, September 1989.

[15] W. Silverman, M. Hirsch, A. Houri, and E. Shapiro. The Logix System User Manual. TR CS 21, Weizmann Institute of Science, Applied Mathematics Department, Nov. 1988.

[16] E. Tick. Comparing Two ParallelLogic-Programming Architectures. *IEEE Software*, 6(4):71–80, July 1989.

[17] K. Ueda. Guarded Horn Clauses. Doctoral dissertation, University of Tokyo, March 1986.

Partial Evaluation

A Partial Evaluation Procedure for Logic Programs

Kerima Benkerimi
John W. Lloyd
Department of Computer Science
University of Bristol
University Walk
Bristol BS8 1TR
kerima@compsci.bristol.ac.uk
jwl@compsci.bristol.ac.uk

Abstract

This paper presents a procedure for the partial evaluation of normal logic programs. Partial evaluation is a transformation technique which, given a normal program P and a normal goal G, produces from P a partially evaluated program P' wrt G. P' is generally more efficient than P in running G. We propose a procedure that guarantees the computational equivalence of P and P' by ensuring that simple syntactic conditions, called the coveredness and independence conditions, are satisfied. We give various computation rules for partial evaluation. Finally, to increase the efficiency of partially evaluated programs, we propose a pre-processing stage which introduces new predicate symbols into the original program P in such a way as to preserve the computational equivalence of P and the transformed program. The transformed program is then partially evaluated instead of P.

1 Introduction

Partial evaluation has attracted great interest in recent years. It was first introduced into Computer Science as an optimisation technique in [5]. In general terms, partial evaluation consists of deriving a specialised version of a program wrt some known input data. Based on this principle, partial evaluators for a variety of applications have been built, all with the same motivation for optimisation. In the functional programming community, interesting results have been obtained using partial evaluation as a systematic method for the generation of compilers and compiler-generators. (See, for example, [7], [8], and [12].) For the logic programming community, partial evaluation has been particularly fruitful when applied to meta-programming. (See, for example, [4] and [15].) In this application, an interpreter is specialised with respect to an object program. The result is a new program with the functionality of the interpreter embedded in it and the extra level of interpretation removed. If the partial evaluator is self-applicable, then it can be used to specialise itself with respect to an interpreter to produce a compiler.

Although some partial evaluators have been put into practice, most of them are experimental and semi-automatic, i.e., require some human assistance in one way or another. One goal of partial evaluation is the production of fully automated partial evaluators, for which the following are important issues.

1. Input data to a program is usually given as partially instantiated arguments in a goal. A partial search tree is constructed for the program and the goal. During this construction, according to certain criteria, atoms are either unfolded or not unfolded. Controlling the process of unfolding is an important task of partial evaluation and it is also one that usually requires human assistance.

2. For some programs, partial evaluation can lead to an exponential explosion of the amount of generated code. Keeping this code to a reasonable size is another issue of partial evaluation. In this respect, recent work in [11] and [14] investigates transformations such as folding and goal replacement [16], which turn out to be useful in reducing the size of the search tree.

More recently, certain theoretical issues have been raised. In [10], the soundness and completeness of partially evaluated normal programs is investigated. *Soundness* of the partially evaluated program P' wrt the original program P and the goal G for the declarative (resp., procedural) semantics means that correct (computed) answers for G and P' are correct (computed) answers for G and P. *Completeness* is the converse of this. In [10], it is shown that partial evaluation for definite programs and goals is always sound, but may not be complete. For normal programs, partial evaluation is found to be, in general, not only incomplete, but also unsound. Two conditions are isolated, the coveredness and independence conditions, under which the programs P and P' are procedurally equivalent wrt G, that is, any answer computed by P wrt G is also computed by P' wrt G, and conversely.

In this paper, we present a procedure for the partial evaluation of normal programs which ensures that the coveredness and independence conditions are satisfied. Furthermore, to increase the efficiency of partially evaluated programs, we define a program transformation which introduces new predicate symbols into the original program P and prove the computational equivalence of P and the transformed program. The transformed program is then partially evaluated instead of P.

An outline of this paper is as follows. In the next section, we introduce the basic concepts of partial evaluation needed throughout. In the third section, we describe the partial evaluation procedure and prove its correctness. We also give various computation rules for partial evaluation. In the fourth section, we introduce the renaming transformation. Finally, we give some conclusions and topics for further research.

2 Basic Concepts of Partial Evaluation

Before presenting the partial evaluation procedure, we give the basic concepts of partial evaluation. Knowledge of the basic theory of logic programming, as can be found in [9], is assumed. In the sequel, Q, subscripted or not, denotes a conjunction of literals.

Definition A *program clause* (resp., *definite program clause*) is a clause of the form

$A \leftarrow L_1, \ldots, L_n$

where A is an atom and $L_1, \ldots, L_n$ are literals (resp., atoms).

Definition A *normal program* (resp., *definite program*) is a finite set of program clauses (resp., definite program clauses).

Definition A *normal goal* (resp., *definite goal*) is a clause of the form

$\leftarrow L_1, \ldots, L_n$

where $L_1, \ldots, L_n$ are literals (resp., atoms).

Definition The *definition* of a predicate symbol p in a normal program P is the set of all program clauses in P which have p in their head.

The following definitions were introduced in [10].

Definition A *resultant* is a first order formula of the form $Q_1 \leftarrow Q_2$, where Q_i is either absent or a conjunction of literals ($i = 1, 2$). Any variables in Q_1 or Q_2 are assumed to be universally quantified at the front of the resultant.

In the following, we will use slightly more general definitions of SLDNF-derivation and SLDNF tree than are given in [9]. In [9], an SLDNF-derivation is either infinite, successful or failed. Here we will also allow it to be *incomplete*, in the sense that at any point we are allowed to simply not select any literal and terminate the derivation. Similar remarks apply to the definition of SLDNF-tree employed here.

Definition Let P be a normal program, G a normal goal $\leftarrow Q$, and $G_0 = G, G_1, \ldots, G_n$ an SLDNF-derivation of $P \cup \{G\}$, where the sequence of substitutions is $\theta_1, \ldots, \theta_n$ and G_n is $\leftarrow Q_n$. Let θ be the restriction of $\theta_1 \ldots \theta_n$ to the variables in G. Then we say the derivation has *length* n with *computed answer* θ and *resultant* $Q\theta \leftarrow Q_n$. (If n=0, the *resultant* is $Q \leftarrow Q$.)

Definition Let P be a normal program, A an atom, and T an SLDNF-tree for $P \cup \{\leftarrow A\}$. Let $G_1, \ldots, G_r$ be (non-root) goals in T chosen so that each non-failing branch of T contains exactly one of them. Let R_i ($i = 1, \ldots, r$) be the resultant of the derivation from $\leftarrow A$ down to G_i given by the branch leading to G_i. Then the set of clauses $R_1, \ldots, R_r$ is called a *partial evaluation of A in P*.

If $\mathbf{A} = \{A_1, \ldots, A_s\}$ is a finite set of atoms, then a *partial evaluation of* $\mathbf{A}$ *in* P is the union of partial evaluations of $A_1, \ldots, A_s$ in P.

A *partial evaluation of P wrt* $\mathbf{A}$ is a normal program obtained from P by replacing the set of clauses in P whose head contains one of the predicate symbols appearing in $\mathbf{A}$ (called the *partially evaluated predicates*) by a partial evaluation of $\mathbf{A}$ in P.

Next we give the definitions of the coveredness and independence conditions.

Definition If A and B are atoms and there exists a substitution θ such that $A\theta = B$, then we say B is an *instance* of A or A is *more general* than B.

Definition Let A and B be atoms. We say A and B have a *common instance* if there exists an atom C such that C is an instance of both A and B.

Definition Let $\mathbf{A}$ be a finite set of atoms. We say $\mathbf{A}$ is *independent* if no pair of atoms in $\mathbf{A}$ have a common instance.

Definition Let S be a set of first order formulas and $\mathbf{A}$ a finite set of atoms. We say S is $\mathbf{A}$*-closed* if each atom in S containing a predicate symbol occurring in an atom in $\mathbf{A}$ is an instance of an atom in $\mathbf{A}$.

Definition Let P be a normal program. The *dependency graph* of P is the directed graph in which the nodes are the predicate symbols in P and there is a directed arc from p to q if there exists a clause C in P in which p is the predicate symbol in the head of C and q is the predicate symbol of a literal in the body of C.

Definition Let P be a normal program and G a normal goal. We say G *depends* upon a predicate symbol p in P if there is a path from a predicate symbol in G to p in the dependency graph for P.

Definition Let P be a normal program, G a normal goal, $\mathbf{A}$ a finite set of atoms, P' a partial evaluation of P wrt $\mathbf{A}$, and P^* the subprogram of P' consisting of the definitions of predicate symbols in P' upon which G depends. We say $P' \cup \{G\}$ is $\mathbf{A}$*-covered* if $P^* \cup \{G\}$ is $\mathbf{A}$-closed.

As the following theorem shows, the coveredness and independence conditions are sufficient to ensure the computational equivalence of the original and partially evaluated programs.

Theorem 2.1 *Let P be a normal program, G a normal goal,* $\mathbf{A}$ *a finite, independent set of atoms, and P' a partial evaluation of P wrt* $\mathbf{A}$ *such that $P' \cup \{G\}$ is* $\mathbf{A}$*-covered. Then the following hold.*

1. *$P' \cup \{G\}$ has an SLDNF-refutation with computed answer θ iff $P \cup \{G\}$ does.*

2. *$P' \cup \{G\}$ has a finitely failed SLDNF-tree iff $P \cup \{G\}$ does.*

The proof of theorem 2.1 appears in [10].

In the sequel, we use the following convention to distinguish constants and variables. A variable is denoted by an identifier beginning with a lower case letter, while constants will be denoted by identifiers beginning with an upper case letter.

3 The Partial Evaluation Procedure

When partially evaluating a program, there are two main reasons why it is desirable not to partially evaluate some predicate symbols. The first one is to avoid an explosion of the search trees for certain programs and the second one is to be able to partially evaluate "open" programs (that is, programs for which the definitions of some predicate symbols are missing). For this purpose, we introduce the following definitions.

Definition Let L be a set of predicate symbols. We say a literal is L-*selectable* if its predicate symbol is in L. We say an SLDNF-tree is L-*compatible* if the predicate symbol of each selected literal in the tree (including subsidiary refutations and trees) is in L.

The procedure described below takes as input a normal program P, a normal goal G, and a set L of predicate symbols, and constructs a set $\mathbf{A}$ of atoms and a partially evaluated program P' of P wrt $\mathbf{A}$. It is devised so that the conditions of theorem 2.1 are satisfied, that is, $\mathbf{A}$ is independent and $P' \cup \{G\}$ is $\mathbf{A}$-covered.

In order to construct an independent set $\mathbf{A}$, we require the well-known concept of most specific generalisation (msg).

Definition Let S be a set of atoms. Then an atom A is an *msg* of S if

- for every atom B in S, A is more general than B, and
- if C is an atom more general than each atom in S, then C is more general than A.

It follows from the above definition that, if A_1 and A_2 are any two msg's of S, then they are variants of each other. It is well-known that a non-empty set of atoms has an msg iff all atoms have the same predicate symbol in their heads. The partial evaluation procedure is as follows.

The Partial Evaluation Procedure

Input: a normal program P, a normal goal G, and a set L of predicate symbols.

Output: a set $\mathbf{A}$ of atoms, a partial evaluation $P_{\mathbf{A}}$ of $\mathbf{A}$ in P, and a partial evaluation P' of P wrt $\mathbf{A}$.

```
PA := ∅;
A := {B : B is an L-selectable atom¹ in G};
mark all atoms in A not_partially_evaluated;
while there are atoms in A which are marked not_partially_evaluated do
  begin
    B := any atom in A marked not_partially_evaluated;
    compute a partial evaluation of B in P using an L-compatible SLDNF-
    tree and add the resultants of this partial evaluation to PA;
    mark B partially_evaluated;
    add to A the L-selectable atoms¹ in the bodies of the resultants of this
    partial evaluation and mark such atoms not_partially_evaluated;
    while A not independent do
      begin
        U := any pair of atoms in A having a common instance;
        replace in A the pair U of atoms by their msg;
        if an atom C of the pair U is marked partially_evaluated² then
          if the msg of the pair U is not a variant of C then
            begin
            delete from PA the partial evaluation of C in P;
            mark the msg not_partially_evaluated;
            end;
          else mark the msg partially_evaluated³;
        else mark the msg not_partially_evaluated;
      end;
  end;
P' := the normal program obtained from P by replacing the definition in P
of each partially evaluated predicate symbol by its definition in PA;
```

End Procedure

[1]The atom may appear in a negative literal.

[2]There can be at most one such atom.

[3]The partial evaluation of such an msg is that of C.

In the procedure, it is only necessary to replace a pair of atoms in **A** having a common instance by an atom that subsumes them. However, the msg is suitable for the purpose of partial evaluation because it is the *least* generalisation in common and can easily be computed. A procedure similar to ours for handling definite programs was given in [3].

Next we show the partial correctness of the procedure, that is, if the procedure terminates, then the partially evaluated program produced is procedurally equivalent to the original program for the goal G. To obtain this result, we require a weak condition on L, defined as follows.

Definition Let P be a normal program and L a set of predicate symbols. We say L is *well-structured* wrt P if, whenever $p \in L$ and there exists a path in the dependency graph for P from a predicate symbol q to p, then $q \in L$.

Definition Let G and H be normal goals. We say G *extends* H if every atom in H is an instance of an atom in G.

Theorem 3.1 *Let P a normal program, G and H normal goals such that G extends H, and L a set of predicate symbols well-structured wrt P. Let P' be a partially evaluated program computed from P by the partial evaluation procedure using G and L. Then the following hold.*

1. *$P' \cup \{H\}$ has an SLDNF-refutation with computed answer θ iff $P \cup \{H\}$ does.*
2. *$P' \cup \{H\}$ has a finitely failed SLDNF-tree iff $P \cup \{H\}$ does.*

Proof: Let **A** be the set of atoms and $P_{\mathbf{A}}$ the set of resultants constructed by the partial evaluation procedure when it terminates. We prove that three properties hold.

- $P_{\mathbf{A}}$ is a partial evaluation of **A** in P.

If, during the construction of **A**, an atom in **A** is marked partially_evaluated, its partial evaluation is added to $P_{\mathbf{A}}$. Also, if a pair of atoms in **A** having a common instance is replaced by its msg, an atom B of the pair is marked partially_evaluated, and the msg of the pair is not a variant of B, then the partial evaluation of B is deleted from $P_{\mathbf{A}}$. Thus, when the procedure terminates, $P_{\mathbf{A}}$ is indeed a partial evaluation of **A** in P.

- **A** is independent.

A is independent, since this is the termination condition of the inner loop.

- $P' \cup \{H\}$ is **A**-covered.

We first show by induction on the length n of a path in the dependency graph for P' that, if H depends upon a predicate symbol $p \in L$, then p is a partially evaluated predicate symbol. If $n = 0$, then p is in H. Since $p \in L$ and G extends H, it follows that p is a partially evaluated predicate symbol. Next suppose that there is a path of length $n+1$ from a predicate symbol r in H to p. Let q be the predicate symbol in the head of a clause in P' containing p in the body such that there is a path of length n from r to q. Since L is well-structured wrt P, we have that $q \in L$. Hence, by the induction hypothesis, q is a partially evaluated predicate symbol. Thus, since $p \in L$, it follows that p is a partially evaluated predicate symbol.

Let P^* be the subprogram of P' consisting of the definitions of predicate symbols in P' upon which H depends. We have to show that $P^* \cup \{H\}$ is $\mathbf{A}$-closed. Since G extends H, it is clear that $\{H\}$ is $\mathbf{A}$-closed. Also, since L is well-structured wrt P, it is clear that the set of definitions in P^* of predicate symbols not in L is $\mathbf{A}$-closed. For each of the other clauses in P^*, the predicate symbol in the head is in L and hence, by the first part of the proof, is a partially evaluated predicate symbol. It follows that this set of other clauses in P^* is also $\mathbf{A}$-closed. Hence $P^* \cup \{H\}$ is $\mathbf{A}$-closed and so $P' \cup \{H\}$ is $\mathbf{A}$-covered.

These three properties ensure that the conditions of theorem 2.1 are satisfied and hence the result follows. □

The following example shows that we cannot drop the condition in theorem 3.1 that L be well-structured.

Example Let P be the normal program

$p \leftarrow \neg q$
$q \leftarrow r(A)$
$r(x) \leftarrow$

G the normal goal $\leftarrow p, r(B)$, H the normal goal $\leftarrow p$, and $L = \{r\}$. Note that L is not well-structured wrt P. Let P' be the normal program

$p \leftarrow \neg q$
$q \leftarrow r(A)$
$r(B) \leftarrow$

Then P' is a partially evaluated program computed from P using G and L. However, $P' \cup \{\leftarrow p\}$ has an SLDNF-refutation, but $P \cup \{\leftarrow p\}$ does not.

Note that the partial evaluation procedure is easily extended to handle the partial evaluation of open programs. Provided that the definitions of predicate symbols in L are known, the computation of the program $P_{\mathbf{A}}$ is the same whether the program P is open or not. There is one difference in the last step of the partial evaluation procedure, where for open programs, it is only possible to compute P' when the definitions which are not known at partial evaluation time become available. Note also that the well-structured condition can be checked for an open program P provided that the dependency graph for P is known.

As the example below shows, the procedure does not always terminate.

Example Let P be the program
$p(x) \leftarrow p(f(x))$
G the goal $\leftarrow p(A)$ and $L = \{p\}$. Suppose we obtain all resultants using SLDNF-trees which contain a single derivation step. Then the atoms added to the set **A** are of the form $p(f^n(A))$, $n \geq 0$, and so the outer loop of the partial evaluation procedure never terminates.

Our approach to handling negation in the partial evaluation procedure is quite flexible. If a negative literal is ground, then it can be evaluated by SLDNF-resolution in the usual way during partial evaluation. Alternatively, a negative literal, whether ground or not, can be left to appear in a resultant and the atom in the literal put into **A** and partially evaluated. Other approaches to handling negation have been suggested. For example, [2] employs an extension of negation as failure called constructive negation, in which non-ground negative literals can be evaluated. In another approach [11], a (possibly non-ground) negative literal $\neg A$ can be partially evaluated by producing the resultants for the atom A. Then the predicate symbol in $\neg A$ and in the heads of the resultants is replaced with a predicate symbol that does not appear in the program. Our approach so far differs from this in that the predicate symbol in the literal $\neg A$ and the heads of the partial evaluation obtained for A is not renamed. However, the renaming transformation presented in section 5 can be applied to negative literals to achieve much the same effect as in [11]. But here this is done "statically" and hence may not be as flexible as the "dynamic" renaming employed in [11]. One advantage of the renaming transformation introduced here is that it is easy to prove its correctness, in contrast to the renaming transformation of [11] whose correctness is an open problem.

We remark that it is not necessary that a programmer actually provide (or even understand the concept of) a well-structured set of predicate symbols. Let us suppose that the programmer merely specifies that certain predicate symbols, say $p_1, \ldots, p_k$, are not to be partially evaluated. Define $L = \{q : q$ is a predicate symbol such that none of $p_1, \ldots, p_k$ depend in P upon $q\}$. Clearly, L is a well-structured set wrt P, which can then be used by the partial evaluation procedure. However, the programmer does need to understand the implication of specifying that $p_1, \ldots, p_k$ not be partially evaluated, which is that no predicate symbol upon which any of $p_1, \ldots, p_k$ depend will be partially evaluated either.

In summary, we envisage programmers using the partial evaluation procedure as follows. First the programmer specifies a normal program P, a normal goal G, and a list of predicate symbols, $p_1, \ldots, p_k$, not to be partially evaluated. Next the partial evaluation procedure is run using P, G and L, where L is defined in the previous paragraph, to produce a partially evaluated program P'. Now the programmer is able to run P' for goals which are extended by G.

We now present four computation rules[4] which can be used by the partial evaluation procedure to construct L-compatible SLDNF-trees. They are motivated by the desire to partially evaluate to as great a depth as possible and yet avoid going down infinite branches. The latter desire suggests a connection with loop trapping and, indeed, the particular computation rules presented here have been motivated by various loop trapping schemes.

Let L be a set of predicate symbols. We will consider four computation rules R_v, R_i, R_g, and R_{ci} defined as follows.

The computation rule R_v selects the leftmost literal whose predicate symbol is in L and which is either a ground negative literal or an atom not a variant of an atom already selected on the branch down to the current goal.

The computation rule R_i selects the leftmost literal whose predicate symbol is in L and which is either a ground negative literal or an atom not an instance of an atom already selected on the branch down to the current goal.

The computation rule R_g selects the leftmost literal whose predicate symbol is in L and which is either a ground negative literal or an atom not more general than an atom already selected on the branch down to the current goal.

The computation rule R_{ci} selects the leftmost literal whose predicate symbol is in L and which is either a ground negative literal or an atom not having a common instance with an atom already selected on the branch down to the current goal.

For each of these computation rules, the computation terminates in deadlock when no literal is available for selection. A resultant at which deadlock occurs then forms part of the partial evaluation of the atom at the root of the tree.

For a variety of examples, the computation rule R_v carried out the partial evaluation as deep as the other computation rules. This suggests that it could be the most useful one. It would be interesting to give a precise definition of the quality of a computation rule for partial evaluation (perhaps, in terms of the number of logical inferences required to run a goal on the partially evaluated program) and compare the various computation rules analytically.

4 The Renaming Transformation

In the partial evaluation procedure, in order to construct an independent set of atoms, two atoms in **A** having a common instance are replaced by their msg. In certain cases, atoms in the original goal are (strictly) subsumed during this process. To avoid this undesirable situation, we introduce a renaming transformation. This is a pre-processing stage whereby new predicate symbols are introduced into the program to be partially evaluated.

[4] We use the term "computation rule" in the sense of [13] rather than the narrower sense of [9] in which a computation rule is a function of the goal alone.

A transformed program is thus obtained which is then partially evaluated instead of the original program.

To motivate the introduction of the pre-processing stage, let us see the effect of applying the partial evaluation procedure to the *append* program wrt the goal $\leftarrow append([A, B|x], [C], y)$ and the set $L = \{append\}$. Suppose the procedure uses the computation rule R_v. The partial evaluation procedure first computes a partial evaluation of $append([A, B|x], [C], y)$. During the construction of an independent set **A**, the atom $append([A, B|x], [C], y)$ is subsumed by the atom $append(u, [C], v)$. The partially evaluated program thus produced is as follows.

$$append([\,], [C], [C]) \leftarrow$$
$$append([x|y], [C], [x|z]) \leftarrow append(y, [C], z)$$

As can be seen, instead of obtaining a program for the specific purpose of appending the list $[A, B|x]$ to $[C]$, we have obtained a partially evaluated program which appends a general list to $[C]$. To avoid this subsumption, we replace the predicate symbol of each atom in the body of a clause in the program having an instance in common with $append([A, B|x], [C], y)$ by $append'$ and give a definition for $append'$. A program equivalent to the original *append* program is thus obtained as follows.

$$append([\,], x, x) \leftarrow$$
$$append([x|y], z, [x|w]) \leftarrow append'(y, z, w)$$

$$append'([\,], x, x) \leftarrow$$
$$append'([x|y], z, [x|w]) \leftarrow append'(y, z, w)$$

We then apply the partial evaluation procedure to the transformed program wrt the goal $\leftarrow append([A, B|x], [C], y)$ and the set $L = \{append, append'\}$, and obtain a new partially evaluated program as follows.

$$append([A, B], [C], [A, B, C]) \leftarrow$$
$$append([A, B, x|y], [C], [A, B, x|z]) \leftarrow append'(y, [C], z)$$

$$append'([\,], [C], [C]) \leftarrow$$
$$append'([x|y], [C], [x|z]) \leftarrow append'(y, [C], z)$$

In the new partially evaluated program, the known elements of the list in the first argument are "passed on" to the list in the third argument. The logical inferences needed to perform this, whose number is linear in the number of the known elements of the list in the first argument, is done at partial evaluation time. In the more general case, when the list in the first argument has n known elements, then n logical inferences would be performed at run time by the first version of the partially evaluated program to "pass on" the known elements of the list in the first argument to the list in the third argument, whereas they are pre-computed by the new partially evaluated program, which is thus more efficient.

Next we give the general framework for renaming transformations.

Definition Let P be a normal program and $p_1, \ldots, p_k$ predicate symbols in P. Then a *renaming* transformation consists of the following steps.

1. Duplicate the definitions of $p_1, \ldots, p_k$ and replace the predicate symbols in the heads of these definitions with predicate symbols $p'_1, \ldots, p'_k$, respectively, where $p'_1, \ldots, p'_k$ do not appear in the language underlying P and p'_i has the same arity as p_i $(1 \leq i \leq k)$.

2. Any occurrence of a predicate symbol p_i $(1 \leq i \leq k)$ appearing in the body of a clause in P or one of the duplicated definitions may be replaced by p'_i.

The main question now is which predicate symbols in P should be renamed to improve the efficiency of partially evaluated programs. We have found the following particular transformation adequate for the example above and for others we have considered.

Definition An atom with predicate symbol p of arity n is in *most general form* if it has the form $p(x_1, \ldots, x_n)$, where $x_1, \ldots, x_n$ are distinct variables.

Definition Let P be a normal program, G a normal goal, and L a set of predicate symbols. Then the *goal specific transformation* is a renaming transformation defined as follows.

1. The predicate symbols $p_1, \ldots, p_k$, whose definitions are duplicated, are the predicate symbols of L-selectable atoms[5] in G which are not in most general form and have a common instance with an msg of all atoms[5] containing the corresponding predicate symbol which appear in the bodies of clauses in P.

2. Each occurrence of a predicate symbol p_i $(1 \leq i \leq k)$ appearing in the body of a clause in P or one of the duplicated definitions is replaced by p'_i.

Note that we are only concerned with atoms in the original goal which might be subsumed. Therefore the predicate symbols of such atoms which are in most general form do not need to be renamed.

Next we show the computational equivalence between the original program and the transformed program.

Theorem 4.1 *Let P be a normal program, P_r a normal program obtained from P by a renaming transformation using predicate symbols $p_1, \ldots, p_k$, and G a normal goal not containing any of the new predicate symbols $p'_1, \ldots, p'_k$. Then the following hold.*

[5] The atom may appear in a negative literal.

1. $P \cup \{G\}$ *has an SLDNF-refutation with computed answer* θ *iff* $P_r \cup \{G\}$ *does.*

2. $P \cup \{G\}$ *has a finitely failed SLDNF-tree iff* $P_r \cup \{G\}$ *does.*

Proof: The proof is a straightforward mutual induction on the ranks of the refutation and finitely failed tree. □

Unfortunately, the desired declarative equivalence does not hold, as the following example shows.

Example Let P be the program

$r \leftarrow p$
$r \leftarrow \neg p$
$p \leftarrow p$

and P_r the program

$r \leftarrow p'$
$r \leftarrow \neg p$
$p \leftarrow p$
$p' \leftarrow p'$

which is obtained from P by a renaming transformation. Clearly, the identity substitution is a correct answer for $comp(P) \cup \{\leftarrow r\}$, but it is not a correct answer for $comp(P_r) \cup \{\leftarrow r\}$.

However, we do have a result in one direction.

Theorem 4.2 *Let* P *be a normal program,* P_r *a normal program obtained from* P *by a renaming transformation using predicate symbols* $p_1, \ldots, p_k$*, and* G *a normal goal not containing any of the new predicate symbols* $p'_1, \ldots, p'_k$*. Then the following hold.*

1. *If* θ *is a correct answer for* $comp(P_r) \cup \{G\}$*, then it is a correct answer for* $comp(P) \cup \{G\}$*.*

2. *If* G *is a logical consequence of* $comp(P_r)$*, then it is a logical consequence of* $comp(P)$*.*

Proof: Let M be a model for $comp(P)$. Extend M to an interpretation M_r for $comp(P_r)$ by defining the assignment of p'_i to be the same as the assignment of p_i, for $1 \leq i \leq k$. Clearly, M_r is a model for $comp(P_r)$. Thus, if W is a closed first order formula not involving the predicate symbols $p'_1, \ldots, p'_k$ and W is a logical consequence of $comp(P_r)$, then W is a logical consequence of $comp(P)$. Both parts of the theorem now follow. □

Next we prove that, by applying the goal specific transformation, no L-selectable atom in the goal will be subsumed by the partial evaluation procedure.

Theorem 4.3 *Let* P *be a normal program,* G *a normal goal in which no pair of atoms have a common instance,* L *a set of predicate symbols, and*

P_r the transformed program obtained from P, G and L by the goal specific transformation. Let $\mathbf{A}$ be the set of atoms produced by the partial evaluation procedure for P_r, G, and L. Then no L-selectable atom in G is (strictly) subsumed by an msg in the set $\mathbf{A}$ by the partial evaluation procedure.

Proof: Let $p'_1, \ldots, p'_k$ be the new predicate symbols introduced corresponding to $p_1, \ldots, p_k$, respectively. Clearly, no L-selectable atom in G containing a predicate symbol p_i $(1 \leq i \leq k)$ will be subsumed. Next note that any atom in the body of a resultant added to $\mathbf{A}$ by the partial evaluation procedure must be an instance of an atom in the body of a clause in P_r. Since the remaining L-selectable atoms in G not in most general form do not have a common instance with an msg of all atoms containing the corresponding predicate symbol which appear in the bodies of clauses in P_r and since the partial evaluation procedure does subsumption by taking an msg, it follows that the remaining L-selectable atoms in G are not subsumed either. □

A common programming technique is to replace a goal $\leftarrow L_1, \ldots, L_n$, containing the variables $x_1, \ldots, x_k$, by the goal $\leftarrow answer(x_1, \ldots, x_k)$ and add the clause $answer(x_1, \ldots, x_k) \leftarrow L_1, \ldots, L_n$ to the program. In such a situation, the goal specific transformation has no effect. This may have the undesirable consequence of atoms in the original goal being subsumed during partial evaluation. We suggest overcoming this problem by simply applying the goal specific transformation as if the goal was indeed $\leftarrow L_1, \ldots, L_n$ instead of $\leftarrow answer(x_1, \ldots, x_k)$.

5 Conclusion

In this paper, we have presented a procedure for the partial evaluation of logic programs based on the theoretical framework established in [10] and proved its correctness. The procedure produces partially evaluated programs which are sound and complete wrt the corresponding original programs for goals of a certain form. We have also given a general framework for renaming transformations which introduce new predicate symbols into the original program. This can improve the efficiency of partially evaluated programs.

A major problem in partial evaluation is that of partial evaluation beyond the pure subset of Prolog and a number of papers (for example, [11], [15], and [17]) have addressed this problem. However, we believe that the long term solution to this problem is not to extend the framework and techniques of partial evaluation to the non-logical features of Prolog, but instead to develop more declarative successors to Prolog which will be more amenable to partial evaluation, as well as other program transformation techniques. There is now a considerable body of research which clearly indicates what form such a successor to Prolog might take. In [1], such a successor to Prolog is presented. This language has declarative replacements for the problematical Prolog meta-logical predicates, such as *var*, *assert*, and *retract*. It also has a pruning operator which is better behaved than Prolog's cut. The pruning operator is similar to the commit operator of the concurrent languages, but is suitably generalised so that the class of programs containing the operator is closed under the typical program transformations such as unfolding. Theorems presented in [6] show that the operator is well behaved wrt partial evaluation.

There are a variety of other interesting open problems in partial evaluation. For example, the general issue of efficiency in partial evaluation has not been sufficiently studied. For this we need to analyze a variety of computation rules. We also need to study renaming transformations other than the goal specific transformation, and related techniques such as folding [16] which can affect efficiency.

Acknowledgements

We would like to thank David Chan, John Gallagher, Pat Hill and John Shepherdson for their helpful comments on drafts of this paper.

References

[1] A.D. Burt, P.M. Hill, and J.W. Lloyd. *Preliminary Report on the Logic Programming Language Gödel.* Technical Report TR-90-02, Department of Computer Science, University of Bristol, 1990.

[2] D. Chan and M. Wallace. A treatment of negation during partial evaluation. In H.D. Abramson and M.H. Rogers, editors, *Meta-Programming in Logic Programming*, pages 299–318, MIT Press, 1989. Proceedings of the Meta88 Workshop, June 1988.

[3] M.H.M. Cheng, M.H. van Emden, and P.A. Strooper. Complete sets of frontiers in logic-based program transformation. In H.D. Abramson and M.H. Rogers, editors, *Meta-Programming in Logic Programming*, pages 283–298, MIT Press, 1989. Proceedings of the Meta88 Workshop, June 1988.

[4] H. Fujita and K. Furukawa. A self-applicable partial evaluator and its use in incremental compilation. In D. Bjorner, A.P. Ershov, and N.D. Jones, editors, *Workshop on Partial Evaluation and Mixed Computation,* Gl. Avernaes, Denmark, pages 69–81, October 1987.

[5] Y. Futamura. Partial evaluation of computation process - an approach to a compiler-compiler. *Systems, Computers, Controls*, 25:45–50, 1971.

[6] P.M. Hill, J.W. Lloyd, and J.C. Shepherdson. *Properties of a Pruning Operator.* Technical Report TR-89-18, Department of Computer Science, University of Bristol, 1989. To appear in the Journal of Logic and Computation, 1990.

[7] N.D. Jones, P. Sestoft, and H. Sondergaard. An experiment in partial evaluation: the generation of a compiler generator. In J.P. Jouannaud, editor, *Rewriting Techniques and Applications*, pages 124–140, Lecture Notes in Computer Science 202, Springer-Verlag, 1985.

[8] N.D. Jones, P. Sestoft, and H. Sondergaard. Mix: a self-applicable partial evaluator for experiments in compiler generation. *Lisp and Symbolic Computation*, 2:9–50, 1989.

[9] J.W. Lloyd. *Foundations of Logic Programming.* Springer-Verlag, second edition, 1987.

[10] J.W. Lloyd and J.C. Shepherdson. *Partial Evaluation in Logic Programming.* Technical Report CS-87-09, Department of Computer Science, University of Bristol, 1987. Revised July 1989. To appear in The Journal of Logic Programming.

[11] S. Owen. Issues in the partial evaluation of meta-interpreters. In H.D. Abramson and M.H. Rogers, editors, *Meta-Programming in Logic Programming*, pages 319–340, MIT Press, 1989. Proceedings of the Meta88 Workshop, June 1988.

[12] P. Sestoft. The structure of a self-applicable partial evaluator. In H. Ganzinger and N.D. Jones, editors, *Programs as Data Objects*, pages 236–256, Lecture Notes in Computer Science 217, Springer-Verlag, 1986.

[13] J.C. Shepherdson. Negation as failure: a comparison of Clark's completed data base and Reiter's closed world assumption. *The Journal of Logic Programming*, 1(1):51–81, 1984.

[14] A. Takeuchi and H. Fujita. Competitive partial evaluation. In D. Bjorner, A.P. Ershov, and N.D. Jones, editors, *Workshop on Partial Evaluation and Mixed Computation,* Gl. Avernaes, Denmark, pages 317–326, October 1987.

[15] A. Takeuchi and K. Furukawa. Partial evaluation of Prolog programs and its application to meta programming. In H.-J. Kugler, editor, *Information Processing 86,* Dublin, pages 415–420, North Holland, 1986.

[16] H. Tamaki and T. Sato. Unfold/fold transformations of logic programs. In *Proceedings of the Second International Conference on Logic Programming,* Uppsala, pages 127–138, 1984.

[17] R. Venken. A Prolog meta-interpreter for partial evaluation and its application to source to source transformation and query optimization. In *ECAI-84: Advances in Artificial Intelligence,* Pisa, pages 91–100, North-Holland, 1984.

Partial Evaluation for Hierarchies of Logic Theories

Michele Bugliesi
ENIDATA S.p.A
Viale Aldo Moro, 38
40121 Bologna, ITALY

Evelina Lamma, Paola Mello
DEIS University of Bologna
Viale Risorgimento, 2
40136 Bologna, ITALY

Abstract

We discuss the impact of Partial Evaluation within the framework of structured logic programming. We define a general scheme for Partial Evaluation to be applied to a wide class of structuring policies for logic programming, capable of supporting both block- and inheritance-based systems. We show how the properties of soundness and completeness of Partial Evaluation in Logic Programming are preserved in this extended scheme.

1 Introduction

Structuring mechanisms have become nowadays a crucial topic in Logic Programming. Several authors have addressed this problem in the literature, on the basis of different approaches: modules and blocks [15,6], inheritance [4,8,5] and viewpoints, [7,13].

Some efforts have recently been devoted, [16,2], to the design of a unifying framework in which a wide range of current proposals can be integrated in a uniform and coherent way. This approach, inspired by [17], is based on the idea that a program can be structured as a collection of elementary components, each component being a separate logic theory called *unit*. Units can be (possibly dynamically) connected into linear hierarchies called *contexts* and contexts, in turn, provide the (possibly dynamic) data base of clauses used for the evaluation of the queries. Depending on the different policies adopted for unit combination, different structuring mechanisms can be identified. Blocks, modules, and inheritance-based systems [2] are easily implemented by means of statically configured hierarchies of units, whereas dynamic configurations provide a natural support for some well-known artificial intelligence techniques such as viewpoints and hypothetical reasoning.

Some interesting results have also been achieved from the implementation point of view. In [10], the authors address the relevance of a compilative approach based on the definition of an extended Warren Abstract Machine

[18], where new instructions and data structures have been introduced to deal with units and contexts.

In this paper we discuss the application of Partial Evaluation as a further enhancement to the compilative approach proposed in [10]. We focus on statically configured systems since they are the best-suited for such a compilative approach. Static configurations allow in fact predicate calls to be directly bound to the corresponding predicate definitions at compile-time thus eliminating most of the run-time overhead due to context handling.

We introduce a definition of Partial Evaluation which extends that given in [11] to capture the notions of unit and unit composition, and which produces a specialization of the source program with respect to a given goal to be evaluated in a given context.

An interesting feature of our technique is that it preserves the original structure of the program so that no collaption of several units into a more compact configuration occurs during the transformation. This ensures non-replication of code for the new program, high generality for it, and finally, full compatibility with the compilation technique addressed in [10].

Furthermore it allows to isolate some closedness conditions for the soundness and the completeness of the transformation, which involve only syntactic checks on the partially evaluated program and the goal. For block-based systems these conditions actually correspond to that introduced in [11] for definite logic programs; for inheritance-based systems, instead, some further checks on the static structure of the program are required.

2 Hierarchies of Logic Programming Theories

Our characterization of structured logic programs originates from the Contextual Logic Programming paradigm introduced by [17]. The key idea is that a program can be conceived as a collection of independent modules called ***units***. A unit is simply identified by the set of clauses it defines and by a unique, atomic name used to denote it. Units can be (possibly dynamically) connected into contexts and contexts, in turn, provide the set of definitions for the evaluation of the queries. As a matter of fact, contexts are represented as ordered lists of units of the form $\lfloor u_N, \ldots, u_i, \ldots, u_1 \rfloor$ and denote the union of the sets of clauses of the composing units.

Example 2.1 *Let P be the program composed by the following units:*

$\textbf{\textit{unit}}(u_1)$:	$\textbf{\textit{unit}}(u_2)$:	$\textbf{\textit{unit}}(u_3)$:
$a(X) : -b(X).$	$b(1).$	$c(X) : -a(X).$

The proof of the goal $c(X)$ in the context $\lfloor u_3, u_2, u_1 \rfloor$ corresponds, in logic programming, to a proof with respect to the set of clauses:

$$\begin{array}{l} c(X) : -a(X). \\ b(1). \\ a(X) : -b(X). \end{array}$$

Different policies for composing units into contexts can be adopted and, accordingly, different classes of structuring mechanisms can be identified as discussed in [16] and [2].

2.1 Static and Dynamic Systems

A first relevant issue concerns the distinction between static and dynamic composition.

Statically configured systems are systems in which each unit has a *fixed* associated context. This means that, if $\lfloor u_N, \ldots, u_1 \rfloor$ is the context associated with a unit u, then, whenever u is asked for the proof of a goal g, the evaluation of g actually takes place in the context $\lfloor u, u_N, \ldots, u_1 \rfloor$. The association of a unit with a context is obtained by establishing explicit inheritance links between units. Therefore, when a unit gets defined, its ***parent*** unit must be also specified and its associated context is obtained by recursively computing the ordered list of its ancestors.

A *top*, empty unit, common to all the hierarchies, is assumed. A switch operator ":" allows us the switching from one hierarchy to the others. The invocation of a goal of the form $u : g$ in the current hierarchy causes a switch to the hierarchy associated with the unit u.

Example 2.2 *Let P be the following structured program:*

$\boldsymbol{unit}(u_1, \boldsymbol{parent}(top))$:	$\boldsymbol{unit}(u_2, \boldsymbol{parent}(u_1))$:	$\boldsymbol{unit}(u_3, \boldsymbol{parent}(u_2))$:
$a(X) : -b(X).$	$b(1).$	$c(X) : -a(X).$

The call $u_3 : c(X)$ enforces $\lfloor u_3, u_2, u_1 \rfloor$ as the new current context for $c(X)$. The unit specified as parameter of the ***parent*** *structure represents the inheritance link for the unit itself.*

Dynamically configured systems, on the other hand, provide a more flexible framework in which a context $\lfloor u_N, \ldots, u_1 \rfloor$ can be dynamically extended during the computation to include new units. Each unit can have therefore a dynamic associated context as in [17].

2.2 Conservative/Evolving Systems

The context can be interpreted as the binding environment for predicate calls. In this setting, an important remark concerns the distinction between the conservative and the evolving policy of predicate binding. Let's suppose that $C = \lfloor u_N, \ldots, u_i, \ldots, u_1 \rfloor$ is the current context.

An *evolving system* is a system in which, for each predicate call g occurring in the unit u_i, the corresponding predicate definition is given by the clauses for g contained in the whole context C. Examples of evolving systems are Miller's one [15] and N-Prolog [7].

A *conservative system* is a system in which, for each predicate call g occurring in the unit u_i, the corresponding predicate definition is given by the clauses contained in the the sub-context $\lfloor u_i, \ldots, u_1 \rfloor$. The definitions *visible* from a unit u, are therefore those found in u and its ancestors in the current context. Examples of conservative systems are blocks and modules [6], Meta-Prolog [1], Contextual Logic Programming [17].

Example 2.3 *Let us consider the program of example 2.2 and the top goal:* $u_3 : c(X)$. *We use the notation* $Ctx \vdash G$, *introduced in [17], to explicitly represent the context associated to each predicate call.*

In an evolving system (see [2], for the operational semantics) we get the derivation steps:

$$\begin{array}{lcl} \lfloor\ \rfloor & \vdash & u_3 : c(X) \\ \lfloor u_3, u_2, u_1 \rfloor & \vdash & c(X) \\ \lfloor u_3, u_2, u_1 \rfloor & \vdash & a(X) \\ \lfloor u_3, u_2, u_1 \rfloor & \vdash & b(X) \\ success & : & \{X \leftarrow 1\} \end{array}$$

Notice that the goal b(X) is proved in the whole context $\lfloor u_3, u_2, u_1 \rfloor$ *even though it is called in the sub-context* $\lfloor u_1 \rfloor$.

By converse, in a conservative system (see [2], for the operational semantics), the context for the call b(X) is $\lfloor u_1 \rfloor$ *and, since* $\lfloor u_1 \rfloor$ *contains no definition for b(X), we get a failure as shown below:*

$$\begin{array}{lcl} \lfloor\ \rfloor & \vdash & u_3 : c(X) \\ \lfloor u_3, u_2, u_1 \rfloor & \vdash & c(X) \\ \lfloor u_2, u_1 \rfloor & \vdash & a(X) \\ \lfloor u_1 \rfloor & \vdash & b(X) \\ failure & & \end{array}$$

2.3 Examples of Statically Configured Systems

Most of the proposals for structuring logic programs found in the literature can be included in the above classification. An interesting discussion about this topic can be found in [2].

In this paper we focus on statically configured systems. The main reason for this choice is that, due to their static configuration, these systems are better-suited for a compilative approach such as the one based on Partial Evaluation. The details about this point will be clarified in the next sections. What is worth mentioning here is that, even though static systems are not powerful enough to cover the whole range of structuring mechanisms, they capture several interesting proposals in this field such as modules, blocks, and inheritance-based systems (see [14]).

2.3.1 Blocks and Modules

In block-based systems, static scope rules determine predicate visibility on the basis of the nesting of blocks in the program. To prove an atomic goal occurring in a clause of a given block, only those clauses defined in that block or in enclosing blocks can be used. In terms of our classification, such a behaviour corresponds to a conservative policy where each block is encapsulated into a separate unit having the enclosing block as its ***parent***.

Example 2.4 *Let us consider the following program presented in [6]:*

$$P = \{r \to q, (((q \to p) \wedge r) \Rightarrow p) \to s\}$$

and structured into two nested blocks: b_1*, the enclosing one, which contains the definitions for* q *and* s*, and* b_2*, the inner one, which contains the definitions for* p *and* r*. Block* b_2 *is nested into the second clause of block* b_1 *and, therefore, its clauses are not visible by the predicates defined in* b_1*.* P *can be mapped to the following conservative system:*

$\textbf{unit}(b_1, \textbf{parent}(top))$:	$\textbf{unit}(b_2, \textbf{parent}(b_1))$:
$q : -r.$	$p : -q.$
$s : -b_2 : p.$	$r.$

Since the system is conservative, the goal $b_1 : s$ *cannot be proved. In fact, the predicate* r*, which is locally defined in* b_2*, is not visible from the external unit* b_1*. Notice that, on the other side, in the case of an evolving system the goal* s *would succeed.*

Such scope rules become more strict in the case of closed modules (see [6]): to prove a goal in a module M, only those predicate definitions which are local to M have to be taken into account. Closed modules are actually a special case of conservative systems, where each unit defines the *top* unit as its parent and therefore it only uses its local definitions.

2.3.2 Inheritance-based systems

Inheritance- and object-based systems can be classified as evolving systems. We can interpret contexts as the explicit representation of a branch in an inheritance tree (for the sake of simplicity we will not consider multiple inheritance). The first unit in the context is the tip node, while the last one is the top of the hierarchy. Inheritance-based systems are intrinsically evolving since, as stated in [19], "a self-reference in a type or class is bound to the object on whose behalf an operation (demonstration) is being executed, rather than on the textual module (unit) in which the self-reference occurs."

Example 2.5 *Let us consider the class template language described in [12]. When we say that a bird is a special case of animal we are stating that whatever is true for animals is also true for birds: the bird theory inherits from the animal theory. In the class template language we express this kind of relationship between classes by means of class rules:*

$$\begin{array}{lcl} bird & \Leftarrow & animal \\ tweety & \Leftarrow & bird \\ horse & \Leftarrow & animal \\ person & \Leftarrow & animal \end{array}$$

where:

$$animal : \left[\begin{array}{l} mode(walk). \\ mode(run) : -self : no\_of\_legs(2). \\ mode(gallop) : -self : no\_of\_legs(4). \end{array} \right.$$

$$bird : \left[\begin{array}{l} mode(fly). \\ no\_of\_legs(2). \\ covering(feather). \end{array} \right.$$

$$horse : \left[\; no\_of\_legs(4). \right.$$

$$human : \left[\; no\_of\_legs(2). \right.$$

$$tweety : \left[no\_of\_wings(2). \right.$$

The call self:g *causes the proof of* g *to be performed in the tip class of the current hierarchy, no matter what the current class is. The use of* self *allows therefore to model the expected behaviour of inheritance.*

This behaviour is intrinsically evolving; in our framework this program can be translated into the following:

$$\textbf{unit}(animal, \textbf{parent}(top)) : \left[\begin{array}{l} mode(walk). \\ mode(run) : -no\_of\_legs(2). \\ mode(gallop) : -no\_of\_legs(4). \end{array} \right.$$

$$\textbf{unit}(bird, \textbf{parent}(animal)) : \left[\begin{array}{l} mode(fly). \\ no\_of\_legs(2). \\ covering(feather). \end{array} \right.$$

$$\textbf{unit}(horse, \textbf{parent}(animal)) : \left[\; no\_of\_legs(4). \right.$$

$$\textbf{unit}(human, \textbf{parent}(animal)) : \left[\; no\_of\_legs(2). \right.$$

$$\textbf{unit}(tweety, \textbf{parent}(bird)) : \left[no\_of\_wings(2). \right.$$

Now the taxonomy is embedded in the parent declaration, and the self label behaviour is automatically expressed by the evolving policy.

3 Extending Partial Evaluation

Partial Evaluation (PE) has been devoted great attention in the last few years since it was introduced in logic programming [9]. PE can be conceived as a source-to-source transformation technique which, given a program P and a goal G, produces a new program P', which is more efficient than P and has the same set of answer substitutions for the goal G or its instances. As stated in [11], "the basic technique for obtaining P' from P is to construct a partial search tree for P and suitably chosen atoms as goals, and then extract the definitions — the *resultants* — associated with the leaves of the tree". P' is then obtained from P by replacing the set of clauses in P, whose head contain one of the predicate symbols appearing in G, with the set of the produced resultants.

The main foundational questions about PE concern soundness and completeness. *Soundness* of the partially evaluated program P' wrt the original program P and the goal G means that each correct (computed) answer for G and P' is a correct (computed) answer for G and P. *Completeness* is the converse of this.

In standard logic programming, soundness follows from the soundness of SLD-resolution. A further closedness condition must be satisfied by the resulting program in order to ensure completeness [11].

The application of these issues to the structured logic systems presented in section 2 involves several major extensions to the basic principles of Partial Evaluation.

In fact, we have to consider that the evaluation of the goal occurs now in a context and, furthermore, we have to take into account the modular configuration of the program.

Given a program P, a goal G and a context C, we should therefore define a new program P' which specializes P with respect to the definition of G found in the context C. Furthermore, in order to ensure the highest level of flexibility and avoid code replication for the resulting program, we should also impose that the transformation preserve the original structure of P.

This raises further problems with respect to the case of logic programming. Given a partial search tree resulting from unfolding, and the corresponding set of resultants, we have first to define an *assignment* function to determine which unit each resultant should be assigned to. Then, the derived program is obtained from the original one by replacing (possibly) all the units in the initial context with their specialized versions. These, in turn, are obtained by erasing the old definitions for the initial goal and by introducing the new ones, according to the assignment function.

In the following, we will denote by $PE(P,G,C)$ the Partial Evaluation of P with respect to a goal G and a context C. A formal definition of $PE(P,G,C)$ can be given, in two steps, in terms of the following notions of *program representation* and of *Partial Evaluation of a goal in a context*:

Definition 3.1 (Program Representation) *Let U(P) be the set of units of a program P. We denote by $|u|$ the set of clauses of a unit u. Then the representation of P is given by:*

$$\mathcal{R}(P) = \{\langle d,u\rangle : \; u \in U(P), d \in |u|\}$$

Definition 3.2 (Partial Evaluation of a goal in a context) *Let P be a program, C a context, G an atomic goal, and R_T the set of resultants of a partial search-tree T for P and $\langle G, C\rangle$. Let also $\mathcal{F}_{ass} : R_T \mapsto U(P)$ be a given assignment function, which assigns the resultants in R_T to the units of P. The Partial Evaluation of G in C is given by:*

$$PE(G,C) = \{\langle d,u\rangle : \; d \in R_T \text{ and } u = \mathcal{F}_{ass}(d)\}$$

Definition 3.3 (Partial Evaluation of P wrt C, G) *Let P be a program, C a context, G an atomic goal. Then:*

$$PE(P,G,C) = P' \quad \text{such that}: \; \mathcal{R}(P') = (\mathcal{R}(P) \setminus \mathcal{D}(C,G)) \cup PE(G,C)$$

where $\mathcal{D}(C,G)$ is the representation of the set of definitions for the goal G contained in the context C.

The definition of the assignment function is a crucial point of our construction. In fact, different choices for the assignment function determine different configurations for the transformed program and, correspondingly, different properties for the transformation.

In logic programming, Partial Evaluation provides a specialization of the program with respect to a goal G; accordingly we cannot expect to be able to have correct answers for calls *more general* (less instantiated) than G.

In the same way, in structured logic programming, since we specialize the program with respect to a goal in a context C, we won't be able to have correct answers for that goal in contexts more *general* than C. In this case *more general* means *logically subsuming*. As a matter of fact, we say that a context C' is logically subsumed by a context C if all the theorems derivable in C are also derivable in C'. Notice that, being the composition of units in contexts a monotonic operation, it is easy to show that C' is logically subsumed by C if C' is an initial sublist ($C' \sqsubseteq C$, i.e. a *sub-context*) of C.

Therefore, what we can expect from the transformation is that it preserves the equivalence between P and P' with respect to instances of G (as in [11]) and *sub-contexts* of C, i.e. with respect to all those computations in which (instances of) G are evaluated in sub-contexts of C.

3.1 Configuring the Transformed Program

Choosing an assignment function that ensures the safety of the transformation is not straightforward. In fact, replacing each clause with the corresponding set of resultants in the same unit, which might appear the obvious choice, leads to unsoundness in some cases, even in sub-contexts of the initial one.

Example 3.1 *Let P be the evolving program:*

$\textbf{unit}(m_1, \textbf{parent}(top))$:	$\textbf{unit}(m_2, \textbf{parent}(m_1))$:
$p :- q.$	$q.$

By partially evaluating P wrt the goal p *in the context* $\lfloor m_2, m_1 \rfloor$ *if this assignment function is assumed, we get the following program*

$\mathbf{unit}(m_1, \mathbf{parent}(top))$:	$\mathbf{unit}(m_2, \mathbf{parent}(m_1)))$:
p.	q.

The transformation is unsound: in fact, in the context $\lfloor m_1 \rfloor$, *which is a sub-context of the initial one, the goal* p *fails in P and succeeds in P'.*

Here the problem is that, while in P the body of the clause $p : -q$ needs the definition of q in m_2 to succeed, the corresponding resultant in P' succeeds in sub-context $\lfloor m_1 \rfloor$without even calling q. In other words, while in P the *deduction context* for $p : -q$ is $\lfloor m_2, m_1 \rfloor$, in P' the *deduction context* for the corresponding resultant $p.$ is $\lfloor m_1 \rfloor$.

On the contrary, in order that the transformation be sound, we should ensure that the deduction context for the clause and the corresponding resultant be kept unchanged.

Generally, given a goal in a context C and a corresponding partial tree, for each resultant R_i in the tree, we have first to identify the *deduction context* $\mathcal{D}c(R_i)$, which is the *minimal sub-context of C, needed to derive* R_i. Then, in order to guarantee the consistency of the deduction contexts, R_i is to be assigned to the *head* unit of $\mathcal{D}c(R_i)$.

A formal definition of an assignment function satisfying theses requirements needs introducing some preliminary notation and definitions. We first consider a restricted class of structured programs in which no dynamic context switch occurs during the evaluation of a query. The problem of dynamic context switches during PE will be considered in section 4.1. Let:

- $\langle G, C \rangle$ denote a *c-atom*, where G is an atomic formula and C a context,
- a *c-goal* be a conjunction of c-atoms
- $\langle (g_1, \ldots, g_n), C \rangle$ be a shorthand for $\langle g_1, C \rangle, \ldots, \langle g_n, C \rangle$.

We give an extented notion of derivability, well-suited for computing the deduction contexts associated to the resultants.

Definition 3.4 (Matching Context Set) *Let G be an atomic goal. The matching context set for* $\langle G, C \rangle$ *is given by:*

$$\mathcal{M}cs(G,C) = \{C' : C' \sqsubseteq C \bigwedge |head(C')| \text{ contains a clause for } G\}$$

Each element of $\mathcal{M}cs(G,C)$ *is therefore a sub-context of C which contains a clause for G in its head unit.*

Definition 3.5 (Derivability) *Let P be a program, CG be the c-goal:*

$$\langle g_1, c_1 \rangle, \ldots, \langle g_i, c_i \rangle, \ldots, \langle g_n, c_n \rangle$$

and let $\langle g_i, c_i \rangle$ the selected c-atom. We say that the new c-goal CG' is derived from CG and P via the substitution σ, the clause Cl and the context L_C, if the following conditions hold:

$$\begin{array}{ll} Cl & = h : -b_1, \ldots, b_m \text{ is a variant of the selected clause in a unit u of } c_i \\ \sigma & = mgu(h, g_i) \\ CG' & = [\langle g_1, c_1 \rangle, .., \langle g_{i-1}, c_{i-1} \rangle, \langle (b_1, \ldots, b_m), C' \rangle, \langle g_{i+1}, c_{i+1} \rangle, \ldots, \langle g_n, c_n \rangle]\sigma \\ L_C & \in \mathcal{M}cs(G, c_i) \text{ is the matching context corresponding to } Cl \\ & (u = head(L_C)) \end{array}$$

The new context C' is computed according to the inference rules (see [2]). Namely:

$$C' = \begin{cases} L_C & \text{if the system is conservative} \\ c_i & \text{if the system is evolving} \end{cases}$$

We will henceforth denote a derivation step from a c-goal CG to a c-goal CG', by $CG \vdash_{L_C} CG'$ where, for the sake of simplicity, we omit mentioning the substitution. We will refer to L_C in the following as the *label context.*

A *C-SLD Derivation* will be, accordingly, a (finite or infinite) sequence of derivation steps $CG_0 \vdash_{c_1} \ldots \vdash_{c_j} CG_j \ldots$

Finally we generalize the notion of resultant and we introduce a constructive definition of *deduction context.*

Definition 3.6 (c-resultant) *Let G_0 be a goal and C_0 a context. Given a finite C-SLD derivation:*

$$\langle G_0, C_0 \rangle \vdash_{c1} \ldots \vdash_{cj} \langle g_1, c_k \rangle, \ldots, \langle g_i, c_i \rangle, \ldots, \langle g_n, c_n \rangle$$

the c-resultant corresponding to the resultant $G_0 : -g_1, \ldots, g_n$, is given by:

$$G_0 : -\langle g_1, c_1 \rangle, \ldots, \langle g_i, c_i \rangle, \ldots, \langle g_n, c_n \rangle.$$

Theorem 1 (Deduction context) *Given a finite C-SLD derivation:*

$$\langle G_0, C_0 \rangle \vdash_{c_1} \ldots \vdash_{c_j} \langle G_j, C_j \rangle$$

the deduction context $\mathcal{D}c(R)$ for the c-resultant $R = G_0 : -\langle G_j, C_j \rangle$ is the maximum element of the set $\{c_j, \ldots, c_1\}$ which is also a sub-context of C_0.
Proof. *By construction from the definition of C-SLD derivation.*

We are now ready to introduce the *assignment function*:

Definition 3.7 (Assignment function: $\mathcal{F}_{ass}$) *Let T be a finite C-SLD tree. Let CR be a c-resultant in T and $\mathcal{D}c(CR) = \lfloor u_k, \ldots, u_1 \rfloor$. Let finally R be the corresponding resultant. Then: $\mathcal{F}_{ass}(R) = u_k$.*

Example 3.2 *In example 3.1, if this assignment function is assumed, we get the following (finite) C-SLD tree. Each branch is marked by the label context used in the derivation step.*

$$\langle p, \lfloor m_2, m_1 \rfloor \rangle \;\vdash_{\lfloor m_1 \rfloor}\; \langle q, \lfloor m_2, m_1 \rfloor \rangle \;\vdash_{\lfloor m_2, m_1 \rfloor}\; \Box$$

$R = p.$ is the only resultant; its deduction context is $\mathcal{D}c(R) = \lfloor m_2, m_1 \rfloor$. Therefore the new clause produced by $PE(P, p, \lfloor m_2, m_1 \rfloor)$ is assigned to m_2 and the previous definition for p is dropped from m_1. Accordingly the following sound *program P' is produced:*

$\boldsymbol{unit}(m_1, \boldsymbol{parent}(top))$:	$\boldsymbol{unit}(m_2, \boldsymbol{parent}(m_2))$:
	$p.$
	$q.$

3.2 Determining the Context for the Residuals

The choice of a well-defined assignment function only partially answers the questions about the soundness and completeness of the transformation. Once the new configuration of the program has been established, there is still the problem of the residuals occurring in the bodies of the resultants created by unfolding. Namely, for each resultant of the form $h : -b_1, \ldots, b_n$, it must be ensured that each of the b_is be evaluated in *equivalent* contexts before and after the transformation. As a matter of fact, two contexts C and C' are equivalent if they have the same success set.

Example 3.3 *In a conservative system, let P be the following program:*

$\boldsymbol{unit}(u_1, \boldsymbol{parent}(top))$:	$\boldsymbol{unit}(u_2, \boldsymbol{parent}(u_1))$:	$\boldsymbol{unit}(u_3, \boldsymbol{parent}(u_2))$:
$q : -r.$	$r.$	$p : -q.$

Let us consider a $PE(P, p, \lfloor u_3, u_2, u_1 \rfloor)$. The corresponding C-SLD tree is:

$$\langle p, \lfloor u_3, u_2, u_1 \rfloor \rangle \;\vdash_{\lfloor u_3, u_2, u_1 \rfloor}\; \langle q, \lfloor u_3, u_2, u_1 \rfloor \rangle \;\vdash_{\lfloor u_1 \rfloor}\; \langle r, \lfloor u_1 \rfloor \rangle$$

Then the resulting program P' is given by:

$\boldsymbol{unit}(u_1, \boldsymbol{parent}(top))$:	$\boldsymbol{unit}(u_2, \boldsymbol{parent}(u_1))$:	$\boldsymbol{unit}(u_3, \boldsymbol{parent}(u_2))$:
$q : -r.$	$r.$	$p : -r.$

Again, the transformation is unsound: r is evaluated in $\lfloor u_3, u_2, u_1 \rfloor$ in P' and in $\lfloor u_1 \rfloor$ in P and these two contexts are obviously not equivalent.

Finding the correct context to be associated with each atom in the body of the resultants is straightforward in our scheme since it can be determined by a direct inspection of the partial search trees. The switch operator can be explicitly used to enforce the right context.

Definition 3.8 (Residuals) *Let $CR = G : -\langle g_i, C_i\rangle$ be a c-resultant for the c-goal $\langle G_0, C_0\rangle$. Then, the corresponding resultant R is determined depending of the the relationship between $\mathcal{D}c(CR)$ and C_i. Namely,*

(i) *if $C_i = \mathcal{D}c(CR)$, then $R = G : -g_i$.*

(ii) *if $C_i \sqsubset \mathcal{D}c(CR)$, i.e. $\mathcal{D}c(CR) = \lfloor u_N, \ldots, u_j, \ldots, u_1 \rfloor$ and $C_i = \lfloor u_j, \ldots, u_1 \rfloor$, then: $R = G : -u_j : g_i$.*

In both cases R is assigned to the head unit of $\mathcal{D}c(CR)$. The general case of a resultant whose body contains more than one atom can be simply obtained by the previous cases, by simply applying (i) *and* (ii) *to each atom in the body.*

Example 3.4 *In example 3.3 condition* (ii) *occurred. Accordingly the transformation produces the following program:*

$\boldsymbol{unit}(u_1, \boldsymbol{parent}(top))$:	$\boldsymbol{unit}(u_2, \boldsymbol{parent}(u_1))$:	$\boldsymbol{unit}(u_3, \boldsymbol{parent}(u_2))$:
$q : -r.$	$r.$	$p : -u_1 : r.$

Notice that now, in both the source and the transformed program, r is evaluated in $\lfloor u_1 \rfloor$.

4 Soundness and Completeness

As already noticed, what we expect from the transformation is that it preserves the equivalence between the source and the resulting programs with respect to all those computations in which (instances of) G are evaluated in sub-contexts of C.

In this section we state the properties of soundness and completeness of Partial Evaluation in the case of structured logic programming. We first extend the notions of soundness and completeness of Partial Evaluation to the framework of structured logic programming. Let P be a program, $\langle G, C\rangle$ a c-atom and P' a partial evaluation of P wrt $\langle G, C\rangle$.

Definition 4.1 (Soundness) *If $\langle G, C\rangle$ has a C-SLD refutation with computed answer θ in P', then $\langle G, C\rangle$ has a C-SLD refutation with computed answer θ in P.*

Definition 4.2 (Completeness) *If $\langle G, C\rangle$ has a C-SLD refutation with computed answer θ in P, then $\langle G, C\rangle$ has a C-SLD refutation with computed answer θ in P'.*

In [3], following the approach proposed in [11], we isolate two conditions which are sufficient to prove the safety of the transformation for different structuring policies, including the static and dynamic one. These conditions just correspond to that given in [11] and, extending that case, they impose some *closedness* properties on the transformed program, the goal and the context in which the goal is to be evaluated.

According to [11], given an atomic formula $A = f(T)$, we say that a program P is $A - closed$ if each occurrence of f in P is an instance of f(T).

Definition 4.3 *($\langle G, C\rangle$-closedness) Let $G = g(T)$; we say that:*

- *P is* weakly $\langle G, C\rangle$-closed *iff each occurrence of g in P is evaluated in a context $C' \sqsubseteq C$ or in a context sharing no unit with C.*
- *P is* $\langle G, C\rangle$-closed *iff it is G-closed and each occurrence of g in P is evaluated in a context $C' \sqsubseteq C$ or in a context sharing no unit with C.*

Theorem 2 (Soundness and completeness) *Let P be a program, G, G' goals, C a context and P' be a Partial Evaluation of P wrt G and C. $P' \cup : -G'$ is sound wrt P if $P' \cup : -G'$ is weakly $\langle G, C\rangle$-closed; it is sound and complete if $P' \cup : -G'$ is $\langle G, C\rangle$-closed.*
Proof. *For the lack of space the proof is omitted. See [3].*

The $\langle G, C\rangle$-closedness conditions are quite strong condition for equivalence which allow the result to be established for all the different classes of systems. Less restrictive conditions can be imposed when considering each specific class. For the class of statically configured systems, in particular, Partial Evaluation turns out to be always sound.

Theorem 3 (Soundness) *Let P be a program, and P' a Partial Evaluation of P wrt a goal and a context C. Then, for any given goal g, each computed answer for g and P' is a computed answer for g and P.*
Proof. *See [3].*

A further important property holds for statically configured conservative systems: given a goal G, Partial Evaluation is also complete provided that the simple $G - closedness$ condition holds for the transformed program and the goal G.

Theorem 4 (Completeness for Conservative Systems) *Let P be a conservative program, and P' a Partial Evaluation of P wrt a goal $G = g(T)$ and a context C. Then, given a goal G', each computed answer for G' and P is a computed answer for G' and P' provided that $P \cup : -G'$ is $\{g(T)\}$-closed.*
Proof. *See [3].*

The result of proposition 4 cannot be extended to evolving systems, as shown below.

Example 4.1 *Let $P \equiv P^0$ be the following evolving program:*

$\textbf{unit}(u_1, \textbf{parent}(top))$:	$\textbf{unit}(u_2, \textbf{parent}(u_1))$:	$\textbf{unit}(u_3, \textbf{parent}(u_2))$:
$p(X) : -q(X).$	$r(1).$	$q(2).$
$q(X) : -r(X).$		

Let $C = \lfloor u_2, u_1 \rfloor$ *be the initial context and* $G = p(X)$ *the initial goal. Then by a single unfolding step we obtain* P^1*:*

$\boldsymbol{unit}(u_1, \boldsymbol{parent}(top))$:	$\boldsymbol{unit}(u_2, \boldsymbol{parent}(u_1))$:	$\boldsymbol{unit}(u_3, \boldsymbol{parent}(u_2))$:
$p(X) : -r(X).$	$r(1).$	$q(2).$
$q(X) : -r(X).$		

Now consider the context $\mathcal{C} = \lfloor u_3, u_2, u_1 \rfloor$*; the transformation is not complete in* $\mathcal{C}$. *In fact* $\mathcal{C}^0 \vdash p(2)$ *but* $\mathcal{C}^1 \not\vdash p(2)$

For evolving systems, it is therefore necessary to maintain the stronger $\langle G, C \rangle$-closedness. However, it is worth mentioning that the completeness of Partial Evaluation is still automatically guaranteed also for evolving systems, if the choice of the initial context corresponds to a whole chain in the unit hierarchy defined by the program. If this is the case, the transformed program is $\langle G, C \rangle$*-closed* by construction.

This provides an effective use of Partial Evaluation in inheritance-based systems. Given the whole inheritance tree for a program P a complete transformation is obtained by specializing P with respect to a goal G and all the inheritance chains corresponding to the branches of this tree.

If $\{C_1, \ldots, C_n\}$ are the contexts corresponding to these branches, we get the set of Partial Evaluations $\{PD(G, C_1), \ldots, PD(G, C_n)\}$. The new program in then obtained by deleting all the original definitions for G, and adding the new ones. This yields to the extended notion of Partial Evaluation with respect to a goal G and a set of contexts $\{C_1, \ldots, C_n\}$, as the union of the set of Partial Evaluations with respect G and to the different C_is. Namely $PD(P, G, \{C_1, \ldots, C_n\}) = P'$ such that:

$$\mathcal{R}(P') = (\mathcal{R}(P) \setminus (\cup_{i \in [1,..n]} \mathcal{D}(C_i, G))) \cup (\cup_{i \in [1,..n]} PD(G, C_i)).$$

For an example see section 5.

4.1 Dealing with Context Switch During Partial Evaluation

Extending the Partial Evaluation scheme we have devised so far to include dynamic context switch is indeed quite straightforward. The only remark concerns the computation of the deduction context for the residuals. In fact, when dynamic context switch is considered, a unique maximum element for the label contexts along each derivation path might not exist. Therefore, the computation of the deduction context needs restating as follows:

Theorem 5 (Deduction context revised) *Given a C-SLD derivation:*

$$\langle G_0, C_0 \rangle \vdash_{c_1} \ldots \vdash_{c_j} \langle G_j, C_j \rangle$$

the deduction context $\mathcal{D}c(R)$ *for the c-resultant* $R = G_0 : -\langle G_j, C_j \rangle$ *is the maximum element of the set* $\{c_k, \ldots, c_1 \mid k \leq j\}$ *where* $\{c_k, \ldots, c_1\}$ *is the set of label contexts which occur before the first context switch in the derivation.*

Finally, the construction of the residuals in the body of the resultants (definition 3.8), immediately extends to the case $C_i \not\sqsubseteq \mathcal{D}c(CR)$. Formally:

Definition 4.4 (Residuals) *Let $CR = G : -\langle g_i, C_i\rangle$ be a c-resultant for the c-goal $\langle G_0, C_0\rangle$. Then, the corresponding resultant R is determined depending of the the relationship between $\mathcal{D}c(CR)$ and C_i. Namely,*

(i) *if $C_i = \mathcal{D}c(CR)$, then $R = G : -g_i$.*

(ii) *if $C_i \neq \mathcal{D}c(CR)$ and $C_i = \lfloor u_j, \ldots, u_1 \rfloor$, then $R = G : -u_j : g_i$.*

5 Applications

For the class of systems we have considered, the transformation technique described in the previous sections provides an effective framework for some relevant applications.

Example 5.1 *Let us consider the inheritance scheme given in example 2.5. Suppose we are interested in specializing the program with respect to the goal mode(X). We have here three inheritance chains:*

$$top \rightarrow animal \rightarrow bird \rightarrow tweety$$

$$top \rightarrow animal \rightarrow horse$$

$$top \rightarrow animal \rightarrow human$$

A Partial Evaluation with respect to the goal mode(X) and the single branch

$$\lfloor tweety, bird, animal, top \rfloor$$

produces the transformed program:

$$\mathbf{unit}(animal, \mathbf{parent}(top)) : \quad \left[\ mode(walk).\right.$$

$$\mathbf{unit}(bird, \mathbf{parent}(animal)) : \quad \left[\begin{array}{l} mode(fly). \\ mode(run). \\ no\_of\_legs(2). \\ covering(feather). \end{array}\right.$$

$$\mathbf{unit}(horse, \mathbf{parent}(animal)) : \quad \left[\ no\_of\_legs(4).\right.$$

$$\mathbf{unit}(human, \mathbf{parent}(animal)) : \quad \left[\ no\_of\_legs(2).\right.$$

$$\mathbf{unit}(tweety, \mathbf{parent}(bird)) : \quad [no\_of\_wings(2).$$

Notice that the goal human : mode(run) *fails now while it succeeded in the original program since $\lfloor animal, human \rfloor \not\sqsubseteq \lfloor tweety, bird, animal, top \rfloor$.*

By converse, if we take into account all the branches, the union of all the resulting Partial Evaluations yields the following complete program:

$\textbf{unit}(animal, \textbf{parent}(top)) : \quad \left[\ mode(walk). \right.$

$\textbf{unit}(bird, \textbf{parent}(animal)) : \quad \left[\begin{array}{l} mode(fly). \\ mode(run). \\ no\_of\_legs(2). \\ covering(feather). \end{array} \right.$

$\textbf{unit}(horse, \textbf{parent}(animal)) : \quad \left[\begin{array}{l} mode(gallop). \\ no\_of\_legs(4). \end{array} \right.$

$\textbf{unit}(human, \textbf{parent}(animal)) : \quad \left[\ mode(run). \right.$

$\textbf{unit}(tweety, \textbf{parent}(bird)) : \quad [no\_of\_wings(2).$

6 Conclusions

In this work we presented a Partial Evaluation scheme that can be suitably applied to different structured logic programming systems. The framework we have devised extends the one presented in [11] for Horn Clause Logic, to capture the notions of units, contexts and contextual evaluation of goals. For the class of systems we have considered the transformation turns out to be always sound; different *closedness* conditions must be satisfied by the partially evaluated program to guarantee completeness.

In particular, for the class of conservative statically configured systems, which represent the traditional, block-based, structured systems, these conditions just correspond to the one introduced in [11] for Horn Clause Logic.

For evolving systems, if Partial Evaluation is performed with respect to all the leaves of the inheritance tree, the condition stated in [11] can be still conveniently applied.

Acknowledgements

This work has been partially supported by the "Progetto Finalizzato Sistemi Informatici e Calcolo Parallelo" of CNR under grant n.890004269. We also would like to thank ENIDATA that partially supported this work.

References

[1] H. Bacha. Meta-prolog design and implementation. In *Proc. 5th Int. Conf. and Symp. on Logic Programming*, 1988. Seattle, The MIT press.

[2] A. Brogi, E. Lamma, and P. Mello. A General framework for Structuring Logic Programs. *C.N.R. Technical Report, "Sistemi Informatici e Calcolo Parallelo"*, N. 4-1, May 1990.

[3] M. Bugliesi, E. Lamma, and P. Mello. Partial Deduction for Structured Logic Programming. *DEIS Technical Report*, April 1990.

[4] K. Fukunaga and S. Hirose. An experience with a prolog-based object-oriented language. In *OOPSLA-86*, 1986. Portland, Oregon.

[5] H. Gallaire. Merging objects and logic programming: relational semantics. In *Proc. AAAI '86*, 1986.

[6] L. Giordano, A. Martelli, and G. F. Rossi. Local definitions with static scope rules in logic languages. In *Proceedings of the FGCS Int. Conf.*, 1988. Tokyo.

[7] D.M. Gabbay and N. Reyle. N-prolog: an extension of prolog with hypothetical implications. In *Journal of Logic Programming, n. 4*, 1984. pages 319-355.

[8] H. Kauffman and A. Grumbach. Multilog: multiple worlds in logic programming. In *Proc. ECAI86*, 1986. North-Holland.

[9] H.J Komorowski. A specification of an abstract Prolog machine and its application to Partial Evaluation. In *Linkoping Studies in Science and Technology Dissertation*, 1981.

[10] E. Lamma, P. Mello, and A. Natali. The design of an abstract machine for efficient implementation of context in logic programming. In *Proc. 6th Int. Conf. on Logic Programming*, Lisbon, The MIT Press, 1989.

[11] J. W. Lloyd and J. C. Shepherdson. *Partial Evaluation in Logic Programming.* Technical Report CS-87-09, Dept. of Comp. Sc. Univ. of Bristol, Dept. of Math., Univ. Walk Bristol, December 1987.

[12] F. G. McCabe. Logic and objects: language, application and implementation. *Doctorat Thesis*, Imperial College, University of London, November 1988.

[13] L.T. McCarty. Clausal intuitionistic logic. 1. Fixed-point semantics. In *Journal of Logic Programming, N. 5*, 1988. pages 1-31.

[14] P. Mello. Inheritance as combination of horn clause theory. In *Inheritance Hierarchies in Knowledge Representation*, 1990. Wiley eds, chapter 14.

[15] D. Miller. Theory of modules for logic programming. In *Proc. 1986 Symp. on Logic Programming*, 1986. Salt Lake City (USA).

[16] P. Mello, A. Natali, and C. Ruggieri. Logic programming in a software engineering perspective. In *Proc. North American Conf. on L.P.*, Cleveland (USA), 1989. The MIT press.

[17] L. Monteiro and A. Porto. Contextual logic programming. In *Proc. 6th Int. Conf. on. L.P.*, Lisbon (P), 1989. The MIT Press.

[18] D. H. D. Warren. An abstract prolog instruction set. In *SRI Technical Note 309*, 1983. SRI International.

[19] P. Wegner and S. B. Zdonik. Inheritance as an incremental modification mechanism or what like is and isnt like. In *in Proc. ECOOP88, and in LNCS, Vol. 322*, 1988. Springer-Verlag.

The Mixtus Approach to Automatic Partial Evaluation of Full Prolog

Dan Sahlin
SICS, Box 1263,
S-164 28, Sweden
electronic mail: dan@sics.se

Abstract

A partial evaluator for Prolog takes a program and a query and returns a program specialized for all instances of that query. The intention is that the generated program will execute more efficiently than the original one for those instances.

This paper outlines the features of "Mixtus", an automatic partial evaluator for *full* Prolog, i.e. including non-logical features such as cut, assert, var, write etc.

Mixtus does not need any annotations to guide it in its process, but will *automatically* generate a program given only an input program and a query.

1 Introduction

This paper gives an outline of the features of Mixtus, an automatic partial evaluator for full Prolog. For a more formal and detailed description see [Sahl90]. Mixtus has been designed with the following objectives:

- Mixtus should be able to handle full Prolog. Many built-in predicates such as var and cut do not behave logically, and are treated with extra care. Even for Prolog programs not containing any non-logical predicates the generated program must present all solutions in the same order as the original program, including duplicates.
- Mixtus should be fully automatic. Most partial evaluators typically need annotations describing when to do "unfolding" of predicates. For an inexperienced user it may be very cumbersome to provide that information. By having all annotations optional and of a general nature, partial evaluation immediately becomes available to all users. With or without annotations, Mixtus is guaranteed to terminate for all input.
- Mixtus should generate reasonably efficient code. As it is the main reason for doing partial evaluation, this is very important. The partial evaluation process must however be constrained so that it does not take too long time or generate too large a program. Many optimizations possible for pure Prolog are not possible for full Prolog, but Mixtus tries to identify the pure parts of the program and handle them separately.
- Mixtus should have a relatively simple structure. This may conflict with the previous goal, generating efficient code. By trying the partial evaluator on a large number of examples we have tried to incorporate only the most important parts for generating efficient code.

All features discussed in this paper have been implemented in SICStus Prolog [Carl88], and are described in more detail in [Sahl90].

1.1 Partial evaluation vs. partial deduction

Lloyd and Shepherdson in [Lloy87] describe partial evaluation for logic programming as follows: "Given a program *P* and a goal *G*, partial evaluation produces a new program *P'*, which is *P* 'specialized' to the goal *G*. The intention is that *G* should have the same (correct and computed) answers wrt *P* and *P'*, and that *G* should run more efficiently for *P'* than for *P*."

Definitions and the conditions for soundness and completeness of partial evaluation for the declarative (the answer is a logical consequence) and procedural (based on SLDNF) semantics are given in that paper. Komorowski who published the first partial evaluator for Prolog [Komo81] has recently [Komo89] named this view on partial evaluation of logic programming "partial deduction", which seems quite appropriate.

A Prolog program may however contain many non-logical features and features relating to the actual execution such as side-effects. This has little to do with deductions, and the term "partial evaluation" seems more appropriate for a system that is capable of handling full Prolog.

1.2 Partial evaluation and mixed computation for full Prolog

Partial evaluation and mixed computation [Ersh88] are closely related as seen from the definitions below, which are modified for full Prolog.

Partial evaluation for full Prolog

Let P be a Prolog program, i.e. a list of clauses.

Let Q be a query to a Prolog program.

Let P[Q] be the results of running the program P with the query Q. By results, we here mean the sequence of side-effects caused by running the program such as reading and writing to the terminal or to files and producing printouts of the bindings of the variables (if any) in Q. It is also assumed that an exhaustive search is made so that the program is forced to produce all solutions. The program may then either terminate, loop or produce infinitely many solutions.

A *partial evaluator* for full Prolog is a function $\Pi_{partial}$ taking a program P and a query Q and returning a new program P'. $\Pi_{partial}$ has the following properties:

For all instances $Q\theta$ of Q:

- P'[$Q\theta$] produces at least all the same results as P[$Q\theta$] and in the same order. It may produce more results only if P[$Q\theta$] starts looping after producing a certain result. Alternatively, it may loop itself when P[$Q\theta$] loops. It will always produce all results, including duplicates, in the same order as P[$Q\theta$].
- The computation of $\Pi_{partial}$(P,Q) will always terminate for all P and Q.

Mixed computation for full Prolog

Most versions of the partial evaluator presented in this paper will use a definition more resembling mixed computation.

Let P, Q and P[Q] be defined as above. A mixed computator for full Prolog is a function Π_{mixed} taking a program P and a query Q and returning a pair $\langle P',Q' \rangle$ consisting of a new program P' and a new query Q' having the following properties:

- The arity of Q' is the number of distinct variables in Q, and all arguments of Q' are distinct variables.
  For example, if Q=q(f(X),3,g(a,X,Y)) we may then have Q'=qx(X,Y).

The remaining conditions on P' are the same as for partial evaluation but with P'[Qθ] replaced by P'[Q'θ].

Relating partial evaluation and mixed computation

Any partial evaluator can be considered a mixed computator by letting

$$\Pi_{mixed}(P,Q) = \langle \Pi_{partial}(P,Q) \cup \{Q' :- Q.\}, Q' \rangle$$

where Q' is related to Q as described above.

Conversely, a partial evaluator may easily be obtained from a mixed computator by extending the returned program by the clause "Q :- Q'.". That is,

$$\Pi_{partial}(P,Q) = P' \cup \{Q :- Q'.\} \quad \text{where } \langle P',Q' \rangle = \Pi_{mixed}(P,Q).$$

This method of converting mixed computation into partial evaluation will be used in most of the systems presented in this paper.

Loops are not preserved

As can be seen from the above definition, a loop in the original program may be removed by partial evaluation. There are two conditions for removing a loop: the loop must not produce any results and it must be followed by a failure. If we are allowed to remove potential improductive loops, composite queries like "p(X), fail" may be replaced by "fail" if "p(X)" does not have any side-effects. This optimization may be very significant if "p(X)" starts a complicated computation. It does not seem feasible to restrict this optimization to the cases where "p(X)" is guaranteed to terminate, as this is a very complex property to deduce, and in general not even decidable. However, it is very straightforward to check if the call may cause any side-effects.

Other important properties not covered by the definitions

As seen from the above definition, one correct partial evaluator is the identity function which simply returns the input program P, ignoring the query Q! Although this is correct, it is not at all what is expected from a partial evaluator. The whole point of making the partial evaluation is to make the program run faster. Unfortunately, the efficiency of a program is difficult to measure without executing the program. Thus any specific claims of speed-up are not part of the definition of partial evaluation above. Instead, the transformations made by the partial evaluator are carefully chosen so that in most reasonable implementations they will normally make the generated program run faster, or at least not slower. Where various implementations may differ in a significant way, the SICStus Prolog implementation [Carl88] based on the Warren Abstract Machine [Warr83] is chosen as the standard.

It is not very difficult to implement a partial evaluator that is guaranteed to terminate for all input programs and queries. The user may however expect more than that; he may ask for a specific maximum execution time. This has not been implemented and it is difficult to predict the time a partial evaluation will take.

1.3 Basic transformations

The three basic transformations used in this partial evaluator are *unfolding*, *folding* and *predicate generation*.

Unfolding. There are several forms of unfolding, and we will return to this issue later. The most basic form of unfolding takes place when a clause and a goal in the body of the clause are given, and a set of new clauses is returned in which the goal has been eliminated by using the defining clauses of the goal.

More formally, if the goal is G, the clause is "F:– Before, G, After" and the clauses defining G are "H_i:–B_i", then an unfolding will yield the clauses

(F:- Before,B_i,After)θ_i if $\theta_i \neq$ fail

where θ_i is the substitution resulting from unifying G and H_i

Predicate generation. This happens when the partial evaluator replaces a predicate call (P_{old}) with a call to a newly generated predicate (P_{new}), which is a specialized version of the old predicate. Semantically, P_{new} is defined by "P_{new} :– P_{old}".

For example, the call p(a,X,Y) is replaced by p1(X,Y), which is semantically defined by p1(X,Y):–p(a,X,Y).

Folding. This is the process by which a goal which is an instance of the body of a predicate is replaced by the corresponding instance of its head. This is a correct transformation if there is only one clause defining the predicate, in which case the head and the body are "equivalent".

In Mixtus, this condition is guaranteed as folding is only applied for predicates created by predicate generation. As predicate generation is not done for composite goals in Mixtus, folding will also never be done for composite goals.

All partial evaluators for Prolog in the literature use unfolding as their basic mechanism, some also have folding, and a few have predicate generation. The main problem in a partial evaluator is to know when to apply the various transformations.

1.4 Sources of performance improvements

The main reason we have for doing partial evaluation is to get a program that runs faster than the original one. The main sources of improved performance in the partial evaluator are the following:

Generation of new, possibly recursive, predicates. The partial evaluator performs a dynamic analysis of how the various predicates are called, and for each instantiation pattern of a predicate, a new predicate specialized for that call pattern is generated. All arguments that are instantiated at partial evaluation time are removed, and only the uninstantiated variables remain.

Unfolding of user-defined predicates. This will remove a predicate call. This transformation is particularly favourable if there are no matching clauses, and the call can be eliminated altogether.

In the conjunction (p,q), if q is found to fail, then the whole conjunct may be replaced by fail, and no call is made at all to p. In real Prolog programs with side-effects not all of these optimizations are possible, and this will be elaborated in detail in this paper.

Most Prolog implementations just do indexing on the first argument outermost functor level[1]. This may counteract the advantages of unfolding as the indexing may be lost. For instance, the query q(A) when partially evaluated with respect to

---

[1] That is, if the outermost structure of the first argument is known when the predicate is called, the right clause(s) will be taken immediately using a jump-table for instance. This

```
q(f(X))  :- f(X).      f(1).      g(a).
q(g(X))  :- g(X).      f(2).      g(b).
                       f(3).      g(c).
```

will normally be totally unfolded generating a program just consisting of the assertions

```
q(f(1)). q(f(2)). q(f(3)). q(g(a)). q(g(b)). q(g(c)).
```

Thus indexing is lost for the inner structure (X) in making all the facts explicit. By preventing unfolding where there are multiple matching clauses it can be guaranteed that no indexing will be lost. But preventing unfolding will also prevent propagation of bindings. Thus there is no clear choice of what to do, and the user is given the possibility of controlling whether unfolding should be done for non-deterministic predicates.

The example above also shows that for real Prolog implementations it is clearly unsatisfactory to use the number of inferences as a measurement of execution complexity.

Evaluating built-in predicates. All built-in predicates that can be evaluated should of course be evaluated at partial evaluation time, and this is also an important source of efficiency improvement. Usually, when a built-in predicate cannot be evaluated, it is because it is insufficiently instantiated. For example, `var(X)` cannot be evaluated, as we do not yet know if `X` will be bound to a non-variable at run time. Some built-in predicates cannot be evaluated as they have side-effects that must be delayed until actual execution time, such as `write(17)` or `read(X)`.

To facilitate unfolding and evaluation, the handling of variable bindings is very important. In the partial evaluator we distinguish between right-propagation and left-propagation of bindings.

Right-propagation of bindings. This takes place for instance when "X=*t*,e[X]" (where *t* is an arbitrary term and e[X] is an expression containing the variable X) is transformed into e[*t*]. Without right-propagation not much can be done by a partial evaluator.

There are however some disadvantages of right-propagation with respect to execution efficiency. If the variable occurs several times in the same predicate call or in conjunctive predicate calls, there is a danger of creating several copies instead of just one of the structure. If the structure is large, this may be a major disadvantage. In most cases the structure is either very small or partial evaluation will totally "consume" and eliminate the structures.

For a disjunction, there is a similar but harder problem of right-propagation. During partial evaluation "X=*t*,(e_1[X]; e_2[X])" becomes transformed into "(e_1[*t*]; e_2[*t*])". Thus there is a danger that backtracking will cause the same structure *t* to be created again, which was not the case in the original code. In contrast to the conjunction case above, it is not clear that it is always better to move the creation of *t* back to right before the disjunction. It may be the case that backtracking will not occur or that a branch fails, so that the structure *t* is just created once or not at all. As the choice is unclear the present partial evaluator does not try to move the

drastically improves performance especially if there are many clauses where indexing can be used to distinguish between the clauses.

bindings out of the disjunction, with the possibility of generating sub-optimal code.

Left-propagation of bindings. In contrast to right-propagation, for full Prolog extreme care has to be taken when propagating bindings left. A non-logical predicate such a "var" makes "var(X),X=3" quite a different thing from "var(3)". For purely logical predicates it is quite safe to move the bindings left. Having more instantiated predicate calls makes it easier for the partial evaluator to do unfolding, so the newly instantiated predicates are examined once again. This may in turn give rise to new left-propagated instantiations, so care has to be taken so that the partial evaluator will not loop.

Left-propagation has the similar problem as right-propagation concerning duplication of terms. For example, it might be disadvantageous to transform "p(X,X), X=bigterm" into "p(bigterm,bigterm)". On the other hand, as "p(bigterm,bigterm)" is reexamined and partially evaluated again, it might be advantageous. Mixtus always performes left-propagation if it is allowed, thereby being potentially sub-optimal.

2 Partial evaluation of pure Prolog

A partial evaluator for pure Prolog, i.e. without non-logical features, will be presented in this section. In contrast to the partial evaluator for full Prolog, the order of the solutions presented will not necessarily be preserved. No explicit code will be given here for the partial evaluation algorithms, but rather the basic ideas will be outlined and motivated. A complete formal specification can be found in [Sahl90], where the system is described in detail using Prolog. The algorithms presented in this chapter are the core of Mixtus, and will remain almost unchanged for the full system.

2.1 Generating residues

The partial evaluator is structured as a specialized meta-interpreter. According to the definition of a partial evaluator it takes a program and a partially instantiated query and returns a program specialized for for all instances of that query. Thus, the meta-interpreter is given the original query and tries to execute as much as possible, consistently obeying the following principle:

In the partial evaluator a term t represents all instances $t\theta$ of t.

For instance, `length([A,B],X)` can safely be evaluated to `X=2`. On the other hand, `length([A|B],X)` cannot be evaluated and must be left as it is. Those remaining goals that cannot be evaluated are called the *residue*, and are used in the construction of the generated program output by the partial evaluator.

2.2 Handling clauses

The procedure Π_{clauses}, takes as input a sequence of clauses defining a predicate, and returns a new sequence of clauses which is the partial evaluation of the predicate. As a side-effect during partial evaluation (using `assert` in the Prolog program), Π_{clauses} may possibly create clauses for other predicates, as explained below.

The result of partially evaluating this sequence of clauses, is the concatenation of the partial evaluations of each single clause.

Each clause is partially evaluated by partially evaluating each goal in the clause, one by one. There are two kinds of goals: calls to built-in predicates and calls to user-defined predicates. The conceptually simplest case is the treatment of built-in predicates.

2.3 Handling built-in predicates

A large and important part of any partial evaluator for full Prolog is the module which takes care of partially evaluating all built-in predicates. The simplest idea is having a database of the conditions for each built-in predicate for being safely evaluated:

```
evaluable(true).
evaluable(X=Y).
evaluable(length(L,X)) :- \+ open_tail(L); integer(X).
open_tail(T) :- var(T)
open_tail([H|T]) :- open_tail(T).
```

That is, `true` and `=/2` can always be evaluated, whereas `length/2` has some conditions guaranteeing that a finite set of solutions will be returned. If the built-in predicate is not evaluable, it will be left as a residue.

An example: The clause `p(X,Y):-X=3,q(X)` when X=3 is evaluated simply becomes `p(3,Y):-q(3)`, as the bindings propagate left and right. If a built-in predicate when executed may return several solutions, several clauses are returned, one for each solution. If a built-in predicate fails, no clauses are returned.

Disjunction (;/2) may be viewed as a built-in predicate. The result of partial evaluation of a disjunction is the concatenation of the partial evaluations of the disjuncts.

A more complex scheme for handling some built-in predicates is implemented in Mixtus. Many predicates get special treatment, e.g. `is/2`, where as much as possible is evaluated even if the whole expression cannot be evaluated. For instance, `X is Y+2*3` is transformed into `X is Y+6`.

2.4 The goal-stack

A stack of goals encountered is maintained, much in the way it is handled in an ordinary Prolog interpreter. If a user-defined goal `A` is encountered, a triple `(A',Anew',Isrec)` is entered into the stack.

The first component `A'`, is a copy of `A`, so that all variables in `A'` are distinct from the variables in `A`. This is necessary so that further instantiations of variables in `A` will not change the triple.

The third component, initially unbound, is set to `true` if a directly or indirectly recursive call to `A` is found. We will return to that situation below.

The second component, `Anew'`, is created by extracting all variables from `A'` and creating a functor which has a name different from all other predicates. For readability in Mixtus the name is formed by concatenation of the names of the first functors, possibly followed by a digit.

For example, if `A'=pred(term(X,Y,3),Y)` we then could have `Anew'= predterm(X,Y)`. Semantically the new relation `Anew'` is defined as `Anew':- A'`.

Only the parts of `A'` that can vary, i.e. the variables, are kept in `Anew'`. As will be shown below, `A'` may be replaced by `Anew'`, thereby eliminating known constants from the arguments of the call.

Mixtus actually goes one step further when creating `Anew'`: If it is known from the context of `A'` that some variables cannot be instantiated or used, then these variables are not included in `Anew'`.

2.5 User-defined predicates

When a used-defined predicate is encountered it may either be unfolded, folded, kept as it is or replaced by a call to a newly generated predicate. This choice is normally made in other partial evaluators by a user annotation for each predicate. Our goal is to have the choice made automatically, and how that is achieved is shown below. This procedure is perhaps the most distinctive feature of Mixtus.

The loop-detection mechanism, which be elaborated in more detail in the next section, will guarantee the termination of the procedure.

Folding	If `A` is an instance of a goal `A'` in a triple in the goal-stack, it is replaced by the corresponding instance of `Anew'`. In this process, the corresponding `Isrec` component of the triple is set to `true`. else
Loop-detection	If by inspecting the goal-stack we suspect an infinite loop has been found, the goal `A` is kept as it is. else
Recursive invocation of partial evaluator	Let the clauses defining A be "H_i:–B_i". Let the substitution resulting from unifying A with a head H_i be θ_i. While extending the goal-stack with `(A',Anew',Isrec)`, $\Pi_{clauses}$ is called with the clauses "(Anew :- B_i)θ_i" as input. The treatment of the partially evaluated clauses returned by $\Pi_{clauses}$ is determined by the `Isrec` component.
Predicate generation	If `Isrec` is set to `true`, as a recursive call is made to `Anew`, no unfolding is done and the goal `A` is replaced by `Anew`. The clauses returned by $\Pi_{clauses}$ define `Anew`, and they are added to resulting program.
Unfolding	If `Isrec` is not set to `true`, unfolding can be done, using `Anew` and the newly generated clauses.

As can be seen from the above procedure, the tests for folding and loop-detection are made before the recursive invocation of the partial evaluator. This will eliminate the danger of going into an infinite recursion since the loop detection will prevent infinite recursion. The test for folding is done before the test for loops as it is better if a call is made to `Anew`, whose clauses are the result of a partial evaluation rather than `A`, which simply uses the original clauses.

2.6 The top-level query

Mixtus only accepts a top-level query that is a call to a user-defined predicate. The above mechanism for handling user-defined goals is used also for the top-level query, but unfolding is always prevented so that it will be guaranteed that a new predicate and a new query are formed.

In the resulting program an additional clause is added relating the original and the new query as described in "Relating partial evaluation and mixed computation" in section 1.2.

2.7 Detection of potential loops

Due to the unsolvability of the halting problem, a loop detection mechanism can never be perfect; it will always be a compromise. In this case, we have chosen to diagnose some non-loops as loops, thereby guaranteeing termination of the program in all circumstances. A loop detection mechanism may be arbitrarily refined and complicated. Here a sequence of increasingly complex alternative loop-detections are presented for a goal-stack `GS` and a goal `A`.

Loop detection version 1

`loop_detection(A,GS)` succeeds if a goal having the same main functor as A occurs at least *depthmax* times in the goal stack. This extremely simple test used with *depthmax*=10 has been surprisingly successful. But there are instances where it succeeds where loop detection preferably should fail. For instance, the query

```
append([1,2,3,4,5,6,7,8,9,a,b,c,d,e,f|A],B,C)
```

is better completely evaluated, rather than being stopped after ten recursions. The following refined loop detection will handle this case correctly.

Loop detection version 2

As long as the arguments shrink in size (in the append-case above: the list gets shorter), it is safe to recurse as this process cannot go on indefinitely. This leads to the second version of loop detection:

`loop_detection(A,GS)` succeeds if the number of calls A' in GS to the predicate A with termsize(A') ≤ termsize(A) is at least *depthmax*.

The function termsize(x) is defined recursively on Prolog terms as

$$\text{termsize}(x) = \begin{cases} 1 \text{ if x is a constant or a variable} \\ 1 + \sum_{i=1}^{\text{arity}(x)} \text{termsize}(\text{argument}(x,i)) \text{ if x is a compund term} \end{cases}$$

where argument(x,i) returns the i:th argument of x

This refined version of loop detection covers most cases encountered in practice.

Loop detection version 3

Sometimes one argument grows during recursion but some other argument gets smaller as for the query `reverse([1,2,3],[],X)` and the program

```
reverse([],A,A).
reverse([A|B],C,D) :- reverse(B,[A|C],D).
```

Most programs exhibiting this behaviour have one argument earlier in the argument list (an input argument) which shrinks whereas the argument later in the argument list (the accumulating argument) grows. A reformulation of the loop detection criterion using a lexical comparison of the sizes of the individual arguments will handle the situation. We get `loop_detection(A,GS)` succeeds if the number of calls A' in GS to the predicate A with lexlesseq(A',A) is at least *depthmax*. lexlesseq is defined so that the first argument not equal in size determines the comparison.

Loop detection version n

As already mentioned, the loop detection may become arbitrarily complex. It is easy to devise various extensions of the variants presented. For instance, the third variant could be made more robust against permutations of the arguments. Two not subsuming loop-detections, such as variants 2 and 3, can be combined into one, which only signals for a potential loop if both tests succeed.

2.8 Some examples of partial evaluation of pure Prolog programs

Some examples will illustrate the basic ideas on how the partial evaluator automatically will choose between folding, unfolding and predicate generation.

All examples are illustrated by a table of the following form. A is the user-defined goal to be partially evaluated. A and Anew are related as described above. For each clause of A a unification is made and the corresponding instance of Anew is created. Partial evaluation then continues with the body of the clause.

<table>
<tr><td>goal-stack</td><td>A</td><td>Anew</td><td></td></tr>
<tr><td>clause i
head H_i</td><td>Aθ (i.e. $H_i\theta$)
head after unification</td><td>Anewθ
new head after unification</td><td rowspan="2">θ = the substitution resulting from unifying A and H_i</td></tr>
<tr><td>body B_i</td><td colspan="2">$B_i\theta$
body after unification</td></tr>
</table>

Example: folding

Let the query be `m(X, [1|Y])` and the program be the member program:

```
clause 1:          m(A,[A|B]).
clause 2:          m(C,[D|E]) :- m(C,E).
```

We then get the following table.

<table>
<tr><th></th><th>A</th><th>Anew</th><th>substitution θ</th></tr>
<tr><td>goal-stack</td><td>m(X,[1|Y])</td><td>m2(X,Y)</td><td></td></tr>
<tr><td>clause 1</td><td>m(1,[1|Y]).</td><td>m2(1,Y).</td><td>{1/X}</td></tr>
<tr><td>clause 2
head</td><td>m(X,[1|Y])</td><td>m2(X,Y)</td><td rowspan="2">{X/C, 1/D, Y/E}</td></tr>
<tr><td>body</td><td colspan="2">:- m(X,Y).</td></tr>
<tr><td colspan="4">As neither folding or loop-detection is applicable, partial evaluation then continues with the goal m(X,Y) in the body.</td></tr>
<tr><td>goal-stack</td><td>m(X,Y)</td><td>m3(X,Y)</td><td></td></tr>
<tr><td>clause 1</td><td>m(X,[X|B2]).</td><td>m3(X,[X|B2]).</td><td>{X/A2, [X|B2]/Y}</td></tr>
<tr><td>clause 2
head</td><td>m(X,[D2|E2])</td><td>m3(X,[D2|E2])</td><td rowspan="3">{X/C2, [D2|E2]/Y}</td></tr>
<tr><td>body</td><td colspan="2">:- m(X,E2).</td></tr>
<tr><td>folding</td><td colspan="2">:- m3(X,E2).</td></tr>
</table>

That is, the new query is `m2(X,Y)` and the generated clauses are

```
m2(1,Y).
m2(X,Y) :- m3(X,Y).
m3(X,[X|B2]).
m3(X,[D2|E2]) :- m3(X,E2).
```

Example: loop-detection and unfolding

The predicate call `r(X,[],3,Z)` will reverse the elements in the list `X`, multiply each element by 3 and return the new list in Z.

```
r([],L,P,L).
r([B|C],D,P,E) :- F is B*P, r(C,[F|D],P,E).
```

A partial evaluation of `r(X,[],3,Z)` is summarized by the following table.

<table>
<tr><th></th><th>A</th><th>Anew</th><th>substitution θ</th></tr>
<tr><td>goal-
stack</td><td><code>r(X,[],3,Z)</code></td><td><code>r2(X,Z)</code></td><td></td></tr>
<tr><td>clause 1</td><td><code>r([],[],3,[]).</code></td><td><code>r2([],[]).</code></td><td><code>{[]/X, []/L,
3/P, []/Z}</code></td></tr>
<tr><td>clause 2
head</td><td><code>r([B|C],[],3,Z)</code></td><td><code>r2([B|C],Z)</code></td><td rowspan="2"><code>{[B|C]/X,
[]/D, 3/P,
Z/E}</code></td></tr>
<tr><td>body</td><td colspan="2"><code>:- F is B*3, r(C,[F],3,Z).</code></td></tr>
<tr><td colspan="4">No folding or loop detection, the partial evaluator is recursively called with <code>r(C,[F],3,Z)</code>.</td></tr>
<tr><td>goal-
stack</td><td><code>r(C,[F],3,Z)</code></td><td><code>r3(C,F,Z)</code></td><td></td></tr>
<tr><td>clause 1</td><td><code>r([],[F],3,[F]).</code></td><td><code>r3([],F,[F]).</code></td><td><code>{[]/C,[F]/L2,
3/P2,[F]/Z}</code></td></tr>
<tr><td>clause 2
head</td><td><code>r([B2|C2],[F],3,Z)</code></td><td><code>r3([B2|C2],F,Z)</code></td><td rowspan="2"><code>{[B2|C2]/C,
[F]/D2, 3/P2,
Z/E2}</code></td></tr>
<tr><td>body</td><td colspan="2"><code>:- F2 is B2*3, r(C2,[F2,F],3,Z)</code></td></tr>
<tr><td colspan="4">No folding but a loop is detected as the goals in the goal stack – <code>r(X,[],3,Z)</code>, <code>r(C,[F],3,Z)</code> – indicate that the goal <code>r(C2,[F2,F],3,Z)</code> may lead to an infinite loop. The goal is therefore kept as it is, referring to the original clauses.</td></tr>
</table>

To summarize, the clauses generated so far are

```
r2([],[]).
r2([B|C],Z)  :- F is B*3, r3(C,F,Z)
r3([],F,[F]).
r3([B2|C2],F,Z)  :- F2 is B2*3, r(C2,[F2,F],3,Z).
```

The call `r3(C,F,Z)` shall now be unfolded as the predicate `r3/3` is not recursive, and we get the final result:

```
r2([],[]).
r2([B],[F]):-F is B*3.
r2([B,B2|C2],F,Z):-
        F is B*3, F2 is B2*3, r(C2,[F2,F],3,Z).
```

As can be seen from the above code, special cases have been generated for lists of length 0 and 1, whereas longer lists are handled by the original predicate `r/4`. By changing the loop detection criterion, we could have generated even more cases for longer lists, but we would always have to resort to using the original predicate for longer lists. It is questionable whether generating more and more clauses actually yields an execution performance improvement in this case. In the next section, we show how to avoid calling the original predicate by generating a predicate further specialized so that the number 3 need not be carried around as an explicit argument.

2.9 Generalized restart

When a loop is detected, the basic algorithm will just keep a call to the original code. By looking at the goal-stack in the previous example more carefully we can do better. The three recursive calls to `r/4` were

```
r(X,[],3,Z), r(C,[F],3,Z), r(C2,[F2,F],3,Z)
```

Clearly the second argument varies and the third argument is constant. In general this can be found out by doing an "anti-unification" [Plot69, Sahl90] between recursive calls. An anti-unification generates the most specific term which is more general than all terms in a set. This term is unique up to renaming of variables. In this case we get the term `r(S,T,3,U)`. A "generalized restart" means that whenever a loop is detected a generalization of the recursive calls is generated, and partial evaluation is restarted with that new goal.

For the above example we get after restart:

	A	Anew	substitution θ
goal-stack	`r(S,T,3,U)`	`r4(S,T,U)`	
clause 1	`r([],T,3,T).`	`r4([],T,T)`	`{[]/S, Y/L, 3/P, T/U}`
clause 2 head	`r([B|C],T,3,U)`	`r4([B|C],T,U)`	`{[B|C]/S, T/D, 3/P, U/E}`
body	`:- F is B*3, r(C,[F|T],3,U).`		
folding	`:- F is B*3, r4(C,[F|T],U).`		

Due to folding, the generated predicate `r4/3` is now recursive

```
r4([],T,T).
r4([B|C],T,U):- F is B*3, r4(C,[F|T],U).
```

The query `r(X,[],3,Z)` now corresponds to the query `r4(X,[],Z)`.

2.9.1 Guaranteeing that folding will eventually apply

Just doing a single generalized restart will not guarantee that we will get an instance of the query so that folding can be applied. But if no folding occurs, the loop-detection will trigger another generalized restart. There is however no danger that the process of loop-detection and generalized restart will go on indefinitely. The reason is simply that at each generalized restart we generate a strictly more general instance of the previous attempted restart, and this sequence of more and more general queries ends with a query where all arguments are distinct variables. Any other call to the same predicate will obviously be an instance of this query, and we can thereby guarantee that folding can be applied.

2.10 Order of solutions

The partial evaluator presented so far does not preserve the order of solutions. For example, the program

```
num(0).
num(s(X)) :- num(X).
```

given the query `num(X), (X=s(0); X=0)` returns `X=0` and `X=s(0)` and then loops. If the query instead is first partially evaluated we get a new query `sx(X)` and a new program

```
sx(s(0)) :- numx(s(0)).
sx(0) :- numx(0).
```

where `numx/1` is defined like `num/1`. When this new program is run we will get `X=s(0)` and `X=0` and no loop as above. Thus the order of the solutions has been changed. The reason is simply that we have allowed the choice point in the query (the semi-colon) to propagate left into the call of `num(X)` which also is non-deterministic. If we want to keep the order of the solutions, more care has to be taken when combining the solutions from a conjunction (i.e. a ',' in Prolog). In the next section it will be shown how this is achieved.

3 Purity of predicates

To efficiently handle partial evaluation of full Prolog, the built-in, user-defined and generated predicates must be classified according to their "purity". A few predicates are so intimately dependent on the original code that they cannot be reasonably handled at all. These predicates are discussed in [Sahl90].

The predicates that are handled are classified into three groups: *side-effect, propagation sensitive* and *logical*. This classification is similar to Lakhotia's in [Lakh89a].

A predicate *P* is considered to belong to the group *side-effect* if "fail,*P*" does not produce at least the same results as "*P*,fail". As expected, `write`, `read`, `assert`, `retract` and "`!`" all belong to this group. The predicates `var`, `nonvar`, "=.." and "=" do not belong to this group.

How should we classify the predicate "loop", defined by the clause "loop:-loop."? Clearly "fail, loop" behaves differently than "loop, fail" but "loop" is not considered a side-effect predicate. The reason is the following. By "produce at least the same results" above we mean the same as in the definition of partial evaluation, that is, we allow the partially evaluated predicate to produce more solutions only if the original program starts looping at a certain point. As a consequence of this view, "fail, loop" will produce at least the same results as "loop, fail". A similar argument will show that the built-in predicate "repeat" is not a side-effect predicate, although "repeat, fail" never terminates.

A predicate *P* not having a side-effect is *propagation sensitive* if a call preceded by a unification does not produce at least the same results as the call followed by this unification, i.e. "`X=t,`*P*" does not produce at least the same results as "*P*`,X=t`". For instance, "`X=3, var(X)`" is clearly not the same as "`var(X), X=3`". A very large group of built-in predicates belong to this category such as `var`, `nonvar`, "==", "\==", "arg" and "functor".

The remaining predicates are *logical*. Here we find all the purely logical predicates such as "=", "=..", "repeat", "loop" (as defined above) and "<".

The following table summarizes the properties of predicates being classified.

	fail,*P* produces at least the same results as *P*,fail	X=t,*P* produces at least the same results as *P*,X=t
logical	yes	yes
propagation sensitive	yes	no
side-effect	no	yes/no

The partial evaluator will use the classification of predicates so that a failure or a unification is moved as far left as possible.

If possible, a predicate should be classified as logical, as the partial evaluator generates much better code in that case. The predicate “<” actually violates the test for being logical as “X<3, X=1” will fail generating an error message whereas “X=1, X<3” succeeds. Nevertheless, the predicate is classified as logical, as this difference is noticeable only for an incorrect program generating an error message. A similar argument is possible for “=..”.

As a general optimization, a nonlogical predicate becomes logical when it is ground, i.e. when it does not contain any variables. This is easily seen from the definition of logical.

When in doubt how to classify a predicate, it is always safe to classify it as “side-effect”. In particular, unknown predicates are always considered side-effect predicates. This makes it possible to run the partial evaluator on one file at a time, thereby reducing the complexity of the partial evaluation procedure. The resulting program generated by the partial evaluator may not be as optimal, but it will always be correct, i.e. the resulting program will produce at least the same results as the original program.

3.1 Classification of generated predicates

All generated predicates are classified on the basis of the classification of the predicates it calls.

A generated predicate containing a call to a predicate having a side-effect (except cut) is always classified as having a side-effect itself. Otherwise, if the predicate contains a call to a propagation sensitive predicate or cut it will be classified as propagation sensitive. Finally, if the predicate only calls logical predicates, it is logical itself.

It may seem odd that a predicate containing a cut, which is considered to have a side-effect, can be classified as propagation sensitive. The reason is that the scope of the cut does not reach outside the predicate. The cut however generally makes the predicate propagation sensitive as for

```
p(a) :- !.
p(X).
```

which succeeds for `b=X,p(X)` and fails for `p(X),b=X`.

4 Partial evaluation of full Prolog

In partial evaluation for full Prolog, the conditions for folding and loop-detection are identical to those for pure Prolog. The main differences concern how to avoid left propagation of bindings, how to unfold and the treatment of all the predicates, cut in particular. The order of the solutions of the generated predicate must also not be different from the original one.

4.1 Avoiding left propagation of bindings

The unfolding mechanism for pure Prolog propagates bindings left and right. As shown in the previous section, left propagation of bindings must not be allowed for side-effect and propagation sensitive predicates if Prolog semantics is to be maintained. Left propagation of bindings is not a problem when unfolding the first goal of a clause.

By generating a new predicate we can temporarily make every goal the first of a clause and perform partial evalution on that clause. To maintain the semantics of cut the clauses produced by partial evaluation must however be unfolded back again.

4.1.1 Generating a temporary predicate

Given a goal G which is to be partially evaluatated in a clause "F:- Before, G, After" the clause is replaced by "F :- Before,Gnew" where Gnew is a call to a new temporary predicate defined by a single clause "Gnew:-G,After". The clause head Gnew has an arbitrary functor name, and the arguments are exactly the variables occurring both in "F:-Before" and in "G,After".

Partial evaluation may then safely continue with the goal G in the newly generated clause "Gnew:-G,After" as it is the first goal. In this process, G may be folded or replaced by a new predicate call as for pure Prolog. There is however one optimization made when unfolding for full Prolog, which is described below separately.

The final result of partial evaluation of "Gnew:-G,After" is a set of new clauses, "$Gnew_i$:- B_i".

The goal-stack is not extended with a triple for Gnew. This will ensure that folding will not apply, that is, no recursive predicate for Gnew will be formed, and thus unfolding can always be applied. To maintain the semantics of potential cuts in "G,After", it is necessary always to perform unfolding for the generated predicate Gnew.

4.1.2 Removing the temporary predicate

The temporary predicate Gnew is removed by forming a disjunction so that the original clause becomes

F :– Before, $\bigvee_i$ (Gnew=$Gnew_i$, B_i)

This will ensure that no bindings are propagated left. If the disjunction is empty, that is no clauses were returned by partial evaluation, it is replaced by "fail". If the "Before" goal is a side-effect goal, this explicit "fail" goal must be kept as it is. If "Before" is a logical or propagation sensitive goal, the whole clause is allowed to fail, and the empty set of clauses is returned.

By keeping the disjunction explicit, no choice-points are moved left, and thereby the above procedure also guarantees that the order of the solutions is preserved.

If the "Before"-part is deterministic (i.e. does not leave any choice-points) and logical, the order of solutions will not be changed by letting bindings from the disjunct propagate left. For instance, `h(X):-p(X),(X=1; X=2)` can safely be transformed into the two clauses `h(1):-p(1)` and `h(2):-p(2)` if `p(X)` is deterministic and logical. However, we now have two calls to `p/1` instead of just one, which might be less efficient. If `p(X)` is a time-consuming calculation which deterministic and logical. However, we now have two calls to `p/1` instead of just one, which might be less efficient. If `p(X)` is a time-consuming calculation which finally ends up with `X=2`, it is clearly disadvantageous to propagate the bindings left. On the other hand, if `p(1)` and `p(2)` fail almost immediately it is probably better to propagate the bindings. We have chosen not to propagate the bindings of the disjunct as we cannot determine in general whether it is an optimization.

Example of partial evaluation of full Prolog: aliasing

It is tempting to incorrectly let the clause

```
p(X,Y) :- var(X), Y=2.
```

be "partially evaluated" into

```
p(X,2) :- var(X).
```

Mixtus will however not let the binding of `Y` pass left over `var(X)`. A call which aliases `X` and `Y`, such as `p(Z,Z)`, will make the two clauses above behave differently.

In [LeSa88], where a partial evaluator for full Prolog is presented, a similar technique seems to be used for creating a predicate. The predicate is however only unfolded if it is defined by a single clause, and the report does not describe how the scope of the cut is maintained. The system described annotates variables occurring in non-logical goals so they are prevented from being further instantiated. It is not clear from the report whether this method is capable of handling the aliasing in the example above.

4.2 No recomputation of variable variants

All generated predicates are stored along with the call that prompted their creation. Whenever a predicate call is to be partially evaluated, this database of generated predicates is consulted and that definition is used instead if the current call is a variable variant of the stored call.

This optimization is crucial to make it viable to apply the partial evaluator on larger programs, especially when propagating bindings left and for unfolding for full Prolog as described below.

4.3 Unfolding for full Prolog

One important optimization is performed when unfolding for full Prolog. The goals formed by unfolding are reevaluated to facilitate propagation of bindings. In pure Prolog this is not necessary as the bindings propagate freely left and right.

An example: Let `p/1` be defined by `p(X):-var(X),X=3`. Unfolding as described for pure Prolog of `p(X)` in `q(X):-p(X),r(X)` gives

```
q(X) :- var(X), X=3, r(X).
```

whereas unfolding for full Prolog makes a reevaluation which propagates the binding X=3

```
q(X) :- var(X), X=3, r(3).
```

This example shows that the reevaluation is essential as instead of just having `r(X)` we now have `r(3)`, which is more instantiated, thereby facilitating partial evaluation.

4.3.1 Making the reevalution efficient

During reevaluation a call to a generated predicate may be encountered. As all generated predicates are semantically defined by a single clause "P_{new}:-P", this call to P_{new} replaced by the corresponding instance of P. The partial evaluation of P will generally be made just by consulting the database of all partially evaluated predicates, as described in section 4.2. Thus a costly full partial evaluation is not invoked on the same goal again, but rather simple efficient database lookup is sufficient.

4.3.2 Unfolding and generalized restart

For predicates produced by the generalized restart mechanism (as described in section 2.9) one precaution has to be taken to avoid loops. The code for these predicates has been produced with a more general instance of the call than the one in the original program to increase the probability of folding. If folding did occur, there is no problem as no unfolding and thereby no recomputation will be made. The problem is when no folding occurred, a rare but possible situation. When unfolding the predicate, the goals encountered are not stored in the database over already partially evaluated goals, and a full partial evaluation will be performed for these goals. This might lead to further generalized restarts and unfoldings, which can make the partial evaluator loop. Mixtus prevents these loops by never unfolding predicates generated by a generalized restart.

4.4 Simplifying unifications without left-propagation

The unifications "Gnew=$Gnew_i$" in the disjunction above should always be simplified as much as possible without any harmful left-propagation of bindings. This means that a variable in Gnew may be unified with a varible in $Gnew_i$, if that variable is not already unified with an other variable in Gnew. The remaining unifications must be kept explicitly.

For example, if "Gnew=$Gnew_i$" is `p(A,B,C)=p(X,X,s(Y))`, then only A may be unified with X, and `B=A`, `C=s(Y)` are kept as explicit unifications.

4.5 Left propagation of bindings

For a logical goal we may propagate the bindings left. As the goal then gets further instantiated, the partial evaluator is restarted on that goal.

For example, `p(X,Y,Z):-append(X,Y,Z),X=[1,2]` may then be partially evaluated into `p([1,2],Y,[1,2|Y])`.

Some care however has to be taken when reevaluating goals: we must ensure that the partial evaluator does not return to the same goal indefinitely with more and more instantiated arguments. This can easily be arranged by maintaining a list of all retried goals.

4.5.1 Using anti-unification to extract common instances

As shown in section 4.1.2, a call Gnew to a set of clauses $Gnew_i$:-B_i can be transformed into a disjunction "$\bigvee_i$ (Gnew=$Gnew_i$, B_i)". By using anti-unification on the heads of the clauses, we can extract all common bindings. Let $Gnew_{anti}$ be the anti-unification of all $Gnew_i$. We can then get the following transformation instead

$$Gnew=Gnew_{anti}, \bigvee_i (Gnew_{anti}=Gnew_i, B_i)$$

As before, the unifications are simplified as much as possible.

Using this transformation means that some bindings only have to be made once, and not for each disjunct. But more important is the fact that left propagation may now be applied.

4.6 Handling cut

Cut is a very important built-in predicate that must be fully supported in any partial evaluator for full Prolog. The first observation we make is that we cannot unfold a predicate containing a cut after partial evaluation, as the scope of the cut would then be changed. Thus we now have three conditions that prevent unfolding: that the predicate is recursive, created by a generalized restart or that the predicate contains cut. Since unfolding is necessary to propagate bindings further, it is crucial that partial evaluation is able to remove as many cuts as possible.

Also notice that in the procedure shown above for temporarily generating new predicates, these new predicates are never kept but always unfolded back using a disjunction. This will ensure that the scope of a cut remains unchanged. Venken in [Venk88] instead suggests that a mark should be used that limits the scope of the cut.

If the disjunction formed just consists of a single disjunct and a cut has been executed in the corresponding clause, the disjunct itself is handled as if it were a cut. Possibly that cut may also be executed.

The problem of how to handle cut is here split up into three parts: how to cut, when to cut, and when to remove cut.

4.6.1 How to cut

Conceptually, this is very simple: just discard the clauses after the clause with the cut that was to be executed.

4.6.2 When to cut

A cut may be performed only if we are sure to reach the cut for all calls to this clause. This means that it must not be possible for the head unification to fail and all goals preceding the cut must not fail in this clause. The first condition is easily checked; all arguments of the head must be distinct variables. The second condition is also easy if all preceding goals are built-in goals. We may then check in a small data-base of built-in predicates whether they may fail. The real problem is to check whether a call to a user-defined or generated predicate cannot fail. A special module in Mixtus analyzes predicates in this respect and tries to estimate the number of solutions a predicate may generate. This module is described in [Sahl90].

These conditions for performing cut generalize the conditions given in [Bugl89].

4.6.3 When to remove cut

A cut may be removed if it is totally unnecessary, that is, it occurs in the last clause, and all predicates preceding it in the clause do not produce any choice-points. The same module mentioned above is also used for the latter analysis. This means that a cut in the first part of a disjunction cannot be removed, but possibly a cut in the second part. Cuts in both the "then"-part and the "else"-part of an "if-then-else"-construct may be removed.

Having removed a cut in a clause, a further improvement may be possible as the partial evaluator earlier was prevented from performing some optimizations as the cut is considered a side-effect goal. The partial evaluator is thus invoked again on the clause, producing a set of clauses. If that set is empty, the previously second last clause is now the last clause, and this procedure for removing a cut is restarted again.

There are other cuts that could be removed: cuts not in the last clause, but in a clause where there already is a cut. The second of two cuts separated only by calls to deterministic predicates may safely be removed. The current partial evaluator does not incorporate this refinement as it cannot be crucial for making a predicate totally free from cuts, which is a necessary condition for unfolding. Also, having two cuts in the same clause, one being redundant is extremely unusual, so it does not seem worth the trouble to check for this condition.

An example

As the following example will show, a cut within a disjunction may trim away the rest of the disjuncts without trimming away the rest of the clauses. Let the query be `p(7,Z)` and the program

```
p(X,Y) :- nonvar(Y), (r(X), !, Y=0; Y=1).
p(X,X).
r(7).
```

When partially evaluating the temporarily generated predicate corresponding to the disjunction above, it is found that the cut may be executed. However, when looking at the whole clause, it is not certain that the cut will be reached as `nonvar(Y)` may fail. The resulting query is `p2(Z)` and the returned program is

```
p2(Y) :- nonvar(Y), !, Y=0
p2(7).
```

4.7 Other features of Mixtus

Space limitations do not permit a full treatment of the following features of Mixtus. They are explained in detail in [Sahl90].

- Many built-in predicates get a special treatment such as `->/2` (if-then-else), `call/1`, `dif/2`, `freeze/1`, `freeze/2`, `is/2`, `copy_term/2` and `findall/3`.
- Some data-structures are moved right in a clause, so they need not be created if the clause would fail before.
- Some variables are classified as “input variables” which facilitates the conditions for taking a cut.
- Two semantically identical generated predicates are mapped into just a single predicate. This might be important as the input variable mechanism may cause the partial evaluator to generate several similar predicates, if calls are made to the same predicate but with different input variables.
- Some simple predicates consisting of a single clause with a single goal are eliminated.
- Cyclic structures are handled.

5 Discussion

The emphasis of Mixtus is as a general program optimization tool by program transformation. Typical speed-ups for normal Prolog programs range from 3% (the already highly optimized SICStus compiler) to 20%. Much better figures are reached for optimizing programs where meta-programming techniques are used; typically 5-10 times faster per interpretation layer. Although Mixtus does not have any special mechanism for restricting the size of the program produced, it is usually no more than 3–4 times larger than the original one.

If possible Mixtus will always fold, even if an unfolding might yield better code. Experience has however shown that this case is very unusual.

Mixtus will never unfold predicates that contain a cut after partial evaluation. Although this might look as a shortcoming of the approach, in reality it prevents code explosion. The cuts in the code are thus actually very helpful in guiding the unfolding process.

The main unsolved (and unsolvable) problem in Mixtus is to create a perfect loop-detection mechanism. Our experiments, however, indicate that the simple tests in this paper usually are quite adequate.

Although Mixtus accepts side-effect predicates such as assert and retract, these are never executed, but rather kept as they are, and it is a question open to future research whether it is feasible to execute them by a partial evaluator.

6 Acknowledgements

I am grateful for the valuable comments on this paper given by Torkel Franzén, Jonas Almgren and Kent Boortz.

7 References

Bjør88 *Partial Evaluation and Mixed Computation*, proceedings from workshop in Gammel Avernæs Oct 1987, Denmark, eds. Bjørner, D., Ershov, A. P. and Jones, N. D., North-Holland

Bugl89 Bugliesi, M. and Russo, F. , *Partial Evaluation in Prolog: Some Improvements about Cut*, Logic Programming, Proceedings of the North American Conference, 1989, MIT Press

Carl88 Carlsson, M. and Widén, J., *SICStus Prolog User's Manual*, Research report R88007, SICS, Sweden, 1988.

Ersh88 Ershov, A. and Jones, N. D., *Two Characterizations of Partial Evaluation and Mixed Computation*, In [Bjør88], pp xv-xxi

Fuch88 *New Generation Computing*, 6 (1988), *Special issue: selected papers from the Workshop on Partial Evaluation and Mixed Computation*, 1987, Ohmsha.Ltd/Springer-Verlag.

Gall86 Gallagher, J., *Transforming logic programs by specializing interpreters*, ECAI86, 7th European Conference on Artificial Intelligence, Brighton, U.K., 1986

Komo81 Komorowski, H.J., *A specification of an abstract Prolog machine and its application to partial evaluation*, PhD theses, No 69, Software Systems Research Center, Linköping University, 1981.

Komo89 Komorowski, H.J., *Synthesis of Programs in the Framework of Partial Deduction*, Ser.A, No 81, Departments of Computer Science & Mathematics, Åbo Akademi, Finland

Lakh89 Lakhotia, A. and Sterling, L., *Development of a Prolog Partial Evaluation System*, Tech. Rept. Department of Computer Engineering and Science, Case Western Reserve University, 1989.

LeSa88 Levi, G. and Sardu, G., *Partial Evaluation of Metaprograms in a "Multiple Worlds" Logic Language*, in Fuch88

Lloy87 Lloyd, J.W. and Shepherdson, J.C., *Partial Evaluation in Logic Programming*, Tech. Rept. CS-87-09, Computer Science Department, University of Bristol, December 1987

Plot69 Plotkin, G.D. *A note on inductive generalisation.* In Machine Intelligence 5, Meltzer, B. and Michie, D., pp. 153-163, 1969.

Sahl90 Sahlin, D., *An Automatic Partial Evaluator for Full Prolog*, SICS 1990

Stan89 *Prolog standard, Draft for Working Draft 2.0, ISO*, National Physical Laboratory, July 1989

Take86 Takeuchi, A. and Furukawa, F., *Partial Evaluation of Prolog Programs and its Application to Meta Programming*, Information Processing 86, Elsevier Science Publishers B. V.

Venk88 Venken, R., *A Partial Evaluation System for Prolog: some Practical Considerations*, In [Fuch88]

Warr83 Warren, D.H.D., *An abstract Prolog Instruction Set*, Technical Note 309, SRI International, Menlo Park, CA, Oct. 1983

Constraints

Computational Complexity and Constraint Logic Programming Languages

Extended Abstract

Jim Cox
Ken McAloon
Carol Tretkoff
Department of Computer and Information Science
Brooklyn College and CUNY Graduate Center
Bedford Avenue and Avenue H
Brooklyn, New York 11210

Abstract

We give a complexity analysis of a variety of languages across the spectrum of the CLP scheme. By varying the logic and memory management, the role of the constraints and the role of the logic can be measured. The analysis clarifies the relation between linear/integer programming and constraint logic programming. We also determine how the power of constraints can easily lead to undecidable queries in Datalog languages with constraints. This work is motivated in large part by the problems of efficient implementation of CLP languages and the concomitant need for low level constraint languages.

1 Introduction

The constraint paradigm has emerged as significant area of research in logic programming and several successful systems, *e.g.* [Colmerauer], [Dincbas *et al.*], [Jaffar Michaylov], [Sakai Aiba], have been developed. In their papers on the CLP scheme [Jaffar Lassez 86], [Jaffar Lassez 87] Jaffar and Lassez provide a formal framework for constraint logic programming language design.

From a high-level point of view, in the formalization of the CLP Scheme the constraints coming from unification and the constraints coming from the applications domain are integrated into a single constraint solving system. However, by varying the logic (*e.g.* propositional, relational, functional) as well as the domain (*e.g.* Rational Numbers as an ordered additive group, Complex Numbers as a field), we obtain a parameterization of CLP languages that allows us to specify languages of subrecursive complexity, which can be tailored for specific applications. Moreover, the logic and the constraints interact in surprising ways. For example, our analysis shows that the introduction of linear arithmetic constraints in Datalog leads to undecidability. Our most precise result in this direction uses the Matiasevitch, Davis, Robinson, Putnam result [Matiasevitch], [Davis Matiasevitch Robinson] on the recursive unsolvability of Hilbert's Tenth Problem for diophantine equations. Our results complement and contrast those of [Kanellakis Kuper Revesz] where it is shown, *in al.*, that bottom-up query evaluation in closed form for relational calculus with polynomial constraints has NC data complexity. It also turns out that storage management is tightly connected with the underlying logic of the CLP language, and it is the handling of local and global variables and parameters that provides a natural uniform classification.

This research is the complexity theoretic foundation of our work on the implementation of constraint logic programming languages. Constraint languages present interesting challenges at the level of compilation and efficient implementation. Communication with the constraint solver and extraction of the constraint programming analogue of the Prolog answer substitution lead one to work with small languages where the constraints have a status which is not overshadowed by that of the surrounding logic. In particular in our implementation of $2LP$ [McAloon Tretkoff] the logic is propositional and the domain is the ordered group of Rational Numbers as a $\mathbf{Z}$-module. Linear and integer programming can be viewed as a subset of $2LP$, Theorem 5 below. The complexity theoretic analysis of this paper unfolds a hierarchy of $2LP$-like languages and points to ways to use program transformation for constraint languages.

Detailed proofs of the results in this paper can be found in [Cox McAloon Tretkoff].

2 Preliminaries and Definitions

A domain $\mathcal{D}$ is given as a tuple $\mathcal{D} = (\mathbf{D}, R_1, \ldots, R_k, f_1, \ldots, f_l, a_1, a_2, \ldots)$ where $\mathbf{D}$ is a nonempty set, the R_i are relations on $\mathbf{D}$, the f_j are operations on $\mathbf{D}$ and the a_i are distinguished elements of $\mathbf{D}$. We also use $R_1, \ldots, R_k, f_1, \ldots, f_l, a_1, a_2, \ldots$ as symbols of the first-order language of the domain $\mathcal{D}$. Terms of this language are defined inductively: variables and individual constants are terms and $f_j(t_1, \ldots, t_n)$ is a term if f_j has arity n and $t_1, \ldots, t_n$ are terms. A term with no free variables is called a *closed* term or a *ground* term. Atomic formulas have the form $R_j(t_1, \ldots, t_n)$ where $t_1, \ldots, t_n$ are terms and R_j is an n-ary relation. Atomic formulas are also called *constraints*. Formulas are obtained from atomic formulas by closure under boolean connectives and quantification. If the free variables of a formula F are $X_1, \ldots, X_n$ we write $F(X_1, \ldots, X_n)$ for F. An assigment is a map from a finite set of variables to $\mathbf{D}$; if the assignment θ is defined on the free variables of F we write $\mathcal{D} \models F\theta$ iff the assignment θ satisfies F in $\mathcal{D}$. The set of closed formulas G of the form $\exists X_1 \ldots \exists X_n C(X_1, \ldots, X_n)$ such that C is a conjunction of constraints and $\mathcal{D} \models G$ is called the *constraint theory* of the domain $\mathcal{D}$.

In what follows, **2** denotes $\{0, 1\}$, **N** the natural numbers, **Z** denotes the integers, **Q** denotes the rational numbers, **R** the real numbers, **C** the complex numbers and **AN** the algebraic numbers. To fix notation in the case of classical logic programming, we consider the language with constant symbol nil and binary functor $cons$ and let **H** be the the Herbrand universe of ground terms in $cons$ and nil. The constraint domain of interest here is $(\mathbf{H}, =, cons, nil)$; a set of constraints is then solvable if the corresponding unification succeeds.

It is also helpful to restrict the typing of certain binary operators. If f is such an operator on a domain, we write $\check{f}$ to restrict the first argument of f to be an individual constant and $\hat{f}$ to restrict the second argument of f to be an individual constant. Thus for multiplication $\check{*}$ allows multiplication by the distinguished coefficients from the domain. Thus for example the domain $(\mathbf{R}, =, +, \check{*}, 0, \pm 1, \pm 2, \ldots)$ is the additive group of the reals as a module over **Z**. This notation is also suitable for dealing with complexity considerations. Thus the domain $(\mathbf{R}, =, +, -, *, /, \widehat{**}, 0, 1, 2, \ldots)$ of the reals as a field allows constraints with exponents written in binary as well as coefficients. It also serves to obviate the need for new notation; thus, $(\mathbf{N}, =, \check{+}, 1)$ denotes the natural numbers with the successor operation.

In the definitions that follow, $p, q_1, \ldots, q_t$ will denote uninterpreted predicate symbols. Their semantics will be determined by inductive definitions given in terms of logic programming rules. A CLP language is specified by a constraint domain $\mathcal{D}$ and conditions on the allowable rules to interpret predicate symbols..

Definition 1 *A* $vanilla - CLP(\mathcal{D})$ *program is given by a finite set of rules of the form*

$$p(X_1, \ldots, X_n) :- c_1(Y_{1,1}, \ldots, Y_{1,k_1}), \ldots, c_s(Y_{s_1}, \ldots, Y_{s,k_s}),$$
$$q_1(Z_{1,1}, \ldots, Z_{1,m_1}), \ldots, q_t(Z_{t,1}, \ldots, Z_{t,m_t}).$$

where the $X_1, \ldots, X_n, Y_{1,1}, \ldots, Y_{s,k_s}$ *are variables and* $Z_{1,1}, \ldots, Z_{t,m_t}$ *are variables or terms of the language of* $\mathcal{D}$.

Note that in the above definition, it is not required that the variables and terms $X_1, \ldots, X_n, Y_{1,1}, \ldots, Y_{s,k_s}, Z_{1,1}, \ldots, Z_{t,m_t}$ be distinct.

The use of the qualifying term "vanilla" is due to the fact that the notation CLP($\mathcal{D}$), in particular CLP($\mathcal{R}$), is used to denote the situation where Prolog structures form part of the constraint domain and the language is a superset of Prolog. Thus if we denote by $\mathbf{H} * \mathbf{R}$ the two sorted universe of structures and Real Numbers with = as shared relation, then CLP($\mathcal{R}$) is vanilla-CLP($\mathbf{H} * \mathbf{R}, =, cons, nil, <=, <, +, -, *, /, 0, 1$). In [Sakai Aiba], the system CAL as defined is vanilla-CLP($\mathbf{AN}, =, +, -, *, 0, 1, \ldots$).

Complexity analysis of constraint logic programming languages with many sorted constraints is a further topic of research.

If the constraint domain $\mathcal{D}$ does not have structures or lists, then vanilla-CLP($\mathcal{D}$) will be called Datalog($\mathcal{D}$). Classical Datalog, *e.g.* [Maier Warren], is a superset of vanilla-CLP($\mathbf{N}, =, 0, 1, 2, \ldots$).

In [Jaffar Lassez 86], [Jaffar Lassez 87] minimal model semantics for the CLP scheme are set out and completeness theorems are proved. Moreover, all examples of constraint systems explicitly considered here are solution compact with satisfaction complete theories and so the completeness results of [Jaffar Lassez 86], [Jaffar Lassez 87] on Negation-as-Failure also hold.

A vanilla-CLP($\mathcal{D}$) program P is interpreted in its minimal model where each predicate symbol $p(X_1, \ldots, X_n)$ is interpreted as an n-ary relation $\bar{p} \subseteq \mathbf{D}^n$. We recall the minimal model construction of [Jaffar Lassez 86]: Inductively, define for each natural number m, and for all predicate symbols p of the program an approximation $\bar{p}^m$ as follows:

Step m = 0.

$\bar{p}^0 = \emptyset$

Step m = k+1.

For $d_1, \ldots, d_n \in \mathbf{D}$, $\bar{p}^m(d_1, \ldots, d_n)$ holds iff $\bar{p}^k(d_1, \ldots, d_n)$ holds or for some rule in P of the form

$$p(X_1, \ldots, X_n) :- c_1(Y_{1,1}, \ldots, Y_{1,k_1}), \ldots, c_s(Y_{s_1}, \ldots, Y_{s,k_s}),\\ q_1(Z_{1,1}, \ldots, Z_{1,m_1}), \ldots, q_t(Z_{t,1}, \ldots, Z_{t,m_t}).$$

and some assignment θ where $d_i = X_i\theta$ for $i = 1, \ldots, n$ we have $\mathcal{D} \models c_j\theta$ for $j = 1, \ldots, s$ and $\bar{q}_j{}^k(Z_{j,1}\theta, \ldots, Z_{j,m_j}\theta)$ for $j = 1, \ldots, t$.

So finally set $\bar{p} = \bigcup_m \bar{p}^m$.

Following [Jaffar Lassez 87] with appropriate change in notation, a *goal* is defined to be a set of the form

$$c_1(X_{1,1}, \ldots, X_{1,s_1}), \ldots, c_r(X_{r,1}, \ldots, X_{r,s_r}),$$

$$p_1(Z_{1,1} \ldots, Z_{1,m_1}), \ldots, p_t(Z_{t,1}, \ldots, Z_{t,m_t})$$

where the $X_{i,j}$ are variables and the $Z_{k,l}$ are terms. Suppose we are given a vanilla-CLP($\mathcal{D}$) program P, a goal Γ, $p_j(Z_{j,1}, \ldots, Z_{j,m_j})$ in Γ and a variant of a rule P with no variables in common with Γ of the form

$$p_j(U_1, \ldots, U_n) :- c_1(Y_{1,1}, \ldots, Y_{1,k_1}), \ldots, c_s(Y_{s,1}, \ldots, Y_{s,k_s}),\\ q_1(T_{1,1}, \ldots, T_{1,n_1}), \ldots, q_t(T_{t,1}, \ldots, Z_{T,n_t}).$$

Set θ to be the substitution $\{U_1/Z_{j,1}, \ldots, U_{m_j}/Z_{j,m_j}\}$ which replaces each U_i by the term $Z_{j,i}$ for $i = 1, \ldots, n$. Then a *derivation step* is made by deleting $p_j(Z_{j,1}, \ldots, Z_{j,m_j})$ from the goal Γ and inserting

$$c_1(Y_{1,1}), \ldots, Y_{1,k_1})\theta, \ldots, c_s(Y_{s,1}, \ldots, Y_{s,k_s})\theta,$$

$$q_1(T_{1,1},\ldots,T_{1,n_1})\theta,\ldots,q_t(T_{t,1},\ldots,T_{t,n_t})\theta$$

to form a new goal. A sequence of goals starting with an initial goal and generated by derivation steps is called a *successful derivation* or simply a *derivation* if the final goal consists of a set of constraints whose conjunction is satisfiable in $\mathcal{D}$. In particular, a successful derivation of a goal $q(Z_1,\ldots,Z_n)$ from a program P yields a set of constraints

$$c_1(X_{1,1},\ldots,X_{1,s_1}),\ldots,c_r(X_{r,1},\ldots,X_{r,s_r})$$

whose conjunction is satisfiable in $\mathcal{D}$ and which are such that the universal closure of the following implication holds in the minimal model of the program:

$$c_1(X_{1,1},\ldots,X_{1,s_1})\wedge\ldots\wedge c_r(X_{r,1},\ldots,X_{r,s_r})\rightarrow q(Z_1,\ldots,Z_n)$$

To fix notation, we define a *query* to be a goal of the form $q(Z_1,\ldots,Z_n)$ where Z_i is either a variable or a ground term, $i=1,\ldots,n$; if every term is a ground term, then the query is a *ground* query.. The query is *accepted* by the program if its existential closure is satisfied in the minimal model of the program. So, the program P accepts the query $q(Z_1,\ldots,Z_n)$ if and only if for some m the approximation $\bar{q}^m$ is not empty. Similarly, the program P accepts the ground query $q(t_1,\ldots,t_n)$ if and only if for some m, we have $\bar{q}^m(d_1,\ldots,d_n)$ where d_i is the denotation of the closed term $t_i, i=1,\ldots,n$.

Thus, given a program P and query $q=q(Z_1,\ldots,Z_n)$, by the Succesful Derivations Lemma of [Jaffar Lassez 86], the existential closure of q is true in the minimal model of P if and only if there is a derivation of q from P. Note that this completeness result establishes a link between satisfiability in the minimal model of a constraint program and alternating Turing machine computation; *cf.* [Chandra Lewis Makowsky], [Shapiro] for the case of classical logic programming.

The *query complexity* of a given CLP language L is the computational complexity of the formal language consisting of all pairs (P,q) such that P accepts q. The *ground query complexity* of a CLP language is the computational complexity of the formal language consisting of all pairs (P,q) such that q is ground and P accepts q.

We will make use of standard complexity theoretic terminology and complexity classes such as P, NP, PSPACE, RE (Recursively Enumerable), etc.

We summarize the discussion thus far with the following:

Theorem 1 (Completeness Theorem) *Let $\mathcal{D}$ be a domain with constraint theory $\mathcal{T}$. Then for every vanilla-CLP($\mathcal{D}$) program P and every query q, P accepts q if and only if there is a derivation of q from P. Moreover, if $\mathcal{T}$ is in RE, then the query complexity of the language vanilla-CLP($\mathcal{D}$) is also in RE.*

For further completeness results for constraint logic programming, see [Maher]; for classical logic programming see [Lloyd].

We now give a classification of CLP languages over a domain $\mathcal{D}$ by means of simple syntactic criteria which turn out to be equivalent to distinctions in storage management and in logic.

Definition 2 *A* minimal-*CLP($\mathcal{D}$) program is given by a finite set of rules of the form*

$$p(X_1, \ldots, X_n) :- c_1(Y_{1,1}, \ldots, Y_{1,k_1}), \ldots, c_s(Y_{s,1}, \ldots, Y_{s,k_s}),\\ q_1(X_1, \ldots, X_n), \ldots, q_t(X_1, \ldots, X_n).$$

where the $X_1, \ldots, X_n$ are variables and for each i, the $Y_{i,1}, \ldots, Y_{i,k_i}$ form a subset of $X_1, \ldots, X_n$.

Note that this means that the variables $X_1, ..., X_n$ are all global variables of the program and that there are no local variables. The condition that the variables appear in the same order in all the procedures of the program makes the unifications trivial and thus the logic reduces to propositional logic. In particular a minimal-CLP program without constraints reduces to a Proplog program. However, the presence of constraints makes minimal-CLP much more powerful than Proplog, *cf.* Theorem 5, below. The restriction on the variables entails, however, that the storage locations $X_1, \ldots, X_n$ are the only ones that can be addressed in the course of a computation. But the memory is not static in the sense that the least size of solutions to the set of constraints generated by a successful computation is not bounded *a priori*. On the other hand, we show that, in the cases of interest here, the size of the storage required for such solutions can be, in fact, bound as a function of the constraint domain and the program itself.

Definition 3 *A* strict-*CLP($\mathcal{D}$) program is given by a finite set of rules of the form*

$$p(X_1, \ldots, X_n) :- c_1(Y_{1,1}, \ldots, Y_{1,k_1}), \ldots, c_s(Y_{s_1}, \ldots, Y_{s,k_s}),\\ q_1(Z_{1,1}, \ldots, Z_{1,n}), \ldots, q_t(Z_{t,1}, \ldots, Z_{t,n}).$$

where the $X_1, \ldots, X_n$ are variables, where for each i the $Y_{i,1}, \ldots, Y_{i,k_i}$ form a subset of $X_1, \ldots, X_n$, and where each $Z_{1,j}, \ldots, Z_{t,j}$ is either X_j or a ground term, $j = 1, \ldots, n$.

Again, the $X_1, ..., X_n$ are global variables in the program but here these variables and constants can be passed as parameters to subroutines. However, when a variable X_i is passed to a subroutine, it must be in position i.

Definition 4 *A* permutation-*CLP($\mathcal{D}$) program is given by a finite set of rules of the form*

$$p(X_1, \ldots, X_n) :- c_1(Y_{1,1}, \ldots, Y_{1,k_1}), \ldots, c_s(Y_{s,1}, \ldots, Y_{s,k_s}),$$
$$q_1(Z_{1,1}, \ldots, Z_{1,n}), \ldots, q_t(Z_{t,1}, \ldots, Z_{t,n}).$$

where the $X_1, \ldots, X_n$ are variables, for each i the $Y_{i,1}, \ldots, Y_{i,k_i}$ form a subset of $X_1, \ldots, X_n$, and the $(Z_{1,1}, \ldots, Z_{1,n}), \ldots, (Z_{t,1}, \ldots, Z_{t,n})$ are permutations of the variables $X_1, \ldots, X_n$.

In this formulation, the situation differs from that of minimal-CLP programs in that only the variables $X_1, ..., X_n$ can be passed as parameters to subroutines but in arbitrary positions.

Definition 5 *A* conservative-*CLP($\mathcal{D}$) program is given by a finite set of rules of the form*

$$p(X_1, \ldots, X_n) :- c_1(Y_{1,1}, \ldots, Y_{1,k_1}), \ldots, c_s(Y_{s_1}, \ldots, Y_{s,k_s}),$$
$$q_1(Z_{1,1}, \ldots, Z_{1,m_1}), \ldots, q_t(Z_{t,1}, \ldots, Z_{t,m_t}).$$

where the $X_1, \ldots, X_n$ are variables, where for each i the $Y_{i,1}, \ldots, Y_{i,k_i}$, form a subset of $X_1, \ldots, X_n$, and where each $Z_{k,l}$ is either a ground term or a variable from among $X_1, \ldots, X_n$.

In the last three cases, the programs are all equivalent to minimal-CLP($\mathcal{D}$) programs which can be obtained by composing the procedures given in the program. Naturally, the resulting minimal-CLP($\mathcal{D}$) program can be exponential in the size of the original program and in fact the complexity results below show to what extent this is indeed the case.

In the next case, subroutines have a certain measure of local storage in that terms in the global variables can be passed as parameters to subroutines.

Definition 6 *A* term-conservative-*CLP($\mathcal{D}$) program is given by a finite set of rules of the form*

$$p(X_1, \ldots, X_n) :- c_1(Y_{1,1}, \ldots, Y_{1,k_1}), \ldots, c_s(Y_{s,1}, \ldots, Y_{s,k_s}),$$
$$q_1(Z_{1,1}, \ldots, Z_{1,m_1}), \ldots, q_t(Z_{t,1}, \ldots, Z_{t,m_t}).$$

where the $X_1, \ldots, X_n$ are variables, for each i the $Y_{i,1}, \ldots, Y_{i,k_i}$, form a subset of $X_1, \ldots, X_n$, and the $Z_{1,1}, \ldots, Z_{t,m_t}$ are terms of the language of $\mathcal{D}$ all of whose variables are among $X_1, \ldots, X_n$.

3 The Transfer Principle

Suppose ϕ is a log-space computable map which sends constants of (the language of) $\mathcal{D}_1$ to closed terms of (the language of) $\mathcal{D}_2$, n-ary operations of $\mathcal{D}_1$ to terms of $\mathcal{D}_2$ with n free variables and k-ary relations of $\mathcal{D}_1$ to a conjunction of constraints of $\mathcal{D}_2$ with k free variables. To fix ideas for complexity analysis, terms and formulas are represented by labeled trees. The function ϕ extends to a map from atomic formulas of $\mathcal{D}_1$ to conjunctions of atomic formulas of $\mathcal{D}_2$ by means of the recursive definition of terms and formulas. If for some natural number k this map satisfies $|\phi(t)| <= |t|^k$ for all terms t of $\mathcal{D}_1$ we say that ϕ is *admissible*. Under the mapping ϕ a constraint $c(X_1, \ldots, X_n)$ of $\mathcal{D}_1$ is sent to a conjunction of constraints $\phi c(X_1, \ldots, X_n)$ of $\mathcal{D}_2$ and every conjunction of constraints of $\mathcal{D}_1$ is sent to a conjunction of conjunctions of constraints of $\mathcal{D}_2$. Moreover, the map ϕ extends canonically to a map from vanilla-CLP($\mathcal{D}_1$) programs to vanilla-CLP($\mathcal{D}_2$) programs and this map sends minimal (*resp.* permutation, strict, conservative, term-conservative) programs to minimal (*resp.* permutation, strict, conservative, term-conservative) programs. It is straightforward to show that when ϕ is admissible, the extension of ϕ to programs remains log-space computable. We say that $\mathcal{D}_1$ is *interpretable* in $\mathcal{D}_2$ iff the map ϕ is admissible and for every conjunction of constraints $C(X_1, \ldots, X_n)$ of $\mathcal{D}_1$ the following equivalence holds:

$$\mathcal{D}_1 \models \exists X_1 \ldots \exists X_n C(X_1, \ldots, X_n) \Leftrightarrow \mathcal{D}_2 \models \exists X_1 \ldots \exists X_n \phi C(X_1, \ldots, X_n)$$

When the domain $\mathcal{D}_1$ is interpretable in $\mathcal{D}_2$ we write $\mathbf{D}_1 \preceq \mathbf{D}_2$.

By way of example, from the theory of Linear Programming, we have with ϕ the identity function,

$$(\mathbf{Q}, =, <=, <, +, -, *, 0, \pm 1, \pm 2, \ldots) \preceq (\mathbf{R}, =, <=, <, +, -, *, /, 0, \pm 1, \pm 2, \ldots)$$

Other examples are

$$(\mathbf{2}, <) \preceq (\mathbf{2}, =, 0, 1) \preceq (\mathbf{N}, =, 0, 1, \ldots) \preceq (\mathbf{R}, =, +, 0, \pm 1, \pm 2, \ldots)$$

and

$$(\mathbf{N}, =, 0, 1, \ldots) \preceq (\mathbf{H}, =, cons, nil)$$

but, assuming P $\neq$ NP,

$$(\mathbf{N}, =, +, 0, 1, \ldots) \not\preceq (\mathbf{H}, =, cons, nil)$$

and, using [Domich Kannan Trotter],

$$(\mathbf{Z}, =, <=, +, -, 0, 1) \not\preceq (\mathbf{Z}, =, +, -, 0, 1)$$

Moreover, by the unsolvability of Hilbert's Tenth Problem [Matiasevitch], for all domains $\mathcal{D}$ with decidable constraint theory,

$$(\mathbf{N}, =, +, *, 1) \not\preceq \mathcal{D}$$

It is also often the case that interpretablility goes both ways. Thus

$$(\mathbf{N}, =, 0) \preceq (\mathbf{C}, =, 0)$$

and

$$(\mathbf{C}, =, 0) \preceq (\mathbf{N}, =, 0)$$

We note that if two domains share the same language and are interpretable in one another, then the same constraint theory *corresponds* in the sense of [Jaffar Lassez 86] to both domains.

Also we have

$$(\mathbf{Q}, =, <=, <, +, -, \check{*}, 0, \pm 1, \pm 2, \ldots) \preceq (\mathbf{R}, =, <=, <, +, -, \check{*}, 0, \pm 1, \pm 2, \ldots)$$

and

$$(\mathbf{R}, =, <=, <, +, -, \check{*}, 0, \pm 1, \pm 2, \ldots) \preceq (\mathbf{Q}, =, <=, <, +, -, \check{*}, 0, \pm 1, \pm 2, \ldots)$$

Another example is given by circular structures and the results of [Maher]:

$$(\textbf{RationalTrees}, =, cons, nil) \preceq (\textbf{InfiniteTrees}, =, cons, nil)$$

and

$$(\textbf{InfiniteTrees}, =, cons, nil) \preceq (\textbf{RationalTrees}, =, cons, nil)$$

The following theorem will allow us to use interpretability to transfer complexity results from CLP languages over one domain to the corresponding languages over another.

Theorem 2 (Transfer Principle) *Suppose $\mathcal{D}_1 \preceq \mathcal{D}_2$. Then in both the ground query case and the general case a lower bound complexity result as coarse as log-space for a CLP language over $\mathcal{D}_1$ transfers to one for the same CLP language over $\mathcal{D}_2$, and an upper bound result for a CLP language over $\mathcal{D}_2$ transfers to one for the same CLP language over $\mathcal{D}_1$. Moreover, the $\preceq$ relation is transitive and lower bounds transfer up through the relation and upper bounds transfer down through the relation.*

Thus a lower bound for minimal-CLP($\mathbf{N}, =, 0, 1$) implies that for minimal-CLP($\mathbf{R}, =, <=, +, -, 0, \pm 1, \pm 2, \ldots$) and an upper bound for the latter implies the same upper bound for the former.

The proof of this theorem is not unrelated to that of the Finite Presentation Lemma and that of Lemma 5.2 of [Jaffar Lassez 86] where ground derivation is connected with derivation relative to the constraint theory for the domain. The proof suggests that the natural link between constraint logic programming and mathematical logic is through Inductive Definitions; also *cf.* [Marek Nerode Remmel].

4 Minimal CLP Languages

We analyze the complexity of minimal CLP languages.

Theorem 3 *The languages minimal-CLP*($\mathbf{N}, =, 0$) *and Proplog have P-Complete query complexity.*

Theorem 4 *The following languages have P-Complete ground query complexity:*

$$\begin{array}{l} \textit{minimal-CLP}(\mathbf{2}, =, 0, 1) \\ \textit{minimal-CLP}(\mathbf{N}, =, <=, <, +, *, \widehat{**}, 0, 1, \ldots) \\ \textit{minimal-CLP}(\mathbf{Q}, =, <=, <, +, -, \check{*}, 0, \pm 1, \pm 2, \ldots) \\ \textit{minimal-CLP}(\mathbf{R}, =, <=, <, +, -, \check{*}, 0, \pm 1, \pm 2, \ldots) \\ \textit{minimal-CLP}(\mathbf{C}, =, +, -, *, /, \widehat{**}, 0, 1, \ldots) \\ \textit{minimal-CLP}(\mathbf{H}, =, cons, nil) \end{array}$$

Theorem 5 *The following languages have NP-Complete query complexity:*

$$\begin{array}{l} \textit{minimal-CLP}(\mathbf{2}, <) \\ \textit{minimal-CLP}(\mathbf{2}, =, 0, 1) \\ \textit{minimal-CLP}(\mathbf{N}, =, <=, <, +, \check{*}, 0, 1, \ldots) \\ \textit{minimal-CLP}(\mathbf{Q}, =, <=, <, +, -, \check{*}, 0, \pm 1, \pm 2, \ldots) \\ \textit{minimal-CLP}(\mathbf{R}, =, <=, <, +, -, \check{*}, 0, \pm 1, \pm 2, \ldots) \\ \textit{minimal-CLP}(\mathbf{H}, =, cons, nil) \end{array}$$

Note that the complexity of minimal-CLP($\mathbf{R}, =, <=, <, +, -, \check{*}, 0, 1, \ldots$) does not change if we allow negative constraints in the sense of [Lassez McAloon 88].

These results clarify the relationship between linear and integer programming, on the one hand, and constraint logic programming on the other. Phase I of linear programming is minimal-CLP($\mathbf{Q}, =, <=, +, -, \check{*}, 0, 1, \ldots$) with only one rule and with only constraints on the right-hand-side. This language has PTIME query complexity. Phase I of integer programming is minimal-CLP($\mathbf{N}, =, <=, +, \check{*}, 0, 1, \ldots$) with only one rule and with only constraints on the right-hand-side. This language has NP query complexity. By Theorem 4, integer programming is embeddable in minimal-CLP($\mathbf{Q}, =, <=, +, -, 0, 1, \ldots$) and this embedding is natural. In fact we are exploiting this in our current work on the $2LP$ system where linear programming techniques are used to extract information from the constraint solver by taking advantage of the simplicity of the logic. On the other hand the $2LP$ logic, albeit simple, is an extension of the techniques available in classical integer programming.

Theorem 6 *The language minimal-CLP*($\mathbf{R}, =, <=, <, +, -, *, /, \widehat{**}, 0, 1, \ldots$) *has query complexity which is NP-hard and in PSPACE.*

Our next theorem gives bounds for the complexity of the minimal version of CAL, [Sakai Aiba].

Theorem 7 *The language minimal-CLP*$(\mathbf{C}, =, +, -, *, /, \widehat{**}, 0, 1, \ldots)$ *has query complexity which is NP-hard and in PSPACE.*

The following theorem is a direct application of [Matiasevitch]:

Theorem 8 *The language minimal-CLP*$(\mathbf{N}, =, +, *, 1)$ *has RE-Complete (hence undecidable) query complexity.*

5 Conservative CLP Languages

In what follows we have DEXP $= \bigcup_{k>0}$ DTIME(2^{n^k}) and similarly for NEXP. By APSPACE is meant the class of languages accepted by an alternating Turing machine in polynomial space. We will make extensive use of the equivalence of APSPACE with DEXP, [Chandra Kozen Stockmeyer].

For the analysis of the complexity of conservative-CLP over various domains, we first prove two lemmas which give lower bounds on strict- and permutation-CLP. Then, the theorems characterizing the complexity of conservative-CLP will follow from these lemmas and the upper bound results we will prove. At this level of complexity, there are far fewer well-understood complete problems that can be used to obtain lower bound results and direct simulations of computation on Turing machines are required instead. The connection between bounded-resource logic programs and alternating Turing machine computation is made in [Chandra Lewis Makowsky] and [Shapiro].

Lemma 1 *The ground query complexity of strict-CLP*$(\mathbf{N}, =, 0, 1, \ldots)$ *is DEXP-hard under log-space reducibility.*

We will now show that the use of constants as parameters to the predicates is not required to simulate an alternating linear-bounded automaton.

Lemma 2 *The ground query complexity of permutation-CLP*$(\mathbf{N}, =, 0, 1, \ldots)$, *is DEXP-hard under log-space reducibility.*

The upper bound proof in the next theorem incorporates some techniques of [Shapiro].

Theorem 9 *The languages conservative-CLP*$(\mathbf{Q}, =, <=, <, +, -, \check{*}, 0, 1, \ldots)$ *and conservative-CLP*$(\mathbf{R}, =, <=, <, +, -, \check{*}, 0, 1, \ldots)$ *have query complexity that is DEXP-Complete. This remains true when negative constraints in the sense of [Lassez McAloon 88] are allowed.*

Theorem 10 *Strict, permutation, and conservative-CLP*$(\mathbf{N}, =, 0, 1, 2, \ldots)$ *all have ground query complexity that is DEXP-Complete.*

We now consider conservative-CLP over the reals as an ordered field. The proof uses work of [Canny], [Renegar] and [Christov Grigor'ev].

Theorem 11 *The language conservative-CLP*$(\mathbf{R}, =, <=, <, +, -, *, /, \widehat{**}, 0, 1, \ldots)$ *has ground query complexity that is DEXP-Complete and query complexity that is in NEXP.*

The next theorem treats conservative-CLP over the field of complex numbers. The proof uses work of [Ierardi] and [Gallo Mishra].

Theorem 12 *Conservative-CLP*$(\mathbf{C}, =, +, -, *, /, \widehat{**}, 0, 1, \ldots)$ *has ground query complexity that is DEXP-Complete and query complexity that is in NEXP.*

Note that this last result gives lower and upper bounds for conservative-CAL. We also have the following result:

Theorem 13 *The language conservative-CLP*$(\mathbf{H}, =, cons, nil)$ *has ground query complexity that is DEXP-Complete and query complexity in NEXP.*

6 Undecidability and Local Storage

The next theorem shows that for linear constraints, even a very restricted use of local storage leads to undecidability. The proof uses the work of [Matiasevitch].

Theorem 14 *The following languages have RE-Complete (hence undecidable) ground query complexity:*

term-conservative-CLP$(\mathbf{Z}, =, +, -, 1)$
term-conservative-CLP$(\mathbf{Q}, =, +, -, 1)$
term-conservative-CLP$(\mathbf{R}, =, +, -, 1)$
term-conservative-CLP$(\mathbf{C}, =, +, -, 1)$

The following shows that Datalog with = and the successor function over numerical domains is undecidable:

Theorem 15 *The following Datalog languages have RE-Complete (and hence undecidable) ground query complexity:*

vanilla-CLP$(\mathbf{Z}, =, \hat{+}, 0, 1)$
vanilla-CLP$(\mathbf{Q}, =, \hat{+}, 0, 1)$
vanilla-CLP$(\mathbf{R}, =, \hat{+}, 0, 1)$
vanilla-CLP$(\mathbf{C}, =, \hat{+}, 0, 1)$

To prove this theorem, one uses the fact that predecessor, addition and multiplication can be defined inductively in terms of successor if there are no restrictions on the use of local variables. The result then follows from the previous theorem; alternatively, further primitive recursive functions could be defined and standard methods used.

The following corollary was first proved directly by Kim Marriott (private communication):

Theorem 16 *Datalog*$(\mathbf{R}, =, +, -, *, 0, 1)$ *is undecidable.*

ACKNOWLEDGEMENTS: We would like to thank J.-L. Lassez, Johann Makowsky, Kim Marriott, Bud Mishra, and Paul Pedersen for helpful discussions. This research was supported in part by PSC-CUNY Grant 669287 and NSF Grant IRI-8902511.

References

[Canny] J. Canny, Some algebraic and geometric computations in PSPACE, *STOC*, 1988.

[Chandra Lewis Makowsky] A. Chandra, H. Lewis, and J. Makowsky, Embedded Implicational Dependencies and their Inference Problem, *STOC*, 1981, 342-354.

[Chandra Kozen Stockmeyer] A. Chandra, D. Kozen and L. Stockmeyer, Alternation, *JACM* **28** (1981) 114-133.

[Colmerauer] A. Colmerauer, Opening the Prolog III universe: a new generation of Prolog promises some powerful capabilities, *BYTE*, Aug. 1987, 177-182.

[Christov Grigor'ev] A.L. Christov and D.Y. Grigor'ev, Complexity of quantifier elimination in the theory of algebraically closed fields, *Journal of Symbolic Computation*, 1988.

[Cox McAloon Tretkoff] J. Cox, K. McAloon and C. Tretkoff, Computational complexity and constraint logic programming languages, Brooklyn College Technical Report, Number 90-4.

[Davis Matiasevitch Robinson] M. Davis, Y. Matiasevitch, and J. Robinson, *Proceedings of Symposia in Pure Mathematics: Mathematical Developments Arising From Hilbert Problems*, Vol. 28 (1976) 323-378.

[Dincbas *et al.*] M. Dincbas, P. Van Hentenryck, H. Simonis, A. Aggoun,T. Graf, and F. Berthier, The Constraint Logic Programming Language CHIP, *Proceedings of International Conference on Fifth Generation Computing Systems*, 1988.

[Domich Kannan Trotter] P. Domich, R. Kannan and L. Trotter, Hermite normal form computation using modulo determinant arithmetic, *Mathematics of Operations Research* **12** No. 1 (1987) 50-59.

[Gallo Mishra] G. Gallo and B. Mishra, Efficient algorithms and bounds for Wu-Ritt Characteristic Sets, N.Y.U.-Courant Institute Technical Report No. 478, 1989.

[Ierardi] D. Ierardi, Quantifier Elimination in the Theory of an Algebraically-closed Field, STOC 89.

[Jaffar Lassez 86] J. Jaffar and J. L. Lassez, Constraint Logic Programming, Monash University Technical Report 1986.

[Jaffar Lassez 87] J. Jaffar and J. L. Lassez, Constraint Logic Programming, *Proceedings of POPL*, 1987, Munich.

[Jaffar Michaylov] J. Jaffar and S. Michaylov, Methodology and Implementation of a CLP System, *Proceedings of the 1987 Logic Programming Conference*, Melbourne, MIT Press.

[Jones Laaser] N. Jones and W. Laaser, Complete problems for deterministic polynomial time, *Theoretical Computer Science* **3** (1977) 107-117.

[Kanellakis Kuper Revesz] P. Kanellakis, G. Kuper, and P. Revesz, Constraint Query Languages, *PODS*, 1990, Nashville.

[Lassez McAloon 88] J-L. Lassez and K. McAloon, Applications of a canonical form for generalized linear constraints, *Proceedings of the 1988 FGCS Conference*, Tokyo, 703-710.

[Lassez McAloon 89] J-L. Lassez and K. McAloon, A canonical form for generalized linear constraints, IBM Technical Report, 1989

[Lloyd] J. Lloyd, *Foundations of Logic Programming*, Springer 1984

[Maher] M. J. Maher, Logic Semantics for a Class of Committed-Choice Programs, *Proceedings of the 1987 Logic Programming Conference*, Melbourne, MIT Press, 858-876.

[Maier Warren] D. Maier and D. S. Warren, *Computing with Logic*, Addison-Wesley 1988.

[Marek Nerode Remmel] V. Marek, A. Nerode and J. Remmel, A theory of non-monotonic rule systems, *LICS '90*, pp 79-94.

[Matiasevitch] Y. Matiasevitch, Enumerable sets are diophantine, *Soviet Math. Dokl.* **11** 354-358.

[McAloon Tretkoff] K. McAloon and C. Tretkoff, $2LP$: A Logic Programming and Linear Programming System, Brooklyn College Computer Science Technical Report No. 1989-21.

[Paterson Wegman] M.S. Paterson and M.N. Wegman, Linear unification, *JCSS* **16** (1978) 158-167

[Renegar] J. Renegar, A faster $PSPACE$ algorithm for deciding the Existential Theory of the Reals, FOCS 88.

[Sakai Aiba] K. Sakai and A. Aiba, CAL: Theoretical Background of Constraint Logic Programming and its Applications, *Journal of Symbolic Computation*, **8** No. 6 (1989), 589-604.

[Shapiro] E. Shapiro, Alternation and the computational complexity of logic programs, *Journal of Logic Programming*, 1984 Vol. 1 (1984) 19-33.

Meta Programming as Constraint Programming

Pierre Lim
Department of Computer Science
Monash University
Clayton 3168, Australia
pierre@bruce.cs.monash.edu.oz.au

Peter J. Stuckey
Department of Computer Science
University of Melbourne
Parkville 3052, Australia
pjs@murtoa.cs.mu.oz.au

Abstract

A meta-program is one which uses another program (the object program) as data. Important applications of meta-programming in logic programming include meta-interpretation, compilation and program transformation. There are a number of problems with the way most PROLOG systems treat meta-programming. They do not make a clear distinction between the object level and meta level. They do not provide an explicit facility for representing object-level expressions at the meta level. Finally they often rely on meta-logical system predicates some of which destroy the logical reading of the program. This paper provides a scheme for meta-programming that overcomes these problems. The approach taken is to define a special purpose structure of computation for meta-programming along with a constraint solver for the structure. Meta-programs are constraint logic programs over this meta-level structure of computation. The scheme is not restricted to logic programming, it is applicable to meta-programming in any constraint logic programming system.

1 Introduction

A meta-program is one which uses another program (the object program) as data. Meta-programming in PROLOG is particularly attractive because the object-language and the meta-language are identical. That is PROLOG programs can be represented by PROLOG terms. This makes meta-interpretation easy and meta-circular interpretation possible. However as pointed out by Hill and Lloyd [4] this approach has a number of problems. Exactly because the object-language and meta-language are identical there is no clear distinction between object level and meta level. Object-level expressions represent themselves and this leads to problems since we cannot distinguish object-level and meta-level variables. Also common meta-logical predicates such as `var/1` prevent a logical reading of the program.

We present an approach similar to Hill and Lloyd's [4] ground approach that overcomes these problems. The basis of the approach is to define a special structure of computation for meta-programming. This allows meta-programs to be understood as constraint logic programs over this specially constructed domain. This approach is not limited to logic programming, it is applicable to meta-programming in any constraint logic programming system.

In the next section we give a brief description of the CLP scheme. In section 3 we describe the meta-level structure of computation and meta-level constraint solver and illustrate them with some examples. In section 4 we compare this approach with similar approachs in the literature.

2 Preliminaries

We assume the reader has some familiarity with the CLP Scheme [5] and meta-programming in logic programming [11]. We give a brief outline of constraint logic programming.

A constraint logic programming system CLP($\mathcal{A}$) exists in the context of a particular structure $\mathcal{A}$. We shall assume for simplicity that $\mathcal{A}$ is single-sorted with domain A. Let Σ denote the collection of function symbols in $\mathcal{A}$, Π denote the collection of relation (or interpreted predicate) symbols in $\mathcal{A}$ and let V denote a collection of variables. Then $\tau(\Sigma)$ and $\tau(\Sigma, V)$ denote, respectively, the ground term and terms of the structure. The structure $\mathcal{A}$ assigns to each n-ary $f \in \Sigma$ a mapping $A \times \cdots \times A \rightarrow A$ and to each n-ary $p \in \Pi$ a mapping $A \times \cdots \times A \rightarrow \{\mathbf{true}, \mathbf{false}\}$.

A program contains a collection of (programmed) predicate symbols Π_p (where $\Pi \cap \Pi_p = \emptyset$). A *constraint* is of the form $p(t_1, \ldots, t_n)$ where p is an n-ary element of Π and $t_1, \ldots, t_n$ are terms. An *atom* is of the form $p(t_1, \ldots, t_n)$ where p is an n-ary element of Π_p and $t_1, \ldots, t_n$ are terms. A constraint logic program is a finite set of *clauses* of the form

$$A \leftarrow B_1, \ldots, B_m$$

where A is an atom, and $B_1, \ldots, B_m, m \geq 0$ are atoms or constraints.

A *derivation step* using CLP($\mathcal{A}$) program P takes a goal

$$(C \; [] \; D_1, \ldots, D_i, \ldots D_n)$$

where C is a satisfiable conjunction of constraints (called the current collected constraint set) and D_i is the selected atom or constraint. If D_i is a constraint then the resulting goal is

$$(C \wedge D_i \; [] \; D_1, \ldots, D_{i-1}, D_{i+1}, \ldots D_n)$$

where $C \wedge D_i$ is satisfiable. If D_i is an atom and there is a clause

$$A \leftarrow B_1, \ldots, B_m$$

where $C \wedge \{A = D_i\}$ is satisfiable ($\{A = D_i\}$ is a set of constraints equating the arguments of A and D_i), then the resulting goal is

$$(C \wedge \{A = D_i\} \; [] \; D_1, \ldots, D_{i-1}, B_1, \ldots, B_m, D_{i+1}, \ldots D_n)$$

A *computation rule* determines at each step which atom or constraint is selected. A *search tree* for goal G (for some computation rule) is the tree rooted at G where the children of each node H are the goals obtained from a derivation step applied to H. For the root node $H = G$. A *derivation* of G is a branch in the search tree of G.

3 Domains for Meta-Programming

We now describe a structure for reasoning about CLP($\mathcal{A}$) programs This meta-level structure incorporates a method of representing object-level ($\mathcal{A}$) terms and interpreted relations for manipulating object-level terms. We describe a method of constraint solving for the meta-level structure and illustrate meta-level programming in this structure with a number of examples.

3.1 Frozen Objects

A new class of meta-level objects called *frozen objects* is introduced. A frozen object is a term over the alphabet including object-level functors (interpreted and uninterpreted), object-level interpreted relation symbols, object-level (programmed) predicate symbols [1], object-level variables and the special symbols {`:-`, `&`, `true`, `false`} i.e. $\Sigma \cup \Pi \cup \Pi_p \cup V \cup$ {`:-`, `&`, `true`, `false`}. Thus a frozen object can represent an object-level program fragment for example. We represent frozen objects at the meta level by terms surrounded by braces, e.g. { `p(X) :- q(X) & true` }.

The signatures of the special symbols and the representation of program clauses by frozen objects are defined by the following rules.

single_goal `::=` *atom* `|` *constraint* `|` `true` `|` `false`
conjunction_list `::=` `true` `|` (*single_goal* `&` *conjunction_list*)

clause `::=` *atom* `:-` *conjunction_list*

Frozen objects respect the signatures of the symbols involved. For example { `X :- g(Y)` } is not a valid frozen object since `X` is an object-level variable (ranges over $\tau(\Sigma, V)$) in the position of an *atom*.

[1] We do not need to know the object-level program beforehand if we restrict object-level predicate symbols to always come from some denumerable set.

A frozen object is atomic at the meta level. It is not constructible or decomposable using meta-level unification i.e. it is always treated as a constant. Two frozen objects are considered to be equal iff they are syntactically identical, e.g. { `f(g(X1, Y))` } $\neq$ { `f(g(X2, Y))` }. Frozen objects may only be created or inspected at the meta level using the interpreted relations in the structure of computation for the meta-program. These will be described fully in the next subsection.

It is important to note that all variables appearing in frozen objects are global at the object level, thus the `X` in { `g(X)` } and { `X > 4` } refers to the same variable. This does not mean that { `g(X)` } is somehow restricted so that $X > 4$, but rather that when we build a frozen object from { `g(X)` } and { `X > 4` }, e.g. { `g(X) & X > 4` }, that the `X` is indeed the same variable.

Frozen objects are closely related to frozen terms that result from the meta-logical system predicate **`freeze/2`** (see e.g. Sterling and Shapiro [11]). **`freeze(Term, Frozen)`** creates a copy of **`Term`** where all free variables are replaced by a new constants e.g. `f(X, g(Y, X))` becomes `f("X", g("Y", "X"))`. **`freeze`** produces exactly the *ground representation* of a term used by Hill and Lloyd [4]. Frozen objects and frozen terms differ in a number of ways. First frozen objects may include meta-level symbols (e.g. **`&`**). Second frozen terms only freeze variables. This is not significant unless we have interpreted functors where for example { `X` }+{ `Y` } and { `Y` }+{ `X` } are equal but { `X + Y` } and { `Y + X` } are not. By far the most important difference is that both a term and its frozen counterpart are available at the same level using **`freeze/2`**. Because of this the order of execution and even the order of binding become important for goals including **`freeze/2`**. Consider

```
freeze(X, F), X = Y, freeze(X, F).
```

Using a left-right order of execution if `X` is bound to `Y` then the second call to **`freeze/2`** fails, but if `Y` is bound to `X` the goal succeeds. Frozen objects avoid these problems since they are meta-level constructs where the object-level variables are not directly manipulable.

3.2 Meta-level Constraint Relations

The meta-level relations are the only way in which the meta-program can manipulate frozen objects (other than treating them as constants). The essential relations are: SOLVABLE to check solvability of conjunctions of constraints, FROZENUNIV to construct and decompose frozen objects, and COPY to produce renamed versions of frozen objects.

SOLVABLE(FrozenObj)

SOLVABLE/1 succeeds if FrozenObj is an expression representing a conjunction-list of object-level constraints that are mutually satisfiable. For example SOLVABLE({ X > 3 & X < 5 & true}) succeeds while SOLVABLE({ X > Y & Y > 7 & X < 5 & true}) and SOLVABLE({ Y }) fail.

FROZENUNIV(FrozenObj, [Functor, Arg1, ..., Argn])

FROZENUNIV/2 is similar to the PROLOG meta-logical predicate =.. or univ/2. It succeeds if FrozenObj is a frozen object (FrozenObj). The second argument is a list whose first element is the principal functor of FrozenObj and the remainder is a list of frozen objects representing the arguments. For example FROZENUNIV({Y < 3 + T}, [<, {Y}, {3 + T}]) succeeds, and FROZENUNIV({ Y }, L) fails. Note also that attempts to construct ill-typed frozen objects using FROZENUNIV also fail. e.g. FROZENUNIV(FO, [:-, {Y}, {3+ T}])

COPY(FrozenObj1, FrozenObj2)

COPY/4 is a relation

```
COPY(FrozenObj1, FrozenObj2, UnusedVars0, UnusedVars)
```

where FrozenObj2 is the frozen object resulting from replacing each variable in FrozenObj1 with a variable from UnusedVars0 which is a frozen (infinite[2]) list of object-level variables. UnusedVars is the frozen list of object-level variables UnusedVars0 excluding those appearing in FrozenObj2. For example

```
COPY({p(X,Y,X)},{p(U,V,U)}, {[U,V,W,T,...]},{[W,T,...]})
```

succeeds.

For convenience we shall also define (and usually use) COPY/2. COPY/2 can be understood as a shorthand notation for COPY/4 where each atom in the program carries two extra arguments representing the accumulator for the unused variables. In practice we can allow the meta-level constraint solver to maintain the information representing the unused object-level variables.

CONSTRAINT(FrozenObj)

CONSTRAINT/1 succeeds if the principal functor of FrozenObj is an object-level relation symbol (interpreted predicate). It fails if its argument is not a frozen object.

[2] Any finite derivation tree only uses a finite number of variables so we could use a finite list of variables which would cause copy to fail by running out of variables sometimes.

`ATOM(FrozenObj)`

`ATOM/1` succeeds if the principal functor of `FrozenObj` is an object-level predicate symbol. It fails if its argument is not a frozen object.

`FUNCTOR(FrozenObj)`

`FUNCTOR/1` succeeds if the principal functor of `FrozenObj` is an object-level function symbol. It fails if its argument is not a frozen object.

Note that ATOM, CONSTRAINT and FUNCTOR can be defined in terms of FROZENUNIV if we know the sets of object-level (programmed) predicate symbols (Π_p), the object-level constraint relations (Π) and the object-level function symbols (Σ) beforehand, and if these sets are finite.

`VAR(FrozenObj)`

`VAR/1` succeeds if `FrozenObj` is a frozen object-level variable. It fails if its argument is not a frozen object.

Note that VAR is no different from the relations ATOM, CONSTRAINT and FUNCTOR. It examines the outermost symbol of a constant, its frozen argument and determines if this a specific class (the object-level variables). Because frozen objects are constants at the meta level, VAR is completely declarative. There is no possibility of the object-level variable `X` in { `X` } becoming bound to `a` and thus making the the frozen object { `X` } equal to { `a` }. In fact there is no notion of object-level substitution unless it is programmed.

3.3 Meta Level Structure of Computation

The meta-level structure of computation $\mathcal{M}$ is dependent upon the object-level structure of computation. The meta-level structure of computation consists of

- the function symbols $\Sigma_{\mathcal{M}} = U \cup F \cup S$. U is a set of meta-level uninterpreted functors, which will contain at least the list functors '.' and *nil*. F is a set of constant symbols; one for each frozen object. S is a set of constants; one for each object-level functor, object-level predicate symbol, object-level interpreted relation symbol and the symbols { **`:-, &, true, false`** }.
- the relation symbols $\Pi_{\mathcal{M}}$ = { =, SOLVABLE, FROZENUNIV, ATOM, CONSTRAINT, FUNCTOR, VAR, COPY}.
- and a set of meta-level variables $V_{\mathcal{M}}$

The interpretation of the symbols in $\Sigma_{\mathcal{M}}$ and the relation = is the usual Herbrand interpretation. The other relation symbols are interpreted as previously described. We assume the existence of a bijective mapping between the set S and object-level functors and predicates and the special symbols {`:-`, `&`, `true`, `false`} for use by FROZENUNIV/2. For example the object-level function symbol `:-` is mapped to the meta-level constant `:-`.

3.4 The Meta-Level Constraint Solver

Solving the meta-level constraints may seem to be quite a difficult task, and in general it is certainly not trivial. But by adding delay conditions to the constraints we are able to achieve a meta-level constraint solver that is quite simple, relying on a local propagation scheme to solve systems of meta-level constraints. Constraint delay conditions are commonly used in constraint logic programming systems to build simple solvers for complex constraints (see [6, 7]).

Firstly note we can solve meta-level equality constraints by unification. The only objects at the meta level are uninterpreted functors, constants (including frozen objects) and meta-level variables. Thus we can use substitutions to remove all the equality constraints.

Now we give the delay conditions for the constraint relations. ATOM/1, SOLVABLE/1, CONSTRAINT/1, FUNCTOR/1 and VAR/1 all delay until their single argument is ground (i.e. ground at the meta level). FROZENUNIV/2 delays until either the first or second argument is ground. COPY/4 delays until the first and third arguments are ground. In practice we use COPY/2 which delays until its first argument is ground. In using COPY/2 we have lost information on which variables are "new" at which point. For simplicity we assume that the variables are created in the order the COPY/2 constraints are added to the (meta-level) constraint set.

Each of the relations SOLVABLE/1, FROZENUNIV/2, ATOM/1, VAR/1, CONSTRAINT/1, FUNCTOR/1 and COPY/2 upon receiving all their inputs will ground all other arguments. Thus our delaying strategy is amenable to solving by local propagation. Efficient techniques for delaying atoms are well known and are incorporated in systems such as NU-Prolog[10] and Sepia [9]. These techniques may equally well be applied when implementing the meta-level solver. This makes the creation of a very fast solver possible, modulo the speed of the object-level constraint solver.

The use of delay in solving constraints in the meta-level structure of computation is not fundamental to the solving of these constraints, rather it is an implementation decision. A delaying constraint solver is fast and easy to produce but may not always determine when a system of constraints is unsatisfiable. For example

FROZENUNIV(`F0, [& | Tail1]`) ∧ FROZENUNIV(`F0, [p | Tail2 ]`)

is unsatisfiable but this will not be determined by a delaying constraint solver, unless more information arrives. A more intelligent constraint solver could be produced that correctly fails this conjunction of constraints.

Note that delaying constraints does not lead to *floundering* since constraints do not require further derivations steps. In the worst case when a derivation finishes with delayed constraints, the answer constraint consists of these delayed constraints. That is, every instance of the goal that satisfies the delayed constraints is a consequence of the program. Of course if the delayed constraints are mutually unsatisfiable then no such instances exist.

We claim that a delaying solver is almost always powerful enough for the fully solving constraints that arise in meta-programming applications. The user is already familiar with ensuring that pre-conditions are met before meta-logical built-in predicates in PROLOG execute correctly, e.g. ensuring `X` is instantiated before executing `call(X)`. Ensuring that constraint relations are eventually sufficiently instantiated is far easier.

3.5 Examples

Although we have only provided a few relations for manipulating frozen objects they are sufficiently powerful for all common meta-programming applications. We illustrate a number of important meta-programming processes in our framework with some abbreviated examples.

As previously mentioned object-level substitution is only possible in our scheme through programming. We can represent substitutions by frozen conjunction-lists of equations, and using FROZENUNIV and VAR we can program `substitute/3` which mimics the application of a substitution to a frozen object. For example

```
substitute({ f(X, Y) }, { X = g(Z) & Z = Y }, T)
```

succeeds with `T` equal to the frozen object { `f(g(Y), Y)` }. Note that `X` is not *bound* to `g(Y)` rather a new frozen object has been built with `X` replaced by `g(Y)`. The following code shows how the essential part of `substitute/3`, replacing a variable with a term, can be written in our language.

```
substitute(Term, Subs, STerm) :-
     VAR(Term),
     subvar(Term, Subs, STerm).
subvar(Var, Subs, Term) :-
     FROZENUNIV(Subs, [&, E, Subs1]),
     ( FROZENUNIV(E, [=, Var, Term]) ;
       subvar(Var, Subs1, Term)     ).
subvar(Var, { true }, Var).
```

For the goal `substitute({ X }, { X = f(Y) & true }, ` *Term*`).` execution proceeds by first checking that { `X` } is an object-level variable. Then { `X = f(Y) & true` } is broken into the equation ($E =$) { `X = f(Y)` } and ($Subs1 =$) { `true` }. Then matching the variable { `X` } with the lhs of the equation sets *Term* to { f(Y) }. The goal substitute({ Y }, { X = f(Y) & true }, *Term*) returns *Term* = { Y } using the second clause of subvar.

One of the crucial parts of meta-interpretation is the resolution step, matching the head of a rule with a goal atom. The following program fragment takes an Atom and Rule and produces the Constraints that result from matching the Atom and head of the Rule.

```
match(Atom, Rule, Constraints) :-
     COPY(Rule, RuleCopy),
     FROZENUNIV(RuleCopy, [:-, Head, Body]),
     equate(Atom, Head, Constraints),
     SOLVABLE(Constraints).

% build a conjunction-list of equations C
% from matching atoms T1 and T2
equate(T1, T2, C) :-
     % check the predicate is the same
     FROZENUNIV(T1, [Pred | A1]),
     FROZENUNIV(T2, [Pred | A2]),
     equate2(A1, A2, C).
equate2([H1 | T1], [H2 | T2], C) :-
     % create equation between arguments
     FROZENUNIV(E, [=, H1, H2]),
     equate2(T1, T2, CR),
     FROZENUNIV(C, [&, E, CR]).
equate2([], [], { true }).
```

The goal ?- match({ p(X,b) }, { p(a, Y) :- q(Y) & true }, *CS*) returns the constraint set {*CS* = { X = a & b = Y & true }}.

Going beyond the standard meta-interpreter we may wish to allow special interpretation for *symmetric* object-level predicates. A fragment of the meta-interpreter[3] handling such predicates is

```
meta(A, Program, CCS0, CCS) :-
     ATOM(A),
     FROZENUNIV(A, [P | Args]),
     symmetric(P),     % Check p is symmetric
     reverse(Args, RArgs),
     % build reversed atom
     FROZENUNIV(RA, [P | RArgs]),
     meta_atom(RA, Program, CCS0, CCS).
symmetric(sibling).
```

[3]See the appendix for the full code

If `Program` contains the fact { `sibling(peter,helen)` } then the goal { `sibling(helen,Who)` } has { `Who = peter & true` } as one of its answers. All of the meta-program fragments above are *pure* constraint logic programs. This contrasts with meta-programs in PROLOG which usually include meta-logical predicates with no logical reading. Our framework provides a language for useful pure meta-programs which are more easily amenable to optimization, transformation, verification and debugging.

4 Comparison with other work

This work was inspired by that of Hill and Lloyd and addresses the same problems pointed out in their paper "Analysis of Meta-Programs" [4]. A basic problem they point out is that variables in a meta program often range over different domains. Another difficult problem is that certain meta-logical predicates behave in such a way that it is impossible to give a logical reading to the program, for example `var/1`. Hill and Lloyd present two solutions to the problems; using a typed representation and a ground representation. Both representations solve the problem of distinguishing object-level and meta-level variables. One of the principal strengths of the ground approach is it is possible to give a declarative definition of `var/1`. This is shared by our approach.

Our approach and the ground approach of Hill and Lloyd are quite similar. We point out some advantages of our approach by examining their example meta-interpreter `solve/2` [4]. The predicate symbol `derive` which they leave unexplained magically creates variant clauses, and also mimics unification on the ground representation of object-level terms. In contrast in our scheme using `COPY/4` we can explicitly create variants of objects, and there is no need to mimic unification because we can invoke the underlying object-level unification algorithm using `SOLVABLE`. When we are concerned with more complex object-level structures like the real numbers the obvious extension of Hill and Lloyd's approach requires a constraint solver for constraints written using the ground representation. This solver is very difficult and inefficient to implement as a logic program since it is not possible to use the underlying object-level solver for constraints represented this way.

4.1 Meta-programming in CLP

Meta-programming for structures other than the Herbrand Universe is not a well-explored area. Heintze et al. [3] outline an approach to meta-programming over the domain of real numbers, and they point out a problem with meta-programming in structures with interpreted functors that does not occur in meta-programming over the Herbrand Universe. This problem arises from the inability to deal with terms purely as uninterpreted objects. For example $X + 3$ will match (equate with) $Y - 2$ since $+$ and $-$ are interpreted. Hence checking that a term has outermost symbol $+$ is not straight-forward. This problem is overcome in our scheme by **FROZENUNIV**. `{ X + 3 }` and `{ Y - 2 }` will not match and have different principle functors which are accessible through **FROZENUNIV**.

Both Heintze et al. [3] and our approach produce a structure of computation for meta-programming over constraint logic programs. The difference in the two approachs stems from their desire for meta-circularity versus our desire for total separation of the object level and meta level. Their approach suffers from common problems with meta-circular schemes, that is object-level variables are represented by (are the same as) meta-level variables, and it includes system predicates like **var/1** which destroy logical properties of the program.

4.2 Object-level variable representation

A number of schemes/languages for meta-programming represent object-level terms where the name of a term is not unique to that term but rather the equivalence class of all variants of the term [1]. For example { `foo(X)` } and { `foo(Y)` } are considered the same object.

This produces difficulties when constructing new object-level terms since we need to be able to determine which variables are the same and which are different. For example constructing the clause

{ `app(A.X, Y, A.Z) :- app(X,Y,Z)` }

from { `app(A.X, Y, A.Z)` } and { `app(X,Y,Z)` } is not straight-forward since for example the last term is equivalent to { `app(Y,Z,X)` }.

One example of a system which takes this approach is Qu-Prolog [12]. Here object-level variables (`"X"`, `"Y"`) are represented by (meta-level) object-vars (**x**, **y**) which are variables which can take the value of any object-level variable. For example **lambda_term(x)** is a clause which states that **lambda_term**(X) is true for X equal to any object-level variable. There is no direct representation of a single object-level variable. They add *apartness* constraints (e.g. $\mathbf{x} \neq \mathbf{y}$) to ensure that different object-vars represent different object-level variables, for example we don't want **p(x,y)** to have an instance `p("X","X")`. This gives them a name for equivalence classes of object-level variables and thus allows the construction of object-level terms.

In contrast with our approach the construction of object-level terms in Qu-Prolog is more difficult. However they do not require explicit variable renaming, this being provided in their resolution step which creates new object-vars. Finally since representing each variable uniquely maintains strictly more information then representing equivalence classes of variables we can always simulate their approach.

4.3 Meta circularity

The consequences of totally separating object level and meta level and restricting object-level computation to a few constraint relations is that direct meta-circularity is unattainable. We accept this restriction because of the considerable difficulties of merging the meta level and object level. Consider Reflective Prolog [2], a language which merges the meta level and object level, allowing both meta-level computation and object-level computation. Reflective Prolog provides a very concise language for many kinds of meta-interpreters. A goal `p(X,Y)` can be solved either through the object-level matching with a clause like `p(a, Z) :- q(Z)`, or through the meta level by matching the *name* of `p(X,Y)`, `"p"("X","Y")` with the argument of a clause `solve(Atom) :- ...`, where `solve` is a special meta-level predicate symbol.

Reflective Prolog allows goals that include both the object-level term and its name (or frozen form). Unfortunately they do not escape all the problems with `freeze`, for example.

```
?- p(X), q(X).
solve("q"("a")).  % q(a) succeeds at the meta level
p(a).
```

If the goal executes in left-right order it succeeds as one might expect, but if `q(X)` is chosen first then the goal fails since then name of `q(X)` is `"q"("X")` does not match with `"q"("a")`. Allowing meta-level and object-level information to interact brings about considerable complication, which we avoid in our scheme. For a framework of meta-programming where the object-level language includes the meta-level language see [13].

Although our scheme is not meta-circular it is possible to write meta-circular interpreters in the following sense. We can write a meta-interpreter that is not dependent on the specific object-level structure[4]. The meta-level structure of computation we have defined is just another structure, hence the same code (albeit executing in a different structure, the meta-meta-level structure) will execute the meta-interpreter code.

5 Concluding Remarks

We have outlined a method for constructing a structure of computation suitable for meta-programming over some object-level structure of computation. We have also outlined a constraint solver for such structures. At present we have two implementations of the scheme we describe herein, both over the Herbrand Universe, the first is a meta-interpreter, while the second is implemented using the Constraint Logic Programming Shell [8].

The advantages of the meta-programming scheme we have outlined are:

- the object level and meta level are totally separated, indeed object-level computation is restricted to simulations by meta-level constraints;

[4] See appendix

- variant terms are provided explicitly in the scheme using COPY, and furthermore we have a purely declarative reading for this relation;
- the scheme is applicable to any constraint logic programming language, rather than just logic programs;
- meta-programs under this scheme have a clear semantics, that is they are constraint logic programs over a special domain;
- the scheme is readily extensible, new constraint relations are easily accommodated by this framework.

Extending the scheme to incorporate new constraint relations is simple, and extending the constraint solver is similarly easy using delaying strategies. One obvious extension to the scheme is allowing meta-level programs (and object-level clauses) to include `not` (evaluated using safe negation as failure).

In essence we have defined a basic structure of computation for meta-programming for which there are many variations, extensions and modifications. All these structures support the thesis of meta-programming as constraint-programming.

References

[1] J. Barklund, "What is a Meta-variable in Prolog?", *Proceedings of the Meta88 Workshop on Meta-Programming in Logic Programming*, Bristol, June 1988, pp. 383–398.

[2] S. Costantini and G. Lanzarone, "A Metalogic Programming Language", *Proceedings of the Sixth Int. Conf. on Logic Programming*, Lisbon, June 1989, pp. 218–233.

[3] N. Heintze, S. Michaylov, P. Stuckey and R. Yap, "On Meta-Programming in CLP($\Re$)", *Proceedings North American Conference on Logic Programming*, Cleveland, October, 1989, pp. 52–68.

[4] P. M. Hill and J. W. Lloyd, "Analysis of Meta-Programs", *Proceedings of the Meta88 Workshop on Meta-Programming in Logic Programming*, Bristol, June 1988, pp. 23–51.

[5] J. Jaffar, J–L. Lassez, "Constraint Logic Programming", *Procs. POPL 87*, Munich, January 1987.

[6] J. Jaffar, S. Michaylov, P. Stuckey and R. Yap, "The CLP($\Re$) Language and System", IBM Technical Report, to appear.

[7] J. Jaffar and S. Michaylov, "Methodology and Implementation of a CLP System", *Proc. Fourth Int. Conf. on Logic Programming*, Melbourne 1987, pp 196–218.

[8] P. Lim and P. Stuckey, "A Constraint Logic Programming Shell", *Workshop on Programming Language Implementation and Logic Programming*, Linkoping, Sweden, August 1990, to appear.

[9] M. Meier, P. Dufresne and D. de Villeneuve, "SEPIA Manual", ECRC Technical Report TR-LP-36, ECRC, 1988.

[10] L. Naish, "Negation and Quantifiers in NU-Prolog", *Proc. Third Int. Conf. on Logic Programming*, London 1986, pp. 624–634.

[11] L. Sterling and E. Shapiro, "The Art of Prolog", MIT Press, U.S.A., 1986.

[12] J. Staples et al., "Qu-Prolog: an Extended Prolog for Meta Level Programming", *Proceedings of the Meta88 Workshop on Meta-Programming in Logic Programming*, Bristol, June 1988, pp. 435–452.

[13] V. S. Subrahmanian, "A Simple Formulation of the Theory of Metalogic Programming", *Proceedings of the Meta88 Workshop on Meta-Programming in Logic Programming*, Bristol, June 1988, pp. 65–101.

Appendix

For the information of the referees we provide a complete listing of a simple meta-interpreter for any underlying object-level structure. The principle relations are `map` which maps frozen conjunction-lists to meta-level conjunction lists and vice versa e.g. { `X = a & Y = b & true` } $\leftrightarrow$ { `X = a` } `&` { `Y = b` } `& true`. `conjoin` appends frozen conjunction-lists e.g. { `X = a & true` } and { `Y = b & true` } go to { `X = a & Y = b & true` }. `equate` creates the conjunction-list of equalities matching two frozen atoms, e.g. { `p(X,b)` } and { `p(a,Y)` } give the equalities { `X = a & b = Y & true` }. `meta/4` takes a frozen goal and list of frozen object-program clauses and frozen conjunction-list of constraints (the current constraint set) and return another frozen conjunction-list of constraints (the answer constraint).

```
meta(true, Program, CCS, CCS).
meta((A&B), Program, CCS0, CCS) :-
     meta(A, Program, CCS0, CCS1),
     meta(B, Program, CCS1, CCS).
meta(A, Program, CCS0, CCS) :-
     ATOM(A),
     meta_atom(A, Program, CCS0, CCS).
meta(C, Program, CCS0, CCS) :-
     CONSTRAINT(C),
     FROZENUNIV(CL, [&, C, { true }]),
     conjoin(CL, CCS0, CCS),
     SOLVABLE(CCS).

meta_atom(A, Program, CCS0, CCS) :-
     member(Clause, Program),
     COPY(Clause, VariantClause),
     FROZENUNIV(VariantClause, [:-, Head, Body]),
     equate(Head, A, C),
     conjoin(C, CCS0, CCS1),
     SOLVABLE(CCS1),
     map(Body, B),
```

```
     meta(B, Program, CCS1, CCS).

% map frozen conjunction-list to meta-level conjunction-list

map(Frozen, (Arg1&Term2)) :-
     FROZENUNIV(Frozen, [&, Arg1, Arg2]),
     map(Arg2, Term2).
map(Frozen, true) :-
     FROZENUNIV(Frozen, [true]).

% append frozen conjunction-lists
conjoin(X, Y, Z) :-
     FROZENUNIV(X, [&, C, T1]),
     conjoin(T1, Y, T2),
     FROZENUNIV(Z, [&, C, T2]).
conjoin({ true }, Y, Y).

% build conjunction-list of equations from matching T1 and T2

equate(T1, T2, C) :-
     FROZENUNIV(T1, [P | A1]),
     FROZENUNIV(T2, [P | A2]),
     equate2(A1, A2, C).
equate2([H1 | T1], [H2 | T2], C) :-
     FROZENUNIV(E, [=, H1, H2]),
     equate2(T1, T2, CR),
     FROZENUNIV(C, [&, E, CR]).
equate2([], [], { true }).
```

We can simply extend this meta-interpreter. For example the clause for handling symmetric predicates, given in section 3.5, can be added to the program, along with information about which object-level predicates are symmetric, to produce a more complex meta-interpreter.

Janus: A step towards distributed constraint programming

Vijay A. Saraswat, Xerox PARC
Ken Kahn, Xerox PARC
Jacob Levy, Technion, Haifa

(Extended Abstract)

Abstract

We propose a new language, Janus, to address shortcomings of concurrent logic programming languages for distributed programming. Unlike parallel computing, distributed computing must facilitate interactions between very large numbers of diverse computations without central coordination or trust. Janus is a member of the dc family of distributed constraint programming languages, a subset of the cc family [11]. dc languages are "failure-free", which is essential if they are to be used for distributed computing. The general cc framework provides a simple yet formal semantics for Janus, and aids in understanding its relationship with other languages.

Janus, along with other concurrent logic programming languages, is based on asynchronous, buffered message passing and provides, in a simple and clean way, unbounded, recursive invocation of agents, indeterministic selection and "private" communication hidden from the "environment". Its main novelty is its simple yet powerful communication and synchronization mechanism based on single-message, point-to-point, directional channels in which reception or transmission rights for channels can themselves be passed in messages. Janus provides operations upon arrays which enable the expression and efficient execution of conventional programming idioms. It also provides bags of unordered elements which are used for many-to-one communication without the need for merge networks. The language design enables data deallocation and memory reuse as soon as the data becomes garbage. Logical errors that arise during computation can be trapped and handled by user code. Communication protocols between Janus implementations and other computations (possibly other nodes executing Janus) are much simpler than those for other concurrent logic programming languages which need to support distributed unification and garbage collection, thus enhancing inter-operability.

1 Introduction

We anticipate a future of immense collections of diverse computations using each other without central coordination, trust, or complete knowledge of each other. These *open systems* change dynamically and cannot be centrally administered since they may cross organizational and even national boundaries. While some of the available services may be purely computational, others may interact with the surrounding world.

If this view of the future is to be believed (e.g. see [4],[6]) the question of developing a coherent conceptual framework for organizing such immense collections of computations arises. Some desiderata for such a framework are: it should "scale well", it should avoid all notions of centralized control, its computations should cope with indeterminism and asynchrony of the world and other computations, it should permit definition and installation of securely encapsulated servers with state, its computations should be reprogrammable despite continuous operation, etc.

Traditionally, these issues have been considered at the operating system rather than the language level. We believe that operating systems like Mach [18] provide good support for open systems at a coarse granularity. However, a distributed implementation of a properly designed programming language can provide the same support in a uniform manner at a much finer granularity [7]. A distributed language system consists of some computational nodes all implementing the same language kernel. Entities are referred to in a uniform manner independent of which nodes defined or created them, or where they are "located"; this means that a program developed on a uni-processor will work in a parallel computer or a distributed network of computers. The semantics of such entities is defined in terms of their interaction with their environment which consists of all other concurrently executing entities; if servers offer the same reactive behaviors to their environments, they are equivalent and clients may switch transparently from one to the other. Entities maintain an "arm's length" relationship with each other, allowing the implementation to use locality considerations to improve performance. We believe that only a programming language framework can provide a uniform notation for describing how services are defined and interact in open systems, and prescribe compile-time enforcable rules which ensure that it is impossible to even define certain kinds of undesirable computations.

In this paper we focus on the concurrent logic programming languages [2,16,10,14] because we believe they provide a computation model which may be suitable for open systems programming. A comparison with other frameworks is given in [12]. A general account of concurrent logic programming languages is given in [11] in the "Ask-and-Tell" cc framework of *concurrent constraint programing languages.* Such languages are fundamentally based on a notion of partial information, together with the notions of consistency and entailment of such information. We treat the (distributed) store as a collection of variables ranging over some domain of interest. Over the life-time of the computation concurrently executing agents may create new variables, and add (*Tell*) constraints relating these variables. Constraints are finitary specifications of possibly infinite sets of values and specify restrictions that any concrete realization of the store must satisfy. A store is *inconsistent* if it is impossible to find a valuation which satisfies the constraints imposed hitherto. Agents synchronize through *a blocking Ask*, by asking whether the store entails another constraint and blocking until—as a result of the execution of other agents—the store entails either the query constraint or its negation. Concurrent logic programming languages such as Parlog, FGHC, *Strand* [15] and Atomic Herbrand [11] (called "FCP(:)" in [9]) are thus concurrent constraint programming languages instantiated over the Herbrand constraint system.

Problems. In the context of distributed computation, a fundamental problem with these languages is that a computation may have multiple producers of information for the same set of variables. Unless these producers are coordinated they may produce conflicting constraints, causing an inconsistency. For example, one agent may impose the constraint `X=3` and another `X=4`, resulting in uncontrolled behavior since an inconsistent store entails any ask condition. This is unacceptable in a distributed setting where aborting the entire networked computation would be disastrous. Indeed, this is the fundamental way in which security of encapsulation of servers can be violated in this computational framework.

Languages such as Atomic Herbrand used atomic publication to avoid the problem: an agent may add constraints to the store only if the resulting store is consistent, and the addition is instantaneous with respect to other attempts. However, in a distributed setting, such a notion is too heavy-weight as a foundational communication mechanism. For Herbrand languages, it requires the implementation of a distributed atomic unification protocol; this additional complexity does not seem motivated for distributed applications and interferes with inter-operability requirements.

Other Herbrand languages such as FGHC ignore the multiple teller problem, trusting the programmer to organize computations so that they will never generate conflicting constraints at run-time. If this trust is violated an inconsistency arises. Mechanisms such as "meta-calls" do not prevent such inconsistencies from occuring and cannot provide any protection if variables are shared across meta-calls.

Distributed constraint programming. For concurrent constraint programming to be used as a conceptual framework for languages for open systems, some restrictions will therefore have to be placed on the use of constraints for communication and control. The principles underlying our approach are:

- Syntactically correct programs should not cause the store to become inconsistent at run-time.

  Consequently constraint-solving is dispensed with at run-time, yielding a style of programming best characterized as "Constraint programming without constraint-solving". The premium is on exploiting the power of *entailment* rather than the power of *consistency*. The role of the run-time system is to put together constraints supplied by various producers and to infer whether some question being asked by a consumer can now be answered.

  Because all possibilities of inconsistency have been removed, notions such as backtracking make no sense, even conceptually.

- The basic communication mechanism should reflect the notion of asynchronous message passing, to be compatible with basic distributed computation concerns.

  Thus computations at a site should be able to progress, producing information, without having to coordinate with agents at other sites.

- Computations in other languages should be able to *inter-operate* smoothly with computations in these languages.
- Languages in this framework should have the potential for performance-efficient implementations competitive with that of conventional (distributed) assignment-based languages.

Specific techniques. We have progressed on two fronts towards these goals.

First, we have identified an efficiently implementable yet expressive constraint system which possesses certain "independence" properties and naturally supports some common idioms in distributed computing.

Suppose `X` and `Y` are two variables unconstrained in the current store, and an agent posts the (consistent) constraint `X=s`, for some (non-variable) term `s` containing `Y`. Then, the constraint system is amenable to a distributed implementation if this constraint imposition *cannot* be construed as a constraint on `Y`. The Herbrand constraint system violates this property, since `s` non-variable and `X=s` implies `X` $\neq$ `Y`. Therefore, Janus cannot be based on Herbrand, but must instead be based on a constraint system in which `X=s` and `X=Y` are consistent, e.g., the domain of infinite trees.

Other than the issue of independence, our paramount concern has been that the constraint system should be expressive enough to allow elegant formulation of standard algorithms over standard data-structures (for example, arrays) and direct enough that these algorithms should be compilable to efficient code. We have also discovered that the concept of unordered collections of objects ("bags") is of great use in directly and cleanly supporting many-to-one communication. Hence, Janus is based on a constraint system defined on top of a domain of infinite (possibly integer-indexed) trees and bags.[1]

Second, we have exploited the idea of syntactic control of interference. The intuitive idea of these restrictions is to allow only two occurrences of a variable in a clause (unless the clause forces the variable to be ground). If every clause in the program satisfies this property, and so does the input clause, then it is guaranteed that every resolvent will also satisfy this property (this we called the *broadcast-free* property in earlier work). Thus, (non-ground) variables are regarded as point-to-point communication channels.[2] The second idea, adapated from [5] is to treat these channels as *directional*, by associating with exactly one of the occurrences of the variable (called the *teller* for the variable) the rights to impose constraints on the variable. Surprisingly, directionality can be introduced without introducing any extra-logical annotations which need to be treated specially at run-time (unlike [5] or Concurrent Prolog). Indeed the annotation is "special" only in that clauses must

---

[1] Bags have to be defined with respect to a non-well-founded set-theory, in order to allow equations like $X = \{X\}$ to have solutions. In particular we use the theory of hypersets developed by Aczel [1]. These technical details are discussed in more depth in [12], but they are not of much practical consequence.

[2] Variables in other logic programming languages such as Prolog or GHC are not point-to-point because of arbitrary fan-out, which may involve multicasting in a distributed setting.

be checked at compile-time to satisfy certain restrictions related to occurrences of the annotation; at run-time the annotation is treated just as any other uninterpreted function-symbol.

Note that it does not make sense to have directional channels and not ban "broadcasting". For, much of the expressiveness of the language arises from the ability to communicate in a message tell rights to a channel, say X, in exactly the same way as other data (e.g., numbers) are communicated. If this message is being communicated to multiple agents (because the variable on which the constraint is being imposed has multiple occurrences), then multiple agents may receive the right to tell constraints on X, thus violating the integrity of the single-teller restriction.

The two occurrence restriction has several ramifications. First, it has the unexpected consequence that cyclic structures created at run-time are always garbage—they cannot be accessed by the rest of the computation, since both occurrences of the variable are used up in creating the cycle. Second, the implementation can detect when the reference to a memory location is no longer valid, since all data has a reference count of one when received by an agent. Hence, it can be reclaimed immediately, without having to incur the overhead of maintaining a reference count (or multiple reference bit). In particular, this means that when an array is modified to a logically new array, the implementation does not need to actually create the new array. Instead, the old array can always be reused and updated in-place. Array sub-sequences can share storage with the original array, and, in some cases, array concatenation can be done in constant time with no additional storage.

In fact, without a garbage collector, a Janus implementation can reclaim garbage as well as a reference count garbage collector. Unreferenced cycles of data or cycles of agents without connections to the main computation can occur and can be reclaimed only by exhaustive garbage collection.

Rest of this paper. Section 2 is devoted to explaining the syntax and semantics of Janus in some more detail and discussing the functionality provided by the underlying constraint system. Section 3 shows that various commonly expressible concurrent logic programming idioms can be expressed straightforwardly in Janus. Section 4 gives a short review of the avenues of research opened up by the design of a practical distributed constraint programming language.

We emphasize that this paper is an extended abstract—for reasons of space, we have been unable to treat many technical details with the attention they deserve. This is repaired in [12].

2 The Janus Language

The syntax used in this paper is a simple variation on the *clausal* syntax common to many concurrent constraint and logic programming languages, and used in [11]. A program is a collection of *clauses*, of the form:[3]

[3]Due to shortage of space, we have omitted discussion of some other features of Janus. In fact, a much richer syntax is allowed for Janus programs, a syntax which admits lexically-scoped

```
behavior_name(ask_term, ..., ask_term) :: agent.
```

where an **agent** is, recursively, a tell-constraint, a simple agent (recursive invocation), a conditional agent (an ask-constraint, followed by an agent), or a parallel composition of agents:

```
agent :: =
  tell_constraint | name(tell_term, ..., tell_term) |
  ask_constraint → agent | agent, agent.
```

This syntax has a few advantages over the more conventional definite clauses. The choice of the syntax "→" for "blocking ask" (conditional agents) is deliberate; this combinator can be construed as a logical entailment operator. It naturally and elegantly allows the specification of nested conditionals thus helping avoid the need for choosing arbitrary procedure names for every branch point in the program.

The operational semantics of Janus is easy to specify. A (non-terminal) configuration consists of a pair $\langle A, \sigma \rangle$, where A is an agent, and σ is the *store*, that is a pair of the form $c : V$, where c is a constraint, and V is the set of variables occurring in A and c. The "telling" of c in a store $c' : V$, terminates in one step, yielding the store $(c \wedge c') : V$. The execution steps of (A_1, A_2) are obtained by interleaving the execution steps of A_1 with those of A_2 in any order. The agent $(c \rightarrow A)$ can, in store σ reduce to the agent A provided that σ entails $\exists X_1, \ldots, X_k.c$ (where $X_1, \ldots, X_k$ are the "local" variables which do not occur in the head of the clause). In this case the store is augmented with an "answer constraint" on the local variables $X_1, \ldots, X_k$ which is conceptually generated by attempting to answer the "query" $\exists X_1, \ldots X_k.c$ given the constraint "database" σ. (Note that because of the presence of bags, there may be more than one answer to any such query. In such a case, any one answer is chosen arbitrarily.)

Similarly, in one step, the agent $p(t_1, \ldots, t_n)$ reduces in a store σ, if there is a clause in the program with head $p(a_1, \ldots, a_n)$ such that the query $\exists Y_1, \ldots Y_k.X_1 = a_1, \ldots, X_n = a_n$ can be answered from the store $\sigma \wedge X_1 = t_1 \ldots X_n = t_n$, where $Y_1, \ldots, Y_k$ are the "local" variables in the query. As for conditional agents, the store is augmented with an answer for the query, on the local variables. Note that more than one clause may be available for reduction—in that case one of them is chosen at run-time, thus yielding the sort of non-determinism generated by Milner's "+" combinator (see [13]). If there is enough information in the store to show that the goal cannot match any clause, then the goal is *removed.* [12] discusses why this is logically defensible—the essential point is to treat the bodies of clauses as certain kinds of implications rather than as conjunctions.

---

variables, block-structure, nested definitions (as in [11]) and definitions of (recursive) functions, while preserving a logical interpretation for the syntax.

2.1 Tellers

In Janus the term !X (called the *teller* for X) is used to indicate the right to tell constraints involving X. An unannotated occurrence of a variable (e.g., the occurrence in p(X)) is called an *asker* for X. Legal Janus clauses must satisfy syntactic restrictions that ensure that:

- a variable can occur at most twice in one "thread of execution" of a clause, unless enclosing ask-conditions ensure that the variable will be ground at run-time,
- at most one of those occurrences (called the *source*) is an occurrence through which bindings can be generated or can flow in from outside the clause, and at most one of those occurrences (called the *sink*) is an occurrence through which bindings are checked or can flow out of the clause,
- in particular, if the body of a clause imposes a constraint on a variable X that occurs in the head of a clause, then the occcurrence in the head must be the teller for X (so that at run-time the goal will be checked to ensure that it has tell rights on X). Here the occurrence in the body is the source and that in the head, the sink.

Thus the teller for X represents the capability to impose (tell) constraints on X, and the asker for X the capability to read (ask) constraints on X. Very importantly, it is possible in Janus to *communicate* these capabilities in messages to other agents. A detailed account of a simple, liberal set of syntactic rules faithful to these intuitions is given in [12]; all programs in this paper satisfy those restrictions, and informally can be seen to satisfy these intuitions.

As a simple example, consider append expressed in Janus:

```
append([], In, !Out) :: Out = In.
append([A | B], In, !Out) :: Out = [A | Out1], append(B, In, !Out1).
```

The clauses obey the Janus restrictions. Intuitively, in the first clause, the first occurrence of Out is the sink and the second the source; and the first occurrence of In is the source and the second the sink. In the second clause, intuitively, the first occurrences of A,B,In and the second occurrences of Out,Out_1 are sources. Operationally, a call append(X,Y,Z) will suspend until the store has some information on X and Z. The first clause can be taken if the store implies X=[] and Z=!S for some term S[4]; and the second clause can be taken if the store implies X=[C | D] (for some terms C and D), and Z=!S, for some variable S. In case both of these clauses are rejected (e.g., because the store entails X=3 or Z=[]), the call terminates, without any constraint being added to the store. Intuitively, such a program defines the behavior of append *only* in those circumstances in which the first argument of the call is a well-formed list, and the last argument is a teller.

[4]It is a property of Janus that in any store generated at run-time, terms such as S will be variables.

2.2 Constraint system

The domain of the constraint system $\mathcal{J}$ underlying Janus consists of a set of constants ("urelements"; these include arithmetic constants) and, recursively, possibly infinite ordered and unordered collections (bags) of such elements. Ask and Tell constraints are interpreted over this domain. The permissible ask constraints include:

- $\mathtt{X} = \mathtt{E}$ where E is any expression.
- Various type and arithmetic tests such as **integer(X)**, $\mathtt{X} \geq \mathtt{Y}$, etc.
- The array operations |A| to obtain the cardinality of A and A.I which obtains the ith element of the array A. These operations also implicitly ask **array(A)**, **integer(I)** and $0 \leq \mathtt{I} \leq |\mathtt{A}| - 1$ (that is, they suspend until the implicit ask conditions can be answered by the store).
- In addition, terms of the form $\{\mathtt{M}\} \cup \mathtt{B}$ may occur in the head of a clause, provided that M and B are variables that do not occur elsewhere in the head of the clause.

  Intuitively, an invocation can "match" a clause-head which contains the term $\{\mathtt{M}\} \cup \mathtt{B}$, if its corresponding argument is known to be a non-empty bag (for example, it may be a non-empty enumerated bag, or a variable A on which a constraint of the form $\mathtt{X}_1 \cup \ldots \cup \mathtt{X}_n = \mathtt{A}$ has been imposed and at least one of the $\mathtt{X}_i$ is an enumerated bag, see below). The match succeeds by equating M to one of the elements in the bag, and B to the "rest" of the bag. (Formally, all this happens in the attempt to answer the query from the constraint database.)

The only tell constraints permitted in Janus are of the form $\mathtt{X} = \mathtt{E}$ where E can be any expression including arithmetic, array, and bag expressions.

Bag expressions are either of the form $\{\mathtt{T}_1, \ldots, \mathtt{T}_n\}$ or $\mathtt{X}_1 \cup \ldots \cup \mathtt{X}_n$. The former denotes the bag that contains n elements, $\mathtt{T}_1, \ldots, \mathtt{T}_n$, and the latter denotes the bag union of the $\mathtt{X}_i$s. For convenience, union is defined in such a way that if any of the $\mathtt{X}_i$ is not a bag it is treated as the singleton bag $\{\mathtt{X}_i\}$.

Array expressions are of the form:

- $\langle \mathtt{T}_1, \ldots, \mathtt{T}_n \rangle$, an array of exactly n elements, $\mathtt{T}_i$ being the ith element,
- **array(N, V)**, an array of N Vs. (This implicitly asks that N is a non-negative integer and V is forced (i.e. ground).)
- A[I..J] the subarray of A between the indices I and J (this implictly asks that I and J be integers in the proper ranges)
- $\mathtt{A}_1 \circ \mathtt{A}_2$, an array which is the concatenation of $\mathtt{A}_1$ and $\mathtt{A}_2$.
- $\mathtt{A}[\mathtt{I}_1 \rightarrow \mathtt{T}_1, \ldots, \mathtt{I}_n \rightarrow \mathtt{T}_n]$, the array different from A only in that each index $\mathtt{I}_j$ has value $\mathtt{T}_j$.

Further details related to $\mathcal{J}$, and the semantics of Janus are contained in [12]. There we prove, among other results, that Janus computations are failure-free, and that variables serve as point-to-point communication channels.

3 Programming in Janus

We lack the space to adequately demonstrate the richness of programming idioms available to the Janus programmer. Instead, we give several examples which we think are representative of various aspects of the language. First we present how to express commonly used concurrent logic programming techniques in Janus. The need to specify a directionality for communication and the restrictions on the ability to share data lead to only small changes in most of the common programming techniques, such as bounded-buffer, incomplete messages, difference lists, short circuits, recursive doubling, buffer synchronization etc.

3.1 Common programming idioms adapted to Janus

The standard bounded-buffer producer-consumer idiom can be programmed in Janus as follows:

```
goal :: producer(!Bs, [demand, demand, ..., demand | Ds]), consumer(Bs, !Ds).
producer(!Bs, Ds) ::
        Ds = [demand | Ds1] → Bs = [produced | Bs1], producer(!Bs1, Ds1),
        Ds = [] → Bs = [].
consumer(Bs, !Ds) ::
        Bs = [produced | Bs1] → Ds = [demand | Ds1], consumer(Bs1, !Ds1),
        Bs = [] → Ds = [].
```

(Note that the `producer` goal is given the teller for `Bs`; this is checked in the head of the clause for `producer`, whose body generates constraints on `Bs`. Similarly for `Ds`.) This producer-consumer pair executes with a bounded buffer between the producer and consumer. *It is very important to note that in a* Janus *implementation that reuses structures, the above program executes in* constant space *if both goals reside in the same address space.* This is possible because each clause in the program is "memory-balanced", that is, each "consumes" as many conses as it "produces"; hence the conses introduced in the initial query are *recycled* for the duration of the computation.

The short-circuit technique can be programmed in Janus as follows:

```
p(..., L, R) :: p(..., L, !M), p(..., M, R).
p(..., L, !R) :: R = L.
```

In the first clause, the first occurrence of `M` is the source and the second the sink. Here, the programmer has to impose a consistent directionality of information flow. An initial query might be `p(done,!D),q(D)`. `q` can wait until `D=done` succeeds, before proceeding. A good implementation of Janus can exploit the directionality of these short-circuits so that it is never the case that `D` is bound to `done` via a long dereference chain.[5]

3.2 Incomplete Messages

A major source of simplicity and elegance in concurrent logic programming is that servers can respond directly to service requests by communicating on ports embedded in the service request. This technique is illustrated by the following "queue-server" program:

```
queue(Input) :: split(Input, !Enq, !Deq), match(Enq, Deq).
split(enqueue(X, Rest), !Enq, Deq) :: Enq = [X | Enq1], split(Rest, !Enq1, Deq).
split(dequeue(!X, Rest), Enq, !Deq) :: Deq = [!X | Deq1], split(Rest, Enq, !Deq1).
match([X | Enq], [!Y | Deq]) :: Y = X, match(Enq, Deq).
```

These rules define a predicate `queue/1`, which will receive a sequence of `enqueue` and `dequeue` messages over time and will be able to respond as if these operations were being performed on a queue.[6] Operationally, a `queue` agent splits into two agents. One monitors the input stream and distributes it into two queues, one consisting of the enqueue requests received (preserving order of arrival) and the other consisting of dequeue requests received. Each enqueue request contains the value to be enqueued. Each dequeue request contains a teller for a variable, the asker for which is retained by the agent sending the request. When an enqueue request arrives, it is communicated via the tell capability directly to the agent which requested that the dequeue operation be performed. (Note that the length of the dequeue list can be greater than the length of the enqueue list, so that the queue may be "negative" for a while.) If we wish to give clients separate "enqueue" and "dequeue" capabilities then only the `match/2` program is needed.

3.3 One to many communication

There are several programming techniques which compensate for the inability to directly share data which is a result of the two-occurrence restriction. As we now show (and as was partly shown in [5]), it is very easy to write a program which can copy the data on one channel into any number of outgoing channels, even if the incoming data contains a teller.

The `distribute` predicate takes `n+2` arguments. The first argument is the channel on which communication is received, and the rest are channels to which the communication is to be copied. (One of these channels, the second argument, is treated specially.) The basic idea is very simple. We illustrate it for the case in which an agent can receive only arrays of length 2.

---

[5] A more detailed exposition, which handles extensions of the usual short-circuit protocol is given in [12].

[6] Typically the input stream is obtained by merging one stream from each client—the handling of many-to-one communication schemes is discussed in more detail below.

```
distribute([X1 | X2], !Y0, ..., !Yn) ::
        Y0 = [Y01 | Y02], ..., Yn = [Yn1 | Yn2],
        distribute(X1, !Y01, ..., !Yn1), distribute(X2, !Y02, ..., !Yn2).
```

However, in addition, it is possible that the agent receives the teller for another stream on its input channel. In this case, we would like to forward this teller to some *one* of the "output" streams, but in such a way that we may continue to monitor the output produced on this channel and copy it to the other streams. To achieve this, we send the teller for a *new* communication channel Z to the selected stream, and then recur with Z as the new "input" stream for the distributor. In this way the role of the asker and teller may ping-pong between the first two arguments of the `distribute` agent:

```
distribute(!X, !Y0, ..., !Yn) :: Y0 = !Z, distribute(Z, !X, !Y1, ..., !Yn).
```

For many programs, explicit calls to a `distribute` predicate can be eliminated in favor of in-line unfolding of the above code.

Other techniques for sharing data are also possible. Frequently the data structure can be passed in a pipelined fashion to avoid all the overhead of copying. Access to the data can, alternatively, be serialized so that only one agent at a time has access. Finally, the data can be made the local state of an agent which has many clients that query the data structure. These issues are further discussed in [12].

3.4 Janus programs using arrays

A major use of arrays is as a random-access data-structure internal to a process, which can be updated sequentially. This is illustrated by the following program for the "Dutch National Flag" problem [3]:

```
dnf(Cols, Sorted) :: dnf(Cols, 0, |Cols| − 1, |Cols| − 1, Sorted).
dnf(In, R, W, B, !Out) ::
        R > W → Out = In,
        R ≤ W → (In.W = red → dnf(In[R → In.W, W → In.R], R + 1, W, B, !Out),
                 In.W = white → dnf(In, R, W − 1, B, !Out),
                 In.W = blue → dnf(In[B → In.W, W → In.B], R, W − 1, B − 1, !Out)).
```

The above program is almost a direct translation of the sequential program in [3]. Note the idiom for swapping two elements of the array, and recall that assignments can be done in place. The code produced by a Janus compiler for this program for a uni-processor machine is not expected to be very different from code produced for the corresponding program in an imperative, sequential language.

In Janus it is possible to quicksort an array in parallel *in place*:

```
qsort(A, !B) ::
        |A| ≤ 1 → B = A,
        |A| > 1 → split(A, !K, !E), qsort2(E, K, !B).
```

The `split(A, !K, !Result)` agent pivots `A` around `A.0`, returning the elements of `A` less than `A.0` in `Result[0..(K − 1)]`, `A.0` in `Result.K`, and elements of `A` not less than `A.0` in `Result[(K + 1)..|A|]`..

```
split(A, K, Result) :: split(A, 1, |A| − 1, K, Result).
split(A, I, Bound, !K, !Result) ::
        (I < Bound →
        (A.0 > A.I → split(A, I + 1, Bound, !K, !Result),
         A.0 ≤ A.I → split(A[Bound → A.I, I → A.Bound], I, Bound − 1, !K, !Result)),
        I = Bound →
        (A.0 > A.I → Result = A[0 → A.I, I → A.0], K = I,
         A.0 ≤ A.I → Result = A[0 → A.(I − 1), (I − 1) → A.0], K = I − 1)).

qsort2(E, K, !B) ::  %Implicitly suspends until E is an array
        0 < K, K < |E| − 1 → qsort(E[0..K], !C), qsort(E[(K + 1)..(|E| − 1)], !D), B = C o D,
        K = 0 → B = E,
        K = |E| − 1 → B = E.
```

Essentially, `split` pivots its input array `A` around `A.0`, in place. The two halves of the array can then be sorted recursively in place, and the results combined in place in constant time since the pieces are contiguous. To our knowledge, it is not possible to obtain such a simple and efficient quick-sort program in other concurrent logic programming languages.

3.5 Bags

The communication mechanism discussed so far has focussed on point-to-point directional communication channels. An agent may have a fixed number of such channels. Such communication schemes are too simplistic, however, to deal elegantly with many to one communication. Consider for example a situation in which an a priori unbounded number of clients may seek service from a server. Many-to-one communication can be achieved in Janus using *bags* which are essentially (possibly infinite) unordered collections.

The reader of a bag suspends waiting for an element to appear in the bag. It then processes that element and typically recurs with the remaining bag. Each writer of the bag `B` has tell rights to a variable X_i and $B = X_1 \cup \ldots \cup X_n$ has been told to the store. A writer can split its reference m ways by telling $X_i = X_{i1} \cup \ldots X_{im}$. A writer can drop its tell rights by imposing the constraint $X_i = \{\}$.

A simple bank account program is an example of a typical use of bags:

```
account({M} ∪ In, Balance) ::
      M = deposit(Amount), Amount ≥ 0 → account(In, Balance + Amount),
      M = withdraw(Amount, !Ack) →
            ((0 ≤ Amount, Amount ≤ Balance) → Ack = ok, account(In, Balance − Amount),
             Amount > Balance → Ack = overdraw_attempt(Amount), account(In, Balance),
             Amount < 0 → Ack = negative_withdrawal(Amount), account(In, Balance))
      M = current_balance(!Reply), number(Balance) → Reply = Balance, account(In, Balance).
```

The guard `number(Balance)` was added to the last behavior of `account` to indicate that `Balance` is forced and can therefore occur multiple times. Straightforward flow-analysis-based compilation techniques can lead to the elimination of this test at run-time.

Note that it is possible to use bags to obtain many-to-one *sequenced* communication: this is done by the client sending to the server a list (array of two elements). The server processes the first element in the list, and places the tail back in the bag. This guarantees that elements in each list are processed in the order in which they occur in the list.

Bags provide a more general and less ad-hoc alternative to the primitive merge servers found in many other concurrent logic programming languages. Bags can support message sending in which messages are unordered as well as those in which the relative order of sends from each client is preserved. Unlike bags, primitive merges force servers to deal with lists of items and clients to follow a system-wide protocol for stream splitting. Rather than provide primitive implementations for a particular library agent, bags provide a more principled and general foundation for accomplishing the same goals.

4 Comparison with Other Work and Conclusions

Our work on distributed constraint programming languages was influenced by [5]. From [5] we learnt how to combine the idea of *broadcast-freedom* with a static annotation scheme. Judiciously defined, the annotation scheme turned out to be enough to obtain failure-freeness, besides having a very intuitive operational flavor. The main difference between Doc and Janus is that Doc programs are not failure-free—even ignoring the "occurs-check" problem. A goal is allowed to reduce without checking that the basic operations in the clause can be executed successfully. In particular, a goal is allowed to reduce without checking that teller rights have been obtained for all the variables on the left hand side of equality goals: hence at run-time, it is possible situations such as `2=3` may occur, requiring the computation to abort. Another major difference is that the annotation scheme in Doc was rather complex and was presented as a modification to the unification algorithm. (Doc annotated every variable with either a "<" annotation or an ">" annotation. Consequently, the most general unification algorithm had to be modified to take into account the proper rules for matching "`X<`" with "`Y>`".) Our contribution here has been to present essentially the same idea (using the notion of tellers) *without* having to modify the unification algorithm at all.[7] Our development has also made it possible to extend the notion of askers and tellers to constraint systems far richer than Herbrand, namely systems with rich functionality for arrays and bags. Also to our knowledge, Doc was never seriously implemented or intended as a language which would be competitive with concurrent imperative languages.

Recently, certain uniprocessor implementation schemes for FGHC have been described [17], for a subset of FGHC similar to Janus. These schemes may have some of the potential for generating tight code that Janus programs have. An advantage of writing code in Janus is that, while the programmer must provide more knowledge about the directionality of communication, this knowledge can be exploited by the compiler. We are skeptical that on comparable code as good a job can be done by a compiler for FGHC as by one for Janus. Also, the concepts of distributed programming match Janus much more closely than other `cc/Herbrand` languages based on run-time constraint solving.

Most Janus programs can be written directly as *Strand* programs. However, a *Strand* program does not have the guarantee that it will not abort at run-time due to "assignment errors". Our work here can be seen as devising liberal compile-time checkable rules that ensure that no "assignment errors" will occur at run-time. In a distributed programming language, it is important that the compiler be able to guarantee that no run-time errors caused by a careless programmer can compromise the integrity of network-wide computations, and this cannot be done in Strand, without restricting the user to a language essentially like Janus.

Future work. The work we describe above is part of a project to investigate language-level support for constructing immense distributed systems. In the context of this project, we wish to examine a set of issues and their interactions with language design, including the design of language extensions for input/output, the development of strong typing schemes for the language, development of an adequate vocabulary for explicit run-time reconfigurability, the development of "fail-safe" implementations that can survive node-failures and network partitions, the implementation of secure implementations which are immune from malicious attempts to compromise the integrity of a node, the development of semantically-based program design, development and debugging tools etc. We believe it will be possible to fruitfully address many of these tasks within this framework because the design of Janus seems to be as simple as it can be, without compromising the usability of the language for distributed computation.

Conclusion. We have introduced a simple distributed programming language based exclusively on the use of constraints for communication and control. Thus the language has a clean logical foundation and a very simple formal semantics (e.g., see [13]). It extends prior concurrent logic programming languages in that computations are guaranteed not to result in inconsistent stores and in that the underlying constraint system is substantially richer than that found in conventional logic pro-

[7] In fact, Janus restrictions imply that unification in Janus can be compiled into simple pattern-matching code.

gramming languages.[8] The restrictions imposed in achieving the failure-freedom property naturally reflect the view of variables as single-message, point-to-point *directional* communication channels, and naturally allow the communication of tell- and ask-rights to channels in messages. At the same time, it seems likely that the language can be implemented so as to be competitive with conventional, distributed assignment-based languages. Indeed, we see this work as being a step on the way towards the establishment of a new paradigm for distributed computing, the distributed constraint programming paradigm.

Acknowledgements. These ideas have been discussed with a number of people over several months. The research underlying this paper has benefitted tremendously from many, many discussions with Mark Miller and Eric Dean Tribble. We also thank Danny Bobrow, Seif Haridi, Fernando Pereira, Julie Basu, Saumya Debray, Mats Carlsson, Volker Haarslev, Bogumil Hausman and David H.D. Warren for discussions and comments.

References

[1] Peter Aczel. *Non well-founded sets.* Number 14 in CSLI Lecture Notes. CSLI, 1988.

[2] K. L. Clark and S. Gregory. Parlog: parallel programming in logic. *TOPLAS*, 8(1):1–49, January 1986.

[3] E. W. Dijkstra. *A Discipline of Programming.* Prentice-Hall, 1976.

[4] Carl Hewitt. *The Ecology of Computation*, chapter Offices are open systems. Elsevier Science Publishers/North-Holland, 1988.

[5] Masahiro Hirata. Programming language Doc and its self-description, or, X = X considered harmful. In *3d Conference Proceedings of Japan Society for Software Science and Technology*, pages 69–72, 1986.

[6] Bernardo Huberman, editor. *The Ecology of Computation.* Elsevier Science Publishers/North-Holland, 1988.

[7] Ken Kahn and Mark S. Miller. *The Ecology of Computation*, chapter Language Design and Open Systems. North Holland, 1988.

[8] Kenneth M. Kahn and Vijay A. Saraswat. Complete visualization of concurrent programs and their execution. In *Proceedings of the IEEE Workshop on Visual Programming.* IEEE, October 1990. Also SSL technical report, Xerox PARC, August 1989.

[9] S. Kliger, E. Yardeni, E. Shapiro, and K. Kahn. The language **FCP(:,?)**. In *Conference on Fifth Generation Computer Systems*, December 1988.

[10] Vijay A. Saraswat. The concurrent logic programming language **CP**: definition and operational semantics. In *Proceedings of the SIGACT-SIGPLAN Symposium on Principles of Programming Languages*, pages 49–62. ACM, January 1987.

[11] Vijay A. Saraswat. *Concurrent Constraint Programming Languages.* PhD thesis, Carnegie-Mellon University, January 1989. To appear, Doctoral Dissertation Award and Logic Programming Series, MIT Press, 1990.

[12] Vijay A. Saraswat, Kenneth M. Kahn, and Jacob Levy. Distributed constraint programming—the dc framework and Janus. Technical report, Xerox PARC, August 1989.

[8] In particular, Janus does not make use of *any* non-logical aspects other than those embodied in the notion of blocking Ask; this in contrast with almost all other concurrent logic programming languages which either introduce gratuitously non-logical operations (Concurrent Prolog, the assignment in Strand), or fail to specify the built-in primitives in enough detail (e.g. GHC).

[13] Vijay A. Saraswat and Martin Rinard. Concurrent constraint programming. In *Proceedings of Seventeenth ACM Symposium on Principles of Programming Languages, San Francisco*, January 1990.

[14] Ehud Shapiro, editor. *Concurrent Prolog, Volume* 1 *and* 2. MIT Press, December 1987.

[15] Strand Software Technologies Inc. *Strand 88 Users Manual*, June 1989.

[16] K. Ueda. *Guarded Horn Clauses.* PhD thesis, University of Tokyo, 1986.

[17] K. Ueda and M. Morita A new implementation technique for Flat GHC. In *Proceedings of the Seventh International Conference on Logic Programming*, June 1990.

[18] M. Young, A. Tevanian, R. Rashid, D. Golub, J. Eppinger, J. Chew, W. Bolosky, D. Black, and D. Baron. The duality of memory and communication in the implementation of a multiprocessor operating system. In *Proceedings of the Eleventh Symposium on Operating System Principles*, November 1987.

Theory

Operational and Denotational Semantics of Rewrite Programs

Maria Paola Bonacina, Jieh Hsiang
Department of Computer Science
SUNY at Stony Brook
Stony Brook, NY 11794-4400 USA
{bonacina,hsiang}@sbcs.sunysb.edu

Abstract

In this paper we present a new operational and denotational semantics for rewrite systems as logic programs. The main feature of our rewrite programs is that they allow us to define predicates not only by implications as in Prolog, but also by equivalences. We give a few examples showing how rewrite programs may turn out to be more effective than Prolog programs in capturing the user's intended semantics, because of this additional feature. Rewrite programs are interpreted by linear completion. Our definition of linear completion differs from the previous one [10, 9], because we allow simplification of goals by their ancestors. If simplification is allowed, programs given by equivalences and programs given by implications show a different behaviour. In the second part of the paper we give a fixpoint characterization of rewrite programs and we show that it captures both the proof theoretic and the model theoretic semantics. Rewrite programs and Prolog programs for the same predicates have the same fixpoint, i.e. the same set of ground true facts, although a rewrite program may give fewer answers. We show that this happens because if predicates are defined by equivalences, distinct Prolog answers turn out to be equivalent with respect to the rewrite program. However, for every Prolog answer there is an equivalent answer given by the rewrite program. This explains why a smaller set of answers covers the same set of ground true facts.

1 Rewrite programs

Term rewriting systems have been widely applied in functional programming [5, 12, 13, 15] and to a less extent in logic programming [8, 10, 9, 11, 18]. In case of functional programs the evaluation mechanism is reduction and a computation consists in reducing a ground input term to an irreducible form, which represents the output. To perform logic programming the evaluation mechanism is extended to reduction and linear superposition. This amounts to a strongly restricted form of Knuth-Bendix completion, termed *linear completion* [9]. A computation consists in generating an answer substitution for a non ground query as it is done in Prolog.

Despite various approaches suggested, there is a common misconception that rewrite programs have the same semantics as Prolog except for a different evaluation mechanism. Surprisingly enough, this is not true in general. In this paper we present a more precise operational and denotational semantics and show how rewrite programs can avoid certain infinite loops which occur in similar Prolog programs.

The main reason for the different behaviour of rewrite programs is the utilization of an inference rule for simplification. We demonstrate its use with a simple example. The following Prolog program:

$append([\,], L, L).$
$append([X|L1], Y, [X|L2]) :- append(L1, Y, L2).$
with the query
$?- append(X, [b|Y], [a, b, c|Z]).$

generates an infinite set of solutions [1]:

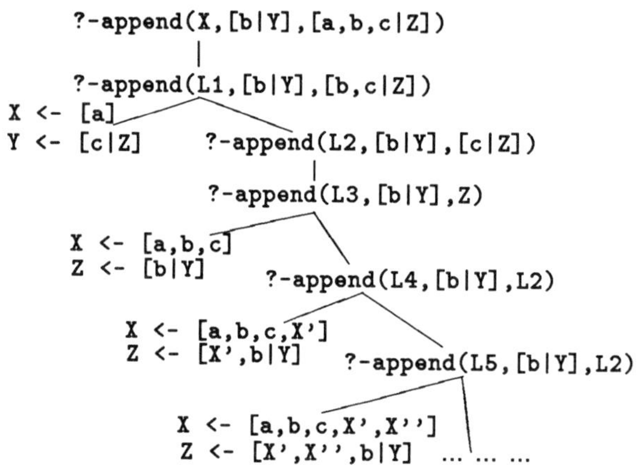

$\{X \leftarrow [a],\ Y \leftarrow [c|Z]\}$
$\{X \leftarrow [a, b, c],\ Z \leftarrow [b|Y]\}$
$\{X \leftarrow [a, b, c, X'],\ Z \leftarrow [X', b|Y]\}$
$\{X \leftarrow [a, b, c, X', X''],\ Z \leftarrow [X', X'', b|Y]\}$
....
$\{X \leftarrow [a, b, c, X', X'', \ldots, X^n],\ Z \leftarrow [X', X'', \ldots, X^n, b|Y]\}$
....

The rewrite program, on the other hand, is defined as

$append([\,], L, L) \rightarrow true$
$append([X|L1], Y, [X|L2]) \rightarrow append(L1, Y, L2)$
and the query is
$append(X, [b|Y], [a, b, c|Z]) \rightarrow answer(X, Y, Z).$

If we execute this program by linear completion we get only the first two answers:

```
                         append(X,[b|Y],[a,b,c|Z]) -> answer(X,Y,Z)
                                          |
                       append(L1,[b|Y],[b,c|Z]) -> answer([a|L1],Y,Z)
answer([a],[c|Z],Z) -> true
                      append(L1,[b|Y],[c|Z]) -> answer([a,b|L1],Y,Z)
                                        |
                 (*)append(L1,[b|Y],Z) -> answer([a,b,c|L1],Y,Z)
answer([a,b,c],Y,[b|Y]) -> true
(**)append(L1,[b|Y],L2) -> answer([a,b,c,X'|L1],Y,[X'|L2])
                                   ↓
answer([a,b,c|L1],Y,L2) <-> answer([a,b,c,X'|L1],Y,[X'|L2])
```

$\{X \leftarrow [a],\ Y \leftarrow [c|Z]\}$
$\{X \leftarrow [a,b,c],\ Z \leftarrow [b|Y]\}$

The last step, labeled by $\downarrow$, is a simplification step where an ancestor goal, labeled by (*) in the above figure, rewrites the current goal (**) to a trivial goal in the form *answer*( ) $\simeq$ *answer*( ). Since no inference can be applied to this goal, the execution halts with just two answers.

The reason for this different behaviour is that the Prolog program and the rewrite program give two different definitions of *append*. The "program units" in a rewrite program and in a Prolog program are interpreted in two different ways. In Prolog, each unit is a clause, where ": –" indicates the logical *if*. In rewrite programs, the logical connective "$\rightarrow$" means *if and only if*. The infinitely many answers in the form

$$\{X \leftarrow [a,b,c,X',X'',\ldots,X^n],\ Z \leftarrow [X',X'',\ldots,X^n,b|Y]\}$$

given by Prolog are not equivalent if *append* is defined by implications, but they all collapse to the second solution

$$\{X \leftarrow [a,b,c],\ Z \leftarrow [b|Y]\}$$

if *append* is defined by bi-implications. The first answer of the rewrite program corresponds to the first answer of the Prolog program. The second answer of the rewrite program corresponds to the second answer of the Prolog program and all the proceeding ones.

We can see why this happens by instantiating the query by using the answer substitutions. If the query is instantiated by the first answer substitution, it is rewritten to *append*$([\ ],[b,c|Z],[b,c|Z])$ and then to *true*. If it is instantiated by the second answer or any of the proceeding ones, it is rewritten to *append*$([\ ],[b|Y],[b|Y])$ and then to *true*. All the answers but the first one yield the same true fact if simplification is applied, i.e. if *append* is defined by equivalences. All those answers are equivalent to the second one with respect to the rewrite program so that they are not generated.

Since the intended definition of *append* is actually

$$append([X|L1], Y, [X|L2]) \ if \ and \ only \ if \ append(L1, Y, L2),$$

the rewrite system is closer to the intended meaning of the definition than the Prolog program.

The interpretation of program units as logical equivalences may also help resolving some loops which may occur in Prolog. For example, consider the following Prolog clause:

$P(X,Y,Z):-append(X,[b|Y],[a,b,c|Z]), non-member(a,X).$
with the query $?-P(X,Y,Z)$.

Prolog falls into an infinite loop when evaluating the first clause for P, since a is a member of X in all the solutions of $append(X,[b|Y],[a,b,c|Z])$. Such potential loops cannot even be prevented beforehand by using *cut*. The rewrite program does not loop and evaluates the second clause of P, since there are only two answers from evaluating the *append* subgoal and none of them satisfies the *non-member* subgoal.

One may suspect that simplification may throw away too many answers and change the intended semantics. For instance, consider the following:

$Q(X,Y,Z):-append(X,[b|Y],[a,b,c|Z]), size(X) > 3.$
with the query $?-Q(X,Y,Z)$.

Since in the two answers for the *append* subgoal generated in the previous examples the size of X is less than or equal to three, it seems that no solution would be provided. This is not the case. When $Q(X,Y,Z) \rightarrow answer(X,Y,Z)$ is given as the query, the execution generates first the two solutions to the *append* subgoal

$$size([a]) > 3 \rightarrow answer([a],[c|Z],Z)$$
$$size([a,b,c]) > 3 \rightarrow answer([a,b,c],Y,[b|Y]),$$

both of which fail to give any solution to the Q problem. Then the execution continues with the goal

$$append(L1,[b|Y],L2), size([a,b,c,X'|L1]) > 3 \rightarrow answer([a,b,c,X'|L1], Y,[X'|L2]).$$

Assuming that *size* is defined as desired, $size([a,b,c,X'|L1]) > 3$ simplifies to *true* and the goal is reduced to

$$append(L1,[b|Y],L2) \rightarrow answer([a,b,c,X'|L1],Y,[X'|L2]) \ (**).$$

Note that this is the same goal (**) generated in the previous execution for the *append* query. In that execution this goal is rewritten by its ancestor (*) and it does not yield any answer. In the execution for the Q query all the ancestors contain a *size* literal too, so that they do not apply to simplify the goal (**), which yields a correct solution

$$answer([a,b,c,X'],Y,[X',b|Y]) \rightarrow true.$$

Then the computation halts as the new goal

$$append(L1,[b|Y],L3) \rightarrow answer([a,b,c,X',X''|L1],Y,[X',X''|L3])$$

is reduced by its ancestor (**) to

$$answer([a,b,c,X'|L1],Y,[X'|L3]) \simeq answer([a,b,c,X',X''|L1],Y,[X',X''|L3]).$$

So far we have seen examples where it is desirable to define predicates by equivalences. However, not all relations are meant to be defined by equivalences. Still, rewrite programs allow us to define predicates by implications. For example, for the *ancestor* relation

$$ancestor(X,Y) :- parent(X,Y).$$
$$ancestor(X,Y) :- parent(Z,Y),\ ancestor(X,Z).$$

both clauses are implications. As it was already pointed out in [9], implications can be written as bi-implications by recalling that $P :- Q$ is equivalent to $P \wedge Q \rightarrow Q$. If we add some facts and a query we get:

$$parent(jb,lc) \rightarrow true$$
$$parent(jb,gg) \rightarrow true$$
$$parent(gg,wm) \rightarrow true$$
$$ancestor(X,Y),\ parent(X,Y) \rightarrow parent(X,Y)$$
$$ancestor(X,Y),\ parent(Z,Y),\ ancestor(X,Z) \rightarrow parent(Z,Y),\ ancestor(X,Z)$$
$$ancestor(jb,Z) \rightarrow answer(Z).$$

This program gives the same answers as Prolog, but the computation is optimized by simplification of goals:

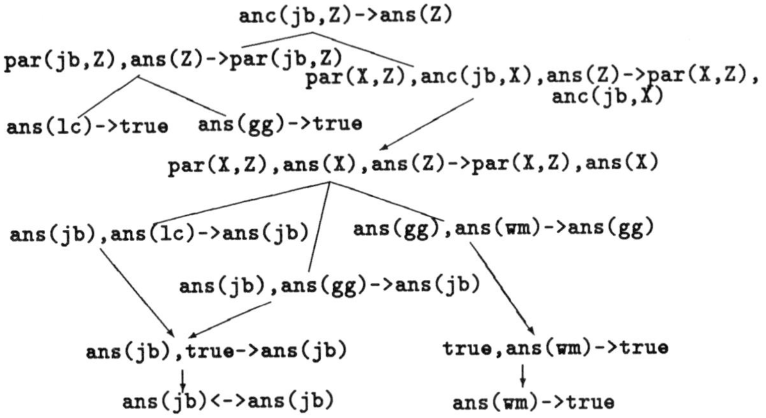

$\{Z \leftarrow lc\}$
$\{Z \leftarrow gg\}$
$\{Z \leftarrow wm\}$

The generation of the first two answers is the same as in Prolog. The third answer is different. Having the goal $parent(X, Z), ancestor(jb, X)$, Prolog first generates $ancestor(jb, jb)$ twice, fails twice, then generates the goal $ancestor(jb, gg)$, which yields the answer $z \leftarrow wm$, and a third failing computation of the goal $ancestor(jb, jb)$. These failing paths are pruned by rewriting. Simplification by previously generated answers reduces the number of recursive applications of the definition of *ancestor* and the amount of backtracking performed by the interpreter. This is not surprising, since simplification is very well known as a powerful way to reduce the search space.

2 Linear completion

As we have seen in the previous section, rewrite programs allow us to distinguish between mutually exclusive definitions and non mutually exclusive definitions. A predicate is *mutually exclusively defined* if it is defined by a set of clauses such that no two heads unify[1]. If a predicate A is defined by a set of clauses

$A(\bar{t}_1)$.
$\dots$
$A(\bar{t}_m)$.
$A(\bar{t}_{m+1}) :- B_{11} \dots B_{1p_1}$.
$\dots$

[1] A more general notion of mutually exclusive clauses appears in [6].

$A(\bar{t}_{m+n}) :- B_{n1} \dots B_{np_n}.$

its rewrite program contains the rules

$$A(\bar{t}_1) \rightarrow true$$
$$\dots$$
$$A(\bar{t}_m) \rightarrow true$$
$$A(\bar{t}_{m+1}) \rightarrow B_{11} \dots B_{1p_1}$$
$$\dots$$
$$A(\bar{t}_{m+n}) \rightarrow B_{n1} \dots B_{np_n}$$

if A is mutually exclusively defined and $\forall i, 1 \leq i \leq n, A(\bar{t}_{m+i}) \succ B_{i1} \dots B_{ip_i}$, where $\succ$ is a simplification ordering [2]. Otherwise A is transformed into

$$A(\bar{t}_1) \rightarrow true$$
$$\dots$$
$$A(\bar{t}_m) \rightarrow true$$
$$A(\bar{t}_{m+1})B_{11} \dots B_{1p_1} \rightarrow B_{11} \dots B_{1p_1}$$
$$\dots$$
$$A(\bar{t}_{m+n})B_{n1} \dots B_{np_n} \rightarrow B_{n1} \dots B_{np_n}$$

We call the rewrite rules representing facts, implications and bi-implications *fact rules*, *if-rules* and *iff-rules*. A *rewrite program* is a rewrite system of if-rules, iff-rules and fact rules. If a program has only if-rules and fact rules, then we also call it an *if-program*. Note that every Prolog program can be transformed into an if-program. Otherwise it is called an *iff-program*. We write $E \equiv P$ and we say that the rewrite program E corresponds to the Prolog program P if they define the same predicates.

Rewrite programs are interpreted by *linear completion*.

A query $\exists \bar{x} Q_1 \dots Q_m$ is negated into $Q_1 \dots Q_m \rightarrow false$ and written as a *query rule* $Q_1 \dots Q_m \rightarrow answer(\bar{x})$, where $\bar{x}$ contains all the free variables in $Q_1 \dots Q_m$. When a rule in the form $answer(\bar{x})\sigma \rightarrow true$ is deduced, $\bar{x}\sigma$ is a solution to the query. The *answer* literal was used by Dershowitz in [9], who refers to [14] for its introduction. The *state* of a computation is defined by a triple

$$(E; L_1 \dots L_l \rightarrow R_1 \dots R_r; S)$$

where E is the program, $L_1 \dots L_l \rightarrow R_1 \dots R_r$ is the current goal and S is the set of *goal simplifiers*. The set S contains all the ancestors of the current goal plus all the previously generated *answer rules*, i.e. the goal rules in the form $answer(\bar{x})\sigma \rightarrow true$. A *goal rule* is any rule generated by the program starting from the query. A computation can be described by a tree, where each node is labeled by a triple. The root represents the initial state

$$(E; Q_1 \dots Q_m \rightarrow answer(\bar{x}); \emptyset)$$

[2] A simplification ordering is an ordering with the following properties: $s \succ t$ implies $s\sigma \succ t\sigma$ for all substitutions σ (stability), $s \succ t$ implies $c[s] \succ c[t]$ for all contexts c (monotonicity), $c[s] \succ s$ (subterm property) and $\succ$ is well founded [7].

A *final state* is a state such that either no inference step can be performed on the current goal or it is an identity. The computation stops when all the leaves in the tree are labelled by final states. A final state in the form

$$(E; answer(\bar{x})\sigma \rightarrow true; S)$$

means that the answer substitution σ for the query is found. An answer rule means a contradiction in the refutational sense, since *answer* means *false* logically. The interpreter builds a refutation starting with the query and ending with a contradiction:

$$E \cup \{Q_1 \ldots Q_m \rightarrow answer(\bar{x})\} \vdash_{LC} answer(\bar{x})\sigma \rightarrow true$$

We also denote it by $E \vdash_{LC} Q_1 \ldots Q_m\sigma$, meaning that $Q_1 \ldots Q_m\sigma$ is proved from program E by linear completion. If a ground query is given, the answer substitution is empty and we write $E \vdash_{LC} Q_1 \ldots Q_m$.

A computation step transforms the current state in one of the following ways:

Simplify:

$$\frac{(E; L_1 \ldots L_l \rightarrow R_1 \ldots R_r; S)}{(E; L'_1 \ldots L'_n \rightarrow R'_1 \ldots R'_s; S)}$$

Overlap:

$$\frac{(E; L_1 \ldots L_l \rightarrow R_1 \ldots R_r; S)}{(E; L'_1 \ldots L'_n \rightarrow R'_1 \ldots R'_s; S \cup \{L_1 \ldots L_l \rightarrow R_1 \ldots R_r\})}$$

Answer:

$$\frac{(E; answer(\bar{x})\sigma \rightarrow true; S)}{(E; —; S \cup \{answer(\bar{x})\sigma \rightarrow true\})}$$

Delete:

$$\frac{(E; L_1 \ldots L_l \simeq L_1 \ldots L_l; S)}{(E; —; S)}$$

where — means "backtrack".

In *Simplify*, $L_1 \ldots L_l \rightarrow R_1 \ldots R_r$ is simplified into a new goal $L'_1 \ldots L'_n \rightarrow R'_1 \ldots R'_s$ using $E \cup S$. The rewritten goal is discarded. Simplification of goals by goals is the basic difference between our definition of linear completion and the one in [9]. In *Overlap* a new goal is generated by overlapping the current goal with a rule in E. The new goal replaces the current one, which is added to the simplifiers set. In *Answer* an answer is found and the answer rule is put into the simplifier set. Then the interpreter backtracks if possible. Similarly, in *Delete* a goal which is an identity is deleted and then the interpreter backtracks.

Note that no overlap between two program rules, no overlap between two goal rules and no simplification of program rules are used. The name linear completion emphasizes that the process is *linear* with respect to superposition.

The simplifiers set is a global variable: its modifications on one path of the computation tree affect the other paths since a current goal at some node can be simplified by an answer rule reached on another path. A linear completion interpreter builds the tree sequentially following some search strategy. For instance a depth first strategy with backtracking as in Prolog can be adopted. If the goal rule in the current state is such that none of the above inference rule applies, the interpreter backtracks. This is the case for instance when the goal rule has the form $answer(\bar{t}) \simeq answer(\bar{s})$. Here we focus on inference rules only, abstracting from the search strategy. In the following we assume that a fair strategy is adopted whenever needed.

The overlap steps in LC are similar to the resolution steps in Prolog. Given a goal rule $A(\bar{u})L_1 \ldots L_l \rightarrow R_1 \ldots R_r$ and a program rule, one of the three overlapping inferences can be used according to the type of the program rule:

Overlap with an if-rule:

$$\frac{A(\bar{s})B_1 \ldots B_n \rightarrow B_1 \ldots B_n,\ A(\bar{u})L_1 \ldots L_l \rightarrow R_1 \ldots R_r}{(B_1 \ldots B_n L_1 \ldots L_l)\sigma \rightarrow (B_1 \ldots B_n R_1 \ldots R_r)\sigma}$$

Overlap with an iff-rule:

$$\frac{A(\bar{s}) \rightarrow B_1 \ldots B_n,\ A(\bar{u})L_1 \ldots L_l \rightarrow R_1 \ldots R_r}{(B_1 \ldots B_n L_1 \ldots L_l)\sigma \rightarrow (R_1 \ldots R_r)\sigma}$$

Overlap with a fact rule:

$$\frac{A(\bar{s}) \rightarrow true,\ A(\bar{u})L_1 \ldots L_l \rightarrow R_1 \ldots R_r}{(L_1 \ldots L_l)\sigma \simeq (R_1 \ldots R_r)\sigma}$$

where σ is the most general unifier of $A(\bar{s})$ and $A(\bar{u})$. In the last case the generated goal is oriented according to a simplification ordering. Here and in the following we assume that the selected literal in a goal $Q_1 \ldots Q_m$ is Q_1. There is no loss of generality, because if the selected literal is Q_j with $j \neq 1$, we can permute the indices so that $j = 1$. The generated goals are oriented by a simplification ordering such that goal rules in the form $B_1 \ldots B_n answer(\bar{t}) \rightarrow B_1 \ldots B_n$ and $B_1 \ldots B_n \rightarrow answer(\bar{t})$ are oriented from left to right. An overlap step replaces a literal in the goal by a proper instance of its predicate's definition. If the defining formula is an implication, the new set of subgoals is added to both sides of the goal equation. If it is a bi-implication, it is added to the left side only. An overlap with a fact deletes a literal in the goal list.

Note that no overlap on an atom different from the head of a rule needs to be considered. If the atom $A(\bar{u})$ in the goal rule $A(\bar{u})\bar{L} \rightarrow \bar{R}$ unifies with an atom $A(\bar{v})$ in an if-rule $CA(\bar{v})\bar{B} \rightarrow A(\bar{v})\bar{B}$ the overlap step generates the goal

$$C\bar{B}\bar{R}\sigma \rightarrow \bar{B}A(\bar{v})\bar{L}\sigma$$

which is reduced by its predecessor to

$$C\bar{B}\bar{R}\sigma \rightarrow \bar{B}\bar{R}\sigma.$$

A following overlap on literal C between this new goal and the same program rule will lead to the identity $A(\bar{v})\bar{B}\bar{R}\sigma \simeq A(\bar{v})\bar{B}\bar{R}\sigma$.

The key feature of rewrite programs is simplification of the current goal by program rules, ancestor goal rules and answer rules. If an if-rule $AB_1 \ldots B_n \to B_1 \ldots B_n$ or a fact $A \to true$ simplifies a query $Q_1 \ldots Q_m$, then the atom Q_j such that $A\sigma = Q_j$ is deleted. If an iff-rule $A \to B_1 \ldots B_n$ applies, the atom Q_j is replaced by $(B_1 \ldots B_n)\sigma$. The rewrite rules $x \cdot true \to x$ and $x \cdot x \to x$ are also implicitly applied. They allow us to delete any repeated atom and any occurrence of *true* in a conjunction. Notice that since the product is associative, commutative and idempotent, we regard conjunctions of atoms as *sets* of atoms: the left side $\bar{L}$ of an if-rule or of an ancestor goal rule matches a side $\bar{R}$ of the current goal rule if there is a subset of $\bar{R}$ which is an instance of $\bar{L}$. Simplification is given higher priority than overlap. The current goal rule is always fully simplified before the next overlap step is performed.

3 A fixpoint characterization of rewrite programs

Rewrite programs have operational, model theoretic and fixpoint semantics like Prolog programs. Let E be a rewrite program, $\mathcal{B}$ be its Herbrand base and $\mathcal{P}(\mathcal{B})$ be the set of all subsets of $\mathcal{B}$, i.e. the set of all the Herbrand interpretations. The operational semantics of E is its *success set*, $\{G \mid G \in \mathcal{B},\ E \vdash_{LC} G\}$. The model theoretic semantics is the set $\{G \mid G \in \mathcal{B},\ E^* \models G = true\}$, where $E^* = E \cup \{x \cdot x \to x,\ x \cdot true \to x\}$. If $E \vdash_{LC} Q_1 \ldots Q_m\sigma$, we say that σ is a *correct answer substitution* for the query $Q_1 \ldots Q_m$ if $E^* \models Q_1 \ldots Q_m\sigma = true$.

We define a *least fixpoint semantics* of rewrite programs on the lattice $\mathbb{B} = \{I' \mid I' = I \cup \{true\}, I \subseteq \mathcal{B}\}$. $\mathbb{B}$ is $\mathcal{P}(\mathcal{B})$ where the element *true* is added to each subset of $\mathcal{B}$. The order relation on $\mathbb{B}$ is set inclusion $\subseteq$, the greatest lower bound operation is intersection $\bigcap$ and the least upper bound operation is union $\bigcup$. The bottom element is $\{true\}$ and the top element is $\mathcal{B} \cup \{true\}$.

A function $T_E : \mathbb{B} \to \mathbb{B}$ is associated to a program E as follows:

Definition 3.1 *Given a rewrite program E, its associated function is the function $T_E : \mathbb{B} \to \mathbb{B}$ such that $P \in T_E(I)$ if and only if there exists in E a rule $A_1 \ldots A_n \simeq B_1 \ldots B_m$ $(n \geq 1, m \geq 1)$ such that $P = A_i\sigma$ and $\{A_1\sigma, \ldots, A_{i-1}\sigma, A_{i+1}\sigma, \ldots, A_n\sigma, B_1\sigma, \ldots, B_m\sigma\} \subseteq I$ for some i, $1 \leq i \leq n$, and some ground substitution σ. (The double arrow $\simeq$ means there is no distinction between the left hand side and the right hand side.)*

Lemma 3.1 *Given a rewrite program E, T_E is continuous, that is for every non decreasing chain $X_1 \subseteq X_2 \subseteq \ldots$ of elements in $\mathbb{B}$, $T_E(\bigcup\{X_i \mid i < \omega\}) = \bigcup\{T_E(X_i) \mid i < \omega\}$.*

It follows that T_E has the properties of continuous functions on a lattice.

Namely the least fixpoint of T_E is an ordinal power of T_E:

$$lfp(T_E) = T_E \uparrow \omega$$

where ordinal powers are defined on $\mathbb{B}$ in the usual way:

$$T \uparrow 0 = \{true\}$$

$$T \uparrow n = \begin{cases} T(T \uparrow (n-1)) & \text{if } n \text{ is a successor ordinal} \\ \bigcup\{T \uparrow k \mid k < n\} & \text{if } n \text{ is a limit ordinal.} \end{cases}$$

For example, the least fixpoint of the rewrite program for the *ancestor* relation is obtained as follows:

$T_E(\{true\}) = \{true, parent(jb, lc), parent(jb, gg), parent(gg, wm)\}$
$T_E^2(\{true\}) = T_E(\{true\}) \cup \{ancestor(jb, lc), ancestor(jb, gg), ancestor(gg, wm)\}$
$lfp(T_E) = T_E^3(\{true\}) = T_E^2(\{true\}) \cup \{ancestor(jb, wm)\}$.

4 Equivalence of proof theoretic, model theoretic and fixpoint semantics

We show now that $lfp(T_E)$ is a fixpoint characterization of both the operational and model theoretic semantics of a program E. These results are obtained through a few steps. The proofs are omitted due to their length and can be found in the full version of the paper [4].

Lemma 4.1 *For all conjunctions of atoms* $Q_1 \ldots Q_m$, $Q_1 \ldots Q_m \leftrightarrow^*_{E^*} true$ *if and only if* $\forall j, 1 \leq j \leq m$, $Q_j \leftrightarrow^*_{E^*} true$.

The following theorem establishes the soundness of linear completion, i.e. that all the answers given by linear completion are correct answer substitutions:

Theorem 4.1 *If* $E \vdash_{LC} Q_1 \ldots Q_m\sigma$ *then* $E^* \models Q_1 \ldots Q_m\sigma = true$.

We now restrict our attention to ground queries. First we prove a lemma which allows us to split the problem of proving a ground conjunction into the subproblems of proving its single atoms:

Lemma 4.2 $\forall Q_1 \ldots Q_m \in \mathcal{B}$, $E \vdash_{LC} Q_1 \ldots Q_m$ *if and only if* $\forall j$, $1 \leq j \leq m$, $E \vdash_{LC} Q_j$.

Intuitively this result holds because since the query is ground, there is no computation of an answer substitution and the processes of reducing to *true* the literals in the query are independent processes. Next we show that all ground queries proved by linear completion from E are equivalent to *true*:

Theorem 4.2 $\forall Q_1 \ldots Q_m \in \mathcal{B}$, $E \vdash_{LC} Q_1 \ldots Q_m$ *if and only if* $Q_1 \ldots Q_m \leftrightarrow^*_{E^*}$ *true*.

These results allow us to relate the fixpoint semantics of a rewrite program E to its operational semantics:

Theorem 4.3 *$\forall Q_1 \ldots Q_m \in \mathcal{B}$, $Q_1 \ldots Q_m \leftrightarrow^*_{E^*} true$ if and only if $\forall i$, $1 \leq i \leq m$, $Q_i \in lfp(T_E)$.*

Therefore, the fixpoint semantics $lfp(T_E)$ captures both the operational and model theoretic semantics of the rewrite program E:

Theorem 4.4 *$\forall G \in \mathcal{B}$, $G \in lfp(T_E)$ if and only if $E \vdash_{LC} G$.*

Theorem 4.5 *$\forall G \in \mathcal{B}$, $G \in lfp(T_E)$ if and only if $E^* \models G = true$.*

5 Denotational semantics of rewrite programs

The above fixpoint characterization of rewrite programs is basically equivalent to the fixpoint characterization of Prolog programs. The fixpoint semantics of a Prolog program P is $lfp(T_P) = T_P \uparrow \omega$, where T_P is the function $T_P : \mathcal{P}(\mathcal{B}) \rightarrow \mathcal{P}(\mathcal{B})$ such that $A \in T_P(I)$ if and only if there exists in P a clause $A' :- B_1 \ldots B_m$ $(m \geq 0)$ such that $A = A'\sigma$ and $\{B_1\sigma \ldots B_m\sigma\} \subseteq I$ for some ground substitution σ [16, 1]. The following theorem shows that the two semantics are indeed the same.

Theorem 5.1 *If $E \equiv P$, then $lfp(T_E) = lfp(T_P)$.*

This theorem shows that a Prolog program and a rewrite program defining the same predicates have the same model. For a ground atom G, $E \vdash_{LC} G$, $G \leftrightarrow^*_{E^*} true$, $E^* \models G = true$, $G \in lfp(T_E)$, $G \in lfp(T_P)$, $P \models G$ and $P \vdash_{Prolog} G$ are all equivalent. However, the behaviour of the two programs P and E may be different. We show in the following that even if a rewrite programs E may generates less answers than the corresponding Prolog program P, for all answers given by P there is an answer given by E which is E-equivalent.

We first prove that all the answers given by linear completion are also given by Prolog. This result follows from completeness of SLD-resolution.

Theorem 5.2 *If $E \equiv P$, if $E \vdash_{LC} Q_1 \ldots Q_m\sigma$, then there exists an answer θ, $P \vdash_{Prolog} Q_1 \ldots Q_m\theta$, such that $\sigma = \theta\rho$ for some substitution ρ.*

We now prove that linear completion is complete as well by proving that all Prolog answers are represented by some answers given by linear completion.

In the following we assume that all queries are single literal queries. There is no loss of generality because a query $Q_1 \ldots Q_m \rightarrow answer(\bar{x})$ can be written as a single literal query by introducing a new predicate symbol N, a new program rule $N \rightarrow Q_1 \ldots Q_m$ or $NQ_1 \ldots Q_m \rightarrow Q_1 \ldots Q_m$ and the query $N \rightarrow answer(\bar{x})$.

First of all we prove that rewrite programs and Prolog programs give the same answers if linear completion is restricted to overlap steps only, i.e. no simplification is performed. This is straightforward, since overlap steps and resolution steps clearly correspond.

Theorem 5.3 *Let LC' be a subset of the linear completion interpreter performing overlap steps only. If $E^* \models G\theta = true$, i.e. θ is a correct answer for G, there exists a computed answer σ, $E \vdash_{LC'} G\sigma$, such that $\theta = \sigma\rho$ for some substitution ρ.*

In order to prove an analogous result for linear completion with simplification we first need to prove two more lemmas.

Lemma 5.1 *If linear completion generates a computation path $(E; G \rightarrow answer(\bar{x}); \emptyset) \vdash_{LC}^{*} (E; \bar{W} \rightarrow \bar{V}; \_) \vdash_{LC}^{*} (E; H; \_) \vdash_{LC} (E; \bar{R} \simeq \bar{R}; \_)$, where the goal H is simplified to an identity by its predecessor $\bar{W} \rightarrow \bar{V}$, then H is $\bar{Z}(\bar{W}\lambda) \rightarrow \bar{Z}(\bar{V}\lambda)$ for some substitution λ and literals $\bar{Z}$. (The hyphen _ in $(E; H; \_)$ means that the third component is not relevant.)*

Lemma 5.2 *Given a query G, if there exists an answer θ generated by LC', i.e. $E \vdash_{LC'} G\theta$, then there exists an answer σ generated by LC, i.e. $E \vdash_{LC} G\sigma$.*

We can finally state our completeness result:

Theorem 5.4 *Let E be an iff-program. If $E^* \models G\theta = true$, i.e. θ is a correct answer for G, there exists a computed answer σ, $E \vdash_{LC} G\sigma$, such that $G\theta \leftrightarrow_{E^*}^{*} G\sigma\rho$ for some substitution ρ.*

Theorem 5.5 *If $E \equiv P$, if $P \vdash_{Prolog} G\theta$, then there exists an answer σ given by linear completion, $E \vdash_{LC} G\sigma$ and a substitution ρ, such that $G\theta \leftrightarrow_{E^*}^{*} G\sigma\rho$.*

6 Discussion

In this paper we have given the operational and denotational semantics of a notion of rewrite programs. We have shown that its operational semantics, via linear completion, is both sound and complete with respect to the denotational semantics.

The main difference between rewrite programs and Prolog programs is that rewrite programs differentiate between predicates which are mutually exclusively defined and those which are not. A predicate is mutually exclusively defined if the head of each of its clauses is logically equivalent to its body. A typical such example is the usual definition of *append.* Rewrite programs, with their simplification power, can take advantage of these definitions to prevent certain infinite loops which are otherwise unavoidable in Prolog.

Rewrite programs and linear completion have already been discussed in [10, 9, 11, 18]. The approach proposed in the first three papers does not allow simplification, thus cannot fully utilize the power of rewriting. Our approach is similar to [18], although they did not study the case where a predicate is defined as an implication and not as a logical equivalence. Neither did they explain the semantics of their method. Techniques for loop detection in the execution of Prolog programs have received considerable attention. In [2, 3] loop checking mechanisms based on subsumption are studied. The basic idea in these loop checks is to eliminate the current goal if it is subsumed by one of its ancestors. The pruning effect of this kind of loop checks can turn out to be similar to the effect of our simplification of goals by ancestors. However, simplification as it is done in linear completion is more powerful in general, since it also includes simplification by program rules and by answer rules. More importantly, we believe that our approach is more natural and easier to understand, since simplification is a natural consequence of writing program units as equations.

Rewrite programs have the curious property of being denotationally equivalent to Prolog on the ground level while yield less answers in general. This is because certain answers equivalent under the equivalence relation defined by the program "collapse" into one. However, rewrite programs are also guaranteed not to lose any necessary answers. That is, they will indeed generate answers where there are some, as we have shown both in the examples and in the theorems. We feel that when a predicate symbol is supposed to be mutually exclusively defined, our semantics is more desirable than Prolog since it captures the intended meaning more accurately.

It should not be too difficult to incorporate our treatment of mutually exclusively defined predicates into a Prolog interpreter. It requires eliminating a few backtracking points and keeping the ancestor goals around for simplification purposes. However, the cleaner semantics and the prevention of certain loops may justify the extra effort spent. We are also interested to see whether *negation* can be incorporated into our framework, since a negative fact $\neg A$ simply means a rule $A \rightarrow false$.

Acknowledgements

This research was supported in part by grants CCR-8805734, INT-8715231 and CCR-8901322, funded by the National Science Foundation. The first author is also supported by Dottorato di ricerca in Informatica, Universitá degli Studi di Milano, Italy.

References

[1] K.R.Apt and M.H.Van Emden. Contributions to the Theory of Logic Programming. *J. ACM*, 29,3:841–862, July 1982.

[2] K.R.Apt, R.N.Bol and J.W.Klop. On the Safe Termination of PROLOG programs. *Proc. of the Sixth Int. Conf. on Logic Programming*, G.Levi and M.Martella eds., 353–368, MIT Press, Cambridge MA, 1989.

[3] R.N.Bol, K.R.Apt and J.W.Klop. On the Power of Subsumption and Context Checks. *Proc. Int. Symp. on Design and Implementation of Systems for Symbolic Computation*, A.Miola ed., 131–140, Capri, Italy, April 1990.

[4] M.P.Bonacina, J.Hsiang. Operational and Denotational Semantics of Rewrite Programs. Technical report, Dept. of Computer Science, SUNY, Stony Brook, NY, March 1990.

[5] R.M.Burstall, D.B.MacQueen and D.T.Sannella. HOPE: An experimental applicative language. *Conf. Record of the 1980 LISP Conf.*, 136–143, Stanford, CA, 1980.

[6] S.K.Debray and D.S.Warren. Functional Computations in Logic Programs. *ACM Trans. on Programming Languages and Systems*, 11,3:451–481, July 1989.

[7] N.Dershowitz. Orderings for term rewriting systems. *J. of Theoret. Comp. Sci.*, 17,3:279–301, 1982.

[8] N.Dershowitz, J.Hsiang, N.A.Josephson and D.A.Plaisted. Associative-commutative rewriting. *Proc. of the Eighth Int. Joint Conf. on Artificial Intelligence*, A.Bundy ed., 940–944, Karlsrue, Germany, 1983.

[9] N.Dershowitz. Computing with Rewrite Systems. *Information and Control*, 65:122–157, 1985.

[10] N.Dershowitz and N.A.Josephson. Logic Programming by Completion. *Proc. of the Second Int. Conf. on Logic Programming*, 313–320, Uppsala, Sweden, 1984.

[11] N.Dershowitz and D.A.Plaisted. Logic Programming Cum Applicative Programming. *Proc. IEEE Symp. on Logic Programming*, 54–66, Boston MA, 1985.

[12] K.Futatsugi, J.A.Goguen, J.P.Jouannaud and J.Meseguer. Principles of OBJ2. *Conf. Record of the 12th Annual ACM Symp. on Principles of Programming Languages*, New Orleans, LA, 1985.

[13] J.A.Goguen and J.Meseguer. Equality, types, modules and (why not?) generics for logic programming. *J. Logic Programming*, 1,2:179–210, 1984.

[14] C.C.Green. The Application of Theorem-proving to Question-answering. Ph.D. Thesis, Dept. of Computer Science, Stanford University, Stanford, CA, 1969.

[15] C.M.Hoffmann and M.J.O'Donnell. Programming with Equations. *ACM Trans. on Programming Languages and Systems*, 4,1:83–112, Jan. 1982.

[16] R.A.Kowalski and M.H.Van Emden. Predicate Logic as a Programming Language. *J. ACM*, 4,23, 1976.

[17] J.W.Lloyd. Foundations of Logic Programming. Second edition, Springer Verlag, Berlin, 1987.

[18] P.Réty, C.Kirchner, H.Kirchner and P.Lescanne. NARROWER: A new Algorithm for Unification and its Application to Logic Programming *Proc. of the First Int. Conf. on Rewrite Techniques and Applications*, J.P.Jouannaud ed., Dijon, France, May 1985.

Towards More Efficient Loop Checks

Roland N. Bol
Centre for Mathematics and Computer Science
P.O.Box 4079, 1009 AB Amsterdam, The Netherlands.
Phone: (+31) - 20 - 592 4080. E-mail: bol@cwi.nl.

Abstract

Loop checking is a mechanism for pruning infinite SLD-derivations. Most loop checks essentially compare the goals in a derivation: a derivation is pruned if 'sufficiently similar' goals are detected. In theory a goal is usually compared with every previous goal in the derivation, but in practice such loop checks are too expensive.

Here we investigate how to alter such loop checks to obtain less expensive ones (notably such that the number of comparisons performed is linear in the number of goals generated) while retaining the soundness and completeness results of the original loop check. To this end we modify Van Gelder's [5] 'tortoise-and-hare' technique and study in detail the number of comparisons performed by a loop check whose checkpoints are placed in accordance with the triangular numbers.

This research was partly supported by Esprit BRA-project 3020 Integration.

1. Introduction

Most loop checking mechanisms for logic programming proposed in the literature ([1], [2], I_G in [3], [4], [5], [6], [9], [10], [11] and 'redundancy' in [13]) are based on comparing goals. In theory, a goal is usually compared with every previous goal in the derivation. For such loop checks, the number of comparisons performed is quadratic in the number of goals generated. An interpreter equipped with such a loop check would not be very useful in practice: the longer a derivation gets, the more time is spent on loop checking instead of generating new goals. For a practical loop check, the number of comparisons should be at most linear in the number of goals generated.

We discuss in this paper two methods for adapting existing loop checks to meet this requirement. Both methods describe which carefully selected pairs of goals are to be compared, using the comparison criterion of the original loop check. For the new loop checks thus obtained we investigate the soundness and completeness (as defined in [2], see also section 2.2) and the number of comparisons performed (relative to the number of goals generated).

The first method, originally proposed by Van Gelder [5], is called the 'tortoise-and-hare technique'. It is discussed in section 3. Roughly speaking, this method compares every newly generated goal in a derivation with only one previous goal, namely the goal that is currently 'halfway' in the derivation. In this way the number of comparisons performed is equal to the number of goals generated. Unfortunately, a loop check thus obtained is generally incomplete.

Then two other closely related techniques are introduced. In both methods an (infinite) number of 'checkpoints' is selected; then every goal that is at such a checkpoint (on account of its level in the SLD-derivation or -tree) is compared with

- every previous goal ('single selected' loop checks), or
- the previous goals at checkpoints ('double selected' loop checks).

The use of single selected loop checks is already suggested in [4]. In section 4 the soundness and (for most cases) completeness of selected loop checks are proved, independently of the selection.

The 'density' of the selection determines the efficiency of a selected loop check. (The original loop check can be described as the selected loop check for which every goal is selected as a checkpoint, which is the most dense selection possible.) A 'linear' loop check is obtained if the increasing number of comparisons at the checkpoints is compensated by a decreasing density of the occurrence of checkpoints among other goals: the further the derivation is developed, the more comparisons are performed at a checkpoint, but the less checkpoints occur.

In [4], Covington argues informally that a single selected loop check with a selection of the form $\{n,n^2,n^3,\ldots\}$ (for some constant $n > 1$) is linear. In section 5 we prove in detail that for a double selected loop check this effect is obtained with the selection $\{\frac{1}{2}i(i+1) \mid i \in \mathbb{N}\}$ (the initial goal is defined to be at level 0). So for single *and* double selected loop checks, an appropriate selection renders the number of comparisons performed linear in the number of goals generated.

2. Preliminaries

In this section we recall the basic notions concerning loop checking, as presented in [2]. Throughout this paper we assume familiarity with the concepts and notations of logic programming as described in [7]. For two substitutions σ and τ, we write $\sigma \leq \tau$ when σ is more general than τ and for two expressions E and F, we write $E \leq F$ if F is an instance of E. An SLD-derivation step from a goal G, using a clause C and an mgu θ, to a goal H is denoted as $G \Rightarrow_{C,\theta} H$. By an SLD-derivation we mean an SLD-derivation in the sense of [7] *or an initial fragment (subderivation) of it.*

2.1 Loop checks

The purpose of a loop check is to prune every infinite SLD-tree to a finite subtree of it containing the root. We define a loop check as a set of SLD-derivations: the derivations that are pruned exactly at their last node. Such a set of SLD-derivations L can be extended in a canonical way to a function f_L from SLD-trees to SLD-trees by pruning in an SLD-tree the nodes in { G | the SLD-derivation from the root to G is in L }. We shall usually make this conversion implicitly.

DEFINITION 2.1.
Let L be a set of SLD-derivations.
RemSub(L) = { D ∈ L | L does not contain a proper subderivation of D }.
L is *subderivation free* if L = RemSub(L). □

In order to render the intuitive meaning of a loop check L: 'every derivation D ∈ L is pruned *exactly* at its last node', we need that L is subderivation free. Note that RemSub(RemSub(L)) = RemSub(L).

In the following definition, by a *variant* of a derivation D we mean a derivation D' in which in every derivation step, atoms in the same positions are selected and the same program clauses are used. D' may differ from D in the renaming that is applied to these program clauses for reasons of standardizing apart and in the mgu used. Thus (see [8]) variants differ only in the choice of the names of the variables.

DEFINITION 2.2.
A *simple loop check* is a computable set L of finite SLD-derivations such that L is closed under variants and subderivation free. □

In [2], loop checks are treated in a more general way. There non-simple loop checks occur: their behaviour may depend on the *program* the interpreter is confronted with. For the topics addressed in this paper, the distinction between simple and non-simple loop checks does not play a role. For simplicity in the presentation, we shall only consider simple loop checks, but usually omit the qualification 'simple'.

DEFINITION 2.3.
Let L be a loop check. An SLD-derivation D of P∪{G} is *pruned by L* if L contains a subderivation D' of D. □

2.2 Soundness and completeness

The most important property is definitely that using a loop check does not result in a loss of success. Even stronger, because we use here a PROLOG-like interpreter augmented with a loop check as the *only* inference mechanism, we may not want to lose any individual solution. That is, if the original tree contains a successful branch (giving some computed answer), then we require that the pruned tree contains a successful branch giving a more general answer.

Finally, we would like to retain only shorter derivations and prune the longer ones that give the same result. This leads to the following definitions, where for a derivation D, |D| stands for its length, i.e. the number of goals in it.

DEFINITION 2.4 (Soundness).

i) A loop check L is *weakly sound* if for every program P and goal G, and SLD-tree T of P∪{G}: if T contains a successful branch, then $f_L(T)$ contains a successful branch.
ii) A loop check L is *sound* if for every program P and goal G, and SLD-tree T of P∪{G}: if T contains a successful branch with a computed answer substitution σ, then $f_L(T)$ contains a successful branch with a computed answer substitution σ' such that $G\sigma' \leq G\sigma$.

iii) A loop check L is *shortening* if for every program P and goal G, and SLD-tree T of $P \cup \{G\}$: if T contains a successful branch D with a computed answer substitution σ, then either $f_L(T)$ contains D or $f_L(T)$ contains a successful branch D' with a computed answer substitution σ' such that $G\sigma' \leq G\sigma$ and $|D'| < |D|$. □

The following lemma is an immediate consequence of these definitions.

LEMMA 2.5. *Let L be a loop check.*

i) If L is shortening, then L is sound.

ii) If L is sound, then L is weakly sound. □

The purpose of a loop check is to reduce the search space for top-down interpreters. Although impossible in general, we would like to end up with a finite search space. This is the case if every infinite derivation is pruned.

DEFINITION 2.6 (Completeness).
A loop check L is *complete w.r.t. a selection rule* **R** *for a class of programs* $\mathcal{C}$, if for every program $P \in \mathcal{C}$ and goal G in L_P, every infinite SLD-derivation of $P \cup \{G\}$ via **R** is pruned by L. □

In general, comparing loop checks is difficult. The following relation comparing loop checks is not very general: most loop check will be incomparable with respect to it. Nevertheless it turns out to be very useful.

DEFINITION 2.7.
Let L_1 and L_2 be loop checks. L_1 is *stronger than* L_2 if every SLD-derivation $D_2 \in L_2$ contains a subderivation $D_1 \in L_1$. □

In other words, L_1 is stronger than L_2 if every SLD-derivation that is pruned by L_2 is also pruned by L_1. Note that the definition implies that every loop check is stronger than itself. The following theorem enables us to obtain soundness and completeness results for loop checks which are related by the 'stronger than' relation, by proving soundness and completeness for only one of them.

THEOREM 2.8 (Relative Strength).

Let L_1 and L_2 be loop checks, and let L_1 be stronger than L_2.

i) If L_1 is weakly sound, then L_2 is weakly sound.

ii) If L_1 is sound, then L_2 is sound.

iii) If L_1 is shortening, then L_2 is shortening.

iv) If L_2 is complete then L_1 is complete.

PROOF. Straightforward. □

2.3. Loop checks comparing goals

After these basic definitions, three groups of simple loop checks are presented in [2]: equality checks, subsumption checks and context checks; a summary of this presentation is given in the Appendix. These loop checks are all based on the comparison of goals: a derivation is pruned as soon as a goal occurs in it that 'is sufficiently similar' to a previous goal.

Obviously the exact criterion for 'being sufficiently similar' is the essence of a loop check. This criterion, in addition to the two goals that are compared, may use some further information about the derivation D, such as the mgu's used, the initial goal (for the resultant-based checks) and the ancestry relation among atoms (for the context checks). However, when too much extra information is used, one may doubt if the loop check really 'compares goals'. It is difficult, if at all possible, to give a precise limit on the amount and the nature of 'other information' that may be used by the criterion. Therefore we refrain from giving a fully exact definition, relying instead on the intuition of the reader.

DEFINITION 2.9.
A *full-comparison* loop check is a loop check of the form

$$L(\varphi) = \text{RemSub}(\{ D \mid D = (G_0 \Rightarrow_{C_1,\theta_1} G_1 \Rightarrow \ldots \Rightarrow G_{k-1} \Rightarrow_{C_k,\theta_k} G_k) \text{ and } \exists\, i < k \text{ such that } \varphi(G_i,G_k,D) \}),$$

where $\varphi(G_i,G_k,D)$ 'essentially compares the goals G_i and G_k':
$\varphi(G_i,G_k,D)$ = true if and only if G_i and G_k 'are sufficiently similar'.
The relation φ is called the *loop checking criterion* of $L(\varphi)$. □

The condition that φ 'essentially compares goals' implies for example that the effort of computing $\varphi(G_i,G_k,D)$ is independent of $|D|$. Therefore the number of φ-computations (*comparisons*) performed by a loop check is a good measure of the overhead caused by the loop check, as was tacitly assumed in the introduction.

LEMMA 2.10 ([4]). *On a finite SLD derivation D, a full-comparison loop check performs* $\frac{1}{2}|D|(|D|-1)$ *comparisons.*

PROOF. Obvious. □

3. The tortoise-and-hare technique

A first attempt to reduce the number of comparisons performed by a loop check is presented in [5]. There every goal G_k is compared with exactly one previous goal, namely the goal $G_{k/2}$ ($G_{(k-1)/2}$ if k is odd) 'halfway' the derivation. The name of the method originates from the technique used to keep track of the goals G_k and $G_{k/2}$ in the derivation: a fast (every derivation step) moving pointer (the hare) points at the 'current' goal G_k, a slow (every other step) moving pointer (the tortoise) points at the goal $G_{k/2}$ 'halfway'. We now formalize this technique.

DEFINITION 3.1 (Tortoise-and-hare technique).
Let φ be a loop checking criterion. The *tortoise-and-hare* loop check of φ is the loop check $L^{th}(\varphi) = \text{RemSub}(\{ D \mid D = (G_0 \Rightarrow_{C_1,\theta_1} G_1 \Rightarrow \ldots \Rightarrow G_{k-1} \Rightarrow_{C_k,\theta_k} G_k)$ and $(k = 2i$ or $k = 2i+1)$ and $\varphi(G_i,G_k,D)$ and $k > 0 \})$. □

The following theorem is an immediate consequence of our previous results.

THEOREM 3.2 (Soundness). *Let φ be a loop checking criterion. If L(φ) is weakly sound (sound,shortening) then $L^{th}(\varphi)$ is weakly sound (sound,shortening).*
PROOF. This follows from the Relative Strength Theorem 2.8, as L(φ) is obviously stronger than $L^{th}(\varphi)$. □

Van Gelder justifies the use of the tortoise-and-hare technique by the observation that due to the use of the leftmost selection rule and the fixed order of clauses in PROLOG every loop must have a fixed length, say *l* (assuming no side-effects occur). As the distance between the tortoise and the hare continuously increases by 1, the loop is detected (after the tortoise enters the looping part of the derivation) as soon as the distance between the tortoise and the hare is a multiple of *l*.

In [5] a looping derivation is not pruned automatically: it is suggested that control should be returned to the user, once a loop is detected. (Which makes sense there: the initial loop checking criterion that is proposed in [5], and to which the tortoise-and-hare technique is added, is not even weakly sound, so it is up to the user to determine whether the derivation is *really* in a loop.) In our setting, a pruned goal is handled as a failed one, giving rise to backtracking. As is implicit in Definition 3.1 (and explicitly mentioned in [5]), during backtracking the tortoise and hare motions are simply 'undone'.

This entails however that the fixed order of clauses in PROLOG cannot be relevant for a demonstration of the completeness of the method: no distinction is made between the application of a clause as a first attempt to solve a goal, or its application as a later attempt after backtracking from previous (failed) attempts. Indeed the tortoise-and-hare technique does not preserve completeness, as the following counterexample shows.

COUNTEREXAMPLE 3.3.
Let P = { p ← p ; p ← q ; q ← p ; q ← q }. Let φ be a loop checking criterion such that φ(p,p,D) = φ(q,q,D) = true and φ(p,q,D) = φ(q,p,D) = false for every derivation D (as one would expect). Let T be the SLD-tree of P∪{←p} pruned by $L^{th}(\varphi)$.
CLAIM. T contains one infinite branch, so $L^{th}(\varphi)$ is incomplete for P.
PROOF. Let G be a goal in T that is not pruned. We prove that G has two immediate descendants, of which only one is pruned. Regardless of G being ←p or ←q, G has two descendants G_1 = ←p and G_2 = ←q, which are both compared with the same 'halfway' goal H. If H = ←p, then G_1 is pruned but G_2 is not; if H = ←q, then G_2 is pruned but G_1 is not. □

4. Selected loop checks

An easy generalization of Counterexample 3.3 shows that a loop check cannot be complete if there exists a maximum N such that every goal is compared with at most N other goals (at least not if N is smaller than the number of ground atoms in the

language). Therefore we adopt a different strategy here: an infinite selection S of natural numbers is made, and a pair of goals (G_i,G_k) is compared if and only if
- $i < k$ and $k \in S$ (single selected loop checks), respectively
- $i < k$ and $i,k \in S$ (double selected loop checks).

DEFINITION 4.1 (Selected Loop Checks).
Let φ be a loop checking criterion and let S be an infinite subset of $\mathbb{N}$.
The *single selected* loop check of φ and S is the loop check

$$L^1(\varphi,S) = \text{RemSub}(\{ D \mid D = (G_0 \Rightarrow_{C_1,\theta_1} G_1 \Rightarrow \ldots \Rightarrow G_{k-1} \Rightarrow_{C_k,\theta_k} G_k) \text{ and } \exists\, i < k \text{ such that } \varphi(G_i,G_k,D), \text{ and } k \in S \}).$$

The *double selected* loop check of φ and S is the loop check

$$L^2(\varphi,S) = \text{RemSub}(\{ D \mid D = (G_0 \Rightarrow_{C_1,\theta_1} G_1 \Rightarrow \ldots \Rightarrow G_{k-1} \Rightarrow_{C_k,\theta_k} G_k) \text{ and } \exists\, i < k \text{ such that } \varphi(G_i,G_k,D), \text{ and } i,k \in S \}).$$

S is called the *selection* of $L^1(\varphi,S)$ or $L^2(\varphi,S)$. □

Clearly, the number of comparisons performed by a selected loop check depends on the selection S. For $S = \mathbb{N}$, we obtain the full-comparison loop checks again, for which the number of comparisons is quadratic in the number of goals generated. In section 5, the efficiency of double selected loop checks with $S = \{\frac{1}{2}i(i+1) \mid i \in \mathbb{N}\}$ is studied in detail. In the rest of this section, we do not consider any specific selection, but rather study the soundness and completeness of selected loop checks in general.

The following lemma enables the use of the Relative Strength Theorem 2.8.

LEMMA 4.2. *Let φ be a loop checking criterion and let S_1 and S_2 be selections.*
Then, *i) $L^1(\varphi,S_1)$ is stronger than $L^2(\varphi,S_1)$ and*
if $S_1 \supseteq S_2$ then ii) $L^1(\varphi,S_1)$ is stronger than $L^1(\varphi,S_2)$ and
iii) $L^2(\varphi,S_1)$ is stronger than $L^2(\varphi,S_2)$.

PROOF. Obvious. □

In particular, the full-comparison loop check $L(\varphi) = L^1(\varphi,\mathbb{N}) = L^2(\varphi,\mathbb{N})$ is stronger than any selected loop check using the criterion φ. This enables us to derive the soundness of a selected loop check from the soundness of the corresponding full-comparison loop check.

THEOREM 4.3 (Soundness of Selection). *Let φ be a loop checking criterion.*
If $L(\varphi)$ is weakly sound (sound, shortening) then for every selection S:
$L^1(\varphi,S)$ and $L^2(\varphi,S)$ are weakly sound (sound, shortening).

PROOF. By Lemma 4.2 and the Relative Strength Theorem 2.8. □

Combining this theorem with the soundness results for the simple loop checks presented in [2] (see the Appendix) yields the following results.

COROLLARY 4.4. *For every selection used,*

i) the (single and double) selected equality, subsumption and context checks based on goals are weakly sound and

ii) the (single and double) selected equality, subsumption and context checks based on resultants are shortening.

PROOF. By Theorem 4.3 and Theorem 7.1. □

Unfortunately, an equally general completeness result cannot be obtained using Lemma 4.2. Instead, generalizing the completeness results from the simple loop checks of [2] to the corresponding selected loop checks requires a detailed analysis of the completeness proofs in [2]. (However, by Lemma 4.2 it suffices to consider only double selected loop checks.)

For the equality checks and subsumption checks, this generalization is straightforward. By definition, a loop check is complete if every 'possible' infinite derivation (given an initial goal and a program satisfying the restrictions) contains two goals that 'are sufficiently similar' for the loop check. However, in the relevant proofs in [2] (notably Theorem 4.18, Lemma 5.15 and Theorem 5.20) a stronger result is proven: every infinite sequence of *unrelated* goals contains two 'similar' goals. Although in [2] this sequence is always taken $\{G_i \mid i \in \mathbb{N}\}$, the sequence $\{G_i \mid i \in S\}$ can be used for any selection S. Hence the completeness results for equality and subsumption checks (see Theorem 7.3) generalize immediately to selected equality and subsumption checks. The classes of programs mentioned below are defined in the Appendix, in Definition 7.2.

COROLLARY 4.5.

i) All (single and double) selected equality checks are complete w.r.t. the leftmost selection rule for function-free restricted programs.

ii) All (single and double) selected subsumption checks are complete w.r.t. the leftmost selection rule for function-free restricted programs.

iii) All (single and double) selected subsumption checks are complete for function-free nvi programs.

iv) All (single and double) selected subsumption checks are complete for function-free svo programs.

PROOF. By the arguments given above. □

For the context checks, the generalization of the completeness results is less straightforward, but still possible.

THEOREM 4.6. *All (single and double) selected context checks are complete for function-free nvi programs and for function-free svo programs.*

PROOF. Let S be a selection. In the completeness proofs for the full-comparison context checks (Theorem 6.14 and 6.16 in the revised version of [2]), an infinite sequence of goals $G_{m_0}, G_{m_1}, \ldots$ $(0 \leq m_0 < m_1 < \ldots)$ is constructed in which 'similar' goals are shown to occur. The selection $M = (m_0 < m_1 < \ldots)$ can be adapted to the selection $S = (s_0 < s_1 < \ldots)$: we define the new selection $T = (t_0 < t_1 < \ldots)$ by:

- $t_0 = s_0$,
- $t_i = \min\{s \in S \mid \exists\, m \in M \text{ such that } t_{i-1} \leq m < s\}$ for $i > 0$.

As in the sequence $G_{m_0}, G_{m_1}, \ldots$, in the goals of the sequence $G_{t_0}, G_{t_1}, \ldots$ atoms $A_0, A_1, \ldots$ occur such that A_{i+1} is the result (directly or indirectly) of resolving A_i. The 'interleaving' with the selection M is needed to ensure that A_{i+1} is not just an instantiated version of A_i, but indeed the result of at least one resolution step performed on A_i. (This follows from the observation that A_i is the selected atom in G_{m_i}; so in Theorem 6.14 exactly one resolution step occurs between A_i and A_{i+1}.)

In the rest of the proof of Theorem 6.14 (and 6.16), the sequence M can be replaced by T without any difficulty. Therefore the double selected CVR check using the selection T is complete for function-free nvi programs and for function-free svo programs. By Lemma 4.2 ($T \subseteq S$) and the Relative Strength Theorem 2.8, the same holds for all (single and double) selected context checks using the selection S. □

Surprisingly, selected context checks are not necessarily complete w.r.t. the leftmost selection rule for function-free restricted programs, as the following counterexample shows.

COUNTEREXAMPLE 4.7.
Let $P = \{\ A(y) \leftarrow B(x),A(x),$
$\quad B(1) \leftarrow \quad \}$
and let $G = \leftarrow B(x_0),A(x_0)$.
Consider the following derivation D of $P \cup \{G\}$ via the leftmost selection rule:

$\leftarrow B(x_0),A(x_0)$
$\quad\downarrow\quad B(1)\leftarrow \quad \{x_0/1\}$
$\leftarrow A(1)$
$\quad\downarrow\quad A(y_1)\leftarrow B(x_1),A(x_1) \quad \{y_1/1\}$
$\leftarrow B(x_1),A(x_1)$
$\quad\downarrow\quad B(1)\leftarrow \quad \{x_1/1\}$
$\leftarrow A(1)$
$\quad\downarrow\quad A(y_2)\leftarrow B(x_2),A(x_2) \quad \{y_2/1\}$
$\leftarrow B(x_2),A(x_2)$
...

D is not pruned by the single selected context checks using the selection $S = \{2i \mid i \in \mathbb{N}\}$. First compare $G_{2j} = \leftarrow B(x_j),A(x_j)$ with $\leftarrow A(1)$. But $A(x_j)$ is not an instance of $A(1)$. Then compare it with $G_{2i} = \leftarrow B(x_i),A(x_i)$ $(i < j)$. $B(x_j)$ is not the result of resolving $B(x_i)$, so we are forced to take $A = A(x_i)$ and $\tau = \{x_i/x_j, x_j/x_i\}$. Then $\theta_{2i+1} = \{x_i/1\}$ and $A(x_j)$ is indeed the result of resolving $A(1) = A(x_i)\theta_{2i+1}$ in G_{2i+1}. But τ and $\theta_{2i+1}\ldots\theta_{2j}$ should agree on x_i, which they do not. □

Concluding, in most cases a selected loop check can be used instead of the corresponding full-comparison loop check, without losing its benefits such as soundness and completeness. In the next section we take a more constructive attitude towards selected loop checks and we investigate how much is gained by using them.

5. Triangular loop checks: a case study

This section presents a detailed study of double selected loop checks with the selection $S = \{\frac{1}{2}i(i+1) \mid i \in \mathbb{N}\}$. Numbers of the form $\frac{1}{2}i(i+1)$ are usually called *triangular* numbers, therefore we call such loop checks *triangular* loop checks. In this section the loop checking criterion is not relevant, as we focus solely on the number of comparisons performed.

THEOREM 5.1. *Let D be a finite SLD-derivation. The number of comparisons performed on D by a triangular loop check is less than |D|.*

PROOF. Let $D = (G_0 \Rightarrow_{C_1,\theta_1} G_1 \Rightarrow \ldots \Rightarrow G_{k-1} \Rightarrow_{C_k,\theta_k} G_k)$. For every triangular number $n = \frac{1}{2}i(i+1)$ $(0 \le n \le k)$, the goal G_n is compared to i previous goals. We may assume that k is a triangular number, say $k = \frac{1}{2}j(j+1)$. The number of comparisons performed on D is then $\sum_{i=0}^{j} i = \frac{1}{2}j(j+1) = k < k + 1 = |D|$. □

The following arrangement of goals may help the intuition:

$$\begin{array}{llllll} G_0 : & G_1 & G_2 & G_4 & G_7 & \ldots \\ & & G_3 & G_5 & G_8 & \\ & & & G_6 & G_9 & \\ & & & & G_{10} & \end{array}$$

Every column contains one 'triangular' goal G (a goal with a triangular number as its index; this index is exactly the level of the goal). The number of goals in the column of G equals the number of columns preceding it (for $G \ne G_0$), which in turn equals the number of comparisons performed at G.

So the presence of G_7, G_8, G_9 and G_{10} 'justifies' the four comparisons performed at G_{10}. This arrangement of goals also explains the word 'triangular'.

When SLD-trees are considered, the situation gets more complicated: two goals G_{10} and G_{10}' may have common ancestors G_7, G_8 and G_9; these five goals cannot completely justify the eight comparisons performed at G_{10} and G_{10}'. We now show that for SLD-trees with a constant (average) branching factor and containing a 'reasonable' number of goals (say $\le 10^{10}$), the number of comparisons performed is less than five times the number of goals generated.

THEOREM 5.2. *Let T consist of the levels 0,...,k of an SLD-tree, have a constant average branching factor b and contain $n \le 10^{10}$ goals. Then a triangular loop check performs less than $5 \cdot n$ comparisons on T.*

PROOF. We may assume that $b > 1$ (for $b = 1$ (or $b < 1$), see Theorem 5.1) and that the depth of T is a triangular number, say $k = \frac{1}{2}j(j+1)$. Then for $0 \le m \le k$, the number of

- goals at level m   is b^m,
- goals in T   is $\sum_{i=0}^{k} b^i = \frac{b^{k+1}-1}{b-1} = n \leq 10^{10}$,
- comparisons at level $m = \frac{1}{2}i(i+1)$ is $i \cdot b^m$,
- comparisons in T   is $\sum_{i=1}^{j} i \cdot b^{1/2 \cdot i(i+1)}$.

We consider two cases.

CASE 1: $b^{j-1} \leq 5$.

In this case the number of goals at level $\frac{1}{2}i(i+1)$ $(1 \leq i \leq j)$ can be at most 5 times the number of goals at level $\frac{1}{2}i(i-1)+1$. Therefore the goals between level $\frac{1}{2}i(i-1)+1$ and level $\frac{1}{2}i(i+1)$ justify at least one fifth of the comparisons at level $\frac{1}{2}i(i+1)$. Formally, $\sum_{i=1}^{j} i \cdot b^{1/2 \cdot i(i+1)} = \sum_{i=1}^{j} b^{i-1} \cdot i \cdot b^{1/2 \cdot i(i-1)+1} \leq b^{j-1} \cdot \sum_{i=1}^{j} i \cdot b^{1/2 \cdot i(i-1)+1} \leq$

$\leq 5 \cdot \sum_{i=1}^{j} \sum_{r=1}^{i} b^{1/2 \cdot i(i-1)+1} \leq 5 \cdot \sum_{i=1}^{j} \sum_{r=1}^{i} b^{1/2 \cdot i(i-1)+r} = 5 \cdot \sum_{l=1}^{k} b^{l} < 5n$. The final equation is justified by the observation that every level-number l $(1 \leq l \leq k)$ can be written as $l = t+r$, where $t = \frac{1}{2}i(i-1)$ is the largest triangular number smaller than l and $1 \leq r \leq i$.

CASE 2: $b^{j-1} > 5$.

In this case the total number of comparisons can be estimated at $\frac{5}{4}$ times the number of comparisons at the last level, since the number of comparisons at level $\frac{1}{2}j(j+1)$ is $j \cdot b^{1/2 \cdot j(j+1)} > b^j \cdot (j-1) \cdot b^{1/2 \cdot j(j-1)} > 5$ times the number of comparisons at level $\frac{1}{2}j(j-1)$ (which is in turn > 5 times the number of comparisons at level $\frac{1}{2}(j-1)(j-2)$; now we have $1 + \frac{1}{5} + \frac{1}{25} + \ldots = \frac{5}{4}$).

Therefore $\frac{\text{the number of comparisons in T}}{\text{the number of goals in T}} = \frac{5 \cdot j \cdot b^k}{4 \cdot n} = \frac{5 \cdot j \cdot b^k \cdot (b-1)}{4 \cdot (b^{k+1}-1)} \approx \frac{5j(b-1)}{4b}$. (Note that $b^{j-1} > 5$ implies $b^{k+1} > 125 \gg 1$.) Finally $k = \frac{1}{2}j(j+1)$ and $\frac{b^{k+1}-1}{b-1} \leq 10^{10}$ implies $j \leq -\frac{1}{2} + \sqrt{-\frac{7}{4} + 2 \cdot {}^{b}\log(10^{10}(b-1))}$. A numeric analysis[1] of the function $\frac{5(b-1)}{4b}\left(-\frac{1}{2} + \sqrt{-\frac{7}{4} + 2 \cdot {}^{b}\log(10^{10}(b-1))}\right)$ shows that its maximum is almost 5 (≈ 4.95 for $b \approx 3.21$). □

[1] Performed using the 'Maple' package, developed by the Symbolic Computation Group of the University of Waterloo, Ontario, Canada.

Finally we consider SLD-trees which do not have a constant average branching factor, but exhibit a kind of 'worst case' behaviour. In these trees only the parents of the 'triangular' goals have more than one descendant. More formally, if b_k is the number of descendants of a goal at level k ($k \geq 0$), then

$$b_k = \begin{cases} b & \text{if } k = \frac{1}{2}j(j+1)-1 \ (j > 0) \\ 1 & \text{otherwise,} \end{cases}$$

for some constant branching factor b.

THEOREM 5.3. *Let T consist of the levels 0,...,k of a 'worst case' SLD-tree with branching factor b, and contain n goals. Then a triangular loop check performs less than $b{\cdot}n$ comparisons on T. Moreover, if $n \leq 10^{10}$, then a triangular loop check performs less than $6{\cdot}n$ comparisons on T.*

PROOF. Let $k = \frac{1}{2}j(j+1)$. The number of goals at level k is then $\prod_{i=0}^{k} b_k = b^j$. Hence the number of comparisons performed at level k is $j{\cdot}b^j$. Each of the levels $\frac{1}{2}j(j-1)+1,\ldots,$ $\frac{1}{2}j(j+1)-1$ consists of b^{j-1} goals, giving $(j-1){\cdot}b^{j-1}$ goals together. So for the $j{\cdot}b^j$ comparisons at level k, there are $(j-1){\cdot}b^{j-1}+b^j$ 'justifying' goals, giving $\frac{j{\cdot}b}{j-1+b}$ comparisons per goal. It is easy to show that $b > 1$ implies $\frac{(j-1){\cdot}b}{(j-1)-1+b} < \frac{j{\cdot}b}{j-1+b}$, so the overall ratio in T is less than $\frac{j{\cdot}b}{j-1+b}$ comparisons per goal. First notice that $b > 1$ implies $\frac{j{\cdot}b}{j-1+b} < b$, which proves the first claim.

Now $n \leq 10^{10}$ implies $b^j < 10^{10}$, so $j < {}^b\!\log(10^{10})$. A numeric analysis of the function $\frac{{}^b\!\log(10^{10}){\cdot}b}{{}^b\!\log(10^{10})-1+b}$ shows that its maximum is almost 6 ($\approx$ 5.76 for $b \approx 21$), which proves the second claim. □

6. Conclusions

The obvious conclusion is that the number of comparisons performed by a triangular loop check is (almost) linear in the number of goals generated. For any realistic number of generated goals n, the number of comparisons performed is at most $6{\cdot}n$. So triangular loop checks satisfy the requirement stated in the introduction. Moreover, unlike the tortoise-and-hare technique, which was motivated by the same requirement, the 'triangular' technique retains the completeness of the corresponding full-comparison loop checks (with the exception of Counterexample 4.7). The only minor disadvantage of the 'triangular' technique might be that the comparisons are not distributed smoothly over the goals, which makes the timing of the interpreter less predictable.

Other selections give rise to other efficiency results: a more sparse selection yields a more efficient loop check, relative to the number of goals generated. However, using a sparse selection is not necessarily the best thing to do: loops are detected later, so the overall effort of generating goals and loop checking may well become larger than with a less sparse selection loop check. A further analysis which selection might be most favorable (or even an investigation of the circumstances on which this depends) is beyond the scope of this paper.

7. Appendix

Here we recall the three groups of simple loop checks that are introduced in [2], together with their respective soundness and completeness results.

7.1 Definitions and soundness results

First we present the weakly sound loop checks of each group.

The first group consists of the equality checks. Their loop checking criterion has the form 'for some substitution τ: $G_k = G_i\tau$' (or in words: 'G_k is an instance of G_i'). Small variations on this criterion give rise to various loop checks within this group. These variations are notably the two interpretations of '=' that are considered (goals can be treated as lists or as multisets) and the possible addition of the requirement 'τ is a renaming' (in other words: 'G_k is a variant of G_i'). Such variations can also be made within the other groups of loop checks, but as it appears that these variations have not much effect on soundness and completeness, we shall not mention them any more.

The second group consists of the subsumption checks. Their loop checking criterion has the form 'for some substitution τ: $G_k \subseteq G_i\tau$' (or in words: 'G_k is subsumed by an instance of G_i'). Although the replacement of = by $\subseteq$ seems to be yet another small variation, it appears that subsumption checks are really more powerful than equality checks.

The third group consists of the context checks, introduced by Besnard [1]. Their loop checking condition is more complicated: 'For some atom A in G_i, $A\theta_{i+1}\ldots\theta_j$ is selected in G_j to be resolved. As the (direct or indirect) result of resolving $A\theta_{i+1}\ldots\theta_j$, an instance $A\tau$ of A occurs in G_k ($0 \leq i \leq j < k$). Finally, for every variable x that occurs both inside and outside of A in G_i, $x\theta_{i+1}\ldots\theta_k = x\tau$.'

For all these weakly sound loop checks, a shortening counterpart is obtained by adding the condition '$G_0\theta_1\ldots\theta_k = G_0\theta_1\ldots\theta_i\tau$' to the loop checking criterion. For reasons explained in [2], the loop checks thus obtained are called 'based on resultants' as opposed to the weakly sound ones, which are 'based on goals'.

Thus the following results were proved in [2].

THEOREM 7.1.

i) The equality, subsumption and context checks based on goals are weakly sound.

ii) The equality, subsumption and context checks based on resultants are shortening. □

7.2 Completeness results

Due to the undecidability of the halting problem, a weakly sound loop check cannot be complete for all programs. In [2] it was shown that a weakly sound *simple* loop check cannot even be complete for all *function-free* programs. Therefore three classes of function-free programs were isolated for which the completeness of (some of) the loop checks mentioned above could be proved. We now present those classes of programs and completeness results.

DEFINITION 7.2.
A program P is *restricted* if for every clause $H \leftarrow A_1,\ldots,A_n$ in P, the definitions of the predicates in $A_1,\ldots,A_{n-1}$ do not depend on the the predicate of H in P. (So recursion is allowed, namely through A_n, but double recursion is not; almost similar to [12].)
A program P is *non-variable introducing* (*nvi*) if for every clause $H \leftarrow A_1,\ldots,A_n$ in P, every variable that occurs in $A_1,\ldots,A_n$ occurs also in H.
A program P has the *single variable occurrence* property (*is svo*) if for every clause $H \leftarrow A_1,\ldots,A_n$ in P, no variable occurs more than once in $A_1,\ldots,A_n$. □

THEOREM 7.3.

i) All equality, subsumption and context checks are complete w.r.t. the leftmost selection rule for function-free restricted programs.

ii) All subsumption and context checks are complete for function-free nvi programs.

iii) All subsumption and context checks are complete for function-free svo programs. □

References

[1] Ph. Besnard. 1989. *On Infinite Loops in Logic Programming*. Internal Report 488, IRISA, Rennes.

[2] R.N. Bol, K.R. Apt and J.W. Klop. 1989. *An Analysis of Loop Checking Mechanisms for Logic Programs*. Technical Report CS-R8942, Centre for Mathematics and Computer Science, Amsterdam; Technical Report TR-89-32, University of Texas at Austin. To appear in Theoretical Computer Science.

[3] D.R. Brough and A. Walker. 1984. *Some Practical Properties of Logic Programming Interpreters*. In Proceedings of the International Conference on Fifth Generation Computer Systems (ICOT eds.). pp. 149-156.

[4] M.A. Covington. 1985. *Eliminating Unwanted Loops in PROLOG*. SIGPLAN Notices vol. 20, no. 1. pp. 20-26.

[5] A. van Gelder. 1987. *Efficient Loop Detection in PROLOG using the Tortoise-and-Hare Technique*. In J. Logic Programming 4. pp. 23-31.

[6] D.B. Kemp and R.W. Topor. 1988. *Completeness of a Top-Down Query Evaluation Procedure for Stratified Databases*. In Proceedings of the Fifth International Conference on Logic Programming (R. Kowalski and K. Bowen eds.), MIT Press, Cambridge Massachusetts. pp. 178-194.

[7] J.W. Lloyd. 1987. *Foundations of Logic Programming* (Second Edition). Springer-Verlag, Berlin.

[8] J.W. Lloyd and J.C. Shepherdson. 1987. *Partial Evaluation in Logic Programming*. Technical Report CS-87-09, Dept. of Computer Science, University of Bristol.

[9] D. Poole and R. Goebel. 1985. *On Eliminating Loops in PROLOG*. SIGPLAN Notices vol. 20, no. 8. pp. 38-40.

[10] D.E. Smith, M.R. Genesereth and M.L. Ginsberg. 1986. *Controlling Recursive Inference*. Artificial Intelligence 30. pp. 343-389.

[11] H. Seki and H. Itoh. 1988. *A Query Evaluation Method for Stratified Programs under the Extended CWA*. In Proceedings of the Fifth International Conference on Logic Programming (R. Kowalski and K. Bowen eds.), MIT Press, Cambridge Massachusetts. pp. 195-211.

[12] O. Štěpánková and P. Štěpánek. 1988. *A Complete Class of Restricted Logic Programs*. In Logic Colloquium '86 (F.R. Drake and J.K. Truss eds.), North Holland, Amsterdam. pp. 319-324.

[13] L. Vieille. 1989. *Recursive Query Processing: The Power of Logic*. In Theoretical Computer Science 69, No. 1. pp. 1-53.

Negative Logic Programs

Sergio Greco
Dipartimento di Sistemi,
Università della Calabria, Rende, Italy
2101gre@icsuniv.bitnet

Domenico Saccà
Dipartimento di Sistemi,
Università della Calabria, Rende, Italy
2101sac@icsuniv.bitnet

Abstract

Negative programs are logic programs where negation may arise also in the head of rules and have been recently introduced to handle exceptions to general rules. In this paper, the semantics of negative programs is given as an extension of the stable model and well-founded model semantics to classical logic programs where negation may arise only in the rule bodies (*seminegative programs*). Also the notion of stratification is extended to negative programs and a stratified fixpoint is presented that computes the total well-founded model of a stratified negative program. Finally, it is shown that a negative program admits an almost "equivalent" seminegative program. However, it is argued that a direct analysis of a negative program can be more effective than considering the seminegative version of it. For instance, it is shown that the seminegative version of a stratified negative program is not necessarily stratified.

1. Introduction

A great deal of researchs are presently involved in providing a clear and effective semantics to logic programs with negation in the rule bodies (*seminegative programs*). Recently, the semantics of well-founded models [20], stable models [6, 15], partial and founded models [15] have introduced a uniform approach to capture the semantics of seminegative programs. In this paper, we extend this approach to cope with logic programs where negation may also arise in the head of the rules (*negative programs*). Possible contradiction is removed by assuming that negative rules (thus the rules with negated head) are a sort of exceptions to general rules. For instance, take the negative program consisting of the following rules:

$$fly(X) :- \ bird(X).$$

$$\neg fly(X) :- \ ground\_animal(X).$$

and of a number of database facts defining *bird* and *ground_animal*. If the database contains "penguin" which is well known in our community to be both a bird and a ground animal[1], a contradiction arises: *the penguin both flies and does not fly*. However, by considering the second rule as sort of refinement to the first general rule, the meaning of the program is rather clear: *all birds fly provided that they are not ground animals*. One could object that the same semantics could be expressed without introducing negative programs. In fact, the above negative program would be replaced by the following seminegative one:

$$fly(X) :- \ bird(X), \neg ground\_animal(X).$$

More in general, as shown later in the paper, given a negative program, there exists a seminegative one which has "almost" the same semantics as the original program. Nevertheless, this results does not affect the relevance of negative programs since they allow to express exceptions in such a structured way that first general rules are defined and then possible refinements are listed. Notice that similar "modular" mechanisms are provided in high-level languages such as Ada and CLU to single out exceptions.

Negative programs have been first introduced in [2] where, following the lines of *paraconsistent logics* the presence of inconsistent information is accepted and, therefore, four-values (*inconsistent* besides to the usual values *unknown*, *false* and *true*) models are used. For instance, in the above example, it is recognized that the penguin both flies and does not fly and no attempt is made to remove such a contradiction. The idea of removing inconsistency using the notion of exception has been introduced in [7, 8, 11]. The novelty of our approach is that the semantics of logic programs with exceptions is given as an extension of well-founded model semantics as well as of other related concepts as they are defined for seminegative programs. Moreover, we recognize a class of negative programs which correspond to stratified programs [1] and for which an effective procedure for constructing the total well-founded model is available. Finally, we point out that, following [11], we treat negation both in the head and in the body of rules in a uniform way, whereas two kinds of negation (namely, "negation as failure" [4] and "classical negation") are considered in [7, 8].

The paper is organized as follows. In Section 2, we describe the semantics of negative programs by introducing the notions of partial interpretation, partial model, founded model, well-founded model, etc. that have been first introduced for seminegative programs. A nice result is that, if a negative program reduces to a seminegative one, then the two semantics coincide. Next, in Section 3, we extend the notion of stratification to negative programs and we prove that stratified negative programs have a total well-founded model that can be computed by means of a stratified fixpoint, that is an extension of the

[1] Every now and then, one of the authors has a nightmare: tired to be present in so many papers around, the penguins have eventually learned to fly!

procedure described in [1]. Later on, in Section 4, we show that, as also pointed out in [7, 8], a negative program can be transformed into an almost "equivalent" seminegative program. Finally, we discuss further work in Section 5.

2. Negative Programs.

Following PROLOG [9], the syntax of negative programs is based on an alphabet consisting of a (possibly infinite) number of constants, variables, function symbols, predicate symbols in addition to connectives symbols ("$\neg$", ",", ":-") and punctuation symbols ("(", ")", ".", ","). As usual, the symbol "," is overloaded for it also stands for the connective "$\wedge$". The basic tokens of the language are terms, predicates, literals and rules.

A *term* is recursively defined as a variable, a constant or $f(t_1, \ldots, t_n)$, where $t_1, \ldots, t_n$ are terms and f is a function symbol.

A *predicate* is of the form $p(\mathbf{t})$, where p is a predicate symbol with arity n ($n \geq 0$) and $\mathbf{t}$ is a sequence of n terms (*arguments* of the predicate).

A *literal* is either a predicate (*positive literal*) or its negation (*negative literal*). A term, predicate or literal is *ground* if it is variable free. Two literals are complementary if they are of the form A and $\neg A$, for some predicate A. In general, given a literal A and a set of ground literals X, $\neg A$ denotes the complement of A and $\neg X$ denotes the set of literals $\{\neg B \mid B \in X\}$. Moreover, X^+ (resp. X^-) denotes the set of all positive (resp., negative) literals in X. Finally, we say that X is *consistent* if there are not two literals A and B in X such that $A = \neg B$

A *negative rule* (or, simply, a *rule*) is of the form:

$$Q_0 :- Q_1, \ldots, Q_m.$$

where $Q_0, \ldots, Q_m$ are literals, Q_0 is the *head* of the rule, and $Q_1, \ldots, Q_m$ is the body of the rule. If Q_0 is positive then the rule is a *seminegative rule*; moreover, if also $Q_1, \ldots, Q_m$ are all positive then the the rule is a *positive rule* (or Horn clause). Given a rule r, $H(r)$ denotes the head of r and $B(r)$ denotes the set of all literals in the body of r. A rule is a *fact* if it has an empty body and is *ground* if it is variable free.

A *negative program* is a set of rules. If all rules are seminegative (resp., positive) then the program is called a *seminegative program* (resp., *positive program*). Let P be a negative program; then, P^+ (resp., P^-) denotes the set of all seminegative (resp., non-seminegative) rules in P.

Let us now turn our attention to the semantics of negative programs.

Let P be a negative program. The Herbrand's Universe of P (denoted by H_P) is the set of all possible ground terms recursively constructed by using constants and function symbols occurring in P. The Herbrand's Base of P

(denoted by B_P) is the set of all possible ground predicates whose predicate symbols occur in P and whose arguments are elements of H_P. A *ground instance* of a rule r in P is a rule obtained from r by replacing every variable X in r by $\phi(X)$, where ϕ is a mapping from the set of all variables occurring in P to H_P. The set of all ground instances of all rules in P is denoted by *ground*(P).

An *(partial) interpretation* for P is any consistent subset of $B_P \cup \neg B_P$. Let I be an interpretation for a negative program P; then $\overline{I}$ denotes the set of predicates $\{A \mid A \in B_P$, and neither A nor $\neg A$ is in $I\}$. Note that, according to the interpretation I, a ground literal is true if and only if it is member of I; therefore, $\overline{I}$ contains all the elements of the Herbrand base for which no value has been assigned in the interpretation (*undefined elements*) [5, 13, 15]. An interpretation is *total* if $\overline{I}$ is empty. Note that, according our notation, I^+ (resp., I^-) denotes the set of all positive (resp., negative) literals in I.

Let I be an interpretation of a negative program P. A rule r in *ground*(P) is (a) *applicable* if $B(r) \subseteq I$, (b) *applied* if it is applicable and $H(r) \in I$, and (c) *blocked* if there exists a literal A in $B(r)$ such that $\neg A \in I$.

We next introduce the notion of model for negative programs. To this end, we remove possible inconsistency introduced because of negative head predicates by assuming that the rules in P^- are stronger than the rules in P^+. In fact, they can be thought of as a sort of exceptions to general rules [7, 8, 11]. We point out that most of the definitions and of the results presented in this section extend those described in [15] for seminegative programs and elaborate on the hints given in [11], where negative programs are shown to be a special case of a larger class of logic programs (namely, *ordered logics*, first introduced in [10]).

Example 1. Consider the following negative program consisting of the following two rules:

$$colored(X) \text{ :- } color(X), \neg colored(Y), X \neq Y.$$

$$\neg colored(X) \text{ :- } ugly\_color(X).$$

and of a number of database facts defining *color* and *ugly_color*. Obviously every *ugly_color* is also a *color*. Possible contradictions can be removed by giving more credit to the non-seminegative rules so that the meaning becomes: *select exactly one of the available non-ugly colors.* □

Definition 1. An interpretation I for P is a *(partial) model for* P if (i) for each A in I^+, every rule r in *ground*(P) with $H(r) = \neg A$ is blocked and (ii) for each $\neg A$ in I^-, either there exists an applied rule r in *ground*(P) with $H(r) = \neg A$ or every rule r in *ground*(P) with $H(r) = A$ is blocked. Moreover, if $\overline{I}$ is empty then the model I is *total.* □

In other words, given a model M, a ground literal may occur in M only if there is no rule that could contradict it (possibly by assigning suitable values to undefined literals in $\overline{M}$). However, a negative literal can be contradicted if it is reconfirmed by an applied non-seminegative rule. This corresponds to say that non-seminegative rules represent a refinement of the knowledge supplied by seminegative rules, thus they are a kind of exceptions to a theory. We point out that the existence of a total model is not guaranteed.

Example 2. For the negative program of Example 1 as well as for the negative program presented in Section 1, their intuitive meaning is now confirmed by the notion of model as for Definition 1. Consider now the following program

$p.$

$\neg p \text{ :- } p.$

The only model is the empty set which, obviously, is not total. Note that this program is rather strange: if we assume that $\neg p$ is true then there is no way to fire an exception to contradict the fact p; on the other side, if p is assumed true then an exception is fired that invalidates p. Therefore, it is safe not to say anything on the value of p. □

Let us now introduce the transformations T_P in the complete lower semi-lattice $<\mathbf{I},\subseteq>$, where $\mathbf{I}$ is the family of all interpretations of a negative program $\boldsymbol{P}$:

$$T_P(I) = \{A \mid \exists r \in ground(P)\ (r \text{ applicable } w.r.t.\ I \wedge H(r) = A)\} -$$
$$\{A \mid \exists r \in ground(P)^-\ (r \text{ non–blocked } w.r.t.\ I \wedge H(r) = \neg A)\}$$

(recall that, according to our notation, $ground(\boldsymbol{P})^-$ contains all non-seminegative rules in $ground(\boldsymbol{P})$).

Note that, for a seminegative program $\boldsymbol{P}$, T_P coincides with the *immediate consequence transformation,* that is well-known to be monotone. We now prove that $T_{\boldsymbol{P}}$ is indeed monotone also for any negative program $\boldsymbol{P}$ so that its least fixpoint, denoted by $T_P^\infty(\emptyset)$, always exists [16].

PROPOSITION 1. *Let* $\boldsymbol{P}$ *be a negative program. Then* T_P *is monotone and* $T_P^\infty(\emptyset)$ *is a model for* $\boldsymbol{P}$.

PROOF. Let X and Y be two interpretations for $\boldsymbol{P}$ and let $X \subset Y$. Let A be a positive element in $T_P(X)$. Then, by definition of T_P, there exists a rule r in $ground(\boldsymbol{P})$ such that $B(r) \subseteq X$ and every possible rule $\hat{r}$ with $H(\hat{r}) = \neg A$ contains at least one literal in the body, say B, such that $\neg B$ is in X. But $X \subset Y$; so $B(r) \subseteq Y$ and $\neg B$ is in Y. Therefore, A is also in $T_P(Y)$. Let $\neg A$ be a negative element in $T_P(X)$. Then, by definition of T_P, there exists a rule r in $ground(\boldsymbol{P})$ such that $B(r) \subseteq X$ and $H(r) = \neg A$. But $X \subset Y$; so $B(r) \subseteq Y$. Therefore, $\neg A$ is also in $T_P(Y)$. Hence, T_P is monotone. Let us now consider the least fixpoint $T_P^\infty(\emptyset)$ of T_P. Let A be a positive element in $T_P^\infty(\emptyset)$. By definition of T_P, every rule r in $ground(P)$ with $H(r) = \neg A$ is blocked. Let $\neg A$ be a negative element in $T_P^\infty(\emptyset)$. Then, by definition of T_P, there exists an applicable rule r in *ground*(P) with $H(r) = \neg A$. Since $\neg A$ is in $T_P^\infty(\emptyset)$, r is also applied. Hence, by Definition 1, $T_P^\infty(\emptyset)$ is a model for P. □

Note that in general, $T_P^\infty(\emptyset)$ is not a total model; it is indeed a rather poor model as it contains only those negative elements that can be derived from the rules and such elements are not in general sufficient to derive all possible positive elements because of negative literals in the rule bodies. It is, however, well known that if P is a positive program then all inferable positive ground literals are derived in $T_P^\infty(\emptyset)$; thus, $T_P^\infty(\emptyset) = M^+$ where M is the unique total minimal model of P and $M^- = \neg(B_P - M^+)$ [9].

Definition 2. Let P be a negative program and M be a model for it. The *enabled instantiation* of P *w.r.t.* M, denoted by P_M^e, is the positive program

$$\{r \mid \exists \hat{r} \in ground(P)^+ \ (\hat{r} \text{ applied } w.r.t. \ M \wedge H(r) = H(\hat{r}) \wedge B(r) = B^+(\hat{r}))\}$$

(again, recall that $B^+(\hat{r})$ contains all positive literals in $B(\hat{r})$). □

PROPOSITION 2. *Let M be a partial model of a logic program P. Then $T_{P_M^e}^\infty(\emptyset) \subseteq M^+$.*

PROOF (sketch). Let A be any element in $T_{P_M^e}^\infty(\emptyset)$. By definition of T_P and because P_M^e is ground, A is the head of some rule, say r, in P_M^e. By Definition 2, there exists an applied rule $\hat{r}$ in *ground*(P) such that $H(\hat{r}) = H(r) = A$. Therefore, A is also in M^+. □

We can say that all positive literals of a model that are also in $T_{P_M^e}^\infty(\emptyset)$ are "founded" in the sense that they are derived from the rules of the programs. On the other side, all other positive ground literals can be considered as a sort of arbitrary assumptions. Note that, due to an implicit closed world assumption [11, 14], a negative ground literal does not need a derivation to be included in a model; it is sufficient that the conditions of Definition 1 are not violated.

Definition 3. Let P be a logic program. A partial model M for P is

(a) *founded* if $T_{P_M^e}^\infty(\emptyset) = M^+$.

(b) *stable* if it is maximally founded (i.e., it is founded and is a proper subset of no other founded model for P). □

PROPOSITION 3. *Let P be a negative program. Then $T_P^\infty(\emptyset)$ is a founded model for P.*

PROOF (sketch). Let $M = T_P^\infty(\emptyset)$ and A be in M^+. By definition of T_P and by Proposition 1, there exists a rule r in *ground*$(P)^+$ such that $H(r) = A$ and r is applied w.r.t. M. It is then easy to see that A is also in $T_{P_M^e}^\infty(\emptyset)$. □

Let us now substantiate the intuition that founded models do not contain (positive) assumptions. To this end, we specialize the definitions of unfounded set [20] and assumption set [15, 11] for negative programs.

Definition 4. Let P be a negative program and I be an interpretation for it. Let X be a non-empty subset of B_P. Then X is an *unfounded set w.r.t. I,* (resp., *assumption set w.r.t. I*) if for each A in X, either there exists an applicable rule (resp., non-blocked rule) r in $ground(P)$ with $H(r) = \neg A$ or every rule r in $ground(P)$ with $H(r) = A$ satisfies one of the following conditions: either r is blocked (resp., non-applicable) or $B(r) \cap X \neq \emptyset$. □

Obviously every unfounded set is an assumption set but the converse is not true. However, for total interpretations, the two concepts coincide. Informally, all predicates in an unfounded set can be declared false because there is no way to derive their truthness. This does not hold for the predicates in an assumption set. However, the truthness of such predicates cannot be derived unless some assumption is made.

Example 3. Consider the following program:

a :- $b, \neg a$.

b :- a.

$c(X)$.

d :- $\neg e$.

e :- $\neg d$.

f :- $g(3)$.

$g(3)$:- f.

$h(1)$.

$h(2)$.

$\neg c(X)$:- $h(X)$.

We have that $M_1 = \{h(1), h(2), \neg c(1), \neg c(2)\}$ is equal to $T_P^\infty(\emptyset)$ and, then, is a founded model. Every non-empty subset of $\overline{M}_1$ is an assumption set w.r.t. M_1. $X = \{a, b, f, g(1), g(2), g(3), h(3)\}$ is the greatest unfounded set w.r.t. M_1, thus all literals in X cannot be derived. Therefore, $M_2 = M_1 \cup \neg X$ is a model for $\boldsymbol{P}$. □

THEOREM 1. *A partial model M is founded if and only if no subset of* M^+ *is an assumption set w.r.t. M.*

PROOF (sketch). *(only-if part).* Suppose that M is founded. We prove by contradiction that no subset of M^+ is an assumption set w.r.t. M. Suppose that $X \subseteq M^+$ is an assumption set w.r.t. M. By definition of $\boldsymbol{P}_M^e$ and of assumption set, for each A in X, every rule r in $\boldsymbol{P}_M^e$ with $H(r) = A$ contains at least one literal in X in its body. Then any element in X cannot be derived in $T_{P_M^e}^\infty(\emptyset)$ until after another element of X has been, in turn, derived. But this means that no element of X can be derived in $T_{P_M^e}^\infty(\emptyset)$, i.e., $T_{P_M^e}^\infty(\emptyset)$ is a proper subset of M^+ as X is not empty by definition of assumption set. We then get a contradiction with the hypothesis that M is founded.

(if part). Suppose that M is a partial model for P and no subset of M^+ is an assumption set w.r.t. M. We show that M is founded. We assume that M^+ is not empty because otherwise the proof would be trivial. Let A be an element in M^+. Since $\{A\}$ is not an assumption set w.r.t. M, both there exists no non-blocked rule r in $ground(P)$ for which $H(r) = \neg A$ and there exists at least one applied rule r in $ground(P)$ for which $H(r) = A$. Therefore, for each A in M^+, there exists a rule r in P_M^e such that $H(r) = A$ and all literals occurring in P_M^e are in M^+. Let $X = M^+ - T_{P_M^e}^{\infty}(\emptyset)$. It is easy to see that X is not empty only if X is an assumption set w.r.t. M. Hence, considering the hypothesis, X is empty and M is founded. □

COROLLARY 1. *A total model M is stable if and only if no subset of M^+ is an assumption set w.r.t. M.*

PROOF. It follows directly from Theorem 1 M and the definition of stable model. □

Note that every negative program P has at least one (possibly partial but not total) stable model as the least fixpoint of T_P is a founded model for P. Total stable models corresponds to the stable models introduced in [6].

Definition 5. Let $\boldsymbol{P}$ be a negative program. A model M for $\boldsymbol{P}$ is

(a) *closed*$^+$ if each non-empty subset of $\overline{M}$ is an assumption set w.r.t. M;

(b) *closed*$^-$ if no subset of $\overline{M}$ is an unfounded set w.r.t. M;

(c) *closed* if it is both closed$^+$ and closed$^-$;

(d) *strongly founded* if it is both founded and closed. □

Informally, a model M is closed$^+$ if no other positive literals can be derived from P using M, unless some other negative literals are added to M. On the other side, M is closed$^-$ if no other negative literals can be added to M without exposing M to a chance of getting a non-removable contradiction (note that unfounded sets remove such a risk). We point out that closed$^+$ models correspond to 3-valued models as defined in [13].

Example 4. Consider the program and the models M_1, M_2 in Example 3. M_1 is closed$^+$ but not closed$^-$ whereas M_2 is closed$^-$ but not closed$^+$. $M_3 = M_2 \cup \{c(3)\}$ is closed as well as founded; so it is strongly founded. If we change $\neg b$ into b in M_3 we obtain a model M_4 that is closed but not founded. □

Let us now introduce the transformation W_P in the complete lower semilattice $<\mathbf{I},\subseteq>$, where $\mathbf{I}$ is the family of all interpretations of a negative program $\boldsymbol{P}$:

$$W_P(I) = T_P(I) \cup \neg U_P(I)$$

where $U_P(I)$ is the *greatest* unfounded set w.r.t. I (note that $U_P(I)$ is the union of all unfounded sets w.r.t I).

THEOREM 2. *Let P be a negative program. Then*

(a) *W_P is monotone;*

(b) *an interpretation for P is a fixpoint of T_P (resp., W_P) if and only if it is a closed$^+$ (resp., closed) model for P;*

(c) *the least fixpoint of W_P is strongly founded.*

PROOF (sketch). (a) T_P is monotone by Proposition 1; moreover, it is easy to see that also U_P is monotone. Therefore, W_P is monotone as well.

(b) *(only-if part)* If M is both an interpretation for P and a fixpoint of T_P then M is a model for P since all conditions of Definition 1 are enabled by the application of T_P. Moreover, M is closed$^+$ because otherwise we could still apply T_P, whereas M is a fixpoint of T_P. Suppose now that the interpretation M is a fixpoint of W_P. Obviously, M is also a fixpoint of T_P and, then, is a closed$^+$ model for P. But M is also a fixpoint of U_P. Therefore, M is also closed$^-$, thus M is a closed model for P. The proof of the *if-part* is routine.

(c) Let M be the least fixpoint of W_P. Then, by Theorem 2 (part b), M is a closed model for P. Since all positive literals in M are all derived in P, M^+ does not contain any assumption set w.r.t. M. Therefore, by Theorem 1, M is founded. It follows that M is strongly founded. □

Definition 6. Let P be a negative program. The least fixpoint of W_P is called the *well-founded model* for P. □

THEOREM 3. *Let P be a negative program. Then*

(a) *every stable model for P is strongly founded;*

(b) *the well-founded model for P is the intersection of all strongly-founded models for P.*

PROOF (sketch). (a) Let M be a stable model. We have that M is closed because otherwise $WP(P)$ would be a larger founded model for P (contradiction with the fact that M is maximally founded). So M is strongly founded.

(b) Every strongly-founded model M for P is closed by definition. Hence, M is a fixpoint of W_P by Theorem 2 (part b). Let N be the well-founded model for P. By definition, N is the least fixpoint of W_P; so $N \subseteq M$. □

Thus, by the above theorem, the well-founded model is the minimal strongly-founded model.

Example 5. Consider the negative program in Example 3 and the model M_3 in Example 4. It is easy to recognize that M_3 is well founded. The other strongly-founded models are $M_3 \cup \{d, \neg e\}$ and $M_3 \cup \{\neg d, e\}$ that are also both stable and total. □

We point out that when a negative program reduces to a seminegative program then all definitions and results of this section coincide with the analogous ones that are presented in [15] for seminegative programs.

3. Stratified Negative Programs

Let us now extend the concept of dependency graph as given for seminegative programs [17] to negative programs. Given a negative program P, the *dependency graph* of P, denoted by G_P, is a directed graph whose nodes are all predicate symbols occurring in P and the arcs are constructed as follows. Given two predicate symbols p and q, there exists an arc from q to p in G_P if there exists a rule r in P such that (i) the head predicate symbol of r is p, (ii) one of the literals in the body of r, say Q, has q as predicate symbol, and (iii) there exists a (not necessarily distinct) seminegative rule whose head predicate is p. Moreover, the arc is marked if either Q is positive and $H(r)$ is negative or Q is negative and $H(r)$ is positive.

Note that, for seminegative programs, the definition of dependency graph coincides with the classical definition as given in [17].

Definition 7. A negative program P is *stratified* if there are no cycles with marked arcs in G_P. □

Again, in case of seminegative programs, the above definition coincide with the definition of stratified programs as given in [1, 3, 12, 18].

Example 6. The following negative program

$a(X,Y) :- \ b(X,Y).$

$a(X,Y) :- \ b(X,Z), a(Z,Y), \neg d(Y).$

$\neg a(X,Y) :- \ c(X,Z), \neg a(Z,Y).$

$\neg d(X) :- a(X,Y).$

where b and c are defined by a number of database facts, is stratified as confirmed by its dependency graph in Figure 1. Note that d is not in the same strong component of a since the arc from a to d is not added as no seminegative rule defines d. It is easy to see that the last rule is redundant and $d(X)$ can be assumed false for each X. □

We next show that stratification can be detected in polynomial time in the size of the program. The size of a negative program P, denoted by $|P|$, is the total number of symbols occurring in P.

PROPOSITION 4. *Let P be a negative program. Testing whether P is stratified can be done in time $O(|P|)$.*

PROOF (sketch). It is easy to see that G_P can be constructed in $O(|P|)$. We then single out the strong components of G_P in time $O(m)$, where m is the number of arcs in G_P. Finally, for each component C, we verify in time

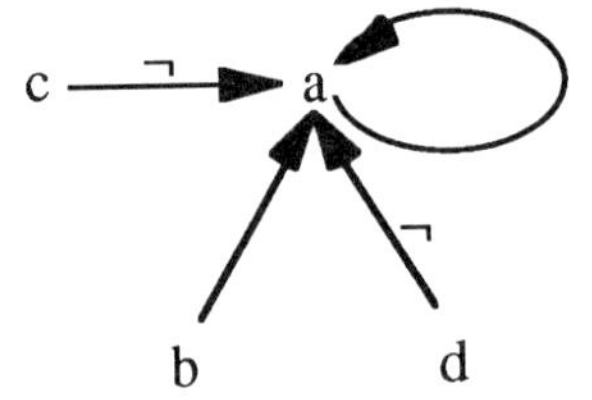

Fig. 1. *Dependency Graph*

$O(m)$ whether there are marked arcs among the nodes in C. Obviously, $m = O(|P|)$. So the overall time complexity of the test is $O(|P|)$. □

We next provide a fixpoint definition of the well-founded model for stratified programs, based on transformations where the operator U_P for the greatest unfounded set does not appear. We point out that the fixpoint definition though the transformation W_P is not very effective because, in general, it is rather hard to recognize unfounded sets. (The alternating fixpoint [19] is a solution — actually, not fully satisfactory because of its complexity — to avoid this problem.) Let us first introduce some preliminary notation.

Let P be a stratified negative program and G_P be the dependency graph of P. Let $C_1, \ldots, C_n$ be the strongly-connected components of G_P. For each C_i, $1 \le i \le n$, P_i denotes the set of all rules r in P such that the predicate symbol of $H(r)$ is in C_i; moreover, B_i is the set $\{A \mid A$ is in B_P and the predicate symbol of A is in $C_i\}$.

The *collapsed dependency graph* of G_P is the directed graph $\hat{G}_P = <N, A>$, where the set of nodes is $N = \{C_1, \ldots, C_n\}$ and the set of arcs is $A = \{(C_i, C_j) \mid (r, s)$ is in G_P, r is in C_i and s is in $C_j\}$. Obviously, $\hat{G}_P$ is acyclic. Then, without loss of generality, we can assume that $<C_1, \ldots, C_n>$ is a topological sort of the nodes of $\hat{G}_P$; thus, they are the *stratified components* of P.

THEOREM 4. *Let P be a stratified negative program. The well-founded model of* **P** *is equal to M_n, where M_n is the total model defined as follows:*

$$M_0 = \emptyset$$

$$\ldots$$

$$L_i^+ = T_{P_i}^{\infty +}(M_{i-1})$$

$$L_i^- = \neg(B_i - M_i^+)$$

$$M_i = L_i \cup M_{i-1}$$

$$\ldots$$

and where $<C_1, \ldots, C_n>$ *are the stratified components of* P.[2]

PROOF. We proceed by induction on n, the number of strong components. The proof is trivial if $n = 0$, i.e., if P is empty (*base of the induction*). Let us now assume that the theorem holds whenever $i < n$, $n > 0$ (*inductive hypothesis*). We prove that it holds also when $i = n$. Consider $M_n = L_n \cup M_{n-1}$. By construction, M_n is a total interpretation of P. We next prove that M_n is indeed a model for P. To this end, we first observe that any element in M_{n-1} satisfies the conditions of Definition 1 since M_{n-1} is a model for $\cup_{1 \le i \le n-1} P_i$ by inductive hypothesis and no element in M_{n-1} occurs in the head of any rule in $ground(P_n)$ by definition of stratification. Let us now consider any element A in L_i^+. Let r be any rule in $ground(P)$ with $H(r) = \neg A$. By definition of stratification, r is in $ground(P_n)$ by definition of stratification. Moreover, since A is in $T_{P_n}^{\infty}(M_{n-1})$ by definition of L_n, r is blocked w.r.t. M_n by definition of T_{P_n}. Hence, A satisfies the conditions of Definition 1. Let us now take an element $\neg A$ in L_n^-. Let r be any rule in $ground(P_n^+)$ with $H(r) = A$ such that r is not blocked w.r.t. M_n. Let us assume that such a rule exists because otherwise $\neg A$ would trivially satisfy the conditions of Definition 1. As M_n is a total interpretation, r is applicable w.r.t. M_n, thus every literal B in $B(r)$ is in M_n. But, because of stratification, B cannot be in L_n^-. Therefore, r is applicable also w.r.t. $M_{n-1} \cup L_n^+$. But A is not in L_n^+; so there must be a rule $\hat{r}$ in $ground(P_n^-)$ such that $H(\hat{r}) = \neg A$ and $\hat{r}$ is not blocked w.r.t. $M_{n-1} \cup L_n^+$. Let B be any literal in the body of $\hat{r}$; by definition of stratification, either B is in M_{n-1} or B is a negative literal whose complement is not in L_n^+, thus B is in L_n^-. It follows that $\hat{r}$ is applicable w.r.t. M_n and, then, applied as $\neg A$ is in M_n by assumption. Again $\neg A$ satisfies the conditions of Definition 1; so we can conclude that M_n is a total model for P. Obviously M_n is founded as positive literals in M_n have been inferred using the rules of P; moreover, as it is total, M_n is *closed* and, then, strongly founded. Let us now prove that M_n is also well founded. Let N be the well-founded model for P, i.e., $N = W_P^{\infty}(\emptyset)$. By inductive hypothesis and because of stratification, $N = M_{n-1} \cup K$, where $K = W_P^{\infty}(M_{n-1})$. Then, by definition of W_P and of T_P, $L_n^+ \subseteq K^+$. But we have shown that M_n is a strongly-founded model; so $L_n^+ = K^+$ and $K^- \subseteq L_n^-$ by Theorem 3 (part b). Let $X = K^- - L_n^-$. We prove that X is empty by contradiction. Suppose, then, $X \neq \emptyset$. Let $A \in X$ such that there exists a rule r in $ground(P_n^+)$ for which $H(r) = A$, r is not blocked

---

[2] Recall that, according to our notation, $T_P^{\infty+}(I)$ denotes the set of all positive literals in $T_P^{\infty}(I)$ and L_i is equal to $L_i^+ \cup L_i^-$.

w.r.t. N and $B(r) \cap X = \emptyset$. If such an A does not exists then X is an unfounded set w.r.t. N (contradiction with the fact that N is closed$^-$). Suppose, then, that A exists with the above properties and let r a rule as above. Consider any (positive or negative) literal B in $B(r)$. $\neg B$ is not in M_{n-1} because otherwise r would be blocked w.r.t. N; B is not in L_n^- because of stratification; B is not in X by assumption. Hence, B must be in $M_{n-1} \cup L_n^+$. But $M_{n-1} \cup L_n^+ \subseteq N$ for $L_n^+ = K^+$; so r is applicable w.r.t. N. Hence, since A is not in N, by Definition 1 there exists a rule $\hat{r}$ in $ground(P_n^-)$ with $H(\hat{r}) = \neg A$ such that $\hat{r}$ is applied w.r.t. N. By Definition 4, X is an unfounded set w.r.t. N (again, contradiction with the fact that N is closed$^-$). It follows that X is empty and, then, $N = M_n$; so this concludes the proof that M_n is a well-founded model for P. □

It turns out that the well-founded model of a stratified negative program is total and, then, stable as well.

We have, then, presented a constructive definition of the total well-founded model for stratified negative programs that seems to coincide with the definition of stratified model for stratified seminegative programs [1]. The actual difference is given by the transformation T_P that is here extended to take into account also rules with negative heads. Notice that such rules are not used to actually infer negative literals but only to filter positive ones.

STRATIFIED FIXPOINT PROCEDURE

- Let P be a stratified negative program;
- Let $<C_1, \ldots, C_n>$ be the stratified components;
- set $M^+ = \emptyset$;

For $i := 1$ **to** n **do**
begin (* Component C_i *)
    $L_i^+ := \emptyset$;
    Repeat
        $Q = L_i^+$;
        $L_i^+ := T_{P_i}^+(M^+ \cup Q)$
    until $L_i^+ = Q$;
    $M^+ := M^+ \cup L_i^+$
end;
- M^+ is the set of all positive literals in the well-founded model of P

Fig. 1. *Stratified Fixpoint for a Negative Program*

The procedure "Stratified Fixpoint for Negative Programs" in Figure 1 is an effective implementation of this definition that only computes the positive literals of L_i (and, eventually, of the overall well-founded model) since negative literals in L_i can be easily stated by complementation at the end of the iteration for the layer i. Therefore, while using the transformation $T_{P_i}(M^+ \cup Q)$, in order to check the truthness of a negative literal in a rule body, we refer to its complement, thus we assume $\neg A$ is true if and only if A is not in $M^+ \cup Q$. This assumption is correct for every seminegative rule for possible negative literals in its body have been already solved in previous layers by definition of stratification. As for a strictly negative rule, the assumption could lead to a wrong inference of a negative literal as $\neg A$ may now refer to some still undefined fact in the layer i. However, since we collect only positive literals at each step of the computation of $T_{P_i}(M^+ \cup Q)$ and the effect of strictly negative rules is to refuse some of such positive literals, the effect of considering $\neg A$ true or undefined is the same (see the definition of T_P).

Note that termination of the procedure is guaranteed for finite Herbrand universes.

We point out that the block **begin** (* Component C_i *) $\cdots$ **end** of the procedure in Figure 1 can be simplified in the following cases:

(a) *P_i^- is empty.* Then the block reduces to

> **begin** (* Component C_i *)
> $L_i^+ := T_{P_i}^{\infty}(M^+)$;
> $M^+ := M^+ \cup L_i^+$
> **end**;

as for the stratified fixpoint for seminegative programs [1].

(b) *P_i^+ is empty.* Then M_i^+ is empty and the computation for C_i can be skipped.

(c) *No predicate symbol in C_i occurs in the body of any rule in P_i^-.* Then the block reduces to

> **begin** (* Component C_i *)
> $L_i^+ := \emptyset$; $L_i^- := \neg(T_{P_i^-}(M^+)$;
> **Repeat**
> $Q = L_i^+$;
> $L_i^+ := T_{P_i^+}(M^+ \cup Q) - L_i^-$;
> **until** $L_i^+ = Q$;
> $M^+ := M^+ \cup L_i^+$
> **end**;

since the rules in P_i^- can be fired only once at the beginning.

It turns out that the well-founded model of a stratified program can be determined using a procedure that is an extension of the stratified fixpoint for classical stratified (seminegative) programs [1].

4. From Negative to Seminegative

In this section we show that a negative program can be transformed into a seminegative one which preserves the original semantics at least as far as founded models are concerned.

Let P be a negative program. Then for every predicate symbol, say q, which occurs in the head of some rule in P^-, we introduce a new predicate symbol $\sim q$, called an *negated predicate symbol,* whose arity is the same as that of q (thus $\sim q(\mathbf{x})$ is to be considered as a predicate). The set of all negated predicate symbols for P is denoted by $\sim \mathbf{q}_P$.

Definition 8. Let P be a negative program. The *seminegative version* of the negative program P, denoted by $SV(P)$, is the seminegative program obtained from P as follows: for each predicate symbol $\sim q$ in $\sim \mathbf{q}_P$, (a) replace the head of each negative rule r with $H(r) = \neg q(\mathbf{x})$ by $\sim q(\mathbf{x})$, and (b) add to the body of each seminegative rule with $H(r) = q(\mathbf{x})$ the literal $\neg(\sim q(\mathbf{x}))$. □

Example 7. Consider the negative program in Example 6. Its seminegative version is:

$a(X,Y) :- \ b(X,Y).$

$a(X,Y) :- \ b(X,Z),\ a(Z,Y), \neg d(Y),\ \neg\sim a(X,Y).$

$\sim a(X,Y) :- \ c(X,Z),\ \neg a(Z,Y).$

$\sim d(X) :- a(X,Y).$

□

We next state without proof the equivalence between P and $SV(P)$. (The proof is rather obvious and requires much space.) To this end, we first need the following notation.

Let I be an interpretation for a negative program P and $\mathbf{q}$ be a set of predicate symbols occurring in P. Then $I_{\mathbf{q}}$ is $\{q(\mathbf{x}) \mid q(\mathbf{x}) \in I \wedge q \in \mathbf{q}\}$.

THEOREM 5. *Let P a negative program.*

(a) *$SV(P)$ can be constructed in time $O(|P|)$.*

(b) *If M is a model for P then there exists a model N for $SV(P)$ such that $N - N_{\sim \mathbf{q}_P} = M$.*

(c) *If M is a founded (resp., strongly-founded, well-founded, stable) model for $SV(P)$ then $M - M_{\sim \mathbf{q}_P}$ is a founded (resp., strongly-founded, well-founded, stable) model for P.*

(d) *If M is a founded (resp., strongly-founded, well-founded, stable) model for P then there exists a founded (resp., strongly-founded, well-founded, stable) model N for $SV(P)$ such that $N - N_{\sim \mathbf{q}_P} = M$.*

(e) *If $SV(P)$ is stratified then also P is stratified.* □

Note that, given a model M for $SV(P)$, $M - M_{\sim q_P}$ is not necessarily a model for $\boldsymbol{P}$, thus $SV(P)$ is less restrictive than P. However, P and $SV(\boldsymbol{P})$ are equivalent as far as all kinds of founded models are concerned. Finally, the converse of Theorem 5.d does not hold.

Example 8. The negative program in Example 6 is stratified whereas its seminegative version (see Example 7) is not as pointed out by the dependency graph in Figure 2.

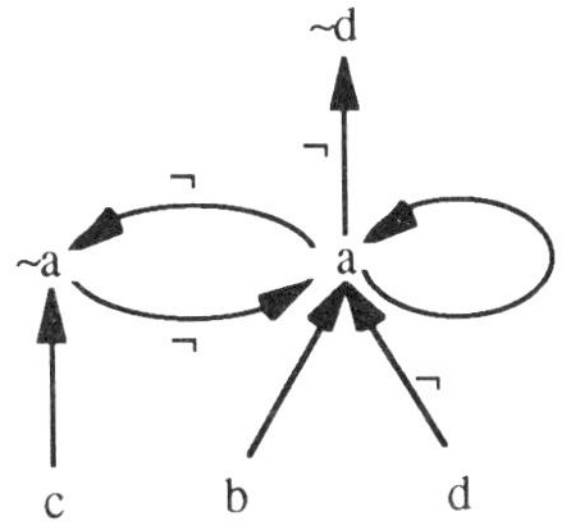

Fig. 2. *Dependency Graph of SV(P)*

Consider now the negative program P in Example 2:

$p.$

$\neg p :- p.$

$SV(\boldsymbol{P})$ is:

$p :- \neg{\sim}p.$

${\sim}p :- p.$

Note that neither P nor $SV(P)$ is stratified. A (non-founded) model of $SV(\boldsymbol{P})$ is $\{p, {\sim}p\}$, that corresponds to a contradiction, but (fortunately!) $\{p\}$ is not a model for $\boldsymbol{P}$. Note that the only founded model for both P and $SV(P)$ is the empty set. Moreover, the empty set is the only model for $\boldsymbol{P}$. □

It turns out that it is more convenient to use the direct fixpoint for stratified negative programs rather than passing through the seminegative version. Furthermore, the seminegative version may include some misleading models. Our belief is that, in general, a direct analysis of a negative program is more convenient under many respects, including the size of representation, than considering the seminegative version of it.

5. Further Research

We have provided well-founded and stable model semantics for an extension of logic programming, called *negative programming,* where negation can arise also in the heads of rules and which has been recently introduced in [2]. Despite the approach of [2], where contradiction is accepted, and following [7, 8, 11], we consider negative programs as a powerful formalism where contradiction is used (and, actually, removed) to express exceptions.

We have also introduced the notion of stratification for negative programs and we have proved that stratified negative programs have the same nice properties as classical stratified programs: the well-founded model is total and can be determined by a stratified fixpoint computation. Finally, we have shown that a negative program can be transformed into an almost "equivalent" classical logic program where negation only occurs in rule bodies.

Following are a number of issues that need further investigation:

(a) Efficient implementation of procedures for finding the well-founded model for stratified programs (e.g., semi-naive method, methods for binding propagation, etc.).

(b) Procedure for finding the well-founded model and stable models in general (for instance, by adapting the alternating fixpoint of [19] or the backtracking fixpoint of [15]).

(c) Investigate larger scenarios where exceptions to exceptions are allowed. Our belief is that updates can be effectively analyzed in this framework.

Acknowledgement

This work has been carried out within the project LOGIDATA that is partially supported by the Italian National Research Council in the framework of the program "Progetto Finalizzato Calcolo Parallelo e Sistemi Informatici".

6. References

[1] Apt, K., H. Blair, and A. Walker. 1987. *Towards a Theory of Declarative Knowledge.* In Foundations of Deductive Databases and Logic Programming, Minker, J. (ed.), Morgan Kaufman, Los Altos, pp. 89-148.

[2] Blair, H., and V.S. Subrahmanian. 1989. *Paraconsistent Logic Programming.* In Theoretical Computer Science 68, pp. 135-154.

[3] Chandra, A., and D. Harel. 1985. *Horn Clauses and Generalization.* In Journal of Logic Programming 2, 1, pp. 320-340.

[4] Clark, K.L. 1978. *Negation as Failure.* In Logic and Data Bases, (Gallaire and Minker, eds), Plenum Press, New York, pp. 293-322.

[5] Fitting, M., and M. Ben-Jacob. 1988. *Stratified and Three-valued Logic Programming Semantics.* IN Proc. 5th Int. Conf. and Symp. on Logic Programming, MIT Press, Cambridge, Ma, pp. 1054-1068.

[6] Gelfond, M., and V. Lifschitz. 1988. *The Stable Model Semantics for Logic Programming.* In Proc. 5th Int. Conf. and Symp. on Logic

Programming, MIT Press, Cambridge, Ma, pp. 1070-1080.

[7] Gelfond, M., and V. Lifschitz. 1989. *Logic Programs with Classical Negation. Stanford University, Stanford, California 94305.*

[8] Kowalski R. A., and F. Sadri. 1989. *Logic Programs with Exceptions.* Department of Computing, Imperial College, London SW7 2BZ.

[9] Lloyd, J.W. 1987. *Foundations of Logic Programming.* Springer Verlag, Berlin.

[10] Laenens, E., and D. Vermeir. 1990. *A Fixpoint Semantics for Ordered Logic.* In Journal of Logic and Computation, to appear.

[11] Laenens, E., D. Saccà, and D. Vermeir. 1990 *Extending Logic Programming.* In Proc. ACM SIGMOD Conference, Atlantic City,NJ, pp. 184-193.

[12] Naqvi, S.A. 1987. *A Logic for Negation in Database Systems.* In Foundations of Deductive Databases and Logic Programming, (Minker, J. ed.), Morgan Kaufman, Los Altos.

[13] Przymusinski, T.C. 1989. *Well-founded models are intersections of three-valued stable models.* Unpublished manuscript.

[14] Reiter, R. 1978. *On Closed World Databases.* In Logic and Data Bases, (Gallaire and Minker, eds), Plenum Press, New York, pp. 55-76.

[15] Saccà, D., and C. Zaniolo. 1990. *Stable models and Non-determinism for logic programs with negation.* In Proc. ACM Symp. on Principles of Database Systems, pp. 205-217.

[16] Tarski, A. 1955. *A Lattice Theoretical Fixpoint Theorem and its Application.* In Pacific Journal of Mathematics 5, pp. 285-309.

[17] Ullman, J.D. 1988. *Principles of Database and Knowledge-Base Systems, Vol. 1 and 2.* Computer Science Press, Rockville, Md.

[18] Van Gelder, A. 1986. *Negation as Failure Using Tight Derivations for Logic Programs.* In Proc. 3rd IEEE Symp. on Logic Programming, Springer-Verlag, pp. 127-138.

[19] Van Gelder, A. 1989. *The Alternating Fixpoint of Logic Programs with Negation.* In Proc. ACM Symp. on Principles of Database Systems, pp. 1-10.

[20] Van Gelder, A., K. Ross, and J.S. Schlipf. 1988. *Unfounded Sets and Well-Founded Semantics for General Logic Programs.* In Proc. ACM SIGMOD-SIGACT Symp. on Principles of Database Systems, pp. 221-230.

Program Analysis

The Benefits of Global Dataflow Analysis for an Optimizing Prolog Compiler

Peter Van Roy

Computer Science Division
University of California, Berkeley

Alvin M. Despain

Department of Electrical Engineering – Systems
University of Southern California

ABSTRACT

We present a simple dataflow analysis scheme for Prolog and measure its effectiveness on a variety of programs. The scheme is based on abstract interpretation and derives ground, nonvariable, dereferenced, and uninitialized variable modes. An uninitialized variable is an unbound variable that is not pointed to by any other variable. Binding uninitialized variables is simpler and more efficient than binding standard Prolog variables. The analyzer has been developed in the context of the Berkeley Abstract Machine (BAM) project. It is integrated into a new optimizing compiler, the Aquarius compiler, which generates code for the BAM, an abstract machine for Prolog implementation. This code is targeted for a new architecture, the BAM processor. We give simulated measurements on the BAM processor showing the effect of analysis on static code size, trailing, dereferencing, and overall performance. We find that our scheme gives a significant improvement in these metrics. We conclude that a simple analysis scheme suffices to remove much of the overhead of the powerful features of logic programming when they are not used.

1. Introduction

The goal of logic programming is to provide programmers with a tool for programming at a high level of abstraction. The most popular logic programming language is Prolog, which attempts to make programming in first order logic practical. However, current Prolog systems are an order of magnitude slower than popular imperative languages such as C. The goal of our work is to narrow that gap. Our hypothesis is that Prolog can be implemented as efficiently as an imperative language: the implementation will replace the powerful features of logic programming with more efficient ones when possible. An important part of such an implementation is a global dataflow analysis scheme.

Little work has been done to measure the effect of global dataflow analysis on the performance of sequential Prolog programs. In this paper we present a simple analysis scheme and measure its effectiveness on a variety of programs.

We measure the analysis time, the effect on performance and static code size, and the percentage of arguments for which the analyzer can derive a mode (i.e. a type).

The analyzer has been developed in the context of the Berkeley Abstract Machine (BAM) project [11]. The goals of the BAM project are to determine a minimal set of extensions to a general-purpose architecture to support Prolog and to build a system with a single-chip implementation of the resulting architecture. The BAM chip is a pipelined load-store processor with 32-bit data and instruction words that is designed to run at 30 MHz. The main extensions for Prolog are fast branch on tag support, tag manipulation (integrated into arithmetic and memory systems), a double-word data port to memory, and several instructions to support our execution model for Prolog.

This paper consists of six parts. In section 2 we give an overview of related work in practical dataflow analysis for Prolog. Section 3 describes the optimizing compiler that is designed to exploit the modes derived by the analysis. Section 4 explains the concept of uninitialized variables, an important part of our analysis scheme. Section 5 introduces our analysis scheme as an example of abstract interpretation, a general technique for deriving global properties of programs. Section 6 gives measurements of performance and code size with and without analysis. Finally, we give conclusions and directions for future work.

Familiarity with Prolog and its execution semantics is assumed. Some familiarity with the basic concepts of abstract interpretation and the Warren Abstract Machine (WAM) [21], a popular execution model for Prolog, is also helpful, although we do make an effort to introduce the relevant concepts.

2. Related work

Beer [1] has suggested the use of a classification of Prolog variables that often allows binding to be simplified. He shows that the frequency of two common Prolog operations, dereferencing (following a pointer chain to its end) and trailing (saving a bound variable so that it can be unbound later on backtracking), is reduced significantly. This idea was a strong influence on our compiler. At the Prolog level, logical semantics are preserved, but at the code level there is now a coherent use of destructive assignment for values that fit in a word. Beer introduces several new tags for this representation, which he calls *uninitialized variables*, and keeps track of them at run-time. Our scheme uses the same tag for both uninitialized and standard Prolog variables. The analyzer finds uninitialized variables at compile-time and the compiler determines when it is safe to use destructive assignment to bind them.

The most comprehensive work measuring the practicality of global dataflow analysis in logic programming has been reported in [22]. This paper describes two dataflow analyzers: (1) MA^3, the MCC And-parallel Analyzer and Annotator, and (2) Ms, an experimental analysis scheme developed for SB-Prolog. MA^3 derives aliasing and ground modes and keeps track of the structure of compound terms, while Ms derives ground and nonvariable modes. Aliasing occurs when two variables are bound to terms that have variables in common. A ground term contains no unbound variables. The paper concludes that both dataflow analyzers are effective and do not overly increase the compilation time. Our dataflow analyzer differs from both MA[3] and Ms in three ways. First, our analyzer works over a different domain. It derives unbound variables and dereferenced modes as well as ground and nonvariable modes. Second, it avoids problems with aliased variables by not deriving mode information for them. Third, it is integrated into a compiler which has been developed to take full advantage of the modes it derives, so that we are able to see the effect of analysis on performance.

For correctness, it is imperative to consider the effects of variable aliasing on dataflow analysis. Finding accurate aliasing information is an important topic in current research [5, 6, 12]. However, aliasing complicates the implementation of dataflow analysis. Our analyzer considers only unaliased variables as candidates for unbound variable modes. Unaliased variables are not pointed to by any other variable. Despite this strong constraint, our measurements show that unaliased variables occur often enough to make the analysis worthwhile. This conservative treatment of aliasing simplifies our implementation, since it is not necessary to explicitly represent and propagate aliasing information.

Taylor has recently developed a Prolog compiler for the MIPS processor that compiles directly to native code [18]. It includes a global dataflow analyzer that explicitly represents type, aliasing, and dereference chain information. His performance numbers confirm our conclusions about the effectiveness of a global dataflow analysis.

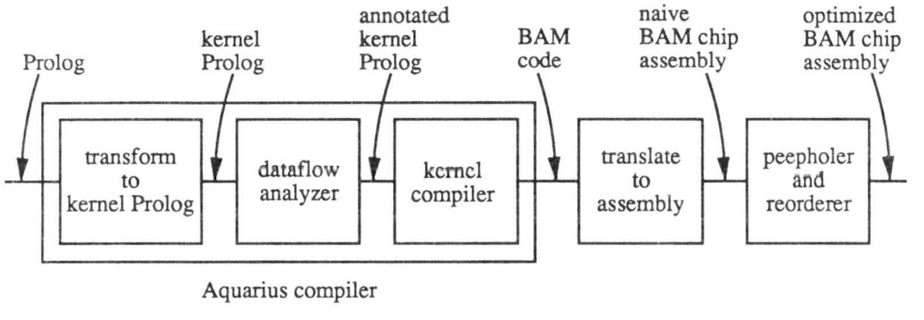

Figure 1 – Compilation of Prolog

3. The Aquarius compiler

Compilation of Prolog for the BAM processor is done in three stages (Figure 1). First, the compiler produces code for the BAM, a simple abstract machine. This is done by transforming Prolog into a simplified internal representation called kernel Prolog, by performing dataflow analysis on the kernel Prolog, and by compiling the resulting annotated kernel Prolog. Second, this code is macro-expanded into assembly code for the BAM processor. Finally, the assembly code is optimized by a peephole optimizer and an instruction reordering stage. Our current system runs on a BAM processor simulator and the MIPS processor and we are porting it to other platforms. Optimizations are still being implemented—we expect the performance numbers (Table 4) to improve.

The compiler is written in Prolog and consists of about 10,000 lines of code.† The run-time system implements a superset of the built-in predicates of C-Prolog. For portability reasons most of the run-time system is written in Prolog. The Prolog component consists of about 6,000 lines of code and is carefully coded to make the most of various optimization possibilities offered by the compiler and thus to reduce the performance penalty for implementing critical built-in predicates in Prolog. The small non-Prolog component is written mostly in code for the BAM, with a very few routines written in the instruction set of the target machine.

The compiler's design is based on the following ideas:

- The compiler's output instruction set, the Berkeley Abstract Machine (BAM), is carefully designed to express the primitive operations of Prolog while allowing extensive optimization. It uses data structures similar to those of the WAM, but it no longer uses the WAM instruction set. The BAM includes:

  (1) Simple instructions. These are register-transfer operations for a tagged load-store architecture.

  (2) Complex instructions. These are evolved from the requirements of environment and choice point handling, and from frequently used operations such as dereferencing, trailing, and general unification.

  (3) Pragmas. These are not executable, but give information that allows a better translation to the assembly language of the target machine.

  This allows extensive low-level optimization as well as compact encoding of operations that are common in Prolog. An early version of part of the instruction set is described in [19].

- The compiler incorporates a simple deduction and learning mechanism which propagates knowledge during compilation. This simplifies the design and makes it more powerful. It extends the usefulness of analysis, which derives information about predicates, by propagating this information inside of predicates.

- The compiler incorporates techniques for compiling predicates into deterministic code. It generalizes the first argument selection of the WAM by creating a decision graph to handle arguments of different types. It exploits type information derived by dataflow analysis to simplify the graph as much as possible.

- The compiler simplifies variable binding through the concept of *uninitialized variables*, unbound variables that are unaliased. Dataflow analysis determines when they can be used safely.

† Not including comments. All Prolog program sizes in this paper exclude comments.

4. Uninitialized variables

A major source of inefficiency in WAM implementations is that variables are often created and then unified soon afterwards. Frequently it is known at compile-time that the variable will be given a value in this fashion. Creating and unifying does much unnecessary work; it would be faster just to reserve a memory location and then write to it.

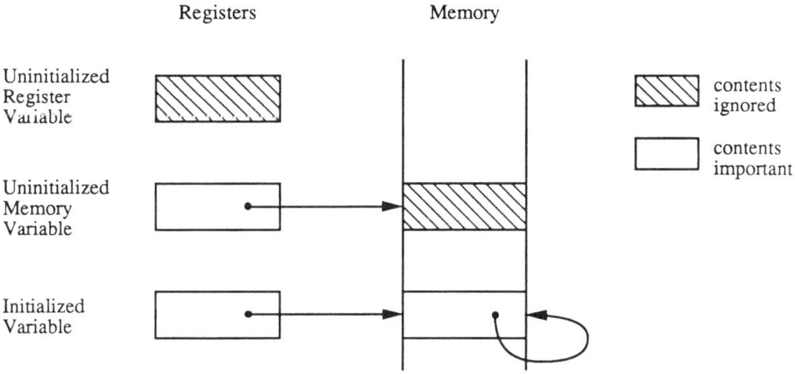

Figure 2 – Classification of Unbound Variables

To solve this problem we introduce a class of simpler unbound variables, called uninitialized variables, which are cheaper to create and bind. An uninitialized variable is a location that is allocated to contain an unbound variable, but the location is not given a value. The location can either be a register or a memory word, resulting in two kinds of uninitialized variables, which we call uninitialized register and uninitialized memory variables. The first are registers whose contents are ignored. The second are pointers to memory locations whose contents are ignored. Standard Prolog unbound variables are called initialized variables; they are pointers to locations pointing to themselves. Figure 2 illustrates the three categories of unbound variables.

Table 1 – The Cost of Unbound Variables

Type of variable	Cost (BAM cycles)			
	Creation	Unification		
		Dereference	Trail	Bind
Uninitialized Register	0	0	0	0
Uninitialized Memory	1	0	0	1
Initialized Variable	2	4	2	1

The dataflow analyzer derives uninitialized memory variables; this is followed by a transformation pass which converts some of them to uninitialized register variables. Table 1 gives the minimum run-time cost in the BAM processor for the creation and unification of the three categories of unbound variables. Unifying an initialized variable is expensive because it consists of three parts: dereferencing the variable, doing a trail check and possibly storing the variable on the trail stack, and storing the value in the variable. Unifying an uninitialized memory variable reduces to a single memory store. Unifying an uninitialized register variable is free if it is created in the register that needs it. The cost of detrailing, restoring a variable to an unbound state on backtracking, is not given in the table because it depends strongly on the effectiveness of the compiler in generating deterministic code. It is zero for uninitialized variables and has an upper bound of 4 cycles per initialized variable.

5. The dataflow analysis scheme

It is difficult to obtain information about a program by executing it in its original form, since the range of possible behaviors is potentially infinite, and Turing has shown that even simple properties of programs may be undecidable. To get around this problem, the idea of *abstract interpretation* is to transform the program into a simpler form which allows practical analysis. After the analysis the inverse transformation gives information about the original program. The fundamentals of a general method based on this approach and its mathematical underpinning are explained by Kildall [13] and Cousot & Cousot [7]. This method has been studied extensively and developed into a practical tool for Prolog [5, 6, 8, 9, 14-17, 22].

Our algorithm relies on Prolog's left-to-right and top-to-bottom execution semantics. However, instead of being allowed to have any value, arguments of predicates are restricted to values which are elements of a small finite set which is constrained to be a *lattice*, i.e. it is partially ordered and every subset has a least upper bound and a greatest lower bound. Each of the elements of the lattice corresponds to an infinite set of possible values in the original program. We call this lattice an *argument lattice* since it is used to represent the value of a predicate argument. We execute the program, constraining variables to lattice values (this is known as *symbolic execution*). If the conditions of abstract interpretation hold, then the least fixed-point of the program's execution over the lattice can be obtained in finite time and is a conservative approximation to the global information, in other words the set of values that a variable can have during execution is a subset of what is derived in the analysis.

In the next section, an example is given to make these ideas concrete and to illustrate the properties of the particular argument lattice we have chosen. This is followed by a description of our entry and exit argument lattices, a discussion of the properties of the lattice elements which simplify the analysis algorithm, and a discussion of our implementation.

5.1. An example of generating an uninitialized variable mode

In this section we show a simple example of the generation of uninitialized variable modes to give an idea of what abstract interpretation does and to introduce our argument lattice. Uninitialized variables are generated whenever the analyzer deduces that an unbound variable cannot be aliased to another. For example, consider the following program fragment:

```
pred(...) :- ..., goal(Z), ...

goal(X) :- X=s(Y), goal(Y).
```

If `Z` is the first occurrence of that variable in the `pred(...)` clause then it is considered a candidate uninitialized variable. This is possible because it is certainly not aliased to any other variable. In the definition of `goal(X)`, if `X` is uninitialized then the argument `Y` of the structure `s(Y)` may be considered uninitialized as well. This `Y` is passed on as an argument to `goal(Y)`. Therefore both calls of `goal(X)` are with an uninitialized argument, so it is consistent to give the argument `X` an uninitialized variable mode.

It may happen that elsewhere in the program there is a call of `goal(X)` where `X` is not uninitialized (for example it may be a compound term, or it may be aliased). In that case, the assumption that `X` is uninitialized is invalidated. This may invalidate assumptions about other arguments of other predicates, so it is necessary to propagate this information. For correctness, it is necessary to iterate until the least fixed-point is reached. At that point symbolic execution of the program does not change any of the derived modes.

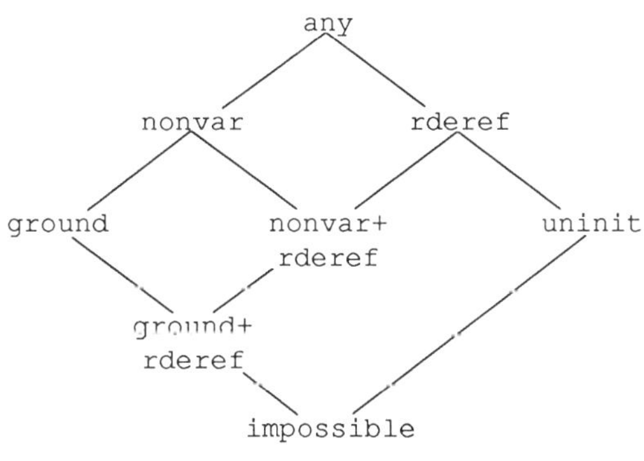

Figure 3 – The Argument Lattice

5.2. The argument lattices

During the analysis our algorithm maintains two lattices for each argument of each predicate in the program. These lattices correspond to the *entry* and *exit* modes of the predicate, i.e. the value of the variable upon entering the predicate and upon successful exit from the predicate. It is understood that the lattice describing the entire program is the product of the predicate lattices, which are themselves products of all the lattices of their arguments. The argument lattice used for entry and exit modes is shown in Figure 3. In this lattice, `any` (the top element) denotes the set of all values, `impossible` (the bottom element) denotes the empty set (i.e. this predicate is unreachable during execution), `uninit` denotes the set of uninitialized variables, `ground` denotes the set of values that are ground, `nonvar` denotes the set of values that are nonvariables, `rderef` denotes the set of values that are recursively dereferenced (i.e. the term is dereferenced, which means that it is accessible without any pointer chasing, and if it is compound then all its arguments are recursively dereferenced), and `ground+rderef` denotes the set of values that are both ground and recursively dereferenced.

The exit lattice differs by one element from the entry lattice: it does not contain `uninit`. This simplifies the design of the analyzer, since to determine that a variable is uninitialized upon exit it would have to determine that there is no execution path inside the predicate on which the variable is used. In practice, a variable that is passed to a predicate is almost always used in some possible execution of the predicate.

5.3. Properties of the lattice elements

The example given above already gives an inkling of the relevant properties of ground, uninitialized, and recursively dereferenced variables that simplify the analysis. Here is a more complete list of these properties:

- The property of being ground, uninitialized, or recursively dereferenced propagates through explicit unifications. The propagation is bidirectional:
  (1) If `X` is ground, uninitialized, or recursively dereferenced, then after executing an explicit unification with a compound term (e.g. `X=s(A,B)`), all of its variables (e.g. `A` and `B`) are ground, all of the new variables (e.g. `A` and `B`) are uninitialized, or all of the new variables are recursively dereferenced.
  (2) In the other direction, if all the variables in the compound term are ground, then `X` is ground. If all the variables are recursively dereferenced, then `X` is recursively dereferenced if it was previously uninitialized or if it is the first occurrence of `X` in the clause.
- The property of being ground is independent of aliasing. For example, if `X` is ground, then it remains ground after executing the unification `X=Y`. This is not true of recursively dereferenced or uninitialized variables.
- An uninitialized variable is not aliased to any other variable. Lattice calculations for uninitialized variables do not affect each other.

5.4. Implementation of the analysis algorithm

The analysis algorithm is written in Prolog as a module in the Aquarius compiler. It accepts an input program in kernel Prolog, along with a set of entry points for the program. It has knowledge of the relevant properties of all Prolog built-in predicates. Integrated in the compiler, it is about 1,200 lines of code. It uses many predicates that are part of the compiler—as a stand-alone program its size would be about 3,200 lines. For efficiency, the fixed-point calculation propagates mode updates according to the algorithm of [16]: in each analysis pass, whenever the exit modes of a goal are changed, then only the predicates which call that goal are symbolically executed in the next pass.

Table 2 – The Benchmarks		
Benchmark	Lines	Description
nreverse	10	Naive reverse of a 30-element list.
tak	15	Recursive integer arithmetic.
qsort	19	Quicksort of a 50-element list.
log10	27	Symbolic differentiation.
ops8	27	Symbolic differentiation.
times10	27	Symbolic differentiation.
divide10	27	Symbolic differentiation.
serialise	29	Calculate serial numbers of a list.
queens_8	31	Solve the eight queens puzzle.
mu	33	Prove a theorem of Hofstadter's ''mu-math''.
zebra	36	A logical puzzle based on constraints.
fast_mu	54	An optimized version of the mu-math prover.
query	68	Query a static database (with integer arithmetic).
poly_10	86	Symbolically raise a polynomial to the tenth power.
crypt	64	Solve a simple cryptarithmetic puzzle.
meta_qsort	74	A meta-interpreter running qsort.
prover	81	A simple theorem prover.
browse	92	Build and query a database.
unify	125	A compiler code generator for unification.
flatten	158	Source transformation to remove disjunctions.
sdda	273	A dataflow analyzer that represents aliasing.
reducer	301	A graph reducer based on combinators.
boyer	377	An extract from a Boyer-Moore theorem prover.
simple_analyzer	443	A dataflow analyzer analyzing qsort.
nand	493	A logic synthesis program based on heuristic search.
chat_parser	1138	Parse a set of English sentences.

In contrast to [22], which uses extension tables to hold mode information about the program during the analysis, our algorithm keeps a table containing only a single mode for each predicate. This results in a loss of information and we intend to determine how much our algorithm will improve with extension tables. Table management is implemented purely logically by means of accumulators, a common technique for applicative programming. An accumulator is a pair of arguments to a predicate that passes the input and output values of a data structure. For example, Prolog's Definite Clause Grammar (DCG) expansion adds one accumulator to each clause. The analyzer has been developed with the aid of a preprocessor that simplifies the use of multiple accumulators [20].

6. Measurements

We have performed three kinds of measurements with the BAM processor simulator. The results of the measurements are given in Tables 4, 5, and 6. Tables 4 and 5 give the effect of dataflow analysis on performance and static code size. Table 6 shows the efficiency of the algorithm by giving the analysis time and the fraction of arguments that get modes. Table 2 describes the benchmarks and their size in lines of code. Table 3 gives the percentage of time that the benchmarks spend executing inside built-in predicates. The benchmarks

Table 3 – Time spent in Built-in Predicates		
Benchmark	Time (%)	Most used built-ins
prover	0	–
meta_qsort	0	–
chat_parser	0	–
nand	<1	–
browse	1	length/2
reducer	40	write/1, compare/3, arg/3
unify	40	arg/3, functor/3, compare/3
crypt	50	div/2, mod/2, */2
boyer	60	arg/3, functor/3
simple_analyzer	70	compare/3, sort/2, arg/3
sdda	70	write/1, =../2, compare/3
flatten	80	write/1, sort/2, compare/3, name/2, functor/3, arg/3

were chosen as examples of realistic programs doing computations representative of Prolog. They are divided into two classes, *small* and *large*, depending on whether the compiled code with analysis is smaller or larger than 1000 words. The benchmarks log10, ops8, times10, and divide10 are grouped together and referred to as *deriv* because they are closely related. The benchmarks are available by anonymous ftp to arpa.berkeley.edu.

Table 3 gives the percentage of time that the large benchmarks spend executing inside built-in predicates. This number does not take into account built-ins that are implemented as in-line code (arithmetic comparison, addition and subtraction, and type checking). The table also gives the most often used built-in predicates for each benchmark in decreasing order of usage. To give an idea how built-ins affect the results of analysis, Table 4 gives two performance averages for the large benchmarks: the first for all programs, and the second for programs that do not use built-ins significantly (the first five of Table 3).

Table 4 gives the execution time in microseconds of the benchmarks for the BAM processor compiled without analysis (No Modes) and with analysis (Auto Modes). Data initialization times are subtracted from deriv, nreverse, qsort, serialise, and prover. For each benchmark we also give the time it spends performing dereferencing (Deref) and trailing (Trail). The last three columns give the ratios of the auto modes to the no modes times. The numbers are obtained from the BAM instruction level simulator and include cache effects [4]. The simulated system has 128 KB instruction and data caches. The caches are direct mapped and use a write-back policy. They are run in warm start: each benchmark is run twice and the results of the first run are ignored. The cache overhead is greatest for poly_10, simple_analyzer, boyer, and the no modes case of tak; for these programs it ranges from 9% to 24%. For meta_qsort, reducer, and chat_parser the overhead ranges from 2% to 3%. For all other programs the overhead is less than 0.5%.

For the small benchmarks we calculate that analysis reduces dereferencing from 17% to 5% of execution time, and trailing from 4% to 0.6% of execution time. This is because they are simple enough that analysis is able to deduce most relevant modes. For the large benchmarks dereferencing is reduced from 11% to

Table 4 – The Effect of Dataflow Analysis on Performance

Benchmark	No Modes (μs)			Auto Modes (μs)			Auto/No Modes		
	Time	Deref	Trail	Time	Deref	Trail	Time	Deref	Trail
deriv	146	18.2	5.5	91.3	0.3	0.1	0.63	0.02	0.02
log10	25.9	2.3	0.7	16.8	0	0			
ops8	28.5	3.3	1.0	18.9	0.3	0.1			
times10	39.7	5.1	1.3	25.7	0	0			
divide10	51.7	7.5	2.5	29.9	0	0			
nreverse	308	79.7	31.1	136	0	0	0.44	0.00	0.00
qsort	378	109	25.1	173	0	0	0.46	0.00	0.00
serialise	512	75.8	12.3	447	44.9	0.7	0.87	0.59	0.05
mu	992	154	48.0	783	139	34.7	0.79	0.90	0.72
fast_mu	1120	148	38.0	932	64.4	7.9	0.83	0.44	0.21
queens_8	1700	271	67.9	1090	33.4	0	0.64	0.12	0.00
query	5180	560	174	3570	0	0	0.69	0.00	0.00
tak	71700	13800	3180	25400	0	0	0.35	0.00	0.00
poly_10	60400	6280	1740	35600	1080	209	0.59	0.17	0.12
zebra	84600	11400	8.6	84100	11400	8.4	0.99	1.00	0.98
average							0.66	0.29	0.19
prover	1070	110	29.4	820	51.2	5.9	0.76	0.47	0.20
unify	1600	198	33.9	1400	138	19.3	0.88	0.69	0.57
flatten	1460	149	9.9	1420	133	6.5	0.97	0.90	0.66
sdda	3180	368	36.9	2940	296	21.3	0.92	0.81	0.58
crypt	4090	319	104	4000	262	104	0.98	0.82	1.00
meta_qsort	5330	674	182	4450	417	63.0	0.83	0.62	0.35
nand	18700	2290	542	13400	902	22.9	0.72	0.39	0.04
simple_analyzer	35400	3880	316	31900	3080	76.2	0.90	0.79	0.24
reducer	48800	6680	1210	44900	5580	731	0.92	0.84	0.61
chat_parser	151000	19400	6990	131000	11200	4360	0.87	0.58	0.62
browse	820000	117000	28600	741000	96700	20400	0.90	0.82	0.71
boyer	1410000	73900	6340	1360000	75000	6270	0.97	1.02	0.99
average							0.89	0.73	0.55
average (no built-ins)							0.82	0.58	0.39

9% and trailing is reduced from 2.3% to 1.3%. These results are less extreme for two reasons: the large benchmarks use built-ins, which are unaffected by analysis, and the analyzer loses information due to its inability to handle aliasing and its limited type domain.

Table 5 gives the static code size (in BAM instructions) for the benchmarks compiled without analysis (No Modes) and with analysis (Auto Modes). The effect of analysis on code size is greater than the effect on performance. This follows from the compiler's implementation of argument selection: when no modes are given, the compiler generates more code to handle arguments of different types. If analysis derives the type then the code becomes much smaller. The code size compares favorably with other symbolic processors, and is low enough that there is no disadvantage to having a simple instruction set. With the analyzer the BAM processor's code size is similar to the KCM [2], about three times the PLM, a micro-coded WAM [10], and about one fourth the SPUR using macro-expanded WAM [3].

Table 6 presents data about the efficiency of the dataflow analyzer. For each benchmark it gives the number of predicate arguments (Args) where a predicate of arity N is counted as N, the number of predicates (Preds), the

Table 5 – The Effect of Dataflow Analysis on Static Code Size			
Benchmark	No Modes (instructions)	Auto Modes (instructions)	Auto/No Modes
tak	80	34	0.42
nreverse	287	139	0.48
queens_8	472	146	0.31
qsort	485	215	0.44
deriv	5891	1123	0.19
log10	1464	272	
ops8	1469	277	
times10	1479	287	
divide10	1479	287	
query	1425	403	0.28
serialise	860	520	0.60
mu	1169	731	0.63
fast_mu	1165	718	0.62
zebra	1271	814	0.64
poly_10	3023	893	0.30
average			0.45
crypt	1239	1027	0.83
browse	1863	1150	0.62
prover	4395	1318	0.30
meta_qsort	2484	1424	0.57
flatten	4267	2335	0.55
unify	6326	4210	0.67
sdda	6526	5031	0.77
simple_analyzer	9057	5836	0.64
nand	23406	6654	0.28
reducer	11726	7682	0.66
boyer	24862	9136	0.37
chat_parser	33557	20516	0.61
average			0.57

analysis time (Time), the fraction of arguments that are uninitialized (uninit), ground (ground), nonvariable (nonvar), or recursively dereferenced (rderef), and the fraction of arguments that have any of these types (any). Analysis time is measured under Quintus release 2.0 on a Sun 3/60. It is roughly proportional to the number of arguments in the program, except for the nand benchmark. The sum of the individual modes columns is usually greater than the any modes column. This is because arguments can have multiple modes—they can be both recursively dereferenced and ground or nonvariable. We see that uninitialized arguments are present in great quantities, even in large programs such as chat_parser and simple_analyzer. Comparing the small and large benchmarks, we see that the fraction of derived modes decreases for each type except nonvariable. For both the small and large benchmarks we find that the compiler transforms one third of the uninitialized modes into uninitialized register modes.

Table 6 – The Efficiency of Dataflow Analysis

Benchmark	Args	Preds	Time (sec)	Modes (fraction of arguments) uninit	ground	nonvar	rderef	any
deriv	12	8	11.9	0.33	0.67	0.00	0.67	1.00
log10	3	2	2.9					
ops8	3	2	3.0					
times10	3	2	3.0					
divide10	3	2	2.9					
tak	4	2	2.3	0.25	0.75	0.00	0.75	1.00
nreverse	5	3	2.2	0.40	0.60	0.00	0.60	1.00
qsort	7	3	3.4	0.43	0.57	0.00	0.57	1.00
query	7	5	4.2	0.86	0.14	0.00	0.14	1.00
zebra	9	5	3.5	0.10	0.00	0.50	0.00	0.60
serialise	16	7	4.2	0.38	0.19	0.06	0.19	0.63
queens_8	16	7	6.0	0.31	0.69	0.00	0.69	1.00
mu	17	8	9.6	0.12	0.47	0.00	0.12	0.65
poly_10	27	11	16	0.33	0.67	0.00	0.67	1.00
fast_mu	35	7	21	0.29	0.55	0.05	0.55	0.89
average				0.35	0.48	0.06	0.45	0.89
meta_qsort	10	7	11	0.30	0.00	0.10	0.00	0.40
crypt	18	9	12	0.00	0.61	0.11	0.56	0.72
prover	22	9	13	0.27	0.09	0.27	0.14	0.68
browse	42	14	20	0.24	0.45	0.05	0.40	0.74
boyer	62	25	31	0.27	0.00	0.06	0.00	0.34
flatten	83	28	34	0.27	0.08	0.16	0.11	0.52
sdda	87	32	45	0.18	0.07	0.17	0.08	0.44
reducer	134	41	50	0.13	0.10	0.05	0.12	0.29
unify	141	29	84	0.18	0.19	0.14	0.21	0.56
nand	180	43	5900	0.26	0.67	0.00	0.28	0.93
simple_analyzer	270	71	77	0.23	0.10	0.08	0.10	0.41
chat_parser	744	156	263	0.44	0.19	0.02	0.09	0.67
average				0.23	0.21	0.10	0.17	0.56

7. Conclusions and further work

We have presented a simple global dataflow analyzer and measured its effect on performance and code size for the BAM processor using the Aquarius compiler. We have also measured the efficiency of the analyzer in terms of its execution time and the percentage of arguments for which types can be deduced. For a representative set of realistic Prolog programs the analyzer is able to find nontrivial modes for 56% of predicate arguments. We measure an average performance improvement of 18% for programs without built-ins and a code size reduction of 43%. Dereferencing is reduced from 11% to 9% and trailing is reduced from 2.3% to 1.3% of the execution time.

There has been much good theoretical work on global analysis for Prolog, but few implementations. Our work shows that a simple dataflow analysis scheme is already quite useful. However, we have imposed many restrictions on its generality to make the implementation practical. As programs become larger, these restrictions limit the quality of the results. We hope the success of our experiment encourages others to relax these restrictions. For example, it would not be too difficult to:

- Extend the domain to represent common types such as integers, proper lists, and nested compound terms. In large programs it seems to be important to be able to look inside of compound terms.
- Extend the domain to represent variable aliasing explicitly.
- Make the analysis more fine-grained by letting the analyzer keep track of the arguments of all goals instead of only predicate arguments.
- Implement other compiler optimizations that rely on analysis such as compile-time garbage collection (replace copying of compound terms by destructive assignment) and multiple specialization (make separate copies of a predicate called in several places with different modes).
- Study the interaction between programming style and the effectiveness of analysis.

Acknowledgements

We wish to thank all the members of the BAM project, in particular Bruce Holmer for BAM software development and his many perceptive comments, Ralph Haygood for the Prolog built-ins and his untiring hunt after superfluous choice points, and Mike Carlton for the BAM and MIPS translators and the cache simulator. We also thank Ashok Singhal for his constructive comments. This work is partially funded by the Defense Advanced Research Projects Agency (DARPA) and monitored by the Office of Naval Research under contract No. N00014-88-K-0579. Equipment and other support for the project has been provided by SUN, DEC, ESL, and Xenologic.

References

1. J. Beer, The Occur-Check Problem Revisited, *Journal of Logic Programming Vol. 5*, 3 (Sept. 1988), pp 243-261.
2. H. Benker, J. M. Beacco, S. Bescos, M. Dorochevsky, T. Jeffre, A. Pohimann, J. Noye, B. Poterie, A. Sexton, J. C. Syre, O. Thibault and G. Watzlawik, KCM: A Knowledge Crunching Machine, *16th International Symposium on Computer Architecture*, May 1989, pp 186-194.
3. G. Borriello, A. Cherenson, P. Danzig and M. Nelson, RISCs vs. CISCs for Prolog: A Case Study, *2nd International Conference on Architectural Support for Programming Languages and Operating Systems (ASPLOS II)*, October 1987, pp 136-145.
4. M. Carlton, J. Pendleton, B. Sano, B. K. Holmer and A. M. Despain, Cache & Multiprocessor Support in the BAM Microprocessor, *4th Annual Parallel Processing Conference*, April 1990.
5. J. Chang and A. M. Despain, Semi-Intelligent Backtracking of Prolog Based on A Static Data Dependency Analysis, *2nd Symposium on Logic Programming*, July 1985.
6. W. V. Citrin, Parallel Unification Scheduling in Prolog, Computer Science Dpt. Report No. 88/415, UC Berkeley, April 1988.

7. P. Cousot and R. Cousot, Abstract Interpretation: A Unified Lattice Model for Static Analysis of Programs by Construction or Approximation of Fixpoints, *4th Symposium on Principles of Programming Languages*, January 1977, pp 238-252.

8. S. K. Debray and D. S. Warren, Automatic Mode Inference for Prolog Programs, *Third Symposium on Logic Programming*, 1986, pp 78-87.

9. S. K. Debray, Static Analysis of Parallel Logic Programs, *5th International Conference on Logic Programming*, August 1988, pp 711-732.

10. T. P. Dobry, *A High Performance Architecture for Prolog*, Kluwer Academic Publishers, 1990.

11. B. K. Holmer, B. Sano, M. Carlton, P. Van Roy, R. Haygood, J. M. Pendleton, T. Dobry, W. R. Bush and A. M. Despain, Fast Prolog with an Extended General Purpose Architecture, *17th International Symposium on Computer Architecture*, May 1990.

12. D. Jacobs and A. Langen, Accurate and Efficient Approximation of Variable Aliasing in Logic Programs, *North American Conference on Logic Programming '89*, October 1989, pp 154-165.

13. G. Kildall, A Unified Approach to Global Program Optimization, *Symposium on Principles of Programming Languages*, January 1973, pp 194-206.

14. C. S. Mellish, *Automatic Generation of Mode Declarations for Prolog Programs (Draft)*, Department of Artificial Intelligence, University of Edinburgh, August 1981.

15. C. S. Mellish, Some Global Optimizations for a Prolog Compiler, *Journal of Logic Programming Vol. 1* (1985), pp 43-66.

16. R. A. O'Keefe, Finite Fixed-Point Problems, *4th International Conference on Logic Programming Vol. 2* (May 1987), pp 729-743, MIT Press.

17. A. Taylor, Removal of Dereferencing and Trailing in Prolog Compilation, *6th International Conference on Logic Programming*, June 1989, pp 48-60.

18. A. Taylor, LIPS on a MIPS: Results from a Prolog Compiler for a RISC, *7th International Conference on Logic Programming*, June 1990.

19. P. Van Roy, An Intermediate Language to Support Prolog's Unification, *North American Conference on Logic Programming '89*, October 1989, pp 1148-1164.

20. P. Van Roy, A Useful Extension to Prolog's Definite Clause Grammar notation, *SIGPLAN Notices Vol. 24*, 11 (November 1989), pp 132-134.

21. D. H. D. Warren, An Abstract Prolog Instruction Set, Technical Note 309, SRI International Artificial Intelligence Center, October 1983.

22. R. Warren, M. Hermenegildo and S. K. Debray, On the Practicality of Global Flow Analysis of Logic Programs, *Fifth International Conference and Symposium on Logic Programming*, August 1988, pp 684-699.

An Algebraic Framework for Abstract Interpretation of Definite Programs

R.S.Kemp and G.A.Ringwood*
Department of Computing
Imperial College
LONDON SW7 2BZ
rsk@doc.ic.ac.uk
gar@doc.ic.ac.uk

Abstract

A general algebraic framework for the abstract interpretation of logic programs, is formulated using partial orders and lattices of tuples of atoms quotiented by variance. This is motivated by a natural extension of the Herbrand semantics of logic programs which incorporates the logic variable. A general method for constructing an abstract domain within the framework is presented and used to give a formal synthesis of Bruynooghe's practical method of abstract interpretation.

1 Introduction

It is claimed that abstract interpretation of programs holds the promise of providing static information about the run-time behaviour of a computation for use by compilers, partial evaluators and debuggers or for program documentation. The archetype rule of signs abstraction of real number multiplication (e.g. [Abramsky & Hankin 1987]) is intuitive and appealing and the example, seems, superficially at least, to be readily generalisable to applicative programs. However, for logic programs abstract interpretation is more difficult and can appear ad hoc.

According to its originators [Cousot & Cousot 1977], an abstract interpretation of a programming language is the homomorphic image of its standard semantics on another (usually simpler) domain. The "standard" semantics of logic programs could be said to be model theoretic but it is not easily apparent how an abstract semantics may be realised from such a concrete semantics. The fact that attention can be restricted to Herbrand models does not help very much since these only include ground terms and so dynamic properties involving variables, such as modes or variable aliasing, cannot be expressed. The logic variable, so crucial to the operational semantics of logic programs, does not explicitly appear in the standard Herbrand model semantics. The fixed point semantics of logic programs, e.g. [Emden & Kowalski 1976] is no better for the same reason.

*Current address: Dept. of Computing, Queen Mary and Westfield College, Mile End Rd, London, E1 4NS

The proof theoretic (operational) semantics of logic programs depend on variable substitutions. For the purpose of abstract interpretation Jones and Sondergaard [1987] adapted denotational semantics for Prolog, with environments capturing the bindings of the logic variables. This is not altogether satisfactory as denotational semantics was designed to give meaning to third generation procedural languages and as such is not particularly sympathetic to the model theoretic or fixed point semantics of logic programming. It is this denotational semantics which [Bruynooghe 1989] appears to appeal to in his practical exposition of abstract interpretation for logic programs.

Following [Clark 1979], Falaschi et al. [1988] give a model theoretic and fixed point semantics for logic programs which better captures the operational role of the logic variable. These semantics holds the promise of a better compromise between the requirements of abstract interpretation and the "standard" semantics of logic programming. The present paper develops a lattice-theoretic framework for the abstract interpretation of logic programs based on the work of Falaschi et al.

Section 2 reformulates and extends [Falaschi et al. 1988, 1989], to provide a concrete semantics, implicitly embodying logic variables, which is abstracted in the following sections. The reformulation is purely algebraic being described in terms of a lattice and, after preliminary definitions, avoids any need to explicitly refer to variable substitutions. In Section 3, a method of constructing abstract domains from relevant subsets of a concrete semantics is given. To justify the usefulness of this framework, in Section 4 a reformulation of Bruynooghe's method of abstract interpretation [Bruynooghe 1989] is attempted, in lattice theoretic terms, as an abstraction of the semantics in Section 2.

2 The Concrete Semantics

The formal description of abstract interpretation requires both a concrete semantics, defining the meaning of programs, and an abstract semantics, in some sense approximating the concrete semantics. The soundness or completeness of the abstract semantics is established with respect to the concrete semantics, by showing that the abstract semantics consistently underestimates or overestimates the concrete semantics. In this section, a concrete algebraic semantics for logic programs is developed, based on [Falaschi et al. 1988], using an instantiation partial order on tuples of atoms; unification is replaced by a join operation and variable substitutions become implicit.

As is usual, TERMS will denote the set of all finite structures composed of functors, constants and variables from the first-order language L generated by a logic program W, and ATOMS = $\{p(t_1,..,t_j,..,t_n)|$ p is an n-ary predicate symbol, $t_j \in$ TERMS$\}$. [Lloyd 1987] will be the default reference for any concepts not explained herein. Define a relation $\sqsubseteq_1$ on ATOMS such that $p \sqsubseteq_1 q$ if q can be formed from p by replacing all occurrences of a single variable from p by a single element of TERMS not containing that variable. If $\sqsubseteq_\infty$ is the transitive closure of $\sqsubseteq_1$, it embodies the usual notion of instance: $p \sqsubseteq_\infty q$ if q is an instance of p. Taking the transitive closure allows any number of variables to be substituted and also gives reflexivity.

It can be shown that $(\text{ATOMS}, \sqsubseteq_\infty)$ is a preorder and from it an equivalence relation can be defined. For atoms p and q, the relation $p \sim q$ will be said to hold if $p \sqsubseteq_\infty q$ and $q \sqsubseteq_\infty p$; this relation embodies the notion of variance. The quotient space of atoms by the variance relation, $\text{ATOMS}/\sim$, will be used as an extended Herbrand Base and denoted by EB. The ground instances of EB form the standard Herbrand Base. The relation $\sqsubseteq_\infty$ on ATOMS generates a partial order $\sqsubseteq \equiv (\sqsubseteq_\infty / \sim)$ on EB. In this way variance has been factored out and the usual renaming of variables which needs to be done when using substitutions is implicit in the formalism.

If $p \in \text{ATOMS}$, the equivalence class with respect to variance of which p is representative will be denoted by [p]. With $[p], [q] \in \text{EB}$, the equivalence class lub$\{[p],[q]\}$, with respect to the partial order $\sqsubseteq$, is the equivalence class of the most general common instance of p and q. This corresponds to unification in the standard formulation of logic programming [Lloyd 1987] when the variables of p and q are standardised apart.

In what follows, it will be necessary to represent goals, clauses and proof trees in the form of (nested) tuples of atoms, and to this end a new set of variables over tuples is introduced. Let V_{expr} be a set of variables ranging over ATOMS and tuples of ATOMS, i.e. distinct from those variables in terms. Now, inductively define the set expr of expressions by $\langle\rangle \in$ expr, $\text{ATOMS} \cup V_{expr} \subseteq$ expr and if $s_1, .., s_n \in$ expr then $\langle s_1, .., s_n\rangle \in$ expr. Tuples can be regarded like functors but with atomic and tuple arguments, i.e. $\langle s_1, .., s_n\rangle \equiv \langle\rangle(s_1, .., s_n)$. In this way the previous instantiation ordering on ATOMS carries over to nested tuples of ATOMS. V_{expr} was introduced so that the variable arguments of tuples can only be substituted by atoms and tuples (i.e. not terms). Now let EXPR denote the quotient set with respect to variance of expr over both term variables and tuple variables, i.e. $\text{EXPR} = (\text{expr}/\sim)$. If s belongs to expr, the equivalence class with respect to variance of which s is a representative will be denoted by $[s]$ as before; likewise, using the same notation as before, the instantiation preorder $\sqsubseteq_\infty$ induces a partial order $\sqsubseteq$ on EXPR. When appropriate, $[s_1] \sqsubseteq [s_2]$ will be written as $[s_2] \sqsupseteq [s_1]$.

The addition of a top element to EXPR makes it into a complete lattice. The following standard theorem [Birkhoff 1967] from lattice theory is used in the proof of this result and it will also be assumed in later sections.

Theorem 1 *If $(R, \trianglelefteq)$ is a poset in which* glb S *exists for all non-empty $S \subseteq R$ and there is a top element $\top \in R$ then $(R, \trianglelefteq)$ is a complete lattice.*

Definition Let $(R, \trianglelefteq)$ be a poset and $S \subseteq R$. If $\forall s \in S\ \forall r \in R\ r \trianglelefteq s \Rightarrow r \in S$ then S will be called a *lower-closed* subset of R. Upper-closed can be defined in a corresponding fashion.

Proposition 1 *Let Q be a lower closed subset of* EXPR *with respect to $\sqsubseteq$. Then $(Q \cup \{\top\}, \sqsubseteq)$, where $\top$ is an added top element, is a complete lattice.*

The proof of this proposition depends on *size*, a monotone mapping from (EXPR, $\sqsubseteq$) to the natural numbers with their usual ordering. The image of size is the number of tuple, functor and constant symbols (a tuple considered as a functor) appearing in any representative of the equivalence class, with repeated symbols counted once for each occurrence. If $e_1 \sqsubseteq e_2$ then size$(e_1) \leq$ size(e_2). Proofs are omitted in this paper but will appear elsewhere in an extended report [Kemp & Ringwood 1990b].

Corollary 1 (EXPR $\cup \{\top\}, \sqsubseteq$) *is a complete lattice.*

The bottom element of (EXPR $\cup \{\top\}, \sqsubseteq$) is $\bot = V_{expr}$, the equivalence class of expression variables. Define a join operation on (EXPR $\cup \{\top\}, \sqsubseteq$) by $e_1 \sqcup e_2 = \text{lub}\{e_1, e_2\}$. Unique atomic variables will be written as an underscore (_) analogous to the Prolog anonymous term variable, i.e. $[\langle \_, \_ \rangle]$ stands for $[\langle \rho, \xi \rangle]$, not $[\langle \rho, \rho \rangle]$, with $\rho, \xi \in V_{expr}$. As an extension of notation, given $[s_1], .., [s_n] \in$ EXPR, the tuple $\langle [s_1], .., [s_n] \rangle$ will be used as an abbreviation for $[\langle s_1, \_, .., \_ \rangle] \sqcup [\langle \_, s_2, \_, .., \_ \rangle] \sqcup .. \sqcup [\langle \_, .., \_, s_n \rangle]$. In view of the explicit use of $[\cdot]$ to distinguish quotient sets there is no ambiguity in this notation.

Projection onto the arguments of tuples induces a mapping from one equivalence class to another. For example, $\{\langle s_1, .., s_{j-1}, s_{j+1}, .., s_q \rangle | \langle s_1, .., s_j, .., s_q \rangle \in [\langle s_1, .., s_q \rangle]\} = [\langle s_1, .., s_{j-1}, s_{j+1}, .., s_q \rangle]$. Likewise, 'lifting' a tuple by inserting a unique atomic variable at a particular argument position in a tuple induces an injection from one equivalence class to another.

The complete lattice (EXPR $\cup \{\top\}, \sqsubseteq$) is the framework for concrete semantics on which this paper builds. Using this basis, the usual Herbrand model and fixed-point semantics of logic programs can be extended to a Herbrand Base containing non-ground atoms.

Definition The *extended Herbrand Base* of a first-order language L generated by a logic program W is EB $=$ (ATOMS$/\sim$) $\subseteq$ EXPR. Furthermore, denote $\text{EB}_n = ((\text{ATOMS}^n)/\sim) \subseteq$ EXPR for $n > 0$.

Using EB, [Falaschi et al. 1988] redefines the usual machinery of logic programming: models, the T operator, etc. This is reformulated below in terms of the lattice over EXPR.

Definition An *extended Herbrand interpretation*, EI, is a subset of EB.

Definition An extended Herbrand interpretation, EM, is an *extended model* for a set of definite clauses, W, if it is an extended model for every clause in W and EM is an *extended model* for:

- a unit clause $h \leftarrow$ in W if $[h] \in$ EM
- a non-unit clause $h \leftarrow b_1, .., b_n$ in W if
  $\forall [b'_1], .., [b'_n] \in \text{EM}, \forall [\langle h'', b''_1, .., b''_n \rangle] \in \text{EB}_{n+1}$
  $[\langle h'', b''_1, .., b''_n \rangle] = \langle [\_], [b'_1], .., [b'_n] \rangle \sqcup [\langle h, b_1, .., b_n \rangle] \Rightarrow [h''] \in \text{EM}$

If, for $S \subseteq$ EB, gi(S) denotes the subset of EB consisting of all singleton sets which are ground instances of elements of the sets of S then this extension can be related to the standard meaning of model in terms of ground instances as follows:

Proposition 2 *If W is a set of definite clauses then W has an extended model. Furthermore, if* EM *is such an extended Herbrand model for W then* gi(EM) *is a model for W in the standard sense.*

Theorem 2 *Let W be a set of definite clauses then there exists an extended minimal Herbrand model, EMM, which is the intersection of all extended Herbrand models for W.*

The significance of the variables in the extended Herbrand Base can be seen from the next theorem.

Theorem 3 *Let W be a set of definite clauses with minimal model EMM. For all $[a] \in EB$, $W \models \forall a$ (universal quantification over all variables of a) iff $\exists [a'] \in EMM\ [a'] \sqsubseteq [a]$.*

Corollary 2 *Let W be a set of definite clauses with minimal model EMM then* gi(*EMM*) *is the standard minimal model.*

Let $S \subseteq$ EB, then an extended T operator, ET:$2^{EB} \rightarrow 2^{EB}$, can be defined by

$$\begin{aligned} \mathrm{ET}(S) \quad = \quad & \{[h''] \in \mathrm{EB} \mid h \leftarrow b_1, .., b_n \in W,\ [b'_1], .., [b'_n] \in S, \\ & [\langle h'', b''_1, .., b''_n \rangle] = \langle [\_], [b'_1], .., [b'_n] \rangle \sqcup [\langle h, b_1, .., b_n \rangle]\} \end{aligned}$$

As with the standard T operator, it can be shown that ET is monotonic and continuous. Then, again as with the standard theory:

Theorem 4 *Let W be a set of definite clauses and* EI *an extended Herbrand interpretation then* EI *is an extended model for W iff* ET(EI) $\subseteq$ EI

Theorem 5 lfp(ET) *exists and* lfp(ET) $= \bigcup_{n \geq 0} \mathrm{ET}^n(\emptyset)$

Theorem 6 *Let W be a set of definite clauses with minimal extended Herbrand model EMM then EMM* = lfp(ET).

The resolvent of a goal $G \equiv [\langle a_1, .., a_k, .., a_m \rangle]$, represented as a tuple, with a clause $\langle h, b_1, .., b_q \rangle$ can be defined as $G' \equiv [\langle a'_1, .., a'_{k-1}, b'_1, .., b'_q, a'_{k+1}, .., a'_m \rangle]$ where $[\langle a'_1, .., a'_{k-1}, a'_k, b'_1, .., b'_q, a'_{k+1}, .., a'_m \rangle] = [\langle a_1, .., a_{k-1}, a_k, \_, .., \_ a_{k+1}, .., a_m \rangle] \sqcup [\langle \_, .., \_, h, b_1, .., b_q, \_, .., \_ \rangle]$ for some argument k. This representation can be modified to represent proof trees, derivations and hence refutations.

Definition A *(partial) proof tree* is either of the form $[\langle h, \_ \rangle]$ or $[\langle h, \langle\rangle \rangle]$ where $h \in$ ATOMS $\cup \{\langle\rangle\}$, or is of the form $[\langle h, \langle \langle b'_1, s_1 \rangle, .., \langle b'_k, s_k \rangle \rangle \rangle]$ where

$[\langle b'_1, s_1\rangle], .., [\langle b'_k, s_k\rangle]$ are partial proof trees, $h \leftarrow b_1, .., b_k$ is a program clause and $[\langle h, b_1, .., b_k\rangle] \sqsubseteq [\langle h', b'_1, .., b'_k\rangle]$.

Leaf nodes of the form $[\langle h, \_\rangle]$ will be said to be *open* and those of the form $[\langle h, \langle\rangle\rangle]$ to be *closed.* A proof tree is *complete* if all its leaves are closed. The *frontier* of a proof tree is the equivalence class of the tuple of atoms labelling open leaves, taken in left to right order.

The *extension* of a proof tree $[s]$ with an open leaf by a clause represented as a proof tree $[\langle h, \langle\langle b_1, \_\rangle, .., \langle b_n, \_\rangle\rangle\rangle]$ is $[s] \sqcup [s']$ where $[s']$ is a tree of the same shape as $[s]$ with all nodes, except the leaf to be expanded, replaced by the anonymous atomic variable and with the subtree rooted at the open leaf replaced by the clause.

Example The proof tree

$$[s] = [\langle p, \langle\langle q_1, \_\rangle, .., \langle q_m, \_\rangle\rangle\rangle]$$

has the frontier $[\langle q_1, .., q_m\rangle]$ and an extension of the tree at q_1 by the clause $[\langle h, \langle\langle b_1, \_\rangle, .., \langle b_n, \_\rangle\rangle\rangle]$ is $[s] \sqcup [s']$ where

$$[s'] = [\langle \_, \langle\langle h, \langle\langle b_1, \_\rangle, .., \langle b_n, \_\rangle\rangle\rangle, \langle \_, \_\rangle, .., \langle \_, \_\rangle\rangle\rangle]$$

Thus the extension of a proof tree is also a proof tree and extending with a unit clause will produce a closed leaf.

By definition the extension, $[s'']$, of a proof tree, $[s]$, is an instance of the original, i.e. $[s] \sqsubseteq [s'']$, and the familiar concept of derivation as a sequence of goals can be defined in terms of a consecutive sequence of frontiers.

Definition Let $[s]$ be a proof tree with frontier $[\langle b_1, .., b_n\rangle]$ and the frontier of an extension of $[s]$ using a clause C be $[\langle b'_1, .., b'_q\rangle]$. Then $[\langle b'_1, .., b'_q\rangle]$ is said to be *derived* from $[\langle b_1, .., b_n\rangle]$ using C. $[\langle b'_1, .., b'_q\rangle]$ is called the *resolvent* of $[\langle b_1, .., b_q\rangle]$ and C.

Definition Let G be the goal $[\langle a_1, .., a_m\rangle]$. A *refutation of length n* for G is then a sequence of clauses $C_0, .., C_{n-1}$, of goals $G = G_0, .., G_n = [\langle\rangle]$ and of proof trees $[s_0], .., [s_n]$ where G_j is the frontier of $[s_j]$, $[s_0] = [\langle\langle\rangle, \langle\langle a_1, \_\rangle, .., \langle a_m, \_\rangle\rangle\rangle]$, $[s_{j+1}]$ is an extension of $[s_j]$ using C_j, and $[s_n]$ is complete. If $[s_n]$ is $[\langle\langle\rangle, \langle\langle a'_1, s'_1\rangle, .., \langle a'_m, s'_m\rangle\rangle\rangle]$ then $[\langle a'_1, .., a'_m\rangle]$ is an instance of G called the *refuted instance.*

As G is the frontier of $[s_0]$, a refutation is, as usual, a derivation of the empty clause. With the definition of refuted instance:

Theorem 7 (Strong Soundness and Completeness)
Let W be a set of definite clauses and G be the goal $[\langle a_1, .., a_n\rangle]$. *G has a refutation with refuted instance* $[\langle a'_1, .., a'_n\rangle] \in EB_n$ *iff there exist* $[b_1], .., [b_n] \in$ *EMM such that* $[\langle a'_1, .., a'_n\rangle] = [\langle a_1, .., a_n\rangle] \sqcup \langle [b_1], .., [b_n]\rangle$

3 Abstract Domains

An abstract domain is informally viewed as a collection of subsets of a concrete domain. Building on the previous section, an abstract algebraic semantics is constructed by considering subsets of EXPR rather than the more usual 'abstract substitutions' in [Jones & Sondergaard 1987], [Mellish 1987], [Kanamori et al. 1989]. A mechanism for the construction of abstract domains is given together with an example of a domain for type inference.

The natural extension of the join operator $\sqcup$ (most general common instance) on EXPR to subsets of EXPR is

$$\mathrm{E}_1 \sqcup \mathrm{E}_2 = \{e_1 \sqcup e_2 \mid e_1 \in \mathrm{E}_1, e_2 \in \mathrm{E}_2\},$$

However $\sqcup$ fails to be a join operation because, in general, it is not idempotent ($\mathrm{E} \not\equiv \mathrm{E} \sqcup \mathrm{E}$). It will usually be the case that not all elements of 2^{EXPR} will be considered as abstractions. Let $\mathcal{S}_0$ be a subset of 2^{EXPR} that is initially of interest as abstractions. For purposes that will become clear later, $\mathcal{S}_0$ will be assumed to include the empty set, $\emptyset$, and $\bigcup \mathcal{S}_0$. Define $\mathcal{S}_1 = \{\rho(\mathrm{s}) \mid \mathrm{s} \in \mathcal{S}_0\}$ where

$$\rho(\mathrm{s}) = \{\sqcup \mathrm{s}' \mid \mathrm{s}' \subseteq \mathrm{s}, \mathrm{s}' \neq \emptyset\}$$

is a closure operation (extensive, monotonic, idempotent) [Birkhoff 1967]. For example, $\rho(\{[p(a,x)], [q(a,x)], [p(y,b)]\}) = \{[p(a,x)], [q(a,x)], [p(y,b)], [p(a,b)]\}$. The closure operator ρ expands the sets of interest so as to include all factors. In this way, the operator $\sqcup$ becomes idempotent on $\mathcal{S}_1$.

For abstract interpretation, it will be necessary to combine the abstractions which arise from different derivations but $\mathcal{S}_1$ will not in general be closed under union. So that the abstractions become an overestimate (rather than an underestimate), $\mathcal{S}_1$ is further closed under intersection. Define the abstract domain $\mathcal{AD} = \{\cap \mathcal{S}' \mid \mathcal{S}' \subseteq \mathcal{S}_1\}$. $\mathcal{AD}$ is a Moore family (a collection of subsets, closed under intersection and including their union) and hence a complete lattice with a join operation

$$\mathrm{A}_1 \cup^{\#} \mathrm{A}_2 = \cap\{\mathrm{A} \in \mathcal{AD} \mid (\mathrm{A}_1 \cup \mathrm{A}_2) \subseteq \mathrm{A}\}$$

and with $\emptyset$ and $\bigcup \mathcal{S}_0$ as top and bottom elements. $\cup^{\#}$ is an approximation to $\cup$ but the advantage of closure under intersection, rather than under union, is that it preserves the closure under factoring (ρ) [Birkhoff 1967] so that $\sqcup$ is idempotent on $\mathcal{AD}$.

However, $\mathcal{AD}$ is not closed under $\sqcup$ and, in general, further closure under $\sqcup$ will destroy closure under $\cap$. For this reason, an approximation $\sqcup^{\#}$ to $\sqcup$, similar to the previous approximation to union, will be defined:

$$\mathrm{A}_1 \sqcup^{\#} \mathrm{A}_2 = \cap\{\mathrm{A} \in \mathcal{AD} \mid (\mathrm{A}_1 \sqcup \mathrm{A}_2) \subseteq \mathrm{A}\}$$

Extending previous terminology, $\mathrm{A}_1 \sqcup^{\#} \mathrm{A}_2$ will be called an abstract instance of A_1 and A_2. Although $\sqcup^{\#}$ is idempotent and commutative it is not associative. Optionally, to achieve a finer-grained abstract domain, $\mathcal{S}_1$ can be closed under $\sqcup$ prior to closure under intersection, i.e. $\mathcal{S}_2 = \{\bigsqcup \mathcal{S}' \mid \mathcal{S}' \subseteq \mathcal{S}_1, \mathcal{S}' \neq \emptyset\}$ and then $\mathcal{AD} = \{\bigcap \mathcal{S}' \mid \mathcal{S}' \subseteq \mathcal{S}_2, \mathcal{S}' \neq \emptyset\}$.

In this way $(\mathcal{AD}, \subseteq, \cup^{\#}, \cap)$ is constructed to be a complete lattice and $\sqcup^{\#}$ gives a safe abstraction (overestimate) of $\sqcup$ on EXPR. Note that for some $\mathcal{S}_0$ $\sqcup^{\#}$ will be identical to $\sqcup$, e.g. if $\mathcal{S}_0 = 2^{\text{EB}}$ then, as noted above, Debray has shown that $(\mathcal{S}_1, \sqcup^{\#})$ is a complete lattice but ρ is a closure operation and so $\mathcal{S}_1$ forms a Moore family. [Debray 1989] has shown that subsets of the powerset can be constructed on which $\sqcup$ is idempotent and indeed is the join operation for a lattice. For the present purposes, a second ordering is also required and Debray's construction cannot be used here.

By construction the abstract domain is a subset of 2^{EXPR}, so the concretisation map for the abstraction is a restriction of the identity on 2^{EXPR} and the abstraction map $\alpha : 2^{\text{EXPR}} \to \mathcal{AD}$, is given by $\alpha(\text{s}) = \cap\{\text{A} \in \mathcal{AD} \mid \text{s} \subseteq \text{A}\}$.

In the following section α will often be applied to a singleton set but, abusing notation, the enclosing set braces will be omitted. In addition, abstractions of the projections and lifts noted in Section 2 will also be needed in the following section and are defined here for convenience. Projection of an abstract tuple onto its j'th argument, $\pi_j^{\#} : \mathcal{AD} \to \mathcal{AD}$, will be defined by

$$\pi_j^{\#}(\text{A}) = \cup^{\#}\{\alpha([s_j]) \mid [\langle s_1, .., s_j, .., s_m \rangle] \in \text{A}\}$$

and the lift function $\lambda_{j,m}^{\#} : \mathcal{AD} \to \mathcal{AD}$ injects an element of EXPR as the j'th argument of an m-tuple

$$\lambda_{j,m}^{\#}(\text{A}) = \cup^{\#}\{\alpha(\langle [s_1], .., [s_j], .., [s_m] \rangle) \mid s_k \in V_{expr}, k \neq j, [s_j] \in \text{A}\}$$

Example The following lattice of types (viewed as subsets of TERMS) can be used to generate $\mathcal{S}_0$, the sets of interest:

$$\begin{aligned} any &= \text{TERMS} \\ list &= nil \mid any.list \\ plist &= nil \mid any.any \\ int &= 0 \mid succ(int) \end{aligned}$$

where '.' is the binary infix list constructor.

Any term of type *list* is also of type *plist* and every term is of type *any* or viewed as a set of terms, *list* is a subset of *plist* is a subset of *any*. The notion of type extends to atoms (two atoms are of the same type if predicate names are identical and corresponding arguments are of the same type) and nested tuples of atoms. These type subsets form a cover of EXPR; add the empty set and EXPR and call it $\mathcal{S}_0$.

There is nothing in principle requiring that the same type abstractions apply to all arguments of all the atoms of all tuples. For example, it might be advantageous to use finer-grained abstractions for the first argument of an atom because of clause indexing. However, for the sake of illustration this will be assumed not to be the case. In the preceding example, every member of $\mathcal{S}_0$ is already closed wrt ρ, so $\mathcal{S}_1 = \mathcal{S}_0$. In fact closure under $\sqcup$ is unnecessary and it is already closed under intersection, so $\mathcal{AD} = \mathcal{S}_2 = \mathcal{S}_1$. The reason why $\mathcal{S}_0$, $\mathcal{S}_1$, $\mathcal{S}_2$ coincide is that the elements of $\mathcal{S}_0$ are upper-closed in $(\text{EXPR} \cup \{\top\}, \sqsubseteq)$.

4 Formalisation of Bruynooghe's Abstract Interpretation

To show the usefulness of the formalism, this section gives an algebraic presentation of the practical abstract interpretation procedure of [Bruynooghe 1989] which generates a finite abstract AND-OR tree representing all possible proof trees of a given query. Bruynooghe effectively associates sets of input and output substitutions, abstract substitutions, with the nodes of the tree. The following algebraic formulation captures the essentials of Bruynooghe's method by associating abstractions of clause instances with each node.

For this section, the program W will be assumed to consist of n clauses C_j^m, for $j \in [1..n]$ where $C_j^m = [\langle h_j, \langle b_{j,1}, ..b_{j,m_j}\rangle\rangle] \in \text{EXPR}$. Occasionally, m_j will also be used to denote the number of body goals of the j'th clause. The operators and orderings defined in the previous section will be assumed and the top and bottom elements of the 'safety' ordering ($\subseteq$) will be written $\top_\subseteq, \bot_\subseteq$ respectively. The abstract domain is further assumed to be over $(\bigcup_{n>0}(\text{ATOMS} \cup V_{expr})^n)/\sim$, i.e. as mentioned in the previous section $\bigcup \mathcal{S}_0 = (\bigcup_{n>0}(\text{ATOMS} \cup V_{expr})^n)/\sim$. AND-OR trees are defined as follows.

Definition Denote $\text{ORTREE}_0 = \{\top_\preceq, \bot_\preceq\}$ and $\text{ANDTREE}_0 = \emptyset$. For $k > 0$,

$$\text{let } \text{ORTREE}_k = \text{ORTREE}_{k-1} \cup \{ \langle A_{in}, \langle R_1, .., R_j, .., R_n\rangle\rangle \mid A_{in} \in \mathcal{AD}, R_j \in \text{ANDTREE}_k\}$$
$$\text{and } \text{ANDTREE}_k = \text{ANDTREE}_{k-1} \cup \{ \langle A_{out}, \langle T_1, .., T_j, .., T_m\rangle\rangle \mid A_{out} \in \mathcal{AD}, T_j \in \text{ORTREE}_{k-1}\}$$

Then let $\text{ORTREE} = \bigcup_{k\geq 0} \text{ORTREE}_k$ and $\text{ANDTREE} = \bigcup_{k>0} \text{ANDTREE}_k$.

It is possible by selecting one child of each OR node to reconstruct a (partial) proof tree. This is done by traversing the AND-OR tree (perhaps partially), at each OR node selecting a clause instance belonging to the abstract call instance at that node or an exit instance from one of the child AND nodes. At each OR node, traverse just one of the children; at each AND node traverse each child node from left to right. In this way an AND-OR tree represents many (usually infinitely many) proof trees.

Based on the safety ordering of $\mathcal{AD}$, the ordering on ORTREE, promised earlier, can be defined whereby trees that are greater in the ordering represent more proof trees (or more complete ones) than lesser trees. It will be convenient to use the same relation symbol for orders on both ORTREE and ANDTREE.

Definition Define $\preceq$ on ORTREE and ANDTREE by

- $\forall T \in \text{ORTREE} \;\; \bot_\preceq \preceq T$

- $\forall T \in$ ORTREE $T \preceq \top_{\preceq}$
- for $R = \langle A, \langle T_1, .., T_m\rangle\rangle$, $R' = \langle A', \langle T'_1, .., T'_m\rangle\rangle \in$ ANDTREE
  $R \preceq R'$ iff $A \subseteq A'$ and for $j \in [1..m]$ $T_j \preceq T'_j$
- for $T = \langle A, \langle R_1, .., R_n\rangle\rangle$, $T' = \langle A', \langle R'_1, .., R'_n\rangle\rangle \in$ ORTREE
  $T \preceq T'$ iff $A \subseteq A'$ and for $j \in [1..m]$ $R_j \preceq R'_j$

Given that each AND-OR tree represents a set of partial proof trees, it should not be a surprise that ORTREE is a complete lattice. The top element, $\top_{\preceq}$, is then an abstraction of all proof trees.

Theorem 8 (ORTREE, $\preceq$) *is a complete lattice.*

Next are presented a set of mutually recursive functions that incrementally build an AND-OR tree. The top level function Query maps from an abstraction of a single atomic goal to an AND-OR tree and is defined in terms of a function that maps from one AND-OR tree to another identical except for having each leaf OR node extended, where possible, and also having abstract values propagated within the tree. For queries with finite AND-OR trees (e.g. not using recursive predicates) the functions will eventually not be able to extend the tree further and it will reach a fixed point; the value of Query is precisely this fixed point. Although the results are defined in terms of a fixed-point they approximate the top-down execution (operational semantics). Bruynooghe has a simple scheme for representing indefinitely large proof trees as AND-OR trees of a fixed maximum size and the changes necessary for this are given at the end of the section.

Query : $\mathcal{AD} \rightarrow$ ORTREE
grow_tree : $\mathcal{AD} \times$ ORTREE $\rightarrow$ ORTREE
Query$(A) = \text{lfp}_{\preceq}(\mathit{grow_tree}_A)$
  where $\mathit{grow\_tree}_A(T) = \pi_2^{\#}(\mathit{and\_eval}(1, \langle \bot_{\subseteq}, \langle T\rangle\rangle, \lambda_{1,2}^{\#}(A)))$

Query maps an abstraction of a single atomic goal to an AND-OR tree that will be shown to include all proof trees for the query. That is, Query(A) is the least fixed point of $\mathit{grow\_tree}_A$, which is one of a family of functions indexed by the elements of $\mathcal{AD}$, that expand a tree at each of the 'leftmost' unexpanded leaves that have not failed. Grow_tree is defined in terms of

and_eval : *Naturals* $\times$ ANDTREE $\times$ $\mathcal{AD} \rightarrow$ ANDTREE
$\mathit{and\_eval}(j, \langle \mathrm{A}_{out}, \langle T_1, .., T_m\rangle\rangle, \mathit{Acl}) =$
  if $j > m$
  then $\langle \mathrm{A}_{out} \cup^{\#} \mathit{Acl}, \langle T_1, .., T_m\rangle\rangle$
  else if $T_j = \bot_{\preceq}$
    then if $\mathit{Acl} = \bot_{\subseteq}$
      then $\langle \mathrm{A}_{out}, \langle T_1, .., T_m\rangle\rangle$
      else $\langle \mathrm{A}_{out}, \langle T_1, .., T'_j, .., T_m\rangle, \rangle$

$$\text{where } R_k = \langle \bot_{\subseteq}, (\bot_{\preceq})^{m_k} \rangle,$$
$$\text{and } \quad T'_j = \langle Acl, \langle R_1, .., R_n \rangle\rangle$$
$$\text{else } and\_eval(j+1, \langle \text{A}_{out}, \langle T_1, .., T'_j, .., T_m \rangle\rangle, Acl')$$
$$\text{where } (T'_j, Acl') = or\_eval(j, T_j, Acl)$$

And_eval is a recursively defined function which maps an element of ANDTREE to a new (possibly extended) tree. The subtree T_j in its second argument is expanded using the abstract clause instance *Acl*. This function is defined in terms of *or_eval* which combines its abstract clause instance argument with calling clause instance of the ORTREE argument and returns an ORTREE reflecting these calling patterns.

$or\_eval : Naturals \times \text{ORTREE} \times \mathcal{AD} \rightarrow \text{ORTREE} \times \mathcal{AD}$
$or\_eval(j, \langle \text{A}_{in}, \langle R_1, .., R_n \rangle\rangle, Acl) = (\langle \text{A}_{in}', \langle R'_1, .., R'_n \rangle\rangle, Acl')$
where $\text{A}_{in}' = \text{A}_{in} \cup^{\#} Acl$
and $\langle \text{A}_1^{in}, .., \text{A}_n^{in} \rangle = \text{Pentry}(j, \text{A}_{in}')$
and $R'_k = and\_eval(1, R_k, \text{A}_k^{in})$
and $Acl' = \text{Pexit}(j, \langle R'_1, .., R'_n \rangle, Acl)$

Or_eval is defined in terms of procedure entry, Pentry, whose image is an abstract instance of each clause for the j'th atomic goal (j+1'th element of tuple). Each of these abstract clause instances is used to extend the child AND nodes, R_j.

Procedure entry
$\text{Pentry}: Naturals \times \mathcal{AD} \rightarrow (\mathcal{AD})^n$
$\text{Pentry}(j, Acl) = \langle Acl_1^{in}, .., Acl_n^{in} \rangle$
where $Acl_k^{in} = \lambda^{\#}_{1,m+1}(\pi^{\#}_{j+1}(Acl)) \sqcup^{\#} \alpha(C_k^m)$

The function Pentry maps the given abstract goal to abstract instances of each clause. The procedure exit function (Pexit) combines the exit patterns from each of the n AND nodes to produce a new abstract instance of the given clause.

Procedure exit
$\text{Pexit}: Naturals \times \text{ORTREE}^n \times \mathcal{AD} \rightarrow \mathcal{AD}$
$\text{Pexit}(j, \langle T_1, .., T_n, \rangle, Acl) = Acl \sqcup^{\#} \lambda^{\#}_{j+1,m+1}(\pi^{\#}_1(\cup^{\#} S))$
where $S = \{\text{A}_k^{out} \mid k \in [1..n], T_k = \langle \text{A}_k^{out}, \langle R_1, .., R_m \rangle\rangle\}$

Definition Let $\text{A} \in \mathcal{AD}$, $j \in Naturals$, C_k^m be the k'th clause and $\text{Pentry}(j, \text{A}) = \langle \text{A}_1, .., \text{A}_n \rangle$. Then *Pentry is safe for* A if $\forall k \in [1..n]$, $\forall \langle h, b_1, .., b_r \rangle \in \text{A}, \forall j \in [1..r], (C_k^m \sqcup \langle [b_j], \langle \_, .., \_ \rangle\rangle) \in \text{A}_k \cup \{\top\}$

In general, *Pentry* will be said to be *safe* if it is safe for all A in $\mathcal{AD}$.

Definition Let $T_1, .., T_n \in \text{ORTREE}$, $Acl \in \mathcal{AD}$, $T_i = \langle \text{A}_i^{out}, \langle R_{i,1}, .., R_{i,m_i} \rangle\rangle$ and $A^{out} = \text{Pexit}(j, \langle T_1, .., T_n \rangle, Acl)$. Then *Pexit is safe for Acl and* T_i if

$\forall\langle h, b_1, .., b_r\rangle \in \mathrm{A}_i^{out}, \forall\langle h', b'_1, .., b'_m\rangle \in Acl, \forall j \in [1..m]$
$[\langle h', b'_1, .., b'_m\rangle] \sqcup \langle\_, .., \_, [h], \_, .., \_\rangle \in A^{out}$.

Pexit will be said to be *safe* if it is safe for all A in $\mathcal{AD}$ and all $T_1, .., T_n \in$ ORTREE.

Clearly, both Pentry and Pexit, as defined above, are safe. This does not though prove that the least fixed point of $grow\_tree_A$ is an AND-OR tree representing all proof trees for the query. However if Pentry and Pexit are safe then, from the overestimation of unification by $\sqcup^{\#}$, the least fixed point of $grow\_tree_A$ does indeed represent all finite proof trees for the query. Recall that $\top_{\preceq}$ is taken to be an abstraction of all proof trees.

Theorem 9 *If Pentry and Pexit are both safe then $grow\_tree_A$ is monotonic.*

Theorem 10 *Let $\alpha(G) \in \mathcal{AD}$. If both Pentry and Pexit are safe then the AND-OR tree* Query($\alpha(G)$) *embodies all complete proof trees for G.*

There is still a problem in that many proof trees will have infinite branches and so Query will map many goals to $\top_{\preceq}$. For this reason, [Bruynooghe 1989] gives a way of representing infinite proof trees as finite AND-OR trees. In order to correctly represent trees with potentially infinite branches, Bruynooghe overestimates (with respect to the safety ordering) the exit pattern of a goal beyond that due to its caller. The resulting tree can be made finite but still embodies all possible call patterns because those subsumed by an ancestor need not be expanded: all call patterns resulting from the success of such a descendant will be described by the existing tree.

If, after procedure entry, the call pattern for a particular node T is the same as that for an ancestor T' then the tree extension functions defined above will repeatedly expand the tree and the result of Query must be $\top_{\preceq}$. The solution is to perform procedure exit at T, after possibly expanding any subtrees known to be finite, and then continue as normal until procedure exit for T' is completed. T' is then recomputed using as exit pattern for the descendant, T, the least upper bound of the last exit patterns of T and T'.

The way in which these altered AND-OR trees represent infinite proof trees is more complicated and based on knowing that the exit patterns are greater to the right of the infinite branch to represent the subsequent branches of the finite proof trees.

Modifying the abstract interpretation functions to produce finite trees requires the addition of an argument *Ancestors* to *and_eval* and *or_eval* of type $2^{\mathcal{AD}^n \times \mathcal{AD}^n}$. In *or_eval* the formal parameters R_k ($k \in [1..n]$) are replaced by $\langle \mathrm{A}_k^{out}, \langle T_{k,1}, .., T_{k,n}\rangle\rangle$ and the definition of R'_k by

$$\begin{aligned} R'_k = {} & \text{if } \exists(\langle \mathrm{A}_1^{in}, .., \mathrm{A}_n^{in}\rangle, \langle \mathrm{A}_1^{out}, .., \mathrm{A}_n^{out}\rangle) \in Ancestors \\ & \text{then } \langle \mathrm{A}_k^{out} \sqcup^{\#} \mathrm{A}_k'^{out}, \langle T_{k,1}, .., T_{k,n}\rangle\rangle \\ & \text{else } \; and\_eval(1, R_k, Acl, Ancestors \cup \{(\langle \mathrm{A}_1^{in}, .., \mathrm{A}_n^{in}\rangle, \langle \bot_{\subseteq}, .., \bot_{\subseteq}\rangle)\}) \end{aligned}$$

where $Acl = \text{A}_k^{in} \sqcup^{\#} \alpha(C_k^m)$

5 Conclusion

The novel features of this work include: the reformulation and extension of Clark and following him Falaschi et al's modification to standard logic programming theory in terms of a lattice over EXPR; the proposal of this extension as a concrete domain for abstract interpretation of logic programs (but see note on Barbuti et al's work, below); a prescription for building an abstract domain from any subsets of EXPR which are considered interesting as abstract concepts; the use of this framework to describe, in a formal manner, an existing practical abstract interpretation scheme (due to Bruynooghe, et al.). Although the current paper restricts itself to definite clauses it should be possible to extend the concrete semantics to handle programs with negation.

Section 4 is not an exact formalisation of Bruynooghe's scheme: when constructing a finite AND-OR tree to represent infinite proof trees the descendant node should "refer back" to the ancestor; there is no (implementation orientated) depth bound on the generated tree and there is no abstract interpretation of builtin predicates (although this could be done). Subsequent extensions made in [Bruynooghe et al. 1988, Janssens & Bruynooghe 1989] are not considered here.

The use of a partial order for safety ($\subseteq$) and a common instance operation ($\sqcup^{\#}$) is similar to [Kanamori et al. 1989] and [Debray & Warren 1988]. Both papers use two partial orders but neither show how to construct them. [Debray 1989] gives a method for constructing a domain with one partial order (instantiation) and uses instantiation-closed abstract domain elements, giving a safety order which is the dual of the instance order. This precludes the analysis of term aliasing, which is needed for some mode analyses and for compile-time garbage collection.

Barbuti et al. use Falaschi's extended system, in [Barbuti et al. 1989], to define abstract equivalents of standard logic programming objects, e.g. Herbrand models, and describe bottom-up abstract interpretation in terms of them. The work of Barbuti only came to the attention of the present authors well after independently initiated work had started and progress been made. This is the first published report of our work. To the best of our knowledge, no-one else has attempted to describe top-down execution, although Barbuti et al's work could possibly be adapted for this.

From Section 4 it appears that a more appropriate concrete semantics would be one based on quotiented proof trees rather than 2^{EXPR}. An extension of the concrete semantics of Section 2 to include proof trees is described in [Kemp & Ringwood 1990a] and [Kemp & Ringwood 1990b]. Future work will centre on extending the declarative semantics to express more aspects of the operational semantics, including failed refutations. A practical application of the theory will be the abstract interpretation of a real-time extension of the concurrent logic language, FGDC [Ringwood 1987], for the purpose of compile-time garbage collection.

6 Acknowledgements

Robert Kemp is supported by a research studentship (8830 3825) from the UK Science and Engineering Research Council.

References

[Abramsky & Hankin 1987] S. Abramsky and C. Hankin. *Abstract Interpretation of Declarative Languages.* Ellis Horwood, 1987.

[Barbuti et al. 1989] R. Barbuti, R. Giacobazzi, and G. Levi. A declarative approach to abstract interpretation of logic programs. Technical Report TR-20/89, University of Pisa, Italy, May 1989.

[Birkhoff 1967] G Birkhoff. *Lattice Theory.* colloquium publications vol 25. American Mathematical Society, 3rd edition, 1967.

[Bruynooghe 1989] M. Bruynooghe. A practical framework for the abstract interpretation of logic programs. Technical Report CW 62 (revised version), Katholieke Universiteit Leuven, Belgium, 1989. To appear in Journal of Logic Programming.

[Bruynooghe et al. 1988] M. Bruynooghe, A. Mulkers, and K. Musumbu. Compile-time garbage collection for Prolog. Technical report, Katholieke Universiteit Leuven, Belgium, 1988.

[Clark 1979] K. L. Clark. Predicate logic as a computational formalism. Research Monograph 79/59, Imperial College, London, UK, December 1979.

[Cousot & Cousot 1977] P. Cousot and R. Cousot. Abstract interpretation: A unified lattice model for static analysis of programs by construction or approximation of fixpoints. In *Proceedings of the 4th Annual ACM Symposium on Principles of Programming Languages*, pages 238–252, 1977.

[Debray 1989] S.K. Debray. Efficient dataflow analysis of logic programs. Technical report, University of Arizona, Tucson, USA, August 1989.

[Debray & Warren 1988] S. K. Debray and D. S. Warren. Automatic mode inference for logic programs. *Journal of Logic Programming*, 5(3):207–229, 1988.

[Emden & Kowalski 1976] M.H. van Emden and R.A. Kowalski. The semantics of predicate logic as a programming language. *Journal of the ACM*, 23:733–742, 1976.

[Falaschi et al. 1988] M. Falaschi, G. Levi, M. Martelli, and C. Palamidessi. A new declarative semantics for logic languages. In *Logic Programming: Proceedings of the 5th International Conference and Symposium*, 1988.

[Falaschi et al. 1989] M. Falaschi, G. Levi, M. Martelli, and C. Palamidessi. Declarative modeling of the operational behaviour of logic languages. *Theoretical Computer Science*, 69:289–318, December 1989. Also Univ Pisa, TR-10/88.

[Janssens & Bruynooghe 1989] G. Janssens and M. Bruynooghe. An application of abstract interpretation: integrated type and mode inferencing. Technical Report CW 86, Katholieke Universiteit Leuven, Belgium, April 1989.

[Jones & Sondergaard 1987] N. D. Jones and H. Sondergaard. A semantics-based framework for the abstract interpretation of Prolog. In *Abstract Interpretation of Declarative Languages*, pages 123–142. Ellis Horwood, 1987.

[Kanamori et al. 1989] T. Kanamori, T. Kawamura, M. Maeji, and K. Horiuchi. Logic program analysis and abstract hybrid interpretation. Technical Report 485, ICOT, Japan, July 1989.

[Kemp & Ringwood 1990a] R. Kemp and G.A. Ringwood. An algebraic Hintikka semantics for logic programs. Tr, Imperial College, London, UK, 1990.

[Kemp & Ringwood 1990b] R. Kemp and G.A. Ringwood. A framework for algebraic abstract interpretation. Tr, Imperial College, London, UK, 1990. In preparation.

[Lloyd 1987] J. W. Lloyd. *Foundations of Logic Programming*. Springer-Verlag, second edition, 1987.

[Mellish 1987] C.S. Mellish. Abstract interpretation of Prolog programs. In *Abstract Interpretation of Declarative Languages*, pages 181–198. Ellis Horwood, 1987.

[Ringwood 1987] G.A. Ringwood. Pattern-directed, Markovian, linear guarded, definite clause resolution. Technical report, Imperial College, London, UK, 1987.

Analysis of Constraint Logic Programs

Kim Marriott
IBM T. J. Watson Research Center,
P. O. Box 704, Yorktown Heights NY 10598, USA

Harald Søndergaard
Dept. of Computer Science,
University of Melbourne,
Parkville 3052 Vic., Australia

Abstract

Increasingly, compilers for logic programs are making use of information from dataflow analyses to aid in the generation of efficient target code. However, generating efficient target code from constraint logic programs is even more difficult than from logic programs. Thus we feel that good compilation of constraint logic programs will require sophisticated analysis of the source code. Here we present a simple framework for the abstract interpretation of constraint logic programs which is intended to serve as the basis for developing such analyses. We show the framework's practical usefulness by sketching two dataflow analyses that are based on it and indicating how they can be used to improve the code generated by a compiler.

1 Introduction

Dataflow analysis is an essential component of many programming tools. Tools such as "debuggers" and type checkers use dataflow analyses to identify errors in a program, while compilers and other program transformers use dataflow analyses to guide various optimizations. Accurate dataflow analyses are usually complex and so they are difficult to design and to prove correct. Fortunately, the theory of abstract interpretation provides some help.

Abstract interpretation formalizes dataflow analysis by viewing it as "approximate" computation, in which computation is performed with descriptions of data rather than the data themselves. P. and R. Cousot [3,4] developed abstract interpretation as a precise framework for discussing approximate computation of imperative programs. The advantage of such a framework is that it serves as a basis for the better understanding of dataflow analyses, and for discussing their correctness. The work of P. and R. Cousot has been extended to functional and logic programming languages. Such extensions are not straightforward. For example, dataflow analysis of logic programs differs markedly from the analysis of programs written in conventional languages because the dataflow is bi-directional, owing to unification, and the control flow is more complex, owing to backtracking.

Abstract interpretation of logic programs was first mentioned by Mellish [16] where it was suggested as a way to formalize mode analysis. Since then, abstract interpretation of logic programs has been an active research area and many general frameworks and applications have been given. Following Marriott and Søndergaard [13], the approaches can be broadly divided into two classes. The first, and most important class for logic program compilers, are top-down analyses (for example [19,17,5,9,2,10,15]). A top-down analysis approximates the SLD-refutation semantics and is intended to give information about "call-patterns". The second class are the bottom-up analyses (for example [10,11,12,1]). These are based on simpler T_P-like semantics and give information about "success-patterns".

In this paper we generalize top-down abstract interpretation of logic programs to the wider class of constraint logic programs (CLP) [8]. A CLP program is a rule-based program in which constraints over some predefined domain are allowed in the rule bodies. Such a program is evaluated similarly to a logic program except that a test for constraint satisfaction replaces unification. Testing for constraint satisfaction may be very expensive, much more so than unification. Thus, it is important that tests for satisfaction be optimized wherever possible in the code generated by a CLP compiler. Thus we feel that any "good" CLP compiler will require non-trivial dataflow analysis of a program to determine when such optimizations are possible. This paper is intended to provide a framework for such analyses.

We now indicate by means of an example program how dataflow analysis of CLP programs can help their efficient implementation.

Example 1.1 Consider the following CLP(R) [7] program to compute mortgage repayments with parameters: x_p, the principal; x_t, the life of the mortgage (in months); x_i, the annual percentage interest rate; x_r, the monthly repayment; and x_b, the outstanding balance.

$$mortgage(x_p, x_t, x_i, x_r, x_b) \leftarrow$$
$$x_t = 1 \wedge \quad (1)$$
$$x_b + x_r = x_p * (1 + x_i/1200). \quad (2)$$
$$mortgage(x_p, x_t, x_i, x_r, x_b) \leftarrow$$
$$x_t > 1 \wedge$$
$$mortgage(x_p * (1 + x_i/1200) - x_r, x_t - 1, x_i, x_r, x_b). \quad \blacksquare \quad (3)$$

This program can be queried in many different ways. The query $Q_1 = mortgage(100000, 360, 12, x_r, 0)$ has answer constraint $x_r = 1028.61$, the query $Q_2 = mortgage(x_p, 360, 12, 1028.61, 0)$ has answer constraint $x_p = 100000$, and the query $Q_3 = mortgage(x_p, 120, 12, x_r, x_b)$ has answer constraint $x_p = 0.303 * x_b + 69.70 * x_r$. In all of these queries the efficiency of the program execution may be improved by taking the form of the query into account.

For example, a "determinacy" analysis akin to that given by Debray and Warren [6] shows that whenever the second argument, x_t, is "ground", no backtracking need take place after (1). This information allows a compiler to generate code in which a redundant choicepoint is not constructed for the first clause. This is true for each of the queries given above. A "freeness" analysis akin to that given by Mellish [16] shows that if the last argument, x_b, is not constrained in the query then it is not constrained in subsequent calls to *mortgage*. In such a case adding the constraint (2) can never lead to unsatisfiability. This information allows a compiler to generate code in which an unnecessary test for satisfiability is not made when executing the first clause. This is true for query Q_1. A "groundness" or "definiteness" analysis akin to that given by Mellish [16] shows that if the first, third and fourth arguments, x_p, x_i and x_r, are uniquely constrained in the query then this holds true in subsequent calls to *mortgage*. This means that the constraints in (3) can be optimized to a sequence of assignments. This is true for query Q_2.

In the remainder of this paper we present a framework for the development of such dataflow analyses. In Section 2 abstract interpretation is introduced. In Section 3 we refine the operational semantics of constraint logic programs to give a semantics which is a suitable for dataflow analysis. In Section 4 we sketch two example dataflow analyses; the first is for "freeness", the second for "definiteness". Finally we summarize the main results of the paper in Section 5. Notation used in this paper is explained in Section 2 of an accompanying paper [14].

2 Abstract Interpretation

Abstract interpretation formalizes the idea of "approximate computation" in which computation is performed with descriptions of data rather than the data itself. Approximate computation is well-known from everyday use, for example the rules of signs, such as "plus times minus yields minus." Approximate computation is formalized as evaluating a formula or a program, not over its standard domain, but by evaluating it over a non-standard domain of descriptions. Of course, when performing approximate computations, one must reinterpret all operators so as to apply to descriptions rather than to proper values.

Abstract interpretation is powerful because it is semantics-based and thus concerned with a programming language as a whole rather than the analysis of particular programs. But, as Nielson [18] observed, the generality of abstract interpretation can be taken further. Assume we are given a language in which one can express the semantics of a wide variety of programming languages. The theory of abstract interpretation may then be developed in the framework of this *meta-language* once and for all. In this way, we need not "reinvent" abstract interpretation for all different programming languages—each is just a special instance of the general theory.

This is the approach we take, and the semantic definitions given here are expressed in a meta-language given by Marriott, Søndergaard and Jones [15]. This meta-language is specifically intended for the definition of the semantics of "logic programming-like" languages and is based on the formalism of denotational semantics. The usefulness and suitability of the meta-language should be apparent from the following sections: both standard and non-standard semantics are easily presented in the meta-language. By choosing the right level of abstraction, they can be made highly congruent: if the standard semantics employs a certain operator on the standard domain, the non-standard semantics should use a very similar operator on the corresponding non-standard domain. We now summarize the main features of the meta-language and the associated abstract interpretation theory.

The meta-language is one of typed lambda expressions, and the types are given by

$$\begin{array}{lcl} T \in \mathit{Type} & ::= & S \mid L \\ L \in \mathit{Lat} & ::= & D \mid T \to L \end{array}$$

where $S \in \mathit{Stat}$, $D \in \mathit{Dyn}$, *Stat* is a collection of *static* types, and *Dyn* is a collection of *dynamic* types. The difference between the two kinds is that (the interpretation of) a static type remains the same throughout all (standard and non-standard) semantics, whereas a dynamic type may change. We call $\mathit{Stat} \cup \mathit{Dyn}$ the collection of *base* types, and *Lat* is the collection of lattice types. The syntax of the meta-language is given by

$$\begin{array}{lcll} e & ::= & c_i & \text{(base functions)} \\ & \mid & x_i & \text{(variables)} \\ & \mid & \lambda\, x\, .\, e & \text{(lambda abstraction)} \\ & \mid & e\ e' & \text{(function application)} \\ & \mid & \mathit{lfp}\ e & \text{(least fixed point operation)} \\ & \mid & \bigsqcup_{x \in e}\ e' & \text{(least upper bound operation)} \end{array}$$

Static types are interpreted as posets (ordered by identity) and dynamic types are interpreted as complete lattices. A *type interpretation* **I** thus assigns a structure $(\mathbf{I}\ E)$ to each base type E. Type interpretations can be naturally extended from the base types to all types. An *interpretation* **I** denotes a type interpretation (by an abuse of notation also called **I**) together with an assignment of an element of $(\mathbf{I}\ T)$ to each base function c of type T. By natural extension this gives the semantics of the meta-language.

By varying the interpretation, one may obtain different semantics from the same set of semantic equations. The *standard interpretation* gives the usual input/output behaviour of the program while dataflow analyses may be expressed as *non-standard* interpretations. The role of abstract interpretation is to give relationships between the standard and non-standard interpretations which guarantee that the analysis safely approximates the standard semantics.

To do this, one must first formalize what the descriptions in the non-standard semantics mean in terms of the elements in the standard semantics. Following P. and R. Cousot [3,4] this is done by means of concretization functions. Intuitively, a concretization function maps a description to the largest object which it describes.

Definition. A *concretization function* γ from A to E is a monotonic function from A to E such that there is a (monotonic) adjoint function $\hat{\gamma}$ from E to A. A *concretization family*, $\Gamma = \{\Gamma_D\}$, from interpretation $\mathbf{I}$ to interpretation $\mathbf{I}'$ is an indexed family of functions such that for each $D \in Dyn$, Γ_D is a concretization function from $(\mathbf{I}\ D)$ to $(\mathbf{I}'\ D)$. ■

Descriptions are ordered according to how large a set of objects they apply to; intuitively, the more imprecise, the "higher" they sit in the ordering. In accordance with this, we now define what it means for a description (or function) to "safely approximate" an object (or function).

Definition. Let Γ be a concretization family from $\mathbf{I}$ to $\mathbf{I}'$. Define the relation *(safely) approximates*, written $appr[\Gamma]_T$, by

$$
\begin{array}{lll}
u\ appr[\Gamma]_S\ v & \Leftrightarrow & v = u \text{ where } S \in Stat \\
u\ appr[\Gamma]_D\ v & \Leftrightarrow & v \leq \gamma_D\ u \text{ where } D \in Dyn \\
u\ appr[\Gamma]_{T \to T'}\ v & \Leftrightarrow & \\
\multicolumn{3}{l}{\qquad\qquad \forall u', v' \,.\, u'\ appr[\Gamma]_T\ v' \Rightarrow (u\ u')\ appr[\Gamma]_{T'}\ (v\ v'). \quad ■}
\end{array}
$$

When the concretization family Γ and type T is clear from the context we write $appr[\Gamma]_T$ as $appr$.

Example 2.1 Assume that the standard interpretation of a dynamic type T is $E = \wp\, Sub$ where Sub is the set of substitutions. In a non-standard interpretation we can interpret T as the set $A = \wp\, Var$ ordered with the superset relation. Intuitively $U \in A$ describes $\Theta \in E$ iff each $\theta \in \Theta$ grounds all variables in U. This intuitive meaning is captured by the concretization function γ from A to E defined by

$$\gamma\ U = \{\theta \in Sub \mid \forall V \in U \,.\, \theta \text{ grounds } V\}.$$

Let $\theta_1 = \{x \mapsto a, y \mapsto z\}$ and $\theta_2 = \{x \mapsto f(a), y \mapsto a\}$. The set $\{\theta_1, \theta_2\}$ is approximated by the description $\{x\}$. Let $restrict : \wp\, Var \to E \to E$ be the function such that $restrict\ U\ \Theta$ is the set of substitutions in Θ restricted to the variables in U. Then $restrict$ is approximated by the function $restrict' : \wp\, Var \to A \to A$ defined by $restrict'\ U\ U' = U \cap U'$. ■

The following fundamental result allows us to argue inductively the correctness of a whole dataflow analysis (or non-standard semantics) once certain base functions are shown to be in the relation safely approximates. This applies not only to constraint logic programming languages as discussed in this paper, but to any language whose semantics can be expressed in the meta-language.

Proposition 2.1 Let $\mathbf{I}$ and $\mathbf{I}'$ be interpretations and let e be a closed expression. If $(\mathbf{I}\ c)$ *appr* $(\mathbf{I}'\ c)$ holds for every base function c, then, $(\mathbf{I}\ e)$ *appr* $(\mathbf{I}'\ e)$. ∎

The following result is also important as it allows the stepwise development of approximations and proof of approximation.

Proposition 2.2 Let $\mathbf{I}$, $\mathbf{I}'$ and $\mathbf{I}''$ be interpretations and let e be a closed expression. Then

$$(\mathbf{I}\ e)\ appr\ (\mathbf{I}'\ e) \wedge (\mathbf{I}'\ e)\ appr\ (\mathbf{I}''\ e) \Rightarrow (\mathbf{I}\ e)\ appr\ (\mathbf{I}''\ e). \quad \blacksquare$$

3 Operational Semantics of CLP

In this section we first give an operational semantics which captures the essence of a CLP interpreter's evaluation of a constraint logic program. We then refine this semantics until we obtain a semantics which is a suitable basis for the abstract interpretation of CLP programs.

First some notation. A *constraint logic program*, or *program*, is a finite set of clauses. A *clause* is of the form $H \leftarrow \pi \wedge B$ where H, the *head*, is an *atom*, π is a *constraint* and B, the *body*, is a finite sequence of atoms. Note that π may be a conjunction of primitive constraints or the vacuous constraint *true*. We let *Var* denote the set of variables, *Atom* the set of atoms, *Con* the set of constraints modulo logical equivalence, *Clause* the set of clauses, and *Prog* the set of CLP programs. *Con* is assumed to contain *true* and to be closed under conjunction and existential quantification.

In the semantic definitions, finite failure is not distinguished from non-termination. For example, the empty program and the program consisting only of the clause $q \leftarrow q$ have the same denotation. This reflects the fact that the statements we want to produce from a dataflow analysis are of the form "whenever execution reaches this point, so and so holds." But in saying so, we do not actually say that execution does reach the point. In particular, "whenever the computation terminates, so and so holds" concludes nothing about termination. As non-termination is not distinguished from finite failure, we can assume a parallel search rule, rather than the customary depth-first rule—this simplifies our task. Owing to the use of a parallel search rule, the execution of a program naturally yields a *set* of answer constraints, as opposed to a sequence. However, note that the usual left-to-right computation rule is assumed.

The semantic definitions make use of renamings. A *renaming* is a mapping $\rho \in Ren \subset Var \to Var$ such that $\rho \circ \rho$ is the identity. Note that this is not the standard definition of renaming, but it simplifies the following presentation. A renaming is not distinguished from its natural extension to atoms, clauses, constraints or sets of constraints. We make use of the function $ren : \wp\, Var \to \wp\, Var \to Ren$ for renaming where $(ren\ U\ W)$ is some renaming, such that the variables in W are renamed away from those in U. For instance, $ren\ \{x, y\}\ \{x\}$ might be $\{x \mapsto z, z \mapsto x\}$.

The definitions also make use of the functions $add : Con \to \wp\, Con \to \wp\, Con$ which adds a constraint to a set of constraints and $exist : \wp\, Var \to \wp\, Con \to \wp\, Con$ which existentially quantifies a set of constraints. They are defined by:

$$\begin{array}{lcl} add\ \pi\ \Pi & = & \{\pi \wedge \pi' \mid \pi' \in \Pi\} \setminus \{false\} \\ exist\ W\ \Pi & = & \{\exists_{\overline{W}}\pi \mid \pi \in \Pi\}. \end{array}$$

where $\exists_{\overline{W}}\pi$ is the existential closure of π for all variables not in W.

We now give a definition of the operational semantics of CLP. It should be clear that this definition is equivalent to the usual operational semantics [8]. The main differences to the standard definition are: it is explicit that the operational semantics is a fixpoint definition; and the semantics operates over sets of constraints rather than single constraints. Note that the test $\Pi' = \emptyset$ corresponds to the usual test for (un)satisfiability. We let :: denote concatenation of sequences. Clauses are implicitly universally quantified, so each call of a clause should produce new incarnations of its variables. This is done by means of the function *ren*, so that the generated clause instance will contain no variables previously met during execution (those in Π) or to be met later (those in $A : G$). The function *vars* takes a syntactic object and returns the set of variables occurring in it.

Definition. The *operational semantics* has semantic domains

$$Sem \;=\; Atom* \to \wp\, Con \to \wp\, Con$$

and semantic functions

$$\begin{array}{l} \mathbf{O} : Prog \to Sem \\ \mathbf{O}' : Prog \to Sem \to Sem. \end{array}$$

The semantic equations are

$$\begin{array}{lcl} \mathbf{O}\, [\![P]\!] & = & \text{lfp}\ (\mathbf{O}'\, [\![P]\!]) \\ \mathbf{O}'\, [\![P]\!]\ S\ nil\ \Pi & = & \Pi \\ \mathbf{O}'\, [\![P]\!]\ S\ (A : G)\ \Pi & = & \end{array}$$

$$\begin{array}{l} \text{let } U = (vars\ \Pi) \cup (vars\ (A : G)) \text{ in} \\ \quad \bigcup_{C \in P} \begin{array}{l} \text{let } [\![H \leftarrow \pi \wedge B]\!] = ren\ U\ (vars\ C)\ C \text{ in} \\ \text{let } \Pi' = add\ (\pi \wedge A = H)\ \Pi \text{ in} \\ \text{if } \Pi' = \emptyset \text{ then } \emptyset \text{ else } exist\ U\ (S\ (B :: G)\ \Pi'). \end{array} \end{array}$$ ∎

Example 3.1 Consider the program P from Example 1.1 and the query $Q_3 = mortgage(x_p, 120, 12, x_r, x_b)$. We have that $\mathbf{O}\,[\![P]\!]\;Q_3$ is $\{x_p = 0.303 * x_b + 69.70 * x_r\}$. ■

Actually the operational semantics does not really give the type of information a compiler requires for the generation of efficient code. This is because we are primarily interested in removing unnecessary tests for satisfiability and unnecessary choicepoints. Therefore, we need information about the constraints at call time. It is straightforward to modify the operational semantics so that it returns the "call constraints" rather than the "answer constraints". However, to aid clarity and brevity we will ignore this modification and only consider the operational semantics. A similar issue arises when analysing logic programs [15].

There is still another problem with using the operational semantics as the basis for dataflow analysis. The problem is that the meaning of a goal may depend on the meaning of an infinite number of other goals; thus termination of analyses based on the operational semantics cannot easily be guaranteed. For instance, assume we are interested in determining which variables are bound to ground terms. As descriptions we choose sets U of variables, with the intention that $V \in U$ means that the current constraint definitely grounds V. Now consider the following program.

$ancestor(x, z) \leftarrow parent(x, z).$
$ancestor(x, z) \leftarrow ancestor(x, y), ancestor(y, z).$

Assume we are given the query $\leftarrow ancestor(a, z)$. An analysis based on the operational semantics must compute an infinite number of query/description tuples, including:

$\langle ancestor(x, z), \{x\}\rangle$
$\langle ancestor(x, y) \wedge ancestor(y, z), \{x\}\rangle$
$\langle ancestor(x, w) \wedge ancestor(w, y) \wedge ancestor(y, z), \{x\}\rangle$
$\vdots$

Clearly such a dataflow analysis will not terminate. What we need is a semantic definition that somehow "merges" information about all incarnations of a variable that appears in a program and is compositional in the sense that the meaning of a goal is given in terms of the meaning of its subgoals.

We now develop such a definition in two stages. The first stage is obtained by observing that

$$\mathbf{O}\,[\![P]\!]\;G\;\Pi = \rho\,(\mathbf{O}\,[\![P]\!]\;(\rho\;G)\;(\rho\;\Pi)) \tag{1}$$

and that

$$\mathbf{O}\,[\![P]\!]\;(A : G)\;\Pi = \mathbf{O}\,[\![P]\!]\;G\;(\mathbf{O}\,[\![P]\!]\;A\;\Pi). \tag{2}$$

Equation (1) means that we can modify the definition so that the calling atom and constraint set are renamed away from the clause rather than the reverse. Equation (2) means that we can rewrite the definition so that the denotation of a goal or clause body is given in terms of the denotation of the constituent atoms. This means that the denotation of a program need only be a mapping from atoms and constraint sets to the answer constraints rather than a mapping from goals and constraint sets.

Definition. The *standard semantics* has semantic domain

$$Den \;=\; Atom \rightarrow \wp\, Con \rightarrow \wp\, Con$$

and semantic functions

$$\begin{array}{lll} \mathbf{P}_{\mathbf{std}} & : & Prog \rightarrow Den \\ \mathbf{C}_{\mathbf{std}} & : & Clause \rightarrow Den \rightarrow Den. \end{array}$$

The semantic equations are

$$\begin{array}{l} \mathbf{P}_{\mathbf{std}}\, [\![P]\!] \;=\; \mathrm{lfp}\ (\bigsqcup_{C \in P} \mathbf{C}_{\mathbf{std}}\, [\![C]\!]) \\ \mathbf{C}_{\mathbf{std}}\, [\![H \leftarrow \pi \wedge B]\!]\ D\ A\ \Pi \;= \\ \qquad \mathrm{let}\ \rho = ren\,(vars\ H \cup vars\ B \cup vars\ \pi)\,(vars\ A \cup vars\ \Pi)\ \mathrm{in} \\ \qquad \mathrm{let}\ W = vars\,(\rho\ A) \cup vars\,(\rho\ \Pi)\ \mathrm{in} \\ \qquad \rho\,(exist\ W\ (\Sigma\ D\ B\ (add\ (\pi \wedge H = \rho\ A)\,(\rho\ \Pi)))) \end{array}$$

where $\Sigma\ F$ is the *folded* version of a function F defined by

$$\begin{array}{l} \Sigma\ F\ nil\ z = z \\ \Sigma\ F\ (x : y)\ z = \Sigma\ F\ y\ (F\ x\ z). \quad \blacksquare \end{array}$$

Proposition 3.1 For every program P, $\mathbf{O}\, [\![P]\!] = \Sigma\, (\mathbf{P}_{\mathbf{std}}\, [\![P]\!])$. $\blacksquare$

We now tailor this definition even closer to the sort of dataflow analyses we are interested in. The motivation for the next change is that in a dataflow analysis we wish to limit the number of atom and abstract constraint pairs whose denotation will need to be computed for a particular abstract query. The idea is to modify the definition so that only atom and constraint set pairs in which the constraint set is restricted to the variables in the atom need be considered. Justification for this modification comes from the observation that:

$$\mathbf{O}\, [\![P]\!]\ G\ \Pi \subseteq meet\ \Pi\ (\mathbf{O}\, [\![P]\!]\ G\ (exist\ (vars\ G)\ \Pi))$$

where the function $meet : \wp\, Con \rightarrow \wp\, Con \rightarrow \wp\, Con$ is defined by

$$meet\ \Pi\ \Pi' = \{\pi \wedge \pi' \mid \pi \in \Pi \wedge \pi' \in \Pi'\} \setminus \{false\}.$$

Definition. The *lax semantics* has semantic domain

$$Den \quad = \quad Atom \rightarrow \wp\, Con \rightarrow \wp\, Con$$

and semantic functions

$$\begin{array}{lll} \mathbf{P_{lax}} & : & Prog \rightarrow Den \\ \mathbf{C_{lax}} & : & Clause \rightarrow Den \rightarrow Den. \end{array}$$

The semantic equations are

$$\begin{array}{lll} \mathbf{P_{lax}}\, [\![P]\!] & = & \mathrm{lfp}\ (\bigsqcup_{C \in P} \mathbf{C_{lax}}\, [\![C]\!]) \\ \mathbf{C_{lax}}\, [\![H \leftarrow \pi \wedge B]\!]\ D\ A\ \Pi & = & ret\ A\ \Pi\ H\ (\Sigma\ D\ B\ (call\ A\ \Pi\ H\ \pi)) \end{array}$$

where

$$\begin{array}{lll} call & : & Atom \rightarrow \wp\, Con \rightarrow Atom \rightarrow Con \rightarrow \wp\, Con \\ ret & : & Atom \rightarrow \wp\, Con \rightarrow Atom \rightarrow \wp\, Con \rightarrow \wp\, Con \end{array}$$

are defined by

$$\begin{array}{lll} call\ A\ \Pi\ H\ \pi & = & ret\ H\ \{\pi\}\ A\ \Pi \\ ret\ A\ \Pi\ H\ \Pi' & = & \\ & & \text{let } \rho = ren\ (vars\ A \cup vars\ \Pi)\ (vars\ H \cup vars\ \Pi')\ \text{in} \\ & & meet\ \Pi\ (exist\ (vars\ A)\ (add\ (A = \rho\ H)\ (\rho\ \Pi'))). \quad \blacksquare \end{array}$$

Proposition 3.2 Letting the concretization function be the identity function, $\mathbf{P_{lax}}$ *appr* $\mathbf{P_{std}}$. ■

We now turn to dataflow analyses. To extract runtime properties of pure CLP programs one can develop a variety of non-standard interpretations of the preceding semantics. To clarify the presentation, we extract from the lax semantics a *dataflow* semantics which contains exactly those features that are common to all the non-standard interpretations that we want. It leaves the interpretation of one dynamic type, *Acon*, and two base functions, c and r, unspecified. These missing details of the dataflow semantics are to be filled in by the interpretations. In the standard interpretation of this semantics, $\mathbf{I_{lax}}$, *Acon* is $\wp$ *Con*, c is *call* and r is *ret*. In a non-standard interpretation, *Acon* is assigned whatever "descriptions" we choose in approximating sets of constraints. *Acon* should thus be a complete lattice which corresponds to $\wp$ *Con* in the standard semantics in a way laid down by some concretization function from *Acon* to $\wp$ *Con*. The interpretation of c and r should approximate *call* and *ret* respectively. The types *Prog*, *Clause*, and *Atom* are static and have the obvious fixed interpretation.

Definition. The *dataflow semantics* has dynamic type *Acon* and semantic domain

$$Den \quad = \quad Atom \to Acon \to Acon,$$

semantic functions

$$\begin{array}{lll} \mathbf{P} & : & Prog \to Den \\ \mathbf{C} & : & Clause \to Den \to Den \end{array}$$

and base functions

$$\begin{array}{lll} c & : & Atom \to Acon \to Atom \to Con \to Acon \\ r & : & Atom \to Acon \to Atom \to Acon \to Acon. \end{array}$$

The semantic equations are

$$\begin{array}{lll} \mathbf{P}\ [\![P]\!] & = & \text{lfp}\ (\bigsqcup_{C \in P} \mathbf{C}\ [\![C]\!]) \\ \mathbf{C}\ [\![H \leftarrow \pi \wedge B]\!]\ D\ A\ \Pi & = & r\ A\ \Pi\ H\ (\Sigma\ D\ B\ (c\ A\ \Pi\ H\ \pi)). \quad \blacksquare \end{array}$$

For convenience we may specify an interpretation $\mathbf{I_Y}$ of the dataflow semantics by the triple $\langle(\mathbf{I_Y}\ Acon), (\mathbf{I_Y}\ c), (\mathbf{I_Y}\ r)\rangle$ and denote $\mathbf{I_Y}\ [\![\mathbf{P}]\!]$ by $\mathbf{P_Y}$. For example, $\mathbf{I_{lax}}$ is given by $\langle \wp\, Con, call, ret\rangle$ and the corresponding semantics is denoted by $\mathbf{P_{lax}}$.

Since the interpretations of c and r are required to be monotonic functions we have:

Proposition 3.3 For every interpretation $\mathbf{I_X}$, $\mathbf{P_X}$ is well-defined. ■

Definition. Let $\mathbf{I} = \langle Acon, c, r\rangle$ and $\mathbf{I'} = \langle Acon', c', r'\rangle$ be interpretations. We say $\mathbf{I'}$ *approximates* $\mathbf{I}$ iff for some concretization function from $Acon'$ to $Acon$, c' *appr* c and r' *appr* r. ■
It follows immediately from Proposition 2.1 that:

Proposition 3.4 If $\mathbf{I_X}$ approximates $\mathbf{I_Y}$, $\mathbf{P_X}$ *appr* $\mathbf{P_Y}$. ■

And then from Proposition 2.2 and Proposition 3.2 it follows that:

Theorem 3.5 If $\mathbf{I_X}$ approximates $\mathbf{I_{lax}}$, $\mathbf{P_X}$ *appr* $\mathbf{P_{std}}$. ■

Developing a dataflow analysis in this framework is therefore a matter of choosing the description domain *Acon* so that it captures the information required for the analysis and defining suitable functions to approximate *call* and *ret*. We give two examples of this in the next section.

4 Example Dataflow Analyses

In this section we show that the dataflow semantics given in the last section is a suitable basis for the analysis of CLP programs by sketching two example dataflow analyses based on it. The first is a freeness analysis, the second is a definiteness analysis.

4.1 Freeness Analysis

In the freeness analysis, descriptions are sets of variables which are read as being "possibly" constrained. The complement of such a variable set are those variables which are "definitely" not constrained, that is, they are free.

Definition. Let $Acon_{free} = \wp\, Var$ with subset ordering and define $\gamma_{free} : Acon_{free} \rightarrow \wp\, Con$ by

$$\gamma_{free}\ W = \{\pi \in Con \mid \forall V \notin W\ .\ V\ free\_in\ \pi\}$$

where $V\ free\_in\ \pi$ is true exactly when π does not constrain V, that is, there is a constraint π' which is equivalent to π and $V \notin (vars\ \pi')$. ■

Lemma 4.1 The function γ_{free} is a concretization function from $Acon_{free}$ to $\wp\, Con$. ■

We can approximate *call* and *ret* as follows.

Definition. Define

$$\begin{array}{lll} call_{free} & : & Atom \rightarrow Acon_{free} \rightarrow Atom \rightarrow Con \rightarrow Acon_{free} \\ ret_{free} & : & Atom \rightarrow Acon_{free} \rightarrow Atom \rightarrow Acon_{free} \rightarrow Acon_{free} \end{array}$$

by

$$\begin{array}{lll} call_{free}\ A\ W\ H\ \pi & = & ret_{free}\ H\ (vars\ \pi)\ A\ W \\ ret_{free}\ A\ W\ H\ W' & = & \end{array}$$
$$\begin{array}{l} \text{let } \rho = ren\ (vars\ A \cup W)\ (vars\ H \cup W') \text{ in} \\ W \cup \{V \in (vars\ A) \mid \neg\, (\exists U \subseteq Var\ .\ alias\ U\ (A = \rho\ H) \wedge \\ \qquad\qquad U \cap (\rho\ W') = \emptyset \wedge U \cap (vars\ A) = \{V\})\} \end{array}$$

where $alias\ U\ \pi$ is true exactly when the only constraint π places on the variables in U is that they are aliases. ■

The reason for this definition of $ret_{free}\ A\ W\ H\ W'$ is that V is *not* possibly constrained, that is free, if:

- $(A = \rho\ H)$ only constrains V to be aliased to other variables, that is, for some $U \subseteq Var$, $alias\ U\ (A = \rho\ H)$ and $V \in U$ are true;

- V is not aliased to any possibly constrained variable, that is, $U \cap (\rho\ W') = \emptyset$; and
- V is not aliased to any other variables in $(vars\ A)$, that is, $U \cap (vars\ A) = \{V\}$.

Lemma 4.2 The following hold:

- $call_{free}$ *appr* $call$, and
- ret_{free} *appr* ret. ■

Definition. Let $\mathbf{I_{free}}$ be the interpretation given by $\langle Acon_{free}, call_{free}, ret_{free}\rangle$. ■

It follows from Lemma 4.2 that $\mathbf{I_{free}}$ approximates $\mathbf{I_{lax}}$. Thus from Theorem 3.5:

Theorem 4.3 $\mathbf{P_{free}}$ *appr* $\mathbf{P_{std}}$. ■

The call version of the freeness analysis can be used to determine that the query description

$$mortgage(x_p, x_t, x_i, x_r, x_b)\ \{x_p, x_t, x_i, x_r\}$$

leads to call constraints of only the same form. It follows that if x_b is not constrained in the initial query, then it will not be constrained in the subsequent calls to *mortgage*. As indicated in Section 1, this information allows a compiler to generate code for *mortgage* without a redundant test for satisfiability in the first clause.

4.2 Definiteness Analysis

In the definiteness analysis, descriptions are sets of variables that are read as being "definitely" constrained to a unique value. This analysis corresponds to a groundness analysis for logic programs.

Definition. Let $Acon_{def} = \wp\ Var$ with superset ordering and define $\gamma_{def} : Acon_{def} \rightarrow \wp\ Cons$ by

$$\gamma_{def}\ W = \{\pi \in Con \mid \forall V \in W\ .\ V\ \mathit{definite\_in}\ \pi\}$$

where V *definite_in* π is true exactly when π constrains V to a unique value. ■

Lemma 4.4 The function γ_{def} is a concretization function from $Acon_{def}$ to $\wp\ Con$. ■

The functions *call* and *ret* are approximated as follows.

Definition. Define

$$\begin{array}{lcl} call_{def} & : & Atom \rightarrow Acon_{def} \rightarrow Atom \rightarrow Con \rightarrow Acon_{def} \\ ret_{def} & : & Atom \rightarrow Acon_{def} \rightarrow Atom \rightarrow Acon_{def} \rightarrow Acon_{def} \end{array}$$

by

$$\begin{array}{l} call_{def}\ A\ W\ H\ \pi \quad = \\ \qquad \text{let } \rho = ren\ (vars\ H \cup vars\ \pi)\ (vars\ A \cup W) \text{ in} \\ \qquad \{V \in (vars\ H) \mid funct\ (\rho\ W)\ (\pi \wedge \rho\ A = H)\ V\} \\ ret_{def}\ A\ W\ H\ W' \quad = \\ \qquad \text{let } \rho = ren\ (vars\ A \cup W)\ (vars\ H \cup W') \text{ in} \\ \qquad W \cup \{V \in (vars\ A) \mid funct\ (\rho\ W')\ (A = \rho\ H)\ V\} \end{array}$$

where *funct* $U\ \pi\ V$ is true exactly when given unique values for the variables in U, the constraint π constrains V to have a unique value. ∎

Lemma 4.5 The following hold:

- $call_{def}$ *appr call*, and
- ret_{def} *appr ret*. ∎

Definition. Let $\mathbf{I}_{\mathbf{def}}$ be the interpretation given by $\langle Acon_{def}, call_{def}, ret_{def}\rangle$. ∎

It follows from Lemma 4.5 that $\mathbf{I}_{\mathbf{def}}$ approximates $\mathbf{I}_{\mathbf{lax}}$. Thus from Theorem 3.5:

Theorem 4.6 $\mathbf{P}_{\mathbf{def}}$ *appr* $\mathbf{P}_{\mathbf{std}}$. ∎

The call version of the definiteness analysis can be used to determine that the query description

$$mortgage(x_p, x_t, x_i, x_r, x_b)\ \{x_t\}$$

leads to call constraints of only the same form. It follows that if x_t is uniquely constrained in the initial query, then it will be uniquely constrained in the subsequent calls to *mortgage*. This information indicates that *mortgage* is locally deterministic because if x_t has a unique value then for a given x_t both of the constraints $x_t > 1$ and $x_t = 1$ cannot be satisfiable. As indicated in Section 1, this information allows a compiler to generate code for *mortgage* without an unnecessary choicepoint in the first clause.

4.3 Other Dataflow Analyses

We have sketched two simple, generic dataflow analyses. We note that more accurate analyses are often constraint domain specific; descriptions which capture properties of constraint sets over the reals are not necessarily going to capture interesting properties of constraint sets over the Herbrand universe. Thus a major topic of future research is to find useful descriptions for specific constraint domains, such as the real numbers.

We feel that it is still useful to classify descriptions into one of two main classes: downward-closed and upward-closed. Not all descriptions are downward- or upward-closed but many are, and often description domains can be decomposed into a product of downward and upward-closed description domains.

Definition. A constraint description domain *Acon* is *downward-closed* iff

$$\forall a \in Acon \,.\, \forall \pi, \pi' \in Con \,.\, (a \ appr \ \pi \wedge (\pi \Rightarrow \pi')) \Rightarrow a \ appr \ \pi'.$$

We define *upward-closed* in the dual manner. ■

The definiteness analysis exemplifies a downward-closed description domain while the freeness analysis exemplifies an upward-closed description domain. In a sense, downward-closed descriptions approximate constraints by weaker constraints and upward-closed descriptions approximate constraints by stronger constraints. In general, downward-closed description domains are useful for analyses which remove redundant choicepoints while upward-closed description domains are useful for analyses which remove redundant tests for satisfiability.

5 Conclusion

We have identified a need for the dataflow analysis of CLP programs and presented a framework for their development. This framework is simple, much simpler than the less general frameworks previously given for the top-down abstract interpretation of definite logic programs. There are two reasons for this. The first is the use of a definition-independent meta-language given by Marriott, Søndergaard and Jones [15] which has allowed results concerning abstract interpretation to be pushed into the metalanguage and facilitated a stepwise, derivational approach to the development of dataflow analyses. The second reason is that constraints are conceptually simpler than most general unifiers and the basic operations required in the semantic definitions may be expressed naturally in terms of logical operations on the constraints.

Acknowledgements

The authors would like to thank Joxan Jaffar who participated in several useful discussions.

References

[1] R. Barbuti, R. Giacobazzi and G. Levi. A declarative approach to abstract interpretation of logic programs. Technical Report 20/89, Dept. of Informatics, University of Pisa, Italy, 1989.

[2] M. Bruynooghe *et al.* Abstract interpretation: towards the global optimization of Prolog programs. In *Proc. Fourth Int. Symp. Logic Programming*, pages 192–204. San Francisco, California, 1987.

[3] P. Cousot and R. Cousot. Abstract interpretation: a unified lattice model for static analysis of programs by construction or approximation of fixpoints. In *Proc. Fourth Ann. ACM Symp. Principles of Programming Languages*, pages 238–252. Los Angeles, California, 1977.

[4] P. Cousot and R. Cousot. Systematic design of program analysis frameworks. In *Proc. Sixth Ann. ACM Symp. Principles of Programming Languages*, pages 269–282. San Antonio, Texas, 1979.

[5] S. K. Debray. *Global Optimization of Logic Programs.* Ph. D. Thesis, State University of New York at Stony Brook, New York, 1986.

[6] S. K. Debray and D. S. Warren. Functional computations in logic programs. *ACM Transactions on Programming Languages and Systems* **11** (3): 451–481, 1989.

[7] N. Heintze *et al.* *The CLP Programmer's Manual.* Dept. of Computer Science, Monash University, Australia, 1986.

[8] J. Jaffar and J.-L. Lassez. Constraint logic programming. In *Proc. Fourteenth Ann. ACM Symp. Principles of Programming Languages*, pages 111-119. San Francisco, California, 1987.

[9] N. D. Jones and H. Søndergaard. A semantics-based framework for the abstract interpretation of Prolog. In S. Abramsky and C. Hankin, editors, *Abstract Interpretation of Declarative Languages*, pages 123–142. Ellis Horwood, 1987.

[10] T. Kanamori and T. Kawamura. Analyzing success patterns of logic programs by abstract hybrid interpretation. ICOT TR-279, ICOT, Tokyo, Japan, 1987.

[11] K. Marriott and H. Søndergaard. Bottom-up abstract interpretation of logic programs. In R. Kowalski and K. Bowen, editors, *Logic Programming: Proc. Fifth Int. Conf. Symp.*, pages 733–748. MIT Press, 1988.

[12] K. Marriott and H. Søndergaard. Bottom-up dataflow analysis of normal logic programs. To appear in *Journal of Logic Programming.*

[13] K. Marriott and H. Søndergaard. Semantics-based dataflow analysis of logic programs. In G. X. Ritter, editor, *Information Processing 89*, pages 601–606. North-Holland, 1989.

[14] K. Marriott, H. Søndergaard and P. Dart. A characterization of non-floundering logic programs. This volume.

[15] K. Marriott, H. Søndergaard and N. D. Jones. Denotational abstract interpretation of logic programs. Submitted for publication.

[16] C. S. Mellish. The automatic generation of mode declarations for Prolog programs. DAI Research Paper No. 163, University of Edinburgh, Scotland, 1981.

[17] C. S. Mellish. Abstract interpretation of Prolog programs. In E. Shapiro, editor, *Proc. Third Int. Conf. Logic Programming* (Lecture Notes in Computer Science 240), pages 463–474. Springer-Verlag 1986.

[18] F. Nielson. Strictness analysis and denotational abstract interpretation. *Information and Computation* **76** (1) : 29–92, 1988.

[19] H. Søndergaard. An application of abstract interpretation of logic programs: Occur check reduction. In B. Robinet and R. Wilhelm, editors, *Proc. ESOP 86* (Lecture Notes in Computer Science 213), pages 327–338. Springer-Verlag, 1986.

Proof Theory

On the Elimination of Redundant Derivations During Execution

Richard Helm
I.B.M. Thomas J. Watson Research Center,
P.O. Box 704, Yorktown Heights, NY 10598, USA
helm@ibm.com

Abstract

We address the problem of determining whether or not a derivation that is known to be redundant can be eliminated during program execution. Through a reduction from the problem of deciding the termination of term-rewriting systems, we show that although this problem is undecidable, results concerning the termination of term-rewriting systems provide many sufficient conditions for the elimination of derivations. Subsumption plays a key rule in the detection and elimination of redundant derivations because it captures, syntactically, the notion of immediate logical consequence. We investigate the relationship between subsumption and immediate logical consequence, and show its subtle dependency on the number of function symbols in the first-order language describing programs. We derive a compactness result for subsumption of sets of rules which implies that operational techniques and syntactic tests based on subsumption are equivalent when there are countably infinite number of function symbols, but that subsumption based techniques are superior when there are a finite number of function symbols, as for example in some definitions of Datalog programs. As part of our analyses, we derive a new sufficient condition for uniform boundedness of linear recursive rules and show that run-time techniques based on "memo-ing" previous goals, such as SLD-AL resolution, cannot in general detect redundant derivations.

1 Introduction

Redundant derivations occur in some very simple, yet typical, programs. Consider the following program

$$\begin{array}{ll} 1: & \mathsf{sibling(X,Z)} \leftarrow \mathsf{sibling(Z,X)} \\ 2: & \mathsf{sibling(X,Z)} \leftarrow \mathsf{sibling(X,Y)} \wedge \mathsf{sibling(Y,Z)} \\ 3: & \mathsf{sibling(X,Z)} \leftarrow \mathsf{parent(X,A)} \wedge \mathsf{parent(Z,A)} \\ 4: & \mathsf{parent(X,A)} \leftarrow \mathsf{sibling(X,Y)} \wedge \mathsf{parent(Y,A)} \end{array}$$

with facts sibling(kate, richard), parent(richard,joy), parent(neil,joy). This program defines many redundant derivations and we have discussed it elsewhere [2, 4]. For example, every instance of sibling(X, Y), sibling(kate,neil) say, has at least two distinct derivations; they can be derived via the second and third rule *and* via the third and fourth rule. This redundancy is readily illustrated in the derivation trees pictured in Figure 1. Notice how the rules used to construct these derivations are different, but their roots and leaves are identical. The detection and elimination of redundant derivations

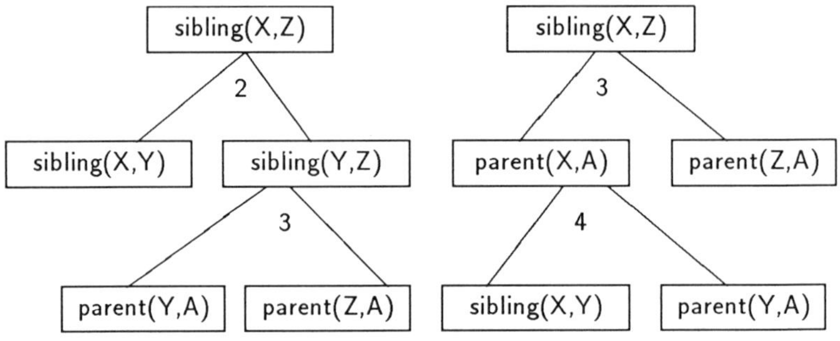

Figure 1:

is an important program optimization as they not only cause significant inefficiency or non-termination during execution, but also indicate if a program has properties which allow it to be more efficiently executed. Recent work[2, 4] has proposed using control languages to modify the operational semantics of programs to eliminate redundant derivations during execution.

However, even though a derivation is redundant, in some pathological cases it cannot be eliminated during program execution without loss of completeness[14]. Redundant derivations must thus be tested to determine if they are eliminable. This paper addresses this issue.

In section 2 and 3, we show how redundant derivations are defined in terms of immediate logical consequence and may be detected syntactically via subsumption, essentially the syntactic equivalent of immediate logical consequence. Because, subsumption plays a key role in detecting redundant derivations, in section 4 we investigate properties of subsumption and its relationship to immediate logical consequence. We show this relationship breaks down when the first-order language in which programs are described contains only a finite number of function symbols. We then derive a compactness result, analogous to compactness results for equation sets [9], which implies firstly, that subsumption based techniques are equivalent to operational techniques when there are countably infinite number of function symbols, and secondly, that subsumption based techniques for detecting redundant derivations are better than operational techniques when there are finite numbers of function symbols. We show how operational tests for redundant derivations for programs defined in this case can give counter-intuitive results, indicating general rules are redundant rather than more specific rules. We also give an alternative characterization of subsumption, which preserves the relationship between subsumption and immediate logical consequence.

Eliminating redundant derivations can be viewed as a process of transforming derivations by the replacement of redundant sub-derivations. This sequence of transformations terminates when all redundant sub-derivations have been replaced by non redundant derivations. A redundant derivation is eliminable, if for every derivation in which it appears, there is a terminating transformation sequence. We show in sections 5 and 6 how the problem of determining the termination of this transformation sequence is closely related to that of termination of a term-rewriting systems. Through a reduction from the halting problem via term-rewriting systems, we show that while in theory, determining whether or not a redundant derivation is eliminable is undecidable, in practice many results concerning the termination of term-rewriting systems, see for example [1], provide sufficient conditions for the elimination of redundant derivations.

The replacement of redundant sub-derivations is also based on the definition of subsumption. Through analysis of the subsumption relationships between derivations obtained via sequences of these transformations, we also obtain two interesting results in section 5. Firstly a new sufficient condition for the uniform boundedness of linear recursive rules[13], and secondly that run-time techniques based on "memo-ing", such as SLD-AL resolution[18], cannot in general detect redundant derivations.

2 Preliminaries

We assume definitions of function symbols, terms, predicates, the Herbrand Base(HB), and substitutions, see for example [9, 10]. We assume that the language L from which a program is constructed contains a countably infinite number of function symbols. We let $\forall X$ denote the universal closure of formula X.

We consider a *program* P as consisting of rules R and facts A. To each *rule* $p(\tilde{t}) \leftarrow p_1(\tilde{t}_1) \wedge ... \wedge p_n(\tilde{t}_n)$, $n > 0$, of a program we associate a *name* r and write $r : p(\tilde{t}) \leftarrow p_1(\tilde{t}_1) \wedge ... \wedge p_n(\tilde{t}_n)$. In the example the last rule is named **4**. For clarity, facts are written $p(\tilde{t}) \leftarrow true$.

We associate an *immediate consequence function* $[\![r]\!] : 2^{HB} \rightarrow 2^{HB}$ with a rule $r : p(\tilde{t}) \leftarrow p_1(\tilde{t}_1) \wedge ... \wedge p_n(\tilde{t}_n)$, such that for all $X \subseteq HB$, $[\![r]\!](X) = \{p(\tilde{t})\theta : \{p_1(\tilde{t}_1)\theta, ..., p_n(\tilde{t}_n)\theta\} \subseteq X$ for some grounding substitution $\theta\}$. We let *id* be the *identity immediate consequence function* and let *ID* be a set of rules of the form $p(\tilde{t}) \leftarrow p(\tilde{t})$ for predicates p appearing in a program such that $[\![ID]\!] = id$. The function T_P[17] is equivalent to $[\![R]\!] + [\![A]\!]$, where $(f + g)(X) = f(X) \cup g(X)$. We let f^{ω} represent the function defined by $f^{\omega}(X) = \bigcup_{n\geq 0}^{\infty} f^n(X)$. Immediate consequence functions are partially ordered by $\leq$ where $f \leq g$ if $\forall X \subseteq HB.f(X) \leq g(X)$ i.e.: they are monotonic, and continuous.

A rule r_1 may be *composed* with a rule r_2 by unfolding an atom in the body of r_1 matching r_2, with the body of r_2. We say a rule composition is *constructed* from a program P if it is composed from rules in P or *ID*. In the previous program, composing the second atom in the body of rule 2 with rule 3 gives the rule

$$\mathsf{sibling}(\mathsf{X},\mathsf{Z}) \leftarrow \mathsf{sibling}(\mathsf{X},\mathsf{Y}) \wedge \mathsf{parent}(\mathsf{Y},\mathsf{A}) \wedge \mathsf{parent}(\mathsf{Z},\mathsf{A}).$$

If a rule composition δ is formed from rule compositions $\{\delta_1, ..., \delta_n\}$, we say δ *contains* each δ_i. We denote a rule compositions by a *rule composition expression(rce)* which is either

1. a *simple rule composition expression* r, for a rule named r, or
2. a *compound rule composition expression* $r.(\delta_1, ..., \delta_m)$ where rule r has m atoms in its body, and where each δ_k is either (a) a rule composition expression signifying that the kth atom in the body of rule r has been composed with the rule defined by δ_k , or (b) an *identity expression* id which signifies that the kth atom in rule r has not been composed with any rule.

The previous rule composition has rule composition expression 2.(id, 3). The Appendix of [4] lists some rule compositions and associated rce's for the example.

A rule composition defines a partial (ie: incomplete) GLD-derivation[19] for the atomic query that is the head of the rule. The partial derivation may be viewed as a derivation tree, whose root is the head of the rule composition, and whose leaf nodes comprise the body of the rule composition. The rule composition expression 2.(id, 3) represents the left-hand derivation tree in Figure 1. Partial derivations and rule compositions are equivalent representations in different mathematical formalisms. Henceforth, we shall use each interchangeably.

3 Redundant Derivations

Intuitively, a derivation(rule composition) δ is redundant if there exists a derivation δ' which derives at least the same set of logical consequences, that is $\forall\delta' \rightarrow \forall\delta$. Although this definition captures our intuition, it has a drawback. Logical consequence, being a declarative concept, does not take into account the lengths of derivations, which are undoubtably important in practice. Consequently, we define redundant derivations in terms of immediate consequence functions[1]. This gives a definition more closely allied to the operational semantics of program execution.

Definition 1 Let the rule composition δ be constructed from rules in a program P. The derivation δ is *redundant* iff it is tautological, or there exists a rule composition δ' constructed from P not containing δ as a sub-composition, such that $[\![\delta']\!] \geq [\![\delta]\!]$. We refer to δ' as a *redundancy eliminating* derivation. If a derivation δ is redundant, we say that the corresponding rule composition δ is *redundant.* ■

[1] This definition of redundant derivations is more refined than that we gave in [4, 2].

Intuitively, if a partial δ derivation is redundant, then whenever it appears within a derivation it may be replaced by the partial derivation δ' with the resulting derivation deriving at least the same facts as before. However, in certain pathological cases, this replacement process can introduce new redundant derivations, which no matter how they are subsequently replaced, result in further redundant derivations being introduced into the derivation. This problem is illustrated in the following example.

Example 1 Suppose that for linear recursive rules, r_1 and r_2, that derivation $r_1.r_2$ is redundant, with corresponding redundancy eliminating derivation $r_2.r_2.r_1.r_1$. Consider the derivation $r_1.r_1.r_2$. Replacing the sub derivation $r_1.r_2$ by $r_2.r_2.r_1.r_1$ gives derivation $r_1.r_2.r_2.r_1.r_1$ which contains a new instance of $r_1.r_2$. Replacing this derivation, gives the derivation $r_2.r_2.r_1.r_1.r_2.r_1.r_1$ which contains yet another new instance of the derivation $r_1.r_2$. Note that it is not possible to eliminate an occurrence of $r_1.r_2$ within all derivations by this replacement process. ∎

This problem, identified in [14], arises because for all derivations containing a redundant partial derivation δ, there may not exist a corresponding redundancy eliminating derivation which does not contain δ. Naively eliminating all derivations which contain the redundant derivation δ may thus result in loss of logical completeness. Before we can discuss this phenomena in more detail, we require a better understanding of the relationship between a redundant derivation and its corresponding redundancy eliminating derivation. This relationship is described in terms of subsumption.

4 Subsumption and Testing for Redundant Derivations

Subsumption[15] captures syntactically the notion of a clause being more general than another clause.

Definition 2 A clause $r_1 : a \leftarrow a_1 \wedge ... \wedge a_n$ *subsumes* a clause $r_2 : b \leftarrow b_1 \wedge ... \wedge b_m$, written $r_1 \geq r_2$, if there exists a substitution θ such that $a\theta = b$ and $\{a_1\theta, ..., a_n\theta\} \subseteq \{b_1, ..., b_m\}$. We refer to θ as a *subsuming substitution.* Two clauses are *subsumption-equivalent* if each subsumes the other. ∎

There is a well known relationship between logical implication and subsumption. If a clause δ' subsumes δ then $\forall\delta' \rightarrow \forall\delta$. The converse is *not* true. Subsumption of definite clauses is important in the study of redundant derivations because it is the syntactic equivalent of immediate logical consequence.

Proposition 3 [11] A rule r_1 subsumes a rule r_2 iff $[\![r_1]\!] \geq [\![r_2]\!]$. A rule r_1 is subsumption-equivalent to a rule r_2 iff $[\![r_1]\!] = [\![r_2]\!]$. ∎

Maher[11] extends this proposition to sets of rules. Using this proposition, the following theorem provides a syntactic test for redundant derivations.

Theorem 4 For a program P and rule compositions δ' and δ constructed from P, if δ' subsumes δ and δ is not a sub-composition of δ', then the derivation δ is redundant. ∎

Note that in Theorem 4, if δ is a tautology, then by the definition of constructed, δ' can be a rule in *ID*.

Example 2 Consider our example program. The rule compositions 2.(id, 3) and 3.(4, id) are subsumption equivalent, both being the rule

$$\text{sibling(X,Z)} \leftarrow \text{sibling(X,Y)} \wedge \text{parent(Y,A)} \wedge \text{parent(Z,A)}.$$

Hence the derivations 2.(id, 3) and 3.(4, id) are redundant with respect to each other. Continuing, the rule 1.1

$$\text{sibling(X,Z)} \leftarrow \text{sibling(X,Z)}$$

is a tautology. Therefore it is subsumed by a rule in *ID* and so derivation 1.1 is redundant. Other equivalent partial derivations are given by the following pairs of subsumption-equivalent rules.

ID	=	1.1	3	=	1.3
2.(1, 1)	=	1.2	2.(id, 3)	=	3.(4, id)
2.(3, id)	=	3.(id, 4.(1, id))	2.(1, 3)	=	3.(4.(1, id), id)
2.(3, 1)	=	3.(id, 4)	2.(2, 3)	=	3.(4.(id, 4), id)
2.(3, 2)	=	3.(id, 4.(1, 4.(1, id)), id)	2.(3, 3)	=	3.(4.(3, id), id)
4.(id, 4)	=	4.(2, id)	4.(id, 4.(id, 4))	=	4.(2, 4)

We have investigated further properties of this program more fully in [2]. ∎

In practice, determining if a derivation is redundant requires repeatedly composing rules and testing for subsumption amongst sets of rules. If a program defines significant numbers of redundant derivations, as does our example, they are found quickly, after only a few rule compositions.

However, when dealing with subsumption over *sets* of rules, the relationship between subsumption and immediate consequence is not as straightforward as proposition 3 suggests. Robinson's original definition of subsumption assumes, as does proposition 3, that L contains a countably infinite number of function symbols. In this case, the rule $p(X) \leftarrow \mathit{true}$ strictly subsumes the rules $p(a) \leftarrow \mathit{true}$ and $p(b) \leftarrow \mathit{true}$. There is a corresponding relationship between the immediate consequence functions of these rules.

In contrast, consider the case when L contains only the constants a, b. The rule $p(X) \leftarrow \mathit{true}$ still strictly subsumes the more specific rules $p(a) \leftarrow \mathit{true}$ and $p(b) \leftarrow \mathit{true}$, but now their respective immediate consequence functions are equivalent over L. Thus when there are only a finite number of constant symbols in L, proposition 3 is false; we have lost the relationship between immediate consequence and subsumption. This problem occurs because a finite set of specific rules can enumerate all instantiations of a more general rule. As we shall see, this disparity has implications for the detection of redundancy in programs which assume a finite number of function symbols in L, as do some definitions of Datalog programs. We now investigate this dependency on the language L.

An alternative characterization of subsumption for the case where L can contain a finite set of function symbols is given by the following definition.

Definition 5 A rule $r_1 : a \leftarrow a_1 \wedge ... \wedge a_n$ *subsumes* a rule $r_2 : b \leftarrow b_1 \wedge ... \wedge b_m$, written $r_1 \geq_g r_2$, if for all ground instances $r_2\theta$, there exists a substitution ϕ such that $a\phi = b\theta$ and $\{a_1\phi, ..., a_n\phi\} \subseteq \{b_1\theta, ..., b_m\theta\}$. A set of rules $\{r_1, ..., r_n\}$ *subsumes* r if and only if for all ground instances $r\theta$, there exists an r_i which subsumes $r\theta$. ∎

Notice the different symbols $\geq$ and $\geq_g$ used to denote these different definitions of subsumption.

By this definition, when there are only a finite set of function symbols in L, a set of specific rules subsume a more general rule if they enumerate all instantiations of the more general rule. The following example illustrates this is for the case when the Herbrand Universe is infinite.

Example 3 If L contains a finite set of function symbols, constants a, b and unary function symbol f say, then the two sets of rules

$$1: \quad p(f(X)) \leftarrow p(X) \qquad\qquad 2: \quad \begin{array}{l} p(f(a))) \leftarrow p(a) \\ p(f(b)) \leftarrow p(b) \\ p(f(f(X))) \leftarrow p(f(X)) \end{array}$$

have equivalent immediate consequence functions in L. However, whereas they are subsumption-equivalent according to definition 5, they are not according to definition 2; no rule in the second set subsumes($\geq$) the rule in the first. ∎

This following proposition shows that when L contains a countably infinite number of function symbols, definition 5 is equivalent to Robinson's original definition of subsumption over single rules.

Proposition 6 Let L contain a countably infinite number of function symbols. A rule r_1 subsumes r_2 if and only if for all ground instances $r_2\phi$, r_1 subsumes $r_2\phi$.

Proof: ($\Rightarrow$) Straightforward.

($\Leftarrow$) Let r_1 be $a \leftarrow a_1 \wedge ... \wedge a_n$ and r_2 be $b \leftarrow b_1 \wedge ... \wedge b_m$. Consider the instance $r_2\phi$ for grounding substitution ϕ which binds distinct variables occurring in r_2 to distinct new constants not occurring in r_1 or r_2. If r_1 subsumes r_2 then there exists a substitution θ such that $a\theta = b\phi$ and $\{a_1\theta, ..., a_n\theta\} \subseteq \{b_1\phi, ..., b_m\phi\}$. Replacing distinct new constants introduced by ϕ with distinct variables, gives $\{a_1\alpha, ..., a_n\alpha\} \subseteq \{b_1, ..., b_m\}$ and $a\alpha = b$. Consequently r_1 subsumes r_2 with subsuming substitution α. ∎

Definition 5 also preserves the relationship between immediate consequence and subsumption over sets of rules.

Proposition 7 A set of rules R_1 subsumes($\geq_g$) a set of rules R_2 if and only if $[\![R_1]\!] \geq [\![R_2]\!]$.

Proof: ($\Rightarrow$) Straightforward.

($\Leftarrow$) It suffices to consider the case when R_2 contains a single rule $r_2 : b \leftarrow b_1 \wedge ... \wedge b_n$ For any grounding substitution θ for r_2, $b\theta \in [\![r_2]\!](\{b_1\theta, ..., b_n\theta\})$ implies $b\theta \in [\![R_1]\!](\{b_1\theta, ..., b_n\theta\})$. This implies that for some rule $r_1 : a \leftarrow a_1 \wedge ... \wedge a_n \in R_1$, $b\theta = a\psi$ and $\{a_1\psi, ..., a_m\psi\} \subseteq \{b_1\theta, ..., b_n\theta\}$. Thus by definition 5, $R_1 \geq_g R_2$. ∎

This result is slightly more general than proposition 3 as it pertains to the case when L contains a finite set of function symbols. This proposition will be important later when we discuss techniques based on immediate consequence functions for detecting redundancy in programs for which L contains a finite number of functions symbols.

Theorem 8 (Compactness) Let L contain a countably infinite number of function symbols. A clause r is subsumed($\geq$) by a finite set of clause R if and only if there exists an $r_i \in R$ such that r_i subsumes($\geq$) r.

Proof: ($\Rightarrow$) By the previous definition, there exists r_i written $a \leftarrow a_1 \wedge ... \wedge a_n$ which subsumes $r\theta$ written $b\theta \leftarrow b_1\theta \wedge ... \wedge b_m\theta$ where θ is a grounding substitution which substitutes distinct variables in r for distinct new constants not occurring in R or r. This means that there exists a substitution α such that $a\alpha = b$ and a substitution ϕ which substitutes distinct variables in r_i for distinct new constants not occurring in R or r such that $\{a_1\alpha\phi\theta, ..., a_n\alpha\phi\theta\} \subseteq \{b_1\theta, ..., b_m\theta\}$. Lifting the distinct new constants to variables, we have that $\{a_1\alpha\phi, ..., a_n\alpha\phi\} \subseteq \{b_1, ..., b_m\}$ and thus clause r_i subsumes r.

($\Leftarrow$) Straightforward. ∎

This theorem gives a result for subsumption of clauses analogous to that concerning the Strong Compactness of equation sets[9]. As theorem 8 and proposition 6 only require a fixed number of new constants, they also hold when L contains a finite and sufficiently large number of function symbols.

Theorem 8 also holds when R contains infinitely many rules, and there exist only a finite number of function symbols occurring in R. In this case it is not possible for the set R to enumerate all possible ground instances of r. In particular the set of all rule compositions of a program, i.e.: derivations, is infinite but contains a finite set of function symbols. If this set subsumes another rule, then by Theorem 8 there exists one rule composition which subsumes it. Consequently, it is sufficient to find one derivation δ' which subsumes a derivation δ to show δ is redundant.

As we have seen, this theorem does not hold when L contains a finite number of function symbols and all these symbols occur in the rules. The number of function symbols is important as some definitions of Datalog programs assume L contains a finite number of constant symbols. In this case, operational techniques to detect redundancy[16, 14], based on the "chase"[12] can give counter-intuitive results. L must contain contain sufficient function symbols for these test to be applied. If not, these techniques will in example 3, determine that rule 1 is redundant. This problem is exacerbated when detecting redundant derivations.

In summary, the operational and subsumption based tests for redundant derivations are equivalent when there are countably infinite, or at least sufficient numbers of function symbols in L, but the subsumption based techniques are superior when there are a finite number of function symbols.

A further consequence of proposition 3 applies to properties of programs [8, 2, 7]. Often conditions which define these properties are expressed in terms of algebraic properties of compositions of immediate consequence functions. In [3] we show that any composition of immediate consequence functions is equivalent to an immediate consequence function associated with a set of rule compositions. Proposition 3 means that using sets of rules corresponding to some functional composition, the conditions which define properties of programs can be tested syntactically using subsumption.

5 Eliminating Redundant Derivations

Earlier we noted that although a partial derivation δ may be redundant, it may not be possible to eliminate all derivations which contain δ without losing completeness. We now discuss this problem in more detail.

The elimination of redundant derivations may viewed as a process of transforming derivations which contain redundant partial derivations into ones which do not. Each transformation step of this process, replaces redundant partial derivations with their corresponding redundancy eliminating derivation. This view is taken in [14]

Suppose that a derivation $\delta' : a \leftarrow a_1 \wedge \ldots \wedge a_n$ subsumes the derivation $\delta : b \leftarrow b_1 \wedge \ldots \wedge b_m$, and that δ appears as a sub-composition of derivation r. We now define how δ may *replaced* in r by δ' to give the transformed derivation r'. A difficulty in performing this replacement arises because more than one atom in δ' may be mapped to an atom in δ by the subsuming substitution θ. This means that one cannot simply substitute δ' for δ in r to get r', the mapping of atoms in δ' by θ must be considered.

The derivation rooted at δ may be represented by the term $\delta.(\delta_1, \ldots, \delta_m)$ where each δ_i is a rule composition expression which represents the derivation of b_i. In forming r', the partial derivation $\delta.(\delta_1, \ldots, \delta_m)$ must be replaced by a new derivation $\delta'.(\delta'_1, \ldots, \delta'_n)$ (see figure 2). The replacement derivation $\delta'.(\delta'_1, \ldots, \delta'_n)$ is constructed a follows. As δ' subsumes δ, there exists a substitution θ such that $a\theta = b$ and for all a_i, there exists a b_j such that $a_i\theta = b_j$. This means that the derivation δ_j for b_j is also a derivation of a_i. Thus

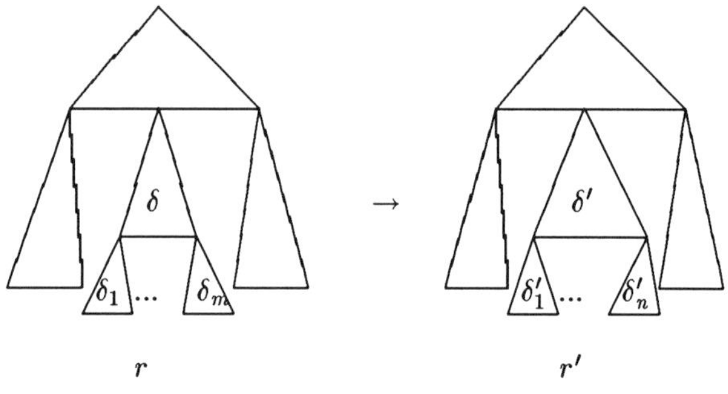

Figure 2: Replacing derivation δ by δ'.

each δ'_i in $\delta'.(\delta'_1, ..., \delta'_n)$ corresponds to some derivation δ_j. Note that, there may exist more than one derivation in $\{\delta'_1, ..., \delta'_n\}$ which corresponds to a particular δ_j because it is possible that for some $a_i, a_k : i \neq k$, $a_i\theta = b_j$ and $a_k\theta = b_j$.

If δ is a tautology, replaced by a rule in *ID*, then the replacement eliminates the subtree rooted at δ. Our notion of transforming derivation trees generalizes that defined for linear recursive rules described in [14].

It is informative to consider what effect the replacement of a derivation in the canonical BF-derivation[19] has on its equivalent SLD-derivations. In our example, consider two SLD-derivations of sibling(X, Y), one containing a partial derivation 2.(3, 1), and the other obtained by replacing 2.(3, 1) by 3.(id, 4).

1.	sibling(X, Y)	sibling(X, Y)
	$\downarrow 2$	$\downarrow 3$
2.	sibling(X, Z), sibling(Z, Y)	parent(X, A), parent(Y, A)
	$\downarrow 3$	$\vdots x$
3.	parent(X, A), parent(Z, A), sibling(Z, Y)	parent(Y, A)
	$\vdots x$	$\downarrow 4$
4.	parent(Z, A), sibling(Z, Y)	sibling(Y, Z), parent(Z, A)
	$\vdots y$	$\vdots z$
5.	sibling(Z, Y)	parent(Z, A)
	$\downarrow 1$	$\vdots y$
6.	sibling(Y, Z)	$\square$
	$\vdots z$	
7.	$\square$	

We let $\downarrow r$ denote resolution of rule r with the underlined, left most atom in a goal, and "$\vdots x$" denote a partial, unspecified derivation sequence x which reduces the leftmost atom of the preceding goal. The length of the unspecified partial derivations, that marked x say, in each of these derivations are identical, and depend on the length of the derivation of the preceding leftmost atom they reduce.

Notice how the replacement of 2.(3, 1) by 3.(id, 4) in an SLD-derivation can be seen to simultaneously replace and reorder multiple sections of the derivation.

We note the following point: the atoms parent(Y,A), parent(Z,A), sibling(X,Y) that constitute the bodies of rules 2.(3, 1) and 3.(id, 4) do not appear all together in any goal in either of these SLD-derivations if a leftmost (or even local) selection function is used. In general if a partial derivation δ' replaces δ, the atoms in in the bodies of the corresponding rules are unlikely to appear together in a goal in an SLD-derivation. As a consequence, run-time techniques that save or "memo" previous goals as lemmas and use subsumption tests over goals to eliminate redundant computation, such as SLD-AL resolution[18], will generally not be able to detect redundant derivations; the goals required for them to do so are simply not generated. Note that for non-trivial selection functions, there do exist SLD-derivations equivalent to both these derivations in which the atoms parent(Y, A), parent(Z, A), sibling(X, Y) do appear together in a goal. However, these selection functions cannot be known *a priori* - they require prescient knowledge of the redundant derivations.

We now show that subsumption is preserved by the replacement of derivations.

Proposition 9 Let rule r_1 subsume r_2. The rule δ' formed by replacing rule r_2 by r_1 in rule δ subsumes δ.

Proof: Let rule $r_1 : a \leftarrow a_1, ..., a_n$ subsumes $r_2 : b \leftarrow b_1, ..., b_m$ with subsuming substitution ϕ. We first show that if r_2 a composed with some rule r, to give rule δ then the result of replacing r_2 by r_1 to give δ' subsumes δ. Suppose that r_2 is composed with r by matching atom b_j with r to give rule δ. There exists atoms $a_i\phi$ in $r_1\phi$ such that $a_i\phi = b_j$. Now r_2 may be replaced by r_1 by composing r with these atoms $a_i\phi$ in $r_1\phi$ to give $\delta'\phi$. All atoms in this rule will appear in δ and thus δ' subsumes δ. It is straightforward to show that r composed with r_1 subsumes r composed with r_2. Repeated application of this result proves the proposition for arbitrary rules δ. ∎

Thus for any derivation δ which contains a redundant derivation, there exists a derivation which subsumes it, and so δ is redundant.

Eliminating a redundant partial derivation from a derivation may introduce further redundant partial derivations. This may require a sequence of replacements to remove all redundancy. A property of the *transformation sequence* obtain by such a sequence of replacements is given by the following corollary to proposition 9.

Corollary 10 Let $\{\delta_i\}$ denote the sequence of derivations $\delta_0, \delta_1, \delta_2, ...$ where for $i > 0$ each δ_{i+1} is formed from δ_i by replacing a sub-derivation δ by a subsuming derivation δ'. For all $i > 0$, δ_{i+1} subsumes δ_i.

By proposition 3, the partial ordering induced by subsumption over sets of rules is equivalent to the partial ordering $\geq$ over immediate consequence functions associated with rules. It forms a complete partial order with greatest upper bound the set of rules of the form $p(x_1, .., x_m) \leftarrow true$ for distinct variables x_i and each predicate symbol p in L. Note the ordering induced by subsumption or immediate logical consequence over rules, does not necessarily correspond to the ordering of arbitrary functions over the Herbrand base. The latter forms a complete lattice, whereas the former may not.

A transformation sequence $\{\delta_i\}$ has the following properties resulting from the subsumption relationship between rules. Firstly, every rule in the sequence has the same predicate symbol, p of arity n say, in the head. Secondly, we may associate the immediate consequence function $[\![\delta_i]\!]$ with each rule δ_i in the sequence. This resulting sequence of functions form a chain ordered by $\geq$ for which there exists a least upper bound. The greatest upper bound of $\{\delta_i\}$ is the rule $p(x_1, ..., x_n) \leftarrow true$ where the x_i are distinct variables. The initial rule in the sequence defines the constant, function and predicate symbols which can appear in the remaining rules in the sequence; no new symbols can be introduced in later rules without violating the subsumption relationships.

Consider the sequence $\{\delta_i\}$ in which every rule in the sequence strictly subsumes all its predecessors. We now show that if there are no function symbols in L, only constant symbols, such sequences must be finite.

For a rule δ_i in the sequence, let $X = [\![\delta_i]\!](HB)$. Some facts in X will contain constants not occurring in δ_i. Replace these constants with new variables. Delete from X facts which are instances of other facts. The resulting set, which we call $immed(\delta_i)$, represents classes of facts which can be computed by δ_i. As L contains only constant symbols, the set $immed(\delta_i)$ is finite.

Theorem 11 Let the rules in the sequence $\{\delta_i\}$ contain only constant symbols. For all i, let δ_{i+1} strictly subsume δ_i. $\{\delta_i\}$ is bounded above by some rule δ_k for some finite k.

Proof: We may associate an immediate consequence function $[\![\delta_i]\!]$ with each rule δ_i in the sequence. Consider $immed(\delta_i)$, the result of applying function $[\![\delta_i]\!]$ to the set of all ground atoms which appear in the body of δ_i.

If δ_{i+1} strictly subsumes δ_i, then by proposition 3, $[\![\delta_{i+1}]\!] > [\![\delta_i]\!]$. This means that that there must exists some atom in $immed(\delta_{i+1})$ which is more general than some atoms in $immed(\delta_i)$. This means that some atom in $immed(\delta_i)$ appears in $immed(\delta_{i+1})$ with some constant appearing within it replaced by some variable. As there are no function symbols, there exist only a finite number of facts in $immed(\delta_i)$ and only a finite number of constant symbols appearing therein. This means that constants in $immed(\delta_i)$ can only be replaced by variables a finite number of times. Consequently, there exists a rule δ_k for some finite k such that δ_k subsumes all rules δ_i where $i \leq k$. ∎

Corollary 12 In a sequence of rules $\{\delta_i\}$ containing only constant symbols, there exists a rule δ_i such that δ_i subsumes δ_{i+1}. ∎

It is an open question whether the previous theorem may be generalized to the case where there exist function symbols.

A special case of transformation sequence is when the initial rule in the sequence is a linear recursive rule r, and all subsequent rules are successive compositions of r. Naughton and Sagiv[13] have shown that if some rule in this sequence subsumes a later rule, then rule r is uniformly bounded. They also give sufficient conditions for uniform boundedness of linear recursive rules. Corollary 12 provides a new sufficient condition for uniform boundedness.

Proposition 13 Consider the transformation sequence of a linear recursive rule r. If some rule in the sequence subsumes a previous rule, then the rule r is uniformly bounded. ∎

Example 4 Consider the following rule from Example 4.1 of [13]

$$r : t(X, Z^0) \leftarrow t(X, Z^1) \wedge e(Z^1, Z^0) \wedge e(Z^1, X) \wedge e(X, X) \wedge e(X, Z^0)$$

In a slight abuse of notation we let $r.r$, $r.r.r$ denote the composition of the rule with itself one and two times respectively. This rule is uniformly bounded, because rule $r.r$ subsumes $r.r.r$. However, this cannot be determined using the sufficient conditions described in [13]. However, by composing this rule with itself, we find that the rule $r.r$.

$$\begin{aligned} t(X, Z^0) \leftarrow t(X, Z^2) \quad & \wedge e(Z^2, Z^1) \wedge e(Z^2, X) \wedge e(X, X) \wedge e(X, Z^1) \\ & \wedge e(Z^1, Z^0) \wedge e(Z^1, X) \wedge e(X, X) \wedge e(X, Z^0) \end{aligned}$$

subsumes r. By the previous proposition, rule r is uniformly bounded. ∎

6 Decidability Results

Recall that the replacement of redundant partial derivations can introduce further redundant derivations, and in some pathological cases, no matter what partial derivations are replaced, further redundant derivations will always be introduced. When this occurs, the replacement process generates an infinite sequence of more general derivations each containing a redundant partial derivation. Consequently, naively eliminating all derivations which contain a redundant partial derivation can result in loss of completeness.

Definition 14 A set of redundant derivation δ is *eliminable* if for all derivations δ' which contain derivation in δ there exists a redundancy eliminating derivation for δ' which does not contain a derivation in δ. ∎

If a derivation δ is eliminable, then every derivation which contains δ is redundant.

The transformation sequences defined by replacing redundant partial derivations by redundancy eliminating derivations may be studied by formulating them as *term-rewriting systems* [6] over terms τ representing partial derivations δ. A term τ, is obtained from rule composition expression δ by replacing each identity expression *id* in δ by a distinct variable X, and by replacing each simple rule composition expression r appearing in δ and which represents a program rule $a \leftarrow a_1 \wedge ... \wedge a_n$, by $r.(X_1, ..., X_n)$ where X_i are distinct variables.

To each redundant/redundancy eliminating pair δ and δ', we associate the rewrite rule $\tau \rightarrow \tau'$ such that (i) all variables in τ' occur in τ and (ii) a variable X in τ corresponding to an atom b_i in the body of rule δ is identical to a variable in τ' corresponding to an atom a_j in the body of rule δ' if and only if $a_j\theta = b_i$ for the subsuming substitution θ. For a set of such rewrite rules, all rules that are instances of others are deleted. The redundant/redundancy eliminating pair $2.(\mathsf{id}, 3)$ and $3.(4, \mathsf{id})$ has the associated rewrite rule $2.(X, 3.(Y, Z)) \rightarrow 3.(4.(X, Y), Z)$.

A transformation sequence *terminates* if for some δ_i, no rewrite rule can be applied; that is, δ_i does not contain a redundant derivation. A rewrite system *terminates* if all transformation sequences from any initial rule δ terminate.

Proposition 15 A redundant derivation δ is eliminable if for every rule which contains δ, there exists a terminating transformation sequence for that rule.

Proof: Note that, by proposition 9, each rule in the transformation sequence obtained from δ subsumes its predecessor. Thus for any rule containing δ we may find redundancy eliminating rule δ' which does not contain δ. Thus δ is eliminable. ∎

We now show that determining whether or not derivations are eliminable is undecidable by reduction from the halting problem for 2-counter machines (2CM)[5]. A 2CM has two non-negative counters, and transition function ψ determined by the current state and whether or not these counters are zero or positive. We represent the counters as terms $o, s(o), s(s(o)), ...$. The transition function can be denoted by $\psi : \Sigma \times \{=, >\} \times \{=, >\} \rightarrow \Sigma \times \{+, -\} \times \{+, -\}$ where $>, =$ represent tests for positive and zero counters respectively, and $+, -$ represent an increment and decrement of the counters. Thus $\psi(a, =, >) = (b, +, -)$ represents a transition from state a to b where in a counter 1 is zero, counter 2 is positive, and in state b these counters have been incremented and decremented respectively. We now encode 2CM's as a set of rewrite rules, and derive from these rewrite rules, a program which has subsumption relationships between rule compositions which defines these rewrite rules.

Each transition of the 2CM may be encoded as a term-rewriting rule, for example $\psi(a,=,>) = (b,+,-)$ may be encoded by $a(..., o(Y), s(X)) \rightarrow b(..., s(o(Y)), X)$ where the ellipses (...) will be described shortly. For this rewrite rule, we must now construct a corresponding redundant/redundancy eliminating pair of rule compositions. Consider the two rule compositions $\delta_1 : a(\bar{t}) \leftarrow a_1(\bar{t}) \wedge ... \wedge a_m(\bar{t})$ and $\delta_2 : b(\bar{t}) \leftarrow b_1(\bar{t}) \wedge ... \wedge b_n(\bar{t})$ such that $\delta_2 \geq \delta_1$. Append to the body of these rules, two new atoms $p(\bar{t}), p(\bar{t})$ to give δ_1' and δ_2'. Define two rules $s : p(\bar{t}) \leftarrow p(\bar{t}) \wedge c(\bar{t})$ and $o : p(\bar{t}) \leftarrow p(\bar{t}) \wedge d(\bar{t})$. The rule composition $\delta_1'.(id, ...m\ times..., id, o.X, s.Y)$ is subsumed by the rule composition $\delta_2'.(id, ...n\ times..., id, s.o.X, Y)$. The subsumption relationship between δ_2' and δ_1' defines the term-rewriting rule $a(X_1, ..., X_m, o(Y), s(X)) \rightarrow b(Y_1, ..., Y_n, s(o(Y)), X)$, where $\{Y_1, ..., Y_n\} \subseteq \{X_1, ..., X_m\}$, and captures the previous transition $\psi(a,=,>) = (b,+,-)$. The transition to the halt state can be defined by a pair of rule compositions δ_1, δ_2 such that $\delta_2 \geq \delta_1$ where δ_2 is of the form $halt : p(\bar{t}) \leftarrow true$.

Let M be a 2CM, Λ the corresponding term rewriting system, and Δ the set of redundant/redundancy eliminating pairs (δ, δ') derived from Λ. Given any initial derivation containing a redundant rule δ from Δ, it is straightforward to show that δ is eliminable if and only if Λ and M terminate. Consequently:

Theorem 16 Eliminability of redundant derivations is undecidable. ∎

We believe similar reductions can be used to show that properties such decomposability and functional composability[8] are also undecidable.

Despite this result, many sufficient conditions for the elimination of redundant derivations can be adapted from the literature concerning termination of rewrite systems (see for example [1]). Finding sufficient conditions involves finding some well-founded partial ordering($\succ$) on terms and showing that the application of rewrite rules system always derives a term u from t such that $t \succ u$.

Example 5 Consider the two rewrite system defined by the redundant derivations in example 2.

System 1	System 2
$1.1.X \rightarrow X$	$1.1.X \rightarrow X$
$1.3.X \rightarrow 3.X$	$1.3.X \rightarrow 3.X$
$1.2.(X, Y) \rightarrow 2.(1.X, 1.Y)$	$1.2.(X, Y) \rightarrow 2.(1.X, 1.Y)$
$2.(X, 3.(Y, Z)) \rightarrow 3.(4.(X, Y), Z)$	$3.(4.(X, Y), Z) \rightarrow 2.(X, 3.(Y, Z))$
$2.(3.(X, Y), Z) \rightarrow 3.(X, 4.(1.Z, Y))$	$3.(X, 4.(Y, Z)) \rightarrow 2.(3.(X, Z), 1.Y)$
$4.(2.(X, Y), Z) \rightarrow 4.(X, 4.(Y, Z))$	$4.(2.(X, Y), Z) \rightarrow 4.(X, 4.(Y, Z))$

We first show that System 1 terminates. Let $n(r, \tau)$ denote the number of occurrences of symbol r in term τ. Observe that for all rules $l \rightarrow r$ in System 1, $n(3, l) = n(3, r)$ and $n(2, l) + n(4, l) = n(2, r) + n(4, r)$. Notice $n(2, l) \geq n(2, r)$ and that the depth of 2's in the term r always decreases (i.e.: rule 2 is always moved higher up the derivation). Note also a term τ may always be reduced by first three rules to a term τ' such that $n(1,\tau') \leq 2 * n(2,\tau') + n(4,\tau')$. Informally system 1 terminates because the rewrite rules reduce the number of 2's and push 1's down the derivation. Eventually, no rules will be applicable and so the rewriting system terminates. More formally, we define the ordering $\succ_1$ over finite terms as follows: term $\tau \succ_1 \tau'$ if $n(2,\tau) > n(2,\tau')$, or if $n(2,\tau) = n(2,\tau')$ then $\tau \succ_1 \tau'$ if $\tau = f(f_1,...,f_n)$ is greater($>$) than $\tau' = g(g_1,...,g_n)$ where $>$ is defined so that $f(f_1,...,f_n) > g(g_1,...,g_n)$ if $f > g$ or if $f = g$, then $\forall i, f_i \geq g_i$ and $\exists i : f_i > g_i$. For System 1, we define $1 > 2 > 3$ and $1 >$ any variable X. The ordering $\succ_1$ is well-founded, monotonic, preserved under substitution(stable) and for all rules $l \rightarrow r$ in system 1, $l \succ_1 r$. Thus by Theorem 7 of [1] System 1 terminates.

We now show System 2 terminates. Once again for all rules $l \rightarrow r$ in system 2, we have that $n(3,l) = n(3,r)$ and $n(2,l) + n(4,l) = n(2,r) + n(4,r)$ and that $n(1,\tau)$ is always reduced, by the first three rules to less than $2 * n(2,\tau) + n(4,\tau)$. The ordering $\succ_2$ on terms having principle functor $1, 2$, or 3 is defined by the ordering $1 > 3 > 2$. For all rules $l \rightarrow r$ where l and r have these principle functors, $l \succ_2 r$. For terms having principle functor 4, $4.(f_1, f_2) \succ_2 4.(g_1, g_2)$ if $n(2, 4.(f_1, f_2)) > n(2, 4.(g_1, g_2))$. The ordering $\succ_2$ is well-founded, monotonic, preserved under substitution(stable) and for all rules $l \rightarrow r$ in system 2, $l \succ_2 r$. Thus system 2 terminates. ∎

Finding appropriate orderings to determine the eliminability of redundant derivations is made more difficult by our desire to determine if a program has any of the previously noted properties. Overly simplistic syntactic orderings such as "length of derivation" are not sufficient for this purpose. At present it appears that finding a suitable well founded-ordering must be done on a case by case basis. However we note the following point.

Syntactic tests for termination make no use of semantic properties of transformation sequences. Suppose that a redundancy eliminating rule is of greater depth then the redundant rule and that the replacement process always introduces a new redundant partial derivation as in example 1. Each rule in a transformation sequence $\{\delta_i\}$ will be of greater degree than and subsume its predecessor. The transformation sequence does not terminate. However, if rules in the sequence do not contain function symbols, then by corollary 12 there exists some rule δ_i which subsumes δ_{i+1}. Now, this pair of rules also defines a transformation sequence which terminates and so δ_{i+1} is eliminable. Thus, semantic properties of rules provide more information about when a rule is eliminable.

7 Conclusion

We have given decidability results and a framework, via term-rewriting systems, for eliminating redundant derivations. These results form the basis for techniques for the automated synthesis of expressions in the control languages described in [2, 4]. The transformations on derivations allowed us to give a new sufficient condition for uniform boundedness and show that "memoing" techniques, such as SLD-AL resolution[18], cannot in general detect redundant derivations. In fact SLD-AL resolution appears complementary to control language based techniques to eliminate redundant derivations; SLD-AL resolution can detect redundancy, such as repeated subgoals arising from a particular resolution strategy, which are not due to redundant derivations, while the control languages, by limiting the number of derivations that need to be generated, reduce the amount of information that needs to be memoed.

8 Acknowledgements

The author acknowledges discussions with Kim Marriott and Laurent Vieille.

References

[1] N. Dershowitz. Termination of rewriting. *Journal of Symbolic Computing*, 3:69–119, 1987.

[2] A.R. Helm. Detecting and eliminating redundant derivations in logic knowledge bases. In *Proceedings of the 1st International Conference on Deductive and Object-Oriented Databases*, pages 247–263, Kyoto, Japan, 1989.

[3] A.R. Helm. *Detecting and Eliminating Redundant Derivations in Logic Programming Systems.* PhD thesis, Dept. of Computer Science, Univeristy of Melbourne, Melbourne, Australia, Forthcoming 1990.

[4] A.R. Helm. On the detection and elimination of redundant derivations during bottom-up execution. In *North American Conference on Logic Programming*, Cleveland, Ohio, 1989.

[5] J.E. Hopcroft and J.D. Ullman. *Introduction to Automata Theory, Languages and Computation.* Addison Wesley, Reading Massachusetts, 1979.

[6] G. Huet and D.C. Oppen. Equations and rewrite rules: a survey. In R. Book, editor, *Formal Language Theory: Perspectives and Open Problems*, pages 349–405, Academic Press, 1980.

[7] Y.E. Ioannides and E. Wong. *Towards an Algebraic Theory of Recursion.* Technical Report 801, Computer Science, University of Madison, Wisconsin, 1988.

[8] J-L Lassez and M.J. Maher. The denotational semantics of horn clauses as a production system. In *AAAI National Conference on Artificial Intelligence*, 1983.

[9] J-L Lassez, K. Marriott, and M.J. Maher. Unification revisted. In Jack Minker, editor, *Foundations of Deductive Databases and Logic Programming*, pages 627–658, Morgan Kaufmann Publishers, 1988.

[10] J.W. Lloyd. *Foundations of Logic Programming.* Springer Verlag, New York, 1984.

[11] M. Maher. Equivalences of logic programs. In Jack Minker, editor, *Foundations of Deductive Database and Logic Programming*, pages 627–658, Morgan Kaufmann Publishers, 1988.

[12] D. Maier, A.O. Mendelzon, and Y. Sagiv. Testing implications of data dependencies. *ACM Transactions on Database Systems*, 4(4):455–469, 1979.

[13] J.F. Naughton and Y. Sagiv. A decidable class of bounded recursions. In *ACM Symposium on Principles of Database Systems*, pages 171–180, San Diego, California, 1987.

[14] R. Ramakrishnan, Y. Sagiv, J.D. Ullman, and M.Y. Vardi. Proof-tree transformation theorems and thier applications. In *ACM Symposium on Principles of Database Systems*, Philadelphia, Pennsylvania, 1989.

[15] J.A. Robinson. A machine-oriented logic based on the resolution principle. *Journal of the Association for Computing Machinery*, 12:23–41, 1965.

[16] Y. Sagiv. Optimising datalog programs. In Jack Minker, editor, *Foundations of Deductive Database and Logic Programming*, pages 659–698, Morgan Kaufmann Publishers, 1988.

[17] M.H. van Emden and R.A. Kowalski. The semantics of predicate logic as a programming language. *Journal of the Association for Computing Machinery*, 23(4):733–742, 1976.

[18] L. Vieille. Recursive query processing: the power of logic. *Theoretical Computer Science*, 68(2), 1989.

[19] D.A. Wolfram, M.J. Maher, and J.L. Lassez. A unified treatment of resolution strategies for logic programming. In *Proc. of the Second International Logic Programming Conference*, pages 263–276, Uppsala, Sweden, 1984.

Avoiding Duplicate Proofs

Bruce Spencer
Faculty of Computer Science
University of New Brunswick
College Hill, Box 4400
Fredericton, New Brunswick, Canada, E3B 5A3
ebspencer@watdragon.waterloo.edu

Abstract

Wos has identified the problem of recomputing redundant information in the general setting of automated reasoning. We consider this problem in two settings: first order logic and default logic. In the first order logic setting we are given a formula and a goal and asked to find the instances of the goal that follow from the formula. In the default logic setting we are given a goal and a set of facts and defaults. We are asked to find a consistent set of instances of defaults that, given the facts, implies the goal. In either setting, whether we are computing substitutions or sets of defaults we can use a proof procedure to find the result. The procedure exhibits redundancy when it finds two results such that one either duplicates or is more specific than the other.

We introduce the foothold format, a variant of linear resolution that admits fewer duplicate proofs than Loveland's popular MESON format. The duplicates arise when reasoning by cases. Applied to settings where results are properties of proofs it leads to proof procedures that compute fewer duplicate results. In the settings above fewer duplicate substitutions and explanations are found. In some of our examples all duplication is eliminated. The foothold refinement depends on a simple condition that can be checked quickly, and can detect redundancy before the proof is completely generated. This is important from a practical point of view, since the earlier redundancy is detected, the more unnecessary work can be avoided. For some examples the speedup is exponential.

1 Introduction

Wos [12] asks

> What strategy can be employed to deter a reasoning program from deducing a clause already retained, or from deducing a clause that is a proper instance of a clause already retained?

Although our procedures in this paper are not computing clauses as such, the question still stands. It takes time to compute a redundant result, and more time to decide if the result should be thrown away.

We consider two settings, first order clausal logic without equality and default logic where the defaults are normal. In the first order setting we are given a goal literal and a set of clauses and we wish to know which instances of the literal follow from the clauses. To do this we use a proof procedure to compute substitutions for the variables in the literal. Prolog is a special case of this setting. A redundant substitution duplicates or is more specific than another substitution.

In the default logic setting described in [2, 8], we are given a set of clauses that represent the known facts, and a distinguished set of literals called hypotheses that represent the assumptions we are prepared to believe, in the absence of contrary evidence. An explanation for the goal is a set of assumptions that is (1) consistent with the clauses and (2) together with the clauses implies the goal. For example, de Kleer's assumption-based Truth Maintenance system[2] (ATMS) computes propositional explanations. A redundant explanation duplicates or is more specific than some other explanation.

These two settings have one feature in common: the results computed are properties attached to a proof of the goal. Redundancy arises in each setting when two proofs give us the same result, or when one result is more specific than the other. In this paper we consider the first variety of redundancy, duplicated results.

We introduce the foothold format for linear resolution proofs that admits fewer duplicate proofs than MESON[5], a well-known proof format. The duplication we avoid arises in MESON when reasoning is done by cases. Reasoning by cases is required to handle clauses with more than one positive disjunct, clauses that do not fall into the Horn subset. Thus this type of duplication does not arise in Prolog, nor in the basic, Horn ATMS. It does arise in non-Horn extensions to Prolog [11], and in non-Horn extensions to the ATMS [10, 3]. It also arises in Theorist[8], a general default reasoning system.

2 Background

In this section we review some concepts in propositional logic, first order logic and default logic.

2.1 Propositional Logic

We assume the reader is familiar with propositional logic, for example as presented in [1].

Much work in automated theorem proving focuses on finding efficient methods for determining whether or not $P \models g$ given a set of clauses P and a literal g. The MESON procedure [5] is one of the simplest and best known. It depends on determining whether a structure that conforms to the MESON format can be built from the clauses. We describe here part of the MESON format, which we call the negated ancestor rule. See Loveland's book for the entire format.

Definition 1 If g is a literal then let $\overline{g}$ be the complement of g. That is, the overbar function adds the $\neg$ connective if it is not present in g, and removes it if it is.

Definition 2 Let P be a set of propositional clauses.

2.1 A **negated ancestor proof** of a literal g from P is a NA proof of g from P with negated ancestor set $\{\}$.

2.2 An NA proof of g from P with negated ancestor set A is either
(case a) nothing if $g \in A$, or
(case b) (1) a clause $g_1 \vee \ldots \vee g_n$ from P where $g_i = g$ for some i, and
(2) an NA proof of $\overline{g}_j$ from P with negated ancestor set $\{\overline{g}\} \cup A$ for each $j = 1, \ldots, i-1, i+1, \ldots, n$.

To reason by cases, a negated ancestor proof uses (case a), where a goal is found among its negated ancestors. As a result the part of MESON we have extracted preserves the important property of completeness. A proof can be adapted from the proof of completeness for the MESON format [5].

Theorem 1 There is a negated ancestor proof of g from P if and only if $P \models g$.

There is a natural graph representation of negated ancestor proofs. It uses alternate forms of the clauses, called contrapositive rules.

Definition 3 For a clause $g_1 \vee \ldots \vee g_n$ there are n **contrapositive rules**:

$$\forall i = 1, \ldots, n \qquad g_i \leftarrow \overline{g}_i \quad \cdots \quad \overline{g}_{i-1} \quad \overline{g}_{i+1} \quad \cdots \quad \overline{g}_n$$

To construct a negative ancestor proof graph of a goal g, begin by constructing a node that contains g. This node will be the root of the graph. Given a partial negative ancestor proof graph, and a goal node containing the literal h (initially h is g) there are two ways to complete the graph. Either (case a) find a node already in the graph containing $\overline{h}$ which is connected to this node by tree edges, and introduce a back edge from the goal node to this ancestor. Or (case b) find a contrapositive rule with h on the left hand side, make a new node for each member of the right hand side, and introduce a tree edge from the goal node to each new node. Recursively prove each new node.

For example, consider the clauses

$$p \vee \neg a$$
$$p \vee \neg b$$
$$a \vee b$$

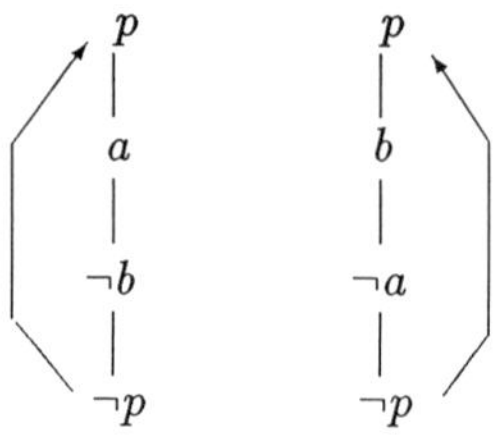

Figure 1: Negated Ancestor Proof Graphs

and the goal p. The contrapositive rules are

$$\begin{array}{lcl@{\qquad\qquad}lcl} p & \leftarrow & a & \neg a & \leftarrow & \neg p \\ p & \leftarrow & b & \neg b & \leftarrow & \neg p \\ a & \leftarrow & \neg b & b & \leftarrow & \neg a \end{array}$$

There are two negative ancestor proof graphs of p, shown in Figure 1. As in the conventional presentation of trees, the root is at the top, child nodes are lower than parent nodes, and tree edges have no arrows. Our back edges point upward.

We shall restrict these trees within these proofs so that no branch from the root contains the same literal twice. As a result from a given goal and set of clauses there are only a finite number of negated ancestor proof graphs.

2.2 First Order Logic

We will assume that the reader is familiar with first order logic, as presented in, for example [1].

Suppose we are given a set P of clauses and a literal g and we want to find the instances of g that follow from P. Procedures that build first order MESON proofs can also build substitutions for the variables in g. For example if $P = \{g(a)\}$ then the proof of $g(x)$ returns the substitution $x := a$. There may also exist indefinite instances of the goal, as defined by a disjunctive set of substitutions. For example if $P = \{g(a) \vee g(b)\}$ then the proof of $g(x)$ should return $x := a \vee x := b$. Green [4] provides a method for computing disjunctive answers. Stickel [11] describes how disjunctive answers can be computed within the MESON format:

> Indefinite answers can be obtained by solving the query with its negation included among the axioms, and examining the proof to find the query's instantiations.

Completeness of the MESON format extends from the propositional case to the first order case [5]. To see why, recall Herbrand's theorem which states:

a set of clauses is unsatisfiable if and only if there is a finite unsatisfiable set of ground instances of these clauses. If $P \models g$ then $P \cup \{\overline{g}\}$ is unsatisfiable, so there is an unsatisfiable set $P' \cup \{\overline{g}_1, \ldots \overline{g}_n\}$ where P' is made up of ground instances of clauses of P, and each g_i is a ground instance of g. Therefore $P \cup \{\overline{g}_2, \ldots \overline{g}_n\} \vdash g_1$. Since ground literals may be treated as propositions, and since the propositional MESON format is complete there is a propositional MESON proof of g_1 from $P' \cup \{\overline{g}_2, \ldots, \overline{g}_n\}$. A lifting argument can now be made to show that from the propositional proof, the appropriate first order proof can be constructed which produces the disjunction of substitutions.

2.3 Default Logic

Commonly in artificial intelligence, conclusions must be drawn despite the absence of complete knowledge about the world. In these cases it may be possible to use knowledge of typical cases that is often true, but may admit exceptions. For example, if we are asked if a specific bird flies, since we know that most birds fly, it may be reasonable to assume that this is one that does. This type of reasoning is called *non-monotonic reasoning* because the set of conclusions we can reach may decrease or increase as we add more knowledge.

Default logic[9] allows us to express that a statement it typically true. The following default rule expresses that birds typically fly:

$$\frac{Bird(x) : \mathrm{M}\ Fly(x)}{Fly(x)}.$$

Here M is to be read as "it is consistent to assume". Defaults of the form

$$\frac{\beta(x) : \mathrm{M}\ \alpha(x)}{\alpha(x)}$$

are called *normal* defaults. A normal default can be represented by a set of ordinary first order formulas and a default of the form

$$\frac{M\ a(x)}{a(x)}$$

where a is a single literal.

The ATMS and Theorist represent a single literal default by designating the literal as an hypothesis. Given a set P of clauses and a set H of the literals in those clauses that are designated as hypotheses, and given a goal literal g, we say that a subset D of H *explains* g if $P \cup D \models g$ and $P \cup D$ is consistent. The bird example would be represented as

$$\{\forall x. Fly(x) \leftarrow Bird(x), Birdsfly(x)\}$$

where $Birdsfly(X)$ is an hypothesis. Given $Bird(tweety)$ an explanation of $Fly(tweety)$ is $\{Birdsfly(tweety)\}$.

A proof procedure can be used to build up explanations as it build the proof, by collecting the hypotheses that are used in the proof. A separate procedure guarantees that the explanation is consistent. The ATMS maintains consistency by finding all minimal inconsistent sets of hypotheses, called *nogoods*, and eliminating any explanation that includes some *nogood*. Theorist interleaves phases that add to the partial proof and partial explanation with phases that check consistency of the partial explanation.

3 The Foothold Format

The basic idea behind the foothold format is to avoid redundant proofs that arise when reasoning by cases by breaking up the symmetry of the cases. In Figure 1, the duplication is due to the symmetry of the two contrapositive rules of $a \vee b$, namely $a \leftarrow \neg b$ and $b \leftarrow \neg a$. In a foothold proof we assign labels from the set $\{-1, 0, +1\}$ to the literals on the right hand side of the contrapositive rules. For this example the symmetry is broken by assigning different labels to $\neg b$ and $\neg a$.

To build the labelled contrapositive rules for a general clause, first separate the positive literals from the negative literals. Put all of the literals of each type into an ordered sequence. Any ordering will do. For each p_i from the positive literals, build a contrapositive rule as follows. To each positive literal that appears before p_i in the ordered sequence assign the label $(+1)$, and to each positive literal that appears after p_i assign (-1). To each negative literal assign (0). Also, build a rule for each negative literal n_i as follows. Assign $(+1)$ to each negative literal that appears before n_i, assign (-1) to each negative literal that appears after n_i and assign (0) to each positive literal.

In the example from Figure 1 the labelled contrapositive rules are

$$\begin{array}{lcl@{\qquad}lcl} p & \leftarrow & a^{(0)} & \neg a & \leftarrow & \neg p^{(0)} \\ p & \leftarrow & b^{(0)} & \neg b & \leftarrow & \neg p^{(0)} \\ a & \leftarrow & \neg b^{(+1)} & b & \leftarrow & \neg a^{(-1)} \end{array}$$

Now, build the negated ancestor proof using these labelled contrapositives. During the search for a negated ancestor, sum up the labels of all of the literals encountered. If the sum is positive when we reach the negated ancestor then accept the proof. Otherwise reject it.

In the example the foothold proofs are

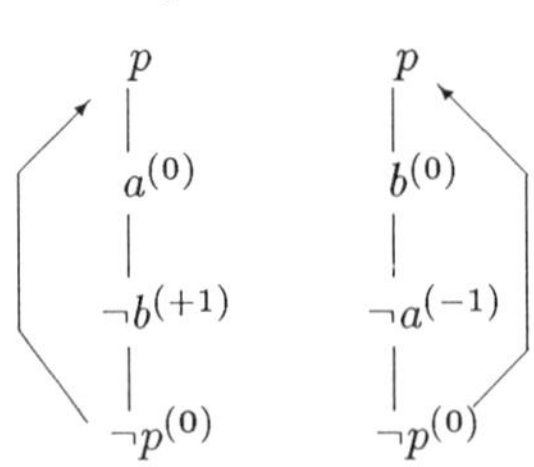

The first of them is accepted and the second is rejected.

The name "foothold" refers to an analogy between reaching the negated ancestor and climbing a tree. The (+1) foothold labels are places where the climber can put his foot, and the (−1) labels are places he must reach over. If he can put his foot down in more places than he must reach over he can climb to the negated ancestor.

This idea is now presented more formally.

3.1 Propositional Foothold Proof Format

In this section we present our foothold format, and show that it admits a proof if one exists. In other words, completeness is preserved.

Definition 4 Let P be a set of propositional clauses.

4.1 The **foothold rule set** of P is the union over clauses C in P of the set of foothold rules of C.

4.2 Let C be a propositional clause. Let $(l_1, \dots l_n)$ be an ordered sequence of the negative literals in C and $(r_1, \dots r_m)$ be an ordered sequence of the positive literals. The **foothold rules** of C with respect to these orderings are

$$\begin{array}{l} \forall i = 1, \dots, n \\ l_i \;\leftarrow\; \bar{l}_1^{(+1)} \;\dots\; \bar{l}_{i-1}^{(+1)} \;\; \bar{l}_{i+1}^{(-1)} \;\dots\; \bar{l}_n^{(-1)} \;\; \bar{r}_1^{(0)} \;\dots\; \bar{r}_m^{(0)} \end{array}$$

$$\begin{array}{l} \forall i = 1, \dots, m \\ r_i \;\leftarrow\; \bar{r}_1^{(+1)} \;\dots\; \bar{r}_{i-1}^{(+1)} \;\; \bar{r}_{i+1}^{(-1)} \;\dots\; \bar{r}_m^{(-1)} \;\; l_1^{(0)} \;\dots\; l_n^{(0)} \end{array}$$

4.3 The superscript (s) on each literal on the right hand side of a foothold rule is called the **foothold label**. A foothold label written $(*)$ is one whose value we disregard (a "don't care").

Definition 5 Let P be a set of clauses, let g be a literal, and let F_P be a foothold rule set of P.

5.1 A **foothold proof** of g from F_P is an FH proof of $g^{(*)}$ with the empty negated ancestor sequence.

5.2 An FH proof of of $g^{(l_g)}$ with negated ancestor sequence S is either
(case a) nothing, if $a_1^{(l_1)} \dots a_n^{(l_n)} g^{(*)}$ is a prefix of S and $l_g + \sum_{i=1}^{n} l_i > 0$, or
(case b) (1) a foothold rule $g \leftarrow g_1^{(p_1)} \dots g_n^{(p_n)}$ and
(2) an FH proof of each $g_i^{(p_i)}$ with negated ancestor sequence $\bar{g}^{(l_g)} S$.

Theorem 2 Let P be a consistent set of propositional clauses. $P \models g$ if and only if for all foothold rule sets F_P of P there is a foothold proof of g from F_P.

Proof ($\Leftarrow$) A foothold proof of g from F_P corresponds to a negated ancestor proof of g from P. Therefore $P \models g$ by Theorem 1.

($\Rightarrow$) Since $P \models g$ there is a negated ancestor proof of g from P. Follow the construction of a negated ancestor proof graph of g in Section 2.1.

The sons for each node are determined by some contrapositive rule of a clause in P. For each rule, there is a foothold rule in F_P that assigns foothold labels to the literals. According to these rules label the literal in each node of the graph (except the root) with its foothold label. To each backedge assign the sum of the foothold labels in the nodes between the source and the destination of that backedge, not including the label in the destination node. Note that no backedge can have a value of zero, since there must be an odd number of switches from positive to negative literals in sequence back to the complement, and each switch introduces either 1 or -1 to the sum. The sum of an odd number of positive or negative 1's is odd, hence non-zero.

If all backedges have positive foothold sums, then the negated ancestor proof was also a foothold proof, and we are done. Otherwise, choose a node N that is pointed to by some backedges with negative sums. These are known as negative backedges. Let p be the number of positive backedges that point to nodes below N. We claim that we can create a new subgraph at N that corresponds to an NA proof of h which has strictly more than p positive backedges. If this claim is true then we can apply it a finite number of times, for the number of negated ancestor graphs is finite, to eliminate all negative backedges. This completes the demonstration.

It remains to demonstrate our claim. Given a backedge B with the value $k < 0$, consider the nodes between the destination N of B and the source of B. Let the literals in these nodes be $h = h_1, h_2, \ldots, h_r = \overline{h}$. This means, without loss of generality, that there are contrapositive rules of clauses in P

$$h_i \leftarrow h_{i+1}\, a_{1i}\, \ldots\, a_{n_i i}$$

Construct new nodes $N_1, \ldots, N_r$ such that N_i contains $\overline{h}_i$ and is the son of N_{i+1}. These correspond to the contrapositive rules

$$\overline{h}_{i+1} \leftarrow \overline{h}_i\, a_{1i}\, \ldots\, a_{n_i i}$$

N_r contains h and it will replace N in the graph.

Remove the negative backedge B and introduce a new backedge B' from N_1 to N_r. Notice that if the foothold rule h_i assigns label l to h_{i+1} then the foothold rule for $\overline{h}_{i+1}$ assign $-l$ to $\overline{h}_i$. Thus the sum of the foothold labels for $h_2, \ldots, h_r$ in the original graph is the additive inverse of the sum for $\overline{h}_{r-1}, \ldots, \overline{h}_1$ in the new graph. Therefore B' is assigned the sum $-k$, which is positive.

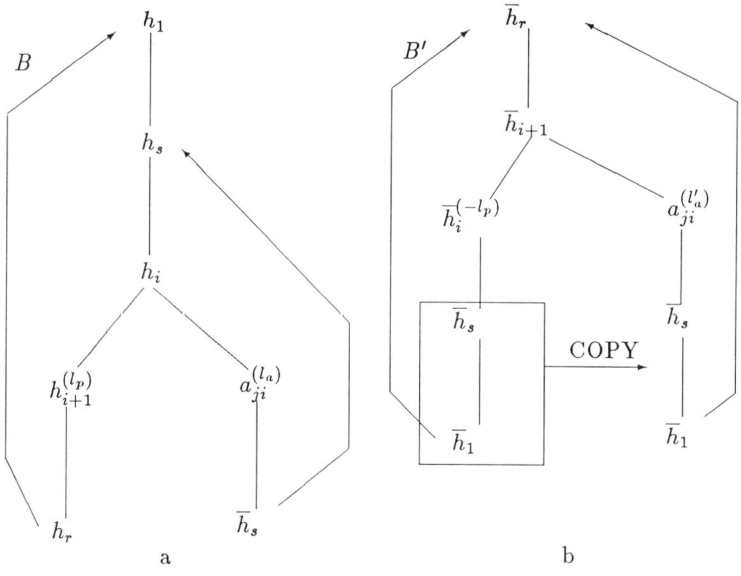

Figure 2: Graphs with Foothold Labels

We now adjust the graph so that it corresponds to an NA proof. Proceed by induction. N_1 contains $\overline{h}$ and since one of its ancestors, N_r contains h, there is an NA proof of $\overline{h}$. Suppose there is an NA proof of $\overline{h}_s$ for $s = 1 \ldots i$. Then there is an NA proof of $\overline{h}_{i+1}$ if there is an NA proof of each $a_{1i} \ldots a_{n_i i}$. There was an NA proof a_{ji} in the original graph and the only change has been to the ancestors of a_{ji}. We make a copy of the old subgraph at a_{ji} in the original graph, and make it a son of the node N_{i+1}, containing $\overline{h}_{i+1}$. We also make the following adjustments. Wherever a descendant of a_{ji} in the original graph had a backedge to the node containing h_s for $s < i$ then that descendant contains $\overline{h}_s$. (See Figure 2.a) In the new graph, remove this backedge from this descendant and make a copy of the subgraph under $\overline{h}_s$, which we know by induction is an NA proof. (See Figure 2.b) By inspection the result is an NA proof of a_{ji}.

We also need to show that for any positive backedge we removed from the original graph, we introduced a corresponding positive backedge in the resulting graph. In Figure 2.a, let X_1 be the sum of the foothold labels below h_1 to h_s, let X_2 be the sum below h_s to h_i, let l_h be the foothold label of h_{i+1}, let l_a be the foothold label of a_{ji}, let X_3 be the sum below h_{i+1} to h_r, and let Y be the sum below a_{ji} to $\overline{h}_s$. We know that $X_1 + X_2 + l_h + X_3 < 0$. We are interested in the case where $X_2 + l_a + Y > 0$. We need to show that the label for the new backedge, $-X_3 + l'_a + Y - X_1$ is positive, where l'_a is the label assigned to a_{ji} by the rule for $\overline{h}_{i+1}$, as shown in Figure 2.b.

$$\begin{array}{rl} \text{Given} & 0 > X_1 + X_2 + l_h + X_3 \\ \text{Then} & -X_1 - X_3 - l_h > X_2 \\ \text{Given} & X_2 + l_a + Y > 0 \\ \text{Then} & X_2 \geq 1 - Y - l_a \\ \text{Transitively} & -X_1 - X_3 + Y > l_h + 1 - l_a \end{array}$$

Now, if the conclusion does not hold then $-X_1 - X_3 + Y + l'_a \leq 0$, but since backedges cannot have zero labels,

$$\begin{array}{rl} & -X_1 - X_3 + Y + l'_a < 0 \\ \text{so} & -X_1 - X_3 + Y \leq -l'_a - 1 \\ \text{From above} & -X_1 - X_3 + Y > l_h + 1 - l_a \\ \text{Transitively} & -l'_a - 1 > l_h + 1 - l_a \\ \text{In other words,} & -l'_a - l_h + l_a > 2 \end{array}$$

Since the l's are restricted to values in $\{-1, 0, +1\}$ we may conclude $l'_a = -1, l_h = -1$ and $l_a = 1$.

Since none of the l's are zero, the literals h_i, h_{i+1} and a_{ji} are either all positive or all negative. The ordering chosen in the foothold rule for h_i must put a_{ji} before h_i since $l_a = 1$ and h_i before h_{i+1} since $l_h = -1$. The ordering chosen in the rule for $\overline{h}_{i+1}$ must put a_{ji} after h_{i+1} since $l'_a = -1$. But these are the same ordering, so a_{ji} is both before and after h_{i+1}. A contradiction has been reached. ∎

3.2 First Order Foothold Proofs

Foothold labels can be assigned to first order clauses in exactly the same way they are assigned to propositional clauses. First order foothold proofs are defined as first order negated ancestor proofs, with the additional restriction that each backedge from a goal to its negated ancestor has a positive foothold sum.

Completeness of first order foothold proofs is also preserved. The argument in Section 2.2 for the completeness of first order negated ancestor proofs also applies to first order foothold proofs. The only property of propositional negated ancestor proofs that was used in that proof was propositional completeness, a property shared by propositional foothold proofs. Since foothold proofs are a special case of negated ancestor proofs, the same lifting lemma may be applied to generate first order foothold proofs.

4 Evaluation

4.1 How easily can foothold proofs be computed?

Like the MESON format, the foothold format leads to proof procedures that are simple to implement. The appendix contains a Prolog procedure for computing foothold proofs. Any theorem prover that is based on the MESON format, such as PTTP [11] can easily be converted to the foothold format.

Procedures that compute MESON proofs can take advantage of an important pruning rule. If a goal is encountered that is the exact duplicate of a goal in the ancestor sequence then this branch of the tree can be ignored and no success is reported. There is no reason to pursue a proof of this goal, because this condition arises when the procedure has entered a loop. Procedures that compute foothold proofs can take advantage of the same pruning rule, for the same reason. The Prolog procedure in the appendix implements this pruning rule.

4.2 When should the foothold format be used?

The foothold format should be used whenever reasoning with clauses that extend beyond the Horn subset and the objective of the search is to find more than one result. If the objective of the search is to find a single solution, or to show that a set of clauses is unsatisfiable, then foothold proof procedures are not necessarily better or worse than MESON proof procedures.

If the objective is to find a proof with minimum height, where the height of a proof is the maximum size of the ancestor set, then the foothold refinement should not be used. The shortest negated ancestor proof may be rejected by the foothold condition, while a longer proof, composed of the same clauses in a different arrangement, meets the condition.

Proof height is an important consideration for "iterative deepening" proof methods. By restricting the search to a preset limit, and iteratively increasing this limit, depth first search strategies can be prevented from running down infinite paths. They will find each proof up to that limit. Thus depth first search achieves the completeness of breadth-first search, without also requiring exponential space.

The iterative deepening strategy can be used with the foothold refinement. Because the minimum height proof may be eliminated, the searcher may be forced to look deeper to generate the same number of distinct proofs. The reduction in search space helps offset the cost of the additional depth.

4.3 How many proofs are avoided?

The amount of redundancy reduced depends on the clauses, but we are guaranteed that the foothold procedure will generate no more redundancy than the negated ancestor procedure, since the foothold format is strictly more specific than the negated ancestor format.

There are some examples where the foothold format still admits an exponential amount of redundancy, in the sense that more than one proof can be built from the same set of clauses. Redundancy in these examples is due to interaction between features, including non-Horn clauses. In the following example different parts of the proof must use different subproofs to prove the same literal. Redundancy arises because in yet another part of the proof the same literal can be proved by any of the subproofs. There are $\Pi_{i=1}^{n} i!$ foothold proofs of p from the following:

$$
\begin{array}{ll}
p \vee \neg p_1 \vee \ldots \vee \neg p_n & \\
p_i \vee \neg p_{i+1} \vee \neg a & \forall i = 1 \ldots n-1 \\
p_n \vee \neg a & \\
p_i \vee a & \forall i = 1 \ldots n
\end{array}
$$

There are some examples where the foothold procedure eliminates all redundancy. Consider the following:

$$
\begin{array}{ll}
p \vee \neg p_1 \vee \ldots \vee \neg p_n & \\
p_i \vee \neg a_i & \forall i = 1 \ldots n \\
p_i \vee \neg b_i & \forall i = 1 \ldots n \\
a_i \vee b_i & \forall i = 1 \ldots n
\end{array}
$$

For each n there is exactly one foothold proof of p from the above, but there are 2^n negated ancestor proofs. In the following table we compare the time to calculate all proofs of p from this program for different values of n. (All programs in this paper were written in Quintus Prolog, and run on a VAX 8600. Times are reported in milliseconds.)

Value of n	Foothold	Negated Ancestor
1	16	017
2	33	033
3	33	100
4	67	216
5	83	417
6	150	1033
7	184	2583
8	200	5483
9	300	12100
10	367	26400
⋮	⋮	⋮
30	3850	$\approx 10^{10}$

As expected, the time to build the 2^n negated ancestor proofs increases exponentially with n, but the time to build the only foothold proof, which has n literals, increases linearly with n.

4.4 How much time is saved?

We compare two procedures for producing proofs. The foothold procedure, FH, uses foothold rules and imposes the foothold condition. The negated ancestor procedure, NA, uses ordinary contrapositive rule. They

	#	Time	Count
FH	1	16	1
NA	1	17	1
FH	2	33	1
NA	2	33	1
FH	3	17	1
NA	3	0	1
FH	4	33	1
NA	4	17	1
FH	5	33	1
NA	5	33	1
FH	6	34	1
NA	6	17	1
FH	7	17	1
NA	7	17	1
FH	8	17	1
NA	8	0	1
FH	9	50	1
NA	9	50	4
FH	11	33	1
NA	11	33	1
FH	12	766	1
NA	12	222450	4096
FH	13	17	1
NA	13	33	1
FH	14	50	1
NA	14	50	4
FH	15	17	1
NA	15	33	1
FH	16	0	1
NA	16	17	1
FH	17	67	1
NA	17	67	2
FH	18	33	1
NA	18	16	1

	#	Time	Count
FH	19	17	1
NA	19	17	1
FH	20	50	1
NA	20	33	1
FH	21	67	2
NA	21	167	12
FH	22	4800	207
NA	22	50167	3782
FH	23	167517	4620
NA	23	1437117	97200
FH	24	100	1
NA	24	200	8
FH	25	2583	5
NA	25	4533	36
FH	27	67	1
NA	27	83	2
FH	28	34	1
NA	28	50	1
FH	30	50	2
NA	30	67	4
FH	31	50	1
NA	31	17	1
FH	32	50	1
NA	32	50	1
FH	35	0	1
NA	35	16	1
FH	36	50	4
NA	36	67	4
FH	37	483	29
NA	37	550	36
FH	39	33	1
NA	39	67	8
FH	44	50	1
NA	44	66	2
FH	45	16683	16
NA	45	1524550	9589

	#	Count at each height							
		3	4	5	6	7	8	9	10
FH	22	1	14	17	23	29	35	41	47
NA	22	4	73	165	298	467	672	913	1190
FH	23	2	10	108	276	516	828	1212	1668
NA	23	8	82	1350	4716	9990	17208	26370	37476
FH	25				2	2	1		
NA	25			5	9	10	6	4	2
FH	37	1	4	4	4	4	4	4	4
NA	37	1	5	5	5	5	5	5	5
FH	45						9		7
NA	45				5	7	147	708	8722

are otherwise identical. They prune branches with identical ancestors, and they prune the search after a height of 10. We have run these programs on the tests suggested by Pelletier[6] that do not include equality axioms. We report on problems for which a proof can be found in the reduced search space in a reasonable amount of time. (Some problems required sound unification, with the occur-check. Because we used Prolog's unification, these could not be run.)

In these tests the foothold refinement is never more expensive than the negated ancestor procedure, except in simple problems, such as 3 and 8, where the times are so small they have little significance. The time saved by the foothold restriction varies from a negligible amount to better than two orders of magnitude. More complex problems exhibit more savings. This suggests that for still larger problems the savings will continue to be significant.

These tables indicate that the foothold format is never slower than the negated ancestor format, and can be much faster.

For some of the more complex problems we report the number of proofs of each height. In Problems 25 and 45 the minimum height proof is rejected. Proofs are found after 1 and 2 more levels, respectively. In these two examples the search spaces are especially reduced.

5 Conclusion

In settings where results are computed from proofs, such as first order logic and default logic, to compute more than one result requires computing more than one proof. Duplicate proofs produce the same result. Time is wasted computing the duplicate proof and checking the result for redundancy. We have presented the foothold format, a refinement of the MESON format that admits fewer duplicate proofs. Procedures that compute these proofs can detect redundancy before the entire proof is constructed. Empirical evidence shows a simple foothold procedure is never slower and sometimes much faster then the same procedure without the foothold refinement. The savings are greater for more complex examples.

References

[1] C.-L. Chang and R. C.-T. Lee. *Symbolic Logic and Mechanical Theorem Proving.* Academic Press, New York and London, 1973.

[2] J. de Kleer. An assumption-based Truth Maintenance System. *Artificial Intelligence*, 28:127–162, 1986.

[3] J. de Kleer. Extending the ATMS. *Artificial Intelligence*, 28:163–196, 1986.

[4] C. C. Green. Theorem-proving by resolution as a basis for question-answering systems. In B. Meltzer and D. Michie, editors, *Machine Intelligence 4*, pages 183–205. American Elsevier Publishing Company, Inc., 1969.

[5] D. Loveland. *Automated Theorem Proving: A Logical Basis.* North Holland, Amsterdam, 1978.

[6] F. J. Pelletier. Seventy-five problems for testing automated theorem provers. *Journal of Automated Reasoning*, 2:191–216, 1986.

[7] D. Poole. A logical framework for default reasoning. *Artificial Intelligence*, 36:27–47, 1988.

[8] D. Poole, R. Goebel, and R. Aleliunas. Theorist: a logical reasoning system for defaults and diagnosis. In N. Cercone and G. McCalla, editors, *The Knowledge Frontier: Essays in the Representation of Knowledge*, pages 331–352. Springer Verlag, New York, 1987.

[9] R. Reiter. A logic for default reasoning. *Artificial Intelligence*, 13:81–132, 1980.

[10] R. Reiter and J. de Kleer. Foundations of assumption-based truth maintenance systems: Preliminary report. In *Proceedings AAAI-87 Sixth National Conference on Artificial Intelligence*, pages 183–188, 1987.

[11] M. E. Stickel. A prolog technology theorem prover. *Journal of Automated Reasoning*, 4:353–380, 1989.

[12] L. Wos. *Automated Reasoning : 33 Basic Research Problems.* Prentice-Hall, Englewood Cliffs, New Jersey, 1988.

Acknowledgements

Thanks go to Robin Cohen and members of the LPAIG at Waterloo. David Poole introduced the problem. Scott Goodwin helped find examples. Bell-Northern Research provided financial support.

A Foothold Proofs in Prolog

```
% Propositional Foothold Proof Procedure

:- op(250, fx, (¬)).

prove(G) :- fh_prove(labelled_literal(G, _), [ ]).

fh_prove(labelled_literal(G, _), Anc) :-
        negate(G, Neg_G),
        member( labelled_literal(Neg_G, _), Anc),
        !, fail. % Cut is allowed when literals are propositions
fh_prove(labelled_literal(G, Label), Anc) :-
        ancestor_search(G, Label, Total, Anc),
        !, %Cut is allowed when literals are propositions
        Total > 0.
fh_prove(labelled_literal(G, Label), Anc) :-
        foothold_contrapositive_rule(G, Body),
        negate(G, Neg_G),
        fh_prove_all(Body, [labelled_literal(Neg_G, Label) | Anc]).

fh_prove_all([ ], _).
fh_prove_all([ G1 | G ], Anc) :-
        fh_prove(G1, Anc),
        fh_prove_all(G, Anc).

ancestor_search(Goal, S0, S0, [labelled_literal(Goal, Label) | Anc]).
ancestor_search(Goal, S0, S2, [labelled_literal(G, Label) | Anc]) :-
        S1 is S0 + Label,
        ancestor_search(Goal, S1, S2, Anc).

negate(X, ¬X) :- \+ X = ¬_.
negate(¬X, X).
```

The Logical Structure of Sequential Prolog

James H. Andrews
Department of Computer Science
University of Edinburgh
Mayfield Road, Edinburgh, Scotland EH9 3JZ
jha@lfcs.ed.ac.uk

Abstract

The standard logical semantics of sequential (left-to-right, depth-first) Prolog does not deal with questions of completeness, and therefore does not adequately describe termination. Denotational characterisations deal with termination properly, but do so in a very functional, non-logical manner. In contrast, this paper presents sound, complete, and logical characterisations of pure sequential Prolog with which termination and correctness properties of programs can be proved. These two characterisations are in the form of proof systems. The first one is sound and fully complete, in the sense that a query formula $\mathbf{A}$ succeeds iff the judgment $S(\exists[\mathbf{A}])$ is a theorem, and fails iff the judgment $F(\exists[\mathbf{A}])$ is a theorem. More generally, $S(\mathbf{A})$ (resp. $F(\mathbf{A})$) is a theorem iff every ground instance of $\mathbf{A}$ succeeds (resp. fails). This first characterisation is infinitary, because no finitary system can have these properties. The second system is finitary and sound, and has a weaker completeness property, but can form the basis for a useable system for proving properties of programs. These characterisations provide further insight into the logical structure that sequential Prolog has as part of the logic programming paradigm.

1 Introduction

Sequential Prolog is a somewhat inadequate logic programming language, because it uses an incomplete strategy for computing queries. Conversely, however, SLD-resolution and fixpoint semantics are somewhat inadequate descriptions of sequential Prolog because they do not precisely characterise the termination of queries: a query which has a solution according to SLD-resolution might cause Prolog to diverge while following an infinite branch of the search tree.

We need to be able to tell when our Prolog programs are going to terminate, however. Moreover, precise characterisations of termination, if they are abstract and logical enough, can act as characterisations of the language itself, and can lead to methods for proving termination and correctness properties of programs. I present such characterisations in this paper.

There have been several approaches to characterising termination in the past. One approach is to analyse the operational semantics directly. For instance, Francez et al. [FGKP85] develop a mathematical description of the search tree that Prolog traverses. They then describe logics which reason about such trees, and about other notions derived from operational semantics. The resultant logics, however, are quite complex and not very abstract, dealing as they do with basic operational notions.

Another, indirect, approach is to give a denotational semantics for the language [JM84, Bau88, NF89]. Such semantics not only help us in proving termination, but also serve as abstract characterisations of the language. Unfortunately, denotational semantics typically give functional denotations for logic programs; in Baudinet, for instance [Bau88], "programs are viewed as functions mapping goals into sequences of answer substitutions." They also tend to reify such notions as unification, which are more properly features of implementations than of logic. Thus denotational semantics, though elegant, do not characterise logical features of programs in a directly logical manner.

So it might seem that sequential Prolog, despite being nominally a logic programming language, can only be accurately described in operational or functional terms. What we need to affirm sequential Prolog's logical nature is to give it a sound, complete, abstract, *and logical* characterisation.

In this paper, I use the technique of proof-theoretic characterisation [HS84, HSH88, And89] to accomplish this. Roughly, a proof-theoretic characterisation of a logic programming language is a proof system which is sound and complete with respect to the language; that is, a proof system such that the set of terminating queries corresponds precisely to the set of theorems of the proof system.

Such systems are relatively easy to find for *parallel* languages. To find such systems for sequential languages, the key concept we seem to need is that of the *disjunctive unfolding* of a formula. I describe this concept here, and, based on that, give two proof-theoretic characterisations of sequential Prolog. One is complete but infinitary; the other has a weaker completeness property but is finitary. Both deal with the connectives and the structure of Prolog programs in a very logical manner.

This paper deals only with pure, negationless, cut-free Prolog, but because it handles the crucial question of sequentiality in a logical way, it should form the basis for logical characterisations of more powerful languages.

The structure of the paper is as follows. Section 2 gives a formal operational semantics, which acts as a reference point for the later soundness and completeness results. Section 3 motivates and describes the idea of disjunctive unfoldings. Section 4 gives the infinitary proof system, and Section 5 gives the finitary proof system. Finally, Section 6 gives a summary and some ideas of where this research might lead.

2 Operational Semantics

First, I must describe exactly what I mean by "sequential Prolog". In this paper, I do not intend this phrase to mean any particular language or implementation, but rather the usual left-to-right, depth-first strategy of computing queries. In this section, I describe an "abstract machine" structured operational semantics which describes this precisely.

Because I wish to study the relationship between logic programming and formal logic, I will define the notions of goal formula and program in a way which expresses the logical connectives more explicitly.

Definition 2.1 A *goal formula* is a formula satisfying the BNF definition

$$\mathbf{G} ::= \mathbf{P}(\mathbf{t}_1, \ldots, \mathbf{t}_n) \mid \mathbf{s} = \mathbf{t} \mid \mathbf{G}\&\mathbf{G} \mid \mathbf{G} \vee \mathbf{G} \mid \exists \mathbf{x}\mathbf{G}$$

where $\mathbf{P}$ is a predicate name and $\mathbf{s}$, $\mathbf{t}$, $\mathbf{t}_i$ are terms. (I assume that we are working in some given first-order language $\mathcal{L}$ with equality and an infinite domain of closed terms.) I will use $\mathbf{A}$, $\mathbf{B}$, $\mathbf{C}$, $\mathbf{G}$ to stand for goal formulae.

A *program* is a set of *predicate definitions* in which the names of all predicates being defined are distinct; a predicate definition of predicate $\mathbf{P}$ is a formula of the form

$$\mathbf{P}(\mathbf{x}_1, \ldots, \mathbf{x}_n) \leftrightarrow \mathbf{A}$$

where $\mathbf{x}_1, \ldots, \mathbf{x}_n$ are pairwise distinct and contain all the free variables of $\mathbf{A}$.

It should be clear that this definition is no loss or gain of power over the clausal form of most Prologs. For instance, a Horn clause program can be transformed into such a program by taking the Clark completion.

The operational semantics, SP, is a straightforward formalisation of the standard "stack-of-stacks" implementation of a Prolog interpreter. Thus, most of the nomenclature surrounding it will be taken from that of interpreter technology.

Definition 2.2 A *goal stack* is just a sequence of formulae. We will generally use α, possibly subscripted, to stand for an arbitrary goal stack. We will write the concatenation of two goal stacks α_1 and α_2 as α_1, α_2.

A *closure* is an expression $(\theta : \alpha)$, where α is a goal stack and θ is a substitution. (In practice, θ will be some syntactic representation of a substitution on a finite number of variables.)

A *backtrack stack* is a sequence of closures. We will generally use β, possibly subscripted, to stand for an arbitrary backtrack stack. We will write the concatenation of two backtrack stacks β_1 and β_2 as $\beta_1; \beta_2$.

ϵ will represent the empty goal stack or backtrack stack (its use will be non-ambiguous).

There will be one operational semantics, called SP_Π, corresponding to each program Π. (Since the particular program being considered will usually not be important, we will usually drop the subscript.) SP is a rewriting system which consists of rules for a binary relation $\overset{\text{SP}}{\Rightarrow}$ between backtrack stacks, and a definition of which backtrack stacks are to be considered "success states" and "failure states". The rewriting rules in SP are as follows:

1. &: $(\theta : (\mathbf{B}\&\mathbf{C}), \alpha); \beta \overset{\text{SP}}{\Rightarrow} (\theta : \mathbf{B}, \mathbf{C}, \alpha); \beta$

2. $\vee$: $(\theta : (\mathbf{B} \vee \mathbf{C}), \alpha); \beta \overset{\text{SP}}{\Rightarrow} (\theta : \mathbf{B}, \alpha); (\theta : \mathbf{C}, \alpha); \beta$

3. $\exists$: $(\theta : (\exists \mathbf{x}\mathbf{B}), \alpha); \beta \overset{\text{SP}}{\Rightarrow} (\theta : \mathbf{B}[\mathbf{x} := \mathbf{x}'], \alpha); \beta$
   where $\mathbf{x}'$ is some variable not appearing to the left of the arrow

4. Defined predicates:
   $(\theta : \mathbf{P}(\mathbf{t}_1, \ldots, \mathbf{t}_n), \alpha); \beta \overset{\text{SP}}{\Rightarrow} (\theta : \mathbf{A}(\mathbf{t}_1, \ldots, \mathbf{t}_n), \alpha); \beta$
   where Π contains the definition $(\mathbf{P}(\mathbf{x}_1, \ldots, \mathbf{x}_n) \leftrightarrow \mathbf{A}(\mathbf{x}_1, \ldots, \mathbf{x}_n))$

5. Unification, success:
   $(\theta : \mathbf{s} = \mathbf{t}, \alpha); \beta \overset{\text{SP}}{\Rightarrow} (\theta\theta' : \alpha); \beta$
   where θ' is the mgu of $\mathbf{s}\theta$ and $\mathbf{t}\theta$

6. Unification, failure:
   $(\theta : \mathbf{s} = \mathbf{t}, \alpha); \beta \overset{\text{SP}}{\Rightarrow} \beta$
   where $\mathbf{s}\theta$ and $\mathbf{t}\theta$ do not unify

The success states of SP are the backtrack stacks of the form $(\theta : \epsilon); \beta$. The single failure state of SP is the empty backtrack stack, ϵ.

To execute a particular goal formula $\mathbf{A}$ in this interpreter, we form the backtrack stack consisting of the single closure $(() : \mathbf{A})$, where $()$ is the empty substitution. If $(() : \mathbf{A}) \overset{\text{SP}*}{\Rightarrow} (\theta : \epsilon); \beta$, we say that $\mathbf{A}$ *succeeds* with substitution θ; if $(() : \mathbf{A}) \overset{\text{SP}*}{\Rightarrow} \epsilon$, we say that $\mathbf{A}$ *fails*. Otherwise (if the computation never reaches a success or failure state), we say that $\mathbf{A}$ *diverges*.

It is straightforward to prove that this operational semantics is equivalent to the depth-first, left-to-right version of SLD-resolution (modulo the translation between Horn clause programs and the form of programs used here); so SP really is just a convenient variant of this form of SLD-resolution. Its convenience for our purpose is in its completely formal structure and its emphasis on the decomposition of formulae, which facilitates the proofs of soundness and completeness.

We can now use SP as the reference point with respect to which all the later soundness and completeness results will apply.

3 Unfoldings of Formulae

The main problem that we come up against in developing a logical characterisation of sequential Prolog is that most logics are very compositional, and Prolog is not: there are some goal formulae whose satisfiability depend not

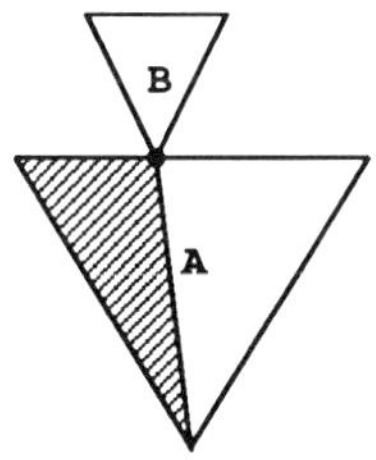

Figure 1: **B** is the key subformula of formula **A**. Informally, the shaded region consists only of =, &, and ∃ formulae.

only on the satisfiability of their constituent subformulae, but on how those subformulae interact.

However, there are some formulae which *do* act compositionally in this sense; and there are two transformations – the predicate unfolding and disjunctive unfolding transformations – that we can apply to *any* formula to get one which acts compositionally. In this section, I describe these transformations. Later, we will see how they in fact capture *all* the non-compositionality of sequential Prolog.

3.1 Non-Compositionality and Unfoldings

When does a conjunctive query **B&C** fail? We would like to be able to say that it does so whenever either **B** fails, or **B** succeeds and **C** fails. But this is not always the case, even for queries with no variables. Any failure in **C** will cause **B** to backtrack, and when **B** backtracks it may go into an infinite loop.

There are queries which do act compositionally, however. For instance, any disjunction **B** ∨ **C** fails if both **B** and **C** fail, and succeeds if either **B** succeeds, or **B** fails and **C** succeeds. Similarly, any conjunction **B&C** *which contains no predicate calls or disjunctions* acts compositionally in the way I just described.

This suggests that some form of disjunctive normal form might help to make problem queries behave better. Because & and ∃ distribute over ∨, we can get a formula that behaves compositionally by "pulling out" some disjunction to the top level. It turns out, however, that this may make the formula behave differently in the operational semantics – unless the disjunction we choose to pull out is the one that is encountered first in a left-to-right, depth-first traversal of the tree of the formula. This whole thing may also be complicated by disjunctions being "hidden" within predicate calls, but we can handle that by expanding the predicate calls with the usual unfold transformation.

This informal discussion motivates the following definitions.

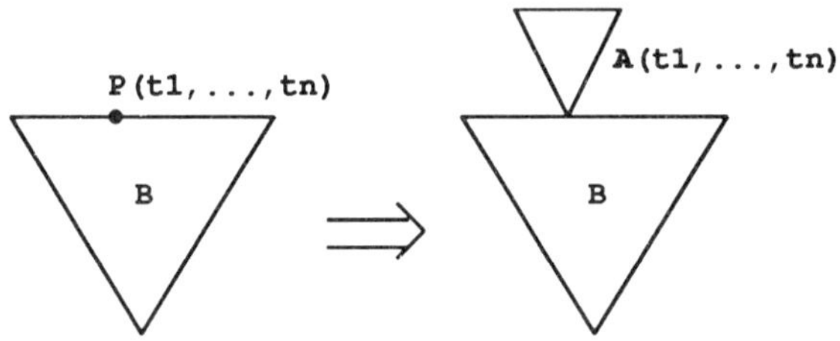

Figure 2: One predicate unfolding of formula **B**, where **P** is defined by $\mathbf{P}(\mathbf{x}_1, \ldots, \mathbf{x}_n) \leftrightarrow \mathbf{A}(\mathbf{x}_1, \ldots, \mathbf{x}_n)$.

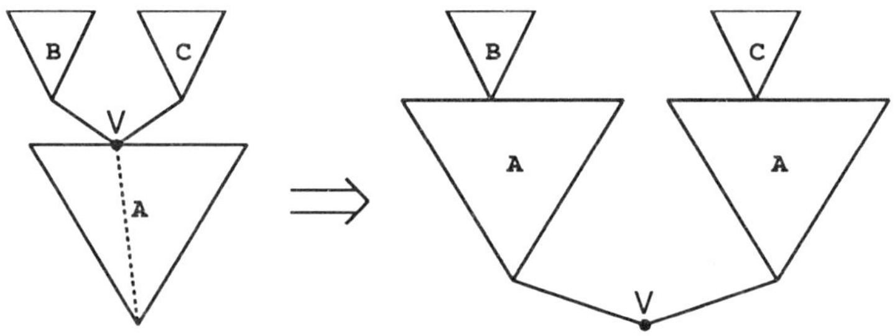

Figure 3: Disjunctive unfolding of a formula. The indicated disjunction, $\mathbf{B} \vee \mathbf{C}$, is the key subformula of **A**.

Definition 3.1 The *key subformula* of a formula is the leftmost disjunction or predicate application subformula which is not inside another disjunction. (See Figure 1.) Not every formula has a key subformula.

A formula $\mathbf{A}'$ is a *predicate unfolding* of a formula **A** if it is obtained from **A** by expanding some predicate application subformula into its body. (See Figure 2.) We write $\mathbf{A} \overset{\text{Pred}}{\Rightarrow} \mathbf{A}'$ if $\mathbf{A}'$ is a predicate unfolding of **A**.

The *disjunctive unfolding* of a formula **A** with key subformula $\mathbf{B} \vee \mathbf{C}$ is the formula $\mathbf{A}^{\mathbf{B}} \vee \mathbf{A}^{\mathbf{C}}$, where $\mathbf{A}^{\mathbf{B}}$ (resp. $\mathbf{A}^{\mathbf{C}}$) means **A** with its key subformula replaced by **B** (resp. **C**). (See Figure 3.) Formulae which do not have a disjunctive key subformula have no disjunctive unfolding; we write $\mathbf{A} \overset{\text{Disj}}{\Rightarrow} \mathbf{A}'$ if $\mathbf{A}'$ is the disjunctive unfolding of **A**.

Examples. The formulae $(\mathbf{B} \vee \mathbf{C})\&\mathbf{s} = \mathbf{t}$, $\exists x(\mathbf{s} = \mathbf{t}\&(\mathbf{B} \vee \mathbf{C}))$, and $\mathbf{B} \vee \mathbf{C}$ all have $\mathbf{B} \vee \mathbf{C}$ as their key subformulae. The disjunctive unfoldings of these formulae are, respectively, $(\mathbf{B}\&\mathbf{s} = \mathbf{t}) \vee (\mathbf{C}\&\mathbf{s} = \mathbf{t})$; $\exists x(\mathbf{s} = \mathbf{t}\&\mathbf{B}) \vee \exists x(\mathbf{s} = \mathbf{t}\&\mathbf{C})$; and $\mathbf{B} \vee \mathbf{C}$ itself. The formula $\mathbf{P}(x)\&(\mathbf{B} \vee \mathbf{C})$ has $\mathbf{P}(x)$ as its key subformula; the formula $\exists x(x = 0\&x = 1)$ has no key subformula.

Now, three classes of formulae which behave compositionally are disjunctions, formulae containing no predicate calls, and conjunctions $\mathbf{B}\&\mathbf{C}$ in which **B** contains no predicate calls. But if a query **A** terminates, then we can apply a finite number of predicate unfoldings to **A**, possibly followed by a disjunctive unfolding, and arrive at a formula in one of these classes. (This property of queries is implied by the soundness and completeness results given later.) To derive a compositional formula from a non-compositional one, therefore, it suffices to apply these transformations.

3.2 Some Facts about Unfoldings

An unfolding of a formula **A** is clearly classically and intuitionistically equivalent to **A** (modulo the given predicate definitions). What is not so clear is that an unfolding of **A** is equivalent to **A** in the weaker logic of sequential Prolog.

It turns out that it is, as stated by the following theorems. Full proofs of these can be found in [And90].

Lemma 3.2 If $\mathbf{A} \overset{\text{Pred}}{\Rightarrow} \mathbf{A}'$, then $\beta_1; (\theta : \alpha_1, \mathbf{A}, \alpha_2); \beta_2$ succeeds with substitution θ (resp. fails) iff $\beta_1; (\theta : \alpha_1, \mathbf{A}', \alpha_2); \beta_2$ succeeds with substitution θ (resp. fails).

Proof. By induction on the length of the computation. The only non-trivial case is when **A** is itself a predicate call, and it is at the left of the leftmost goal stack. In this case, it should be clear that a predicate call expansion step can be inserted or deleted to form one computation from the other.
□

Theorem 3.3 If $\mathbf{A} \overset{\text{Disj}}{\Rightarrow} \mathbf{A}'$, then $(\theta : \mathbf{A}, \alpha); \beta$ succeeds with substitution θ (resp. fails) iff $(\theta : \mathbf{A}', \alpha); \beta$ succeeds with substitution θ (resp. fails).

Proof. By induction on the depth of the key subformula (which is a disjunction) in the tree of the formula **A**. The proof is a long but straightforward case analysis.
□

4 A Complete, Infinitary Proof System

With the notion of unfoldings in hand, we can give a sound and complete proof system for sequential Prolog. This section presents and discusses that system, and sketches the proofs of soundness, completeness, and related results.

This complete proof system, however, is *infinitary*: there is a rule with an infinite number of premisses. It must be infinitary because the problem we have set ourselves turns out to be vulnerable to a version of Gödel's incompleteness theorem. This incompleteness is not specific to the proof-theoretic approach, but turns up in other guises in all methods for proving properties of Prolog programs. It is annoying, but not really a problem from a mathematical point of view. The system exhibits a well-known form of incompleteness, which can be handled exactly by giving the kind of infinitary rule we have here.

The incompleteness of the system is a *practical* problem, of course, since in general infinitary derivations cannot be written down or represented on a computer. In the next section I give a proof system which is finitary and has a limited form of completeness, although it is not fully complete.

4.1 The Proof System SPndi

Our goal is to give natural-deduction-style rules for each connective that characterise the behaviour of that connective with respect to success or failure in the sequential Prolog interpreter (for instance, like the informal "$\mathbf{B} \vee \mathbf{C}$ fails iff both **B** and **C** fail" description of the last section). We therefore need two kinds of judgment, one for failure and one for success of a query formula. These "signed formulae" will be the judgments of the complete proof system, SPndi ("Sequential Prolog, natural deduction, infinitary").

Definition 4.1 A *signed formula* is an expression of the form $S(\mathbf{A})$ (read "**A** succeeds") or of the form $F(\mathbf{A})$ (read "**A** fails"). We use $\sigma(\mathbf{A})$ to denote an arbitrary signed formula.

I have chosen this notation, rather than use **A** and $\neg\mathbf{A}$ for $S(\mathbf{A})$ and $F(\mathbf{A})$ respectively, to avoid confusion with the issue of negation as failure in programs (not addressed by this paper).

The rules for SPndi are in Figure 4. SPndi is sound and complete for sequential Prolog, in a sense to be defined more precisely below. First, let me make some informal observations about the rules. The rules for the connectives and equality do reflect the informal kinds of descriptions that we want of success and failure of queries. They are also closely related to the corresponding rules in first order natural deduction proof systems; the only things which make them weaker are the non-commutativity of & and $\vee$, and the extra side-conditions.

Side-condition $(*a)$, "**B** contains no predicate calls", would seem at first glance to be so restrictive as to make the system incomplete. However, any terminating formula which does not meet this condition can be transformed by applications of the unfoldings rule, which expands predicate calls and separates the halves of disjunctions. This is the side-condition that restricts conjunctions and existential formulae to be in one of the classes of compositional formulae mentioned in Section 3.1. Formulae which cause an infinite sequence of predicate expansion steps are those which diverge by calling left-recursive predicates, so accordingly, they have no derivations. Similar remarks apply to side-condition $(*c)$ on the $F(\exists)$ rule.

Note particularly the rules $S(\exists)$ and $F(\exists)$. These rules are almost identical to the rules for $\exists$ on the right- and left-hand side of sequents in the

1. Success rules.

$S(=)$: $\dfrac{}{S(\mathbf{t} = \mathbf{t})}$ $\qquad$ $S(\exists)$: $\dfrac{S(\mathbf{B}[\mathbf{x} := \mathbf{t}])}{S(\exists \mathbf{x} \mathbf{B})} (*a)$

$S(\&)$: $\dfrac{S(\mathbf{B}) \quad S(\mathbf{C})}{S(\mathbf{B} \& \mathbf{C})}$

$S(\vee), 1$: $\dfrac{S(\mathbf{B})}{S(\mathbf{B} \vee \mathbf{C})}$ $\qquad$ $S(\vee), 2$: $\dfrac{F(\mathbf{B}) \quad S(\mathbf{C})}{S(\mathbf{B} \vee \mathbf{C})}$

2. Failure rules.

$F(=)$: $\dfrac{}{F(\mathbf{s} = \mathbf{t})} (*b)$ $\qquad$ $F(\exists)$: $\dfrac{F(\mathbf{B}[\mathbf{x} := \mathbf{y}])}{F(\exists \mathbf{x} \mathbf{B})} (*c)$

$F(\&), 1$: $\dfrac{F(\mathbf{B})}{F(\mathbf{B} \& \mathbf{C})}$ $\qquad$ $F(\&), 2$: $\dfrac{F(\mathbf{C})}{F(\mathbf{B} \& \mathbf{C})} (*a)$

$F(\vee)$: $\dfrac{F(\mathbf{B}) \quad F(\mathbf{C})}{F(\mathbf{B} \vee \mathbf{C})}$

3. Unfolding rule.

Unf: $\dfrac{\sigma(\mathbf{A}')}{\sigma(\mathbf{A})}$

where $\mathbf{A}'$ is a predicate or disjunctive unfolding of $\mathbf{A}$

4. Infinitary rule.

Inf: $\dfrac{\sigma(\mathbf{A}[\mathbf{x} := \mathbf{t}_1]) \quad \sigma(\mathbf{A}[\mathbf{x} := \mathbf{t}_2]) \quad \ldots}{\sigma(\mathbf{A})}$

where $\mathbf{t}_1, \mathbf{t}_2, \ldots$ is an enumeration of all the terms in the language

Side-conditions:
$(*a)$: $\mathbf{B}$ contains no predicate calls
$(*b)$: $\mathbf{s}$ and $\mathbf{t}$ are non-identical closed terms
$(*c)$: the derivation of the upper signed formula contains no predicate unfolding steps, and $\mathbf{y}$ does not occur free in $\mathbf{B}$

Figure 4: The complete, infinitary proof system SPndi.

sequent calculus. This is significant, because it means that we have managed to obviate the need to use substitutions (or syntactic representations thereof) as an essential part of the characterisation. SPndi therefore affirms that Prolog computations really *are* talking about witnesses for existentially quantified variables, and are not just functions on substitutions.

Note also that the only rule which is non-compositional is the unfoldings rule. This affirms that the notions of predicate and disjunctive unfolding capture all of the non-compositionality of sequential Prolog, and do so in a way that allows the rest of the characterisation to be compositional.

Finally, consider the infinitary rule. The non-existence of a finitary, complete proof system arises, in part, from the presence of free variables in judgments – which is, in turn, required by the logical form of the $F(\exists)$ rule. The exact statement of the incompleteness theorem is somewhat technical (see [And90] for the statement and proof); however, it is the same kind of incompleteness that arises in proof systems for first order arithmetic, for example, and there it can be handled by the analogous infinitary rule. (For more discussion about the use and implications of infinitary rules in the logics of programs, see section 1.7 of Goldblatt's book [Gol82]).

4.2 Soundness and Completeness

SPndi is sound: if a closed formula is derivable, it is "valid". The notion of validity here, however, comes not from first order logic, but from the operational semantics. There is a more general semantic notion, analogous to truth in a model; I use the verb "to work" for this, in order to make the operational connection clear.

Definition 4.2 A signed formula *works* with respect to a substitution θ just in the following two cases: $S(\mathbf{A})$ works wrt θ if the backtrack stack $(\theta : \mathbf{A})$ succeeds in the operational semantics SP; and $F(\mathbf{A})$ works wrt θ if $(\theta : \mathbf{A})$ fails in SP.

A signed formula $\sigma(\mathbf{A})$ is *valid* if, for every substitution θ which maps all free variables of $\mathbf{A}$ onto closed terms, $\sigma(\mathbf{A})$ works with respect to θ.

Theorem 4.3 (Soundness of SPndi)
1. If $F(\mathbf{A})$ has an SPndi-derivation with no predicate unfolding steps, then for all θ, $(\theta : \mathbf{A})$ fails without performing any Defined Predicate steps.
2. If $F(\mathbf{A})$ is derivable in SPndi, then it is valid.
3. If $S(\mathbf{A})$ is derivable in SPndi, then it is valid.

Proof. By induction on the structure of the SPndi-derivation. The only really difficult cases are for unfoldings, for which we use the operational equivalence of unfoldings. Note that because of the $F(\exists)$ rule the proof of (2) depends on the proof of (1), and because of the $S(\vee), 2$ rule the proof of (3) depends on the proof of (2). (See [And90] for full proofs of this and other theorems in this paper.)
□

Theorem 4.4 (Completeness of SPndi)
1. If **A** is a closed formula and $\sigma(\mathbf{A})$ is valid, then $\sigma(\mathbf{A})$ is derivable.
2. If $\sigma(\mathbf{A})$ is valid, then $\sigma(\mathbf{A})$ is derivable in SPndi.

Proof. (1.) By induction on the length of the SP-computation. There are three separate stages, to deal with formulae which fail without performing Defined Predicate steps, general failing formulae, and general successful formulae. We must make use of the equivalence of unfoldings, and the fact that an unfolding of **A** has a shorter computation than **A**. (2.) By induction on the number n of free variables in **A**. The case $n = 0$ is the previous theorem. The case $n > 0$ can be handled by eliminating one variable with the infinitary rule.
□

I end this section with the main comprehensive result concerning SPndi: that it is an exact (sound and complete) characterisation of terminating sequential Prolog computations.

Corollary 4.5 (Characterisation)
1. For every formula **A**:
$S(\mathbf{A})$ is derivable in SPndi iff every closed instance of **A** succeeds.
$F(\mathbf{A})$ is derivable in SPndi iff every closed instance of **A** fails.
2. For every formula **A**:
A succeeds (resp. fails) iff $S(\exists[\mathbf{A}])$ (resp. $F(\exists[\mathbf{A}])$) is derivable in SPndi.

Proof. A straightforward consequence of the Soundness and Completeness theorems, and the operational rules for the existential quantifier.
□

It should be pointed out that although SPndi is infinitary and thus not very useful for practical purposes, it is unique in being an exact and logical characterisation of sequential Prolog (one which treats the connectives in a logical manner). For this, it merits attention independent from its practical use.

5 A Weakly Complete, Finitary Proof System

In this section, we study a finitary (and thus more useful) proof system which is sound and has a limited form of completeness, but is not complete in the fuller sense of SPndi.

This system is called SPndf (Sequential Prolog, natural deduction, finitary), and the form of completeness that it has is the following: any valid signed formula *containing no calls to recursive predicates* is derivable in SP-ndf. This result, though not very useful practically, does show that the incompleteness of SPndf arises exclusively from the possibility of divergence, and not from inadequacies in how it describes the connectives or equality. In any case, I also suggest how we might add more power to the proof system, in order to get closer to the (unattainable) goal of full completeness in a finitary system.

5.1 The Proof System SPndf

SPndf can be regarded as being derived from SPndi by first using a more general form of judgment, then removing the infinitary rule, and then adding some rules about equality to ensure weak completeness.

The more general form of judgment that SPndf uses is a set of signed formulae, interpreted disjunctively. Because a set of signed formulae interpreted in this way behaves like the right-hand half of a sequent, we call these objects "semi-sequents".

Definition 5.1 A *semi-sequent* is a finite set of signed formulae. We write a semi-sequent $\{\sigma_1(\mathbf{A}_1)\ldots\sigma_n(\mathbf{A}_n)\}$ as a sequence $\sigma_1(\mathbf{A}_1),\ldots,\sigma_n(\mathbf{A}_n)$.

The disjunctive interpretation is reflected in the validity condition for semi-sequents.

Definition 5.2 A semi-sequent $\sigma_1(\mathbf{A}_1),\ldots,\sigma_n(\mathbf{A}_n)$ is *valid* if, for every substitution θ mapping free variables of the semi-sequent onto closed terms, there is some $i, 1 \leq i \leq n$, such that $\sigma_i(\mathbf{A}_i)$ works wrt θ.

If we used semi-sequents in SPndi instead of sequents, we could use the same rules, just augmenting every occurrence of a signed formulae $\sigma(\mathbf{A})$ by a set of signed formulae Γ. We would then be able to write some of the rules in a different way: the implicit disjunction in semi-sequents allows us to combine the two $S(\vee)$ rules, for instance, like this:

$$\frac{\Gamma, S(\mathbf{B}), F(\mathbf{B}) \quad \Gamma, S(\mathbf{B}), S(\mathbf{C})}{\Gamma, S(\mathbf{B} \vee \mathbf{C})}$$

SPndf uses semi-sequents and these "amalgamated" versions of the $S(\vee)$ and $F(\&)$ rules. As will become clear, this structure is necessary so that we can give rules for equality which compensate for the loss of the infinitary rule.

The rules for SPndf are listed in Figure 5. In all rules, the order of signed formulae within the semi-sequent is unimportant. The main difference from SPndi is the presence of the equality rules, which replace the infinitary rule. Signed sentences of the form $F(\mathbf{s} = \mathbf{t})$ behave as assumptions that $\mathbf{s}$ and $\mathbf{t}$ are equal. This behaviour can be explained by noting that, if we interpret the semi-sequent "comma" as "or" and failure as negation, we can view $F(x = 0), S(x = 0)$ as meaning $\neg(x = 0) \vee x = 0$; that is, $x = 0 \rightarrow x = 0$.

5.2 Soundness and Completeness

SPndf is sound according to the new definition of validity.

1. Equality.

Eq: $$\frac{}{\Gamma, S(\mathbf{t} = \mathbf{t})}$$ Occurs: $$\frac{}{\Gamma, F(\mathbf{s} = \mathbf{t})}(*a)$$

Ineq: $$\frac{}{\Gamma, F(\mathbf{f}(\mathbf{s}_1, \ldots, \mathbf{s}_n) = \mathbf{g}(\mathbf{t}_1, \ldots, \mathbf{t}_m))}(*b)$$

Comp: $$\frac{\Gamma, F(\mathbf{s}_1 = \mathbf{t}_1), \ldots, F(\mathbf{s}_n = \mathbf{t}_n)}{\Gamma, F(\mathbf{f}(\mathbf{s}_1, \ldots, \mathbf{s}_n) = \mathbf{f}(\mathbf{t}_1, \ldots, \mathbf{t}_n))}$$

Subst: $$\frac{\Gamma, F(\mathbf{s} = \mathbf{t}), \sigma(\mathbf{A}(\mathbf{s}))}{\Gamma, F(\mathbf{s} = \mathbf{t}), \sigma(\mathbf{A}(\mathbf{t}))}$$

2. Structural.

Thin: $$\frac{\Gamma}{\Gamma, \sigma(\mathbf{A})}$$ Cut: $$\frac{\Gamma, S(\mathbf{A}) \quad \Gamma, F(\mathbf{A})}{\Gamma}$$

3. Connectives.

$S(\&)$: $$\frac{\Gamma, S(\mathbf{B}) \quad \Gamma, S(\mathbf{C})}{\Gamma, S(\mathbf{B}\&\mathbf{C})}$$ $F(\&)$: $$\frac{\Gamma, S(\mathbf{B}), F(\mathbf{B}) \quad \Gamma, F(\mathbf{B}), F(\mathbf{C})}{\Gamma, F(\mathbf{B}\&\mathbf{C})}(*c)$$

$S(\vee)$: $$\frac{\Gamma, S(\mathbf{B}), F(\mathbf{B}) \quad \Gamma, S(\mathbf{B}), S(\mathbf{C})}{\Gamma, S(\mathbf{B} \vee \mathbf{C})}$$ $F(\vee)$: $$\frac{\Gamma, F(\mathbf{B}) \quad \Gamma, F(\mathbf{C})}{\Gamma, F(\mathbf{B} \vee \mathbf{C})}$$

$S(\exists)$: $$\frac{\Gamma, S(\mathbf{B}[\mathbf{x} := \mathbf{t}])}{\Gamma, S(\exists \mathbf{x} \mathbf{B})}(*c)$$ $F(\exists)$: $$\frac{\Gamma, F(\mathbf{B}[\mathbf{x} := \mathbf{y}])}{\Gamma, F(\exists \mathbf{x} \mathbf{B})}(*d)$$

4. Unfoldings.

Unf: $$\frac{\Gamma, \sigma(\mathbf{A}')}{\Gamma, \sigma(\mathbf{A})}$$

where $\mathbf{A}'$ is a predicate unfolding or disjunctive unfolding of $\mathbf{A}$

Side-conditions:
$(*a)$: $\mathbf{s}$ is a proper subterm of $\mathbf{t}$ or vice versa
$(*b)$: $\mathbf{f} \not\equiv \mathbf{g}$
$(*c)$: $\mathbf{B}$ contains no predicate calls
$(*d)$: the proof of the upper semi-sequent does not contain any predicate unfolding steps, and $\mathbf{y}$ does not appear in the lower semi-sequent

Figure 5: The finitary, weakly complete proof system SPndf.

Theorem 5.3 (Soundness of SPndf) Every semi-sequent derivable in SPndf is valid.

Proof. By induction on the structure of the SPndf-derivation.
□

SPndf is not, however, complete as it stands: given the usual recursive definition of "*append*", for example, there are semi-sequents such as $S(append(X, [\,], X))$ which are valid but not derivable because every instance of them has different shape of derivation. However, every valid semi-sequent *which does not contain calls to recursive predicates* is derivable. We can prove this by first proving that valid semi-sequents with no predicate calls at all are derivable.

Theorem 5.4 Every valid semi-sequent $\sigma_1(\mathbf{A}_1)\ldots\sigma_n(\mathbf{A}_n)$, in which the $\mathbf{A}_i$'s contain no applications of predicates other than $=$, is derivable in SPndf.

Proof. A variant of Henkin's proof of the completeness of the sequent calculus for first order logic. We begin by assuming the opposite, and proving a contradiction. That is, we assume that there is a valid, underivable semi-sequent $\mathcal{S}$; we prove a contradiction by proving, in stages, that the existence of $\mathcal{S}$ implies the existence of such a semi-sequent in a smaller and smaller class of semi-sequents – and then proving that there is no such semi-sequent in the smallest class.
□

As it turns out, this proof does not involve the thinning and unfoldings rules to any essential degree, and if we were to add the rule

$$\frac{\Gamma, F(\mathbf{t} = \mathbf{s}), \sigma(\mathbf{A}(\mathbf{s}))}{\Gamma, F(\mathbf{t} = \mathbf{s}), \sigma(\mathbf{A}(\mathbf{t}))}$$

we would not need the Cut rule either (which is only needed to prove the commutativity of equality). So even a much weaker system would be complete in this very weak sense.

The "weak completeness" result is stronger than this last theorem, and states that valid semi-sequents with no calls to *recursive* predicates are derivable. We can prove this through defining the class of programs that have no recursion or mutual recursion.

Definition 5.5 A *hierarchical* program is one in which each predicate $\mathbf{P}$ can be assigned a natural number $n_{\mathbf{P}} > 0$ such that if $\mathbf{P}$ calls $\mathbf{Q}$, $n_{\mathbf{Q}} < n_{\mathbf{P}}$.

Corollary 5.6 (Weak Completeness of SPndf) If Π is a hierarchical program, then every semi-sequent which is valid with respect to SP_Π is derivable in SPndf_Π.

Proof. Every predicate call in such a semi-sequent can be expanded via the unfoldings rule. After a finite number of such expansions, the semi-sequent will contain no predicate calls, at which point the previous theorem

applies.
□

Finally, we have a characterisation result which corresponds to the one of the last section.

Corollary 5.7 If Π is hierarchical, then:

1. $S(\mathbf{A})$ $(F(\mathbf{A}))$ is derivable in SPndf_Π iff every closed instance of $\mathbf{A}$ succeeds (fails).
2. $\mathbf{A}$ succeeds (fails) iff $S(\exists[\mathbf{A}])$ $(F(\exists[\mathbf{A}]))$ is derivable in SPndf_Π.

Proof. A consequence of the Soundness and Weak Completeness theorems.

5.3 Strengthening SPndf

How can we strengthen SPndf to prove more, and more useful, theorems? Some of the valid semi-sequents which are not derivable in SPndf are those which require inductive proofs: for instance, $S(append(X, [\,], X))$. We can alleviate this problem to a large extent by deriving a full sequent calculus from SPndf, and then adding induction rules to it. In this section, I suggest one possible course of development in this direction, which will be explored more fully in my thesis.

Definition 5.8 A *sequent* is an expression of the form

$$\sigma_1(\mathbf{A}_1), \ldots, \sigma_n(\mathbf{A}_n) \rightarrow \sigma_{n+1}(\mathbf{B}_1), \ldots, \sigma_{n+m}(\mathbf{B}_m)$$

The signed formulae on the left are called the *antecedents* and those on the right the *consequents* of the sequent.

A sequent $\mathcal{S}$ is valid if, for every θ which maps free variables of $\mathcal{S}$ onto closed terms, if all of the antecedents work wrt θ, then one of the consequents works wrt θ.

We can define a finitary sequent calculus for these sequents by using the rules for SPndf and adding rules for antecedent signed formulae. What completeness properties such a calculus will have is unclear; however, since full sequents give us the power of implication, we can now give induction rules.

Definition 5.9 Let $\mathcal{S}$ be of the form $\Gamma \rightarrow \Delta, \sigma(\mathbf{A}(\mathbf{x}))$, where $\mathbf{A}(\mathbf{x})$ is the only formula in $\mathcal{S}$ to have $\mathbf{x}$ free. Let $\mathbf{f}$ be an n-ary function symbol. Then $IH(\mathcal{S}, \mathbf{f})$ is the sequent

$$\Gamma, \sigma(\mathbf{A}(\mathbf{y}_1)), \ldots, \sigma(\mathbf{A}(\mathbf{y}_n)) \rightarrow \Delta, \sigma(\mathbf{A}(\mathbf{f}(\mathbf{y}_1, \ldots, \mathbf{y}_n)))$$

where $\mathbf{y}_1, \ldots, \mathbf{y}_n$ are n variables not free in $\mathcal{S}$.

The induction rule (or more properly rule schema) for the sequent calculus now takes the form

$$\frac{IH(\mathcal{S},\mathbf{f}_1) \quad \ldots \quad IH(\mathcal{S},\mathbf{f}_m)}{\mathcal{S}}$$

where $\mathcal{S}$ is any sequent of the form $\Gamma \rightarrow \Delta, \sigma(\mathbf{A}(\mathbf{x}))$, and $\mathbf{f}_1 \ldots \mathbf{f}_m$ are all the function symbols in the language $\mathcal{L}$. This rule is sound in the same sense that the other rules for SPndf are sound, as stated by the following theorem.

Theorem 5.10 If each premiss of an application of the induction rule is valid, then the conclusion is valid.

Proof. If $\Gamma \rightarrow \Delta$ is valid, then the result holds trivially. Otherwise, there is some substitution $\theta[\mathbf{x} := \mathbf{t}]$ with respect to which all of the Γ signed formulae work, and we must prove that $\sigma(\mathbf{A})$ works with respect to it. We can do this by induction on the structure of $\mathbf{t}$; each subcase corresponds to one of the premisses of the rule application.
□

Example. If the language $\mathcal{L}$ has only the nullary function symbol [ ] and the binary function symbol [_|_], then $S(append(X,[\,],X))$ could be proven by using the rule application

$$\frac{\begin{array}{c}\rightarrow S(append([\,],[\,],[\,])) \\ S(append(Y,[\,],Y)), S(append(Z,[\,],Z)) \rightarrow S(append([Y|Z],[\,],[Y|Z]))\end{array}}{\rightarrow S(append(X,[\,],X))}$$

Other approaches to induction in program logics, such as well-founded induction [MW78], might also prove useful in strengthening such a sequent calculus.

6 Summary and Future Work

SPndi and SPndf are two proof systems which characterise the behaviour of sequential Prolog computations in a sound, complete and logical manner. SPndi is infinitary but fully complete, and SPndf is finitary and has weak completeness properties. Both have rules which use the predicate and disjunctive unfolding transformations on formulae, allowing them to come much closer to the strength of sequential Prolog than traditional logical characterisations. Since both are highly compositional, treat the connectives in a logical manner, and avoid manipulating substitutions directly, both are more "logical" in nature than denotational characterisations.

This presentation of a logical characterisation for pure, negationless sequential Prolog brings this programming language firmly into the realm of logical analysis, and should allow us to apply other techniques from mathematical logic to study its properties.

The model theory of these proof systems deserves some study. The equivalence relation induced by the disjunctive unfolding operation would probably be an important element of such a model theory. Following Fitting [Fit85], we might define models via the notions of upward- and downward-saturated sets of signed sentences.

SPndf may be able to be strengthened in order to prove more useful completeness properties, such as completeness for all closed semi-sequents (and thus all existential closures of queries). It may also be interesting to experiment with different validity conditions on formulae and semi-sequents, such as validity with respect to all substitutions rather than just ground substitutions.

One great advantage of Baudinet's and other denotational semantics over these characterisations is that those are able to handle negation by failure and cut. Though the well-known non-logical nature of these features would suggest that no logical characterisation is possible, it should be possible to add other weaker forms of them in a logical manner: for instance, negation restricted to input variable formulae, inequality, and if-then-else.

The addition of such features would make the language under consideration fairly powerful and practical. Combining this with the addition of induction rules to a full sequent calculus version of SPndf would form a good basis for a system for proving or formally developing practical Prolog programs.

7 Acknowledgements

My thanks to Paul Voda, who saw the importance of trying to find logical ways of characterising sequential Prolog long ago, and who suggested to me the course of research which led to this paper; and to my advisors at Edinburgh, Don Sannella and Stuart Anderson, who made many valuable comments. Thanks also for helpful suggestions to Inge-Maria Bethke, Lars Hallnäs, Gordon Plotkin, David Walker, and the referees.

References

[And89] James H. Andrews. Proof-theoretic characterisations of logic programming. In *Proceedings of the 14th International Symposium on the Mathematical Foundations of Computer Science*, volume 379 of *Lecture Notes in Computer Science*, pages 145–154, Porąbka-Kozubnik, Poland, August-September 1989. Springer.

[And90] James H. Andrews. The logical structure of sequential prolog. Technical Report LFCS-90-110, Laboratory for the Foundations of Computer Science, University of Edinburgh, Edinburgh, Scotland, April 1990.

[Bau88] Marianne Baudinet. Proving termination properties of Prolog programs: A semantic approach. In *Proceedings of the Third Annual IEEE Symposium on Logic in Computer Science*, pages 336–347, Edinburgh, Scotland, July 1988.

[FGKP85] N. Francez, O. Grumberg, S. Katz, and A. Pnueli. Proving termination of Prolog programs. In Rohit Parikh, editor, *Logics of Programs*, volume 193 of *Lecture Notes in Computer Science*, pages 89–105, Berlin, July 1985. Springer-Verlag.

[Fit85] Melvin Fitting. A Kripke-Kleene semantics for logic programs. *Journal of Logic Programming*, 4:295–312, 1985.

[Gol82] Robert Goldblatt. *Axiomatising the Logic of Computer Programming*, volume 130 of *Lecture Notes in Computer Science*. Springer-Verlag, Berlin, 1982.

[HS84] Masami Hagiya and Takafumi Sakurai. Foundation of logic programming based on inductive definition. *New Generation Computing*, 2:59–77, 1984.

[HSH88] Lars Hallnäs and Peter Schroeder-Heister. A proof-theoretic approach to logic programming. Technical Report R88005, Swedish Institute of Computer Science, 1988.

[JM84] Neil D. Jones and Alan Mycroft. Stepwise development of operational and denotational semantics for Prolog. In *Proceedings of the 1984 International Symposium on Logic Programming*, February 1984.

[MW78] Zohar Manna and Richard Waldinger. The logic of computer programming. *IEEE Transactions on Software Engineering*, SE-4:199–229, 1978.

[NF89] Tim Nicholson and Norman Foo. A denotational semantics for Prolog. *ACM Transactions on Programming Languages and Systems*, 11:650–665, October 1989.

Parallelism I

Optimizing And-Or Parallel Implementations

Gopal Gupta
Department of Computer Science
University of Bristol
Bristol BS8 1TR, U.K.

Bharat Jayaraman
Department of Computer Science
State University of New York at Buffalo
Buffalo, NY 14260, U.S.A.

Abstract

This paper describes ways of improving the performance of combined and-or parallel implementations. The class of implementations we consider supports or-parallelism using any environment representation that provides constant-time variable access and task-creation, e.g., binding arrays [W87] and versions vectors [H87], and supports independent and-parallelism e.g., the RAP [D84] and CGE methods [H86]. The major run-time overhead in such and-or parallel implementations can be traced back to the overhead for or-parallelism, namely, non-constant-time task-switching. We present a number of techniques for reducing this overhead by exploiting and-parallelism to reduce the number of conditionally bound variables whose bindings need to be installed during task-switching. These techniques can be easily incorporated in a compiler, and can lead to substantial savings in execution time.

1. Introduction

The obvious reason for combining and-parallelism and or-parallelism in a single framework is that any implementation that supports either alone is suboptimal compared with one that supports both. Another important reason is that when there is potential for both and- and or-parallelism in a single program, not exploiting either form of parallelism can lead to unnecessary over-computation. For a trivial example, the pair of goals `?- append(X, Y, [1,..,m]), append(P, Q, [1,..,n])`, leads to a `O(m*n)` computational cost under a pure or-parallel or pure and-parallel or even a sequential implementation, because all `n + 1` solutions for `P` and `Q` are re-computed for each of the `m + 1` solutions for `X` and `Y`. Instead of re-computing the solutions, if we compute the solutions only once and then combine them through a cross product, the computational cost would only be of the order `O(m + n)` (assuming that the time it takes to compute the cross-product of solutions is insignificant compared to the time it takes to re-compute the solutions). Note that goals where such solution sharing is possible frequently arise in database searching, symbolic integration, etc.

In earlier papers [GJ89a, GJ89b], we presented an and-or parallel execution model that integrates the binding arrays method for or-parallelism

[W84, W87] and the RAP method [D84, H86] for independent and-parallelism In this paper, we first show that the proposed model is more general in that it can work with certain other environment representation schemes, especially version vectors [H87]. The main focus of this paper, however, is on techniques for improving the performance of a combined and-or parallel implementation, especially for the case when goals exhibit both and-parallelism and or-parallelism. The major run-time overhead in our and-or parallel model can be traced back to the overhead incurred for or-parallelism, i.e., the cost of task-switching. We present a number of techniques for reducing this overhead, by exploiting and-parallelism and the semantics of CGEs [H86]. Essentially, these techniques reduce the overhead by reducing the number of conditionally bound variables† (also called *conditional variables* in this paper) whose bindings need to be installed during task-switching. This is achieved by the following set of actions:

(i) separating the local conditional variables from global conditional variables in the binding lists‡ and installing only global conditional variables during task-switching;

(ii) recognizing conditional variables which are installed again immediately after they are removed from a processor's environment—a phenomenon which arises due to solution sharing as we shall shortly see—and saving the removal/installation steps altogether for them; and

(iii) taking advantage of the groundness information in CGEs to avoid installation of certain conditional variables.

These optimizations are such that they can be introduced by a compiler. Thus, and-parallelism and or-parallelism are more efficient in our combined and-or parallel model compared to purely or-parallel [CH86, H87, W84, W87] or purely and-parallel models [D84, H86, LK88].

In order to show the generality of our and-or parallel execution, we first note that there are three important criteria for an ideal or-parallel implementation: constant-time access to all variables, constant-time task-creation, and constant-time task-switching. By constant-time, we mean that the time taken is independent of the depth of the execution-tree and the size of the goal arguments. We have shown in [GJ90b] that it is not possible to satisfy all three criteria simultaneously. Since an or-parallel implementation can satisfy at most two criteria, this can be used as a basis for classifying the various or-parallel systems proposed. For example, the Binding Arrays method [W84, W87] and the Version Vectors method [H87] offer constant-time task creation and variable access; the Directory Tree method [CH86] offers constant-time variable access and constant time task-switch; and the Hash Windows method [B84] offers constant time task-creation and constant time task-switch. In our opinion, methods offering constant-time perfor-

† conditionally bound variables are those variables which can receive more than one binding during execution.

‡ Note that binding lists are implemented as trail stacks in most parallel systems.

mance for variable access and task-creation are better than the others. This is because variable access and task-creation are the two most frequently performed operations and are entirely program-dependent, while task-switching depends on the scheduling strategy chosen and thus can be optimized by the run-time system. Our and-or parallel model has been implemented using the binding arrays approach, but we show that it can be used just as easily with the version vectors approach. Furthermore, although we use CGEs for and-parallelism, our technique can be used to implement languages such as Andorra Prolog [W90].

The rest of the paper is organized as follows: Section 2 briefly presents our model for combined and-or parallelism; section 3 shows that the model can be used with either binding arrays or version vectors; section 4 presents the optimization techniques for reducing task-switch time; and finally section 5 presents conclusions. We assume that the reader is familiar with or-parallel models [W84, W87, H87], Restricted And-Parallelism [D84, H86], and the Warren Abstract Machine (WAM) [W83].

2. A Model for Combined And-Or Parallelism

Figure 1 shows an extended and-or tree for expressing and-or parallelism in a simple example. The extended and-or tree is an extension of the basic and-or tree. In addition to *and* nodes and *or* nodes, it has *cross-product* nodes to hold the cross-product of solutions from and-or parallel goals†, and *sequential* nodes which indicate the beginning of execution of *sequential goals* following the execution of a CGE. Nodes have space for their subgoals (also called goal-list), and or-nodes have space for the bindings of the variables occurring in the subgoals. The binding of a conditional variable, along with its address, is also stored in a *binding list* associated with the node in which the binding is produced. The binding list serves the purpose of the trail stack during backtracking—all variables which appear in the binding list are marked to unbound—and also helps in updating the environment of a processor when it switches tasks and selects work at some other site in the tree.

Cross-product nodes are introduced to facilitate sharing of solutions of and-parallel goals and serve to avoid the over-computation alluded to earlier. They are analogous to join-nodes in the PEPSys model [WR87], and are parents of and-nodes and sequential nodes. Each element in the cross-product set is a *tuple* which corresponds to one specific solution for the and-parallel goals. Thus the cross-product set corresponding to the cross-product node labeled `e X f` is $\{\langle e^1,f^1\rangle,\langle e^2,f^1\rangle,\langle e^1,f^2\rangle,\langle e^2,f^2\rangle\}$. The components of each tuple are addresses of terminal nodes of the and-branches. An and-branch is a branch rooted at an and-node, and consists of those nodes lying along a path from the and-node to a leaf node (which represents *one* solution

† Note that in the extended and-or tree the the solutions to and-parallel goals are computed only once, and to produce all solutions the solutions of individual and-parallel goal have to be combined by a cross-product.

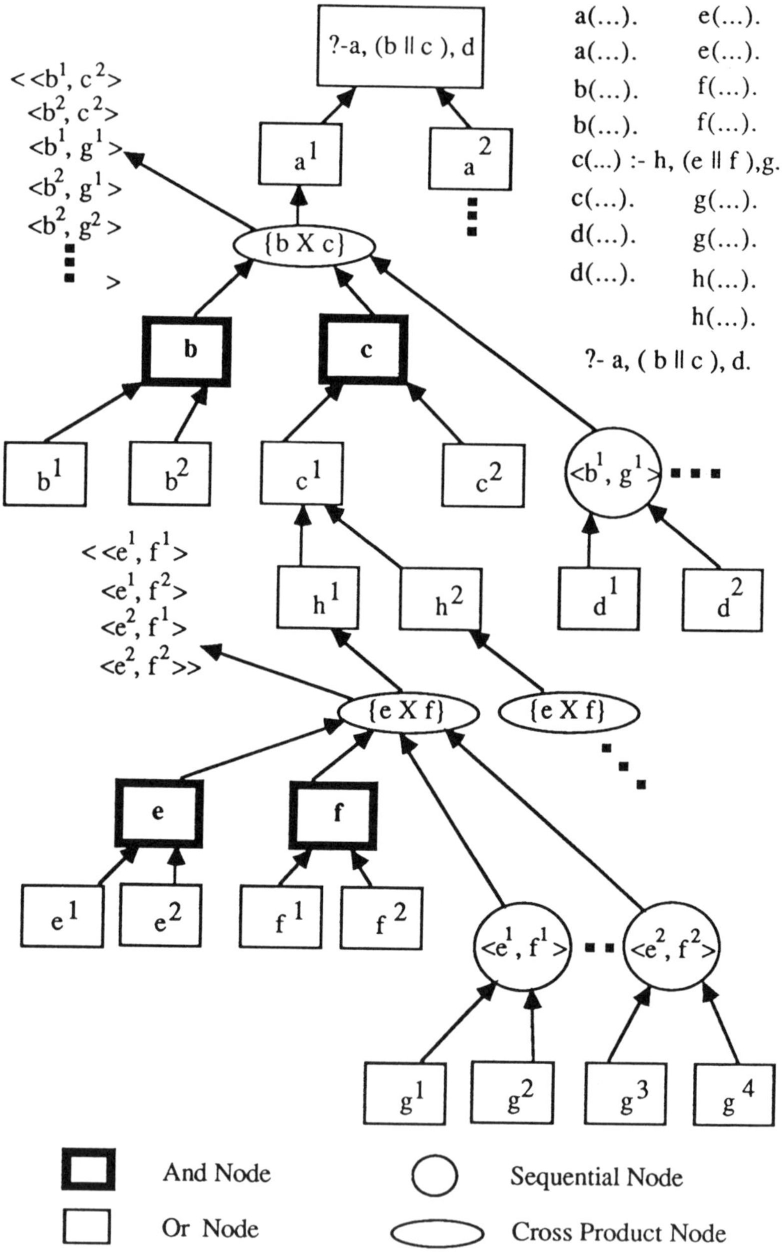

Figure 1. An Example of an Extended And-Or Tree

for the associated and-parallel subgoal). For example, nodes labeled b and b^1 form an and-branch rooted at b. Note that we avoid an explicit join of bindings produced for variables in the and-parallel subgoals. Instead, we represent the cross-product set using addresses of terminal nodes.

The structure of the extended and-or tree, except perhaps for the sequential nodes, should be self-evident from figure 1 (note that in the figure (b || c) indicates that b and c can be executed in and-parallel). We therefore clarify the role of sequential nodes. For example, suppose that the and-nodes e and f have produced solutions e^1 and f^1 respectively. A tuple $\langle$e^1, f$^1\rangle$ would then be inserted in the cross-product set associated with cross-product node labeled e X f, and a sequential node labeled $\langle$e^1, f$^1\rangle$ would be created corresponding to this tuple to solve goal g, where g is the next (sequential) goal to be solved after the execution of CGE containing e and f is over. The sequential nodes are inserted as children nodes of the corresponding cross-product node. The creation of other tuples $\langle$e^1, f$^2\rangle$, $\langle$e^2, f$^1\rangle$, etc., results in the creation of the corresponding sequential nodes. Similarly, when goals g^1, g^2, etc. are solved, tuples $\langle$b^1, g$^1\rangle$, $\langle$b^1, g$^2\rangle$, etc. are inserted in the cross-product set of the cross-product node b X c, and sequential nodes labeled $\langle$b^1, g$^1\rangle$, etc. are created as children of that cross-product node for the execution of goal d.

Three points should be noted in the above discussion : (a) Since the cross-product set is represented using address of terminal nodes, before a processor executes a goal corresponding to sequential node labeled with the tuple $\langle t_1, t_2, \ldots, t_n \rangle$, it should first update its environment with the bindings made in the and-branches corresponding to $t_1, t_2, \ldots, t_n$. (b) Initiating the execution of each sequential goal, such as $\langle$e^1, f$^1\rangle$, depends only on the completion of e^1 and f^1 and not on other and-branches of e and f. Hence execution of a sequential goal may be initiated, even though all the solutions to preceding and-parallel goals may not have been found yet. (c) There are many sources of parallelism: (i) two or more or-nodes could be executed in parallel giving rise to or-parallelism; (ii) two or more and-nodes could be executed in parallel giving rise to and-parallelism; (iii) two or more cross-product tuples could be executed in parallel, or an or-node and a cross-product tuple could be executed in parallel, giving rise to *consumer instance parallelism* (using the terminology in [RK89]).

The above is a general scheme for exploiting and-or parallelism in logic programs. An abstract machine architecture similar to the WAM, using an extension of binding arrays for representing multiple or-parallel environments, has been designed for this model, more details of which can be found in [GJ89b, G90]. The data areas of this abstract machine consist of a local stack, for allocating space to various nodes and local variables, and a global stack (or heap), for allocating the heap variables. The extended and-or tree lies in node stacks accessible to all processors. Execution is started by placing the root node in the node stack of one of the processors. Processors traverse the branches of the tree, executing subgoals in the nodes, and growing and contracting the tree in the process. Since the number of branches in the and-or tree would be much larger than the number of processors, each processor ends up executing more than one branch of the tree. This is accomplished through backtracking on success/failure. The movement of a processor from its current site to the place where work is available is called *task switching*. Task switching involves updating the environment so that all the bindings can be correctly accessed at the new site of work.

Before we describe how environment can be represented in our model, we show that solution sharing indeed incurs less overhead than re-computing solutions. Consider two independent and-parallel subgoals `a, b` where both `a` and `b` have more than one solution each. If we re-compute each solution for `b` for every solution of `a`, then all the variables (conditional or unconditional) appearing in subgoals `a` and `b` would be accessed *at least once* during unification. In general they would be accessed more than once: first, to be initialized with a value, and perhaps later for unification with another value. (For example, in the WAM, a conditional variable is accessed once during the `put_variable` instruction to allocate space and later again when it receives a binding value). If, instead of re-computing the solutions for subgoals, a processor shares the and-branches produced for `a` and `b` by other processors, then the only overhead it incurs is in installing bindings from binding-lists of the nodes in the and-branches. Since every conditional variable in the and-branch would be accessed only once during binding installation, and, in general, the number of conditional variables is much smaller than the total number of variables in the and-branch, the number of variable accesses are much less during installation than during re-computing. Note that we have not even considered the overheads arising out of environment and node allocations during re-computing, which are not incurred during solution-sharing and which make it even more efficient.

3. Environment Representation

In the next two subsections, we show how the two most well known environment representation schemes with constant time task-creation and variable-access but non-constant task-switching time [W87, H87] can be extended to incorporate and-parallelism. The extensions ensure that bindings to all variables are accessed in constant-time even in the presence of and-parallelism.

3.1. Extending the Binding Arrays Method

It should be first noted that the binding arrays method [W84, W87] will not work correctly in the presence of and-parallelism. To see the problem, consider the goals (p, (q1 || q2), r), where q1 and q2 also exhibit or-parallelism. Suppose further that goal p has been completed. In order to execute goals q1 and q2 in and-parallel, it is necessary to maintain separate binding arrays for them. As a result, the binding-array offsets for any conditional variables that come into existence within these two goals will overlap. Thus, when goal r is attempted, we are faced with problem of merging the binding-arrays for q1 and q2 into one composite binding-array or maintaining fragmented binding-arrays.

To solve the above problem, first recall that in the binding-array method [W84, W87] an offset-counter is maintained for each branch of the or-parallel tree for assigning offsets to conditional variables. However, offsets to the conditional variables in the and-parallel branches cannot be uniquely assigned, since there is no implicit ordering among them; at run-time a processor can traverse them in any order.

We introduce one more level of indirection in the binding array to solve this problem. In addition to the binding array, each processor also maintains another array called the *base array*. As each and-node is created, it is assigned a unique integer id. When a processor encounters an and-node, it stores the offset of the next free location of the binding array in the ith location of its base array, where i is the id of the and-node. The offset-counter is reset to zero when an and-node is created. Subsequent conditional variables are bound to the pair $\langle i, v\rangle$, where v is the value of the counter. The counter is incremented after each conditional variable is bound to this pair. The dereferencing algorithm is described below:

```
deref(V)        /*unbound variables are bound to themselves*/
term *V {
    if V→tag == VAR
            if not V→value == V
                    deref(V→value)
            else V
    else if V→tag == NON-VAR
            V
        else {          /*conditional var bound to <i, v>*/
            val = BA[v + base[i]];       /*BA is the binding array.*/
            if val→value == val
                    V
            else deref(val) }}
```

Note that access to variables is constant-time, though the constant is somewhat larger compared to the binding-arrays method for pure or-parallelism. Also note that now the base array is also to be updated on a task-switch. More details of this extension can be found in [GJ89b, G90].

When bindings to conditional variables are made they are recorded in the binding array as well as in the binding list. There are two situations where a processor needs to update its binding array: The first is when the processor decides to continue with the execution of a sequential node, after the completion of an and-branch and generation of a tuple thereafter. Before it can do so, it needs to update its binding array with the bindings created for the conditional variables in other and-branches in the tuple. Note that this updating overhead is in lieu of re-executing the and-branches. The second situation where the binding array needs to be updated arises when a processor runs out of work. The processor then selects a site in the tree where work is available and task-switches to start execution from that site. Task-switching involves removing from the binding array those bindings made to conditional variables between the current node and the common ancestor node of the current node and the new site, and installing those bindings made to conditional variables between the new site and the common ancestor (we call the former operation binding *removal* and the latter binding *installation*). Note that if a sequential node (with associated tuple $\langle t_1, t_2, \ldots, t_n \rangle$) is encountered during task-switching then all the bindings made to conditional variables in the and-branches $t_1, t_2, \ldots, t_n$ are either removed from or installed into the binding array depending upon where the sequential node lies.

3.2. Extending the Version Vectors Method

In the version vectors method [H87], conditional variables are bound to a vector of values. The length of the vector is n, where n is the number of processors. A processor with processor id i stores its corresponding binding in the ith slot of the associated vector. During task-switching processors install the correct binding of all the conditional variables, which appear in the binding lists of the intervening nodes, in the appropriate slot in the corresponding version vectors.

The problem that arises in the versions vectors model due to the presence of and-parallelism is the following: Given the goal and the tree shown in fig. 1, if a processor with id i is working on the and-parallel subgoal b and another processor with id j is working on subgoal c, then conditional bindings imparted by any one of them are not visible to the other. This is because binding generated by processor i is stored in the ith slot of the version vector, while that generated by j is stored in the jth slot. Since during variable access processors look up only their associated slot, bindings produced by i are not visible to j and vice versa. Thus, before processor i or j can continue with the sequential goal d (whose associated tuple is, say, $\langle b^1, c^1 \rangle$) processor i must update its slots in the version vectors for conditional variables which have been imparted a binding by processor j during execution of and-branch c^1, while processor j must update its slots in the version vectors for conditional variables which have been imparted a binding by processor i during execution of and-branch b^1. The dereferencing algorithm remains the same as in pure or-parallel case. The version vectors are needed to be updated in a manner similar to the binding arrays method during task-switching. For the extended versions vectors method the operations of *binding removal* and *binding installation* are taken to mean removal and installation, respectively, of bindings from version vectors of conditional variables rather than from the binding array.

It is perhaps obvious now, given an environment representation method for implementing or-parallelism with constant-time task creation and variable access, but non-constant time task-switching, how to incorporate it in the extended and-or tree. The part of the environment which is maintained privately by each processor, i.e. bindings of conditional variables, would have to be updated for each of the and-branches $\mathtt{t}_1$, $\mathtt{t}_2$, ..., $\mathtt{t}_n$ before a processor can continue with a sequential node labeled with the tuple $\langle \mathtt{t}_1, \mathtt{t}_2, \ldots, \mathtt{t}_n \rangle$. In addition, if such a sequential node is encountered during task-switching, all the conditional bindings along and-branches $\mathtt{t}_1$, $\mathtt{t}_2$, ...,

t_n would also have to be installed in, or removed from, the private part of the environment depending on where the sequential node lies. For example, the private part of a processor in case of the binding arrays method is its private binding array while in case of the versions vectors method it consists of its private slots in the version vectors.

4. Optimizations

In this section we present techniques for reducing the major source of overhead in our combined and-or model, namely, task-switching, an operation that involves traversing the tree and updating the environment. Earlier attempts to reduce task-switching overheads can be found in [H87, W87]. Although these techniques (known as *variable promotion* and *delayed installation*) were originally designed for purely or-parallel systems, they are also applicable to and-or parallel systems. However, in this paper we focus only on techniques that are possible due to the presence of and-parallelism. These techniques are (i) not very difficult to implement, (ii) can result in substantial gain in time, (iii) can be easily incorporated in a compiler [G90], and (iv) are independent of the work-scheduling strategy chosen. Examples illustrating these optimizations can be found in [GJ90].

4.1. Splitting the Binding List

The first optimization is based on the observation that after an and-parallel subgoal `G` has been solved, subsequent goals need only the bindings produced for `G`'s unbound variables. For example, in the CGE

`(independent(X, Y) | a(X, 2) || b(Y, 8)), d(0, X, Y),`

if `independent(X,Y)` evaluates to true because both `X` and `Y` are unbound variables, then the subgoal `d`, as well as other following subgoals, use only the bindings produced for `X` and `Y`. Thus, once all the solutions for `a` and `b` have been produced, the processors picking up sequential subgoal `d` for execution need install only those conditional variables which appear in the arguments of the subgoals `a` and `b` and not those which may have come into existence within the and-branches of `a` and `b` during execution. However, there are two difficulties with this approach.

(i) The variables in the top-level goal (for example, variables `X` and `Y` above) may dereference to a conditional variable which may get bound within the and-branch (fig. 2). That is, the bindings of such conditional variables may lie in the binding list of nodes within in the and-branches. Since we cannot tell *a priori* the node which is going to bind a variable, accessing the binding of these variables for binding installation or removal requires traversing all the binding lists within the and-branch.

(ii) Conditional variables present in structures occurring in the and-branches may be accessed indirectly later, e.g., when that structure is accessed from some other goal not in the and-branch during unification (Fig. 3). Installing or removing the bindings of such conditional variables again requires traversing all the binding lists within the and-branch.

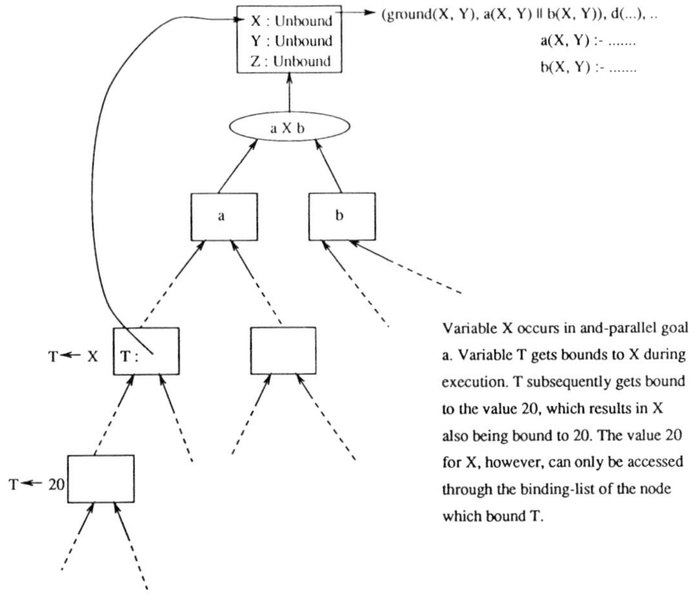

Figure 2 : Problems with Local Conditional Variables

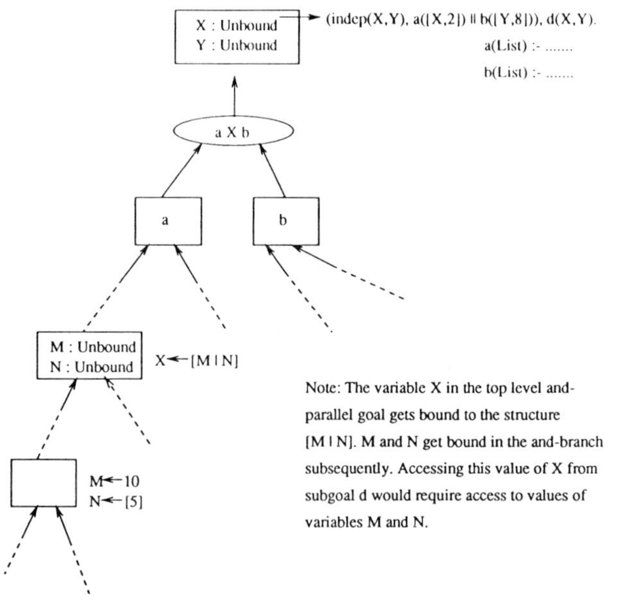

Figure 3 : Problems with Structure Variables

It turns out that although we cannot completely avoid traversing binding lists, we can considerably reduce the amount of work that is involved in installing the conditional variables in the and-branches.

If we follow WAM conventions, then in case (ii) all conditional variables occurring within structures would be global variables and would be allocated space on the heap. Thus, if we maintain separate binding lists for global conditional variables and local conditional variables and install bindings appearing only in the binding list of global variables, then the problem mentioned in (ii) would be eliminated. (Note that in an implementation that represents binding lists as trail stacks, the trail stack would be split in two.) As a result of maintaining separate binding lists the amount of work done during binding installation would be decreased since we only have to install global conditional variables, saving the work for local conditional variables.

However, splitting the binding list and installing bindings from only global binding lists solves the problem mentioned in case (ii) but it doesn't solve the problem mentioned in case (i). Re-considering case (i), we observe the following:

(a) A variable in the argument of an and-parallel subgoal (e.g., `X` and `Y` above) cannot dereference to a variable (conditional or unconditional) which comes into existence within the and-branch, because of the WAM convention that "newer" variables always point to "older" ones.

(b) If a variable in the argument of an and-parallel subgoal (e.g., `X` and `Y` above) dereferences to an unbound conditional variable `U` in its ancestor node and gets bound within the and-branch, then this binding would be imparted to variable `U`, because, in the WAM, variables are dereferenced before they are bound. The address-value pair for this binding would be kept in the global or local binding list within the and-branch depending on whether the conditional variable is global or local.

Examining case (b) further, if the conditional variable is global and the pair is kept in the global binding list, no problems arise since bindings in global binding lists are installed during task-switching. If the conditional variable is local, it will *not* be installed during task-switching since processors do not install from local binding lists. To remedy this situation, we "globalize" such local conditional variables before initiating the execution of the subgoal, so that if it gets bound within the and-branch its address-value pair is kept in the global binding list and gets properly installed. By globalizing, we mean that the variable is moved from local stack to the heap. The globalization step can be carried out when the argument variable is being loaded into argument registers (during WAM `put_value` instruction). This results in a new instruction, which we call `put_and_value` and which is similar to WAM's `put_value` instruction, but which also globalizes the variable to which the argument variable dereferences to. This new instruction is more similar to WAM's `put_unsafe_variable` instruction except that in the latter a local variable is globalized only if it is allocated space in the *current* environment.

As a special case if the argument variable dereferences to itself (i.e., it is the first occurrence of a local conditional variable), then the variable itself is globalized. As in the previous case, the globalization step can be carried out when the argument variable is being loaded into argument registers (during WAM `put_variable` instruction). This results in a new instruction, which we call `put_and_variable` and which is similar to WAM's `put_variable` instruction, but which also globalizes the argument variable.

The net effect of the above two new instructions is to globalize local conditional variables to which variables in the arguments of an and-parallel subgoal might dereference to. As a result of globalization, if a processor picks a sequential goal labeled $\langle t_1, t_2, \ldots, t_n\rangle$, it need install only the bindings in global binding lists of and-branches $t_1, t_2, \ldots, t_n$. Similarly, if this sequential node is encountered during task-switching, binding installation/removal need be done for only bindings occurring in global binding lists of and-branches $t_1, t_2, \ldots, t_n$. Thus the work of installing local conditional variables is saved. Empirical studies [TD87] have shown that in many benchmark programs the number of local conditional variables is a significant percentage of the total number of variables which come into existence during execution (approximately 20% on average, for large benchmarks). Thus, not having to install bindings from local binding-lists during task-switching leads to considerable savings in time.

One should, however, note that binding installation from the local binding lists of an and-branch cannot be avoided if the processor task-switches to a node in the and-branch for the purpose of finding a solution for the associated and-parallel subgoal. This is because these bindings may be needed during execution of the subgoal. Thus, installation of bindings from the local binding list for an and-branch can be avoided only if a solution has already been found and the processor wants to continue with the execution of sequential node or a node below the sequential node. For example, in figure 1 if a processor switches to node labeled **e X f** it needs to install bindings from both local and global binding lists along the and-branch c-c^1-h^1, while a processor switching to node $\langle b^1, g^1\rangle$ needs to load only from the global binding lists along and-branches b-b^1 and c-g^1.

4.2. Common Tuple-Elements

The second optimization is concerned with reducing the number of conditional bindings to be installed during task-switching by recognizing those and-branches that are immediately re-installed after removal.

When a processor is backtracking and possibly removing bindings of conditional variables bound in the and-branches of a cross-product tuple, it is very likely that after getting to the cross-product node it will pick up another tuple to continue execution (the tuple set is recorded as a sequence of tuples in the cross-product node). The bindings of conditional variables bound in the and-branches corresponding to the new tuple would be installed before execution is begun. However, the new tuple might have some elements common with the old tuple whose bindings were just removed, which we would have to install again. Thus, a natural improvement would be to save the removal/installation steps for the common elements in the current tuple and the next. This improvement has two advantages – not only less work is done, the contention for the node-stacks and binding lists is also reduced.

For example, suppose we have the following goal `?- (true, a || b)`, during whose execution `a` and `b` are executed in and-parallel. Let us assume that solutions a^1, a^2 and a^3 are found for subgoal `a` and solutions b^1 and b^2 are found for subgoal `b`. Using a straightforward algorithm (the one Prolog uses to find all solutions) the cross-product tuple sequence would be generated with the following ordering: $\langle\langle a^1, b^1\rangle, \langle a^1, b^2\rangle, \langle a^2, b^1\rangle, \langle a^2, b^2\rangle, \langle a^3, b^1\rangle, \langle a^3, b^2\rangle\rangle$. We refer to the algorithm which generates this set as the naive algorithm. Suppose further that the tuple $\langle a^1, b^1\rangle$ is picked by a processor to continue the execution of the sequential goal. Once the execution of the sequential goal is done, the processor starts to backtrack. When the processor reaches the sequential node corresponding to $\langle a^1, b^1\rangle$ during backtracking, it further backtracks through the tuple and removes the conditional bindings along the and-branches a^1 and b^1. After the binding removal is done it picks another tuple from the cross-product node and continues with the execution of the sequential goal to find another solution. Now suppose that the tuple $\langle a^1, b^2\rangle$ is selected as the next tuple for execution. Since bindings along the and-branch a^1 are being re-installed, the effort spent in removing them during backtracking is wasted. A more efficient strategy when a sequential node is reached during backtracking would be for the processor to select the tuple it wants to execute next and then remove and install bindings from only those and-branches *in which the two tuples differ.* Thus, in our example, we should simply remove bindings in and-branch b^1 and install those along b^2 and continue with the execution of the sequential goal. Note that this saves the work of installing and removing bindings along a^1, thus saving some time in switching from one tuple to another. The savings can be even more if the arity of the tuples is larger and more elements are common among the two tuples.

The incorporation of the optimization described above poses one problem. When we backtrack to a sequential node, we would like to choose the tuple which has the maximum number of elements common with the current tuple. This can be a non-trivial task since it would involve comparing the current tuple with all the existing tuples in the cross-product node. However, there is an efficient method of generating the cross-product tuple sequence such that two adjacent tuples differ in their component elements *only in one position.* When a processor reaches a sequential node during backtracking, it selects the tuple after the current one in the tuple sequence. In this way the processor just has to remove/install bindings from only one and-branch. If we generate the above tuple set in a way such that adjacent tuples differ only in one element then it would look as follows : $\langle\langle a^1, b^1\rangle, \langle a^1, b^2\rangle, \langle a^2, b^2\rangle, \langle a^2, b^1\rangle, \langle a^3, b^1\rangle, \langle a^3, b^2\rangle\rangle$.

After a processor finishes executing its current tuple and picks the next one in the tuple-sequence, hoping that it would have to remove/install variables only along one and-branch, it is possible that that tuple may have already been picked up by another idle processor. In such a situation, the processor picks the next available untried tuple in the tuple-sequence. The next tuple obtained thus may differ in more than one element position, but still it would be the untried tuple "nearest" to the current one, and hence would require least amount of removal/installation steps (because tuples in the tuple-sequence are arranged in a fashion that consecutive tuples differ in only one element position). However, now the processor has to do an element-wise comparison of the current tuple and the chosen tuple to determine the elements in which the two differ before removing/installing variables along the corresponding and-branches. Note that the processors never wait for the generation of the optimal tuple which will minimize binding array update; rather, the tuples in the tuple-sequence are generated in such a way that if a processor picks up the next tuple in the tuple-sequence after processing the current tuple, then the next available tuple in the tuple-sequence will be such that the binding array updates would be minimized.

We now give an algorithm for generating the cross-product set with the tuples in the order desirable for common tuple-elements optimization. The algorithm has the same complexity as the naive algorithm. We assume that solutions to each and-parallel subgoal are organized as separate circular lists in the corresponding and-nodes. Also assume that the first tuple is arbitrarily generated by selecting one arbitrary element from each solutions list. (Actually, in a practical system there are some advantages in choosing the first tuple carefully which we will not discuss here to keep matters simple). To understand how the algorithm works, we first describe the naive algorithm informally through a series of steps below:

(i) Copy first tuple into current tuple. Let the rightmost element position in the current tuple be the current position. Print current tuple.

(ii) If the elements at the current position have gone through one complete cycle in their solution list, move current position one element to the left in the current tuple. Repeat this step until a position is found whose elements have not gone through one complete cycle in the solution list. If we move beyond the leftmost position, the entire cross-product set has been generated and the algorithm terminates.

(iii) Replace all elements at positions to the right of the current position in the current tuple by elements at corresponding position in the first tuple.

(iv) Replace the element in current position in current tuple by the next element in the corresponding solution list. Print current tuple. Move current position to the rightmost element in current tuple. Go to step (ii).

As a result of step (iii) in the above naive algorithm, adjacent tuples differ in their elements in more than one position. If we omit this step then step (i), (ii) and (iv) would give an algorithm which generates the cross-product set with the desired characteristic. We call this derived algorithm the optimized algorithm. Note that in the optimized algorithm, determining that a position in the current tuple has cycled through the solution list is difficult because in each iteration the cycle starts from a new element. To overcome this problem we have to remember the element from where the cycle of a particular solution list started.

Below we give precise program code for the optimized algorithm. Note that `next` is a function which, given a solution, returns the next element in that solution's corresponding circular solution list. The variable `arity` is initialized to the size of the tuple (number of subgoals being executed in and-parallel). Array variable `first_tuple` is used for storing the first tuple, while array variable `ctuple` is used for remembering where the cycle started in different solutions lists during each iteration. The elements of the cross-product set appear in an array called `tuple_set` once the program terminates. Variables `top` and `base` are pointers into the tuple_set array and serve as pointers to current position and current tuple respectively. We use the programming syntax of C to describe the algorithm. Figure 4 illustrates how this algorithm works by a simple example.

```
    /*ele_t is the type of tuple elements*/
ele_t ctuple[arity], first_tuple[arity], tuple_set[MAXSIZE];
ele_t *top, *base, *temp; int j,k;
compute_tuple_set()
  {base = tuple_set;
  top = base + arity - 1;
  for (j = 0 ; j < arity ; j++)
     {
     tuple_set[j] = first_tuple[j];        /* Copy the first tuple into tuple_set*/
     ctuple[j] = first_tuple[j];          /* Start the cycle from the first tuple*/
     }
  while(true)
   { while(next(*top) == ctuple[top - base]) /*Starting from top element*/
       { ctuple[top - base] = *top;       /*in tuple_set for each element */
         top = top - 1; check if the cycle is completed*/
        if (top < base)                   /*If cycles completed for all elements, exit.*/
           { printf("Cross-Product Set Enumeration Over");
             return;
           }
       }
     temp = base; base = base + arity; /*Start generating next tuple in tuple_stack.*/
     for (k = 0 ; k < arity ; k++)
          base[k] = temp[k];        /*Create copy of most recent tuple in tuple_stack.*/
     top[arity] = next(*top);         /*Modify the top element of the copied tuple.*/
     top = base + arity - 1;          /*Update top and repeat the cycle.*/
   }
}
```

Program 1: Optimized Generation of the Cross-product Set

4.3. Ground CGEs

A commonly occurring form of CGEs is as follows.

`(ground(X,Y) | b(X,Y) || c(X,Y) || d(X,Y,Z)).`

In such cases, all variables appearing in some of the and-parallel subgoals

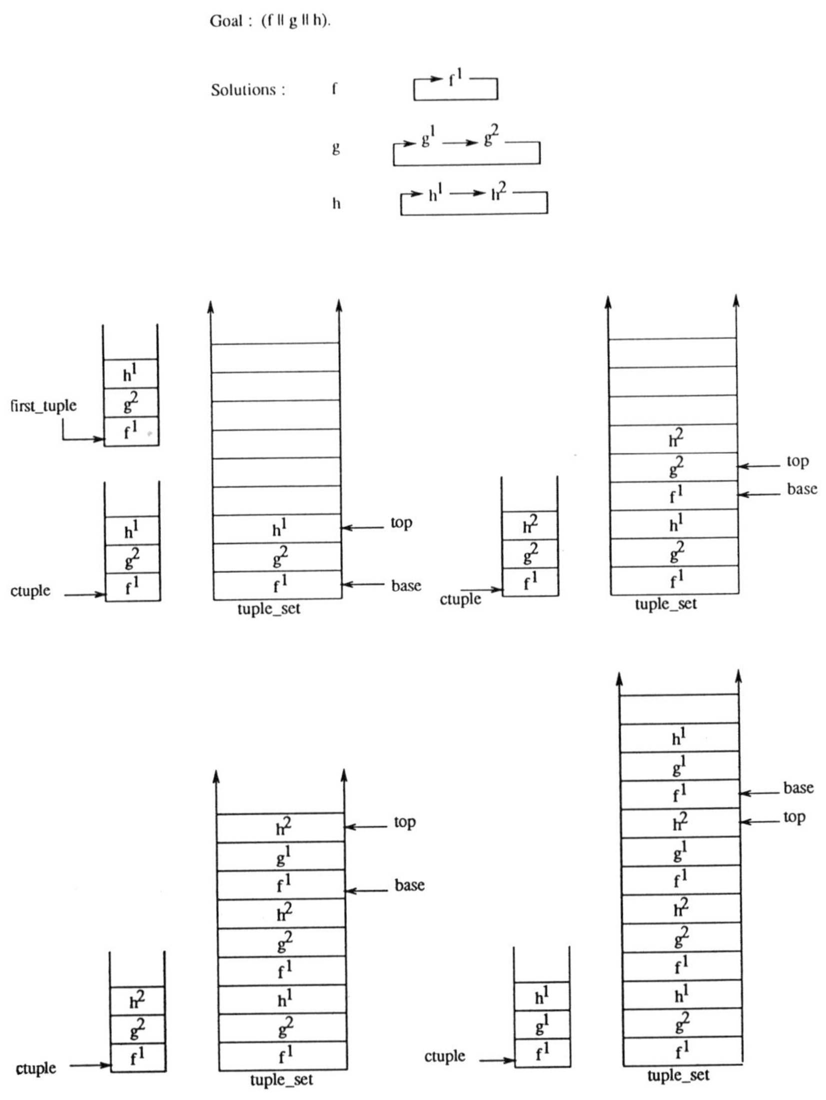

Fig. 4: Optimized Generation of Cross Product Set

(e.g. subgoals b and c) would be bound to *ground* values if the condition succeeds. Here, there is no need for processors to install bindings from binding lists (global or local) of and-branches of such subgoals. This is due to the following reasons:

(i) As mentioned before, a subgoal uses bindings of only those variables of another sibling subgoal which appear in the sibling subgoal's arguments. Thus, a sequential subgoal accesses only the bindings of variables appearing in the arguments of and-parallel subgoals.

(ii) If a conditional variable is ground before the condition in the CGE is evaluated, then the node where the variable is bound to ground value would be an ancestor node of the cross-product node corresponding to the CGE. The bindings of such a conditional variable, thus, would already have been installed by a processor before it reaches the cross-product node corresponding to the CGE.

(iii) Semantics of CGEs require that only variables occurring to the left of a CGE can occur in its condition part.

Hence, if we can infer from the evaluation of the condition of a CGE that all variables in arguments of an and-parallel subgoal in the CGE are ground, then, during task-switching, by (ii) and (iii) the bindings of such variables must already have been installed when a processor reaches the cross-product node corresponding to the CGE. Now, since there are no unbound variables in arguments of the subgoal, by (i) there is no need for a processor to install bindings from binding lists (global or local) within the subgoal's and-branch.

Hence, if all variables appearing in the arguments of a subgoal are ground, the processor need not install bindings from that subgoal's and-branch at all. Thus, in the CGE above there is no need for a processor to install bindings for subgoals b and c because all the variables present in their arguments have to be bound to ground values in order for the condition in the CGE to evaluate to true. The same, however, cannot be said for subgoal d. Thus, a processor does need to install bindings from d's branch, since d has a potential conditional variable, Z, as its argument (note that work in installing bindings in d can be reduced by splitting the binding lists). We believe that the ground-CGEs optimization would greatly improve the performance of the system, since the ground condition would be frequently found in CGEs.

There are many cases for which we can detect at compile-time that all arguments of a predicate would be ground if the condition in the CGE evaluates to true (for example, if the set of variables appearing in arguments of a subgoal is a subset of set of variables being checked for groundness in the condition, such as in the example above). In general, however, it is not always possible to gather this information at compile time, especially if the condition has occurrences of the boolean operator *or* in it. For example, given the condition (ground(X, Y) or independent(X, Y)) we cannot conclude at compile time that if this condition evaluates to true, then variables X and Y would be bound to ground values. The only way to find out if all variables of a subgoal are grounded is to check their bindings explicitly at run time. This can easily be incorporated in a compiler which generates appropriate code to check for the groundness of the bindings of variables appearing in the subgoal. The check can be conducted, for example, by using the `check_ground` instruction of RAP-WAM [H86]. At run time if all variables occurring in a subgoal are found to be ground, this information can be stored in the and-node by setting a bit. When a processor encounters an and-branch whose and-node's bit is set, it doesn't install bindings from binding lists of that branch.

Note again, however, that if a processor task-switches to a node in an and-branch to continue its execution, bindings have to be installed from both the global and local binding list, similar to the case of splitting binding-lists optimization.

This optimization can also be viewed as a special case of split-trail optimization where no binding installation/removal is necessary for an and-branch all variables in whose corresponding subgoal are bound to ground-terms.

5. Conclusion

In this paper we presented several techniques for improving the performance of a combined and-or parallel implementation. Because our combined and-or model is based on an environment representation that incurs a high overhead in task switching (but offers constant-time variable access and task creation), our main focus was on techniques for minimizing the cost of task-switching. The proposed techniques take advantage of and-parallelism and significantly reduce this overhead by reducing the number of conditional variables whose bindings need to be installed during task-switching. The techniques we have presented are quite general and can easily be implemented through WAM like instructions [G90]. An implementation of a system based on an extended WAM and incorporating these optimization is under way. Although our implementation uses the binding arrays method (suitably extended), we showed in this paper that our model for and-or parallelism can also work with other similar environment representation methods, including the version vectors method.

Acknowledgements

We thank D.H.D. Warren, P. Szeredi, F. Kluźniak and the anonymous referees for their comments and suggestions. This work was supported in part by NSF grant DCR 8603609 and U.K. Science and Engineering Research Council grant GR/F 27420, and originated when the authors were at the University of North Carolina at Chapel Hill.

References

[B84] P. Borgwardt, "Parallel Prolog using stack segments on shared memory multiprocessors," In *Proc. of the 1984 Int'l Symp. on Logic Prog.*," pp. 2-11.

[CH86] A. Ciepielewski, B. Hausman, "Performance Evaluation of a Storage Model for OR-Parallel Execution of Logic Programs," In *1986 IEEE Symp. on Logic Prog.*, pp. 246-257.

[D84] D. DeGroot. "Restricted AND-parallelism," *Int'l Conf. on Fifth Generation Computer Systems*, Tokyo, Nov., 1984.

[G90] G. Gupta, "And-Or Parallel Execution of Logic Programs: Abstract Machine Design and Implementation," Ph.D. Thesis, Univ. of N. Carolina at Chapel Hill, In preparation.

[GJ89a] G.Gupta and B. Jayaraman, "A Model for And-Or Parallel Execution of Logic Programs," *Proc. of the 18th Int'l Conf. on Parallel Processing,* 1989.

[GJ89b] G. Gupta and B. Jayaraman, "Compiled And-Or Parallel Execution of Logic Programs," In *Proc. of NACLP '89*, MIT Press.

[GJ90] G. Gupta and B. Jayaraman, "Optimizing And-Or Parallel Implementations,", University of Bristol, TR-90-15.

[GJ90b] G. Gupta and B. Jayaraman, "On Criteria for Or-parallel Execution Models of Logic Programs," In *Proc. 1990 NACLP*, Austin, TX.

[H86] M. V. Hermenegildo, "An Abstract Machine Based Execution Model for Parallel Execution of Logic Programs," Ph.D. thesis, The University of Texas at Austin, 1986, TR-86-20.

[H87] B. Hausman *et. al.*, "Or-Parallel Prolog made efficient on shared memory multiprocessors," in *1987 IEEE Int'l Symp. in Logic Prog.*

[LK88] Y-J. Lin and V. Kumar, "AND-parallel execution of Logic Programs on a Shared Memory Multiprocessor : A Summary of Results," in *Fifth Int'l Logic Prog. Conf.,* Seattle, WA, 1988.

[RK89] B. Ramkumar and L. V. Kale, "Compiled Execution of the REDUCE-OR Process Model," In *Proc. of NACLP '89*, MIT Press.

[TD87] H. Touati and A. Despain, "An Empirical Study of the Warren Abstract Machine," In *Symp. on Logic Prog.*, 1987, pp. 114-124.

[W83] D. H. D. Warren, "An Abstract Instruction Set for Prolog", Tech. Note 309, SRI International, 1983.

[W84] D. S. Warren, "Efficient Prolog Memory Management for Flexible Control Strategies," In *The 1984 Int'l Symp. on Logic Prog.,* Atlantic City, pp. 198-202.

[W87] D. H. D. Warren, "The SRI-model for Or-Parallel execution of Prolog - Abstract Design and Implementation Issues," *1987 IEEE Int'l Symp. in Logic Prog.*

[W90] D. H. D. Warren, "Extended Andorra Prolog", Internal PEPMA report.

[WR87] H. Westphal, P. Robert, *et. al.*, "The PEPSys Model: Combining Backtracking, AND- and OR-parallelism," In *1987 IEEE Symp. in Logic Prog.*, San Francisco, pp. 436-448.

Joining AND Parallel Solutions in AND/OR Parallel Systems

Laxmikant V. Kalé
kale@cs.uiuc.edu

Balkrishna Ramkumar
ramkumar@cs.uiuc.edu

Department of Computer Science,
University of Illinois at Urbana-Champaign,
Urbana, IL 61801, USA

Abstract

When two or more subgoals in the body of a Prolog clause are solved in (AND) parallel, their solutions need to be *joined* to compute solutions for the clause. This is often a difficult problem in parallel Prolog systems that exploit OR and independent AND parallelism in Prolog programs. In several AND/OR parallel systems proposed recently, this problem is side-stepped at the cost of unexploited OR parallelism in the program, in part due to the complexity of the backtracking algorithm beneath AND parallel branches. Furthermore, the data dependency graphs used by these systems cannot always represent all the exploitable independent AND parallelism known at compile time.

In this paper, we describe the compile time analysis for an optimised *join* algorithm for supporting independent AND parallelism in logic programs efficiently without leaving any OR parallelism unexploited. We then discuss how this analysis can be used to yield very efficient run time behaviour. We also discuss problems associated with a tree repesentation of the search space when arbitrarily complex data dependency graphs are permitted. We describe how these problems can be resolved by mapping the search space onto the data dependency graphs themselves. The algorithm has been implemented in a compiler for parallel Prolog based on the Reduce-OR process model which does not require any backtracking. The algorithm is suitable for implementations of AND/OR systems on both shared and nonshared memory machines.

1 Introduction

In recent years, there has been considerable interest in exploiting both AND and OR parallelism in logic programs. For reasons of efficiency, the research has been largely confined to independent AND parallelism. The main problem with implementing OR and independent AND parallelism together is the interaction between the two, which manifests itself when solutions for AND parallel subgoals in the body of the clause need to be combined. In this case, since each of the AND parallel goals may themselves be solved in OR parallel, they may each produce several solutions. Therefore, the 'combine' operation involves a *relational join* of the consistent solutions from all the AND parallel goals in the body of a clause.

Our approach is one that exploits both OR and independent AND parallelism that exists in Prolog programs and is based on the Reduce-OR process model (ROPM) [13] for the parallel execution of logic programs. Like the other AND and OR parallel process models discussed in Section 2, only independent AND parallelism is exploited in our implementation of ROPM[1]. It supports full OR parallelism, including a form of OR parallelism called *consumer-instance* parallelism where different instances of a consumer literal in a clause can be evaluated in parallel.

In this paper, we describe an optimised algorithm for performing the *join* of AND parallel goals in the body of a clause and the compile time analysis required for its successful implementation in a compiler that supports both OR and independent AND execution of logic programs. The algorithm performs the relational join *incrementally*, and fires consumer goal instances that depend on the join *as soon* as the join is computed. This permits the extraction of another form of OR parallelism, which we call *pipeline* parallelism[2]. The algorithm also permits the representation of the data dependencies in the program (detected at compile time) using arbitrary directed acyclic graphs. The algorithm thus permits the exploitation of more parallelism in Prolog programs than other schemes that use series-parallel data dependency graphs (like CGEs when run-time checks are not used[3]), without sacrificing efficiency. The compiler has been implemented on both shared and nonshared memory machines [17].

2 Related Work

Recently, several models have been proposed for exploiting both OR and independent AND parallelism in logic programs. The underlying assumptions for each of these models differ somewhat. We discuss each of these approaches briefly.

The ANDORRA model originally proposed by D.H.D. Warren and discussed in [8] exploits OR parallelism and a limited form of AND parallelism. The subgoals evaluated in AND parallel may be dependent, but they must be deterministic. This scheme permits stream parallelism between AND

[1]We use hand-annotated graphs to represent clauses. Recently proposed techniques for detecting strict and non-strict independence [10] can be used to generate these annotations.

[2]Note the distinction between *consumer instance* parallelism and *pipeline* parallelism. The former can be exploited even if a full-relational join is used. To exploit *pipeline* parallelism, however, it is necessary to perform the join operation incrementally. In *consumer instance* parallelism consumer instances are evaluated in parallel, whereas in *pipeline* parallelism consumer instances are evaluated in parallel with producer instances.

[3]In practice, for efficiency reasons, most schemes using CGEs choose not to perform run time checks. As for expressiveness, nodes in a Data Join Graph are capable of containing run-time checks like CGEs. This is not currently implemented.

parallel subgoals. This is the original ANDORRA model; a more general scheme is currently being designed [19]; the details were unavailable at the time of writing of this paper.

A scheme similar to the Reduce-OR process model is the Sync model proposed by Peggy Li [15]. It too is designed to exploit independent AND and OR parallelism on distributed memory machines, and uses a data dependency graph similar to the Data Join Graph used by ROPM. Consumer instance parallelism pipeline parallelism are exploited, although the latter is only partially exploited. This is because solutions arriving at join nodes arrive as solution sets enclosed by *sync* signals and pipelining is not done across sync signals. The Sync model solves only a restricted version of the problem addressed in this paper. This is discussed further in in Section 7.

Another scheme that is similar to the Reduce-OR process model is the PM model proposed by Vineet Singh [18] for backward-chaining deductions. It too supports independent AND parallelism and full OR parallelism and is somewhat similar to the Sync Model. The description of this scheme does not discuss any optimisations for the join operation. The scheme described in this paper can be used to optimize the join operation in the PM model.

Biswas' scheme [1] is designed to extract *limited-OR* and *restricted-AND* parallelism from logic programs. In this scheme the OR parallel execution is demand driven. As a consequence, the join operation is quite simple since an AND node in the AND/OR search tree contains only one active tuple at any point in time. Their join operation does not have to deal with multiple solutions on each AND parallel branch participating in the join. The exploitation of all detectable parallelism in logic programs is not the primary objective in this scheme.

Conery's approach [2], like our approach [14], is also suitable for non-shared memory machines. However, his scheme, as described in [2], is quite inefficient and may not be practical on shared memory machines. The optimisations proposed by us in [14] can be used in Conery's scheme to render it efficient. Like Biswas' scheme, Conery's AND/OR process model does not exploit *consumer instance* parallelism, and as a result the join operation is far simpler in his scheme.

Like ROPM, Wise's model [21] uses a *relational join* approach to dealing with solutions from AND parallel branches. However, the scheme discussed in [21] does not perform the join incrementally leading to a loss of *pipeline* parallelism.

The PEPSys approach [3] uses *join cells* to implement the "joining" of AND parallel branches. However, due to the complexity of the backtracking algorithm, they do not exploit OR parallelism under AND parallel subgoals in their implementation. Also, the use of hash windows in their binding scheme suggests that their scheme may be difficult to implement efficiently on a nonshared memory machine like a hypercube.

Like ROPM, the scheme proposed by Gupta and Jayaraman [6] exploits both consumer instance parallelism and pipeline parallelism. However, the implementation is restricted to shared memory machines. They use binding arrays [20] and, in addition, a *base array* to implement OR and independent AND parallelism in their model. *Cross product* nodes similar to the *join cells* used by the PEPSys approach are used to represent a join. The shared memory assumption permits this scheme to avoid performing explicit joins as is done in our scheme; instead a join is performed symbolically by using addresses of the solutions to be joined. This cost is incurred, in part, during the loading of binding and base arrays in a task switch to an instance of a literal which can be evaluated as a result of availability of the computed joined tuple.

Besides the suitability of our algorithm for implementation on both shared and nonshared machines, another principal difference from the above mentioned schemes, is the ability of our scheme to handle arbitrarily complex data dependency graphs. The above schemes use a parenthetical notation (like Conditional Graph Expressions (CGEs) proposed in [5] or [11]), which are not as expressive as arbitrary data dependency graphs[4] As a result, these schemes cannot always represent all the parallelism possible using static data dependency graphs. This is discussed in greater detail in Section 6.

3 The Join Algorithm

Before we describe the join algorithm, we first establish some terminology. Each rule (clause) is represented by a graph called a Data Join Graph (DJG). The difference between a data dependency graph and a DJG is that in DJGs arcs represent literals and nodes represent the joining points for the data produced by literals on its incoming arcs. Partial solution tuples at a node in the DJG are called *node tuples* and reside in *node-relations*, whereas those at an arc in the DJG are called *arc tuples* and reside in *arc-relations*.

In order to support AND parallelism, it is necessary to handle the join of two (or more) AND parallel solutions efficiently. A naive solution is to consider a cross product of all the solutions in the AND parallel branches. That is clearly an overkill, since only AND parallel solutions that descend from the same 'common ancestor' tuple need to be joined.

In this section, we first provide a brief description of the optimised join algorithm. Following that, in Section 4, we discuss algorithms for computing common ancestors and other related information. This information is computed during compile time analysis of the program. We briefly discuss some optimisations that reduce the run time overhead and describe the run time behaviour of the algorithm. Finally, we discuss some of the advantages of our algorithm over those proposed in the literature.

3.1 The Algorithm

[4]It is possible to generalize CGEs to make them as expressible as arbitrary graphs using semaphores[9]. However, it is not clear whether this representation is suitable for AND and OR parallel execution.

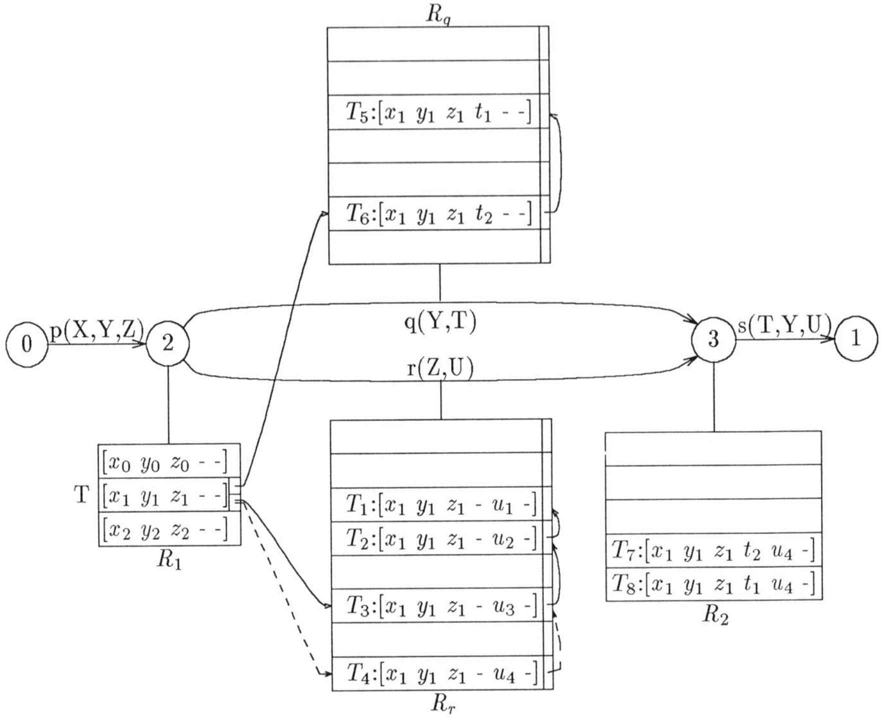

Figure 1: The Optimised Join Algorithm: a simple example

In the naive algorithm, when a tuple is inserted in an arc-relation, it is joined with all the tuples in the other arc-relation(s) that join at the same successor node. The process of joining two tuples involves first checking if the tuples are compatible (i.e. they have the same values for the variables bound in both of them) and then combining the bindings to create a 'joined' tuple. There are two sources of overhead in this algorithm: visiting tuples that are not compatible, and performing the consistency checks. The optimised algorithm makes it possible to visit only the relevant (compatible) tuples in the other join arc and thereby also avoids the consistency checks.

Consider the DJG in Figure 1. With every tuple T inserted in the node-relation for node 2 in this example, one *forward* pointer is created for each arc emanating from node 2. In general, at node N, there is one *forward* pointer for each arc that participates in a join for which N is a common ancestor. Each *forward* pointer in T points to a (initially empty) list of tuples that are extensions of T in the arc-relations to be joined.

When a subgoal G is fired, a (pointer to its) *context* tuple CT (the partial set of bindings used to fire G) is carried by a 'solve G' request. (CT resides in the node-relation of the node immediately preceding the arc representing G in the DJG.) CT is thus available to every response created for G. In Figure 1, for response tuple T_4 for subgoal r, the context tuple $CT(= T)$ happens to be the common ancestor tuple itself. In general, the context tuple is used to obtain the common ancestor tuple for the join operation (see below). T_4 is now inserted into the linked list of all tuples in R_r that are extensions of T, as indicated by the dotted lines. To compute the additions to the joined relation R_2, we *do not* join T_4 with the whole of R_q. Instead, we now follow the q-pointer from the context tuple T into the linked list of extensions of T in R_q. This leads us to tuples T_5 and T_6. The join of T_4 with T_5 and that of T_4 with T_6 result in two new tuples T_7 and T_8 in the node-relation R_2.

As can be seen, the whole arc-relation (R_q here) is not traversed, only the relevant tuples are visited. In addition, if the DJGs ensure independent AND-parallelism (as is the case in our implementation), there is no need for any consistency checks for the tuples visited.

In general, the situation can be far more complex than that of the example in Figure 1. We wish to remind the reader at this point that arbitrarily complex data dependency graphs are being considered. We discuss these cases with the aid of a complex example (see Figure 2), and describe how they are handled by the algorithm. For convenience, in the following discussion we use 'node-relation i' to refer to the node-relation at node i.

Multiple Common Ancestors: There may be more than one common ancestor for a join in the DJG. Here, before a join, a consistency check needs to be made to ensure that the tuples being joined both share the same (multiple) common ancestors. Consider the join at node 1 in the DJG in Figure 2. A closer look at the DJG reveals two lowest[5] common ancestors for this join: nodes 5 and 6. When a response tuple T arrives at arc (12,1), a backpointer from T's context tuple to one of its lowest common ancestors (say, in node-relation 5) is traversed, and a forward pointer is followed from the common ancestor tuple in node-relation 5 into the arc-relation at arc (13,1). For every tuple T_i in the arc-relation at (13,1) that is to be joined with T, a check is first made to ensure that both T and T_i are extensions of the same common ancestor tuple in node-relation 6. If so, T and T_i are joined, otherwise they are not.

Distant Common Ancestors: The context tuple may not itself be a common ancestor of the tuples in both the arc-relation tuples being joined as was the case in Figure 1. In this case, the intermediate node-relation tuples carry additional *backpointers*. In such a case, the context tuples would carry a back pointer to the common ancestor tuple. For example, consider node 11 in the DJG for the map colouring example in Figure 2. Node 11 has lowest common ancestor 2. Let T_{ca} be a tuple in

[5]For arcs incident at a join-node J in a DJG, a common ancestor node N_{ca} is called a lowest common ancestor, if $\neg\exists$ a path from N_{ca} to any other common ancestor of J in the DJG.

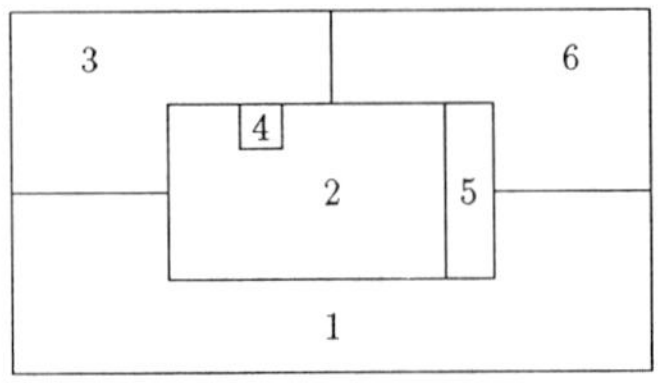


```
colour(R1,R2,R3,R4,R5,R6) :- next(R1,R2), next(R1,R3), next(R1,R5),
                             next(R1,R6), next(R2,R3), next(R2,R4),
                             next(R2,R5), next(R2,R6), next(R3,R4),
                             next(R3,R6),  next(R5,R6).
next(blue,green).    next(blue,red).     ......
```

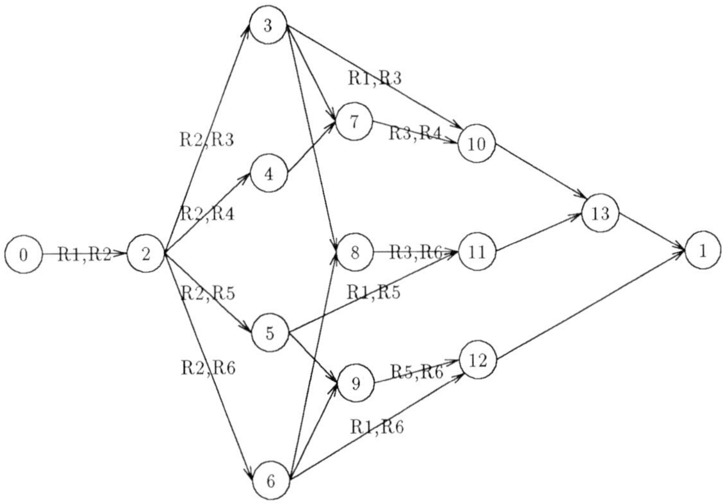

Figure 2: A possible data join graph (DJG) for a simple map colouring example. The labels (x,y) on the arcs are an abbreviation for `next(x,y)`. The unlabelled arcs in the DJG correspond to *null* arcs.

node-relation 2. Any tuple inserted in one of the node-relations 3, 5 or 6 having T_{ca} as a parent carries a backpointer to T_{ca}. This backpointer is propagated to any extension tuples of T_{ca} inserted in node-relation 8. The context tuples for the tuples being joined at node 11 belong to node-relations 5 and 8. The context tuples that are extensions of T_{ca} thus have a pointer to T_{ca}, their lowest common ancestor.

In general, a node may be an intermediate node for more than one join node. Tuples in such node-relations may end up carrying several backpointers. For example, node 8 in the DJG in Figure 2 is an intermediate node for the joins at node 11, node 13 and node 1. So, in addition to carrying a backpointer to a common ancestor tuple in node-relation 2 for node 11, a tuple in node-relation 8 would also carry backpointers to common ancestor tuples in node-relations 3 and 6. This is because node 3 is a lowest common ancestor for the join at node 13, and node 6 is one of the lowest common ancestors for the join at node 1.

One Common Ancestor for Multiple Joins: In this case, the tuples in the node-relation for node N need to carry two forward pointers for each join for which N is a common ancestor. This is clearly evident in the DJG in Figure 2. Node 2 is a common ancestor for join operations at node 7, 8, 9 and 11. Therefore each tuple in node-relation 2 has to carry eight forward pointers corresponding to the eight arc-relations that join at these nodes.

Nodes have in-degree > 2: N-ary joins can be easily be transformed automatically to binary joins by adding null arcs. This has been done in Figure 2. We assume DJGs with binary joins in the rest of the paper.

4 Lowest Common Ancestor Analysis

In the description of the join algorithm in Section 4, it is clear that for two tuples in AND parallel arcs to be joined, it is necessary for them to know their lowest common ancestor *tuples*. This can be determined only at run time. However, it is possible to determine, at compile time, the nodes at which the common ancestor tuples reside. It is also possible to determine which pointers to lowest common ancestors propagate forward to the respective AND parallel arcs (see above). We now describe algorithms to compute the common ancestor nodes for every pair of AND parallel arcs that need to be joined, and the tuple backpointers that need to be carried by tuples at the various nodes in the graph. Further details can be found in [7].

4.1 The Algorithm

We first set up some additional terminology for ease of exposition. The set of nodes in the DJG for a clause C is *nodes(C)*. Similarly, the set of arcs is *arcs(C)*. The set of successor arcs of a node N (i.e. arcs emanating from node N) in a DJG is *succ-arcs[N]*; the set of predecessor arcs is *pred-arcs[N]*. A *join node* is a node in the DJG that has more than one arc incident on it. An arc incident on a join node is called a *join arc*. A *node-tuple* is a tuple that resides in a node-relation in a DJG.

Let us consider a DJG for a clause C. The steps in the common ancestor analysis are as follows:

1. *Label the graph:* Sort the nodes of the graph topologically. The sorted nodes are stored in an array called *node-order*. For each node and arc in the DJG, compute the set of nodes on every path from the start of the graph to the node or arc in question. For node N and arc A, we will refer to these sets as *node-path[N]* and *arc-path[A]* respectively. By convention, we let $Node \in$ *node-path[Node]*.

```
PROCEDURE Reduce-Common-Ancestors(C, node-order, node-path,
                                   common-ancestors)
FOR each Node ∈ nodes(C)
    IF JOIN-NODE(Node)
        LCA ← {}
        /* traverse common ancestors in reverse topological order */
        FOR i = num-nodes(C) TO 1 BY -1
            IF node-order[i] ∈ common-ancestors[Node]
                CA = node-order[i]; /* found an l.c.a.  */
                LCA ← LCA ∪ {CA}
                common-ancestors[Node] ← common-ancestors[Node] -
                                          node-path[CA]
        common-ancestors[Node] ← LCA
```

Figure 3: The algorithm to compute *lowest* common ancestors sets for the join nodes in a DJG C.

2. *Compute Common Ancestors:* For each pair of arcs leading to a join node J, compute the set of common ancestors. This information is stored with the join-node to prevent duplication. We refer to this set as *common-ancestors[J]*.

3. *Reduce to Lowest Common Ancestors:* For each join node J in the DJG, *common-ancestors[J]* is trimmed down to contain only the *lowest* common ancestors for J.

4. *Compute the tuple backpointers carried by each node:* For each node in the graph, determine the set of backpointers that need to be carried by each node.

If A_1 and A_2 are any two arcs incident on a join node J, it is easy to see that $\textit{common-ancestors}[\mathrm{J}] = \textit{arc-path}[A_1] \cap \textit{arc-path}[A_2]$. In Figure 3, we describe how, for a join-node J in the DJG C, *common-ancestors[J]* is reduced to containing only the lowest common ancestors of J. The algorithm constructs the lowest common ancestor set for each join-node $J \in \textit{nodes}(C)$ as follows:

Let LCA denote the lowest common ancestor set for J. Initially, LCA = {}. We traverse the common ancestors of J in *reverse* topological order. Let $CA \in$ *common-ancestors[J]* be the next common ancestor of J found. It is easy to see that CA is a lowest common ancestor. CA is inserted in LCA. Now, any common ancestors of J in *node-path[CA]* are removed from *common-ancestors[J]* set using set difference (*common-ancestors[J]* ← *common-ancestors[J]* - *node-path[CA]*). When all the common ancestors of J have been examined, LCA contains all the lowest common ancestors of J.

```
PROCEDURE Compute-Tuple-Backpointers(C, node-order, arc-path,
                                     common-ancestors)
Initialise all node-backpointers and arc-backpointers to {}
FOR i = num-nodes(C) TO 1 by -1
    Node ← node-order[i]; /* reverse topological order */
    node-backpointers[Node] ← ⋃_{sa∈ succ-arcs[Node]} arc-backpointers[sa]
                                     - {Node}
    needed ← node-backpointers[Node]
    FOR pa ∈ pred-arcs[Node] /* predecessor arcs of Node */
          carried ← needed ∩ arc-path[pa]
          arc-backpointers[pa] ← carried ∪ common-ancestors[Node]
          needed ← needed - carried
```

Figure 4: The algorithm to compute the tuple backpointers for node-tuples in the DJG.

We now have the necessary information about the lowest common ancestors of nodes in the DJG to be able to compute what backpointers need to be carried by node-tuples at run time. As explained earlier, for a join operation to proceed, the two tuples being joined need access to their lowest common ancestor tuples. Any tuple being joined has access to its context tuple. As explained when distant common ancestors were discussed, if the context tuple is itself not the lowest common ancestor, then it must carry backpointers to the lowest common ancestors. So a backpointer is copied from one node-tuple to the next along a path to where it is needed.

Using the lowest common ancestor information we compute the backpointers to be carried by each node and arc. This algorithm is given in Figure 4. We emphasise here that it is only necessary for node-tuples to carry backpointers. In order to simplify the compile-time algorithm, we compute the pointers that will logically be carried by the nodes *and arcs* and throw away the information about the *arcs* after static analysis. For a given DJG C, the algorithm proceeds as follows:
Initialise node-backpointers for every $N \in nodes(C)$ and arc-backpointers for every $A \in arcs(C)$ to $\{\}$. Visit the nodes in reverse topological order. For each node N, node-backpointers[N] is simply the set union of the arc-backpointers of N's outgoing arcs. (Also, we do not allow N to belong to node-backpointers[N].) We then compute the arc-backpointers for each of N's predecessor arcs. Initially, the backpointers *needed* by N are node-backpointers[N]. We need to ensure that each node in node-backpointers[N] is supplied by atleast one of the predecessor arcs. So, for each $pa \in$ pred-arcs[N], the backpointers pa can supply is given by the common elements between *needed* and arc-path[pa]. It is also necessary for each incoming arc to carry the common ancestors of N to be able to perform the join operation

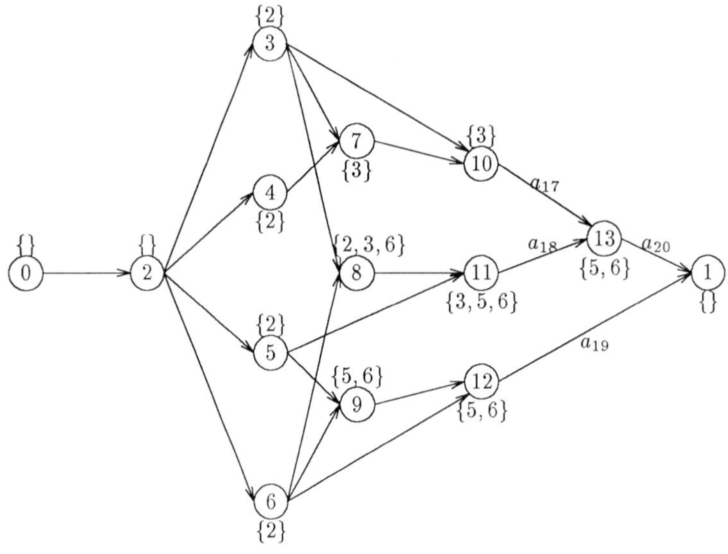

Figure 5: Computing tuple backpointers for the map colouring problem. The numbers in curly brackets associated with a node N denote the node-backpointers carried by N.

---

at node N. It is clearly not necessary (nor always possible) for every incoming arc to carry all the backpointers required by N. Therefore, after the arc-backpointers for each *pa* are computed, the backpointers supplied by *pa* are filtered out of *needed* (*needed* = *needed* − arc-path[*pa*] in Figure 4).

The result of running this algorithm on the map colouring example in Figure 2 can be seen in Figure 5.

5 Optimisations

It is possible to reduce the number of backpointers that need to be carried in some cases. For example, consider situations where the tuple backpointers that need to be carried by a join node J are available at J's common ancestor node CA. It is not necessary for these tuple backpointers to be carried by the intermediate nodes, since the common ancestor tuple at CA is always available at J. This optimisation has been implemented; for reasons of space, we omit the details here.

Another optimisation arises out of a practical consideration. The implicit assumption in the above discussion has been that all arcs (representing literals) in the DJG are treated equally. It is often preferable to evaluate builtin predicates inline as and when they are encountered in the DJG, rather than create subgoals to solve them. This creates some potential problems. First, the prospect of evaluating builtin predicates inline opens up the possibility of sharing tuples between node- and arc-relations in the DJG. i.e. an existing tuple could be used to evaluate a builtin inline. Second, the algorithms discussed above to compute the lowest common ancestors assume that all tuples are distinct. It is now possible, for example, for a tuple being joined to be the same as its context tuple even if the preceding node is not the common ancestor as was the case in Figure 1. Third, if a tuple T is shared by two (or more) distinct join arcs in a DJG, T may now belong to several linked lists (i.e. several arc-relations in the DJG). It is thus necessary to make provisions to permit the same tuple to belong to several arc-relations. Fourth, the information computed by the above algorithms may result in a tuple carrying a backpointer to itself due to the sharing of tuples.

It turns out that all these problems can also be detected and resolved at compile time by tagging inline predicates. Once again space considerations limit the discussion of these optimisations. These optimisations have also been implemented. For a more detailed exposition of the optimisation issues, we refer you to [16].

6 Run-Time Behaviour

In Figure 6 we provide a code fragment that describes how the information computed in the above sections is used. We describe below how the computed information results in an efficient run-time behaviour.

In Figure 6, the arrival of a solution tuple T at arc (5,11) triggers off the following behaviour: The *SetUpJoin* instruction stores T in the arc-relation (5,11) and extracts the lowest common ancestor CA of T. In this example, CA belongs to node-relation 2. Using the forward pointers stored in CA, a pointer to the list of relevant tuples in arc-relation (8,11) are obtained. Note that each of these operations can be performed in constant time given the information computed during static analysis.

Assuming there exist tuples that need to be joined, the *JoinTuples* instruction performs the join operation. The details of the join operation can be found in [14]. Once the join tuple J is computed, the propagation of backpointers is carried out with the aid of *CopyBackPtr* instructions. In this example, according to Figure 5, backpointers to ancestor tuples at nodes 3, 5 and 6 need to be copied. This is done on lines 120-122 in Figure 6. This too is a constant time operation.

The tuple J is now used in the join operation at node 13. The *PushStack* instruction makes it possible to save the context of the join operation (i.e. the tuples currently being joined and the ancestor tuple) for subsequent joins at node 11 involving the incoming tuple T. The *PopStack* instruction restores this context. Finally, the *NextTuple* instruction sets up the next pair to tuples to be joined. If there are no more tuples to be joined, we step out of the loop.

In Figure 5, we see that the two arcs being joined at node 1 share lowest common ancestors at nodes 5 and 6. One of these is arbitrarily designated the primary common ancestor and is used by the *SetUpJoin* instruction as

```
                :
--> 117     CheckResponse  node 11
    118     SetUpJoin    <back/fwd ptr indices>, fail=140
    119     JoinTuples             /* join tuples at node 11      */
    120     CopyBackPtr <ptr to ancestor tuple at node 3>
    121     CopyBackPtr <ptr to ancestor tuple at node 5>
    122     CopyBackPtr <ptr to ancestor tuple at node 6>
    123     Nop                    /* for the null arc (11,13)    */
    124     PushStack    Join Stack /* save join node 11's env.   */
    125     SetUpJoin    <back/fwd ptr indices>, fail=138
    126     JoinTuples             /* inner join at node 13       */
    127     CopyBackPtr <ptr to ancestor tuple at node 5>
    128     CopyBackPtr <ptr to ancestor tuple at node 6>
    129     Nop
    130     PushStack    Join Stack /* save join node 13's env.   */
    131     SetUpJoin    <back/fwd ptr indices>, fail=136
    132     MCACheck     <backptr indices to other l.c.a> fail=136
    133     JoinTuples             /* innermost join at node 1    */
    134     SendClauseResp         /* solution found for clause!  */
    135     NextTuple    jump=132  /* next tuple for join node 1  */
    136     PopStack     Join Stack /* join complete at node 1 -
                                  restore join env. for node 13 */
    137     NextTuple    jump=126  /* next tuple for  node 13     */
    138     PopStack     Join Stack /* join complete at node 1 -
                                  restore join env. for node 13 */
    139     NextTuple    jump=119  /* next tuple for node 11      */
    140     Suspend
                :
```

Figure 6: A code fragment that describes the action taken upon the arrival of a solution S at arc (5,11) incident on node 11. The arrow indicates the entry point associated with the arrival of S.

---

described above. The *MCACheck* instruction is used to check that the other lowest common ancestor of the tuples being joined is the same. In general, one such instruction will be generated for each multiple common ancestor. This too is a constant time operation. Thus, the total overhead per join operation imposed by this algorithm is constant.

To demonstrate this point empirically, consider the performance of the simple map colouring example in Figure 2. Quintus Prolog on the Sun 3/60 took 415 ms to execute the program. If the AND parallelism was not exploited (i.e. the program was run using a sequential DJG) our compiler took 1320 ms on the Sun 3/60. However, using the DJG in Figure 2, the sequential execution time was 360 ms. Of course, this problem is much too small to execute in parallel. In addition to the effectiveness of the join algorithm, this experiment also demonstrates the usefulness of the arbitrary graph representation.

7 Advantages Over Other Schemes

One of the obvious criticisms that can be levied at the proposed algorithm is its apparent complexity. It is necessary at the outset to distinguish between descriptive complexity and run-time complexity. Although the description of the algorithm may appear complex, the run time behaviour is very efficient. Moreover, we believe that, for an efficient solution to the problem addressed in this paper, this complexity is inevitable regardless of the execution model. In this section, we attempt to justify these statements and demonstrate the advantages of the proposed algorithm over other schemes. We discuss why some of the analysis presented in this paper is also useful for the efficient execution of other AND/OR parallel models like PEPSys [3] and that proposed by Gupta and Jayaraman [6].

One of the principal limitations of the schemes proposed in the literature is that they cannot handle arbitrarily complex data dependency graphs. Series-Parallel graphs are often limiting and unable to express the maximum possible parallelism in a program. The DJG representation, however, is capable of representing all the possible parallelism in a Prolog program (see [12].). But, this prompts another question: Is it important to try and exploit all the available parallelism in a program? We believe that the decision of whether or not to exploit the maximum possible parallelism in a program is best postponed until run time; however, the compile time representation of the program must not preclude the exploitation of all available parallelism. For example, grainsize analysis[4] can be used to laterally partition the Reduce-OR tree into its parallel and sequential components. Furthermore, the DJG can still be used during sequential execution to avoid recomputation of literals during backtracking.

Peggy Li' scheme [15] is similar to that proposed here but with a some significant restrictions. First, the Sync model does not permit multiple common ancestors for a join, thus limiting some possible parallelism. Second, it is necessary for the partial solution lists being joined to be finite and complete. This makes it possible to group the AND-solutions on each join arc into distinct sets each having a unique lowest common ancestor tuple (sync signal). It is now sufficient to take cross-products of solution sets that share the same sync signal (one from each join arc). This is neither possible in the presence of multiple common ancestors nor in the presence of infinite solutions. In the former case, the uniqueness property of the lowest common ancestor tuple is destroyed, and in the latter, the sets of AND parallel solutions on each join arc are infinite and therefore cannot be bounded by sync signals.

Consider, for example, the simple data dependency graph in Figure 7. If CGEs are used, this example cannot be expressed without loss of parallelism [13, 12]. In addition, even if DJGs were used to represent the program, if the tree representations of the search space as proposed by Gupta and Jayara-

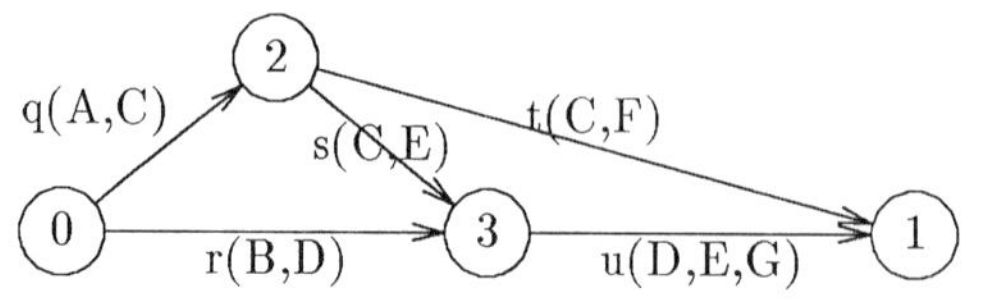

Figure 7: A data dependency graph which cannot be explored using the AND/OR search trees proposed by Gupta and Jayaraman or the PEPSys group.

man [6] or PEPSys [3] are chosen, the graph *cannot* be explored without loss of parallelism. For arbitrary graphs, we believe that compile time analysis similar to that proposed in this paper is necessary in order to exploit the parallelism effectively. The tree representation is effective in representing graphs using a parenthetical notation (like CGEs) but is too weak to represent the search space of complex graphs as in Figure 7 without substantial modification. This observation has led us to map the search space on to the representation of the program, i.e. onto the DJGs themselves.

We now use a simple example to study other differences between our scheme and those recently proposed in the literature. With this in mind, we now restrict the discussion to a parenthetical representation of data dependency graphs. We also assume the existence of a global address space. Let us consider the program in Figure 8. A tree representation of this problem, using the scheme proposed in [6], will create a cross product node at the top level and evaluate $(P_1, P_2, \ldots, P_n)$ and $(Q_1, Q_2, \ldots, Q_m)$ in AND parallel (see Figure 8). For each solution found for P_i (Q_j), an instance of P_{i+1} (Q_{j+1}) is fired. Thus when a solution S for any instance of P_n (Q_m) is found, the tree is traversed up to the lowest cross product node (in this case, the root) and S is deposited there. A join is then performed with any solutions for Q_m (P_n) in the cross product node.

Another algorithm would be to pass the address of the cross product node down the tree from P_i to P_{i+1} (Q_j to Q_{j+1}). When a solution for P_n is found, the address of the cross product node is immediately available and the node can be accessed directly and the join operation performed. The algorithm described in this paper can be viewed as a variant of this algorithm, where the *CopyBackPtr* instruction passes the address of the lowest common ancestor from P_i to P_{i+1}. But which (if either) is the better algorithm?

In a shared memory context the algorithms are simply duals of each other. One incurs the cost of walking up the tree looking for the lowest cross product node whereas the other incurs a comparable cost in copying the address of the cross product node while going down the tree. However, on a distributed memory machine, it is very likely to be far more expensive to traverse up the tree to the cross product node, since it may involve several dereferences across processor boundaries. In general it is not possible to de-

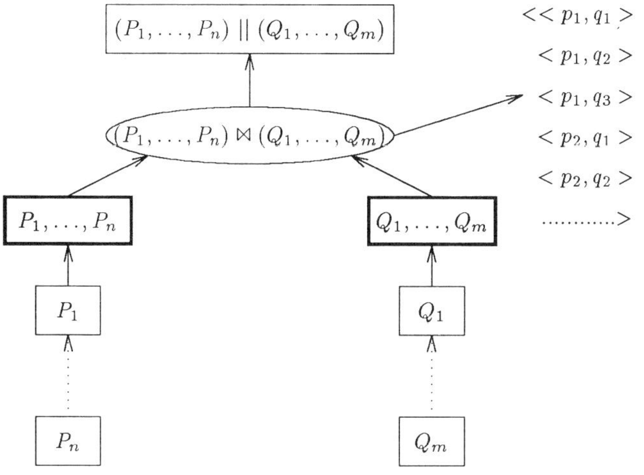

Figure 8: An AND/OR tree representation of the search space for the OR goal $(P_1, P_2, \ldots, P_n) \mid\mid (Q_1, Q_2, \ldots, Q_m)$ where P_i and Q_j are literals (which may have AND/OR subcomponents), "," is a sequential operator and "||" is an AND parallel operator. "p_i" and "q_j" are partial solutions satisfying $(P_1, P_2, \ldots, P_n)$ and $(Q_1, Q_2, \ldots, Q_m)$ respectively.

termine the processor on which a particular goal is serviced. Thus the latter approach is clearly the more efficient approach. The algorithms proposed in this paper can be easily adapted to suit the tree representation of the search space. If we restrict ourselves to a parenthetical notation, the algorithms would obviously be much simpler.

It is also possible to modify the tree representation of the search space to handle arbitrary graphs. The simple algorithm of traversing up the tree to look for the lowest cross product node will no longer work. To see this, consider again the example in Figure 7. Partial solution tuples at node 2 are used to fire both *s(C,E)* and *t(C,F)*. Node 2 represents a cross product node for the join at node 1, and at the same time, it is an intermediate node (*not* a cross product node) for the join at node 3. It is difficult to recognize this distinction when traversing up the tree. However, during the growth phase of the search tree, at node 2 it is possible to notify subgoal *s(C,E)* that its cross product node is 0, whereas for subgoal *t(C,F)* the cross product node is 2. Thus, the additional compile-time complexity is necessary in the join algorithm to accomodate arbitrary data dependency graphs. Also, it is important to note that in the algorithms described in this paper, the complexity of the algorithms is restricted to the compile time analysis, and this analysis yields extremely efficient run time behaviour.

8 Conclusion

We have described algorithms that perform compile time analysis for an efficient join algorithm for combining solutions from AND parallel branches in AND/OR parallel systems. The algorithm is suitable for implementations on both shared and nonshared memory machines. It also permits the representation of static data dependencies in the program using arbitrary directed acyclic graphs. It thus enables the exploitation of the maximum possible parallelism representable using static data dependency graphs, including consumer instance parallelism and pipeline parallelism.

We use the output from the compile time analysis discussed in this paper to generate abstract machine code for the optimised join algorithm. The run time overhead of this algorithm per join operation is constant.

We plan to extend the graphs that are supported by the current implementation to include conditional expressions, which can be tested at run time. This will make it possible to extract potential parallelism that can only be detected at run time. The data dependency graphs are currently supplied to the system via user annotations. To automate the graph generation, we intend to use 'off the shelf' graph generation packages and adapt them as required.

References

[1] Biswas P., Tseng C-C. A Data-Driven Parallel Execution Model for Logic Programs. In *International Conference on Logic Programming*, pages 1204–1222, Seattle, August 1988.

[2] Conery J.S. Binding Environments for Parallel Logic Programs in Non-shared Memory Multiprocessors. In *Symposium on Logic Programming*, pages 457–467, September 1987.

[3] de Kergommeaux J.C. and Robert P. An Abstract Machine to implement efficiently OR-AND Parallel Prolog. In *International Conference on Logic Programming*, Seattle, August 1988. addendum to proceedings.

[4] Debray S.K., Lin N-W., Hermenegildo M. Task Granularity Analysis in Logic Programs. In *ACM SIGPLAN-90 Conference on Programming Language Design and Implementation. Also SIGPLAN Notices vol. 25, no. 6*, October 1990.

[5] DeGroot D. Restricted AND Parallelism. In *International Conference on Fifth Generation Computer Systems*, pages 471–478, November 1984.

[6] Gupta G., Jayaraman B. Compiled And-Or Parallelism on Shared Memory Multiprocessors. In *North American Conference on Logic Programming*, pages 332–349, Cleveland, October 1989.

[7] Hamburg K.A. *Graph Analysis, Determinacy Analysis, and Annotations for Parallel Execution of Logic Programs*. Master's thesis, Dept.

of Computer Science, University of Illinois at Urbana-Champaign, August 1988.

[8] Haridi S., Brand P. ANDORRA Prolog: An Integration of Prolog and Committed Choice Languages. In *International Conference on Fifth Generation Computer Systems*, pages 745–754, Tokyo, Japan, November 1988.

[9] Hermenegildo M. Using Semaphores to Generalize CGEs. personal communication.

[10] Hermenegildo M. and Rossi F. On the Correctness and Efficiency of Independent AND parallelism in Logic Programs. In *North American Conference on Logic Programming*, pages 369–389, October 1989.

[11] Hermenegildo M.V. *An Abstract Machine based Execution model for Computer Architecture Design and Efficient Implementation of Logic Programs in Parallel.* PhD thesis, Dept. of Computer Science, University of Texas at Austin, 1986.

[12] Kale L.V. 'Completeness' and 'Full Parallelism' of Parallel Logic Programming schemes. In *Symposium on Logic Programming*, pages 125–133, San Francisco, September 1987.

[13] Kale L.V. Parallel Execution of Logic Programs: The REDUCE-OR Process Model. In *International Conference on Logic Programming*, pages 616–632, Melbourne, May 1987.

[14] Kale L.V., Ramkumar B. and Shu W. A Memory Organization Independent Binding Environment for AND and OR Parallel Execution of Logic Programs. In *The 5th International Conference/Symposium on Logic Programming*, pages 1223–1240, Seattle, August 1988.

[15] Li Peggy. *A Parallel Execution Model for Logic Programming.* PhD thesis, Dept. of Computer Science, California Institute of Technology, Pasadena, California, April 1986.

[16] Ramkumar B. and Kale L.V. An Optimised Join Algorithm for Efficient Exploitation of AND-parallelism in AND/OR Parallel Systems. in preparation for journal publication.

[17] Ramkumar B. and Kale L.V. Compiled Execution of the REDUCE-OR Process Model on Multiprocessors. In *North American Conference on Logic Programming*, October 1989.

[18] Singh V. and Genesereth M.R. *PM: A Parallel Execution Model for Backward-Chaining Deductions.* Technical Report KSL-85-18, Dept. of Computer Science, Stanford University, May 1985.

[19] Szeredi P. Current Status of ANDORRA. personal communication.

[20] Warren D.S. Efficient Prolog Memory Management for Flexible Control Strategies. In *Symposium on Logic Programming*, pages 198–202, 1984.

[21] Wise M.J. *Prolog Multiprocessors.* Prentice Hall, International Edition, 1986.

Scheduling and Variable Assignment in the Parallel Parlog Implementation

Jim Crammond

Dept. of Computing,
Imperial College,
London SW7, England.

jac@doc.ic.ac.uk

Abstract

This paper describes three different algorithms for distributing work among processors in a shared memory multiprocessor implementation of Parlog. The performance of each scheme is analysed, running on some benchmark programs and some comparisons made; in particular, focusing on issues of distribution of work and locking.

A simple scheme is proposed for reducing the amount of locking required for variable assignment in the Parallel Parlog system, which can be implemented in conjunction with one of the scheduling schemes described above. This is compared with a locking scheme that uses the atomic exchange facility available on some multiprocessors.

1. Introduction

This paper considers the scheduling aspects of the Parallel Parlog system which has been developed for running on shared memory multiprocessors. At the centre of this system is an emulator (written in C) which implements a parallel abstract machine for Parlog known as the JAM [3]. This abstract machine defines abstract processors (or workers) which execute processes (work) that in turn executes the Parlog goals.

A process executes a Parlog goal by finding a clause whose head arguments match those of the goal call and whose guard goals (if any) succeed; the process commits the goal to the successful clause and is said to *reduce* the goal to the evaluation of its clause body. If this clause has one or more goals in its clause body then a new process is created for each body goal except the last one and these are added to a "work pool". The executing process then executes the remaining body goal directly - this is a form of tail recursion optimisation (TRO).

A process can suspend on a variable in an input goal call argument if the argument is insufficiently instantiated[1]. Another process sharing that variable may bind it during *output unification*, performed after commit and before executing the clause body, and thereby *wake* the suspended process by adding it to the work pool.

---

[1] in a nondeterministic predicate like *merge/3*, the process can suspend on a number of variables - waiting until *one* of them is instantiated.

Scheduling - where an abstract machine processor looks for work (a process) in the work pool - takes place when a process executes a unit clause with no body goals to execute directly, or when it executes a goal which suspends on a variable.

Scheduling can also arise as a result of a *timeslice* - where a processor is forced to place the process it is executing into the work pool after executing a fixed number of goals and to find another process. In this system, however, a timeslice only occurs if a process has executed a 1000 reductions through TRO and this does not occur in any of the test programs tried here.

The abstract machine defines various data areas and an instruction set for the execution of these processes. However, it does not specify precisely how the "work pool" should be realised, allowing alternative forms of implementation such as those described in this paper.

The next section gives an overview of the features of the abstract machine relevant to the implementation of the "work pool" and to the scheduling algorithms which follow.

2. Background

In the abstract machine definition, each processor has the following main data area stored in shared memory:

- **heap** contains tagged words representing structure terms, lists and variables created during program execution. This area is managed by the use of a general semi-space garbage collection scheme to reclaim space [1].
- **process stack**
  stores process structures that correspond to abstract machine processes. The process structure is a fixed size data structure (the variable length extensions being stored on the argument stack), thus this area is managed by maintaining a free list within the stack.
- **argument stack**
  contains tagged words representing goal arguments for a process that has been added to the "work pool" or is suspended on some variable(s). This area is managed as a stack with *holes* - items can be deallocated even if they are not on the top of stack by marking them as "free cells". A hole is reclaimed when cells on the top of stack are popped off, exposing the hole. A simple garbage collector is occasionally used when large holes develop in the stack.

These areas are *managed* by the processor which *owns* them, but items stored in these areas are readable and potentially writable by any processor.

In addition to these areas, there is a **code** area that contains the instructions (and other data) comprising the compiled form of the program. This can be in shared memory and/or have copies in private memory for each processor.

A process itself can be in one of four states at any one time: **executing** when it is currently being executed by some processor, **runnable** when it is currently in the work pool waiting to be executed, **suspended** when it is in a *suspension list* associated with some variable or **free** when it is deallocated and perhaps in some process free list.

A suspension list is a linked list which starts in the unbound variable's value field, pointing to the most recent process suspended on it, and is continued through a suspension list field in the process structure[2]. Each processor has a *free list* register that points to the first free process structure and this is continued by a free list field in the process structure (which can be overlaid with the suspension list field since a process cannot be suspended and free at the same time).

In the emulator, abstract machine processors take the form of Unix™ processes which have shared memory and locks allocated between them; it is left to the operating system (e.g. Dynix™ for Sequent machines) to map these Unix processes to real processors. Each Unix process executes the main loop of the emulator which essentially co-routines between the *execute* routine that executes a process, emulating abstract machine instructions, and the *search for work* routine, that locates the next process to execute - i.e. the scheduler.

In this context, tail recursive optimisation means being able to execute potentially several goals within one call to the *execute* routine, before switching to the scheduler. To achieve this, it is important to try and select a goal which will not immediately suspend on a variable that would be instantiated by another goal in the same clause body.

Where there are dependencies (shared variables) between body goals, the usual programming convention is to specify the producer goals to the left of the consumer goals, giving a left to right *direction of data flow*. Hence, the compiler can use this heuristic to arrange that the leftmost body goal is executed directly by the process.

The compiler can also order the remaining goals so that they are taken from the work pool in the order given in the program, this may reduce the number of suspensions that occur during execution.

Finally, note that for simplicity, the description of Parlog execution given above has assumed a *flat* language, with only simple guard tests which are executed directly by the process, and only parallel conjunctions of goals in the body. The Parlog system in fact supports a process tree structure which enables *deep guards* and sequential conjunctions to be supported. However, the scheduler makes no distinction between these processes, so this aspect is not significant. This also means that the algorithms given in this paper should equally apply to other flat committed choice logic languages, particularly FCP and FGHC.

---

[2] where a process is suspended on more than one variable the linked list is slightly more complicated [3], but this is not significant here.

3. The Scheduling Algorithms

The basic idea behind the first algorithm described here is that each processor has its own local work pool into which it places all processes that it creates or wakes up during execution, and when it requires new work the processor first looks in its local pool. If its pool is empty then the processor examines the work pool of other processors until it finds a non-empty pool, whereby it "steals" a process from that pool. This approach minimises the overhead of scheduling on *busy* processors of making processes available - all processes in all work pools are "stealable" - and puts the onus on *idle* processors to find work.

The second algorithm extends the first one by maintaining a certain number of stealable or *public* processes in its work pool. Other processes are *private* to this processor, but as public processes are "stolen" from its pool, the processor can turn private processes into public ones. This algorithm puts a slight overhead on busy processors but has benefits from requiring less locking to take work from the local work pool.

The third algorithm has completely private local work pools together with a single global work pool. Processors add work to the global pool if it is not sufficiently full, or otherwise add to their own local pools. The advantage of this algorithm is that finding work is easier - work may only be found in one of two places: the local pool or the global one.

The *search for work* routine must also have a mechanism to detect deadlock - when there are no runnable processes in the system and the program evaluation is incomplete. A description of the deadlock algorithm used in all three schemes is given in the context of the first algorithm in the next section.

Now the three algorithms are discussed in more detail.

3.1. Algorithm 1: Local Run Queues

This algorithm was implemented in the first prototype Parallel Parlog emulator described in [2]. The local work pools are realised in the form of circular *run queues*, allocated as an additional data area in shared memory for each processor. A circular queue has two pointers associated with it: a queue front pointer **QF** and a queue back pointer **QB** (see figure 1). Processes are added to the back of the queue by the local processor only, while they can be taken off the front of the queue by any processor. Both QF and QB must be accessible to *all* processors (to test for an empty queue) but the significant advantage of the queue is that locking is only required when removing a process from the queue and *not* when adding a process to the queue - only the local processor can modify the QB pointer.

When the local processor locks its run queue to take a process off, it can choose from which end of the queue to take off a process, since it is obviously not about to add a process to the queue concurrently. This allows two possible *local scheduling* schemes to be implemented:

- **local queue** When work is taken from the front of the queue, the oldest work is taken off first, which tends to be more "top level" goals, giving a breadth first search bias to exploring the search tree.

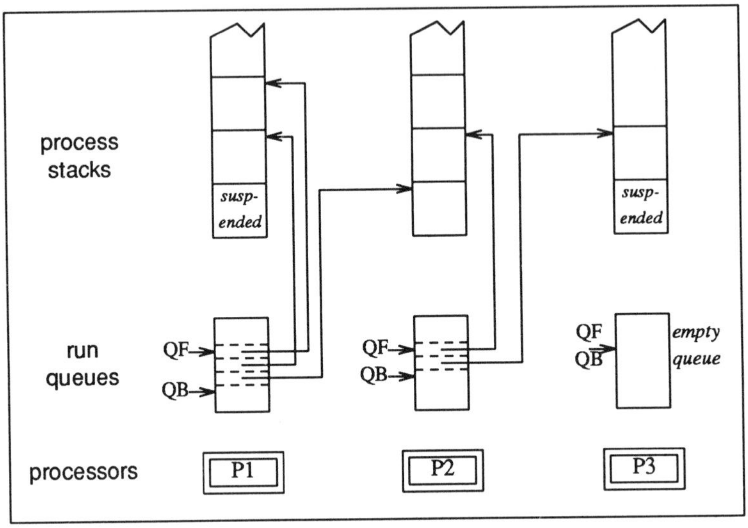

Figure 1: Processors with local run queues.

- **local stack** When work is taken from the *back* of the queue (i.e. accessed like a stack), the most recently created work tends to be taken off first, giving a depth first bias to exploring the search tree (but note that the process taken may be an "old" process that has just been woken up).

In [2] comparisons were made between these two approaches, which found that on some benchmarks the stack approach resulted in fewer suspensions, leading to slightly better performance. However, the main benefit of the stack approach was in better utilisation of process and argument stacks; in some cases the savings in memory usage were substantial. For certain benchmarks the local queue approach tended to result in a far greater number of active processes (runnable or suspended) in the system at one time - a result of the breadth first search - thus demanding greater process and argument stack space. Therefore the *local stack* scheme is used in the *search for work* routine which is now described.

The processor first examines its own run queue pointers to see if it can take work from there. If so, a lock is set which prevents other processors from writing to QF (i.e. stealing a process). Once locked, the test for empty queue is repeated - another processor may have stolen the last process before the lock was obtained - then a process is taken from the back of the queue (adjusting QB) and the lock is released.

If no work is found, remote queues are interrogated in the same manner, except that a process is taken from the front of a remote queue (adjusting QF). The scan of remote queues begins from an "adjacent processor" *i+1* and cycles through, visiting processors in the order *i+1, i+2,..., n, 1, 2,..., i-1*. Intuitively, this should produce better load balancing than if all processors start their search from the same processor (such as processor *1*), although this is difficult to prove.

It should at least avoid unnecessary contention for one queue when there is plenty of work in other run queues.

If the scan of all run queues fails to find work, then a check for deadlock is made. To detect deadlock, the emulator requires a *state* register associated with each processor. This normally has one of two values: **execute** and **search**. A processor changes to *search* state when it enters the scheduler and changes to *execute* state on leaving the scheduler to execute a process.

The deadlock detection algorithm distinguishes processor 1 as the **master** processor and the other processors as **slaves.** On failing to find work, the *master* enters a third processor state: **deadlock**, and then waits for each slave to follow suit. If all processors enter *deadlock* state then deadlock has occurred; otherwise, if one of the slaves enters *execute* state instead then the master re-enters *search* state and waits for all slaves in *deadlock* state to undeadlock before proceeding to rescan the remote run queues.

Slave processors cannot enter *deadlock* state unless the master has done so; therefore if the master is not deadlocked the slave makes another scan of the remote run queues. Otherwise, the slave enters *deadlock* state and waits for the master's state to change.

When deadlock occurs in the current system, the master processor creates a process to invoke a predefined "deadlock" goal; thus it leaves *deadlock* state and so other processors re-enter *search* state. Termination is not handled in the scheduler directly, rather it happens as a result of executing a "halt" instruction, or if a (top level) process fails.

3.2. Algorithm 2: Local Run Queues with Private Part

This algorithm is very similar to the first one, but it exploits the property of local stack scheduling that the local processor removes work from the opposite end of the run queue to remote processors. A third pointer is introduced to each run queue: the public queue back pointer **QP**, which divides the run queue into a public part between QF and QP and a private part between QP and QB. Whenever a processor adds a process to its run queue (incrementing QB), it checks to see whether there are a sufficient number of public processes by comparing QP with QF. If not, then QP is incremented, making the oldest private process in the queue public.

The scheduler first looks for a process in the private part of the local queue; if this is empty (i.e. QP = QB) then the back of public part is tried and if this is also empty then the front of the public parts of the remote queues are scanned for work.

With this scheme, remote processes use the QP pointer instead of the QB pointer to test for an empty queue, thus the QF and QP pointers must be accessible to all processors, but each processor can maintain QB as a private pointer (i.e. an abstract machine register).

No locking is required to add a process to the local queue, as before; also no locking is required to make another process public. But the significant advantage of this scheme is that no locking is required to *remove* a process from the private part of the local run queue, thus reducing the cost of taking local work.

The next point to consider is how many public processes should each processor attempt to maintain in its run queue. This can be regarded as a matter of tuning, but one important consideration is the overhead of the actual test for the number of processes currently in a run queue.

Since the run queue is a circular queue, the test for the length of the public part, which is done by comparing address values of QP and QF, should include a check for wrap around, as illustrated in figure 2. However, a special case that yields a very efficient test is when the number of public processes to maintain is set to 1. In this case it is sufficient to compare QF with QP. If they are the same - the public part is empty - then QP is incremented.

The overhead incurred by this scheme then is very small, particularly when each processor maintains just one public or "stealable" process. The only disadvantage of doing this is that some potential loss of parallelism may occur as a result of not enough public processes available, particularly when there is only sufficient work to keep some processors busy, and not all of them.

```
q_len = QP - QF;
if (q_len < 0)     /* wraparound? */
        q_len = Queuesize - q_len;

if (q_len < threshold)
        increment(QP)
```

Figure 2: Test for making a process public.

3.3. Algorithm 3: Local Pools with a Single Global Pool

This scheme is based on one described in [6]. Each processor has a private work pool in this algorithm, and there is a single global work pool that is shared by all processors. When a processor wishes to add a process to a work pool, it first checks the number of processes in the global pool. If this number is below a *threshold* value, then the new process is added to the global pool. Otherwise, it is added to the local pool.

With this scheme, scheduling is slightly simpler: the processor looks first in its local pool, then in the global pool. If no process is found in either, then the deadlock detection algorithm is applied, after which the global pool may be retried if deadlock was not detected.

The local work pools can be implemented by a simple *run list*. Within each process there is a run list field which links together all private runnable processes and a pointer (or abstract machine register) **RP** points to the first process on the run list. The run list field can be overlaid with the free list field and the suspended list field, therefore requiring no additional memory. New private processes are added to the front of this run list and processes are taken from the front, thus retaining the *local stack* scheduling behaviour of the previous algorithms.

The global pool can also be implemented by a run list, having the advantage of saving space over a circular run queue[3]. However, to maintain the "take oldest work first" behaviour of the previous schemes a run list with front and back pointers is required (see figure 3); work is added by appending to the back of the run list, and taken by removing from the front of the run list. A global counter is maintained which contains the current length of the queue, so it can be compared with the *threshold* value. A single lock is used for both adding and removing from the queue since both actions require exclusive access to update this counter.

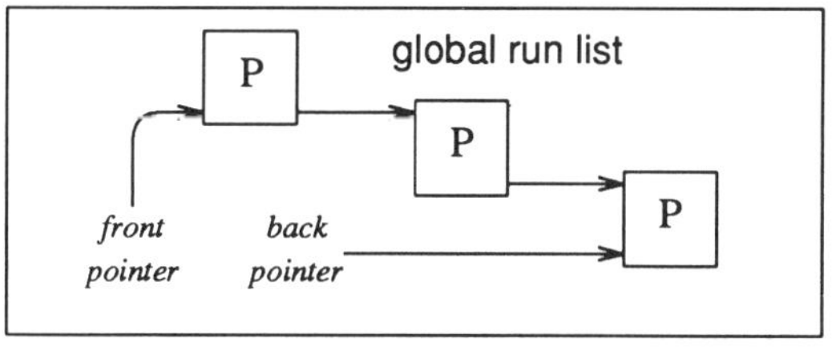

Figure 3: Processes in a Global Run List

4. Performance

This section examines the performance of these algorithms on a number of benchmark programs on two multiprocessors: a Sequent Symmetry S81 and a BBN Butterfly II. The Symmetry is a "conventional" shared memory multiprocessor with processors (Intel 80386's) and memory connected to a common bus. Each processor board has a large cache which can store shared memory locations as well as private ones; this considerably reduces bus traffic.

The BBN Butterfly II is a virtual shared memory machine in that the hardware presents a global address space to the software, but physically each processor (Motorola 88000) has its own local memory that is also linked to an interconnection network to enable access from all other processors. Unlike the Symmetry, access times to memory are not uniform - accessing local memory is about 3 times faster than accessing remote memory over the network (although access times to all remote memories are about the same). Another difference with the Butterfly is that shared memory is not cached once shared between two or more Unix processes; access times to cache are about 3 times faster than to local memory, so when shared data areas are not cached the benchmarks run around 20-35% slower on one processor.

The benchmarks were taken from a series of programs developed by Tick to compare concurrent logic language systems and Or-parallel Prolog systems [7, 8]. The *pascal* and *semigroup* programs are single solution benchmarks, *pascal* computes the *n*th row of Pascal's triangle - here we use n = 400 - and *semigroup* computes a Bradt semigroup with 1450 tuples from a generator set of 5 tuples [4]. The other benchmarks are search oriented, finding all solutions to a given problem. The *turtles* problem is scaled up from the one described in [7], having 8 solutions rather than 4; also the *triangle* problem used here is the "full" problem with 775 solutions given in [5].

[3] the benefit of no locking when adding to a run queue cannot be applied here.

4.1. Symmetry Results

Tables 1(a), 1(b) and 1(c) show the results of running the benchmarks on the Sequent Symmetry. The execution times represent the best times obtained from a series of runs. The 1 processor times were remarkably consistent - with no more than 0.5% deviation from the best times. 8 and 16 processor times varied by about 2% and 4% respectively, except for *puzzle*, *semigroup* and *turtles* where greater variations occurred - this is explained later. The local work figures show the percentage of work taken from the local run queue in algorithms 1 and 2; for algorithm 3 it is the proportion of work taken from the local run list.

The following observations can be made from the execution times given in these tables:

- on one processor algorithms 2 and 3 were about the same, both being slightly better than algorithm 1, particularly on the *triangle* benchmark.
- in general, algorithm 2 remained slightly better than algorithm 1 on 8 and 16 processors, although it was significantly better on the *turtles* benchmark.
- algorithm 3 was slightly poorer than the other algorithms on 8 and 16 processors on most benchmarks, with the notable exception of the *mastermind* benchmark.

On one processor all of the algorithms process the work in the same order, thus memory management behaviour is identical throughout execution. The difference in performance between algorithm 1 and the others can be accounted for by its extra locking overhead - it requires a lock operation each time it removes work from a run queue, whereas algorithm 2 has negligible locking and algorithm 3 has no locking as all of its work is in a local run list. However, the performance cost of this locking was at most only 4% on the *triangle* benchmark.

To account for the trends on the parallel runs, we need to examine more closely the speed up and locality of work figures. Most of the benchmarks are highly parallel and this was reflected in excellent speed ups of around 7.5 or better on 8 processors and 14.5 or better on 16 processors. The speed ups for *puzzle* and *semigroup* were poorer indicating a slight limitation in the amount of available parallelism; for the *turtle* benchmark, this limitation was more marked. Associated with the poorer speed up figures were poorer locality figures - as processors ran out of work locally, they started to search remote run queues or the global pool for work.

Algorithm 2 had the best locality figures as a result of the constrained way that work is made public - only one process can be stolen from a given run queue between the times that the owner processor adds two processes to it. In comparison, *all* processes in the run queue may be stolen during such period with algorithm 1. We might then have expected algorithm 1 to outperform algorithm 2 on benchmarks with limited parallelism for this reason, but this was not the case. Instead, algorithm 1 suffered from *contention* problems which are described below.

The locality figures for algorithm 3 were notably worse than the other algorithms. This was despite having a small threshold value - the formula $(n + 2)/4$ was used, where n is the number of processors. The explanation for this is that a processor places "new" work in the global pool, whereas the other

benchmark	1 processor execution time *(secs)*	8 processors time *(secs)*	8 processors speed up	8 processors % local work	16 processors time *(secs)*	16 processors speed up	16 processors % local work
cube	59.0	7.8	7.6	98.7	4.0	14.8	95.9
puzzle	83.6	12.0	7.0	98.7	6.2	13.5	93.7
kkqueen	106.5	13.8	7.7	99.8	7.0	15.3	99.0
semigroup	223.0	30.2	7.4	99.3	17.1	13.0	96.8
pascal	182.8	23.6	7.8	99.6	11.8	15.6	99.2
turtles	226.8	42.8	5.3	98.5	32.3	7.0	92.6
mastermind	238.4	31.8	7.5	99.3	16.2	14.7	98.7
triangle	1465.6	197.0	7.4	99.9	100.4	14.6	98.7

Table 1(a): Symmetry Statistics for Algorithm 1: Local Run Queues.

benchmark	1 processor execution time *(secs)*	8 processors time *(secs)*	8 processors speed up	8 processors % local work	16 processors time *(secs)*	16 processors speed up	16 processors % local work
cube	57.9	7.6	7.6	98.9	3.8	15.1	97.2
puzzle	83.3	11.8	7.1	99.5	6.3	13.1	98.4
kkqueen	105.5	13.6	7.7	99.8	6.9	15.1	99.5
semigroup	220.3	29.5	7.5	99.5	16.9	13.0	97.9
pascal	178.7	23.0	7.8	99.7	11.6	15.4	99.3
turtles	220.2	38.6	5.7	99.3	22.9	9.7	97.1
mastermind	236.6	31.3	7.6	99.6	16.3	14.5	98.7
triangle	1418.5	187.2	7.6	99.9	94.1	15.1	99.9

Table 1(b): Symmetry Statistics for Algorithm 2: Run Queues with Private Part.

benchmark	1 processor execution time *(secs)*	8 processors time *(secs)*	8 processors speed up	8 processors % local work	16 processors time *(secs)*	16 processors speed up	16 processors % local work
cube	58.1	8.0	7.3	87.8	4.3	13.6	78.8
puzzle	82.7	12.2	6.8	95.4	6.3	13.1	87.3
kkqueen	105.4	13.5	7.8	95.7	6.8	15.5	94.6
semigroup	219.7	32.8	6.7	91.9	22.1	9.9	81.5
pascal	178.0	23.7	7.5	95.7	12.1	14.7	91.4
turtles	220.8	43.1	5.1	81.1	26.2	8.4	76.9
mastermind	236.1	29.4	8.0	97.7	14.8	16.0	96.4
triangle	1417.8	197.1	7.2	91.1	103.9	13.6	88.8

Table 1(c): Symmetry Statistics for Algorithm 3: Local Pools with a Global Pool.

algorithms involve releasing "old" work to other processors. In the case of *mastermind* there seems to be a benefit from doing this, but in general new work tends to be associated with "bottom level" goals which are less likely to generate a significant amount of subsequent work to solve, resulting in more accesses to the global pool. Furthermore, the new work placed in the global pool can depend on other new work created by the same processor but placed in the local run list - in which case the work taken from the global pool may suspend.

Another problem that arose from this poor locality was that it tended to produce greater imbalances in heap and stack sizes between the processors. This was particularly acute with the *triangle* benchmark which required a considerable increase in the process stack size to run on 8 and 16 processors. Process stack size does not particularly effect execution time, but if one processor's heap is much greater than others then this can degrade the performance of the parallel garbage collector.

Table 2 shows the number of calls to the scheduler and the number of scheduler related locking operations performed for each algorithm on 16 processors. The number of scheduler calls for algorithm 3 was greater than the others (except for *mastermind*) confirming that less productive work was often taken. This table also shows that algorithm 1 used substantially more locking operations than the other algorithms and that algorithm 2 used the least number. For the highly parallel benchmarks these differences did not translate to big differences in execution times because the overhead of locking on the Symmetry is very small - when there is no contention for a lock. However, contention affected algorithm 1 for *turtles* where the best time was 40% worse than that of algorithm 2. In this case many processors, including the local one, may have been "fighting" to get work from one run queue; with algorithm 2 a busy processor may have been able to obtain work from its private region without having to join the fight. For algorithm 3, the global pool can be a source of contention when parallelism is limited.

A good indicator of possible contention is the *variation* in execution times for different runs of the same program. As stated above, the highly parallel benchmarks showed very small variations in execution times on 8 and 16 processors; for *puzzle* and *semigroup* variations of up to 10% on 16 processors were observed and thus still quite small, but the *turtle* benchmark showed wide variations, particularly on algorithms 1 and 3, where some runs were over 50% slower than the best times given in table 1.

		algorithm #1		algorithm #2		algorithm #3	
benchmark	no. of reductions	sched. calls (×1000)	no. of locks (×1000)	sched. calls (×1000)	no. of locks (×1000)	sched. calls (×1000)	no. of locks (×1000)
cube	291206	150	155	145	10	155	73
puzzle	283432	75	81	75	3	75	24
kkqueen	695863	146	149	146	3	146	19
semigroup	735543	314	329	313	47	332	149
pascal	1074731	519	526	504	42	540	96
turtles	1482041	602	648	584	38	655	324
mastermind	1525307	294	299	315	12	262	26
triangle	6125680	5641	5715	5641	6	5641	1290

Table 2: Locking Statistics for the Algorithms on 16 Processors.

To summarise, the overall trend indicates that algorithm 2 produces the most stable results; algorithm 1 can suffer from contention for run queues when there is limited parallelism; algorithm 3 usually has poorer locality which results in poorer memory usage and smaller speed ups.

4.2. Butterfly Results

Table 3 gives the best execution times for the three algorithms on 1 and 8 processors. In raw speed terms the Butterfly executed the Parallel Parlog System over 4 times faster than the Symmetry on one processor, but this advantage was generally lost on 8 and 16 processors as the Symmetry produced much better speed ups. On the Butterfly speed ups of 3.5 and 4.5 on 8 processors were achieved on the highly parallel benchmarks, the best speed up on 16 processors was 8.6 on *triangle* (using algorithm 2). A significant factor here is that shared memory is *not* being cached on the multiprocessor runs, thus distorting the speed up figures obtained from one processor times. Another factor that affects the Butterfly performance is *memory contention* (and in particular "hot spot" contention) where processors suffer delays in accessing remote memory due to the volume of requests over the network to one memory.

The variations in execution times were more exaggerated on the Butterfly, with differences of up to 8% on 8 processors on the highly parallel benchmarks, 20% on *puzzle* and *semigroup* and well over 50% for *turtles* on all algorithms[4]. Again, memory contention was a probable factor here; also locking is more expensive on the Butterfly and contention for locks will produce more memory contention.

The locality figures were the same as for the Symmetry (they were slightly better on algorithm 3); the figures for calls to the scheduler and locking operations were very similar to those for the Symmetry. The savings in locking operations had a more noticeable effect on the *triangle* benchmark, where algorithm 2 was 9% faster than algorithm 1 on one processor and 26% faster on 8

	1 processor execution times *(seconds)*			8 processor execution times *(seconds)*		
benchmark	alg. #1	alg. #2	alg. #3	alg. #1	alg. #2	alg. #3
cube	13.4	12.6	12.7	4.8	4.7	6.2
puzzle	19.4	18.9	19.0	5.1	5.4	6.3
kkqueen	23.8	22.9	22.9	5.5	5.2	5.5
semigroup	50.8	48.4	48.6	13.6	13.7	18.2
pascal	45.2	41.2	42.1	13.7	12.7	14.3
turtles	53.2	49.7	50.0	28.9	22.7	32.3
mastermind	54.8	52.4	53.5	19.0	17.0	14.8
triangle	389.2	356.6	361.0	97.8	77.8	136.6

Table 3: Execution Times on the BBN Butterfly II.

[4] 16 processors figures are not given in table 3 because variations on some benchmarks were too severe to produce reliable "best" times.

processors (and over 40% faster on 16 processors).

The figures for algorithm 3 are generally a bit worse than the others because the global pool is stored in the memory of the first processor, thus accesses to it take longer from other processors. For *triangle* there was a lot of contention for access to the global pool resulting in a very poor execution time. However, once again algorithm 3 was the best for *mastermind.*

These figures essentially confirm the results produced on the Symmetry. Some improvements to the Parlog implementation *independent of scheduling* may be able to reduce memory contention and improve speed ups, but the results obtained indicate that algorithm 2 is the best scheduler on the Butterfly.

5. Variable Assignment

In the Parlog implementation there are two forms of assignment: *local assignment* of clause variables which occurs during input matching (or certain guard functions) before commit, and *global assignment,* where variables in the goal call are instantiated during output unification, after commit.

No other goal can access local clause variables before commit, so local assignment is a straightforward simple assignment of the variable cell. For global assignment the variable being assigned may be shared by other goals and could therefore have a suspension list attached to it.

In a sequential Parlog system, global assignment involves checking whether the variable being assigned has a suspension list and if so, waking the processes up. In a parallel system, global assignment is more complicated; another goal (process) may attempt to add itself to the suspension list for this variable - updating its value field - between the time this process reads the unbound variable and attempts to instantiate it. This race condition makes it possible for the suspended process to be left un-woken. A similar but much less common situation is that another process may also bind the variable at the same time, during its output unification and perhaps to a different value!

Therefore, parallel global assignment requires locking the variable to gain exclusive access during the assignment. From analysis, the number of global assignments done per reduction is typically 1 or 2. This is therefore one of the main sources of locking in the Parallel Parlog system.

On the Sequent Symmetry and BBN Butterfly II machines, this assignment can be achieved efficiently using *atomic exchange* instructions. On the Butterfly, the atomic exchange facility is used via the `xmemui` function:

```
oldvalue = xmemui(address, newvalue)
```

which atomically sets the contents of *address* to *newvalue* and returns the previous contents of *address*. On the Symmetry this function can be written as an “asm function”.

With this function, global assignment can be implemented as follows:

```
oldvalue = xmemui(variable, newvalue);
if (oldvalue is not an unbound variable)
      unify(newvalue, oldvalue);
else if (the value field of oldvalue contains a suspension list)
      wake(oldvalue);
```

A similar approach is used for suspending on a variable; essentially, the variable is exchanged with an unbound cell with value field pointing to the suspending process and the old variable value is copied to the process's suspension list field. If the old value is *not* unbound then it is reassigned to the variable using a global assignment.

This *locking* global assignment can be avoided if it can be determined that all other processes which reference the variable are stored in the local run queue so that no other processor can access the variable at this time. Using the first scheduling algorithm this can not be achieved without a locking operation, since a remote processor can steal a process from the local queue at any time, thus defeating the purpose of any avoidance test.

With algorithm 2 a relatively simple, conservative test can be applied to decide whether the variable lies in the area of the local heap that only processes containing in the private part of the local run queue can also reference. If this test succeeds then a non-locking global assignment can be done, like in a sequential Parlog system.

A processor requires two pointers for this test: the heap top pointer, **HT**, and a *public heap pointer* **HP**. The HP pointer is set to the value of HT each time a process in the local run queue is made public, thereby making the whole local heap public.

As execution proceeds, consider the situation before the next process is made public. The HT pointer will grow as new terms are created on the heap thus developing a private region between HP and HT. No other processor will be able to access cells in this private region unless the local processor binds a variable that is *not* in this region to a pointer term (i.e. a variable reference, list or structure pointer) that points into it. So, when a *locking* global assignment is done, the *value* being assigned must be checked; if it is a pointer to the private area, again HP is reset to HT making the whole heap public.

Clearly, this is conservative since the term being made public may not be at the top of the private region of the heap; but since it could point to a structure whose arguments contain further pointers, calculating exactly where the HP pointer should be positioned would be too expensive.

The parallel global assignment algorithm is then extended to the following:

```
if (variable lies between HP and HT)
{       oldvalue = *variable;
        *variable = newvalue;
}
else
{       if (newvalue is a pointer to a cell between HP and HT)
                HP = HT;
        oldvalue = xmemui(variable, newvalue);
}
if (oldvalue is not an unbound variable)
        unify(newvalue, oldvalue);
else if (the value field of oldvalue contains a suspension list)
        wake(oldvalue);
```

One minor complication with this scheme is that HP must be repositioned after a garbage collection. In the current implementation HP is simply reset to HT once HT has been adjusted.

Table 4 gives figures indicating the proportion of assignments that avoided locking using this technique for the benchmarks running on the Butterfly on 8 processors. Execution times are given, together with the execution times from table 3 of algorithm 2 using atomic exchange. This table shows that a high percentage of assignments avoided locking assignments, particularly when a high proportion of local work was executed. Surprisingly perhaps, the execution times were very similar with the most significant improvement being 15% for the *mastermind* benchmark. In the case of *turtles* the time was apparently worse, although there were wide variations in times for this benchmark. The reason for the small differences can probably be attributed to the efficiency of the atomic exchange instruction.

On the Sequent Symmetry, the overhead of atomic exchange is very small - about 2% over a sequential global assignment. Therefore it is not surprising that this technique had little effect on the performance; indeed on one processor, the benchmarks ran about 1% slower using this technique and the best improvement on 16 processors, for *triangle*, was only 2%.

benchmark	no. of global assignments (×1000)	percentage non locking assignments	execution time *(seconds)*	execution time from table 3 *(seconds)*
cube	130	85.3	4.4	4.7
puzzle	209	90.6	5.5	5.4
kkqueen	195	99.3	5.2	5.2
semigroup	734	93.6	13.0	13.7
pascal	1511	95.4	12.8	12.7
turtles	531	88.6	28.0	22.7
mastermind	1227	97.8	14.8	17.0
triangle	5641	98.4	74.5	77.8

Table 4: Non-locking Assignments using the Locking Avoidance Scheme.

6. Conclusion

Three scheduling algorithms have been described in this paper, and some performance figures have been produced from execution runs on a Sequent Symmetry and BBN Butterfly II. This showed that using local run queues with private regions produced the best results in terms of locality - i.e. proportion of work taken from the local run queue - and in terms of locking overhead. This algorithm tended to produce the most consistent execution times and speed ups.

A scheme to avoid variable locking on global assignment was described in association with this scheduling algorithm. It was shown that this technique could avoid a substantial number of locking operations. However, when compared to global assignment using atomic exchange, the resulting differences in execution time were small. Therefore, it would seem that such a scheme will only benefit machines where atomic exchange is not available (such as the

Encore Multimax) and where a locking operation is more expensive.

Acknowledgements

The performance results were produced on the Sequent Symmetry and BBN Butterfly multiprocessors at Argonne National Laboratory. My thanks to the members of the MCS and EES divisions who made this possible.

References

1. J. Crammond, ''A Garbage Collection Algorithm for Shared Memory Parallel Processors,'' *International Journal of Parallel Processing* **17**(6)(December 1988).

2. J. Crammond, ''Implementation of Committed Choice Logic Languages on Shared Memory Multiprocessors,'' Research Report PAR 88/4, Dept. of Computing, Imperial College, London (May 1988). PhD Thesis, Heriot-Watt University, Edinburgh

3. J. Crammond, ''The Abstract Machine and Implementation of Parallel Parlog,'' Research Report, Dept. of Computing, Imperial College, London (June 1990).

4. T. Disz, E. Lusk, and R. Overbeek, ''Experiments with OR-Parallel Logic Programs,'' pp. 576-600 in *Proc. of the Fourth International Conference on Logic Programming*, MIT Press, Melbourne (May 1987).

5. R.P. Gabriel, *Performance and Evaluation of Lisp Systems*, MIT Press (1985).

6. T. Ozawa, A. Hosoi, and A. Hattori, ''An Evaluation of FGHC on a Shared Memory Multiprocessor,'' Technical Report,, Fujitsu Limited, Kawasaki (1989).

7. E. Tick, ''A Performance Comparison of AND- and OR-Parallel Logic Programming Architectures,'' pp. 452-467 in *Proc. of the Sixth International Conference on Logic Programming*, MIT Press, Lisbon, Portugal (June 1989).

8. E. Tick and J. Crammond, ''Comparison of Two Shared-Memory Emulators for Flat Committed Choice Logic Programs,'' in *Proc. of the International Conference on Parallel Processing*, Penn State Press, St. Charles, IL (August 1990).

Negation

A Characterization of Non-Floundering Logic Programs

Kim Marriott
IBM T. J. Watson Research Center,
P. O. Box 704, Yorktown Heights NY 10598, USA

Harald Søndergaard
Dept. of Computer Science,
University of Melbourne,
Parkville 3052 Vic., Australia

Philip Dart
Information Technology Division, DSTO,
P. O. Box 1600, Salisbury SA 5108, Australia

Abstract

SLDNF resolution provides an operational semantics which (unlike many Prolog implementations of negation) is both computationally tractable and sound with respect to a declarative semantics. However, SLDNF is not complete, and it achieves soundness only by discarding certain queries to programs because they "flounder."

We present dataflow analyses that for a given normal logic program detect (1) whether naive Prolog-style handling of negation is sound and (2) whether SLDNF resolution avoids floundering. The analyses are presented in a language-independent framework of abstract interpretation based on denotational definitions. To our knowledge they are more precise than any of their kind. In particular we obtain a characterization of a class of non-floundering programs larger than any other that we know of.

1 Introduction

There are a number of problems associated with the operational semantics of logic programs that have negative literals occurring in clause bodies. Such programs are called *normal* [7] and, as this name suggests, are very common in practice. Prolog systems typically apply one of two approaches to the operational semantics of such programs. In both approaches a default left-to-right computation rule is used, but in addition, one of the approaches uses a delay mechanism.

In the semantics without delay, negative literals are evaluated using negation-as-failure as soon as they are met. The problem with this approach is that it is unsound with respect to the declarative semantics given by the program's Clark completion [4]. The operational semantics *with* delay was developed to overcome this problem. The idea is to process a negative literal only after it has been made ground. If it is not ground then evaluation of the literal is "delayed" until future bindings ground it. This is the approach taken in languages such as NU-Prolog [12]. The problem with this approach is that negative literals may never resume, since subsequent bindings do not ground them fully. The situation where there are delayed literals, but no literals to select for processing is referred to as *floundering.*

It should be reported to the programmer when a computation flounders, since otherwise the approach would be unsound. But even when floundering is reported, the approach lacks completeness with respect to the declarative semantics, since the groundness criterion is stronger than necessary to guarantee soundness. Given these problems and the importance of normal logic programs, it is natural to investigate conditions which guarantee that the problems do not arise for particular programs and goals. This is the issue which we address in this paper.

Floundering, or the evaluation of a non-ground literal, is usually a sign of some mistake on the programmer's part. Floundering is not a decidable property of programs [3], but there exist a number of "syntactic" characterizations of programs that will not flounder. These characterizations, however, are very restrictive and rule out many programs that are both useful and non-floundering. For this reason our approach is "semantic" in the sense that it is based on dataflow analysis of normal logic programs. Throughout this paper we adopt the point of view that a dataflow analysis is just a non-standard semantics. That is, the analysis can be thought of as a (finitely computable) approximation to the semantics of the language. This is a useful way to look at things, because it makes analyses firmly semantics-based, thus rendering their correctness relatively easy to establish. Furthermore, it allows for a generic approach to dataflow analysis, in which variant analyses (differing in precision) can be obtained by simply changing a few parameters in a common definition.

The paper is organized as follows. In Section 2 we recapitulate some useful notions from lattice theory and denotational semantics. In Section 3 we recapitulate basic ideas and results from abstract interpretation theory. In Section 4 we give the semantic definitions that serve as the basis for the dataflow analyses. In Section 5 we give two dataflow analyses. The first determines whether non-ground negative literals may be evaluated when using the operational semantics without delay. The second determines whether floundering may occur when using the operational semantics with delay. We then discuss the use of such dataflow information. In Section 6 we compare our dataflow analyses with other work in the area. We summarize the main contributions of the paper in Section 7.

2 Preliminaries

A *preordering* on a set is a binary relation that is reflexive and transitive. A *partial ordering* is a preordering that is antisymmetric. A set equipped with a partial ordering is a *poset.*

Let $(X, \leq)$ be a poset. A (possibly empty) subset Y of X is a *chain* iff for all $y, y' \in Y, y \leq y' \vee y' \leq y$. Let Y be an arbitrary subset of X. An element $x \in X$ is an *upper bound* for Y iff $y \leq x$ for all $y \in Y$. Dually we may define a *lower bound* for Y. An upper bound x for Y is the *least upper bound* for Y iff $x \leq x'$ for every upper bound x' for Y. When the least upper bound exists, we denote it by $\bigsqcup Y$. Dually we may define the *greatest lower bound* $\bigsqcap Y$ for Y. A poset of which every subset possesses a least upper bound and a greatest lower bound is a *complete lattice.* In particular, equipped with the subset ordering, the powerset of X, denoted by $\wp X$, is a complete lattice.

We use functions in their Curried form and, as usual, function space formation $X \rightarrow Y$ associates to the right, and function application to the left.

Let $(X, \leq)$ and $(Z, \preceq)$ be posets and let $f : X \rightarrow Z$ be a function. The function $f : X \rightarrow Z$ is *monotonic* iff $x \leq x' \Rightarrow f\ x \preceq f\ x'$ for all $x, x' \in X$. In what follows, monotonicity of functions is essential, so much so that it is understood throughout this paper that $X \rightarrow Y$ denotes a space of monotonic functions. A *fixpoint* for a function $f : X \rightarrow X$ is an element $x \in X$ such that $x = f\ x$. If X is a complete lattice, then the set of fixpoints for (the monotonic) $f : X \rightarrow X$ is itself a complete lattice. The least element of this lattice is the *least fixpoint* for f, denoted by *lfp* f.

For a set X we let $X*$ denote the set of finite sequences of elements of X. The empty sequence is denoted by *nil* and we use the operator ":" for sequence construction.

A *normal program,* or just *program,* is a finite set of clauses. A *clause* is of the form $H \leftarrow B$ where H, the *head,* is an *atom* and B, the *body,* is a finite sequence of literals. A *literal* is either an atom, in which case it is *positive,* or the negation of an atom in which case it is *negative.* A program is *definite* iff all literals in the program's clause bodies are positive. We let *Var* denote the (countably infinite) set of variables, *Term* the set of terms, *Pred* the set of predicate symbols, *Lit* the set of literals, *Atom* the set of atoms, *Clause* the set of clauses, and *Prog* the set of (normal) programs for some given alphabet.

3 Abstract Interpretation

Abstract interpretation formalizes the idea of "approximate computation": computation performed with descriptions of data rather than the data themselves. Everyday examples of approximate computations are the casting out of nines to check numerical computations and application of the rules of signs, such as "plus times minus yields minus." Approximate computation is formalized as evaluating a formula or a program, not over its standard domain, but over a non-standard domain of descriptions. The standard domain may consist of sets of terms, substitutions, or whatever, depending on how the semantics is modeled, and the non-standard domain is determined by the sort of program properties we want to expose. Of course, when performing approximate computations, one must reinterpret all operators so as to apply to descriptions rather than to proper values.

Abstract interpretation is powerful because it is semantics-based and thus concerned with a programming language as a whole rather than the analysis of particular programs. But, as advocated by Nielson [11], the generality of abstract interpretation can be taken further. Assume we are given a language in which one can express the semantics of a wide variety of programming languages. The theory of abstract interpretation may then be developed in the framework of this *meta-language* once and for all. In this way, we need not "reinvent" abstract interpretation for all different programming languages—each is just a special instance of the general theory.

Here we recapitulate the language-independent approach to abstract interpretation given by Marriott, Søndergaard and Jones [10]. Following Nielson, we use the formalism of denotational semantics. This gives us a meta-language which is simple but powerful, well-understood, and widely used. In part, its versatility is due to the ease with which it accommodates semantic definitions at any level of abstraction one may want. This is useful in a basis for dataflow analysis, because there are many details of an operational semantics that only tend to obscure the cardinal point of propagation of dataflow information.

Our meta-language is one of typed lambda expressions, and the types are given by

$$\begin{array}{lll} T \in \mathit{Type} & ::= & S \mid L \\ L \in \mathit{Lat} & ::= & D \mid T \to L \mid L \times L \end{array}$$

where $S \in \mathit{Stat}$, $D \in \mathit{Dyn}$, *Stat* is a collection of *static* types, and *Dyn* is a collection of *dynamic* types. The difference between the two kinds is that (the interpretation of) a static type remains the same throughout all (standard and non-standard) semantics, whereas a dynamic type may change. We call $\mathit{Stat} \cup \mathit{Dyn}$ the collection of *base* types, and *Lat* is the collection of lattice types.

The syntax of the meta-language is given by

$$
\begin{array}{lll}
e & ::= & c_i & \text{(base functions)} \\
 & | & x_i & \text{(variables)} \\
 & | & \langle e, e' \rangle & \text{(pair construction)} \\
 & | & \text{fst } e & \text{(left projection)} \\
 & | & \text{snd } e & \text{(right projection)} \\
 & | & \text{if } e \text{ then } e' \text{ else } e'' & \text{(conditional)} \\
 & | & \lambda\ x : T\ .\ e & \text{(lambda abstraction)} \\
 & | & e\ e' & \text{(function application)} \\
 & | & \text{lfp } e & \text{(least fixed point operation)} \\
 & | & \bigsqcup_{x \leftarrow e} e' & \text{(least upper bound operation)}
\end{array}
$$

In addition we use the standard extension of "let clauses."

Static types are interpreted as posets (ordered by identity by default) and dynamic types as complete lattices. A *type interpretation* **I** thus assigns a structure **I** E to each base type E. Type interpretations can be extended naturally from the base types to all types. An *interpretation* **I** denotes a type interpretation (by an abuse of notation also called **I**) together with an assignment of an element of (**I** T) to each base function c of type T. By natural extension this gives the semantics of the meta-language. For details see Marriott, Søndergaard and Jones [10] or Nielson [11].

By varying the interpretation, one may obtain different semantics from the same semantic equations. The *standard interpretation* gives the usual input/output behavior of the program while dataflow analyses may be expressed as *non-standard* interpretations. The role of abstract interpretation is to give relationships between the standard and non-standard interpretations which guarantee that the analysis safely approximates the standard semantics, that is, is sound.

To do this one must make precise what the descriptions in the non-standard semantics denote in terms of the elements in the standard semantics. This is done by means of concretization functions. A concretization function maps a description to the largest object which it describes.

Definition. A *concretization function* γ from X to Y is a monotonic function from X to Y such that there is a (monotonic) adjoint function $\hat{\gamma}$ from Y to X. A *concretization family*, $\Gamma = \{\Gamma_D\}$, from interpretation **I** to interpretation **I**$'$, is an indexed family of functions such that for each $D \in Dyn$, Γ_D is a concretization function from (**I** D) to (**I**$'$ D). ■

Descriptions are ordered according to how large objects they apply to. Since "objects" are often sets ordered by inclusion, "larger" in general means the "applying to more elements," so descriptions are more imprecise the "higher" they sit in the ordering. In accordance with this, we define what it means for one description (or function) to safely approximate an object (function).

Definition. Let Γ be a concretization family from $\mathbf{I}$ to $\mathbf{I}'$. The relation $appr[\Gamma]_T$ is defined by

$$
\begin{array}{lcl}
x \; appr[\Gamma]_S \; y & \Leftrightarrow & y = x \\
x \; appr[\Gamma]_D \; y & \Leftrightarrow & y \leq \Gamma_D \; x \\
\langle x, x' \rangle \; appr[\Gamma]_{T \times T'} \; \langle y, y' \rangle & \Leftrightarrow & (x \; appr[\Gamma]_T \; y) \wedge (x' \; appr[\Gamma]_{T'} \; y') \\
x \; appr[\Gamma]_{T \to T'} \; y & \Leftrightarrow & \forall\, x', y' \,.\, x' \; appr[\Gamma]_T \; y' \Rightarrow \\
 & & \quad (x \; x') \; appr[\Gamma]_{T'} \; (y \; y')
\end{array}
$$

for $S \in Stat$ and $D \in Dyn$. ∎

Usually the concretization family Γ and type T of an expression are clear from the context, so we write $appr[\Gamma]_T$ simply as $appr$.

Example 3.1 Assume that the standard interpretation of a dynamic type D is $\wp\, Sub$ where Sub is the set of substitutions. In a non-standard interpretation we may interpret D as the set $\wp\, Var$ ordered by the superset relation. The intention is that $V \in \wp\, Var$ describes $\Theta \in \wp\, Sub$ exactly when each $\theta \in \Theta$ grounds all variables in V. This is captured by the concretization function $\gamma : \wp\, Var \to \wp\, Sub$ defined by $\gamma\; V = \{\theta \in Sub \mid \forall\, v \in V \,.\, \theta \; grounds \; v\}$.

Let $\theta_1 = \{x \mapsto a, y \mapsto z\}$ and $\theta_2 = \{x \mapsto f(a), y \mapsto a\}$. The set $\{\theta_1, \theta_2\}$ is approximated by the description $\{x\}$. The function $restrict$: $\wp\, Var \to \wp\, Sub \to \wp\, Sub$, where $restrict\; V\; \Theta$ contains the substitutions in Θ restricted to the variables in V, is approximated by the function $restrict'$: $\wp\, Var \to \wp\, Var \to \wp\, Var$ defined by $restrict'\; V\; V' = V \cap V'$. ∎

The following fundamental result immediately allows us to argue inductively the correctness of a whole dataflow analysis (or non-standard semantics) once certain base functions are shown to be in the relation "safely approximates." This applies not only to the logic programming languages discussed in this paper, but to any language whose semantics can be expressed in the meta-language.

Proposition 3.1 Let Γ be a concretization family from $\mathbf{I}$ to $\mathbf{I}'$. If, for every base function c, it holds that $(\mathbf{I}\; c)\; appr[\Gamma]\; (\mathbf{I}'\; c)$, then $(\mathbf{I}\; e)\; appr[\Gamma]\; (\mathbf{I}'\; e)$ for every closed expression e.

4 Semantic Definitions

In this section we give a number of semantic definitions which we shall use in the next section as the basis for a floundering analysis. The first definition captures the essence of a left-to-right evaluation of definite programs.

The second definition is an extension of the first which captures a left-to-right evaluation of normal programs in which negative literals are evaluated when they are first met. The third definition is a variant of the second which captures a left-to-right evaluation in which non-ground negative literals are delayed until ground. These definitions are made simpler by our use of "parametric substitutions" rather than standard substitutions. We first explain what a parametric substitution is.

4.1 Parametric Substitutions

Traditionally a *substitution* is an idempotent, almost-identity mapping $\theta \in Sub \subseteq Var \rightarrow Term$ from the set of variables *Var* to the set of terms over *Var*. A substitution is not distinguished from its natural extensions to $Atom \rightarrow Atom$. Our notation for substitutions is standard. For instance $\{x \mapsto a\}$ denotes the substitution θ such that $(\theta\ x) = a$ and $(\theta\ V) = V$ for all $V \neq x$.

Classical substitutions have some drawbacks when used in a denotational definition. First, most general unifiers are not unique, even when idempotent. For example, when unifying $p(x)$ and $p(y)$, it is not clear whether the result should be $\{x \mapsto y\}$ or $\{y \mapsto x\}$, and it is hard to guarantee that a semantic definition is invariant under choice of unification function. Second, renaming causes problems. To overcome these problems we use "parametric" substitutions which are similar to substitutions but, instead of mapping atoms to atoms, map atoms to classes of atoms which are equivalent modulo variable renaming. Parametric substitutions have previously been studied by Maher [8] though for a different purpose and under the name "fully parameterized substitutions."

To formalize the idea we need to introduce a set of "parameters" *Par* which is disjoint from the set of variables *Var*. The reason for the distinction is that variable names are significant, while parameter names are not. The set of terms over *Par* is denoted by *Term*[*Par*], and the set of atoms over *Par* is denoted by *Atom*[*Par*]. A *substitution into Par* is a total mapping $\sigma : Var \rightarrow Term[Par]$ which is "finitely based" in the sense that all but a finite number of variables are mapped into distinct parameters. We do not distinguish substitutions into *Par* from their natural extension to $Atom \rightarrow Atom[Par]$. The set of substitutions into *Par* is denoted *Sub*[*Par*].

Let us for the time being denote *Atom* by *Atom*[*Var*] to stress its distinction from *Atom*[*Par*], and let X be either *Var* or *Par*. We define the *instantiation preordering*, $\unlhd$, on *Atom*$[X]$ by

$$A \unlhd A' \text{ iff } \exists\, \tau : X \rightarrow \mathit{Term}[X]\,.\, A = (\tau\ A').$$

The instantiation preordering clearly induces an equivalence relation on *Atom*[*Var*] (or *Atom*[*Par*]) which is "consistent variable (or parameter) renaming." We denote the resulting quotient by $\mathit{Atom}[X]_{\unlhd}$ and use $\unlhd$ to denote the induced partial ordering on $\mathit{Atom}[X]_{\unlhd}$ as well.

For $A \in \overline{A}$, where $\overline{A} \in \mathit{Atom}[X]_{\unlhd}$, we may denote $\overline{A}$ by $[A]$. In fact we think of $[\cdot]$ as the function from $\mathit{Atom}[X]$ to $\mathit{Atom}[X]_{\unlhd}$ that, given A, yields the equivalence class of A.

A *parametric substitution* is a mapping from *Atom* to $\mathit{Atom}[\mathit{Par}]_{\unlhd}$. We will not allow all such mappings, though: the mappings we use are "essentially" substitutions. More precisely, the set $\mathit{Psub} \subseteq (\mathit{Atom} \rightarrow \mathit{Atom}[\mathit{Par}]_{\unlhd})$ of parametric substitutions is defined by

$$\mathit{Psub} = \{[\cdot] \circ \sigma \mid \sigma \in \mathit{Sub}[\mathit{Par}]\}.$$

That is, application of a parametric substitution can be seen as application of a substitution that has only parameters in its range, followed by taking the equivalence class of the result. Extended with a least element $\bot_{\mathit{Psub}}$, *Psub* becomes a complete lattice [8].

We use a notation for parametric substitutions similar to that used for substitutions; however, square rather than curly brackets are used, to distinguish the two. For example, the parametric substitution $\pi = [x \mapsto x', y \mapsto f(x')]$ will map $p(x, y, z)$ to $[p(x', f(x'), z')]$. So π corresponds to the substitution $\{y \mapsto f(x)\}$. An alternative way to think of π is as an existentially quantified (over parameters) conjunction: $\exists\, x'\,.\, x = x' \wedge y = f(x')$ [8]. We let ϵ denote the "identity" parametric substitution which maps atoms to their equivalence class. Every substitution θ has a corresponding parametric substitution given by $\epsilon \circ \theta$. However, not all parametric substitutions have a corresponding substitution. For example, there is no substitution θ such that $\epsilon \circ \theta = [x \mapsto f(y', z')]$.

The semantic definitions make use of three functions involving parametric substitutions:

- *meet* corresponds to "composition";
- *unify* corresponds to renaming, computation of a most general unifier, and subsequent restriction to variables of interest; and
- *grounds* tests whether a set of parametric substitutions all make a given atom ground.

Definition. The function *meet* : $\wp\, Psub \to \wp\, Psub \to \wp\, Psub$ is defined by

$$meet\ \Pi\ \Pi' = \{\pi \sqcap \pi' \mid \pi \in \Pi \wedge \pi' \in \Pi'\} \setminus \{\bot_{Psub}\}.$$

The function *unify* : $Atom \to Atom \to \wp\, Psub \to \wp\, Psub$ is defined by

$$unify\ H\ A\ \Pi = \{\bigsqcup\{\pi' \mid \pi'\ H \trianglelefteq \pi\ A\} \mid \pi \in \Pi\} \setminus \{\bot_{Psub}\}.$$

The function *grounds* : $\wp\, Psub \to Atom \to Bool$ is defined by

$$grounds\ \Pi\ A \Leftrightarrow \forall \pi \in \Pi\, .\, \pi\ grounds\ A. \quad \blacksquare$$

Example 4.1 Let $\pi = [y \mapsto y', z \mapsto f(y')]$ and $\pi' = [y \mapsto a]$. Then $meet\ \{\pi\}\ \{\pi'\} = \{[y \mapsto a, z \mapsto f(a)]\}$. $\blacksquare$

Example 4.2 Let $A_1 = p(a, x)$, $A_2 = p(y, z)$, and let $\pi = [y \mapsto y', z \mapsto f(y')]$. Then we have that $unify\ A_1\ A_2\ \{\pi\} = \{[x \mapsto f(a)]\}$. Notice that this parametric substitution does not constrain y or z, only variables in A_1 may be constrained. On the other hand we have that $unify\ A_2\ A_1\ \{\pi\} = \{[y \mapsto a]\}$, in which both x and z are unconstrained. Notice also that $unify\ A_1\ A_1\ \{\pi\} = \{\epsilon\}$, while $unify\ A_2\ A_2\ \{\pi\} = \{\pi\}$.

Let $A_3 = p(f(y), z)$. Then $unify\ A_3\ A_2\ \{\epsilon\} = \{\epsilon\}$. There is no "occur check problem," because the names of placeholders in $(\epsilon\ A_2)$ have no significance. One can think of this as an automatic renaming being performed by *unify*.

Finally $unify\ A_3\ A_1\ \{\epsilon\} = \emptyset$, corresponding to failure of unification. $\blacksquare$

The idea behind *unify* should be clear from this example: not only does the function *unify* perform renaming "automatically," it also restricts interest to certain variables, namely those of its first argument.

We now make use of parametric substitutions to give semantic definitions that are suitable as a basis for the analysis of normal logic programs.

4.2 Semantics of Definite Programs

To aid exposition, we first give a semantic definition which captures the left-to-right evaluation of a definite program. It is essentially the definition given by Marriott, Søndergaard and Jones [10] and is similar to the definition of Winsborough [13]. We later extend this definition to normal programs. Note that in this, and subsequent semantic definitions, finite failure is not distinguished from non-termination. For example, the empty program and the program consisting only of the clause $p \leftarrow p$ have the same denotation. This is a standard approach in semantic definitions used for dataflow analysis.

The definition is best understood by considering the standard interpretation in which *Asub* is $\wp\, Psub$, m is *meet* and u is *unify*. The essential idea is that a program's denotation is a mapping from an atom and initial set of parametric substitutions to the set of "answer" parametric substitutions.

Definition. The *definite semantics* has dynamic domain $Asub$, semantic domain

$$Den \quad = \quad Atom \to Asub \to Asub,$$

semantic functions

$$\begin{array}{lll} \mathbf{P} & : & Prog \to Den \\ \mathbf{C} & : & Clause \to Den \to Den \\ \mathbf{B} & : & Atom* \to Den \to Asub \to Asub \\ \mathbf{L} & : & Atom \to Den \to Asub \to Asub, \end{array}$$

and base functions

$$\begin{array}{lll} m & : & Asub \to Asub \to Asub \\ u & : & Atom \to Atom \to Asub \to Asub. \end{array}$$

The semantic equations are

$$\begin{array}{lll} \mathbf{P}\, [\![P]\!] & = & \text{lfp}\, (\bigsqcup_{C \in P} (\mathbf{C}\, [\![C]\!])) \\ \mathbf{C}\, [\![H \leftarrow B]\!]\; D\; A\; \Pi & = & m\; \Pi\; (u\; A\; H\; (\mathbf{B}\, [\![B]\!]\; D\; (u\; H\; A\; \Pi))) \\ \mathbf{B}\, [\![nil]\!]\; D\; \Pi & = & \Pi \\ \mathbf{B}\, [\![A : B]\!]\; D\; \Pi & = & \mathbf{B}\, [\![B]\!]\; D\; (\mathbf{L}\, [\![A]\!]\; D\; \Pi) \\ \mathbf{L}\, [\![A]\!]\; D\; \Pi & = & D\; A\; \Pi. \quad \blacksquare \end{array}$$

Definition. The *definite semantics*, $\mathbf{P_{def}}$, is the interpretation of the definite semantics in which $Asub$ is assigned $\wp\, Psub$, m is assigned *meet*, and u is assigned *unify*. ■

Example 4.3 Consider the following list concatenation program P:

$$append(nil, y, y)$$
$$append(u : x, y, u : z) \leftarrow append(x, y, z).$$

Let A be the atom $append(x, y, z)$ and let Π be the set of parametric substitutions $\{[z \mapsto a : nil]\}$. Then $\mathbf{P_{def}}\, [\![P]\!]\; A\; \Pi = \{[x \mapsto nil, y \mapsto a : nil, z \mapsto a : nil], [x \mapsto a : nil, y \mapsto nil, z \mapsto a : nil]\}$. ■

4.3 Normal Program Semantics without Delay

The following definition extends the previous definition to normal programs by capturing the standard Prolog left-to-right evaluation in which negative literals (possibly non-ground) are evaluated when they are first met. It differs from the preceding definition in two important aspects.

The first is that the denotation of a program is now a mapping from an atom and set of parametric substitutions to a tuple whose first component is the set of answer substitutions, and whose second component is a flag $F \in Flo$ which is *false* if no non-ground negative literal could have been evaluated for that query and *true* otherwise.

The second difference is that the semantic function **L** has been extended to handle negative literals. The semantic definition "approximates" Prolog evaluation in the sense that negative literals are always assumed to succeed[1]. The idea behind the definition is that if the current substitution set Π does not fully ground the negative literal $\neg\ A$ then there is a possibility that a non-ground negative literal may have been evaluated. Even if $\neg\ A$ is fully ground by Π there is still a possibility that the evaluation of $\neg\ A$ will lead to the evaluation of a non-ground negative literal. This is possible exactly when the evaluation of A leads to such an event.

The definition is best understood by considering the standard interpretation in which *Asub* is $\wp\,Psub$, m is *meet*, u is *unify* and g is *grounds*. The domain *Flo* is ordered by *false* $\leq$ *true*.

Definition. The *normal semantics* has dynamic domain *Asub*, semantic domains

$$\begin{array}{lcl} Flo & = & Bool \\ Den & = & Atom \rightarrow Asub \rightarrow (Asub \times Flo), \end{array}$$

semantic functions

$$\begin{array}{lcl} \mathbf{P} & : & Prog \rightarrow Den \\ \mathbf{C} & : & Clause \rightarrow Den \rightarrow Den \\ \mathbf{B} & : & Lit* \rightarrow Den \rightarrow Asub \rightarrow (Asub \times Flo) \\ \mathbf{L} & : & Lit \rightarrow Den \rightarrow Asub \rightarrow (Asub \times Flo), \end{array}$$

and base functions

$$\begin{array}{lcl} m & : & Asub \rightarrow Asub \rightarrow Asub \\ u & : & Atom \rightarrow Atom \rightarrow Asub \rightarrow Asub \\ g & : & Atom \rightarrow Asub \rightarrow Bool. \end{array}$$

The semantic equations are

$$\begin{array}{lcl} \mathbf{P}\ [\![P]\!] & = & \text{lfp}\ (\bigsqcup_{C \in P}(\mathbf{C}\ [\![C]\!])) \\ \mathbf{C}\ [\![H \leftarrow B]\!]\ D\ A\ \Pi & = & \text{let}\ \langle \Pi', F\rangle = \mathbf{B}\ [\![B]\!]\ D\ (u\ H\ A\ \Pi)\ \text{in} \\ & & \quad \langle m\ \Pi\ (u\ A\ H\ \Pi'),\ F\rangle \\ \mathbf{B}\ [\![nil]\!]\ D\ \Pi & = & \langle \Pi, \mathit{false}\rangle \\ \mathbf{B}\ [\![L : B]\!]\ D\ \Pi & = & \text{let}\ \langle \Pi', F'\rangle = \mathbf{L}\ [\![L]\!]\ D\ \Pi\ \text{in} \\ & & \quad \text{let}\ \langle \Pi'', F''\rangle = \mathbf{B}\ [\![B]\!]\ D\ \Pi'\ \text{in} \\ & & \qquad \langle \Pi'',\ \text{if}\ F'\ \text{then}\ \mathit{true}\ \text{else}\ F''\rangle \\ \mathbf{L}\ [\![A]\!]\ D\ \Pi & = & D\ A\ \Pi \\ \mathbf{L}\ [\![\neg\ A]\!]\ D\ \Pi & = & \langle \Pi,\ \text{if}\ g\ A\ \Pi\ \text{then snd}\ (D\ A\ \Pi) \\ & & \qquad \text{else}\ \mathit{true}\rangle.\ \blacksquare \end{array}$$

Definition. The *standard normal semantics*, $\mathbf{P_{std}}$, is the interpretation of the normal semantics in which *Asub* is assigned $\wp\,Psub$, m is assigned *meet*, u is assigned *unify* and g is assigned *grounds*. ■

[1] To do otherwise requires a more complex definition and the use of Plotkin-like power-domains. For such a definition see Marriott and Søndergaard [9].

Example 4.4 Consider the following program P_1 to compute proper prefixes of a list:

$$prefix(x, y) \leftarrow append(x, z, y) \wedge \neg\, eq(x, y)$$
$$eq(x, x).$$

The predicate *append* is defined in Example 4.3. Let $A = prefix(x, y)$ and let $\Pi = \{[y \mapsto a : nil]\}$. Then $\mathbf{P_{std}}\, [\![P_1]\!]\, A\, \Pi =$

$$\langle \{[x \mapsto nil, y \mapsto a : nil], [x \mapsto a : nil, y \mapsto a : nil]\}, false\rangle$$

indicating that the query $\leftarrow prefix(x, a : nil)$ cannot cause the evaluation of a non-ground negative literal. Now consider the program P_2 in which *prefix* is defined by

$$prefix(x, y) \leftarrow \neg\, eq(x, y) \wedge append(x, z, y).$$

We have that $\mathbf{P_{std}}\, [\![P_2]\!]\, A\, \Pi =$

$$\langle \{[x \mapsto nil, y \mapsto a : nil], [x \mapsto a : nil, y \mapsto a : nil]\}, true\rangle$$

indicating that with P_2, the same query *may* lead to the evaluation of a non-ground negative literal (as indeed it will). ■

4.4 Normal Program Semantics with Delay

We now modify the previous definition so that it captures the operational semantics in which negative literals are evaluated only when ground, as in SLDNF resolution. As before, the denotation of a program maps an atom and a set of parametric substitutions to a pair whose first component is the set of answer substitutions. However, the second component is no longer an element of *Flo*, but rather a mapping from sets of substitutions to *Flo*. To understand the use of this component, consider what happens when a negative literal $\neg\, A$ is first reached with current substitution set Π which does not ground A. At this stage there may not be enough information to tell whether $\neg\, A$ will ever get woken up since this depends on the context and the future evaluation of positive literals. This problem of the denotation of an object depending upon the context is well-known in denotational semantics and is usually handled using "continuations." The idea is that when $\neg\, A$ is reached, it contributes a function $E : \wp\, Psub \rightarrow Flo$ to the program's denotation. The function E is defined in such a way that if the current substitution set later becomes instantiated to Π' then $(E\ \Pi')$ is *false* if the evaluation of $\neg\, A$ with Π' definitely does not lead to floundering. Otherwise $(E\ \Pi')$ is *true*.

Now consider the application of the denotation of some program to the query composed of atom A and substitutions Π. Let $\langle \Pi', E\rangle$ be the result. The idea is that the function E is the least upper bound of the functions contributed by the negative literals that have been reached during evaluation of the query. Thus $(E\ \Pi'') = false$ if every negative literal would be grounded by Π'' (without its evaluation floundering). It follows that if $(E\ \Pi')$ is *false* then the initial query will not lead to floundering, otherwise it may.

Again this definition is best understood by considering the standard interpretation in which *Asub* is $\wp$ *Psub*, m is *meet*, u is *unify* and g is *grounds*.

Definition. The *delay semantics* has dynamic domain *Asub*, semantic domains

$$\begin{array}{lcl} \mathit{Flo} & = & \mathit{Bool} \\ \mathit{Env} & = & \mathit{Asub} \rightarrow \mathit{Flo} \\ \mathit{Den} & = & \mathit{Atom} \rightarrow \mathit{Asub} \rightarrow (\mathit{Asub} \times \mathit{Env}), \end{array}$$

semantic functions

$$\begin{array}{lcl} \mathbf{P} & : & \mathit{Prog} \rightarrow \mathit{Den} \\ \mathbf{C} & : & \mathit{Clause} \rightarrow \mathit{Den} \rightarrow \mathit{Den} \\ \mathbf{B} & : & \mathit{Lit}* \rightarrow \mathit{Den} \rightarrow \mathit{Asub} \rightarrow (\mathit{Asub} \times \mathit{Env}) \\ \mathbf{L} & : & \mathit{Lit} \rightarrow \mathit{Den} \rightarrow \mathit{Asub} \rightarrow (\mathit{Asub} \times \mathit{Env}), \end{array}$$

and base functions

$$\begin{array}{lcl} m & : & \mathit{Asub} \rightarrow \mathit{Asub} \rightarrow \mathit{Asub} \\ u & : & \mathit{Atom} \rightarrow \mathit{Atom} \rightarrow \mathit{Asub} \rightarrow \mathit{Asub} \\ g & : & \mathit{Atom} \rightarrow \mathit{Asub} \rightarrow \mathit{Bool}. \end{array}$$

The semantic equations are

$$\begin{array}{lcl} \mathbf{P}\ [\![P]\!] & = & \mathrm{lfp}\ (\bigsqcup_{C \in P}(\mathbf{C}\ [\![C]\!])) \\ \mathbf{C}\ [\![H \leftarrow B]\!]\ D\ A\ \Pi & = & \mathrm{let}\ \langle \Pi', E \rangle = \mathbf{B}\ [\![B]\!]\ D\ (u\ H\ A\ \Pi)\ \mathrm{in} \\ & & \quad \langle m\ \Pi\ (u\ A\ H\ \Pi'), \\ & & \qquad \lambda\,\Pi''\,.\,(E\ (m\ \Pi'\ (u\ H\ A\ \Pi'')))\rangle \\ \mathbf{B}\ [\![nil]\!]\ D\ \Pi & = & \langle \Pi, \lambda\,\Pi\,.\,\mathit{false} \rangle \\ \mathbf{B}\ [\![L : B]\!]\ D\ \Pi & = & \mathrm{let}\ \langle \Pi', E' \rangle = \mathbf{L}\ [\![L]\!]\ D\ \Pi\ \mathrm{in} \\ & & \quad \mathrm{let}\ \langle \Pi'', E'' \rangle = \mathbf{B}\ [\![B]\!]\ D\ \Pi'\ \mathrm{in} \\ & & \qquad \langle \Pi'', \lambda\,\Pi.\ \mathrm{if}\ E'\ \Pi\ \mathrm{then}\ \mathit{true}\ \mathrm{else}\ E''\ \Pi \rangle \\ \mathbf{L}\ [\![A]\!]\ D\ \Pi & = & D\ A\ \Pi \\ \mathbf{L}\ [\![\neg\ A]\!]\ D\ \Pi & = & \langle \Pi,\ \lambda\ \Pi'.\ \mathrm{if}\ \ g\ A\ \Pi'\ \ \mathrm{then\ snd}\ (D\ A\ \Pi')\ \Pi' \\ & & \qquad \mathrm{else}\ \ \mathit{true} \rangle. \end{array}$$ ∎

Definition. The *standard delay semantics*, $\mathbf{P}_{\mathbf{del}}$, is the interpretation of the delay semantics in which *Asub* is assigned $\wp$ *Psub*, m is assigned *meet*, u is assigned *unify*, and g is assigned *grounds*. ∎

Note that the base functions are exactly those used in the standard normal semantics.

Example 4.5 Consider the two programs P_1 and P_2 from Example 4.4, let $A = \mathit{prefix}(x, y)$, and let the substitution set $\Pi = \{[y \mapsto a : nil]\}$. Then

$$\mathbf{P}_{\mathbf{del}}\ [\![P_1]\!]\ A\ \Pi = \langle \Pi', E \rangle$$

where $\Pi' = \{[x \mapsto nil, y \mapsto a : nil], [x \mapsto a : nil, y \mapsto a : nil]\}$ and $(E\ \Pi') = \mathit{false}$, indicating that the query $\leftarrow \mathit{prefix}(x, a : nil)$ definitely does not lead to floundering. The same holds true for the program P_2. ∎

5 Dataflow Analyses

In this section we give non-standard interpretations of the normal (delay) semantics. These can be used to detect possible floundering or evaluation of non-ground negative literals.

We will only be interested in dataflow analyses in which descriptions describe sets of "downwards closed" parametric substitutions. This is a natural restriction in the present context because the properties we are interested in determining, such as definite groundness, are "downwards closed." The advantage of restricting our attention to such analyses is that *meet* can be approximated by the greatest lower bound operator on the description lattice [10].

Definition. Let γ be a concretization function from description domain X to $\wp\, Psub$. Then γ is *downwards closed* iff $\forall\, x \in X \,.\, \forall\, \pi, \pi' \in Psub \,.\, \pi \in \gamma\, x \wedge \pi' \trianglelefteq \pi \Rightarrow \pi' \in \gamma\, x$. ■

Proposition 5.1 Let γ be a downwards closed concretization function from D to $\wp\, Psub$. Then $\sqcap_D$ *appr meet* (and in fact is the best approximation). ■

Developing a dataflow analysis is therefore a matter of choosing the description domain so that it captures the information required for the analysis and then defining suitable functions to approximate *unify* and *grounds*.

We shall primarily be interested in analyses in which some "allowed" propositional formulas, or more precisely, equivalence classes of allowed propositional formulas, are the descriptions. Such descriptions are related to those used by Dart [5]. A parametric substitution π is approximated by a formula F if, for any instance π' of π, the truth assignment given by "V is true iff π' grounds V" satisfies F. For example, the formula $x \leftrightarrow y$ approximates the parametric substitutions $[x \mapsto a, y \mapsto b]$ and $[x \mapsto u', y \mapsto u', u \mapsto u']$ but not $[x \mapsto a]$, while $x \wedge y$ approximates $[x \mapsto a, y \mapsto b]$.

Different choices of the allowed propositional formulas lead to different analyses. For example, one choice is just the formulas consisting of conjunctions of propositional variables and the constant *false*, another is obtained by adding bi-implication. Of course there is a tradeoff between the complexity of the formulas allowed and the cost of the analysis. In the remainder of this section we develop the most precise analysis possible in this context in which all monotonic propositional formulas are allowed as descriptions.

Let *Prop* be the poset of equivalent propositional formulas ordered by implication over some suitably large finite variable set. We can represent an equivalence class in *Prop* by a canonical representative for the class, perhaps a formula which is in disjunctive or conjunctive normal form. We shall abuse notation and apply logical connectives both to propositional formulas and to classes of equivalent formulas.

Lemma 5.2 The poset *Prop* is a finite (complete) lattice with (distributed) conjunction, $\bigwedge$, as the greatest lower bound operation and (distributed) disjunction, $\bigvee$, as the least upper bound operation. ■

Definition. Let $\gamma : Prop \to \wp\, Psub$ be defined by

$$\gamma\ F = \{\pi \in Psub \mid \forall\, \pi' \trianglelefteq \pi\, .\, (assign\ \pi')\ satisfies\ F\}$$

where $assign : Psub \to Var \to Bool$ is given by $(assign\ \pi\ V)$ is true exactly when π grounds V. ■

Example 5.1 Let $F = [x \leftrightarrow y]$. Then $[x \mapsto a, y \mapsto b] \in \gamma\ F$ and $[y \mapsto b] \notin \gamma\ F$. ■

Lemma 5.3 The function γ is a downwards closed concretization function from *Prop* to $\wp\, Psub$. ■

Since γ is downwards closed, *meet* is simply approximated by the greatest lower bound operator on the descriptions, that is, (distributed) conjunction. The function *grounds* is straightforward to approximate.

Definition. Let $grounds_{prop} : Atom \to Prop \to Bool$ be defined by

$$grounds_{prop}\ A\ F \text{ iff } \forall\ V \in (vars\ A)\, .\, F \Rightarrow V. \ ■$$

Lemma 5.4 $grounds_{prop}$ *appr grounds*. ■

To approximate *unify* is more complex. We first give an alternative definition of *unify* in terms of restriction, renaming and most general unifiers.

Let $res\ U\ \pi$ be the parametric substitution that acts like π when applied to variables in U, but maps variables outside U to distinct parameters. The function $mgp : Atom \to Atom \to \wp\, Psub$ is the analogue of the unification function, *mgu*, for standard substitutions. It is defined by

$$mgp\ H\ A \quad = \quad \{\bigsqcup\{\pi \in Psub \mid \pi\ H = \pi\ A\}\} \setminus \{\bot_{Psub}\}.$$

An alternative characterization is that $mgp\ H\ A = \{\epsilon \circ \mu \mid \mu \in mgu\ H\ A\}$. The lemma makes use of renamings. A *renaming* is a mapping $\rho \in Ren \subset Var \to Var$ such that $\rho \circ \rho$ is the identity. We do not distinguish a renaming from its natural extension to atoms and clauses. We use a function $ren : \wp\, Var \to \wp\, Var \to Ren$ for renaming where $(ren\ V\ W)$ is some renaming, such that the variables in W are renamed "away from" the variables in V. We may also "apply" a renaming to a parametric substitution, $app : Ren \to \wp\, Psub \to \wp\, Psub$ is defined by $app\ \rho\ \Pi = \{\pi \circ \rho \mid \pi \in \Pi\}$.

Lemma 5.5 Let atoms H and A and set Π of parametric substitutions be given. Let $\rho = ren\ (vars\ H)\ ((vars\ A) \cup (dom\ \Pi))$. Then

$$unify\ H\ A\ \Pi \quad = \quad res\ (vars\ H)\ (meet\ (app\ \rho\ \Pi)\ (mgp\ H\ (\rho\ A))). \ ■$$

We can now develop an approximation to *unify*. Note that we already know that *meet* can be approximated by conjunction. We must find approximations to *res*, *app* and *mgp*.

Definition. Let *tass* W be the set of truth assignments to the variables in $W \subseteq Var$. Let $res_{prop} : \wp\, Var \rightarrow Prop \rightarrow Prop$ be defined by

$$res_{prop}\ W\ F \quad = \quad \bigvee\{\psi\ F \mid \psi \in tass\ ((vars\ F) \setminus W)\}. \quad \blacksquare$$

Example 5.2 $res_{prop}\ \{x, y, z\}\ [x \wedge (y \leftrightarrow v) \wedge (z \leftrightarrow v)] = [x \wedge (y \leftrightarrow z)]$. $\blacksquare$

Lemma 5.6 res_{prop} *appr res*. $\blacksquare$

Definition. Let $mgp_{prop} : Atom \rightarrow Atom \rightarrow Prop$ be defined by

$$\begin{aligned} mgp_{prop}\ H\ A \quad = \quad & \text{if } (mgu\ H\ A) = \emptyset \text{ then } false \\ & \quad \text{else let } \{\mu\} = (mgu\ H\ A) \text{ in} \\ & \qquad \bigwedge\{V \leftrightarrow (\bigwedge(vars\ (\mu\ V))) \mid V \in dom\ \mu\}. \quad \blacksquare \end{aligned}$$

Example 5.3 $mgp_{prop}\ p(x, y)\ p(a, f(u, v)) = [x \wedge (y \leftrightarrow (u \wedge v))]$. $\blacksquare$

Lemma 5.7 mgp_{prop} *appr mgp*. $\blacksquare$

It is straightforward to verify that $(\rho\ F)$ *appr* $(app\ \rho\ F)$. Thus we define the approximation to *unify* as follows:

Definition. Let $unify_{prop} : Atom \rightarrow Atom \rightarrow Prop \rightarrow Prop$ be defined by

$$\begin{aligned} unify_{prop}\ H\ A\ F \quad = \quad & \text{let } \rho = ren\ (vars\ H)\ ((vars\ A) \cup (vars\ F)) \text{ in} \\ & res_{prop}\ (vars\ H)\ (\rho\ F \wedge (mgp_{prop}\ H\ (\rho\ A))). \quad \blacksquare \end{aligned}$$

It follows from Lemma 5.5, Proposition 3.1, Lemma 5.7 and Lemma 5.6 that:

Lemma 5.8 $unify_{prop}$ *appr unify*. $\blacksquare$

Example 5.4 Let $A = append(x, y, z)$, $H = append(nil, y, y)$, and $H' = append(u : x, y, u : z)$. Then

$$\begin{aligned} unify_{prop}\ H\ A\ [true] \quad &= \quad [true] \\ unify_{prop}\ A\ H\ [true] \quad &= \quad [x \wedge (y \leftrightarrow z)] \\ unify_{prop}\ H'\ A\ [true] \quad &= \quad [true] \\ unify_{prop}\ A\ H'\ [false] \quad &= \quad [false] \\ unify_{prop}\ A\ H'\ [x \wedge (y \leftrightarrow z)] \quad &= \quad [(x \wedge y) \leftrightarrow z]. \end{aligned}$$

(These are the applications of $unify_{prop}$ needed to compute $\mathbf{P_{gro}}\ [\![P]\!]\ A\ [true]$, where P is the append program from Example 4.3). $\blacksquare$

We are now in a position to define the dataflow analyses.

Definition. $\mathbf{P}_{\text{prop}}$ and $\mathbf{P}'_{\text{prop}}$ are those interpretations of the normal semantics and the delay semantics, respectively, in which *Asub* is assigned *Prop*, m is assigned conjunction, u is assigned $unify_{prop}$, and g is assigned $grounds_{prop}$. ■

The interpretation of the definite semantics in which *Asub* is assigned *Prop*, m is assigned conjunction, and u is assigned $unify_{prop}$ is the groundness analysis given by Marriott, Søndergaard and Jones [10]. The next two theorems follow immediately from Lemma 5.8, Lemma 5.7, and Proposition 3.1.

Theorem 5.9 $\mathbf{P}_{\text{prop}}$ *appr* $\mathbf{P}_{\text{std}}$. ■

Theorem 5.10 $\mathbf{P}'_{\text{prop}}$ *appr* $\mathbf{P}_{\text{del}}$. ■

Consequences of Theorem 5.9. We have given a dataflow analysis $\mathbf{P}_{\text{prop}}$ which takes as input a program and a query description. If the dataflow analysis returns *false* then we are guaranteed that whenever a query matching the description is processed, using a left-to-right computation rule without delaying of non-ground negative literals, no non-ground literal will be evaluated. If the analysis returns *true*, this conclusion may not be valid. The analysis may even be useful when the semantics *can* delay negative literals, since *false* indicates that groundness tests and delaying will not be needed, allowing a compiler to produce more efficient target code.

Example 5.5 Consider P_1 from Example 4.4. Let $A = prefix(x, y)$. Then

$$\begin{aligned} \mathbf{P}_{\text{prop}}\ [\![P_1]\!]\ A\ [y] &= \langle [x \wedge y], \mathit{false} \rangle \\ \mathbf{P}_{\text{prop}}\ [\![P_1]\!]\ A\ [x] &= \langle [x], \mathit{true} \rangle. \end{aligned}$$

This tells us that a call in which the second argument is ground definitely does not lead to evaluation of non-ground negative literals, whereas a call in which only the first argument is ground *may* cause such a problem (as in fact it will in this case). ■

Consequences of Theorem 5.10. The analysis $\mathbf{P}'_{\text{prop}}$ also takes as input a program and a query description. If it returns *false* then we are guaranteed that whenever a query matching the description is processed using a left-to-right computation rule with delaying of non-ground negative literals (SLDNF resolution), no floundering will occur. If the analysis returns *true*, that conclusion may not be valid.

Example 5.6 Consider P_2 from Example 4.4. Let $A = prefix(x, y)$. Then

$$\begin{aligned} \mathbf{P}'_{\text{prop}}\ [\![P_2]\!]\ A\ [y] &= \langle [x \wedge y], E_1 \rangle \\ \mathbf{P}'_{\text{prop}}\ [\![P_2]\!]\ A\ [x] &= \langle [x], E_2 \rangle \end{aligned}$$

where (E_1 $[x \wedge y]$) is *false* and (E_2 $[x]$) is *true*. This tells us that a call in which the second argument is ground definitely will not lead to floundering, whereas a call in which the first argument is ground may. ■

6 Related Work

The first methods to ensure that floundering does not occur consisted in checking simple syntactic conditions. Such conditions include "allowedness" [7]: a clause is allowed if every variable in the clause occurs in a positive literal. This is far too strong a condition, ruling out for example every program with a non-ground unit clause. Decker and Cavedon [6] suggest several ways of weakening the allowedness condition, but the proposed characterizations are still syntactic by nature and generally stronger than a condition based on abstract interpretation. That is, our method characterizes a strictly larger class of non-floundering programs.

Dart [5] gives an analysis in which the descriptions are propositional formulas that are conjunctions of implications. These descriptions are strictly less expressive than ours since disjunction is not allowed. For example, Dart's analysis cannot be used to show that the program

$$\begin{array}{l} p \leftarrow q(x,y) \wedge r(x,y) \wedge \neg\, s(y) \\ q(a,x) \\ q(x,a) \\ r(x,x) \end{array}$$

will not flounder for any positive query, while the method given here can. Delayed negative literals are not explicitly handled in Dart's analysis; this is not necessary because the analysis actually detects the much stronger property that *all* literals will eventually become ground. Thus Dart's analysis cannot be used to show that the program

$$\begin{array}{l} p(x) \leftarrow r(x,y) \wedge \neg\, q(y) \\ r(x,a) \end{array}$$

will not flounder for any positive query, while the method given here can. Thus the present method is intrinsically more accurate.

Barbuti and Martelli [2] have suggested a dataflow analysis for the problem, based on abstract interpretation. However, this dataflow analysis was unsound because it assumed that evaluation of a ground negative literal cannot lead to floundering. Thus for example, given the program

$$q \leftarrow \neg\, p(x)$$

Barbuti and Martelli's analysis erroneously concluded that the query $\leftarrow \neg\, q$ cannot lead to floundering. This flaw has later been corrected [1].

The descriptions used in Barbuti and Martelli's analysis correspond to conjunctions of variables plus *false*, and they are thus strictly less expressive than the descriptions used here. However, the analysis partly overcomes this lack of precision by "re-evaluating" a positive literal whenever its arguments become more instantiated by the evaluation of other literals. We conjecture that this gives the same precision as if the propositional descriptions of Dart had been used, though less precision than that given by our descriptions.

Finally, both Dart and Barbuti and Martelli tie groundness information to argument positions of predicates, rather than to variables, as done here. Consider the program

$$p(f(x, b)) \leftarrow \neg\, q(x).$$

Given the query $\leftarrow p(f(a, y))$, both methods funnel groundness information about x and y through the argument position of p. Since $f(a, y)$ is not ground, nothing is concluded about x, so it is not discovered that floundering cannot occur. The method presented in this paper will discover absence of floundering in this case.

To give an impression of the limitations of the suggested method, we finally give two examples where absence of floundering will *not* be detected. Consider the program

$$q(x) \leftarrow p(x) \wedge \neg\, r(y)$$
$$p(b)$$

and the query $\leftarrow q(a)$. The failure of p will not be detected, so floundering is deemed possible. In this case the problem could be overcome by also propagating principal functors, but obviously no such type inference provides a general solution. As another example consider the program

$$q \leftarrow \neg\, p \wedge \neg\, r(x)$$
$$p$$

and the query $\leftarrow q$. The failure of $\neg\, p$ is not detected. Again, simple enhancements of the method could solve this particular problem, but the undecidability of floundering excludes a general solution.

7 Conclusion

We have presented two novel dataflow analyses for normal logic programs. The first determines whether non-ground negative literals will definitely not be evaluated when using the operational semantics without delay (this is a common Prolog implementation of negation). The second determines whether SLDNF resolution may lead to floundering. They are both useful for detecting possible errors in a program and the first analysis also has applications for the compilation of normal programs into efficient code. The analyses should also be of use in partial evaluation of normal logic programs. They are more precise than previously suggested analyses. In particular we obtain a characterization of a class of non-floundering programs larger than any class previously suggested.

Two contributions of this paper are the frameworks given for the development of dataflow analyses for normal logic programs. These frameworks are based on a notion of parametric substitutions. The frameworks allow other analyses to be quickly developed and proved correct by instantiating three parametric functions.

References

[1] R. Barbuti and M. Martelli. A characterization of non-floundering logic programs and goals based on abstract interpretation techniques. To appear in *Foundations of Computer Science.*

[2] R. Barbuti and M. Martelli. A tool to check the non-floundering logic programs and goals. In P. Deransart *et al.*, editors, *Programming Language Implementation and Logic Programming (Lecture Notes in Computer Science 348)*, pages 58–67. Springer-Verlag, 1988.

[3] E. Börger. Unsolvable decision problems for Prolog programs. In E. Börger, editor, *Computation Theory and Logic (Lecture Notes in Computer Science 270)*, pages 37–48. Springer-Verlag, 1987.

[4] K. Clark. Negation as Failure. In H. Gallaire and J. Minker, editors, *Logic and Databases*, pages 293–322. Plenum Press, 1978.

[5] P. Dart. On derived dependencies and connected databases. To appear in *Journal of Logic Programming.*

[6] H. Decker and L. Cavedon. Generalizing allowedness while retaining completeness of SLDNF-resolution. Technical Report IR-KB 52, ECRC, Munich, FRG, 1990. Extended abstract to appear in *Proc. Third CSL Workshop (Lecture Notes in Computer Science)*, Springer-Verlag.

[7] J. W. Lloyd. *Foundations of Logic Programming.* Springer-Verlag, second edition 1987.

[8] M. Maher. On parameterized substitutions. Unpublished note, 26 pages. IBM T. J. Watson Research Center, Yorktown Heights, New York, 1986.

[9] K. Marriott and H. Søndergaard. Top-down abstract interpretation of normal logic programs. In preparation.

[10] K. Marriott, H. Søndergaard and N. D. Jones. Denotational abstract interpretation of logic programs. Submitted for publication.

[11] F. Nielson. Strictness analysis and denotational abstract interpretation. *Information and Computation* **76** (1): 29–92, 1988.

[12] J. Thom, and J. Zobel, editors. NU-Prolog reference manual. Technical Report 86/10, Dept. of Computer Science, University of Melbourne, Australia, revised edition 1987.

[13] W. Winsborough. Source-level transforms for multiple specialization of Horn clauses (extended abstract). Technical report 88-15, Dept. of Computer Science, University of Chicago, Illinois, 1988.

Adding Negation-as-Failure to Intuitionistic Logic Programming

Anthony J. Bonner
L. Thorne McCarty

Rutgers University
Department of Computer Science
New Brunswick, NJ 08903
bonner@paul.rutgers.edu
mccarty@cs.rutgers.edu

Abstract

Intuitionistic logic programming is an extension of Horn-clause logic programming in which implications may appear "embedded" on the right-hand side of a rule. Thus, rules of the form $A(x) \leftarrow [B(x) \leftarrow C(x)]$ are allowed. These rules are called *embedded implications*. In this paper, we develop a language in which negation-as-failure is combined with embedded implications in a principled way. Although this combination has been studied by other researchers, Gabbay has argued in [10] that the entire idea is logically incoherent since modus ponens would not be valid in such a system. We show how to solve this problem by drawing a distinction between *rules* and *goals*. To specify the semantics of rules and goals, we then develop an analogue of Przymusinski's perfect model semantics for stratified Horn-clause logic [20]. Several modifications are necessary to adapt this idea from classical logic to intuitionistic logic, but we eventually show how to define a *preferred model* of a *stratified intuitionistic rulebase*, and this enables us to specify the semantics of such a rulebase by reference to its preferred models. Finally, we prove a soundness and completeness theorem. Throughout the paper, we discuss various examples of the use of intuitionistic embedded implications plus negation-as-failure, to demonstrate the utility of the language.

1 Introduction

Intuitionistic logic programming is an extension of Horn-clause logic programming in which implications may appear "embedded" on the right-hand side of a rule. Thus, rules of the form $A(x) \leftarrow [B(x) \leftarrow C(x)]$ are allowed. Several researchers have investigated the properties of these "embedded implications" [11, 10, 14, 15, 17, 2], and have shown them to be useful for hypothetical reasoning [3], for legal reasoning [16], for modular logic programming [17], and for lexical scoping [18].

In a series of prior papers [2, 4, 6], Bonner, et al., have established various theoretical results on the complexity and expressibility of intuitionistic embedded implications in the function-free (Datalog) case. For the full language, in which universal quantifiers may also appear "embedded" on the right-hand side of a rule, the query problem is undecidable [6], but if embedded universal quantifiers are barred from the language, the query problem is decidable and its data-complexity is PSPACE-complete [2]. If negation-as-failure is added to the language, these complexity results can be extended to expressibility results. Thus, as shown in [6], the unrestricted language with embedded universal quantifiers plus negation-as-failure can express any typed, generic, computable database query in the sense defined by Chandra and Harel in [7, 8]. If the language includes negation-as-failure, but no embedded universal quantifiers, then it can express any typed, generic database query in PSPACE [2]. Additional syntactic restrictions yield additional complexity classes. If the rules are at most linear recursive, then the language can express any database query in NP, and if linear recursion alternates with negation-as-failure in a stratified manner, then the language can express the database queries at each level in the polynomial time hierarchy above P [4]. It is interesting that these complexity classes can all be generated by a single language with a natural sequence of syntactic restrictions.

Note the role played by negation-as-failure in these results. Without negation-as-failure, we can state complexity results, but we cannot state expressibility results since we cannot represent non-monotonic queries. Also, for many applications, negation-as-failure turns out to be a very useful addition to the language of embedded implications, just as it has been shown to be a very useful addition to the language of definite Horn clauses. Several examples are discussed in Sections 2 and 3.5 below. Thus a theory of negation-as-failure in the context of intuitionistic logic programming seems essential. In our prior papers [2, 4, 6], the treatment of negation-as-failure was entirely proof-theoretic. In this paper, to round out the picture, we develop a semantic theory and prove a soundness and completeness theorem.

There are reasons to think that the addition of negation-as-failure to intuitionistic logic programming will lead to serious semantic difficulties. Gabbay studied the problem in [10], and concluded that the entire idea was logically incoherent, since modus ponens would no longer be valid. We address this problem in Section 3.2. More recently, Harland [12] has proposed a semantics for negation-as-failure within intuitionistic logic programming, based on the fixed-point construction of Miller [17]. Harland's approach seems to overcome some of Gabbay's objections. However, Harland's semantics requires that we label predicates as "completely defined" or "incompletely defined", and this requirement precludes the use of the very rules that are needed for our expressibility results. This point is discussed further in Section 3.5. Our approach, instead, is based on Przymusinski's *perfect model semantics* for stratified Horn-clause logic augmented by negation-as-failure [20]. Although this approach requires that we restrict our attention to *stratified intuitionistic rulebases*, a term defined in Section 3.3, this restriction turns out to be acceptable for our intended applications.

In the case of classical logic programming, Przymusinski's idea was to define a *preference relation* on the classical models of a rulebase, and then to identify the *minimal* elements in the preference ordering as the intended models of the rules [20]. In the case of intuitionistic logic programming, the natural generalization would be to define a preference relation on the intuitionistic models of the rulebase, which are usually taken to be Kripke models [13]. However, it turns out that we need to make two modifications of Przymusinski's original idea in order to generalize it to intuitionistic logic. First, we need to generalize the notion of a Kripke structure, which is monotonic, to the notion of a *non-monotonic structure*, which is not. Second, we need to modify the definition of a preference relation. Przymusinski's preference relation minimizes atomic goals stratum by stratum, and this automatically maximizes negative goals stratum by stratum, since the logic is classical. For intuitionistic logic programming, we need to consider a broader class of goals, and within this broader class we need to minimize positive goals and maximize negative goals simultaneously, since intuitionistic logic lacks the law of excluded middle. These points are developed in Sections 4.2 through 4.4. Once these definitions have been modified, however, we can follow the perfect model analogy quite closely by using the preferred models of a rulebase to specify its intended meaning. In fact, as in the classical perfect model semantics, we show that every stratified intuitionistic rulebase has, up to equivalence, a single preferred model.

The development in this paper is for a language without function symbols. This is the kind of language typically used in database applications, and it is exactly the language needed for the expressibility results in [2, 4, 6]. Although it is function-free, we allow the language to have an *infinite* set of constant symbols. It should therefore be straightforward to generalize the development given here to include function symbols, since in a logic with function symbols but without equality (e.g., Prolog), each Herbrand term can be treated as a distinct constant symbol. The intuitionistic logic programming language discussed in [14, 15] treats function symbols in precisely this way.

2 Examples

In this section, we present two examples of the use of intuitionistic embedded implications combined with negation-as-failure. The reader will note the appearance of two implication symbols in these examples: $\leftarrow$ and $\Leftarrow$. The distinction between these two symbols will be explained in Section 3.2, but for the moment it should be ignored. More examples will be provided in section 3.5, after inference with negation-as-failure has been formally defined.

Example 1. Assume a database of atomic formulas $TAKE(s, c)$ asserting that student s has taken course c, and a rulebase that states the graduation requirements for a university. Thus $GRAD(s)$ means that student s is eligible to graduate. We can then define a predicate $NEAR\_GRAD(s)$, meaning that student s is within one course of satisfying the graduation requirements, as follows:

$$NEAR\_GRAD(s) \leftarrow COURSE(c),\ [GRAD(s) \Leftarrow TAKE(s,c)].$$

Intuitively, this rule states that student s is nearly a graduate if there exists some course c such that, if the student took this course, then he could graduate. In [3], it is shown that there is a precise sense in which such rules cannot be expressed in classical logic, even in full classical logic. However, the embedded implication in this rule has a natural interpretation in intuitionistic logic. It means simply: Add the formula $TAKE(s, c)$ to the database and then try to prove $GRAD(s)$.

Now imagine a set of rules defining a student's eligibility for financial aid, as follows:

$$STIPEND(s) \leftarrow ADMITTED(s),\ NEAR\_GRAD(s),\ \sim GRAD(s).$$
$$FELLOWSHIP(s) \leftarrow ADMITTED(s),\ \sim NEAR\_GRAD(s),\ \sim GRAD(s)$$

Intuitively, a student s who has been admitted to the university is eligible for a stipend if he is a near-graduate but not yet a graduate. On the other hand, if he is neither a near-graduate nor a graduate, then he is eligible for a fellowship. □

In this example, the symbol '$\sim$' denotes negation-as-failure. Thus, in applying the rule for $FELLOWSHIP(s)$, we would ask if there exists some course c such that, if $TAKE(s,c)$ were assumed to be true then $GRAD(s)$ would also be true. We would conclude that s is eligible for a fellowship only if this hypothetical test fails. Conversely, we would conclude that s is eligible for a stipend only if this hypothetical test succeeds. Note that $NEAR\_GRAD(s)$ is vacuously true if $GRAD(s)$ is true (as long as there exists a course somewhere in the database!). But we do not want to give a stipend to a student who has already graduated, so we also include the test $\sim GRAD(s)$ in the rule for $STIPEND(s)$. This means that a stipend is available to those students who need to take *exactly* one course in order to satisfy the graduation requirements. This observation becomes important in the following example.

Example 2. In [19], Pareschi studies the use of intuitionistic embedded implications in a definite clause version of Categorical Grammar. Classical Categorical Grammar (CG) encodes linguistic information by assigning syntactic types to lexical items. A translation of CG into first-order logic represents these type assignments by definite clauses in which lexical items appear inside a special predicate *CONN*. For example, the Horn rule below encodes the English rule for 'put'. This rule, along with appropriate rules for other lexical items, allows the derivation of the sentence: "Mary put a book on the table."

$$S(x,w) \leftarrow NP(x,y),\ CONN(\text{put},y,y+1),\ NP(y+1,z),\ PP(z,w).$$

In this rule, the variables x, y, z and w represent positions in a string of words. The rule states that a sentence occurs between positions x and w if a noun phrase ("Mary") occurs between x and y, the word 'put' connects positions y and $y+1$, another noun phrase ("the book") occurs between $y+1$ and z, and a prepositional phrase ("on the table") occurs between z and w.

Although this particular example can be handled adequately with Horn-clause logic, intuitionistic embedded implications are needed to represent the type assignments for relative pronouns. For example, the rule for 'which' might be written as follows:

$$\begin{aligned} REL(v-1,w) \quad \leftarrow \quad & CONN(\text{which},v-1,v),\ v \le y,\ y \le w, \\ & [S(v,w) \Leftarrow NP(y,y)]. \end{aligned}$$

Here, the relative clause is assumed to have a noun phrase of null length at some position y representing the "extraction site" for the relative pronoun. Intuitively, the rule states that if the word 'which' connects string positions

$v-1$ and v, and if there exists some position y between v and w such that, if a noun phrase were inserted at y then there would be a sentence between v and w, then it follows that there is a relative clause between string positions $v-1$ and w. These rules thus allow the derivation of the following relative clauses:

which Mary put a book on ↑,
which Mary put ↑ on the table,
which ↑ put a book on the table,

where the symbol ↑ marks the extraction site. But there is a problem. These rules also allow the derivation of the following string as a relative clause:

which Mary put a book on the table,

since the embedded implication $[S(v,w) \Leftarrow NP(y,y)]$ is vacuously true whenever $S(v,w)$ is true. Pareschi considers several possible solutions to this problem, including a modification of the intuitionistic proof theory and a filtering of certain kinds of proofs [19]. But there is an obvious solution using negation-as-failure. If we simply redefine the rule for relative pronouns as follows:

$$\begin{aligned} REL(v-1,w) \quad \leftarrow \quad & CONN(\text{which}, v-1, v),\ v \leq y,\ y \leq w, \\ & [S(v,w) \Leftarrow NP(y,y)], \\ & \sim S(v,w). \end{aligned}$$

then the ungrammatical derivation is blocked. □

These examples show the possible uses of intuitionistic embedded implications plus negation-as-failure in very simple cases. More complex examples are discussed in Section 3.5 below. However, in order to analyze these more complex examples, it is necessary to formulate the inference system of our language with greater precision. This is the subject of the following section.

3 Inference

A number of researchers have developed inference systems for intuitionisitic logic programming [11, 15, 17, 2]. However, most of this work has focused on the negation-free case. As pointed out by Gabbay in [10], negation-as-failure introduces subtle problems for intuitionistic logic.

In this section, we first review the negation-free case and discuss the problems of introducing negation. We argue that the problems pointed out by Gabbay can be resolved if one distinguishes two types of logical implication, one for rules and one for goals. Using this idea, we develop an inference system for intuitionistic logic programming plus negation-as-failure.

3.1 The Negation-Free Case: Review

This section defines a logical inference system for intuitionistic logic programming. Such systems have been developed by several researchers, and the one presented here is a simplified version which retains many of the essential properties of the more elaborate systems while admitting a clean theoretical analysis. It is an extension of function-free Horn logic (i.e., Datalog), both syntactically and proof theoretically. In [2], it is shown that the data complexity of this system is complete for polynomial space.

The syntax of the logic is first order. It includes three (possibly infinite) sets: a universe of constant symbols $a, b, c, \ldots$, a set of variables $x, y, z, \ldots$, and a set of predicate symbols $A, B, C, \ldots$. Note that the logic, as defined here, does not include function symbols.

As in Horn logic, a rule has the form $A \leftarrow \phi$, where ϕ is a conjunction of goals. However, because our inference system is hypothetical, we have a larger class of goals. In general, if ϕ is a legal goal (i.e., a query), then so is $\phi \leftarrow A_1, \ldots, A_n$, where each A_i is atomic. These considerations are summarized by the following rules, which define the syntax of our language:

$$\begin{aligned} \mathit{rule} &:= \mathit{atom} \mid \mathit{atom} \leftarrow \mathit{goal}_1 \ldots \mathit{goal}_m \\ \mathit{goal} &:= \mathit{atom} \mid \mathit{goal} \leftarrow \mathit{atom}_1 \ldots \mathit{atom}_m \end{aligned}$$

where the terminal symbol *atom* refers to atomic formulas. Goals thus include the formulas B and $B \leftarrow C, D$ and $(B \leftarrow C) \leftarrow D$. When interpreted either classically or intuitionistically, a goal is equivalent to a definite Horn clause. Rules include the formulas $A \leftarrow B$ and $A \leftarrow (B \leftarrow C, D)$ and $A \leftarrow [(B \leftarrow C) \leftarrow D]$. Such rules are called *embedded implications* [14, 15]. A rulebase is defined to be a finite set of rules, and a database is defined to be a finite set of ground atomic formulas.

Definition 3.1 (Inference) *Suppose R is a rulebase. Then we define the following inference system, where DB is an arbitrary database,*

Axioms: *$R + DB \vdash A$ is an axiom for every atomic formula $A \in DB$.*

Inference Rules:

1. *for any rule $A \leftarrow \phi_1 \ldots \phi_m$ in R, and for any ground substitution θ,*

$$\frac{R + DB \vdash \phi_i\theta \quad \text{for each } i}{R + DB \vdash A\theta}$$

2. *for any goal ϕ,*

$$\frac{R + DB + \{B_1, \ldots, B_m\} \vdash \phi}{R + DB \vdash \phi \leftarrow B_1 \ldots B_m}$$

In this inference system, each inference rule has the following interpretation: If the formulas above the the horizontal line can be inferred, then those below the horizontal line can also be inferred. The following elementary example shows how inference can be performed in a "top-down" manner by inverting these rules.

Example 3. Suppose that R consists of the following three rules:

$$A \leftarrow (B \leftarrow D).$$
$$B \leftarrow C.$$
$$C \leftarrow D.$$

Then $R \vdash A$. This can be proved by a straightforward, top-down argument:

$$\begin{array}{ll} & R \vdash A \\ \textit{if} & R \vdash B \leftarrow D \\ \textit{if} & R + D \vdash B \\ \textit{if} & R + D \vdash C \\ \textit{if} & R + D \vdash D \end{array}$$

But the last line is trivially true since it is an axiom. □

It is implicit in Definition 3.1 that the variables of a rule are universally quantified. Furthermore, as in Horn logic, if a variable does not appear in the head of a rule, then the universal quantifier can be moved inside the rule body and converted to an existential. For example, in the embedded implication $A(x) \leftarrow [B(x,y) \Leftarrow C(x,y)]$, the variable y does not appear in the head. If this rule appears in a rulebase R, then the inference system above implies that for any constant symbol x,

$$R + DB \ \vdash \ A(x) \quad \textit{if} \quad R + DB \ \vdash \ B(x,y) \Leftarrow C(x,y) \quad \textit{for some } y.$$

Consequently, the rule can be read in two equivalent ways:

$$\begin{array}{l} \forall_x \forall_y \ A(x) \leftarrow [B(x,y) \Leftarrow C(x,y)] \\ \forall_x \ A(x) \leftarrow \exists_y \ [B(x,y) \Leftarrow C(x,y)] \end{array}$$

The latter interpretation enables our logic to represent the notion of being "within one course of graduation," as defined in Example 1.

3.2 Negation-As-Failure: Paradoxes

We now extend the syntax of our rules to allow negated goals. Thus, rules of the form $A \leftarrow \sim B$ are allowed. Operationally, the expression $\sim B$ is interpreted as the failure to prove B; that is, $R \vdash \sim B$ iff $R \nvdash B$. As in Horn logic, difficult problems arise if rulebases with negation are not stratified. Section 3.3 develops the notion of stratification for intuitionistic rulebases. Even when they are stratified, however, embedded implications display interesting paradoxes, as originally pointed out by Gabbay [10]. This section examines some of these paradoxes and proposes a syntactic solution. Section 4 proposes a semantic solution.

If implicational queries are allowed, then paradoxes arise even for stratified Horn rulebases. The following example, for instance, shows that for such rulebases, implication is not transitive.

Example 4. Suppose that R consists of the following two rules:

$$\begin{array}{l} A \leftarrow B, \ \sim C. \\ B \leftarrow C. \end{array}$$

Then $R \vdash A \leftarrow B$ and $R \vdash B \leftarrow C$, but $R \nvdash A \leftarrow C$. Each of these points is straightforward. For instance, to infer $A \leftarrow C$, we would have to add C to the rulebase and then infer A; that is, we would have to derive the expression $R + C \vdash A$. However, once C is in the rulebase, the first rule is permanently blocked, so there is no way to derive A. Thus, $R + C \not\vdash A$. Hence $R \not\vdash A \leftarrow C$. □

The next example shows that stratified embedded-implications violate a very basic property of logical systems: modus ponens.

Example 5. Suppose that R consists of the following two rules:

$$B \leftarrow \sim C.$$
$$D \leftarrow (B \leftarrow C).$$

Then $R \vdash D \leftarrow B$ and $R \vdash B$, but $R \not\vdash D$. Each of these points is straightforward. For instance, to infer D, we would have to infer $B \leftarrow C$. We would thus have to add C to the rulebase and infer B; that is, we would have to derive the expression $R+C \vdash B$. Once C is in the rulebase, however, the first rule is blocked, so there is no way to derive B. Thus $R+C \not\vdash B$ so $R \not\vdash B \leftarrow C$. Hence $R \not\vdash D$. □

Examples 4 and 5 show that stratified rulebases lack some basic properties that we normally associate with logical implication. It might seem, therefore, that embedded implications augmented with negation-as-failure cannot be treated logically. After all, if implication is not transitive, and if modus ponens is not valid, then what makes the system logical?

A solution to the problem is suggested by our distinction between rules and goals. Syntactically, rules and goals are implications, but these implications are treated differently by the inference system of Definition 3.1: Inference rule 1 deals with rules, and inference rule 2 deals with goals. Since they are treated differently, it should not be too surprising that they have different properties. The real surprise is that this difference does not make itself apparent until the system is augmented with negation-as-failure. It is the different treatment of rules and goals that is the source of the apparent problem with implication.

The problem can be resolved by a simple syntactic device: We distinguish between the two types of implication by using two types of implication symbols. Rules will continue to have the form $A \leftarrow B$, but goals will have the form $A \Leftarrow B$. Rules are transitive and can be used for modus ponens, whereas goals cannot. Proof theoretically, the expression $R \vdash A \Leftarrow B$ means simply that $R+B \vdash A$. Semantically, as shown in Section 4, goals and rules also have two distinct interpretations.

With this is mind, we now define the syntax of our language with negation-as-failure. As in Horn logic, we distinguish between positive and negative goals. If ϕ is a positive goal (i.e., it contains no negation signs), then $\sim \phi$ is a negative goal. Furthermore, because the inference system is hypothetical, if ϕ is a legal goal, then so is $\phi \Leftarrow A_1, ..., A_n$, where each A_i is atomic. These considerations are summarized by the following rules, which define the syntax of our language:

$$\begin{array}{lll} rule & := & atom \leftarrow goal_1 ... goal_m \\ goal & := & pgoal \mid ngoal \\ pgoal & := & atom \mid pgoal \Leftarrow atom_1 ... atom_m \\ ngoal & := & \sim pgoal \mid ngoal \Leftarrow atom_1 ... atom_m \end{array}$$

Negative goals include the formulas $\sim B$ and $\sim (B \Leftarrow C)$ and $(\sim B) \Leftarrow C$. If interpreted classically, a negative goal is equivalent to a negative Horn clause. Rules include the formulas $A \leftarrow \sim B$ and $A \leftarrow \sim (B \Leftarrow C)$ and $A \leftarrow (\sim B \Leftarrow C)$.

3.3 Stratified Inference

Aside from the paradoxes mentioned above, inference involving negation-as-failure is not always well-defined. For instance, given the two rules $A \leftarrow \sim B$ and $B \leftarrow \sim A$, it is not clear whether A should be inferred, or B, or both, or neither. As in Horn logic, however, it is not difficult to provide an operational semantics for negation-as-failure as long as there is no recursion through negation. In particular, a rulebase can be stratified, or layered, as described in [1]. This section develops the notion of stratification for intuitionistic rulebases.

Given a goal $P(x) \Leftarrow Q(x)$, we call the predicate symbol P the *head predicate* of the goal. Head predicates are central to our notion of stratification. They are defined recursively in the following definition.

Definition 3.2 *The predicate symbol in an atomic formula is its head predicate. The head predicate of a formula ϕ is also the head predicate of the formulas $\sim \phi$, $\phi \Leftarrow \psi$, and $\phi \leftarrow \psi$.*

Definition 3.3 (Stratification) *Let R be a rulebase. R is stratified iff it is the disjoint union of rulebases $R_0, ..., R_k$, where for each rule in R_i,*

- *If the rule has a negative premise whose head predicate is P, then every rule with head predicate P is contained in $\cup_{j<i} R_j$*
- *If the rule has a positive premise whose head predicate is P, then every rule with head predicate P is contained in $\cup_{j<i} R_j$*

In this case $R_0, ..., R_k$ is called a stratification of R, and R_i is its i_{th} stratum.

This definition guarantees that if recursion occurs, then it occurs only within a single stratum and that it never occurs through negation. In the rest of this section, we consider only stratified rulebases, and we always assume that we have a particular stratification in mind.

Notice that a predicate may be defined by many rules in many strata. We say that a predicate *belongs* to the highest stratum in which it is defined.

Only head predicates play a role in the definition of stratification. Thus, in the rule $A \leftarrow (B \Leftarrow C)$, the rules defining C can appear in any stratum. In particular, they can appear above the strata in which A and B are defined. Thus $\leftarrow$ affects the possible stratifications of a rulebase, but $\Leftarrow$ does not. Intuitively, in the formula $A \leftarrow B$, the atom B is "executed" in order to prove A, while in the formula $A \Leftarrow B$, the atom B is "assumed" to be true in order to prove A. This is why, in the latter case, B is not considered for the stratification; i.e., because B is not "executed", the formula $A \Leftarrow B$ cannot lead to recursion through negation.

We now define the operational semantics of stratified rulebases. The idea is to derive expressions of the form $R \vdash \phi$ stratum by stratum, using the derivations of one stratum as the starting point for the derivations of the stratum above.

Given a stratified rulebase R, we define a set of inference systems, one for each stratum. These systems generalize the inference system of Definition 3.1 in two ways. First, each inference system corresponds to a particular stratum of R, where the jth inference system uses only the rules in the jth stratum. Second, each inference system is provided with an unspecified set of axioms $\mathcal{A}$. Each inference system thus defines a mapping cl_j that takes a set of axioms $\mathcal{A}$ as input, and returns a set of inferred expressions $cl_j(\mathcal{A})$ as output. These mappings encapsulate inference as a single operation, thus providing a convenient separation between inference, which occurs within strata, and negation-as-failure, which occurs between strata.

The operational semantics of R are defined stratum-by-stratum in terms of these mappings: Given the output from cl_j, we apply the closed world assumption to it, and use the resulting expressions as the input to cl_{j+1}. In this way, the derivations of one stratum are the starting point for the derivations of the stratum above. The rest of this section makes these ideas precise.

Definition 3.4 *Suppose R is a stratified rulebase. An inference expression for R is an expression of the form $R + DB \vdash \phi$ where DB is a database and ϕ is a goal. The inference expression is positive iff ϕ is positive, and negative iff ϕ is negative.*

Definition 3.5 (Inference) *Let R be a stratified rulebase, and let $\mathcal{A}$ be a set of inference expressions for R. For each stratum of R, we define a distinct inference system, in which $\mathcal{A}$ is the set of axioms. The inference system associated with the jth stratum is defined as follows, where DB is an arbitrary database:*

Axioms:

1. *The expression $R+DB \vdash A$ is an axiom for every atomic formula $A \in DB$ such that A belongs to the jth stratum.*
2. *Each expression in $\mathcal{A}$ is an axiom.*

Inference Rules:

1. *for any rule $A \leftarrow \phi_1 ... \phi_m$ in the jth stratum of R, and for any ground substitution θ,*

$$\frac{R + DB \vdash \phi_i\theta \quad \textit{for each } i}{R + DB \vdash A\theta}$$

2. *for any goal ϕ,*

$$\frac{R + DB + \{B_1, ..., B_m\} \vdash \phi}{R + DB \vdash \phi \Leftarrow B_1 ... B_m}$$

$cl_j(\mathcal{A})$ denotes the set of inference expressions derivable in this system.

Like all Gentzen-style inference systems, this system is monotonic in the set of axioms. It is also idempotent and inflationary. We thus have the following basic results.

Lemma 3.1 *cl_j is a function which maps sets of inference expressions for R into sets of inference expressions for R. Furthermore, this function has the following properties:*

- *Monotonicity: If* $\mathcal{A} \subseteq \mathcal{B}$ *then* $cl_j(\mathcal{A}) \subseteq cl_j(\mathcal{B})$.
- *Idempotence:* $cl_j(\mathcal{A}) = cl_j(cl_j(\mathcal{A}))$
- *Inflationaryness:* $\mathcal{A} \subseteq cl_j(\mathcal{A})$

Given a set of inference expressions $\mathcal{A}$, we define a new set $\overline{\mathcal{A}}$. Informally, $\overline{\mathcal{A}}$ is the result of applying the *closed world assumption* to $\mathcal{A}$; i.e., if an expression is not true, then assume it is false. This is the basis of negation-as-failure.

Definition 3.6 *Let $\mathcal{A}$ be a set of inference expressions for R. Then $\overline{\mathcal{A}}$ is another set of inference expressions for R, where for any database DB and any positive goal ϕ,*

- $R + DB \vdash \phi \in \overline{\mathcal{A}}$ *iff* $R + DB \vdash \phi \in \mathcal{A}$
- $R + DB \vdash \sim\phi \in \overline{\mathcal{A}}$ *iff* $R + DB \vdash \phi \notin \mathcal{A}$

We have now assembled the main components of our operational semantics of stratified rulebases: (i) Definition 3.6 captures the idea of negation-as-failure, which occurs between strata, and (ii) Definition 3.5 captures the idea of inference, which occurs within strata. It remains to combine these ideas into a unified semantics of stratified rulebases. The following definition does exactly this. By alternating inference with negation-as-failure, it constructs a set of inference expressions stratum-by-stratum in a bottom-up fashion.

Definition 3.7

- $\mathcal{A}^0 = \{\}$
- $\mathcal{A}^{j+1} = \overline{cl_{j+1}(\mathcal{A}^j)}$ *for* $j \geq 0$.

Intuitively, $\mathcal{A}^j$ is the set of inference expressions derived by the first j strata of the rulebase. Using $\mathcal{A}^j$ as a starting point, $\mathcal{A}^{j+1}$ is generated by applying the rules in the $j+1^{st}$ stratum until saturation, after which the closed world assumption is applied. Because a rulebase has a finite number of strata, this process eventually terminates. If a rulebase R has only k strata, then for $j \geq k$, the closure operator cl_{j+1} does not add any positive inference expressions to $\mathcal{A}^j$. However, the second inference rule of Definition 3.5 is still applicable to negative inference expressions. For instance, if the expression $R + B \vdash \sim A$ is in $\mathcal{A}^k$, then the expression $R \vdash (\sim A) \Leftarrow B$ is in $\mathcal{A}^{k+1}$. For this reason, $\mathcal{A}^k$ is a proper subset of $\mathcal{A}^{k+1}$. Note, however, that $\mathcal{A}^{k+j} = \mathcal{A}^{k+1}$ for $j \geq 1$. This prompts the following definition.

Definition 3.8 *Let R be a stratified rulebase with k strata. Then, for any database DB and any goal ϕ,*

$$R + DB \vdash_j \phi \quad \textit{iff} \quad \textit{the expression } R + DB \vdash \phi \textit{ is in } \mathcal{A}^j.$$
$$R + DB \vdash \phi \quad \textit{iff} \quad R + DB \vdash_{k+1} \phi.$$

This completes the definition of the operational semantics of stratified embedded-implications.

3.4 A Special Case

In the case of stratified Horn rules, the semantics developed above reduce to the semantics of Apt, Blair and Walker [1] and of Przymusinski [20]. It is worth noting, however, that these semantics differ from the semantics of Prolog in a special case: for rules of the form $A \leftarrow \sim B(x)$. Because of the possibility of floundering, Prolog gives such rules a special interpretation. This section discusses this interpretation and argues that by introducing intermediate predicates, our semantics can be forced to interpret rules as Prolog does, and vice-versa.

As in the negation-free case (Section 3.1), our operational semantics imply that the variables of a rule are universally quantified. Furthermore, if a variable does not appear in the head of a rule, then the universal quantifier can be moved inside the rule body and converted to an existential. For example, in the rule $A \leftarrow B(y), \sim C(y)$, the variable y does not appear in the head. This rule can thus be read in two equivalent ways:

$$\forall_y \ A \leftarrow B(y), \ \sim C(y)$$
$$A \leftarrow \exists_y \ [B(y), \ \sim C(y)]$$

Note that Prolog interprets this rule in the same two ways. In this respect, our semantics treats Horn rules with negation in the same way that classical logic programming does.

However, our semantics, like those of [1] and [20], differ from the semantics of Prolog in one respect: In Prolog, rules such as $A \leftarrow \sim C(y)$ are given a special interpretation. In such rules, the value of the variable y is unguarded, that is, it is not constrained by a positive literal, such as the literal $B(y)$ in the previous example. Unguardedness can cause the Prolog interpreter to flounder. For this reason, Prolog does *not* interpret this rule in either of the following ways:

$$\begin{array}{c} \forall_y \ A \leftarrow \sim C(y) \\ A \leftarrow \exists_y \sim C(y) \end{array} \qquad (1)$$

Instead, Prolog interprets it this way:

$$A \leftarrow \sim \exists_y \ C(y) \qquad (2)$$

That is, the existential quantifier is brought inside the negation sign.

This attempt by Prolog to avoid floundering is only partially successful however. Both in Prolog and in our semantics, we can effectively obtain either interpretation (1) or interpretation (2) by introducing intermediate predicates. For instance, by introducing a unary predicate $E(y)$, the following two rules effectively give us interpretation (1):

$$A \leftarrow E(y) \qquad\qquad E(y) \leftarrow \sim C(y)$$

This is true both in Prolog and in our semantics. Furthermore, in both systems, these rules cause floundering during top-down inference. Likewise, by introducing a zero-ary predicate D, the following two rules effectively give us interpretation (2):

$$A \leftarrow \sim D \qquad\qquad D \leftarrow C(y)$$

This is true both in Prolog and in our semantics. Furthermore, in both systems, these rules do not cause floundering during top-down inference. Prolog's special interpretation of unguarded rules is therefore a convenience that does not provide any additional expressive power and does not eliminate floundering.

Conceptually, then, the operational semantics described in Section 3.3 provides a uniform interpretation of stratified rulebases. In the special case of stratified Horn rulebases, this semantics is equivalent to others in the literature [1, 20]. In the very special case of unguarded Horn rules, this semantics can be translated into the semantics of Prolog in a straightforward way.

3.5 Examples

This section shows that stratified rulebases of embedded implications can solve some familiar problems. Note that in both the examples given, the predicate *SOMELEFT* acts as an "intermediate predicate" as described in Section 3.4.

Example 6. Suppose R is the following stratified rulebase:

$$\begin{aligned}&EVEN \leftarrow SELECT(x),\ [ODD \Leftarrow MARK(x)].\\&ODD \leftarrow SELECT(x),\ [EVEN \Leftarrow MARK(x)].\\&EVEN \leftarrow\ \sim SOMELEFT.\\&SOMELEFT \leftarrow SELECT(x).\\&SELECT(x) \leftarrow D(x),\ \sim MARK(x).\end{aligned}$$

Then $R, DB \vdash EVEN$ iff DB contains an even number of entries of the form $D(x)$. □

In this example, the rulebase determines the parity of a relation D.[1] This rulebase is best understood from the top-down perspective. During inference, the first two rules select elements one-by-one from the relation D. Each time an element x is selected, the formula $MARK(x)$ is hypothetically added to the database. In this way, a record is kept of which elements have been selected, so that they are not selected again. (Note that the last rule selects only unmarked elements.) As elements are selected and marked, the first two rules "flip back and forth" between the two queries $EVEN$ and ODD. At each point in this computation, the predicate $EVEN$ is true iff the set of unmarked elements has even parity. The third and fifth rules terminate the recursion, stating that $EVEN$ is true when there are no unmarked elements left.

[1]It is worthwhile noting that this problem cannot be solved in Datalog (function-free Horn logic) even when stratified negation is allowed [8].

Example 7. Suppose that DB is a database representing a directed graph. That is, $NODE(a) \in DB$ iff a is a node in the graph, and $EDGE(a, b) \in DB$ iff there is an edge in the graph from a to b. Suppose also that R is the following stratified rulebase:

$$YES \leftarrow SELECT(x),\ [PATH(x) \Leftarrow MARK(x)].$$
$$PATH(x) \leftarrow SELECT(y),\ EDGE(x,y),\ [PATH(y) \Leftarrow MARK(y)].$$
$$PATH(x) \leftarrow \sim SOMELEFT.$$
$$SOMELEFT \leftarrow SELECT(x).$$
$$SELECT(x) \leftarrow NODE(x),\ \sim MARK(x).$$

Then $R, DB \vdash YES$ iff the graph represented by DB has a directed Hamiltonian path. □

The rulebase in this example is best understood from the top-down perspective. During inference, the rulebase tries to construct a Hamiltonian path one node at a time. The first rule selects a node x at which the path is to begin. The second rule is then applied repeatedly, selecting a node y connected by an edge to the last node in the path. Each time a node is selected, it is marked. In this way, no node is selected twice. The third and fourth rules say that a Hamiltonian path has been found when every node has been marked, that is, when every node has been visited exactly once. Note that node selection is non-deterministic, so in effect, the rulebase searches the graph for all possible Hamiltonian paths.

It is the ability to record facts, such as which nodes are marked, that distinguishes this logic from (function free) Horn logic and accounts for its computational complexity [2, 4].

In [12], Harland develops a semantics for intuitionistic embedded implications augmented with negation-as-failure. The two examples above highlight the differences between Harland's treatment and our own. Harland's approach does not depend on stratification, and assigns a meaning even to the rule: $A \leftarrow \sim A$. On the other hand, Harland's semantics cannot handle the rulebases above. To see this, we need to examine the operational semantics in [12] more closely. Harland draws a distinction between "completely defined" predicates, such as $APPEND$, and "incompletely defined" predicates, such as $CARCINOGEN$. Negation-as-failure is available only for completely defined predicates, while goals must have incompletely defined predicates in their premises. But look at the definition of $EVEN$ and ODD in Example 6 above. The predicate $MARK$ appears inside the negation-as-failure symbol in the fifth rule, and yet it also appears in the premise of a goal in the first two rules. This dual role for the predicate $MARK$ is crucial. A similar observation applies to the rulebase that computes Hamiltonian paths in Example 7, and to the Turing machine encodings that are needed for the expressibility results in [2, 4]. It does not appear that these rulebases would be handled correctly by Harland's semantics. Note, however, that the rules in Examples 1 and 2 of Section 2 cause no such problems. This suggests that it may be useful to develop distinct semantic theories for distinct species of negation.

4 Model-Theoretic Semantics

Section 3 provided a proof-theoretic development of intuitionistic logic programming with negation-as-failure. This section provides a model-theoretic development.

In classical Horn logic programming, the semantics is truly classical only in the negation-free case. When negation is introduced, new semantic devices are needed to account for the non-monotonicity of the resulting system. A common approach, due to Przymusinski, is to introduce a preference relation on the classical models of the rulebase, and then to focus on the most preferred, or *perfect*, models [20]. It is now well known that stratified Horn rulebases have a unique perfect model [20].

Similarly, in intuitionistic logic programming, the semantics is truly intuitionistic only in the negation-free case. When negation is introduced, a natural approach would be to introduce a preference relation on intuitionistic models to account for the non-monotonicity. When we attempt to do this, however, two difficulties emerge. First, a preference relation by itself does not fully account for non-monotonicity. Second, because intuitionistic logic is not a two-valued logic (i.e., it lacks the law of the excluded middle), the preference relation developed in [20] is not strong enough. The rest of this section addresses these two difficulties and proposes novel solutions.

This first section below provides a brief development of intuitionistic semantics. The following sections then show how this semantics can be modified to account for negation-as-failure.

4.1 Intuitionistic Semantics

The following is a simplified development of the Kripke semantics of intuitionistic logic. A complete development may be found in [9, 13].

Definition 4.1 (Structures) *An intuitionistic structure is a triple* $M = \langle S, \leq, \pi \rangle$, *where*

- S *is a non-empty set,*
- $\leq$ *is a transitive, reflexive relation on* S,
- π *is a mapping from elements of* S *to sets of ground atomic formulas,*
- *for any two elements* s_1 *and* s_2 *in* S, *if* $s_1 \leq s_2$ *then* $\pi(s_1) \subseteq \pi(s_2)$.

The elements of S *are called the substates of* M.

In a complete development of intuitionistic semantics, each substate may have its own distinct domain of constant symbols. We have assumed here, however, that the domain of each substate is equal to the universe of all constant symbols. In [6], we show that for embedded implications, these are the only kind of structures that one needs to consider. We continue to use these simplified structures in this paper, since they simplify the theoretical development.

Truth in an intuitionistic structure M is defined relative to its substates. Thus, one can ask whether a formula ψ is true at a particular substate s of M, written $s, M \models \psi$. The following definition makes this idea precise.

Definition 4.2 (Satisfaction) *Suppose M is an intuitionistic structure and s is a substate of M. Then,*

$$
\begin{array}{llll}
s, M \models A & \textit{iff} & A \in \pi(s) & \textit{when } A \textit{ is atomic.} \\
s, M \models \psi_1 \wedge \psi_2 & \textit{iff} & s, M \models \psi_1 \ \textit{and} \ s, M \models \psi_2 & \\
s, M \models \forall_x \psi(x) & \textit{iff} & r, M \models \psi(b) \ \textit{for all } r \geq s & \\
 & & \textit{and all constant symbols } b. & \\
s, M \models \psi_2 \leftarrow \psi_1 & \textit{iff} & r, M \models \psi_1 \ \textit{implies} \ r, M \models \psi_2 & \textit{for all } r \geq s
\end{array}
$$

Note that unlike classical logic, intuitionistic implication is not defined in terms of disjunction and negation. Rather, it has an independent semantic definition. An intuitive interpretation of this semantics may be found in [13] and [9].

Definition 4.3 (Models) $M \models \psi$ *iff* $s, M \models \psi$ *for all substates s of M. If $M \models \psi$, then M is a model of ψ.*

Definition 4.4 (Validity) *A formula ψ is valid iff $M \models \psi$ for all intuitionistic structures M.*

Definition 4.5 (Entailment) *Suppose ψ_1 and ψ_2 are formulas. Then $\psi_1 \models \psi_2$ iff the formula $\psi_2 \leftarrow \psi_1$ is valid.*

The following theorem is a central result of [6]:

Theorem 4.1 (Soundness and Completeness) *Let R be a negation-free rulebase and ϕ be a goal. Then $R \vdash \phi$ iff $R \models \phi$.*

4.2 Non-Monotonic Structures

In the tradition of logic programming, we would like to identify a single model that characterizes all the inferences sanctioned by a rulebase R. That is, we would like to find a single intuitionistic structure M_R that is a model of R and for which $M_R \models \phi$ iff $R \vdash \phi$ for all goals ϕ. We call such a structure a *canonical model* of R. In [6], it is shown that negation-free rulebases have a canonical intuitionistic model.

When intuitionistic logic is augmented with negation-as-failure, it is not possible to construct a canonical model. Let us forget for the moment that we have introduced two types of implication in the proof theory of stratified rulebases. Suppose that R is the rulebase consisting of the single rule $A \leftarrow B, \sim C$. Then $R \vdash A \leftarrow B$ but $R \not\vdash A \leftarrow B, C$. For any intuitionistic structure M, however, if $M \models A \leftarrow B$ then $M \models A \leftarrow B, C$. In general, therefore, a stratified rulebase does not have a canonical, intuitionistic model.

The problem is that intuitionistic structures are "biased" towards monotonicity. This is due to the fourth item in Definition 4.1. This could be called the *monotonicity condition*: Intuitively, it requires that substates get larger monotonically as they get higher in the structure. The simplest way of eliminating the monotonic "bias" in intuitionistic structures is to eliminate this condition. We say that the resulting structures are non-monotonic.

Definition 4.6 (Structures) *A non-monotonic structure is a triple* $M = \langle S, \leq, \pi \rangle$, *where*

- S *is a non-empty set,*
- $\leq$ *is a transitive, reflexive relation on* S,
- π *is a mapping from elements of* S *to sets of ground atomic formulas.*

The elements of S *are called the substates of* M.

Note that intuitionistic structures are a special case of non-monotonic structures. For brevity, we often refer to non-monotonic structures simply as *structures*. We shall show that every stratified rulebase has a canonical, non-monotonic structure. First, however, we must define what it means for a non-monotonic structure to be a model of a stratified rulebase.

4.3 Non-Monotonic Satisfaction

In Section 3, we argued that stratified rulebases really demand two types of implication: Implications of the form $A \leftarrow B$ to denote rules, and implications of the form $A \Leftarrow B$ to denote goals. The inference systems in Definitions 3.1 and 3.5 treat these two forms of implication differently. Inference rule 1 deals with rules, and inference rule 2 deals with goals. It is an interesting coincidence that in the negation-free case, rules and goals have the same semantic interpretation, i.e., they both correspond to intuitionistic implication. The situation with stratified rulebases is more complex. We have already shown that rules and goals have different proof-theoretic properties. They must, therefore, have different semantic definitions.

This section defines a notion of satisfaction for non-monotonic structures. There are a number of equivalent ways to do this. The formulation below is chosen because of its similarity to classical logic. In particular, except for $\Leftarrow$, every logical connective has a classical interpretation. The connective $\Leftarrow$ can thus be viewed as a modal operator that causes inference to shift from one classical world to another. For instance, to determine whether $s, M \models A \Leftarrow B$, we move to the closest worlds above s in which B is true, and then we ask whether A is true in these worlds. The idea of "closest", or minimal, worlds captures the non-monotonic nature of the connective $\Leftarrow$. The semantics of the two connectives $\leftarrow$ and $\Leftarrow$ are thus quite different.

Definition 4.7 (Satisfaction) *Suppose that* $M = \langle S, \leq, \pi \rangle$ *is a non-monotonic structure and that* s *is a substate of* M. *Then*

$s, M \models A$	*iff*	$A \in \pi(s)$, *when* A *is atomic.*
$s, M \models \psi_1 \wedge \psi 2$	*iff*	$s, M \models \psi_1$ *and* $s, M \models \psi_2$.
$s, M \models \sim \psi$	*iff*	$s, M \not\models \psi$
$s, M \models \forall_x \psi(x)$	*iff*	$s, M \models \psi(b)$ *for all constant symbols* b.
$s, M \models \psi_2 \leftarrow \psi_1$	*iff*	$s, M \models \psi_1$ *implies* $s, M \models \psi_2$.
$s, M \models \psi_2 \Leftarrow \psi_1$	*iff*	$r, M \models \psi_2$ *for all minimal substates* $r \geq s$ *such that* $r, M \models \Box\psi_1$.
$s, M \models \Box\psi$	*iff*	$r, M \models \psi$ *for all substates* $r \geq s$.

In this definition, we have introduced a convenient box notation. Intuitively, anything that is "boxed" represents a monotonic truth: If $\Box\phi$ is true at a substate s, then it remains true as we climb to higher substates. This corresponds to the proof-theoretic notion of adding a formula to a rulebase: If B is added to a rulebase R, then B remains true no matter how many other formulas we add to R. In this way, the semantic notion of minimal substates corresponds nicely to the proof-theoretic notion of hypothetical insertion.

Definition 4.8 (Models) *Let M be a non-monotonic structure. Then*

- *If ϕ is a goal, then $M \models \phi$ iff $s, M \models \phi$ for all minimal substates s of M.*
- *If ψ is a rule, then $M \models \psi$ iff $s, M \models \psi$ for all substates s of M.*

If $M \models \psi$, then we say that M is a *model* of ψ. M is a model of a rulebase R iff it is a model of every rule in R.

Because of its emphasis on minimal substates, this semantics differs from intuitionistic semantics in several important respects. First, it is not monotonic. That is, if $M \models \phi$ then it is not necessarily the case that $M \models \phi \Leftarrow \psi$. This is exactly the kind of behavior that we want to capture. Second, a non-monotonic structure may be inconsistent: If M has no minimal substates, then $M \models (\sim \phi \wedge \phi)$ for all goals ϕ. Such inconsistencies will exist if, for instance, M consists of an infinite descending chain of substates with no minimal element. Even if M has minimal substates, a subtler inconsistency may exist. For instance, if M has no substates such that $M \models \Box\psi$, then $M \models (\sim \phi \wedge \phi) \Leftarrow \psi$ for all formulas ϕ. These considerations prompt the following definition.

Definition 4.9 (Inconsistency) *A structure M is inconsistent iff $M \models \phi \Leftarrow \psi$ and $M \models (\sim \phi) \Leftarrow \psi$ for some goal $\phi \Leftarrow \psi$. M is consistent iff it is not inconsistent.*

The following lemma is a basic result about consistency.

Lemma 4.2 *A structure M is consistent iff for every database DB, there is a minimal substate s of M for which the set $\{r \geq s \mid r, M \models \Box DB\}$ has a minimal element.*

4.4 Preferred Models

Section 4.2 defined a generalization of intuitionistic structures, called non-monotonic structures. Section 4.3 then defined what it means for such a structure to be a model of a stratified rulebase. This section defines a preference relation on structures. Development of a preference relation is the final step in the semantics of stratified Horn rulebases, and it is also the final step in the semantics of stratified, intuitionistic rulebases.

In the perfect model semantics of stratified Horn rulebases, the preference relation minimizes the number of true atomic facts in a disciplined way.

First, those atoms defined in the lowest stratum of the rulebase are minimized; then those defined in the second-lowest stratum are minimized; then those in the third-lowest stratum, etc. This process is a generalized version of the closed world assumption.

In Horn logic programming, it is natural to minimize atomic facts, since these are the only inferences that one makes. In intuitionistic logic programming, however, one infers a more general class of formulas, including goals of the form $A \Leftarrow B$. It is therefore natural to generalize the notion of minimizing atoms to that of minimizing positive goals.

It turns out, however, that minimizing positive goals is not enough. In classical logic, minimizing the set of true atoms automatically maximizes the number of false atoms. This is because, in a classical structure, an atom is either true or false. In a non-monotonic structure, however, an atom may be neither true nor false: It may be true in some minimal substates of the structure, and false in others. For this reason, our preference relation must do two things simultaneously: It must minimize positive goals and maximize negative goals. Furthermore, it must do this stratum by stratum, from the bottom up. These ideas are formalized by the following definitions.

Definition 4.10 (Projection) *Suppose G is a set of goals. Then $G|_j$ is the set of goals in G whose head predicates belong to the jth stratum. In addition, $G|_j^+$ and $G|_j^-$ denote the positive and negative goals in $G|_j$, resp.*

Using this notation, we define a preference relation on sets of goals. Within each stratum, this relation prefers the set that has the fewest positive goals and the most negative goals. Furthermore, the comparison is lexicographic in that two sets of goals are compared at the jth stratum only if they are identical at all lower strata. In this way, lower strata are given higher priority.

Definition 4.11 (Preference) *Let G and H be two sets of goals. Then $G \preceq H$ iff for each stratum j,*

$$\begin{array}{ll} \textit{if} & G|_i = H|_i \ \textit{for all} \ 1 \leq i < j, \\ \textit{then} & G|_j^+ \subseteq H|_j^+ \ \textit{and} \ H|_j^- \subseteq G|_j^-. \end{array}$$

Note that $\preceq$ is transitive and reflexive and that $G = H$ iff $G \preceq H$ and $H \preceq G$. This preference relation on sets of goals induces a preference relation on structures, as follows.

Definition 4.12 *If M is a structure, then goals(M) denotes the set of goals satisfied by M. That is, goals$(M) = \{\phi \mid M \models \phi\}$, where each ϕ is a goal.*

Definition 4.13 *Let M_1 and M_2 be two structures. Then, $M_1 \preceq M_2$ iff goals$(M_1) \preceq$ goals(M_2). In addition, $M_1 \simeq M_2$ iff $M_1 \preceq M_2$ and $M_2 \preceq M_1$.*

Note that $\preceq$ is a transitive, reflexive relation on structures and that $\simeq$ is an equivalence relation. Two structures are equivalent iff they satisfy exactly the same goals. If $M_1 \preceq M_2$ then we say that M_1 is *preferable* to M_2. As in the perfect model semantics of stratified Horn rulebases, we focus on the minimal elements of this relation.

Definition 4.14 (Preferred Models) *Let R be a stratified rulebase, and let $\mathcal{M}_R$ be the set of consistent models of R. A preferred model of R is a minimal element of $\mathcal{M}_R$, that is, minimal with respect to the preference relation $\preceq$.*

The following definition completes our generalization of the classical, perfect-model semantics.

Definition 4.15 (Entailment) *Let R be a stratified rulebase and ϕ be a goal. Then $R \models \phi$ iff $M \models \phi$ for all preferred models M of R.*

5 Soundness and Completeness

We have now assembled the main components of our theory of intuitionistic logic programming augmented by negation-as-failure: (*i*) the inference system of Section 3, and (*ii*) the semantics of Section 4. The remaining task is to equate these two components by proving a soundness and completeness theorem.

We do this in two steps: We first construct a *canonical model*, M_R, of a stratified rulebase R. We then show that the canonical model M_R is a preferred model of R, and, up to equivalence, the only preferred model of R. Soundness and completeness then follow immediately. Because of space limitations, all proofs are omitted. The interested reader is referred to [5] for details.

To construct the canonical model, we first define a box notation for our inference system analogous to the box notation introduced in Section 4.3.

Definition 5.1 (Monotonic Inference) *Let R be a stratified rulebase and let ϕ be a closed goal. Then $R \vdash \Box\phi$ iff $R + DB \vdash \phi$ for all databases DB. If Φ is a set of goals, then $R \vdash \Box\Phi$ iff $R \vdash \Box\phi$ for each goal $\phi \in \Phi$.*

Note that if $R \vdash \Box\phi$ then $R + DB \vdash \Box\phi$ for any database DB. For this reason, if $R \vdash \Box\phi$ then we say that R *infers ϕ monotonically*. We use monotonic inference to define a binary relation on databases. We then use this relation to construct a non-monotonic structure M_R, which we call the *canonical model* of the stratified rulebase R.

Definition 5.2 *Let R be a stratified rulebase and let DB_1 and DB_2 be two databases. $DB_2 \geq DB_1$ iff $R + DB_2 \vdash \Box DB_1$.*

Definition 5.3 (Canonical Model) *Let R be a stratified rulebase. The canonical model of R is the tuple $M_R = \langle S, \leq, \pi \rangle$, where*

$$S = \textit{The set of all databases.}$$

$$\leq \textit{ is the binary relation given by Definition 5.2.}$$

$$\pi(DB) = \{B \mid R + DB \vdash B \textit{ where } B \textit{ is atomic}\}$$

It is not hard to show that $\leq$ is transitive and reflexive [5]. The canonical model is therefore a valid, non-monotonic structure, by Definition 4.6. The following theorem is our first major result about canonical models.

Theorem 5.1 *Let R be a stratified rulebase. Then for any goal ϕ,*

$$R + DB \vdash \phi \quad \textit{iff} \quad DB, M_R \models \phi$$

Corollary 5.2 *The canonical model M_R is a model of R.*

Corollary 5.3 $M_R \models \phi$ *iff* $R \vdash \phi$ *for all goals ϕ.*

Using Corollary 5.3, we get the theorem below, which is our second major result about canonical models.

Theorem 5.4 *Suppose that N is a model of a stratified rulebase R such that $goals(M_R)|_i = goals(N)|_i$ for all $1 \leq i < j$. Then $goals(M_R)|_j^+ \subseteq goals(N)|_j^+$.*

Theorem 5.4 gives us half of what we need to prove that M_R is a preferred model of R. In addition, we need to show that $goals(N)|_j^- \subseteq goals(M_R)|_j^-$. The notion of consistent models makes this task possible.

Lemma 5.5 *Suppose that N is a consistent model of R such that $goals(M_R)|_j^+ \subseteq goals(N)|_j^+$. Then $goals(N)|_j^- \subseteq goals(M_R)|_j^-$.*

The following result is an immediate consequence of Theorem 5.4 and lemma 5.5.

Corollary 5.6 *If N is a consistent model of R, then $M_R \preceq N$.*

Corollary 5.6 shows that the canonical model M_R is a preferred model of R. Thus, every stratified rulebase has at least one preferred model. Furthermore, if N is any other preferred model of R, then $N \simeq M_R$. Thus, up to equivalence, the canonical model is the *unique* preferred model of R. Soundness and completeness follow immediately from of this uniqueness.

Corollary 5.7 (Soundness and Completeness) *Let R be a stratified rulebase and ϕ be a goal. Then* $R \vdash \phi$ *iff* $R \models \phi$.

6 Conclusion

This paper has developed a semantics for the addition of stratified negation-as-failure to intuitionistic logic programming, as a complement to the proof-theoretic treatment in our earlier work [2, 4, 6]. Several difficulties were encountered along the way, and overcome. Problems pointed out by Gabbay in [10] were handled by drawing a distinction between rules: $A \leftarrow B$, and goals: $A \Leftarrow B$. The "bias" of intuitionistic Kripke structures towards monotonic rules was handled simply by dropping the monotonicity condition, and satisfaction in non-monotonic structures was then defined separately for the connectives $\leftarrow$ and $\Leftarrow$. Our basic approach was inspired by Przymusinski's perfect model semantics for stratified Horn-clause logic [20], but with various modifications dictated by the intuitionistic setting. Thus, we defined a preference ordering on non-monotonic structures that minimizes positive goals and maximizes negative goals simultaneously, a more complex criterion than was needed in classical logic. Finally, we defined the semantics of a rule base R in terms of the preferred models of R, and we proved a soundness and completeness theorem using this definition. Note that the class of rules for which this approach works, namely, stratified intuitionistic rulebases, as given by Definition 3.3, is exactly the class of rules needed for the expressibility results in [2, 4]. Harland's proposal for the semantics of negation-as-failure [12], discussed in Sections 1 and 3.5, is complementary to our proposal in this respect.

There are several directions in which the work of the present paper might be extended. First, the logic could be extended to include function symbols. The development in this paper assumes that the logic includes constants but no function symbols. Since we allow the set of constants to be infinite, however, incorporating function symbols without equality, as in Prolog, should be straightforward. See [14, 15] for an example of how this might be done. Second, the requirement that an intuitionistic rulebase be globally stratified could be relaxed to the requirement of *local stratification* [20]. In fact, the rules in Example 2 are not globally stratified, since a relative clause may appear inside the derivation of a sentence, but such rules would be locally stratified by virtue of the usual constraints on string positions. This extension to locally stratified rulebases also seems straightforward. Third, although the full language of intuitionistic logic programming described in [14, 15, 6] includes embedded universal quantifiers, we have considered in this paper only the restricted (and decidable!) sublanguage in which universal quantification is confined to the top level of the rules. Adding negation-as-failure to the full language raises additional problems, and requires another subtle adjustment of the semantics. We will develop these ideas further in subsequent papers.

References

[1] K.R. Apt, H.A. Blair, and A. Walker. Towards a Theory of Declarative Knowledge. In Jack Minker, editor, *Foundations of Deductive Databases and Logic Programming*, chapter 2, pages 89–148. Morgan Kaufmann, 1988.

[2] A.J. Bonner. Hypothetical Datalog: Complexity and Expressibility. To appear in a special issue of *Theoretical Computer Science (TCS)*. Also appears in abridged form in volume 326 of *Lecture Notes in Computer Science*, pages 144–160. Springer Verlag, 1988.

[3] A.J. Bonner. A Logic for Hypothetical Reasoning. In *Proceedings of the Seventh National Conference on Artificial Intelligence*, Saint Paul, Minnesota, August 21–26 1988. American Association for Artificial Intelligence (AAAI). Published in expanded form as Technical Report TR-DCS-230, Department of Computer Science, Rutgers University, New Brunswick, NJ 08903.

[4] A.J. Bonner. Hypothetical Datalog: Negation and Linear Recursion. In *Proceedings of the ACM Symposium on the Principles of Database Systems (PODS)*, pages 286–300, Philadelphia, PA, March 1989.

[5] A.J. Bonner and L.T. McCarty. Adding Negation-as-Failure to Intuitionistic Logic Programming. Technical report, Department of Computer Science, Rutgers University, New Brunswick, NJ 08903, 1990.

[6] A.J. Bonner, L.T. McCarty, and K. Vadaparty. Expressing Database Queries with Intuitionistic Logic. In *Proceedings of the North American Conference on*

Logic Programming (NACLP), pages 831–850, Cleveland, Ohio, October 16–20 1989.

[7] A.K. Chandra and D. Harel. Computable Queries for Relational Databases. *Journal of Computer and System Sciences (JCSS)*, 21(2):156–178, 1980.

[8] A.K. Chandra and D. Harel. Structure and Complexity of Relational Queries. *Journal of Computer and System Sciences (JCSS)*, 25(1):99–128, 1982.

[9] M.C. Fitting. *Intuitionistic Logic, Model Theory and Forcing.* North-Holland, 1969.

[10] D.M. Gabbay. N-Prolog: an Extension of Prolog with Hypothetical Implications. II. Logical Foundations and Negation as Failure. *Journal of Logic Programming*, 2(4):251–283, 1985.

[11] D.M. Gabbay and U. Reyle. N-Prolog: an Extension of Prolog with Hypothetical Implications. I. *Journal of Logic Programming (JLP)*, 1(4):319–355, 1984.

[12] J. Harland. A Kripke-like model for negation as failure. In *Proceedings of the North American Conference on Logic Programming (NACLP)*, pages 626–642, Cleveland, Ohio, October 16–20 1989.

[13] S. Kripke. Semantical Analysis of Intuitionistic Logic. I. In J.N. Crossley and M.A.E. Dummett, editors, *Formal Systems and Recursive Functions*, pages 92–130. North Holland, Amsterdam, 1965.

[14] L.T. McCarty. Clausal Intuitionistic Logic. I. Fixed-Point Semantics. *Journal of Logic Programming (JLP)*, 5(1):1–31, 1988.

[15] L.T. McCarty. Clausal Intuitionistic Logic. II. Tableau Proof Procedures. *Journal of Logic Programming (JLP)*, 5(2):93–132, 1988.

[16] L.T. McCarty. A Language for Legal Discourse. I. Basic Features. In *Proceedings of the Second International Conference on Artificial Intelligence and Law*, pages 180–189. ACM Press, June 1989.

[17] D. Miller. A Logical Analysis of Modules in Logic Programming. *Journal of Logic Programming (JLP)*, 6:79–108, 1989.

[18] D. Miller. Lexical scoping as universal quantification. In G. Levi and M. Martelli, editors, *Logic Programming: Proceedings of the Sixth International Conference*, pages 268–283, Cambridge, MA, 1989. MIT Press.

[19] R. Pareschi. A definite clause version of categorial grammar. In *Proceedings, 26th Annual Meeting of the Association for Computational Linguistics*, pages 270–277, Buffalo, NY, June 1988.

[20] T. Przymusinski. On the Declarative Semantics of Deductive Databases and Logic Programs. In Jack Minker, editor, *Foundations of Deductive Databases and Logic Programming*, chapter 5, pages 193–216. Morgan Kaufmann, 1988.

On Constructive Negation for Disjunctive Logic Programs

Jorge Lobo
Institute for Advanced Computer Studies
University of Maryland
College Park, Maryland 20742
jorge@cs.umd.edu

Abstract
Answers for queries in logic programs, can be seen as formulas involving only equality and inequality predicates. This representation permits the extension of proof-procedures as SLDNF-resolution to handle non-ground negative queries. In this paper, we extend these ideas to the class of disjunctive logic programs.
Keywords: Theory, Constructive Negation, Disjunctive programs.

1 Introduction

Procedural interpretations for rules of negation in logic programming generally have been confined to ground literals [2, 19]. The restriction is imposed since answers for queries provided by these procedures are based solely on substitutions and most general unifiers. However, recently a new approach to the form of an answer, termed constructive negation [3], has permitted the extension of some of these procedures to more general queries. The underlying idea behind this new technique is to answer queries using formulas involving only the equality predicate. To illustrate the approach, consider the program $P = \{p(X) \leftarrow \neg q(X);\ q(X) \leftarrow r(X);\ r(a);\ r(b)\}$. We know that $q(X)$ is true either when $X = a$ or $X = b$. Then, a possible answer for $q(X)$ may be the equality formula $X = a \vee X = b$. In the case of p, $p(X)$ will be true whenever $q(X)$ is false. Using the Negation as Failure rule [4] we are able to conclude that $q(X)$ is false if X is bound to a term not equal to a and not equal to b. From this information, we conclude that a possible answer for $p(X)$ may be the equality formula $X \neq a \wedge X \neq b$. In general, given a (positive) logic program P and a query $Q(X_1, \ldots, X_m)$, a correct answer substitution θ for Q can be transformed to the equality formula:

$$E_\theta = (X_1 = X_1\theta \wedge \cdots \wedge X_m = X_m\theta)$$

which indicates that $P \models \forall(E_\theta \Rightarrow Q)$. We refer to E_θ as a partial answer for Q. A *full answer* for the query is an equality formula E_Q such that E_Q satisfies the condition: $P \models \forall(E_Q \equiv Q)$ (see [15] for more details of partial and full answers). For general (sometimes referred to as normal) programs, individual and full answers can also involve inequalities as the previous example shows. For disjunctive logic programs the situation is slightly more complex. In this case, we can have a situation where no individual answer can be given as a simple substitution over variables occurring in the query. For example, given the program $\{p(a) \vee p(b)\}$ and the query $Q(X) \equiv p(X)$, an answer for Q can be described making multiple copies of the query to answer with the formula $X = a \wedge Y = b \Rightarrow Q(X) \vee Q(Y)$, and there is no "simpler" formula that represents a possible answer for Q. An alternative reading of the answer is $P \models \forall X(X = a \Rightarrow Q(X)) \vee \forall X(X = b \Rightarrow Q(X))$. This representation does not introduce new variable names for the query. In the next section we present some basic definitions and a precise description for queries and answers in disjunctive programs. We also describe how we use constructive negation to answer queries that involve negated atoms in positive disjunctive programs. In Section 3, we extend the concepts to stratified disjunctive programs. Section 4 contains some concluding remarks.

2 Negation in Positive Programs

A disjunctive logic program P consists of a finite set of universally quantified clauses of the form $A_1 \vee \cdots \vee A_n \leftarrow B_1, \ldots, B_m$, where $n \geq 1$, $m \geq 0$ and the As and Bs are atoms. $A_1 \vee \cdots \vee A_n$ is called the head of the clause and $B_1, \ldots, B_m$ is called the body. The definition of a predicate Q in a program P is the set of clauses in P such that Q appears in the head of the clauses. Given two terms t_1 and t_2, an equality literal is either a literal of the form $t_1 = t_2$ or a formula of the form $\forall(t_1 \neq t_2)$, where $\forall$ quantifies some (perhaps none) of the variables occurring in t_1 and t_2 [3]. We consider *true* and *false* especial cases of equality literals. These equality literals are called positive and negative equality literals respectively. Given a substitution θ for the free variables in the negative literal $\forall(t_1 \neq t_2)$, $\forall(t_1 \neq t_2)\theta$ is valid if and only if $t_1\theta$ and $t_2\theta$ are not unifiable. $\forall(t_1 \neq t_2)\theta$ is satisfiable but not valid if free variables have to be bound in the literal to make $t_1\theta$ and $t_2\theta$ not unifiable. By Clark's Equational Theory for a program P ($CET(P)$) we refer to the following set of universally quantified axioms:

$X = X$.

$X = Y \Rightarrow Y = X$.

$X_1 = Y_1 \wedge \cdots \wedge X_n = Y_n \Rightarrow (f(X_1, \ldots, X_n) = f(Y_1, \ldots, Y_n))$ for each function symbol f in the language of P.

$X_1 = Y_1 \wedge \cdots \wedge X_n = Y_n \Rightarrow (p(X_1, \ldots, X_n) \equiv p(Y_1, \ldots, Y_n))$ for each predicate symbol p in the language of P.

$f(X_1, \ldots, X_n) \neq g(Y_1, \ldots, Y_n)$ for each pair of distinct function symbols f and g in the language of P.

$t \neq X$ for each term t different from X in which X occurs.

Similar to Horn programs, we use metarules of negation like the Closed World Assumption (CWA) to derive negative information from disjunctive programs. In this paper we describe constructive negation for disjunctive programs based on the Generalized Closed World Assumption (GCWA) of

Minker [9], a sound rule of negation for disjunctive programs.

Definition 2.1 *([9])*
Given a program P. The set of negated ground atoms assumed to be true under the generalized closed world assumption is the set:
$GCWA(P)=\{\neg A : A \in HB(P) \mid$ *for every (possibly empty) positive ground clause* C, *if* $P \models (A \vee C)$ *then* $P \models C\}$. □

Minker and Rajasekar define in [10, 11] a more constructive (procedural) definition of a rule of negation based on the GCWA called Support-for-Negation[1]. Before presenting the rule we need some definitions.

Definition 2.2 *[12]***(SNgoal)**
A SNgoal is a clause of the form :
$C \leftarrow A_1, \ldots, A_n$ *where* $n \geq 0$ *and* C *is a positive (possibly empty) clause and the* A_i *are atoms. If* $n = 0$ *a SNgoal is called a bottom-SNgoal* □

Definition 2.3 *[12]***(SN-derivation)**
Let P *be a disjunctive logic program,* $G = C \leftarrow A_1, \ldots, A_m, \ldots A_k$ *be a SNgoal. A SN-derivation from* P *with top-SNgoal* G *consists of a (possibly infinite) sequence of SNgoals* $G_0 = G, G_1, \ldots$ *such that for all* $i \geq 0$, G_{i+1} *is obtained from* G_i *as follows:*

(1) A_m *is an atom in the body of* G_i. A_m *is called the selected atom.*
(2) $C' \vee A \leftarrow B_1, \ldots, B_q$ *is a program clause in* P
(3) $A_m\theta = A\theta$ *where* θ *is a substitution (most general)*
(4) G_{i+1} *is the SNgoal*
$(C \vee C' \leftarrow A_1, \ldots, A_{m-1}, B_1, \ldots, B_q, A_{m+1}, \ldots, A_k)\theta$ □

Definition 2.4 *[12]***(SN-refutation)**
An SN-refutation from P *with top-SNgoal* G *is a finite SN-derivation* $G_0 = G, G_1, \ldots, G_n$ *of a bottom-SNgoal* G_n. *Let* θ_i, $i > 0$, *the substitution applied at step i of the refutation. We say that* θ *is the substitution associated with the refutation if* θ *is the composition of substitutions* $\theta_1 \cdots \theta_n$. □

Definition 2.5 *[12]***(SN set)**
Let P *be a disjunctive program and* A *be a ground atom. The Support-for-Negation set of* A *with respect to the program* P *is defined by:*
$SN(A, P) = \{C \mid C$ *is the bottom-SNgoal in an SN-refutation from* P *with top-SNgoal* $G = \leftarrow A\ \}$ □

In [12] SNgoal, SN-derivation, SN-refutation and SN set are referred as DC-goal, SLOC-derivation, SLOC-refutation and SNSLOC respectively.

Assume we would like to know if a ground atom A can be deduced to be false from a program P using the Support-for-Negation rule. Then, it is

[1]The description of Support-for-Negation that we present here is a simpler definition presented first in [12]

sufficient to show that for every clause C in $SN(A, P)$, C is provable from P, given that all the clauses in $SN(A, P)$ are ground. The following theorem establishes the relation between the GCWA and the Support-for-Negation rule.

Theorem 1 *[12]*
Given a disjunctive program P and a ground atom A. If we can assume $\neg A$ using the Support-for-Negation rule then $\neg A \in GCWA(P)$. □

The SN set reduces the number of clauses to be checked before concluding if a ground atom can be assumed to be false using the GCWA.

Queries in general Horn programs are universally quantified clauses of the form $\leftarrow L_1, \ldots, L_n$ where the L_s are literals. Since we are dealing with disjunctive programs one might believe that a more general type of query is necessary. However, any query of the form $\leftarrow F$ where F is any first order formula can be transformed easily into a query $\leftarrow L_1, \ldots, L_n$ in a modified program P obtained from the original program and F (see [6]). To simplify presentation we restrict our queries to a conjunction of literals.

Definition 2.6 *A query $Q(X_1, \ldots, X_m)$ is a formula of the form $L_1 \wedge \cdots \wedge L_n$ where the L_i are literals and $X_1, \ldots, X_m$ are the only free variables that occur in the query. A query is positive if all the L_i are atomic formulas.* □

Answers for a query depend directly upon the semantics associated with the logic program. If we parametrize the semantics we can develop a general theory of correct answers for a query independent of the semantics associated with the program. This requires the definition of what we consider an appropriate semantics for a logic program. Such a definition of semantics was given by Przymusinski in [15].

Definition 2.7 ([15]) *A semantics $Sem(P)$ for a program P is a set of first order sentences such that:* $\quad Sem(P) \models P \cup CET(P)$. □

In the case of disjunctive programs, the concept of full answer as described in the introduction is too strong. There are many queries without full answers but with answers that completely characterize the query with respect to the semantics chosen for the program. Moreover, the concept of an answer has to be adapted to cover the presence of indefinite information where not all answers can be represented as a unique substitution for some variables in the query.

Definition 2.8 *Let P be a disjunctive program and $Sem(P)$ be the semantics associated with P. An answer to a query $Q(X_1, \ldots, X_n)$ is a set of equality formulas $E_Q = \{E_1, \ldots, E_m\}$ such that $Sem(P) \models \forall X_1, \ldots, X_n(E_1 \Rightarrow Q) \vee \cdots \vee \forall X_1, \ldots, X_n(E_m \Rightarrow Q)$. We denote the formula $\forall X_1, \ldots, X_n(E_1 \Rightarrow Q) \vee \cdots \vee \forall X_1, \ldots, X_n(E_m \Rightarrow Q)$ by $\overline{E_Q \Rightarrow Q}$.* □

This definition for answers allows the set $\{false\}$ to be an answer to any query. Indeed, this definition corresponds to partial answers in general Horn programs [15]. Complete answers, defined below, are the counterpart to full answers for general Horn programs.

Definition 2.9 *Let P be a disjunctive program, let $Sem(P)$ be the semantics associated with P, and let E_{Q_1} and E_{Q_2} be two answers for the query $Q(X_1, \ldots, X_n)$. We say that E_{Q_1} is more general than E_{Q_2} ($E_{Q_2} < E_{Q_1}$) iff $(\overline{E_{Q_1}} \Rightarrow Q) \Rightarrow (\overline{E_{Q_2}} \Rightarrow Q)$. An answer E_Q of Q is complete iff for any other answer E of Q, $E < E_Q$. Q is completely definable if it has a complete answer. A program P is completely definable with respect to the semantics $Sem(P)$ if all possible queries are completely definable with respect to $Sem(P)$.* □.

Example 2.1 *For the disjunctive program $P = \{p(a) \vee p(b);\ p(c)\}$, the sets $E_1 = \{false\}$, $E_2 = \{X = a,\ X = b\}$ and $E_3 = \{X = a \vee X = c,\ X = b \vee X = c\}$ are answers for the query $p(X)$, and $E_3 > E_2 > E_1$. E_3 is a complete answer for $p(X)$.* □

A direct result of this definition is that every full answer is complete. In the rest of the paper we assume that the programs are completely definable.

Support-for-Negation suggests a procedure to answer a negative query $\neg A$, where A is a ground atomic formula: From a disjunctive program P, construct the set $SN(A, P)$ by producing all SN-refutations with top-SNgoal $\leftarrow A$ and use any theorem prover to prove that every clause in $SN(A, P)$ is a logical consequence of P. In [10], this procedure is described using SLI-resolution [13] as a theorem prover. In [12] the procedure is defined in terms of SLO-resolution [8]. The effectiveness of these procedures depends upon the size of the set $SN(A, P)$. We want to extend Support-for-Negation to cover more cases and bring the definition closer to the definition of the GCWA. The first extension that we consider will not require clauses in $SN(A, P)$ to be ground. For this extension, we will need to decide whether or not a universally quantified formula is a logical consequence of the program. This leads to a problem discussed by Lloyd in [5] and that Przymusinski refers to as the universal query problem [16]. Suppose we have the program $P = \{p(a),\ q(a),\ q(b)\}$. If we want to prove if $\forall x q(x)$ is a logical consequence of the program based on minimal model semantics we obtain different results if we use only minimal Herbrand models instead of all (not necessarily Herbrand) minimal models. From the minimal Herbrand model of P we can conclude that $\forall x q(x)$ is a logical consequence of P but there are many minimal models of P where $\forall X q(X)$ is false.

Definition 2.10 *A universal query $\forall Q(X_1, \ldots, X_n)$ is the universal closure of the query $Q(X_1, \ldots, X_n, Y_1, \ldots, Y_m)$ over the variables $Y_1, \ldots, Y_m$ with $X_1, \ldots, X_n$ the only free variables occurring in $\forall Q(X_1, \ldots, X_n)$.* □

Here, we are not interested in discussing what semantics is more appropriate to answer universal queries. We will assume that we have a semantics S to answer universal queries based on either minimal models or minimal Herbrand models. Given a positive clause C, if $\forall C$ is a logical consequence of a program P under the semantics S we will write that $S(P) \models \forall C$. Although the GCWA is defined in terms of Herbrand models an alternative definition can be described depending on the semantics used to evaluate universal formulas.

Definition 2.11 *Given a program P and a sound semantics S for universal queries, the set of negated ground atoms assumed to be true under the generalized closed world assumption and S is the set:*
$GCWA_S(P)=\{\neg A : A \in HB(P) \mid$ *for every positive clause* C, *if* $S(P) \models \forall(A \vee C)$ *then* $S(P) \models \forall C\}$. □

This new definition can be applied to extend the Support-for-Negation rule where a ground atom A can be assume to be false if $S(P) \models \forall C$ for each positive clause C in $SN(A, P)$. This extension makes the rule complete with respect to the $GCWA_S$.

Lemma 1 $\neg A \in GCWA_S(P)$ *iff* $S(P) \models \forall C$ *for all* $C \in SN(A, P)$.

Proof: Follows directly from Theorem 1. □

The next extension will lift the restriction of the GCWA to queries with only negated ground atoms. As in constructive negation for general Horn programs, an answer to a query will be an equality formula.

Definition 2.12 *Given a program P and an atom A, the general Support-for-Negation set of A with respect to the program P is defined by:*
$GSN(A, P) = \{(C, \theta) \mid C$ *is the bottom-SNgoal in a SN-refutation from P with top-SNgoal $G = \leftarrow A$ and associated substitution* $\theta\}$ □

The substitutions in the GSN set can be transformed to equality formulas to obtain correct answers for a query as follows.

Example 2.2 *Let P be the disjunctive program* $\{ p(f(X)) \vee q(X), q(a)\}$. *Then,* $GSN(p(Y)) = \{ (q(X), \{Y/f(X)\}) \}$. *A correct answer for the query* $\exists Y \neg p(Y)$ *is* $\{\{\forall X(Y \neq f(X))\}\}$. □

In general, a correct answer for a negative query can be obtained by taking the conjunction of the negation of the equality formulas associated with the substitutions in the GSN set. However, this answer does not correspond to a complete answer for the query. Consider the program and the query in Example 2.2. The answer $\forall X(Y \neq f(X))$ is not a complete answer for $q(X)$ since if $\forall X(Y \neq f(X))$ is *false*, (i.e $Y = f(X)$), and $X = a$ then $\neg q(Y)$ is also a consequence of P and the $GCWA_S(P)$ independent of the semantics S. The complete answer for $\exists Y \neg p(Y)$ is given by $\{\{(\forall X(Y \neq f(X)) \Rightarrow$

$(X = a))\}\}$. This indicates that if the the conjunction of the negation of the equality formulas associated with the substitutions in the GSN set is *false* it is necessary to check for which substitutions the (positive) clauses in the GSN set are *true* and incorporate these substitutions into the answer. The two parts of the answer can be written as an implication.

The *most general substitution set* for a positive clause C, defined below, contains the substitutions for the variables in C that makes the clause *true* with respect to the program.

Definition 2.13 *Let P be a disjunctive logic program. Let $C(Z_1, \ldots, Z_n)$ be a positive clause (possibly) containing the free variables $Z_1, \ldots, Z_n$. Let S be a semantics to evaluate universal queries in P. The* most general substitution set *for C, $\mathcal{MGS}(C(Z_1, \ldots, Z_n))$, is the set of most general substitutions θ over the free variables in C such that*

$$S(P) \vdash \forall C(Z_1, \ldots, Z_n)\theta.$$

□

Example 2.3 *Let $C(X)$ be the clause $p(X, Z) \vee q(Z, X)$ and let P be the program:*

$$\{p(X, f(W)) \leftarrow m(f(W), X);$$
$$m(X, Y) \vee q(X, Y);$$
$$p(X, a) \vee q(a, Y)\}.$$

$\mathcal{MGS}(C(Z)) = \{\{Z/f(W)\}, \{Z/a\}\}$.
If $C(Z)$ is $p(X, Z)$ and the program is $\{p(X, a) \vee p(Y, b)\}$, then $\mathcal{MGS}(C(Z)) = \emptyset$. We assume that we are considering all the minimal models of the programs. □

The next theorem describes how to obtain complete answers from the GSN and the $\mathcal{MGS}$ sets.

Theorem 2 *Let P be a disjunctive logic program. Let $Q = \exists X_1 \cdots \exists X_n \neg A$, with A being an atom. Let S be the semantics associated to P to evaluate universal queries. Let $GSN(A)$ be the finite set:*

$$GSN(A) = \{(C_1, \theta_1), \ldots, (C_j, \theta_j)\},\ j \geq 0$$

Let X_{θ_i} be the variables occurring in the substitution θ_i, $i \leq j$. A complete answer for Q with respect to $P \bigcup GCWA_S(P)$ is the singleton set $\{E\}$ where E is the equality formula:

$$E = [(E_{\theta_1} \Rightarrow \bigvee_{\theta'_1 \in \mathcal{MGS}(C_1(X_{\theta_1}))} E_{\theta'_1}) \wedge \cdots \wedge (E_{\theta_j} \Rightarrow \bigvee_{\theta'_j \in \mathcal{MGS}(C_j(X_{\theta_j}))} E_{\theta'_j})].$$

An empty disjunction represents false. An empty conjunction represents true.

Proof: We want to prove that for all ground substitutions θ of A,

$$CET(P) \models E\theta \text{ iff } \neg A\theta \in GCWA(P).$$

($\Rightarrow$) Let θ be such a substitution that $CET(P) \models E\theta$. Any clause in $GSN(A\theta, P)$ is an instance of a clause in $GSN(A)$ since any SN-refutation

of $\leftarrow A\theta$ is an instance of a SN-refutation of A. Let $(C,\varepsilon) \in GSN(A\theta, P)$, where ε is the identity substitution since $A\theta$ is ground. We need to prove that $S(P) \models \forall C$. Assume that C is an instance of a clause C_i, for some $(C_i, \theta_i) \in GSN(A)$. Then $A\theta$ is an instance of $A\theta_i$. Therefore, $E_{\theta_i}\theta$ is satisfiable. But there is a unique substitution for the variables in $E_{\theta_i}\theta$ that makes the equality equation true since E_{θ_i} is of the form $(X_1 = t_1 \wedge \cdots \wedge X_n = t_n)$, with $t_1, \ldots, t_n$ terms; and the substitution θ replaces all the variables x_k by ground terms, for $1 \leq k \leq n$. Let ρ be such a substitution. This substitution replaces the free variables in $A\theta_i$ by ground terms. Hence, $C = C_i\rho$ by the definition of C and C_i. Now, since $E_{\theta_i}\theta\rho$ is valid, $\bigvee_{\theta_i' \in \mathcal{MGS}(C_i(X_{\theta_i}))} E_{\theta_i'}\rho$ has to be satisfiable. Moreover, there is a $E_{\theta_i'}\rho$ that is satisfiable. Similar to E_{θ_i}, $E_{\theta_i'}$ is of the form $(Y_1 = t_1 \wedge \cdots \wedge Y_m = t_m)$, with $t_1, \ldots, t_m$ terms; and the substitution ρ replaces all the variables y_k by ground terms, for $1 \leq k \leq m$. That makes C an instance of $C_i\theta_i'$. We know that $S(P) \models \forall C_i\theta_i'$. $S(P) \models \forall C_i\theta_i'$ implies that for any instance D of $C_i\theta_i'$ $S(P) \models \forall D$. In particular, when $D = C$, $S(P) \models \forall C$. Since this result does not depend on the pair (C, ε) chosen from $GSN(A\theta, P)$ it implies that $\neg A\theta \in GCWA(P)$.
($\Leftarrow$) Let $\neg A\theta$ be in $GCWA(P)$ and assume that $E\theta$ is not satisfiable. Then, there is an i, $1 \leq i \leq j$, such that $(E_{\theta_i} \Rightarrow \bigvee_{\theta_i' \in \mathcal{MGS}(C_i(X_{\theta_i}))} E_{\theta_i'})$ is false. In a manner similar to the first part, there is a unique substitution γ for the variables in $E_{\theta_i}\theta$ that makes $E_{\theta_i}\theta$ valid. Therefore, $E_{\theta_i}\theta\gamma$ is valid and $\bigvee_{\theta_i' \in \mathcal{MGS}(C_i(X_{\theta_i}))} E_{\theta_i'}\gamma$ is not satisfiable. If $E_{\theta_i}\theta$ is satisfiable then there is a pair (C, ε) in $GSN(A\theta, P)$ such that C is an instance of C_i. If $\bigvee_{\theta_i' \in \mathcal{MGS}(C_i(X_{\theta_i}))} E_{\theta_i'}\gamma$ is not satisfiable, it implies that there is no substitution θ_i' in $\mathcal{MGS}(C_i(X_{\theta_i}))$ such that C is an instance of $C_i\theta_i'$ and $S(P) \models \forall C_i\theta_i'$. Hence, For any substitution ρ such that C is an instance of $C_i\rho$, $S(P) \not\models C_i\rho$. Therefore $S(P) \not\models \forall C$. Then, $\neg A\theta \notin GCWA(P)$, contradicting the hypothesis. □

Example 2.4 *Let S be a general (not necessarily Herbrand) model semantics to evaluate universal queries, and let P be the disjunctive program:*

$\{p(X) \leftarrow r(X);$
$r(X) \vee q(X,Y) \leftarrow m(X,Y);$
$r(X) \leftarrow m(X, f(X));$
$m(g(Z), f(g(Z)));$
$m(X, g(Y));$
$q(g(W), U)\}.$

$GSN(p(X), P) = \{(q(g(Z), f(g(Z))), \{X/g(Z)\}),$
$(q(X, g(Z)), \varepsilon),$
$(\square, \{X/g(Z)\})\}.$

$E = (X \neq g(Z)) \wedge$ *true* $\wedge (X \neq g(Z))$.

Then, $GCWA_S(P) \bigcup P \models \forall Z(X \neq g(Z)) \Rightarrow \neg p(X))$. □

In the next section we extend constructive negation to programs with negation in the body of a clause and describe how to obtain complete answers in these programs.

3 Constructive Negation and Stratified Programs

In this section we extend the rule of Support-for-Negation to infer negative information from stratified disjunctive programs. A disjunctive program P is called *stratified* if there is a partition $P = P_1 \dot{\bigcup} P_2 \dot{\bigcup} \ldots \dot{\bigcup} P_n$ such that the following conditions hold for $i = 1, \ldots, n$

1. if a predicate symbol occurs positively in a clause in P_i, then its definition is contained within $\dot{\bigcup}_{j \leq i} P_j$
2. if a predicate symbol occurs negatively in a clause in P_i, then its definition is contained within $\dot{\bigcup}_{j < i} P_j$

P_1 can be empty. The Support-for-Negation is defined using an extended version of the Generalized Closed World Assumption. This extension is described by Minker and Rajasekar in [18] and is based on Definition 2.1 of the GCWA.

Definition 3.1 *Let* $P = P_1 \dot{\bigcup} P_2 \dot{\bigcup} \ldots \dot{\bigcup} P_n$ *be a stratified disjunctive program. Then,*

$GCWAS_1 = GCWA(P_1)$
$GCWAS_{i+1} = GCWAS_i \bigcup GCWA(P'_{i+1} \bigcup MS_i)$, *for* $i < n$
$GCWAS(P) = GCWAS_n$

where P'_i *is a positive disjunctive program constructed from* $ground(P_i)$ *by deleting*

1. *Each program clause that has a negative literal* $\neg B$ *in its body such that* $B \vee C \in can(MS_{i-1})$ *where* C *is a (possibly null) ground positive clause.*
2. *All negative literals in the bodies of the remaining program clauses.*

Where $ground(P_i)$ *consists of all the ground instances of clauses in* P_i *obtained from the Herbrand Universe of* P.

MS_1 *is the set of all positive ground clauses derivable from* P_1.

MS_{i+1} *is the set of all positive ground clauses derivable from* $P_i \bigcup MS_i$.

□

The stratum of a predicate symbol Q is the largest stratum in which a clause defining Q appears. The stratum of an atom A is the stratum of the predicate symbol occurring in A. The stratum of a negated atom $\neg A$ is the stratum of A plus 1. The stratum of the equality predicate is 1.

Example 3.1 *For the program* $P = \{r \leftarrow s \; ; \; r \vee s \; ; \; p \vee q \leftarrow r, \neg s \; ; \; q\}$, *a stratification is defined by* $P = P_1 \dot{\bigcup} P_2$ *where,*

$P_1 = \{r \leftarrow s\ ;\ r \vee s\}$ *and* $\quad P_2 = \{p \vee q \leftarrow r, \neg s\ ;\ q\}$. *Then,*
$GCWAS_1 = GCWA(P_1) = \{s\}$ *; and* $MS_1 = \{r,\ r \vee s\}$
Now, $P_2' = \{p \vee q \leftarrow r\ ;\ q\}$ *and*
$GCWAS_2 = \{s\} \cup GCWA(\{p \vee q \leftarrow r\ ;\ q\} \cup \{r,\ r \vee s\}) = \{s,\ p\}$
$GCWAS(P) = \{s,\ p\}$ □

The definitions of Support-for-Negation is described in terms of normal equality formulas. A normal equality formula is a (possible empty) disjunction of formulas of the form $\exists(E_1 \wedge \cdots \wedge E_n)$, $n \geq 0$, where the E_i are equality literals and $\exists$ quantifies some of the variables occurring in the formula [3]. We do not lose generality with this assumption since Przymusinski [15] shows that there is an algorithm that transforms any equality formula into an equivalent normal formula, i.e. for any equality formula $E(X_1, \ldots, X_n)$ there is normal formula E' such that $CET(P) \models \forall X_1, \ldots, X_n(E \equiv E')$. In order to define the Support-for-Negation set for an atom A in a stratified program we will follow the same steps as for the Support-for-Negation set in positive programs (see Section 2)

Definition 3.2 (SNCgoal)
A SNCgoal is a clause of the form: $\quad C \leftarrow L_1, \ldots, L_n$, *where* $n \geq 0$, C *is a positive clause (possibly empty) and the* L_i *are (possibly equality) literals. A SNCgoal is called a bottom-SNCgoal if all the* L_i *are equality literals which are satisfiable but not valid.* □

The stratum of a SNCgoal $C \leftarrow L_1, \ldots, L_n$ is the maximum stratum among the strata of the literals $L_1, \ldots, L_n$.

Definition 3.3 (SNC-derivation)
Let P *be a completely definable stratified disjunctive program,* $G = C \leftarrow L_1, \ldots, L_m, \ldots L_k$ *be a SNCgoal. If the stratum of* G *is 1, an SCN-derivation is any SN-derivation of* G. *If the stratum* n *of* G *is larger than 1, assume that all the SNC-derivations for SNCgoals in a stratum less than* n *are defined. A SNC-derivation for goal* G *consists of a (finite or infinite) sequence of SNCgoals* $G_0 = G, G_1, \ldots$, *such that for all* $i \geq 0$, G_{i+1} *is obtained from* G_i *as follows:*

(1) Let L_m *be literal in* G_i. L_m *is called the selected literal.*
(2) If L_m *is a non-equality positive literal* A, *then*
  (a) $C' \vee A \leftarrow B_1, \ldots, B_q$ *is a program clause in* P
  (b) $A_m\theta = A\theta$ *where* θ *is a substitution (most general)*
  (c) G_{i+1} *is the SNCgoal*
  $(C \vee C' \leftarrow L_1, \ldots, L_{m-1}, B_1, \ldots, B_q, L_{m+1}, \ldots, L_k)\theta$.
(3) If L_m *is a non-equality negative literal, let* $\exists F_1 \vee \cdots \vee \exists F_q$ *be the normal equality form of the complete answer for* L_m, *then* $G_{i+1} = C \leftarrow L_1, \ldots, F_j, \ldots L_k$ *for any* j *such that* $1 \leq j \leq q$.
(4) If L_m *is the equality literal* $(t_1 = t_2)$ *and* t_1 *and* t_2 *unify with mgu* θ *then* $G_{i+1} = (C \leftarrow L_1, \ldots, L_{m-1}, L_{m+1}, \ldots, L_k)\theta$.

(5) If L is the negated equality literal $(\forall(t_1 \neq t_2))$ *and* $\forall(t_1 \neq t_2)$ *is valid then* $G_{i+1} = (C \leftarrow L_1, \ldots, L_{m-1}, L_{m+1}, \ldots, L_k)$. □

Example 3.2 *Given the disjunctive program P:*

$\{p(X) \leftarrow r(X);$
$r(X) \vee q(X,Y) \leftarrow m(X,Y);$
$r(X) \leftarrow m(X, f(X));$
$m(g(Z), f(g(Z)));$
$m(X, g(Y));$
$q(g(W), U);$
$h(X,Y) \leftarrow t(X), n(Y);$
$n(Y) \leftarrow \neg p(Y);$
$t(X) \vee s(f(X));$
$s(f(g(X)));$
$s(f(f(X)))\}.$

For the SNCgoal $\leftarrow h(X,Y)$ *the following sequence is a SNC-derivation:*

$G_0 = \leftarrow h(X,Y),$
$G_1 = \leftarrow t(X), n(Y),$
$G_2 = s(f(X)) \leftarrow n(Y),$
$G_3 = s(f(X)) \leftarrow \neg p(Y),$
$G_4 = s(f(X)) \leftarrow \forall Z(Y \neq g(Z))$

The complete answer for $\neg p(Y)$ *is obtained as shown in Example 2.4.* □

The existence of a complete answer for L_m is assured since the stratum of G is larger than the stratum of L_m and we are assuming that the program P is completely definable.

Definition 3.4 (positive SNC-derivation)
A positive SNC-derivation from P with top-SNCgoal G is a finite SNC-derivation $G_0 = G, G_1, \ldots, G_n$ *of a bottom-SNCgoal* G_n. *Let* θ_i *be the substitution applied at step i of the derivation. We say that* θ *is the substitution associated with the positive derivation if* θ *is the composition of substitutions* $\theta_1 \cdots \theta_n$ *restricted to the variables in G.* □

The Example 3.2 shows a positive derivation for $\leftarrow h(x,y)$.

Definition 3.5 (SNC set)
Let P be a stratified disjunctive program and let A be an atom with free variables $(X_1, \ldots, X_n)$. *The Support-for-Negation set of A with respect to the program P is defined by:*
$GSNC(A,P) = \{(D,\theta) \mid$ *D is a bottom-SNCgoal in a positive SNC-derivation from P with top-SNCgoal* $G = \leftarrow A$ *and associated substitution* $\theta\ \}$. □

The difference between the elements of a GSN set and a $GSNC$ set is that the elements D in $GSNC(A,P)$ are of the form $C \leftarrow E$ where C is a positive clause and E is a conjunction of equality literals. In GSN set the E part is empty.

Theorem 3
Let P be a stratified disjunctive logic program. Let $Q(x_1, \ldots, x_n) = \neg A$ be a negative query and let S be a sound semantics for P to evaluate universal queries. Let $GSNC(A, P)$ be the finite set:

$$GSNC(A,P) = \{(C_1 \leftarrow F_1, \theta_1), \ldots, (C_j \leftarrow F_j, \theta_j)\},\ j \geq 0$$

Let X_{θ_i} be the variables occurring in the substitution θ_i, $i \leq j$. A complete answer for Q with respect to $P \bigcup GCWA(P)$ is the singleton set $\{E\}$ where E is the equality formula:

$$[((E_{\theta_1} \wedge F_1) \Rightarrow \bigvee_{\theta_1' \in \mathcal{MGS}(C_1(X_{\theta_1}))} E_{\theta_1'}) \wedge \cdots \wedge ((E_{\theta_j} \wedge F_j) \Rightarrow \bigvee_{\theta_j' \in \mathcal{MGS}(C_j(X_{\theta_j}))} E_{\theta_j'}))]$$

Where an empty disjunction represents false *and an empty conjunction represents* true.

Proof: We prove the theorem by induction on the stratum of $\neg A$. By definition of the stratum of a literal, the minimum stratum for $\neg A$ is 2. The base case, $n = 2$, follows directly from Theorem 2 since P_1 is a positive program and in this case the F_is in E are empty. The induction hypothesis establishes that for any query $\neg A$ in a stratum n, $2 \leq n \leq k$, the equality formula

$$[((E_{\theta_1} \wedge F_1) \Rightarrow \bigvee_{\theta_1' \in \mathcal{MGS}(C_1(X_{\theta_1}))} E_{\theta_1'}) \wedge \cdots \wedge ((E_{\theta_j} \wedge F_j) \Rightarrow \bigvee_{\theta_j' \in \mathcal{MGS}(C_j(X_{\theta_j}))} E_{\theta_j'}))]$$

is a complete answer for $\neg A$. Assume the stratum of $\neg A$ to be $n + 1$. By the induction hypothesis we can obtain a positive disjunctive program P_i^* by replacing each rule in $\bigcup_{1 \leq i \leq n} P_i$ of the form:

$$C \leftarrow L_1, \ldots, L_{m-1}, L_m, L_{m+1}, \ldots, L_r$$

by the equivalent collection of rules:

$$C \leftarrow L_1, \ldots, L_{m-1}, E_1, L_{m+1}, \ldots, L_r$$

$$\vdots$$

$$C \leftarrow L_1, \ldots, L_{m-1}, E_j, L_{m+1}, \ldots, L_r$$

where L_m is a negative literal and $\exists E_1 \vee \cdots \vee \exists E_j$ is the normal form of the answer for L_m. A ground instance $C' \leftarrow L_1', \ldots, L_{m-1}', L_{m+1}', \ldots, L_r'$ of $C \leftarrow L_1, \ldots, L_{m-1}, L_{m+1}, \ldots, L_r$ produced by a substitution θ will appear in P_i^* if and only if a ground instance of $L_m\theta$ is in $GCWA_n(P)$. Therefore, $C' \leftarrow L_1', \ldots, L_{m-1}', L_{m+1}', \ldots, L_r'$ will appear in P_i' if and only if for some i, $1 \leq i \leq j$, $E_i\theta$ is valid. Now, given an atom A, a clause C belongs to the Support-for-Negation set $GSN(A, P_i')$ iff it is a ground instance of a clause C' such that $(C' \leftarrow F)$ is in $GSNC(A, P_i^*)$, where $C = C'\theta$ and $F\theta$ is satisfiable, for some substitution θ. From this observation and Theorem 2 we can conclude that

$$[((E_{\theta_1} \wedge F_1) \Rightarrow \bigvee_{\theta_1' \in \mathcal{MGS}(C_1(X_{\theta_1}))} E_{\theta_1'}) \wedge \cdots \wedge ((E_{\theta_j} \wedge F_j) \Rightarrow \bigvee_{\theta_j' \in \mathcal{MGS}(C_j(X_{\theta_j}))} E_{\theta_j'}))]$$

is a complete answer for $\neg A$. □

Example 3.3 *Let S be a general (not necessarily Herbrand) model semantics to evaluate universal queries. Let P be the program in Example 3.2:*
$GSNC(h(X,Y),P) = \{(s(f(X)) \leftarrow y \neq g(Z), \varepsilon)\}$.
$\mathcal{MGS}(s(f(X))(X)) = \{\{X/g(W)\},\{X/f(g(W))\}\}$. *Then,*
$GCWAS_S(P) \bigcup P \models \forall((Y \neq g(Z) \Rightarrow ((X = g(W)) \vee (X = f(g(W))))) \Rightarrow \neg h(X,Y))$.
The computation of $\neg p(Y)$ is given in Example 2.4 □

The semantics described in this paper for stratified programs is based on the GCWA. Minker and Rajasekar also describe in [18] a semantics for stratified programs based on the Weak Generalized Closed World Assumption (WGCWA) [17]. Similar theorems for constructive negation based on the WGCWA can be proven under the same lines of the proofs presented here. A description of these theorems can be found in [7].

4 Conclusions

The Generalized Closed World Assumption was originally defined in terms of ground atoms [9]. In this paper, we present a definition described over atoms in general using the concepts of constructive negation developed for general Horn programs [3]. Based on this extension and the definition of the GCWA for stratified disjunctive programs given in [18] we define constructive negation in stratified disjunctive programs. The extensions of constructive negation to other semantics as perfect models [14] or generalized disjunctive well-founded semantics [1] are interesting topics of future research. One of properties that characterizes theses semantics is that the negative information assumed is not only atomic, i.e we can deduce $\neg p \vee \neg q$ without knowing if $\neg p$ is true or $\neg q$ is false. The basic assumption of the GCWA for stratified programs is that all the negative information that can be assumed is atomic. Therefore, the answer for negative literals is always a single substitution which transformed in the appropriate equality formula can replace the negative literal in the body of the clauses. This replacement can not be directly achieved when the answer is not definite as is the case in perfect models and generalized disjunctive well-founded semantics. For these semantics, the definition of constructive negation might require algorithms similar to the ones described in [1].

A proof-procedure that incorporates constructive negation can be obtained by modifying SLI-resolution of Minker and Zanon [13]. A description of this algorithm can be found in [7].

Acknowledgements

I wish to thank Jack Minker for his support and his useful discussions during the development of the paper. I also thank Arcot Rajasekar for his comments on earlier drafts of this paper. This research was supported by the National Science Foundation under grant number IRI-86-09170 and the Army Research Office under grant number DAAG-29-85-K-0-177.

References

[1] C. Baral, J. Lobo, and J. Minker. Generalized disjunctive well-founded semantics for logic programs : Declarative semantics. In *Proc. of Fifth International Symposium on Methodologies for Inelligent Systems*, Charlotte, NC, 1990.

[2] L. Cavedon and J.W. Lloyd. A Completeness Theorem for SLDNF-resolution. Technical Report CS-87-06, Computer Science Department, University of Bristol, Bristol, 1987.

[3] D. Chan. Constructive Negation Based on the Completed Databases. In R.A. Kowalski and K.A. Bowen, editors, *Proc. 5th International Conference and Symposium on Logic Programming*, pages 111–125, Seattle, Washington, August 15-19, 1988.

[4] K. L. Clark. Negation as Failure. In H. Gallaire and J. Minker, editors, *Logic and Data Bases*, pages 293–322. Plenum Press, New York, 1978.

[5] J.W. Lloyd. *Foundations of Logic Programming.* Springer–Verlag, 1984.

[6] J.W. Lloyd and R.W. Topor. Making prolog more expressive. *Journal of Logic Programming*, 1(3):225–240, 1984 October 1984.

[7] J. Lobo. *On the Semantics of Disjunctive Logic Programs with Negation.* PhD thesis, University of Maryland, Department of Computer Science, 1990. (under preparation).

[8] J. Lobo, J. Minker, and A. Rajasekar. Extending the Semantics of Logic Programs to Disjunctive Logic Programs. In G. Levi and M. Martelli, editors, *Proc. 6th International Conference on Logic Programming*, Lisbon, Portugal, June 19-23 1989.

[9] J. Minker. On Indefinite Databases and the Closed World Assumption. In *Lecture Notes in Computer Science 138*, pages 292–308. Springer-Verlag, 1982.

[10] J. Minker and A. Rajasekar. Procedural Interpretation of Non-Horn Logic Programs. In E. Lusk and R. Overbeek, editors, *Proc. 9th International Conference on Automated Deduction*, pages 278–293, Argonne, IL, 23-26, May 1988.

[11] J. Minker and A. Rajasekar. A Fixpoint Semantics for Disjunctive Logic Programs. *Journal of Logic Programming*, 1990. To appear.

[12] J. Minker, A. Rajasekar, and J. Lobo. Theory of Disjunctive Logic Programs. In J. Lassez, editor, *Computational Logic: Essays in honor of Alan Robinson.* MIT Press, 1990.

[13] J. Minker and G. Zanon. An Extension to Linear Resolution with Selection Function. *Information Processing Letters*, 14(3):191–194, June 1982.

[14] T.C. Przymusinski. On the declarative semantics of deductive databases and logic programming. In J. Minker, editor, *Foundations of Deductive Databases and Logic Programming*, pages 193–216. Morgan Kaufmann Pub., Washington, D.C., 1988.

[15] T.C. Przymusinski. On Constructive Negation in Logic Programming. In E. Lusk and R. Overbeek, editors, *Proc. of the North American Conference of Logic Programming*, Cleveland, Ohio, October 16-20, 1989. Extended Abstract.

[16] Teodoro C. Przymusinski. On the Declarative and Procedural Semantics of Logic Programs. To appear in Journal of Automated Reasoning.

[17] A. Rajasekar, J. Lobo, and J. Minker. Weak Generalized Closed World Assumption. *Journal of Automated Reasoning*, 5:293–307, 1989.

[18] A. Rajasekar and J. Minker. On Stratified Disjunctive Programs. Technical Report CS-TR-2168 UMIACS-TR-88-99, Department of Computer Science, University of Maryland, College Park, December 1988. To appear in the Annals of Mathematics and Artificial Intelligence Vol. 1, 1990.

[19] K. Ross. A procedural semantics for well founded negation in logic programs. In *"Proceedings of the 8th ACM SIGACT-SIGMOD-SIGART Symposium on Principle of Database Systems"*, Philadelphia, Pennsylvania, March, 29-31, 1989.

Parallelism II

Handling of Speculative Work in OR-Parallel PROLOG: Evaluation Results

Bogumil Hausman
Swedish Institute of Computer Science
Box 1263, S-164 28 Kista
Sweden

Abstract

To improve efficiency of OR-parallel execution we proposed new schemes for pruning speculative work (work in any branch which can be cut away is speculative). And as the current Aurora system makes no distinction between speculative and nonspeculative work, we proposed different schemes for scheduling speculative work. The new strategies for pruning and scheduling speculative work are implemented and evaluated in the Argonne scheduler of the Aurora system. The results show that the new strategies minimize the amount of speculative work performed and increase efficiency of OR-parallel execution.

1 Introduction

As hardware prices dramatically drop, parallel computers become more and more common. There are many of them available commercially, from 2-32 processors accessing a shared memory (Sequent Symmetry, Encore Multimax) to the massively parallel machines up to 64k processors (Connection Machines). As the multiprocessing market grows there is an urgent necessity to develop parallel algorithms that exploit multiprocessors. PROLOG with its implicit nondeterminism seems to be the perfect tool for parallel programming.

Members of the Gigalips project, an informal research collaboration among different individuals from Argonne National Laboratory, the University of Bristol, and the Swedish Institute of Computer Science, chose to construct an OR-parallel PROLOG system run on shared memory multiprocessors.

One of the main goals of the Gigalips project was to provide an implementation of the full PROLOG language. In this way some portability problems are avoided and it is possible to port existing PROLOG applications. As the implementation was treated as porting PROLOG to yet another machine, the sequential semantics of PROLOG extralogical predicates had to be defined and implemented in the OR-parallel setting (Hausman et al. 88). The implementation effort resulted in the Aurora OR-parallel PROLOG system (Lusk, Warren, and Haridi et al. 88) run currently on Sequent and Encore machines.

To improve efficiency of the Aurora system we defined new schemes for pruning speculative work (work in any branch which can be cut away is speculative). And as the current Aurora system makes no distinction between speculative and nonspeculative work, we proposed different schemes for scheduling speculative work. The new strategies were defined and discussed in (Hausman 89, Hausman 90).

In this paper the new strategies for pruning and scheduling speculative work are implemented and evaluated in the Argonne scheduler of the Aurora system.

The paper is organized as follows. In Section 2 we present required prerequisites. In Section 3 we discuss briefly problems caused by OR-parallel execution of predicates containing cut and show some implementation options for cut. In Section 4 we discuss different scheduling schemes for speculative work. Section 5 summarizes evaluation results of the new strategies for pruning and scheduling speculative work mentioned in Sections 3, and 4.

2 Prerequisites

2.1 The SRI Storage Model

The specific problem with OR-parallel implementations is the management of simultaneous multiple bindings of variables. D.H.D. Warren proposed the SRI storage model (Warren 87). The idea is to record all the conditional bindings in a binding array specific for each worker. When a worker starts a new task, the conditional bindings inherited from the worker from which the task is stolen must be placed (installed) in the binding array of the starting worker. When a worker backtracks some conditional values are removed from the worker's binding array (deinstalled). In order to implement installation/deinstallation, the trail contains address-value pairs.

The SRI model is very simple to implement and provides variable accesses which are constant-time operations. At the same time the non-constant time for task creation can be kept relatively small by an appropriate scheduling strategy (see the following section).

2.2 Scheduling in Aurora

In the SRI model, the overhead is caused by the cost of installation/deinstallation of bindings. One way to minimize this cost is to attempt to maximize the granularity of tasks (thus minimizing the frequency of task switching in general). A scheduler should provide the topmost available tasks first, as the tasks with larger granularity usually reside in the topmost part of the tree. Another way to minimize the overhead is to minimize the number of required installations/deinstallations. A scheduler should provide tasks which are closer (reside closer in the tree) to a worker searching for work, as locality minimizes the number of bindings which have to be updated in the worker's binding array.

To minimize the overhead of the SRI model the following heuristics were proposed (Warren 87, Hausman et al. 87, Butler et al. 88). The worker which has exhausted its subtree walks up the path towards the root until it either finds an open node (and claims an alternative from it), or finds a closed node with open nodes under it. In the second case the worker usually has several open nodes to choose from. The worker always claims an alternative from the topmost open node.

To win efficiency the scheduling should approximate the sequential processing whenever feasible. Each worker has zero or more open nodes on the path from the tip it is working on to the root of the tree. The open node closest to the root is called the *dispatching node* of a worker. A dispatching node can be shared among many workers. Only the part of the tree above and including the dispatching nodes is actually shared among several workers, and this part is called *public*. A worker looking for work can claim alternatives only from the dispatching nodes. When the dispatching node of some worker is closed (all alternatives taken), the nodes immediately below it (if any) become the new dispatching nodes. The subtree below a dispatching node consists of simple branches which are private to the workers working on them, thus while working on its private branch a worker can manage memory efficiently and has no need for locking (see Figure 1). The oldest private node is called the *sentry* node. It is assumed that at the tip of each branch there is a node showing the current position of an executing worker (be it process or processor), and such nodes are called *embryonic*. An embryonic node is converted into an ordinary node when a nondeterministic predicate is invoked, and then a new embryonic node is created.

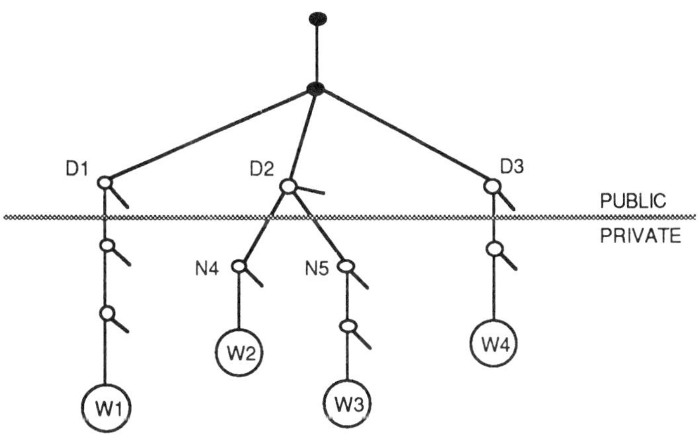

Figure 1. The public and the private parts of a search tree. Nodes $D1$, $D2$ and $D3$ are the dispatching nodes of the corresponding workers. When a dispatching node $D2$ is closed, nodes $N4$ and $N5$ (sentry nodes of respectively workers $W2$, and $W3$) become new dispatching nodes.

The scheduling strategy (picking the nearest of the topmost available tasks in the public part of the tree) resulted in different schedulers which use various data structures to decide which available task is the nearest one and shall be picked by a worker searching for work. The schedulers are described and compared in (Lusk, Warren, and Haridi et al. 88), here we are going to discuss briefly only the Argonne scheduler.

2.3 The Argonne Scheduler

The Argonne scheduler allows workers to make their own local decisions based on the information stored in the tree. A bit (called the *work bit*) in each node indicates whether or not there are available alternatives below, and idle workers migrate towards available tasks attracted by the bits. After reaching a node with its work bit set, a worker moves down into one of the branches leading to work with the lowest number of active workers. The strategy of choosing a branch with the lowest number of active workers ensures that idle workers distribute themselves evenly over the tree. If there is no available work in the tree, workers try to position themselves in the parts of the tree where work might appear. Idle workers make their decisions step by step, i.e. a worker positioned at some particular node can process the node's available alternative (if there are any) or, depending on the information stored in the tree, move along an arc to a nearby node and repeat the decision process. When a task becomes available, all the nodes in a branch with the task have their work bits set. When a dispatching node is closed (last alternative taken) the corresponding work bits leading to the node are cleared.

3 Pruning Speculative Work in the Scope of a Cut

3.1 Scope

As during OR-parallel execution there are many branches being executed simultaneously we have to define the scope of a cut in the new setting. On the WAM instruction level the cut predicate has an argument which is a reference to the last node created before the predicate containing the cut is invoked. We shall call a child of the argument node the *cut boundary node* (it is a root of the subtree belonging to the predicate containing the cut). The scope of a cut consists of nodes in the path between the place on the branch where the cut is invoked and its cut boundary node (the node included), and nodes in the subtrees to the right of the path (see Figure 2). Execution of a cut prunes all nodes in its scope.

3.2 Overlapping Scopes

The main difficulty in implementing cut correctly on an OR-parallel system is caused by the case of several workers executing cuts pruning overlapping parts of the execution tree (see Figure 2).

In Figure 2, if the cut $!^{(1)}$ in node G or E is reached before the cut $!^{(2)}$ in node F, care must be taken that the cut $!^{(1)}$ does not prune the second branch in p. If that happened, the semantics of cut would be violated, since the choose(a1) succeeds during the sequential execution and the cut $!^{(1)}$ in the first clause of p is not reached due to the failure of validate(a1). Looking at the execution tree, when the cut $!^{(1)}$ is reached it is in the scope of the cut $!^{(2)}$. The cut $!^{(1)}$ has a larger scope than the cut $!^{(2)}$, as it cuts to a higher node in the tree, and their scopes overlap.

The general rule is that, if a cut is in a scope of another cut, the cut with the larger scope must not prune branches that would not be pruned anyway by the cut with the smaller scope. Those branches can be pruned when the branch leading to the cut with the smaller scope fails (Hausman et al. 88).

If correctness is the only consideration, then the cut's semantics can be implemented simply by pruning all the branches rooted at the right siblings of a worker's sentry node and then suspending the execution of cut until the branch becomes leftmost in the subtree belonging to the predicate containing the cut (Calderwood 88, Carlsson 88). We will call this solution *local leftmost* scheme.

```
p :- q, !(1).
p :- speculative1.
q :- choose(X), !(2), validate(X).
q :- speculative2.

choose(a1).
choose(a2).
validate(a2).
```

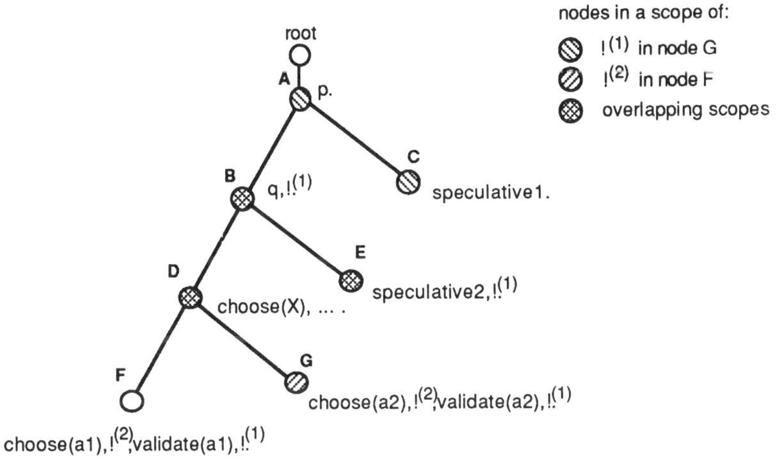

Figure 2. Cuts with different overlapping scopes. Active tasks are associated with the tip (embryonic) nodes.

Another consideration is speculative work. Work in any branch which can be cut away is speculative. The simple solution proposed above lets computations in all branches in the scope of the suspended cut go on until the branch containing the suspended cut becomes leftmost. The restarted cut then prunes away branches in its scope. Notice that in this solution, execution of a cut might be suspended even if it is not in the scope of any other cut, which is clearly sub-optimal.

A better solution (Hausman et al. 88) would be to prune at once all branches which would be pruned anyway by cuts with smaller scopes. The difference between this and the previous alternative is that the execution of cut will be suspended only if it is in the scope of a cut with a smaller scope, and first when the scope boundary of the "smaller" cut is crossed. We will call this solution *scope information based.*

The scope information based scheme is better with respect to the amount of speculative work performed, and we proposed different implementation options for the scheme in (Hausman 89). The key to the implementation was to decorate a search tree with scope information, which could be used by workers to detect a scope boundary of a "smaller" cut. We started with one piece of scope information per node: the cut boundary flag indicating whether the corresponding node is a cut boundary. As the cut boundary flags can become out of date and could cause unnecessary suspensions, we extended the scope information by cut counters. Each worker has a cut counter containing a current number of cuts in the worker's continuation. A worker decrements a cut counter by one when a cut is executed, and when a clause containing cuts is entered the counter is incremented by the number of cuts in the clause. The cut counters are stored in nodes when the nodes are created and are not changed afterwards.

A third solution (Ali 87) would be to delay execution of any branch until it can no longer be affected by cuts. The solution prevents all speculative work, but at the same time limits the amount of parallelism severely.

There is yet another solution (Kalé et al. 88) where the part of the tree pruned by a larger cut is not discarded and is restarted when the larger cut is pruned later by a smaller cut, i.e. the larger cut should not have been done. The main problem with the solution is that the pruned region cannot be discarded even it is not restarted in future, causing a large space overhead.

The *local leftmost* and *scope information based* schemes are implemented and evaluated in Section 5.2.

4 Scheduling Speculative Work

As the Argonne scheduler does not make the distinction between speculative and nonspeculative work, we proposed a more optimal scheduling strategy which gives preference to nonspeculative work or, failing that, to the least speculative work available (Hausman 89, Hausman 90).

We showed that in a subtree which is in the scope of a cut tasks with the lowest speculativeness (meant as the probability of being pruned) reside in the leftmost branch and speculativeness of the tasks decreases with the depth of the subtree. We showed also that if the scheduler can provide only topmost available tasks, speculativeness of the tasks can be assessed by counting the number of branches leading to cuts that could prune the work.

These two conclusions became a basis of different strategies for scheduling speculative work (Hausman 89, Hausman 90). In general all the proposed schemes can be divided into two groups: the first group of methods tries to assess speculativeness of available tasks (*delayed release* of speculative work with delay time proportional to speculativeness of tasks), while the second group makes local decisions based on checking if available tasks are speculative (*local less speculative preferred*, *delayed release of speculative work* with constant delay time, *depth-first search*). To detect and schedule speculative work we used a more precise kind of scope information: when a worker enters a clause which ends in a fail, the number of cuts in the worker's continuation is reset to the number of control predicates in the clause (as control predicates in the worker's continuation cannot be reached any longer).

In the *local less speculative preferred* scheme a worker backtracking to a node with speculative work available below traverses down into the leftmost branch leading to work and takes the topmost available task in that branch.

In the *delayed release* scheme if available work is speculative it is made available to other workers less frequently than nonspeculative work. The delay time can be made constant or proportional to speculativeness of tasks.

In the *depth-first search* when available work is speculative, the idle workers try to take the bottom-most available task in the leftmost branch.

All the mentioned above schemes for scheduling speculative work are implemented and evaluated in Section 5.3.

5 Evaluation Results

The new strategies for pruning and scheduling speculative work introduced in Sections 3 and 4 are supposed to minimize the amount of speculative work allowed and increase the efficiency of OR-parallel execution. To show that this is really the case, the strategies were implemented in the Argonne scheduler of the echo version of Aurora OR-parallel PROLOG system (based on SICStus Prolog version 0.3). The corresponding evaluation results are shown and discussed here in this section. The system was run under DYNIX on a Sequent Symmetry S81, a shared memory multiprocessor equipped with sixteen Intel 386 (16 MHz clock) processors and 32 Mbytes of memory. To attempt to guarantee that each worker was assigned the full power of a CPU, the system was run with at most 14 workers, i.e. two processors were left aside to run the operating system. To avoid variations caused by the operating system, the run times given are the shortest obtained from eight runs.

5.1 Benchmarks

To evaluate the new strategies we used three programs: the Mastermind program, the Numbers program for generating the two largest numbers consisting of given digits and fulfilling the specified requirements, and the Chat-80 natural language query system. As our intention was to test different search trees, the Mastermind program was run with four different secret codes residing in different parts of the search tree, the Numbers program was run with four different queries each generating numbers in different parts of the search tree, Chat-80 was run with two database search queries followed by cut. For the evaluation we used the average for all the queries, more detailed evaluation results can be found in (Hausman 90).

The three programs represent three different types of search space. The Mastermind program produces a large search tree (generated by five positions in the secret code each having six possible colors) which is repeatedly pruned by each consistent guess, and after each pruning the search tree is expanded to generate the next guess. The Numbers program produces a more shallow search tree (each generated number consists of three digits each having five possible values) pruned each time a new number fulfilling the specified requirement is generated, and after each pruning (generation of the first number required) the tree is expanded only once to generate the second number. The Chat-80 database search queries produce very broad search trees due to a large amount of facts in the Chat-80 database.

To increase granularity of tasks each query was run with granularity 10, i.e. a worker made some work available to other workers on each 10th executed CALL instruction.

5.2 Pruning Speculative Work

Three different schemes for pruning speculative work were implemented and evaluated in the Argonne scheduler of the Aurora system.

The first one is the implementation of the *local leftmost* scheme mentioned in Section 3.2, where a worker invoking a cut immediately prunes all the branches rooted at the right siblings of the worker's sentry node and then suspends the execution of the cut until its branch becomes leftmost in the subtree belonging to the predicate containing the cut. To avoid suspensions due to the branches rooted at the cut boundary node (they contain cuts with the same scope) the execution of a cut suspends only if the worker is not leftmost in the subtree rooted at a child node of the cut boundary node.

The second and the third of the implemented schemes are *scope information based*, i.e. a worker invoking a cut prunes immediately all branches which would be pruned anyway by cuts with smaller scopes, and suspends only when the scope boundary of a "smaller" cut is crossed. The second scheme uses cut boundaries flags to detect "smaller" cuts, while the third scheme uses both cut boundaries flags and cut counters.

The evaluation results of the three schemes for pruning speculative work are depicted in Figure 3. The presented speedups are the average for all the queries. The figure shows the relative speed of the schemes compared with the local leftmost scheme run on one worker.

The performance results are encouraging. On one worker the scope information based schemes are only about 2% slower, the overhead caused by decorating the search tree with scope information. For a larger number of workers the scope information based schemes are generally much better and for fourteen workers improve the results up to 40%.

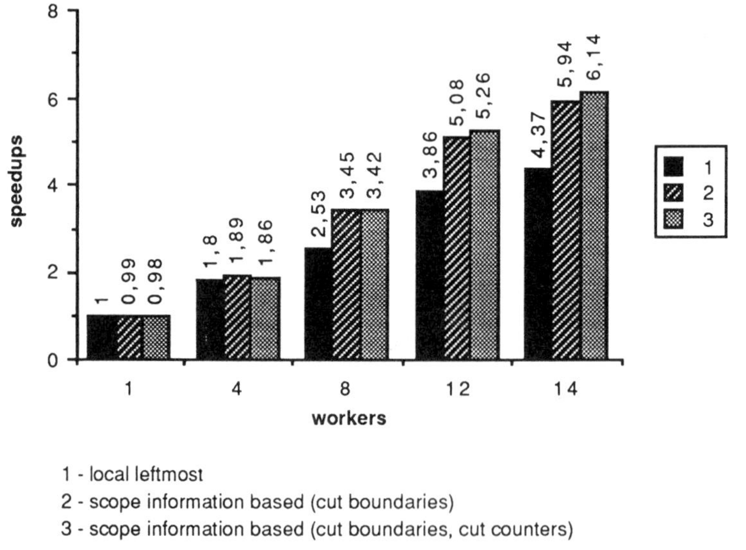

Figure 3. Comparing speed of the different pruning schemes. The speedups are the average for all run queries.

For the Mastermind program the scope information based schemes remove all the suspensions of cut (see Figure 4). The corresponding amount of created nodes is shown in Figure 5. In the Mastermind program the unnecessary suspensions of the leftmost scheme are due to the fact that the scheme cannot detect that cuts in different branches have the same scope and do not have to suspend. For the same reason the leftmost scheme causes unnecessary suspensions for the Numbers program, and for the Chat-80 database queries.

The results show that the scope information based schemes avoid unnecessary suspensions of cut and thus minimize amount of speculative work performed (assessed in Figure 5 by amount of created nodes).

Notice that even having the best strategy the speedups are modest (6 for 14 workers) which is due to a fact that the programs are inherently less parallel because of cuts.

5.3 Scheduling Speculative Work

The following schemes for scheduling speculative work were implemented and evaluated in the Argonne scheduler of the Aurora system:

- the local less speculative preferred
- the delayed release of speculative work with constant and nonconstant delay time
- the depth-first search

The last two schemes were in addition combined with the local less speculative preferred scheme.

All the schemes used the best strategy for pruning speculative work (scope information based with cut boundaries and cut counters).

To simplify the description of our implementation, we will call the leftmost branch in speculative parts of the search tree (a speculative part of the tree is a subtree rooted at the local highest cut boundary node) a *boundary branch*. Notice that the branch is not speculative (a worker active at the tip node of the branch is not in the scope of pending cuts) but the branch's available work is speculative (as the worker's continuation contains pending cuts). As mentioned in Section 4 available work in a boundary branch is less speculative than available work in other parts of the same speculative part of the tree.

5.3.1 Local Less Speculative Preferred

The implementation of the local less speculative preferred scheme is rather straightforward in the Argonne scheduler. When a worker searching for work detects available work below (work bit set), the worker traverses down into the local leftmost branch leading to work if the work is speculative, or if the work is nonspeculative the worker traverses down into one of the branches leading to work with the lowest number of active workers. The scheme is compared with the other schemes in Section 5.3.4.

5.3.2 Delayed Release of Speculative Work

The delayed release of speculative work was implemented by increasing the granularity of speculative work. As mentioned before the basic granularity of all work was 10, i.e. a worker made some work available to other workers on each

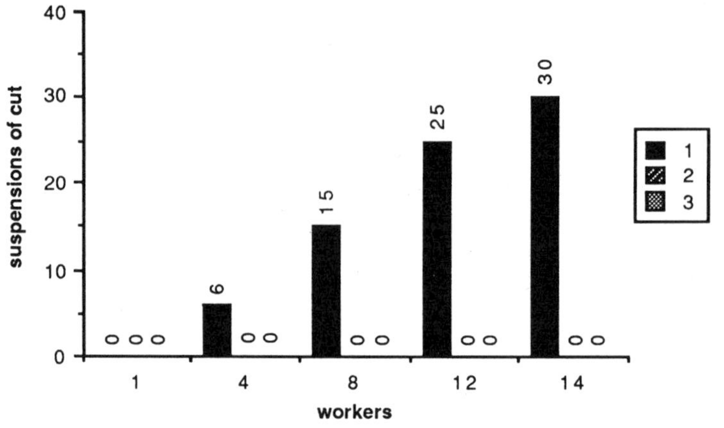

1 - local leftmost
2 - scope information based (cut boundaries)
3 - scope information based (cut boundaries, cut counters)

Figure 4. Comparing the number of suspensions of cuts for the different pruning schemes, a query of the Mastermind program.

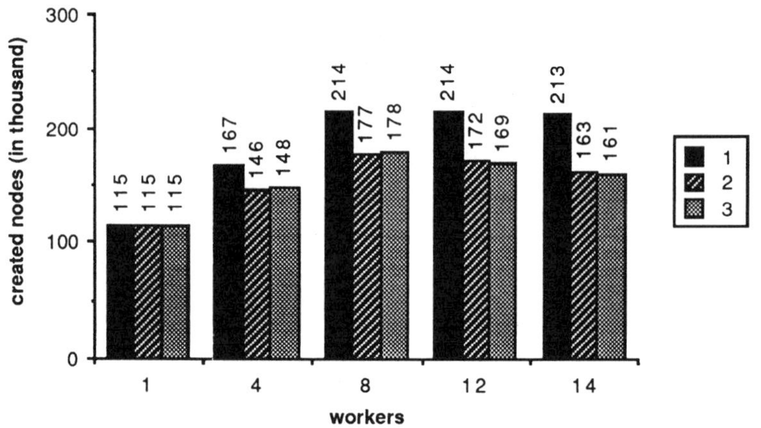

1 - local leftmost
2 - scope information based (cut boundaries)
3 - scope information based (cut boundaries, cut counters)

Figure 5. Comparing the number of created nodes for the different pruning schemes, a query of the Mastermind program.

10th executed CALL instruction. In the delayed release scheme with constant delay time the granularity of speculative work was increased by a constant factor (the scheme was run with granularity 20, 100, 1000, and 10000). In the delayed release scheme with nonconstant delay time the granularity of speculative work was increased by a factor proportional to the number of pruning branches, N, (the scheme was run with granularity N * 20, N * 100, N * 1000, and N * 10000). In addition all the schemes were combined separately with the local less speculative preferred strategy. The results showed that for all run queries the optimal value was 1000 for the pure delayed release schemes (both constant and nonconstant delay time), while for the schemes extended with the local less speculative preferred strategy the optimal value was 100. To attract idle workers to process less speculative work, available work residing in a boundary branch had granularity 10.

The evaluation results of four delayed release schemes (constant delay time, nonconstant delay time, and their extensions by the local less speculative preferred strategy) run with their optimal granularities of speculative work are summarized in Figure 6. The presented speedups are the average for all the queries.

The results show that all the schemes with nonconstant delay time give worse performance than the corresponding schemes with constant delay time. The difference is due to the overhead caused by counting of pruning branches.

The best scheme is the delayed release of speculative work with the constant delay time combined with the local less speculative preferred strategy. The scheme is compared with the other schemes for scheduling speculative work in Section 5.3.4.

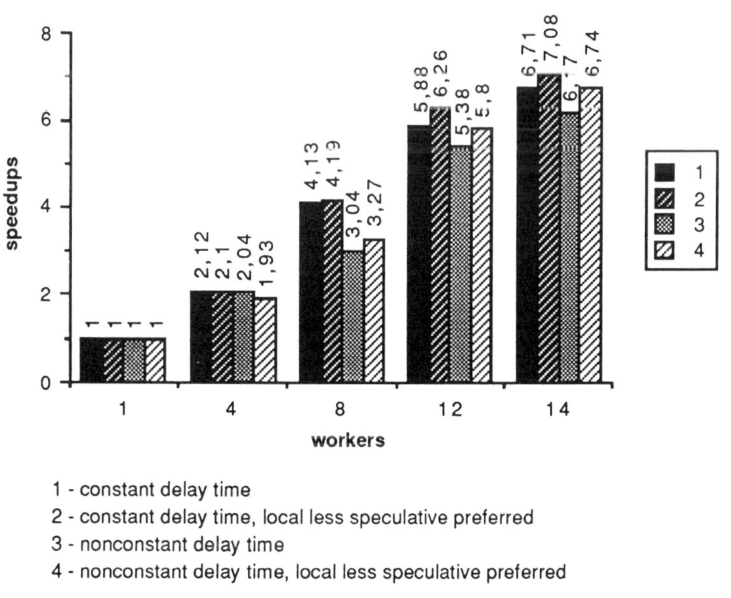

Figure 6. Comparing the speeds of different delayed release schemes. The speedups are the average for all run queries.

5.3.3 Depth-first Search

The depth-first search of speculative parts of the search tree was implemented simply by keeping all nodes in a boundary branch public, i.e. all created nodes were made public on each executed CALL instruction. The depth-first search required another scheduling strategy: a worker searching for work was obliged to take the bottom-most available task instead of the topmost one as before. As available work no longer resided only in dispatching nodes, clearing and setting of work bits were redefined to take account of the new situation. To avoid unnecessary overhead a worker active in a private part of the tree checked if its branch was a boundary branch only when there were idle workers searching for work. If the branch happened to be a boundary branch then from that moment onward all its nodes were made public.

The evaluation results of the depth-first search scheme and its extension by the local less speculative preferred strategy are summarized in Figure 7. The presented speedups are the average for all the queries.

The results show that the best scheme is the depth-first search combined with the local less speculative preferred strategy. The scheme is discussed and compared with the other schemes in the next section.

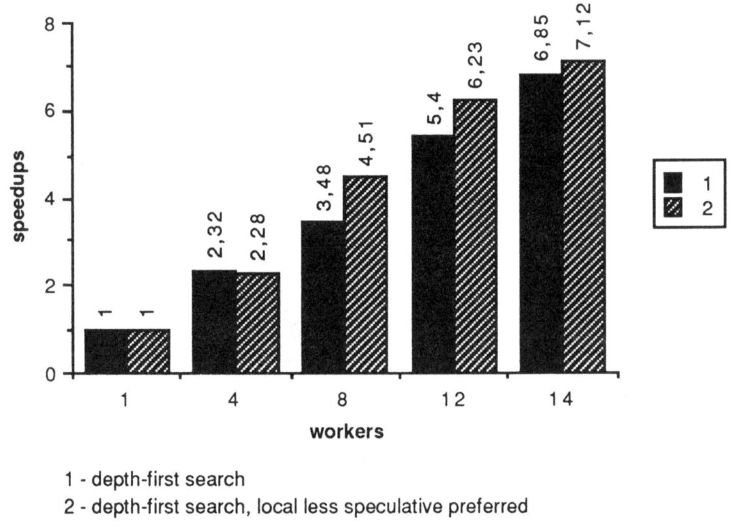

Figure 7. Comparing the speeds of different depth-first search schemes. The speedups are the average for all queries.

5.3.4 The Best Scheme

The best schemes for each group of strategies are compared in Figure 8. The figure shows the relative speed of the schemes compared with the basic scheduling strategy which makes no distinction between speculative and nonspeculative work. To make a fair comparison the basic strategy was run with the scope information based (cut boundaries, cut counters) algorithm for pruning speculative work.

The performance results show that all the proposed schemes for scheduling speculative work have improved efficiency of OR-parallel execution for the run set of benchmarks.

The best scheme is the depth-first search combined with the local less speculative preferred strategy, but the differences between the depth-first and delayed release schemes are relatively small.

The best delayed release and depth-first search schemes are the ones combined with the local less speculative preferred strategy. This shows that the strategy is very useful, as it explicitly forces idle workers to migrate to the less speculative parts of the search tree.

The small differences between performance of the depth-first and delayed release schemes can be explained by the fact that the depth-first search is better at reaching cuts residing deeper in the tree, while the delayed release scheme is not that good at reaching the deeper cuts but avoids a distinct extension of the public part of the tree (the overhead of the depth-first search). The amount of public nodes for the extended depth-first search and the delayed release schemes for the Numbers program is shown in Figure 9.

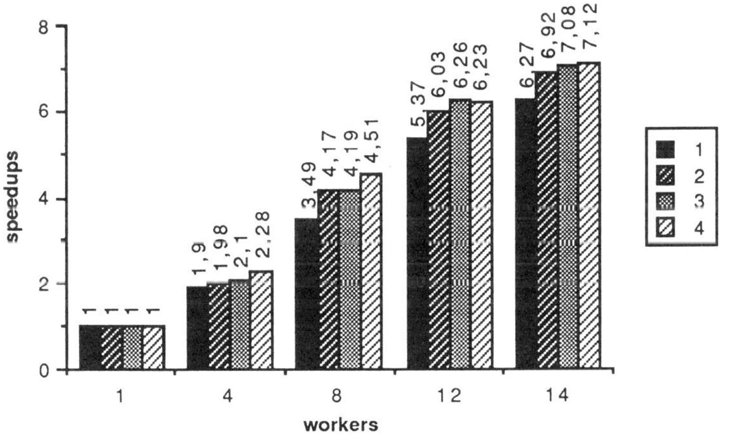

1 - no distinction between speculative and nonspeculative work
2 - local less speculative preferred
3 - delayed release (constant delay time), local less speculative preferred
4 - depth-first search, local less speculative preferred

Figure 8. Comparing the speeds of all the schemes for scheduling speculative work. The speedups are the average for all run queries.

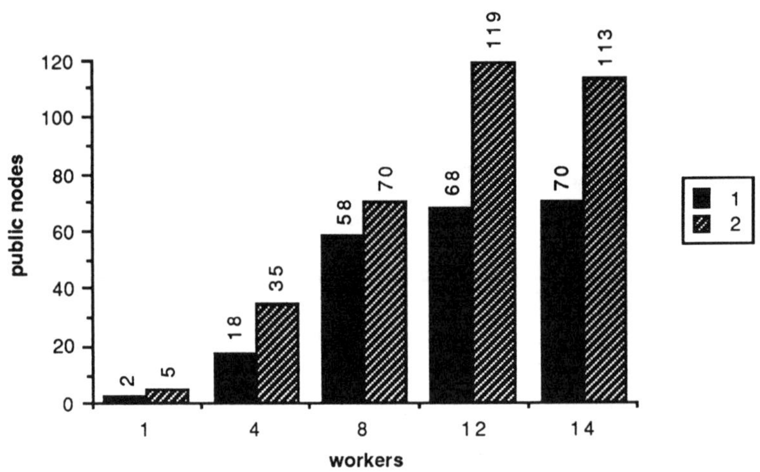

1 - delayed release (constant delay time), local less speculative preferred
2 - depth-first search, local less speculative preferred

Figure 9. Comparing the number of public nodes for the delayed release and the depth-first search schemes, a query of the Numbers program. Both schemes are combined with the local less speculative preferred strategy.

6 Conclusions

To increase the efficiency of OR-parallel execution of PROLOG we have investigated different schemes for pruning and scheduling speculative work. We have proposed new algorithms and implementation techniques for achieving this goal.

The *scope information based* schemes for execution of cut have been implemented in the Argonne scheduler of the echo version of the Aurora system. The strategies have been compared with the *local leftmost* scheme. The performance results for the run set of benchmarks have shown that for one worker the schemes based on scope information are only about 2% slower (the overhead caused by decorating the search tree with scope information), and for a larger number of workers they are generally much better and for fourteen workers improve the results up to 40%. The better performance is due to avoiding some unnecessary suspensions of cuts, i.e. the speculative parts of the search tree are pruned earlier, and this minimizes the amount of speculative work performed.

The new schemes for scheduling speculative work: the *local less speculative preferred*, the *delayed release of speculative work* with constant and nonconstant delay time, and the *depth-first search* schemes have been implemented and evaluated in the Argonne scheduler of the echo version of the Aurora system. In addition, the last two schemes have been combined with the *local less speculative preferred* strategy. The schemes have been compared with the basic scheduling scheme of the Argonne scheduler which makes no distinction between speculative and nonspeculative work.

The performance results have shown that all the proposed schemes have improved the efficiency of OR-parallel execution for the run set of benchmarks.

The best *delayed release* and *depth-first search* schemes have been the ones combined with the *local less speculative preferred* strategy. The strategy minimizes the amount of speculative work performed as it explicitly forces idle workers to migrate to the less speculative parts of the search tree.

Generally the best scheme has been the *depth-first search* combined with the *local less speculative preferred* strategy. The *depth-first search* minimizes the amount of speculative work performed because the pending cuts residing deeper in the tree can be reached and executed more quickly. The differences between the *depth-first search* and the *delayed release* schemes have been relatively small: this shows that the *delayed release* scheme is not that good at reaching the deeper cuts but avoids a distinct extension of the public part of the tree (the main source of overhead in the *depth-first search*).

The results show that the scheduling strategies which give preference to less speculative work are relatively easy to implement, and improve the efficiency of OR-parallel execution.

Acknowledgements

We wish to thank all colleagues within the Gigalips Project and SICS for useful remarks and discussions.

References

[Ali 87] Ali, K. A. M., *A Method for Implementing Cut in Parallel Execution of PROLOG*, in Proceedings of the 1987 Symposium on Logic Programming, San Francisco, pp. 449-456 (1987).

[Butler et al. 88] Butler, R., Disz, T., Lusk, E. L., Olson, R., Overbeek, R. and Stevens, R., *Scheduling OR Parallelism: an Argonne Perspective*, in Proceedings of the Fifth International Logic Programming Conference and Fifth Symposium on Logic Programming 1988, MIT Press (August 1988).

[Calderwood 88] Calderwood, A., *Cut, Commit and Side Effects in OR-Parallel PROLOG*, Internal Report, Gigalips Project/personal communication (1988).

[Carlsson 88] Carlsson, M., *Implementation of Cut in OR-Parallel PROLOG*, personal communication (April 1988).

[Hausman et al. 87] Hausman, B., Ciepielewski, A. and Haridi, S., *OR-Parallel PROLOG Made Efficient on Shared Memory Multiprocessors*, in Proceedings of the 1987 Symposium on Logic Programming, pp. 69-79 (1987).

[Hausman et al. 88] Hausman, B., Ciepielewski, A. and Calderwood, A., *Cut and Side-Effects in OR-Parallel PROLOG*, in Proceedings of International Conference on Fifth Generation Computer Systems 1988, pp. 831-840, ICOT (November 1988).

[Hausman 89] Hausman, B., *Pruning and Scheduling Speculative Work in OR-Parallel PROLOG*, in Proceedings of PARLE 89, Conference on Parallel Architectures and Languages Europe, Springer-Verlag, Vol. 2, pp. 133-150 (June 1989).

[Hausman 90] Hausman, B., *Pruning and Speculative Work in OR-Parallel PROLOG*, Ph.D. Dissertation (in preparation), The Royal Institute of Technology, Stockholm, Sweden (March 1990).

[Kalé et al. 88] Kalé, L.V., Padua, D.A. and Sehr, D.C., *OR Parallel Execution of PROLOG Programs with Side Effects*, Journal of Supercomputing, Vol. 2, No 2, pp. 209-223 (1988).

[Lusk, Warren, and Haridi et al. 88] Lusk, E., Warren, D. H. D., Haridi, S., Brand, P., Butler, R., Calderwood, A., Carlsson, M., Ciepielewski, A., Disz, T., Hausman, B., Olson, R., Overbeek, R., Stevens, R. and Szeredi, P., *The Aurora OR-Parallel PROLOG System,* New Generation Computing, Vol 7 (2, 3), pp. 243-271, also in Proceedings of International Conference on Fifth Generation Computer Systems 1988, pp. 819-830, ICOT (November 1988).

[Warren 87] Warren, D.H.D., *The SRI Model for OR-Parallel Execution of PROLOG - Abstract Design and Implementation Issues*, in Proceedings of 1987 Symposium on Logic Programming, San Francisco, pp. 92-102 (1987).

On Criteria for Or-Parallel Execution Models of Logic Programs

Gopal Gupta

Dept. of Computer Science
University of Bristol
Bristol BS8 1TR, U.K.

Bharat Jayaraman

Dept. of Computer Science
SUNY at Buffalo
Buffalo, NY 14260

Abstract

Three important criteria for an ideal or-parallel execution model for logic programs are constant-time access to variables, constant-time task creation, and constant-time task switching. We prove in this paper that all three criteria cannot be simultaneously realized by any execution model for or-parallelism based on a finite number of processors but unbounded memory. We then categorize the various or-parallel methods proposed in the literature based on these criteria.

1. Introduction

A number of methods have been proposed for or-parallel implementation of logic programs [H87, W84, W87a, TL87, B84, DLO87, CH83, CH86, C87, L84, K86, A87]. Although extremely efficient or-parallel systems have been realized [LWH88], not much has been done to study these methods in an organized fashion, with the exception of the works of D.H.D. Warren [W87b], who examined a few or-parallel methods, especially those that are variants of the Argonne Model [DLO87] and the SRI model [W87a], and also Hausman and Ciepielewski [CH86], who examined several variations of their directory tree method [CH83]. In this paper we attempt to give a more general treatment, encompassing a larger class of methods. We propose that an ideal or-parallel implementation model should satisfy the following three criteria:

1. the cost of *environment creation* should be constant-time;
2. the cost of *variable access and binding* should be constant-time; and
3. the cost of *task switching* should be constant-time.

We use the term constant-time to mean that the time for these operations is independent of the number of nodes in the or-parallel search tree, as well as the number of goals and the size of terms that appear in goals. These criteria are derived from a consideration of the three important operations in any logic programming system (sequential or parallel): allocation of space for variables (environment creation), unification (variable access and binding), and resumption after success or failure (task switching). While it would be ideal if an or-parallel execution model could satisfy all three criteria, we show in this paper that this ideal cannot be achieved by any or-parallel model using a finite number of processors and constant-time addressable memory.

To appreciate our negative result, observe that a sequential, WAM-like execution model—which can be viewed as a special case of an or-parallel model—provides constant-time environment creation and constant-time variable access and binding, but not constant-time task switching. The latter operation, also known as backtracking in sequential implementations, requires untrailing variables, and the number of such variables is not a constant in general. An or-parallel model, however, does not have to perform backtracking, and hence it might appear that all three criteria can be satisfied. But this reasoning is not correct because of the finite processor assumption; the or-parallel tree can have more or-parallel tasks available than processors, and hence there is a need for task switching. One can make task switching a constant-time operation, as in the directory tree [CH86] or other methods, but only at the expense of the other two operations. Unlike a sequential implementation, an or-parallel implementation must support multiple bindings (or values) for the same variable, corresponding to different branches of the or-parallel search tree. These multiple bindings are the main cause for non-constant time variable access, because it is not obvious, without additional bookkeeping, which binding is applicable when a variable is accessed from an arbitrary node of the or-parallel search tree. Attempts to make variable access a constant-time operation lead to non-constant overheads in the other operations. For example, in order to facilitate constant-time variable access, if we record the binding of a variable applicable to a given node in the node itself, then environment creation is affected because there are in general a non-constant number of variables for which this information must be recorded.

The fact that at least one of the criteria must be sacrificed partly explains why so many or-parallel execution models have been proposed in the literature. Based on which criteria one chooses to satisfy one has a different execution model for or-parallelism. This also suggests a natural scheme for classifying various execution models for or-parallelism. We classify these or-parallel execution models according to which (proper) subset of the three criteria they satisfy . Our treatment based on the above three criteria is more general than those found in [W87b] and [CH86] in that it encompasses all or-parallel methods that are based on the or-parallel search tree. While these criteria have been briefly mentioned in works of other researchers [W87a, H87, CH86], the main contribution of our work is firstly in formulating these criteria in the form presented above, secondly, in proving that these criteria cannot all be satisfied together, and lastly, in using them as a basis for classification.

The rest of the paper is organized as follows: section 2 introduces the essential concepts and terminology in the form of definitions and remarks; section 3 proves the main result with aid of a few lemmas, and discusses the result in the context of a few specific or-parallel implementations; section 4 presents our classification of or-parallel execution models based on these criteria; and section 5 presents conclusions.

2. Notation and Terminology

To keep the presentation self-contained we provide in this section definitions for all terms used and also introduce notation that will be employed in later sections. In the following definitions, N stands for the set (possibly infinite) of nodes in the or-parallel tree, V the set (possibly infinite) of all variables, T the set of terms (possibly non-ground) in the logic program, P the set of processors, and M the set of memory locations in the multiprocessor system. Let $\mathcal{P}(S)$ denote the power set of a set S and $|S|$ its cardinality.

Definition: *logic program, query*

A *logic program* is a conjunction of definite *relational* clauses over first-order *terms.*

A *query* is a list of *goals*, where a *goal* is a positive literal of the form *p(terms)*.

2.1. Or-parallel Tree

Definition: *or-parallel tree, local environment*

An *or-parallel tree* for a query Q and logic program LP is a tree of nodes, each with an associated *goal-list* and *local environment*, such that:

1. the root node of the tree has Q as its associated goal-list and the set of variables appearing in Q as its local environment; and
2. each non-root node n is created as a result of successful unification of the first goal in (the goal-list of) n's parent node with the head of a unique variant of a clause in LP, H :- $B_1, B_2, \ldots, B_n$, and:
   a. the goal-list of node n is $(B_1, B_2, \ldots, B_n, L_2, \ldots, L_m)\theta$, if the goal-list of the parent of n is $L_1, L_2, \ldots, L_m$ and $\theta = mgu(H, L_1)$.
   b. the *local environment*, $l(n)$, of n is the set of all variables present in the unifying clause, where $l : N \rightarrow \mathcal{P}(V)$.

Remarks:

i. All nodes of an or-parallel tree need *not* have the same number of offspring nodes, i.e., the *branching factor* is not the same for all nodes.
ii. The branching factor is bounded by a constant, determined by the logic program.
iii. We assume there is an unbounded supply of variables, and variables in a clause are uniquely renamed before unification so that the sets of variables in any two local environments are disjoint from one another.

Definition: $\leq$

For two nodes n_1 and n_2 of an or-parallel tree, we say $n_1 \leq n_2$ iff n_1 and n_2 lie on the same path from the root of the tree and either $n_1 = n_2$ or n_1 is closer to the root than n_2. In the latter case, we say $n_1 < n_2$.

Remarks:

i. $\leq$ is a partial order.

ii. We will sometimes write $m \geq n$ instead of $n \leq m$.

Definition: *global environment*

The *global environment*, $g(n)$, of a node n in an or-parallel tree is the union of the set of variables in all local environments lying on the path from the root of the tree to n. That is, $g : N \rightarrow \mathcal{P}(V)$, and $g(n) = \{v \mid (\exists x)\ x \leq n$ and $v \in l(x)\}$.

Remarks:

i. We assume that $n_1 \neq n_2 \Rightarrow g(n_1) \neq g(n_2)$, since we may introduce one distinct dummy variable in the local environment of each node.

Definition: *owner node, access node, binding node*

For each variable v in the local environment of a node n:

1. There is a unique *owner node* for v, $o(v) = n$, where $o : V \rightarrow N$.
2. There is a subset of N called *access nodes* for v, where each access node m is such that $m \geq n$.
3. There is a subset of access nodes called *binding nodes* for v, which can be characterized in terms of a partial function $b : V \times N \rightarrow N$ that specifies the binding node of a variable v in the *global environment* of a node n. The set of binding nodes for v =

   $$\{m \mid b(v, m) = m\},$$

   where b satisfies the requirement that if there is a node m such that $b(v, m) = m$, then $b(v, y)$ is undefined for all $y < m$ and $b(v, y) = m$ for all $y \geq m$.

Remarks:

i. At each access node m of a variable v, the value of v is accessed during the unification operation associated with the creation of m; at each binding node k of a variable v, v gets bound to a value during the unification operation associated with the creation of k.

ii. The characterization of the or-parallel tree in terms of owner, binding and access nodes is based on the observation that there are three operations performed on variables—variable creation, variable binding and variable access. Corresponding to these 3 operations we have 3 kinds of nodes in the or-parallel tree, namely, owner nodes, binding nodes and access nodes.

iii. Every binding node is an access node since a variable must be accessed before being bound; i.e., variable binding is a special case of variable access.

Proposition: *uniqueness property of binding nodes*

If a variable v has two distinct binding nodes n_1 and n_2, then $n_1 \not< n_2$ and $n_2 \not> n_1$, i.e., n_1 and n_2 do not lie on the same path from the root.

Proof: Let n_1 and n_2 be two distinct binding nodes, i.e., $n_1 \neq n_2$. Suppose $n_1 \leq n_2$, to derive a contradiction. By the definition of a binding node, for all $y \geq n_1$, we have $b(v, y) = n_1$. Hence $b(v, n_2) = n_1$. But $b(v, n_2) = n_2$, since n_2 is a binding node. Hence $n_1 = n_2$, a contradiction. **End of Proof.**

Corollary: The binding node of a variable in a global environment is unique.

Definition: *value cell, value*

For each variable v in the local environment of a node n:

1. There is a set of *value cells* for v, where each value cell is a memory location that is used for storing the value of v created by the corresponding binding node. We use a partial function $vc : V \times N \rightarrow M$, which defines the value cell for v in the global environment of a node n, where the function vc satisfies the requirement that $vc(v, y)$ is undefined for all $y < o(v)$.
2. There is a one-to-one correspondence† between the set of binding nodes for v and a set of *values*, where each value is a *term.* This set of values can be specified by a partial function $val : V \times N \rightarrow T$, which defines the value for v in the global environment of a node n. For each binding node m for v, we have (a) for all $y < o(v)$, $val(v, y)$ is undefined; (b) for all $o(v) \leq y < m$, $val(v, y)$ is unbound; and (c) for all $y \geq m$, $val(v, y) = val(v, m)$.

Remarks:

i. Contrary to common convention, the value cell does not always refer to the cell allocated for v in the local environment of the owner node of v; rather, the value cell is the memory cell allocated for holding the binding generated by a binding node.

ii. The function $val(v, n)$ cannot be described analytically because then we would be able to predict the value of a given variable in a particular environment even before that variable gets bound, which amounts to solving the halting problem.

Definition: *conditional binding, conditional variable*

A binding for a variable v is said to be *unconditional* iff either $b(v, o(v)) = o(v)$ or the branching factor of every node from $o(v)$ down to and excluding the binding node of v is one; in this case, the variable v is said to be *unconditionally bound.* Otherwise, the binding is said to be *conditional* and v is referred to as a *conditionally bound variable* or a *conditional variable.*

---

† We assume that two identical bindings generated by different binding nodes are distinguishable from each other.

Definition: *complete or-parallel tree*

A *complete or-parallel tree* is one where:

1. for each leaf node l, the goal-list of l is either empty (*success leaf node*) or the first goal in l does not unify with any clause (*failure leaf node*); and
2. for each non-leaf node n, a child node is present in the or-parallel tree corresponding to each successful unification of the first goal in n's goal-list with every clause head in LP.

Remarks:

i. An *incomplete or-parallel tree* is one in which some leaf or non-leaf node can be extended by creating an offspring node.

ii. It is possible that there is no complete or-parallel tree for a given query and logic program (because of nontermination).

2.2. Computational Model

We assume a model of computation in which there is an unbounded number of memory locations, each of which can be accessed in constant-time. We assume that a finite number of processors (i.e. $|P|$ is finite) cooperatively construct the or-parallel tree, by creating offspring nodes as long as the tree is incomplete. In order to create an offspring node at some node n, a processor must first move from its current node to the location of node n. All processors may be assumed to be located at the root of the or-parallel tree initially. The following definitions focus on three important operations in this model of computation: task creation, task switching, and variable access.

Definition: *task site*

A *task site* in an incomplete or-parallel tree is a node n for which there is at least one untried candidate clause for the first goal in n's goal-list.

Definition: *task creation*

If n is a task site, a processor is said to *create a task* at node n when it constructs the global environment and goal-list for an offspring node corresponding to an untried clause at n. The time taken to construct the *global environment* of the offspring node of n is called the *cost of task creation.*

Remarks:

i. A lower-bound on the cost of task creation is the cost of creating the local environment for the offspring node of n.

ii. In certain parallel schemes, such as *environment closing* [C87] and *variable importation* [L84], variable bindings are copied from a child node's local environment to the parent node's local environment after completion of a sub-goal. We regard this work as part of task creation for the next sub-goal, since it is done in order to prepare for the next call.

Definition: *current environment*

The *current environment* of a processor located at node n is $g(n)$.

Definition: *task switching*

A processor is said to *switch tasks* when it moves from node n_1 to node n_2 in an or-parallel tree. The time taken by the processor to change its current environment to that at n_2 is called the *cost of task-switching.*

Definition: *access cell*

For every variable v accessible to a processor p at a node n, there is a memory location called an *access cell* that is used for looking up the binding of v during variable access. A partial function $ac : V \times P \times N \rightarrow M$ defines the access cell for v in the environment of a processor p at node n. The function ac satisfies the requirement that $ac(v, p, y)$ is undefined for all $y < o(v)$.

Remarks:

i. The difference between an access cell and a value cell is that the former is used for *looking up* the binding of v during variable access, whereas the latter is used for *storing* the binding of v during variable binding.

ii. Each value cell of a variable has to be accessible to all processors since it contains the binding generated for the variable. Hence, value cells cannot be maintained privately by any processor. On the contrary, each processor can maintain its own access cell for any particular binding of any variable v. Hence vc is not a function of p, but ac is.

iii. For every v, n, and p the value associated with the access cell $ac(v, p, n)$ is identical to that of value cell $vc(v, n)$. Thus, any or-parallel model has to make sure that the contents of value cells are reflected in the access cells in a given environment. Some methods ensure this by having the value cell and access cell share the same physical memory location, e.g. directory tree method [CH83] and the hashing window method [B84]; other methods keep them physically separate but copy the binding in both the value cell and access cell during variable binding generation, e.g. binding arrays [W84, W87] and versions vectors method [H87] (these methods allocate access cells in the binding array and versions vector respectively, while allocating value cells in the binding list or trail).

Definition: *variable access*

The process of locating the access cell $ac(v, p, n)$ by a processor p at node n for a variable v in $g(n)$ is called *variable access.* The time taken by the processor for this operation is called the *cost of variable access.*

Remarks:

i. Locating the final binding of a variable is a two-step process: (a) variable access, in which the applicable access cell is located, and (b) dereferencing, in which the contents of the binding cell are used to obtain the final binding. Dereferencing may involve indirection and thus in general would be non-constant time. Our definition of variable access does not include dereferencing.

We conclude this section by re-stating our three our criteria for an ideal or-parallel implementation in the light of the discussion above:

1. the cost of task creation should be constant-time;
2. the cost of variable access should be constant-time; and
3. the cost of task switching should be constant-time.

By constant-time, we mean that the time taken by these operations do not depend either on the depth or the size of the or-parallel tree or the size of the goal-list or the size of terms created during execution. Similarly, we consider the size of a set to be non-constant if its cardinality is proportional to the depth or size of the or-parallel tree, the size of the goal-list or size of terms created during execution. For example, the size of set of conditional variables in a global environment of a node is non-constant, since its cardinality is proportional to the depth of the tree.

3. The Main Result

In this section we prove that the three criteria cannot be simultaneously satisfied. Perhaps the most conventional way to devise this proof would be to construct a constant-time reduction of a known problem having the desired property to the problem at hand, such that the known problem is solved if and only if the problem at hand is solved. We present an alternative approach: essentially we consider all possible ways in which the problem could be solved and show that one or more of our criteria is violated. The proof is a bit long, but can be divided into two main parts:

1. *Access cells and value cells are identical.* Since there is a one-to-one correspondence between values and binding nodes, accessing a value reduces to that of determining binding nodes (this will be proved in corollary 1). For such methods we show that, in general, no binding node can be determined without violating one of the criteria. Lemma 1 considers the case when the information needed to locate a binding node is kept somewhere in the or-parallel tree, i.e., in some combination of owner nodes, binding nodes, and access nodes; and lemma 2 considers the case when the information is maintained in a data-structure independent of these nodes. Theorem 1 puts lemma 1 and lemma 2 together.
2. *Access cells and value cells are separate.* For such methods we show in Lemma 3 that task-switching is always a non-constant time operation.

Finally, the conclusions of Lemmas 1, 2 and 3, and Theorem 1 are organized in Theorem 2, which proves our assertion.

In the lemmas below we assume that a variable is treated uniformly in all environments. For example, if a particular binding of a variable in a particular environment is stored in a value cells allocated in the binding node, then all other bindings for v in other environments are also stored in value cells allocated in respective binding nodes and so on. It is easy to extend the proofs to include non-uniform treatment of variables in different environments, but we don't include it here for reasons of simplicity and space.

Lemma 1 : *Let access cells and value cells be identical. If the information regarding binding node b(v, n) (of a variable v in the global environment of a node n) is associated with either the owner node, the binding node or the access nodes, then either b(v, n) cannot be determined in constant-time by a processor at node n, or non constant overhead is incurred during task-creation.*

Proof: We first consider the three cases when the information is maintained exclusively in one of these three nodes, and then consider when the information is maintained in some combination of these cases:

i. *The association between v, n, and $b(v, n)$ is kept in the binding node:* In this case, the only way for a processor to locate the binding node $b(v, n)$ is to traverse the tree upwards from node n until it reaches the binding node. This is a non-constant time operation since the number of intervening nodes between node n and node $b(v, n)$ is not constant in general. If the processor reaches the owner node of v during this upward traversal then the binding node is undefined (i.e., v is unbound in $g(n)$). Since the number of nodes between $o(v)$ and n is also not constant in general, determining that the binding node for a variable v in environment $g(n)$ doesn't exist is also a non-constant time operation.

ii. *The association between v, n, and $b(v, n)$ is kept in the owner node:* Given an arbitrary variable v, its owner node $o(v)$ is unique. Therefore, the owner node of v maintains the set of binding nodes for v, $B(v) = \{m \mid b(v, m) = m\}$. If a processor at n wants to determine $b(v, n)$, it must find an $x \in B(v)$ such that $x \leq n$. The different binding nodes for v in $B(v)$ are not related to node n in any way that would enable n to serve as an index to a data-structure for constant-time access to the binding node $b(v, n)$. Hence, the set $B(v)$ has to be explicitly searched in order to find an $x \in B(v)$ such that $x \leq n$. Since $B(v)$ is a set of non-constant size, searching for an x such that $x \leq n$ is a non-constant time operation†.

iii. *The association between v, n, and $b(v, n)$ is kept in the access nodes:* Since access nodes cannot be determined in advance, the association would have to be maintained in every node, i.e., each node k would need to store the binding pair $\langle w, b(w, k)) \rangle$ for each (conditional) variable w accessible from it. Since the number of conditional variables accessible

† Although it is not required for the proof of the lemma, given a node x in a dynamically changing tree, even determining that $x \leq n$, i.e. node x is an ancestor of node n, and therefore the correct one, is not possible in constant-time [M79, SV88].

from a particular k would not in general be constant, creation of k would become a non-constant time operation, because all the binding pairs of k's parent would have to be copied into k. If, instead of copying these pairs, node k shares them with its parent node, then access to these pairs (and hence access to the binding nodes) would become a non-constant time operation, since k's parent can share the binding pairs of its parent, etc. In the worst case, to determine the binding node of a variable, all ancestors of k would also have to be searched, and thus this case degenerates to case (i). Thus, either binding node determination becomes a non-constant time operation or non-constant overhead is incurred during task-creation.

iv. *The association between v, n and $b(v, n)$ is stored in some combination of binding, owner, and access nodes:* Let C be the set of all conditional variables in the global environment of a node n. In general C would be a set of a non-constant size. Let C_1 be the set of conditional variables for which case (i) is true, C_2 the set of conditional variables for which case (ii) is true, and C_3 the set of conditional variables for which case (iii) is true. Thus, $C = C_1 \cup C_2 \cup C_3$. Since C is of non-constant size, at least one of C_1, C_2 or C_3 is of non-constant size, and thus the reasoning of cases (i), (ii) or (iii) can be used to prove this case. **End of Proof.**

Lemma 2: *Let access cells and value cells be identical, and let C be the set of conditional variables in the global environment of a node n. If the information regarding binding node $b(v, n)$ of a variable $v \in C$ is recorded in a data structure independent of the or-parallel tree, then either accessing the binding node is a non-constant time operation or non-constant time overhead is incurred during task-creation or task-switching.*

Proof: Suppose $b(v, n)$ can be found in constant time. A processor has to record in a data-structure‡ the value for $b(v, n)$ for all variables $v (\in C)$ accessible from n. There are three ways this data-structure can be organized:

i. *As a global data-structure common to all processors.* Here, either task-creation of node n or accessing $b(v, n)$ will be a non-constant time operation. If $b(v, n)$'s for all variables in set C accessible from node n are recorded in the global data-structure during the creation of that node, then task-creation is a non-constant time operation since in general a non-constant sized subset of variables in C would be accessible from n. If $b(v, n)$'s are recorded incrementally as they are needed, then accessing them would be a non-constant time operation because we would then have to find an ancestor node m of n such that $b(v, n) = b(v, m)$ and an entry for $b(v, m)$ exists in the global data-structure. Finding such an m would obviously be a non-constant time operation since it would involve searching the tree upwards from n until such an m is found. Hence, determining the binding node is a non-constant time operation.

‡ No assumption about this data-structure is made: it could be an array, hash table, etc.

ii. *As a private data-structure, one for each processor.* Here, task-switching will be a non-constant time operation, since each time a processor switches tasks, it has to record entries for all variables accessible from the new nodes now in processors path. The number of new nodes accessible to a processor on a task-switch, as well as the number of variables accessible from these newly accessible nodes, is dependent on the depth of the node corresponding to the new task, and thus is not a constant. Hence task-switching is a non-constant time operation. Alternatively, if this private data-structure is constructed incrementally, then accessing binding nodes is a non-constant time operation because of reasons similar to those given in case (i).

iii. *As a data-structure, part of which is global and part private to each processor.* Since C is of non-constant size, either the set of variables recorded in the global data-structure or the set of variables recorded in the private data-structures would be of non-constant size. Hence this case can be proved using the reasoning of case i or case ii. **End of Proof.**

Theorem 1: *Let access cells and value cells be identical and let C be the set of conditional variables in the global environment of a node n. The binding node $b(v,n)$ of a variable $v \in C$ cannot be determined by a processor at node n in constant time without incurring non-constant overhead during task-creation or task-switching.*

Proof: The function b cannot be analytically defined since doing so would allow us to predict the binding node of a given variable in a particular environment even before that variable gets bound, which amounts to solving the halting problem. This means that to evaluate the function $b(v,n)$ the association between a variable v and its binding node in environment $g(n)$ has to be explicitly maintained. There are two ways to maintain this association: either in the or-parallel tree (in some combination of owner, binding and access nodes) or independent of the or-parallel tree (in a data-structure independent of the tree).

Let C_{in} be the set of variables for which the association information is stored in the tree and let C_{out} be the set of variables for which the association information is stored independent of the tree. Since C is a set of non-constant size, and $C = C_{in} \cup C_{out}$, at least one of C_{in} or C_{out} is also of non-constant size. If C_{in} is of non-constant size, by lemma 1 either binding nodes cannot be accessed in constant time or non-constant overhead is incurred during task-creation. If C_{out} is of non-constant size, by lemma 2 either binding nodes cannot be accessed in constant time or non-constant overhead is incurred during task-creation or task-switching. Thus, in either case non-constant overhead is incurred. **End of Proof.**

Corollary 1: *Let access cells and value cells be identical and let C be the set of conditional variables in the global environment of a node n. It is not* *possible for a processor at an access node n to access $val(v, n)$ (for $v \in C$) in $vc(v, n)$ in constant time without incurring non-constant overhead during task-creation or task-switching.*

Proof: Since the relation between functions b and val is one-one, finding $val(v, n)$ in constant time without incurring non-constant time task-creation or task-switching overheads means $b(v, n)$ can also be found in constant time without incurring non-constant-time task-creation or task-switching overheads†. Clearly this is not possible according to theorem 1. **End of Proof.**

Lemma 3: *If access cells are distinct from value cells, task-switching is a non-constant time operation.*

Proof: Let C be a non-constant set of conditional variables. During task-switch by an arbitrary processor p, the bindings applicable to conditional variables in C may change due to a change of current global environment of p. Hence, p should make sure that the access cells are correctly established for all such conditional variables. Suppose p switches from node k_1 to node k_2. Let k be the least common ancestor node of k_1 and k_2. Let K be the set of all nodes in the path from k_1 to k_2 via k. Let $C' = \{v \mid v \in C \wedge b(v, k_1) \in K\} \cup \{v \mid v \in C \ \wedge \ b(v, k_2) \in K\}$. A variable w is *affected* by a task switch if $w \in C'$.

The set C can be partitioned into two subsets C_1 and C_2 such that:

i. $C_1 = \{v \mid ac(v, p, k_1) = ac(v, p, k_2)\}$. That is, for conditional variables in C_1, the processor uses the same physical memory location for the access cell irrespective of the environment it is in (i.e., it does not allocate a new one).

ii. $C_2 = \{v \mid ac(v, p, k_1) \neq ac(v, p, k_2)\}$. That is, a new physical memory location is allocated in the environment at k_2 for the access cell for each conditional variable in set C_2.

Since C is of non-constant size, at least one of C_1 or C_2 is also of non-constant size. In case (i) the access cells have to be *updated* for each conditional variable in C_1 (at the very least for *affected* conditional variables in $C' \cap C_1$); similarly, in case (ii) the access cells have to be *created and updated* for each conditional variable in C_2 (at the very least for *affected* conditional variables in $C' \cap C_2$). Since either C_1 or C_2 is of non-constant size and in general C' would be of non-constant size, task-switching will be a non-constant time operation. **End of Proof.**

Theorem 2: *There is no implementation method for a bounded number of processors which satisfies all three criteria.*

---

† For example, when a binding is generated we can record (the address of) its binding node with it in the value cell. Then, access to a variable's binding in the value cell means automatic access to that binding's binding node at no extra cost.

Proof: Let C be the (non-constant sized) set of conditional variables in the or-parallel tree at any given moment. Partition the set C into two disjoint sets C_a and C_b, where C_a is the subset of C for which access cells and value cells are distinct, and C_b the subset of C for which these cells are identical. Clearly, either C_a or C_b must have a non-constant number of variables. By lemma 3, if C_a were of non-constant size, task-switching will be a non-constant time operation. Hence, consider the case that C_b is of non-constant size. C_b corresponds to the set where access cells and value cells are identical. For such variables variable-access amounts to accessing the values in value-cells. By corollary 1 if C_b is of non-constant size then the values of variables in C_b cannot be accessed in constant time without incurring non-constant overhead during task-creation or task-switching. **End of Proof.**

Discussion

From the above lemmas and theorems, it appears that the main task in an or-parallel system is to determine the binding node during variable access. Once the binding node is identified, the binding it created can be accessed in constant time. Different methods differ in how they identify the binding node, but a central aim of all the methods is to identify the binding node efficiently so that the value cells can be accessed in constant time during variable access or for environment update during task-switching. For example, some methods simplify the operation of finding the binding node of a variable by allocating the value cells in the binding node itself (e.g. binding arrays method [W84, W87a], version vectors method [H87], hashing windows method [B84]). Some schemes assign a unique id to the binding node and record this id with each binding. For example, in the time stamping method [TL87], the variable bindings are organized in a fashion that once the binding node is known the corresponding binding can be efficiently accessed.

In most methods proposed in the literature, either set C_a or C_b (described in theorem 2) is an empty set. However, the proof above is more general and subsumes even those methods which may have both C_a and C_b non-empty. We consider a few methods and see why they satisfy theorem 2; in the process, we will see an illustration of the proof of the lemmas and the theorem.

Binding Arrays Method

In the binding arrays method [W84, W87], value cells and access cells are allocated memory space separately. Access cells are allocated space in the binding array private to the processor while value cells are allocated space in the binding lists in the binding node. Since the slot used in the access cell for a particular conditional variable is fixed irrespective of which global environment it is in, its content has to be updated on a task-switch. This results in task-switching time becoming non-constant in accordance with lemma 3. Thus, theorem 2 holds for the binding arrays method. (By a similar reasoning, we can see that the version vectors [H87] method also has non-constant task-switching time and thus satisfies theorem 2.)

For the binding arrays method, the value of sets C_a and C_b described in theorem 2 are: $C_a = C_v$ and $C_b = \phi$, where C_v is the set of all conditional variables in the or-parallel tree at a given time. Also, the value of sets C_1 and C_2 described in lemma 3 are: $C_1 = C_v$ and $C_2 = \phi$. Note that lemma 3 is parameterized by p, k_1, k_2, C_1, C_2. Thus, a variation of the standard binding arrays method can be conceived where for certain pair of nodes k_1 and k_2 a processor decides to update its binding array in place ($C_1 \neq \phi$), whereas for certain other pair of nodes k_3 and k_4 it leaves its old binding array stationed at k_3 and constructs a new one for k_4 ($C_2 \neq \phi$). This corresponds to the case where there are more binding arrays than the number of processors and the ownership of a binding array can change from time to time. In this case, in order to optimize task-switching time, a processor may build a new binding array for a branch when it sees that the or-parallel tree has become too big. Obviously this modified binding array method satisfies lemma 3 and thus theorem 2.

Note that it is not necessary for the binding arrays and versions vectors method to record the value cells in the binding nodes. Value cells can be recorded using a different scheme, say, for example, as in the time stamping method [TL87]. This will give us a variation of the binding arrays and the versions vector method. More variations of the binding arrays method (Manchester-Argonne and Argonne-SRI models), which also satisfy theorem 2, are given in [W87b].

Muse System

In the Muse system [AK90] the binding environment of each processor is distinct, i.e. it is not shared with others. When a processor switches to another node in the or-parallel tree, it constructs the whole stack from that node to the root node in its memory. As a result, due to subcase (ii) of lemma 2 and corollary 1, task-switching becomes a non-constant time operation. The same holds true for Kabu-Wake method [K86].

Directory Tree Method

In the directory tree method [CH83], the binding environment is represented using directories and contexts. Each node has its own directory which contains a number of contexts, one for each of its ancestor nodes. A context corresponds to a clause and has space for variables in the clause. When a node branches it has to create new directories (with copies of the node's contexts) for each of its children nodes.

In this method value cells and access cells are identical and are allocated space in access nodes. Each node has its own copy of all the contexts. Hence, by lemma 1 and corollary 1, task creation is a non-constant time operation. Thus, theorem 2 holds for the directory tree method. Note that for this method the value of sets C_a and C_b described in theorem 2 are: $C_a = \phi$ and $C_b = C_v$.

For similar reasons, theorem 2 holds for the environment closing method [C87] and the environment representation scheme used in ROPM [RK89]. They both have non-constant task-creation time.

Hashing Window Method

In the hashing windows method [B84], the access cell and value cell are identical and allocated space in the binding node. Hence, by lemma 1 and corollary 1, variable access is a non-constant time operation. (To insure fast access to variable bindings within a binding node, a value cell is allocated a cell in a *hash window* whose address is obtained by hashing on the variable address). Thus, the hashing window method also satisfies theorem 2.

For similar reasons, theorem 2 holds for the Argonne Model [DLO87, W87b]. However, in the Argonne Model, the hash window is of constant size (= 32) and the contents of the hash window of a node are shared with its children, which results in each bucket in the hash-window having a largc number of variables mapped to it (which are stored as a list). Thus, the non-constant cost of traversing the tree upwards (towards the root) and finding the binding node is reflected as the cost of locating the value cell in the bucket. The further up the tree the binding node of v is, the more towards the end of the list in the bucket would be the value cell of v.

Theorem 2 also holds for the variation of the hashing windows method adopted for representing environments in the PEPSys model [WR87]. In this model, when a conditional variable is accessed from a node, its binding is copied into the hashing window of the access node, so that future accesses to this variable from the descendent nodes have to traverse fewer nodes. Thus, this scheme also satisfies theorem 2 by virtue of lemma 1 (case iii) and corollary 1.

Time Stamping Method

The time stamping method [TL87] records the id of the processor and a unique time stamp with each variable binding. The ⟨pid, time-stamp⟩ pair can be regarded as the id of the binding node which created the binding. The id is later used in accessing the bindings. The value cells (which are identical to access cells in this method) are organized in a data-structure independent of the or-parallel tree. Thus, in accordance with lemma 2 and corollary 1, variable access is a non-constant time operation. Actually, in the time stamping method, task-switching too is a non-constant time operation because the *ancestor stack* (which can be viewed as representation of the association between variables and their binding nodes) has to be constructed during task-switching from information recorded in the nodes. Thus, due to lemma 2 and corollary 1 task-switching too is a non constant time operation in this method.

And-Or parallel Methods

The theorem also holds for the or-parallel component of and-or parallel systems. For example, consider the following three methods for incorporating independent and-parallelism and or-parallelism in a single framework: (i) the Reduce-Or Parallel Model [RK87] (ii) the PEPSys model [WR87] and (iii) the authors' own and-or parallel model [GJ89]. Note that the environment representation scheme used in the three methods sacrifice the task-creation, variable-access and task-switching criteria respectively.

4. Classification of Or-Parallel Models

In the previous section we proved that the three criteria cannot be satisfied together. The fact that all three criteria cannot be simultaneously satisfied is partly the reason why so many methods have been proposed in the literature for or-parallel execution of logic programs. Based on which criteria one chooses to satisfy one has a different execution model for or-parallelism. One can also use this as a basis for classifying the various or-parallel execution models. Since there are three criteria to be satisfied, in principle there are $2^3 = 8$ classes of methods according to this classification (see figure 1). We have proved that no methods exists in Class 1, which corresponds to methods providing constant-time for all three operations, i.e. task creation, variable access and task switching. Class 8 methods are uninteresting since all three operations are non-constant time. None of the methods proposed in the literature fall in class 7, which corresponds to non-constant task creation as well as non-constant task-switching time. Although it is theoretically possible to create an or-parallel method which would fall in this class, this is unlikely in practice, because, if task creation is non-constant time, it is very likely that the environment has already been replicated during node-creation; thus there is no need for any environment updating during task-switch since each branch in the or-parallel tree has its own private environment.

Theoretically, there is no reason why any method should sacrifice more than one criterion, although some methods do, e.g., the variable importation method [L84] and the time stamping method [TL87]. This is because they distribute the cost of multiple environment representation over two operations rather than one, possibly for reasons of efficiency. The overall performance may eventually remain unchanged (or even improve). For example, in the time stamping method [TL87], in the worst case variable bindings would have to be accessed in the global data-structure by searching the entire data-structure. However, by keeping the ancestor stack, which results in non-constant time task-switching, only a fraction of the global data-structure has to be accessed. Thus, although two criteria may be sacrificed by a particular method, it does not necessarily mean that it is inferior to a method which sacrifices only one criterion.

In table 1 we give a table showing which particular criteria are satisfied by different methods. A $\surd$ in a column indicates that the criterion corresponding to that column is satisfied by the method.

Discussion

Methods falling in the same class can be directly compared with each other, and the best one among them determined. It makes more sense to compare methods within the same class, rather than methods belonging to different classes. (Later we compare the different class of methods and argue that one class of methods is inherently superior to other classes of methods.) For example, both the directory tree method and the environment closing

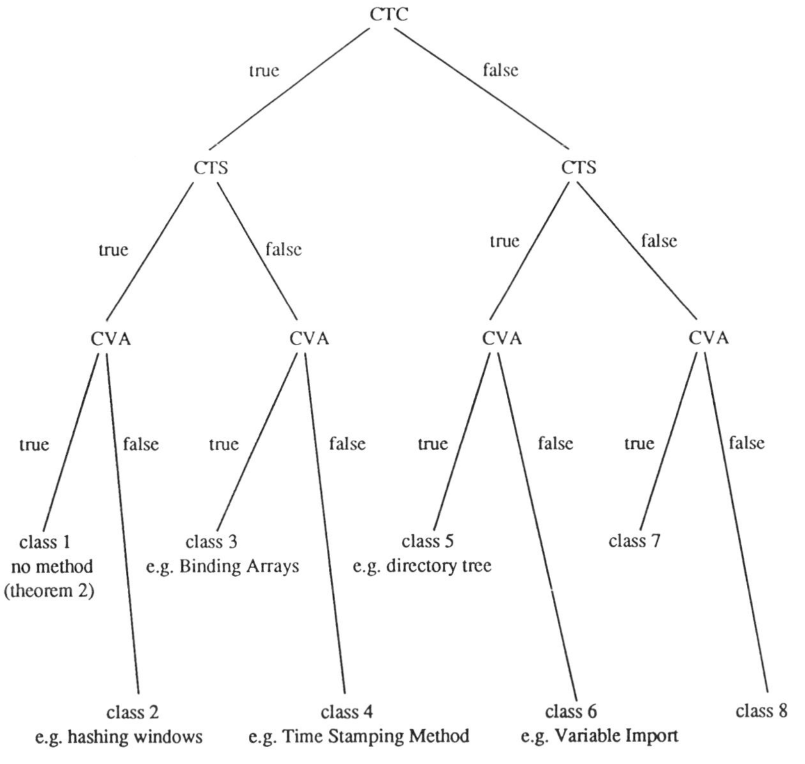

CTC = Constant Time Task Creation

CTS = Constant Time Task Switch

CVA = Constant Time Variable Access

Figure 1 : Classification of Or-parallel Methods

method duplicate the environment during task-creation. However, environment closing duplicates a smaller fraction of the environment since it does not duplicate variables which are already bound, while the directory tree method does. Thus, although two or-parallel methods might be theoretically equivalent, in practice one may be more efficient than the other. For similar reasons the binding arrays method is superior to versions vectors methods as far as executions costs are concerned (the reasons are given in [W87a]).

Method	CTC	CVA	CTS
Version Vectors [H87]	√	√	
Binding Arrays [W84, W87a]	√	√	
Argonne-SRI Model [W87b]	√	√	
Manchester-Argonne [W87b]	√	√	
Time-Stamping [TL87]	√		
Hashing Windows [B84]	√		√
Naive Model [W87b]	√		√
Argonne Model [DLO87]	√		√
Directory Tree [CH83]		√	√
Environment Closing [C87]		√	√
Variable Import [L84]			√
Kabu-Wake [K86]	√	√	
BC-Machine [A87]	√	√	
Muse [AK90]	√	√	
Abstract Model [W87b]		√	√

CTC = Constant-time Task Creation; CVA = Constant-time Variable Access;
CTS = Constant-time Task Switch

Table 1: Criteria Satisfied by Various Methods

For shared-memory multiprocessors, methods that sacrifice constant time task-switch tend to be superior to those that sacrifice constant-time task-creation and variable-access. This is because the number of task-creation and variable-access operations is program dependent while the number of task-switching operations is dependent on the scheduling policy employed by the run-time system. Thus, the cost of task-switching can be carefully controlled by the implementor (by optimizing granularity, for instance), while this is not possible for task-creation and variable access. This has been demonstrated by the Aurora system [LWH88] which employs sophisticated schedulers [CS89, S89, B90] to minimize the cost of task-switching.

For distributed memory systems, methods with non-constant time task-creation are likely to perform better. This is because the whole environment can be made available locally by copying during task-creation. However, the advent of *distributed shared memory systems* [WH88, LH89] may make methods sacrificing constant-time task-switching as competitive on distributed systems as those sacrificing constant-time task-creation. And, as mentioned earlier, since performance of the methods in the former class is less dependent on the behavior of the logic programs, they might even out-perform the methods in the latter class on distributed memory sytems.

5. Conclusions

In this paper we have presented three criteria which an ideal or-parallel system should satisfy: (i) constant-time access to all variables, (ii) constant-time task creation, and (iii) constant-time task-switching. We formulated and proved a theorem that given only a bounded number of processors, there is no or-parallel execution method which can satisfy all three criteria simultaneously. We used the three criteria as a means of classifying the various or-parallel methods proposed in the literature. The classification is quite useful since it provides greater insight into the various or-parallel methods, and also allows more meaningful comparisons between them.

Acknowledgements: Thanks to David H.D. Warren, Feliks Kluźniak and the anonymous referees for their comments and suggestions. This work was supported in part by NSF grant DCR 8603609 and U.K. Science and Engineering Research Council grant GR/F 27420.

References

[A87] K. Ali, "Or-parallel execution of Prolog on BC-machine," In *Proceedings of 5th International Conference and Symposium on Logic Prog.*, Seattle, 1988.

[AK90] K. Ali, R. Karlsson, "The Muse Or-parallel Prolog Model and its performance," In *NACLP '90.*

[B90] A. J. Beaumont, et. al., "The Bristol Scheduler for Aurora," Technical Report TR-90-04, University of Bristol, 1990.

[B84] P. Borgwardt, "Parallel Prolog using stack segments on shared memory multiprocessors," In *Proceedings of the 1984 Int. Symp. on Logic Prog.*, Atlantic City, NJ, 1984, pp. 2-11.

[C87] J. S. Conery, "Binding Environments for Parallel Logic Programs in Non-Shared Memory Multiprocessors," *1987 IEEE Int. Symp. in Logic Prog.*, San Francisco, pp. 457-467

[CH83] A. Ciepielewski and B. Hausman, "A Formal Model for Or-parallel Execution of Logic Programs," In *IFIP 83, North Holland, P.C. Mason (ed.).*

[CH86] A. Ciepielewski and B. Hausman, "Performance Evaluation of an Or-parallel Execution Model for Logic Programs," In *Symposium on Logic Prog.*, 1986, pp. 246-255.

[CS89] A. Calderwood and P. Szeredi, "The Manchester Scheduler," ICLP '89.

[DLO87] T. Disz, E. Lusk, and R. Overbeek, "Experiments with OR-parallel Logic Programs," In *1987 IEEE Int. Symp. in Logic Prog.*, San Francisco.

[GJ89] G. Gupta and B. Jayaraman, "Compiled And-Or Parallel Execution of Logic Programs," In *NACLP '89.*

[H87] B. Hausman, et. al., "Or-Parallel Prolog Made Efficient on Shared Memory Multiprocessors," in *1987 IEEE Int. Symp. in Logic Prog.*, San Francisco, CA.

[K86] K. Kumon *et al*, "Kabu-wake : A New Parallel Method and Its Evaluation," Proceedings of CompCon '86, 1986, pp. 168-172.

[L84] G. Lindstrom, "Or-Parallelism on Applicative Architectures," in *2nd International Logic Prog. Conf.,"* Uppsala, Sweden, 1984.

[LH89] K. Li and P. Hudak, "Memory Coherence in Shared Virtual Memory Systems," In *ACM Transactions on Computer Systems*, **7**(4), November 1989, pp. 321-359.

[LWH88] E. Lusk, D. H. D. Warren, S. Haridi, et. al., "Aurora Or-parallel Prolog System," In FGCS 1988.

[M79] D. Maier, "An Efficient Method for Storing Ancestor Information in Trees," In *SIAM J. Computing* Vol 8, No. 4, Nov. 1979.

[RK89] B. Ramkumar and L. V. Kale, "Compiled Execution of the REDUCE-OR Process Model," In *NACLP '89.*

[S89] P. Szeredi, "Performance Analysis of the Aurora Or-Parallel Prolog System," In NACLP '89.

[SV88] B. Scheiber and U. Vishkin, "On Finding Lowest Common Ancestors: Simplification and Parallelization," In *SIAM Journal of Computing*, Vol. 17, No. 6, Dec. 1988.

[TL87] P. Tinker and G. Lindstrom, "A Performance Oriented Design for Or-parallel Logic Programming," *1987 IEEE International Symposium in Logic Programming*, San Francisco.

[WH88] D.H.D. Warren and S. Haridi, "The data diffusion machine – a shared virtual memory architecture for parallel execution of logic programs," In *Proceedings of FGCS '88*, pp. 943-952.

[W87a] D. H. D. Warren, "The SRI-model for Or-Parallel execution of Prolog – Abstract Design and Implementation Issues," *1987 IEEE Int. Symp. in Logic Prog.*, San Francisco.

[W87b] D. H. D. Warren, "Or-Parallel Execution Models of Prolog," TAPSOFT '87, Springer Verlag, LNCS 250.

[W84] D. S. Warren, "Efficient Prolog Memory Management for Flexible Control Strategies," In *The 1984 Int. Symp. on Logic Prog.,* Atlantic City, pp. 198-202.

[WR87] H. Westphal, P. Robert, J. Chassin and J. Syre, "The PEPSys Model: Combining Backtracking, AND- and OR-parallelism," In *1987 IEEE Int'l Symp. in Logic Prog.*, San Francisco, pp. 436-448.

The Muse Or-Parallel Prolog Model and its Performance

Khayri A. M. Ali and Roland Karlsson
Swedish Institute of Computer Science, SICS
Box 1263, S-164 28 Kista, Sweden
khayri@sics.se and roland@sics.se

Abstract

Muse (*Mu*lti-*se*quential Prolog engines) is a simple and efficient approach to Or-parallel execution of Prolog programs on shared memory and a class of distributed memory multiprocessor machines. Based on the Muse approach, a 7-processors distributed memory multiprocessor prototype system has been constructed, which is running a variant of Prolog with good performance results in absolute and relative terms. Similar performance results, and better, have been achieved on a shared memory multiprocessor machine, the Sequent Symmetry with 16 processor. The sequential Sicstus Prolog system has been adapted to Or-parallel implementation on both systems. Extra overhead associated with this adaptation is very low, around 5%. The speed-up factor is very close to the number of processors in the system for a large class of problems.

The goal of this paper is to present the Muse execution model, some of its implementation issues, and some experimental results obtained from two different multiprocessor systems.

1 Introduction

1.1 History of BC-Machine Research

In 1986, a research project at SICS, called BC-machine, was started with the goal of finding a suitable approach to Or-parallel execution of Prolog on distributed memory multiprocessor machines. This class of machines is able to be more scalable and to utilize faster processing units. Or-parallelism is easy to detect and exists in a large class of applications (e.g., natural language processing [11], expert systems [13], theorem proving [12], meta-interpreters [9], etc.).

Two ideas have been proposed by the BC-machine group; the Multi sequential-machines approach [1] and the BC-machine approach [2]. Both ideas are based on having multiple sequential Prolog engines. This allows keeping all advantages of the sequential Prolog technology, e.g., efficient implementation, garbage collection, etc. The main drawbacks of the former approach [1] are the overhead of 1) copying an engine state, and 2) load balancing. In the BC-machine approach [2], the load balancing problem has been solved assuming some shared memory in the system and copying overhead is reduced by using a special broadcast network for parallel copying.

1.2 Motivations to the Muse Approach

The initial thought was that copying overhead is very high and hardware support, as broadcast network in BC-machine, is essential for efficient implementation. When we did our first experiment by implementing an Or-parallel Prolog system based on the BC-machine model on a simple prototype system without having any broadcast network, we obtained a very surprising result about copying overhead. Copying overhead is actually much lower than people could expect. It ranges from 0.01% to 25% of processors' time depending on programs. This percentage is small in comparison with the corresponding overhead (total task switching overhead) in other Or-parallel execution models. In Muse we reduce the copying overhead further to make the model suitable for a larger class of multiprocessor machines.

1.3 Current Implementations and Results

We have implemented an Or-parallel Prolog system based on the Muse approach on a 7-processors distributed memory multiprocessor prototype system constructed at SICS. The architecture is similar to ACE of IBM [8]. It consists of a number of processing units, each provided with local memory, some shared memory, and a common bus. The performance results are encouraging in both absolute and relative terms. The sequential Sicstus Prolog [7], a fast, portable system, has been adapted to Or-parallel implementation. The extra overhead associated with this adaptation is low, around 5%. The speed-up factor is very close to the number of processors in the system for a large class of problems. The same Or-parallel Prolog system has been ported to the Sequent Symmetry with 16 processors, a shared memory multiprocessor machine, with similar and better performance results. Recently, we have developed a portable version of Muse system on Sequent. That version is being ported to uniprocessor Unix workstations and to the hardware prototype.

The current Muse system supports, so far, a variant of Prolog, called Commit Prolog, with cavalier commit [5] instead of cut and asynchronous (parallel) side-effects instead of synchronous (sequential) ones. The standard Prolog semantics of cut and sequential side-effects can be obtained on the current system by following a few rules that restrict the degree of Or-parallelism. Supporting directly the Prolog semantics of cut and sequential side-effects operations without restricting the parallelism is our next step. We have developed efficient mechanisms for supporting such operations that will be implemented in the near future.

1.4 Structure of the Paper

The paper is organized as follows. Section 2 describes the Muse execution model. Section 3 shows how the Muse model can be implemented as a minimal extension to the WAM. Section 4 discusses very briefly scheduling work principles of Muse. Section 5 specifies a version of Prolog that we call Commit Prolog. Section 6 discusses very important optimizations of copying overhead. Section 7 presents some experimental results on two different multiprocessor systems. It also compares our results with the results obtained from related approaches. Section 8 concludes the paper and discusses our plans for the continued development of Muse.

2 Muse Execution Model

In this section, we describe the Muse Or-parallel execution model in two steps: first the basic model, and then a method for reducing the main source of overhead in the basic model.

2.1 Multiprocessor System Assumptions

We assume a multiprocessor system having a number of processors or processes, called *workers*[1], with identical local address spaces, and some global address space shared by all workers. Operating systems like DYNIX (a parallel version of Unix) on Sequent machines and MACH on a number of multiprocessor machines support these requirements. We also assume that each worker is a sequential Prolog engine with its own local four stacks: *a choicepoint stack, an environment stack, a term stack, and a trail.* The first two correspond to the WAM local stack and the second two correspond to the WAM heap and trail respectively [18]. The stacks are not shared between workers. The Prolog program is either stored in the shared space or in each worker's space. It is assumed that the reader is familiar with the WAM [18].

2.2 Execution Model

1. When execution of a Prolog program starts, one worker P processes the top level query creating all data structures in its own stacks. The other workers are idle until P creates local nodes (choicepoints).

2. One of the idle workers Q interrupts P requesting work.

3. P allows Q to get a piece of work by sharing its local nodes with Q. P makes its local nodes shared with Q as follows.

[1]We use the name worker to represent process or processor exactly as it is used in Aurora [13].

(a) For each local node, P creates a shareable frame in the shared space.

(b) P moves information describing the unprocessed alternatives from the local nodes to the corresponding shareable frames.

(c) Each local node acquires a pointer to the corresponding shareable frame.

(d) P copies its state to Q. At this moment, P and Q have identical states and both share all of P's nodes (see Figure 1).

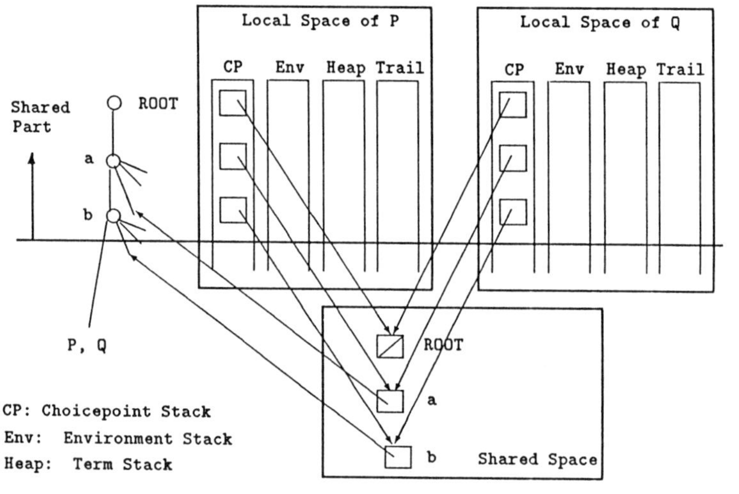

Figure 1: Sharing Work.

4. P and Q work together to finish processing the shared unprocessed alternatives (tasks). They process the shared nodes from the bottom-most up to the root node using the built-in backtracking mechanism of Prolog. P proceeds with its current task while Q simulates failure to release the next alternative (task) from the bottom-most shared node. Releasing an alternative from a shared node is done while locking the corresponding shared frame.

5. When a worker gets a task, it processes that task exactly as a standard sequential Prolog engine with the normal backtracking mechanism.

6. When a worker P creates local nodes and there is an idle worker Q, P makes its local nodes shareable with Q as in step (3).

7. When all work on a Prolog search tree is processed, all workers become idle and the execution terminates.

So far, this model is the same as the BC-machine model [2] with only one difference in step (3.d). In the BC-machine model, P copies its state not only to Q but to all idle workers in one operation assuming a broadcast copying network in the system.

Copying the whole worker state on every copy is expected to be an expensive operation. In the following section, we will illustrate how the copying overhead can be reduced substantially.

2.3 Incremental Copying

The main drawback of the above model is the overhead of copying a worker state in step (3.d). Actually, what we would like to get in step (3.d) is simply that Q gets the same state as P. The idea of incremental copying is to make Q keep the part of its state which is consistent with P's state, and to have P copy to Q only the difference between the two workers' states. Before showing how this can be supported efficiently, we would first like to briefly review the backtracking mechanism of Prolog.

On creation of a choicepoint c, the current state of computation is stored in c. The state of computation is represented by contents of the WAM registers. On processing an alternative which is not the last one from c, addresses of variables created before c, that get bound during execution of the alternative, are stored in the trail stack. On backtracking to c for getting the next alternative, the state of computation is restored from c and all modifications to variables created before c are undone by going through the trail stack.

Now we can show how to implement efficiently the incremental copying idea. Assume that there is no work available at any shared node on the current branch[2] of a worker Q and that there is another worker P with local nodes. Assume also that Q has selected P for sharing its local nodes. First, the worker Q backtracks to the youngest shared node n with P (see Figure 2). Then P makes its local nodes shareable with Q and copies to Q only the differing parts between the two states. The differing parts are the top segments of stacks corresponding to nodes younger than n and the local modifications that are made on the common parts after creating n. These modifications are known to P by accessing the top segment of its trail stack (see Figure 2). Now, P and Q have identical states and both share all of P's nodes exactly as in step (3.d) in the above section. Copying overhead is further reduced in Section 6.

3 Extending the WAM

In this section we describe the memory organization of the system and show how the Muse Or-parallel execution model has been implemented as a min-

[2]The current branch is the path from the current node up to the root of the search tree.

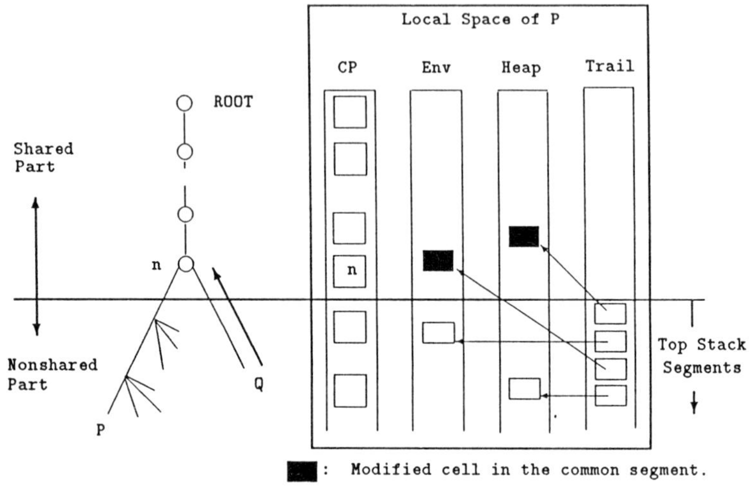

Figure 2: Incremental Copying Idea.

imal extension to the WAM [18].

The Muse Or-parallel execution model is based on having multiple sequential Prolog engines, each with its own local address space, and some global address space shared by all engines. Each sequential Prolog engine is a worker with its own four stacks. Workers share a segment of memory for storing frames associated with shared nodes, global tables (e.g., symbol table, predicate table, etc), asserted rules, buffering instances of terms generated during parallel execution of *setof* and *bagof*, and some global registers. The shared memory segment is administrated as a general heap.

Part of the shared memory segment is maintained as a free list of fixed size blocks for frames associated with the shared nodes. Such frames are allocated by a worker who is going to make its local (nonshared) nodes shareable with another worker and are deallocated by the last worker backtracking from the node. There is one shared frame associated with every shared node. Each shared frame is referenced from the corresponding (local) choicepoint frames. Each shared frame basically contains a pointer to the next alternative of the associated shared node, a bit-map indicating workers which are at and below the node, and a lock for synchronizing accesses to the node.

The only modification to the WAM stacks is that one extra field (word) is added to each choicepoint frame. This word is used for two different purposes depending on whether the node is shared or not. For a shared node, the word contains a pointer to the child choicepoint frame in order to find quickly the child node on cut/commit operations. (Notice that a shared node has logically many children but from a single worker perspective, there is only one child which corresponds to the current branch.) For a nonshared node

n, the word contains the number of remaining alternatives of the nonshared nodes older than n. This number is used as a measure of the local load of each worker for guiding the scheduler to make good decisions on selecting a busy worker for sharing when there is an idle worker in the system. (There is a global register associated with each worker containing the current load of the corresponding worker.)

Another modification to the WAM is that on every procedure call, a worker checks for interrupt signals sent by other workers. The two possible interrupt signals are a request to make local nodes shareable, and abort the current task[3] as part of cut/commit operation.

All the WAM stacks are located at a fixed address in local address space of every worker. This allows copying a segment of a stack from one worker to another without relocation of pointers.

A nice feature of the two operating systems that are available to us (DYNIX on Sequent Symmetry and a mini Unix on our hardware prototype), is that the local address space of each process (worker) could be mapped into a separate part of the global address space of the system. This enables any worker to copy data directly into the local address space of another worker by using the global address of the latter. For most bus based multiprocessors, this copying operation is supported efficiently, and more importantly no extra storage is needed to buffer the copied information.

4 Scheduling Work

Nodes on the search tree are either shared or nonshared. The nodes of the search tree correspond to WAM choicepoints. These nodes divide the search tree into two parts: a shared, upper, part and a nonshared, lower, part. Each shared node is accessible only to workers within the subtree rooted by the node. Nonshared (local) nodes are only accessible to the worker that created them. Each worker can be in either engine mode or in scheduler mode. The worker enters scheduler mode when it enters the shared part of the tree, or when it executes side-effects or *setofs*. In scheduler mode, the worker establishes the necessary coordination with other workers. The worker enters engine mode when it leaves scheduler mode. In engine mode, the worker works exactly as a sequential Prolog engine on local nodes, but is also able to respond to interrupt signals from other workers.

The main function of the scheduler is to match idle workers with the available work with minimal overhead. The sources of overhead in the Muse model include (1) copying a part of worker state, (2) making local nodes shareable, (3) grabbing a piece of work (a task) from a shared node, (4) selecting a busy worker for sharing when there is no available work in the shared nodes on the current branch, and (5) selecting a position on the tree for an idle worker when there is (temporarily) no work available for it.

[3]Current task is the local work.

Our principal strategy decisions are the following:

- The scheduler attempts to share a chunk of nodes between workers on every copy. This maximizes the number of shared tasks and reduces the frequency of copying, which in turn reduces copying overhead. The cost of grabbing a shared task is almost in the same order as the cost of getting a local alternative.

- Tasks are released from the bottom-most shared node with available work on the current branch. This allows taking the nearest piece of available work on the current branch.

- An idle worker is responsible for selecting the best busy worker and positions itself at the right position on the tree before interrupting the busy worker for requesting sharing. This allows a busy worker to concentrate on its task and to response only for interrupts that have to be handled by it.

The basic algorithm of our schedulers for matching idle workers with available work is as follows. *When a worker finishes a task, it attempts to get the nearest piece of available work on the current branch. If none exists, it attempts to select a busy worker with excess local work for sharing. If none exists, it becomes idle and stays at a suitable position on the tree.* More detailed information about scheduling issues will be presented in another paper; space limitations do not permit us to discuss these issues here.

5 Commit Prolog

There are two main approaches concerning Prolog language for multiprocessor implementations:

1. Developing a new version of Prolog language suitable for multiprocessor systems as advocated by the ECRC group [4]. The main motivation is that the standard Prolog language is developed for uniprocessor systems.

2. Using the standard Prolog language as advocated by David H. D. Warren. The main motivation is that standard Prolog semantics is well accepted by the logic programming community.

Each approach has its own advantages and disadvantages. For instance, an advantage of the first approach is that simpler and more efficient implementations could be obtained. One disadvantage of the first approach is that not all existing Prolog programs can be executed with the standard Prolog semantics. In general, the user has to rewrite parts of his program in order to get the required semantics.

On the other hand, the second approach allows existing Prolog programs to be executed without modifications and getting the same standard Prolog semantics. It does not mean at all that all existing Prolog programs can get significant speed-ups when executed on multiprocessor systems. For Prolog programs that heavily use synchronous side-effects and cuts with large scopes, it is very difficult to get any speed-up. Supporting synchronous side-effects and cut with large scope always requires more complex implementations on multiprocessor systems.

So far, we have implemented a parallel version of Prolog, called *Commit Prolog*. It is a Prolog language with cavalier commit[4] instead of cut, asynchronous (parallel) side-effects and internal database predicates instead of the synchronous (sequential) counterparts, and sequential and parallel annotations. Commit Prolog is simply an Or-parallel version of Sicstus Prolog [5]. So, constructs like *setarg*, *freeze* and *undo*, that are supported by Sicstus, are also supported in Commit Prolog with the same semantics. Supporting directly the standard Prolog language is our next step.

The parallel annotation is used to annotate any predicate to allow clauses of the predicate to be executed in parallel whereas the sequential annotation is used to enforce clauses of a predicate to be processed sequentially. In our current system, by default all predicates are annotated sequential.

Cut and Sequential side-effect semantics could be obtained on Commit Prolog by following some rules described in a longer version of this paper [3].

6 Reducing Copying Overhead

In this section we are going to reduce further the copying overhead which represents the main source of overheads associated with the Muse model. In Section 6.1, we show how to reduce copying overhead when the youngest local nodes are sequential nodes. In Section 6.2, we discuss a method that reduces copying overhead on a shared memory multiprocessor machine like Sequent Symmetry.

6.1 Reducing Overhead when Youngest Nodes are Sequential

A node on the search tree is either sequential or parallel. Parallel nodes have potential for Or-parallelism and could be processed in parallel while alternatives on a sequential node must be processed sequentially. That is, no alternative is utilized in the sequential node until all paths generated by an earlier alternative in the node have been completely processed.

A significant improvement of sharing and copying overhead is obtained when the youngest (local) nodes of the selected busy worker are sequential nodes. To illustrate the idea, assume that P is the selected busy worker which has the youngest nodes sequential and Q is an idle worker that has selected P for sharing. In this case, if P shares all its nodes with Q and copies

[4] Cavalier commit prunes branches both to the left and right of the committing branch, and is not guaranteed to prevent side-effects from occurring on the pruned branches [5].

the difference between the two workers states, and then P proceeds with its current task and Q simulates failure for getting a task from the nearest shared node, the worker Q will backtrack from all bottom-most sequential nodes and get an alternative from the bottom-most parallel node with available alternatives (the node *par* in Figure 3). So, sequential nodes, such as node *seq* in Figure 3, should not be shared and the corresponding state should not be copied from P to Q.

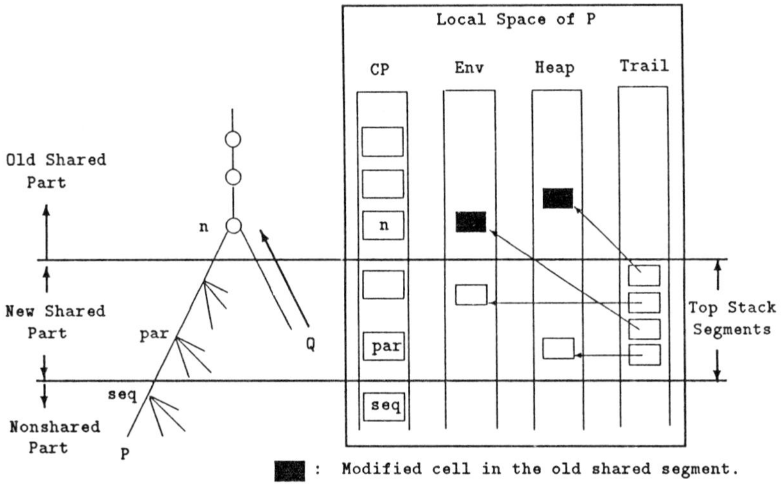

Figure 3: Reducing Copying Overhead.

This optimization is possible only when no *setarg* is invoked by P after taking the current alternative from the youngest parallel node. *setarg* is a backtrackable destructive assignment supported by Sicstus Prolog [7]. The *term stack* contains a goal for undoing *setarg* on backtracking. In this case, P copies the whole top segment of the *term stack*.

6.2 Parallel Copying

In Section 2.3, when an idle worker Q requests sharing from a busy worker P with excess local load, P performs the following operations while Q is waiting until P completes these operations (see also Figure 3):

1. Makes nonshared nodes with Q shareable (sharing).

2. Copies the top segments of its own stacks to Q (copying).

3. Installs bindings from its local *environment stack* (Env) and *term stack* (Heap) associated with (old) shared nodes into Q's corresponding stacks (installation).

Copying overhead is represented by the time spent by P performing the last two operations and the time spent by Q waiting until P completes performing these operations.

A method, called *parallel copying*, has been developed for minimizing P's time spent on copying and installation operations, and for utilizing Q's waiting time, as much as possible, on performing those operations. It also allows Q to perform copying while P is performing sharing. This method could only be used in a system that allows a local address space of each process (worker) to be mapped into a separate part of the global address space. (The DYNIX operating system on Sequent Symmetry is an example of such a system.) In such a system, local space of the worker P could be accessed by the worker Q. Thus, copying and installation operations could be performed by Q while P is performing sharing. The method is further described in [3].

7 Experimental Results

In this section we present results of our experiments for a large group of benchmarks running on a shared memory multiprocessor machine (the Sequent Symmetry with 16 processors), and on a constructed distributed memory machine with 7 processors.

7.1 Benchmarks

The group of benchmarks used in this paper can be divided into two sets: the first set (*8-queens1, 8-queens2, tina, salt-mustard, parse2, parse4, parse5, db4, db5, house, parse1, parse3, farmer*) are relatively well understood granularity and ideal speed-up characteristics and which have been used by other researchers in previous studies [4, 6, 17]. Thus, they allow measurement of basic overheads and comparison with previous results. This set contains benchmarks with coarse grain parallelism (*8-queens1, 8-queens2, tina, salt-mustard*), with medium grain parallelism (*parse2, parse4, parse5, db4, db5, house*), and with fine grain parallelism (*parse1, parse3, farmer*). *8-queens1* and *8-queens2* are two different 8 queens programs from ECRC. *tina* is a holiday planning program from ECRC. *salt-mustard* is the "salt and mustard" puzzle from Argonne. *parse1* – *parse5* are queries to the natural language parsing parts of Chat-80 by F. C. N. Pereira and D. H. D. Warren. *db4* and *db5* are the data base searching part of the fourth and fifth Chat-80 query. *house* is the "who owns the zebra" puzzle from ECRC. *farmer* is the "farmer, wolf, goat/goose, cabbage/grain" puzzle from ECRC.

The second set of benchmarks (*pundit, semigroup, satchmo, andorra-interp*) contains large (except *satchmo*), real, programs with very interesting Or-parallelism. *pundit* is a natural language system from the Unisys Paoli Research Center [11]. *semigroup* is a theorem proving program for studying the R-classes of a large semigroup from Argonne National Laboratory [12].

satchmo is a little theorem prover for proving theorems in Predicate Logic. The original *satchmo* is written by Rainer Manthey and Francois Bry from ECRC, and modified by Mats Carlsson from SICS and Lee Naish from the University of Melbourne. *andorra-interp* is an interpreter for the Andorra computational model written by Seif Haridi at SICS [9]. All the benchmarks look for all solutions of the problem.

7.2 Performance Results: Timings and Speedups

7.2.1 On Sequent Symmetry

Table 1 presents the run times (in milliseconds) from the execution of the first set of benchmarks (described in Section 7.1) on a 16 processors Sequent Symmetry S81 with 32 Mbytes of memory. The run times given are the shortest obtained from several runs (as measured in [6, 17]). Times are shown for 1, 4, 8, 12, 15 workers with speed-ups (relative to the 1 worker case) given in parentheses. The last column shows running times on Sicstus version 0.6 (Sicstus0.6) with the ratio of running times on Muse for the 1 worker case and the Sicstus0.6 times. For benchmarks with small run times the timings shown refer to repeated runs, the repetition factor being shown in the first column. *all-goals* in the last row corresponds to the goal: (*8-queens1, 8-queens2, tina, salt-mustard, parse2*20, parse4*5, parse5, db4*10, db5*10, house*20, parse1*20, parse3*20, farmer*100).* That is, the timings shown in the last row correspond to running the whole first set of the benchmarks as one benchmark.

Goals *repetitions	Muse Workers 1	4	8	12	15	Sicstus0.6
8-queens1	6910	1740(3.97)	880(7.85)	599(11.53)	490(14.10)	6770(1.02)
8-queens2	17540	4419(3.97)	2240(7.83)	1510(11.61)	1209(14.51)	16450(1.07)
tina	14580	3730(3.91)	1920(7.59)	1330(10.96)	1099(13.27)	13780(1.06)
salt-mustard	2120	531(3.99)	270(7.85)	189(11.22)	159(13.33)	2020(1.05)
parse2 *20	5980	1780(3.36)	1329(4.50)	1160(5.16)	1149(5.20)	5870(1.02)
parse4 *5	5510	1500(3.67)	920(6.00)	770(7.15)	740(7.45)	5400(1.02)
parse5	3900	1049(3.72)	589(6.62)	459(8.50)	449(8.69)	3820(1.02)
db4 *10	2440	669(3.65)	400(6.10)	309(7.90)	289(8.44)	2240(1.09)
db5 *10	2970	819(3.63)	480(6.19)	370(8.03)	341(8.71)	2730(1.09)
house *20	4390	1331(3.30)	840(5.23)	721(6.09)	689(6.37)	4220(1.04)
parse1 *20	1579	620(2.55)	579(2.73)	610(2.59)	640(2.47)	1570(1.01)
parse3 *20	1360	581(2.34)	519(2.62)	540(2.52)	569(2.39)	1340(1.01)
farmer *100	3199	1399(2.29)	1419(2.25)	1419(2.25)	1429(2.24)	3060(1.05)
all-goals	72478	20390(3.55)	12599(5.75)	10219(7.09)	9461(7.66)	69350(1.05)

Table 1: Run Times (in milliseconds) of Muse for the First Set of Benchmarks on Sequent Symmetry.

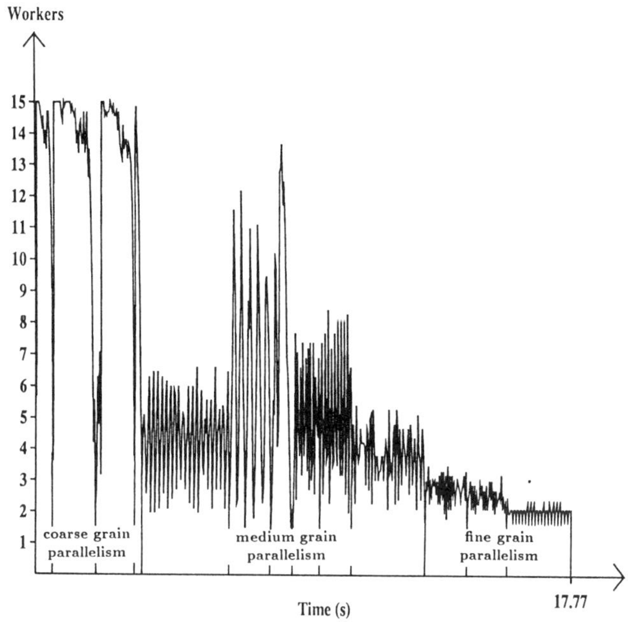

Figure 4: Exploited Parallelism by 15 Workers for the *all-goals* Benchmark.

Benchmark (or Goal)	Muse Workers 1	15
pundit:		
1.1.1	64.31	4.54(14.17)
4.1.1	406.98	27.88(14.60)
4.1.3	49.81	3.73(13.35)
5.1.2	35.56	2.62(13.57)
6.1.2	130.02	9.16(14.21)
9.1.1	180.25	12.42(14.51)
9.1.4	368.89	25.43(14.00)
22.1.1	61.78	4.41(14.01)
25.1.3	35.64	2.87(12.42)
28.1.1	145.22	10.92(13.30)
31.1.3	63.16	4.49(14.07)
31.1.4	67.30	4.87(13.82)
satchmo	112.38	7.83(14.35)
semigroup	4503.64	300.56(14.98)
andorra-interp	96.24	6.93(13.95)

Table 2: Run Times (in seconds) of Muse for the Second Set of Benchmarks on Sequent Symmetry.

Figure 4 shows the exploited parallelism by 15 workers over time for the *all-goals* benchmark, measured by *Mus*e graphical *t*racing facility (*Must*) [16]. The whole area under the curve is divided into 13 parts corresponding to the 13 subgoals in the *all-goals* benchmark with the same order as they are listed above. Figure 4 shows also subareas corresponding to coarse, medium, and fine grain parallelism. (The reason of having 17.77 seconds in Figure 4 and 9.461 seconds in Table 1 is simply that the former time corresponds to a version of Muse with extra run-time overheads associated with the generation of trace information.)

Table 2 presents the run times (in seconds) for 1 and 15 workers from the execution of the second set of the benchmarks on Sequent Symmetry. The test sentences of the *pundit* program are listed in Table 3.

Test Sentences	
1.1.1	starting air regulating valve failed.
4.1.1	while diesel was operating with sac disengaged, the sac lo alarm sounded.
4.1.3	pump will not turn when engine jacks over.
5.1.2	disengaged immediately after alarm.
6.1.2	inspection of lo filter revealed metal particles.
9.1.1	sac received high usage during two becce periods.
9.1.4	loud noises were coming from the drive end during coast down.
22.1.1	loss of lube oil pressure during operation.
25.1.3	suspect faulty high speed rotating assembly.
28.1.1	unit has excessive wear on inlet impellor assembly and shows high usage of oil.
31.1.3	erosion of impellor blade tip is evident.
31.1.4	compressor wheel inducer leading edge broken.

Table 3: Test Sentences of *pundit* Benchmark.

7.2.2 On Constructed Hardware Prototype

Tables 4 and 5 present the Muse run times from the execution of the benchmarks on a 7-processors hardware prototype constructed at SICS. The results shown in these tables correspond to a portable version of Muse on Sequent after porting to the hardware prototype without any significant modifications. That is, better results could be obtained than those in Tables 4 and 5 when the Muse system takes advantages of the hardware prototype.

The hardware prototype consists of 7 68020 CPUs, 7 2.5 MBytes (local memory), 4 MBytes (global memory) and VME bus as a common bus in the system. We have a plan to build a copying network to study the percentage of performance improvements when such a network exists in the system. All our results reported in Tables 4 and 5 are from the prototype without the copying network. The VME bus is used to access global memory and for copying.

Goals *repetitions	Muse Workers 1	4	6
8-queens1	11411	2873(3.97)	1943(5.87)
8-queens2	28955	7274(3.98)	4890(5.92)
tina	24039	6186(3.89)	4267(5.63)
salt-mustard	3520	1034(3.40)	913(3.86)
parse2 *20	9094	2723(3.34)	2470(3.68)
parse4 *5	8416	2310(3.64)	1820(4.62)
parse5	5931	1599(3.71)	1165(5.09)
db4 *10	3711	1033(3.56)	820(4.53)
db5 *10	4524	1275(3.55)	963(4.70)
house *20	7085	2196(3.23)	1775(3.99)
parse1 *20	2421	950(2.55)	1007(2.40)
parse3 *20	2073	883(2.35)	931(2.23)
farmer *100	5226	2318(2.25)	2683(1.96)
all-goals	116757	33142(3.52)	26438(4.42)

Table 4: Run Times (in milliseconds) of Muse for the First Set of Benchmarks on the Hardware Prototype.

Benchmark (or Goal)	Muse Workers 1	6
pundit:		
1.1.1	94.47	16.54(5.71)
4.1.1	596.27	102.21(5.83)
4.1.3	74.09	12.98(5.71)
5.1.2	52.68	9.31(5.66)
6.1.2	188.35	33.20(5.67)
9.1.1	264.00	45.30(5.83)
9.1.4	540.05	92.63(5.83)
22.1.1	89.73	15.67(5.73)
25.1.3	51.65	9.14(5.65)
28.1.1	211.90	37.60(5.64)
31.1.3	92.22	16.10(5.73)
31.1.4	98.55	17.35(5.68)
satchmo	157.53	27.36(5.76)
semigroup	–	–
andorra-interp	140.71	23.97(5.87)

Table 5: Run Times (in seconds) of Muse for the Second Set of Benchmarks on the Hardware Prototype.

7.2.3 Discussion of Performance Results

The performance results that Tables 1,2,4 and 5 illustrate are encouraging: almost ideal speed-ups for programs with coarse grain parallelism, reasonable speed-ups for programs with medium grain parallelism, and low speed-ups for programs with fine grain parallelism.

The main reason for having some better results in Tables 1 and 2 than those in Tables 4 and 5 is that the capacity of the Sequent Symmetry bus is much higher than the capacity of the VME bus. The VME bus is slower than Sequent Symmetry bus by a factor around 20. It neither supports caching nor simultaneous locking (test-and-set) operations. That is, in our hardware prototype the ratio between communication speed to processor speed is much lower than in the Sequent Symmetry machine. *salt-mustard* in Table 4 has lower speed-ups in comparison with that in Table 1. The reason for this is that *salt-mustard* heavily uses meta-calls which require looking up the predicate table which resides in global memory, and that the VME bus does not support caching. Table 6 shows better results for a version of *salt-mustard*, called *sm-mixtus*, without meta-calls. This version is a direct translation of *salt-mustard* generated by the Mixtus partial evaluator [15]. We could not run the *semigroup* benchmark on the hardware prototype because the *semigroup* code size is larger than the available memory.

	Muse Workers		
Program	1	4	6
sm-mixtus	735	194(3.79)	144(5.10)

Table 6: Run Times (in milliseconds) of Muse for a Version of *salt-mustard* without Meta-calls on the Hardware Prototype.

On one processor, Muse is about 5% slower than Sicstus0.6 (shown in Table 1), the sequential Prolog system from which it is derived. This overhead is smaller than in Aurora, 24% [13] (see also below), and in PEPSys, 30% [14]. The 5% extra overhead of Muse is divided into two parts. 2.5% is for maintaining the current value of the local load in each worker, and for checking arriving requests from the other workers in the system. We do not know yet the source of the other 2.5% overhead; it may be due to the C compiler or to the DYNIX operating system.

7.3 Comparison with Aurora

We have chosen the Aurora Or-parallel Prolog system [13] to compare with our performance results for the following reasons: Aurora is one of the best Or-parallel Prolog systems existing today for shared memory multiprocessor machines; Aurora runs on the same Sequent Symmetry which is available to us; and Aurora is based on the same sequential Prolog system (Sicstus).

It is too early to do a full comparison between the Muse and Aurora systems at this stage of development. The Aurora system supports parallel implementation of cut and sequential side-effects whereas Muse does not support them yet. Additionally, the Muse system supports garbage collection [3] but Aurora does not. However, a preliminary comparison between the performance results of Muse and Aurora would be possible. We compare our results with the Aurora results for the first set of benchmarks (described in Section 7.1). Aurora results based on Sicstus0.3 are found in [6, 13, 17]. The Muse system is based on Sicstus0.6 which is faster than Sicstus0.3 by a factor around 1.5. (Sicstus0.6 is only about 1.8 times slower than Quintus Prolog, one of the fastest commercial Prolog system.) The current version of

Aurora is also based on Sicstus0.6. Since no new results are published on the current version of Aurora, we have measured the run times given in Table 7 (with the Manchester scheduler) on the same Sequent Symmetry and under the same conditions as the results in Table 1.

Goals *repetitions	Aurora Workers 1	4	8	12	15	Sicstus0.6
8-queens1	7831	2000(3.92)	1010(7.75)	689(11.37)	559(14.01)	6770(1.16)
8-queens2	20700	5179(4.00)	2600(7.96)	1750(11.83)	1411(14.67)	16450(1.26)
tina	18270	4700(3.89)	2400(7.61)	1680(10.88)	1370(13.34)	13780(1.33)
salt-mustard	2490	630(3.95)	319(7.81)	229(10.87)	189(13.17)	2020(1.23)
parse2 *20	7029	2310(3.04)	1689(4.16)	1601(4.39)	1669(4.21)	5870(1.20)
parse4 *5	6520	1770(3.68)	1280(5.09)	1090(5.98)	1020(6.39)	5400(1.21)
parse5	4599	1331(3.46)	890(5.17)	770(5.97)	669(6.87)	3820(1.20)
db4 *10	2880	800(3.60)	460(6.26)	380(7.58)	340(8.47)	2240(1.29)
db5 *10	3500	980(3.57)	570(6.14)	469(7.46)	419(8.35)	2730(1.28)
house *20	5021	1480(3.39)	940(5.34)	809(6.21)	769(6.53)	4220(1.19)
parse1 *20	1851	740(2.50)	710(2.61)	770(2.40)	829(2.23)	1570(1.18)
parse3 *20	1590	699(2.27)	699(2.27)	740(2.15)	790(2.01)	1340(1.19)
farmer *100	3620	2110(1.72)	2110(1.72)	2260(1.60)	2390(1.51)	3060(1.18)
all-goals	86211	25020(3.45)	16020(5.38)	13490(6.39)	12740(6.77)	69350(1.24)

Table 7: Run Times (in milliseconds) of Aurora for the First Set of Benchmarks on Sequent Symmetry.

It can be seen from Tables 1 and 7 that Muse is faster than Aurora in all benchmarks. Table 8 shows in the last row the ratio of the running times on Aurora to the running times on Muse for *"all-goals"* benchmark. Aurora timings are longer than Muse timings by 19% to 35% between 1 to 15 workers. These results could be changed when Muse supports parallel implementation of cut and sequential side-effects, and when Aurora supports garbage collection. We believe that on shared memory multiprocessor machines like Sequent Symmetry Aurora will be faster than Muse for other classes of benchmarks in which sharing of the WAM stacks is more efficient than copying.

System	Workers 1	4	8	12	15
Aurora	86211	25020	16020	13490	12740
Muse	72478	20390	12599	10219	9461
Aurora / Muse	1.19	1.23	1.27	1.32	1.35

Table 8: Run Times (in milliseconds) of Aurora and Muse, and the Ratio between them for the *"all-goals"* Benchmark on Sequent Symmetry.

Since the Muse model does not require sharing of the WAM stacks, it is more suitable for a larger class of multiprocessor machines. That is, the Muse model is also suitable for multiprocessor machines that do not support caching like BBN Butterfly machine, and for machines with local/global memory like ACE-IBM machine [8].

8 Conclusions

We have presented a simple and efficient execution model, named Muse, to support Or-parallel Prolog on shared memory machines and on a class of distributed memory multiprocessor machines. The Muse model is suitable for any multiprocessor system supporting local and global address spaces, and copying memory blocks from one local address space to another. Operating systems like DYNIX and MACH support these functions on a wide range of multiprocessor machines.

The Muse execution model provides a very high degree of locality of references. This property is crucial to any efficient execution model. There are two main reasons for the good locality of references in the Muse model. First, the WAM stacks, which represent the dominating part of accesses, are not shared among workers. Secondly, on incremental copying, top stack segments, which will be copied from a processor P to another processor Q, are always in P's cache before copying. After copying, each processor will work on its own copy of these segments in its own cache.

The Muse approach keeps all advantages of the sequential Prolog technology, e.g., efficient compilation, indexing, unification with constant access time, stack based storage management, garbage collection, etc. So, it is very easy to adapt any sequential Prolog implementation to Or-parallel execution with very low extra overhead and with minimal effort. (The Melbourne group is using the Muse model for adapting the Nu-Prolog.)

Based on the Muse approach, a 7-processors distributed memory multiprocessor prototype system has been constructed and running a variant of Prolog with good performance results in absolute and relative terms. Similar performance results, and better, have been achieved on a shared memory multiprocessor machine, Sequent Symmetry with 16 processor. The sequential Sicstus Prolog system has been adapted to Or-parallel implementation on both systems. The extra overhead associated with this adaptation is very low, around 5%. The speed-up factor is very close to the number of processors in the system for a large class of problems. We have also ported the Muse system to uniprocessor workstations (Sun3 and Sun4). One advantage of that is that timing bugs could be discovered very early.

The performance results are compared with the results of the related approaches. Muse has the lowest extra overhead per worker and has similar or better relative speed-ups for a large group of benchmarks.

Several small and large Prolog programs have been ported to the current Muse system with annotating parts of the programs that contain Or-parallelism. The standard Prolog semantics of cut and sequential side-effects has been obtained on the current system by following some rules that restricts the degree of Or-parallelism. Directly supporting the Prolog semantics of cut and sequential side-effects operations without restricting the parallelism is our next step.

Space limitations do not permit us to discuss in depth three important issues in this paper. The first issue is the garbage collection in Muse and its interaction with incremental copying. This issue is discussed in [3]. The second issue is the scheduler which is responsible for coordinating the activities of multiple workers looking for work in a Prolog search tree. The third is an elaborated performance evaluation study of all sources of overhead associated with the Muse model. The latter two issues will be discussed in more detail in another paper.

We are working on improving the capabilities and performance of Muse. We have a plan to port Muse to other machines like the BBN Butterfly machine and to Encore machine.

An interesting issue would be to investigate the integration of the Muse Or-parallel model with an And-parallel model in order to exploit more parallelism in Prolog programs [9, 10].

Acknowledgments

We are grateful to Mats Carlsson and Seif Haridi for many useful discussions. We would like also to thank Torbjörn Granlund for his help in the implementation of Muse, Jan Sundberg and Claes Svensson for constructing the graphical tracing facility for Muse.

References

[1] Khayri A. M. Ali. Or-parallel Execution of Prolog on a Multi-Sequential Machine. International Journal of Parallel Programming, Vol. 15, No. 3, pages 189 – 214, June 1986.

[2] Khayri A. M. Ali. Or-parallel Execution of Prolog on BC-machine. In Proceedings of the Fifth International Conference and Symposium on Logic Programming, pages 1531 – 1545, 1988.

[3] Khayri A. M. Ali and Roland Karlsson. The Muse Approach to Or-Parallel Prolog. SICS Research Report, 1990.

[4] Uri Baron, et al. The Parallel ECRC Prolog System PEPSys: An Overview and Evaluation Results. In Proceedings of the International Conference on Fifth Generation Computer Systems 1988. pages 841 – 850, ICOT, November 1988.

[5] Ralph Butler, Terry Disz, Ewing Lusk, Robert Olson, Ross Overbeek, and Rick Stevens. Scheduling OR-parallelism: an Argonne perspective. In Proceedings of the Fifth International Conference on Logic Programming, pages 1590 – 1605, MIT Press, August 1988.

[6] Alan Calderwood and Péter Szeredi. Scheduling Or-parallelism in Aurora – the Manchester scheduler. In Proceedings of the sixth Interna-

tional Conference on Logic Programming, pages 419 – 435, MIT Press, June 1989.

[7] Mats Carlsson and Johan Widén. Sicstus Prolog User's Manual. October 1988. SICS Research Report R88007B.

[8] Armando Garcia and Richard F. Freitas. The ACE Multiprocessor Workstation. IBM Research Division, Thomas J. Watson Research Center, Hawthorne, NY 10598, 1988.

[9] Seif Haridi and Per Brand. Andorra Prolog, an Integration of Prolog and Committed Choice Languages. In Proceedings of the International Conference on Fifth Generation Computer Systems 1988. pages 745 – 754, ICOT, November 1988.

[10] Manuel Hermenegildo. An Abstract Machine for Restricted And-parallel Execution of Logic Programs. In Ehud Shapiro, Editor, Third International Conference on Logic Programming, London, pages 25 – 39, Springer–Verlag, 1986.

[11] Lynette Hirschman, William Hopkins, and Robert Smith. OR-parallel Speed-up in Natural Language Processing: A Case Study. In Proceedings of the Fifth International Conference on Logic Programming, pages 263 – 279, MIT Press, August 1988.

[12] Ewing Lusk and Robert McFadden. Using Automated Reasoning Tools: a study of the semigroup F2B2. Semigroup Forum, 36(1): 75 – 88, 1987.

[13] Ewing Lusk, David H. D. Warren, Seif Haridi, et al. The Aurora Or-parallel Prolog System. New Generation Computing, 7(2,3): 243 – 271, 1990.

[14] Michael Ratcliffe. A progress report on PEPSys. July 1988. Presentation at the Gigalips Workshop, Manchester.

[15] Dan Sahlin. The Mixtus Approach to Automatic Partial Evaluation of Full Prolog. In Proceedings of the 1990 North American Conference on Logic Programming, MIT Press, October 1990.

[16] Jan Sundberg and Claes Svensson. MUST: A graphical tool for observing the behavior of Or-parallel logic programs. In preparation as SICS Research Report.

[17] Péter Szeredi. Performance analysis of the Aurora Or-parallel Prolog System. In Proceedings of the 1989 North American Conference on Logic Programming, pages 713 – 732, MIT Press, March 1989.

[18] David H. D. Warren. An Abstract Prolog Instruction Set. Technical Note 290, SRI International, 1983.

Abstracts of Invited Lectures

Hyperproof: An excursion in situated logic

Jon Barwise
Departments of Philosophy and Mathematics
Sycamore 120
University of Indiana
Bloomington, IN 47405
barwise@iuvax.cs.indiana.edu

Abstract

To the extent that logic programming is based on first-order logic, it is buying into an idealized view of logic, one where logic is seen as an autonomous activity. This idealization was intended to simplify the study of inference by setting aside certain problematic aspects of real world reasoning. However, in setting these aside, the idealization also ignores some positive aspects of logic that are computationally of some significance, and so deserve to be re-examined. This talk will touch on a number of such issues. It will concentrate, however, on *Hyperproof*, a computational project that has grown out of the study of situated logic.

1 What is situated logic?

Let's start off with a modest thought experiment. Imagine you are at home, sitting in your favorite chair, doing whatever you like to do there. You feel being pretty autonomous and otherwise self-sufficient. But imagine that you are about to be transported to a distant place: Austin, Tokyo, Bloomington, or some other unlikely but inhabited spot. There are a number of things you would want to take with you, no doubt: clothes, money, toothbrush, reading material, and the like. Still, though, life goes on there and you can adapt. But suppose you are being transported to a less benevolent environment, say Antarctica. Now life becomes genuinely problematic. You will need a whole range of support, including food and shelter. Next, go to an even more hostile environment: outer space. You need to take your own atmosphere along, together with ways of coping with the lack of gravity. And finally, suppose you were somehow taken right out of space and time itself. What would could you conceivably take along to cope? Your life processes take place within time and space in an essential way.

This point of this experiment is just to remind you that human life has evolved within a certain sort of environment, and that it depends on that environment to sustain it in countless ways we do not even need to think about. Any feeling of autonomy we have quickly disappears as we move further and further from the environment to which we are naturally adapted. The further we remove ourselves, the more difficult it becomes to sustain life as we know it. Every part of the organism depends for its survival on its fit with the environment.

I want to suggest that since this is true of our physical processes, it is likely to be true of their mental counterparts. It seems almost certain that evolution took advantage of our environment as we evolved into speaking, reasoning, and planning creatures. Indeed, it would be the most amazing of miracles if our cognitive processes did not exploit our embedding in the world. It seems almost certain that your mental life is just as dependent on a fit with its environment as is the rest of you.

Modern logic, however, has been preoccupied with the eternal: logical truth and logical consequences are seen as residing outside of space and time, let alone gravity and temperate zones. Typical, and the original motivation for the approach, are logical relationships of the sort that arise in doing mathematics. One attempts to discover what claims follow from what assumptions about numbers, functions, sets, and the like. But mathematicians, those doing the mathematics, are not themselves numbers, functions, or sets. Neither do they have a causal impact on such mathematical objects, at least not on most philosophical accounts of mathematics, those that motivated modern logic. Consequently, the viewpoint of modern logic is that of an idealized observer outside of space and time, outside of any environment at all, reasoning about a situation from which it is causally isolated. The machinery of modern logic, both proof theory and model theory, adopts this perspective. As different as they are in other ways, both the formalist and the realist traditions in modern logic have bought into the view of logic as an autonomous, unsituated activity.

By contrast, people, robots, and computers reside in the world, they view and reason about the world from a perspective within it, and they interact with the very situations about which they reason. By *situated logic* I mean the study of logic when these aspects are brought into account.

Situated logic has to do with the fact that language and thought are situated activities, activities carried out by physically embodied agents situated in a complex environment about which they reason. The situatedness of language and thought includes effects of context, but it goes beyond context in various ways. It is the view that motivated Barwise and Perry [2], and which I have tried to expand on more recently in Barwise [1].

There are two sides to the situatedness of ordinary reasoning, a down side and an up side. The down side has to do with limitations it imposes on the reasoner, limitations having to do with computational resources available to the reasoner, and the enormous complexity of the real world. The reasoning of an agent residing in time cannot take too long and it cannot take up too much of the agent's resources. Furthermore, the complexity of the world typically far outstrips an agent's ability to grasp it. These limitations complicate the reasoning task. Tracking them can also complicate the story the theorist needs to tell, since a host of seemingly non-logical issues impinge. No doubt this down side was partially responsible for the idealization away from situatedness in the first place.

But there is also a positive side to the situatedness of everyday logic, a side that has gone under appreciated in logical theorizing. Just as you live at home by taking advantage of your supporting environment, so too the situated reasoner has many resources available to it, resources that the idealized, disembodied reasoner lacks. Two of these bear special mention in connection with *Hyperproof.*

One advantage of the situated reasoner should be obvious from our thought experiment. It is that the environment in which we evolved, or for which the robot or computer is designed, and toward which the reasoning is directed, is richly structured and law-like. It obeys "constraints." The agent can exploit these constraints in countless ways. Just as we can breathe whether or not we know about air, so too the situated reasoner can exploit constraints even if he, she, or it is unaware of them.

The other advantage is the fact that the situated reasoner can control and manipulate his environment, changing it in ways that he cannot change the structures of mathematics. Indeed, his ability to have an effect on his environment is the major motivation for his reasoning about it. Controlling the environment and reasoning about it are complimentary activities: the ability to do one enhances our ability to do the other.

It is these positive aspects of situated logic that interest and excite me. It seems that in idealizing away from situatedness of logic we cut ourselves off from some very powerful logical mechanisms that are used to good effect by people and could be used to better effect by robots and other computers of the future. But first we need to understand them and to develop mathematical tools for modeling them. These are not easy tasks, but I think they are worth the effort.

In this expository talk, I will briefly review some recent probes into the region of situated logic, probes that seem promising as we look for new contributions that logical theory can make to computational practice in the future. I will concentrate on *Hyperproof.*

2 Hyperproof

Hyperproof is a project initiated and directed by John Etchemendy and me. It is a joint project of CSLI, at Stanford University, and CICA, at Indiana University. (The acronyms are for the Center for the Study of Language and Information, and the Center for Innovative Computer Applications, respectively.) Other people who are (or have been) involved with it include: Gerard Allwein, Alan Bush, Doug Felt, Mark Greaves, Michael Lenz, Christopher Phoenix, and Sun-Joo Shin. It is this project I would like to describe to you in this lecture.

Hyperproof is, in most ways, a very modest relaxation of the idealization from first-order logic. In other ways, though, it is quite a radical departure. I will begin by giving you the motivation for and feel of the project. Then I will point out the connection with situated logic, in case it is not obvious. I will conclude by speculating about some potential connections between *Hyperproof* and logic programming.

Motivation

Psychologists tell us that an enormous fraction of inference in our day-to-day life takes place within the perceptual system. Indeed, it is called "perceptual inference." As we view and reason about our environment, a lot of information extraction goes on before things ever get to the stage of conscious, controllable, thought. We have a wealth of implicit knowledge of the world that we cannot articulate, but that we use as we extract information about the world around us. With a few notable exceptions (Euler, Venn, Peirce, for example), logicians have steadfastly ignored the visual dimension in reasoning. We are trying to remedy this.

One way to think about *Hyperproof* is as an attempt to design inferential tools that reflect and build on this observation. At the level of theory, we want to be able to have a theory of mind and inference that accounts for the interplay of perceptual information extraction with the kinds of reasoning more typically studied in logic. At the level of tools, we want to design computational artifacts for use in reasoning, tools that allow the user to shift part of the burden from the language back to the perceptual domain.

The *Hyperproof* system

In more concrete terms, *Hyperproof* is an attempting to design a representational system that allows for two distinct kinds of representation: visual (e.g., diagrammatic or pictorial) representations, on the one hand, and linguistic representations, on the other. For our linguistic representations, we are sticking with the notation of first-order logic, more out of expedience than out of a conviction that it will be the most useful in the long run. For visual representations, our current system is based on pictures of simple blocks worlds. The reasoning tasks we are currently able to handle are confined to those that can be conveniently represented within such a framework.

The two positive aspects of situated logic mentioned above are both exploited in *Hyperproof.* The user is able to exploit constraints that hold of the diagrams created, in order to reason about the block world the diagrams describe. And the user is able to alter these diagrams during the reasoning process, incorporating information into them as it becomes available.

Different kinds of information are best represented in different ways. Sentences and diagrams are both good at representing partial information, but they are good at different aspects. Contrast the information in a map with some linguistic representation of it. Or contrast the information in a legal document with what could be conveyed in a picture. And in between we find things like blueprints that use both forms of representation mixed together in crucial ways. In *Hyperproof*, we attempt to use the most efficient form of representation, and to find systematic ways of moving information between the two during inference.

This means that there are, in principle, at least four sorts of rules of inference in a system like *Hyperproof*:

1. Sentences $\rightsquigarrow$ Sentences
2. Diagrams $\rightsquigarrow$ Diagrams
3. Diagrams $\rightsquigarrow$ Sentences
4. Sentences $\rightsquigarrow$ Diagrams

The rules of type 1 are the usual rules we are used to from logic. Thus *Hyperproof* is an extension of classical, first-order logic. It has all the usual rules of inferences involving sentence to sentence transformations.

Rules of type 2 allow us to extract information from diagrams in the form of other diagrams. An example is the rule of **Merge** where one has two or more diagrams representing different possible situations and form the diagram that represents the information they have in common.

An example of a rule of type 3 is the rule **Observe**, which lets you simply read off (using the strong Kleene evaluation scheme) facts from a diagram. Another is the rule of **Inspect**, which allows one to inspect a number of open cases, to see if some sentence is true in all of them.

In many ways, the most important and most powerful rules are those of type Sentences $\rightsquigarrow$ Diagrams, rule that allow you to express information in sentences in the form of diagrams. Let me discuss one of the sentence $\rightsquigarrow$ diagram rules in our current system, the so-called rule of **Cases Exhaustive**. This rule allows the user to compare a single piece of sententially presented information against an arbitrary number of cases that are represented visually, to see if the cases displayed exhaust the information presented by the sentence. (An important special case of this is the rule **Apply** which lets you add information to the diagram if the information is implicit in the sentence cited as support.) Since sentences are good at representing disjunctive information, this is one of the most important rules of the system for getting information from sentences into diagrams, where the characteristic features of diagrams can be taken advantage of.

The situatedness of *Hyperproof*

Without giving a visual demonstration of *Hyperproof*, it is hard to give a feel for the flavor of the system, especially in words, which the system transcends. Equipment cooperating, I will give a demonstration of the system in the lecture. Here I will instead list some of the features of diagrams that the system exploits, features that exploit situatedness of reasoning in at least a couple of ways. The following list of features is taken with minor modifications from the paper Barwise and Etchemendy [4]. This paper also contains a much fuller description of *Hyperproof*, with illustrations.

Perceptual inference

We have already dwelt on this, but it bears repeating. While strictly speaking, the eyes are part of the brain, from the cognitive point of view, the perceptual apparatus is fairly independent of our controllable cognitive activities. The sorts of things it does are automatic and so fairly well insulated from the forms of reasoning we engage in at a conscious level. Moreover, the perceptual system is an enormously powerful inferential system. This is not surprising, given the fact that visual situations satisfy their own family of constraints. Indeed, it is the fact that visual situations do satisfy constraints that has made it possible for our perceptual system to evolve so as to recognize regularities in the world. And so it is not surprising that people use the tools this system provides in reasoning.

Closure under constraints

Diagrams are physical situations. They must be, since we can see them. As such, they obey their own set of constraints, constraints we can exploit in reasoning with them. This is, of course, one of the themes of situated logic. And we can modify the diagrams, just as the situated reasoner can modify the situation it is in. When we add a couple objects to a diagram, a host of other facts become supported by the diagram. By choosing a representational scheme appropriately, so that the constraints on the diagrams have a good match with the constraints on the described situation, the diagram can generate a lot of information that the user never need infer. Rather, the user can simply read off facts from the diagram as needed. This situation is in stark contrast to sentential inference, where even the most trivial consequence needs to be inferred explicitly.

Conjunctive *vs* disjunctive information

It is often said that a picture is worth a thousand words. The truth behind this saying is that even a relatively simple picture or diagram can support countless facts, facts that can be read off the diagram. Thus a diagram can represent in a compact form what would take countless sentences to express. By contrast, sentences come into their own where one one needs to describe a variety of mutually incompatible possibilities. This is what makes the rule of **Cases Exhaustive** so important in our system.

Isomorphic *vs* non-isomorphic representation

Another advantage of diagrams, related to the preceding two, is that a good diagram is isomorphic to the situation it represents, at least along certain crucial dimensions. This is what makes the one a picture, or diagram, of the other. By contrast, the relationship between the linguistic structure of a sentence and that of its content is far more complex. It is certainly nothing like an isomorphism in any obvious way.

Symmetry arguments

As we have looked at the use of diagrams in various sorts of reasoning tasks, we have been struck by the fact that in almost all such solutions, there is some sort of symmetry argument. These symmetry arguments often go unnoticed by the user. And they bear a striking similarity to the rule of universal generalization, or ∀ Introduction, in first-order logic.

Universal generalization, when applicable, results in an enormous (often infinite) reduction in inferential overhead over the alternative of establishing each and every case individually. Similarly, symmetry arguments often result in a drastic lowering of inferential overhead, by cutting down on the number of cases that need to be explicitly considered, in cases where universal generalization is not applicable. And for some reason symmetry arguments are often quite transparent with visual representations. The eye seems remarkably good at spotting equivalent diagrams, with respect to symmetry arguments. We cannot claim to understand just why this is so, but as a result diagrams greatly facilitate proofs that use symmetry arguments. In any case, it seems clear that the ability to shortcut the number of cases that need to be considered by appealing to symmetries in the diagrams and the situations they represent is a significant aspect of the power of diagrams in reasoning.

This is one place where our computer system currently falls short of what the user would like it to do. In using the rule **Cases Exhaustive**, a good system needs to be able to tell that a few representative cases are in fact sufficient, by means of symmetry considerations, to cover a vast number of cases. People are able to do this, but finding a computationally tractable algorithm to implement in *Hyperproof* has, so far, eluded us.

3 Hyperproof and Logic Programming

Does *Hyperproof* (or situated logic more generally) have anything to contribute to logic programming? Or vice versa? Time will tell. But it does seem at least plausible to me that there is room for fruitful interactions. That is why I was pleased to be asked to address this group.

One indication of potential interaction comes from the increasing role of constraints in logic programming. Constraints are just the sorts of things that diagrams satisfy automatically. Perhaps programming languages with diagrammatic components will be able to take advantage of new constraint satisfaction techniques. Or perhaps it will allow one to pose problems in ways that circumvent the need for explicitly represented constraints. Just make sure the diagrams of the programming language satisfy the constraints in question.

A very suggestive line of work in this direction come from the work on visual programming languages. I am thinking in particular of the work reported in Kahn and Saraswat [6], though I am aware that there is other work along similar lines.

This work starts with the observation that concurrent logic programs have a very simple and elegant visual representation, one that allows the user to visualize the program and its execution. The basic operation (unification) corresponds to simple operations on these representations. Indeed, unification of terms can be depicted quite simply as the visual unification of the contours representing the terms. And so program execution allows a simple visualization. The hope, of course, is that such visual representations of concurrent logic programs will be easier to create and understand.

This is strikingly familiar to anyone who has taught students to build Turing machines. Flow diagrams are easy to create and understand, whereas the more linguistic 4-tuple representations are cognitively impenetrable. Indeed, this realization is what led Etchemendy and me [3] to develop *Turing's World*, a program that allows users to build Turing machines by drawing their flow chart on the screen of a Macintosh. This program turned out to be so powerful that students can now design and run universal Turing machines without great difficulty.

What does all this have to do with *Hyperproof*? Imagine a program verification system that allowed the user to represent a Turing machine or logic program visually, as well as information about the input, output, and state of the machine or variables at run time. Claims about the program's behavior would be analogous to the sentences in *Hyperproof*. Proofs of program correctness could contain as parts actual runs of the program, under special assumptions about the input and state. Under such a regime, each of our four rule types makes perfectly good sense. The analog of **Observe** would be **Execute**. **Cases Exhaustive** would verify that the programmer did not forget the sorts of special cases that are typically overlooked in programming.

This is all wild speculation, of course. Time will tell whether these particular directions pan out. But it does seem safe to say that the power of the computer to help us visualize more easily is going to change the way we program, and the way we reason about programs, and the very way we think about reasoning.

Acknowledgments

As indicated above, *Hyperproof* represents joint work with John Etchemendy and the other members of the team listed above. I would like to thank all of them for their contributions to the project and to improving this paper. It also owes a lot to feedback that Etchemendy and I have gotten in giving talks on *Hyperproof* around the world.

References

[1] Jon Barwise, *The Situation in Logic*, CSLI Lecture Notes, 1989, University of Chicago Press.

[2] Jon Barwise and John Perry, *Situations and Attitudes*, Bradford Books, M.I.T. Press, 1983.

[3] Jon Barwise and John Etchemendy, *Turing's World*, Chariot Software, San Diego, 1986.

[4] Jon Barwise and John Etchemendy, Visual information and valid reasoning, *Visualization in Mathematics*, ed. by Walter Zimmerman and Steven Cunningham, Mathematical Association of America, to appear, 1990?

[5] Robin Cooper, Kuniaki Mukai and John Perry, eds, *Situation Theory and its Applications*, CSLI Lecture Notes, 1990.

[6] Ken Kahn and Vijay Saraswat, "On the complete visualization of concurrent programs and their executions", to appear in the IEEE Workshop on Visual Languages, 1990.

An Algebraic Semantics of Logic Programs as Structured Transition Systems

Andrea Corradini and **Ugo Montanari**
Dipartimento di Informatica
Corso Italia 40
I - 56125, Pisa, Italy
andrea@dipisa.di.unipi.it

Abstract

In this paper a general methodology for the definition of an algebraic semantics of a wide class of formalisms is presented. The methodology generalizes the algebraic description of Petri nets proposed by J. Meseguer and U. Montanari in [MM88], and its generality and expressiveness are tested through its application to Horn Clause Logic. The resulting algebraic semantics associates to each logic program a class of models, i.e. of (small) categories whose arrows are the abstract computations of the program, equipped with a rich algebraic structure. The various models differ for the level of abstraction: the initial one is the most concrete, and has partial orderings of resolution steps as arrows, while in the final one (the most abstract) all the refutations for the same goal are identified. The classic semantics of logic programs and of some extensions can be easily recovered from the final model.

1 Introduction

In their LICS '88 paper "Petri Nets are Monoids" [MM88], J. Meseguer and U. Montanari proposed a new algebraic definition for Place/Transition Petri nets. A net is simply a graph with a commutative monoidal structure on states: this way, a net is regarded as an object of a suitable category of graphs, called **Petri**, where the morphisms are required to preserve the monoidal structure of nodes. Then two categories are defined, among others, having as objects reflexive graphs (resp. small categories) with a monoidal structure on both nodes and arcs (resp. on objects and arrows). Those categories are called **CMonRPetri** and **CatPetri**. Since the obvious forgetful functors from these categories to **Petri** have left adjoints, two free constructions can be defined which associate to each net N its free reflexive graph C[N], and its free *Petri category* T[N]. It turns out that both structures have a relevant meaning in Petri net theory: C[N] is the *marking graph* of N, while T[N] is a category whose arrows are isomorphic to the *non sequential processes* of N, as defined in [BD87]. Furthermore, the new categorical framework makes easy the definition for Petri nets of a notion of implementation morphism, of a closed monoidal structure, and of new invariants.

The relevance and the practical usefulness of category theory in theoretical computer science has been emphasized by several authors (see for example [AL89, Go89]), and the successful algebraic treatment of Petri nets is a further evidence of this fact. An immediate, impressive consequence of the use of general categorical tools, is that the semantics of nets is automatically *compositional* in a strong sense: in fact, any composition operation defined in terms of *colimits* in the category of nets is automatically preserved by the free constructions, since they correspond to left (free) adjoint functors. Moreover, as argued in [Me89, Me90], the categorical setting allows to encompass the traditional distinction between *operational* and *declarative* semantics: the same construction can be operationally defined through inference rules and equations, or can be declaratively characterized by a universal property.

These considerations naturally led to some attempts to generalize the approach proposed in [MM88], in order to apply the same guidelines and similar categorical constructions to the definition of the semantics of other formalisms. In this line of research, recently J. Meseguer proposed a categorical semantics for *concurrent rewriting systems*, which are considered as a unified model of concurrency [Me90]. It is shown that the programs of a wide class of paradigms (including functional, logical, and object oriented programming, Turing Machines, Petri Nets, Chemical Abstract Machines, and much more) can be represented as concurrent rewriting systems over a suitable equational signature $\langle\Sigma, E\rangle$, which depends on the specific formalism. Such systems can also be regarded as *theories* of the so-called *directed equational logic*. Then a notion of *model* for such systems is proposed, which is essentially a category having a similar algebraic structure on both objects and arrows. The arrows of a model are abstract, concurrent computations of the rewriting systems, and the initial model is generated by a free construction, which defines a left adjoint functor between the category of rewriting systems and that of models. The algebraic treatment of Petri nets of [MM88] can then be obtained by instantiating the general definitions for a specific signature.

A different approach, which will be presented in this paper, has been taken in [Co90], where the algebraic treatment of nets in [MM88] has been considered as a guideline for the definition of a general methodology which allows to define an algebraic semantics for a wide class of formalisms. The characterizing issue of this proposal is to consider the programs as *internal* structures (typically graphs) in a universe category **C**, possibly more structured than **Set**. Then, all the categorical constructions are performed *inside* that category. For example, the models are still (small) categories, but this time *internal* to **C**. In particular, choosing **CMon**, the category of commutative monoids, as universe, one gets a semantics of nets equivalent to that of [MM88].

The resulting methodology seems, at a first look, more general than the framework proposed by [Me90], because the states of a system are not bounded to be the elements of an algebra, but can form an object of an (almost) arbitrary category. For example, in the treatment of Horn Clause Logic discussed later, the states are the arrows of a (small) cartesian category: it is not clear how an analogous treatment could be done in the other framework. However, the analysis of the precise relationships between our approach and that of [Me90] requires further investigation.

The paper is organized as follows. In Section 2 we discuss the basic rationale of the methodology proposed in [Co90], and introduce the categorical constructions which define them. Next, in Section 3, we apply the methodology to Petri nets, in order to test it in a simple case. Finally, in Section 4, Horn Clause Logic is considered. A new, very rich algebraic semantics is proposed, which associates to every logic program a class of 'acceptable' models, corresponding to different levels of abstraction. The initial (free) model of a program includes all its (abstract) computations as arrows, while the terminal one is sufficient to recover the classical semantics of Horn Clause Logic. Partial results about this topic are reported in [CM89-90]. A certain basic knowledge about categories is helpful. For the definitions of the category theoretic notions used in the paper we refer to [ML71, AL89].

2 The methodology

In this section we discuss the main ideas of the general methodology for the analysis of computational models, first presented in [Co90]. The methodology can be applied to a wide class of formalisms (including Phrase Structured Grammars, Rewriting Systems, Petri Nets, and Logic Programs), and associates to each program of those formalisms a class of *acceptable models*. A model is a (small) category whose arrows represents *abstract computations* of the program, and every model corresponds to a different level of abstraction.

In order to guarantee the generality of the methodology, we had to look for a uniform representation of both the static and the dynamic aspects of the programs belonging to formalisms like the ones mentioned above. Since such programs are endowed with a natural notion of *states* and *transitions*, one could think to regard them as *transition systems*, and thus to generate all their computations as paths of elementary transitions. However, this approach would lead to incorrect results, since such programs cannot be considered, as they are, as *true* transition systems. In fact, while in the standard definition of transition systems a transition $t: u \rightarrow v$ can be applied only to state u, usually a more permissive *matching rule* is either implicitly or explicitly associated with such programs, stating when and how a transition can be applied to a state, and which the resulting new state is. For example, in the case of a Petri net a transition can be fired at a marking (i.e. at a global state) if its preconditions are included in the marking itself; in the case of a logic program, a clause can be applied to a goal if its head unifies with an atomic formula of that goal.

Nevertheless, it is often the case that a *structured* transition system (i.e. a system with a similar, typically algebraic, structure on both states and transitions) can be defined, which, incorporating the matching rule into the structure of transitions, is able to suitably model the behaviour of the original program. This will be called the *induced transition system* of the program. For example, in the case of Petri nets the induced transition system of a net is its marking graph. If certain conditions are satisfied, the induced transition system can be generated from the program it simulates with a free construction which lifts the algebraic structure of states to transitions.

The fundamental advantage of considering transition systems with an algebraic structure on both states and transitions (while for example in [Pl81] just the algebraic structure of states is put in evidence), resides in the fact that often the same structure can automatically and consistently be extended to the set of computations of the system, through a free construction which generalizes the well-known generation of the free category of a graph. Thus every program can be associated (through this two step construction) with a *structured* category (called its *free model*) whose arrows are not simple sequences of elementary transitions, but are instead *abstract* computations, equipped with an algebraic structure.

The methodology individuates suitable categories for each of the levels of description of a system (i.e. programs, structured transition systems, and models), and relates these categories with free adjoint functors, which generate from a given program its induced transition system and its free model of computations. Moreover, in general a class of *acceptable* models can be associated to a given program, which is a subcategory of all possible models: the free model is initial among them, and sometimes a final (most abstract) model can be determined, too.

The generality of our methodology comes from the fact that all the definitions and results are parametric with respect to the algebraic structure of states and transitions: for example we will show in the next sections that the algebraic treatment of Petri nets (resp. Logic Programs) can be obtained as an instantiation of the methodology, if we choose commutative monoids (resp. strict cartesian categories) as the structure of states and transitions.

In the following subsection we introduce the main definitions and results of category theory needed to formalize the methodology, which is then defined in Section 2.2.

2.1 Categories of internal structures

The technique we use to abstract from the actual structure of the states and transitions of a system is that of *internalization*. A simple example will explain the basic rationale. A *(directed) graph* is a tuple $G = \langle V, T, \partial_0, \partial_1 \rangle$, where V is a set of *nodes*, T is a set of *arcs*, ∂_0 and ∂_1: T → V are the *source* and *target* functions, respectively (as usual, we often write t: u → v if $\partial_0(t)$ = u and $\partial_1(t)$ = v). A *graph morphism* f: ‹V, T, ∂_0, ∂_1› → ‹V', T', ∂'_0, ∂'_1› is a pair ‹f_0, f_1› of functions, with f_0: V → V', f_1: T → T', and such that for all t ∈ T, $\partial'_0(f_1(t)) = f_0(\partial_0(t))$ and $\partial'_1(f_1(t)) = f_0(\partial_1(t))$. The category having all (small) graphs as objects and graph morphisms as arrows is called **Graph**.

Presented this way, a graph can be considered as described *internally* to the category **Set**, which has *sets* as objects and *total functions* as arrows. In fact, T and V are both objects of **Set**, while ∂_0 and ∂_1 are arrows of **Set**: thus a graph is just a diagram with the following shape in **Set**:

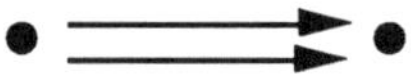

Moreover, graph morphisms are pairs of arrows of **Set**, which commute when composed in the right way with the source and target arrows.

Let us consider now *structured graphs*, i.e. graphs whose collections of arcs and nodes have a richer structure than a simple set. In many situations, the algebraic structure of arcs and nodes is similar, and the source and target mappings are required to preserve that structure. If **C** is the category of those algebraic structures, then the structured graph can be regarded as a diagram having the same shape as above, but this time in category **C**. This yields to the definition of *internal* graphs.

2.1 Definition *(Internal Graphs)*

Let **C** be a category. An *internal graph of* **C** is a tuple G = ‹c_0, c_1, ∂_0, ∂_1›, where:

- c_0 and c_1 are objects of **C** (shortly, $c_0, c_1 \in |\mathbf{C}|$)
- ∂_0, ∂_1: $c_1 \to c_0$ are arrows in **C**.

Let G = ‹c_0, c_1, ∂_0, ∂_1› and G' = ‹c'_0, c'_1, ∂'_0, ∂'_1› be two internal graphs of **C**. Then an *internal graph morphism* f: G → G' is a pair ‹f_0, f_1› of arrows of **C** (f_0: $c_0 \to c'_0$, f_1: $c_1 \to c'_1$), such that $f_1;\partial'_0 = \partial_0;f_0$, and $f_1;\partial'_1 = \partial_1;f_0$ (where _;_ is the operation of arrow composition of **C**, see the definition of categories below).

Graph(C) is the category having internal graphs of **C** as objects, and internal graph morphisms as arrows. ♦

Analogously, the notions of *reflexive graph* and of *category* can be generalized to their corresponding *internal* versions, too. A *reflexive graph* R = ‹V, T, ∂_0, ∂_1, id› is a graph ‹T, V, ∂_0, ∂_1›, equipped with a function id: V → T such that for each v ∈ V, $\partial_0(id(v)) = \partial_1(id(v))$ = v. Therefore an *internal reflexive graph of* **C** is defined as an internal graph of **C** having an additional arrow id: $c_0 \to c_1$ such that $id;\partial_0 = id;\partial_1 = id_{c_0}$ (the identity arrow of object c_0). **RGraph(C)** is the category having internal reflexive graphs of **C** as objects, and *internal reflexive graph morphisms* as arrow, that is internal graph morphisms which preserve identities (i.e. such that $id;f_1 = f_0;id'$)

A *category* C = ‹V, T, ∂_0, ∂_1, id, _;_› is a reflexive graph equipped with a partial binary operation _;_ on arcs (*arrow composition*). If t, t' ∈ T, then t ; t' is defined iff $\partial_1(t) = \partial_0(t')$. In this case, $\partial_0(t ; t') = \partial_0(t)$, and $\partial_1(t ; t') = \partial_1(t')$. Moreover, the following axioms must be satisfied for all arrows t, t', and t'' in T:

Associativity: (t ; t') ; t'' = t ; (t' ; t'')

Identity: t ; id(∂_1(t)) = t and id(∂_0(t)) ; t = t

In a category C = ‹V, T, ∂_0, ∂_1, id, _;_›, V are the *objects* (usually denoted by |C|), and T are the *arrows*.

As for graphs, a category can be regarded as a suitable diagram in category **Set**: in fact the operation of arrow composition can be regarded as a *total* function having as domain the set {<t, t'> | $\partial_1(t) = \partial_0(t')$} which can be categorically defined as a *pullback* in **Set**. Moreover, the axioms of associativity and identities can be rephrased as a requirement of commutativity for suitable diagrams in **Set** [AL89]. Then an *internal category of* ***C*** can be defined simply by substituting category **Set** with **C**. **Cat**(**C**) is the category having all (small) internal categories of **C** as objects, and *internal functors* as arrow, i.e. internal reflexive graph morphisms which preserve arrow composition.

As we will see in the next sections, in the general case we want to define the structured transition systems simulating the dynamic behaviour of the programs as internal (reflexive) graphs of a suitable universe category **C**, and the categories of computations of the programs (i.e. the models) as internal categories of the same universe **C**, since we want to extend the same algebraic structure of transitions to computations. Moreover, we require that the free category of computations of a program be uniquely determined through a free construction; in categorical terms we are looking for a *free adjunction* [ML71] between the categories [**R**]**Graph**(**C**) and **Cat**(**C**).

In the case of unstructured graphs (i.e. graphs internal to **Set**) it is well known that between categories **Graph**, **RGraph**, and **Cat** there exist the obvious forgetful functors **Cat** → **RGraph** and **RGraph** → **Graph**, with their free adjoints R: **Graph** → **RGraph** and C: **RGraph** → **Cat**. Informally, if G is a graph, R[G] is obtained by adding one reflexive arc to each node of G. On the other hand, C[G] is obtained by adding to G a new arc $t_1; \ldots; t_n: \partial_0(t_1) \rightarrow \partial_1(t_n)$ for each sequence ‹$t_1, \ldots, t_n$› of 'composable' arcs of G (i.e. such that $\partial_1(t_i) = \partial_0(t_{i+1})$).

In the case of structured graphs, it is natural to ask under which conditions these free constructions can be generalized. More precisely, we want to point out which properties a category **C** must satisfy, in order to guarantee the existence of the free adjoints for the obvious forgetful functors **Cat**(**C**) → **RGraph**(**C**) and **RGraph**(**C**) → **Graph**(**C**). Let us summarize the results that will be used in the following. Proofs can be found in [Co90].

2.2 Theorem *(from Internal Graphs to Reflexive Graphs and Categories)*

a) If **C** is a category with binary coproducts, then the forgetful functor **RGraph(C)** $\rightarrow$ **Graph(C)** has a free adjoint R_C: **Graph(C)** $\rightarrow$ **RGraph(C)**. If G $\in$ |**Graph(C)**|, then $R_C[G]$ has as arcs the coproduct of the arcs and the nodes of G.

b) If **C** is the category of models in **Set** of a left-exact sketch, then the obvious forgetful functor **Cat(C)** $\rightarrow$ **RGraph(C)** has a free adjoint C_C: **RGraph(C)** $\rightarrow$ **Cat(C)**. ♦

The definition of *left-exact sketches* and of their models goes beyond the scope of the paper: we refer to [BW85] for an introduction of these notions. For the goals of this paper, it is sufficient to notice that many interesting categories can be characterized as categories of models of a left-exact sketch. For example, many categories of algebras (like rings, groups, (commutative) monoids, etc.) enjoy this property, and also **Graph**, **RGraph**, **Cat**, **PreOrd** (the category of preorders), **PO** (the category of partial orders), and **Cart** (the category of small cartesian categories).

2.1.1 Heterogeneous graphs

Although internal graphs are a good formalization of the notion of structured transition systems, in many situations we have to consider graphs where the structure of nodes is richer than the structure of arcs. A typical example is a Petri net, which, as defined in [MM88], has a free commutative monoid as nodes, but just a *set* as transitions (cf. Definition 3.1 below). We will call this kind of graphs *heterogeneous graphs.*

2.3 Definition *(Heterogeneous Graphs)*

Let **C** and **B** be two categories, such that a forgetful functor U: **C** $\rightarrow$ **B** exists. Then G = ‹c, b, ∂_0, ∂_1› is a *heterogeneous graph with arcs in **B** and nodes in **C*** iff c $\in$ |**C**|, b $\in$ |**B**|, and ∂_0, ∂_1: b $\rightarrow$ U[c] are arrows in **B**. A *heterogeneous graph morphism* f: ‹c, b, ∂_0, ∂_1› $\rightarrow$ ‹c', b', ∂'_0, ∂'_1› is a pair ‹f_0, f_1› where f_1: b $\rightarrow$ b' is an arrow in **B**, f_0: c $\rightarrow$ c' is an arrow in **C**, and such that $f_1;\partial'_0 = \partial_0;U[f_0]$ and $f_1;\partial'_1 = \partial_1;U[f_0]$. **Graph(B, C)** is the category having heterogeneous graphs with arcs in **B** and nodes in **C** as objects, and heterogeneous graph morphisms as arrows. ♦

Practically, a heterogeneous graph ‹c, b, ∂_0, ∂_1› $\in$ |**Graph(B, C)**| can be considered as an internal graph ‹U[c], b, ∂_0, ∂_1› $\in$ |**Graph(B)**|, but the morphisms are required to preserve the richer structure on nodes. The following result shows that if the forgetful functor U: **C** $\rightarrow$ **B** has a free adjoint, then one can safely enrich the structure of arcs of a heterogeneous graph in order to get an internal graph of the more structured category.

2.4 Proposition *(Enriching the Arcs of a Heterogeneous Graph)*

Let **C** and **B** be two categories such that there exists a forgetful functor U: **C** $\rightarrow$ **B** with free adjoint F: **B** $\rightarrow$ **C**. Then the forgetful functor U': **Graph(C)** $\rightarrow$ **Graph(B, C)**, obviously induced by U (i.e. U'[‹c_0, c_1, ∂_0, ∂_1›] = ‹c_0, U[c_1],

$U[\partial_0], U[\partial_1]\rangle$ on objects, and $U'[\langle f_0, f_1\rangle] = \langle f_0, U[f_1]\rangle$ on arrows), has a free adjoint F'. ♦

2.2 Defining the methodology

Putting together all the above definitions and results, we can introduce the steps of our methodology for the analysis of computational systems. For a given formalism, the methodology recognizes the existence of three levels (namely programs, structured transition systems, and models) which correspond to three different categories of internal structures, related by adjunctions. An additional, fourth level is often necessary to focus the attention on the acceptable models of a program, i.e. on a suitable subcategory of all possible models. In a simplified but quite general situation, the methodology can be summarized as follows.

2.5 Definition *(Guidelines for the Methodology)*
Suppose we have a class of 'programs' **Prog**. The following steps define a methodology which associates each program in **Prog** with a class of models.

1) Determine the 'natural' structure of the states and of the transitions of programs in **Prog**, and what the morphisms among systems in **Prog** are, in order to regard **Prog** as a category. This category has the form **Graph**(**B**,**C**), i.e. it is a category of heterogeneous graphs with states in **C** and transitions in **B**. Since **C** is more structured than **B**, there exists a forgetful functor U: **C** → **B**: to be able to apply the next steps, one has to look for its free adjoint F: **B** → **C**.

2) Define a category of *transition systems* which model the dynamic behaviour of the programs of **Prog**. This category usually has the form **RGraph**(**C**), i.e. it is the category of reflexive internal graphs having both transitions and states in **C**. If **C** has binary coproducts, by Theorem 2.2a and Proposition 2.4 the forgetful functor U: **RGraph**(**C**) → **Graph**(**B**,**C**) has a free adjoint F: **Graph**(**B**,**C**) → **RGraph**(**C**), which associates to a system its *induced transition system*.

3) Define a category of *models* for transition systems. This category usually has the form **Cat**(**C**), i.e. it includes internal categories of **C**. If **C** satisfies the hypotheses of Theorem 2.2b, the forgetful functor **Cat**(**C**) → **RGraph**(**C**) has a free adjoint C_C, which associates to each transition system its *free model*.

4) Define the category **Mod**(P) of *acceptable models* of a program P ∈ **Prog**, i.e. a suitable subcategory of **Cat**(**C**), rooted at the free model of P. Some models of **Mod**(P), corresponding to different semantics of P at various levels of abstraction, can be determined via suitable categorical techniques. For example, the final object of **Mod**(P), if it exists, is the most abstract semantics of P. ♦

This methodology can be considered as an excellent example of the way category theory provides guidelines for formulating definitions, as stressed in [Go89]. Having characterized the constructions as left adjoint functors, the generation of the free models for the programs belonging to a given formalism simply reduces to the definition of the category of point 1) above, i.e. to the choice of the right structure for states (**C**) and transitions (**B**). In fact, if category **C** satisfies the hypotheses of Theorem 2.2, everything else is uniquely determined, thanks to the uniqueness of left adjoints.

The 'universe' category is actually the parameter of the methodology (see [Co90] for a deeper discussion of this point). Taking category **Set** as universe, one gets the classic (unstructured) transition systems; **CMon** (the category of commutative monoids) is the right universe for the treatment of Petri Nets, as shown in the next section; **Mon** (that of non-commutative monoids) serves for Phrase Structured Grammars (which are not discussed here); and finally **SCart** (the category of (small, strict) cartesian categories) is shown to be the right universe for the treatment of logic programs, as discussed in Section 4 (see also [CM89-90]).

As the last point, it should be stressed that in many real situations the steps of the methodology defined above cannot be applied directly, but some 'ad hoc' solutions have to be found. Nevertheless, the methodology summarized above still remains a useful guideline. In particular, in order to satisfy the (strong) requirements on category **C**, often one has to choose a category which is bigger than the one which, at a first glance, could seem natural to consider. The following fact ensures that widening the category of the structures of states we do not go into troubles, since the states are preserved by the construction of the free model.

2.6 Proposition *(Generation of the Free Category Preserves the States)*
Let **C** be a category with all pullbacks, and G be an internal graph of **C**. Then the free internal category of **C** generated by G, if it exists, has exactly the nodes of G as objects. ♦

3 Petri Nets

Petri Nets [Pe62] are the first and maybe the most popular formalism for specifying and modelling distributed activities. In this section we briefly recall their algebraic presentation, first proposed in [MM88], as a particular instantiation of our methodology. As the title *Petri Nets are Monoids* suggests (and as anticipated above), the algebraic structure which in some sense 'characterizes' the nets is that of commutative monoids.

A Place/Transition Petri Net [Rei85] is classically defined as a set of *places*, a set of *transitions*, and a *flow relation* connecting each transition to two multisets of places, called its *preset* and *postset*, respectively. The dynamic behaviour of a net is described by the *token game*. Each place can contain a set of *tokens*, and a transition is *enabled* if all the places contain at least as many tokens as their multiplicity in the preset of the transition. An enabled transition can *fire*, moving the tokens from the places in its preset to the places in its postset. Several transitions can be enabled at the same time, and can fire concurrently.

The tokens can be regarded as distributed components of a global state (called a *marking*): since transitions involving disjoint parts of the global state are independent, a natural notion of *concurrent* computations arises for Petri nets. As a consequence many different notions of *net computations* have been defined, including *firing sequences* (total orderings of elementary transitions), *step sequences* (total orderings of multisets of concurrent transitions), and *non sequential processes* (partial orderings of transitions).

Clearly, only the last kind of computations is sufficient to capture the relevant aspects of the concurrent behaviour of nets, and to be the basis for a *truly concurrent* semantics for Petri nets. The relevant point of the presentation which follows is that the non-sequential processes are *automatically* generated as the arrows of the free model of a net, thanks to the fact that the algebraic structure of the transitions of the system induced by the net (i.e. its *marking graph*) is made explicit. On the contrary, forgetting the (monoidal) structure of transitions, one gets as computations just the step sequences.

The first step of the methodology consists of defining a category of heterogeneous graphs representing Petri nets. This can be easily done, following [MM88] where the isomorphism between the elements of a free commutative monoid, and the finite multisets of its generators is exploited.

3.1 Definition *(A Category of Petri Nets as Heterogeneous Graphs)*

A Petri net is a heterogeneous graph $N = \langle S^{\otimes}, T, \partial_0, \partial_1 \rangle$, where $S^{\otimes}$ is the free commutative monoid generated by the set of *places* S, T is a set of *transitions*, and $\partial_0, \partial_1 \colon T \to S^{\otimes}$ are functions associating to each transition its *preset* and its *postset*, respectively. The category of Petri nets, called **Petri** in [MM88], is exactly **Graph(Set, FCMon)** in the terminology of Definition 2.3, where **FCMon** is the category of *free* commutative monoids. ♦

Category **FCMon** does not satisfy the hypotheses of Theorem 2.2, but its super-category **CMon** (obtained by removing the freedom requirement) does. This is the reason why we will consider **CMon** as the universe corresponding to category **C** of Definition 2.5.

For the second step of the methodology, we take as the category of structured transition systems for Petri nets simply **RGraph(CMon)**, having as objects reflexive graphs with a commutative monoidal structure on both nodes and transitions. Intuitively, the monoidal operation on transitions means concurrency, while the identity transitions given by the reflexive structure allow a token to stay idle during the firing of a transition involving other tokens; thus a single arc of such a graph corresponds to a step, i.e. to a multiset of elementary transitions, plus some idle tokens. Since the hypotheses of Theorem 2.2a and Proposition 2.4 are satisfied, there exists a free adjoint functor from **Petri** to **RGraph(CMon)**, which associates to each net its marking graph, i.e. the graph having the global states of the net (the markings) as nodes, and the steps as arcs. It is easy to check that this functor is exactly the functor C[_]: **Petri** $\to$ **CMonRPetri** defined in [MM88], and that **CMonRPetri** is the full subcategory of **RGraph(CMon)** including all graphs whose monoid of nodes is free.

The next step consists of defining the category of models for Petri nets. Accordingly to requirement that the algebraic structure of transitions should be extended to the entire computations, we take as models the objects of **Cat(CMon)**, i.e. the (small) categories with a commutative monoidal structure on both objects and arrows: these are (when the monoid of states is free) the *Petri categories*, as defined in [MM88]. Since category **CMon** satisfies the hypothesis of Theorem 2.2b, there exists a free adjoint functor C_{CMon}: **RGraph(CMon)** $\to$ **Cat(CMon)**, which, composed with functor C[_], gives the left adjoint functor T[_]: **Petri** $\to$ **Cat(CMon)**, i.e. the one which associates to each net its free Petri category. As for any free construction, the internal category T[N] can be defined by inference rules and equations.

3.2 Definition *(The Petri Category of a Net)*

Given a net $N = \langle S^{\otimes}, T, \partial_0, \partial_1 \rangle$, its *free Petri category* $T[N] = \langle S^{\otimes}, T', \partial'_0, \partial'_1, id, ; \rangle$ is generated via the following inference rules and equations:

GEN: $\dfrac{t: u \to v \text{ in } N}{t: u \to v \text{ in } T[N]}$ OP: $\dfrac{t: u \to v,\ t': u' \to v' \text{ in } T[N]}{t \otimes t' : u \otimes u' \to v \otimes v' \text{ in } T[N]}$

ID: $\dfrac{u \in S^{\otimes}}{id_u : u \to u \text{ in } T[N]}$ COMP: $\dfrac{t: u \to v,\ t': v \to w \text{ in } T[N]}{t\, ;\, t' : u \to w \text{ in } T[N]}$

ASSOC: $(t_1 \otimes t_2) \otimes t_3 = t_1 \otimes (t_2 \otimes t_3)$

COMM: $t \otimes t' = t' \otimes t$

IDOP: $id_{u \otimes v} = id_u \otimes id_v$

UNIT: $t \otimes id_0 = t$ where 0 is the unit of $S^{\otimes}$

IDENT: $id_u\, ;\, t = t$ and $t\, ;\, id_v = t$

ASSOC': $(t_1\, ;\, t_2)\, ;\, t_3 = t_1\, ;\, (t_2\, ;\, t_3)$

EXCH: $\dfrac{t_1: u_1 \to v_1,\ t_2: v_1 \to v_2,\ t_3: u_3 \to v_3,\ t_4: v_3 \to v_4}{(t_1; t_2) \otimes (t_3; t_4) = (t_1 \otimes t_3)\, ;\, (t_2 \otimes t_4)}$ ♦

The above rules and equations state that the arrows of T[N] are obtained by taking the arcs of N as generators (GEN), by adding the identities (ID), and by closing them under a commutative monoidal operation (OP, ASSOC and COMM) and a sequentialization operation (COMP). Identities and sequential composition must satisfy the axioms for categories (UNIT, ASSOC'). Furthermore, since T[N] is an internal category of **CMon**, all its arrow components (i.e. ∂'_0, ∂'_1, id, and ';') have to be monoid homomorphisms. This is forced by OP for ∂'_0 and ∂'_1, and by IDOP and UNIT for *id*.

The most interesting axiom is EXCH, which forces ';' to be a monoid homomorphism, stating a relationship between the sequential and parallel composition of transitions: if all the compositions are defined, it says that the parallel composition of two sequences of transitions can be regarded as the sequence of the parallel compositions of their elementary steps. As anticipated above, it turns out that the arrows of the free Petri category T[N] are related to the non sequential processes of N, and in particular coincide with the processes defined in [BD87]. We refer to [DMM89] for a deep analysis of these relationships.

Finally, let us consider the fourth step of the methodology, i.e. the definition of a class of *acceptable models* of a Petri net. A reasonable choice is to define the category of acceptable models of a net N, **Mod**(N), as the subcategory of **Cat**(**CMon**) including all the internal categories M such that there exists an internal functor f: T[N] $\rightarrow$ M, which is epi and preserves the states. With this definition, the terminal model of N is a preorder, P[N], which is the *reachability relation* among markings, i.e. M $\leq_{P[N]}$ M' iff there exists a step (or firing) sequence from M to M'.

It should be stressed that the requirement that all models have the same objects is satisfactory for systems (like Petri nets and logic programs) where the transitions are not labeled, and thus no observation mechanism has to be taken into account. On the contrary, this definition would be too restrictive for formalisms like *process description languages* (e.g. Milner's CCS [Mi89]) where a notion of equivalence of states can be defined, based on sophisticated observation mechanisms.

With respect to this last point, it should be stressed that in [FM90, Fe90] a new algebraic semantics has been proposed for CCS, which follows some of the hints of our methodology (like the definition of two categories related by a free adjunction, corresponding to the transition systems and to the models, respectively). However, there are several reasons why the methodology defined in Section 2 cannot be directly applied, as it is, to CCS.

The first, minor point, is that CCS is defined directly as a transition system, and thus the first step of the methodology (the definition of the category of programs) does not make any sense for it. The second point is that CCS transitions (and computations) are *labeled*: the methodology proposed in Definition 2.5 does not allow to deal with this feature. In [FM90, Fe90] the labeling of transitions (resp. computations) is obtained through a comma category construction in the category of transition systems (resp. models).

The last (most problematic) point is that although both transition systems and models for CCS are defined in [Fe90] with a similar algebraic structure on arcs and arrows, respectively, the construction of the free model cannot be performed *internally* to the category of such algebras, because the operations on computations are not *compatible* extensions of the corresponding operations on transitions. We refer to [Fe90] for a deeper discussion of this point, showing for example why the *synchronization* of transitions cannot be extended to computations.

In spite of these problems, the algebraic framework still provides useful techniques for the semantic analysis of process description languages. For example, it allows to define a free functor which generates the free model of a transition system, and allows to associate a language with a class of models corresponding to different levels of abstractions. This last point is very valuable for formalisms like CCS, where the actual level of abstraction to consider strongly depends on various assumptions, and for which several semantics has been proposed in literature, corresponding to different notions of equivalence. The algebraic approach allows to characterize a specific model by imposing some equations, stating which computations have to be considered equivalent. This technique has been fruitfully exploited in [Fe90, FM90], where a model for CCS which faithfully represents its truly concurrent semantics as defined in [Wi82] is characterized through suitable axioms. The fourth step of our methodology is very meaningful for CCS. yIn fact, the notions of observational equivalence and congruence (in several of the versions proposed in the literature) can be defined in a quite natural way via finality.

4 Horn Clause Logic

In this section we apply our methodology to logic programs [Ll87]. This will equip logic programs with a new algebraic semantics, which associates a category of models to each program. The final model of a program corresponds, roughly speaking, to its classic semantics, while the initial one has a much richer structure, since as expected it includes all the (abstract) computations as arrows.

Although we focus on the operational semantics of logic programs, which can more easily be simulated by a transition system, in [CM90] it is shown (in a more set-theoretic setting) that also their declarative semantics (i.e. the model-theoretic and the fixpoint ones) can be defined for arbitrary transition systems. Thus, analyzing the behaviour of logic programs through their induced transition systems, one is able to preserve the existence of three distinct, although equivalent, semantics.

The full treatment of the algebraic semantics of logic programs can be found in [Co90], while partial results are reported in [CM89, CM90]. Here we just try to summarize the basic ideas, reporting the main definitions and results: all proofs are omitted. In the following subsections we will essentially use the standard definitions of logic programs and of their operational semantics, as reported for example in [Ll87]. However, some definitions are suitably adapted in order to fit better into our categorical approach:

- Non-ground terms and atomic formulas are considered over a *canonical tuple* (not a *set*) of variables $T^n \equiv \langle x_1, \ldots, x_n \rangle$, uniquely determined by its length.

- If T^n and T^m are canonical tuples of variables, a *substitution from T^m to T^n* is a function σ: $T^n \rightarrow T_\Sigma(T^m)$, also represented as a tuple $\langle x_1/\sigma(x_1), \ldots, x_n/\sigma(x_n)\rangle$. Since the names of variables are inessential, σ can be written as $\langle\sigma(x_1), \ldots, \sigma(x_n)\rangle$, thus a substitution is just a tuple of terms.

- Substitution application and compositions are *partial operations*. A substitution σ from T^m to T^n can be applied only to a term (or formula) t over T^m, yielding the instantiated term (resp. formula) $t \circ \sigma$. Similarly, σ can be composed with another substitution σ' from T^i to T^j only if $j = m$: in this case their composition $\sigma \circ \sigma' \equiv \langle\sigma(x_1)\circ\sigma', \ldots, \sigma(x_n)\circ\sigma'\rangle$ is from T^i to T^n.

In the next subsections we apply the steps of the methodology of Definition 2.5 to logic programs. In Section 4.1 and 4.2 we define suitable categories having as objects the structures of states and of transitions of logic programs. Therefore a program will be represented as a heterogeneous graph. Next, in Section 4.3 we define the category of structured transition systems for logic programs, and show how to automatically construct the induced transition system of a program. Finally in Section 4.4 we consider the generation of the free model of a logic program, and the definition of the class of acceptable models of a program. Some results relating the terminal acceptable model of a program with its classic semantics close the section.

4.1 The structure of logic program states

As stressed in Section 2.2, the main point in the application of our methodology to a class of programs is the choice of the right structure for the states and the transitions, in order to regard a program as a heterogeneous graph. A logic program can be represented in a natural way as a graph, where the arcs represent the program clauses, and the nodes are *goals*, i.e. tuples of atomic formulas. For example, the clause $c = (A \text{ :- } B_1, \ldots, B_n)$ is represented as an arc c: $\langle B_1, \ldots, B_n\rangle \rightarrow \langle A\rangle$.

In fact, the behaviour of a logic program P (with respect to an initial goal G) is operationally described as a sequence of resolution steps: each step transforms a goal into a new one (thus the goals are the 'global' states) through the application of a clause of P. The *matching rule* states that a clause c can be applied to a goal G iff the head of c unifies with an atomic formula in G with a most general unifier θ; the resulting goal is obtained by substituting in G the head of c with its body, and by instantiating the resulting formula with θ.

Regarding a logic program as a graph, its nodes have a quite rich structure: the main (possibly partial) operations we can define over tuples of formulas (goals) are

- *projections,* to extract atomic formulas out of a tuple,
- *tupling,* to build a tuple from its component atomic formulas,
- *application* of a term substitution to a formula,
- *unification* of two formulas.

Moreover, since also substitutions are involved, we have to consider *substitution composition*, too. Formulas and substitutions constructed over a given logic program signature $\langle \Sigma, \Pi \rangle$ (where Σ is a ranked set of function symbols, and Π is a ranked set of predicate symbols) can be easily represented as the arrows of a suitable *(strict) cartesian category*, in such a way that all the above operations directly correspond to basic categorical constructions. Let us give the precise definition of a strict cartesian category.

4.1 Definition *(Strict Cartesian Categories)*

A *cartesian category* C is a category with a terminal object $\mathbf{1} \in |C|$, and with a product diagram for every pair of objects X, Y $\in |C|$. A cartesian category is *strict* if its objects form a monoid with the product as monoidal operation, and the terminal object as unit. More formally, a *strict cartesian category* is a 12-tuple

$$C = \langle O, A, \partial_0, \partial_1, id, comp, \_\times\_, \mathbf{1}, fst, snd, \langle\_,\_\rangle, ! \rangle$$

where $\langle O, A, \partial_0, \partial_1, id, comp\rangle$ is a category, $\_\times\_: O\times O \to O$ is the product of objects, $\mathbf{1}: 1 \to O$ gives the terminal object, fst and snd: $O\times O \to A$ give the projections, $\langle\_,\_\rangle: A\times A \to A$ is the pairing function, and $!: O \to A$ maps every object X to the unique arrow $!X: X \to \mathbf{1}$. All these components have to satisfy the following axioms, including those of categories (CAT), those about products and terminal object (PROD), and those of monoids (MON):

CAT: $id_Y \circ t = t,\ \ t \circ id_X = t,\ \text{if } t: X \to Y;\qquad (t \circ t') \circ t'' = t \circ (t' \circ t'');$

PROD: $!Y \circ t = !X,\ \text{if } t: X \to Y;$
$\langle fst_{X,Y} \circ t, snd_{X,Y} \circ t\rangle = t,\ \text{if } t: Z \to X\times Y;$
$fst_{X,Y} \circ \langle t,t'\rangle = t,\ \ snd_{X,Y} \circ \langle t,t'\rangle = t',\ \text{if } t: Z \to X, t': Z \to Y;$

MON: $(X \times Y) \times Z = X \times (Y \times Z),$
$X \times \mathbf{1} = X,\ \ \mathbf{1} \times X = X,\ \text{if } X, Y, Z \in O.$ ♦

Given a logic program signature $\langle \Sigma, \Pi \rangle$, it is possible to build a strict cartesian category $\mathbf{SCC}(\Sigma,\Pi)$, called the *category of formulas and substitutions* of $\langle \Sigma, \Pi \rangle$, having as arrows all terms, formulas, and substitutions built over $\langle \Sigma, \Pi \rangle$. In particular, the objects of the category represent canonical tuples of variables; the tupling operation allow to construct substitutions (i.e. tuples of terms) and goals (tuples of formulas); arrow composition models both the application of substitutions to terms (or goals), and the composition of substitutions (thus they are naturally partial); and finally the unification of two formulas is the pullback of the corresponding arrows, if it exists.

4.2 Example *(Formulas and Terms as Arrows of a Category)*

As a running example, let us consider the following simple program for the *append* predicate

$c_1 = append(x_1, [], x_1).$
$c_2 = append(x_1, [x_2 | x_3], [x_2 | x_4]) \text{ :- } append(x_1, x_3, x_4).$

For this program we have $\Sigma_0 = \{[]\}$, $\Sigma_2 = \{[\_|\_]\}$, $\Pi_3 = \{append\}$, and all others Σ_i, Π_j are empty: we call Σ_{AP} this logic program signature.

The following picture shows some arrows of category $\mathbf{SCC}(\Sigma_{AP})$.

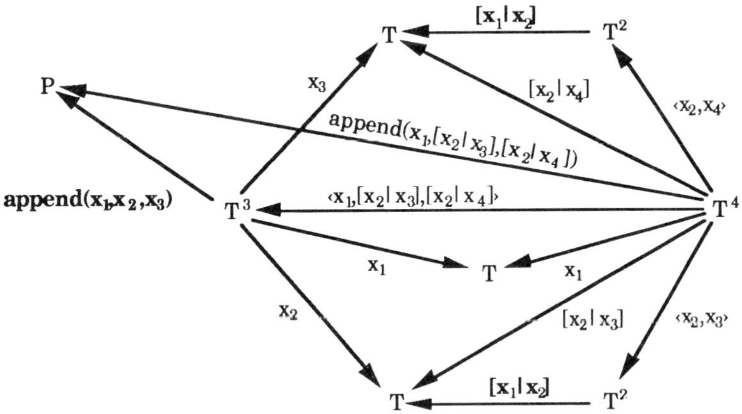

For example, the formula *append*(x_1, $[x_2/x_3]$, $[x_2/x_4]$) is represented as an arrow from T^4 (representing the canonical tuple $\langle x_1, \ldots, x_4 \rangle$) to P. That formula is obtained as the application of substitution $\langle x_1, [x_2/x_3], [x_2/x_4] \rangle$ to the formula *append*(x_1, x_2, x_3). On the other hand, $\langle x_1, [x_2/x_3], [x_2/x_4] \rangle$ is the tupling of three distinct arrows from T^4 to T. The projections faithfully correspond to variables [AM89]: for example x_i: $T^n \rightarrow T$ is a shorthand for the composition of projections $snd_{T^{i-1},T} \circ fst_{T^i,T} \circ \ldots \circ fst_{T^{n-1},T}$: $T^n \rightarrow T$ which extracts the i-th component of the canonical tuple of variables T^n. In the picture some objects have many distinct occurrences, to avoid unnecessary confusion. ♦

It is worth stressing that **SCC** is actually a (free adjoint) functor (see Lemma 4.7), and thus it defines a free construction which generates a strict cartesian category from the operators of a signature. In the above example, the arrows whose name is in bold type (i.e. the operators of signature Σ_{AP}) can be considered as the *generators* of category **SCC**(Σ_{AP}).

Summarizing, we showed that the algebraic structure of the 'states' of a logic programs (i.e. of the goals) naturally corresponds to the structure of the arrows of a strict cartesian category. Therefore we take **SCart**, the category of all such categories, as the universe which corresponds to category **C** in the outline of the methodology (Definition 2.5).

4.2 The structure of arcs of a program

In order to represent logic programs as heterogeneous graphs we still have to look for a suitable representation of program clauses. To this aim, we must observe that every clause of a program cannot be regarded simply as a pair of independent formulas (its head and its body), since it also carries an additional information, namely which are the variables shared by the head and the body. To take this fact into account, we will represent the clauses of a logic program essentially as if they were distinct operators of a many-sorted signature: each clause has a distinct sort, and its arity is the number of the distinct variables appearing in it.

A (many-sorted) signature $\underline{\Sigma}$ is usually defined as a pair $\langle S, \Sigma\rangle$, where S is a set of *sorts*, and Σ is a family of sets of *operators*, indexed by $S^* \times S$. For example, $\sigma \in \Sigma_{w,s}$, with $w = s_1 \cdot \ldots \cdot s_n$, denotes an operator of n arguments of sorts (types) $s_1, \ldots, s_n$, respectively, which returns a value of sort s; w is called the *arity* of σ, and s its *type*. A *signature morphism* $h: \langle S, \Sigma\rangle \to \langle S', \Sigma'\rangle$ is a pair $h = \langle f, g\rangle$, consisting of a map $f: S \to S'$, and a family of maps g_{ws}: $\Sigma_{w,s} \to \Sigma'_{f^*(w),f(s)}$, where $f^*: S^* \to S'^*$ is the obvious extension of f to strings. In our framework, it is convenient to look at signatures as particular graphs, having a free monoidal structure over nodes, and satisfying some additional requirements.

4.3 Definition *(the Category of Many Sorted Signatures)*

A signature $\underline{\Sigma}$ is a heterogeneous graph $\underline{\Sigma} = \langle S^*, \Sigma, ary, typ\rangle$, having a free monoid S^* of *sorts* as nodes, and a set Σ of *operators* as arcs. The functions ary, typ: $\Sigma \to S^*$ map each operator to its arity and to its type, respectively. The type of each operator is required to be a generator, i.e. $typ(\sigma) \in S$, for each $\sigma \in \Sigma$. A signature is therefore an object of **Graph(Set, FMon)** (where **FMon** is the category having free monoids as objects and monoid homomorphisms as arrows), satisfying that additional requirement. A *signature morphism* is a morphism in **Graph(Set, FMon)**, which, on nodes, is restricted to be the free extension of a function between the sets of generators. **Sign** is defined as the subcategory of **Graph(Set, FMon)** whose objects and morphisms satisfy the restrictions just listed. ♦

It is worth noticing that an element $s_1 \cdot \ldots \cdot s_n$ of the free monoid of sorts S^* faithfully represents a (canonical) n-tuple of sorted variables $\langle x_1{:}s_1, \ldots, x_n{:}s_n\rangle$. From this point of view, an operation $\sigma: s_1 \cdot \ldots \cdot s_n \to s$ can be considered as represented by an 'abstract' term in n variables $\sigma(x_1, \ldots, x_n)$.

4.4 Example *(A Signature as Heterogeneous Graph)*

Let us show how the lp-signature Σ_{AP} of Example 4.2 is represented as a heterogeneous graph. Since Σ_{AP} is two-sorted, its nodes will form the free monoid $\{T, P\}^*$. Thus $\Sigma_{AP} = \langle \{T, P\}^*, \{append, [\_|\_], []\}, ary, typ\rangle$, with append: $T \cdot T \cdot T \to P$, $[]: 0 \to T$, and $[\_|\_]: T \cdot T \to T$. Graphically (just relevant nodes are depicted),

$$P \xleftarrow{\text{append}} T \cdot T \cdot T \qquad T \cdot T \xrightarrow{[\_|\_]} T \xleftarrow{[]} 0$$

On the other hand, since the program for the *append* predicate includes two clauses, with one and four distinct variables respectively, we define its *signature of clauses* $\Sigma_{Cl(AP)}$ as

$$\Sigma_{Cl(AP)} = \langle \{T, C_1, C_2\}^*, \{c_1, c_2\}, ary', typ'\rangle,$$

where $c_1: T \to C_1$, and $c_2: T^4 \to C_2$.

For technical reasons, it is convenient to consider as the universe from which the structures of arcs of logic programs can be taken, the larger category **Graph(Set, Mon)** (shortly **MGraph**) instead of **Graph(Set, FMon)** or **Sign**. Thus **MGraph** will play the role of category **B** of Definition 2.5. In fact, it is easy to check that there exists a forgetful functor U: **SCart** $\rightarrow$ **MGraph**, which is exactly the functor we need for defining a logic program as a heterogeneous graph (by Definition 2.3). Eventually, we are ready to show how a logic program can be represented as a heterogeneous graph having as nodes a strict cartesian category (i.e. an object of **SCart**), and as arcs a signature determined by its clauses (regarded as an object of **MGraph**).

4.5 Definition *(The Graph Representing a Logic Program)*

Given a logic program $P = \{c_i = A_i :- B_{i1}, \ldots, B_{in_i}\}_{i \leq n}$ over an lp-signature $\langle \Sigma, \Pi \rangle$, its representation as heterogeneous graph, G_P, is defined as

$$G_P = \langle \mathbf{SCC}(\Sigma,\Pi), C_P, \partial_0, \partial_1 \rangle$$

where $\mathbf{SCC}(\Sigma,\Pi) \in |\mathbf{SCart}|$ is the category of formulas and substitutions of $\langle \Sigma, \Pi \rangle$ informally described in Section 4.1, while graph $C_P \in |\mathbf{MGraph}|$ and the graph morphisms ∂_0, ∂_1 are defined as follows.

1) C_P (the *signature of clauses* of P) is the representation as graph of the (n+1)-sorted signature (if n is the number of clauses in P), having the set $\{C_i\}_{i \leq n} \cup \{T\}$ as sorts, and the clauses $\{c_i\}_{i \leq n}$ as operators. Each clause c_i has type C_i and arity T^m, if m is the number of distinct variables appearing in the clause. Thus it is represented by arc $c_i: T^m \rightarrow C_i$.

2) By Definition 2.3, ∂_0 and ∂_1 are graph morphisms from C_P to the underlying graph of $\mathbf{SCC}(\Sigma, \Pi)$, and have to be monoid homomorphisms on the nodes. Informally, ∂_0 maps an arc $c_i: T^m \rightarrow C_i$ of C_P to the arrow of $\mathbf{SCC}(\Sigma, \Pi)$ which represents the body of clause c_i, while ∂_1 maps c_i to the arrow representing its head.

On the nodes of C_P, ∂_0 and ∂_1 are determined by their definition on generators, as follows: $\partial_0(T) = \partial_1(T) = T$ (i.e. the sort of terms is preserved); $\partial_0(C_i) = P^{n_i}$, if n_i is the number of atomic formulas in the body of clause c_i; and $\partial_1(C_i) = P$ (since the clauses are definite). ♦

It must be observed that a logic program has been regarded in the last definition as an object of category **Graph(MGraph, SCart)**. This is however a quite large category, where many graphs live which cannot be considered as logic programs at all. The definition of a suitable category including *all and only* graphs which really represent logic programs goes beyond the scope of the paper; an attempt in this direction is reported in [Co90].

4.6 Example *(The Program for* ***append*** *as a Heterogeneous Graph)*

Let us consider again the program for the *append* predicate of Example 4.2. It can be represented as the following heterogeneous graph of **Graph(MGraph, SCart)**, where Σ_{AP} and $\Sigma_{Cl(AP)}$ are as in Example 4.4:

$$AP = \langle \mathbf{SCC}(\Sigma_{AP}), \Sigma_{Cl(AP)}, src, trg \rangle$$

Graphically, we have the following situation, where the higher part of the diagram shows the arcs of $\Sigma_{Cl(AP)}$, while the lower part includes the relevant arrows of **SCC**(Σ_{AP}). The dashed arrows labeled *src* and *trg* are sufficient to uniquely determine those graph morphisms.

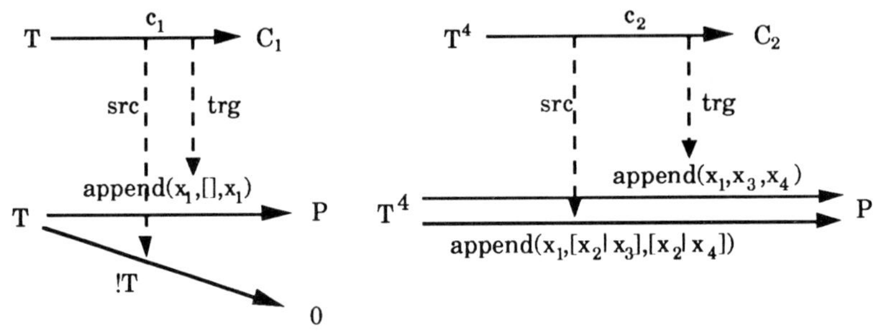

It is worth noting that since both *src* and *trg* must preserve sort T, both *append(x1, [x2/x3], [x2/x4])* and *append(x1,x3,x4)* are represented as arrows from T^4 to P, although the second formula includes just three different variables. Moreover, the source of clause c_1 is arrow !T: $T \to 0$, i.e. the unique arrow to the terminal object in SCC(Σ_{AP}), representing the empty formula. ♦

4.3 From programs to transition systems

Following the outline of our methodology, till now we just defined the first level of structures (that of 'programs') for the case of Horn Clause Logic. The next step is to define the category of structured transition systems for logic programs. Let us informally justify (in the specific case of logic programming) the implicit, fundamental assumption on which the second step of the methodology of Definition 2.5 is based, namely the fact that the transition system induced by the program must have the same structure on states and transitions.

Having represented a logic program P as a graph, we are looking now for a transition system TS[P] which faithfully mimics the behaviour of P in the following sense: a goal G is refutable in P with an answer substitution θ iff there is a computation of TS[P] from the empty goal to (a suitable representation of) the goal $G \circ \theta$. Let us show that TS[P] can be obtained by adding to the arcs of the graph representing P the same algebraic structure as that of nodes. Let P be the following logic program:

P = { c_1 = q(x,y) :- p(x), r(y).
c_2 = p(a).
c_3 = r(b).}

Representing P as a graph, we get something like Gp = {c_1(x, y): ‹p(x), r(y)› → ‹q(x,y)›, c_2: ‹› → ‹p(a)›, c_3: ‹› → ‹r(b)›}, where '‹›' is the empty goal, and the variables occurring in the first clause are regarded as arguments of the 'operator' c_1. Now, suppose we want to mimic the refutation of the goal

g_1 =‹q(a,b)› with a transition system computation. To be consistent with the usual definition of refutations, we build our computations starting from the final state. Since in a transition system a transitions t: u → v can be (backward) applied only to state v, we cannot apply transition c_1 as it is to state g_1, because the target of c_1 is not identical to g_1. We must use instead an *instantiation* of the original clause, that is c_1(a, b): ‹p(a), r(b)› → ‹q(a,b)›; applying it to g_1 we get the next goal g_2 = ‹p(a), r(b)›. For the same reason, we cannot apply either c_2 or c_3 to g_2; however, we can apply them in parallel, using the tupled clause (‹c_2, c_3› : ‹› → ‹p(a), r(b)›), or we can apply the parallel composition of, for example, c_2 and the *idle* transition ‹r(b)›: ‹r(b)› → ‹r(b)›, that is c_2 × ‹r(b)›: ‹r(b)› → ‹p(a), r(b)›, and then reduce the resulting goal with c_3.

Summarizing, a transition system which faithfully mimics a logic program can be obtained by closing the arcs of the corresponding graph under substitution application and tupling, and by adding all identity clauses. In categorical terms, we have to lift the structure of cartesian category from nodes to transitions, too, and we have to make the graph reflexive. The immediate consequence of these considerations is that the category of structured transition systems we are looking for is simply **RGraph(SCart)**, i.e. the category of internal reflexive graphs having a strict cartesian category on both nodes and arcs.

Let us show now how the induced transition system of a logic program can be freely generated by the program itself. We perform this construction in two steps: for the first step we need the following lemma.

4.7 Lemma *(Functor U: **SCart** → **MGraph** has a Free Adjoint)*

The functor U: **SCart** → **MGraph** has a left adjoint **SCC**: **MGraph** → **SCart**. If G is a heterogeneous graph of **MGraph**, **SCC**(G) has as objects the nodes of G, while as arrows it includes the arcs of G (as generators), identities, projections, and arrows to the terminal object, and its arrows are closed under composition and tupling. All these operations are subjected to the axioms for strict cartesian categories reported in Definition 4.1. ♦

It is worth stressing that the category of formulas and substitutions of a logic program signature **SCC**(Σ, Π) is exactly the free strict cartesian category generated by the representation of signature ‹Σ, Π› as a graph of **MGraph**. This is due to the fact that the terms of a logic program are considered as uninterpreted, syntactical items.

Coming back to the generation of the induced transition system, by Lemma 4.7 and Proposition 2.4 there exists a free adjoint functor F: **Graph(MGraph, SCart)** → **Graph(SCart)**. If G_P = ‹**SCC**(Σ,Π), C_P, ∂_0, ∂_1› is the graph representing a logic program P, F[G_P] is the internal reflexive graph of **SCart** F[G_P] = ‹**SCC**(Σ,Π), **SCC**(C_P), ∂'_0, ∂'_1›, where ∂'_0, ∂'_1: **SCC**(C_P) → **SCC**(Σ,Π) are two functors which freely extend ∂_0 and ∂_1.

To complete the construction, we still have to make the internal graph F[G_P] reflexive. Since **SCart** has binary products (actually it is finite cocomplete, as a direct consequence of Proposition 4.9 below), by Theorem 2.2a the free reflexive graph of F[Gp] exists and is obtained by taking as arcs the coproduct of **SCC**(Cp) and **SCC**(Σ,Π). However, it is shown in [CM89] that the resulting reflexive graph, when regarded as a transition system, does not simulates program P correctly: intuitively, the problem is that the sort T of terms, occurring in both categories **SCC**(Σ,Π) and **SCC**(Cp), originates two distinct sorts in their coproduct in **SCart**. On the contrary, the two occurrences of T should be identified. In order to force this identification, we can take as induced transition system the free internal reflexive graph, but in the subcategory of **SCart** where the functors are required to preserve sort T.

4.8 Definition *(The Transition System Induced by a Logic Program)*
Let Gp = ‹**SCC**(Σ,Π), Cp, ∂_0, ∂_1› be the representation as graph of a program P, and F[Gp] = ‹**SCC**(Σ,Π), **SCC**(Cp), ∂'_0, ∂'_1› be its free internal graph of **SCart**. Moreover, let $\mathbf{SCart_T}$ be the subcategory of **SCart** including as objects all the strict cartesian categories with an object T, and as arrows the functors which preserve T. Since $\mathbf{SCart_T}$ has binary coproducts, by Theorem 2.2a there exists a free functor $R_{\mathrm{SCart_T}}$, mapping each internal graph to its free reflexive graph of $\mathbf{SCart_T}$.

Then the *induced transition system of P* is defined as TS[Gp] ≡ $R_{\mathrm{SCart_T}}$[F[Gp]]. ♦

TS[Gp] has category **SCC**(Σ, Π) as nodes, and (by Theorem 2.2a) category **SCC**(Σ, Π) $+_T$ **SCC**(Cp) as arcs, where '$+_T$' denotes the coproduct in $\mathbf{SCart_T}$. Since **RGraph**($\mathbf{SCart_T}$) is a subcategory of **RGraph**(**SCart**), in the next section we will consider TS[Gp] as a internal reflexive graph of **SCart**.

4.4 The models of a logic program

Following the guidelines of the methodology, after defining the structured transition system induced by a program, we have to look for the existence of its free model, and to define the category of acceptable models for a logic program. A model of a logic program will be an internal category of **SCart**, accordingly to the requirement that the algebraic structure of the transitions should be extended to the entire computations. Thanks to Theorem 2.2b, the following fact is sufficient to ensure the existence of the free adjoint functor C_{SCart}: **RGraph**(**SCart**) → **Cat**(**SCart**), which associates to each structured transition system of **RGraph**(**SCart**) its free model of computations.

4.9 Proposition *(**SCart** is the Category of Models of a LE-sketch)*
Category **SCart** is the category of models in **Set** of a left exact sketch. Informally, the sketch of strict cartesian categories can be obtained by suitably composing the sketch of cartesian categories, and the one of monoids (see [BW85] for some examples of LE-sketches). ♦

In the following, we denote by $[\![P]\!]_F$ the free model of a logic program P, i.e. $[\![P]\!]_F \equiv C_{\mathrm{SCart}}$[TS[Gp]]. Let us shortly analyze the structure of $[\![P]\!]_F$. Since it is an internal category of **SCart**, having the same states as P (by Proposition 2.6), it must have a structure like

$$[\![P]\!]_F = \langle \mathbf{SCC}(\Sigma,\Pi), X, dom, cod, id, \_;\_ \rangle,$$

where $\mathbf{SCC}(\Sigma,\Pi)$ is the category of formulas and substitutions of the signature of P, and X is the strict cartesian category of the computations of the transition system TS[Gp]. Moreover, by the definition of internal category, dom and cod: $X \to \mathbf{SCC}(\Sigma,\Pi)$, id: $\mathbf{SCC}(\Sigma,\Pi) \to X$ and $\_;\_ : X \times_0 X \to X$, are arrows of **SCart**.

The rich structure of category X provides some interesting operators on computations, i.e. on sequences of composable transitions in TS[Gp]. For example, arrow composition in X models the application of substitutions to computations; and two computations involving the same variables can be tupled in a sort of parallel composition. The behaviour of these operations is regulated by some axioms, enforced by the structure, which provide a rich, modular proof system, where (pieces of) computations can be managed exactly as if they were original clauses of the program. For a deeper discussion of this topic we refer to [Co90]; we only want to stress here that the abstract computations of a program automatically turn to be *partial orderings*, since, for example, two computations differing just for the order in which two clauses are applied to two independent goals are identified. This could provide the basis for a 'truly concurrent' semantics of AND-parallelism.

For what concerns the definition of the category of *acceptable models* for a logic program P, more abstract models can be obtained by identifying some of the computations of $[\![P]\!]_F$. Since the classical semantics of a logic program (i.e. its least Herbrand model [Ll87]) can be rephrased in our framework as a suitable subset of the global states (i.e. goals) which are reachable through a computation starting from the empty goal, it seems natural to require that the structure of states be the same in all the models for P. This yields to the following definition.

4.10 Definition *(The Acceptable Models of a Logic Program)*

Let P be a logic programs and $[\![P]\!]_F$ be its free model. An *acceptable model* of P is a pair $\langle h, C\rangle$ where $C \in |\mathbf{Cat}(\mathbf{SCart})|$, and h: $[\![P]\!]_F \to C$ is an internal functor of **SCart**, which is an isomorphism of objects, and an epimorphism on arrows.

The *category of acceptable models of P*, called **Mod**(P), is the category having acceptable models of P as objects, and such that f: $\langle h, C\rangle \to \langle h', C'\rangle$ is an arrow of **Mod**(P) if f is an internal functor of **SCart**, and h' = h;f. ♦

Therefore the structure of the states of all the acceptable models of P is required to be the same (up to isomorphism), namely $\mathbf{SCC}(\Sigma,\Pi)$. **Mod**(P) has obviously an initial object, which is $\langle id_{[\![P]\!]_F}, [\![P]\!]_F\rangle$; moreover, it also has a terminal object, denoted by $\langle po, [\![P]\!]_{IO}\rangle$, which is the most abstract model of P [Co90]. $[\![P]\!]_{IO}$ (also called the *input/output model*) is actually an *internal preorder* of **SCart**, thus it can be regarded as representing a reachability relation among goals: this implies that all the refutations for the same goal are identified.

Since the classical semantics of a logic program P if defined as the set of (ground, atomic) goals which have a refutation in P, and thus does not distinguish among two different refutations for the same goal, it turns out that the terminal model of P is sufficient to recover its classic semantics, and some simple extensions of it. In fact, since the states $[\![P]\!]_{IO}$ also includes non-atomic, non-ground goals, also other semantics can be recovered, like the one proposed in [FLMP88] (where Herbrand models including non-ground atomic formulas are considered), and that of [FLP84] (where clauses with multiple heads are introduced, and models include non-atomic goals). The following theorem summarizes these results (see also [CM90, Co90]).

4.11 Theorem *(Recovering the Classic Semantics of Programs)*

Let P be a logic program. Then

1) The set of arrows of $[\![P]\!]_{IO}$ from the empty goal to the collection of arrows of $\mathbf{SCC}(\Sigma, \Pi)$ which represent ground-atomic formulas is isomorphic to the minimal Herbrand model of P [Ll87].

2) The set of arrows of $[\![P]\!]_{IO}$ from the empty goal to the collection of arrows representing atomic (possibly non-ground) formulas is isomorphic to the minimal C-model of P as defined in [FLMP88], up to the naming of variables.

3) The set of arrows of $[\![P]\!]_{IO}$ from the empty goal to the collection of arrows of $\mathbf{SCC}(\Sigma, \Pi)$ which represent ground (possibly non-atomic formulas) is isomorphic to the free (non commutative) monoid generated by the minimal Herbrand model of P (while the minimal model of [FLP84] is (up to a closure) the corresponding free *commutative* monoid).

4) If g is a goal, the set of arrows of $[\![P]\!]_{IO}$ from the empty goal to the collection of arrows of the form $g \circ \theta$ (where θ is a substitution) is isomorphic to the set of all *correct answer substitutions* of g [Ll87]. ♦

5 Conclusions and future work

In this paper we presented a general algebraic framework for the semantic analysis of a wide class of formalisms. The main contribution is the definition of a methodology, completely described in categorical terms, and its application to Petri Nets and Logic Programming.

In the case of logic programs, the resulting semantics associates to each program a class of models, that is of (small) categories having abstract computations as arrows, equipped with a rich algebraic structure. The arrows of the free (initial) model are partial orderings of resolution steps, and could provide a 'truly concurrent' semantics for AND-parallelism.

As briefly discussed at the end of Section 3, presently a limitation of the methodology is that it can be satisfactorily applied only to programs whose induced transition systems are not labeled. This class includes many interesting formalisms, like Petri Nets, Horn Clause Logic, Phrase Structure Grammars, and Term Rewriting Systems. However, process description languages, like Milner's CCS, do not fall in this class, because the labels play a fundamental role in them, being the basis of the definition of complex observational mechanisms.

As a future topic of research, we intend to integrate some categorical mechanisms for the handling of labels (for example the comma category constructions used in [Fe90, FM90]) within the general methodology of Section 2, in order to deal with *labeled* transition systems and their associated observational mechanisms as well. This should allow us to integrate some results about the semantics of concurrency, already developed for process description languages, in the framework of the methodology, possibly leading to the development of some new techniques for providing concurrent logic programming languages with a truly concurrent semantics.

6 References

[AL89] Asperti, A., Longo, G., *Applied Category Theory,* Technical Report TR-18/89, Dipartimento di Informatica, Università di Pisa, 1989. Forthcoming by MIT Press, 1990.

[AM89] Asperti, A., Martini, S., *Projections instead of variables, A category theoretic interpretation of logic programs*, Proc. 6th Int. Conf. on Logic Programming, Lisboa, 1989, pp. 337-352.

[BD87] Best E., Devillers R., *Sequential and Concurrent Behaviour in Petri Net Theory*, Theoretical Computer Science, **55** (1), 1987, pp. 87-136.

[BW85] Barr, M., Wells, C., *Toposes, Triples and Theories*, Grundlehren der mathematischen Wissenschaften 278, Springer Verlag, 1985.

[CM89] Corradini, A., Montanari, U., *An Algebraic Representation of Logic Program Computations,* Technical Report TR-36/89, Dipartimento di Informatica, Università di Pisa, Dec. 1989. Also in Lassez, J., Editor, *Festschrift in Honor of J. A. Robinson*, to appear.

[CM90] Corradini, A., Montanari, U., *Towards a Process Semantics in the Logic Programming Style*, in Proc. 7th Symposium on Theoretical Aspects of Computer Science, STACS '90, LNCS 415, 1990, pp. 95-108.

[Co90] Corradini, A., *An Algebraic Semantics for Transition Systems and Logic Programming*, Ph.D. Thesis TD-8/90, Dipartimento di Informatica, Università di Pisa, March '90.

[DMM89] Degano, P., Meseguer, J., Montanari, U., *Axiomatizing Net Computations and Processes*, in Proc. 4th Annual Symposium on Logic in Computer Science, Asilomar, CA, USA, 1989, pp.175-185.

[Fe90] Ferrari, G., *Unifying Models of Concurrency*, Ph.D. Thesis TD-4/90, Dipartimento di Informatica, Università di Pisa, March '90.

[FM90] Ferrari, G., Montanari, U., *Towards the Unification of Models for Concurrency*, in Proc. CAAP 1990, LNCS 431, pp.162-176.

[FLMP88] Falaschi, M., Levi, G., Martelli, M., Palamidessi, C., *Declarative Modeling of the Operational Behaviour of Logic Languages*, TR-10/88, Dipartimento di Informatica, Univ. of Pisa, 1988. Also as: *A new declarative semantics for logic languages*, in Proc. 5th Int. Conf. Symp. on Logic Programming, MIT Press, 1988, pp. 993-1005.

[FLP84] Falaschi, M., Levi, G., Palamidessi, C., *A Synchronization Logic: Axiomatics and Formal Semantics of Generalized Horn Clauses*, in Inf. and Control, **60** (1-3), Academic Press, 1984, pp. 36-69.

[Go89] Goguen, J.A., *A Categorical Manifesto*, Technical Monograph PRG-72, Oxford University Computing Laboratory, Programming Research Group, March 1989.

[Ll87] Lloyd, J.W., *Foundations of Logic Programming*, Springer Verlag, 1984, (Second Edition 1987).

[Me89] Meseguer, J., *General Logics*, in Proc. Logic Colloquium '87, H.-D. Ebbinghaus et al. (eds), North-Holland, 1989, pp. 275-329.

[Me90] Meseguer, J., *Rewriting as a Unified Model of Concurrency*, Tech. Rep. SRI-CSL-90-02, SRI International, February '90.

[Mi89] Milner, R., *Concurrency and communication*, Prentice Hall, 1989.

[ML71] Mac Lane, S., *Categories for the Working Mathematician*, Springer Verlag, New York, 1971.

[MM88] Meseguer, J., Montanari, U., *Petri Nets are Monoids: A New Algebraic Foundation for Net Theory*. Proc. Logics In Computer Science, Edinburgh, 1988, pp. 115-164. Also SRI-CSL-88-3, Jan. 88, to appear in *Info and Co.*

[Pe62] Petri, C.A., *Kommunication mit Automaten*, Schriften des Institutes für Instrumentelle Mathematik, Bonn 1962.

[Pl81] Plotkin, G., *A Structural Approach to Operational Semantics*, Technical Report DAIMI FN-19, Aarhus University, Department of Computer Science, Aarhus, 1981.

[Rei85] Reisig, W., *Petri Nets: An Introduction*, EACTS Monographs on Theoretical Computer Science, Springer-Verlag, 1985.

[Wi82] Winskel, G., *Event Structures for CCS and Related Languages*, Proc. 9th ICALP, LNCS 140, 1982, pp. 561-576.

Prolog and Natural-Language Analysis: into the Third Decade

Fernando C. N. Pereira
AT&T Bell Laboratories
Murray Hill, NJ 07974

Abstract

Algorithmic analysis and interpretation of natural language provided the needs and ideas underlying the invention of Prolog by Colmeraurer and his colleagues. Now, eighteen years later, it seems appropriate to examine Prolog's success in addressing those needs. I will argue that Prolog made it possible for certain problems of language analysis and interpretation to be formulated and solved in simple cases, but that further progress has been hampered by expressive and algorithmic weaknesses of Prolog. Recent advances in logic programming such as richer notions of term and term unification, higher-order logic programming and memoization-based techniques of query evaluation may help overcome those weaknesses if they are well incorporated into a single logic programming language.

1 A Bit of History

The birth of logic programming and Prolog is indissociably bound with the problems and techniques of language analysis and interpretation [16]. The first Prolog-based grammar formalism, Colmerauer's metamorphosis grammars [15], was inspired on Colmerauer's earlier Q-system rewrite-rule language [14], which had been designed for natural language analysis and translation applications.

In an earlier paper [71], David H. D. Warren and I argued the advantages of Prolog-based grammar formalisms, in particular definite-clause grammars (DCGs), relative to what was then the foremost computational formalism for natural-language analysis, augmented transitions networks (ATNs) [88]. Briefly, the argument centered on the declarativeness of DCGs, the conciseness of unification for expressing constraints on analysis and structure-building in semantic interpretation, the use of the "logical variable" in incrementally building complex structures, and the efficiency of compiled Prolog as the implementation of Prolog-based grammar formalisms. Those advantages underwrote much of the growth of Prolog-based language analysis, yielding a large set of techniques and formalisms now described in detail in various textbooks [19, 27, 70].

2 The Poverty of Terms

It is a remarkable case of convergent evolution that logic programming cannot claim for itself the sole credit for the development of language-analysis techniques based on unification. The developments of the linguistic theory of lexical-functional grammar (LFG) [9] and of the grammar formalism of functional-unification grammar (FUG) [46, 47] were both partly motivated by the weaknesses of ATNs, in particular their lack of declarativeness and their awkward structure matching and building primitives. According to Martin Kay (personal communication) the unification basis of FUG, and even the use of the word "unification" to refer to it, were conceived quite independently from notions of unification in automated deduction. The intuition behind FUG is that linguistic objects (eg. phrases) are naturally described in terms of certain linguistic *features*, whose values are themselves objects described in terms of their features. This yields directly a hierarchical notion of *functional description* (or, in more theory-neutral terminology, *feature structure* [79]), for which the natural mechanism of structure matching and construction is akin to unification. An important difference between FUG unification and logical unification, though, is that in FUG there is no distinction between rules and terms: everything is a functional description. As a result, FUG unification must deal with *disjunctive* descriptions, representing alternations in grammar rules or lexical items.

LFG is an attempt to move away from the dominant linguistic theories of the 1970s, based on rules and transformations, by placing most of the burden of linguistic description in the lexicon and in equational constraints between the fillers of *grammatical functions* of linguistic objects. Unsurprisingly, the solution process for those equational constraints turns out to be formally related to unification. However, more recent versions of LFG include further expressive devices that increase the expressive power of the formal component of LFG beyond that of a notational variant of term unification.

The development of linguistic theories such as LFG, GPSG [26] and HPSG [73], and of grammar formalisms such as FUG and PATR-II [78], led to a substantial body of theoretical and practical research on various notions of constraint-satisfaction and unification in grammar. These include the feature structure unification and unification of disjunctive descriptions mentioned above [44, 41, 45, 76], as well as negative descriptions [61, 20, 38] functional uncertainty [40] and a variety of other devices. More details on those linguistically-motivated notions of unification can be found in various surveys [48, 67, 79]. As usual, increases in expressiveness and notational economy have computational costs. For instance, disjunctive and negative descriptions are asymptotically intractable, but clever algorithms [44, 53] alleviate this in many useful cases.

The main lesson of the above developments is that linguists find Prolog terms notationally and expressively inadequate to represent linguistic information. First, most linguistic theories assign a rich set of features to linguistic objects. In some cases these feature structures may be encodable as terms, with loss of perspicuity, or grammar preprocessors and prettyprinters may be used to carry out the encoding and decoding behind the scenes [5, 35]. Particular cases of disjunctive and negative constraints can also be encodable into terms [5, 55]. However, the general case cannot be treated in that way, and even the special cases require for convenience a lot of ancillary machinery that deters from the original simplicity of logic grammars.

So far, the argument has centered on the difficulties of describing grammatical objects and rules in Prolog. However, similar problems arise in semantic interpretation. In the next section, I will consider separately the question of how to correctly manipulate meaning representations involving bound variables. Here, I will consider the problem of representing *selectional restrictions* in lexical semantics, which is connected to the general issues of the expressiveness of terms identified above.

Selectional restrictions encode constraints on the use of certain words as arguments to other words. These constraints are essential in blocking the derivation of nonsensical analyses for sentences. For example, the sentence

(1) A sensor is attached to every component of the system to measure its motion

is many ways ambiguous. However, common sense selectional restrictions, such as that only measuring instruments (eg. sensors) can be used to measure something, and that sensors can measure only the motion of things they are attached to, can eliminate the nonsensical readings. Of course, such restrictions are in general defeasible, but they are a useful first approximation for limited domains. Selectional restrictions can be encoded by specifying for each word taking arguments (for instance, verbs, adjectives) the types of objects that can meaningfully fill those argument positions. The encoding requires some notion of subtyping, as shown in the example with the inference from sensors (subtype) to measuring instruments (supertype).

Restricted forms of subtyping can be encoded with term unification, for instance single inheritance [18] and certain cases of multiple inheritance [5, 55]. However, more direct solutions are desirable, such as that provided by LOGIN [3].

Subtyping is also useful for other purposes in linguistic description, for instance to organize lexical information in a modular fashion [25, 78].

The foregoing discussion suggests the need for object descriptions in terms of object features and their values, allowing disjunctive and negative descriptions and subtype relationships between descriptions. Logic programming systems providing some of those facilities, together or separately, have been under theoretical and experimental investigation for a number of years [1, 2, 3, 82]. Additional mechanisms, such as arbitrary constraints on the values of features, have also been experimented with [62]. However, a coherent practical package is not yet available that achieves the efficiency of Prolog when restricted to Prolog-like rules and objects. The critical problem

```
s(Sent) --> np(Subj), vp(Subj, Sent).
vp(Subj, Sent) --> v(Subj, Obj, Sent), obj(Subj, Obj).
obj(_, Obj) --> np(Obj).
obj(Subj, Subj) --> [himself].
np(john) --> [john].
np(mary) --> [mary].
```

Figure 1: Pseudoabstraction in DCGs

is how to avoid paying too much for disjunctive and negative constraints if they are used only sparsely.

3 Loose Variables

One of the very attractive features of logic grammars is the way the semantic interpretation of sentences can be carried out in a syntax-directed fashion by associating each phrase with an open term representing the meaning contribution of the phrase, and combining the meaning contributions of phrases by appropriate unification of the variables in those open terms. For example, a grammar might associate the open term `loves(X,Y)` to the verb form "loves", the constant `john` to the proper noun "John" and whatever the subject meaning is to the reflexive pronoun "himself". The sentence

(2) John loves himself

would be interpreted by unifying the object meaning `Y` with the subject meaning `X`, producing the verb phrase meaning `loves(X,X)`. The subject meaning `X` is then unified with the subject filler meaning `john` to yield the sentence meaning `loves(john,john)`. This technique, which for lack of an official name I will term *pseudoabstraction*, goes back to the earliest metamorphosis grammar examples written by Colmerauer and his colleagues [15]. Grammar nonterminals will have a *result* argument for the nonterminal meaning and *filler* arguments for the meanings it depends on. The DCG on Figure 1 shows just enough of a grammar to derive the interpretation of (2) by pseudoabstraction.

Pseudoabstraction can be understood more systematically as a simulation through unification of certain cases of β-reduction [70, 58]. The result argument is an open term and the filler arguments are λ-abstracted variables. Unification with a filler variable performs one β-reduction step. However, this correspondence is not generally sound.

First, unification with a filler argument "poisons" the result argument so that it cannot be used again. This problem arises for example in the analysis of coordination. Consider the sentence "John and Mary ate" with the verb phrase meaning represented by `ate(X)` with `X` the subject filler variable. We would like to apply this interpretation separately to the meanings of "John" and "Mary" to yield two sentence meanings, which would then be conjoined into the final **ate(john)&ate(mary)**. But this is not possible without extralogical operations (such as term copying). Alternatively, one might use explicit abstraction and application in the problematic cases, leaving to a postprocessor the normalization of the meaning representation [58]. However, this negates the simplicity of doing semantic interpretation on the fly that made pseudoabstraction attractive in the first place.

Second, variable-scope restrictions cannot be expressed. A usual and convenient byproduct of pseudoabstraction is that the quantified variables in the resulting interpretation are represented by logical variables. For example, the meaning of the sentence "Every child ate" might be represented by the term **every(X,child(X),ate(X))**. This seems superficially reasonable, but it is crucially flawed in that the variable **X** is not scoped. For instance, incorrect grammar rules might well later unify **X** with some other term. More subtly, interpretation fragments may be moved in the interpretation process outside the intended scope of the variables they contain. Although it is not possible to discuss this problem in detail here, its main manifestation is that careful accounting for (encodings of) bound and free variables, inexpressible in pure Prolog, is required for the soundness of scoping algorithms in logic grammars [5, 36, 60]. Attempts at expressing quantifier scoping alternatives in pure first-order unification frameworks are unsound in the general case [32], because they can move the representations of the meanings of quantified noun phrases outside the scopes of free variables they contain, leading to ill-formed interpretations. This question has interesting theoretical ramifications in the theory of semantic interpretation, which I have addressed elsewhere [68].

The alternative of adding true λ-abstraction and reduction to logic grammars instead of the elegant but unsafe pseudoabstraction technique has been noted for a number of years [86]. However, the extent of the problems with pseudoabstraction became evident only as larger interpretation problems were attempted in logic grammar or unification frameworks. Furthermore, the alternative awaited a suitable integration of λ-terms with Prolog, now available in λProlog [56]. The expressive possibilities of λProlog for language interpretation have already received some investigation [57, 63], but I believe that the crucial advantage to be still exploited comes from the combination of universal quantification in goals with higher-order unification. Although doing justice to that potential requires a paper on its own, I will try to sketch it here.

As I have discussed elsewhere [68, 69], natural language interpretation requires the expression of dependencies between phrase meanings and *assumptions* as to the (as yet unspecified) meanings of some of some of their parts. For example, the meaning of a relative clause depends on the relative trace it contains; the meaning of a sentence with a quantified noun phrase depends on the unscoped quantified noun phrase; the meaning of a bound-anaphora pronoun depends on its antecedent. Thus, the mean-

```
s (P2 P1) Store G0 G S0 S :-
    np P1 Store1 G0 G1 S0 S1,
    vp P2 Store2 G1 G S1 S,
    shuffle Store1 Store2 Store.
s (Q P) Store G0 G S0 S :-
    pi X \ (s (P X) [(quant Q X)|Store] G0 G S0 S).

np X [(quant (Q N) X)|Store] G0 G S0 S  :-
    det Q S0 S1,
    nom N Store G0 G S1 S.
np X [] G G S0 S :- pn X S0 S.
np X [] (gap X) nogap S S.

vp X\(R X Y) Store G0 G S0 S :-
    tv R S0 S1,
    np Y Store G0 G S1 S.
vp P [] G G S0 S :- iv P S0 S.

nom (M N) Store G0 G S0 S :-
    n N S0 S1,
    npmod M Store G0 G S1 S.

npmod P\P [] G G S S.
npmod M Store G0 G S0 S :- relcl M Store G0 G S0 S.

relcl P1\U\((P1 U) & (P2 U)) Store G G [that|S0] S :-
    pi X \ (s (P2 X) Store (gap X) nogap S0 S).
```

Figure 2: Assumption Discharge in Semantic Interpretation

ing derivation for a phrase will in general depend on certain assumptions. Discharging those assumptions yields λ-abstractions over the appropriate positions in the phrase, for instance the property which is the meaning of a relative clause (abstracted over the trace) or the scope of a quantified noun phrase. Universal quantification in goals is the mechanism that allows the correct expression of the dependency of phrase meanings on assumptions, and (a restricted form of) higher-order unification allows the extraction of the appropriate abstraction from the dependency as is also done in λProlog presentations of sequent calculi [23, 24]. The scoping constraints that I noted above were not representable with pseudoabstraction fall out directly from the use of universal quantification, without explicit mention of bound and free variable occurrences.

The λProlog program fragment in Figure 2 is a simplified example of the use of assumptions and abstraction in semantic interpretation. Each predicate it defines represents a grammar nonterminal. The six arguments of the defined predicates are, respectively, the interpretation of a phrase, the quantifier store it depends on [17], the incoming and outgoing gap information, and the starting and ending string positions. The quantifier store of a phrase P represents the meanings of quantified noun phrases in P whose scope has not yet been determined. The gap arguments are used for a *gap threading* analysis of WH-movement [42, 64, 70]. If a phrase contains a gap associated to a pronoun outside the phrase, the phrase's incoming gap argument must be `(gap X)` for some `X` and its outgoing gap argument must be `nogap`. With the exception of `shuffle`, all the predicates used but not defined in Figure 2 represent lexical categories, for instance `iv` for intransitive verbs. The `shuffle` predicate nondeterministically merges two quantifier stores to generate all possible quantifier scopings.

Universal quantification is used in the second and in the last clauses of the program. In the second clause, an element is removed from the store and scoped. Each store element `(quant Q X)` represents an unscoped quantified noun phrase. The noun phrase appeared as an argument of some predicate in the sentence, and `X` is the variable that fills that argument position. The quantified noun phrase meaning `Q` is a function mapping properties to propositions. For example, the meaning of "every child" might be represented by

```
P\(every U \((child U) => (P U)))
```

that is, a second-order predicate that is true of `P` if `P` is a property that every child has. The interpretation of the whole sentence, before the store element `(quant Q X)` is removed, is `(P X)` for some property `P`. The universal quantification over `X` ensures that `P` does not depend on `X`. In other words, `P` is the abstraction of `X` from the interpretation of the sentence, which will form the scope of the quantifier `Q` being removed from the store. The application `(Q P)` represents then the interpretation of the sentence with `Q` given its scope `P`.[1]

The last clause operates in a similar way to analyze relative clauses. The relative clause must contain a gap `(gap X)` where `X` is the meaning for the gap itself. `(P2 X)` is the meaning of the relative clause, and the universal quantification over `X` forces `P2` to be exactly the property obtained by abstracting `X` from the relative clause meaning.

Although the grammar of Figure 2 is too simple to exhibit potential scoping conflicts, in general universal quantification is crucial in guaranteeing the soundness of the generated scopings. For instance, the meaning of a quantified noun phrase dependent on a gap would not be allowed to rise above the scope of the gap defined by the universal quantification in the last clause, while such an unsound movement would be allowed in a DCG

[1] As shown, this program is sound but has an infinite search space under λProlog because the second clause is not constrained to apply only when there are quantified noun phrases to be discharged. A simple depth bound can be used to prune the search space.

with pseudoabstraction. Thus, this use of higher-order logic in semantics is not just a matter of convenience, but rather a matter of *soundness* of the interpretation rules. Certain higher-order extensions of Prolog with a first-order semantics may address the convenience issue [4, 10], but only a system with universal quantification and an abstraction mechanism can logically enforce the soundness of semantic derivations.

4 Save It or Lose It

Much early work on logic grammars depended on the direct execution of grammars by Prolog. For DCGs, direct execution by Prolog corresponds to recursive descent backtrack parsing. This parsing method does not terminate for left-recursive grammars, but some natural language constructions are best expressed with left-recursive rules. Furthermore, backtrack parsing time is asymptotically exponential on input length, even for CFGs. It would thus seem that direct grammar execution in Prolog is a very bad idea, and certainly critics of Prolog are rather predictable in bringing those problems up.

Good reasons nevertheless exist for direct execution of grammars in Prolog. With respect to left recursion, standard techniques exist to transform it into right recursion, although a straightforward extrapolation of those techniques from CFGs to DCGs will not quite work because the set of ground instances of rules in a logic grammar is in general infinite. Furthermore, an idea of Rosenkrantz and Lewis [75] for relating left corner to recursive descent parsers can be easily extended to DCGs, as was done in the BUP system [52]. Strictly speaking this is no longer direct execution, but the transformation is so simple that it can be performed automatically by partial execution [70], and is often done by hand just for the troublesome parts of a grammar.

With respect to parsing speed, we should consider its three main factors: input length, grammar size and efficiency of each parsing step. In the past, input length was effectively bounded by small constants in the sentence corpora used in most computational linguistic work, for instance natural-language database queries. Grammar sizes were bounded by limitations in linguistic knowledge, and also, in much early work, by how much grammar could be written by one researcher in a relatively short period.[2] Nevertheless, even those relatively small grammars would be too inefficient without some means to control systematic syntactic ambiguities, such as those of postmodifier attachment. Techniques used for this include the use of selectional restrictions to limit possible attachments [18, 54] and encoding

[2]The influence of the usual style of linguistic work plays also an important role here: a small set of complex but sharply distinguishable phenomena get most attention in grammar writing while the greater bulk of language, whose parsing and interpretation is word- or idiom-specific, is hardly considered.

all possible attachments in one single normalized analysis [65]. Finally, individual parsing steps in direct execution were very efficient compared with the equivalent steps in alternative parsing algorithms [65]. For the typical natural-language interface prototype, direct interpretation won handsomely.

However, the conditions that encouraged direct execution would not last forever. Grammar writers became more ambitious, grammars became larger and test corpora included longer and more complex sentences. Some sources of ambiguity, such as coordination, ellipsis and gapping, cannot be restricted by the techniques successful with attachment ambiguity. Systematic ambiguities typically make the number of analyses, and thus parse time in a backtrack parser, grow exponentially with input length.

In the simpler area of context-free parsing, the above problems have long been solved by the adoption of *tabular* parsing algorithms based on dynamic-programming principles. The crucial observation underlying these algorithms is that the number of distinct phrases of some nonterminal category within a string of length n grows at most with n^2. In the Cocke-Kasami-Younger algorithm [89], the simplest and earliest of the tabular algorithms, a nonterminal N is placed in cell $t[i, j]$ of a parsing table just in case a phrase of type N extends from position i to position j in the input string. By building longer phrases from shorter ones by rule application, the algorithm can fill the parsing table in time proportional to n^3. Better algorithms, such as Earley's [22] or Graham-Harrison-Ruzzo's [29] take advantage of left context in the form of predictions to decrease the lower the n^3 bound for particular kinds of grammars. For instance, Earley's algorithm with k words of lookahead will parse sentences from any LR(k) grammar in linear time. More generally, dynamic programming can be applied to any context-free parsing scheme expressible as a pushdown transducer (eg. top down, LR(k), left corner) using Lang's dynamic-programming pushdown transducer interpreter [50].

The apparent similarity between definite clauses and context-free rules, and between context-free parsing algorithms and definite-clause proof procedures, was recognized early on [49]. However, there has been relatively little in-depth investigation of the connection, in particular in what concerns the application of generalizations of tabular methods to definite clauses, and hence, to grammar formalisms based on definite clauses. David H. D. Warren's Earley deduction proof procedure [84] is one of the few exceptions to that lack of results, but its relative lack of exposure in print meant that it has been studied only for its applications to language parsing [72]. I will review Earley deduction here as an example of the connection.

Earley deduction extends Earley's algorithm to definite clauses in the most direct way. Ignoring the left-to-right order of the computation, parsing string $w = w_1 \ldots w_n$ can be seen as the derivation of a table of all possible *items* $[A \to \alpha \cdot \beta, i, j]$ where $A \to \alpha\beta$ is a rule in the grammar G, by applying the rules of inference in Figure 3 to an initial set of items containing just $[S' \to S, 0, 0]$ where S is the start symbol of the grammar and S' is a new

$$\text{Predict:} \quad \frac{[A \rightarrow \alpha \cdot B\beta, i, j] \qquad \langle B \rightarrow \gamma \rangle \in G}{[B \rightarrow \cdot\gamma, j, j]}$$

$$\text{Complete:} \quad \frac{[A \rightarrow \alpha \cdot B\beta, i, j] \qquad [B \rightarrow \gamma\cdot, j, k]}{[A \rightarrow \alpha B \cdot \beta, i, k]}$$

$$\text{Scan:} \quad \frac{[A \rightarrow \alpha \cdot w_j\beta, i, j-1]}{[A \rightarrow \alpha w_j \cdot \beta, i, j]}$$

Figure 3: Earley's Algorithm

$$\text{Predict:} \quad \frac{[A \leftarrow \alpha\underline{B}\beta] \qquad \langle B' \leftarrow \gamma \rangle \in \mathcal{P} \qquad \sigma = \text{mgu}(B, B')}{[B' \leftarrow \gamma]\sigma}$$

$$\text{Complete:} \quad \frac{[A \leftarrow \alpha\underline{B}\beta] \qquad [B' \leftarrow] \qquad \sigma = \text{mgu}(B, B')}{[A \leftarrow \alpha\beta]\sigma}$$

Figure 4: Earley Deduction

dummy start symbol. The string w is accepted if the process terminates having found the item $[S' \rightarrow S\cdot, 0, n]$.

In Earley's algorithm, the dot in an item separates the symbols (phrases or terminal symbols) to its left, which have been already found, from those to its right, which still have to be found. The next symbol that needs to be recognized to extend the item follows the dot. In Earley deduction, definite clauses are used in the place of items. These are called *derived* clauses, and the algorithm consists of applying certain rules of inference to generate derived clauses until no new ones are built. The symbols to the left of the dot in Earley's algorithm correspond to goals already proved in Earley deduction, and the symbol following the dot corresponds to the *selected* goal.[3] String positions and scanning are not needed. The Earley deduction inference rules for a program $\mathcal{P}$ are shown in Figure 4. Underlining marks the selected goal. If S is the goal to be proved, the process is seeded with a clause $S' \leftarrow S$ for some new dummy literal S'. The proof is successful if the final set of derived clauses contains $S' \leftarrow$. Variables in S whose bindings are sought are repeated in S', which becomes an "answer literal".

Earley deduction can be used as a version Earley's algorithm for DCGs. The usual translation of DCGs to definite clauses is used [71], in which grammar symbols are represented by predicates with two additional arguments for string positions. Goal selection picks the goal corresponding to the leftmost symbol still to be found. The string to be parsed is represented by unit clauses connecting successive string positions. A similar approach can be applied to parsing with certain classes of unification grammars [81].

[3] The soundness or search completeness of Earley deduction do not depend on the choice of goal selection method, but efficiency and termination of course do.

The connection between Earley's algorithm, Earley deduction and Earley parsing of DCGs has been generalized by B. Lang [51]. Starting from his dynamic programming interpreter for pushdown transducers [50], he defines *logical* pushdown automata (LPDAs) and a corresponding dynamic programming scheme. As might be expected, the stack symbols of an LPDA are first-order terms, and the transitions involve unification between transition templates and stack symbols. LPDA formats can be chosen to simulate under the dynamic programming interpreter a wide variety of tabular definite clause interpreters. For example, Earley deduction with leftmost literal selection is simulated by applying dynamic programming to the pushdown automaton corresponding to the usual top-down execution of Prolog.

The simplicity of Earley deduction comes from the fact that all the information about the progress of computation is kept in a uniform tabular format: derived clauses. However, this can be quite costly, and more specialized tabular mechanisms taking advantage of the control mechanisms of Prolog can be more practical. For example, a left-corner parser [5, 52] can be combined with an extension table mechanism [21] to save proved goals representing already parsed phrases.

A crucial aspect of tabular parsing algorithms is that a new derived object (e.g., phrases or items) will be added to the table only if it is not already there. This guarantees termination and irredundancy (the same object will not be derived twice). For definite clause counterparts of these algorithms, however, the identity check must be replaced by a *subsumption* check to determine whether the new object is subsumed by an existing one.[4] Subsumption checking is of course more expensive than the identity check for CFGs. Furthermore, the subsumption check may not be sufficient to ensure termination.[5] In particular, the prediction step of Earley deduction may generate an infinite sequence of incresingly large instances of an input clause, even in cases in which a purely bottom-up procedure would terminate. However, the problem can be solved by restricting the amount of instantiation allowed in the prediction step so that only a finite number of instances of any input clause are generated. Such techniques have been studied for some definite-clause proof procedures [77] and for unification parsers [31, 80, 81].

The tabular nature of the algorithms just outlined, that is, the ability to save intermediate results (lemmas) is their greatest strength. Unfortunately, it is also their greatest weakness. The problem is that much more complicated term and substitution representations, or extensive copying of derived clauses, are required. Thus the speed gains of tabular algorithms can be swamped by the costs of individual execution steps except for large grammars and input strings.

[4]Given the monotonicity of unification, for certain algorithms it is also possible to remove from the table objects subsumed by an object being added: all the consequences of the old objects will be subsumed by consequences of the new one.

[5]Of course, in general this must be the case, since definite clauses are only semidecidable.

The clause representation problems in tabular algorithms arise from three sources. First, in the very nature of dynamic programming, intermediate results must be exchanged between alternative branches of the search space. Second, non-input resolution steps may be required, for example the completion step in Earley deduction, and thus derived clauses may have to be renamed apart. Third, alternative instantiations of the same derived entity (clause, goal) must be kept. Techniques for managing alternative bindings in or-parallel Prolog [85, 87] are not directly applicable here, because environments and binding arrays do not coexist well with result saving or non-input resolution.

The common practical solution for the above problem is to use Prolog's **assert** primitive to copy and store derived clauses. The cost of this copying is then typically the dominant factor in the parser. Nevertheless, that cost may be partly offset in practice by the efficiency of the individual unification and subsumption steps in a high-performance Prolog implementation.

Alternatively, one may consider applying structure-sharing methods. Boyer-Moore structure sharing [8] was designed for arbitrary resolution theorem provers, so it can be used for tabular parsing [31]. Unfortunately, its access cost for a variable binding is in the worst case proportional to proof length. It is possible to do somewhat better by using copying just when necessary to avoid non-input resolutions. Then renaming apart is not necessary, and schemes with logarithmic binding access costs are possible [66].

In another remarkable case of convergent evolution, researchers in deductive databases have developed a variety of tabular proof procedures for definite clauses [7], some of which have strong similarities to tabular parsing algorithms. In particular, the *magic templates* method of Ramakrishan [74] may be seen as an optimized version of Earley deduction in which the information created by the prediction step in Earley deduction for a particular goal clause is precompiled in the form of *magic template* predicates. Bernard Lang (personal communication) has used LPDAs to establish this connection rigorously.

Most work on deductive databases has concerned itself with Datalog, the function-free subset of definite clauses. Clearly, the cost of copying a clause instance or goal in Datalog is bounded by a small constant factor, analogous to the cost of adding a tuple into a relation in a relational database. In contrast, tabular parsing for logic or unification grammars will in general involve derived clauses and goals whose size grows with the length of the derivation, for instance from arguments representing semantic interpretations.

The importance of sharing is that, without it, the size of parsing tables may grow exponentially with input length. Indeed, consider the simple ambiguous grammar in Figure 5, in which the sole argument represents the interpretation of the parsed string as an arithmetic expression. Of course, given the associativity of sum and product, the above grammar can as usual be transformed into an unambiguous one. But similar situations arise in language interpretation, for instance with postmodifier attachment, in which

```
expr(Expr) --> prim(Expr).
expr(plus(Expr1,Expr2)) -->
   expr(Expr1), [+], expr(Expr2).

prim(Expr) --> const(Expr).
prim(Expr) --> ['('], expr(Expr), [')'].
prim(times(Expr1,Expr2)) -->
   prim(Expr1), [*], prim(Expr2).
```

Figure 5: Ambiguous DCG

associativity does not hold. The number of derived clauses generated with that grammar by a complete tabular parser will, for suitable choice of ambiguous input strings, grow on input length as the Catalan numbers [13, 28]. Furthermore, the size of each derived clause is proportional to the length of the string whose analysis it represents. However, a tabular parser for context-free skeleton of the DCG will only create polynomially many items, because it will not distinguish among different analyses of the same string as the same nonterminal. In fact, a similar degree of sharing would be possible for the DCG with a parser that would represent derived clauses implicitly in terms of the substitutions necessary to construct a derived clause from its parents, rather than explicitly as the straightforward Prolog implementation through `assert` allows. The potential of sharing for curbing combinatorial explosion, and what classes of grammars it applies effectively to, have not to my knowledge been much investigated. However, the sharing technique called *packing* has been used to control combinatorial explosion in the representation of analysis trees and semantic interpretations in the parser for the SRI Core Language Engine grammar formalism [5, 6]. Structure-sharing schemes for unification grammar [43, 66] have also been described, but their properties have not been analyzed rigorously.

5 Where Next?

The promise of Prolog computational linguistics has been only partly realized. It is conceivable that a logic programming language addressing the weaknesses of Prolog identified in this paper could be built, although the question of whether it could be made efficient enough for practical use is very much an open problem. In the meanwhile, the insights from the kind of analysis I outlined here can be used to discipline our use of Prolog in linguistic problems. In particular, restricted forms of feature notation with disjunction, negation and inheritance can be made effectively part of grammar formalisms translatable into Prolog [55, 5]; uses of pseudoabstraction can be restricted to avoid certain unsound semantic derivations [58]; and relatively efficient tabular parsing techniques with specialized sharing can be applied [5]. From this perspective, Prolog is being used not as a logic programming language but as a symbolic programming language with convenient features — unification, nondeterminacy and lemma storage — for manipulating parsing configurations.

I believe the problems discussed here are worth investigating further. However, we should not let our current tools obscure our perception of the larger questions we ultimately seek to answer. Logic grammar and unification formalisms for the most part support a phrase-structure view of linguistic structure and a phrase-structure parsing view of language analysis and interpretation. However, much linguistic [11, 33] and computational [12, 34, 37, 83] research undermines the primacy of phrase structure, and, piece by piece, suggests a radically different view of language, which I will hazard to state as follows: a system in which a multitude of language use contingencies, only analyzable by statistical means, are wrapped over a skeleton of subtle and abstract regularities in syntactic and semantic structure. Language analysis, in this view, is the construction of those interpretations that satisfy the underlying constraints with highest probability with respect to the string under analysis and the contingent facts of language use. Work on logical representation of syntactic and semantic constraints in language [39, 59, 83] may help in this endeavor, although it quite unclear at the moment how to mesh statistical regularities and structural constraints in a single decoding mechanism.

6 Acknowledgments

I would like to thank Stuart Shieber for his detailed comments and David S. Warren for his help with references.

References

[1] H. Aït-Kaci. *A Lattice Theoretic Approach to Computation based on a Calculus of Partially Ordered Type Structures.* PhD thesis, University of Pennsylvania, Philadelphia, Pennsylvania, 1984.

[2] H. Aït-Kaci, R. Boyer, P. Lincoln, and R. Nasr. Efficient implementation of lattice operations. *ACM Transactions on Programming Languages and Systems*, 11(1):115–146, 1989.

[3] H. Aït-Kaci and R. Nasr. LOGIN: A logic programming language with built-in inheritance. *Logic Programming*, 3(3):185–217, 1986.

[4] H. Aït-Kaci and R. Nasr. Residuation: A paradigm for integrating logic and functional programming. Technical Report AI-359-86, MCC, Austin, Texas, 1986.

[5] H. Alshawi, D. M. Carter, J. van Eijck, R. C. Moore, D. B. Moran, F. C. N. Pereira, S. G. Pulman, and A. G. Smith. Research programme in natural language processing. Final report, Cambridge Research Centre, SRI International, Cambridge, England, July 1989.

[6] H. Alshawi, D. M. Carter, J. van Eijck, R. C. Moore, and S. G. Pulman. Overview of the Core Language Engine. In *Proceedings of the International Conference on Fifth Generation Computer Systems*, pages 1108–1115, Tokyo, Japan, 1988. Institute for New Generation Computer Technology.

[7] F. Bancilhon and R. Ramakrishnan. An amateur's introduction to recursive query processing strategies. In M. Stonebraker, editor, *Readings in Database Systems*, section 8.2, pages 507–555. Morgan Kaufmann, San Mateo, California, 1988.

[8] R. S. Boyer and J. S. Moore. The sharing of structure in theorem-proving programs. In B. Meltzer and D. Michie, editors, *Machine Intelligence 7*, pages 101–116. John Wiley and Sons, 1972.

[9] J. Bresnan and R. Kaplan. Lexical-functional grammar: A formal system for grammatical representation. In J. Bresnan, editor, *The Mental Representation of Grammatical Relations*, pages 173–281. MIT Press, 1982.

[10] W. Chen, M. Kifer, and D. S. Warren. HiLog: a first-order semantics for higher-order logic programming constructs. In E. L. Lusk and R. A. Overbeek, editors, *Logic Programming: Proceedings of the North American Conference, 1989*, pages 1090–1114, Cleveland, Ohio, 1989. MIT Press.

[11] N. Chomsky. *Barriers*. MIT Press, 1986.

[12] K. W. Church and P. Hanks. Word association norms, mutual information, and lexicography. *Computational Linguistics*, 16(1):22–29, 1990.

[13] K. W. Church and R. Patil. Coping with syntactic ambiguity or how to put the block in the box on the table. *Computational Linguistics*, 8(3–4):139–149, 1982.

[14] A. Colmerauer. Les systèmes-Q ou un formalisme pour analyser et synthétiser des phrases sur ordinateur. Internal Publication 43, Département d'Informatique, Université de Montreal, Canada, 1970.

[15] A. Colmerauer. Metamorphosis grammars. In L. Bolc, editor, *Natural Language Communication with Computers*, pages 133–187. Springer-Verlag, 1978. First appeared as "Les Grammaires de Metamorphose", Groupe d'Intelligence Artificielle, Université de Marseille II, November 1975.

[16] A. Colmerauer, H. Kanoui, R. Pasero, and P. Roussel. Un système de communication homme-machine en Français. Rapport, Groupe d'Intelligence Artificielle, Université d'Aix-Marseille II, 1973.

[17] R. Cooper. *Quantification and Syntactic Theory*, volume 21 of *Synthese Language Library*. D. Reidel, Dordrecht, Netherlands, 1983.

[18] V. Dahl. Translating Spanish into logic through logic. *Computational Linguistics*, 7(3):149–164, 1981.

[19] V. Dahl and H. Abramson. *Logic Grammars*. Springer-Verlag, 1989.

[20] A. Dawar and K. Vijay-Shanker. An interpretation of negation in feature structure descriptions. *Computational Linguistics*, 16(1):11–21, 1990.

[21] S. W. Dietrich. Extension tables: Memo relations in logic programming. In *Proceedings of the 1987 Symposium on Logic Programming*, pages 264–272, San Francisco, California, August 31–September 4 1987. IEEE Computer Society Press.

[22] J. Earley. An efficient context-free parsing algorithm. *Communications of the ACM*, 13(2):94–102, February 1970. Reprinted in [30].

[23] A. P. Felty. *Specifying and Implementing Theorem Provers in a Higher-Order Logic Programming Language.* PhD thesis, Department of Computer and Information Science, University of Pennsylvania, Philadelphia, Pennsylvania, 1989.

[24] A. P. Felty and D. Miller. Specifying theorem provers in a higher-order logic programming language. In E. L. Lusk and R. A. Overbeek, editors, *9th International Conference on Automated Deduction*, Argonne, Illinois, 1988.

[25] D. Flickinger, C. Pollard, and T. Wasow. Structure-sharing in lexical representation. In *23rd Annual Meeting of the Association for Computational Linguistics*, pages 262–267, Chicago, Illinois, 1895. Association for Computational Linguistics, Morristown, New Jersey.

[26] G. Gazdar, E. Klein, G. Pullum, and I. Sag. *Generalized Phrase Structure Grammar.* Harvard University Press, 1985.

[27] G. Gazdar and C. S. Mellish. *Natural language processing in Prolog : an introduction to computational linguistics.* Addison-Wesley, 1989.

[28] R. L. Graham, D. E. Knuth, and O. Patashnik. *Concrete Mathematics.* Addison-Wesley, 1989.

[29] S. L. Graham, M. A. Harrison, and W. L. Ruzzo. An improved context-free recognizer. *ACM Transactions on Programming Languages and Systems*, 2(3):415–462, July 1980.

[30] B. J. Grosz, K. S. Jones, and B. L. Webber, editors. *Readings in Natural Language Processing.* Morgan Kaufmann, Los Altos, California, 1986.

[31] A. Haas. A parsing algorithm for unification grammar. *Computational Linguistics*, 15(4):219–232, 1989.

[32] P.-K. Halvorsen and R. M. Kaplan. Projections and semantic description in lexical-functional grammar. In *Proceedings of the International Conference on Fifth Generation Computer Systems*, pages 1116–1122, Tokyo, Japan, 1988. Institute for New Generation Computer Technology.

[33] Z. S. Harris. *Language and Information.* Columbia University Press, 1988.

[34] D. Hindle. Noun classification from predicate-argument structures. In *28th Annual Meeting of the Association for Computational Linguistics*, pages 268–275, Pittsburgh, Pennsylvania, 1990. Association for Computational Linguistics, Morristown, New Jersey.

[35] S. Hirsh. P-PATR, a compiler for unification based grammars. In V. Dahl and P. Saint-Dizier, editors, *Natural Language Understanding and Logic Programming, II.* Elsevier Science Publishers, 1987.

[36] J. R. Hobbs and S. M. Shieber. An algorithm for generating quantifier scopings. *Computational Linguistics*, 13:47–63, 1987.

[37] J. R. Hobbs, M. Stickel, P. Martin, and D. Edwards. Interpretation as abduction. In *26th Annual Meeting of the Association for Computational Linguistics*, pages 95–103, Buffalo, New York, 1988. Association for Computational Linguistics, Morristown, New Jersey.

[38] M. E. Johnson. *Attribute-Value Logic and the Theory of Grammar*. Number 14 in CSLI Lecture Notes. Center for the Study of Language and Information, Stanford, California, 1988. Distributed by Chicago University Press.

[39] M. E. Johnson. Deductive parsing with multiple levels of representation. In *26th Annual Meeting of the Association for Computational Linguistics*, pages 241–248, Buffalo, New York, 1988. Association for Computational Linguistics, Morristown, New Jersey.

[40] R. M. Kaplan and J. T. Maxwell, III. An algorithm for functional uncertainty. In *Proceedings of the 12th International Conference on Computational Linguistics*, pages 297–302, Budapest, Hungary, 1988. Association for Computational Linguistics, Morristown, New Jersey.

[41] L. Karttunen. Features and values. In *Proceedings of Coling84*, pages 28–33, Stanford, California, 1984. Association for Computational Linguistics, Morristown, New Jersey.

[42] L. Karttunen. D-PATR: A development environment for unification-based grammars. Report CSLI-86-61, Center for the Study of Language and Information, Stanford, California, 1986.

[43] L. Karttunen and M. Kay. Structure sharing with binary trees. In *23rd Annual Meeting of the Association for Computational Linguistics*, pages 133–136A, Chicago, Illinois, 1985. Association for Computational Linguistics, Morristown, New Jersey.

[44] R. T. Kasper. *Feature Structures: A Logical Theory with Application to Language Analysis*. PhD thesis, University of Michigan, Ann Arbor, Michigan, 1987.

[45] R. T. Kasper and W. C. Rounds. A logical semantics for feature structures. In *24th Annual Meeting of the Association for Computational Linguistics*, pages 257–266, Columbia University, New York, 1986. Association for Computational Linguistics, Morristown, New Jersey.

[46] M. Kay. Functional grammar. In *Proceedings of the Fifth Annual Meeting of the Berkeley Linguistic Society*, pages 142–158, Berkeley, California, February 17-19 1979. Berkeley Linguistic Society.

[47] M. Kay. Parsing in functional unification grammar. In D. R. Dowty, L. Karttunen, and A. M. Zwicky, editors, *Natural Language Parsing*, chapter 7, pages 251–278. Cambridge University Press, 1985.

[48] K. Knight. Unification: A multidisciplinary survey. *ACM Computing Surveys*, 21(1):93–124, 1989.

[49] R. A. Kowalski. Logic for problem solving. DCL Memo 75, Department of Artificial Intelligence, University of Edinburgh, Edinburgh, Scotland, March 1974.

[50] B. Lang. Deterministic techniques for efficient non-deterministic parsers. In J. Loeckx, editor, *Proceedings of the 2nd Colloquium on Automata, Languages and Programming*, pages 255–269, Saarbrücken, Germany, 1974. Springer-Verlag.

[51] B. Lang. Complete evaluation of Horn clauses: an automata theoretic approach. Rapport de Recherche 913, INRIA, Rocquencourt, France, November 1988.

[52] Y. Matsumoto, H. Tanaka, H. Hirakawa, H. Miyoshi, and H. Yasukawa. BUP: a bottom-up parser embedded in Prolog. *New Generation Computing*, 1(2):145–158, 1983.

[53] J. T. Maxwell, III and R. M. Kaplan. A method for disjunctive constraint satisfaction. Unpublished manuscript, 1990.

[54] M. C. McCord. Using slots and modifiers in logic grammars for natural language. *Artificial Intelligence*, 18(3):327–367, 1982.

[55] C. S. Mellish. Implementing systemic classification by unification. *Computational Linguistics*, 14(1):40–51, 1988.

[56] D. A. Miller and G. Nadathur. Higher-order logic programming. In E. Shapiro, editor, *Third International Conference on Logic Programming*, London, England, 1986. Springer-Verlag.

[57] D. A. Miller and G. Nadathur. Some uses of higher-order logic in computational linguistics. In *24th Annual Meeting of the Association for Computational Linguistics*, pages 247–256, Columbia University, New York, 1986. Association for Computational Linguistics, Morristown, New Jersey.

[58] R. C. Moore. Unification-based semantic interpretation. In *27th Annual Meeting of the Association for Computational Linguistics*, pages 33–41, Vancouver, British Columbia, 26-29 June 1989. Association for Computational Linguistics, Morristown, New Jersey.

[59] M. Moortgat. *Categorial Investigations: Logical and Linguistic Aspects of the Lambek Calculus.* PhD thesis, University of Amsterdam, Amsterdam, Holland, October 1988.

[60] D. B. Moran. Quantifier scoping in the SRI Core Language Engine. In *26th Annual Meeting of the Association for Computational Linguistics*, pages 33–47, Buffalo, New York, 1988. Association for Computational Linguistics, Morristown, New Jersey.

[61] M. D. Moshier and W. C. Rounds. A logic for partially specified data structures. In *ACM Symposium on the Principles of Programming Languages*, Munich, Germany, 1987. Association for Computing Machinery.

[62] K. Mukai and H. Yasukawa. Complex indeterminates in Prolog and their application to discourse models. *New Generation Computing*, 3(4):441–466, 1985.

[63] R. Pareschi. *Type-Driven Natural Language Analysis.* PhD thesis, University of Endinburgh, Edinburgh, Scotland, 1989.

[64] F. C. N. Pereira. Extraposition grammars. *Computational Linguistics*, 7(4):243–256, 1981.

[65] F. C. N. Pereira. *Logic for Natural Language Analysis.* PhD thesis, University of Edinburgh, Edinburgh, Scotland, 1982. Reprinted as Technical Note 275, January 1983, Artificial Intelligence Center, SRI International, Menlo Park, California.

[66] F. C. N. Pereira. A structure-sharing representation for unification-based grammar formalisms. In *23rd Annual Meeting of the Association for Computational Linguistics*, pages 137–144, Chicago, Illinois, 1985. Association for Computational Linguistics, Morristown, New Jersey.

[67] F. C. N. Pereira. Grammars and logics of partial information. In J.-L. Lassez, editor, *Logic Programming: Proceedings of the Fourth International Conference*, pages 989–1013, Melbourne, Australia, 1987. MIT Press.

[68] F. C. N. Pereira. Categorial semantics and scoping. *Computational Linguistics*, 16(1):1–10, 1990.

[69] F. C. N. Pereira and M. E. Pollack. Incremental interpretation. *Artificial Intelligence*, 1990. Forthcoming.

[70] F. C. N. Pereira and S. M. Shieber. *Prolog and Natural-Language Analysis*. Number 10 in CSLI Lecture Notes. Center for the Study of Language and Information, Stanford, California, 1985. Distributed by Chicago University Press.

[71] F. C. N. Pereira and D. H. D. Warren. Definite clause grammars for language analysis—a survey of the formalism and a comparison with augmented transition networks. *Artificial Intelligence*, 13:231–278, 1980. Reprinted in [30].

[72] F. C. N. Pereira and D. H. D. Warren. Parsing as deduction. In *21st Annual Meeting of the Association for Computational Linguistics*, pages 137–144, Cambridge, Massachusetts, June 15–17 1983. Association for Computational Linguistics, Morristown, New Jersey.

[73] C. Pollard and I. I. Sag. *Information-Based Syntax and Semantics: Fundamentals*. Number 13 in CSLI Lecture Notes. Center for the Study of Language and Information, Stanford, California, 1987. Distributed by Chicago University Press.

[74] R. Ramakrishnan. Magic templates: A spellbinding approach to logic programs. In R. A. Kowalski and K. A. Bowen, editors, *Logic Programming: Proceedings of the Fifth International Conference and Symposium*, pages 140–159, Seattle, Washington, 1988. MIT Press.

[75] D. J. Rosenkrantz and P. M. Lewis, II. Deterministic left corner parsing. In *IEEE Conference Record of the 11th Annual Symposium on Switching and Automata Theory*, pages 139–152, 1970.

[76] W. C. Rounds and R. Kasper. A complete logical calculus for record structures representing linguistic information. In *Symposium on Logic in Computer Science*. IEEE Computer Society, 1986.

[77] T. Sato and H. Tamaki. Enumeration of success patterns in logic programs. *Theoretical Computer Science*, 34:227–240, 1984.

[78] S. M. Shieber. Criteria for desigining computer facilities for linguistic analysis. *Linguistics*, 23:189–211, 1985.

[79] S. M. Shieber. *An Introduction to Unification-Based Approaches to Grammar*. Number 4 in CSLI Lecture Notes. Center for the Study of Language and Information, Stanford, California, 1985. Distributed by Chicago University Press.

[80] S. M. Shieber. Using restriction to extend parsing algorithms for complex-feature-based formalisms. In *23rd Annual Meeting of the Association for Computational Linguistics*, pages 145–152, Chicago, Illinois, 1985. Association for Computational Linguistics, Morristown, New Jersey.

[81] S. M. Shieber. *Parsing and Type Inference for Natural and Computer Languages.* PhD thesis, Department of Computer Science, Stanford University, 1989.

[82] G. Smolka and H. Aït-Kaci. Inheritance hierarchies: Semantics and unification. *Journal of Symbolic Computation*, 7:343–370, 1989.

[83] E. P. Stabler, Jr. The logical approach to syntax: Foundations, specifications and implementations of theories of government and binding. Unpublished manuscript, 1989.

[84] D. H. D. Warren. Earley deduction. Unpublished note, 1975.

[85] D. H. D. Warren. The SRI model for or-parallel execution of Prolog — abstract design and implementation issues. In *Proceedings of the 1987 Symposium on Logic Programming*, pages 92–102, San Francisco, California, August 31–September 4 1987. IEEE Computer Society Press.

[86] D. S. Warren. Using λ-calculus to represent meanings in logic grammars. In *21st Annual Meeting of the Association for Computational Linguistics*, pages 51–56, Cambridge, Massachusetts, 1983. Association for Computational Linguistics, Morristown, New Jersey.

[87] D. S. Warren. Efficient Prolog memory management for flexible control strategies. In *Proceedings of the IEEE International Symposium on Logic Programming*, Atlantic City, New Jersey, 1984. IEEE Computer Society Press.

[88] W. A. Woods. Transition network grammars for natural language analysis. *Communications of the ACM*, 13:591–606, October 1970.

[89] D. H. Younger. Recognition and parsing of context-free languages in time n^3. *Information and Control*, 10(2):189–208, 1967.

Abstracts of Advanced Tutorials

Parallel Implementations of Prolog

Andrzej Ciepielewski

Abstract

There are two distinct prongs in the field of parallel logic programming. One is concerned with parallelizing Prolog, a language with no notions for expressing concurrency, and the other with committed-choice logic programming languages designed for concurrent programming. In this tutorial I will only be concerned with the first subfield. The intention of the tutorial is not to give a historical or geographical summary of the field. It is rather to provide a unified view of the different approaches and issues they are concerned with. The following topics will be surveyed:

(1) The main models for AND-, OR- and AND/OR- parallel execution.

(2) Different approaches to multiple bindings management.

(3) Shared versus distributed memory implementation techniques.

(4) Scheduling.

(5) Speculative work and search strategies.

(6) Side-effects.

(7) Compile time analysis and automatic parallelization.

(8) Programming for efficiency.

(9) Performance evaluation.

(10) Putting it all together or overview of few systems.

The participant are expected to know at least one of the logic programming languages.

Types for Logic Programs (Abstract)

Uday S. Reddy
Department of Computer Science
The University of Illinois at Urbana-Champaign
Urbana, IL 61801.

1 Introduction

The value of static type checking in program development has long been recognized. It allows many clerical programming errors to be automatically detected. Further, the type information that is available at compile time can be used to generate highly optimized code during compilation.

There has been a great deal of research in designing type systems for Prolog, so that the benefits of type checking can be realized in logic programming. Following the pioneering work of Bruynooghe [Bru82], Mycroft and O'Keefe [MO83] and Mishra [Mis84], a number of other researchers proposed a variety of type systems. In this survey, we review the fundamental concepts behind these type systems using the established conventions in formal logical systems.

It appears that one of the major distinctions between the various type systems is whether they assume a *typed* language or an *untyped* language. The situation is somewhat confused because even untyped languages can have type systems "added on" so that they may appear rather similar to typed languages. However, the distinction is important to understand the formal properties of the type systems. In [Red88], the two kinds of type systems were termed *prescriptive* and *descriptive* type systems respectively.

A second major distinction underlying the type systems is whether they use the usual "typed" approach to data objects. In a typed approach, there is no single Universe containing all data objects, but there are separate domains of objects for different types. An alternative approach is to assume that there is a single Universe of all objects and that different types form different subsets of the Universe. The theory of regular tree sets is often used to describe such sets, but there are also other approaches. These distinctions naturally lead to three different kinds of type systems: (1) conventionally typed languages, (2) typed languages with Universe, and (3) untyped languages. In sections 2, 3 and 4, we formulate three type systems for logic programs along these lines.

2 Typed Prolog

Typed Prolog is a formal language representing a rational reconstruction of the type system of Mycroft and O'Keefe [MO83]. The type system of Lambda Prolog is also similar to this type system.

The expressions of Typed Prolog are constructed using three alphabets of symbols:

1. A set T of *type constructors.* Each type constructor $\sigma \in T$ has an *arity* denoting the number of type parameters it accepts.

2. A set F of *functor symbols.* Each functor $f \in F$ has a type signature of the form $\tau_1 \times \cdots \times \tau_k \to \tau'$ (for $k \geq 0$) indicating the types of its arguments and result.

3. A set P of *predicate symbols.* Each $p \in P$ has a type signature of the form $Pred(\tau_1, \ldots, \tau_k)$ indicating the types of its arguments.

A type term τ is either a type variable α or a term of the form $\sigma(\tau_1, \ldots, \tau_k)$. Terms and atoms are written as usual. Clauses are of the form

$$[\forall X_1 : \tau_1, \ldots, X_n : \tau_n](A \leftarrow B_1, \ldots, B_k)$$

such that $X_1, \ldots, X_n$ are all the variables appearing in the atoms $A, B_1, \ldots, B_k$.

In addition to these syntactic considerations, the well-formed programs of Typed Prolog should also obey the "context-sensitive syntax" represented by type rules. Three important type rules are the following:

$$H \vdash X : \tau \qquad \text{if } (X : \tau) \in H$$

$$\frac{H \vdash t_1 : \theta(\tau_1) \quad \ldots \quad H \vdash t_k : \theta(\tau_k)}{H \vdash p(t_1, \ldots, t_k) \text{ Atom}} \qquad \text{if } p : Pred(\tau_1 \times \cdots \times \tau_k)$$

$$\frac{H \vdash t_1 : \theta(\pi_1) \quad \ldots \quad H \vdash t_k : \theta(\pi_k) \quad H \vdash \phi \text{ Formula}}{[\forall X_1 : \tau_1, \ldots, X_n : \tau_n]\ (p(t_1, \ldots, t_k) :- \phi) \text{ Clause}} \qquad \begin{array}{l}\text{if } H = \{X_1 : \tau_1, \ldots, X_n : \tau_n\},\\ p : Pred(\pi_1 \times \cdots \times \pi_k), \text{ and}\\ \theta \text{ is a renaming substitution}\end{array}$$

In the above, H denotes a set of type hypotheses of the form $X : \tau$. The first rule says that the type of a variable is whatever is assumed in H. The second rule says that $p(t_1, \ldots, t_k)$ is a well-formed atom if there is an instance of the type of p such that the arguments t_i have the argument types in the instance. The third rule says that a clause is well-formed if, assuming the given type declarations for variables, the argument terms t_i can be shown to have the same types as given by the type signature of p and the body is a well-formed formula.

Polymorphism is supported by the presence of type variables in signatures. For instance, if $append : Pred(list(\alpha), list(\alpha), list(\alpha)$ is a type signature, $append([1],[2],Z)$ is a well-formed atom in a type environment containing $Z : int$.

Semantics The semantics of Typed Prolog is based on many-sorted logic extended with polymorphism. We choose a collection $\mathcal{D}$ of *domains* and interpret each type constructor as a function over $\mathcal{D}$. This associates a domain with each type term. A predicate symbol $p : Pred(\tau_1 \times \ldots \times \tau_k)$ is interpreted as a *family* of predicates. For each valuation v of type variables as domains, the family contains a predicate p_v over $D_{v(\tau_1)} \times \cdots \times D_{v(\tau_k)}$. Interpretations are defined by a straightforward generalization of one-sorted interpretations. An interpretation satisfies a clause iff it satisfies the clause for all valuations v of type variables. The conventional results for untyped Prolog regarding Herbrand models, least models, and least fixed points generalize to Typed Prolog.

Type consistency This property states that the standard untyped operational semantics of Prolog is correct for Typed Prolog. This shown by induction on the size of SLD-derivation trees [MO83].

Type reconstruction A Typed Prolog program, formally speaking, needs to include all the declarations in alphabets and clauses. Type reconstruction is the problem of determining these declarations automatically, given a program without declarations. Regarding this problem, the following facts are easy to verify based on [Mil78]. The variable declarations in clauses are can be uniquely reconstructed. The type signatures for predicate symbols can be uniquely reconstructed given the type signatures for functor symbols, but under the assumption that a predicate is not used polymorphically within its own definition. Neither the Mycroft-OKeefe type checker nor Lambda Prolog perform this form of type reconstruction at the present time.

Extensions Typed Prolog can be easily extended to include most of the non-logical features of Prolog including cuts, negation, asserts and retracts. Because types in this framework are merely used to designate well-formed formulas, the lack of adequate semantics for these features is not a problem. Overloading can be permitted as in the programming language Hope, but type declarations may be needed to eliminate ambiguities. Adding subtyping is a nontrivial extension. In particular, the type consistency property does not hold warranting the operational semantics to take types into account.

3 Regular Tree Typed Prolog

This language is a typed language in the vein of Typed Prolog, but assumes a Universe and dispenses with the notion of types for functor symbols. It is similar to some aspects of the type system of Yardeni and Shapiro [YS87] but incorporates polymorphism.

The function symbols in Prolog are uninterpreted constructors. So, it is meaningful to treat them as untyped symbols and assume that any functor can be applied to any arguments. This retains the notion of a Universe, as in untyped Prolog. Types are still obtained as certain subsets of the Universe and predicate symbols are assigned type signatures using such types. An important benefit of this type system is that it allows us to talk about one type being a *subtype* of another because types denotes sets with a well-defined inclusion relation.

Pragmatically, the most attractive feature of such a type system is that a functor can be used for constructing more than one type of values. For instance, the functors 0 and *succ* can be used to construct natural numbers, and they can be reused, together with another functor *pred*, to construct integers. It is then immediate, by set inclusion, that natural numbers form a subtype of integers.

Regular tree sets In principle, any language can be used to describe types in this framework as long as type terms in the language have decidable equality and inclusion relationships. Regular tree sets, introduced in [Mis84, MR85] under the name "regular trees", are an especially useful formalism because they capture most sets commonly thought of as "types". Formal definition and properties of these sets may be found in the above references as well as [YS87]. It suffices to say that they form a family of sets closed under functor application, union and recursion. As an example, the set of lists over integers can be defined by

$$X = \{nil\} \cup int.X$$

Language The language of regular tree typed Prolog is similar to Typed Prolog with only a few modifications. The alphabet of type constructors is not needed. Functor symbols are assinged arities instead of type signatures. The type rules are modified by replacing the functor application rule with the first rule below, and adding the second rule for type inclusion:

$$\frac{H \vdash t_1 : \tau_1 \quad \ldots \quad H \vdash t_k : \tau_k}{H \vdash f(t_1, \ldots, t_k) : f(\tau_1, \ldots, \tau_k)}$$

$$\frac{H \vdash t : \tau}{H \vdash t : \tau'} \qquad \text{if } \tau \subseteq \tau'$$

Semantics Choose a Universe $\mathcal{H}$ and interpret each type term τ is a subset $S_\tau \subseteq \mathcal{H}$. Each functor symbol f is assigned a family of interpretations $f_{\tau_1,\ldots,\tau_k} : S_{\tau_1} \times \cdots \times S_{\tau_k} \rightarrow S_{f(\tau_1,\ldots,\tau_k)}$. Predicates are interpreted as in Typed Prolog.

Type consistency property is available just as for Typed Prolog. Hence, there is no run-time overhead for types.

Type reconstruction It is possible to uniquely reconstruct most general variable declarations in clauses. A set of type declarations $X_1 : \tau_1, \ldots, X_k : \tau_k$ is considered more general than another set $X_1 : \tau_1', \ldots, X_k : \tau_k'$ iff there is a type substitution θ such that $\tau_i \subseteq \theta(\tau_i')$ for all i. So, most general declarations yield smallest types which nevertheless include all the cases mentioned in the clause. Unfortunately, this kind of type reconstruction introduces a great deal of type insecurity. If the above reconstruction is performed by the system, it would always *find* the types which form acceptable inputs to predicates. Thus, many type errors would go unnoticed. The only detectable type errors would be clauses for which no types can be declared (called "useless" clauses [YS87]).

The problem of the reconstruction of predicate type signatures is open.

4 Descriptive type systems

In contrast to the approach of typed languages, where types are used to designate well-formed programs, the approach of descriptive type systems starts with an untyped language and derives types as semantic properties of the program. The task of designing a descriptive type system for Prolog was begun by Mishra [Mis84]. On pragmatic grounds, it is decided that "the type of a predicate describes all terms for which the prodicate may succeed". In other words, the type of a predicate is a superset of its success set. The particular choice of the superset is important as it determines which atoms are to be considered well-formed. Further considerations suggest that the sets assigned as types of predicates must form a model of the program, and that the sets must be *cartesian closed.* A set of terms is said to be cartesian closed if, whenever it includes two terms $t[u_1, v_1]$ and $t[u_2, v_2]$, it also includes the terms $t[u_1, v_2]$ and $t[u_2, v_1]$. In other words, such a set ignores the dependencies between the subterms of the member terms.

Polymorphism The treatment of polymorphism in a descriptive type system is rather intricate. The pragmatic purpose of polymorphism is to propagate type information between different variables in a clause. For instance, if an atom $X = Y$ appears in a clause, it must be possible to infer that both X and Y have "the same type". To express such propagation, an implication type constructor was proposed in [Red88]. Using this, the type of the equality predicate is expressed as $Pred(\alpha_1 \times \alpha_2 \supset (\alpha_1 \cup \alpha_2) \times (\alpha_1 \cup \alpha_2))$. This type may be interpreted as follows: if $t = u$ is a true atom and α_1 and α_2 types such that $t : \alpha_1$ and $u : \alpha_2$, then it is also the case that $t : \alpha_1 \cup \alpha_2$ and $u : \alpha_1 \cup \alpha_2$.

Type inference Descriptive type systems are expressly formulated to allow automatic type inference assuming no type declarations provided by the user. An algorithm for inferring monomorphic types was given in [Mis84] and recently improved by [HJ90]. An algorithm for inferring polymorphic types is found in [PR89].

5 Conclusion

The different approaches reviewed here have varying strengths. Typed Prolog is attractive for its simplicity, but is somewhat inflexible in the use of functor symbols. Moreover, adding subtyping leads to complications. On the other hand, regular tree typed Prolog supports flexibility and subtyping. However, it sacrifices type security and no method is available for type reconstruction. Descriptively type systems solve most of these problems, but at the cost of simplicity. The inferred types are hard to understand, especially in the presence of polymorphism. All the approaches are, however, available for adoption in practice with their characteristic limitations.

The expanded version of this abstract may be found in [Red90].

References

[Bru82] M. Bruynooghe. Adding redundancy to obtain more reliable and more readable Prolog programs. In *First Intern. Logic Program. Conf.*, pages 129–133, 1982.

[HJ90] N. Heintze and J. Jaffar. A finite presentation theorem for approximating logic programs. In *ACM Symp. on Princ. of Program. Languages*, pages 197–209, ACM, Jan 1990.

[Mil78] R. Milner. A theory of type polymorphism in programming. *Journal of Computer and System Sciences*, 17:348–375, 1978.

[Mis84] P. Mishra. Towards a theory of types in prolog. In *International symposium on logic programming*, pages 289–298, IEEE, 1984.

[MO83] A. Mycroft and R. A. O'Keefe. A polymorphic type system for Prolog. In *Logic Programming workshop*, pages 107–122, Universidade Nova de Lisboa, 1983.

[MR85] P. Mishra and U. S. Reddy. Declaration-free type checking. In *ACM Symp. on Princ. of Program. Languages*, pages 7–21, 1985.

[PR89] C. Pyo and U. S. Reddy. Inference of polymorphic types for logic programs. In E. L. Lusk and R. A. Overbeek, editors, *Logic Programming: Proceedings of the North American Conference 1989*, pages 1115–1134, MIT Press, 1989.

[Red88] U. S. Reddy. Notions of polymorphism for predicate logic programs. In *Logic Programming: Proc. Fifth Intern. Conf. and Symp.*, pages (addendum) 17–34, MIT Press, August 1988.

[Red90] U. S. Reddy. A perspective on types for logic programs. In F. Pfenning, editor, *Types in Logic Programming*, MIT Press, 1990. (to appear).

[YS87] E. Yardeni and E. Shapiro. A type system for logic programs. In E. Shapiro, editor, *Concurrent Prolog*, chapter 28, pages 211–244, MIT Press, 1987.

Constraint Logic Programming: From Theory to Applications

Pascal Van Hentenryck
Department of Computer Science
Brown University
Box 1910
Providence, RI 02912

Abstract

Constraint Logic Programming (CLP) is a generalization of logic programming (LP) where unification, the basic operation of LP, is replaced by the more general concept of constraint-solving over a computational domain. CLP defines a class of language parametrized by the computational domain. Defining a CLP language amounts to choosing a computational domain (e.g. rational numbers), selecting a set of allowed constraints (e.g. linear equations and inequalities), and designing a constraint-solver for the constraints. CLP combines the advantages of LP (declarative semantics, nondeterminism, partial answer) with the efficiency of special-purpose constraint-solving algorithm. As a consequence, it reduces the programming effort for numerous applications, yet preserves most of the efficiency of specialized tools. Especially attractive for combinatorial problems is the combination of nondeterminism and constraint-solving.

This tutorial aims at giving a comprehensive overview of this area, from the theory to the design of CLP languages and their applications to industrial problems. The tutorial is divided into four main parts: theory, languages, applications, and extensions.

The theory part describes the declarative, operational, and fixpoint semantics of CLP languages and studies their connections.

The languages part studies various languages that are instantiations of the scheme. Studying these languages amounts to describing their computation domains and their associated constraint-solvers. Computation domains investigated so far include Linear Rational (Real) Arithmetics, Boolean Algebra, Finite Domains, and Presburger Arithmetics as well as data-structures like lists, strings, and arrays. Computation domains are studied from two perspectives: expressiveness and algorithms.

The application part reviews some successful applications in areas like combinatorial optimization, hardware design, and finance.

The extension part presents some recent proposals to enrich the framework including concurrent constraint programming, constraint hierarchies, and meta constraint programming.

Deductive Database Systems: Applications and Programming

Carlo Zaniolo
Microelectronics and Computer Technology Corporation
3500 West Balcones Center Drive
Austin, TX, 78759
carlo@mcc.com

Abstract

While it is tempting to view deductive databases as Prolog with secondary store facilities, they are in fact very different in terms of language syntax, semantics, execution model, enabling technology, programming style, development environment, and application forte. In this tutorial, we will review these differences with the objective of providing attendees with an understanding of applications that are best developed in a deductive database environment, and with the programming skills needed to do so.

1 Declarative and Procedural Programming

Deductive databases share with Prolog and other logic-based systems the use of Horn clause logic as a common conceptual basis. But advanced deductive database prototypes, as exemplified by $\mathcal{LDL}$ [NaTs], are very different in terms of syntax, semantics, architecture and environment—with many of these differences due to their emphasis on declarative programming. This is manifested when writing Horn clause programs in systems such as [Ceta, Meta, NaTs]. In these systems, the order in which goals appear in the rules need not determine their actual execution order, which is controlled by the system rather than the programmer. This extends the non-navigational paradigm of relational query languages, where select/join expressions are executed in an order chosen by the query optimizer according to performance estimates. As in relational databases, this results in ease of use, since the programmer is relieved from performance related concerns, such as navigating through the database and using access structures; furthermore, data independence is much enhanced since the resulting code can be reused even after physical changes have occurred in the database.

The most novel declarative aspect of deductive databases is their ability to make applications less dependent on a particular execution model, such as forward-chaining or backward-chaining. Indeed, a Prolog programmer can only write rules that work with backward chaining, an OPS5 programmer can only write rules that work in a forward chaining mode. In systems such as $\mathcal{LDL}$ [NaTs] and NAIL! [Meta], instead, the system will select the proper mode. Thus, the user can now focus on the logical correctness of the rules rather than on the underlying execution strategy. The significance of this point is better illustrated by an example.

A methane molecule consists of a carbon atom linked with four hydrogen atoms. Then, an ethane molecule can be constructed by replacing any H of a methane, by a carbon with three Hs. Therefore, the respective structure of methane and ethane molecules are as follows:

```
          H                      H    H
          |                      |    |
     H -- C -- H            H -- C -- C -- H
          |                      |    |
          H                      H    H
```

More complex alkanes can then be obtained inductively, in the same way: i.e., by replacing an H of a simpler alkane by a carbon with three Hs. We can now define alkanes using Horn clauses. A methane molecule will be represented by a complex term, `carb(h, h, h)`, and an ethane molecule by `carb(h, h, carb(h, h, h))`. In general, alkane molecules can be inductively defined as follows:

```
all_mol(h, 0, Max).
all_mol(carb(M1, M2, M3), N, Max) ←
                        all_mol(M1, N1, Max),
                        all_mol(M2, N2, Max),
                        all_mol(M3, N3, Max),
                        N= N1+N2+N3+1, N <= Max.
```

In addition to defining alkanes of increasing complexity, these non-linear recursive rules count the carbons in the molecules, and ensure finiteness in their size and number by checking that the tally of carbons never exceeds Max. This alkane definition can be used in different ways. For example, to generate all molecules with no more than four carbons one can write:

```
? all_mol(Mol,Cs, 4).
```

To generate all molecules with exactly four carbons one will write:

```
? all_mol(Mol, 4, 4).
```

Furthermore, if the relation `alk(Name, Str)` associates the names of alkanes with their structure, then the following rule will compute the number of carbons for an alkane given its name (assume that 10000 is a large enough number for all molecules to have a lower carbon complexity).

```
find(Name, Cs) ← alk(Name, Str), all_mol(Str, Cs , 10000).
```

The first two examples can only be supported through a forward chaining computation, which, in turn, translates naturally into the least-fixpoint computation that defines the model-theoretic based semantics of recursive Horn clause programs [NaTs]. The least fixpoint computation amounts to an iterative procedure, where partial results are added to a relation until a steady state is reached. The simplicity of this execution model makes it more suitable for handling data on secondary store than backward chaining that leads to main-memory-based, stack-oriented implementations. The simpler execution model also allow systems such as [Ceta] to achieve fast execution with abstract machines simpler than the WAM.

Therefore, deductive databases support well the first two examples via forward chaining, while Prolog and other backward chaining systems would flounder. In the last example, however, the first argument, `Str`, of `all_mol` is bound to the values generated by the predicate `alk`. Thus a computation, such as Prolog's backward chaining, that recursively propagates these bindings is significantly more efficient than forward chaining. Now, deductive databases solve this problem equally well, by using techniques such as the *Magic Set Method*, or the *Counting Method*, that simulate backward chaining through a pair of coupled fixpoint computations [CGT, Ull].

Since fixpoint computations check newly generated values against the set of previous values, cycles are handled automatically. This is a most useful feature since cyclic graphs are often stored in the database; furthermore, derived relations can also be cyclic. For instance in our alkane example, there are many equivalent representations for the same alkane. To generate them, equivalence-preserving operations, such as rotation and permutation on the molecules are used—but repeated applications of these operations bring back the initial structure. In deductive databases, there is no need to carry around a bag with all previous solutions, since cycles are detected and handled automatically and efficiently by the system.

The declarative semantics and programming paradigm of deductive data bases, extend beyond Horn clause programming to include negation and nondeterminism. In particular, negated goals in rules are efficiently supported according to their declarative semantics, which is based on the notion of stratification [NaTs]. Prolog's operational construct, called *cut*, is not part of $\mathcal{LDL}$. Instead, there is a construct known as `choice` that supports the expression of non-determinism, while retaining a declarative logic-based semantics [NaTs].

For all its merits, however, declarative programming is not the approach of choice for all applications. For instance, there are specific well-known problems, for which no declarative formulation can compete with textbook algorithms in terms of cogency or optimality. In languages such as $\mathcal{LDL}$, updates represent the main vehicle for expressing algorithms based on imperative operators that change the states of objects. Database updates have a formal semantics which models the notions of a before-state and an after-state, and are amenable to efficient implementations that support the notion of database transactions [Ceta, NaTs]. In addition, there are also constructs to express simple conditionals and iterations.

This tutorial will cover both the declarative and non-declarative aspects of programming with deductive databases, illustrating the semantics and use of the constructs through several examples.

2 Systems and Applications

An important trend emerging in the architecture of deductive database prototypes is their close coupling with external computing environments. Thus, for example, the NAIL! system is built on top of an SQL server [Meta], while $\mathcal{LDL}$ can work either as a stand alone system, or with an SQL server [Ceta]. In addition, $\mathcal{LDL}$ compiles query templates into equivalent C programs that are linked with external routines with a close coupling of data structures. This leads to a smaller kernel language, where meta-level predicates are not in the language, but they can often be replaced by, or defined as, external procedures in C. This close connection with databases and support for bilingual declarative/procedural programming was found very useful in many applications. In addition to database applications, these include scientific applications in the molecular biology area [Tsur], semantic prototyping from E-R based specifications [Teta], and complex analysis on data [Tsur].

In reviewing the experience gained so far, this tutorial will help clarifying the pros and cons of deductive database systems in different application areas, and discuss possible directions for the evolution of future systems.

References

[Ceta] Chimenti, D. et al., "The LDL System Prototype," IEEE Journal on Data and Knowledge Engineering, March 1990.

[CGT] Ceri, S., G. Gottlob and L. Tanca, "Logic Programming and Deductive Databases," Springer-Verlag, 1989.

[Meta] Morris, K. et al. "YAWN! (Yet Another Window on NAIL!), Data Engineering, Vol.10, No. 4, pp. 28–44, Dec. 1987.

[NaTs] S. Naqvi, and S. Tsur. "A Logical Language for Data and Knowledge Bases," W. H. Freeman Publ., 1989.

[Teta] Tryon, D., et al. "System Analysis for Deductive Database Environments: an Enhanced role for Aggregate Entities," Procs. 9th Int. Conference on Entity-Relationship Approach, Lausanne, CH, Oct. 8-10, 1990.

[Tsur] Tsur S., "Applications of Deductive Database Systems," Proc. IEEE COMCON Spring '90 Conf., San Francisco, Feb 26-March 2.

[Ull] Ullman, J.D., Database and Knowledge-Based Systems, Vols I and II, Computer Science Press, Rockville, Md., 1989.

Author Index

The MIT Press, with Peter Denning as general consulting editor, publishes computer science books in the following series:

ACM Doctoral Dissertation Award and Distinguished Dissertation Series

Artificial Intelligence
Patrick Winston, founding editor
J. Michael Brady, Daniel G. Bobrow, and Randall Davis, editors

Charles Babbage Institute Reprint Series for the History of Computing
Martin Campbell-Kelly, editor

Computer Systems
Herb Schwetman, editor

Explorations with Logo
E. Paul Goldenberg, editor

Foundations of Computing
Michael Garey and Albert Meyer, editors

History of Computing
I. Bernard Cohen and William Aspray, editors

Information Systems
Michael Lesk, editor

Logic Programming
Ehud Shapiro, editor; Koichi Furukawa, Jean-Louis Lassez, Fernando Pereira, and David H. D. Warren, associate editors

The MIT Press Electrical Engineering and Computer Science Series

Research Monographs in Parallel and Distributed Processing
Christopher Jesshope and David Klappholz, editors

Scientific and Engineering Computation
Janusz Kowalik, editor

Technical Communication
Ed Barrett, editor